SO-BIH-225

Motives in
Fantasy, Action, and Society

THE UNIVERSITY SERIES IN PSYCHOLOGY

Editor

DAVID C. McCLELLAND
Harvard University

BEARDSLEE, DAVID C. and WERTHEIMER, MICHAEL (Editors)— *Readings in Perception*

FISHER, SEYMOUR and CLEVELAND, SIDNEY E.—*Body Image and Personality*

ATKINSON, JOHN W. (Editor)—*Motives in Fantasy, Action and Society: A Method of Assessment and Study*

McCLELLAND, DAVID C., BALDWIN, ALFRED L., BRONFENBRENNER, URIE, and STRODTBECK, FRED L.—*Talent and Society: New Perspectives in the Identification of Talent*

BASS, BERNARD M. and BERG, IRWIN A. (Editors)—*Objective Approaches to Personality Assessment*

Motives in
Fantasy, Action, and Society

A METHOD OF ASSESSMENT AND STUDY

Edited by

JOHN W. ATKINSON

Associate Professor of Psychology
University of Michigan

D. VAN NOSTRAND COMPANY, INC.

PRINCETON, NEW JERSEY

TORONTO   LONDON

NEW YORK

D. VAN NOSTRAND COMPANY, INC.
120 Alexander St., Princeton, New Jersey (*Principal office*)
24 West 40 Street, New York 18, New York

D. VAN NOSTRAND COMPANY, LTD.
358, Kensington High Street, London, W.14, England

D. VAN NOSTRAND COMPANY (CANADA), LTD.
25 Hollinger Road, Toronto 16, Canada

First published June 1958
Second prepublication printing June 1958
Reprinted January 1963, September 1964

Preface

Motives in Fantasy, Action, and Society is offered to serve a variety of different needs among students of motivation. It presents a method for assessment of human motives through analysis of the content of thematic apperceptive stories and other kinds of samples of imaginative thought. The method of analysis is described in complete manuals and in extensive pretested practice materials for three important social motives: achievement, affiliation, and power. Hence, the book will serve as a useful handbook for anyone who wants to learn how to employ these methods or one of the alternative techniques that are included. The book also contains a representative survey of the different kinds of empirical investigations that have been conducted during the past decade to establish the validity of the method and to explore various uses that can be made of it. Thus it offers a varied set of interesting readings that can be readily adapted to courses in motivation, personality, social psychology, and projective methods. The material, both old and new, is arranged in a way that should convey to the reader who approaches this work for the first time a sense of the interrelatedness of results from studies of many different kinds of motivational problems.

The psychology of human motivation, falling as it does at the crossroads of many different scholarly interests, has long needed an integrative method of study. There have been notable gains on a number of separate fronts: conventional experimental investigations of motivation, the development of techniques for assessing individual differences, and analysis of motivational problems at the level of society. However, the bundles of facts which have been gathered do not hang together, and the incompleteness of theoretical conceptions which have arisen from these disparate approaches is everywhere obvious. We cannot expect the general principles of human motivation to emerge from simple experimental analysis, modeled after the study of lower animals, which ignores the fact that the subjects of study have already acquired many different kinds of motivating dispositions which can, and often do, produce diametrically opposite reactions to the same experimental treatment. Cronbach[1], in a

---

[1] Cronbach, Lee J. The two disciplines of scientific psychology. *American Psychologist,* 1957, **12**, 671-684.

brilliant analysis of the deficiencies of the two disciplines of scientific psychology, has put his finger on this fallacy of the traditional experimental approach while also calling attention to the weakness of the traditional individual-differences, or correlational, approach. The correlational psychologist, in magnifying the importance of measuring individual differences and a limited search for correlates, has forgotten the essential role of controlled experimentation in discovering causal relations.

The task of developing systematic principles of human motivation does demand simultaneous interest in assessment of individual differences and experimentation to discover the principles of interaction between personality disposition and environmental influence. But even this is not enough. The domain of human motivation also encompasses the many different kinds of relevant observations that can be made only in studies of society. Hence the constant task of the psychology of motivation must be to develop methods and concepts which will serve to unify the facts and insights developed in experimental inquiry, in consideration of individual differences, and in societal studies. This book will show how assessment of human motivation through content analysis of imaginative thought samples can serve such an integrative function.

The forty-six chapters represent a collection of separate studies, half of which appear for the first time in this volume. Most of the studies were accomplished by individuals who were in a position to interact frequently and to co-ordinate their efforts as one-time members of research teams or seminars at the University of Michigan or at Wesleyan University, where this work began under the tutelage of David C. McClelland. The book provides an occasion for taking stock of this collective effort. In addition, several other investigators who have worked independently of these face-to-face groups have kindly contributed papers which strengthen the book a great deal.

I wish to express my thanks to each of these co-workers who have made the book possible by contributing papers and willingly suffering the fate of having them arranged, edited, and introduced by one in their midst granted the temporary power of editorial license. In this connection, a special word of gratitude is due the contributors to this volume who have worked independently of the loosely organized research teams and seminars at Michigan and Wesleyan: Irvin L. Child, Elizabeth M. Douvan, Seymour Feshbach, Elizabeth G. French, Robert H. Knapp, Charles McArthur, Paul H. Mussen, Bernard C. Rosen, Alvin Scodel, and Thomas Storm. I sincerely hope that in embedding their work in the context of so many papers from the places which happen to have been the loci of most of this work I have not distorted the fact of its independence.

The editor, from his vantage point as a participant in this research from the time of its inception in 1947, has attempted to focus attention upon important issues and to supply a theoretical thread in the introductory statements to each part of the book. These theoretical ideas are most fully developed in Chapters 20, 22, and 42. It would be far from accurate, however, to suggest that all of the contributors share the same theoretical conception. The reader will discover this for himself as he moves from one paper to the next. Each man speaks his own mind. Earlier reports and discussions of some of this research by McClelland (258, 259), McClelland, Atkinson, Clark, and Lowell in *The Achievement Motive* (272), and by Atkinson (24) and McClelland (261) in the *Nebraska Symposium on Motivation* reflect changes and developments in theoretical interpretation. The current views of these writers and of others who have contributed papers to the volume will appear in the chapters bearing their names.

The book assumes no responsibility for coverage of the varied research activity or divergent theory in the field of motivation nor of other uses of thematic apperception, even though it is a focal point of interest throughout. The book has its own particular story to tell. Its organization into separate parts represents a compromise between straight historical presentation to give the flavor of the development of ideas and the discovery of problems in a decade of work, and the arrangement of studies according to particular questions they seek to answer.

The six parts of the book deal with six basic questions: I. Does the arousal of motivation have any effect on the content of imaginative thought? II. What, in detail, is the nature of this influence? III. How do individual differences in the kind and strength of motivation influence behavior? IV. What factors influence the growth and development of a motive? V. Can content analysis of "thought samples" be employed to study problems of motivation in society? VI. How can thematic apperceptive measures of motivation be improved?

The appendices contain extensive practice material, and other information which will be of practical value to anyone who might want to employ the method himself. The bibliography contains a list of references to many other persons who have made important contributions in their use of the thematic apperceptive method. I have made use of a mimeographed bibliography prepared by Ralph Haber and Richard Alpert to call attention to studies which have employed the measures of motivation presented in this book. These are designated by an asterisk (*) in the list of references.

This is likely not to be a book one will read through from beginning to end. The student of society, for example, may find it most desirable to begin with Parts V and IV, which deal with motivation and society and the social origins of human motives. He can then turn to Parts I and III for other evidence of the validity of the method, and to Part II for detailed descriptions of the kind of content analysis that has been made in the societal studies. The table of contents will undoubtedly suggest other alternative beginnings.

ACKNOWLEDGMENTS

It is difficult to express adequately my appreciation of the help offered me, in one form or another, by students, friends, and colleagues, during the ten-year span of research covered in this book —there has been so much of it. The sustained interaction with David C. McClelland over the tactics and strategy of this research, which began in 1946-1947 when I was his student, has been the source of many of the ideas reflected in the selection and organization of material and in chapters bearing my name. The same can be said of my experiences in collaboration with Russell A. Clark, Roger W. Heyns, Joseph Veroff, and Edward L. Walker over periods of several years at a stretch, and of recent theoretical discussions with Daniel R. Miller, and of other frequent contacts with colleagues who have contributed insights and criticism or wise guidance of some of the Michigan dissertations using methods described in this volume: J. David Birch, C. R. Brown, Clyde Coombs, Daniel Katz, E. Lowell Kelly, Wilbert J. McKeachie, Theodore M. Newcomb, Helen Peak.

I want especially to express my gratitude to Donald G. Marquis, who, as chairman of the Department of Psychology at Michigan throughout this decade of research, offered constant encouragement and help in providing the time and special opportunities for research and the growth of ideas, the kind of support which is the *sine qua non.*

Appropriate acknowledgment of financial assistance from various agencies is made in each chapter of this volume. Here, however, I want to express my own personal indebtedness to the following: the Office of Naval Research, which, in a grant to McClelland (1947-1950), supported the early efforts dealing with hunger and achievement motivation; the Horace H. Rackham School of Graduate Studies (1951) for a grant to begin work on the need for affiliation; the Social Science Research Council (1952-1955) for a three-year Faculty Research Fellowship, which provided an opportunity for half-time commitment to this work and funds for extending it in the realm of interpersonal motivations; and the Ford Foundation, which currently provides a five-year research grant for further extensions of this work in the realm of personality dynamics. I speak also for several collaborators and students who with me have benefited from this support in expressing to these agencies our thanks for the freedom to follow new leads as they have become apparent rather than having to be tied to particular prescribed lines of investigation during the period of their support.

The decision to put together a book such as this, which would argue the value of an integrative method of studying human motivation, can be attributed to my experience during 1955-1956 at the Center for Advanced Study in the Behavioral Sciences. Constant contact with persons in other fields of behavioral science, who were also free for a year from the usual academic demands on time, helped me to develop an appreciation of what other disciplines concerned with human behavior expect and deserve from the psychology of motivation. Without blaming any of them for the use I have made of their ideas and criticisms, I should like to acknowledge the help of several colleagues of that delightful year who read and commented on some of the things I have said in this volume: Raymond A. Bauer, Urie Bronfenbrenner, Louis Guttman, Bert F. Hoselitz, Gardner Lindzey, S. Martin Lipset, Alex Inkeles, Jacob Marschak, James N. Morgan, Roy Radner, Frank Restle, and Patrick Suppes.

Finally, my sincere thanks to those who have spent the recent months with me, slashing through and out from under the sheafs of copy and proofs: Judith G. Perloe, who carried the lion's share, with the help of Lucy M. Strong, Elaine C. Hatfield, Sheila C. Feld, Mary Jane Atkinson, Charles P. Smith, and the littlest helper, Ann Mina Atkinson, who cut slips for the index.

Permission to reprint selections from books or journals was kindly granted by the following publishers: American Psychological Association, Inc; American Sociological Society; Appleton-Century-Crofts, Inc; Dryden Press, Inc; Duke University Press.

JOHN W. ATKINSON

Ann Arbor, Michigan
May, 1958

Table of Contents

xi

APPENDIX I

APPENDIX II

APPENDIX III

INTRODUCTION

The Point of View

THE INTEGRATING THEME of this book is the search for a method of assessment and study of human motivation having a trio of virtues —validity, flexibility, and generality. The method must yield valid descriptions of how people differ in strength of motivation. But it must, at the same time, be flexible enough to be adapted both to experimental investigations which seek the general principles of motivation, and to studies of man in society which seek to unravel the social origins of human motives and to discover their social consequences. Finally, the method must have generality; it must cut a broad swath across the domain of substantive problems we have come to think of as problems of motivation. It must, in other words, be applicable to the study of the different kinds of motives that are important in human affairs.

Most of the work reported in this book grows directly out of investigations initiated a decade ago under the direction of David C. McClelland, investigations which have been reviewed in an earlier book, *The Achievement Motive* (272). But the guiding ideas and the techniques employed have a much longer history. Their present-day advocates are particularly indebted to Sigmund Freud and Henry A. Murray, the pioneers who planted and nurtured the seeds. In the 1930's, Henry A. Murray (313, 314) and his colleagues at the Harvard Psychological Clinic invented a technique for assessing motivation which concretized the rich insight of Freud that human motives are most clearly expressed in free-associative thought. This technique, *The Thematic Apperception Test* (*TAT*) (315), requires the individual to create imaginative stories in response to a series of pictures; the content of his fantasy is then analyzed to reveal the underlying aims of his behavior. A decade of exploratory empirical work and wide clinical usage provided numerous encouraging indications of the ultimate potentialities of this method (e.g., 36, 81, 178, 335, 345, 352, 361, 401, 416). However, in 1947 when our search began, there was hardly any firm factual evidence to justify the many intuitive inferences that were commonly being made from thematic apperception in clinical assessments of personality. There had been virtually no contact between the use of this method and the employment of experimental procedures, to control motivation, of the kind which had evolved as an adjunct to the study of learning in lower animals. Nor did the early uses of thematic apperception and other similar projective methods reflect sufficient awareness of the canons of psychometric rigor which had been developed in the steady advance of seemingly more objective tests of individual differences. These other important influences will, we trust, be apparent in the approach to the study of motivation presented in this book.

The pages which follow bring together a variety of investigations, all of which employ the same or very similar methods for assessing human motivation. There are studies which search for systematic principles relating motivation and performance, a topic which too often interests only the learning theorist. There are discussions of the internal consistency and other properties of a test of individual differences in strength of motivation, issues which normally spark off real excitement in the heart of only the measurement specialist. Then, with a turn of the page, there are to be found investigations dealing with the possible substitutive function of fantasy, or with the characteristics of symbolic expressions of inhibited sexual motivation, or with an attempt to assess motivation in children through graphic expression. These are issues which have somehow gotten to be the special concern of the clinical psychologist. In close proximity to these problems of clinical interest are presented discussions of the role of achievement motivation in social mobility and an analysis of a motivational problem in economic history. In point of emphasis, these and other investigations illustrate various focal points of restricted interest which too often are like so many isolated islands within contemporary psychology. Here, however, these various investigations of motives in fantasy, action, and society are linked by a common method for assessing the kind and strength of motivation.

What is the plan, or intention, behind the selection and organization of material? We mean to decry the artificial separation of interests which has held back the psychology of motivation for so long. We mean to say that the search for general principles relating stimulating situation and response and measurement of individual differences are not isolated problems, the one to be attempted only or mainly with animals, the other only with what appears to be most easily accomplished with humans. We mean to say, also, that it makes no scientific sense to try to understand the behavior of a person through global assessment of the subtle interplay of his various motives—no matter how insightful the method of analysis—unless there is some rigor in the assessment and some principle which relates it to behavior. We mean to say, furthermore, that the ambitions which propel men upward in a social structure and which may contribute to the gradual rise and fall of a civilization are to be considered motivational problems of man in his natural habitat which we should seek to interpret and understand in terms of the same general principles that experimental analysis tries to uncover and refine. We feel, in other words, the need for adequate instruments to measure how individuals differ in the important motivational variables that are usually referred to in general explanatory principles, and the need to constantly rephrase these principles so they will fit the kinds of observations it is possible to make using instruments which encompass the problems. Our hope, naturally, is to present a persuasive argument for the potential *integrative* value of a particular method for assessment of human motivation.

This book, then, presents a method of inquiry and a point of view concerning what is needed to advance the psychology of motivation. It will review the development of a method for assessing motivation which seems capable of overcoming the disease of *ad hocitis* that afflicts methodology in the broad domain conventionally labeled "human motivation." The book is organized to present a picture of a rather loosely knit body of research (but a fabric nevertheless) spanning the past decade. This program first sought a valid method for assessing motivation and then, finding it, has begun to test its usefulness and range of applicability to problems which excite the curiosity of most behavioral scientists: How do the motives of an individual influence his behavior? What are the social origins of various human motives? What are the social consequences of certain motives?

The book is the work of many authors, most of whom at one time or another have been members of loosely organized teams or research seminars at Wesleyan or Michigan. I know that these co-workers will not feel it amiss if, in a brief scanning of the content of the book, I call particular attention to the additional contributions to this volume by investigators who have worked in complete independence of what, earlier, I have referred to as a "program."

The book begins with an introductory survey and comparison of alternative methods for assessing motivation by McClelland. He reviews the methodological and theoretical issues that must be faced in trying to develop measures of motivational variables and in trying to discover what it is that is being measured.

Part I surveys experimental results which now can be mobilized to show that motivation does have an influence on the content of imaginative thought and that the influence of motivation is encouragingly similar as one studies different kinds of motivating states.

This section contains a study of sexual motivation contributed by Paul H. Mussen and Alvin Scodel, and an analysis of the drive-reducing function of fantasy contributed by Seymour Feshbach.

Part II presents detailed manuals for content analysis of imaginative protocols to produce indices of the strength of three important social motives: the achievement motive (n Achievement), the affiliation motive (n Affiliation), and the power motive (n Power). A report of the adequacy of these manuals and practice materials, the latter contained in Appendix I, is also presented here, as are two promising alternative methods for assessing the strength of achievement motivation. This section contains the first of three papers dealing with a modified apperception test, the "insight questionnaire," which were contributed by Elizabeth G. French.

Part III examines the ahistorical issue, the arousal of motivation and its influence on behavior in a given situation. This section deals specifically with the difficult problem of conceptualizing the interaction between personality and situation as it has been confronted in this research. Since most of the work to date has been concerned with the behavioral effects of achievement motivation, theoretical interest has turned to the nature of the relationship between the need for achievement and risk-taking behavior turned up by McClelland in studies of the role of achievement motivation in economic development. A theoretical model is presented to explain the motivational determinants of risk-taking behavior. This represents the high-water mark in our attempt to state explicitly how the motives of an individual and factors in the momentary situation influence his behavior.

Part III also moves on to new explorations. Persons are classified according to the strength of both need for achievement and need for affiliation in a step towards a conception of personality in terms of configuration of motives, that is, motive types. Robert H. Knapp has contributed the initial results of his studies of achievement motivation and aesthetic preference; and French and others have contributed the results of studies dealing with complex interactions between the motivation of the individual and the momentary situation he confronts.

Part IV turns attention to the historical issue. How are motives acquired? Why is childhood experience so important? This section includes a theoretical discussion of the importance of early learning in the formation of motives and a study of parental attitudes towards child training in relation to the achievement motivation of children. Also contained in this section is a cross-cultural analysis of achievement imagery in folktales in relation to indices of child-training practice contributed by Irvin L. Child, Thomas Storm, and Joseph Veroff.

Part V should be of special interest to sociologists, economists, historians, and others whose main interests lie in the problems of society. Studies contributed by Elizabeth Douvan and Bernard C. Rosen assess the strength of achievement motivation in middle- and working-class Americans. And a third paper, by McClelland, carries the method of content analysis to Greek literature and surveys the questions which arise when one is so bold as to suggest that a motivational analysis of literary documents and artifacts uncovers some new facts for the historian to wrestle with.

Part VI turns attention specifically to the measuring instrument and the methodological questions which arise in assessing motivation through content analysis of imaginative thought. The thematic apperceptive instrument is subjected to close experimental scrutiny. It is placed in a theoretical context as any instrument which purports to be like a thermometer should be. Some of its strengths and weaknesses are laid open to view in a series of papers which seek to identify the various factors in addition to the motive of the individual which can influence the content of a story. Among these studies is one contributed by Charles McArthur calling for re-examination of the effects of achievement motivation on thematic apperception. The book ends with a springboard for more sophisticated research to refine the method of assessing motivation, a turn of events I hope it will serve to encourage. The book ends asking questions more clearly than when it started.

If the investigations presented are scrutinized from the point of view of the tenets of criticism which have evolved through more than fifty years of experimentation on learning and motivation in lower animals, the relative lack of clarity in theoretical conception and in operational definition of some important variables will often be patently clear. But so too, we must remind ourselves, do many of the studies of animal motivation of thirty years ago seem relatively naive by modern standards of experimentation with animals. Our state of relative ignorance in the realm of human motivation enables us to take our present experiments seriously and to argue our theoretical hunches with great zest—but not without a decent sense of humor about how all this will seem years hence if we are lucky enough to make some progress.

So also may some of the investigations which follow seem to oversimplify the problems of human motivation to those who have worked most intimately with the whole conflicted person in the modern clinic. But many of the subtleties in our theoretical conceptions of human motivation, which are by now part of the common lore of most psychologists, have acquired a specious kind of clarity and concreteness they do not deserve, have they not? We have all heard the same arguments and discussion of issues so often that we often come to accept certain ways of thinking about motivation by virtue of sheer repetition of argument rather than as a consequence of convincing factual evidence. It is time to turn to the facts and to let them speak for themselves.

The psychometrician may be tempted to look askance at some of our relatively modest reliability coefficients or to harbor suspicions of multidimensionality! In answer, we assert our conviction that in the not too distant future content analysis of imaginative thought, as a general method for assessment of individual differences, will be as razor sharp as the preference scale—when more who know how to count decide to join the quest.

This book has been written for the person who is sensitive to the need for methodological advance if there is to be the initial accumulation of "integratable" factual information that must be the foundation of theoretical inference. This book is for the person who is appalled that there seem to be nearly as many methods for measuring motivational variables and motivational concepts as there are researchers and problems, the person who knows it would be better if the same instruments and procedures were used to study a variety of problems, as a thermometer is used in the study of heat. We search for an integrative method. We presume that this is the only way we shall ever arrive at a general and testable theory of human motivation. Editor.

CHAPTER 1

∎∎

Methods of Measuring
Human Motivation

DAVID C. MCCLELLAND

HUMAN MOTIVATION has always been a topic of key interest to psychologists, but the lack of adequate methods for measuring it has seriously hampered the development of systematic knowledge of the subject. Complex "theories" of motivation from Freud to Hull are plentiful since they can spring full-blown from the creative fancies of their authors, unchecked by precise measurement *at the human level.* The difficulty is two-fold. On the one hand, "tough minded" animal psychologists complain that clinical methods of assessing human motivation are not methods of measurement at all, but at best simply codified subjective impressions of doubtful reliability. On the other hand, "tender-minded" clinical psychologists object that however tough-minded the experimental psychologists may be, they for the most part duck the problem of measuring human motivation altogether or try to handle it by unchecked (and often uncheckable) extrapolations from studies of the white rat. Evidently if we are to make much headway, we need to focus our resources and energies on the measurement problem. Here, as elsewhere in science, real theoretical advance has to wait on methodological developments.

The present collection of papers represents an attempt to see what could be done by employing a particular method of measuring human motivation—a method which involves content analysis of imaginative thought sequences. The choice of this method was not completely fortuitous but was the product of some preliminary consideration of the advantages and disadvantages of other possible methods of measurement and of the criteria which would determine whether a particular method was scientifically promising or not. It seems worth presenting that consideration here more explicitly if only to make it possible for others to propose different criteria for evaluating the promise of a method of measurement or to make a different judgment of a particular method in terms of the same criteria. Such a procedure

7

will have the additional advantage of allowing us to compare the results obtained from different methods of measurement.

But what is a motive? Is it not desirable to define what is being measured before trying to discuss ways of measuring it? There are theorists who have proceeded this way—particularly the learning theorists like Brown (48) and Farber (126), who define what the characteristics of a drive *must be* in terms of the variables in Hull's learning theory and then set about finding a measure that will have those characteristics. The approach to be followed here is more empirical, less prejudicial in advance as to what the characteristics of a motive will turn out to be. At the outset, it takes no position as to whether, for example, there are certain primary (unlearned) and secondary (learned) drives, whether motives drive (provide a source of energy) or direct (release energy in certain directions), or whether they are temporary states or enduring dispositions of the organism (cf. Baldwin, 30). To a certain extent, such questions can be answered only *after* one has a measure of motivation, not before. Such a loosely empirical procedure is certain to prove confusing to those who have definite theoretical ideas as to what such terms as *drive, need, motive,* and *value* mean, but, as will presently become clear, the position taken here is that the decision as to which of these terms to use should depend not so much on the author's theoretical dispositions as on the method of measurement which provides the operational definition for the term. That is, in concrete terms, more failure of communication occurs if two authors call their variable *"n* Achievement" (Edwards 112, McClelland *et al.,* 272) when they are using uncorrelated methods of measurement than if, though they use the same method of measurement and the same title for it, one prefers to think of the variable as "driving" and the other as "directing" the organism.

But surely *some* ideas as to what a motive is must guide research planning. Otherwise how would one know that he was working on motivation at all? Precisely so: there must be such ideas, but they should begin by being general and become precise through measurement. Thus, physicists began with a very general idea of heat based on sensory experiences of warmth and cold, developed measures which corresponded roughly with those experiences, and ended, through increasingly precise measurement, with scientific constructs of heat and temperature which went far beyond vague subjective impressions in the precision of what Cronbach and Meehl (85) call "the nomological network." It would certainly have been a mistake to have decided *in advance* of measurement precisely what the connection of heat and temperature was going to be with other variables and then to have chosen one's methods of measurement accordingly.

So in studying motivation, one starts with general ideas as to the nature of the variable, tries to get a measure of it, and determines whether he has succeeded in terms of such criteria as the following, which appear to be general in the sense that they determine whether any scientific measurement has a claim to be taken seriously.[1]

CRITERION A

The measure of a motive should sensitively reflect the presence or absence of a motive or its variations in strength. This requirement seems so elementary that it is hardly worth stating; yet the fact of the matter is that many alleged methods of measuring motivation (such as the Taylor Scale of Manifest Anxiety, 402) have not satisfactorily met this criterion. The difficulty is, of course, to determine *independently of the measure* whether the motive is present or absent or varies in strength. Here one runs immediately into the problem of what one means by a motive; otherwise, how can one determine its presence or absence? But again the problem is more difficult in theory than it is in practice. One can start with a general idea as to presence-absence and find out ultimately whether it was correct in terms of the "payoff" of the measure based on it. The question boils down, then, to listing the various ways in which experimentalists feel they can produce presence-absence of a motive or find two groups of people which differ in the average amount present of the motive in question. The problem is analogous to the one originally faced by the physicist who may have tried to determine how to measure heat by the expansion of liquids in a tube. He could vary the amount of heat applied (e.g., by bringing a lighted match closer) or he could place the tube in water at different end states (either boiling or freezing) and could observe the effects on the liquid in the tube on the assumption that it should reflect sensitively the assumed differences in the amount of heat present in the two procedures.

Psychologists have tried to vary the amount of motivation present in human beings in a number of ways. The first two are direct carry-overs from a large group of animal experiments:

(1) They *deprive* the human subject of something (usually food or water) in order to manipulate the strength of his hunger or thirst. The effects of such deprivation on perception and association have been extensively studied (329, 332). Unfortunately many of the results are not strictly comparable because experimenters have varied in the degree to which they let subjects know the purpose of the experiment. At one extreme, McClelland and Atkinson (270) went

---

[1] I owe much in this discussion to a treatment of this problem given by Professor Paul Lazarsfeld of Columbia University.

to unusual lengths to conceal from their subjects the fact that hunger was the variable being studied; at the other extreme, Levine, Chein, and Murphy (226) asked subjects to volunteer for a study of the effects of hunger on perception. In the first instance the fact that the subjects did not eat was quite incidental and involuntary, whereas in the second they consciously went without food at the request of the experimenter. Either procedure is, of course, justifiable, depending on what the researcher wants to know. What is not justifiable is trying to reconcile the results of the procedures as if they were identical, since the latter certainly involves many more complex learning sets and conflicts of motives than the former. Here is a clear instance where the unthinking application of techniques worked out originally with animals has led to considerable confusion at the human level. For example, it has sometimes been assumed that the perceptual and associative effects of prolonged starvation on conscientious objectors voluntarily depriving themselves amidst plenty (376, pp. 80-81) would parallel the effects of starvation when food was simply scarce.

(2) Psychologists have also applied strong *persistent stimuli* to the subjects in order to change their motivational state. Electric shock has usually been the weapon of choice for producing such a stimulus, although, of course, there is no reason why other "weapons," such as needle point showers (325), cannot also be employed. The effect of electric shock on conditioning and maze learning has long been the subject of study, but without any very tangible result, at least so far as the understanding of psychodynamics is concerned (127). One reason is that it soon became apparent that the meaning of shock to the subject was important and had to be controlled in order to get consistent results. Sometimes the shock served as information, sometimes as punishment, sometimes as a source of anxiety. As in the case of food deprivation, the experimenter was faced not only with the problem of simple manipulation of an environmental factor but also with attempting to control the perceived effect of the manipulation. Another reason for the apparent lack of significance of the shock experiments may be that strong stimuli in general, or electric shock in particular, may not be appropriate "models" of adult motivation, at least as observed in normal people.

More promising has been the whole line of research which used electric shock, not directly as a source of stimulation, but indirectly as a source of anxiety (292), since anticipation of shock seems to produce many of the behavioral characteristics of anxiety as observed in the clinic where it derives from quite different sources. Nevertheless the enthusiasm for this analogy has probably exceeded the degree of operational similarity on which it is based. Fear of physical, localized pain (as from shock) is not necessarily identical with fear of vaguer psychic traumata. Since fear of physical injury does not loom large in motivational systems of most people, research done on it has only indirect value for understanding other more important types of human anxiety. This has not prevented theorists from making derivations or extrapolations rather extensively from animal studies (Brown, 48; Miller and Dollard, 295; Mowrer, 308), but one would be more impressed if there were some actual research results reported on the derived motives in question. For example, Brown (48) speculates at length about how people might acquire a "need" for money on the basis of research which has demonstrated that cues associated with injury have the capacity to evoke anxiety, since money may eliminate such cues. Yet apparently neither he nor anyone else has as yet done any research which involves direct measurement of this supposedly important human need.

(3) Lewin and his co-workers (229) have been most closely identified with the attempt to vary human motivation by the presentation of *objects of different attractiveness* ("reward value" or "valence"). For example, barrier behavior of children can be observed under the stimulus of "toys present" in the visual field (motivation aroused) and compared with barrier behavior when no toys are present (motivation not aroused). This approach has not led to the development of any generalized measures of particular motives useful in assessing individual differences. That is, the "barrier behavior" does not yield an index of strength of the "toy motive" which can be obtained in the absence of the incentive or which can be taken to represent a more general "play" motive not tied to a particular stimulus. What results is not a picture of the subjects' motives which can be used to predict what he will do in a new situation. Instead, he must be put in the situation to find out what he will do: the motive is tied to a specific situation and a specific incentive. There seems to be no *a priori* reason why the Lewinian approach could not be used to develop measures of generalized motives if one could, for example, demonstrate that a subject showed a particular type of reaction to a *class of incentives*. If so, then the test reaction to one instance of the class would have predictive power for the remainder. Some of the experiments on level of aspiration appear to fall partly in this category, the only difficulty being that so far levels of aspiration for varieties of incentives have not shown very much generality. Perhaps the inherent difficulty with this method of arousing motivation is that it is too "stimulus bound"—

and bound, for the most part, to visual stimuli at that. The same visual cues may arouse different motives in different people so that generality is hard to obtain.

(4) Attempts to manipulate human motives are also made directly by *special instructions* given the subjects or by experiences that are experimentally induced. Historically the most important of these attempts were those initiated by Sears (370) and others to induce ego involvement, success, and failure by various types of instructions and by manipulation of reported performance scores relative to levels of aspiration or norms reported for other competing individuals or groups. In the same tradition were many of the studies reported by the Yale group in *Frustration and Aggression* (102) in which attempts were made to induce frustration experimentally by such techniques as taking a bottle away from a baby, preventing Boy Scouts from seeing a movie they expected to see, keeping college students up all night, producing direct conflict between two overt motor responses, and the like.

The experiments reported in subsequent chapters have followed in this tradition. They were designed to arouse human motives in as life-like a way as possible. For example, in trying to increase the achievement motive (Ch. 3) every attempt was made to provide a setting which, in males at least, would genuinely arouse achievement strivings. References were made to "intelligence" or "leadership capacity," and in some cases doing well or poorly at actual tasks was arranged. Furthermore, it was not assumed that the relationship of the administrator to the subjects could be disregarded, that mechanical recitations of obviously "phony" instructions by anyone —even a pretty co-ed or a confused graduate student—about any task—even cancelling x's and o's—would succeed in producing achievement striving. (See also 272.)

The advantage of this approach would appear to be that every attempt is made to manipulate the variable as it occurs in life and not as one would think it should occur by analogy with animal experiments or as deduced from theoretical assumptions, as in the first two procedures. So far as human beings are concerned, neither strong stimuli nor tissue needs to be the way in which motives are normally aroused. Perhaps such a "common sense" approach will turn out to be incorrect, but that can fortunately be determined by whether or not it pays off ultimately in terms of accounting for the variance in human behavior. The evidence presented subsequently is that the payoff has been quite substantial.

To date, human motives more or less successfully aroused in addition to the achievement motive include the following: *the affiliation motive,* aroused by exposing subjects to public sociometric judgment and by rejection from fraternities which students wanted to join (Chs. 4 and 5); *the sexual motive,* aroused in males by nude female slides and by proximity to an attractive female "lure" and in females by musical stimulation (Chs. 7, 8, 9); *the power motive,* presumably aroused among candidates for an election during the suspense of waiting for the ballots to be counted (Ch. 6). Attempts to arouse security needs by threats of physical harm (a visit to the dentist's chair (138), or escape through a hundred-foot column of water at the Submarine School in New London (18)) have not been conspicuously successful to date in producing detectable variations in fantasy behavior. But Walker *et al.* (Ch. 10) have found temporal and geographic proximity to an atomic explosion produces increased expression of fear-related motivation.

That the type of arousal technique so far used may not be limited to a particular culture and therefore of restricted general usefulness is suggested by the fact that Angelini (16) has repeated the basic achievement arousal techniques in Brazil among Portuguese-speaking subjects with results on fantasy very similar to those obtained in the United States except that he was able to arouse his female subjects by references to intelligence and leadership capacity, whereas three or four attempts to do this in the United States had previously failed (272, 302). The only method of arousing an achievement motivation in U. S. women which has affected their achievement fantasies is reported by Field (133, 272) when he defined success and failure largely in sociometric terms as "social acceptability." The discrepancy between these results and Angelini's has yet to be explained.

The other major method of working with differences in motive strength is to go out and find these differences in nature, rather than to attempt to produce them experimentally, as in the preceding four procedures. That is, one finds two groups of subjects who differ in some conspicuous way and treats them as representing two different arousal stages of the motive. For example, it can be assumed that ministers as a group have higher average religious motivation than men in general, an assumption which can then be used as a basis for testing the extent to which a measuring instrument like the Allport-Vernon Scale of Values accurately reflects such differences in motivation. It is essentially this method which is proposed by McArthur in criticizing the *n* Achievement score (Ch. 38) because some components of it do not correlate with grades in college. That is, one can assume that academic overachievers have higher achievement motivation than academic underachievers, treat the two groups as representing two levels of strength in achievement motivation, select those aspects of fantasy, for example, which characterize the one more than the other, and assume they reflect the difference in motivation. The difficulty with the group differences method is that the groups may differ on more variables than the motive in question: overachievers differ from underachievers in other ways than in achievement motivation, and these other differences may be picked up in the measure. Ideally a motivational variable should be under experimental control so that it can be manipulated independently of all other correlated factors, and its "pure" effects detected.

So far we have spoken of the first criterion only in most general terms, stating that the measure should reflect changes in motive strength *in some way*. It should, of course, do more than this if possible: it should reflect them monotonically at least, if not linearly; it should respond over the whole range of motive strength; it should provide equal units, the way a thermometer does in responding to heat. And so forth. But some of these are counsels of perfection. Being so near the beginning of measurement in this area, we shall be fortunate if an index can be had which is monotonic over *part* of the range, equal units or not. Thus it is possible that the fantasy measure of motivation reported here drops down again through some repressive mechanism at the highest levels of arousal, but we can still use it over a wide portion of the range.

CRITERION B

The measure of a motive should reflect variations in only that motive. Such a criterion is a logical necessity. If a (variations in motive strength) leads to c (some behavioral signs), then c can be used to infer the presence of a, if and *only if* a is the one way to produce c. It is for this reason that a great deal of energy has been expended trying to decide what characteristics of behavior or behavior sequences can be *uniquely* attributed to the presence of motivation. Another way of putting the question is: What is there about what an organism does which makes psychologists want to use such a concept as motivation anyway?

Traditionally motives are supposed to drive, direct, or select behavior (285). That is, they are used to account for variations in activity level, for the sequence of responses, and for the capacity to acquire new responses. In each of these instances, the crucial fact is that past behavior does not seem adequate by itself to account for what the organism does. For instance, an organism may have demonstrated its capacity to make a certain response many times (run through a maze, remember someone's name), but on occasion it does not make the response even though the cues to elicit the response seem adequate. Why not? We invoke the motive concept to explain why. We say the person or the animal is not motivated to go through the maze because his motive is low or satiated. Or, if we are clinicians, we invoke the same kind of explanation to account for his forgetting a name—e.g., he is motivated to avoid remembering. Or, once again, the organism may make some responses which tend *not* to be repeated under similar circumstances and others which are. What explains the difference since frequency of past occurrence of the response may be the same? Again, the answer involves the motive concept. We say the person has had some motive satisfied in the one case and not in the other, to restate the familiar Law of Effect. Or, finally, the organism may have demonstrated its capacity to make certain responses many times, but sometimes it puts them together in one sequence and sometimes in another. Why? Again, we find the motive concept useful to explain the chaining of responses, the organization of behavior, or in particular, the emergence of *new* responses such as one finds in dreams, fantasies, and symptomatology.

These are the usual "unique" characteristics of the behavior stream which have been by one theorist or another attributed to motives, but unfortunately none of them has turned out to be a foolproof sign that a motive is present. Take the first criterion, for example. Thorndike, Hull, and other functionalists pictured the organism under the influence of drive as being more active, as restless. Technically, of course, Hull was more specific than this and stated that a drive would activate habits according to their relative strength in the habit family hierarchy. This would mean that if the strongest habit in the hierarchy was that of doing nothing or "freezing" (see Brown and Jacobs, 50), then the sign of the presence of a drive would be inactivity rather than activity. Consequently it would be possible to make inferences about the presence of motivation only if one had prior knowledge of the exact composition of the habit family hierarchy, a prerequisite impossible to fulfill in most human situations. It is still conceivable that motivation might increase energy output as measured at the physiological level despite inhibition of overt responses, but this possibility has not been extensively explored up to the present time.

To turn to the second criterion, since rewards obviously "stamp in" or select certain types of behavior (the so-called "empirical law of effect"), the presence of learning (or "selected" responses) is often advocated as an indication that motivation must also have been present (126, 292). Such an inference is valid, of course, if learning takes place *only* when motivation is reduced, a proposition which it is extremely difficult to prove. That is, if learning can occur merely through contiguity, then learning cannot be used as a foolproof indicator of the presence of motivation. Furthermore, learning, defined as the increased probability of a response occurring in a given situation, may also be facilitated by other conditions, such as positive transfer, so that there are other reasons for regarding improvement in performance with suspicion as a foolproof sign of the presence or strength of a motive.

The third traditional behavioral criterion for inferring the presence of motivation—namely, the organization of a series of acts or its directedness—stands close inspection hardly better than the other two. For example, Hull (187) invokes the motive concept to account (a) for choice behavior, as when rats choose to turn right or turn left, depending on whether they are hungry or thirsty, and (b) for chaining of responses, as in the patterning of successive turns in a maze, relying largely on the stimulus characteristics of the drive state or anticipatory goal responses to do so. But he would not argue that therefore either choice behavior or behavior sequences are uniquely determined by a motive so that whenever one or the other occurs one can safely infer the presence of the motive. The excitatory potential of a particular choice may reflect not only the motive in question but also previous reinforcement—other motives acting simultaneously—and many other variables in Hull's or anyone's system. To illustrate the problem at the human level: if a person works hard (performs a connected sequence of achievement-related acts), it might be taken to indicate that he had a strong achievement motive except it might also mean that he has a *habit* of working hard (reinforced, for example, by extraneous rewards, such as earning money) or that he has a strong desire to marry a certain girl who insists on a hard-working husband. Brown and Farber (49) have made a similar point in arguing that behavior is so complexly determined it would be difficult to pick out any descriptive characteristic of it as uniquely signifying the presence and strength of a motive.

Nevertheless, further attempts to do so have been made. For example, Frenkel-Brunswik (144) has argued for the importance of "alternative manifestations" as an index of the presence of motivation. She found that while rated exuberance and rated irritability both correlated positively with rated need for aggression, these outward behavioral signs actually correlated negatively with each other. The explanation would appear to be that the same person was unlikely to be both exuberant and irritable, though each of these characteristics was taken to be a sign of *n* Aggression. As Wittenborn (438) points out, eating large amounts of chicken or of steak might signify the presence of a strong hunger drive, and yet they might not be correlated responses across persons. That is, one individual might satisfy his drive one way, and another in another way. If one were dealing with ordinary habits, one would expect some generalization of response tendencies to edible stimuli (chicken and steak); if one finds a low correlation between two such responses and a similar pattern of correlations of each with other responses, one might be justified in deciding that a motive rather than a habit is involved. Wittenborn demonstrates how this would mean operationally (1) a low or even negative correlation between responses a and b and (2) a high correlation between the columns of correlations of a and b with other variables. A habit might then alternatively be defined as requiring a *high* correlation between a and b. It is interesting to note that this relatively recent approach to inferring the presence of a motive is similiar to one proposed by Murray some time ago (314) to differentiate his motive concept from Allport's trait concept (6). He felt that the need construct was necessary to account for the inconsistencies (alternative manifestations?) in behavior whereas the trait concept was needed to account for the obvious consistencies of behavior.

One final attempt to find response characteristics uniquely indicating the presence of a motive may be mentioned. It starts with the observation that so far as animals are concerned there are some "unique signs" of the presence of a motive in the patterns of consummatory behavior (272, Ch. 2). Eating may be taken as evidence for the presence of hunger, though not always (294); biting in dogs and rats, for aggressive tendencies; purring in cats, for pleasure. It would certainly be useful if there were such unique signs in humans for the presence of various social motives. The research reported in this book looked for such signs in fantasy or more generally in the associative processes. If, for example, one could demonstrate that certain associations (ideas, images) appeared more frequently *if and only if* the subject was under the influence of heightened achievement motivation, then one might safely infer that the presence of those associations signified the presence of the achievement motive. One of the reasons for search for such signs in fantasy, rather than, say, among autonomic responses, was the expectation that the possibility of identifying unique and differentiable signs for different motives was greater considering the variety and subtleties of human verbal behavior. Exactly the same reasoning has led other investigators to search for unique signs of the presence of a motive in verbal questionnaires—for example, the Taylor Scale of Manifest Anxiety (402), Murray's questionnaires for assessing human needs (314).

CRITERION C

The measure of a motive should give the same reading for an individual or a group under the same or nearly the same conditions. In short, it should be reliable. Reliability refers in the first place to the ability of two observers to come up with the same reading on the same occasion (recording reliability) and in the second place to a high agreement of scores obtained on one occasion with those obtained on another similar occasion (test-retest reliability). As far as the first requirement is concerned, it is of such fundamental importance in science that it would hardly be worth mentioning except that there are still large numbers of professional persons interested in motivation (largely psychiatrists and psychoanalysts untrained in scientific method) who neglect it altogether. That is, the signs, symptoms, or whatnot that they use to infer the presence or strength of a motive are often not reported or recorded well enough for measures of interobserver agreement even to be computed. To this extent their science remains a private affair, agreement on the principles of which must depend on personal predilection and the persuasive powers of the observer, rather than on operations public for all to see and check.

So far as the stability of measures of motivation from one occasion to another is concerned, some special problems arise which have often been overlooked. One of the most crucial has to do with the way in which subjects are obtained for observation. If one is interested in conditioning the eyelid response, or mapping retinal color zones, or studying proactive interference, it does not apparently matter much whether the subject is a volunteer or a patient, is paid for his services or is drafted, or whether he is poor or rich, male or female, old or young, Catholic or Protestant. Yet it has been demonstrated that all of these variables influencing motivational measures are important sources of variance. Consequently, a research design must consider very carefully just what subjects ought to be used as a sample. For example, Burdick (58) reports the n Achievement score of volunteers is higher than for nonvolunteering subjects, Davids (88) that there are important differences in motivational measures depending on whether the subjects were volunteers for "scientific research" or "for a competition for a desirable paid position," Lazarus (223) that high school students who volunteered to be subjects in response to a notice posted on the bulletin board had higher average n Achievement scores than a group of college student volunteers, while other research has amply demonstrated that for *total* samples of high school and college students the average n

Achievement score is significantly lower among high school students.[2] Several studies have shown important sex differences in motivational variables (129, 237, 272), and age differences are perhaps best illustrated by the fact that exactly the same experiment repeated on high school and college students give *opposite* results (272, Ch. 9). In short, the problem of reliability of group results in motivation depends in large part on the care which is taken to test the same kind of subjects obtained in the same way under the same kind of conditions.

The same kind of considerations apply to test-retest reliability of the score of an individual: his motives, his views of the test and the administrator must be the same on the second occasion as they were on the first. Even to state the requirement so explicitly shows how difficult it may be to fulfill in practice. With characteristics under voluntary control, like adding $2 + 2$, it may be possible to ask the subject again and again, and get the same response because the same conditions can be voluntarily reinstated by the subject. With characteristics not under voluntary control, like motivation, it may be difficult to reinstate a former set of conditions. One test may "spoil" the subject for a retest. If a child, for example, has just kicked another child on the playground, and the psychologist goes up to him and asks him to do it again, to make sure that it was not an "accidental" expression of aggression, he would not be likely to give the same response, partly because the first expression of the motive changed the motivational situation, and partly because asking him to do it again changes the motivational situation.

That some such alteration in conditions on successive projective tests of motive strength occurs has been demonstrated by Atkinson (22), who found evidence for a cyclical variation in the level of a given motive from story to story within a test, and by Birney (43), who, in an unpublished study of achievement imagery in successive stories to the same picture, also has obtained an alternation effect. The tables presented by Rogers and Dymond (347, pp. 132-134) for readings on a number of TAT variables on successive administrations also show a cyclical effect. What is high on Test 1 for the group tends to be lower on Test 2 (20 out of 21 scales) and higher again on Test 3 (16 out of 21 scales). Theoretically, the subjects

---

[2] Unpublished results obtained in Ricciuti (340) and by McClelland show, for example, that large random samples of male college freshmen have scored higher on 14 out of 17 pictures administered under similar conditions to large random samples of male juniors in high school, a result which is consistent with Rosen's finding (Ch. 35) that *n* Achievement is positively associated with social class.

could maintain their rank order on successive tests and a high test-retest reliability be obtained, but since high test-retest reliabilities are not usual—at least for associative, involuntary measures of motivation (Ch. 45, 237)—a more likely hypothesis is that making a certain associative response tends to introduce resistance to giving it again, as demonstrated by Telford (406) years ago. So while a subject who has just told an achievement-related story may, if he has a strong achievement motive, be predisposed to tell another, this predisposition is counteracted to some extent by associative refractory phase, thus reducing internal consistency and test-retest reliability.

The practical effect of this is that, so far as projective measures of motivation are concerned, it would not appear wise to insist on high test-retest reliability before using such measures because it is so hard to replicate testing conditions—to put the subject back in the condition he was in before he made the first response. Instead, one can rely on other criteria, such as validity, for inferring stability of motivational dispositions indirectly.

CRITERION D

The measure of a motive should have relational fertility. It should correlate with many other variables or account for much of the variance in human behavior. In some sense this is the ultimate criterion of whether a measure survives in the competition for attention in the market place of scientific variables since the purpose of science is to account for as much of what takes place with as few variables and assumptions as possible. "Relational fertility" is not quite the same thing as validity, as that term is commonly understood, although validity, properly speaking, is *an instance* of relational fertility. If one thinks of validity as meaning something measures "what it is supposed to measure," it is incorrect to make such a decision in terms of the correlation with some one other measure which is somehow more apt to be a "true" measure than the one you are "validating," but it is correct to assess the validity of the measure in terms of the *number and extent* of its connections to other theoretically-related variables, *among which may be* the "truer" measure (see 266). Properly speaking, it is "the extent or richness of the network of associations within which a construct occurs" (85) that determines its validity, not that it happens to correlate with something which may be regarded as a "truer" measure. For example, the thematic apperceptive measure of *n* Achievement proposed in subsequent chapters was found to be uncorrelated with a certain type of clinical estimate of *n* Achievement strength (272). As a shorthand statement, one might say that the new measure had low "validity," not because clinical ratings are in some ultimate sense a "truer" measure, but because they have an established network of empirical associations and the new test does not. However, further research demonstrated that the new test of *n* Achievement was *more valid* (had more relational fertility) than clinical estimates of *n* Achievement because it was empirically related to more variables in theoretically meaningful ways.

Two further aspects of relational fertility are worth special mention. At its crudest level it refers to the network of empirical relationships of a measure, but obviously "crude empiricism" is not enough. The relationships should be "theoretically meaningful"— that is, *ultimately* the construct must be tied into a general system of behavior theory in some logically consistent way, and the various empirical relationships must make sense in terms of such a theory. However, there is room for disagreement as to how soon this criterion has to be met. In terms of the variables in Hull's learning theory, for example, the characteristics of a drive are already spelled out and it only remains to find a measure which has those characteristics. The approach recommended here is to put off such ultimate theoretical decisions until one has accumulated a sufficient body of empirical knowledge about human motivation to make the decisions informed.

Another aspect of relational fertility which seems worth special mention is the extent to which the relationships are known which account for the way the measure changes in the developmental history of the individual. Under the first criterion, we have stressed that the measure should vary as the motive varies here and now: if it does, we have confidence it is reflecting the motive and not something else. An analogous confidence arises if we can actually discover the ways in which the motive can be made to vary in strength among individuals with different developmental histories. The confidence comes from the fact that we know the antecedents which influence the motive measure, and to this extent we have it "under control" and can "synthesize it," so to speak. Such knowledge is part of the relational fertility of a construct, but a very special part in that it enables us to understand the "make-up" of the motive better and to check our ideas about its "make-up" by predicting what antecedents would lead to variations in its strength. To the extent that we can find factors in parental attitudes or other background characteristics which are significantly associated with *n* Achievement scores (272, Ch. 9), manifest anxiety scores, or whatnot, we gain important knowledge as to what produces the motive in question and therefore increased confidence that our measure is "really" measuring it.

Armed now with some general criteria of evaluating methods of measuring motivation, it is time to check the methods that have been used against the criteria.

SELF-RATINGS BY THE SUBJECT

The oldest and simplest method of measuring human motivation is simply to ask the subject what his motives are, either directly or indirectly. In the *direct* method the subject either fills out a rating scale as to how strong his n Achievement is (for example) or indicates the degree of his acceptance of such statements as "I enjoy relaxation wholeheartedly only when it follows the successful completion of a substantial piece of work" (96, 314). In the *indirect* method the subject is typically asked to express his like or dislike for a variety of activities, objects, or situations; inferences are then drawn—either *a priori,* as in the Allport-Vernon *Study of Values,* or by factor analysis (161)—about his motives from the pattern of likes and dislikes. In addition to Murray's early questionnaires (314) for measuring various motives, several recent inventories have been couched in more directly motivational terms. For example, Edwards (112) has a Personal Preference Scale which derives a score for various personality needs by forcing the subject to make a choice between two statements expressing alternative needs. Cohen *et al.* (80) have used a similar approach to derive a measure of the need for cognition. A group working with Farber at Iowa has developed a picture interpretation test in which the subjects rank four alternative interpretations of each of ten TAT cards (192). Consistent preferences for a certain kind of interpretation yield measures of achievement imagery, insecurity, blandness, and hostility, characteristics which have sometimes been interpreted as motives and sometimes as habits. By far the most widely used self-descriptive inventory sometimes thought to measure human motivation is the Taylor Manifest Anxiety Scale (cf. 68, 126, 264, 402). Its popularity probably results in part from the fact that anxiety is the human motive most easily understood by learning theorists and in part from the fact that it is easy to administer and score.

How do such measures satisfy the criteria we have set up? Many of these measures do have high reliability, the criterion they satisfy best. To some extent this may reflect the fact that they are conscious reports under voluntary control of inner states, and the subject ordinarily tries to give answers like the ones he gave last time, provided the conditions of test administration are the same. One might argue on theoretical grounds that since motives (as opposed to "sets") represent unconscious states not under voluntary control, such stable measures could not be measuring motivation, but the fact remains that so far as this criterion is concerned, the measures are satisfactory: they are reliable.

The evidence on relational fertility (Criterion D) is mixed, as one would expect from lumping so many measures under one heading. The relationships of Murray's original questionnaire measures of needs were not extensive (314), and he was discouraged with them. Furthermore, recent reviews of replications of research on the Taylor Manifest Anxiety Scale (129, 264) report an inability to get stable, meaningful patterns of results despite large-scale attempts to use it. Sometimes it is related to faster reaction time, for example, and sometimes not (129). Some of the difficulties in these studies may arise from insufficient attention to the problem of what subjects were used and what motives they had for serving, since the investigators often do not even bother to control or consider the relevance of these variables, despite the fact that, for instance, differences between the sexes (129) and between volunteers and "draftees" (23) regularly show up in motivation research. On the other hand, standardized preference scales like the Strong Vocational Interest Blank (396) and the Allport-Vernon *Study of Values* (10, 108) have been related significantly to a number of different variables; the Iowa Picture Association Test has shown some promising relationships to performance under a variety of conditions (435); and deCharms *et al.* (96) have suggested that a self-descriptive measure of motivation (which they label *v* Achievement for "valuing" achievement) may have important correlates which are different from those which a fantasy measure of the achievement motive has.

So far as the other aspects of its relational fertility criterion are concerned—for example, theory and developmental history—the questionnaire measures of motivation have been most explicitly discussed theoretically by the Iowa group working with the Taylor Anxiety Scale. They have argued (126) that if the A-score is a measure of drive in Hull's sense, it should facilitate responses like reaction time, lead to increased responsiveness to generalization stimuli, etc. Other users of questionnaire measures of motives or values have generally been unconcerned with the theoretical status of what they are measuring, and neither group has apparently done any substantial work on developmental variations of such self-descriptive measures in an attempt to discover how one happens to get a high or low score on them. There are exceptions of course (Dukes, 108) but, by and large, investigators have simply not worried much about tracing the developmental origins of, for example, a high "Aesthetic" score on the Allport-Vernon Scale of Values.

It is with respect to the first two criteria that self-descriptive measures of motivation are weakest. It is difficult to find studies in the literature which have attempted to show that such measures vary with experimental changes in the strength of the motive they purport to measure. For example, how do ratings of hunger or n Achievement increase (or change) as either of these motives is experimentally induced? Do individuals score higher on any of the various questionnaire measures of anxiety as experimentally-induced anxiety increases? It has been demonstrated that "sets" will readily influence results on such questionnaires. For example, Strong showed that individuals trying to score high on the engineer scale of his Blank could easily do so (396). On the other hand, induced motives, not under conscious control, do not appear to have as marked an effect on self-descriptive and preference measures (see 102, though, for an instance in which induced frustration *does* have an effect on descriptions of feelings toward others).

The evidence for such a conclusion comes largely from studies showing how difficult it is to influence performance under voluntary control, especially if it is "reality-oriented," by induced motivational states. For example, the resistance of voluntary performance to deterioration under extreme fatigue or frustration is well-known (60). Furthermore, the research on the effects of motives on perception has clearly demonstrated that the less ambiguous the stimulus, the harder it is to find any effects of motivation (332, 333). For example, in unpublished research in our laboratory we found that induced achievement motivation did not increase (a) the choice of achievement alternatives to complete stories about pictures (as in the Iowa Picture Interpretation Test) or (b) the frequency of achievement completions of skeleton words like STRI_E (which could be "strive" or "strike"). Even in a less reality-oriented task like the Rorschach, Cox and Sarason (84) have been unable to demonstrate that induced threat increased the frequency of Rorschach signs of anxiety. Apparently the task has to involve a minimum of reality determinants, either in the stimuli or in the instructions as in fantasy, for the effects of induced motivation to be marked. Yet this is precisely the requirement that self-descriptive or preference measures of motivation ordinarily do not meet.

Further evidence on this point comes indirectly from studies showing that a fantasy measure of a given motive (e.g., n Achievement) which is easily influenced by induced states is not correlated with self-descriptive or preference measures of the same motive (96, 272). The logic is by no means foolproof: induced states *might* have two effects on different behavior systems, but to the extent that the measures from the different systems are uncorrelated, such an eventuality would appear unlikely. And there is a lot of evidence on this point, gathered because the content analysis method of measuring motivation described in subsequent chapters is so laborious that it was obviously to everyone's advantage to try to find a simple set of preferences or self-descriptions which could serve as a machine-scored substitute for content analysis. All the evidence reviewed at the end of this chapter points to low or insignificant relationships between fantasy measures of motivation and measures based on choice or self-description.

The reason for the lack of correlation between the two kinds of measures may lie in the failure of the choice measure to satisfy the remaining criterion of a good instrument—namely, its capacity to reflect differences in motivation *and only* motivation (Criterion B). If, for the sake of the argument, one assumes for the moment that the fantasy measure of motivation is "purer," then the lack of correlation could be explained if it can be shown that the choice or self-descriptive measures are influenced by extraneous factors. And they obviously are. By definition they involve choice, and choice can easily be influenced by sets and intentions (380). Subjects rate themselves or answer questions about themselves differently, depending on what they think the purpose of the experiment to be, as the ability to fake high scores in the Strong Blank (396) or any rating scale demonstrates. The desire to appear in a good light, which distorts such self-description of motives (82), can be corrected to some extent by forcing the subject to choose between two equally desirable or undesirable alternatives, as in the Edwards Personal Preference Scale (112), but even here one has no assurance that the ultimate choice is dictated by motives only and not by, say, the conscious (and often inaccurate) self-picture. Such an assurance can be had, of course, as soon as the scores on such a test begin to relate to behavior as a measure of motivation should. The point here is that one would not predict such relationships because the measure is likely to reflect the way the subject has learned to view himself or reality, a perceptual picture which has many determinants beside the motive supposedly being measured. The same point has been made about the Taylor Manifest Anxiety Scale, both by its proponents and by its opponents: it reflects a good many other things than the anxiety drive it presumably measures (116, 264).

Another nonmotivational variable which influences many preference measures is the acquiescence factor—the tendency to "go along" with any statement even if it contradicts one formerly agreed to (34). It may be so influential that even to counterbalance it would produce the meaningless result of the subject saying at one moment that he is hard working and the next that he is pretty lazy.

On balance, self-descriptive or choice measures of motivation do not appear very promising. They fail to measure up to the criteria of a good measure at a number of points. But perhaps the argument from history is the most persuasive of all: if they had been good measures of motivation, why has the psychology of motivation been so slow in developing as compared, for instance, with the psychology of learning, especially when such measures have been in use for a long time? Why has a whole psychoanalytic view of unconscious motivation developed entirely independently of such measures if they were really adequate?

RATINGS OF MOTIVATION BY OUTSIDE OBSERVERS

If it is unsafe to ask a subject to report on his motives either directly or indirectly because he may dissemble or not know much about them, it is possible to turn to someone else who knows him well and who is better qualified to judge than he. Nearly all the key figures in the development of the study of motivation from Freud to Murray (314) and Frenkel-Brunswik (144) have employed this method, particularly for getting at unconscious motives that the subject cannot tell us about. As a method it has contributed greatly to our current understanding of motivation, but it has such serious drawbacks that it probably should not be used except in exploratory studies where no other method can be employed. It has what Cronbach and Meehl (85) so aptly call "bootstraps value" in that it helps the investigator discover what variables are worth studying more precisely. It helps establish the "lay of the land." But since some psychologists, perhaps particularly those who have been influenced by psychiatry, have seemed to feel that it is the *best* method of measuring human motivation—indeed, the final criterion against which all other measures must ultimately be evaluated—it is worth stating some of its methodological weaknesses in detail without meaning to disparage its use altogether for exploratory studies.

To begin with the most obvious weakness, the method of clinical assessment has been seldom, if ever, used to measure the effects of induced motivational states (Criterion A). A typical experiment might involve calibrating judges' ratings of how anxious subjects were against differences in experimentally-induced anxiety. A more common procedure is to compare ratings or estimates of anxiety in two contrasting groups, assumed to differ in anxiety (e.g., those who go to a psychiatrist for help vs. those who do not). The difficulty with such an approach is standard with this method: the behavioral effects judged to be associated with anxiety may in fact be due to other differences in the two groups. Also the argument may become circular: the two contrasting groups may be selected partly on the basis of judgments of the key factor (anxiety) with which one is then going to validate the same kind of judgments.

The unreliability (Criterion C) of over-all assessments of motive strength is sometimes considered an objection to their use, and of course if two judges cannot agree, there is no basis for deriving any kind of measure at all from the procedure. It was at least an advance when psychologists insisted that clinical judgments such as psychoanalysts make about motivation be subjected to the simple test of observer agreement. But the fact is that such agreement *can* become fairly high after sufficient training (Ch. 15, 272), and the objection misses the main point.

The real problem with clinical assessment is that, even though the judgments are reliable, no method is available for determining to what extent they reflect the motive in question—*and only* that motive (Criterion B). In fact, one of the major disadvantages of the method, scientifically speaking, is precisely the advantage it is supposed to have over other methods—namely, the property of being able to synthesize in a single measure conflicting results which may come from a variety of sources. To be specific, suppose a person rates himself high on the "drive to succeed," shows little evidence of achievement motivation on the TAT, does somewhat less well in his school work than would be expected from his IQ, and works hard on the school newspaper but not outside school to earn the extra money his family obviously needs. A judge could be asked to combine these or other such behavioral clues into an over-all rating of the subject's achievement drive. At the least the judge should be able to rank the subject with respect to other subjects on whom he has similar information. A clinician rating motives on the basis of data supplied by the subject in a series of interviews is performing essentially the same synthetic act of judgment.

The objection to such a procedure is that it involves a synthesis in which it is not known just what factors the judge used in arriving at his final estimate. The fact that another judge can follow the same procedure and come out with the same result is no guarantee that either one of them is assessing the motive in question *and only* that motive. An analogy from physics may be helpful. It might be argued that the best instrument for measuring how hot it is outside today is a human judge because he can synthesize temperature and humidity into an over-all temperature estimate that an ordinary thermometer cannot make (cf. 266). Such a method of measurement would have its uses for certain practical purposes, such as predicting how many people would faint if exposed to such weather conditions, but it would scarcely be adequate as a measure of either temperature or humidity. The human temperature sense has Cronbach and Meehl's "bootstraps value" (85) in developing more precise measures of temperature (e.g., the thermometer), but few people would argue, once the thermometer has been set up with its network of relations to other variables, that it should continue to be checked and corrected against subjective estimates of temperature. Clinical assessments of motive strength are like subjective estimates of temperature: they may combine various factors into a single measure so that it is impossible to tease out the exact degree to which they reflect a single variable—that is, the motive they are supposedly assessing.

Clinical estimates of motive strength may be a product of irrelevant factors not only in the subject but also in the judge because they are notoriously a function of the judge's own motives and own special orientations. Some data from the psychotherapy research project at the Menninger Clinic (242) provide as good an example as any of the influence of the judge's background on the estimates he makes. They show that judges can make reasonably reliable rankings (r above .87 for 9 out of 11 instances) on a number of variables, but that the rankings are not independent. For example, three variables were intercorrelated as follows:

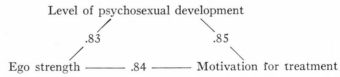

Level of psychosexual development

.83   .85

Ego strength ——— .84 ——— Motivation for treatment

What is the ranking "motivation for treatment" measuring? It is impossible to say. One possibility is that such motivation is in fact a function of the subject's level of psychosexual development; another is that the judge was unable to discriminate between these two factors so that his ranking was "contaminated" by several variables; still another—and the one of primary concern here—is that according to the judge's training and belief as a good psychiatrist, motivation for treatment *must be* a function of level of psychosexual development. In terms of contemporary psychoanalytic theory it would simply be difficult to conceive of a person with a low level of psychosexual maturity or ego strength who had a high motivation for treatment. The relationship between the variables is to some extent in the judge's head before he makes the rankings so that the "discovered" correlation cannot be taken to mean anything certain about the empirical relationship between the variables in the patients. So the obtained measure of the subject's motivation for treatment cannot unambiguously be taken to mean anything about his motivation, since it may be determined almost wholly by the judge's opinion of the level of the patient's psychosexual maturity or ego strength. On the other hand, the judge's estimate *may* be quite correct, the relationship *may* be as obtained, etc.; the tragedy of the situation is that *it is impossible to determine the true state of affairs so long as complex judgments of human motives are used as methods of measurement.*

For the fact of the matter is that the judge must perceive what is a particularly ambiguous stimulus—namely, the supposed motives the subject has for doing what he does and thinking what he thinks. In making a judgment, the observer's own training, his own motives, may influence it as much as or more than the objective stimulus material. Two types of solutions to this problem have been suggested, neither of them completely satisfactory. The first is simply to use more than one judge so that any particular bias may be corrected by the random biases of a group of judges (Murray, 314). Two heads should be better than one, but of course two heads may also simply compound an error. Even high agreement among several judges may mean only that their projective systems (or cultural values) are similarly organized because they come from similar backgrounds or have had similar training, as in the example from the Menninger Clinic study.

The other way of removing or correcting some of the bias of judges is to use only judges who have been well trained and can claim some special degree of objectivity, usually on the grounds that they have been personally psychoanalyzed. While a study by Sears (369) does demonstrate that awareness of one's characteristics tends to shift one's bias in judging others, there is very little reason to suppose that the judge thereby becomes somehow neutral or "decultured." In fact, the psychiatrists making the judgments in the Menninger study may have confounded the variables all the more because of their psychoanalytic training in which a personal analysis is a key part in organizing their thinking about "what goes with what." More specific, concrete evidence on this point has recently been supplied by Cutler (86), who has shown that therapists, even after an analysis, continue to misperceive the behavior of their patients primarily in those areas where they themselves show unconscious conflicts.

Do estimates of motive strength in others satisfy the criterion of relational fertility? They often do if they are correlated with other subjective judgments of further variables, as in the example given from the Menninger Clinic study, because both sets of judgments may be complexly determined by the same factors. Whether subjective estimates correlate extensively with objective measures of other variables is another question harder to answer in terms of the data. Murray (314) reports many such correlations, but they are difficult to replicate exactly because the original judgments were made in such a complex manner. For the same reason it is hard to work out a systematic theory from the relationships: too many variables are confounded.

To summarize, ratings of human motivation by judges are at best very imperfect methods of measurement which should be used only in the "bootstraps" stage of research for their suggestive value. On no account should they be used as criteria against which other measures are finally "validated." Cronbach and Meehl have recently made the same point (85, p. 285) in another connection.

BEHAVIORAL MEASURES OF MOTIVATION

Another approach to the problem of measuring human motivation is to try to detect its presence from something a person does—from some unique set of response characteristics. Relevant here are all the studies which have demonstrated the effect of a motive state on some kind of behavior—e.g., physiological response systems, performance, learning, perception, memory, association—because if these effects are unique enough, they can be used to infer the presence of the motive. If one were to start with such a finding—with the effects of threat, for example, on autonomic responses—then the first criterion of a good measure of motivation would already have been met: it would have been demonstrated that the measure varies with a known variation in the motive.

Investigators working in this area, however, have not been much interested in using their findings to assess individual differences in motive strength. So there is not a great deal of data to provide answers as to whether the other criteria are satisfied. For example, much work has been done on the effect of drives like anxiety on learning (127), of drives like hunger or the need for money on perception (270, 329, 332). But neither speed of learning nor apparent size has been seriously proposed as a measure of individual differences in the strength of particular motives. Perhaps the chief reason is that such behavioral effects do not appear to be unique enough to the motive in question. Fear may speed up learning or performance but so do many other variables—other drives, past reinforcements, responses yielding positive transfer. What chance is there then that rate of learning could be used as a "pure" measure of the strength of fear in a person? The same point may be made to those who want to consider performance the final criterion against which to validate a measure of motivation. For example, McArthur (Ch. 38) has proposed that the measure of n Achievement derived from fantasy be refined by eliminating those characteristics which do not predict performance in college. But good performance in college almost certainly reflects not only the strength of the achievement motive but other motives, values, social pressures, and situational effects as well. So to tailor the motive measure to this criterion would simply make it more "impure" than ever.

Similarly, estimates of coin size either from memory or under certain viewing conditions might be considered a measure of the individual's need for money, but apparently this has never been done, perhaps because "apparent size" is also determined by too many other nonmotivational variables. So it is difficult to say whether such a measure is reliable, reflects *only* or *largely* the "money motive," and has relational fertility. Certainly it would seem to be worth the effort to explore a little more systematically a number of such response systems to discover whether one or more of them could satisfy the criteria of a good measure of motivation.

The only response system which has been extensively explored to date for unique motivational effects is *organized fantasy* in stories, and it is this exploration which is presented in subsequent chapters. Perhaps the chief reason why it has been studied before other response systems is because it capitalizes on the generalization, repeatedly confirmed in studies of the effects of motivation on behavior, that the more ambiguous the situation, the greater the effect of motivation. What is more, it makes use of the kind of ambiguity which is essential—namely, the ambiguity as to what responses the subject is to make, an ambiguity which Postman and Crutchfield (332) confuse with conflict between two well-defined responses of equal probability. The distinction is important for motivational research because *choice* of one of two equally probable responses to a stimulus does not seem to reflect the effects of motivation very sensitively,[3] whereas *production* of new responses in an unstructured situation does (270, 272).

To summarize the results of subsequent chapters as to how well a fantasy measure of motivation has succeeded is premature and unnecessary. Instead, it will suffice to make two very general points as to its success: (a) Subsequent chapters present ample evidence that fantasy is easily influenced by induced motivational states and that motive measures based on such alterations in fantasy satisfy the criterion of relational fertility—such measures are responsible for the creation of a larger body of empirically-based knowledge about human motivation than any other method. It has been the aim of this chapter to argue that this superiority is not accidental, that measuring motivation in fantasy has certain intrinsic methodological advantages over self-descriptions or judgments by others, both of which

---

[3] See the failure to find any effects of induced achievement motivation on word completions (unpublished study) already referred to.

as methods of measurement present such serious difficulties, if our analysis has been correct, that it is hard to see how they could lead to the accumulation of a systematic body of knowledge about motivation. (b) What is not perhaps sufficiently clear either in subsequent chapters or previous discussion is that fantasy also has its weaknesses as a method of measurement, weaknesses directly related to our other two criteria of a good measure—uniqueness and reliability. To anticipate a little, the *sensitivity* of fantasy is both its greatest strength and its greatest weakness: strength because it picks up slight motivational variations, weakness because it picks up variations in other factors as well, making it difficult to get stable and replicable results. What can be said about its reliability and the uniqueness with which it reflects motives as opposed to other factors?

To dispose of the easiest question first, What is the evidence that coding of story content can be done with high interobserver agreement and low projection by the judges? In the coding systems presented in this book an attempt is made to solve both problems by "unitizing" what is to be scored and getting an over-all score by summing the frequency of the coded units rather than by making a final synthetic judgment. Ideally the judge simply "points to" an identifiable phrase and classifies it according to a scoring definition as belonging in a category, just as he might classify a movement of a rat as a "right turn" or a certain visual image under the microscope as a "red blood corpuscle." There is little room for projection because the judge is asked for a classificatory response, not a complex judgment based on a number of cues. With proper training the method yields interscorer agreement coefficients of .90 or better for total scores (Ch. 15, 22, 272). Frequently the interscorer reliabilities reported are higher within the group which developed the scoring system than for other investigators who try to learn the system from published scoring manuals. For example, both Hedlund at Iowa (173) and Lindzey and Heinemann (237) at Harvard report considerably lower scoring reliabilities for the n Achievement score ($r = .64$ to $.85$) than those reported by people trained personally in the McClelland-Atkinson group ($r = .85$ to $.98$). The explanation appears to lie in the fact that in the past the published scoring manual simply did not convey all the information needed to become a reliable scorer. Certainly it does not lie in the fact that scoring reliability is generally low in these other groups as Lindzey and Heinemann report much higher reliabilities for some of their own variables. The comparative difficulty in communicating coding systems from one laboratory to another is a practical rather than a theoretical handicap, holding back the general use of this method of measuring motivation. It can be overcome by personal contacts and better scoring manuals of pretested practice materials of the sort included in the Appendix of this book for n Achievement, n Affiliation, and n Power.

Other questions having to do with stability of the fantasy measures of motivation and replicability of results ultimately boil down to problems of uniqueness. Or, to put the question the other way: What variables *other than the motive to be assessed* may influence the fantasy measure of it? One such variable has already been discussed —namely, associative refractory phase: once a given associative response has been made, there is less likelihood that it will appear again immediately (406). This fact automatically sets some limits on fantasy as a reliable measure of motive strength. At least sufficient time and opportunity for alternative responses must be allowed to reduce the inhibition against repeating a fantasy response. An allied variable has also been discussed: the lack of voluntary control over the response system. That is, since the subject does not know how different responses are scored, he is not in a position to re-establish a set which will produce the same result from occasion to occasion. Hence it is up to the experimenter to try to re-establish exactly the same set—an intrinsically more difficult thing to do.

Aside from these variables there are those relating (a) to the type of cue used to elicit the fantasy, (b) to the social context in which the testing is done, and (c) to the type of fantasy response elicited from the subject. Changes in any of these factors affect the frequency and functional significance of the type of imagery theoretically supposed to reflect uniquely a given motive. If one knows what the effects of other factors are, then it is possible to control for them and get comparable results either from time to time on the same subject or from one group of subjects to another for the same experiment. If one does not control for such effects, results may be unstable and perhaps not due to motivational factors in individuals at all, but to other factors which can also produce the fantasy response characteristic of the motive.

What effects has the cue used to elicit fantasy? This question involves comparisons among picture cues and between picture cues and other types of cues. It is known that not all picture cues are equivalent in the sense of producing achievement imagery which increases with induced achievement motivation (341) and which correlates with that produced by other pictures (173, 272) or with such outside variables as performance in school (340). Nevertheless, on balance, as Reitman and Atkinson (Ch. 46) conclude, there is a wide area of equivalence, and the problem seems to be the partly empirical, partly theoretical, one of determining why certain pictures and not others yield equivalent measures of a given motive. Two of the variables known to modify picture equivalence are serial position and percentage imagery elicited by the picture. Reitman and Atkinson report that n Achievement score will predict arithmetic performance if based on the first four pictures in a series and not if based on the last four pictures. They also report that it doesn't seem to matter much whether the n Achievement score is based on pictures which yield a high or a low amount of achievement imagery. It predicts performance about equally well in either case. However, there are obviously the two limiting cases in which a picture elicits either near 100% or near 0% achievement imagery from the sample, cases making it impossible to find individual differences in motive score to relate to any other response variable.

The same general equivalence of cues exists when stories to pictures are compared to fantasy elicited in other ways. Verbal cues suggesting a story plot ("a father talking to his son seriously," 272) or asking the subject to explain the motives for someone's behavior (the French Insight Test, 141, 142, 143) yield results which are highly comparable to those obtained through picture cues. On the other hand, if the verbal cue is a portion of a sentence which the subject must complete, the content of his completions is not related to the content of his stories to pictures (237, 272). Perhaps the reality component is larger in the sentence-completion than in the picture-story or "motive-insight" methods. It is possible to elicit stories by musical cues too (see Beardslee and Fogelson, Ch. 9), but a systematic comparison of these stories with those produced to pictures by the same subjects has not been made, although one would not expect the comparison to be close under certain circumstances since some of the music has very specific arousal effects in the sexual sphere, at least for women. Finally, it is possible to work with material for which there have been no external cues at all—namely, with folk tales (274) or with literary documents (39), both of which have yielded results predictable in terms of work with the standard method of suggesting stories with pictures. Although really systematic work in this area has not been completed, the safest practical generalization appears to be that cues will tend to be equivalent so long as they suggest vaguely the content area of the motive being measured but *do not elicit strong or specific associations based on particular cultural or personal past associations*. This is simply another way of stating the general rule that in order for the story content to be more or less uniquely determined by motivational factors, it must not be largely determined by other factors, such as past associations. Since it is conceivable that the pictures used might elicit individual differences in motivation only within the framework of American cultural assumptions, it is worth recording that the same pictures have produced results in Germany, Brazil, Italy, and Japan which are at least initially comparable in many respects to those found in the United States. This is probably because the most successful pictures are those which tap important foci in the general "human condition"—for example, a man at his work, the son in relation to his father or a friend, etc.

The type of associative material obtained will be influenced not only by the cues specifically introduced to elicit it, but also by *contextual cues* present when the test is administered. The most obvious instance of this is the effect of the instructions or tasks given the subjects beforehand on the imagery content of stories written subsequently, for it is in this manner that changes in story content are induced to develop the scoring system. Yet the problem is that individual differences in imagery produced under relaxed or aroused conditions have different correlates (74, 272), although the extent of these differences has not as yet been extensively explored. Even when the test administrator is not particularly trying to arouse the subjects, the conditions under which the testing is done may be sufficiently motivating to produce marked changes in the level of achievement or affiliation imagery for the group as a whole. For example, it is known that the prestige or status of the experimenter can by itself increase the average *n* Achievement score and influence the relationship of such scores to performance (42) and that *n* Achievement scores obtained under group administration do not correlate significantly (r = .12) with those obtained under individual administration (237). Perhaps it was because they used individual administration that Parrish and Rethlingshafer (323) failed to replicate some of the results with *n* Achievement found previously. Group administration gives more anonymity and decreases variability in score due to the nature of the interpersonal relationship established, at least so far as *n* Achievement and "dominance" are concerned, but not for other variables tested by Lindsey and Heinemann like "sex" and "happiness" (237). Even using a female graduate student as administrator of the *n* Achievement test given to about 70 male college freshmen has in one instance markedly and significantly increased the average *n* Achievement score as compared with two other equivalent groups of subjects to which the tests were administered by other, slightly older, male students. Obviously such variables must be carefully controlled or included in the experimental design when one works with fantasy measures of motivation. Again the simplest, most practical rule is to remember that nearly all the results in this book were obtained (a) under group testing conditions (b) with male administrators of about the same age and status as the late adolescent males used as subjects. Departures from this set of contextual cues should either be part of the experimental design or, if not, should be made consistent with the general rule that the situation for the subjects should be a relaxed, "normal" one, a situation not eliciting any *special* associations based on past experience. A case in point was the decision by McClelland, reported in a subsequent chapter, to use a young female adult to test nursery school children. Either a male administrator or the teacher herself might have evoked very special attitudes or associations in the children.

The nature of the fantasy response elicited from the subject may also vary. He may be asked for anything from a series of discrete associations to a connected story sequence. The rule again appears to be that the more specific the response called for—the greater the "reality" determinants—the less its content correlates with more imaginative content. At least, adjective check list associations (96) and sentence completions (237, 272) do not correlate with n Achievement scores in full-blown imaginative stories. Within the story method itself one can vary the number of stories called for at a sitting, the amount of time per story, the mode of producing the story (orally or in writing), or, if in writing, the number of queries on the paper designed to guide the subject in what he writes. It is difficult to demonstrate that any of these variables is really crucial, a circumstance indicating a fairly wide equivalence range with respect to such procedural variables. For example, neither increasing story time allotted from 5 to 8 minutes (237) nor decreasing it from 5 to 2 minutes (340, 341, 342) seemed to make much difference, although the latter change may have been responsible for introducing a significant correlation between n Achievement score and number of words in the story. Meaningful results have been reported with scores based on both oral and written stories (272), though no direct comparison has been made. On the response side must also be included the question as to whether the same story can be scored for more than one motive without introducing artifactual correlations among the scores. Reitman and Atkinson (Ch. 46) find that correlations of n Achievement and n Affiliation based on the same pictures are insignificant and not different in trend from scores based on different pictures, and they recommend using multimotive scoring of the same pictures.

A nonverbal "fantasy response" has recently been discovered by Aronson (Ch. 17) which correlates with the verbal n Achievement score in several cross-validating populations. Some of the early results with it are presented in this volume. Besides being a more practical measure under certain conditions (cross culturally and in working with young children), it supports the generalization already discussed that correlation is more likely to occur among fantasy or expressive responses than between those responses and others more determined by cognitive or perceptual reality factors.

Even this brief review of variables affecting imaginative behavior demonstrates how sensitive it is to influences which one may not be interested in measuring. If one may generalize at this early stage of standardization research at all, the conclusion which seems most justifiable is that variables of a motivational nature (e.g., relationship to the administrator, "volunteer error," changed attitude toward the task as it produces serial position differences, apparent intent of the test) are most influential in causing instability and unreliability, whereas minor procedural variations (e.g., type of cue, time allotted to produce a story) are least influential. As a technique of measuring motivation, fantasy is intrinsically less stable and reliable than other methods like self-ratings. But its advantages in terms of the other criteria are so great that the extra effort needed to attain stable results by controlling the extraneous factors that influence it seems eminently worth while.

COMPARISON OF RESULTS OBTAINED BY DIFFERENT METHODS OF MEASUREMENT

What is the relationship among the three main methods of measuring motivation? Do different methods of measurement yield the same results? The answer seems to be "no," difficult as the data are to interpret in any consistent way. To simplify matters, let us confine our discussion largely to the achievement motive because the most is known about it, although in doing so we must also recognize that the findings for it cannot be completely generalized to other variables like n Dominance (237).

To begin with the relationships among various measures, the n Achievement score based on content analysis of stories (McClelland *et al.*, 272) is *not* related to *direct* self-ratings of achievement drive (237, 272), though it has a very low *positive* correlation with one set of questions about achievement—the so-called v Achievement scale (deCharms *et al.*, 96)—and a nearly significant *negative* correlation with another such set of questions for males (237). Its relationship to two multiple choice forms of the picture-story test developed at Iowa (including the Iowa Picture Interpretation Test) is very low and insignificant (173, 435). Nor are the two multiple choice forms for obtaining an achievement imagery score significantly related to each other (173), though the IPIT achievement score does appear to be significantly related to certain other questionnaire measures of drive such as the Taylor Anxiety Scale and the ITQ (435). The n Achievement score has been found in two separate investigations (237, 272) to be *negatively* related to achievement-related sentence completions for males, but the relationship is positive for females, and different, depending on whether the TAT was administered in a group or individually (237, p. 47). Surely this is confusion confounded! At the very least, it suggests caution in calling different measures by the same name and thinking they measure the same thing.

Much effort has gone into trying to develop a choice-type instrument which would accurately reflect the n Achievement score because such a measure would be so much simpler to use than one based on content analysis. But the results just reviewed are certainly not encouraging, and there are many more such failures to report. For example, the n Achievement score based on fantasy has low, insignificant, or variable relationships not only to multiple-choice alternatives for story completions and self-descriptive achievement sentiments but also to (a) a variety of standard personality test measures (272, p. 274), including all the Strong Vocational Interest Blank scales (263) and the n Achievement score on the Edwards Personal Preference Scale ($r = -.002$, $N = 300$, courtesy R. C. Birney); (b) each of the 400 items on the Strong Vocational Interest Blank on successive cross-validations, though there may be some relationships to groups of items (263); (c) about 50 attitude items on current events answered Agree, Disagree or ? (unpublished study using the attitude toward the Korean War questionnaire developed at Cornell, 397); (d) the rank order assigned by male college students to 10 different characteristics a person might like in a job (e.g., "opportunity to use one's talents," "adventure," "freedom from supervision") despite the fact that many of these characteristics might be supposed on theoretical grounds to tap values associated with n Achievement (also from 397); (e) the choice of which of two out of three pictures, varying in achievement cue value, go together (unpublished study); (f) the choice of certain industrious animals as "totems" or identification figures (e.g., "bee" over "wasp," "ant" over "beetle," "eagle" over "parrot," "beaver" over "dog"—unpublished study); (g) preference for pictures displaying live characteristics appearing more often in doodles (Ch. 17) by subjects with high n Achievement (unpublished study). Some day a consistent relationship of n Achievement score with a choice or interest or self-descriptive measure of motivation may show up, but it has not to date despite some fairly extensive attempts to find it. *The conclusion seems inescapable that if the* n *Achievement score is measuring anything, that same thing is not likely to be measured by any simple set of choice-type items.*

Finally, n Achievement score was not related significantly to composite clinical judgments of n Achievement (272), though this result was probably in part due to the fact that the judges at that time could not be instructed very accurately as to just what it was they were supposed to be looking for. More recently Groesbeck (Ch. 28) has found significant correlations between n Achievement scores and ratings of competence as future clinical psychologists made by staff members. The relationship between motive measures obtained by self-description and by judgments of outside observers tends to be significant (cf. 272, p. 279) because the judge to some extent uses what the subject says about his motives in assigning a rating to him.

Where the various measures of achievement motivation are compared, not with each other, but with respect to their relationship to other variables, the picture is a little different. Though Hedlund's multiple choice test of achievement imagery did not correlate with anagrams output (173) the way either his or Clark and McClelland's n Achievement scores had (74), the achievement imagery score (AI) from the Iowa Picture Interpretations Test has shown significant positive relationships with various performance measures, including verbal learning (192), addition (435), and maze learning (201). It is true that the relationships are not impressively large and are of borderline significance in some cases, but two aspects of these relationships are particularly impressive. One is that, just as with the n Achievement score (28, 141), the positive relationship of AI to performance disappears when special incentives like shock are introduced (Johnston, 201). The other is that Williams (435) reports subjects with high AI gain most in performance under the effects of failure (provided they were working for goals set by themselves), a finding which is quite similar to one reported in *The Achievement Motive* (272, p. 224) where a greater gain is shown for subjects with high n Achievement as the instructions became more ego-involving. All these results point in the opposite direction of those based on intercorrelating the measures. They suggest that AI (based on multiple choice) and n Achievement score (based on fantasy), though uncorrelated, have *some* similar functional relationships to other variables! Two possible explanations suggest themselves: either we are dealing here with a true case of alternative manifestations of the same motive or the low positive relationships between the two measures reflect enough variance in common to account for the results.

While two methods of measurement may yield similar relationships to other variables, it also seems worth while to look for differences in these relationships as deCharms *et al.* (96) have done systematically. They found that while n Achievement scores (based on content analysis of fantasies) were positively related to memory and performance, v Achievement scores (based on the degree to which the person subscribed to achievement sentiments) were not related to these measures but were related to the tendency of subjects to be influenced by the opinions of experts in an ambiguous situation. Such functional *differences* stress the need for using different terminology for describing different methods of measuring motivation to avoid confusion.

SUMMARY

As an introduction to a collection of papers using a particular method of measuring human motivation, an attempt has been made to evaluate the method as compared with other methods in the light of certain general criteria as to how one decides whether a method of measurement is adequate or not. The first criterion—that the measure must be shown to vary with known variations in the motive —led to a consideration of at least five different ways psychologists have had for believing that they were dealing with known variations in human motive strength, the so-called "stimulus" definitions of motivation. The second criterion—that the measure must be shown to reflect the motive uniquely—led to a review of various response systems which might be considered the unique sign of the presence of a motive, the so-called "response" definitions of motivation. The third and fourth criteria were the more traditional criteria of reliability and validity, although each was interpreted as presenting some special problems for motivation research. Reliability in the sense of evoking the same response under identical conditions is particularly difficult to establish for responses signifying the presence of a motive for the simple reason that once having made the response, the person is in a different condition than he was before he made it. A particular danger in this kind of research lies in the fact that stable results may not be obtained in a replication of an experiment because it is not a replication of the motivational conditions of the first experiment: the subjects may have different motives for serving, or a different relationship to the test administrator, etc. Validity in the sense of comparing one response measure against another better one is meaningless for motivation research because there is no "better measure." Instead, validity in this sense is seen as a special case of the broader criterion that the measure must have *relational fertility*. Its worth is judged by the number of other variables to which it relates in meaningful ways both with respect to the general theory of behavior and to the way in which individual differences in the motive can be empirically ascribed to developmental differences in the life histories of individuals.

Three main methods of measuring human motivation have been reviewed in the light of these criteria—asking the subject either directly or indirectly, obtaining an over-all judgment by outside observers, and recording specific behavioral signs of motivation in physiological responses, in performance, in perception, in association, or in expressive movements. Self-descriptive methods are generally reliable, but little evidence exists to demonstrate that they vary with the motive in question and only that motive. In consequence, the relations they show to other variables are difficult to interpret in exclusively motivational terms and exist largely for other measures derived from questionnaires (see 69) where there has been a similar confounding of the determinants of the responses. Judgments by others can also be reliable although they are less likely to be, but they, too, suffer from being multidetermined, in this case not only by a variety of factors in the subject but also in the judge, since he may project his own motives into his estimate if it is a complex one. Both of these methods suffer because the means *par excellence* for demonstrating they are reflecting uniquely a particular motive—namely, the experimental method—has seldom, if ever, been applied to them.

The same is not true of the third method of measuring motivation based on distinctive response patterns in the subject because it takes as its starting point motivationally-induced variations in those response patterns. The system of responses worked with most extensively to date involves some sort of imaginative chain of associations, usually stories suggested by pictures. A number of results of the application of this method are contained in this volume and constitute evidence that it has real promise as far as the criteria of unique variation and of relational fertility are concerned. The criterion of reliability is harder to satisfy because it is difficult to set up two exactly comparable motivational situations: either the subject has changed motivationally or the incentive conditions have. And, since fantasy has been demonstrated to be peculiarly sensitive to motivational influences, it is also sensitive to those changes and tends to give somewhat variable results from time to time on the same subject or on comparable occasions with different subjects unless great care is taken to equate the motivational situation.

Finally, the three methods of measuring human motivation yield essentially uncorrelated results, and it would therefore seem wise for research workers to employ terminology which will communicate immediately which method of measurement they are using. For example, the authors representing the tradition in this book use v Achievement to describe self-ratings of motivation and n Achievement to describe a measure of achievement motivation derived from content analysis of fantasy. The final outcome as to how useful these various methods of measurement are or as to what each one is measuring will of course depend on further research, but it is to be hoped that the vigorous exploration of the value of one such method according to a set of criteria of a good measure will stimulate others to explore other methods in the light of the criteria or at least to propose a better set of criteria.

The Effect of the Experimental Arousal of Motivation on Thematic Apperception

THIS SECTION tells the story of the search for validity in making inferences about motivation from the content of imaginative stories. A decade ago, when systematic study of the effects of motivating states on thematic apperception was begun, the theoretical conception of human motivation seemed only a little less fuzzy than the logic of available methods for assessing it. Hence, in the search for a valid method of measurement it made some sense to start with at least one known quantity, a condition that seemed familiar, manipulable, and conventionally accepted as a motivating state: hunger.

Earlier explorations by Sanford (359, 360) and Levine, Chein, and Murphy (226) had uncovered suggestive evidence of the influence of hunger on imaginal and perceptual processes. And in the initial study of a series entitled "The projective expression of needs," McClelland and Atkinson (270) found a number of clues as to how motivation might influence apperception in an analysis of the effect of different intensities of hunger on perceptual responses when the stimulus determinants had been reduced to a minimum.

We begin with a study of the effects of hunger on thematic apperception. It shows that a simple analysis of the goal-directed action sequence can be applied with high scoring reliability to behavior attributed to the characters of imaginative stories. A counting operation can provide a frequency index of the strength of motivation in the author of the stories. In the study of hunger, the primary task is to develop and clarify categories for content analysis which meaningfully embrace the kinds of changes in imaginative content that actually accompany the arousal of motivation.

In subsequent parallel studies of three important social motives—achievement, affiliation, and power—the problem is threefold. First, a good deal of ingenuity is required to design lifelike experimental situations to arouse these motives. Then the scoring categories developed in the study of hunger have to be adapted and modified to accommodate a change in the content of imaginative response. Finally, the experimenters have to infer from the empirical findings a unifying definition of the aim or goal of the motive being studied.

Clark's investigation of sexual motivation turns the method to a substantive problem which had initially interested Freud and for which he had found analysis of free-associative thought to be the most fruitful method of investigation. Clark's study confronts the problem of conflict of motives. In another paper (72), he has applied the logic of Miller's approach-avoidance conflict model to explain the inhibition of manifest sexual responses in thematic apperception. The further analysis of his results, which is presented here, points the way for systematic investigation of disguised expressions of motives.

The subsequent studies of sexual motivation by Mussen and Scodel and by Beardslee and Fogelson bring the reader up-to-date on progress that has been made in this approach to codifying thematic material for both manifest and latent expressions of a particular motive. Whether or not there are codable *symbolic* expressions of achievement, affiliation, and power motives is an obvious question for future research.

A study of fear turns the method towards the kind of motivation which has been most systematically studied in the animal laboratory and which, it has been suggested by some, may be the master motive which provides the initial impetus for behavior directed towards achievement, affiliation, power, and other social goals. The unique problem in the study of fear is the application of a method of content analysis developed in terms of approach or goal-seeking tendencies to a motivating condition which instigates avoidance. The study by Walker, Atkinson, *et al.* faces, in addition, several difficult methodological problems which arise when a projective technique is employed under adverse field conditions, namely, having soldiers write stories shortly after the explosion of an atomic bomb. Another study of fear, by Scott, which utilizes thematic apperceptive data obtained in a national survey, is presented in Part VI. Together, these two studies strengthen the argument that thematic apperception can be effectively used to investigate motivational problems in large scale studies, in the social field as well as in the laboratory.

The final paper of this section, contributed by Feshbach, raises the question of the functional significance of imaginative or fantasy behavior. His method of content analysis in obtaining indices of the strength of the impulse to aggression, while not the same as that developed in the other studies, is sufficiently similar to provide convincing evidence that anger, too, can be experimentally aroused and measured in thematic apperception. In addition, evidence is presented which suggests that motivation is reduced by thematic apperceptive expression. Perhaps the assessment of any motive through thematic apperception is to be considered an assessment of the strength of a motive in terms of one of the forms of motive-gratifying behavior.

The most significant implication of these studies is that disciplined content analysis of thematic apperceptive stories can be considered a generally valid method to be exploited in the investigation of any kind of motivating condition. While not by any means exhausting the list of the springs of human action, hunger, achievement, affiliation, power, sex, fear, and aggression represent as comprehensive a list of the kinds of motivation studied *by the same method* as can be found anywhere in psychological literature.

CHAPTER 2

The Effect of Different Intensities of the Hunger Drive on Thematic Apperception*

JOHN W. ATKINSON AND DAVID C. McCLELLAND[1]

THE FIRST EXPERIMENT in this series (270) attempted to measure the effects of different intensities of the hunger drive on perception for which the objective determinants had been reduced to a minimum. Its purpose was to seek any principles which might govern the relationship between need intensity and its expression in perception. The results provided clues as to how perceptual material should be interpreted to diagnose the strength of a drive such as hunger.

But most so-called projective methods do not deal with perceptual material unless, like the Rorschach, they are concerned more with the formal than the contentual aspects of phantasy. Therefore, the next step is to see whether the findings with perceptual material apply to a projective method more nearly like those ordinarily employed—the Thematic Apperception Test, for example. Several previous attempts have been made to measure the effect on imaginative productions of specific experimentally induced conditions (36, 81, 345), but none has dealt with the problem very extensively or attempted to control the amount of the variable, the effect of which is to be measured.

In the present experiment the intensity of the hunger drive was controlled as in the previous experiment by depriving the subjects of food for one hour, four hours, and 16 hours. They then wrote out

* Reprinted with minor abridgement by permission of author and publisher from the *Journal of Experimental Psychology,* 1948, **38**, 643-658. Copyright 1948 by the American Psychological Association, Inc.

[1] This project was made possible by a grant from the Office of Naval Research. The authors are grateful for this aid and particularly for the cooperation of Captain C. W. Schilling, formerly director of the Medical Research Laboratory, U. S. Naval Submarine Base, New London, Conn., and his staff.

short stories about pictures drawn mostly from Murray's Thematic Apperception Test (referred to hereafter as the TAT). This design permitted the direct comparison of contentual aspects of the stories told under the influence of three degrees of intensity of the hunger drive.

PROCEDURE

The Ss were drawn from Naval personnel attending the submarine training school at the U. S. Navy Submarine Base at New London, Conn. and were obtained as previously described. Food deprivation was also controlled as before. In fact, some of the Ss used in the previous experiment participated in this experiment after concluding the tests of perception. In all there were 44, 22, and 37 Ss in the one, four, and 16 hour deprivation groups respectively who took the entire test and whose records were analyzed; 30 more Ss had to be discarded because they did not meet the experimental hunger conditions or because their stories were too incomplete to work with. Of the 103 Ss whose stories were analyzed, 22 had to be discarded for most of the results reported in the paper because they did not see two of the pictures.

The pictures used are described in Table I with the code letter used to identify them. They were chosen to suggest all types of situations

TABLE I. DESCRIPTION OF PICTURES, GIVING CODE LETTER AND SOURCE

A. Four 'bums' resting (TAT 9 BM in 1943 edition)
B. 'Beachcomber' (TAT earlier edition, cf. 314, p. 542)
C. 'Father' talking to 'son' (TAT 7 BM)
D. Woman looking into room (TAT 5)
E. Restaurant balcony scene—man and woman looking out window, table in foreground (Meier-Seashore Art Judgment Test picture No. 84)
F. Older man in black hat, younger blond man, piece of raw meat with knife beside it (especially designed for this experiment—three picture elements in color not joined together in a single scene)
G. Man standing under lamp (TAT 20)
I. Men in tavern or coffee shop talking (especially designed for this experiment)

relating to hunger—satiation (A), deprivation (B), invitation to eat (D), place of eating (E), food (F), etc. Slides were made of all these pictures (except F) and were visibly projected under conditions described elsewhere (270). F was projected by reflection. There were two orders of presentation as follows: pictures A B C D E F G I and D A F B E G I (picture C was dropped as it gave no food responses). As stated above, 22 subjects did not see pictures G and I, but their results are included in the analysis of characteristics of various pictures. Most of the Ss saw the pictures in the second order but 13 in the one hour group and 15 in the 16 hour group saw them in the first order.

The procedure is best described from the instructions given the subjects after they had entered the room in groups of 7-15 and taken seats facing the screen.

"Please fill out the information blank on the top of your answer sheet [which asked simply for name, rank, dates of birth and induction].

"This is a test of your creative imagination. Six pictures will be projected on the screen. You will have twenty seconds to look at the picture and then five minutes to write what you think about it. Notice that on each of the six pages on your answer sheet corresponding to the six pictures to be shown, the same four questions are asked. Try to spend about one minute answering each question. I'll help you keep track of the time so that you can answer all four questions for each picture. I'll tell you when to go on to the next question. You'll have time to go back and finish up before the next picture is shown.

"Obviously there are no right or wrong answers, so you may feel free to make up any kind of a story about the picture that you choose. The more vivid and dramatic the better. I would suggest writing as fast but as legibly as you can in order to make your story about the picture as vivid and detailed and imaginative as you can. Remember this is a test of creative imagination. Do not merely describe the picture. Anyone can do that. Make up a story about it. The four questions will guide your thinking so that you may cover all the ground in the time required.

"You may start writing as soon as you like after the picture is projected. The lights will be turned on after twenty seconds. Don't wait more than 15 seconds to start or you won't have time to do a complete job. The four questions are:

1. What is happening? Who are the persons?
2. What has led up to this situation? That is, what has happened in the past?
3. What is being thought? What is wanted? By whom?
4. What will happen? What will be done?

"These questions cover the whole plot of the story pretty well. If you need more room for any question use the back of the paper. Make the stories as interesting as you can. Work as fast as you can—feel free to make up any kind of story at all. Be as imaginative as you are able to be. Does every one understand the directions? No questions will be answered after we once start. Also please do not say anything when the pictures are shown."

Special instructions were necessary to introduce picture F which was made up of three disconnected parts. The following comment was therefore made just before it was shown in the third or sixth position.

"This picture is a little different. There will be a number of disconnected pictures, persons, or objects that you can fit into a story. On the basis of what you see in this next picture, work out a story including what you see and anything else you might want to bring into it. Be imaginative."

In choosing the materials and in following the procedure just outlined every attempt was made to follow previous practices so far as possible in order to eliminate results peculiar to a different technique. For instance, the four questions spaced apart on the record sheets are those ordinarily raised at the beginning of a TAT session (314, p. 532). They were repeated here to remind the Ss of the various aspects of a story which were wanted and to facilitate the scoring of the records.

Scoring the records proved to be the major difficulty in obtaining results, as seems always to be the case with the experimental use of projective methods. There are any number of solutions to the difficulty which have been proposed (77, 313, 364), but there is no standard method of scoring which could be adopted. This is particularly unfortunate because the results obtained by one method of scoring cannot be compared with those from any other method. Since there was no adequate methodological basis for choosing a system, one was finally worked out for use here which was based in part on Murray's need analysis, in part on the customary analysis of a behavior sequence (need, instrumental act, goal response), and in part on results obtained in the first experiment in the series.

More than 50 stories were read and considered before any category of analysis was formulated. The effort was to construct categories which could be identified by the Ss' actual words with a minimum of inference on the part of the judge. The categories finally used follow with a brief description of each:

F I   *Food-related imagery.* Any reference to anything having to do with food or eating. This is the criterion for further analysis. It indicates that food is at least incidental to the story being told. All stories not checked in this category were not analyzed any further.

F th   *Food thema.* Food-getting or food-enjoying activity is the central plot of the story. Someone goes to the store to buy meat for supper. A family is getting ready to eat, etc.

D th   *Food deprivation thema.* Deprivation of food is the central plot of the story. The deprivation story dwells on the threatening situation, the shortage (the black market), the down and out person on the verge of starvation etc.[2] Instrumental acts are aimed at removing the deprivation. In food stories there may be difficulties in getting food but unless they constitute the primary theme or emphasis of the story, they were not scored D th (but were scored D).

O th   *Other themas.* All themas not classified as F or D, i.e. food, were not central to their plot.

N   *Need food.* Someone in the story wants food (as actually stated,

[2] There were scoring difficulties with picture B because many Ss wrote severe deprivation stories for it (shipwreck, airplane crash etc.) but it was hard to decide whether food deprivation was primary. A general rule of thumb was finally established that it would be scored D th if only *one* other need beside food was mentioned (e.g., water or rest). If two or more other needs were mentioned it was scored D but not D th.

not inferred). This category includes most food themes and also all cases where someone wants food; the central thema of the story is about something else. The need must be stated and is not inferred from instrumental food-getting activity.

D   *Food deprivation.* Any shortage, scarcity, blocking by external agent, etc. leading to food deprivation, temporary, or permanent. This includes all Deprivation Thema stories and also all other cases of food deprivation whether food is central to the plot or not.

I, f or d, +, −, or 0. *Instrumental activity* aimed at getting food (I f) or at removing deprivation (I d) which is successful (+), unsuccessful (−) or of unknown outcome (0). Someone in the story must do something either to get food (I f) or to overcome the deprivation such as the black market (I d).

G   *Goal activity* (terminal behavior). Someone is eating, will eat immediately after the action or has just finished eating. Mealtime words such as lunch and dinner were scored G.

H, i, s or p. *Hostility,* either instrumental (i), subjective (s), or pressive (p). In the first instance, aggression (stealing, violent action) is used as the instrumental activity to get food or overcome the deprivation. In the second, one or more characters in the stories feels angry or aggressive, but doesn't do anything about it. In the third, there is a hostile or aggressive press (either actual or imagined), usually the source of the deprivation. If someone stole food (H i) and was met with defensive hostility, this was not scored H p. This category contains only easily identifiable hostility and aggression.

A, s or g. *Anxiety* over survival (s) (fear of death or starving) or over guilt (g) as when food has been stolen, black market purchases made, etc.

P   *Phantasy.* Someone wishing for or dreaming about getting food. This does not include the ordinary thoughts or intents that precede action.

WF   *Wish fulfillment.* The person in need of food is satisfied by chance, an act of fate, a handout, etc. but not by his own efforts.

S   *Substitution.* Some other need is satisfied at the end of the story in place of the blocked or partly blocked need for food. This does not include satisfactions from overcoming food deprivation.

F p   *Friendly press.* Someone in the story is invited to eat or helped to get food.

This system of categories was designed to cover the major aspects of a behavior sequence involving food—to wit, the motivating state, the kind of situation (deprivation or food-seeking), the instrumental activities (active or passive wish fulfillment, real or unreal, hostile or problem solving) and the goal response activity (amount of eating and enjoyment of food). Its utility can perhaps best be illustrated by its application to three typical sample stories. All of the following occurred in response to picture F in the 16 hour deprivation group.

Story 1

"The persons are a man from the black market and an honest citizen of a small Southern town. The citizen hasn't had any meat for a couple of weeks and the man from the black market knows it. The man from the black market thinks he can sell the meat for twice what it is worth. The citizen doesn't want to buy from the black market but he is wanting the meat. The citizen doesn't buy the meat and reports it to the police."

There is food-related imagery (F I). The central thema is clearly the need of the 'honest citizen' for the meat (F th) which he wants (N). Deprivation (D) is stated in the words 'hasn't had any meat for a couple of weeks.' The instrumental acts do not get food (I f −) but do get rid of at least part of the reason for the shortage—the black marketer (I d +). There is also some substitute satisfaction (S) implied for doing the right thing ('doesn't want to buy . . . reports it to the police').

Story 2

"The man in black is a detective and he is studying the meat to see if he can get a clue to the black marketer who is the man in grey. There has been a shortage of meat and also a large cost when available. The detective thinks he can catch the crook—he wants a clue. The detective will investigate anything that arouses his suspicion and he will catch the crook."

This story has the necessary food related imagery (F) but it is clearly about the shortage of meat and is therefore a deprivation story (D th). No food need is stated and the action is simple. He catches the crook (I d +).

Many of the stories were more complicated than these which have been chosen to illustrate some of the essential differences in the classification categories. Story 3 illustrates some of the difficulties in scoring that occurred.

Story 3

"The man on the top was a preacher in a Catholic Church and the younger man a member of his parish. It being Friday, all Catholics should sustain (sic) from eating any flesh of any animal. Upon visiting the member's home and discovering that they are having meat to eat he is shocked. The pastor will tell the younger man his fault, and how he is not a good Catholic. The man will outwardly say he's sorry, but he will do it again because he wants what he wants when he wants it."

This is a food thema story which involves actual eating (G) as well as the need for food (N). There is interference on the part of the priest (D) but the response is successful in overcoming it (I d +). The problem here lies partly in deciding that this is not centrally concerned with a threatened deprivation (a decision based mostly on the actual eating as compared with absence of real deprivation) and partly in deciding that the priest's intervention is deprivation and not hostile press (a decision based on the absence of actual aggression). Most classification problems were of this sort and usually they could be resolved on some such bases as these.

To arrive at the final scores, one E (JWA) first classified all the stories. The other E (DCM) then classified independently all the stories in response to picture F (which accounted for nearly half the food stories given). A running tally showed there was agreement on about 75-80 percent of the classifications. However, most of the disagreements came in the hostility category in trying to decide whether it was i, s, or p. In the main categories (F I, N, G, etc.) there was disagreement in less than five percent of the cases. Then the two judges decided together which of two classifications a response should receive. During discussion the hazier definitions were clarified so that there was ready agreement on practically all classifications, once the definitions were fully understood by both judges in the same way. Finally the same procedure was adopted with the remainder of the stories. In general only the most obvious points were scored—that is, there had to be actual words that supported each tally. The scores should therefore be considered as conservative estimates of the most obvious trends. The judges knew to which group the Ss belonged, but could not have easily influenced the results as they had no clear-cut expectations as to how the results would come out.

RESULTS

The major results of the experiment are presented in Tables II (for the situation) and III (for the reactions) in terms of the

TABLE II. NUMBER AND PERCENTAGE OF Ss SHOWING VARIOUS KINDS OF SITUATIONAL STORY CHARACTERISTICS AT LEAST ONCE IN THE TOTAL TEST OF SEVEN PICTURES

Characteristic	1 Hour Deprivation $N = 38$		4 Hour Deprivation $N = 21$		16 Hour Deprivation $N = 22$		Chi-square of Differences		
	N	%	N	%	N	%	1-4 hr.	4-16 hr.	1-16 hr.
Food imagery	35	92.1	18	85.7	20	90.9			
Food central	25	65.8	13	61.9	20	90.9		3.52*	4.69
F thema	19	50.0	13	61.9	13	59.1			
D thema	7	18.4	3	14.3	11	50.0		6.24	6.62
Block**	2	5.3	1	4.8	2	9.1			
Need food	21	55.3	18	85.7	18	81.8	5.60		4.32
F deprivation	19	50.0	11	52.4	18	81.8		4.24	5.97

Chi-square = 3.8 and 6.6 at the 5 percent and 1 percent levels of significance.

* Yates's correction used.

** Blocks do not include Ss who blocked on more than half the picture and hence were voided.

percentage of the subjects in each deprivation group showing a given characteristic at least once in the seven stories told. This method of tabulating the data is somewhat insensitive, as it does not count the times beyond the first that a characteristic appears. Other methods were tried, such as the number of times a characteristic appeared out

TABLE III. NUMBER AND PERCENTAGE OF Ss SHOWING VARIOUS KINDS OF REACTIONS IN THEIR STORIES AT LEAST ONCE IN THE TOTAL TEST OF SEVEN PICTURES

Characteristic	1 Hour Deprivation $N = 38$		4 Hour Deprivation $N = 21$		16 Hour Deprivation $N = 22$		Chi-square of Differences		
	N	$\%$	N	$\%$	N	$\%$	1-4 hr.	4-16 hr.	1-16 hr.
Instrumental									
Activity	23	60.5	14	66.7	20	90.9		2.83*	6.33
f+	12	31.6	10	47.6	9	40.9	1.49		
d+	5	13.2	2	9.5	12	54.6		10.89	11.75
f− or d−	5	13.2	5	23.8	8	36.4			3.08
fo or do	7	18.4	4	19.1	4	18.2			
Goal activity	28	73.7	13	61.9	8	36.4	.89	2.81	8.09
Hostility	17	44.7	12	57.1	11	50.0			
Instr.	8	21.1	6	28.6	7	31.8			
Subj.	5	13.2	4	19.1	2	9.1			
Press	6	15.8	5	23.8	3	13.6			
Friendly									
Press	9	23.7	7	33.3	0	0.0		6.56*	4.39*
Wish phantasy	11	29.0	4	19.1	4	18.2			
Wish fulfill-									
ment	8	21.1	4	19.1	4	18.2			
Anxiety									
Guilt	8	21.1	3	14.3	4	18.2			
Survival	5	13.2	3	14.3	7	31.8			1.99*
Substitution	2	5.3	3	14.3	2	9.1			

Chi-square = 3.8 and 6.6 at 5 percent and 1 percent levels of significance.
* Yates's correction used.

of the total possible number of times, but they yielded such small percentages that, although the results were the same, the major trends in the data were more difficult to see. Furthermore the differences among the groups obtained by the method used in Tables II and III, when compared with mean scores wherever there were enough cases to calculate a mean, were the same as obtained by the use of mean scores when the total number of appearances of a characteristic were taken into account.[3]

Table II, which summarizes the data on the statement of the situation, shows that there is no overall increase in food imagery as hunger increases. Since this is a case where the percentages are high and therefore possibly insensitive to small differences, the mean number of times food imagery appeared in the seven pictures for each of the three groups was also calculated. The means for the one hour, four hour and 16 hour groups were respectively: 2.32, $\sigma_m = .20$; 2.29, $\sigma_m = .28$; and 2.23, $\sigma_m = .28$. The differences are slight and insignificant. When, however, the relevance of food to the central plot of the story is considered, a very different picture appears. Here there is a decided increase in the number of times the plot revolves around food as hunger increases. Further analysis[4] reveals that the increase lies in the food-deprivation plots and not in the food-getting plots. This last point is confirmed by the increase in food deprivation, whether central or not, which appears in the last line of the table. In general, these differences appear only between the one and four hour groups and the 16 hour group. The only difference of any significance between the one hour and the four hour groups was in the number of times the need for food was expressed.

Table III continues the comparison for some of the reactions of the characters in the stories to a behavior sequence involving food. The differences which are significant or fairly large are checked by means of chi-square. As hunger increases, there is an increase in instrumental activity which is focussed not on food getting but on removing the source of deprivation of food. On the other hand, there is a marked decrease in goal activity (eating) and in press actively promoting goal activity (invitations to eating). None of the other differences is reliable, though several are in an understandable direction (e.g., increase in anxiety over survival, increase in instrumental hostility as a means of getting food, decrease in phantasies just wishing for food, etc.).

---

[3] A rough check on the stability of these percentages was made by dividing the 38 Ss in the 1 hour group into two groups of 19 Ss and correlating the frequencies obtained by the two groups for each of 21 categories. The product moment correlation was .89 (uncorrected) which indicates a fair degree of reliability of the data as far as results on groups of around 20 Ss are concerned. This also provides some check on the ability of the judges to classify the characteristics consistently.

[4] Note that the sum of the percentages of the two subcategories is usually more than the percentage in the overall category. This is because the overall category includes those Ss who show *either* F th *or* D th, while some may show *both,* a fact which appears separately in the subclassifications.

Some of the major results are presented graphically in Fig. 1, which shows, first, the failure of food imagery to increase; second, the complementary shift from goal to instrumental activity; and third, the flatness of the food-getting thema curve as compared with the sharp increase between four and 16 hours deprivation for the deprivation thema curve, which is characteristic of all deprivation related measures (D th, D, I d+, f— or d—).

On the basis of these shifts a scoring method was devised for summarizing each person's standing in relation to his projected need for food. The following categories were scored +1: D th, N, D, and

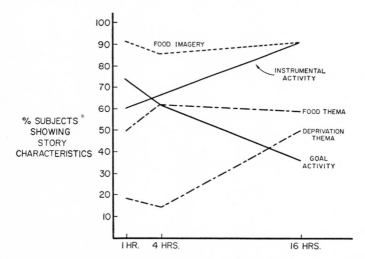

Fig. 1. Percentage of Ss showing selected food related story characteristics as a function of increasing hunger.

I f— or d—. I d+ was scored +2 (because of the size of its chi-square) and G and F p were scored —1. A characteristic was scored each time it appeared in the total test. The resulting total will be referred to as the *Need Food score* (NF Score). Table IV summarizes the mean NF scores for the three deprivation groups. As far as means are concerned, the one and four hour groups are significantly lower on the NF scale than the 16 hour group.

Table V presents a breakdown of scores for some of the main categories on five of the pictures for which data were available on the larger number of Ss.[5] Also for the sake of simplicity only the

---

[5] The results on pictures G and I show identical trends but the frequencies are so small it was decided not to include them in the table.

56 *Motivation and Thematic Apperception*

TABLE IV. MEAN NEED FOOD (NF) SCORES OF THE THREE DEPRIVATION
GROUPS WITH ESTIMATED RELIABILITIES OF THE
DIFFERENCES AMONG THEM

Hours Food Deprivation	Mean NF Score	σ_m	Difference and Probability of Its Occurring by Chance with			
			4 hr.	P	16 hr.	P
1 hour........	.74	.36	.83	<.10	3.31	<.01
4 hour........	1.57	.52	—	—	2.48	<.01
16 hour.......	4.05	.66	—	—	—	—

percentages of Ss showing a characteristic in the one hour and 16
hour groups are presented. Several facts immediately emerge from
these data. In the first place, the pictures differ widely in the extent
to which they evoke food-related stories. By far the most successful
picture in this respect was F, which was constructed especially for

TABLE V. PERCENTAGE OF ALL THE Ss IN THE ONE HOUR DEPRIVATION
GROUP ($N = 44$) AND IN THE 16 HOUR GROUP ($N = 37$) SHOWING
SELECTED CHARACTERISTICS FOR DIFFERENT PICTURES

	F I	N	D	I	I d	G	Fp	Mean NF Score
Picture A (Four 'bums' resting)								
1 hour.................	50.0	6.8	2.3	9.1	2.3	27.3	0.0	−.14
16 hour.................	35.1	10.8	8.1	5.4	0.0	18.9	0.0	.03
Picture B ('Beachcomber')								
1 hour.................	27.3	15.0	18.2	11.4	5.4	4.6	0.0	.45
16 hour.................	32.4	21.6	32.4	24.3	16.2	2.7	0.0	1.03
Picture D (Woman looking into room)								
1 hour.................	13.6	2.3	0.0	2.3	0.0	6.8	0.0	−.11
16 hour.................	18.9	5.4	0.0	10.8	0.0	8.1	10.8	−.16
Picture E (Restaurant balcony scene)								
1 hour.................	22.7	2.3	0.0	2.3	0.0	18.2	2.3	−.21
16 hour.................	13.5	2.7	0.0	5.4	0.0	10.8	0.0	−.08
Picture F (Two men and piece of meat)								
1 hour.................	81.8	36.4	27.3	43.2	2.3	27.3	18.2	.39
16 hour.................	83.8	54.1	40.5	64.9	21.6	10.8	2.7	1.62
Chi-square...............		2.6		3.8	5.8*	3.4	3.4*	

* Yates's correction used.

this test. It was unique in two respects. It was the only picture that had food in it—i.e., a piece of meat—and it was the only picture which was 'unstructured'—i.e., which was not a single scene, but three isolated picture elements which had to be combined into a plot. There was no other picture which approached it in any category except perhaps picture B in the D category.

In the second place, the data do not reveal any very great differences among the pictures in their sensitivity to changes in the hunger drive. The best pictures should be those which give enough food-related responses to be scored and which give the largest differential for different degrees of hunger. The size of the differential does not seem to vary markedly with the food-evoking capacity of the picture or with the nature of the picture, though obviously some pictures fail to evoke a certain characteristic at all. The rule seems to be that if a picture evokes a characteristic moderately frequently (in at least 15-20 percent of the Ss), it will discriminate the two groups regardless of its other properties. It should be noted, however, that though this holds true for the size of the differential it does not hold true for its reliability. Only the differences for picture F approach statistical significance.

Furthermore there is an interesting exception to the rule. Picture E and picture A are both suggestive of satiation or at the very least of meal times (supper and lunch). The 16 hour group reacted to both pictures by producing less overall food imagery than the one hour deprivation group. If the data on F I for pictures A and E are combined so that the percentage of Ss who produced F I on either picture is recorded, the difference approaches significance (chi-square = 3.50). This suggests that with pictures implying goal activity there is a blockage of the normal food associations for hungry Ss, a fact which is clearly in line with the decrease in their production of goal responses (G). The difference probably did not appear in picture F because the piece of meat was supposed to be fitted into the plot which almost required that food imagery be used by all Ss.

The final fact to be gathered from Table V is that all the pictures except D showed a shift in mean NF score in the correct direction (more positive for the hungrier group). The discriminative power of the various pictures as reflected by the critical ratios of the differences was as follows: first, picture F (C. R. = 4.50); second, picture B (C. R. = 1.81); third, picture E (C. R. = 1.63); and fourth, picture A (C. R. = 1.00). Picture D showed small and insignificant, if consistent, reversals in most categories and in NF score. It is difficult to draw any general conclusion from this except that, since it was the least food related of the five pictures, a certain minimal relation between a picture and the need it is supposed to reflect is absolutely necessary before it will accurately reflect that need.

DISCUSSION

The apperceptive expression of a need. The present experiment makes some important contributions to the central problem of this series of papers—namely, how a need expresses itself in perception and apperception. It has collected the first real data showing how thematic apperception stories are related to a known condition of the subjects. Murray (313) in his list of the ways in which story interpretations can be validated does not mention the technique used here. He is chiefly concerned with how an interpretation can be checked against biographical data, against the results of different tests, or against future behavior. Here the approach has been to discover *how* a need expresses itself so that the judge will have some actual basis for making or improving his interpretations of thematic stories.

Of course, judges have always used, consciously or unconsciously, certain clues for deciding whether or not a story or a series of stories indicated the presence of a need. The present results suggest that some of these clues may have been misleading. For instance, it has commonly been assumed (cf. 62, p. 189) that phantasies serve the function of partially gratifying unfulfilled desires. One might therefore expect that hungry subjects would project more food objects which could serve to gratify an unfulfilled wish for food. The present data clearly indicate that this assumption (which Murray also makes—314, p. 260) is wrong, at least so far as these data are concerned. Or again, on the basis of Bellak's finding (36) that criticism increases aggressive words in such stories, one might suppose that hunger would increase the overall number of food-related words and images, but it does not.[6] There must be many other such clues that clinicians use in making their interpretations, but not many of them have been made explicit. Since the only check on whether the clues used are correct is the checking of the total impression against some other source of knowledge, it is extremely difficult to improve the basis of such judgments because it is almost impossible to know what factors formed the total impression and to vary them systematically as they are validated against an outside criterion.

The present method promises better results. It can now be stated with some certainty that a person trying to diagnose hunger from thematic stories should look for (1) food deprivation, both as the

---

[6] There is the possibility, of course, that the method of scoring used here—presence of food imagery in a story—is less sensitive than the method used by Bellak of counting every need-related word.

Hunger 59

central plot of the story and as a secondary characteristic; (2) instrumental activities which successfully overcome the source of food deprivation but which often do not get the person food; (3) statements implying hunger or a need for food in the characters; (4) a fewer than normal number of references to goal activity such as eating, to friendly press such as an invitation to eat; and (5) a decreased responsiveness in terms of food imagery to pictures strongly implying satiation or the recent termination of eating.

These are the primary characteristics of 'hungry' stories. There are some secondary ones which are not as well established. For instance, the judge should not expect an increase in successful food-getting activity, but he might look for an increase in anxiety over survival, and a decrease in thinking about food at an unreal level (wish phantasy or fulfillment).

It has been shown how these clues can be combined into a composite numerical score which gives a pretty good indication for most of the Ss of how long they have been without food. Naturally it is hoped that this procedure will have a much wider significance than could be attached to the determination of hunger from the Ss' stories. It would be much simpler to ask the Ss when they last ate! The results become of major importance only if changes occur in the same way in the same categories of response with other experimentally induced needs—particularly psychogenic ones. Other experiments in the series tackle this problem.

Theoretical considerations. The data also shed some light on the nature of the processes involved in thematic apperception. The first point of theoretical interest is that the results are much the same as those obtained in the first experiment (270) on the effect of hunger on perception. Perception and apperception apparently respond to a need in much the same way. The chief difference lies in the greater freedom of the apperceptive processes to show a variety of changes under the conditions of the experiment. For instance, the first experiment showed an increase in the perception of objects instrumental to eating with an increase of hunger. The second experiment elaborates this finding by showing that instrumental activities as well as objects are concerned but the activities are not so much connected with food getting as with eliminating deprivation. One might even argue that the Ss in the first experiment saw plates rather than oranges, not because the plates were instrumental, but because they were empty. That is, the increase in perception of food-related objects rather than actual food may have signified not instrumentality but the deprivation so characteristic of the 'hungry' stories.

Or again, in the first experiment, the Ss failed to perceive an increased number of food objects, but in the second experiment, the more sensitive apperceptive processes reflected an actual significant *decrease* in goal activity. Also, perception did not clearly differentiate the four hour from the 16 hour deprivation group. Apperception did, though it did not reflect many significant changes between the one and four hour groups.

Even if it is granted that apperception is merely reacting more sensitively than perception but according to the same underlying process, the problem remains as to what the process is and why it functions in this particular way. Cattell suggests (62, p. 180) that there are three processes involved in what is ordinarily called 'projection.' The first, 'naive inference from limited personal experience,' could be illustrated in the present experiment by the Ss' 'naively' inferring that people in the pictures have been deprived of food because they have been. The second, 'unconscious, immediate, or true projection,'[7] can probably not occur as a defense mechanism against such a non-ego-involving drive as hunger, but a case could be made for the fact that the hungry Ss' tendency to attribute the hunger motive to others in the pictures objectifies the need so that it can be handled more effectively. The third, 'projection of press required by emotional state,' is illustrated perhaps by the refusal of the Ss to give goal activity responses to situations normally evoking them. That is, since they feel hungry, they see the world as a place with less food in it, which 'explains' how they feel.

The data indicate that a number of such processes occur and the writers feel that there is little to be gained by trying to label certain processes projection and others something else. It is all behavior and should be treated like any other behavioral attempt at adjustment by the organism. That is, perception and apperception are determined like any other behavior is—partly by the state of the S (including needs and drives), partly by his past experience, and partly by the objective situation. The major difference between this and any other situation is that the objective cues have been reduced or nearly eliminated so that the behavior must be determined mostly by needs and past experience.[8]

The view that the cognitive and perceptual processes involved here do not function essentially differently from any behavioral attempts at adjustment is supported by Knapp's (218) and Allport and Postman's (8) similar conclusions from studies of rumor and by the nature of the changes that actually occurred here. That is, in general it is to the obvious advantage of the organism to concern itself more and more with instrumental rather than goal activity as the need increases. It is also useful to emphasize the problem (deprivation) and ways of overcoming it (I d +). Perhaps the only surprising element in the situation is that this mobi-

---

[7] The distinction between this and the third process is essentially the same as that Murray makes (312) between supplementary and complementary apperceptive projection.

[8] The difference between this and the situations in which Freud described projection is that he was dealing with cases in which the need was so strong as to render ordinary objective determinants relatively unimportant. In phantasy situations the objective determinants are rendered unimportant by the experimenter so that behavior can be more completely reflective of needs. The end result is often the same except that the Freudian projection will only occur in cases of such extreme need that the ordinary objective determinants of an interpretation are overridden.

lization at the imaginative level of the resources of the organism toward solving or handling the problem of food deprivation goes on apparently very largely without the S's knowledge or conscious intent.

Secondary implications. The data bear on several problems that have been raised insistently by previous research in this field. For instance, what is the effect of recent experiences on the validity of projective tests such as the TAT? As Coleman says, "the TAT should not be subject to such day-to-day fluctuations" (81, p. 257). Both he and Bellak (36) conclude that it is not—at least not at any very fundamental level. The present data do not support this conclusion entirely. If, for instance, an S takes a TAT at 11 A.M. in the morning and he has missed his breakfast (a situation comparable to the 16 hour deprivation group), there is much greater likelihood of his telling a general deprivation story to picture A (the 'beachcomber' from an early TAT edition) than if he takes the TAT shortly after lunch. This does not mean, of course, that the basic picture of the man's personality structure will be altered. There may be alteration only in the manifest and not in the latent content, as in Freud's dream analyses. But it does suggest caution to the extent at least of finding out what significant things have happened to a person in the last few hours or even days before administration of a projective test.

What kinds of pictures are most effective in eliciting the needs of the S? Here again there have been several studies (364, 399), most of which conclude that they should be vague and contain characters with whom the person can identify. The basis for choosing these characteristics has not been any demonstrated discriminative power of such pictures but rather the quality of the stories they produce. So far as any conclusion can be drawn from the few pictures used here, it would seem that the projection pictures should contain objects or situations related to the need one is interested in measuring. This is to insure a sufficient frequency of responses related to the need under consideration to get differential reflections of it. To be more explicit, the pictures should contain goal objects in an unstructured relationship to a person with whom the S can identify. In this connection, the technique of presenting three or more elements which the S must weave into a story seems particularly promising. They should also present situations suggestive of terminal or goal activity and of deprivation or blockage of instrumental activity. The present set of TAT pictures is particularly deficient in the first characteristic. That is, they do not contain goal objects around which themes can be woven but present instead situations which may be so ambiguous that, like picture D in the present series, they fail to evoke much of any response (and hence no differential response) related to the needs which the experimenter is interested in measuring. These points, it must be emphasized, are merely suggestions which arise from a very limited number of pictures viewed under the influence of a simple physiological drive and yield no firm factual support for wide generalization. However, they have seemed worth making, since this is one of the first attempts which has been made to determine the effectiveness of pictures in terms of their actual discriminating power for the need being measured.

SUMMARY

A group of 81 men, applicants for admission to Naval submarine training school, wrote out brief stories in response to seven projected pictures, 38 after one hour, 21 after four hours, and 22 after 16 hours of food deprivation. Results from 22 more men who wrote stories in response to five of the seven pictures were used in the analysis of the comparative merit of the pictures in eliciting responses reflecting hunger. The stories were analyzed by two judges independently for 23 characteristics relating to the hunger drive. The following conclusions appear justified:

1. The judges were able to agree in categorizing story content in a large percentage of cases. The correlation between the categories for two groups of 19 Ss under the same condition was .89, indicating a considerable degree of stability for group percentages in various categories.

2. As hunger increased, there was no overall increase in the percentage of Ss showing food imagery or food themas, but there was a decided increase in the percentage showing food deprivation themas, characters expressing a need for food, and activity successful in overcoming deprivation, but not always instrumental in getting food. On the other hand, as hunger increased, there was a decided decrease in the amount of goal activity (eating) and in friendly press favorable to eating.

3. A composite need food score was devised by scoring $+2$, $+1$, or -1 for all instances in each record of categories which showed reliable increases or decreases for the groups as hunger increased. The mean need food score differentiated reliably the three deprivation groups with little overlap in score between the one and 16 hour deprivation groups.

4. No outstanding differences in sensitivity to reflecting hunger was discovered for the various pictures used provided the picture was enough related to hunger to produce a sufficient number of food-related responses to show a differential. The most successful picture in differentiating the three food deprivation groups was one containing a goal object (food) in a completely unstructured relationship to a young man with whom the Ss could identify.

The application of these findings to the clues used in interpretation of Thematic Apperception Test records is discussed. It is suggested in particular that the amount of need deprivation and of instrumental activity present in stories is a better index of the strength of a need than is the amount of goal activity. If the results are confirmed at more complex need levels, it should be possible to obtain a single score measuring need strength which would combine the shifts occurring in story content as the strength of the need increases.

Consideration of the theoretical implications of these results indicates that it is desirable to treat apperceptive behavior as functioning like any other type of behavior rather than to attempt to fit it under the limited principles governing Freudian or defensive projection, which appears to be a special case.

CHAPTER 3

The Effect of the Need for Achievement on Thematic Apperception*

DAVID C. McCLELLAND, RUSSELL A. CLARK, THORNTON B. ROBY,

AND

JOHN W. ATKINSON[1]

A NUMBER of shifts in perception and in the thematic content of stories have been established, shifts which provide important clues for the detection of the strength of the hunger drive from projective records (Ch. 2, 270). But the crucial experiment in the series remains to be performed. No one is particularly interested in diagnosing hunger from projective responses. The point is, do the same kinds of shifts occur for an experimentally controlled psychogenic need, or are the clues which have been discovered applicable only to some simple physiological tension like hunger?

The present experiment was designed to answer this crucial question. It was decided to choose a psychogenic need which could be aroused experimentally and to see whether it produced perceptive and apperceptive changes similar to those already noted for hunger. The need chosen was 'need achievement' or 'need mastery,' the need which *presumably* is aroused by experimentally inducing ego-involvement, according to a technique which by now is fairly well standardized among psychologists experimenting in the field of personality (12, 320, 370). The word 'presumably' is used advisedly. No one knows for certain that there is a unitary n Achievement[2]

* Reprinted with minor abridgement by permission of author and publisher from the *Journal of Experimental Psychology,* 1949, 37, 242-255. Copyright 1949 by the American Psychological Association, Inc.

[1] This project was carried out at Wesleyan University and was made possible by a grant from the Office of Naval Research for which the authors are very grateful.

[2] The convention adopted by Murray (314) of shortening need to n will be followed throughout this paper.

which can be satisfied by success and aroused by failure in the same way that hunger is satisfied by food and aroused by deprivation of food. However, if manipulation of the conditions of ego-involvement produces the same kinds of effects on projection as manipulation of hours of food deprivation, there will be some basis for considering the psychogenic state aroused as a need, at least to the extent that it functions like a physiological one. It was to establish this kind of parallelism of function that work began in this series with a simple physiological tension which nearly everyone would accept as a need or drive. Consequently, if the results in this experiment are in substantial agreement with those obtained in earlier ones in the series, it will provide evidence for the existence of higher order psychogenic needs which at least function like those at a simpler physiological level.

One of the crucial problems in this type of experiment is to find a scoring system for thematic stories which is objective enough to provide high observer agreement and sensitive enough to reflect changes in motivational states. So a further purpose of this experiment is to develop further the scoring system which was found useful for hunger (Ch. 2) and to test its applicability to a more complex psychogenic need. The standardization of an objective scoring system for projective records should ultimately make possible some general principles for interpreting them. What is even more important, it should open up for experimentation the whole field of imagination, which has been more or less neglected, except by the clinicians, since introspection was discredited as a fruitful approach to arriving at psychological principles.

PROCEDURE

The materials used in the experiment consisted of some simple paper and pencil tests and some slides for thematic apperception. There were seven short tests, in each of which the subject performed a writing task as often as possible in the normal manner for one min. and then backwards or in some unusual manner for one min. The total time taken including pauses between tests for instructions was about 25 min. Their chief function here was to provide the basis for inducing ego-involvement. That is, there were two main, fundamentally different conditions under which the tests were administered. In one (hereafter referred to as *relaxed*), the test administrators were introduced by the instructor at a regular class session as some graduate students who were trying out some tests. This orientation was reinforced by further remarks by the 'graduate student' to the effect that these tests had been recently devised, were still in the developmental stage, and that data were being collected in order to perfect them. Throughout, the emphasis was clearly on the fact that the experimenters were interested in testing the tests and not the students. These instructions were designed to create an easy relaxed atmosphere in which the need for achievement was at a minimum.

In the other main condition (hereafter referred to as *failure*), the administration of the preliminary tests was quite different. After the experimenters had been introduced to the class by the instructors, they began passing out the test booklets with no explanation as to the purpose of the experiment. The only remarks made dealt with the first test—anagrams—and the necessity of paying close attention to directions as the tests were timed. After completing the first test, the subjects calculated and recorded their scores on it. Then they filled out a short questionnaire which asked for: name, high school and college attended with estimated class standing in each, IQ (if known), and an estimate of their general intelligence (above average, average or below average). The purpose of the questionnaire was only incidentally to obtain information. It was primarily to get a subject ego-involved in the situation by making his test score known to himself and outsiders in relation to a lot of other achievement-related facts about him.

This aim was further supported by the following remarks then made by one of the experimenters (RAC) given from memory so as to give the impression of spontaneity:

> The tests which you are taking directly indicate a person's general level of intelligence. These tests have been taken from a group of tests which were used to select people of high administrative capacity for positions in Washington during the past war. Thus in addition to general intelligence, they bring out an individual's capacity to organize material, his ability to evaluate crucial situations quickly and accurately; in short, these tests demonstrate whether or not a person is suited to be a leader.

> The present research is being conducted for the Navy to determine which educational institutions turn out the highest percentage of students with the administrative qualifications shown by superior scores on these tests. For example, it has been found that Wesleyan University excels in this respect. You are being allowed to calculate your own scores, so that you may determine how well you do in comparison with Wesleyan students.

At this point the experimenter quoted norms for Test 1 that were so high that practically everyone in the class failed and placed in the lowest quarter of the Wesleyan group. It was then explained that Test 1 was the single most diagnostic test in the battery and thus an individual's standing on this first test would be a good indication of how well he might expect to do on the test as a whole.[3]

---

[3] It goes without saying that the instructions contained nothing that was true, or for that matter nothing that was completely false. The references to the Navy and to the Washington administrators (cf. 410) were all partly true and could be checked by over-curious psychology students. Every other precaution was taken to prevent leaks about these instructions since they were crucial to the whole experiment. Different classes at the same institution were run on the same day and the procedure was not 'exposed' to the students at the end or even to

After this the subjects went on and completed all the paper and pencil tests. At the end they added up individual test scores to obtain a total score and again were given falsely high norms "so that they could see how well they had done as a whole in comparison with Wesleyan students."

That these instructions succeeded in producing very different effects on the students was obvious to even the most casual observer. Under the ego-involving instructions, they worked hard and quietly, and there were various obvious expressions of dismay when the norms were announced. There was no indication that the instructions were disbelieved. Under relaxed conditions the subjects were as a whole more relaxed and gave the impression of enjoying the tasks as they would a series of parlor games.

At the conclusion of the paper and pencil tests used to arouse different need states the other experimenter (JWA) read the following instructions:

This next test is a test of your creative imagination. A number of pictures will be projected on the screen before you. You will have 20 seconds to look at the picture and then five minutes to make up a story about it. Notice that there is one page for each picture. The same four questions are asked. They will guide your thinking and enable you to cover all the elements of a plot in the time allotted. Plan to spend about a minute on each question. I will keep time and tell you when it is about time to go on to the next question for each story. You will have a little time to finish your story before the next picture is shown.

Obviously there are no right or wrong answers, so you may feel free to make up any kind of a story about the pictures that you choose. Try to make them vivid and dramatic, for this is a test of creative imagination. Do not merely describe the picture you see. Tell a story about it. Work as fast as you can in order to finish in time. Make them interesting. Are there any questions? If you need more space for any question use the reverse side.

The results from two other variants on the major conditions proved meaningful and will be reported. In the first of these a group of students was run in a *neutral* but not 'relaxed' atmosphere. That is, they were task-oriented rather than ego-oriented (cf. 12), but they were asked to cooperate seriously and to work hard on the tasks so that adequate norms for them could be established. The reason for these instructions was to get a somewhat higher n Achievement tension than under the relaxed condition in order to maximize individual differences as part of another experiment (74). In the final group an attempt was made to get an intenser n Achievement aroused by giving the Ss a taste of success by quoting low norms after the first test followed by an even greater failure at the end induced by quoting high norms. This will be referred to as the *success-failure* group.

There was no indication in the ego-involved groups that the projective tests were not still part of the program of testing for administrative

---

the instructors (whose kindness in cooperating under the circumstances is greatly appreciated).

ability. The slides used for eliciting the written stories consisted of two especially chosen for this experiment (two men in overalls looking or working at a machine; a young man looking into space seated before an open book), followed by two taken from the Murray Thematic Apperception Test ('father' talking to 'son'—TAT 7 BM; boy and surgical operation—TAT 8 BM). The pictures were chosen to suggest achievement—either at a specific task or general level and in school-related and unrelated situations.

The Ss were all male, a majority veterans, and all college students taking various psychology courses. They were run in regular classroom periods either in the summer of 1947 or the Spring of 1948. The entire testing time, which included some tests of perceptual inference reported elsewhere (271), took from 70-80 min., except for the *success-failure* condition in which it was necessary to cut out the last three of the motor perseveration tests to finish within a normal 50-min. class period.

Scoring.—The stories were scored according to the same general system used in the hunger experiment (Ch. 2) with additions and modifications necessitated by the more complex nature of the need involved. Detailed scoring criteria cannot be given here for lack of space, but they have been reported in full elsewhere.[4] The following brief descriptions will serve at least to identify the major categories used.

g, t, or u I: Achievement imagery is scored either general (g I) or task (t I); stories with no achievement imagery are scored as unrelated (u I). To be general, achievement imagery must deal with some long term problem of getting ahead at the ego ideal level (career, schooling, inventing something, etc.). Everything else, particularly the specific task situation, was classified as t I.

Ach or D th: Themas or plots are scored if the achievement imagery is central to the story. If the plot is concerned with someone who is in an achievement difficulty which has or is anticipated as having serious long term effects, it is scored as deprivation thema (D th); otherwise it is an achievement thema (Ach th), though there may be many difficulties in the way of the goal.

d p or w: Deprivations or blocks in the path of progress or indications of past failures, i.e., things not running smoothly. If the trouble is with the person himself, it is scored d p; if it is with the world, it is scored d w. D th was not also scored for d unless there was some secondary and separate source of hindrance.

N p or g: Need for achievement is stated in the story either at the personal level ("He wants to be a doctor") or at the general level ("He wants to serve humanity").

I +, —, or o: Instrumental activity which is either successful (I +). unsuccessful (I —) or of doubtful outcome (I o). The person in the story must do something (even if only think or decide) about achieving his

---

[4] Further analysis has produced some modification of these original definitions of achievement imagery and the various subcategories (designated as Scoring System A in 272). See Ch. 12.

goal which is separate from the statement of the situation and the statement of outcome: e.g., "the boy graduates from school" is scored for outcome but considered too passive to represent instrumental activity.

Ga +, −, *or o:* Anticipations of outcomes (goal responses) which may be either of success (Ga +, "He is thinking of the day when he'll be famous") or failure (Ga −, "He is worried about what will happen") or neither (Ga o, "He is wondering what will happen").

nu or ho P: Nurturant or hostile press. Some person in the story is either actively helping or hindering the person working for achievement. The hindrance must be more hostile than a static block (see d w above).

S: Substitution. A person who meets with an obstacle in his achievement instigation-action sequence adopts a substitute instrumental act or substitute goal response ("He drowns his sorrows in a tavern").

G or G′ + *or* −: Goal responses which occur either within the story (G) or at the end (G′) and which may be either positive affect ("He was happy in his new job") or negative affect ("The boy is worried over having flunked his exam").

O +, −, *or o:* Outcomes of the whole story are judged according to whether they are happy (O +), unhappy (O −), or doubtful (O o). Finer breakdowns were made but did not prove useful. The total outcome was not necessarily the same as that for the instrumental activity and was also separate from the final affect (G′). For example, "They fixed the machine" is scored O + but not G′ +, because it doesn't say they were pleased about it.

The following story illustrates how the scoring was used. After each word or phrase scored is written in parenthesis the scoring symbol applicable:

1. What is happening? Who are the persons?—"The boy is being talked to by his father, maybe something about what has happened in school, or he may be planning to get married."

2. What has led up to the situation—that is, what has happened in the past?—"He may have flunked out of school (D th) and is being lectured on what is expected of him (nu P)."

3. What is being thought—what is wanted? By whom?—"The father wants the boy to make good (N p), he is thinking that he wants his son to follow in his footsteps and make good in life (Ga +, g I)."

4. What will happen? What will be done?—"The boy will do his best, will go back to school because he has learned a lesson he will never forget (I +). He will make good this time and be a success (O +)."

As this example shows, the scoring was not done from the viewpoint of a single character with whom the writer supposedly identified, although this is the usual method of procedure. Thus the father's wish for the son's success is scored N p (father's viewpoint), and the father's help is scored nu P (son's viewpoint). The rationale for this was the conviction that determination of the person with whom the writer identified was often difficult and that it was not necessary—e.g., in this instance it is just as possible to suppose that the writer is projecting his wish to do well into the father figure as into the son. Note also that the second statement of the father's wish is not scored again. A given category is scored only once per story no matter how many times it appears.

This example shows how decisions on the scoring of a specific item were affected by the total context and by the scoring of other items. Thus, it is not until the whole story is read that the thema is clearly one of achievement and not marriage, and it is not until the third paragraph that the decision can be made that the imagery is general and the thema one of deprivation. The factors which lead to this decision are the presence of Ga + and N p (see above definitions). It was recognized that the interdependence of scoring categories was not wholly desirable from the statistical viewpoint, but it soon became obvious that the interdependence existed at the intuitive level for categories like g I and D th, no matter how discretely the definitions might be drawn. Hence, it seemed best to state as explicitly as possible any other categories that were usually taken into account in the normal process of arriving at a judgment on a given category.

TABLE I. THE NUMBER AND PERCENTAGE OF ACHIEVEMENT-RELATED STORIES WRITTEN UNDER RELAXED, FAILURE, AND SUCCESS-FAILURE CONDITIONS

The number of stories in each condition is 156
(39 $Ss \times 4$ stories)

		Relaxed		Failure		Chi-square	Success-Failure	
		N	$\%$	N	$\%$		N	$\%$
Imagery								
task	t I	73	46.8	56	35.9	3.82	47	30.1
general	g I	26	16.7	75	48.1	35.16	85	54.5
unrelated	u I	57	36.5	25	16.0	16.94	24	15.4

Chi-square is 3.84 and 6.64 at the .05 and .01 levels of significance, respectively.

The way in which all the stories were scored will be described in full under results in the section on reliability of the scoring. It involved two judges working together without knowledge of which of three groups (neutral, failure, and success-failure) the stories belonged to.

RESULTS

The main results of the experiment are shown in Tables I, II, III, and IV, which summarize the frequency of appearance of various scoring categories for the relaxed, failure, and success-failure conditions. The results from the neutral condition, which generally fell between the relaxed and failure conditions, will be reported only in summary form. In all the tables increases or decreases from the relaxed to the failure condition are tested for significance by means of chi-square[5] Table I shows that there is a large and very significant increase in the number of stories dealing with general or long term achievement while there is a decrease in the number of stories with no achievement imagery and of those with task achievement imagery.

Because of this shift the method of computing percentages in Tables II, III, and IV has been changed. Since there were significantly more stories with achievement imagery in the two failure conditions, there is a correspondingly greater opportunity for other achievement-related characteristics to appear in these conditions. But the important question is: given an achievement story, are there significant differences in its internal characteristics when written under different conditions? Hence, the results for further characteristics are presented as percentages not of all stories but only of the achievement stories in each condition.

TABLE II. THE NUMBER AND PERCENTAGE OF THE ACHIEVEMENT-RELATED STORIES WRITTEN UNDER DIFFERENT CONDITIONS SHOWING VARIOUS STORY CHARACTERISTICS RELATED TO THE DESCRIPTION OF THE SITUATION

Number of Stories:	Relaxed 99		Failure 131		Chi-square	Success-Failure 132	
	N	$\%$	N	$\%$		N	$\%$
Plot Ach th	59	59.6	83	63.4		98	74.2
D th	6	6.1	25	19.1	8.11	14	10.6
Obstacles d p	12	12.1	23	17.6		24	18.2
d w	22	22.2	17	13.0	3.41	21	15.9

Chi-square is 3.84 and 6.64 at the .05 and .01 levels of significance, respectively.

Table II shows only a significant increase in the number of deprivation themas. A comparison of the failure with the success-

---

[5] It should be noted that the population considered here is number of stories, rather than, as in the hunger experiment, the number of Ss showing a characteristic at least once. The latter measure, while easier to interpret statistically, is not as applicable to the data of this experiment because of the much greater frequencies obtained for many of the need-related categories. The authors realize that a chi-square test of significance applied to repeated measures from the same Ss is hard to interpret because of the peculiar nature of the universe to which the inference is made, but have decided to use it for two reasons: (1) other statistics appear to have even more serious objections and (2) the differences found to be significant for all four pictures and used in calculating the final n Achievement score were also significant when only the results from the single most diagnostic picture (TAT 7 BM) were used.

failure results suggests that the former reflect sensitively the Ss'
greater failure experience since the combined thema totals are nearly
identical for the two conditions (82.5 and 84.8 percent respectively),
both being considerably larger than the same figure for the relaxed
condition (65.7 percent).

TABLE III. THE NUMBER AND PERCENTAGE OF THE ACHIEVEMENT-RELATED
STORIES WRITTEN UNDER DIFFERENT CONDITIONS SHOWING
VARIOUS STORY CHARACTERISTICS RELATED TO THE
CHARACTERS' REACTION TO THE SITUATION

Number of Stories:	Relaxed 99		Failure 131		Chi-square	Success-Failure 132	
	N	$\%$	N	$\%$		N	$\%$
Need stated:							
N p&/or g	21	21.2	58	44.3	13.30	64	48.5
Instrumental acts							
I +	9	9.1	41	31.3	16.29	31	23.5
I −	7	7.1	3	2.3		6	4.5
I o	6	6.1	10	7.6		7	5.3
Anticipatory goal response							
Ga + &/or Ga −	15	15.2	47	35.9	12.33	60	45.5
Ga o	6	6.1	11	8.4		15	11.4

Chi-square is 3.84 and 6.64 at the .05 and .01 levels of significance, respectively.

Table III shows a larger number of significant shifts in the
forward-looking, striving aspects of the stories. This table indicates
that an aroused n Achievement increases the likelihood that characters in the story will be described as wanting to get ahead (N p),
as doing something successful about getting ahead (I +), and as
thinking in advance about success or failure (Ga + or Ga −). In
Table IV the shifts appear in the number of people seen as aiding
or hindering achievement (nu or ho P) and in the frequency with
which positive affect is specifically mentioned, either in the course
of the story or at the end (G or G′ +). It is interesting to note that
there are no significant changes in the outcome category, despite
the fact that most of the present *a priori* systems for scoring the
TAT (36, 314, 416) lay emphasis on this characteristic and despite
the fact that a far more elaborate breakdown of different types of
endings was actually made than is reported here. There is one shift
in outcomes, however, for the success-failure group, which gives
significantly fewer doubtful outcomes to its stories than does the
failure group. This suggests that repeated failure may cause an

TABLE IV. THE NUMBER AND PERCENTAGE OF THE ACHIEVEMENT-RELATED STORIES WRITTEN UNDER DIFFERENT CONDITIONS SHOWING VARIOUS STORY CHARACTERISTICS RELATED TO THE OUTCOME OF THE SITUATION

Number of Stories:	Relaxed 99		Failure 131		Chi-square	Success-Failure 132	
	N	$\%$	N	$\%$		N	$\%$
Press:							
ho P &/or nu P	10	10.1	29	22.1	5.82	20	15.2
Substitution:							
S	2	2.0	11	8.4	3.20*	7	5.3
Goal response:							
G &/or G′ +	4	4.0	33	25.2	18.61	31	23.5
G &/or G′ −	18	18.2	34	26.0		32	24.2
Outcomes:							
o +	47	47.5	63	48.1		69	52.3
o −	16	16.2	12	9.2		24	18.2
o o	36	36.2	56	42.8		39	29.5

* Corrected for continuity.
Chi-square is 3.84 and 6.64 at the .05 and .01 levels of significance, respectively.

unwillingness to state the outcome of an achievement sequence, especially an unfavorable (O −) outcome, since this is the category which is reduced in the failure group.

A tabulation of the frequency of appearance of each story characteristic for each S was made as a basis for obtaining a single summary n Achievement score. The characteristics which showed a significant increase in Tables I-IV from the relaxed to the failure condition were scored +1 and those which decreased were scored −1. Thus, there were seven positive characteristics (g I, D th, N, I +, Ga + or −, nu or ho P, and G or G′ +) and two negative characteristics (t I and u I). The results from the success-failure group were not taken into account in developing the scoring system because it was felt that the need state aroused might be more complex than in the straight failure group.

Table V presents the mean n Achievement scores for each condition. The means for the relaxed and failure conditions differ very significantly as they should from the way the scoring system was devised. The success-failure condition was almost exactly equal to the failure condition as had been indicated by the comparisons in Tables I-IV. The neutral condition showed a moderate need strength, by this scoring system, which was significantly greater than the relaxed condition and significantly less than the two failure conditions.

TABLE V. MEAN n ACHIEVEMENT SCORES FOR THE RELAXED, NEUTRAL, FAILURE, AND SUCCESS-FAILURE CONDITIONS

N	Relaxed 39	Neutral 39	Failure 39	Success-Failure 39
Mean............	-1.00	3.13	5.82	6.00
σ_m...............	.46	.69	.82	.73
Diff.............		4.13	2.69	.18
σ_{diff}.............		.83	1.07	1.14
Critical ratio.......		4.98	2.51	.16
P...............		<.01	<.02	>.50

This last comparison is particularly important methodologically because the papers from these three groups had been mixed together and were all scored together without the judges' knowing to which group any paper belonged. Thus, with all possibility of bias removed, there is still a significant mean difference in n Achievement score between a presumed low and high intensity of induced n Achievement.

Reliability of the scoring. A matter of considerable methodological importance, in view of the present tendency of experimentalists to eschew free verbal reports, is the reliability of the scoring system used here. Consequently, reliability was studied intensively from three different angles. First, an attempt was made to determine the extent to which the judges agreed on a given category for a particular story. Since agreement is almost certainly a function of amount of the judges' experience with the scoring system, a measure of it was taken at the end of the scoring, after one of the judges had had a year's previous experience with the system amounting to the scoring of at least 3000 stories and the other had scored at least 1000 stories. The two judges always worked together, one reading the story aloud so that both could independently form tentative judgments, which were discussed, if they differed, in making the final decision. At the time the test was made they were spending on the average of two to three min. per story, or at the most from five to ten min. per S. The test consisted of drawing 10 records at random from the neutral, failure, and success-failure groups and rescoring them. The index of agreement was computed by dividing twice the agreements by the sum of the items scored on each of the two occasions. It turned out to be 291/321, or 91 percent.

Secondly, reliability was approached from a less conservative viewpoint by attempting to measure the extent to which the totals are stable for a given category on two judgments of the same records.

This is more to the point in estimating the dependability of group shifts, since judges may quite possibly miss a category in one story and pick it up somewhere else, leaving the total the same, though not the percentage agreement. To check this, the stories written by the 39 relaxed *S*s were completely rescored after all the other stories had been finished.[6] There was a nearly significant increase in the proportion of stories scored as containing achievement imagery, due to a conscious liberalization in the judges' set, but this increase did not change the ratio of general to task imagery or any of the other categories scored. Seventeen out of 22 of the category totals were within three points of each other.

Also relevant to this point is the comparability of the totals for various categories for the failure and success-failure groups. They are very close in nearly every case in Tables I-IV, and the mean overall n Achievement scores are practically identical. This shows that category totals are apt to be quite stable even when obtained on two different groups of *S*s, and even when there are minor differences in the method of arousing n Achievement.

In the third place, the reliability of an individual's overall n Achievement score was tested by correlating the scores obtained for 30 individuals on two different scoring occasions. The product moment correlation was .946, indicating fairly high stability of an individual's score for his whole record. Furthermore, this correlation is probably conservative, since 20 of the 30 *S*s came from the relaxed group, which reduced the range of scores, and since the scoring was done much more hastily on both occasions than it normally would be in a clinical situation.

DISCUSSION

Validity of n Achievement score. No one can deny that there are differences in the story characteristics which appear in the relaxed as compared with the failure condition, but is it proper to assume that these differences represent a difference in the need for achievement in the two groups? This is the central problem of validity, of whether the score derived from these differences measures anything of importance, or more particularly of whether it measures the n Achievement which it is supposed to measure. There are two kinds of evidence which argue that it is a valid measure of n Achievement.

The nature of the procedure used to arouse the need provides the

---

[6] An attempt was made to mix the relaxed stories with others in the rescoring but it was not continued beyond the first 10, since the judges who had scored these same stories several times before easily recognized them as being very different from the others with which they were mixed. Any further attempt to conceal their identity seemed a waste of time.

first basis for assuming that n Achievement was more intense in the two failure conditions. In discussing what we have labelled n Achievement, after Murray (314, p. 164), Sears states: "There are many names for this learned drive: pride, craving for superiority, ego-impulse, self-esteem, self-approval, self-assertion; but these terms represent different emphases or different terminological systems, not fundamentally different concepts. Common to all is the notion that the feeling of success depends on the gratification of this drive, and failure results from its frustration" (370, p. 236). This suggests that the experimental operations which will satiate and arouse the drive are success and failure. However, the success and failure must be in relation to some achievement goal which the Ss have set for themselves. That is, in the case of a physiological need like hunger, it is only necessary to deprive the Ss of food to arouse the drive, since the organism automatically by the consumption of energy produces in time a need for food. But in the case of a psychogenic need it is necessary first to induce Ss to want some goal like achievement. In the present experiment that was supposedly done by giving the Ss an opportunity to perform on some tests which were described to them in such a way that doing well should lead them to feel increased pride, self-esteem, self-approval, feelings of success, etc. Since these terms define what is commonly meant by the striving for success or n Achievement, if the instructions and the tests were such as to arouse these feelings, then by definition n Achievement was aroused in the failure and success-failure groups.[7] And it does seem reasonable to assume that the attainment of high intelligence and leadership as suggested in the instructions are two goals which in our society would lead to the feelings mentioned.

Granted that n Achievement was aroused by the instructions, it further seems reasonable to suppose that failure-frustration would lead to a heightened need. Although this assumption is supported by experimental evidence (131) and by the deprivation method of arousing physiological drives, we recognize that it may complicate the resulting picture here. That is, granted that failure does heighten n Achievement, it may also lead to the projection of material which is specific to the experience of failure rather than characteristic of a 'pure' heightened need.[8] It was this conviction that led to the

---

[7] Since these instructions are also the ones commonly called 'ego-involving' by other workers in the field (cf. 12), it is apparent the authors believe that ego-involvement and n Achievement arousal are the same thing under certain conditions.

[8] The fact that the failure group showed more deprivation themas than the success-failure group, while both showed about the same high number of themas as compared with the relaxed group, would support this proposition. That is, one could argue that heightened need tension results in more achievement

Achievement 77

collection of stories from an ego-involved group which had had neither success nor failure. Unfortunately, for reasons given fully elsewhere (cf. 271), the Ss in this group were too inhibited to write stories which could be readily analyzed. So the main comparisons had to be made between a relaxed condition and a condition in which n Achievement was augmented by failure.[9]

The comparison with the effect of hunger on similar stories (Ch. 2) provides the second basis for arguing that a need has been aroused by the experimental conditions. However unwise it may prove to be to have used failure to heighten the need intensity, it serves to make the need-arousal method more nearly comparable to the deprivation used to increase hunger (Ch. 2). Consequently, it becomes more legitimate to ask, What is the evidence that food-deprivation and achievement-deprivation affect imagination in the same way?

Table VI provides the positive evidence that the two needs have the same general effect. The case rests largely on the first three items (D th, N and I +), since failure of categories to shift may mean failure of the scoring system at some point. Even so the evidence is im-

---

imagery central to the plot, but that failure as a method of increasing this tension shifts some of this plot or thema imagery to the deprivation category.

[9] Intensive reanalysis of the data of this experiment and of other subsequent experiments has led to refinements in the definition of achievement-related imagery and the various subcategories. Later experiments, for example, show that n Achievement can be aroused by achievement-orienting instructions without inducing feelings of failure. Chapters III, IV, and V of *The Achievement Motive* (272) deal at length with descriptions of various test conditions, the development of a more general conception of what constitutes achievement imagery (reproduced here as Ch. 12), and a more conservative statistical analysis of the validity of the various categories of imaginative response. Chapter 45 of this volume illustrates how n Achievement can be directly aroused by achievement-orienting instructions.

Perhaps the most persistent unresolved problem in research on n Achievement concerns the observed sex differences. Veroff, Wilcox, and Atkinson (420) found the average n Achievement score of American college women to be already as high under relaxed conditions as it is for men or women under aroused conditions. Nevertheless, individual differences in n Achievement showed the same relation to performance in women as in men.

Field (133) has reported an increase in n Achievement in women following the arousal of concern about social acceptance. Morrison (302) has attempted to differentiate career orientation and social-achievement orientation in women. But Vogel (421) has discovered the same problem in trying to produce experimental arousal of need for affiliation in women. However, Angelina (16), replicating the present experiment in Brazil, reports a significant increase in n Achievement scores of both men and women following experimental arousal procedures.

The question of sex differences and other questions concerning the general applicability of the n Achievement scoring system are dealt with at length in Chapter VI of *The Achievement Motive* (272). Editor.

TABLE VI. A COMPARISON OF THE STORY CHARACTERISTICS SHOWING SIGNIFICANT CHANGES FOR BOTH INCREASED n FOOD AND INCREASED n ACHIEVEMENT

1. An increase in the number of plots dealing primarily with deprivation of the goal in question (D th).
2. An increase in the number of times that characters in the stories were said to want or wish for the goal in question (N)
3. An increase in the mention of instrumental activities which are successful in dealing with the need-related problem (I+)
4. No change in the number of plots dealing with direct attainment of the goal (F th or Ach th)
5. No change in the amount of substitute activity, in instrumental activity of unsuccessful or doubtful outcome, or in negative affect (represented by subjective hostility in the food experiment)

pressive, considering the fact that a complex psychogenic need like that for achievement might be supposed on *a priori* grounds to differ extensively from a simple primary need like hunger.

There is also some negative evidence, i.e., instances of categories which shift in one experiment but not in the other. But these can rather easily be explained in terms of differences in procedure in the two experiments. For example, the biggest lack of correspondence in the two experiments was in the way a higher need decreased the favorable aspects in the food stories and increased them in the achievement stories. A case in point is the decrease in friendly press for hunger and the increase in nurturant press for n Achievement. This can be explained by the fact that the two control groups were not equivalent. The one-hour hunger group was *satiated* with respect to hunger, whereas the relaxed group in the present experiment could best be described as *unmotivated* with respect to n Achievement. Satiation undoubtedly carries over to increase the frequency of appearance of favorable story aspects, as has been shown for the n Achievement situation when success is given the Ss (269, 271). Since the low need groups therefore doubtless differed initially in the amount of favorable material projected, it is not surprising that high need groups in the two experiments produced different or even opposite effects. Other incongruencies between the two experiments are largely due to changes in the scoring system necessitated by the greater complexity of n Achievement (e.g., the general imagery category).

If one notes the major agreements and explains away in this manner the disagreements, Table VI can be said to supply considerable support for the argument that the conditions of this experiment induced a state in the Ss which affected their imagination in the same general way as an increase in hunger. To the extent

Achievement 79

that one accepts hunger as a need, it would therefore seem valid to refer to the state induced by ego-involvement and failure as a need. Even if one grants this, however, it must of course still be shown that the situationally induced need affects apperception in the same way as a strong character need would, as clinically or otherwise defined. This ultimate problem of validity must await further study.

Clinical applications. In the meantime, the data are sufficiently clear-cut to provide some guidance for the person working with the TAT clinically. They suggest in the first place what story characteristics are apt to be important as indicators of need strength. Although the validity of these indicators is by no means finally established, they do represent an advance over the logical or *a priori* validity earlier workers in the field have been forced to assume for their scoring systems. In the second place, the data suggest to the clinician that the conditions of adminis-tration of the TAT are of considerable importance in determining the dynamic content of the stories. Stories written under relaxed, neutral, and failure conditions differed so much in the present experiment as to suggest more caution than has heretofore been indicated in assuming that the basic personality picture given by the TAT is not influenced by recent experiences (36, 81). Our results suggest strongly that the clinician should be careful to investigate such matters as how the sub-ject conceives of the test, his reason for taking it, his relation to the tester who may or may not have given him other tests that have involved success or failure, etc.

Nature of motivation. One of the most important implications of this experiment is suggested by a consideration of the categories which shifted in frequency when the need was presumably aroused. Most, if not all of them, appear to have a future reference—for instance, the stated wish for achievement, successful instrumental striving, anticipatory goal responses, and positive affect at the end of the story. Two other im-portant characteristics—the increase in general imagery and the increase in deprivation themas—also appear to refer to the future on further scrutiny, the former because it is defined as involving a person's career or life work, and the latter because it is defined as a situation in which forces are at work against a person that would make him worse off in the future. In both instances the presence of stated need or anticipatory goal response was often useful in defining the category. On the other hand categories did not change which seemed to involve more of an objective description of the situation (plots, obstacles and outcomes) without the striving or anticipatory dimension. This, taken with similar earlier evidence (271), suggests that it is one of the major characteristics of motivation—at least achievement motivation—to be anticipatory or forward looking. This might seem to be a somewhat radical departure from the usual conception of a motive as a persisting deficit stimulus, but oddly enough Hull (186), working from entirely different data, has come to much the same conclusion—namely, that fractional anticipatory goal responses are the key to understanding purposeful and motivational phenomena. In fact, one can argue that the anticipatory goal responses observed in this experiment supply a kind of direct confirmation of Hull's view which has been very difficult to obtain with animals.

Methodological considerations. Last but not least these results have an important bearing on the experimental methodology of handling verbal material. They report a method for scoring written thematic apperception stories which is sensitive enough to distinguish between the conditions under which the stories are written, which is objective enough to yield high agreement on a repeat scoring by two trained judges working together, and which is easy enough to apply quickly to an individual record. This in itself is of considerable importance in a field in which prior scoring systems have either been so complex or so dependent on clinical insight (36, 314, 416) that they are of little use to the experimental psychologist interested in studying imaginative processes.

The potential value to psychological theory of an objective scoring method for free verbal behavior is illustrated by the fact that its application in this experiment clearly indicates that phantasy does not always serve the purpose of wish-fulfillment or substitute gratification for pleasures denied in reality, an assumption which has been rather frequently made (cf. 222, p. 93). Instead, a study of the variety of story characteristics which shifted in this experiment with an increase in need supports the parsimonious assumption that imaginative behavior is governed by the same general principles as govern any behavior. For example, a variety of experiments show the same increase in instrumental activity with increased drive at the gross motor level; others, as in the standard Pavlovian conditioning, show the same increase in anticipatory goal responses (salivation). If one grants that the principles governing imaginative behavior are no different from those governing performance when both are analyzed according to the same categories of response, then the method used here becomes a more subtle and flexible approach to the establishment and extension of those principles than the ordinary method of studying performance. Thus, for example, it would be difficult to get a performance response which would correspond to the anticipation of deprivation which follows drive arousal at the imaginative level. One might even go so far as to suggest that by the use of this method Tolman could study much more directly the 'cognitive maps' which the behavior of his rats has led him to infer are the important intervening variables in determining behavior (412).

SUMMARY

Over 200 male college students wrote five-min. stories in response to four slides depicting achievement-related situations under the influence of various interpretations of the meaning of the story writing and several short pencil and paper tests taken just previously. The stories were analyzed completely for 39 Ss from each of four conditions: (1) a *relaxed* condition, in which all the tests were in-terpreted as being in an experimental stage, (2) a *neutral* condition, in which the tests were described as experimental but in which the *S*s were urged to do their best to establish some norms, (3) a *failure* condition, in which the tests were interpreted as standardized measures of intelligence and leadership and in which the *S*s wrote their stories after failing on the paper and pencil tests, and (4) a *success-failure* condition, which was the same as the failure condition except that the *S*s succeeded on the first part of the paper and pencil tests and then failed on the whole test. The stories from a group who wrote under ego-involving instructions but without suc-cess and failure proved too inhibited to analyze, and those from a group who succeeded throughout are not reported because the mean-ing of the situation to the *S*s did not seem clear. The scoring fol-lowed in general the usual analysis of an overt behavioral sequence with adaptations from Murray. The following results were obtained:

1. The scoring method, when used by two experienced judges working together, could be quickly applied (two to four min. per story), was sensitive enough to discriminate among the stories writ-ten under different conditions even when mixed together before judging, and was objective enough to yield on rescoring a 91 per-cent agreement for individual categories and a rescoring reliability coefficient for the n Achievement score developed of .948.

2. On the assumption that the relaxed and failure conditions represented a low and high degree of induced need for achievement, a comparison was made of the category shifts between these two groups. The following changes occurred at least at the .05 level of significance: a *decrease* in unrelated and task achievement imagery, an *increase* in general achievement imagery, achievement-related deprivation themes, stated needs, successful instrumental acts, anticipatory goal responses, nurturant or hostile press, and positive affective states. In nearly every case the success-failure condition showed the same percentages as the failure condition pro-viding a category total stability check.

3. A single n Achievement score was computed for each indi-vidual by summing the characteristics he showed which increased reliably for the group and subtracting those which decreased re-liably. The mean n Achievement scores computed in this way in-creased significantly in accordance with the presumed increase in induced need from relaxed, to neutral, to the failure conditions.

The validity of these results as true measures of n Achievement is discussed particularly as it derives from a comparison with similar trends obtained with hunger and from a consideration of the ex-perimental operations performed on the *S*s. The data are further interpreted as pointing to the dynamics of the test situation as an important determiner of TAT content, as supporting a theory of motivation based on anticipatory goal responses, and as providing a method for investigating such important theoretical constructs as 'cognitive maps' and 'anticipatory goal responses'—a method which is more sensitive than that based on the usual inferences from performance responses.

CHAPTER 4

*A Projective Measure of Need for Affiliation**

THOMAS E. SHIPLEY, JR., AND JOSEPH VEROFF[1]

THE PROBLEM of finding a valid method of measuring the strength of the need for affiliation (*n Affiliation*) has arisen out of the attempts to study the need for security (344). Birney (40) found that a group of college men whose need for security had been experimentally aroused by leading them to believe that they had scored poorly on a personality inventory showed significantly more imagery related to affiliation than a control group. The system that Birney used for scoring *n Affiliation,* however, did not seem general enough. The present study, therefore, was initiated to extend his work by arousing the affiliation motive more specifically and by finding a more generally applicable measure of it.

This paper will present the procedure adopted to arouse *n Affiliation* experimentally, the final scoring system for measuring *n Affiliation,* the results of applying the scoring system to experimental groups and to groups supposedly differing naturally in need for affiliation, and finally some additional indications of the validity of the measure of *n Affiliation* obtained.

PROCEDURE

Two studies were designed to obtain a valid measure of *n Affiliation.* The first study was a comparison of the stories written in response to pictures by one group whose affiliation motivation had been experimentally aroused with stories written by a control group whose affiliation moti-

---

* Reprinted with minor abridgement by permission of author and publisher from the *Journal of Experimental Psychology,* 1952, **43**, 349-356. Copyright 1952 by the American Psychological Association, Inc.

[1] This report is the product of a series of exploratory studies into the nature of security motivation financed by grants from the United States Public Health Service under the general direction of Dr David C. McClelland, to whom the authors are indebted. Data used in these studies have also been collected with the aid of grants from the Office of Naval Research for a study of achievement motivation which are also gratefully acknowledged.

vation was not specifically engaged. It was hoped that a valid measure could be developed by comparing the types of affiliation imagery produced by the two groups. The second study, designed to substantiate the validity of the measure obtained in the first study, was a comparison of the stories written by two groups whose affiliation motivation could reasonably be assumed to be of different intensity. In this study the affiliation motivation was assumed to be stronger in a group of college freshmen rejected from fraternities as compared to a similar group accepted into fraternities.

Experiment I. The study concerned with the experimental arousal of *n Affiliation* was performed at the University of Pennsylvania. Two fraternities were selected which seemed most nearly the same in respect to social backgroud, status on the campus, and size of actual membership. They were told that it was a study of group behavior and that $25 would be donated to the fraternity treasury for their cooperation.

Fraternity A was chosen arbitrarily as the experimental group (Aroused Group). From this fraternity 37 out of 60 members served as Ss. A sociometric test was given to arouse *n Affiliation*, and this was followed by the TAT from which it was hoped a measure of *n Affiliation* could be derived. Forty-five out of 60 members of Fraternity B (Control Group) were given a food preference test prior to the story-writing procedure.

Both groups were tested in their respective fraternity houses. Some members in both groups were excluded to adapt the N's to the experimental procedures. The Ss were selected on the basis of their order of appearance in the room used for the testing procedure.

In the introduction to the sociometric procedure,[2] E (TES) told the Ss that the following test was concerned with the problem of morale; that the Navy was interested in the friendship patterns of groups and how members of a group describe one another. The sociometric test for the Aroused Group was so arranged that each S was described by every other S from a list of 15 adjectives. These adjectives were: *aggressive, anti-social, argumentative, conceited, cooperative, entertaining, friendly, independent, intolerant, modest, self-assured, sincere, submissive, sympathetic,* and *timid.* On the top page of a booklet given to each S was a list of the adjectives arranged in alphabetical order. The Ss first rated these adjectives from 1 to 15, i.e., the rating 1 was to be given to that adjective which when ascribed to an individual would make him most attractive to the rater, etc. Then the first S stood up, and the other Ss were instructed to write his number, 1, at the top of the second page, which also contained the same adjectives and to check the two adjectives on that page which best described him. There was one page listing the adjectives for each S present. This procedure was continued until all of the Ss present had stood up and been rated. Each S was also requested to rate himself when his turn for standing occurred. A separate

---

[2] We are indebted for this procedure to Dr. Roger W. Heyns and Dr. John W. Atkinson of the University of Michigan.

list of names corresponding to the order of standing of each S was kept by all Ss, and from this list the Ss were also requested to pick the numbers of those three individuals from the group whom they would choose as close personal friends. It was felt that these cues in the sociometric procedure—rating fraternity brothers, being rated by fraternity brothers, and choosing friends—would arouse the Ss' *n Affiliation* to a greater intensity than would the cues ordinarily present in a fraternity group.

The TAT was introduced immediately following the sociometric test by a second E (JV). The standard instructions (314) for the group form of the TAT were then presented. The five pictures included four from the TAT (No. 6BM, 3BM, 20, 10) and a fifth picture showing a group of young men seated around a table with another young man in the background. After they wrote their stories, the Ss were told to write their numbers used in the sociometric test on the top of their story forms. At this point the group was told that both these tests were to be anonymous, and hence the Ss were requested to destroy their pages listing the names corresponding to the numbers.

The Control Group wrote stories to the same five pictures after having taken the food preference test. Each S was presented with two lists each containing 20 common foods. The Ss were told to check those foods on the first list which they would refuse to eat under most circumstances. On the second list they were to indicate by an L or a D whether they liked or disliked a particular food.

Experiment II. This study was done at Wesleyan University. One month following the college's rushing program, 33 freshmen were randomly selected from all those who had been accepted into fraternities. These men constituted the Accepted Group. A Rejected Group was composed of 16 freshmen selected from those freshmen who had signified their desire to be pledged to a fraternity but had been rejected. In the judgment of the Dean of Freshmen and/or the college doctor each man who was finally selected for the Rejected Group had shown some indication that he had been disappointed by the rejection. Because of the limitation of information and the number of Ss available, no systematic attempt was made to match the Ss of these two groups on additional variables that might conceivably affect the affiliation motivation. However, a check indicates that the two groups were comparable with respect to minority-group membership and socioeconomic status.

These 49 freshmen were sent a letter from the Dean of Freshmen requesting them to meet in a lecture hall to take a test that had not been included with the other tests given when they had matriculated. These Ss were given only the written TAT with no previous arousal as in Exp. I. The standard instructions were used with the same pictures shown in Exp. I, except that a sixth picture from the TAT (No. 14) was included at the end.

SCORING SYSTEM FOR *n* AFFILIATION

The stories of the two groups in the arousal experiment were compared for types of imagery related to affiliation. The kind of imagery that seemed to discriminate the Aroused Group from the Control Group was brought together in a scoring system adopted to measure *n Affiliation*.

The subcategories employed for scoring the stories are similar to those successfully adopted by McClelland *et al.* for achievement (Ch. 3) and hunger (Ch. 2). That is, the subcategories seem to have general applicability for a wide variety of motives. The problem here was to define an affiliation-related story so that one could look for the presence of the subcategories which have been shown to reflect the motive strength for other needs.

Imagery. Affiliation imagery is considered to be present where there is an objective statement in the story that a person is separated from another and is concerned about it or concerned about possible separation. This means that a story to be scored for *Imagery* should contain at least one of the following types of imagery: (*a*) concern with rejection, being jilted, "stood up," left out, outcast, or ignored; (*b*) concern with loneliness, being without former friends or relatives, including mere mention of the word "lonely"; (*c*) concern with physical departure (e.g., negative affective concern over the death of a loved one); (*d*) concern with psychic separation (i.e., a quarrel, fight, or disagreement); (*e*) concern with no reciprocal love (i.e., one loves another, and is concerned because the other does not love him); (*f*) reparation (i.e., seeking forgiveness, repenting, or changing one's ways to preserve an interpersonal relationship).

A clue which frequently but not always indicates concern over separation is the introduction into the story of some person not in the picture used to elicit the story. This lead, which by itself yields too narrow a definition of affiliation imagery, has been followed up more extensively by Birney (40).

Unrelated Imagery. The imagery in a story is considered to be unrelated if there is no mention of an affiliative loss or separation as defined above. Once a story has been scored *Unrelated Imagery* it is not, of course, scored for any of the subcategories below.

The following subcategories are scored if there is affiliation imagery present in a story. Each subcategory can be scored only once per story. Following each definition a brief example is given.

Need. When there is a statement of a desire for the recovery, maintenance, or attainment of a friendly or loving relationship, *Need* is scored. Not scored *Need* are statements of a need for help, money, respect, etc. from a person. Some indications of a statement of *Need* are: "dreaming of," "prays for," and "desires his return." *Example:* Her son has been sent to Korea. She wants him to return quickly.

Instrumental Activity. When there is a statement that someone in the story plans or acts to preserve or gain a friendly or loving relationship, the story is scored for *Instrumental Activity. Example:* He is trying to get the girl's mother to permit her to marry him.

Goal Anticipation. This category is scored when someone is anticipating the recovery, loss, or gain of the friendly or loving relationship. *Goal Anticipation* is also scored when someone in the story anticipates the results of the recovery, loss, or gain. *Example:* He feels sure that his girl will consent to marry him.

Obstacle. When the individual concerned about a relationship has personal shortcomings, such as jealousy or bad character, which stand in his way of preserving, obtaining, or recovering the personal relationship in question, the story is scored for *Obstacle.* The obstacle can also be in the environment. When something or someone (other than the desired person) stands in the way of the individual concerned, the story is also scored for *Obstacle. Example:* Her fiancé was killed in a train wreck.

Affective Goal State. A story is scored for *Affective Goal State* when there is a statement of affect (positive or negative) over the attainment, preservation, or loss of the goal relationship, or when there is a statement of affect over any activity involved in gaining, preserving, or losing the goal relationship. Affect may be inferred from statements of marriage, making up, etc., culminating a relationship that had been scored for *Imagery. Example:* When he heard that Sally had jilted him, he wept and tore his hair.

Thema. When the main plot of a story or one of two equally predominant plots in a story is concerned with the gain, preservation, or loss of a friendly or loving relationship, the story is scored for *Thema. Example:* A girl is slumped over her bed, weeping. She feels that there is little to live for since her father has just been reported killed in Korea. She wants him to return but realizes that this is now impossible. She will always miss him and resent the fact that he had to be called up for such service.

It should be pointed out that the scoring system is fairly easy and highly reliable. Reliability has been checked by two different methods. First, two scores were compared for *Imagery* and subcategory agreement. For 294 stories there was 91% agreement over *Imagery* and an average of 88% agreement over the subcategories. The index of agreement was computed by dividing twice the number of agreements of a given category by the sum of the number of times the category was scored by the two scorers. Secondly, the reliability was checked by correlating over-all *n Affiliation* scores given to 49 *S*s by two scorers. The *n Affiliation* scores were calculated algebraically for each *S* by summing one point for each appearance of *Imagery* and any of the subcategories in his stories, and subtracting one point for each appearance of *Unrelated Imagery.* This interscore product-moment correlation was .93, indicating a fairly high stability of an S's score obtained by different scores.

RESULTS

The scoring system was applied to the stories of the Control and Aroused Groups. Two Es scored all the stories not knowing from which group a given story came. In the case of disagreements the final scoring was the result of a joint decision by the two scorers.

For each S in the arousal study the number of stories containing a particular category was determined. This number was converted into a percentage by dividing by five (the total number of stories written by each S). Therefore, an S could receive a percentage score of 0, 20, 40, 60, 80, or 100. These percentage scores were then converted into degrees by the *arc-sin* $\sqrt{percentage}$ transformation procedure. This was done in order to normalize the distribution of scores so that t tests might be applied to the data.

Table 1 contains the results of the category comparisons of the

TABLE 1. MEAN NUMBER OF STORIES CONTAINING IMAGERY AND SUB-CATEGORIES WRITTEN UNDER AROUSED AND CONTROL CONDITIONS

	Aroused Group $N = 185$ (37 $Ss \times 5$ stories)	Control Group $N = 225$ (45 $Ss \times 5$ stories)	Mean Difference	t^* $N = 82$	p^{**}
Imagery..............	3.35	2.53	.82	3.21	<.01
Unrelated Imagery.....	1.65	2.47	−.82	3.21	<.01
Need................	2.14	1.07	1.07	3.56	<.001
Instrumental Activity..	1.08	.62	.46	1.99 at	.05
Goal Anticipation......	.41	.47	−.06	.37	>.50
Obstacle..............	2.16	1.56	.60	2.22	<.05
Affective Goal State....	2.43	2.07	.36	1.62	<.11
Thema...............	2.65	2.15	.50	2.12	<.05

* Although the raw data are presented in the first three columns, the actual t-tests and resulting p values are based on an analysis of percentages that have been transformed by the arc-sin $\sqrt{percentage}$ procedure. The degrees of freedom for the t-tests, of course, are based on the number of subjects and not the total number of stories.

** These and all subsequent p values are for both tails of the distribution.

Control and Aroused Groups. Five out of the seven categories appear significantly more often in the stories of the Aroused Group than in the stories of the Control Group. Only *Unrelated Imagery* and *Goal Anticipation* appear more frequently in the Control Group, but only the difference for *Unrelated Imagery* is significant.

To check upon the validity of the scoring measure of *n Affiliation*, the *E*s scored the stories of the Accepted and Rejected Groups in the same manner as they scored the stories of the Aroused and Control Groups, and the same statistical treatment was employed. Table 2 reports the results of this study.

TABLE 2. MEAN NUMBER OF STORIES CONTAINING IMAGERY AND SUBCATEGORIES WRITTEN BY COLLEGE MEN ACCEPTED AND REJECTED BY FRATERNITIES

	Rejected Group $N = 96$ (16 Ss × 6 stories)	Accepted Group $N = 198$ (33 Ss × 6 stories)	Mean Difference	t^* $N = 49$	p
Imagery	3.69	2.61	1.08	2.37	<.05
Unrelated Imagery	2.31	3.39	−1.08	2.37	<.05
Need	2.06	1.33	.73	1.63	<.11
Instrumental Activity	1.69	1.06	.63	1.73	<.10
Goal Anticipation	1.25	.67	.58	1.08	<.30
Obstacle	2.88	2.15	.73	1.83	<.10
Affective Goal State	2.94	1.91	1.03	2.40	<.05
Thema	3.38	1.97	1.41	3.62	<.001

* Again the reader is reminded that although the raw data are presented in the first three columns, the actual t tests and resulting p values are based on an analysis of percentages that have been transformed by the arc-sin $\sqrt{\text{percentage}}$ procedure. The degrees of freedom for the t tests, of course, are based on the number of subjects and not the total number of stories.

They are not as significant as those found in the arousal study. Nevertheless, three of the seven categories appear significantly more often in the stories of the Rejected Group at or beyond the .05 level of confidence. Three other categories in this study (*Need, Instrumental Activity,* and *Obstacle*) differ at approximately the .10 level but in the same direction previously obtained for the Aroused vs. Control Groups comparisons. Again *Goal Anticipation* did not differ significantly in either direction, while *Unrelated Imagery* appears significantly more often in the Accepted Group.

Perhaps it should be pointed out that because the various subcategories are not completely independent of the *Imagery* category, the p values obtained from the t tests are not accurate. However, the fact that the general procedure has been repeated at least once with confirmation of the direction of changes lends additional confidence to the findings.

The over-all effectiveness of the scoring system was tested by computing total n *Affiliation* scores for each S in all groups. For a given S, $+1$ was counted for each appearance of *Imagery* and for any appearance of the subcategories with the exception of *Goal Anticipation*, the one category which did not successfully discriminate between the two groups in either study. Also, -1 was counted for any of the stories scored *Unrelated Imagery*. This category appeared significantly less often in the Aroused Group for the first study and in the Rejected Group for the second study. An S's final n *Affiliation* score was the algebraic sum of these points. In Table 3 the significance of the differences between the mean n *Affiliation*

TABLE 3. MEAN n *Affiliation* SCORES FOR AROUSED VS. RELAXED GROUPS AND FOR REJECTED VS. ACCEPTED GROUPS

	Experimental Arousal Study		Fraternity Rejection Study	
	Aroused Group $N = 37$ (5 stories each)	Relaxed Group $N = 45$ (5 stories each)	Rejected Group $N = 16$ (6 stories each)	Accepted Group $N = 33$ (6 stories each)
Mean............	12.11	7.51	14.31	7.64
σ_m	1.04	.99	2.00	1.37
Mean diff.........	4.60		6.67	
$\sigma_{M\ diff}$...........	1.47		2.46	
t...............	3.13		2.71	
p...............	$<.01$		$<.01$	

scores of the Aroused Group compared to the Control Group and of the Rejected Group compared to the Accepted Group are presented.

The mean n *Affiliation* score of the Aroused Group is significantly higher than the mean n *Affiliation* score of the Control Group, as is also the case for the Rejected Group as compared to the Accepted Group ($p < .01$ in both cases).

DISCUSSION

Theoretical considerations. McClelland has suggested a two-factor theory of motivation (258). He says that there may be two types of motives—one characterized by approach behavior and the other by avoidance behavior. He notes that there are behavioral indications that there are men whose achievement motivation is characterized by the hope of success and other men whose achievement motivation is characterized by the fear of failure. It has been shown (258) that the TAT stories of the men presumably motivated primarily by the hope of success contain achievement imagery with positive anticipation of the goal $(Ga+)$, while men presumably motivated primarily by the fear of failure write stories containing achievement imagery with negative anticipation of the goal $(Ga-)$. Other tentative indications of the two-factor theory applied to the achievement motive may be found in Atkinson (23) and McClelland and Liberman (275).

One may likewise argue for two aspects of affiliation motivation: (a) seeking affiliation because of the pleasant stimulus reward value of the affiliative relationship (approach behavior) and (b) seeking affiliation because of the painful stimulus value of rejection. With this theoretical orientation the present scoring system can be viewed as measuring predominantly that aspect of *n Affiliation* characterized by fear of rejection, i.e., the type of imagery scored is separation from objects of affiliation—primarily a statement of deprivation. Nevertheless, there are certain characteristics of the scoring system which may be related to approach behavior, such as positive affect or positive instrumental activity. However, these positive aspects of the affiliation imagery were not isolated in the present study because their incidence did not permit statistical treatment.

The results obtained may be readily understood by the deprivation theory of motivation, i.e., that behavior is motivated by the avoidance of a painful stimulus. Hence the Aroused Condition of this experiment probably threatened the men temporarily with possible deprivation of affiliation, and the rejected freshmen were in fact so deprived. Therefore, the separation imagery reflects the heightened deprivation state in the two studies. Although the results follow from this theoretical orientation, a two-factor theory of motivation has been discussed because the writers believe that a future experiment specifically designed to arouse the hypothesized approach aspect of the affiliation motive would present an opportunity to isolate a type of imagery different from the separation imagery herein presented. If such a factor should be isolated, different behavioral correlations would be expected as in the case of the achievement motive.

Validity of the n Affiliation measure. The validity of the scoring system as a measure of *n Affiliation* primarily in its fear of rejection aspect can be indicated by two sets of data:

1. Rejection from a fraternity after one has indicated his desire to pledge must certainly be considered a rejection situation for freshmen in college. When rejected freshmen's stories were compared to accepted freshmen's stories, the rejected freshmen should show more *n Affiliation* imagery than the accepted freshmen since all of these men had been turned

down fairly recently by at least one peer group and had shown some concern about it. The results show that the Rejected Group as a whole did write more stories with fear of rejection imagery than the Accepted Group, although the category differences were not so great as in the arousal study. It was to be expected that the experimental study should show greater differences than those obtained in the fraternity rejection study. In fact, it may seem surprising that differences were obtained in the fraternity rejection study since one month had passed since the freshmen had been rejected by the fraternities before the testing was done. Also it should be noted that these boys in the fraternity rejection study probably perceived the testing situation as connected with Wesleyan's admission policy and not connected with the psychological experimentation done at the University. One might expect, therefore, that their affiliation motivation might be overshadowed by situationally aroused achievement motivation. Despite these two factors working against the possibility of discriminating the difference in the intensity of n *Affiliation* between the two groups, significant differences were found between the stories of the two groups. Consequently, not only has the validity of the scoring measure of n *Affiliation* been confirmed, but also a surprising sensitivity of the measure has been demonstrated.

2. It will be remembered that a sociometric procedure had been used to arouse n *Affiliation* in the Aroused Group. With the sociometric results the Es were able to obtain two different measures of popularity (popularity poll and a measure of social approval) to which the n *Affiliation* scores can be related. Inasmuch as it is maintained that the scoring system measures predominantly the fear of rejection aspect of n *Affiliation,* one would expect that an S who had a high n *Affiliation* score should be unpopular. An S who has been rejected by his group or considered unpopular should have a high n *Affiliation* score. If this hypothesis is born out, there would be further confirmation of the validity of the n *Affiliation* measure. Moreover, the differences between the Accepted Group and the Rejected Group, which may be considered a popular and an unpopular group, respectively, would also be confirmed.

The first measure of popularity was the number of times an individual was chosen by his fraternity brothers as a close personal friend. The correlation between the number of votes for each S and his n *Affiliation* score computed by Kendall's *tau* rank-order technique (210) was $-.27$ ($p <$ .05). If one S who had the greatest number of votes and the highest n *Affiliation* score is not considered in the correlation, *tau* becomes $-.40$ ($p < .01$).

The second measure of popularity or social approval was more complicated. A popularity score was computed in the Aroused Group by summing the ratings given each of the two traits used to describe each S by every other S. The sociometric procedure demanded that each S rate 15 adjectives from 1 to 15 as described in the procedure. Furthermore, each S selected two adjectives to describe every other S. What this popularity of social approval score indicates, therefore, is the extent to which the adjectives used to describe a given S were favorable or unfavorable. The lowest absolute score obtained by an S, as computed by summing up each of the ratings given each adjective to describe that S, indicates that this S is the most popular or has the characteristics most approved. The *tau* obtained by correlating the *n Affiliation* score rankings with these popularity score rankings was $-.33$ ($p < .01$). Here again popularity is negatively correlated with *n Affiliation*. Both the first popularity correlation and the differences found between the Accepted and Rejected Groups in the fraternity rejection study are confirmed.

Nature of the arousal condition. Since there is evidence that the scoring system measures predominantly the defensive aspect of the affiliation motive, or a deprivation state, one must consider the sociometric arousal situation in this light. What was there about this arousal situation that would elicit more imagery reflecting either an increase in the fear of rejection type of affiliation motivation or a heightened state of affiliation deprivation? The cues used to arouse the motive were describing others on personality traits, being described by others, and choosing personal friends. This situation was sufficiently ambiguous at the outset to raise doubts about an S's final rating and to allow him to anticipate the possibilities of rejection. Although an S may have been overtly accepted by other Ss in the group outside the experimental situation, in this covert situation, many Ss would probably anticipate rejection. Also it will be recalled that Ss were not informed specifically that resulting description of Ss and the popularity of Ss would not be reported. Perhaps this is one reason why Ss in the Aroused Group wrote more stories with separation imagery than the Control Group.

SUMMARY

Two studies were conducted to obtain a valid measure of the affiliation motive by scoring stories written in response to pictures. In one study 37 college fraternity brothers wrote stories in response to pictures after their affiliation motivation had been aroused by a sociometric procedure. A control group of 45 college fraternity brothers wrote stories after taking a food preference test. In the second study 16 college freshmen rejected from fraternities and 33 college freshmen accepted by fraternities wrote stories in response to pictures.

A scoring system for the affiliation motive was developed. The basic imagery of the stories scored by the system centered about the separation from affiliative objects. Applying the scoring system to the stories in the two studies yielded the following results:

1. In the first study, five out of the seven categories of the scoring system appeared significantly more times in the stories of the group aroused by the fear of rejection compared to the stories of the control group.

2. In the second study, three out of the seven categories of the

scoring system appeared significantly more times in the stories of the rejected freshmen than they appeared in the stories of the accepted freshmen. Three other categories approached significance in the same direction.

3. An over-all measure of *n Affiliation,* derived by combining the categories that discriminated the two groups in at least one study, showed a significantly higher mean score for the group aroused in the first study and for the rejected freshmen in the second study.

An additional indication of the validity of the scoring measure of *n Affiliation* is that significant negative correlations exist between the over-all measure of *n Affiliation* for the *S*s in the group aroused in the first study and two different measures of popularity obtained from the sociometric procedure.

Theoretical considerations about the nature of the affiliation motive are discussed.

CHAPTER 5

The Effect of Experimental Arousal of the Affiliation Motive on Thematic Apperception*

JOHN W. ATKINSON, ROGER W. HEYNS, AND JOSEPH VEROFF[1]

SHIPLEY AND VEROFF (Ch. 4) have reported scoring criteria for thematic apperception stories to provide an index of strength of the affiliation motive (n Affiliation). Following the logic of earlier motivation studies (Ch. 2, Ch. 3, 72, 272), they found that experimental arousal of n Affiliation increased the frequency of imaginative stories dealing with affective concern over separation from another person. In the present experiment, conducted for the same purpose with several differences in experimental procedure and a different set of pictures, *separation imagery,* as a criterion for designating affiliation-related stories, did not by itself discriminate between experimentally aroused and control conditions. This paper presents the experimental findings which support a broader definition of affiliation imagery and scoring procedures for obtaining a measure of strength of n Affiliation, and a reconciliation of the differences between the two studies.

The theoretical basis for the procedures employed is elaborated elsewhere (72; 258, Ch. 12; 272, Chs. 2, 7; 420). A series of pictures was selected to which male college students might be expected to reveal motivation for social acceptance (n Affiliation). Then, since the aim of this research is to define clearly the kinds of imaginative responses that are symptomatic of n Affiliation, two test situations were designed: one in which affiliation-motivating cues prior to the

Reprinted by permission of author and publisher from *The Journal of Abnormal and Social Psychology,* 1954, **49,** 405-410. Copyright 1954 by the American Psychological Association, Inc.

[1] We wish to acknowledge the initial support of this research by a grant from the Horace H. Rackham School of Graduate Studies, support of its continuation by a Social Science Research Council Fellowship to JWA, and the portion of RWH's time made available during 1952-53 as a result of a Ford Foundation grant for related research on conformity.

95

writing of stories would be maximized, and one in which such cues would be minimized. A 20-minute period of sociometric ratings conducted in the dining room of a fraternity house (also used in the Shipley-Veroff study) met the requirement for a situation containing many cues which would arouse anticipations of affective changes contingent upon being liked and accepted by others or disliked and rejected. A college classroom in which the subjects (Ss) performed a 10-minute anagrams task following a task-orientation-type instruction fulfilled the theoretical requirement for a situation having fewer affiliation cues and, if anything, incompatible cues. It is assumed that this control condition contained fewer affiliation-motivating cues than the fraternity dining room setting without the sociometric procedure which constituted the control condition of the Shipley-Veroff experiment.

METHOD

Procedure

Aroused condition. The Ss were 31 members of a fraternity at the University of Michigan (spring, 1951), which received $25.00 for participation in this experiment. They congregated in the dining room following an evening meal. The rationale offered for the sociometric procedures included reference to research findings on conferences which showed how important interpersonal relations were in relation to satisfaction with group performance. The sociometric procedure is described in detail elsewhere (Ch. 4). It consisted of ranking traits according to the degree to which possession of the trait would make a person likeable, description of self and members of one's own class delegation in terms of these traits, and finally choice of *at least three* persons as most desirable close personal friends.

After about 20 minutes of activity of this sort (assumed to arouse n Affiliation), the imaginative measure of motivation was administered according to the procedures described in earlier work on the achievement motive (Ch. 3, 272). Each S wrote four-minute stories in response to six pictures. The pictures used were the five originally developed by Henry and Guetzkow (179) for use in research with small groups and a sixth from the n Achievement series. The pictures in order of presentation with their code designations for the present study were (a) the heads of two young men facing each other in conversation, (b) a man standing in an open doorway looking away from the viewer at the landscape outside, (c) six men seated about a table as if in conference, (d) an older woman with a troubled expression looking away from a younger man, (e) four men sitting and lounging informally in a furnished room, and (f) a boy seated at a desk holding his head in one hand (H of the n Achievement series).

Control condition. The 36 Ss were male students in an introductory psychology course (spring, 1951). The E was introduced during a class period as a person engaged in collecting preliminary data for some other work.[2] Prior to administration of the six pictures, the classroom group was given an anagrams task (272). They were instructed to make as many words out of the word "generation" as they could during the limited time period. No particular emphasis was put on the importance of this task. Its purpose was to reduce the influence of any affiliation-motivating cues in the classroom situation by introducing incompatible achievement-related cues. After 10 minutes of this, the measure of motivation was introduced.

n *Affiliation Scoring System*

The breakdown of imaginative behavioral sequences into the categories developed earlier for hunger (Ch. 2) and achievement motivation (Ch. 3, 272) was accomplished for these stories in terms of affiliation. The affiliation imagery criterion, which defines the concept of n Affiliation, is given in detail. A complete scoring manual with illustrative examples is presented in Ch. 13.

Affiliation Imagery (Aff Im) is scored when a story contains evidence of concern, in one or more of the characters, over *establishing, maintaining, or restoring a positive affective relationship with another person(s)*. Concern of this sort is immediately evident if the relationship is described as friendship.

In the absence of a clearly stated relationship of friendliness, affiliation concern can be inferred from statements about how one person feels about another or their relationship. Statements of liking, wanting to be liked, accepted, forgiven, or wanting understanding or sympathy indicate the desire for an affiliative relationship.

When no statement of feeling or wanting is present, the nature of the relationship can be inferred from companionate activities such as parties, reunions, visits, or relaxed small talk as in a bull session. These are regarded as affiliative activities from which affiliative feelings can be inferred.

Often the reaction of some character in a story to separation or disruption of an interpersonal relationship is indicative of affiliative concern (Ch. 4). Negative feelings such as sorrow in parting or grief over some action which has led to separation imply the desire to restore the affiliative relationship.

Unrelated Imagery (UI) is scored when there is no evidence of affiliative concern as defined above, and the remaining categories are then not scored.

The following categories are scored when the behavorial sequence has been identified as affiliation related. Each is scored only once per story.

Need (N) is scored when someone in the story expresses a desire for the establishment, maintenance, or restoration of an affiliative relationship.

Instrumental Activity is scored when there is evidence in the story that a person is doing something (including thinking) to bring about an affiliative goal state. The instrumental act is scored successful $(I+)$, unsuccess-

---

[2] We wish to acknowledge the assistance of David Klaus in running this condition.

ful (I—), or of doubtful success (I?), depending on the over-all outcome of instrumental activity in the story.

Anticipatory Goal State is scored when someone in the story is anticipating goal attainment or frustration. When a person in the story thinks about the pleasantness accompanying an affiliative relationship or its restoration, the anticipatory state is scored positive (Ga+). Negative anticipations (Ga—) are indicated by thoughts about pain of rejection or future separation. Doubtful anticipations are scored Ga—.

Obstacle or Block is scored when goal-directed activity is blocked or interfered with. The obstacles may be in the environment (Bw) or within the person (Bp).

Affective State is scored when some statement indicates an affective (emotional) state associated with an affiliative activity. When someone in the story experiences joy and satisfaction in affiliation, the affective state is scored positive (G+). When pain over separation or rejection is present, the affective state is scored negative (G—).

Affiliation Thema (Aff Th) is scored when the main plot of the story has to do with establishing, maintaining, or restoring an interpersonal relationship characterized by friendship, mutual interest, and sympathetic understanding. If there is a competing behavioral sequence, this category is not scored. The thema category is an indication that affiliation-related thoughts dominated the *S*'s thinking to the exclusion of other thoughts during the four-minute period in which he was writing the story.

Scoring reliability. The total scores assigned to the five story records of 20 *S*s (not previously scored) by two coders working independently correlated .96. The percentage agreement in scoring affiliation imagery (twice the number of agreements divided by the total number of times the category was scored by both coders) was 95 per cent. The percentage agreement in scoring subcategories appearing in stories already scored for affiliation imagery was 90 per cent.

RESULTS

Comparisons between the control and aroused conditions were accomplished by breaking the combined control-aroused distribution of frequencies per *S* for a particular category as near to the median as possible. Table 1 shows that the expected increases in frequency of Imagery, Successful Instrumental Activity, Positive Anticipatory Goal State, Environmental Obstacle, Positive Affective State, and Thema are significant. Four categories—Unsuccessful Instrumental Activity, Negative Anticipatory Goal State, Personal Obstacle, and Negative Affective State—failed to increase.

For the Need category, an alternative breaking point which took cognizance of the sizable number of *S*s in the control condition who showed this category only once yielded clearer evidence of a difference than did the approximate median break (Table 1). While recognizing that a comparison suggested by examination of the data favors ac-

TABLE 1. NUMBER OF SS IN CONTROL AND AROUSED CONDITIONS ABOVE AND BELOW BREAKING POINT OF COMBINED CONTROL-AROUSED DISTRIBUTION OF FREQUENCIES FOR VARIOUS AFFILIATION-RELATED IMAGINATIVE CATEGORIES

Imaginative Category	Breaking Pt. (Range 0-6)	Control ($N = 36$)		Aroused ($N = 31$)		χ^2	p^*
		Above	Below	Above	Below		
Affiliation Imagery (Im)..	2-3	11	25	23	8	12.69	.001
Need (N)..............	0-1	21	15	22	9	1.16	.15
	(1-2)**	(5)	(31)	(11)	(20)	(4.27)	(.025)
Instrumental Activity							
Successful (I+)........	1-2	7	29	12	19	3.04	.05
Doubtful or unsuccessful							
(I−)..............	0-1	11	25	12	19	.49	
Anticipatory Goal State							
Positive (Ga+)........	0-1	5	31	12	19	5.42	.01
Negative (Ga−).......	0-1	11	25	12	19	.49	
Obstacle							
Personal (Bp).........	0-1	11	25	8	23	.18	
Environmental (Bw)...	1-2	6	30	13	18	5.23	.025
Affective State							
Positive (G+).........	0-1	15	21	20	11	3.49	.05
Negative (G−)........	0-1	22	14	18	13	.64	
Thema (Th)............	1-2	9	27	15	16	3.96	.025
n Affiliation score (based on Im, N, I+, Ga+, Bw, G+, Th).......	7-8	10	26	21	10	10.70	.001

* In the predicted direction.
** Figures in parentheses indicate alternative breaking point, not the approximate median.

ceptance of a chance difference, we nevertheless accept this category as symptomatic of n Affiliation pending further experimentation.

An over-all index of strength of the affiliation motive in each S, the *n Affiliation score,* was computed by assigning a value of +1 for each occurrence in an S's stories of the seven categories of response which discriminated between presumed low and high motivation conditions. The median n Affiliation scores of the control and aroused conditions were 6.14 (range 1-15) and 9.75 (range 2-18), respectively. The expected difference between the two conditions is significant at the .001 level (see Table 1).

DISCUSSION

Shipley and Veroff (Ch. 4) defined affiliation imagery exclusively in terms of separation anxiety, i.e., affective concern over separation from another person or persons. The present results argue for a broader definition of affiliation imagery and hence a broader conception of the affiliation motive. Any evidence of concern over establishing or maintaining a positive affective relationship with another person(s) (in addition to concern over restoring broken relationships) is viewed as symptomatic of motivation to affiliate according to the present results.

The difference between the two scoring systems can be attributed to (*a*) differences in the pictures used to elicit stories in the two studies and (*b*) differences in the presumed low motivation control conditions.

Effect of picture differences. Five pictures used by Shipley and Veroff were selected from the TAT, noted for its ability to arouse fantasies concerning basic interpersonal problems. A fifth picture was especially designed by them to elicit thoughts concerning separation from others. The present pictures, on the other hand, portray a greater variety of common everyday situations. From this we expect and find important differences in the kinds of stories elicited. When the Shipley-Veroff stories were rescored according to the present criteria, comparison of the frequencies of various imaginative categories in the almost identical aroused conditions of the two experiments showed that the earlier pictures elicited disproportionately more Needs, Obstacles, and Negative Affective States than the present pictures[3] The pictures of the earlier investigation, in other words, were structured to favor perception of them as affiliation-deprivation situations. This accounts in part for the relatively restricted definition of affiliation imagery growing out of the earlier experiment.

As might be expected, the more restricted scoring procedures did discriminate between the control and aroused conditions of the present experiment, but less adequately than the more comprehensive criteria proposed here. The median score obtained for the control condition of the present experiment was 3.86 and for the aroused condition 5.00 ($\chi^2 = 3.23$, $p = .05$ in the predicted direction).[4]

---

[3] Tables showing the frequency of imaginative responses to different pictures in the two studies have been deposited with the American Documentation Institute. Order document 4095 from the ADI Auxiliary Publications Project, Photoduplication Service, Library of Congress, Washington 25, D. C. remitting in advance $1.25 for 35 mm. microfilm or $1.25 for photostats. Make checks payable to Chief, Photoduplication Service, Library of Congress.

[4] The earlier report (Ch. 4) recommends scoring +1 for Affiliation Imagery, Instrumental Activity (+, —, or ?), Affective States (positive or negative), Obstacles (personal or environmental), and Thema; and —1 for Unrelated Imagery. In this comparison, Unrelated Imagery was scored 0 instead of —1 since the frequency of Unrelated Imagery is completely dependent upon the frequency of Affiliation Imagery, and scoring —1 is gratuitous, equivalent to weighting the imagery category twice as heavily as any other category.

To expect, in addition, that the broader scoring system proposed here would discriminate between the two conditions of the earlier experiment as adequately as the earlier scoring system would ignore the effect of an important difference between the control conditions of the two experiments on the scoring procedures that were developed by comparing the particular control and aroused groups in each experiment.

Effect of differences between control conditions. Figure 1 contains our conceptualization of the motivating effects of the cues in the sociometric arousal and control conditions of the two experiments. The general logic of the usual diagrammatic presentation of approach-avoidance conflict is implied in this conceptualization (72, 293).

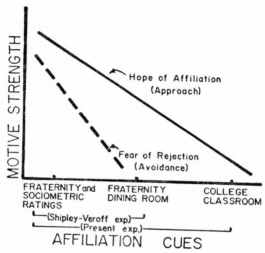

Fig. 1. Assumed motivating effect of cues in the aroused and control conditions of the two experiments.

The approach gradient (positive motivation to affiliate, or hope of affiliation) is presumed to be at its maximum as a result of the combined effect of cues in the fraternity dining room settings and the sociometric rating procedures in the nearly identical aroused conditions of the two experiments. The Shipley-Veroff control condition, a fraternity dining room after supper and a food preference inventory administered before the imaginative measure, is assumed to have contained more cues which would arouse motivation to affiliate than the more neutral college classroom condition of this experiment which included some incompatible achievement-motivating cues.

A fear of rejection or avoidance gradient is also plotted. It represents the degree to which anticipations of painful rejection are aroused by the situational cues. It is strongest in the aroused conditions of both experiments and falls off sharply since it is assumed to be primarily determined by the sociometric rating procedure which virtually guaranteed a certain amount of rejection for all Ss.

In the present study, the arousal of both hope of affiliation (approach) and fear of rejection (avoidance) is low in the control condition and high in the aroused condition. In the earlier study, the difference between control and aroused conditions was relatively greater for fear of rejection than for hope of affiliation. As a result, the Shipley-Veroff scoring system based on pictures already favoring affiliation-deprivation imagery should be sensitive to the expression of affiliation motivation when rejection is threatened, but rather insensitive to the effect of an increase in positive motivation alone because their control condition was already, to a certain extent, positively motivated.

Since the present control group was not influenced by either the positive-motivating cues of the fraternity dining room or the fear-producing cues of the sociometric arousal procedure, the present scoring criteria should be sensitive to positive motivation aroused by the fraternity dining room cues in the Shipley-Veroff control condition. This expectation is confirmed. Our scoring of the Shipley-Veroff aroused condition for affiliation imagery was virtually identical with the original scoring of it. However, where they report a mean (per S) imagery count of only 2.53 in their control condition, the more comprehensive imagery criteria suggested here produce a higher mean of 2.93. As a result, the total number of subcategories scored in their control stories is also increased, and the over-all difference between the control and aroused conditions is found to be much less than when separation imagery alone was the basis for comparison.

The scoring procedures developed in the present experiment are recommended as a more general definition of affiliation motivation than those developed in the earlier study in which the particular properties of the pictures and the nature of the difference between control and aroused conditions may be assumed to have had the effect of restricting the definition of affiliation imagery to separation anxiety as outlined in the arguments above.

n Affiliation and popularity. There is one bit of evidence to indicate that both scoring procedures were measuring the same variable in the aroused conditions of the two studies. During the sociometric rating procedure of both studies, Ss were asked to rank a number of traits in order of the degree to which possession of that trait would make a person likeable, and later they were to assign two of the traits on the list to each member of their delegation. The mean rank of traits assigned to a person is an index of the degree to which he is considered likeable by his associates. In the Shipley-Veroff study, the rank correlation (tau) between individual n Affiliation scores and this popularity index was $-.33$ ($p = .05$). In the present study, the rank correlation (tau) between these same measures was $-.27$ ($p = .05$) and rose to $-.36$ when the one case having the lowest n Affiliation score and the least likeable ratings was eliminated.

n Affiliation is an approach tendency. Analysis of the traits used to describe Ss during the sociometric rating procedure supports a conception of the affiliation motive as a disposition to move toward others to elicit positive affective responses from them. The Ss above the median n Affiliation score in the aroused condition were described as *approval seeking* by at least one other person significantly more frequently than Ss below the median n Affiliation score ($\chi^2 = 7.43$, $p = .01$). They were, in addition, described as *self-assertive and confident* (indicative of positive anticipations) by at least one other person more frequently than Ss low in n Affiliation ($\chi^2 = 2.88$, $p = .10$). Unanticipated by us was the additional finding that they were also more often rated by at least one other person as egotistical than were Ss low in n Affiliation ($\chi^2 = 7.43$, $p = .01$).

The correspondence of these results with the Blum and Miller (46) findings on children that indices of orality are positively related to approval seeking and negatively related to sociometric status provides a promising lead concerning the origins of the affiliation motive.

SUMMARY

The purpose of this study was to develop a method of scoring thematic apperception stories to measure strength of motivation for social acceptance, or n Affiliation. Imaginative stories were written in response to pictures by two groups of male Ss under experimental conditions designed to differ in the degree to which motivation to be accepted and liked by others would be aroused. The presumed high motivation condition consisted of a sociometric procedure conducted in a fraternity dining room before stories were written. The low motivation control condition was a college classroom.

Behavioral sequences dealing with attempts to establish, maintain, or restore positive affective relationships with other persons occurred more frequently in the imaginative stories of the group in which n Affiliation had been aroused. The differences between the scoring definitions proposed here and a more restricted set growing out of a similar experiment by Shipley and Veroff are reconciled in terms of an analysis of differences between the pictures and low motivation control conditions in the two experiments.

CHAPTER 6

··

Development and Validation of a Projective Measure of Power Motivation*

JOSEPH VEROFF[1]

THE PURPOSE of this study was to develop a valid measure of power motivation. McClelland and his associates have shown that scoring stories written in response to pictures can be used as a basis for measures of strength of the achievement (272) and the affiliation (Ch. 4, Ch. 5) motives. Following the same general procedures of these studies, the experimenter anticipated that a parallel measure of another motive—the power motive—could be developed.

What is meant by power motivation? Numerous social theorists have used a concept of power. In some cases, the concept is relegated to the part it plays in the analysis of social structure. In other cases, social power is a dimension to be considered in the analysis of interpersonal relationships. In the latter sense the power motive will be considered that disposition directing behavior toward satisfactions contingent upon the control of the means of influencing another person(s). In the phenomenal sphere of the power-motivated individual, he considers himself the "gatekeeper" to certain decision-making of others. The means of control can be anything at all that can be used to manipulate another person. Overt dominance strivings can be considered one kind of control execution. The definition of the power motive offered here, however, is meant to include more than dominance. The importance of this kind of social motivation has been

---

* Reprinted with minor abridgement by permission of author and publisher from *The Journal of Abnormal and Social Psychology,* 1957, **54,** 1-8. Copyright 1957 by the American Psychological Association, Inc.
[1] The research reported in this paper was submitted to the faculty of the University of Michigan in partial fulfillment of the requirements for the Ph.D. degree. The author would like to acknowledge the assistance of Dr. Daniel Katz in directing this work. The project was carried out while the author was a Research Training Fellow of the Social Science Research Council. He is indebted to the Council for its financial aid.

elaborated by Adler (2) and Sullivan (398) and has been brought to bear upon some of the recent research in group dynamics (61).

Before one can make these predictions about the relationship of power motivation to behavior, a means of measuring the strength of the motive has to be established. The design of this research to develop such a measuring instrument falls into two steps.

First, written stories are obtained in response to pictures from two groups, for one of which it can be assumed that power motivation is aroused and for the other it can be assumed the concern about power is not specifically aroused. A scoring system isolating the kind of imagery presumably reflecting power motivation can then be applied to these two sets of stories. The stories from the aroused group should contain more imagery in the categories scored for power motivation than those from the nonaroused group. Differences in imagery obtained between the two groups provide an empirical clarification of how power motivation is expressed in thought processes.

Second, the expected differences in imagery produced in these two experimental groups are used as the basis for a measure of individual differences in power motivation. Scores so derived should predict individual differences in other behaviors related to satisfying power motivation.

EXPERIMENTAL DESIGN AND HYPOTHESES

Step 1: Group Differences in Power Motivation. For the *arousal condition* the experimenter was able to take advantage of a natural situation: the election of student leaders at the University of Michigan. The candidates must petition for their candidacy. Once having declared candidacy, they have a month's time for campaigning before the actual election. After two days of balloting, the candidates congregate at the polls to see what the balloting has decided. At least two hours elapse after they have congregated before any official returns are announced. It was therefore decided to employ this waiting period for the study. All candidates who had at least one other opponent were previously asked by mail to cooperate in a research project designed to get at important social variables. The only information given was that the experimenter was interested in them as campus leaders and was interested in the effects of social situations upon imagination. Because the candidates were presumably extremely concerned about the control of the means of influence—being elected to office—the situation was thought to meet the requirements for arousal of the motive as it was defined.

Since not all the candidates participated, volunteering bias may have been introduced. Such bias, however, would seem irrelevant to the problem under investigation. All 34 male Ss who appeared were used. No differentiation within this group was made on the kind of office for which they were candidates, since all the contested offices involved the responsibility of making decisions and influencing others.

To heighten the relevance of the cues of the ballot-counting situation to the story-writing procedure, the candidates were asked to judge their chances of winning the election, on the following scale: 0/5, 1/5, 2/5, 3/5, 4/5, 5/5 chances. The whole procedure was done anonymously.

The Ss in the *nonaroused condition* were 34 male students in an undergraduate course in psychology at the University of Michigan. The procedure was introduced as one about which some graduate students were interested in obtaining some normative data. After the procedure, the Ss were asked to sign their names in order that further measures could be correlated with their story-writing performance. It seemed reasonable to regard this group as one for whom the concern about control of the means of influence was not specifically engaged.

One may argue that differences in respects other than aroused power motivation underlie such differences between these two groups as may be obtained in their stories. Perhaps Ss in the aroused group have had peculiar learning experiences predisposing them to write power-related imagery for reasons having nothing to do with power motivation as defined. The validity of this argument is granted; there is no means of isolating this factor in the present design. Greater reliance is placed on the second step in the design—predicting power-motivated behavior from a measure derived from the first step—for establishing the tentative validity of the measure of power motivation. This problem will be more fully treated in discussion of the results.

Story-writing procedure. All Ss wrote stories for five pictures in a manner outlined in *The Achievement Motive* (272). The only procedural difference is that the pictures were reproduced in booklets rather than projected on a screen, and instructions modified accordingly. The five pictures are listed below in the order in which they were presented:

1. Two men in a library; Picture E in the Achievement series (272).
2. Instructor in classroom; Picture 21 in Birney's study (41).
3. Group scene; Picture E in the Affiliation series (Ch. 5).
4. Two men on campus; Picture 41 in Birney's study (41).
5. Political scene; from magazine, *Woman's Day.*

Step 2: Individual Differences in Power Motivation. Since the stories of the nonaroused Ss could be identified, other measures possibly related to a derived score of power motivation were obtained in this group: (a) Allport-Vernon Scale of Values (9), (b) Vocational Goals Inventory (66), (c) questionnaire on siblings, and (d) ratings by instructors of classroom behavior. The Vocational Goals Inventory required Ss to rank-order ten listed possible satisfactions on a job: being leader, interesting job, recognition from fellow men, being boss, surety of keeping job, self-expression, high pay, fame, helping others, working on one's own. The sibling questionnaire asked Ss to list their siblings and their ages, to permit reconstruction of birth order. The ratings by instructors pertained to the following classroom behavior: (a) argumentative in the classroom—likes to argue and contradict; (b) eager to get points across in the classroom in order to convince either the instructor or other students of a point of view. They were made on a three-point scale of frequency: 1 = "very frequently," 2 = "at times," and 3 = "never or rarely." The following hypotheses were advanced concerning the relationship between individual differences in power-motivation scores derived from the projective instrument and the variables measured by the preceding measures:

Hypothesis 1. Power motivation is positively related to Political and Economic and negatively to Social, value orientation, as measured by the Allport-Vernon Scale of Values. A person highly interested in controlling the means of influence should value those ideas having to do with such control within the culture—namely, the political and economic values. Being interested in controlling a person in a sense negates his sympathy for this person's feelings, and therefore the negative relationship with the Social dimension was anticipated.

Hypothesis 2. Power motivation is positively related to the intensity of interests in the job satisfactions of being boss and being leader. These job satisfactions can be interpreted as positions in which the potentiality for controlling the means of influence is high.

Hypothesis 3. Power motivation is positively associated with the number of siblings in the S's family. Furthermore an association was hypothesized between birth order and strength of power motivation, though no prediction about the direction of the association is made. Power satisfactions are perhaps derived from many experiences in which being manipulated by others and manipulating others were in evidence. One would expect that the high power-motivated individuals would come from larger families where this type of experience is more likely to occur. Birth order would seem to be an important variable in further shaping these experiences.

Hypothesis 4. Power motivation is positively associated with instructors' ratings of argumentativeness and trying to convince others. These behaviors are presumably instrumental in satisfying the power motive in the classroom.

SCORING STORIES FOR POWER MOTIVATION

In scoring a story, it is first identified as being related to power motivation or not. If a scorer decides that the story is related to power motivation (i.e., the story meets the Power Imagery criteria given below), it is then further scored for the presence or absence of the categories in the behavioral sequence. If the scorer decides that the story is not related to power motivation (Unrelated), no further scoring is done. The Power Imagery criteria are given in detail below. A complete scoring system with examples is available (See Ch. 14).

Power Imagery is scored when a story contains a reference to the thoughts, feelings, or actions of one of the characters which indicates that the character is concerned with the control of the means of influencing a person. Evidence of concern can come from one or more of three sources: (*a*) statements of affect, (*b*) statements of control activity, and (*c*) statements of superior-subordinate role relations. These three criteria are elaborated below.

a. There is some statement of affect surrounding the maintenance or attainment of the control of the means of influencing a person. A character can be feeling good about winning an argument or feeling bad because he was unable to have his way. Also statements showing dominance or about wanting to win a point, gain control (such as by a political or executive position), convince someone of something, or put a point across can be interpreted as implicit statements of affective concern about the control of the means of influence. Affective concern can also be found in statements of wanting to avoid weakness. Examples of this are: being humiliated in a status position, being ashamed of an incapacity to assert one's self or become dominant, and resenting the influence of another and wanting to overcome this.

Some very weak statements of concern over control of the means of influence are scored. Statements of desires to teach another person something, to interest another person in something, to inspire someone—although apparently weak in obvious power significance—should be scored. The only times when these statements would not be scored are in cases where the teaching, inspiring, or interesting is solicited by the person being influenced.

Statements of a person wanting another person to gain control of the means of influence—such as a person wanting someone else to win an election—should not be scored as Power Imagery. The only exception is a case in which there is a very clear identification of the person with the preferred candidate. This kind of imagery may appear in election stories where John wants to win the election, although John is not the candidate.

b. There is a definite statement of someone doing something about maintaining or attaining the control of the means of influence. Something that the character is actually doing in the story is the only kind of imagery that can qualify as Power Imagery under this criterion. The character has to dispute a position, argue something, demand or force something, try to put a point across, try to convince someone of something (and theoretically any activity in order to obtain control of the means of influencing someone).

Three special considerations should be noted under Criterion b. The two special considerations noted under Criterion a are applicable to Criterion b. Statements which involve trying to teach, interest, or inspire someone are scorable under Criterion b. Trying to win an election for someone else will not be scorable unless there is a close identification between the person campaigning and the candidate for office. Sometimes, moreover, it will be clear that an activity, although it meets the criterion listed in the preceding paragraph, is only for the purpose of arriving at the goal of another motive. In such a case, the story should not be scored for Power Imagery.

c. A story can be scored for Power Imagery if there is a statement of an interpersonal relationship which in its execution is culturally defined as one in which there is a superior person in control of the means of influencing a subordinate person. Examples of this are boss-worker and judge-defendant. Mere mention of superior-subordinate relationship is not enough to score. There has to be some mention of the activity involved in carrying out this relationship. Mere mention of a given person being influential would be enough to allow this story to be scored for Power Imagery.

Unrelated Imagery is scored when there is no evidence of power motivation concern in the stories as defined under Power Imagery.

When the story has been identified as one containing Power Imagery, it is scored for the presence or absence of the subcategories similar to those outlined for achievement motivation (272): Need; Instrumental Activity; Goal Anticipation; Block; Affective State; Thema.

In the final coding the coder did not know whether a given story came from one or the other of the two groups. To check on the reliability of this coding, a second coder scored a random set of twenty-four Ss from the total sample. The percentage of agreement for a given category between the two scorers ranged from 57 to 97. Furthermore, need for power scores (n Power scores) were tallied for each S by adding the number of categories appearing in his stories. The n Power scores obtained from the two coders were rank-ordered for the subsample. The rank-order correlation (rho) between the ranks obtained on these Ss by the two judges was $+.87$.

RESULTS

Step 1: Group Differences in Power Motivation. Imagery in the stories written by the aroused and nonaroused groups was compared by dichotomizing the frequency distributions of the combined groups as near to the median as possible. Table 1 gives for each category the number of Ss in each group above and below the median of the combined distribution. Exact tests were computed for each instance that

TABLE 1. NUMBER OF SUBJECTS IN AROUSED AND NONAROUSED GROUPS ABOVE AND BELOW MEDIAN* FOR VARIOUS POWER-RELATED IMAGINATIVE CATEGORIES

Imaginative Category	Aroused Group ($N = 34$)		Nonaroused Group ($N = 34$)		$p\ddagger$
	Above†	Below	Above	Below	
Power Imagery...........	27	7	15	19	.0023
	Breaking point between 1 and 2				
Need....................	21	13	14	20	.047
Instrumental Activity					
Positive...............	22	12	15	19	.047
Negative..............	12	21	8	26	.090
Questionable...........	16	18	13	21	n.s.
Any sign..............	24	10	13	21	.0056
	Breaking point between 1 and 2				
Goal Anticipation					
Positive...............	3	31	1	33	n.s.
Negative..............	3	31	3	31	n.s.
Any sign..............	6	28	3	31	n.s.
Block					
Personal...............	4	30	1	33	n.s.
Environmental.........	3	31	2	32	n.s.
Affective State					
Positive...............	4	30	1	33	n.s.
Negative..............	3	31	2	32	n.s.
Any sign..............	6	28	3	31	n.s.
Thema.................	28	6	17	17	.0044

* Median based on combined frequencies of both the aroused and the nonaroused groups.

† Except where indicated *S*s were divided as to whether the category appeared once or not at all in the five stories, this procedure approximating the combined median most closely.

‡ All the probabilities were computed by Exact Test, one-tailed hypothesis, 1 *df*.

potentially represented a significant deviation from a chance distribution. Power Imagery, Need, Instrumental Activity, and Thema appeared significantly more often in the aroused group's stories than in the nonaroused group's stories. These results, incidentally, are comparable to those obtained in similar comparisons in respect to the achievement and affiliation motives, except that the categories Goal Anticipation, Block, and Affect failed to differentiate the groups.

An over-all check on the differences in imagery can be made by comparing the n Power scores for the *S*s in the two groups. Table 2 shows the number of *S*s in each group above and below the combined groups' median n Power score. The probability of obtaining this distribution by chance is .0013, again as estimated by an Exact Test.

TABLE 2. NUMBER OF SUBJECTS IN AROUSED AND NONAROUSED GROUPS ABOVE AND BELOW MEDIAN* OF n POWER SCORES

Group	n Power Score	
	Above 6	Below 6
Aroused group ($N = 34$)............	22	12
Nonaroused group ($N = 34$).........	9	25

Note.—$p = .0013$, one-tailed hypothesis, 1 df.
* The approximation to the median was computed by combining the n Power scores of both the aroused and the nonaroused groups.

Step 2: Individual Differences in Power Motivation. Scores of the nonaroused group for n Power were dichotomized as near as possible to the group median. The resulting division into High and Low n Power scores is retained through all comparisons to be made in this section. The results of the comparisons made between the n Power scores and the variables for which relationships were predicted appear in Table 3. In most cases the other variables are dichotomized near the median into high and low categories.

This table supports the following observations which confirm predicted hypotheses. High n Power scorers, as compared to low n Power scorers, tend to have lower scores on the Social Value Dimension of the Allport-Vernon Scale of Values, show a significantly stronger interest in the job satisfaction of being leader, and were rated significantly higher by their instructors on the frequency of argumentation and the frequency of trying to convince others of their points of view in the classroom.

Other hypotheses were not confirmed. High n Power scorers as compared to low n Power scorers did not differ significantly in their scores on the Economic and Political value orientations, on their ratings of the job satisfaction of being boss, and on the number or order of siblings in their families.

Table 3 also includes an unpredicted result, that high n Power scorers rated the job satisfaction of obtaining recognition from their fellows significantly higher than low n Power scorers. No other comparison between the motive measure and the Vocational Goals Inventory yielded any positive results.

DISCUSSION

The results obtained comparing the imagery produced by the aroused and nonaroused groups are similar to parallel results found with the measures of achievement and affiliation motivations. In the

TABLE 3. FREQUENCIES OF HIGH-LOW N POWER SCORERS IN VARIOUS CATEGORIES ON MEASURES RELATED TO POWER MOTIVATION

Measure	Dimension	High n Power	Low n Power	Chi square	p	df
Allport-Vernon Scale of Values	Political					
	High*............	8	5	—	n.s.	—
	Low.............	8	8			
	Economic					
	High............	6	5	—	n.s.	—
	Low............	10	8			
	Social					
	High............	7	9	—	.12	1
	Low............	9	4			
Vocational Goals Inventory	"A job where you could be leader"					
	High............	9	4	—	.096†	1
	Low............	7	10			
	"A job where you could be boss"					
	High............	8	8	—	n.s.	—
	Low............	8	6			
	"A job where you could be looked upon very highly by fellow men"					
	High............	10	3	—	.049	1
	Low............	6	11	(2 tailed hypothesis)‡		
Sibling Questionnaire	No. of Siblings					
	0..............	0	1			
	1..............	7	4	—	n.s.	—
	2..............	4	3			
	3 or more........	5	3			
	Has older sibling					
	Yes............	9	5	—	n.s.	—
	No............	7	6			
Instructor's Ratings	Argumentativeness Frequency					
	High............	7	1			
	Medium.........	7	7	5.62§	<.05	2
	Low............	4	7			
	Frequency of Trying to Convince Others					
	High............	9	1			
	Medium.........	7	6	11.02	<.001	2
	Low............	2	8			

* High and Low division on Allport-Vernon Scale of Values based on deviation from normative data (2).

† The probabilities of the 2 × 2 tables were computed by the Exact Test.

‡ All other probabilities were estimated under a one-tailed hypothesis.

§ Chi squares where reported were estimated by the Mood Maximum Likelihood Ratio (9).

113

present design, however, there is an ambiguity in the nature of the arousal condition which was not present in the earlier studies. This ambiguity—the fact that the power arousal group was different from the nonaroused group not only in presumed level of arousal of some motivational pattern but also in whatever dispositions are salient in discriminating candidates and noncandidates for college offices— forces one to make only tentative conclusions about these results. It may be that the group differences uncovered in the analysis of the stories are due to motivations which are distinct from the power motive as defined.

Two other reasonable interpretations of the obtained differences between the two groups attribute them to differences in the level of achievement or recognition motivation. Fortunately it was possible to check the former possibility. The two sets of stories were scored for achievement motivation as outlined in *The Achievement Motive* (272). No significant difference in mean n Achievement scores of the groups was found.

The other interpretation, that the group differences are accountable in terms of recognition rather than power motivation, is a distinct possibility. The only basis for thinking otherwise is that the scoring system was built around a conceptualization of power motivation as distinct from strivings for recognition. Recognition themes in stories were not scored unless they fulfilled the criteria for power motivation as well. That is, if a story brought up problems of recognition as a way of obtaining control of the means of influence, then and only then was it scored. There is, however, no experimental way in the present study to rule out the interpretation of the power-motive measure in terms of recognition. In further use of the measure of power motivation, caution to recognize this possible contamination is recommended.

There seemed to be no difference between the aroused and nonaroused groups on certain of the affected categories (Goal Anticipation, Affect, and Obstacle), which proved valuable in discriminating groups with the other measures. An explanation for this discrepancy should be offered. Perhaps this particular motive does not permit the arousal of associated affective thoughts. There might be good cause to inhibit the expression of affect surrounding the power area, since there are many recognized taboos for expressing power in this culture —especially the expression of overt satisfactions derived from power behavior. Support for this explanation comes from the observation that these categories appeared very infrequently in the stories of both groups. Another reason for the lack of differential appearance of these categories might be that the particular pictures used in this study did not provide cues to the kind of thinking that would reflect the affective component. This possibility can be tested in further research.

That the measure reflects not only the group differences in assumed motivation level but also individual differences in variables related to aspects of power concern as defined is a fact suggesting that the instrument can be used with success in researches in which such a measure of motivation would be needed. The measure of power motivation, if some of its ambiguities are clarified, can be potentially used for exploring dimensions of control behavior exhibited in interpersonal relationships. Researchers using concepts of power different from the one presented here should be cautious in the use of this measure.

Some of the hypothesized relationships, particularly with the Allport-Vernon scales, were not substantiated in this study. These value measures can perhaps reflect many *different* motivational orientations, and it may thus be naive to expect a positive relationship between a fairly specific motivational pattern and values that can service many different needs.

Lack of support for the prediction that Ss high in n Power would rate the job satisfaction of being boss higher than Ss low in n Power may indicate that re-evaluation of the meaning of being boss for them is in order. "Boss" can be thought of as a negative word in this culture, and, indeed, there was little variability in the Ss' ranking of job satisfaction in this respect. Nearly everyone ranked this alternative low.

The simple prediction that high n Power Ss would come from large families was not substantiated. This finding would seem to indicate that any relationship between the power motive and the family structure depends on more complex considerations than simple frequency of contact with other family members. When the distribution of n Power score is divided into thirds (high, medium, and low), a trend was uncovered. Eight out of twelve high n Power scorers had at least one older sibling whereas this was true for only one out of six medium n Power scorers and five out of nine low n Power scorers. (Chi square $= 4.34$, $p < .15$, 2 df, two-tailed hypothesis.) Perhaps some fruitful distinctions can be made in the area of family structure which may be useful in understanding the development of the power motive.

The finding that high n Power Ss rated the job satisfaction of gaining recognition from their fellow men higher than do low n Power Ss points to the possibility that the satisfactions of prestige may be intimately tied with the satisfactions of power. This point of view has been elaborated by Murphy (311). There is also the possibility that the measure includes, at least partially, some aspects of recognition motivation. Indeed, all of the significant findings can be theoretically accounted for by considering the motive measured to be the recognition motive.

The relationship between achievement and power motivation. The product-moment correlation between the n Achievement and n Power scores was $+.27$ ($p < .05$). An attempt was made to use the n Achievement scores, however, to predict the same variables with which n Power scores had been related. No significant findings with these variables were obtained. In short, there seems to be a slight positive association between the two motives, but what is measured in scoring for the power motive is that process which seems to be directly related to power rather than achievement strivings.

SUMMARY

Two groups of Ss wrote stories in response to five pictures. One was tentatively considered to be aroused by cues relevant to power motivation; the other was not aroused. A scoring system paralleling the coding methods which had been fruitful in measuring the achievement and affiliation motives was applied to the stories and succeeded in differentiating the two groups. Four of the seven categories coded appeared significantly more frequently in the stories of the aroused group.

Individual differences in power motivation were estimated for Ss in the nonaroused group by the n Power scores (based on the coding categories). High n Power scorers differed from low n Power scorers in this group on a number of other factors relevant to power motivation. Some hypotheses relating strength of power motivation to other variables were not confirmed.

Although there was a significant positive correlation between n Power scores and n Achievement scores, the n Achievement score distribution does not predict the same relationships with power-related variables.

In conclusion, the results indicate that the projective measure of power motivation developed here not only can successfully isolate the presumed differential level of motivation in groups but also can successfully predict attitudes and overt behavior which are presumably related to the processes involved in power motivation. It is cautioned, however, that the measure may be conceived also in terms of recognition motivation.

CHAPTER 7

The Relationship Between Symbolic and Manifest Projections of Sexuality with Some Incidental Correlates*

RUSSELL A. CLARK AND MINDA RAE SENSIBAR

THIS PAPER will be concerned with a further analysis of the data collected from two of the experiments (experiments A and C) described in greater detail in an earlier article by Clark (72). In brief, experiment A consisted of collecting TAT stories from one group of subjects (Ss) after they had been exposed to photographic slides of attractive nude females. The control group for this experiment consisted of comparable Ss who wrote stories after having been exposed to slides of a nonsexual nature. Experiment C was essentially a repetition of experiment A with the addition that the TAT stories were written under the influence of alcohol in a beer-party setting. That is, the experimental group took the TAT during a fraternity beer party after having been exposed to slides of attractive nude females. The control group in this experiment took the TAT during a beer party without prior exposure to such slides. Hereafter experiment A will be referred to as the nonalcoholic condition and experiment C as the alcoholic condition.

The TAT stories were scored for the presence of manifest sexual content. This sexual content was partitioned into three components: (a) primary—explicit or implicit evidence for sexual intercourse; (b) secondary—evidence for the occurrence of such secondary sex activity as kissing, dancing, fondling, etc.; (c) tertiary—characters in the stories perceived as sweethearts, on a date courting, in love, etc., but not engaged in either primary or secondary sexual activity.

*Reprinted by permission of author and publisher from *The Journal of Abnormal and Social Psychology,* 1955, **50**, 327-334. Copyright 1955 by the American Psychological Association, Inc.

117

Sexual activity was scored only once for each story, and that which was biologically most sexual received priority.

The analysis of the data from the nonalcoholic condition revealed that the sexually aroused group expressed significantly *less* manifest sex content in their stories than did the unaroused control group. The analysis of the data from the alcoholic condition showed that the aroused group expressed significantly *more* manifest sex than did their unaroused controls. These results along with others described in the previous article led to the conclusion that under normal conditions increased anxiety or guilt accompanying the increased sexual arousal accounts for the inhibition of the manifest sex content. However, under conditions involving alcohol and the permissive beer-party setting the guilt or anxiety over expressing manifest sex is so reduced that the aroused group expresses significantly more sex than does the control.

PROBLEM AND PROCEDURE

With these foregoing results in hand a Freudian hypothesis immediately came to mind. When the manifest expression of sexuality is being inhibited, as seems to be the case for the aroused group under nonalcoholic conditions, perhaps a disguised form of expression such as symbolism will be exhibited. Freud's discussion of this situation with respect to dreams is too well known to require any elaboration here. Therefore, it was decided to score for the presence of sexual symbolism. This presented certain difficulties. The major difficulty was encountered when we tried to score merely for the presence of all separate objects that are considered to be potential symbols. The reason for our difficulty was that the TAT pictures which were employed clearly depicted objects that are considered classical sexual symbols. For example, picture 12BG clearly shows a boat resting in a pond under a tree in a general wood setting. The boat, tree, and rolling landscape are sexual symbols mentioned by Freud and others. Picture 14 shows the silhouette of a boy in a window. A window or portal is, of course, another sexual symbol. Other such examples could be cited. Thus, we were getting large numbers of symbols that were merely mentions of objects that were clearly depicted in the pictures. This did not seem to be a sensible procedure. Our final decision was not to score for the presence of symbolism if there was only the mere mention of a given classical symbol that was clearly depicted in the TAT picture. In fact, we did *not* score the mere mentioning of a classical symbol even if it was not clearly depicted in the picture. In order to be scored for symbolism a story had to meet the following criterion: The classical symbol or symbols mentioned had to be utilized or involved in some action which in and of itself could be interpreted as being symbolic. That is, isolated objects which fulfilled the requirements for sexual symbols were scored only if they appeared in a symbolic context that could be interpreted as signifying intercourse, masturbation, tumescence-detumescence cycles, etc. For example, if in response to picture 14 a person wrote that this was a boy looking out of his dormitory window, this was *not* scored as symbolic, but if it was a thief *climbing up* to go through the *window* in order to steal the *jewels* in the *house,* this *was* scored as symbolic. In this latter statement the window, which is a classical symbol and clearly represented in the picture, is also a part of a classically symbolic action sequence, i.e., climbing, breaking into house, stealing jewels. In essence what we scored for was not the mere presence of isolated objects that could or could not be symbols, but for themata that could be interpreted in a symbolic fashion. These themata, of course, involved objects which are considered to be the symbols for the male or female genitals, breasts, etc.

In scoring, the stories were given weights of two, one, or zero. A weight of two indicated that symbolism was strongly present in the story, a weight of one indicated that some symbolism was present, and zero indicated that no symbolism could be detected. An individual's total score was the sum of the weights given his five separate stories. The scoring was done independently by two scorers after they had familiarized themselves with the literature on sexual symbolism. The product-moment correlation between the initial two sets of total scores for both the alcoholic and nonalcoholic conditions was $+.82$. The scoring used for the present analysis represents a joint scoring in which differences in the two sets of scores were reconciled.

RESULTS AND DISCUSSION

A t test of the difference between the two groups of the nonalcoholic condition (cf. also Table 1) demonstrated that the aroused group exhibited a significantly higher symbolic sex score than did the control group ($t = 2.19$, $p < .05$). It will be recalled, of course, that this aroused group showed significantly less manifest sexual content than its control group. This finding, then, is in line with Freud's general hypothesis that anxiety can cause manifest sex content to be inhibited, but that sexual motivation can find expression in symbolic form. Also if Freud's hypothesis is correct, one would expect the groups in the alcoholic condition to express little symbolism because of the fact that once anxiety was reduced by the consumption of alcohol and the permissive party atmosphere most of the sexual expression would be manifest in nature. This, in fact, turned out to be the case. In this condition both the control and the aroused group expressed very little symbolism and in almost identical amounts. The average symbolism score for the combined groups in this condition was .45. This value is lower than that obtained for either the control group ($t = 1.79$, $p < .08$) or the aroused group ($t = 3.87$, $p < .01$) of the nonalcoholic condition. These findings, of course, are in complete accord with the classical Freudian contention. That is, if anxiety is present, the libido finds expression in a disguised or symbolic fashion. When anxiety is absent, sexual expression is channeled directly in manifest form.

A recent paper by Hall (168), however, takes exception to this Freudian contention. In general Hall maintains that sexual symbolism in dreams is not a disguised expression of sex, the purpose of the disguise being to smuggle the content past the censor, but rather a means of representing as clearly as possible the particular conception of sexuality that the dreamer has in mind. One of several cogent reasons that Hall has for offering his alternative theory is that in his collection of dreams he often found both manifest and symbolic expression of sexual activity in the same dream or same sequence of dreams. The question that Hall raises concerns the efficacy of disguising the sexual content if at the next moment it is revealed in manifest form.

Hall's theory was of particular interest because the same phenomenon was noted in this study in the TAT stories. That is, an individual would give both strong manifest and symbolic sex in the same story or series of stories. To throw additional light on this somewhat paradoxical question we decided to examine the intragroup relationship between symbolic and manifest expression of sex. If Freud's contention is correct, you would again expect a negative relationship between the two as was the case with the intergroup comparisons. If Hall's formulation is correct, one might possibly expect even a positive relationship. It was feasible to do this only for the two groups of the nonalcoholic condition. The frequency of appearance of symbolism was so very low under conditions of alcohol that any kind of intragroup trend analysis was meaningless. The obtained relationship for the nonalcoholic condition can be seen in Table 1. Table 1 presents the results of an analysis of variance in which both the aroused and control groups were divided into thirds as equally as possible based on the *manifest* sex score. This manifest sex score was derived by giving the weight of two to a primary sex story, a weight of one to a secondary or tertiary sex story, and a weight of zero to a story containing no manifest sex. The breakdown into thirds of the distribution was made separately for the control and aroused groups. That is, the "highs" in the aroused group represent those with the highest manifest sex content in their own group, but they have significantly lower manifest sex scores than the highs in the control group. Lastly, the entries in the cells represent averages based on the total symbolic sex score previously described.

It can be seen from Table 1 that the relationship between manifest and symbolic sex is neither positively nor negatively linear but rather a curvilinear one with those individuals who write either strong manifest sex stories or very weak manifest sex stories exhibiting the greatest amount of symbolism. That this trend is probably not a random one is evidenced by the F test involving the variation due to the

TABLE 1. MEAN SCORE ON SEXUAL SYMBOLISM AS A FUNCTION OF
EXPERIMENTAL CONDITION AND MANIFEST SEX SCORE
(NONALCOHOLIC CONDITION)*

Experimental Condition	High Manifest Sex Group		Moderate Manifest Sex Group		Low Manifest Sex Group	
	N	Mean	N	Mean	N	Mean
Aroused........	15	1.87	14	.64	10	1.70
Control........	9	.89	16	.56	13	1.00

Analysis of Variance†

Source	Sums of Squares	df	Variance Estimate
Total..	38.20	76	
Experimental treatment.....................	2.15	1	2.15
Manifest sex score.........................	3.18	2	1.59
Error.......................................	32.87	73	.45
Experimental treatment × Manifest sex score	0.51	2	.26
Within cells...............................	32.36	71	.46

* In the statistical treatment of the data in this table the means are based on the raw data. However, the actual t tests or F tests were based on transformed data using the square-root technique. This was done because the variance estimates were not homogeneous and seemed to be proportional to the means. Also, in the analysis of variance adjustment was made for the disproportionate subclass frequencies. This was done according to the method offered by Johnson (200).

$$† F = \frac{\text{Experimental treatment}}{\text{Error}} = 4.78 \quad p < .05;$$

$$F = \frac{\text{Manifest sex score}}{\text{Error}} = 3.53 \quad p < .05.$$

different levels of manifest sex score. Also the fact that the interaction between the experimental treatment and manifest sex score is insignificant indicates that there is no evidence that the trends in the two groups are dissimilar.

This curvilinear relationship is rather a curious finding. The large amount of symbolism in the high manifest group is, of course, the major deviant finding and in need of explanation. This follows because according to a Freudian formulation the writing of strong sex stories would seem to preclude the possibility of the presence of much anxiety. There are a number of ways in which to account for our finding. One way is to assume that if sexual motivation becomes sufficiently high, there is the tendency for symbolism to be expressed without regard to the presence of anxiety. With this added assumption an interpretation which is in line with Hall's general formulation could also account for the increased amount of symbolism in the aroused group.

One other possibility is, of course, that both Hall and Freud are correct. It may well be that symbolism is used as an alternative means of expressing sex even in the absence of anxiety but becomes more preferred to the extent that anxiety is involved. However, an examination of the data from the alcoholic condition should help clarify this issue. The aroused group from this experiment represents a sexually aroused group presumably with much of the anxiety reduced by the alcohol and permissive party atmosphere. This group gave a large number of manifest sex stories. If Freud's formulation is correct, you would *not* expect much symbolism in this group because of the presumably low anxiety level. If the formulation which is more in line with Hall's theorizing is correct, you would expect a large amount of symbolism. As indicated previously from the comparisons involving the combined groups from the alcoholic condition this is not the case. The average symbolism score for the aroused group alone was .41, which is lower than the aroused group ($t = 3.88$, $p < .01$) and control group ($t = 1.83$, $p = .07$) of the nonalcoholic condition.

It would thus seem that to the extent that anxiety is lacking, symbolism is lacking, and that Freud's formulation is supported. However, there still remains the apparently paradoxical fact that in the intragroup breakdown for the nonalcoholic condition those with high manifest scores also have high symbolism scores. This seems paradoxical because, as mentioned before, the writing of sex stories, especially of a primary nature, would seem to preclude the possibility of the presence of anxiety. However, there is one possibility that should not be ignored, and this involves the *response-produced* guilt that stems from writing stories of a sexual nature. The individuals who write strong sex stories must normally have a fairly low anxiety level which permits them to do this, but writing sexual stories, especially if primary in nature, may cue off enough guilt to channel the expression into symbolic form. This certainly did seem to be what was happening in some cases in which a primary manifest sex story was followed immediately by one containing symbolism.

The solution to this very paradox has been handled by Miller (290) in slightly different terms in his treatment of approach-avoidance conflicts. Miller points out, "Similar paradoxical effects may be deduced when the attractiveness of the goal is held constant and its repulsiveness varied within the limits allowing the two gradients to cross. As the strength of avoidance at the goal is weakened, the subject will be expected to move forward. But as he moves forward, the strength of approach increases so that stronger avoidance must be aroused before his advance is stopped. The fact that the subject moves nearer to the dangerous goal more than compensates for its reduction in unattractiveness" (p. 440).

In this instance going closer to the goal would involve writing stories of a more primary nature. Therefore, it would be individuals with the initial low gradients of avoidance who would write the most sexual stories and thus be apt to experience the most *response-produced* guilt.

Therefore, what may possibly be happening is something like this. The individuals in the *low* manifest group (both aroused and control) through past training are highly anxious about expressing sex. For the aroused Ss this anxiety is, of course, reinforced by the stimulation of the nude slides to which they were exposed. These individuals, therefore, would tend to express most of their sexuality in symbolic terms. The individuals in the *high* manifest group through past training have acquired less anxiety over sexuality and therefore approach close enough to the goal to write stories of a primary nature which in turn cues off quite a bit of guilt resulting in symbolic expression of sexuality. Now what about the individuals in the moderate manifest category? They could be individuals with a moderate amount of anxiety who write stories with mild sexuality in them, but this is not enough to cue off much guilt, so they have only a moderate amount of symbolism in their stories.[1]

There still remains at least one apparent inconsistency: Why is it that in the intragroup comparisons the individuals with the highest manifest sex scores give high symbolism, whereas in the intergroup comparisons just the reverse holds true? Why should not the control group of the nonalcoholic condition give as much or more symbolism than the aroused group in view of the fact that they give significantly

---

[1] Although the foregoing analysis makes pretty good sense, it should be obvious that this is an oversimplification. A tacit assumption has been that although individuals varied in the amount of anxiety over sex (avoidance motive), their sex drives (approach motives) were relatively the same. This is probably not a warranted assumption even though it is likely that the variability in anxiety is far greater than the variability in the sex drive. If one allows for variability in the approach motive, it might be that the individuals who wrote primary stories, for example, did so *not* because of an initially lower avoidance motive, but because of a high approach motive. This complicates even further an already highly complicated picture. We regard the *ad hoc* interpretations presented above as mainly serving the function of highlighting the necessity of considering the various pertinent factors. To do definitive work, ideally one would have to have independent measures of the approach tendency, both the stimulus-produced and response-produced avoidance tendencies, plus a knowledge of how these three interacted to produce both manifest and symbolic expressions of sexuality.

more manifest sex? That is to say, is it not possible that the increased response-produced guilt of the control group is enough to offset the stimulus-produced (nude slides) anxiety of the aroused group? One possible answer to this is that in the aroused group nearly *everyone* should have experienced a certain high level of anxiety as a function of examining the slides of attractive nude females, whereas, in the control group perhaps an equivalent level of guilt was reached by only those individuals who wrote stories of a primary manifest nature.

Perhaps an analogy involving the rat in a maze would simplify the entire picture. Assume that hungry rats have in the past been both shocked and fed in the goal box of a straight maze. If one group of rats is put in a maze near the goal box where the fear is great, they will start making avoidance responses. Also assume that in the past the rats have been fed in side alleys, that they have not received very much food there but also little or no shock. So in addition to retreating down the alley they may also duck into a side alley and get some partial gratification without anxiety. The other group of rats is placed in the far end of the maze where fear is low. These rats will start to make approach responses. Some of these rats, as Miller (290) points out, will "overshoot" into the territory where the anxiety is high enough to cause them to beat a retreat or duck into the side alleys. However, on the average one would expect both more avoidance behavior and substitute gratification on the part of the first group than the second.

This is analogous to what might be taking place in the sex experiment with sex and anxiety replacing hunger and fear. The side alleys would correspond, of course, to the symbolic expression of sexuality. Avoidance behavior would be comparable to expressing less anxiety-laden sexuality or no sexuality.

Although much of the foregoing has been *ad hoc* conjecture, a few tentative conclusions seem justifiable: (*a*) It does seem that classical symbolism serves as a disguised expression of sexuality. (*b*) Symbolism as a mode of expression seems to be preferred only to the extent that anxiety over sex is present. (*c*) The amount of symbolism in a story is not necessarily a direct measure of the "normal" level of anxiety. For example, if an individual's normal level is quite low, he may approach so close to the goal that this engenders a high level of response-produced guilt which may in turn produce symbolic expression of sexuality. (*d*) The above is a possible explanation of the seemingly paradoxical fact that both strong manifest and symbolic expressions of sexuality appear in the same fantasy sequences.

Incidental Correlates of the Inhibited Expression of Sexuality

In view of the evidence of the inhibited sexual expression obtained under nonalcoholic conditions it seemed worth while to examine the data from this condition to see if a similar finding held for the perception of the sex of the characters depicted in the TAT pictures. A second relationship was investigated because of the vast evidence for a linkage between sex and aggression (see next section).

Perception. Three of the five pictures used in the nonalcoholic condition were sufficiently ambiguous to make possible a misinterpretation of the sex of the characters. Picture 14 from Murray's 1943 series shows the silhouette of a figure standing at a window. This figure is usually perceived as a male by male Ss but it is sometimes perceived as a female. Picture 20 from this same series depicts a shadowy figure standing under a lamp post. This again is more often perceived as a male than as a female. Picture 10 is also somewhat indistinct and is usually described as a man and a woman in an embrace or confronting one another, but sometimes it is perceived as two men or two women. The contribution of picture 10 to the results was negligible because it was misperceived so rarely, but to be consistent it was counted in the analysis if anyone described the two figures as female. Table 2 demonstrates that the aroused

TABLE 2. PERCENTAGE OF SUBJECTS PERCEIVING AT LEAST ONE OUT OF THREE AMBIGUOUS FIGURES AS FEMALE

Condition	N	Percentage Perceiving at Least One Female	Chi Square
Aroused...............	39	64.1	6.87*
Control...............	38	34.2	

* Significant at the .01 level.

group perceived all of these characters as female significantly more often than did the control group.

This actually is not what one might expect. Bruner and Postman (56), for example, discuss two general effects of emotionality, value, etc. on perception. One is a *defense* process in which the individual fails or is slow to perceive an anxiety-laden stimulus. The other is a *sensitization* process in which the stimulus is perceived more readily. In light of the previous findings which show the aroused group being defensive by expressing sex symbolically rather than manifestly, one might expect the defensive process to be dominant and operate such that ambiguous figures would *not* be perceived as female. This was not the case. However, in a further analysis it was found that for the aroused group in only 23.1 per cent of the stories in which misperceptions occurred was the female involved in any kind of manifest sex activity. The same percentage for the control group was 50.0. Thus, it would appear that sensitization is occurring at the perceptual level, but that defensive processes intervene to prevent the involvement of the female figure in any kind of sexual activity.

Aggression. Throughout the psychological literature there appear scattered conjectures and evidence that sexuality and aggression are somehow intimately linked. Freud writes, "That cruelty and the sexual instinct are most intimately connected is beyond doubt taught by the history of civilization, but in the explanation of this connection no one has gone beyond the accentuation of the aggressive factors of the libido" (147, p. 570). Dollard *et al.* (102) report a study by Sollenberger in which there was shown to be a very marked relationship between aggressive behavior and male hormone content of adolescent boys. Ford and Beach (140) cite numerous examples of aggressive behavior occurring during copulation up and down the phylogenetic scale. In a recent study Lindner (233) found that sexual offenders showed more aggression on a projective test than did a control group of nonsexual offenders.

A similar finding exists with the present data. The stories for both groups were scored for the presence of overt aggression. There were five general categories that constituted the scoring system for aggression: (*a*) all occurrences of death except by suicide;[2] (*b*) physical violence—beatings, auto accidents, combat, etc.; (*c*) personal tragedies and misfortunes—homes burning to the ground, loved ones ill, loss of life savings, etc.; (*d*) crimes—theft, breaking and entering, embezzlement, etc.; (*e*) quarrels—disagreements in which anger, hatred, resentment, tension, etc. are involved. Punishment or imprisonment for crimes committed was *not* considered as aggression. The crimes were scored, of course, but not any attendant punishment. Finally, only aggressive acts directed against persons were considered in this present analysis.[3] The scoring was done inde-

---

[2] For the purposes of the present analysis and a later analysis, it was considered expedient to omit suicides because their theoretical significance is quite complex. A check was made, however, and it was found that their inclusion would not have altered the nature of the findings.

[3] Those Ss who had no aggression in any of their stories could not, of course, be included in this analysis.

pendently by two separate scorers. A product-moment reliability coefficient was calculated using as the score for each individual the total frequency of appearance of aggressive incidents in his five stories. This correlation was .91.

Table 3 shows that the aroused group expresses significantly less aggression than the control group. It will be recalled that the aroused group under this condition (nonalcoholic) also expressed significantly less manifest sex. This would again seem to show a close linkage between sex and aggression. However, it is not at all

TABLE 3. PERCENTAGE OF SUBJECTS EXHIBITING AT LEAST THREE INSTANCES OF OVERT AGGRESSION

Condition	N	Percentage Giving at Least Three Aggressive Responses	Chi Square*
Aroused............	39	10.2	17.57**
Control.............	38	57.9	

* Corrected for continuity.
** Significant at the .01 level.

clear what the exact nature of this linkage is. If there had been *more* aggression in the aroused group instead of less, this would have been consonant with the frustration-aggression hypothesis expounded by such writers as Dollard *et al.* (102). That is to say, the aroused group can be considered to have been frustrated in that they were aroused but had no opportunity for release. A distinct possibility is that there were greater aggressive tendencies in the aroused group, but these suffered the same fate for the same reason as the sexual tendencies discussed in the previous sections. That is to say, it might easily be that the expression of any frustration-produced aggression would be inhibited by the presence of anxiety over expressing aggression. It might be that some measure of a disguised or substitute form of aggression would show a higher frequency in the aroused group as was the case with expression of sexuality.

Although it is a little difficult to conceive of something like symbolic aggression, there is a somewhat different approach that is pertinent. McClelland (258) in his discussion of aggression cites evidence that if there is strong anxiety present, aggressive tendencies appearing in fantasy will be projected into impersonal, vague, or unspecified agents. That is, a person is killed not at the hands of another person but by an animal, through sickness, accident, etc.

Following this lead all instances of aggression appearing in the stories were scored as to whether the agent of the aggression was personal in source or whether the agent was impersonal or unspecified. In most cases this was a straightforward judgment made with little hesitancy. However, two general categories were somewhat equivocal. The first involved auto accidents, railroad accidents, etc. It could be argued that because there must be a person behind the wheel this type of aggression should be considered, in the last analysis, to be personal in source. Nevertheless, because in this general situation intent to harm is absent, and because the emphasis is definitely on the vehicle as the instrument of harm, we felt strongly that this situation belonged in the impersonal category. The second situation which was not completely clear involved mere statements that an individual had been killed in the war.[4] These statements are to an extent depersonalized, but because war usually involves interpersonal conflict with intent to harm, these instances of aggression were scored as personal. The scoring was again done independently by two individuals and product-moment reliability coefficients were calculated. An individual's score consisted of the total number of personal or impersonal aggressions. Separate reliabilities were calculated for the two types of aggression. For aggression which was personal in source the correlation was .93; for impersonal aggression the correlation was .88.

The results of this analysis showed that for the control group 30.2 per cent of the aggression was impersonal or unspecified whereas the aroused group exhibited 53.6 per cent as impersonal or unspecified. The analysis in Table 4 demonstrates that this is a reliable difference. Therefore, although the aroused Ss express significantly less aggression than the control group, an appreciably greater per-

TABLE 4. PERCENTAGE OF SUBJECTS GIVING AT LEAST 50 PER CENT OF THEIR AGGRESSIVE RESPONSES AS IMPERSONAL IN SOURCE

Condition	N	Percentage Giving at Least 50% Impersonal Aggressive Responses	Chi Square
Aroused	30	66.6	6.70*
Control	35	34.3	

* Significant at the .01 level.

[4] There may be some doubt as to whether "deaths in war" should be considered as personal or impersonal aggression. Analyses omitting these relatively few instances altogether or scoring them as impersonal in source still yield results significant beyond the .05 level of confidence.

centage of their aggression is impersonal in source. Thus, a reasonable conclusion would seem to be that the aroused Ss were not only anxious about expressing manifest sex, but also anxious about expressing manifest aggression; and when they did express manifest aggression, there was a tendency to project it into impersonal or unspecified sources.

The possibility that *displaced* aggression might show the above trend was entertained, but it is difficult to decide what figure should be the primary target of the aggression from which displacement could be measured. We did score for aggression that was displaced to animals or inanimate objects. There were more of these in the aroused group, but the frequency of occurrence was so low that statistical analysis was precluded.

SUMMARY

This study involved scoring TAT stories for the presence of sexual symbolism. The stories scored came from two different experiments. In one experiment the experimental group was sexually stimulated before taking the TAT, while the control group received no such prior stimulation. The second experiment was conducted in the same fashion except that it was carried out in a beer-party atmosphere under the influence of alcohol. The results showed that under non-alcoholic conditions the aroused group expressed significantly more symbolism than the control group. It had been shown previously that this aroused group inhibited the manifest expression of sex. Under conditions of alcohol both groups gave very little symbolism. It had previously been shown that these two groups expressed large amounts of manifest sexuality. These results are, of course, in line with the Freudian hypothesis that inhibited sexuality finds an outlet symbolically in fantasy. However, a second, intragroup, analysis showing the amount of symbolism, expressed as a function of the amount of manifest sex expressed, revealed the relationship to be curvilinear with both low and high manifest sex corresponding to high symbolism. Various interpretations are discussed for this latter finding. A further incidental finding revealed that the aroused group perceived ambiguous figures in the TAT as female more often than did the control. However, a smaller percentage of these "misperceived" females became engaged in sexual activity in the aroused group than in the control group. Another finding dealt with the expression of manifest aggression. The aroused group which expressed significantly less manifest sex in their stories also expressed significantly less manifest aggression. It was also found that the aggression which did appear in the stories of the aroused group was more apt to be attributed to impersonal or unspecified sources.

CHAPTER 8

●●

The Effects of Sexual Stimulation Under Varying Conditions on TAT Sexual Responsiveness*

PAUL H. MUSSEN AND ALVIN SCODEL[1]

THE PRESENT STUDY is concerned with the effects of sexual stimulation in different situational contexts on subsequent TAT sexual responsiveness. Our hypothesis states that these responses will be more inhibited following sex arousal in the presence of a stern father figure than following such arousal in the presence of a young, permissive individual.

A procedure almost identical with the one described by Clark (72) was used. The subjects were two groups of male students in an introductory psychology course. Both groups took the TAT after having been exposed to sex-arousing stimulation. In the Formal group (33 subjects), a series of eight photographic slides of attractive nude females was presented by a formal, professorial, and somewhat stern man in his sixties. Subjects were told that the research was related to Sheldon's body-type theories. They were instructed to rate the attractiveness of each of the eight nudes and to indicate the criteria for their judgments.

Using the same instructions, a young-looking, informal, permis-

* Reprinted by permission of author and publisher from the *Journal of Consulting Psychology,* 1955, **19,** 90. Copyright 1955 by the American Psychological Association, Inc.

[1] An extended report of this study may be obtained without charge from Paul Mussen, University of California, or Alvin Scodel, Ohio State University, or for a fee from the American Documentation Institute. To obtain it from the latter source, order Document No. 4439 from ADI Auxiliary Publications Project, Photoduplication Service, Library of Congress, Washington 25, D. C., remitting in advance $1.25 for microfilm or $1.25 for photocopies. Make checks payable to Chief, Photoduplication Service, Library of Congress.

sive graduate student presented the slides to the Informal group (38 subjects).

In both groups, the first examiner left the room immediately after the ratings were completed. At this point, another experimenter stepped forward, explained that he was attempting to standardize a test of creative imagination, and then administered eight TAT cards from the Murray series (7BM, 12BG, 3BM, 14, 20, 6GF, 6BM, 13MF) to the group.

The manifest and implied sexual content of each TAT story was scored according to a seven-point scale, ranging from 0 to 6, depending on the intensity of sexual activity. The subject's total sexual response score was the sum of the scores on the eight stories.

The mean sexual response score of the Informal group was 9.55, while the mean for the Formal group was 7.12 (SD's, 5.18 and 4.26, respectively). The difference between means yielded a t value of 2.13, significant between the 2 and 5 per cent levels of confidence.

Thus, it would seem that arousal of socially disapproved needs in the presence of an authority figure results in greater inhibition of subsequent expression of that need than arousal of the same need in a permissive situation.

CHAPTER 9

Sex Differences in Sexual Imagery Aroused by Musical Stimulation

DAVID C. BEARDSLEE AND R. FOGELSON

THE PURPOSE of the present research has been to investigate and measure the differences in the sexual motivation of males and females by means of content analysis of "imaginative" stories written in response to TAT pictures and to short musical selections. The experiment attempts to extend Clark's (72; 73; Clark and Sensibar, Ch. 7) research in this area. Both overt or manifest sexual imagery and sexually symbolic imagery were studied.

There have been few psychologically-oriented studies concerning the effects of music on male and female sexual motivation. The experimental literature on "affective qualities of music" has depended either on preference judgments or on conscious evaluations and ratings (Sopchak, 387). In view of the important role of unconscious sexual motivation and Clark's findings as to the inhibition of sexual imagery by sexual arousal, it is difficult to interpret these studies.

Havelock Ellis (115) asserts that considerable importance can be attached to the voice and to music generally as a method of sexual appeal. He feels that sexual stimulation from the voice and music has a greater effect on women than on men. It is suggested that since the change of voice at puberty is greater in the male than in the female, "a woman's voice retains childlike qualities and is therefore less specifically feminine than a man's voice is specifically masculine" (p. 52). This line of argument suggests the use of music to obtain differential sexual arousal of male and female subjects.

PROCEDURE

Four groups of subjects were used: two groups of males and two of females. All groups were first presented with the same two pictures as stimuli for "creative" stories. Subsequently, four short musical selections were played as stimuli for imaginative productions. One group of males (Group MN) and one group of females (Group FN) were presented with four "neutral" musical selections, while the remaining groups (MA and FA) were presented with "active" or "arousing" musical selections.

The stories written to the two pictures served as a control test for group differences. The first depicts a couple, arm in arm, gazing at an imaginary dream house. The second, from the standard TAT series (No. 20), portrays a vague figure of indeterminate sex standing under a streetlight.

The musical selections were chosen from within the framework of what might loosely be called "movie music." Six of the eight compositions were themes from motion pictures; the other two musical selections employed the same basic instrumentation as the "movie music." "Movie music," by virtue of the fact that it is used as a background for portrayals of human action, is quite versatile in that it must strive to represent a wide variety of human emotions and situations. Vocal music was not used in this study because male and female voices are easily recognizable and this would create a "halo effect." To eliminate specific personal associations and recollections, an effort was made to select music which had not achieved a high degree of popularity.

The assembling of "movie music" into two series, "neutral" and "arousing," was done in cooperation with a musicologist. Some of the criteria used for classifying a piece of music as active or arousing were that the music should contain a pronounced emphasis on rhythm, themes with comparatively large tonal ranges, and a gradual buildup to a climax. In contradistinction, the neutral music could be characterized as having very little rhythmic emphasis and a general evenness in melody and over-all construction.

The subjects were undergraduate elementary psychology students at two central New England liberal arts colleges. Four classes were available at the men's college, two of these constituting group MN and two group MA. The largest of the three classes available at the women's school was used as group FA, the other two comprised group FN. The two institutions are comparable in that they are both liberal arts colleges, their students are recruited from essentially similar geographic areas, and the students of the two institutions come from comparable socioeconomic backgrounds. Both collegiate groups were approximately equal in age, and neither had formally studied projective testing methods.

The subjects were given 30 seconds to observe each of the pictures, followed by four minutes to write the story suggested by the picture. The same procedure was followed for the musical selections except that each of the musical selections was approximately three minutes in duration. The subjects were permitted to write notes while the music was playing, but they were instructed not to begin the actual writing of a story until the musical selection was completed.

The subjects were given the usual instruction that "this is a test of creative imagination," etc., and were instructed to sign their names to the test booklet. The test was administered to the male subjects by one of the experimenters. It was administered to the female subjects by their regular teacher, since the presence of a strange male might have influenced the result.

The sexual imagery of subjects was scored in three different ways: (a) Manifest or Overt Sex Imagery, (b) Symbolic Sex Activity, and (c) Sex Symbolism (as discussed by Freud). The first and third scoring techniques were adopted from Clark, who made available his scoring criteria and stories.[1]

Clark defines Overt Sex Imagery as (a) *primary*—explicit or implicit evidence for sexual intercourse [score of 3]; (b) *secondary*—evidence for the occurrence of such secondary sex activity as kissing, dancing, or fondling [score of 2]; (c) *tertiary*—characters in the stories perceived as sweethearts, on a date, courting, in love, etc., but not engaged in either primary or secondary activity [score of 1]. This scoring system was used unchanged. The interscorer reliability in this study was 96 per cent agreement on categorization with "agreement on absence" ignored.

The second score, which is referred to as Symbolic Sex Activity to distinguish it from Sex Symbolism (clinically defined), is an attempt to create a public scoring definition for sexual symbolism along the lines of the definition of achievement imagery and of affiliation imagery. The basis of the definition is Freud's presentation of the fundamental characteristics of sexual activity as rhythmic self-stimulation (147, p. 585 ff). Four variables[2] are scored, each for presence or absence. These are *Motion, Rhythm, Peak,* and *Penetration.*

Motion is scored if the story contains reference to gross bodily movement of an animate organism. Head, arm, or hand movement is not scored. Mere change of place is not scored. Examples: "he walked" or "he was lifting a bag" is scored; "he went" or "he was lifted in the elevator" is not scored.

Rhythm is scored if the story contains action which demonstrates a repetitive quality or character of continuous or serial nature. A single repetition is not scored. No distinction is made between animate and inanimate objects. Examples: "clapping," "swinging," and "the tree nodded" are scored. "He jumped across the brook" is not scored as rhythm.

Peak is scored whenever the story involves a general increase in tension or activity followed by a letdown. An increase without a decrease is not scored. Examples: "he climbed on up the mountain, then descended" and "he became increasingly worried over the exam; when it was over he relaxed" are scored as peak.

Penetration is scored whenever the story contains reference to the entrance into or movement through a resisting surface. Examples: "he dove into the water" or "he 'busted' his way through the door" is scored

---

[1] We are especially indebted to David C. McClelland for advice in the development of this system of scoring.

[2] Detailed definitions of these categories, together with scoring definitions for the other two variables, are available from the Psychology Department, Wesleyan University.

penetration. "He went through the door" or "the arrows bounced off his armor" is not scored.

A story was scored as containing sexually symbolic activity if *any two* of the four variables were present in the story. The individual's score was the sum of the scores on his stories. The interscorer agreement was 95 per cent.

The scoring of Sex Symbolism was done with a clinical approach—that is, the scorer's intuition, operating with his knowledge of Freudian theory and his experience with projective materials, guides his judgment as to what is sexually symbolic. Following Clark, the *mere mention* of a classical symbol was not scored, but the classical symbol or symbols mentioned had to be utilized or involved in some action which in and of itself could be interpreted as being symbolic. Stories were given a weight of two to indicate that symbolism was strongly present, one to indicate that some symbolism was present, and zero if no symbolism was present. An individual's score was the sum of his scores on each story. The reliability was 89 per cent agreement between Clark's scoring of his own data and the scorers in this study.

All three scoring systems focus on sexual *activity*. Overt Sex Imagery is scored principally on the basis of occurrence of interpersonal love relations, Symbolic Sex Activity on the basis of intercourse-type activity, and Sex Symbolism (clinically defined) only when classically symbolic objects are embedded in a sexlike activity.[3]

RESULTS

Control Pictures. Since all groups had the same two pictures, groups MN and MA are combined into a single group, as are groups FN and FA. Table I shows no significant differences between the mean scores of males and females on the two control pictures. The differences are all very small. None of the four experimental groups (MN, MA, FN, FA) differs significantly from any other on any of the three mean scores. However, if the scores for primary Overt Sex Imagery (explicit or implicit evidence for intercourse) are studied separately, it is found that 5 males wrote stories fitting this category while no females did ($p < .10$, two-tail Fisher Exact test). If the stories involving primary Overt Sex Imagery are rescored on the basis of the story *exclusive* of the particular phrase which led to the primary score, no major changes occur. If the stories are rescored only on the basis of tertiary Overt Sex Imagery, the t's are almost unchanged. It may be concluded that college males and females show virtually no differences in Overt Sex Imagery to pictures except females may show less primary imagery. The male group is significantly more variable. In fact, groups MN and MA

---

[3] In line with Nichol's (319) failure to obtain differential GSR's to male and female symbols, none of these scores attempt to separate male and female symbols.

individually are significantly more variable than either of the female groups.

Sex Differences in Response to Music. Table I also presents the scores of the four groups in response to musical selections. The males show significantly more Overt Sex Imagery than do females

TABLE I. SEX DIFFERENCES IN THREE KINDS OF SEX IMAGERY IN STORIES TO PICTURES AND MUSIC

Stimulus	Group	N	Imagery		
			Overt Sex Imagery	Symbolic Sex Activity	Sex Symbolism (clinically defined)
Two	Females	71	1.10	.20	.46
Control	Males	84	1.15*	.18	.49
Pictures	Diff. (F-M)		−.05	.02	−.03
	t		.50	.07	.12
	p		NS	NS	NS
Four	Females	43	1.65	.93	.67
Neutral	Males	38	2.50	.61	.74
Music	Diff. (F-M)		−.85	.32	−.09
Selections	t		2.44	1.88	.39
	p		<.02	<.10	NS
Four	Females	28	1.96	1.93	2.50
Arousing	Males	46	2.20	1.20	1.80
Music	Diff. (F-M)		−.24	.73	.70
Selections	t		.68	2.81**	1.84
	p		NS	<.01**	<.10

* Male scores significantly more variable (p <.05).
** p corrected for significant difference in variance (Walker & Lev, 423, p. 157). Females more variable.

in response to neutral music, but this difference disappears when arousing music is used.

As with the pictures, primary Overt Sex Imagery, separated from the remaining overt categories, shows a strong female inhibition. Five of group MN and 6 of group MA wrote stories involving it, some writing more than one such story. One member of group FA and none of group FN yielded any primary Overt Sex Imagery. Combining the neutral and aroused groups, $\chi^2 = 5.82$, $d.f. = 1$, $p < .02$. A similar result was obtained in a pilot study involving a comparison of male and female groups at two other colleges and using six diverse musical selections. Five of 25 males and none of 35 females wrote stories containing primary Overt Sex Imagery ($p < .02$, two-tail Fisher Exact test). It seems possible then to interpret the difference in this same direction on the control pictures as suggestive of a general tendency for women in this culture to inhibit more than men explicit or implicit reference to intercourse. That this is not wholly obvious is indicated by the fact that explicit reference to intercourse was very rare for males in these data. Most of the scores were for mention of illegitimate conception, discussion of a lecture on "the facts of life," or any mention of a mistress or prostitute. Overt-Sex-Imagery scores based on secondary and tertiary imagery only, or on tertiary imagery only, yield approximately the same results as total Overt-Sex-Imagery scores. The size of the difference between MN and FN decreases, but it remains significant at the five per cent level.

On Symbolic Sex Activity, the females score almost significantly higher than the males in response to neutral music, and very significantly higher in response to arousing music. In the neutral music groups, the female scores exceed the male scores on three of the four categories (Motion, Rhythm, Peak). In the case of Motion, the difference is statistically significant. In the aroused music groups, the females exceed the males in these same three categories and are significantly higher on Peak. The differences are insignificant for Penetration, but this category has been left because Clark's groups were significantly different on this variable. No significant difference is observed for Sex Symbolism in response to neutral music, but arousing music produces a near-significant difference between the two sexes, the females scoring higher.

In contrast to the results for the control pictures, it is clear that musical stimuli lead to different amounts of symbolic imagery in the two sexes. Females differ most from males in expressing more Symbolic Sex Activity than the males. The categories of Symbolic Sex Activity (Motion, Rhythm, Peak, and Penetration) all involve the kinesthetic aspect of sex.

Differences in Response to Types of Music. If, in Table I, the arousing and neutral music groups are compared, holding sex constant, the differences in Overt Sex Imagery are insignificant ($t = .81$ for males and .93 for females). The nature of the music used makes no significant difference in Overt Sex Imagery. For Symbolic Sex Activity the t is 3.47 for males and 3.83 for females ($p < .01$). For Sex Symbolism (clinically defined), the t is 4.33 for males and 5.44 for females ($p < .01$). Thus both men and women show significantly more symbolic activity and symbolism to arousing music than to neutral music.

When the neutral and aroused groups are compared for Symbolic Sex Activity on each of the four records separately, the mean score for every one of the arousing records is higher than for any of the neutral records. This difference in effects of types of music is highly consistent in both sexes.

Interaction of Sex Differences and Music Differences. The data of Table I may also be analyzed for sex differences in the differential effects of the two kinds of music. The difference between neutral and aroused males may be compared with the difference between neutral and aroused females. The difference between the differences is insignificant ($t = 1.19$) for Overt Sex Imagery, but this comparison yields a t of 2.41 for Symbolic Sex Activity and a t of 2.03 for Sex Symbolism.[4] We conclude from these data that for both ways of scoring symbolism, the females show a significantly greater difference in amount of imagery to neutral and arousing music. The same trend is present for Overt Sex Imagery.

Comparison of Music and Nude Slides as Arousers of Sexual Imagery. The difference between neutral and "movie music" discussed in the preceding section may be thought of as an "arousal effect" attributable to the difference in type of music. Clark's (73) study compares the sexual imagery in stories to pictures of a control group and a group of males who were shown slides of nude females prior to writing stories to neutral pictures. His "arousal effect" is the difference between a control group and a group with prior exposure to nude slides. Figure 1 compares these "arousal effects." Scores have been reduced to a four story basis. In addition, the stories of Clark's nonalcohol groups have been scored in terms of our Symbolic Sex Activity categories. The mean of his neutral group is .37 ($N = 38$); the mean of his group that was aroused by prior nude slides is .023 ($N = 39$). The difference yields a t of 2.73, so that for prior nude slides, a significant decrease ($-.347$) of Symbolic Sex Activity is observed in males.

Prior exposure to nude slides under non-alcohol conditions leads to significantly less Overt Sex Imagery and Symbolic Sex Activity, and more Sex Symbolism (see bars numbered "1" in Figure 1).

---

[4] The exact p levels are unavailable. The formula for t here assumes equal variances of all four groups (Walker and Lev, (423), p. 158). The effect of unequal variances on the ordinary t tests in these data is to reduce the degrees of freedom by about $\frac{1}{3}$. Since 151 degrees of freedom are here involved, the reduction in degrees of freedom would be unimportant; however, the true effect of unequal variances is apparently unknown.

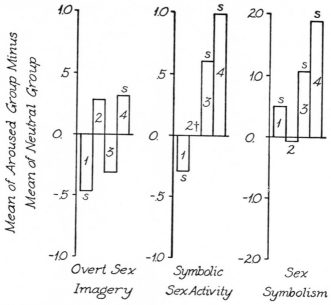

Fig. 1. Arousal effects of music and of prior exposure to nude slides.
1. Males, non-alcohol, prior exposure to nude slides.*
2. Males, alcohol, prior exposure to nude slides.*
3. Males, arousing versus neutral music.
4. Females, arousing versus neutral music.
s—These effects are significantly different from zero.

* Data from Clark (1955) multiplied by 4/5. Symbolic Sex Activity scored for this study; † data not available.

Arousing vs. neutral music for both males (bar "3") and females (bar "4") leads to insignificant change on Overt Sex Imagery, and significantly more Symbolic Sex Activity and Sex Symbolism. That is, arousing music increases Symbolic Sex Activity without increasing Overt Sex Imagery.

Relations between the Three Types of Imagery within Groups. Clark (See Table 1, 72) reports a very interesting relationship between Overt Sex Imagery and Sex Symbolism (clinically defined) in his nonalcohol groups. When the groups are divided into thirds on the basis of Overt Sex Imagery, then Clark's high and low groups both exceed the medium group in Sex Symbolism scores. The breakdown was made separately within each group, and analysis of variance showed the relationship to be significant.

This relationship did not occur in any of the four groups of the present study.[5] Nor was there any consistent relationship between Overt Sex Imagery and Symbolic Sex Activity. However, Symbolic Sex Activity and Sex Symbolism were found to be positively related in the present study. The product moment correlations calculated for each group are all positive, ranging from .20 in the MN group to .47 in the FA group.

DISCUSSION

Since there are no indications that women produce more sexually symbolic material in response to pictures than do males, the first question these findings raise is why do women show more symbolism than men in response to music? In four comparisons involving two types of music and two scoring systems for sex symbolism, women score very significantly higher on one, almost significantly higher on two, and slightly but not significantly lower on the fourth (Table I). Furthermore, women are significantly more sensitive to the difference in type of music.

One possibility is that music as a stimulus innately arouses responses (percepts, images) in women characteristic of the sexual response. Such aspects of the musical stimulus as rhythm and dynamic changes may lead, by the nature of the female physiology and neurology, to such "pseudosexual responses." Ellis' speculations, cited earlier, as to the effect of the difference in change of voice would be consistent with this view. One might account in a similar manner for the finding of Kinsey *et al.* (213) that males tend to report sexual arousal by visual stimuli much more than women, while women tend to be more sexually aroused than men by motion pictures. Modern motion pictures depend on such auditory stimuli as background music, and it is from such background music that the musical selections used in the present study were drawn. This conception of an innate difference in the effectiveness of music as a "releasing" stimulus (Tinbergen, 411) seems to be difficult to establish at the present time without cross cultural data.

It is also possible that the difference in sexually symbolic imagery is a function of learning. It might be argued that women listen to music more and therefore the images it arouses are higher in the habit family hierarchy and appear more readily in their stories. It has been noted that females score lower on the Penetration category than the males. Thus the Symbolic Sex Activity categories which do differentiate males and females are Motion, Rhythm, and Peak.

---

[5] Clark's alcohol groups displayed so little sex symbolism that this relation could not be studied.

Imagery of this type could conceivably be conditioned to music more in females than in males. The result would then be interpreted as indicating that arousing music elicits more "kinesthetic" imagery and accounts for the higher scores on Symbolic Sex Activity. The explanation would be sought in differential amounts of time spent listening to music and demonstration that the conditions under which listening occurred would, in fact, lead to the establishment of the appropriate conditioned imagery.

Razran (338) has shown that stimulus materials presented during eating come to evoke food-related verbalizations but not hunger sensations. He concludes that "what was conditioned in the study was more an unconscious cognition" (p. 282). In the case of musical stimuli, the most obvious "conditioned imagery" would be "dancing."

All stories were scored for any mention of dancing. In the neutral music groups 11 per cent of the males and 12 per cent of the females wrote one or more stories involving dancing. In the arousing music groups, 52 per cent of the males and 54 per cent of the females mentioned dancing. This does not support a "conditioned imagery to music" explanation of the sex difference. Furthermore, Clark has shown that for males, at least, the Symbolic Sex Activity score is significantly altered (decreased) by nonrhythmic stimulation (nude slides). Since these pictures have quite different stimulus properties, it seems difficult to believe that imagery conditioned to music would be tripped off by them.

Finally, in the present study the females respond with almost significantly more Sex Symbolism and with a significantly larger arousal effect on this score than the males. It is hard to explain why the classical Freudian symbols (snakes, jewels, balconies, etc.) should have become conditioned to music. The nude slides of Clark's study brought about a significant increase in Sex Symbolism similar to the increase due to arousing vs. neutral music of the present study. The fact that music and pictures have equivalent effects on Sex Symbolism is strong evidence that in dealing with the effects of music, Sex Symbolism, and not happenstance conditioned imagery, is involved.

The increase in Sexual Symbolism and Symbolic Sex Activity scores produced by the arousing music might be viewed as an instance of an increase in level of activation, a construct introduced by Woodworth and Schlosberg (442) to account for changes in emotion. The Symbolic Sex Activity score is based largely on activity imagery, and the scoring of classical symbols was conditioned by Clark's restriction that these be embedded in an activity. But this sort of explanation does not account for the *decrease* in males and the lack of significant *increase* in females in Overt Sex Imagery.

Since secondary and tertiary Overt Sex Imagery involve activity, general activation would be expected to increase it.

If, then, the *opposite* effects of music and nude pictures on the Symbolic Sex Activity score are to be regarded as evidence that in both cases one is dealing with sex, it becomes necessary to consider the relationship between the three scores studied. Figure 1 suggests a gradient from overt to covert levels of consciousness, a gradient of indirectness of sexuality. Clark hypothesized that nude slides arouse sexual motivation and also anxiety in order to explain the decrease of Overt Sex Imagery and increase of Sex Symbolism (clinically defined) in his nonalcohol group. He hypothesized lowered anxiety in the alcohol groups to explain the higher level of Overt Sex Imagery and significant increase in sexual imagery following arousal by nude slides. In our scoring of Clark's data, the direct arousal of sexual motivation and anxiety by nude slides seems to suppress the intermediate category of Symbolic Sex Activity. We might hypothesize that music arouses sexual imagery but less anxiety therewith. The contrasted types of music studied would be expected to differ in the degree to which they aroused sexual motivation, but it would not be expected that arousing music would produce as widely generalized anxiety as nude slides. Hence, arousing music might produce a *decrease* (although not significant) of Overt Sex Imagery in males and an increase of both symbolism scores in males. The insignificant increase of Overt Sex Imagery in females is consistent with the general interpretation that music is more motivationally arousing to females but does not arouse correspondingly greater anxiety.

CHAPTER 10

....

The Expression of Fear-Related Motivation in Thematic Apperception as a Function of Proximity to an Atomic Explosion

EDWARD L. WALKER AND JOHN W. ATKINSON[1] WITH THE
COLLABORATION OF JOSEPH VEROFF, ROBERT BIRNEY,
WILLIAM DEMBER, AND ROBERT MOULTON

CURRENT EFFORTS at bridging the gap between research in animal motivation and the study of human motives have centered largely around the concept of fear (292). The arousal of fear in animals is usually accomplished through the use of electric shock, in some instances at intensities of just subtetanizing levels (385). Such methods are, for obvious ethical and practical reasons, rarely available for use with human subjects. As an alternative to experimental arousal, recent investigators have utilized individual differences in fear already present in their subjects (403). This procedure, of course, sets rather narrow limits on the degree of fear which may be studied and on the experimenter's freedom to manipulate this variable.

The conditions under which the present experiment was carried out provided an almost unique opportunity to set up, for human subjects, situations which would *a priori* seem highly fear arousing. Further, for these subjects the situations were completely realistic; there was little of laboratory-artificiality about them.

The fear-arousing agent in this study was an atomic explosion.

---

[1] This investigation was conducted under contract with the Human Resources Research Office during the summer of 1952 (Subcontract No. HumRRO 650-009 [95-65-6-52-9]). The views expressed are those of the authors and not those of the sponsoring agency.

The experimental subjects were soldiers who were to be or who had been placed in very close proximity to the explosion.

It was the major purpose of the present experiment to investigate the possibility of measuring fear by a projective method similar to that employed successfully by McClelland and others for measuring hunger, achievement, and affiliation motivation. The present study affords an opportunity to judge the feasibility of using thematic apperceptive instruments under trying field conditions and in a large scale investigation which presents a number of novel methodological problems never confronted in carefully circumscribed laboratory experimentation.

The measure of fear in this study is based upon the same general rationale underlying the previously developed measures of motivation. A subject is presented with a series of pictures (in this case two) containing cues related to the motive in question and is asked to write an imaginative story in response to each picture. A time limit is set (in this case approximately four-six minutes) in order to limit the amount of variability in length of stories obtained from different subjects. The imaginative response of a particular subject is viewed as jointly determined by his present state of motivation, which may be influenced by situational cues, and the cues contained in the picture.

If a particular motive is aroused by cues in the situation immediately preceding the administration of the measure, certain response tendencies—those related to that motive—will increase in strength and as a result appear more frequently. The measure of the strength of motivation obtained is the total number of imaginative responses related to the motive in question. A total score is obtained by summing the scores obtained in separate stories.

The general procedure outlined above involves two major methodological problems: 1) situations must be created which are clearly differentially motive-arousing and 2) it must be possible to identify reliably the imagery that should reflect the motive under investigation. With respect to the first problem, differential temporal proximity to the previously mentioned atomic explosion was used.

From the point of view that fear is a motive, the behavioral-sequence notion—upon which the scoring systems for the hunger, achievement, and affiliation measures are built—becomes an appropriate basis for imagery analysis. The major difficulty in applying the behavioral-sequence analysis to fear lies in the exact specification of scorable imagery. In short, fear may be conceived as a general aspect of all motives (e.g., fear of failure, fear of rejection). If, however, the measure is to differentiate among the variously aroused groups of this experiment, then scorable imagery should be relevant only to the particular arousal conditions used. Thus, "fear" in this study is restricted in its denotation to "fear of bodily harm."

A suggestive lead for developing a scoring system to measure fear-related motivation in thematic apperception is provided by Murray (312). In a simple experiment with young children he found that fear-provoking stimulation increased estimates of the maliciousness of faces appearing in pictures. With this as a guiding hypothesis, that fear would increase the tendency to react to the pictorial environment as threatening, a set of scoring categories were *a priori* developed for the behavioral sequence instigated by some threat of bodily harm and directed towards avoidance or escape from such a threat. It is assumed that fear constitutes a state of motivation producing action directed towards relief, or reduction of fear, and that this tendency will be expressed in thematic apperception in terms of the same elements of the behavioral sequence (e.g., need, instrumental activity, anticipatory goal states, obstacles, etc.) that have been found symptomatic of other motivating states. As in the case of other motives (e.g., Ch. 3), an individual's score is the total of all fear-related imaginative responses. This score is made up of the imaginative equivalents of both adaptive responses (e.g., instrumental acts which successfully avoid or overcome the threat, anticipation of being able to cope with the threat) and nonadaptive responses which imply a state of anxiety and helplessness (e.g., unsuccessful attempts to avoid the threat, anticipations of great harm, obstacles in the way of successful adaptive action). Hence it is necessary to call attention to the distinction between fear as a source of adaptive motivation and fear arising "from a sense of helplessness" as described by Mowrer and Viek (309). Since these two different tendencies—one implying the activation of previously learned skills for coping with a threatening situation, the other implying fright and panic—are not isolated in the present analysis, the total score will be referred to as the *fear-related motivation score*. This score can be interpreted as an index of the frequency of imaginative responses which represent reactions to situations which pose a threat to bodily harm and attempts to cope with such a situation.

The major hypothesis of this investigation is that fear-related motivation will be greater, the greater the proximity to an atomic explosion.

METHOD

Description of Pictures

Form A. The first picture of Form A contained an ambiguous figure looking at the sky, which contained a number of dots.[2] In an earlier study, the figure was often interpreted as that of a woman, and the dots as a flight of ducks or planes.

The second picture portrays a group of persons that very clearly are soldiers in the partial ruins of a city during some kind of attack. A building is crumbling, and the sky is darkened as if by smoke.

Form B. The first picture of Form B contains a young woman and two children running. The dark background suggests either rain or smoke.

The second picture contains three human figures who might be wearing helmets (and hence be perceived as soldiers) in the street of a city. The background, darkened in one portion, suggests smoke rising from a building.

The first picture in each form contained a figure that could be perceived as a woman. These were deliberately chosen in order to minimize the extent to which soldiers might generalize a tendency *not* to attribute fear to themselves. Presumably the inhibition of expression of fear would be less likely to occur if the central character were female.

A preliminary analysis of results revealed that our hope that the first picture of Form A would be interpreted as a female character was very rarely fulfilled. This plus the ambiguity of what was seen in the sky of the picture rendered this picture much more similar to an actual threat situation for a soldier than we had intended.

Each Form of the thematic apperceptive test comprised a little booklet. The cover contained space for relevant identification data and a brief paraphrase of the standard instruction for writing stories. The first page contained the first picture. This was followed by a page containing the four leading questions, printed at spaced intervals, which were used in earlier research with other motives (Ch. 3). Then followed another picture and another page for writing a story.

Experimental Groups. There were four groups of men who formed experimental groups and who received a complete indoctrination course. These groups were labeled Groups 1, 2, 3, and 4.

---

[2] We wish to acknowledge the cooperation of the Survey Research Center of the University of Michigan for allowing us to use both this picture and the first picture of Form B.

Conditions of Administrations. For experimental groups there were five different conditions of administration. They were as follows:

Condition A. Tests were administered to the men in an Army camp in a part of the country remote from the atomic maneuvers. These men had not yet learned that they were to participate in the forthcoming maneuver. The projective tests were administered before there was anything to suggest an association with atomic matters of any kind. Group 1 was tested at this time with half of the group receiving Form A and half Form B.

Condition B. Tests were administered approximately ten hours before the explosion at the camp where the maneuver was held. By this time the men in the indoctrinated groups had received extensive lectures in atomic matters in general and in atomic weapons and their effects in particular. They had also participated in a rehearsal of the maneuver which omitted the explosion. Group 2 was tested for the first time and Group 1 for the second at this time. Men who had had Form A at Test Condition A were now given Form B, and those who had had Form B were now given Form A. This pattern of form reversals was followed throughout wherever appropriate.

Condition C. This was by far the most dramatic administration. The men were stationed in trenches 4000 yards from the point of the detonation. They were given necessary maneuver instructions, and the count which precedes the explosion proceeded 10 - 9 - 8 - 7 - 6 - 5 - 4 - 3 - 2 - 1 - XXXX. As soon as it was safe to leave the trenches, the men did so. They were immediately handed a questionnaire which required approximately 15 minutes to fill out. Then they wrote their projective stories. While they were doing this, the atomic cloud was boiling up directly overhead into its characteristic shape. During the entire period the men were in a state of acute alertness for the wail of a siren which would announce, if necessary, the declaration of Condition Black. This condition required everyone to leave the area with the greatest possible haste. All testing was completed within the first 30 minutes after the detonation. Group 3 was first tested at this time, while Group 2 received its second test.

Condition D. This testing period followed the detonation by approximately 10 hours and was carried out at the desert camp in the evening. Group 4 was first tested at this time, while Group 3 received its second test.

Condition E. This testing period came approximately two weeks after the maneuver and was carried out at the remote regular army post from which the men originally came. Group 4 received its second test at this time.

Control Groups. Several other groups (Groups 11, 12, 13, and 14) were control groups to whom the tests were administered as near as possible in the same pattern as they were administered to Groups 1, 2, 3, and 4. These tests were, however, carried out in Army posts many miles distant from the site of the bomb test. Hence these groups constitute a "neutral" control condition comparable to Condition A.

The Scoring System for Fear-Related Motivation. The projective measure of fear of physical harm will be presented in this section. The content analysis of imaginative stories to be discussed closely parallels the scoring systems developed for the achievement and affiliation motives. There is only one crucial problem facing a scorer: to decide whether a given story is related or unrelated to the affective process in question—in this case, fear of physical harm. Once this can be established, the scorer then can follow through in scoring subcategories which are elements of the behavioral sequence. For this reason only the criteria for identifying a fear-related story will be presented in detail. The subcategories will only be briefly defined. One can refer to Chapter 12 for a detailed discussion of the categories modeling the behavioral sequence and their significance in scoring imaginative stories.

Criteria for Identifying a Fear-Related Story (Threat Imagery)

Somewhere in the story an external condition poses a threat to the physical welfare of a person(s). Evidence of threat can be provided by the appearance of one or more of the following kinds of imagery:

1. a direct statement of fear
2. negative affect surrounding an external situation, such as tenseness
3. statement of need to avoid the situation
4. instrumental activity directed at avoiding a harmful situation, such as attempting to escape.

If the external situation poses a threat which does not clearly involve potential physical harm, an appearance of a statement of fear or negative affect is enough to justify scoring the story. An example of this would be: "there is a storm coming up and the mother and children are afraid." The storm mentioned by itself does not clearly involve potential physical harm, but in view of the statement of fear the story would be scored. A statement of need and instrumental activity would also justify scoring a story which does not clearly involve potential physical harm, if the need and instrumental activity statements clearly refer to attempts at avoiding physical harm. "There is a fire in the town and these people want to put it out" is an example of a story which would not be scored, although there is a statement of need. Here the need does not clearly involve avoiding physical harm. However, "There is a fire in the town and these people want to escape injury" would be scored.

In the absence of the above criteria, however, imagery may still be scored if the total context of the story indicates that there is *a high probability of personal injury from a mere statement of the objective situation.* That is, when the people in the story have a definite connection to an external situation which can very probably result in the personal injury of the people, the story can be scored. Examples of this are listed below:

1. *Bombing.* In most circumstances a bombing story will be scored. A bombing story can be interpreted as indicating a high probability of physical harm. Even a bomb dropping on a city implies that people are likely to be killed or injured. A person thinking that bombs will be dropped should be interpreted as a person thinking of potential physical harm, as in the story below:

> The girl is looking at airplanes.
> There is a lot of them around. It really looks like the planes
>   are going to drop something.
> They are going to drop some bombs, that is, the planes are
>   going to drop them.
> They will drop their bombs and then be on their way home.

This is a "weak" bomb story, but since there is a statement that they are going to drop some bombs in answer to the question, "What is being thought?", this story sets up a definite connection between a person in the story and a potentially harmful situation. However, just a statement that bombs are being dropped, even if it is mentioned that the people are soldiers, cannot be scored because this may be interpreted as a test run. Also, someone getting an aesthetic experience from an A-bomb burst would not be scored.

2. *Attack.* Most attack stories will not be scored. It will be assumed that the writer is identifying with the attacking troops, and so an attack story will not be scored as an external situation threatening to the enemy unless one of the four criteria—affect, fear, instrumental activity, or need—appears in reference to the enemy. An attack story will be scored, however, if there is some evidence of danger to the attacking troops, such as flying bullets or enemy barrages. The following story will not be scored:

> There's a battle in progress. Soldiers.
> One country has started aggression against another.
> The town is wanted by the soldiers.

If in the above story mention was made of the soldiers thinking about how they could return to the safety of the lines, this story would be scored because the danger is made more explicit and hence scorable.

3. *Preventative measures.* Stories showing decontamination imagery will be scored. Preventative measures with regard to diseases will also be scored.

TABLE 1. THE FOLLOWING ARE THE SUBCATEGORIES SCORED ONLY IF THE STORY CONTAINS THREAT IMAGERY

Category	Brief Definition	Example
Need (N)	Someone wants something which, if attained, would remove threat of physical harm.	"They want shelter from the bomb."
Instrumental Activity (I)	Someone performs or thinks of performing an act the function of which is to reduce the threat of physical harm. If the outcome of the act is successful, score $I+$; if unsuccessful, score $I-$; and if doubtful, score $I?$.	"They are running away from the fire."
Nurturant Press (NUP)	Forces from the environment provide relief.	"First aid will be given."
Anticipation of Pain (GA$-$)	Statement of fear or anxiety, or statements of thoughts about an unsuccessful outcome of events.	"He is afraid." "She thinks she will be killed."
Anticipation of Relief (GA$+$)	Statements of thoughts of escaping or obtaining relief.	"He thinks he will be safe there."
Doubtful Anticipation (GA?)	Statements of uncertainty about the future.	"They wonder what will happen."
Obstacles (B)	Anything interfering with successful avoidance of threat. Score BP if the interference comes from within the person concerned with the threat. Score BW if the interference comes from the environment.	"They are running for shelter and pieces of slack hit them." Score BW. "They become very confused after the bomb explodes." Score BP.
Positive Affective State (G$+$)	Statements of experiencing relief from threat.	"He breathed easier after the fire was under control."
Negative Affective State (G$-$)	Statements of experiences of pain.	"He was tense during the battle."

In addition, distinctions about the over-all outcome of a story are coded. *Anxiety Outcome* is scored when the outcome gives no evidence of relief. The story is scored *Relief Outcome* if the threat is overcome, *Doubtful Outcome* if there is a specific statement of ignorance of outcome, and *Incomplete Outcome* when no final outcome is given. A particular category is scored only once per story.

The *fear-related motivation score* represents the number of times *Threat Imagery* and each of the subcategories listed above (with the exception of *Incomplete Outcome*) appeared in the two-story record of a particular subject. It represents the gross amount of preoccupation with threat.

Several other indices were obtained from the two-story records of all subjects. First, the number of words per story was obtained to provide a basis for determining whether or not the length of protocol influenced the fear-related scores obtained from analysis of the content of stories. Secondly, it often happened that the subject did not write an imaginative story but instead gave a response that could be classified under one of the following headings: attitudinal response, personalized reaction, I don't know, or no response. If a story was classified as one of these five categories, it was not scored further. Only subjects who wrote two imaginative responses are included in the analysis of results.

Reliability of Scoring. The general procedure for scoring the stories was to randomize the several hundred protocols drawn from several groups at a time and to distribute them to each of the five judges participating in the scoring. In this way systematic differences between judges can be considered randomly distributed among groups, forms, and administrations.

Each of the judges scored the same set of 31 protocols for a check on interjudge agreement during the scoring process and without knowledge of which stories were being used for the reliability check. Percentage of agreement between a given pair of judges was defined as the number of agreements on a category divided by the sum of the frequencies with which each judge scored the given category. For *Threat Imagery* the lowest percentage of agreement between any two judges was 89%, the highest was 97%. Subcategory agreement was lower, but the lowest percentage of agreement for any category for any two judges was 65%. Most of the percentages were in the 80-90% range.

Another check on reliability was to compute the fear-related motivation scores obtained for each subject in this same subsample according to the scoring of each of the five judges. The average intercorrelation (rank-order) for the fear-related motivation scores was .85.

Adjustment of raw fear-related motivation scores to account for differences in length of imaginative stories. The measure had been administered under highly variable field conditions. And the sample of subjects covered a wide range of verbal aptitude. It was decided, therefore, to check any possible relationship between length of protocol and fear-related motivation scores. In one experimental condition, the number of words ranged from 0 to 344. The product moment correlation between fear-related motivation scores and length of protocol for 41 subjects in the first administration of Form B in Test Condition C was $+.41$ ($p < .01$). Some adjustment had to be made. The alternative chosen was to adjust raw scores of all subjects to give them scores indicating where they stood in the distribution of scores obtained from protocols having nearly the same number of words as their own.

Any protocol containing fewer than 30 words was eliminated from further analysis since there was practically no variability in fear-related motivation scores among protocols of this length. Then four of the control groups were chosen as a standard population. They were minimally affected by the influences which affected the motivation of the participant groups. The total number of words per protocol ranged from 30 to over 200, with a median of 98 in this population. This range was divided into five intervals, each having a range of 30 words, and a sixth group which included all protocols having 180 words or more. Form A and Form B were equally represented in each of these subgroups. The Ns of these subgroups varied from 30 (a minimum) to 130. The adjustment was to calculate Z scores for each subject in all groups dependent upon the mean and standard deviation of scores in the standard population for protocols the same length as his own. To eliminate negative numbers, a constant of $+5$ was added to each Z score. To eliminate decimal points, this score was then multiplied by 10. Thus a person whose raw fear-related motivation score was right at the mean for stories of a given length in the standard population would have an adjusted score of 50. The effect of these adjustments was to lower the correlation between length of protocol and fear-related motivation score from .41 to .02.

The effect of form of the test and order of administration. To establish the effect of differences between the two forms of the test and of first versus second administrations, we turn to the data obtained from one of the control groups (12 H) who had taken both forms on the same day under neutral conditions at an army base temporally and geographically distant from the bomb test. Tables 2 and 3 show quite clearly that the fear-related motivation score is higher in response to Form B than to Form A and that, irrespective

TABLE 2. COMPARISON OF FORMS A AND B UNDER NEUTRAL CONDITIONS*

	First Administration		Second Administration	
	Below	Above	Below	Above
Form A.......	40	22	38	26
Form B.......	24	41	26	38
	$\chi^2 = 9.04, p < .01$		$\chi^2 = 4.50, p < .05$	

* Number of Ss whose fear-related motivation scores were above and below the approximate median of a combined distribution of scores from Forms A and B.

of form, the score is higher on the second administration than on the first administration.

A picture by picture analysis further reveals that the difference between first and second administrations is accounted for by the fact that scores obtained on the first story of each form are significantly higher ($p < .05$) on the second administration. No such difference occurs in response to the second picture in each form. The effect of a prior administration can be summarized as a general increase in

TABLE 3. COMPARISON OF FIRST AND SECOND ADMINISTRATIONS UNDER NEUTRAL CONDITIONS*

	Form A		Form B	
	Below	Above	Below	Above
Administration 1.......	40	22	43	32
Administration 2.......	25	29	26	38
	$\chi^2 = 8.17, p < .01$		$\chi^2 = 4.50, p < .05$	

* Number of Ss whose fear-related motivation scores were above and below the approximate median of a combined distribution of scores from two administrations.

readiness to respond on the first story of the second administration.

Further analysis reveals that even on the first administration the fear-related motivation score in response to the first picture of Form A, the ambiguous figure looking at the sky, is significantly lower ($p < .01$) than the score obtained in response to the first picture on Form B, a woman and children running from something. The minimal sensitivity of the first picture on Form A, particularly on a first administration, should be kept in mind as a possible source of the difference between the two forms in sensitivity to the fear "aroused" by various conditions to be described shortly.

A second question has to do with the equivalent form reliability of the two tests. Is a person likely to score high or low on both of them? This question is dealt with in Table 4 in a way that takes cognizance of the increase in readiness to respond on a second administration. When Form B is administered first, there is good agreement between the two forms in placing persons in the same third of the distribution of scores ($p < .05$).

TABLE 4. THE EQUIVALENCE OF FORMS A AND B IN ORDERING THE SAME INDIVIDUALS UNDER NEUTRAL CONDITIONS*

Form B		Form A—2nd Administration		
		High	Middle	Low
1st Administration	High..........	10	6	4
	Middle.........	6	11	5
	Low..........	2	5	8
		$\chi^2 = 8.58, p < .05$**		

Form A		Form B—2nd Administration		
		High	Middle	Low
1st Administration	High..........	11	7	3
	Middle.........	2	9	8
	Low..........	7	5	2
		$\chi^2 = 11.07, p < .05$**		

* Number of Ss appearing in High, Middle, and Low thirds of distribution of scores on each form.
** One-tail values of p for chi-squares approximated by the Mood Test of Maximum Likelihood (299, p. 276).

However, when Form A is administered first, the relationship is not as clear. A number of individuals who fail to respond at all on the first administration of Form A, apparently to be considered "false lows," show a much greater response to the second administration. We attribute this result to a combination of the ambiguity of the first picture in Form A and the ambiguity of the test situation itself on a first administration.

The effect of proximity to an atomic explosion on fear-related motivation in thematic apperceptive stories. It is assumed that fear-related motivation should be increasingly aroused with increasing proximity to an atomic explosion. It is further assumed that fear-related motivation will be manifested in thematic apperceptive stories as coded. Hence, we expect the fear-related motivation score to be higher in Conditions B, C, and D than in the neutral or control test conditions conducted at an army installation distant from the atomic test and higher in Condition C than in either B or D.

Group 1 in Test Condition A and the four nonparticipant groups are alike in having been tested at a distant army installation without prior knowledge of the impending bomb test. But one of these groups (Group 12) and part of another (Group 11 O) had engaged in some other research activities which may have in some way contaminated their results. And Group 14 had inadvertently been scored by only one of the five judges. Hence only Groups 11 H and 13 H can be combined with Group 1, Test Condition A, to provide a stable estimate of fear-related motivation elicited by the picture cues under relatively neutral, nonthreatening and uncontaminated conditions. This combined group will be referred to as the Control Group in subsequent comparisons. Since none of the participating groups took the test a second time under "neutral" conditions, the Control Group for the second administration is composed only of the two nonparticipating groups 11 H and 13 H.

To simplify the comparisons, each of the experimental conditions is compared with a control condition tested with the same form and on the same administration (i.e., first versus second). The percentage of subjects whose fear-related motivation scores are above the median of the Control Group are shown in Table 5. The significance of the difference between each experimental condition and its control is tested by means of chi square in a 2×2 contingency table. Since on any one administration, the persons taking Form A and Form B are different, the two forms represent independent tests of the same hypothesis. The chi squares are therefore combined following the procedure recommended by Cochran (78), which takes account of the direction of the difference to provide an over-all estimate of the statistical significance of the observed differences. These are given at the bottom of Table 5. This procedure was repeated for the second administration. It should be appreciated, however, that except in cases of legitimate exclusion of data the same persons are involved in both first and second administrations. Hence the second tests of significance are not independent of the first.

Table 5 shows quite conclusively that fear-related motivation scores were higher in test conditions B, C, and D than in the control condition. For every form-administration combination, the percentage of subjects having high fear-related motivation scores is greater under conditions which, on an *a priori* basis, are more fear-arousing than under neutral control test conditions. The combined probabilities for results with Form A and Form B are given at the bottom of the table. On the first administration, the stories written immediately after the explosion (Condition C) and several hours

TABLE 5. PERCENTAGE OF SUBJECTS IN EXPERIMENTAL CONDITIONS WHOSE FEAR-RELATED MOTIVATION SCORES WERE ABOVE THE MEDIAN SCORE OF THE CONTROL CONDITION

(B = ten hours before atomic explosion; C = within half-hour after atomic explosion; D = 10 hours after atomic explosion; E = about two weeks after atomic explosion.)

Form A		First Administration						Second Administration						
	Control	B	C	D	χ^2	p	Control	B	C	D	E	χ^2	p
	N: 192	55	34	34			N: 95	24	30	35	32		
	53.1	63.6	—	—	1.91	.20	50.5	75.0	—	—	—	4.65	.05
	(53.1)	—	67.6	—	2.46	.20	(50.5)	—	63.3	—	—	1.50	.40
	(53.1)	—	—	67.6	2.46	.20	(50.5)	—	—	71.4	—	4.54	.05
							(50.5)	—	—	—	65.6	2.20	.20

Form B		Control	B	C	D	χ^2	p	Control	B	C	D	E	χ^2	p
		N: 197	35	38	34			N: 92	21	58	33	28		
		53.8	68.0	—	—	1.81	.20	51.1	61.9	—	—	—	.80	
		(53.8)	—	84.2	—	12.15	.001	(51.1)	—	70.7	—	—	5.64	.05
		(53.8)	—	—	79.4	7.78	.01	(51.1)	—	—	72.7	—	6.12	.05
								(51.1)	—	—	—	57.1	.58	

Forms A and B Combined

	Normal Deviate	Combined Prob.		Normal Deviate	Combined Prob.
B > Control	1.93*	<.06	B > Control	2.16	<.05
C > Control	3.58	<.001	C > Control	2.55	<.02
D > Control	3.09	<.01	D > Control	2.81	<.01
			E > Control	1.59	<.10

* According to the method for combining probabilities from 2×2 contingency tables presented by Cochran (78), the square root of each of the χ^2 are summed and divided by the square root of the number of 2×2 tables involved. The resultant test criterion is the approximate normal deviate. Probability is obtained from the normal deviate table.

later (Condition D) clearly contained more frequent expressions of fear-related motivation than the stories of the control condition ($p < .001$ and $p < .01$). The difference between control stories and those written the evening before the bomb test (Condition B) is more tenuous ($p < .06$). Again on second administration, all three groups produced significantly more imagery having to do with fear-related motivation than the Control Groups. But the soldiers in Condition E, back at their army base approximately two weeks later, did not produce significantly more fear-related motivation in their stories than the Control Groups.

Condition E may be considered a second low-motivation control condition since the soldiers in it were then removed from the potential threats of the bomb-test situation. Table 6 presents comparisons between each of the experimental conditions (B, C, and D) and Condition E. Since no groups were administered the TAT device for the

TABLE 6. COMPARISON OF THREE THREAT CONDITIONS (B, C, AND D)
WITH CONDITION E, TWO WEEKS AFTER ATOMIC EXPLOSION

Percentage of Ss above the median of combined distribution of scores.

	Second Administration			
			Forms A and B Combined	
Conditions	Form A	Form B	Normal Deviate	p
B	54.2	61.9	B > E	
E	43.8	42.9	1.50	<.14*
C	46.7	62.1	C > E	
E	53.1	25.0	3.54	<.005
D	60.0	66.7	D > E	
E	53.1	25.0	2.70	<.01

* Combined probabilities obtained as described in Table 5.

first time in Condition E, the comparisons are restricted to results obtained on the second administration. The combined probabilities of the differences separately observed on Form A and Form B again clearly indicate that fear-related motivation was more frequently expressed in the stories written by soldiers under threat conditions. Again, the difference between Condition B and a control condition is most tenuous. In this case it fails to reach the conventional level of statistical significance ($p < .14$).

Table 7 presents comparisons among the three experimental conditions. If there were significant differences between the three conditions, our measuring instruments fail to produce any conclusive evidence of such differences. None of the combined probabilities allow rejection of the null hypothesis. Condition C, closest in proximity to the actual explosion, should be expected to produce the most fear-related motivation. But only on the first administration of Form B is this hypothesis sustained. Here Condition C is significantly higher than Conditions B ($p < .05$) and D ($p < .05$). However, on all the other combinations of form and administration the trend is reversed.

DISCUSSION

The results demonstrate the feasibility of using the thematic apperceptive method even under the most trying field conditions. In comparison with previous studies of motivation, the measuring instrument was of minimal length and control over the testing conditions was ex-

TABLE 7. COMPARISONS AMONG THE THREE THREAT CONDITIONS
(B, C, AND D)

Percentage of Ss above the median of combined distribution of scores.

Conditions	First Administration		Second Administration	
	Form A	Form B	Form A	Form B
B	52.7	40.0	54.1	52.4
C	47.1	68.4*	46.7	48.3
B	49.1	40.0	54.1	52.4
D	50.0	52.9	51.1	45.5
C	47.1	68.4**	46.7	50.0
D	52.9	44.1	60.0	51.5

Forms A and B Combined

	First Administration		Second Administration	
	Normal Deviate	p	Normal Deviate	p
	C > B 1.38	<.17	B > C .62	—
	D > B .76	—	B > D .49	—
	C > D 1.12	<.26	D > C .83	—

* χ^2 4.97, $p < .05$
** χ^2 4.32, $p < .05$

tremely hard to manage. Yet, an *a priori* scoring system, derived from the results of earlier work, does detect a difference between the level of fear-related motivation expressed in thematic apperceptive stories by soldiers under fairly normal conditions of army life and by those under a rather unique situation which can hardly be challenged as one which should be expected to arouse some degree of fear-related motivation.

In addition to demonstrating that the behavioral sequence analysis of thematic apperceptive stories can be applied to fear, the present investigation shows how two important technical problems can be met in a large-scale study. First, the problem of great heterogeneity in verbal facility, which produced a statistically significant correlation between motivation score and length of protocol, was removed by converting the raw score to a standard score representing the position of that score in a distribution of scores from protocols of the same length. This technique can undoubtedly be applied to other large-scale field studies facing the problem of great differences in verbal ability. Second, the present investigation shows that a team of scorers can be quickly trained in a novel scoring system without any great sacrifice in the reliability of the coding, which condition is the *sine qua non* of successful research with thematic apperceptive instruments.

SUMMARY

Groups of soldiers wrote short thematic apperceptive stories at various degrees of temporal and geographic proximity to an atomic explosion. Stories were analyzed for evidence of fear-related motivation as expressed in behavioral sequences having to do with attempts to cope with some threat of physical harm. The results show that the behavioral sequence type of analysis developed in studies of approach tendencies (hunger, achievement, affiliation, etc.) can be usefully applied to analysis of fear-related motivation and that the thematic apperceptive method can be adapted for use under trying field conditions with groups that are very heterogeneous in verbal ability.

CHAPTER 11

....

*The Drive-Reducing Function of Fantasy Behavior**

SEYMOUR FESHBACH[1]

THE PRIMARY OBJECT of this research is to investigate the hypothesis that fantasy will reduce the strength of a motive by means of symbolic satisfaction. Current interest in fantasy as a form of behavior stems primarily from: (a) the emphasis placed by psychoanalysis on the role of fantasy in human adjustment, (b) the widespread use of the Thematic Apperception Test as a diagnostic instrument, and (c) recent studies exploring the effects of experimentally induced drives upon various cognitive processes including fantasy. These latter investigations have in general confirmed the assumption that ungratified needs are reflected in fantasy. However an unresolved and neglected problem is whether fantasy behavior to any degree satisfies these needs.

Psychoanalysts have long maintained that fantasies including dreams, daydreams, myths, and artistic productions represent wish fulfillment. According to Freud, "unsatisfied wishes are the driving power behind phantasies; every separate phantasy contains the fulfillment of a wish, and improves on unsatisfactory reality" (148, p. 176). More recently Symonds (400), writing from the psychoanalytic standpoint, clearly suggests that goal responses expressed in fantasy may be drive reducing. The latter hypothesis is compatible with a behavior theory which holds that self-initiated verbal responses may have secondary reward value and thus reinforce the tendency to repeat those responses when stimulated by the drive which had

---

* Reprinted by permission of author and publisher from *The Journal of Abnormal and Social Psychology,* 1955, **50,** 3-11. Copyright 1955 by the American Psychological Association, Inc.

[1] The study was carried out while the author was a United States Public Health Service Research Fellow. The present study was undertaken as a doctoral dissertation in the Department of Psychology at Yale University. The author wishes to express his appreciation to Professors Child, Janis, and Sarason of Yale University for their interest and assistance.

originally occasioned them. Some such hypothesis is suggested by a reinforcement theory in explaining the persistence of certain forms of fantasy behavior as, for example, that found in obsessional neurosis.

Although the hypothesis that fantasy behavior has a substitute or compensatory function is widely entertained (6, 145, 416), it is by no means universally accepted. McClelland *et al.* (Ch. 2, Ch. 3) have explicitly doubted its validity on the basis of indirect inference from the content of TAT-type fantasies. A study by Wittenborn and Eron (439), also based on TAT fantasies, finds some substantiation for a drive-reduction hypothesis in the pattern of intercorrelations among certain features of TAT responses. However, positive or negative evidence directly bearing upon the hypothesis is lacking.

Experimental studies of substitute behavior, conducted chiefly by Lewin and his students, have touched upon this problem (98, 122, 229, 246). Some of their results suggest that, with the exception of "play" situations, fantasy completion of interrupted or insoluble tasks has little, if any, substitute value. However, the exclusive use of the resumption technique as a measure of drive strength and of the interrupted-task technique as the primary method of inducing motivation (in addition to inadequate experimental procedures) greatly limits the generality of their findings. An experimental approach using more sensitive and direct measures of drive strength, and inducing drives with possibly wider theoretical and practical implications, seems necessary.

In addition, in order to demonstrate the phenomenon of drive reduction as an effect of fantasy behavior, it seems desirable to use a drive which by reason of theory and experience seems likely to be measurably reduced by fantasy; i.e., a psychogenic as contrasted to a physiologically rooted drive. With these considerations in mind, the present research is designed to test the following hypothesis: Fantasy expression of hostility will partially reduce situationally induced aggression. Ideally, this hypothesis might be tested by inducing aggressive drive, measuring the strength of the drive induced and, after an interpolated fantasy activity, measuring the strength of aggressive drive a second time. The decrement in aggression from the first occasion to the second would provide the most direct test of the hypothesis. There are practical difficulties in carrying out this design. For one thing, it is difficult to find measures of aggression that can be meaningfully applied twice within a short period of time. Secondly, in preliminary work, the subjects (*S*s) would not accept the situation when the measures of aggression were given directly after aggression was aroused.

For these reasons the drive-reduction hypothesis is to be tested by comparing the strength of aggressive drive (at the end of the experimental session) in two groups, one of which receives the opportunity to express hostile fantasy while the other engages in nonfantasy or control activities. The actual test is then simply a measure of the subsequent difference in aggression between these two groups. The specific prediction is that the fantasy group will be less aggressive than the control group. The predicted difference is just as pertinent to the drive-reduction hypothesis as the ideal test previously described, even though the measure is one of end effect and relative difference rather than of absolute change in each group.

METHOD

The Ss were all members of introductory psychology classes at a large metropolitan college. Classes were randomly assigned to one of three experimental treatments: (a) arousal of aggression and interpolation of fantasy activity (Insult Fantasy group); (b) arousal of aggression and interpolation of nonfantasy activities (Insult Control group); (c) nonarousal of aggression and interpolation of fantasy activities (Noninsult Fantasy group). The Insult Fantasy group consisted of 123 Ss (five classes), the Insult Control group of 56 Ss (three classes), and the Noninsult Fantasy group of 78 Ss (three classes).[2] In the total group there were approximately twice as many men as women. However, the sex ratio from class to class varied considerably.

Aggression was aroused by the experimenter (E), who assumed an insulting attitude toward a class of college students. The interpolated activities provided one group of insulted Ss the opportunity to express their hostility in fantasy (Insult Fantasy group), whereas the activities in which a comparable group of insulted Ss were engaged permitted little or no opportunity for fantasy (Insult Control group). These two groups were then compared on subsequent measures of hostility toward E and the experiment to determine if the fantasy experience resulted in less aggression than did the nonfantasy activity.

The Noninsult Fantasy group engaged in the same fantasy activity as did the Insult Fantasy group and received the same measures of aggression as did the two Insult groups. Comparison between the Noninsult and Insult groups on these measures would indicate whether E's insulting attitude actually did arouse aggression in the insulted groups and at the same time would establish the validity and usefulness of the measures of aggression with respect to the principal comparison between the Insult Fantasy and Insult Control groups.

---

[2] These are the Ss who remained after eliminating from all Insult groups 23 Ss who in class discussions held several days after the experiment said they knew the insulting attitude of E was feigned. Because of administrative limitations, classes, not Ss, were assigned at random to the various experimental treatments.

Procedure. Two Es were used in carrying out the study. The individual who acted as the principal E [3] was carefully selected for his ability to arouse the hostility of Ss in the Insult groups without their realizing that his remarks were deliberately intended to achieve that end. The writer acted as his assistant in each of the 11 classes which participated in the study.

The E was briefly introduced to the class by its instructor, who left the classroom and did not return until near the end of the period. Administration of the experimental procedures consumed one 50-minute class period and all the classes were seen within a four-day period.

After the instructor left the classroom, E, in an authoritarian, arrogant manner, made several derogatory remarks about the motivation, ability, and level of maturity of the student body of the college. For example, he made such comments as "Now I realize that you ——— College students, or should I say ——— College grinds have few academic interests outside of your concern for grades . . . if you will try to look beyond your limited horizons, your cooperation will be useful. In other words, I'd like you to act like adults rather than adolescents." [4] The Noninsult classes received a friendly introduction designed to gain their cooperation.

Fantasy-nonfantasy variable. The E who acted as insulter did not know whether the insulted class was to be in the Fantasy or Control group until after he made his insulting comments. After making his introductory remarks, he opened a folder from which he read the instructions for the particular activity to be given. This procedure was followed so as to eliminate the possibility that E's behavior could be biased by foreknowledge of whether the class was to be in the Fantasy or Control group.

Four TAT pictures (103, 18GF, 7BM, and 12M) were presented by means of a slide projector to the Noninsult Fantasy and Insult Fantasy groups. The order in which the pictures were given was systematically varied. The instructions and procedure for administration of the group TAT followed those used by McClelland, Clark, *et al.;* these instructions present the TAT as an achievement task which involves the construction of an interesting and dramatic story under specific time limitations. The TAT was given as a test of ability, and in this respect is like the nonfantasy activities administered to the Control group.

The Insult Control classes received tests which offered little, if any, opportunity for fantasy. Each class was given a different nonfantasy ac-

---

[3] The writer is very much indebted to John Dickinson, at the time a graduate law student, whose caustic skills and courtroom demeanor were very effective in antagonizing the students and at the same time restraining them from overt aggressive behavior.

[4] A full account of all procedures including measures of aggression has been deposited with the American Documentation Institute. Order Document No. 4244 from the ADI Auxiliary Publications Project, Photoduplication Service, Library of Congress, Washington 25, D. C., remitting in advance $2.50 for 6×8 in. photoprints or $1.75 for 35 mm. microfilm. Make checks payable to Chief, Photoduplication Service, Library of Congress.

tivity which consumed the same amount of time as the TAT procedure. The nonfantasy activity was varied in an attempt to control for possible differences in preference for the fantasy vs. the nonfantasy activity. Had only one nonfantasy activity been used in all three classes in the Control group, then one might argue that if the Fantasy group subsequently displayed less aggression than the Control group, the difference could be due to the negative characteristics of the nonfantasy activity. Two of the Control classes were given standard tests; one Series AA of the Revised Minnesota Paper Form Board Test, and the second, Parts 1 through 4 of the General Clerical Aptitude Test. The instructions for the tests were abridged so as to correspond in length with those given for the TAT. The remaining class was given a "picture description test" which required a one-sentence description of each of a series of slides projected on a screen. These slides consisted of scenic photographs and paintings in which architectural forms predominated.

Measures of aggression. Subsequent to the interpolated activity all groups were administered a slightly modified version of the Rotter-Willerman (355) form of the Sentence Completion Test. The instructor then returned, and the Es left the classroom. The instructor informed the class that the faculty was interested in reactions of the students to having research take up class time. He then administered to the class a questionnaire consisting of eight items dealing with attitudes toward the experimenter, experiment, and psychological research.

RESULTS

Effects of the Insulting Behavior of E

The attitude questionnaire. The attitude questionnaire administered by the instructor at the close of the class hour is the most explicit and direct measure of aggression toward E. If the insulting attitude assumed by E had the intended effect of arousing hostility toward him, then this effect should be reflected by the responses of the insulted Ss on the questionnaire.

The Insult and Noninsult groups[5] were initially compared on each question separately. For the first six items, each of which had six alternatives, comparisons are based on the proportion of Ss selecting the most aggressive alternatives, points 5 and 6 on the six-point scale. Preliminary experiments had indicated that the best discrimination between insulted and noninsulted groups would probably be obtained in this way. For the remaining questions, which had only two possible answers, "yes" and "no," the differences are based on the proportion

---

[5] In order to avoid repetition of tables, the Noninsult Fantasy group data are presented in the section of the results concerned with differences between the Insult Fantasy and Insult Control groups. For those interested in the specific numerical results pertinent to the responses of the Noninsult Fantasy group on the questionnaire, reference can be made to Tables 1 and 2.

of people who gave the more aggressive of the two answers. The Insult groups display considerably more aggression on the questionnaire than the Noninsult group. The differences between the Noninsult and Insult Fantasy groups are significant for five of the eight questions, and differences between the Noninsult and Insult Control groups are significant for seven of the eight questions.

In addition to the item analysis, a more general measure of aggression was obtained based on the first six items by assigning scores to each response, the least aggressive choice receiving a score of 1 and the most aggressive choice receiving a score of 6. A second measure was based only on the three questions dealing with attitudes toward E (items 3, 5, and 6). The third measure was based on the two questions concerning evaluation of the experiment (items 2 and 4).[6] On all three of these measures there are highly significant differences between the Insult groups and the Noninsult group.

The results of both the item comparisons and the over-all scores confirm the existence of the intended effect of the insult variable. As anticipated, the insulted Ss are much more critical of the study and much more hostile toward E than Ss who were not insulted.

The Sentence Completion Test. The responses to this test were scored for aggression according to a detailed scoring scheme[7] based primarily on distinctions according to the object of aggression and the form in which the aggression was expressed. The most important categories were: (*a*) aggression toward E; (*b*) aggression expressed toward possible substitutes for E (teachers, research workers); (*c*) aggression toward the test situation; (*d*) aggression expressed toward possible substitutes for the test situation (tests in general, experiments, college); (*e*) general aggression (aggression toward people, institutions, or practices). Within each of the above categories a distinction was made between emotional and objective aggression. The former was denoted by such terms as hate, dislike, detest, while the latter referred to criticism of the objects specified in each category. Emotional aggression was conceived to be a more direct expression of hostility than objective aggression.

An analysis was made of the percentage of Ss having one or more responses in each scoring category.[8] Only three categories yielded

---

[6] Question 1 was omitted from these two more specific measures because it could not be unambiguously assigned to either one.

[7] A study of the reliability of the scoring categories based on 30 Ss selected at random was carried out with another psychologist. The tests were independently scored. There was disagreement in scoring of only seven sentences.

[8] Due to lack of time, one class in the Noninsult Fantasy group and one class in the Insult Fantasy group failed to complete the test. These classes are not included in the analysis of the results for the Sentence Completion Test. A

TABLE 1. PERCENTAGE OF SUBJECTS IN EACH GROUP GIVING EXTREME AGGRESSIVE RESPONSES ON THE ATTITUDE QUESTIONNAIRE

Question	Response	Non-insult Fantasy ($N = 78$)	Insult Fantasy ($N = 107$)	Insult Control ($N = 56$)	Diff. IC-IF	t	p
1. How much did you like participating in the study just recently conducted?	very irritated and extremely irritated	0	9.3	25.0	15.7	2.7	$<.004$
2. How worthwhile was it to participate in the study just recently conducted?	considerable complete waste of time	6.4	15.9	19.7	3.8	0.62	$<.27$
3. If you were asked by the Experimenter to volunteer for another study he was conducting, would you volunteer?	probably not, definitely not	6.4	32.7	50.0	17.3	2.15	$<.02$
4. In your opinion, how much of a contribution will this study make to the field of psychology?	very little, none	11.5	26.1	30.4	4.3	0.63	$<.27$
5. In your opinion, how competent was the psychologist who conducted the experiment in which you participated?	very incompetent and extremely incompetent	3.8	21.5	35.7	14.2	1.95	$<.03$
6. What is your reaction now to the psychologist who conducted this experiment? How much do you like or dislike him?	dislike very much	0	42.0	57.2	15.2	1.85	$<.04$
7. Is there anything you disliked about the experiment?	yes	42.0	73.0	82.0	9.0	1.3	$<.10$
8. Several experiments are going to be conducted by the psychology department. Are you willing to volunteer?	no	56.0	56.0	66.0	10.0	1.2	$<.12$

differences in aggression between the Noninsult group and either of the Insult groups significant at the .05 level or above.[9] These categories—1, 2Em, and 3—deal, respectively, with aggression toward E, emotional aggression toward possible substitutes for E, and aggression toward the test. There is no significant difference in category 5 which represents aggression toward individuals who do not show any mani-

second class in the Insult Fantasy group was eliminated from this analysis in order to equate the proportion of the two sexes in each experimental group.

[9] The data are presented in Table 4. Yates's correction for continuity was used in all chi-square tests of independence.

fest similarity to E. The results provide tentative evidence of a gradient of generalization—aggression toward objects being a decreasing function of their similarity to the original instigator of the aggression in this situation.

The analysis of the attitude questionnaire and the Sentence Completion Test has demonstrated that both are sensitive to the arousal of aggression by the insulting comments of E and can therefore be used to test differences in aggression between the Insult Fantasy and Insult Control groups.

Effect of Fantasy

The attitude questionnaire. The results of the item analysis of the attitude questionnaire are presented in Table 1. Inspection of the table reveals that on every item the Insult Control group is more aggressive than the Fantasy group.[10] The smallest differences, not statistically significant, are on questions which deal with attitudes toward the study. The differences on questions which deal explicitly with attitudes toward E are much larger and are also statistically significant.[11] The consistently lower amount of aggression displayed by the Insult Fantasy group is in accord with the hypothesis that aggression expressed in fantasy behavior will reduce aggressive motivation.

The means of the Insult Fantasy and Insult Control groups on the more general measures based on the attitude questionnaire are given in Table 2. The differences between the two insulted groups indicated by the item comparisons are borne out by this method of analysis. The over-all aggression scores of the Insult Control group are significantly higher than those of the Insult Fantasy group. For the measure reflecting only aggression toward E this difference is significant at the .01 level. For the measure based on the criticism of the experiment, the difference is in the same direction but is small and not statistically significant.

The conclusions stated thus far about the statistical significance of

---

[10] The number of women in the Insult Fantasy group was reduced in order to equate the proportion of the two sexes in each experimental group. Since the women displayed less aggression than the men, a higher proportion of women in the Insult Fantasy group would tend to lower the mean aggression scores of that group. Cases to be eliminated were selected by use of a table of random numbers.

[11] The p values reported in this paper, with the exception of the Sentence Completion Test analysis, are based on a one-tailed test of significance. The one-tailed test is used where specific predictions of the direction of the anticipated difference were made. In the case of the Sentence Completion Test, the predictions were not specific enough to indicate on which of the scoring categories the Fantasy group would show less aggression than the Nonfantasy group.

TABLE 2. MEAN AGGRESSION SCORES OF EACH GROUP ON THE ATTITUDE QUESTIONNAIRE

Group	Total Aggression (all 6 items)	Personal Aggression toward E (items 3, 5, 6)	Aggressive Evaluation of the Experiment (items 2 and 4)
Noninsult Fantasy ($N = 78$)...	14.92	7.04	5.96
Insult Fantasy ($N = 107$)......	21.17	11.47	7.03
Insult Control ($N = 56$).......	23.09	12.88	7.23
Difference (IC $-$ IF)..........	1.92	1.41	.20
t	2.02	2.49	.56
p	$<.025$	$<.01$	$<.29$

TABLE 3. MEAN AGGRESSION SCORES ON THE ATTITUDE QUESTIONNAIRE OF MEN IN EACH CLASS IN THE INSULT GROUPS

Group	Total Aggression (all 6 items)	Personal Aggression toward E (items 3, 5, 6)	Aggressive Evaluation of the Experiment (items 2 and 4)
Insult Fantasy			
Class D....................	23.04	11.83	7.15
Class E....................	21.95	11.81	7.00
Class F....................	20.14	11.00	6.85
Class G....................	22.19	12.62	7.06
Class H....................	18.10	9.60	6.70
Mean....................	21.08	11.37	6.95
Insult Control			
Class J....................	23.13	12.47	7.33
Class K....................	23.13	12.88	7.25
Class L....................	23.80	13.40	7.50
Mean of classes..........	23.35	12.92	7.36
Difference between mean of classes....................	2.27	1.55	0.41
t	1.91	2.01	3.37
p	$<.06$	$<.05$	$<.01$

the results have been reached by treating each individual as an independent case. However, it is possible that differences in E's behavior, in the several classes in which he tried to keep his behavior constant, may have caused all the members of one class to vary from the others uniformly. To control for this possibility, another significance test of the difference between the two Insult groups was made using only the class means to constitute the sample. The comparison was based on the class means of the men only because of the varying proportions of women in different classes, and their tendency to have lower aggression scores than the men. The results of this analysis are presented in Table 3. All differences are in the predicted direction, thus confirming the findings reported above. The difference in over-all aggression between the Insult Fantasy and Insult Control groups approaches significance, while the difference based on attitudes to-

TABLE 4. PERCENTAGE OF SUBJECTS IN EACH GROUP HAVING ONE OR MORE AGGRESSIVE RESPONSES IN EACH SCORING CATEGORY ON THE SENTENCE COMPLETION TEST

Scoring Category	Noninsult Fantasy $(N = 51)$	Insult Fantasy $(N = 76)$	Insult Control $(N = 55)$	χ^2 (IF, IC)	p^*
1. Aggression toward E					
Emotional	2	13	24		
Objective	0	3	2		
Combined	2	13	25	2.46	>.13
2. Aggression toward E substitute					
Emotional	4	5	18	4.31	>.05
Objective	18	18	7	2.47	>.13
Combined	21	23	25		
3. Aggression toward test					
Emotional	0	8	11		
Objective	4	13	18		
Combined	4	17	25	.95	>.35
4. Aggression toward test substitute					
Emotional	6	5	4		
Objective	24	32	16	3.13	>.09
Combined	26	32	20		
5. Aggression toward individuals other than those included under categories 1 and 2					
Emotional	21	24	24		
Objective	16	22	15		
Combined	28	34	36		

* The p values are based on two-tailed tests of significance.

ward E is significant at the .05 level of confidence. Also, the difference based on evaluation of the study is significant at the .01 level.

The Sentence Completion Test. The results of a chi-square analysis of the percentage of Ss having one or more responses in each of the aggression categories are reported in Table 4. The most relevant measures for comparing the two Insult groups are categories 1, 2Em, and 3, which, since they discriminate between the Insult and Noninsult groups, are the most indicative of aggression. On each of these three measures, the Insult Control group displays more hostility than the Insult Fantasy Ss. The difference is significant at the .05 level for category 2Em and is not statistically significant for the other categories. If one computes for each individual the number of aggressive responses based on all three categories, the differences between the Insult Control and Insult Fantasy groups are considerably enhanced. The results of this comparison are presented in Table 5 and show

TABLE 5. PERCENTAGE FREQUENCY DISTRIBUTIONS OF INSULT GROUPS FOR SCORES BASED ON CATEGORIES 1, 2E, AND 3 ON SENTENCE COMPLETION TEST

Aggression Score	Insult Fantasy ($N = 76$)	Insult Control ($N = 55$)
0	71	45
1	17	22
2	5	15
>2	7	18

Note: Dichotomizing between 0 and 1, $\chi^2 = 7.7$; $p < .01$; dichotomizing between 1 and 2, $\chi^2 = 7.3$; $p < .01$.

the Insult Fantasy group to have significantly less hostility than the Insult Control group. Thus the differences in aggression found between the two groups on the attitude questionnaire are confirmed by the Sentence Completion Test.

Fantasy Data

The effect of the insults upon the fantasy responses. The TAT stories were coded to conceal identity of Ss and the experimental treatment and then rated on a five-point rating scale of aggression, a rating of five being given to the most aggressive fantasy. The results of the ratings are presented in Table 6. The stories of the Insult Fantasy group are consistently more aggressive than those of the Noninsult Fantasy group. However, the differences are small and only for Card 18 GF is the mean difference significant. The difference between the two groups in total mean aggression

TABLE 6. COMPARISONS BETWEEN INSULT FANTASY AND NONINSULT FANTASY GROUPS ON MEAN AGGRESSION RATINGS ON THE TAT STORIES

Picture	Noninsult Fantasy	Insult Fantasy	t	p
4...................	2.07	2.23	1.0	<.17
18GF................	2.09	2.44	2.2	<.02
7BM.................	1.72	1.89	1.3	<.10
12M.................	1.95	2.06	0.7	<.25
Total (all 4 pictures)..	7.83	8.62	2.1	<.02

scores based on all four cards is also small but is statistically significant.

The insulted Ss did then express more hostility in fantasy than the noninsulted Ss. This difference is consistent with an interpretation of the main findings, reported in the previous section, as due to reduction of aggressive drive by aggressive fantasy.

The relationship between aggression in fantasy and aggression toward E. A negative correlation between aggression in fantasy and subsequent aggression toward E would tend to support the major hypothesis but is not a critical test. A Pearson r was calculated between over-all aggression on the attitude questionnaire and aggression as rated from the TAT fantasies. The correlation for the Insult Fantasy group is $-.25$ and is significant at the .01 level of confidence. The corresponding correlation for the Noninsult Fantasy group is $-.15$ which is not significantly greater than zero. The two correlations are not, however, significantly different from each other.

The relationship between aggression in fantasy and subsequent aggression toward E is in a direction, then, which tends to support the hypothesis of a drive-reducing effect of fantasy.

DISCUSSION

The experimental findings confirm the major prediction based on the drive-reduction hypothesis, namely, that those Ss who were insulted by an E and were given the opportunity to express their aggression in fantasy would subsequently display less hostility toward E than a comparable insulted group which engaged in nonfantasy activities. The fact that two different and independent measures of drive strength, the attitude questionnaire and the Sentence Completion Test, yielded similar results increases confidence in the genuineness of the phenomenon. These measures are different in several important respects. The expression of aggression on the attitude questionnaire was sanctioned for all groups by the instructor, who encouraged the students to reveal their feelings about experiments in which they had been participants. In addition, the range of alternatives to each question gave tacit sanction to the holding of extreme attitudes about E. On the other hand, the Sentence Completion Test involved the spontaneous expression of aggressive feelings toward E despite the knowledge that the test responses would be available to him.

The question arises as to possible alternative explanations of the difference in hostility between the two insulted groups. One might argue that the difference is a result of an increment in hostility in the Control group rather than a decrement in the Fantasy group. Such an increment could conceivably arise from differences in the frustrating qualities of the control and fantasy activities, the former supposedly being more frustrating. An effort was made to control this factor in the experimental design by varying the nature of the nonfantasy task. There is no a priori reason for assuming that the control activities are any more or less demanding than the activity of constructing TAT stories which is presented as an achievement task. Moreover, because the variation of class means in the Insult Control group is very small and the statistical analysis based on class means takes account of the effect of possible differences in the frustrating character of the particular task used in each class, the obtained difference cannot be attributed to an assumed frustrating quality of just one or two of the control tasks.

Any obvious frustration produced by the control activities should be reflected on the measures of aggression. In response to a question on the attitude questionnaire requesting the students to indicate if there was anything about the experiment they disliked, 82 per cent of the Insult Control group and 73 per cent of the Insult Fantasy group expressed dislike of some aspect of the experiment including the E. An analysis of these spontaneous comments revealed that, of those who expressed some criticism, 16 per cent of the Insult Fantasy group criticized the fantasy activity while only 11 per cent of the Insult Control group criticized the control activities.[12] Thus, in addition to the a priori argument, there is no empirical evidence to indicate that the control tasks are more frustrating than the fantasy task.

One must look then to the fantasy activity as the cause of the significant difference in aggression between the Fantasy and Control

---

[12] Even in the Noninsult Fantasy group, 14 per cent of Ss (33 per cent of those who expressed some dislike of the experiment) criticized the fantasy task. They complained of insufficient time in which to complete the stories and of having to do too much writing.

groups. The most direct explanation of this difference is the reduction of hostility by means of aggressive fantasy. A possible alternative to the drive-reduction hypothesis is one that assumes that guilt and not drive reduction is the primary mechanism responsible for the lowered aggression in the fantasy group. Here it would be supposed that the evocation of aggressive fantasy aroused guilt responses which generalized to subsequent expressions of hostility on the tests of aggression and tended to inhibit aggressive responses on those tests.

The experimental data provide some basis for rejecting the assumption that guilt is the important mediating mechanism. If guilt were the crucial factor, then one would expect the increase in hostile fantasy in the Insult group to be associated with an increase in expression of guilt. The TAT stories were analyzed for indications of guilt in regard to aggressive expression. The difference in expression of guilt between the Insult Fantasy and Noninsult Fantasy groups was slight and insignificant. In addition, the Sentence Completion Test was scored for self-aggressive responses, which might be taken as an index of guilt. The frequency of such responses was very low in all experimental groups, and the small differences among the groups were insignificant.

The drive-reduction hypothesis seems the simplest and also the most suited to account for the differences between the Fantasy and Control groups. A basic assumption underlying this hypothesis is that fantasy expression is a form of behavior that follows the same behavioral principles that have been derived from motor phenomena. Fantasy or imaginative behavior, like other forms of behavior, can serve as a substitute goal response when the most adequate goal response cannot be made. In the present experiment, *S*s could not give vent to their hostility directly because of social inhibiting factors, fear of possible punishment from an authority figure, or lack of adequate opportunity. The Fantasy group *S*s, however, were given an opportunity for indirect expression of hostility in their fantasy contructions.

Fantasy responses may acquire reward value, i.e., become drive reducing in at least two ways: (*a*) through response generalization from direct, overt aggression or (*b*) through a gradient of reward; if in the past covert aggressive thoughts and wishes preceded and/or accompanied overt aggressive responses which were reinforced, these preceding covert verbal responses may acquire secondary reinforcing properties.

This interpretation is compatible with a more general hypothesis relating verbal behavior and drive reduction which has been developed by Dollard and Miller (103). In explaining various abnormal phenomena such as delusional fantasies, these authors emphasize the reduction of anxiety as the primary reinforcement of the delusional responses. The results of the present study suggest that these delusional responses may also reduce the drive, e.g., aggression, which is eliciting anxiety.

As viewed here, fantasy behavior is an adjustment mechanism which can serve to reduce tensions and provide substitute goal satisfactions. It may function as an outlet for socially unacceptable motives and frustrated achievement strivings. The effects of fantasy are likely to depend on a number of factors such as the particular drive, the type of fantasy, and individual predisposition. For example, one might expect that fantasy behavior would be less effective in reducing such primary drives as pain, hunger, and thirst. Spontaneous fantasy, as in daydreams, may be more effective than induced fantasy, as represented by TAT stories, in reducing motivation. This might occur because, in the former case, the fantasy responses are more similar to those present in the real-life situation. Finally, in some individuals fantasy might conceivably increase rather than decrease drive. Thus rehearsal of undisguised aggressive thoughts might augment the aggressive motives of people who characteristically express their hostility in direct, overt behavior and consequently have not learned to use fantasy as a means of discharging their aggression. The extent of drive reduction produced by fantasy under various circumstances is a problem to be solved by future research.

SUMMARY AND CONCLUSIONS

The purpose of this study was to investigate the hypothesis that the expression of aggression in fantasy will serve to partially reduce aggressive drive.

This hypothesis was tested by experimentally inducing aggression by insulting a group of students, interpolating a fantasy or nonfantasy activity, and subsequently measuring the strength of the aggressive drive. Another group was not insulted but was administered the fantasy activity and the subsequent tests of aggression in order to provide a means of validating the measures of aggression used.

The results are consistent with the drive reduction hypothesis:

1. The insulted group which had an opportunity to express aggression in fantasy subsequently displayed significantly less aggression toward E than did the control group which engaged in nonfantasy activities. This difference was found with two independent and valid measures of aggression.

2. A significant negative correlation was found between the amount of aggression expressed in fantasy and subsequent aggression toward E for the insulted group which had engaged in fantasy.

3. The insulted Ss expressed significantly more aggression in their fantasies than did the noninsulted Ss.

PART TWO

....

The Method for Assessment
of Motivation

IN THIS SECTION, detailed scoring manuals are presented for analysis of imaginative protocols to obtain indices of the strength of n Achievement, n Affiliation, and n Power. The manuals serve two functions. First, they describe in great detail what is meant by n Achievement, n Affiliation, and n Power in specifying what kinds of imagery should and should not be taken as symptomatic of these motives. Second, the manuals may be used in conjunction with extensive practice materials collated by Sheila Feld and Charles P. Smith, which are presented in Appendix I. Also presented in Appendix I are complete instructions in how to use the manuals and practice materials.

The present section contains the report of a methodological study by Feld and Smith which shows that very high scoring reliabilities may be expected of novice coders who have learned to score by the prescribed method *without the help of an already-trained tutor*. This demonstration of the degree of precision that is possible in coding thematic material, even by novice coders who have had only the minimum training prescribed in the practice materials, leaves little room in the future for the kind of shabby, hit-and-miss use of projective techniques that has too often been allowed to mar their respectability as scientific methods in the past.

The editor has added a number of footnotes to the original scoring manuals in order to call to the reader's attention some important issues that have arisen in past use of the manuals. Some scoring decisions may seem rather arbitrary. These decisions are either rooted in the empirical evidence of the validation experiments presented in Part I, or, in the absence of clear evidence, may be taken as conservative injunctions to the novice to assure high scoring reliability.

The scoring criteria for any of the motives are not to be taken as final in any sense. They represent the method as it is presently applied in the research studies of this book. But if we have anticipated correctly the course of research in years to come, we may expect that as the theoretical conception of motivation becomes more clear it will be possible to construct more appropriate validation experiments from which more refined methods of content analysis will emerge.

Also presented in this section are two alternative methods for assessing individual differences in the strength of achievement motive. The "insight inventory" developed by French, instead of asking the subject to write a story in response to a picture, confronts the subject with descriptions of behavioral incidents, e.g., "Bill always lets the other fellow win," and requires that he give an explanation of the behavior. This method, which circumvents the need for pictures to elicit projective responses, has been employed by French and Chadwick (143) to assess the affiliative motive as well. The correspondence between experimental results obtained by French using the "insight inventory" (See Part III) and those obtained in parallel studies using thematic apperception argues strongly for the equivalence of measures obtained with the two methods.

The final chapter in this section, by Aronson, presents evidence of a stable relationship between n Achievement scores derived from thematic apperception and graphic expression in the form of doodles which can be reliably scored. The possibility that analysis of graphic expression may provide a means of circumventing the inhibition of verbal expression of motivation when there is conflict, as for example in Clark's study of sexual motivation (72), argues for including it as a potential alternative method deserving careful follow-up and development. Uses of this method for analysis of graphic expression to assess achievement motivation in very young children and from artifacts are presented in Chapters 21 and 37. Appendix II contains a set of prescored "doodles" for practice in this method.

CHAPTER 12

....

A Scoring Manual for the Achievement Motive*,1

DAVID C. McCLELLAND, JOHN W. ATKINSON,
RUSSELL A. CLARK, AND EDGAR L. LOWELL

RELATION OF SCORING CATEGORIES TO THE ADJUSTIVE BEHAVIORAL SEQUENCE

OUR CLASSIFICATION of many of the aspects of the behavior and experiences of characters in imaginative stories reveals an implicit acceptance of the kind of descriptive categories elaborated by many different psychological theorists in conceptualizing adjustive overt behavior. Thus, we perceive the behavioral sequence originating when an individual experiences a state of need or a motive (N). (The symbols in parentheses are used throughout to denote the various scoring categories.) He may also be anticipating successful attainment of his goal $(Ga+)$ or anticipating frustration and failure $(Ga-)$. He may engage in activity instrumental (I) to the attainment of his goal which may lead to the attainment of the goal $(I+)$ or not $(I-)$. Sometimes his goal-directed activity will be blocked. The obstacle or block (B) to his progress may be located in the world at large (Bw) or it may be some personal deficiency in himself (Bp). He may experience strong positive and negative affective states while engaged in solving his problem, i.e., in attempting to gratify his motive. He is likely to experience a state of positive affect $(G+)$ in goal attainment, or a state of negative affect $(G-)$

---

* Abridged and reprinted by permission of author and publisher from Chapter IV of McClelland, D. C., Atkinson, J. W., Clark, R. A., and Lowell, E. L. *The Achievement Motive*. Copyright 1953 by Appleton-Century-Crofts, Inc.

1 The numbered passages which follow are the editor's footnotes to the original text of the *n* Achievement scoring manual. These footnotes are amplifications and revisions of the text which are based on seminar discussions of difficult scoring decisions.

The scoring criteria presented here constitute "Scoring System C" (272, p. 147). See Ricciuti and Clark (341) for the latest evidence of the validity of these criteria and for several important suggestions for further refinement of the method.

179

when his goal-directed activity is thwarted or he fails. Often some-one will help or sympathize with him—[nurturant press (Nup)]—aiding him in his goal-directed behavior. This, in brief, is our analysis of the behavioral sequence. It is presented schematically in Figure [1]. Note that the five states an individual may experience (Need, Positive or Negative Anticipatory Goal States, Positive or Negative Affective States) are located within the person in this diagram. Instrumental Activity is denoted by the arrows suggestive of trials and errors in the problem-solving attempt. A

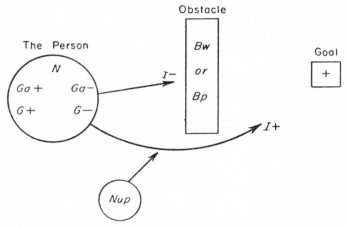

Fig. 1. Position of the scoring categories in the adjustive behavioral sequence.

Block (which also may be located within the person) is denoted as a barrier that must be overcome if the goal is to be attained. The symbol for Nurturant Press is another person with an arrow in the direction of the goal indicating aid of some sort. And finally, the goal is indicated by a plus sign. The goal defines whether or not the various anticipations, affective states, instrumental acts, and so forth of the person are achievement-related or are related to some other motive. Presumably these categories may be used to describe the behavioral sequence no matter what the goal of the individual. For this reason, major attention must be directed to the definition of what constitutes an achievement goal.

DEFINITION OF ACHIEVEMENT IMAGERY (AI)

The scorer must first decide whether or not the story contains any reference to an achievement goal which would justify his scoring the sub-categories (Need, Instrumental Activity, and so on) as achievement-related. By achievement goal is meant *success in competition with some standard of excellence*. That is, the goal of some individual in the story is to be successful in terms of competition with some standard of excellence. The individual may fail to achieve this goal, but the concern over competition with a standard of excellence still enables one to identify the goal sought as an achievement goal. This, then, is our generic definition of n Achievement. In the definitions of criteria for scoring Achievement Imagery that follow, it will become apparent that we include certain types of imagery in which there is no explicit statement in the story concerning competition with a standard of excellence. For these particular criteria it is our feeling that the evidence is sufficient for a fairly safe *inference* that competition with a standard of excellence is implicitly involved.

Competition with a standard of excellence is perhaps most clear when one of the characters is engaged in competitive activity (other than pure aggression) where winning or doing as well or better than someone else is the primary concern. Often, however, competition with a standard of excellence is evident in the concern of one of the characters with how well a particular task is being done, regardless of how well someone else is doing. Any use of adjectives of degree (good, better, best) will qualify so long as they evaluate the excellence of performance. Stories are scored for Achievement Imagery *only* when one of the criteria listed below is met. Although competition with a standard of excellence is implicit in all three criteria, as pointed out above, the phrase is used to denote the first criterion in which concern over how well the activity is being done is most explicit.

1. *Competition with a standard of excellence. a.* One of the characters in the story is engaged in some competitive activity (other than pure cases of aggression) where winning or doing as well as or better than others is *actually stated* as the primary concern. Wanting to win an essay contest, or an apprentice wanting to show the master that he, too, can fix the machine, are typical examples.

b. If one of the characters in the story is engaged in some competitive activity (other than pure cases of aggression), but the desire to win or do as well as or better than others is *not explicitly* stated, then (1) affective concern over goal attainment, and (2) certain types of Instrumental Activity are considered as indicating that the desire to compete successfully with a standard of excellence is implicit in the story. Examples of (1) would be: "The boy wins the essay contest and feels *proud.*" "The boy loses the contest and becomes *bitter.*" "The boy *anticipates* the *glory* that will be his if he should win." An example of (2) would be: "The boy is working *very carefully* on his essay." [2]

c. Often the standard of excellence involves no competition with others but meeting self-imposed requirements of good performance. In this case, in order to score for *AI* what is needed are words to the effect that a good, thorough, workmanlike job, and so forth is desired, or statements showing the affective concern or Instrumental Activity that will allow such an inference. Typical examples are: "The boy is *studiously* and *carefully* preparing his homework." "The

---

[2] Stories are not always scored for Achievement Imagery (AI) when the evidence of affective concern is largely negative. When a person is in achievement-related difficulty, it is normal to experience negative affect (G−). This is not enough to justify scoring Achievement Imagery. There must be independent evidence of a *positive achievement orientation.* The story must indicate, either by a direct statement of need (N) or by a sufficiently descriptive instrumental activity (I), that the person stays in the field and is realistically concerned about overcoming the deficiency. In most cases, both G− and N must appear, or G− paired with a *clearcut* achievement-related instrumental act. The following story is an excellent example of *what not to score.* Here the person leaves the field—a fine example of a failure-avoidance motive but not of an achievement motive. (Score Doubtful Imagery.)

The young student *seems to be perplexed* with some problem and then finding no solution appears to daydream. The young student was asked a question about which he *didn't know the answer,* so he *felt rather discouraged and disgusted.* The student is *wondering whether school work is necessary "stuff"* or not. He hopes he *were doing something else.* He will continue in school, perhaps graduate; if not, he will soon quit school and look for adventure elsewhere perhaps in a trade school.

In the next story, there is negative affect following an obstacle, but there is no evidence of achievement concern in any statement of need nor is there any instrumental act which implies achievement concern. (Score Doubtful Imagery.)

Machine has broken down and is being fixed. Man fixing it is the boss of the shop. Other man is *worker who broke machine.* Boss has told worker to be careful in handling machine because it operates with difficulty. Man fixing the machine thinks breakage could have been avoided. The worker *is just plain angry because the damn thing broke* and he is watching with disgust. The machine will be repaired. Worker will be fired if it happens again.

In the following two stories, there is both negative affect (regret) and a statement of need to overcome the obstacle. Both these stories are scored for Achievement Imagery and also for other categories.

Peter is in class and he has to write a quiz. The day before Peter *instead of studying for the quiz went to the movies* with some friends. Peter *thinks now how foolish it was to go to the movies,* he *wants now to know the answers for the quiz.* Peter will have a poor grade in his quiz and *should work harder to make up* his grade.

An engineer is taking an open book exam and he is *finding the exam too* difficult. The student is not stupid, but he has a girl and *didn't study as hard as he should have.* He *wishes that he had studied harder* and *wishes the correct answers.* He would cheat, but it is an honor exam and he has too much character. He will get a "D" in the exam and *will turn over a new leaf* and devote the proper time to study.

boy is *worried* because he cannot quite grasp the meaning in the textbook assignment."

In the above criteria, distinction is made between statements of the *intensity* and *quality* of instrumental acts. Working hard, or working fast would be evidence of concern over achievement only when excellence at the task demanded speed or intense effort. But one may work hard to complete a task for reasons other than personal achievement. For instance, "The boy is working hard to finish his homework," may indicate only that he wants to go out and play or perhaps that he is late with his term paper and is rushing to get it in. In neither of these examples is there evidence of concern over a standard of excellence, and so there is no basis for scoring Achievement Imagery. However, a statement such as "He is working slowly with great thoroughness" implies concern with accuracy, a standard of excellence. In this instance and in ones like it, Achievement Imagery would be scored.

2. *Unique accomplishment.* One of the characters is involved in accomplishing other than a run-of-the-mill daily task which will mark him as a personal success. Inventions, artistic creations, and other extraordinary accomplishments fulfill this criterion. There need be no explicit statement of concern over the outcome or direct statement that a good job is wanted when someone is working on a new invention or is in the process of doing something unique which will be generally accepted as a personal accomplishment. Here we make the inference that the individual is competing with a standard of excellence, and that unless his goal is reached he will also experience feelings of failure.[3]

---

[3] The manual focuses attention chiefly on the distinction between the story in which two men are simply working at a machine versus two inventors in the process of developing something new and socially useful. The scorer, however, must be sensitive to what would constitute a unique accomplishment in other fields of endeavor. For example, a boy practicing at the piano versus the young composer struggling with a new composition, a reporter finishing an article versus a reporter getting the beat on everyone else, etc. In the story below, the unique accomplishment imagery is embedded in a story that is loaded with ideological content. It should be scored as a unique accomplishment in terms of the underlined imagery.

These two men are working with a machine, perhaps a printing press. It might be Tom Paine and an assistant *working on the publication of his famous booklet* advocating freedom for America. Oppression by the British has angered Paine into writing a pamphlet expressing the grievance of the Americans *which is destined to make history.* The two men are perhaps disturbed by the failure of their primitive press and are discussing possibilities of repairing it so that *their important document* can be published. The pamphlet of T. Paine *is destined to become one of the greatest of revolutionary documents* and was instrumental in arousing the colonists to fight for their freedom.

3. *Long-term involvement.* One of the characters is involved in attainment of a long-term achievement goal. Being a success in life, becoming a machinist, doctor, lawyer, successful businessman, and so forth, are all examples of career involvement which permit the inference of competition with a standard of excellence *unless it is made explicit that another goal is primary,* e.g., food for the kids, personal security.[4]

Often, one of the characters may be involved in attainment of some limited achievement goal, i.e., a specific task. When rather routine and limited tasks or performances are shown definitely to be related to long-term achievement interests, Achievement Imagery *is* scored. Studying for an exam would *not* be scored unless there was evidence of concern over doing well or over the possibility of failure as outlined under criterion (1) listed above, *or* unless the exam were explicitly related to "going on to medical school" or "graduating from college"—both being long-term achievement goals. *The relationship of a specific task to a long-term achievement goal must be clearly stated and not inferred by the scorer when it does not fulfill criterion (1) above.*

It is worth noting that we are able to include long-term involvement as evidence of achievement motivation only because we have knowledge that in contemporary American society, success in the career usually demands successful competition with a standard of excellence. Not everyone can be a doctor, lawyer, successful businessman, or expert machinist. Attainment of these goals is accompanied by feelings of personal success which we believe to be historically related to the pleasure associated with independent accomplishment in early childhood, in which reward (hence pleasure) is contingent upon mastery, viz., doing a good job. *In scoring the stories of other cultures without knowledge of the culture, it would be necessary to adhere to the criterion of an explicit statement of concern over successful competition with a standard in order to define the achievement goals of that culture. Only with growing knowledge of the culture could other criteria be added which involve the inference that competition with a standard of excellence is inherent in certain cultural activities.* (Editor's Italics).

Only stories which fulfill at least one of these above three criteria are scored for the achievement-related subcategories.[5]

---

[4] If other motives are contributing to the striving toward a long-term achievement but are not primary, so that *some part* of the striving is attributable to *n* Achievement, Achievement Imagery should be scored.

[5] The same phrase may be scored for Achievement Imagery and any other category. But the same phrase may *not* be scored for *two* subcategories.

DOUBTFUL ACHIEVEMENT IMAGERY (TI)

Stories containing some references to achievement but which fail to meet one of the three criteria for Achievement Imagery are scored Doubtful Achievement Imagery (*TI*) and are not scored further for achievement-related subcategories. The *T* chosen as a symbol for this category indicates that most frequently the stories to be classified as doubtful are ones in which one of the characters is engaged in a commonplace *task* or solving a routine problem. Whenever there is doubt about whether or not one of the three criteria for Achievement Imagery has been met, and the story is not totally unrelated to achievement, it is classified *TI*.

UNRELATED IMAGERY (UI)

Stories in which there is no reference to an achievement goal are scored unrelated and not scored further. The difference between a story scored *TI* and one scored *UI* is simply that the *TI* story usually contains reference to some commonplace task goal and often contains other task-related subcategories, but fails to meet one of our three criteria for scoring Achievement Imagery; whereas the story scored *UI* fails to have any reference whatsoever to achievement.

The three imagery categories (*UI, TI,* and *AI*) comprise a continuum of increasing certainty that the story contains imagery related to achievement motivation. Often the scorer may feel that a story that must be scored *TI* because it fails to meet any one of the criteria for *AI*, should have been scored for *AI* and the other achievement-related subcategories as well. Our experience indicates that while undoubtedly some achievement stories are lost according to the present criteria, in the long run, rigid adherence to the stated criteria is the only means of assuring high scorer reliability. The rationale for distinguishing between stories with doubtful achievement imagery and those unrelated to achievement will become clear when the method of computing the *n* Achievement score is discussed.

STORIES ILLUSTRATING VARIOUS TYPES
OF ACHIEVEMENT IMAGERY

Competition with a Standard (AI)

1. One fellow is the supervisor and the other the machine operator. There has been trouble with the machine, and the supervisor is attempting to repair it. The machine operator has been turning out faulty equipment and after having been called down by the supervisor, he explained what he thought has been wrong. Upon inspection by the supervisor, this theory

has been proven correct. The operator has his doubts about the ability of the supervisor to repair the machine. The boss realizes this and is determined to repair it. *He wants to prove that he is capable of making minor repairs.* The boss will do part of the repairs, but due to the technicalities of the machine will be unable to complete the job, and he will have to either call in the maintenance men or a specialized repair man from the outside.

2. An operation is taking place. The persons are the doctor, patient, nurse, and a student. The patient must have been sick at one time to be on the table. The student is observing the doctor doing his job along with the nurse. The doctor is concentrating on his work. The student is attending the doctor's movements, the nurse probably thinking of her boy friend. *A good job is wanted by the doctor* and student. The doctor will complete the operation, give a lecture on it, the student will ask questions on the work, the nurse will take off on her other duties.

(The clearly stated desire to meet a standard of excellence enables one to score these two stories *AI* instead of *TI*.)

3. The boy is taking an examination. He is a college student. He is trying to recall a pertinent fact. He did not study this particular point enough although he thought it might be on the examination. He is trying to recall that point. He can almost get it but not quite. It's almost on the tip of his tongue. Either he will recall it or he won't. If he recalls it, he will write it down. *If he doesn't, he will be mad.*

(Evidence of affective arousal as a result of non-attainment of the achievement goal in this specific task situation is all that keeps the imagery from being considered *TI*.)

4. A group of medical students are watching their instructor perform a simple operation on a cadaver. A few of the students are very sure they will be called on to assist Dr. Hugo. In the last few months they have worked and studied. The skillful hands of the surgeon perform their work. The instructor tells his class *they must be able to work with speed and cannot make many mistakes.* When the operation is over, a smile comes over the group. Soon they will be leading men and women in the field.

(The instructor's interest in accuracy and perfection is evidence of a desire for mastery in this specific task.)

5. The student is *worrying about his two exams* coming up Friday, the first night of the May frolic. The student has spent most of his time previous to this, studying information for his research paper in English 108. He is *wondering how he can ever manage to study sufficiently enough to be able to pass the exams* while he is so preoccupied with thoughts of the Frolic. He will study "like mad" for a few hours, and then "knock off," hoping for the best.

(Note that it is the student's affective arousal [worrying] concerning the threat of not reaching his achievement goal [passing the exam] which leads to the decision to score this story *AI* and not the vigorous Instrumental Activity of the last sentence [studying "like mad"]. A distinction must be made between evidence of intense Instrumental Activity [working hard] and evidence of concern over mastery. Stories with only intense

Instrumental Activity will not be scored *AI* unless one of the three criteria for Achievement Imagery is met.)

Unique Accomplishment (AI)

6. Something is being heated in a type of furnace which appears to be of metal. The men are blacksmiths. The men have been doing *research* on an alloy of some type and *this is the crucial test* that spells success or failure of the experiment. They want a specific type of metal. They are working for government interests. They may be successful this time. They have *invented* a metal that is very light, strong, durable, heat resistant, etc. A *real step in scientific progress.*

7. The boy is a student and during a boring lecture his mind is going off on a tangent, and he is daydreaming. The instructor has been talking about medieval history, and his reference to the knights of old has made the lad project himself into such a battle arrayed with armor and riding a white stallion. The boy is thinking of riding out of the castle, waving good-bye to his lady fair, and *going into the battle and accomplishing many heroic deeds.* The boy will snap out of it when the instructor starts questioning the students on various aspects of the lecture, and the boy will become frantic realizing he has not been paying attention.

8. Gutenberg and his assistant, Flogman, are working on an edition of the Bible. They are working hard to get as many printed as possible. Together *they have worked on Gutenberg's idea of a printing press and now, together, they are attempting to prove its worth.* Gutenberg thinks, "Will that fifth lever in the back of the joint hold up?" Flogman thinks, "If the Cardinal approves, we are in, but it is not likely that he will." The Cardinal disapproves, but the City Council approves, and Gutenberg and Flogman receive their contracts.

9. The boss is talking to an employee. The boss has some special job that he wants done, and this man is an expert in that particular phase. The boss wants the employee, an engineer, to start *working on a specially designed carburetor for a revolutionary engine.* The employee is thinking out the problem. The job will come off "O.K.," and the engine will *revolutionize* the automobile industry.

10. *Two inventors are working on a new type of machine.* They need this machine in order to complete the work on their new invention, the automobile. This takes place some time ago. They are thinking that soon they will have succeeded. They want to improve transportation. Their *invention* will be successful and they will found a great industrial concern.

Long-term Involvement (AI)

11. *The boy is thinking about a career as a doctor. He sees himself as a great surgeon performing an operation.* He has been doing minor first aid work on his injured dog, and discovers he enjoys working with medicine. He thinks he is suited for this profession and sets it as an ultimate goal in life at this moment. He has not weighed the pros and cons of his own ability and has let his goal blind him of his own inability. An adjustment which will injure him will have to be made.

12. A boy, Jim Neilson, 18 years old, is *taking an examination for entrance in the Army Air Corps.* He has studied very hard in high school *hoping all along that he will some day be a fighter pilot.* Now that he sees how difficult the examination is, he is very worried that he may fail it. He is thinking so much about his failing it he cannot concentrate on the test itself. He will just barely pass the test and will later become a cadet, then finally a pilot.

(The first sentence of this story is an example of a specific task being related to a long-term achievement goal. The second sentence reiterates the long-term concern. There is also affective concern over the possibility of failing the test that would warrant scoring this story *AI.*)

13. The boy is a thinker, bored with his schoolwork he is attempting to do. His mind wanders. He thinks of his future. The boy has completed all but the last of his high school career. The boy is eager to graduate. He has faith in his capabilities and *wants to get started on the job he has lined up, dreaming of advancements.* The boy will graduate ranking near the middle of his class. He will do all right on the outside.

14. The boss is inquiring about a story that the young man wrote in the paper. He had claimed evidence in a murder trial that didn't actually exist. Reporter reported false evidence, and the police have raised quite a stink about it. Public opinion is clamoring for conviction. The boss wants the reporter to find new evidence which will take pressure off the paper. *Reporter is thinking he'll lose his job if he doesn't.* Reporter will find new evidence but police get conviction anyway so pressure is off paper. Man doesn't lose job.

(Here there is concern about a long-term goal, the job. The specific task of finding new evidence is related to this long-term goal of the reporter.)

15. This is a father and a son. The father is an immigrant, and his son has stopped to see his father. *The son has been successful in his business* largely because of the training he received in his home as a child and youth. The old man is looking with a feeling of pride at his son and feels that he is very fortunate to have many things he himself never had. The son realizes this *pride* in his father's thoughts. The son will try to give his father some of the things he gave up in order to educate him.[6]

Doubtful Achievement Imagery (TI)

16. There are two men working in some sort of machine shop. They are making some sort of a bolt or something. One of the men's car broke down, and he has discovered that a bolt is broken. So, being a fairly good forger, he is making a new bolt. He is discussing with the other man just how he

---

[6] The following story is an example of involvement which is too specific to be scored long-term involvement.

There are two men here, John the younger, Bill the older. The machine on which John is working has broken in some way. Bill will try to fix it. John has worked in this lab only 6 months and is unfamiliar with the machine except to run it. John wants to learn to fix the machine. Bill wants the machine fixed so that he may do it himself (J.) next time. The machine will be fixed. John will go back to work. Bill will return to his supervising job.

is making the bolt and telling him about all of the details in making this bolt. When he is finished, he will take the bolt and replace the broken bolt in the car with it. He will then be able to get his car going.

(This is an example of a specific task story in which there is no stated need for mastery and no evidence of affective arousal concerning the possibility of personal success or failure. There is, however, a specific achievement goal, namely, making the bolt. Therefore, the story is scored *TI* rather than *UI*.)

17. Two workmen are trying to remove one lead pig from a small blast furnace. This action was to be completed months before, but only now did the necessary material arrive. One young man is showing the other just how to handle the pig, and perhaps a little theory is presented while they are waiting for the finished product. During the conversation, a distant bell is heard, the men quickly stop their work and prepare to adjust a number of tools before taking the pig from the furnace.

18. Jim is in the midst of deep thought trying to pick the answer to a problem on his exam out of the thin air. He is evidently having a difficult time with it. Jim probably didn't prepare himself too well for his exam and therefore doesn't have necessary things at his fingertips. Jim is trying to remember some formula. If he could just remember it, he could solve his problem immediately. Jim will skip to the next problem in a short while and then return to this one.

(Note that being in an exam situation is not scored *AI* in this instance, since there is no evidence of concern over the outcome either in the form of a stated need to do well, working carefully, affective arousal over the possibility of success or failure, and so forth.)

19. The persons are students in a school. They were studying until a distraction occurred which was the teacher who attracted their attention. The students were studying. The teacher had disciplined them for their actions in class telling them to study a story for repetition later. The students are looking at the teacher with dislike in their eyes. They don't think much of her this day and dislike her for her ways of teaching. The students will not do too well in the repetition exercise, and as a result further punishment will be applied.

(The achievement goal of the story is studying. There is no evidence of concern over mastery, perfection, or the possibility of failure, so the story is scored *TI*.)

20. An elderly man and young man with their heads together in conference. The older one is giving advice to the younger man perhaps on a matter of law. The young man, who has just entered the field of law, has come up with a difficulty in a recent case and has turned to the senior and wiser partner of his firm. They go over the situation and facts from which the elderly man will then advise. The advice will be taken by the young lawyer, and he will then proceed to form his case around the advice.

(Two lawyers are engaged in a specific, routine task, that of solving a particular problem. The mere mention of the profession of law is not sufficient to classify this story as long-term involvement. Becoming a lawyer is not the goal of the story. Rather, the solution to a specific legal problem is the goal. Unless there is evidence that perfection, the best possible solution, and so on, is wanted, the story is scored *TI*.)

21. Doctor Ingersoll is making a very difficult operation on Frank Briston's left kidney. Another doctor and nurse are present. Frank has been a drunkard most of his life which has poisoned his kidneys. The doctor is concentrating on the operation. The nurse is thinking that it is futile to try to save him. He will just go to drink again. He will recover, but as the nurse thought he will die of drinking.

(A doctor performing a routine operation is scored *TI*, unless there is direct evidence of concern over mastery, perfection, and so forth.)

22. It looks like a painting that has not been completed. The boy in the bottom of the picture is the artist. The painting has been started but has not been completed. The canvas was prepared and the rough drawing made. The boy (in the lower right-hand corner) is thinking about what to do next. He has already begun to shade in the left-hand side of the painting. The painting will be completed by the boy.

(This story is clearly not an example of a unique accomplishment. The boy is not creating a work of art. Rather he is engaged in the specific task of painting a picture, therefore, this story is scored *TI*.)

Unrelated Imagery (UI)

23. A young fellow is sitting in a plaid shirt and resting his head on one hand. He appears to be thinking of something. His eyes appear a little sad. He may have been involved in something that he is very sorry for. The boy is thinking over what he has done. By the look in his eyes we can tell that he is very sad about it. I believe that the boy will break down any minute if he continues in the manner in which he is now going.

24. The boy is daydreaming of some picture he may have seen or is projecting himself into the future, putting himself into the situation as it would be if he were a man. The boy has seen a movie. The boy is thinking of how he would like to be in the situation as seen. The daydream, if not too vivid or realistic, will be terminated so that he can engage in activity more related to his present needs.

25. An elderly man is talking to a much younger man in the study of the older man. A problem has presented itself in which the older man needs the younger man's help or advice. The younger man is listening to what is being said and seriously thinking over the situation at hand. A conclusion will be reached in which there will appear some of the advice of the younger man. But the older man will not accept everything presented by the younger.

(Here the solution of the problem is in no clearly stated way related to achievement, and hence it is scored *UI*. In Example 20 the solution of a problem related to achievement was the goal.)

STATED NEED FOR ACHIEVEMENT (N)

Someone in the story states the desire to reach an achievement goal. Expressions such as "He *wants* to be a doctor," "He *wants* to finish the painting," "He *hopes* to succeed" are the clearest examples. Very strong indications of the presence of the motive in phrases like "He is *determined* to get a good mark" are also scored. The accomplishment desired may be specific, "He wants to finish the invention"; may refer to personal status, "He wants to become a successful businessman"; or may be more general and altruistic, "He wants to be of service to mankind." Need is scored only once per story, even when it appears more than once in varying forms. *Need is not inferred from Instrumental Activity.* It may seem quite obvious to the scorer that the characters who are working furiously toward an achievement goal must want to succeed. Need is scored, however, only when there is a definite statement of motivation by one of the characters.

Not all statements of desire that appear in an achievement-related story are evidences of the presence of Need (N). If, for example, an inventor "wants his assistant to hand him the hammer," N is not scored. The scorer may imagine the stated need satisfied and then determine whether or not an achievement goal has been attained. Obviously, having the hammer in hand is no personal accomplishment. If the inventor had stated that, "He hopes to get the lever in place so that the machine will be complete," N would be scored. Having the machine completed is an achievement goal of the inventor. Another kind of statement of need which is *not* scored is a statement by one character which defines an achievement goal for another character. Examples of this are: "The teacher wants the students to study their lesson," "A man wants the machinist to fix his car," "The machine has probably gone on the 'bum' and now needs to be fixed."

Illustrative Stories

(Note that all the examples which follow also fulfill one of the criteria for scoring Achievement Imagery.)

26. A man is experimenting with a new alloy of iron, while his assistant looks on. Many years of research have lead up to this situation. The two men have experimented and failed many times over but have stuck to their job. *Both men are hoping that at last they have succeeded* in making the strongest steel possible. They will test their alloy and find that it meets with their expectations. It will then be refined in great quantities for use the world over.

27. A young person *wishes to become a doctor.* He can visualize himself performing an operation. He received a toy doctor's kit for a present several years ago, and several of his friends are planning to be doctors. He is thinking of the pleasant or glamorous side of the picture and not the long years of study. He will be unable to pass pre-medical school. He decides to become a lab. technician as he wants to stay in that field.

28. Watt and an assistant are working on the development of the steam engine. There has been a *need* for mechanical power, time, and labor saving machinery to increase production. A *need* for better and faster transportation. It looks as though they are fitting a valve or piston.

(*N* is *not* scored in this story, because the need stated does not refer to a need for achievement on the part of the characters but rather to a lack in the world.)

29. A skilled craftsman is working at his machine. A townsman *wanted* a basket woven in a certain way and asked the craftsman to make it. The craftsman is absorbed in his work and thinks that this will be another fine product worthy of his reputation. He will work far into the night until it is finished and display it with pride the next day when the townsman calls for it.

(*N* is *not* scored in this story, since the statement of need for a basket by the townsman defined the achievement goal of the craftsman. When the townsman's need was satisfied, i.e., the basket handed to him finished, he did not experience feelings of personal accomplishment. Had the *craftsman* "wanted a basket woven in a certain way" and then gone on to weave it, N would be scored.)

INSTRUMENTAL ACTIVITY WITH VARIOUS OUTCOMES (I +, I ?, I −)

Overt or mental activity[7] by one or more characters in the story indicating that something is being done about attaining an achievement goal is considered Instrumental Activity and is scored $I+$, $I?$, or $I-$ to indicate whether the outcome of the Instrumental Activity is successful, doubtful, or unsuccessful. Instrumental Activity is scored only once per story even though there may be several instrumental acts stated. The outcome symbol scored reflects the net effect of all the instrumental acts which have occurred. *There must be an actual statement of activity within the story independent of both the original statement of the situation and the final outcome of the story*. If the first sentence of a story describes such a situation as "Two men are working on a new invention" and there is no further statement of Instrumental Activity in the story, I would *not* be scored. Neither would I be scored if a story went on with no statement of Instrumental Activity and ended "They will finish the invention." [8]

---

[7] Covert or mental activity such as *thinking* about how to attain the goal, *planning, scheming,* etc., should be scored I if instrumental to the attainment of an achievement goal.

[8] Instrumental Activity appearing in the initial clause of the first sentence which is sheer description of the picture is not scored—e.g., "Here are two men working." Nor is Instrumental Activity inferred from the final clause of the last sentence which states the outcome—e.g., ". . . and he goes on to college." However, a clearcut statement of an instrumental act appearing either later in

The instrumental act sometimes may be successful even though the over-all outcome of the *story* is not a success. Also, a statement of Instrumental Activity within the story in the past tense may be scored so long as it is more than a statement of the outcome of previous instrumental acts. For example, after the statement of the situation "Two men are working on an invention," a statement such as "They have *worked diligently* night and day in the past with repeated trials yielding only failures" may appear. It would be scored *I* and then $+$, ?, or $-$, depending upon the rest of the story. However, if after the statement of the situation, a statement such as "They completed two important phases of their work yesterday" appeared, *I* would *not* be scored. This is considered as a description of the outcome of previous acts with no word indicating actual striving.[9]

Stories Illustrating Successful Instrumental Activity (I+)

30. James Watt and his assistant are working on the assembly of the first steam engine. They are working out the hole for a slide valve of the first successful steam engine. All previous experiments have failed. Successful use of steam has not been accomplished. If the slide valve works, the first compound steam engine will be harnessed. *James Watt is pulling the pinion in place for the slide valve.* His assistant is watching. The purpose is to make a pinion to hold the yoke in place which will operate the slide valve. If the slide valve works satisfactorily, they will perfect it for use in factories and for use on the railway. *It will work.*

(Not until the end of the story do we learn that the Instrumental Activity which occurred earlier in the story is successful.)

31. A boy is dreaming of being a doctor. He can see himself in the future. He is hoping that he can make the grade. It is more or less a fantasy. The boy has seen many pictures of doctors in books, and it has inspired him. *He will try his best* and hopes to become the best doctor in the country. He can see himself as a very important doctor. He is performing a very dangerous operation. He can see himself victorious and is proud of it. He gets world renown for it. He will become the *best doctor in the U. S.* He will be an honest man too. His name will go down in medical history as one of the *greatest men.*

32. The two men are mechanics and are making parts for a racer. (Statement of situation.) They have found a future in driving midget cars at various tracks and are intent on trying their skill. They are think-

---

the first sentence or earlier in the last sentence may be scored. Just avoid scoring *I* when it is sheer initial statement of situation or final statement of outcome of the story. This does *not* mean to avoid first and last sentences *in toto.*

[9] A statement of Instrumental Activity in the future tense may also be scored so long as it is more than a statement of outcome. For example, "They will succeed" would *not* be scored I+, while "They will continue to work diligently and will succeed" would be scored I+.

ing about the money they will get when they enter the races. A superior racing car is wanted by both men. They will eventually go to the races and will make their money. The car will be just another homemade job, but the fans will enjoy seeing the hometown boys come through.

(This story has not been scored *I*, because there is no statement of Instrumental Activity independent of the statement of the situation and the final outcome. This story illustrates a conservative use of the manual which has been effective in producing high scorer reliability.)

Stories Illustrating Doubtful Instrumental Activity (I?)

33. The older man is a well-known pianist giving the younger man lessons in advanced piano. He is not satisfied with his student at the moment. In the past, *the young man has worked hard* on the piano, *studying long hours,* and all his family noticed how well he was doing. He is *thinking hard and trying hard* to put into his music just what his teacher wants him to. Just because he has a famous teacher, it doesn't necessarily mean that he will be famous. *He may not do very well or also he may.*

34. The boy is in an art studio. He is probably learning to be a sculptor. Behind him is a picture of a sculptor at work. *By looking at work done before his time and by great artists, he can learn much* from their styles and mistakes. He is probably thinking someday he'll be doing great artistic work like that. The boy wants all the information he can get to better himself. *He will observe and then go to work* on some artistic work himself. He may accomplish something great and maybe not. Anyway, he is learning.

(In these two examples the outcome of the Instrumental Activity is scored doubtful, because the writer presents alternatives of both success and failure without choosing between them.)

35. The men are metal workers and they are working on a new tool for the shop. They need a sharp-edged tool and are doing work which requires tempering. A tool for the shop has worn out or broken and needs to be replaced. In the period that this picture depicts, tools couldn't be purchased but must be made in the shop. The men are probably wondering if their work will be flawless or if the tool will replace the one that has broken. *After the metal has been removed from the flame, it will be dipped into some cold water.* Doing this repeatedly serves to temper and harden the new tool.

(In the above example the outcome of the Instrumental Activity is scored doubtful, because the writer does not present an ending to his story.)

Stories Illustrating Unsuccessful Instrumental Activity (I−)

36. The scene is a workshop. Two men are doing a very important job. They are grinding an important cog for a new jet engine which will attempt a flight to the moon. The inventor who doesn't want to let his secret out has hired these two men to work secretly for him. They are not very well known, but if the job is a success, they will be famous.

They are both very tense, each knowing that one little mistake will mean *months of hard work* lost and wasted. When they are finished, they find that the piece is too small for the engine, and they have *failed* and must start again.

37. The boy is thinking that he does not know whether he can cover the material the night before the test. His roommate, seen at the right, is working. The boy is trying to decide whether to go to bed or to study all night. He has been swamped with work and has been delayed from study until a late hour because of another activity which he could not miss. He finds that the work is difficult and hasn't enough time for it. If I stay up, I'll miss much in reading later. If I go to bed, I'll get up early but maybe won't have time to finish the work. He wants to get the work covered thoroughly to pass with a good grade. He goes to bed and *gets up early and studies*. Then he covers the work, but not well enough and consequently he *doesn't do well* on the test and *shoots his average out the window*.

ANTICIPATORY GOAL STATES (GA+, GA−)

Someone in the story anticipates goal attainment or frustration and failure. The Anticipatory Goal State is scored positive $(Ga+)$ when someone is thinking about the success he will achieve, expects that the invention will work, dreams of himself as a great surgeon. The Anticipatory Goal State is scored negative $(Ga-)$ when someone is worried about failure, is concerned over the possibility that the invention won't work, expects the worst, or is wondering whether or not he will succeed. Both $Ga+$ and $Ga-$ may be scored in the same story, but each may be scored only once. The $Ga-$ category includes all achievement-related anticipations that are not clearly positive. Thus, doubtful statements such as, "He is wondering what the outcome will be" are scored $Ga-$.

Achievement-related anticipations must be related to the achievement goal of the story.[10]

Stories Illustrating Positive Anticipatory Goal State (Ga+)

38. A research man is forming a bar. Both men are extremely interested in the operation. These two men are working together on a research problem. They have been working tirelessly up to now to get the correct ingredients for the material being used now. They are feeling satisfied with their work. A stronger metal is desired by both men. The experiment has been a successful one. They will attempt to sell their new

---

[10] Distinction between *instrumental thought* (I) and *goal anticipation* (Ga+). When a person is thinking or planning or wondering *how* to attain the goal, score *I*. When he is dreaming or pondering about the completion of his task, e.g., whenever he has a mental picture of the circumstances which define the attainment of the goal, score Ga+.

Recollecting a past goal state or goal activity is also scored Ga+ since we have no past-oriented category for thought processes.

discovery *with a feeling of surety that they will become rich.* This work has meant much in their lives.

39. The older man is advising the younger one on the choice of occupation. The older man is a doctor and *he sees prospects in the young man to become a great surgeon.* The younger man has just returned from the Army, and he is disappointed with the attitude of the civilians and has given up hope of being a surgeon. The young man is thinking that it is useless to become a great healer if people are going to fight wars which amount to nothing more than mass murder. The older man will convince him that the world is not as bad as he believes, and he will return to medical school.

(Note that the Anticipatory Goal State need not refer to the person who is ultimately going to achieve the goal in question. In this story the old doctor is anticipating a successful future for the young man.)

Stories Illustrating Negative (*or Doubtful*) Anticipatory Goal State (*Ga−*)

40. A father is telling his son not to worry while in college because his health is more important, but to become a professional man and carry on in his father's footsteps. The son has flunked a few exams and feels very bad about it. His father has noticed his unusual behavior and thinks he should talk with his son. *The boy thinks he just can't make it through college,* but he really wants to. His father wants him to continue and become a professional man. The boy will go back to college full of resolution for better studying, and he won't let the work get the best of him, for "it is not life that matters, but the courage you bring to it."

41. Two men trying out their invention for the first time. One man is tightening the last bolt on the machine before the test, while the other is giving the machine a careful eye check. These two men worked in a factory where the machines were constantly breaking down, so they decided to invent a new process for doing the work. A new machine is wanted by the factory owner, and the people who are successful will receive a boost in pay. *The two men are thinking now whether or not their efforts and time have been spent in vain.* The invention will work, and the men will receive their reward—a story-book ending.

42. The boy is doing homework. He is a student at some college. He is encountering a very difficult problem. Perhaps he has not been faced with anything as difficult as this problem. The boy is searching for a solution. *He wonders if he will succeed in solving this and future problems of college curriculum.* He will probably solve this situation but become permanently baffled by other situations.

(The above anticipation is doubtful in nature, and according to the present system would be scored *Ga−*.)

43. The older man has just told the younger one that he has a very important job he wants him to do. The younger man has had a very good record in his previous work, and the older man believes that he is

the only one capable of doing the job. *The younger man is wondering if he is capable of performing this* task, and he *realizes what the results will be if he fails.* The older man knows that he is asking a great deal, but feels the younger man will come through "O.K." The young man will have a great deal of trouble with this, but he is very determined and will succeed. (In the above story a doubtful anticipation is followed by a clearly negative anticipation. In the next sentence, a positive Anticipatory Goal State appears, "feels the younger man will come through 'O.K.' " This story would be scored both $Ga-$ and $Ga+$.)

OBSTACLES OR BLOCKS (BP, BW)[11]

Stories are scored for obstacles when the progress of goal-directed activity is blocked or hindered in some way. Things do not run smoothly. There are obstacles to be overcome before the goal may be attained. The obstacles may be a previous deprivation, i.e., failure, which must be overcome before further progress towards the goal is possible, or the obstacle may be a present environmental or personal factor. If the obstacle is located within the individual (lack of confidence, a conflict to be overcome, inability to make decisions, responsibility for some breakdown in equipment, or some past failure), it is scored Personal Obstacle (Bp). When the block to be overcome is part of the environment, i.e., when it may be located in the world at large such as: "The invention was almost finished when the gasket broke," "His family couldn't afford to send him to medical school," "Competition was too keen for him"; or *when there is some doubt about whether it is located in the individual or in the world,* Environmental Obstacle (Bw) is scored. Both Bp and Bw may occur and be scored in the same story, but each is scored only once per story.

It is necessary to make a distinction between "apparent obstacles" which really define the achievement goal of the story and real obstacles to on-going goal-directed behavior. If a story began with the statement "The skilled craftsman is fixing with great care the old antique which broke," Bw is not scored, since the breakdown which has already occurred defines the achievement goal of the story. However, if the craftsman has the chair nearly finished when the wood snaps, then Bw is scored. In this latter case, the breakdown interrupts goal-directed activity in progress. This distinction is made only in the case of Bw. Indications of past failures are scored Bp whether or not they interfere with the immediate goal-directed activity.

---

[11] Bp stands for "block within the person"; Bw stands for "block in the world," i.e., external to the person.

Stories Illustrating Personal Obstacle (Bp)

44. A new man is being taught how to run a machine in a factory. He is interested in the work, but he is nervous. He has been hired quite recently and has *made a mistake*. The foreman is helping him to realize what he has done. The new man is hoping that with practice he will become a skilled worker. The foreman is bored teaching him. He is required to do this every day as work hands come and go, and he feels he is wasting his time. The foreman will show the man how to do the work and then will walk off. The hired man will look around to see if anyone is watching. Then he will start to do the required work as best he can.

45. A boy is daydreaming. He is a student who knows he has to study. *In the past he has had poor marks*. Now he realizes he must study harder or else his schoolwork will just be a waste of time. He thinks of the last mark and what will happen if he doesn't improve. This man will really study and prove to himself he is not a failure but will make good.

46. Father is giving advice to his son. The son has been faced with some *trying situation or problem*. Perhaps he *is trying to decide whether to stay in college or accept a business position*. The son wants guidance. His father is trying to utilize his greater experience in life in order to help his son. The father will probably persuade the son to stay in college and reap the advantages of a higher education that he was deprived of.

(The block to be overcome in this last story is the problem of coming to a decision.)

Stories Illustrating Environmental Obstacle (Bw)

47. Two workmen in a small garage. They have just completed an experiment which they hope will revolutionize the rubber industry. They have been conscious of the need for better rubber. They have worked for years at this and now have their results before them. They are wondering if success is theirs. They want success because of the remuneration to get them back on their feet. They will not be successful. *They have not the equipment needed for rubber improvements*. The improvement of rubber by merely adding a compound and heating is over. They will not give up.

48. Lawyer and client in conversation. The younger man came in for advice. He had a going business and was prospering, but a *new industry is driving his product off the market*. "Shall I be forced to give up?" "Shall I sue?" "What are my chances of success?" The lawyer explains that competition is legitimate and can't be sued. The man will go out and instead of selling, will convert his industry to a specialty along the same line only one which is not jeopardized. He will try to sell out.

49. Student is sitting at his desk worrying over his grades. *He has had poor high school preparation for college,* and as a result poor semester grades. He wishes he could settle down and make a go of his college

without constant failing. He eventually makes a go of his college after finding courses in which he is interested.

(In this last example the obstacle is scored *Bw* and not *Bp*, because it seems clear that the high school was to blame for the inadequate preparation and not the student.)

NURTURANT PRESS (NUP)

Forces in the story, personal in source, which aid the character in the story who is engaged in on-going achievement-related activity are scored Nurturant Press (*Nup*). Someone aids, sympathizes with, or encourages the person striving for achievement. The assistance must be in the direction of the achievement goal and not merely incidental to it. For example, "The experienced machinist is trying to straighten things out for the apprentice and is encouraging him." Press must always be considered from the point of view of the character or characters in the story who are striving for achievement.

Stories Illustrating Nurturant Press (Nup)

50. *An old experienced man is giving a young green kid a little helpful advice on how to improve his work.* The kid has been slow and has had a little trouble getting into the swing of things, and the old gentleman has noticed it. The kid is thinking maybe the old boy has some good ideas, and it may help him improve and maybe even impress someone enough for a raise. The kid will take all the advice to heart and go back to work with better methods or ideas suggested by the older man.

51. The young boy is dreaming of what he hopes to do for the future. He is thinking of a great surgeon who saved his father's life and wishes to become such a man. His father needed an emergency operation. He watched the surgeon save his father's life. He is thinking he must work hard to reach his goal. But he is sure that is what he wants to do in life. He will see the surgeon again and *will be encouraged in his ambitions by the great man.*

AFFECTIVE STATES (G+, G−)

Affective (emotional) states associated with goal attainment, active mastery, or frustration of the achievement-directed activity are scored *G*. When someone in the story experiences: (1) a positive affective state associated with active mastery or definite accomplishment ("He *enjoys* painting," "He is *proud* of his accomplishment," "They are very *satisfied* with their invention"), or (2) *definite objective benefits* as a result of successful achievement which allow the inference of positive affect ("His genius is acknowledged by millions," "The people are proud of the inventor," "Fame and fortune were his," "He received a raise in pay"), *G+* is scored. G+ *indicates more than mere successful Instrumental Activity.* "He works his way through college and becomes a doctor" is scored $I+$. Positive Affect $(G+)$ would be scored only when a statement of positive affect was included, i.e., "He becomes a successful doctor and experiences a deep sense of satisfaction," or if there were *adequate* indications of objective benefits associated with his success from which positive affect might be inferred with little doubt, i.e., "He becomes a *famous surgeon*." This is another example of an arbitrary distinction which was necessary to make in order to insure an objective scoring system.[12] Positive Affect may occur within the story, or it may be associated with the outcome of the story. *It is scored only once per story and should only be scored when there is a definite statement of positive affect associated with the achievement-directed activity or a statement of objective benefits above and beyond the statement of successful instrumental activity.*[13]

When someone in the story experiences: (1) a negative affective state associated with failure to attain an achievement goal ("He is disturbed over his inability," "He is discouraged about past failures," "He is disgusted with himself," "He is despondent, mad, and sorry"), or (2) *the objective concomitants of complete failure and deprivation* which allow the inference of negative affect ("He became a drunken bum," "He became the laughing stock of the community"), $G-$ is scored. As in the case of positive affect, negative affect must not be inferred merely from the unsuccessful outcome of instrumental activity. Negative Affect may occur within the story or at the end, but it is scored only once per story.[14] Both Positive and Negative Affect may appear in the same story, in which case both are scored.

Mere mention of famous persons is not sufficient evidence for scoring $G+$. The Affective State categories are only scored when associated with the achievement-related activities of the story, as is the case with all subcategories.

---

[12] *Objective benefits.* A descriptive statement, in a word or phrase, of the objective state of affairs accompanying success or failure sufficient to warrant your inference that the outcome falls in the upper 10% (G+) or lower 10% (G−) of all possible outcomes for that sort of activity should be scored G. For example: "He becomes a doctor" (no G+), "He becomes a successful doctor" (no G+), "He becomes a famous doctor" (yes G+), "He becomes a very successful doctor" (yes G+), "He fails" (no G−), "He fails and is a broken man" (yes G−).

[13] *Affective states.* Any affective word, positive or negative, associated with *activity, attainment,* or *nonattainment* will be scored G+ or G− unless it is scored Ga+ or Ga−. G+ can come in the *middle* of the story when positive affect regarding *progress toward the goal* is evinced. For example: "He is interested in his work."

[14] G− can be scored on the basis of negative affect over an *obstacle which causes lack of progress toward the goal.*

Stories Illustrating Positive Affective State (G+)

52. This is the story of the invention of a machine. One man is showing another one of his new inventions. The man approves but is recommending that some changes be made. The inventor has spent the greater part of his life working on this invention. At last he finds that his work and dream is realized. *The men are both happy* due to the new discovery. The inventor is not interested in money that can be made out of it but only the benefit it will be to mankind. The inventor, on the advice of his friend, will sell the invention to a manufacturer. He will receive little reward and will die a sick man.

(Note that $G-$ would also be scored in this story because of the negative concomitance associated with the outcome.)

53. A father is talking to his son. *He is telling him that he is proud of him because he is doing so well in school.* He wants his son to stay on the ball and keep getting good marks. He just knows his son will be a very successful businessman. The son has just come home from college after pulling honors all through the year. He never goes out and is always in his room studying. He never partakes in sports. They are both dreaming of what the son will be in the future, a successful businessman. The son can just see himself as the president of the biggest baby rattle company in the U. S. The boy will become meagerly and puny because of his studying. He will never have any fun out of life. He will always be a mope. Is it worth it?

54. Goodyear and his young son are getting near the end of the experiment on uses of rubber. They have been pressing different objects from rubber. They spilled a tub of rubber on the stove. Goodyear is thinking that now he is close to his goal. *They will be hailed in later years as great inventors and saviors of our country.*

(The above story is an example of our practice of scoring so-called *objective benefits* as indicating the presence of $G+$.)

Stories illustrating Negative Affective State (G−)

55. This is the night before the big economics exam, and Johnny Jones is worried. He's got to get an A. He has been taking it easy all year and now wants to bring his average up with a good grade. He is *thinking what a damn fool he has been,* and why didn't he study the months before. He must get an A or he will have to take the course over. If he has to take the course over, he knows his father will give him the devil for not working hard the first part of the year.

(Note that the phrase "Johnny Jones is worried" has a future reference and so would be scored $Ga-$ rather than $G-$.)

56. The older man is about 60, and the younger man, his son, who is a writer, about 30. He is trying to encourage his son to continue. He is successful in writing. The father is a well-known writer who struggled to get where he is. The son so far has had very little work accepted, and it doesn't seem as if he ever will. The father knows that if the boy tries, he can do it. The young man has his doubts but is beginning to feel that

perhaps his father is right. The boy will struggle some more. He will get work accepted, but some will come back. Because he *feels inferior to his father*, he has an emotional block and is never as successful as he might otherwise have been.

57. The man is a professor of astronomy, and the younger person is a student. They have just discovered a new planet that is headed for the earth and will end the world. These two men have been fearing this for many months and have just proved their findings. They are thinking that the earth will soon be no more and that all life must end. They want to find a way to escape from this so that they may save a few people on earth and become heroes. The planet will change course. Their blunder will be discovered, and *they will become outcasts for putting people on earth in a dither.*

(This illustrates the scoring of *G—* for negative objective concomitances of failure.)

ACHIEVEMENT THEMA (ACH TH)

Achievement Thema (*Ach Th*) is scored when the Achievement Imagery is elaborated in such a manner that it becomes the central plot or thema of the story. Striving for an achievement goal and eventual attainment of the goal may be the central plot of the story. On the other hand, the plot may be primarily concerned with someone who is in need-related difficulty and never does succeed. In any case, the decision to be made by the scorer is whether or not the whole story is an elaboration of the achievement behavior sequence. If there is a major counter plot, or if there is any doubt about the achievement imagery being central to the plot, *Ach Th* is not scored. It does happen that *AI* and some of the subcategories will be scored in stories having another *leitmotif.* These stories are *not* scored *Ach Th.*[15]

Stories Illustrating Achievement Thema

58. The boy is contemplating running away from home. He has just been badly whipped, and being quite an introvert, he declines to show his emotions. This boy has been reprimanded because he has failed to conform to social approval in regard to taking a small stone belonging to another lad who has evidently attached a good deal of sentimental value to it. The boy in the picture had recognized this stone as a

---

[15] To compute the *n* Achievement score, give +1 for Achievement Imagery (AI), O for Doubtful or Task Imagery (TI), and —1 for Unrelated Imagery (UI). Subcategories can be scored only if AI has been scored. Each subcategory scored counts +1. Since each category may be scored only once, the maximal score possible for a single story would be +11 (AI, N, I, Ga+, Ga—, Bp, Bw, Nup, G+, G—, and Th). The *n* Achievement score for a particular person is the sum of the scores obtained on all of the stories written by that person. *N* Achievement scores on different persons are only comparable when the scores are obtained from the same pictures.

diamond, and he likes it so much that he wants to obtain more. He is determined to leave and go to South Africa and *get a fortune* and is now laying mental plans for his lone expedition.

(This story is *not* scored *Ach Th*. Not until the last few lines is there any evidence to justify scoring it Achievement Imagery (*AI*). This Achievement Imagery is peripheral to the central concern of the story which appeared earlier.)

59. Father and son are discussing the future of the world. The boy has just returned from overseas combat duty, looking older and wiser than when he left four years ago. Before entering the Army, the boy never gave much time to his father and had spent most of it with the gang. Now he is changed and considers a talk with his father of extreme importance. They are discussing the peace treaties that are being drawn up, each wanting peace fervently. No matter how much they desire peace, the answer is not given them. They can only surmise as to the best way of concluding a lasting peace. Time will tell whether the son's generation will *do better than* the father's.

(Once more, the Achievement Imagery ("do better than") appears very late in the story and is hardly central to the plot of this story. Therefore, *Ach Th* would *not* be scored.)

60. The boy and his father have had a serious accident and the boy's father is being operated on. The boy and his father were having a quarrel about the boy's marks in school, and the boy accidentally caused an automobile accident by stepping on the gas pedal. The boy is thinking that if his father dies, he will be to blame. He fervently wants his father to recover and be well again so he can prove to his father that he can do schoolwork. The father dies on the operating table, and the boy makes a vow to himself that he will become a great surgeon and save lives. He does and saves many lives, but his conscience never lets him alone. At the height of his career he commits suicide.

(In this example the Achievement Imagery appears as a counter plot. Because there is a strong alternate theme, *Ach Th* is *not* scored.)

61. A young boy is daydreaming about the past wars in which doctors have participated. He is not sure of the course to follow. He cannot decide whether or not to become a doctor. He is thinking about John Drake, the great surgeon of World War I, and his great feats in it. He was certainly a remarkable man. The boy will finally become a famous surgeon himself and in turn will be an incentive to the future doctors of the world to work hard and be interested only in the welfare of mankind.

(By way of contrast, this story illustrates the Achievement Thema. No other interest is introduced.)

62. Father and son are having a serious talk. They are going into bankruptcy because of a railroad strike. They are trying to remedy the situation by borrowing money from bankers. They do get some money but not as much as they need to get the business running successfully again. The business continues but does not make money as usual until ten years later.

(This example of *Ach Th* illustrates the fact that by Achievement Thema we do not necessarily mean a "success story." In this example the achievement-related activity central to the plot of the story is not very successful. Rather, the whole story is about an unsuccessful attempt to overcome achievement-related difficulties.)

CHAPTER 13

....

A Scoring Manual for the Affiliation Motive[1]

ROGER W. HEYNS, JOSEPH VEROFF, AND JOHN W. ATKINSON

WHAT FOLLOWS is a revision of the scoring procedures developed by Shipley and Veroff (Ch. 4) for n Affiliation. These revisions are based on analysis of additional data obtained under very similar experimental conditions with different pictures and reanalysis of their data (Ch. 5). The definitions which follow *include* and extend those developed by Shipley and Veroff and purport to be a more general statement of what is meant by n Affiliation or motivation to be socially accepted. This revision, however, is probably not final. Future refinements are anticipated if the experience with the achievement motive is taken as an example. Therefore, this measure of the affiliation motive should be considered more as a research tool than as a formal test.

DEFINITION OF AFFILIATION IMAGERY (AFF IM)

The single most important decision the scorer of a particular imaginative story has to make is the one which enables him to identify a particular sequence of imaginative behavior as affiliation related. Said another way, the scorer must first decide whether or not there is any imagery in an imaginative story which would allow the inference that the person writing the story was at all motivated to affiliate. Minimal evidence of the motive, then, is what is meant by Affiliation Imagery.

Affiliation Imagery (Aff Im) is scored when the story contains some evidence of concern in one or more of the characters over *establishing, maintaining, or restoring a positive affective relationship*

---

[1] The numbered passages which follow are the editor's footnotes to the original text of the n Affiliation scoring manual. These footnotes are amplifications and revisions of the text which are based on seminar discussions of difficult scoring decisions.

The introductory passage of The Scoring Manual For The Achievement Motive serves to introduce the general meaning of the categories for n Affiliation as well. Editor.

205

with another person. This relationship is most adequately described by the word friendship. The minimum basis for scoring would be that the relationship of one of the characters in the story to someone else is that of friendship.

Certain interpersonal relationships, in and of themselves, do not meet this criterion. For example, father-son, mother-son, brothers, lovers, etc., are all descriptive of a relationship between two people, but they do not necessarily imply that the relationship has the warm, companionate quality implied in our definition of affiliation. These must be further characterized by concern about maintaining or restoring a positive relationship.[2] Sex, achievement, dominance, or

---

[2] In other words, the bare statement of the existence of a mother-child or father-child relationship is not grounds for scoring Aff Im. In addition, if the mother or father or child is doing something *affiliative* that might be *expected only* because she is the mother (father or child), don't score unless further Aff Im is given.

The following are instances of stories concerning parent-child relations, and explanations of the imagery scoring in each case.

The son who left home at 18 to make a place for himself—the son has just returned. It is the first time his mother has seen him in 20 years. He got in a fight with his father when 18—his father wouldn't allow him to go to college; he wanted him to stay in the small town and work at the gas station. Mother thinks how long it's been since she last saw him. How he's aged and how it's too bad he wasn't at home for his father's funeral. Son wishes he hadn't come home. He no longer knows his mother; she's a stranger to him. Son will stay in small town for a few weeks. Then say he has urgent business. Big city—leave and again pound the streets in the B.C. looking for a job.

The above story is not scored for Aff Im. There is no clearcut indication of warmth of feeling on the part of either mother or son.

A boy has gotten into an argument with his mother. He wanted to get married and she didn't like the idea. He is thinking that she doesn't understand and she is thinking he is too young. He still wants his mother's approval. He will finally get his mother's permission and will marry the girl.

The above story is scored for Aff Im. The son wants his mother's approval, this implies a need for a positive response from another person, and thus is a basis for scoring Aff Im.

The guy is feeling low. It is mother and son. The son told his mother something that he did which wasn't very ethical. The boy got into trouble and didn't know how to get out of it. He kept getting in deeper and finally was in too deep not to do anything more about it. The boy is feeling sad and disheartened. He wants his mother to do something, forgive him if she would. The boy will lose his job and the mother will forgive him. He will start anew and never more get into trouble.

The above story is similar to the one just before it, the child wishes forgiveness in this case rather than approval. The basis for scoring Aff Im is the same in both cases; there is an expressed need for a positive response from another person. Similar situations would be a child seeking understanding from a parent, being ashamed of hurting his parent, etc.

other motives might better describe the nature of the relationship in cases of this sort when there is no explicit statement of the precise nature of the relationship.

Affiliative concern is also readily inferred from some statement of how one person *feels* about another or their relationship. Some statement of *liking,* or the *desire to be liked* or *accepted* or *forgiven* reveals the nature of the relationship.

The affiliative concern of one of the characters may be apparent in his *reaction to a separation or some disruption of an interpersonal relationship.* Feeling bad (negative affect) following a separation or disruption implies concern with maintaining or restoring the broken relationship. For example, sorrow in parting, shame or grief over some action that has led to a separation, or similar instances imply the desire to restore the affiliative relationship of the past.[3] But we must bear in mind that a sheer factual description of a disrupted interpersonal relationship is no guarantee that either member of the relationship wants it restored. Families are broken up, sons and fathers argue and part, lovers quarrel—these and many similar instances occur frequently with no evidence that there is a desire for restoration of the relationship or forgiveness. Such instances do not allow the inference of affiliative concern and are hence *not scored* as Affiliation Imagery.

When there is no statement in the story of a friendship relationship, nor an indication of feeling or wanting, there is a third kind of story content which permits the scoring of imagery. We infer the existence of affiliative feelings from generally accepted affiliative, companionate activities such as parties, reunions, visits, relaxed small talk as in a bull session.[4] In addition, friendly, nurturant acts

---

[3] In other words, any word that implies feeling bad about some action that has led to separation, such as shame, guilt, would be the basis for scoring Aff Im.

[4] However, not all bull sessions involve relaxed small talk. Thus mere mention of a bull session is not sufficient ground for scoring Aff Im. Sharing experiences, conversation which is an end in itself, i.e., nonproblem-solving oriented talk, can be considered the goal of the affiliation motive. Thus its occurrence constitutes a basis for scoring Aff Im.

The following story is scored for Aff Im; the phrase bull session is here clearly being used to describe relaxed small talk.

A discussion is being held in our house by a bunch of brothers—a bull session—all are amused—some walk in, others walk out—but all do not disagree seriously. Nothing in particular—*just a desire to "blow off" steam and "sound off" with a bunch of guys we all get along with fairly well.* Hard to say—women, girls, alcoholic beverages, nothing desired—just shooting off all talking—mostly one at a time but occasionally all at once. Nothing —will gradually break off when we move on to our studies or the sack—no hard feelings some blowhards and liars but all in good feelings.

such as consoling, helping, being concerned about the happiness or well-being of another are regarded as evidence of affiliative feelings provided they are not culturally prescribed by the relationship between the persons. Thus, for example, protecting the child on the part of the father to the son would not necessarily be indicative of affiliation, while the same sort of behavior between nonrelatives would be. There must, in these ambiguous instances, be evidence that the nurturant activity is not motivated by a sense of obligation.[5]

Also *not scored* are those instances in which the characters are engaged in what might normally be viewed as a companionate activity such as a fraternity reunion, but the affiliative nature of the situation is counterindicated by elaborations of the story which *deny* the affiliative concerns of the characters, i.e., the whole story is about a business meeting, a debate in which tempers fly in an effort to maintain dominance, etc.

Excluded from our definition of Affiliation Imagery are descriptions of normally close interpersonal relationships which are not always characterized by companionship, mutual interest, and sympathetic understanding. In such cases when there is no additional support for the assumption that the relationship is an affiliative one, Affiliation Imagery is not scored. Heterosexual relationships are usually the most ambiguous on this score. *Dating behavior* may or may not imply affiliation. There must be evidence of the sort outlined above before it is scored Affiliation Imagery. Some dating stories which seem to involve concern over disruption are not scored if the relationship is not clearly established as an affiliative one. Concern over marriage, however, is a heterosexual relationship that normally implies more than sex and hence *is* scored Affiliation Imagery unless elaborated in such a way as to make it certain that there are not any affiliative concerns in this relationship.[6]

The next story, on the other hand, is not scored for Aff Im since the point of the conversation is to solve a problem, to reduce anxiety and uncertainty about a threat.

A bull session in a fraternity house is going on. The people are brothers. The war in Korea led up to this situation. They are thinking of what the future will hold. They want a chance to do something along their line of study. Someone may be stirred up enough to enlist for fear of not getting a good deal.

[5] There must, in other words, be explicit evidence of an affiliative concern to augment what might be no more than the acting out of a culturally-defined role.

[6] Mere mention of the existence of a marriage relationship is not sufficient grounds for scoring Aff Im. There must be concern about getting married, being happily married, etc. before Aff Im is scored.

The following story is not scored for Aff Im; marriage is mentioned, but nobody expresses concern about it.

To summarize, Affiliation Imagery is scored when the relationship between two or more individuals is friendly. If the nature of the relationship is not spelled out this clearly for us by the author of the story, we must infer affiliative concerns by examining the way one or more of the characters[7] feel about the other or the relationship between them. Often the concern for affiliation is evident in a character's reaction to separation or disruption of a relationship. If there is no clear evidence of affiliative concern in statements about how the characters feel, we must examine their actions to see whether or not their behavior in the particular situation implies the kinds of feeling from which we might infer concern over establishing, maintaining, or restoring a warm, companionate interpersonal relationship. Loving, nurturing, and friendly actions on the part of one character towards another imply a desire that similar actions be reciprocated.

We realize that some things are escaping us and that some fairly doubtful instances may be included, but experience has taught us that scoring reliability is only possible by sticking to the written definitions of the categories and not scoring what doesn't clearly fit. When there is *reasonable doubt* of the fit of a particular instance it should be scored Doubtful Imagery. Re-examination of these provides a basis for clarifying category definitions. If the story clearly qualifies, Affiliation Imagery is scored and *then* a further analysis of the behavioral sequence related to the Affiliation Imagery is undertaken. It

---

Father is talking to his son—son is going to college. Son is just ready to leave for his first year at college. His father is thinking how his son is grown up so quickly. He wants (the father) to assure himself that his son will make the new adjustment at college and continue making his father proud of him. He will give his son some advice about buckling down, working hard at school and continue making his father proud of him—However, the son left alone at school will begin drinking, going out with girls and *finally get married in his first year*—after first flunking out.

The next story, on the other hand, is scored for Aff Im since there is concern about marriage. They were planning for the marriage, and are now arguing over just when it should occur.

Apparently a tense moment, or a moment of clash has occurred between the man and his girl. They seem to be arguing over something. The two have gone together for some time and are *planning to be married*—it is the first time there has ever been a radical difference of opinion between them. They each have different plans—*The man feels he should go into the service before they are married and the girl wants to marry now.* They will work out a happy solution; some sort of a compromise on taking the step after they know definitely what will happen to him in the service.

[7] It is important to note that the basis for scoring Aff Im can be the wishes, feelings, actions of *any* character, one or more, in the story. We do *not* attempt to determine with whom the author of the story seems to have identified, and then score only for the motives of that character.

may be that no other category will be scored. Most often, however, one or more of the subcategories defined below will also be present when imagery is scored. Stories that clearly do not meet the stated criteria are scored Unrelated Imagery (U Im) and not scored any further. Doubtful Imagery stories are also not scored any further.

Illustrations of Affiliation Imagery

1. Two college *buddies* who haven't seen each other in a long time. A chance meeting and they are *glad to see each other*. It is probably a class *reunion* or frat founders day. They were very *close friends* in college. They are probably reminiscing. They will have an evening *together* and make arrangements for *future meetings*.

(This story is saturated with a number of bases for scoring Aff Im.)[8]

2. A younger man is approaching a man older than himself for help or advice on a problem. The younger man is *worried about his lack of acceptance in the new social group* he just became acquainted with. The young man seeks restoration of his confidence. He knows his problem. A short conversation will ensue in which the older man will restore the young man's confidence in himself.

(Here is concern over separation from an affiliative object, in this case a group.)

3. The people involved are a baby and his brother. The older fellow is baby sitting. The parents have gone out for the evening. The older fellow is *thinking of how nice it would be down at the corner with the gang*. He seeks escape. He will spend a lonesome, uneventful evening with the baby, but perhaps witnessing and experiencing many uneasy moments caused by the baby's crying.

(Once more concern over separation from the affiliative object, the gang.)

4. The boys are just *getting up from a fraternity dinner table*. The one standing with the glasses is the pledge. They have eaten dinner and the pledges entertained the actives with their jokes, etc. The pledge is wondering what might happen next and is relieved that dinner is over. He *wants to* complete training and *become an active*. He will probably complete his training and become a good leader.

(Here we have an example of convivial, companionate activity, and also the desire to affiliate.)[9]

---

[8] The following story has the minimum basis for scoring Aff Im, the relationship described is one of friendship.

The fellows are having an argument. The one on the left seems to be angry with the one on the right. The one on the right has done something the one on the left didn't like. The one on the right is puzzled by the accusation. The boys will *still be friends* after the argument.

[9] The following story illustrates an instance where the normally convivial, companionate fraternity situation is presented as an aggressive situation, and thus Aff Im is not scored.

An active is raising the devil with a pledge. These are two fraternity men as indicated above. The pledge has probably done something that irked the

STATED NEED FOR AFFILIATION (N)

This category is scored when someone in the story desires to affiliate with some other person or a group of persons. The bare statement of a need is provided by expressions such as "he wants to," "he hopes . . . ," "he is determined . . . ," etc. To identify the motivational state as that of *n* Affiliation, what is wanted must fit the general criterion of Affiliation Imagery, i.e., establishment, maintenance, or restoration of an interpersonal relation characterized by warmth, mutual liking, and understanding. Wanting understanding implies wanting a positive affective reaction from another person.[10] Selected examples follow: he wants to be forgiven (for some action which interrupted a friendly relationship), he wants understanding, he wants to marry his girl, he doesn't want to lose her, he wants to see the visitors he expects, he wants people to accept him and want him around, he wishes there were someone to chum with, he *longs for* the old companionship, he wants *to join* a fraternity, his only desire is to blow off steam and sound off with a bunch of guys in a bull session, they want to hold the spring prom.

Prayer for maintaining or establishing an interpersonal relationship is scored Need. Also scored Need is a statement of unrequited love.

These examples share this characteristic: what is wanted is a relationship with others, or the kind of activity (bull session, junior prom) in which there can be a relationship with others that is described by the words *friendly* or *accepting*.

INSTRUMENTAL ACTIVITY (I+, I?, I-)

This category refers to overt acts or thoughts of a problem-solving nature by one or more of the characters in the story directed towards establishing, maintaining, or restoring an interpersonal relationship characterized by friendship, mutual interest, and sympathetic under-

active. The active is thinking of doing something "dirty" for the pledge, i.e. the pledge is in for the devil. The pledge is very defiant. The pledge will probably get a bad opinion of the active from this incident and will probably have hostile feelings against him forever throughout activeship.

[10] Wanting to nurture someone implies wanting to induce positive reactions and a warm relationship. The following story is scored for N.

A grandchild is giving his grandmother a present for his 85 birthday. She is obviously pleased and surprised. When he was younger his grandmother always made cookies etc. He liked her and they became quite close. *So on her birthday he wants to give her something.* The grandmother is feeling very proud of her grandchild because of his thoughtfulness. *The grandchild is hoping she likes the gift.* She will accept the gift, thank and kiss him for it, and probably give him some of the cookies that he always liked.

standing. They are scored $I+$, $I?$, $I-$, depending upon the ultimate outcome of the activity. The three symbols correspond to successful, doubtful, and unsuccessful instrumental acts. The decision concerning the outcome of a particular instrumental act must be postponed until the final outcome of the story is known. Instrumental Activity is scored only once per story even though several separate instrumental acts may appear. The outcome scored will be the overall outcome of all the instrumental acts in the story.

There are a number of types of instrumental acts which can be enumerated. Such acts as giving advice or helping another are not sufficient to warrant scoring I. These particular acts must be accompanied by evidence of concern for the feelings of the person being advised or helped. Certainly they should not be scored when they could be construed as instrumental to some other goal than that of a positive relationship, e.g., dominance or meeting obligations.[11]

The most clearcut type of affiliative instrumental act consists of *convivial, companionate activities:* they decided to play a game of poker, they were having their usual Saturday night party, they were shooting the bull between classes, they went for a walk together and enjoyed each other's company.

Another common type of affiliative instrumental act consists of *acts or thoughts directed towards restoring a broken relationship:* he went for advice concerning his inability to get along with people, he thought about how he would ask for forgiveness, he asked for forgiveness, after three long years he decided to return to his wife.

Positive nurturant actions on the part of one person towards an-

---

[11] Seeking help or advice is not scored *I* unless the help or advice sought concerns an affiliative problem. The following story is scored *I* since the help the boy seeks concerns his acceptance in the new social group.

A younger man is approaching a man older than himself for help or advice on a problem. The younger man is worried about his lack of acceptance in the new social group he has just become acquainted into. The young man seeks a restoration of his confidence. He knows his problem. A short conversation will ensue in which the older man will restore the young man's confidence in himself.

The next story is not scored for *I* since it is not clear whether or not the problem the pledge wants help with is an affiliative one.

Two people are having a serious conversation with each other. They are fraternity brothers and are probably talking about something very close to themselves or their house. A problem has developed or *perhaps one needs advice.* Maybe a pledge is talking to his big brother. *The pledge is thinking that in his big brother he can find understanding and worthwhile advice. The younger fellow wants to be put straight and make himself a better fellow and thus wants his big brother to help him in this.* The pledge will be enlightened and will proceed to develop into a worthwhile individual

other are also viewed as affiliative acts, e.g., he tried to cheer up his friend, he offered sympathy. The assumption made is that such actions have previously been instrumental in establishing and maintaining a positive relationship with other persons.

By convention, neither the initial statement of a story nor the final statement of outcome is scored as an instrumental act. This convention is dictated by the fact that the writer of the story is asked the questions: What is happening? and What will be done? The scorer should look for statements of activity independent of an initial statement of a situation and final statement of an event in the story. The statement must be of someone actually *doing* something.[12]

A statement of Instrumental Activity *in the past tense* is scored so long as it is more than a statement of the results of previous acts. For example, "they went together to the movies yesterday" would be scored, while "they had a good time at the movies yesterday" would not be scored Instrumental Activity.[13]

Sometimes the activity scored instrumental will seem almost to be goal activity. The scorer should keep in mind that *all* activity which contributes to bringing about certain positive affective feelings (the actual goal of any behavioral sequence) is scored Instrumental Activity. Thus, "they shook hands warmly" may seem to be the goal activity itself. We, however, view the *warm feelings* of affiliation as the goal of the whole sequence. The handshaking is instrumental action, i.e., it is directed towards the production of those warm affiliative feelings, the goal state.

---

[12] Instrumental Activity appearing in the initial clause of the first sentence which is sheer description of the picture is not scored, e.g., "Here are two men talking." Nor is Instrumental Activity inferred from the final clause of the last sentence which states the outcome, e.g., ". . . and he gets the girl."

However, a clearcut statement of an instrumental act appearing either later in the first sentence or earlier in the last sentence may be scored. Just avoid scoring *I* when it is sheer initial statement of the situation or final statement of outcome of the story. This does not mean to avoid the first and last sentence *in toto*.

[13] A statement of Instrumental Activity in the future tense is scored providing it is not a mere statement of outcome. The following story is scored Aff Im on the basis of the boy wanting forgiveness, and feeling guilty. The italicized statement concerns activity in the future that will avoid disruption to the affiliative relationship, or so it is hoped. Since the effect of this action is not clear, that is, we do not know if the caution will avoid disruption, I? is scored.

It seems a father is telling his son what to do and what not to do. The boy appears to be guilty of doing something undesirable and is being reprimanded in a man-to-man talk. Apparently the boy did something that did not comply with the desire of the father. The son feels guilty and wants forgiveness by his father. *The son will be more cautious next time.* Probably no further punishment will be inflicted on the boy at this time.

ANTICIPATORY GOAL STATES (GA+, GA−)

This category is scored when someone in the story anticipates goal attainment or frustration and deprivation. The Anticipatory Goal State is scored Positive (Ga+) when *someone in the story* is thinking of the happiness accompanying an affiliative relationship or some affiliative activity or is thinking of the activity itself, e.g., he is thinking of how nice it would be to be with the gang, his thoughts are with his friends, he is dreaming of the fun he had last summer with his friends,[14] he is dreaming of the day he will be initiated into the club. Note the difference between this kind of thinking and the kind of problem-solving thinking that is scored instrumental activity. In the illustrations just given, the thoughts of the character are not directed towards bringing about the affiliative relationship. Rather they contain imagery associated with the attainment of the goal state itself.[15]

The Anticipatory Goal State is scored Negative (Ga−) when someone is thinking of the pain of separation or rejection or the fact of possible future separation or rejection itself. For example, he is thinking of how much he will miss his parents; he is worried about how his friends will react to his behavior; he wonders whether or not he will be liked at college.

Conventions and Special Discriminations

1. Doubtful or uncertain anticipations are scored negative.
2. Often, the author of the story does not tell us directly what one of the characters is thinking. He may, however, describe the state of the person objectively in such a way that we are justified in inferring the state of anticipation, e.g., he is waiting expectantly for his friends

---

[14] Recollecting a past goal state or goal activity is also scored Ga+ since we do not have a past-oriented category for thought processes (at present).

A college boy is home for spring vacation. He is standing in the doorway of a not now used summer cottage. The previous summer this boy met, dated, and fell in love with a girl whose parents were staying at this cottage near his home town. The girl is now far away in Hawaii and the boy is seeking to recapture the previous summer. *The boy dreams of last summer and longs for those happy days.* Does the girl still love him or does she think it a summer romance? He wishes he knew for sure. She writes that she does but it's been so long and she's young and pretty and so far away. The boy will turn, lock the door and leave. He will feel better somehow but the unanswered question will remain until she comes home.

[15] When a person is thinking or planning or wondering *how* to attain the goal, *I* is scored. When he is dreaming or pondering about the completion of his Instrumental Activity, i.e. whenever he has a mental picture of the circumstances which define the attainment of the goal, score Ga.

to arrive (Ga+), he is nervous and uncertain as he walks into the fraternity (Ga−).[16]

3. The anticipations must be intimately related to the affiliation behavioral sequence in order to be scored. Both Positive (Ga+) and Negative (Ga−) anticipations may appear. They may both be scored, but each type of anticipation is scored only once per story.

OBSTACLES OR BLOCKS — PERSONAL (BP) AND ENVIRONMENTAL (BW) [17]

Categories Bp and Bw are scored when goal-directed activity is hindered or blocked in some way. Things do not run smoothly for the person concerned with establishing, maintaining, or restoring an affiliative relationship. The obstacle may be some previous separation or interference with an interpersonal relationship that must be first overcome, or the obstacle may be some contemporary environmental or personal factor.

Actual physical separation is the most frequent Environmental Obstacle (Bw), e.g., someone is alone and wants companionship, someone dies. However, two persons who might have been expected to affiliate may be in close physical proximity but separated by some flare-up or disagreement. Unless the fault is clearly attributed to the character concerned with affiliation, as in the case of misbehavior leading to a disruption of a relationship, disagreements are scored Bw.

Most frequently, Personal Obstacles (Bp) take the form of past actions or present attributes of one character which disrupt a relationship or prevent a positive relationship, e.g., he is ashamed of what he did and wants his friend to forgive him, his own inability to get along with others reduces the chances of his being accepted in the club, he doesn't have the same interests (as the affiliative object).

What has been said before is worth repeating here: the mere occurrence of some disruption to a relationship is not sufficient evidence of an affiliative behavioral sequence. Before Obstacle can be scored,

---

[16] Anticipations of success of a nurturant act would be scored Ga+.

The persons in the picture appear to me to be older brother talking to his younger brother about an interesting experience. The older brother had, perhaps, been a star athlete and hence is relating an exciting anecdote. *The older brother feels that maybe his relating this experience will liven the younger boy's spirit* because the latter is entering an important event or contest. The younger brother will give his all to follow in his brother's footsteps, whom his expression shows signs of idolization.

[17] Bp stands for Block within the person, Bw for Block in the external world.

it must be ascertained that some character in the story is concerned with restoring the positive affiliative relationship.

Both types of obstacles may be scored but only once per story for each.

AFFECTIVE STATES—POSITIVE (G+) AND NEGATIVE (G−)

Affective (emotional) States associated with attainment of affiliative relationships, affiliative activities, or their frustration are scored G. When someone in the story experiences the joys and satisfactions of affiliation, e.g., he is happy over being accepted into the club, or companionate activity, e.g., they enjoyed the poker game, the Affective State is scored Positive (G+). When the pain of separation or rejection is experienced, the Affective State is scored Negative (G−), e.g., he feels *lonely,* he is *depressed* over his inability to make friends, he *feels bad* about what he did that led to his friends' anger.[18]

It should be noted that the Affective States (G+ and G−) differ from the anticipations (Ga+ and Ga−) in being linked to the immediate circumstance of the character in the story. The anticipations (Ga+ and Ga−) are Affective States having a future reference. One may feel miserable at the moment of being lonely or rejected by his friends (G−) or may feel anxious over the possibility in the future (Ga−). Similarly, one may enjoy the conversation with friends (G+) or think how nice it would be to have some friends in for conversation (Ga+).[19]

---

[18] Any affective word associated with activity, i.e., they will work out a *happy* solution; attainment or nonattainment of a goal, i.e., he feels *happy,* will be scored G+ or G− unless it is scored Ga+ or Ga−.

[19] While one may in general say that G+ and G− are linked to the immediate circumstances of the characters in the story, and that Ga+ and Ga− have future reference, a description by the author of the story of how a character will feel in the future, or has felt in the past, would be scored G, not Ga. Ga is scored when there is an anticipation by one of the characters of how he expects to feel.

The following story is scored G+. The author describes the affective outcome of a future *I*, a walk.

A fellow is looking out the door, at leisure. He is a young fellow. It is spring, and he is wanting to go out in the open. He is waiting for his girl. He is thinking of going for a walk with her. He is waiting for her to come, so they can leave, but is in no hurry. His posture would indicate relaxation and expectancy to going out. *They will go for a walk and enjoy each other's company.* They like being together.

The next story is also scored G+. The author is describing the feeling of one of the characters in the past.

Both Positive and Negative Affective States may appear in the same story. They are both scored, but *each* is scored only once per story as in the case of the anticipatory states.

Often the author of the story doesn't tell us directly how the character feels. If the objective description of his current circumstance is so complete and vivid as in the case of *he is the best liked person in the club* or *he doesn't have one friend in the world,* the inference of Affective State is allowed and G+ or G− is scored. This type of inference is very rare and should not lead to a confusion between Successful or Unsuccessful Instrumental Activity and Affective State. A simple statement of the outcome of Instrumental Activity is not sufficient evidence to warrant scoring Affective State.

AFFILIATION THEMA (TH)

Thema (Th) is scored when the behavioral sequence in question is the central plot or *leitmotif* of the imaginative story and does not share the stage with any other behavioral sequence. When the Affiliation Imagery is so elaborated that the whole story (independent of the number of subcategories scored) is about establishing, maintaining, or restoring an interpersonal relationship characterized by friendship, mutual interest, and sympathetic understanding, Thema is scored.

The assumption made in scoring Thema at all is this. The subject is asked to write a four minute story in response to a picture. If his thoughts are saturated with imagery concerning one particular goal for a period of four minutes, it is assumed that his motivation for that particular goal is sufficiently strong to prevent competing associations in his imaginative story for that period of time. The Thema category, then, is an estimate of motive strength based on the unidimensionality of the associations which make up the imaginative story. If there is a strong alternative behavioral sequence in the story, Affiliation Thema is not scored. The scorer should keep in mind that Thema may be scored even though no other subcategory is scored. Thema is not, in other words, dependent upon the presence of instrumental acts, anticipations, or the outcome of a story. Occasionally a story is written in such a way that only Imagery and Thema are scored. The scoring of Thema in such an instance reveals that the story was saturated with imagery about affiliation none of which was stated in the form required for scoring the various sub-

---

The boy is the son of a deceased person probably father. He is thinking alone at the door. *The boy has had a very happy family life* and the death is a great shock. He is thinking of his childhood and also wondering of the future. He will go on in his father's business and try to make good.

categories. Similarly, it often occurs that several subcategories are scored in stories *not scored* for Thema since there was in the story a competing behavioral sequence, i.e., evidence of other kinds of motivation imagery.[20]

[20] The n Affiliation score is obtained for each story by counting $+1$ for each of the following categories: Affiliation Imagery (Aff Im), Need (N), Successful Instrumental Activity (I+), Positive Anticipatory Goal State (Ga+), Positive Affective State (G+), Environmental Obstacle (Bw) and Thema (Th). The maximum possible score in one story is $+7$. Both Doubtful and Unrelated Imagery are here scored 0. However, it is advisable to note all of the categories described even though in light of current evidence (See Ch. 5) not all of the categories should enter into the determination of the n Affiliation score. The question of whether to score and count all the categories, as in the case of n Achievement, or only those which indicate positive (approach) interest has yet to be answered definitively. See Part VI for further discussion of the distinction between approach and avoidance motives and their expression in thematic apperception.

CHAPTER 14

....

A Scoring Manual for the Power Motive

JOSEPH VEROFF[1]

THE METHOD of scoring stories written in response to pictures for power motivation closely parallels the pattern established for the hunger, achievement, and affiliation motives. Essentially what has been involved in measuring these motives and what will be involved in measuring power motivation is a content analysis of the written protocols for evidence of thought processes related to a conceptual behavioral sequence.[2] In order to analyze a story for power motivation, therefore, a person has to decide that the story presents some evidence of concern with the satisfactions characteristic of the motive, as it will be defined, and then must understand how the motive is manifested in imagery relevant to the analysis of the behavioral sequence.

It is of crucial importance for scoring stories for power motivation that the scorer understand the behavioral sequence. Once a person is able to identify the presence of imagery in a story that is related to power motivation, then the subcategory system of coding logically follows from the behavioral sequence. The means of identifying Power Imagery in a story will be discussed in the following section, as will the way in which Power Imagery is manifested in the categories derived from the behavioral sequence. Once a scorer decides that a story is unrelated to power motivation, he no longer has to be concerned with the subcategories. If he decides that a story does contain the category Power Imagery, then he must check over the story for imagery that can be subcategorized according to the behavioral sequence. A story is scored either Power Imagery (Pow Im) or Unrelated (U Im). One additional category not falling in the behavioral sequence analysis is the Thema category. The latter is a category

---

[1] From Veroff, J. Validation of a Projective Measure of Power Motivation. Unpublished doctors thesis, University of Michigan, 1955.
[2] See the introductory passage of the scoring manual for the achievement motive, Ch. 12.

which is scored if the story containing Power Imagery is saturated with imagery relevant to the power motive.

DEFINITION OF POWER IMAGERY (POW IM)

In order for the over-all code of Power Imagery to be scored, there has to be some reference to the thoughts, feelings, and actions of one of the characters in a story which indicates that the character is concerned with the control of the means of influencing a person. Power Imagery can be indicated in the imagery about any character mentioned in the story. Evidence of concern can come from any one of three sources.

1. *There is some statement of affect surrounding the maintenance or attainment of the control of the means of influencing a person.* A character can be feeling good about winning an argument or feeling bad because he was unable to have his way about something. Also statements about wanting to win a point or show dominance, gain control (such as by a political or executive position), convince someone of something or put a point across can be interpreted as implicit statements of affective concern about the control of the means of influence. Affective concern can also be found in *statements of wanting to avoid weakness.* Examples of this are being humiliated in a status position, being ashamed of an incapacity to assert one's self or become dominant, resenting the influence of another and wanting to overcome this.

Special considerations under Criterion 1. Some very weak statements of concern over control of the means of influence are scored. Statements of desires to teach another person something, to inspire another person, to interest another person in something—although apparently weak in obvious power significance—should be scored. The only times when statements like those above would not be scored would be in cases where the teaching or inspiring or interesting is solicited by the person being influenced, such as statements of teachers wanting to answer questions that students have raised. Solicited advice or opinion would be scored if there is evidence for Power Imagery over and above mere mention of answering requests. A person "trying to put across a point" within a solicited advice-giving story would make the story scorable for Power Imagery.

Statements of a person wanting another person to gain control of the means of influence—such as a person wanting someone else to win an election—will not be scored as Power Imagery. The only case like this which can be scored is where there is a very clear identification of the person wanting and the candidate. This kind of imagery may appear in election stories where John *wants to win* the election, although John is not the candidate.

Examples of Criterion 1

1. It is a family scene of "The Late George Apley" type. The patriarch of the family is explaining a business decision to his son. The son has *resented* his father's maintaining his position as head of the business in his old age. The son wants an explanation of why he does not have control of the procedure and still must let his father decide. The father will maintain the family business and will be in charge of all investments, 'till his death at which time his son will take over.

(The statement of the son's resentment of his father's position is an example of direct affective concern about the means of influence.)

2. Father and son. The son has just told his dad that he has enlisted. The father is not pleased. The son has been dominated by his parents since his youth and *wants to get away from it*. The father can't understand it. The son wants understanding. The son will come out a better man. The parents will have reconciled themselves to the fact that the son is able to stand on his own two feet.

(Here is an example of a statement of *wanting* to avoid the influence of someone else, from which affective concern over control of the means of influence is inferred. This is a sufficient reason for scoring this story under Criterion 1. Note that there is a close tie between feelings of dependence and feelings of being dominated. These feelings will be hard to separate in stories and should be scored for evidence of Power Imagery.)

3. It has been proposed at a board of directors meeting that Jones Paper Clips, Inc. be merged with Acme Wire Products Co. Both companies started out following World War II, competed stiffly for local control of the paper clip market. Both companies are deep in debt, losing money. Joe White who has dreamed of being a big executive has sunk his life's savings in Jones P. C., Inc. *He doesn't want to lose control*. The merger will be accomplished. Joe will be V.P. of a new company which will prosper. He will later sell out, found new company which will run old one out of business.

(Again, the direct statement of need for maintaining control is an indication of affective concern that can be scored for Power Imagery.)

4. A group of boys, possibly those who are on some committee, are in the process of holding a meeting. The chairman who is at the table has asked a question and two boys are debating heatedly. Probably, one boy *feels strongly that his point of view should be recognized* while the boy standing opposite him objects. The boy at the window is disgusted by this bickering and the boy on the left side of the table *wants his ideas to be accepted*. There will be a confusing and heated discussion among the boys because the argument is apparently startling and vital. Probably a compromise between the two boys will result if disgust can be avoided with the members.

(There are many instances of affective concern about the control of the means of influence in this story.)

5. Students in some classroom with the instructor asking questions. A discussion probably started the class off and then the teacher started asking questions to get the points of his lecture across. The instructor *wants to teach the class*. Information is wanted by the students. The information wanted will be gotten by answering questions.

(The italicized phrase makes this story scorable for Power Imagery.)

6. Two men are talking. One is a teacher. The other is his student. The student has a problem in choosing a career and has come to the teacher for advice. The student wants sound advice. The teacher *wants to advise him correctly*, and is thinking about how to put his suggestions. They will come up with a temporary idea which the student will try out.

(Although the italicized imagery seems to meet Criterion 1, it is not used as evidence for Power Imagery because the advice in this story was solicited. The story is *not* scored for Power Imagery.)

2. There is a definite statement about someone doing something about maintaining or attaining the control of the means of influencing another person. Something that the character is actually doing is the only kind of imagery that can qualify as Power Imagery under this criterion. The character has to be disputing a position, arguing something, demanding or forcing something, trying to put a point across, giving a command, trying to convince someone of something, punishing someone, (and theoretically any activity) in order to obtain control of the means of influencing someone. Statements that are either in the passive voice or in the past or future tense are scorable. But the mere mention of dissension or of a shift in opinion in a story is not sufficiently explicit for it to be scored. Someone must be explicitly dissenting or trying to influence opinion in these cases. Physical power can be used as a means of influencing, but does not by itself imply power concern. Power Imagery would not be scored, for example, if it were clear that the utilization of physical power was mainly in the service of expressing hostility.

Three special considerations should be noted under Criterion 2. The two special considerations noted under Criterion 1 are applicable to Criterion 2 also. Trying to interest, teach, inspire someone will be statements that are scorable for Power Imagery under Criterion 2. Trying to win an election for someone else would not be scored unless there is a close identification of the person campaigning and the person up for office. A third consideration should be recognized. Sometimes it will be clear that the activity of the characters in the stories, although it meets the criteria listed in the previous paragraph, is *only* for the purposes of arriving at the goal of some other motive. When this is so, the story should not be scored for Power

Imagery. However, *if it is not clear* whether power motivation or some other motivation is the ultimate concern of the imagery, *score the story for Power Imagery.*

Examples of Criterion 2

7. These two men are planning a break from the political party to which they both belong. The elder man is the instigator. Noticing the disapproval the young man has shown with the party policy, *he is convincing him to join with him. The elder man was pushed into the party.* At first, he thought it was a good idea. As he saw the workings of it he became more against it. The elder man is going to break from the party and wants the younger man to join. He is convincing the younger man. *The two will start a new opposition party.* Both will prove workers and a steadfast friendship will evolve.

(This story contains many instrumental activities with someone actually doing something in order to control the means of influence. Hence, it would be scored under Criterion 2 for Power Imagery. *Convincing someone* is perhaps the best example of the kind of imagery which is to be scored by this criterion.)

8. It is a board meeting of a large corporation. The characters are the chairman and the board of directors. It is a crucial meeting because a minority group *is trying to seize control.* The minority group, under the direction of a young, able, financial wizard, *has been gaining strength in order to upset the old-wing control of the corporation.* The leader of the new revolutionary group is mad because he has first been thwarted by a neat parliamentary trick of the "old guard" chairman. The new group *will take control,* unseating the old guard because they represent progress and initiative. The new always wins out over the old.

9. It seems as if two men are having a discussion of a very important problem and the older of the two seems to find it hard *to convert* the other. A long argument must have happened to account for the expression of the man. *The older seems to be trying to get a favorable answer from the reluctant younger man.* I believe the older man who seems the most calm will *win the argument.*

(The above two stories are filled with statements of specified instrumental acts in the service of power concerns, as defined.)

10. These are students in a classroom. *A student is expounding* on a theory which he thinks is correct. This is a physics class. The teacher has asked a question, and this student thinks he has the answer. The rest of the students are waiting for the teacher's reaction. Some do not think the answer given is correct. The teacher will say this is almost the correct answer, and then he will give the complete answer.

(In this story the only statement which makes the story scorable is the italicized one. A term "expounding" should be taken as a behavior implying an influence attempt.)

11. This looks like a political rally with campaigners present. Time has come for town elections. They are preparing for candidates and the

campaign. Ideas and suggestions are being given for publication, etc. Dates will be set for speeches, etc. The election will be held after all the campaigning and publicizing. *One of the men will win.*

(This story is entirely composed of instrumental behavior for an election. It would not be scored if the last sentence were not present. The statement that one of the men will win implies that he was doing the campaigning also. Without this statement one would not know whether one of the campaigners was a candidate or not. And in that case the story would not have been scored.)

12. Four older men are lounging in the living room telling sea stories. They were all at a dinner party with their wives and have retired to smoke while the wives clear the tables and wash the dishes. The man on the left is a republican unknown to the others who are democrats. He will blast Truman and the others except the one with his back toward us will *pounce on him verbally*. The one with his back toward us is a Commie who will agitate the rest until they find out what he is saying. All *will pounce on the Commie* and the wives' nice bridge-dinner party will end up in a fight and the cops are called.

(The term "pounce on" used in this story stands for behavior directed toward controlling the means of influence. Often aggressive statements will appear in the context of power imagery. Again it might be difficult to separate aggression and power. Aggressive statements would not be scored if the aggression is obviously just for the sake of destruction without any regard to its implications for controlling the means of influence.)

13. Four top union men are meeting at one of the men's home. *They are arguing on a policy.* There has been intense friction between the union and the management at the factory over a wage dispute. The man sitting at the left in the picture *is demanding the other's support* in the backing of a venture. They will meet the next day with management and *have a bitter quarrel over settling the wage dispute.* The appearance of their faces indicates that they are firm in their convictions and *will stand up for the union.*

(This story contains many statements of instrumental activity that service the means of control of influence. One might question whether the instrumentality is directly related to the control orientation. But there is enough evidence here that it is when one notes that the imagery has to do essentially with a dispute for the control of decisions.)

14. *Old maid is trying to get her way with her supporting nephew.* The man's parents were killed when he was young and the aunt raised him. She was an old maid. The aunt thinks that her nephew owes her more than respect. She wants devotion. He wants a release from it all. He wants to get married and she doesn't approve. He will assert himself and get married, but he will always wonder whether he did the right thing.

(The only imagery in this story scorable for Power Imagery is the first sentence. It is an example of Criterion 2.)

15. Seems to be a classroom; either a discussion or lecture is taking place. Persons involved are students and one instructor. The student

seems to be answering or asking a question of the instructor. This has been done and now the student is responding. An answer to the question is being thought by student or instructor, as the case may be. An answer will be given and possibly the whole class will assume a more wide awake feeling.

(This story is not scored for Power Imagery. Although it is a teaching situation, no one is trying to teach, inspire, put a point across. It is only a matter of getting answers to questions that were asked.)

16. Two men are discussing something seriously. The persons are a middle-aged man and a very elderly gentleman. It is possible that the middle-aged man is seeking advice from the elderly gentleman about some family business as they appear well-to-do. They are thinking about a problem. The younger man wants advice from the elderly gentleman. The older gentleman will give the young man advice and he will accept it or he might not.

(This story is not scored for Power Imagery either. Although one person is giving advice to another, it was solicited advice and, hence, does not meet Criterion 2.)

3. A story can be scored for Power Imagery *if there is a statement of an interpersonal relationship which in its execution is culturally defined as one in which there is a superior person having control of the means of influencing another one who is subordinate.* Examples of these are: boss-worker, judge-defendant. Mere mention of a superior-subordinate relationship is not enough. There has to be some mention of the activity involved in carrying out this relationship. Indeed, if a story about a boss and a worker goes on to elaborate about the affiliative bond between the two men, the story should not be scored. Mere mention of the fact that a given person was influential would be enough to allow the story to be scored. For a story to be scored Power Imagery under this criterion, there has to be some mention of the subordinate as well as of the superior position. Either the subordinate is directly involved in the imagery, or the effect of the superior on the subordinate has to be clear, for the story to be scored. The parent-child relationship is not in itself considered a power relationship. The use of culturally defined channels of influence by the subordinate in a story of a superior-subordinate relationship will be scored.

Examples of Criterion 3

17. A campaign headquarters with the big boss talking with the people who are to do the heavy campaigning for "their man." The campaign means a lot to the man running, for in the past years their side has lost by very few votes. If the campaign is carried out with the utmost in ideas and enthusiasm, they will be able to win. But, however, the campaign is not an easy one to win. All are considering this viewpoint.

The big boss will lead the others in a big band box campaign so that they will be victors. That campaigning is to be considered as one of the most important parts.

18. A boss is talking to her secretary, telling her what has to be done. The secretary came in to find out what there had to be done for the day. She is thinking that she ought to do the work promptly. She wants to do a good job. She will carefully do what is expected of her.

(In both of these stories, the main reason for scoring these stories for Power Imagery is the statement of the role relationships which are culturally defined as power-related, viz., relationships between bosses and workers. Furthermore, the activities in the stories bear out the underlying power relationships.)

Subcategories

These categories unless otherwise specified are scored only once per story. If Unrelated Imagery (U Im) is scored, no subcategory will be scored. Any sentence can be scored for more than one subcategory. The same phrase may be scored for Imagery and any other category, but the same phrase may *not* be scored for *two* subcategories.

NEED (N)

If in the story there is an *explicit* statement of someone wanting to attain or maintain control of the means of influence, then the story should be scored for Need. Most of these statements will be prefaced by such phrases as "he wants to," "he wishes to," or "he would like to." However, some phrases such as "is determined to" can be taken as implying a state of need. One should be careful to code stories Need only if the goal state related to power is the one which is inherently connoted by the condition or object which is wanted in the statement. For example, if a story is about a person trying to convince someone of doing something in order to attain money and, if within the story the imagery "he wants money" appears, then this story would not be scored for Need. It would be scored for Need if the subject had written "he wants to convince this person." The person in the story can be wanting either to attain the goal of control or to avoid the feeling of weakness or being dominated.

Examples of Need

19. Two men are discussing a situation. They apparently disagree. The man on the right is trying to convince the other of something. They have realized they disagree on something. And now they are arguing it out. The man on the right is trying to convince the other. The other man by the window seems not to be convinced. *The man on the right wants to*

convince him and the other is unwilling to be convinced. They won't reach a decision. The man by the window refuses to be convinced.

20. Two boys have met after taking a law test. They are discussing various problems on the test and the answers they gave. Debating their own answers as most logical. They are now arguing. They have just come from this previously mentioned law test for which they have both studied hard and have both interpreted a question differently. One thinks that his answer was correct while the other also believes his is. *They both wish their point to be recognized by the other.* Probably both boys will end up saying, "Well, we'll see when we get those tests back," meaning there will be no compromise of ideas at this meeting.

(In the two examples above the italicized phrases are clear statements of Need.)

21. The younger man is the son of the older, a prominent lawyer. (The young man wishes to get out and start a practice of his own.) The father does not approve. The father has taken great pride in the son and always assumed he would carry on his name. The father is telling the son how silly it is to go out on his own. Although *the son would like to get out from under his father's rule,* he is being swayed. The son will remain in business with his father. He will, however, never feel completely independent of his father. He will not be a forceful person.

(This story is likewise scored for Need. Note, however, that it is not scored on the basis of the second sentence in the story. This is not a statement of need for control of the means of influence. The italicized phrase is what makes this story scorable for Need. It is a statement of need to avoid being dominated or influenced.)

INSTRUMENTAL ACTIVITY (I)

This category is scored for a story if there is a statement in the story about someone actually *doing something* to control the means of influence. Actually any kind of behavior can theoretically be scored if there is a connection between that behavior and the attainment or maintenance of control within the context of the story. Usually the kind of behavior scored as Instrumental Activity is someone trying to convince someone, put a point across, teach something, interest someone in something. Many times thinking behavior is scorable. For example, someone is thinking of the best means to convince his audience.

One should be careful to avoid scoring stories that imply Instrumental Activity but by the nature of the wording merely describe situations. One would not score, "There is an argument going on," but one would score "Jim is arguing with Bill over a point of view."

The Instrumental Activity is further scored I+, I−, or I?. It is scored I+ if the total activity is *ultimately* successful in arriving at a goal. The Instrumental Activity is scored I− if it is unsuccessful and I? if it is questionable in attaining the goal (e.g., "He *probably* will win"). If there are several instrumental activities mentioned and they vary in the sign one can attribute to them, they are scored I?. This is also true if there is more than one character who shows power concern in the story, and one wins and the other loses out. If there is a compromise, score I?. Activities occurring in the past, present, or future can be scored for instrumental activity.

Examples of Instrumental Activity

22. The man with the brief case has come as a salesman to see the elder man, a prominent businessman. The elder man hardly notices him because he is thinking thoughts of his own. The elder man has always been dominant in the firm. In the board meeting the other day he was opposed by a new board member. *He is thinking of how he is going to overcome this obstacle,* a situation in which he has been often. *He will continue to plot against the man who opposes him until he gets his resignation.* After the man has resigned, the elder man will find no satisfactions in his group of yes men.

23. Fellow at the window is a college president, the other guy is a regent *demanding in a friendly way that some policy be carried out.* Seems the students are disturbed by a proposed new form of student government. The regent wants the president to quiet them down somehow. President feels he must concur, although it may be against his moral convictions. Regent wants non-interference from lowly students. Actually he thinks that president is capable but too liberal. President will give in. *Regent will invite him to his house for dinner.* President forgets incident and again becomes willing pawn.

(The two stories above would be scored I+ because of the italicized phrases in them.)

24. A college undergrad, a senior, *is speaking to a neophyte and presumably a freshman about his fraternity and its glories.* He hopes to get the guy to pledge his fraternity. The freshman has been to this fraternity, but wonders whether he should pledge it. *The senior has been badgering him for a few days.* The freshman is wondering if what the senior is saying is bull. The senior hopes he is getting his points across. The freshman will give the question a lot of thought and won't get too much sleep. *The senior and the other brothers will continue to hound the guy.* Eventually he will say no to them.

(All the italicized phrases are examples of the instrumental acts. The story is scored I— because the acts were not successful.)

GOAL ANTICIPATION (GA)

Goal Anticipation (Ga) is scored for a story if within the story there are statements of characters thinking about the goal—controlling the means of influence—or thinking or anticipating about whether they will or will not be successful in reaching the goal. It should be noted carefully that this means that a *character in the story* has to be doing the thinking. Comments by the author of the story about whether or not the goal will be reached are not scorable.

Examples of Ga are someone worried about whether he is going to win an election, someone thinking about the fact that he is going to win an argument, someone merely thinking about winning a point or showing superiority.

Ga can be scored Ga+ if the anticipation is goal attainment (he thinks he will win the election), and it is scored Ga− if the anticipation is either doubt about goal attainment (he is worried about his chances of winning the election) or concern about losing (he thinks he will lose the election). Both Ga+ and Ga− can be scored for the same story.

Examples of Goal Anticipation

25. It is a business meeting. The members are officials of a board with equal standing. The man (left, standing, clenched fist) is angry. The board has voted on a measure and the angry man has lost a former supporter, so his plan is thwarted. The angry man wants them to reconsider *as he thinks that their plan will be disastrous to his plans*. The opposition, seemingly quite friendly, will not back down. The rest of the group are non-committal.

(The man thinking that their plan will be disastrous to his is a negative goal anticipation. The story would be scored Ga−.)

26. There is a boy and a young man. The man is telling the boy something rather serious. Perhaps they are talking about school or one of the boy's friends. The man has stopped the boy to talk with him. He wants to convince him of something. Perhaps about doing his schoolwork. The boy is listening patiently maybe a little annoyed at having to listen to what the man says. He is listening though and will probably remember some of what the man says. The man will leave *feeling that he has accomplished something*. The boy will probably learn from what was said but not necessarily follow it.

(This story would be scored for Ga+. In this story the word "feeling" seems to mean "thinking." The phrase "feeling that he has accomplished something" is interpreted to mean "thinking about the goal." Thus it is scored Ga+. Although the term "anticipation" is used to define this category, the goal does not have to be in the future. The goal can be in the past or present, as in this example. That is, a statement about a goal already accomplished which the character is thinking about is scored Ga.)

BLOCKS IN THE PERSON OR IN THE WORLD (BP AND BW)

If within a power-related story, there are instances of disruptions to ongoing behavior toward attaining or maintaining control of the means of influence, then the story is scored for Block. It will be important to make a distinction between ongoing disruption and disruption which in fact establishes the power-related concern to begin with. Almost all power-related stories contain blocks in the sense that people are to be convinced or taught or influenced in some way. This kind of imagery is not scored for Block because it is too intimately connected to the power concern. What is scored for Block, however, is an instance of further disruption to the power-seeking behavior in a story already established as a power-related story. For example, one would not score an argument in which one is trying to convince another of a point of view if all that was mentioned was that there was this kind of argument going on. If, however, the story goes on with the argument situation and elaborates the difficulties encountered by the first person in convincing the second, then the story would be scored for Block. Mere failure to obtain the goal would not be scored for Block.

If the obstacle lies in some weakness or difficulty of the person concerned with establishing the control of the means of influence, then the story is scored Block Person (Bp). If the obstacle lies in the world—either in another person or in a given situation—then the story is scored for Block World (Bw). Both Bp and Bw can be scored within the same story. Each can be scored only once per story.

Example of Block Personal

27. The secretary has come in for an appointment with the boss. She has been a little slow in her work and the boss has called her in for a pep talk. He wants her to get on the ball and is trying to persuade her to do more work on time. *He is not very tactful* about it, which the secretary resents. She finally quits the job to take on a better one.

Example of Block World

28. These men are gathered together for a discussion. They are trying to work out a solution to the best means of handling their failing business in which they are partners. Business has turned for the worse so the leader of the partners has called a meeting at his home. The man on the left is trying to convince the others that they need a new sales force. The other men are dubious. He wants them to accept his plan. *The man standing will disagree violently with this man.* No decision will be reached.

AFFECTIVE STATES: POSITIVE (G+) AND NEGATIVE (G−)

Affective states associated with the reaching or not reaching the goal of control of the means of influence are scored G. When someone in the story experiences happiness with having convinced someone of something, dominated some situation, and influenced another person's behavior, then the story is scored for Positive Affect (G+). There has to be an explicit statement of these feelings, and they should not be inferred from mention of successful outcome alone. A story is scored for Negative Affect (G−) if someone feels upset or angry about either being weak or not having successfully influenced someone. These affective statements can appear in the sequence preceding final goal attainment or frustration. But the distinction between anticipations of future events which can contain some affective words (e.g., being worried about an election or being satisfied that he will gain control of the business) should be kept clear from immediate affective statements (e.g., he is glad to have won the argument). The former are scored Ga and the latter are scored G.

An important thing to remember in scoring a story for Affect is that the affective statement has to be *connected to the power concern*. Just because clear affective imagery appears within a story scorable for Power Imagery, it does not mean that this affective imagery is scorable for G. A story in which there is a character who is depressed and who at the same time shows power concern scorable for Power Imagery is not automatically scored for G−. The depression has to be related to lack of power satisfaction.

On occasion there will be no direct affective statements surrounding control of the means of influence, but the story still should be scored for G because the statement of the outcome is so vivid that the implication of affect is obvious. For example, if a man were to be running for office and he wins and becomes the most influential governor the state ever had, then the scorer should feel free to score the G+ category because of this statement. Note that becoming a *good* governor would not be scored. This is a statement which has no direct relevance to the power concern. Both G+ and G− can be scored in the same story.

Examples of Affective States

29. An older and younger man are conversing. They are talking about the young man's future. He has reached a point in his career where he has to decide whether he should take a job that holds no interest but pays well or take a job that holds his interest but is financially inferior. The older man is trying to talk the younger man into taking the poorer paying job. He wants him to take the job. The younger man cannot decide about it. Under the guidance of the older man the younger man takes the poorer paying job. The older man *feels satisfied* that he was able to convince him into this decision.

30. A teacher is instructing a class in political science. It is an ordinary classroom in a leading university. The teacher has prepared himself for the class, having gone over the points that he wanted to get

across for that day. The students want clarification of his lecture. They do not understand what the teacher has talked about. *The teacher is disgruntled because he thinks he has been ineffective.* He will try to go over the points one by one. The students may or may not understand this time.

(The first example is scored for G+; the second for G—.)

THEMA (TH)

Thema is a subcategory which requires a judgment independent of the scheme of the behavioral sequence. When the behavioral sequence of the power concern is the central plot of the story and does not have competition from other concerns for being the predominant source of imagery in a story, then the subcategory Thema should be scored. That is, when the power concern is elaborated in such a way that most of the story deals with attaining or maintaining control of the means of influence, then Thema is scored. In a sense, the judgment of presence of Thema is a judgment of the intensity of the power motivation concern in a given story. The assumption in regard to this judgment is that the stronger the motive the less likely will other motive thoughts appear in the story.

Scoring Thema should be independent of the number of subcategories scored. Although it is likely that a story containing elaborations of many of the subcategories would be unidimensional with respect to showing power concern predominantly, the scorer should not use the frequency of subcategories as the criterion for scoring Thema. Indeed, a story can be written in such a way that few of the subcategories are scored, and yet it would be obvious that the power motivation concern is the *leitmotif* of that story. And what is more, a story can contain a number of subcategories in one or two sentences, but the rest of the story can be unrelated to power motivation. In that case, then, Thema would not be scored. Do not score Thema if there was some question of scoring Power Imagery to begin with.

Examples of Thema

31. Two college students are conversing somewhere on campus. They are discussing whether or not _____ State College should be titled a university. The one speaking is trying to convince the other that it should. He is pointing out that it has many various colleges. He is a logical and sensible person. His friend, however, will never be convinced simply because he thinks _____ is better than _____ State and, thus, cannot give up the idea that _____ State should not become a university. The two persons will go on being friends. The first student will always be the more open-minded.

(Although this story can be scored for only one subcategory, I—, the story is still scored for Thema, because there are no other predominant behavioral sequences in the story.)

32. Here are a number of workers for the Republican party. They have gathered together to outline the campaign. Each of them has been nominated for a post in the City Elections. Since they want to win the election, they have come together to plan the campaign. They are thinking of their chances for election and would like to win very much. After careful planning they win the election. To celebrate they throw a party.

(This story has very little reference to anything outside the behavioral sequence related to the election. Hence, it would be scored for Thema.)

33. An older man is trying to convince the younger man into running for office in the coming election. The older man has lost his power in the party, and since the younger man is very popular in town, he wants to persuade the man to run for mayor, because he thinks he can maintain some of his influence behind this man. The younger man is very enterprising. He recently moved to town, set up his business, and would like to settle down to a comfortable life. The prospects of being in politics do not intrigue him. The younger man likes talking with the older man and he just would like things to be on a friendly basis. The older man cannot convince the younger man to run, which makes the older man unhappy. The younger man settles down, has lots of children and lots of friends.

(Although this story is scored for Need, I—, Ga+, G—, it would not be scored for Thema, because the competing imagery about the desires and thoughts of the younger man cuts down the saliency of the Power Imagery in this story.)

If Power Imagery is scored, then the greatest possible number of subcategories which can be scored in a single story is: Need $(+1)$; I, either I+, I?, or I—, $(+1)$; Ga+ $(+1)$; Ga— $(+1)$; Bp $(+1)$; Bw $(+1)$; G+ $(+1)$; G— $(+1)$; and Th $(+1)$. Together with $+1$ for Imagery, this would make the maximal score possible $+10$.

CHAPTER 15

....

An Evaluation of the Objectivity of the Method of Content Analysis[1]

SHEILA FELD AND CHARLES P. SMITH

THIS STUDY was conducted to evaluate a method of training persons to score TAT-type stories for n Achievement, n Affiliation, and n Power. The system of content analysis developed for each of these needs, like any other objective method of analysis, can be employed by investigators other than the originators of the system. To date, most scorers have learned the systems by scoring practice sets of stories and by attending seminars in which scoring problems were discussed with an "expert" who knew the system definitively. Interjudge scoring reliabilities of .83 (356, p. 17), .87 (Ch. 46), and .90 (272, p. 187) have been reported for this type of training procedure. However, since it is not always practicable for a person to learn a scoring system as apprentice to an "expert," it seemed desirable to perfect a training procedure which would not require the presence of an "expert" tutor. The present study was conducted to evaluate a training procedure in which the scoring systems are learned with only the aid of scoring manuals and specially compiled sets of practice materials.

To evaluate the results of this training procedure a criterion level of interjudge scoring reliability acceptable for research purposes is necessary. A review of published research using the three systems of content analysis revealed that interjudge scoring reliabilities of .66 (300), .89 (301), .95 (420), .89 (96), .91 (Ch. 36), .80 (Ch. 27), .96 (206), and .82 (Ch. 23) and score-rescore reliabilities of .95 (Ch. 3), .93 (23), .95 (420), .88 (28), and .94 (Ch. 36) have been reported for n Achievement. For n Affiliation, interjudge scoring reliabilities of .93 (Ch. 4) and .96 (Ch. 5) and score-rescore re-

---

[1] This study was supported by a grant from the Ford Foundation (J. W. Atkinson, Project Director). The study was conducted during the term of a grant from the United States Public Health Service to C. P. S.

liability of .89 (28) have been reported. The single published piece of research utilizing the n Power measure reports an interjudge reliability of .87 (Ch. 6). These reported reliabilities provide a standard of scoring reliability acceptable for research purposes which may be used to evaluate the results of the training procedures which are proposed.

Two preliminary studies which utilized training procedures not requiring consultation with an "expert" scorer were conducted by the authors. In the first study, each of eleven Ss learned one of the three scoring systems by studying the appropriate scoring manuals, scoring one set of 40 practice stories, scoring another set of 120 practice stories, and comparing his scores with those of an "expert" at specified intervals. A criterion set of 120 stories (four stories written by each of 30 persons) was then scored to provide an index of scoring competence. Rank-order correlations between each S and the "expert" on the total four-story scores of the 30 persons were as follows: from .71 to .84 (Median $= .815$) for n Achievement, from .57 to .64 (Median $= .58$) for n Affiliation, and from .54 to .65 (Median $= .62$) for n Power.

These results were clearly not satisfactory, and a second study was designed with changes in the procedure suggested by the first study. The training procedure for the second study dealt only with the n Achievement scoring system. It consisted as before of studying the scoring manual, scoring sets of practice stories, and comparing scores with those of an "expert." But this time there were seven sets of 30 stories each, and the three Ss compared their scoring with that of the "expert" more frequently than in the previous study. In addition, the "expert" scoring of the first set of practice stories consisted of *written explanations* of all scoring decisions instead of a simple listing of the categories scored.

When the Ss completed six practice sets, scoring competence was checked on two criterion sets. The first criterion set, Set VII, was composed of 30 stories written to the same pictures as the stories in the six practice sets. The second criterion set was composed of 59 stories written to novel pictures. Rank-order correlations between each S and the "expert" on the total scores of the 30 stories of the first criterion set ranged from .75 to .87 (Median $= .84$). For stories written to novel pictures, correlations ranged from .72 to .76 (Median $= .75$). The results showed an expected decrease in scoring reliability for stories written to pictures with which the Ss had no previous scoring experience. While these results represented a small improvement over those of the first study, further improvement in the training procedure seemed necessary.

In the present study, the general procedure of the second study was followed, but several important modifications were introduced. An appendix, consisting of clarifications and extensions of the original manual, was prepared for each of the three scoring manuals. Written explanations of the "expert's" scoring decisions were provided for an additional 30 stories. The amount and distribution of time spent scoring was carefully controlled to provide maximum benefit from practice. The S was asked to note the absence as well as the presence of categories as he scored. And a systematic review of errors was added to the training procedure.

METHOD

Subjects. The 12 Ss, all volunteers, were psychology majors at the University of Michigan. Eleven were graduate students. Before this study none of the Ss had scored stories using these scoring systems.

Incentives. Each S was told he would be paid five cents for each story scored correctly. A story was considered correctly scored when the S agreed with the "expert" on the scoring of the Imagery category and (in cases scored for motive-related Imagery) when the difference between the S's and the "expert's" total score for that story was not more than one point. If an S scored at least 30 stories an hour, he could earn up to $1.50 an hour. It was hoped the incentive system would encourage Ss to score each story with care. In addition, Ss were told that those who learned to score well would have opportunities to score stories for research purposes at a rate of $1.75 an hour. Perhaps more important than these extrinsic incentives was the interest of each S in learning one of the scoring systems in order to be proficient with a research technique which he could use for his own purposes.

Procedure. Each of the three coding systems was learned by four Ss. Each S worked individually throughout the experiment with no assistance from the experimenters and no discussion with the other Ss. An attempt was made to control the relative ability of the Ss and the time and effort expended in practice. Serious interest was induced by the monetary incentives mentioned above. Variations in ability were restricted by accepting as Ss only psychology majors who were graduate students or advanced undergraduates. Time was controlled by having the Ss come to the laboratory at specified times for scoring sessions.

Before the first scoring session, Ss were given a scoring manual to read. After studying the manual, each S answered questions about its content. (These "Self-Tests" and all of the other materials used are presented in the appendix of this book. The reader is referred there for fuller details.)

At the first scoring session, Ss were given a set of 30 stories (Set A) which they scored one category at a time. That is, all 30 stories were scored for motive-related Imagery, then for Need, Instrumental Acts, and all the other categories. The S checked the "expert's" written explanations after each scoring decision. Twenty of the 30 stories contained motive-related Imagery. These were preselected to include several instances of each type of subcategory, even those categories which appear very rarely in typical samples of protocols. The first session lasted about three hours.

At the second scoring session, the *S*s were given a second set of 30 stories (Set B). Each story was scored for every category before the next story was scored. Both presence and absence of a category were to be noted. The *S* checked the "expert's" written explanations after every ten stories. This session lasted about two hours.

At the third session, the *S* scored a third set of 30 stories (Set C) and then checked the "expert" scoring. Following this, he scored a fourth set of 30 stories (Set D) and then checked with the "expert" scoring. The third session lasted about two hours.

At the fourth session the *S* scored a fifth set of 30 stories (Set E), checked with the "expert" scoring, and then reviewed his errors beginning with Set B to see if he was making mistakes systematically. This session lasted about two hours.

At the fifth session, the *S* scored a criterion set of 60 stories (Set F) written to the same pictures as those in Sets A-E. Then he checked with the "expert" scoring. This session lasted about an hour and a half.

At the sixth session, the *S* scored a second criterion set of 60 stories (Set G). These stories were written to different pictures from those in Sets A-F. A measure of transfer of training to novel material was obtained. This session lasted about an hour and a half. Thus, the *S*s spent a total of approximately 12 hours in systematic practice spread over a period of about three weeks.

The stories used in the training procedures were selected from files of earlier research data. All stories had been scored by more than one "expert" scorer. Stories were not assigned to a particular set on any systematic basis, except that Sets B-G were selected to include approximately an equal number of stories which had been scored for motive-related and unrelated Imagery. These were presented in random order. The *S*s did not realize that the percentage of stories with motive-related Imagery was constant from set to set. By controlling the percentage of stories with motive-related Imagery, we equated the sets of stories on one of the variables which influence interjudge scoring reliability. Scores on different sets of stories were thus more nearly comparable.

RESULTS

Two indices of interjudge (*S* and "expert") agreement are presented in Table 1: first, percentage agreement on the presence of motive-related Imagery, and second, rank-order correlation on total score assigned each story. Both measures have been commonly used in reporting scoring reliabilities for these systems of content analysis. Regarding the first index, the scoring of the Imagery category is the single most important scoring decision to be made; other categories can be scored only if motive-related Imagery is present. Particular attention is therefore paid to agreement in the scoring of this category. Regarding the second index, rank-order correlations

TABLE 1. PERCENTAGE AGREEMENT IN SCORING IMAGERY AND RANK-ORDER
CORRELATIONS BETWEEN n ACHIEVEMENT, n AFFILIATION, AND
n POWER SCORES OBTAINED BY NOVICE CODERS AND EXPERTS

Motive	$S\#$	Reliability Index	Story Set					
			B *	C	D	E	F**	G
n Achievement	1	%***	.93	.88	.93	.93	.95	.92
		Rho****	.95	.79	.83	.92	.90	.84
	2	%	.81	.90	.80	.89	.85	.71
		Rho	.81	.84	.80	.91	.87	.82
	3	%	.74	.86	.77	.90	.83	.81
		Rho	.59	.77	.66	.87	.87	.80
	4	%	.84	.94	.88	.80	.84	.86
		Rho	.76	.82	.71	.89	.83	.81
	Median	%	.82	.91	.84	.895	.845	.835
		Rho	.785	.805	.755	.90	.87	.815
n Affiliation	5	%	.69	.91	.89	.90	.95	.84
		Rho	.68	.84	.86	.88	.92	.83
	6	%	.87	.88	.97	.90	.93	.84
		Rho	.84	.90	.95	.83	.86	.78
	7	%	.79	.88	1.00	.93	.90	.90
		Rho	.75	.87	.97	.94	.88	.84
	8	%	.93	.88	.90	.91	.89	.91
		Rho	.90	.85	.81	.91	.86	.86
	Median	%	.83	.88	.935	.905	.915	.87
		Rho	.795	.86	.905	.895	.87	.835
n Power	9	%	.93	.62	.80	.81	.86	.78 *****
		Rho	.87	.55	.67	.70	.79	.69
	10	%	.79	.88	.85	.87	.82	.81
		Rho	.69	.78	.86	.77	.78	.69
	11	%	1.00	.94	.93	.79	.93	.92
		Rho	.94	.89	.85	.59	.89	.91
	12	%	.80	.68	.82	.82	.79	.84
		Rho	.74	.63	.74	.67	.73	.68
	Median	%	.865	.78	.835	.815	.84	.825
		Rho	.805	.705	.795	.685	.785	.69

* Results from Set A are not included because it was not scored in the same
manner as Sets B-G. N = 30 stories for Sets B-E.

** N = 60 stories for Sets F and G.

*** % = percent imagery agreement. This index is computed as follows:

$$\frac{2 \text{ (number of agreements between } S \text{ and Expert on the presence of imagery)}}{\# \text{ of times } S \text{ scored imagery present} + \# \text{ of times Expert scored imagery present}}$$

**** Rho = rank-order correlation between S and Expert on total score assigned
each story.

***** Due to an error, only two of the three pictures used in Set G Power Stories
were novel pictures.

238

are used since most studies using these systems of content analysis categorize Ss as high or low on a given motive on the basis of a median break in the distribution of total scores for the Ss. A reliable ordering of individuals is therefore essential.

Set F is the criterion set for familiar pictures. Both indices of scoring reliability indicate that the Ss learned to use the three scoring systems with median interjudge agreement above .78. Correlations on Set F for n Achievement scoring range from .83 to .90, and the percentage agreement on the presence of motive-related Imagery ranges from .83 to .95. For n Affiliation scoring, the correlations on Set F range from .86 to .92, and percentage agreement on the presence of motive-related Imagery ranges from .89 to .95. Correlations on Set F for n Power scoring range from .73 to .89, and percentage agreement on the presence of motive-related Imagery ranges from .79 to .93.

Set G is the criterion set for novel pictures. For the n Achievement and n Affiliation scoring systems, median scoring reliabilities were still in the .80's for this set of novel stories. Correlations on Set G for n Achievement scoring range from .80 to .84 and percentage agreement on the presence of motive-related Imagery ranges from .71 to .92. For n Affiliation scoring, correlations on Set G range from .78 to .86 and percentage agreement on the presence of motive-related Imagery ranges from .84 to .91. Correlations on Set G for n Power scoring range from .68 to .91 and percentage agreement on the presence of motive-related Imagery ranges from .78 to .92.

Comparisons of the performance of all Ss on Set G (novel material) and Set F (familiar material) indicate that there is a significant decrease in scoring proficiency from familiar to novel pictures on the correlational index of proficiency ($p = .025$), and a decrease in the same direction for the percentage agreement index.[2]

DISCUSSION

The results of this study are very encouraging. They indicate that with this training procedure, which entails only about twelve hours of independent practice, high interjudge scoring reliabilities can be obtained for scoring systems applied to projective test data. The reliabilities obtained by our Ss compare favorably with those reported in the literature for experimental uses of the three scoring systems. On the criterion set of stories written to familiar pictures (Set F), median reliabilities of .87 (Achievement), .87 (Affiliation),

---

[2] The Mann-Whitney U test was used (423, p. 434). For the correlational index of scoring proficiency, $Z = 1.96$, $p = .025$; for the percentage agreement index, $Z = 1.27$, $p = .10$. A one-tailed test was used.

and .78 (Power) were obtained. On the criterion set for novel pictures (Set G), median reliabilities above .80 were obtained for the n Achievement and n Affiliation scoring systems. Reliabilities for scoring novel pictures for n Power were somewhat lower, the median reliability being .69, but it should be pointed out that the n Power scoring system is the most recently developed of the three and has had the least refinement through use in research.

The reliabilities reported here, it should be noted, are more stringent than those reported in the introductory section of this article. The present correlations are based on a single-story score for each person whereas the published reliabilities are based on scores of from four to six stories for each person. The range of scores is greatly restricted when single-story scores are used. Therefore the correlation is an attenuated estimate of scoring reliability. Another sense in which the reliabilities reported here may be conservative estimates has to do with the fact that any research team learning the scoring systems can combine this training procedure with group discussion and thereby may increase scoring reliability still further.

As might be expected there seems to be some variation among individuals in ability to use the coding systems. One possible source of variation stood out. Several of the Ss in the present study had some previous experience coding interviews obtained by survey techniques. These individuals seemed able to use the motive coding systems more proficiently than Ss with no previous coding experience.

The drop in reliability from the conventional to the novel pictures is probably due to the greater feedback the Ss had regarding scoring decisions on the conventional pictures. Themes recur with surprising consistency in stories written by different persons to the same picture. A S having trouble with a scoring decision on a particular picture in Set A or Set B would probably have a number of occasions in Sets C and D to see how the "expert" dealt with that problem. This sort of feedback was not available to the Ss for any new themes which may have turned up in the stories written to novel pictures.

The decrement in scoring proficiency with novel pictures raises the important problem of how to learn to score stories written to new pictures. Two suggestions may be made with respect to this problem. First and most important is the scoring of the pictures together with repeated discussions and consultation of the scoring manual. Second, where the manual leaves some room for doubt, difficult themes may be scored consistently in a particular way for all Ss. Then the scores obtained for this picture may be correlated either with the scores on a performance criterion or scores on other pictures or both. If such correlations are not satisfactory, a new scoring convention may be tried. For a discussion of this problem see McClelland *et al.* (272, p. 190 ff.) It should be noted, however, that despite the decrement in scoring proficiency found with the novel pictures used in this study, reliabilities are still in the .80's for n Achievement and n Affiliation. We would therefore anticipate that with a minimum amount of additional effort new pictures could be scored with satisfactory reliabilities.

Irrespective of the distinction between novel and conventional pictures, it is important to note some of the reasons why stories written to some pictures are scored with higher reliabilities than stories written to other pictures. First, the examples in the scoring manuals may represent certain themes and pictures better than others. Second, some pictures elicit a larger variety of themes than others. Such pictures are usually more ambiguous or give less information than pictures which elicit a smaller variety of themes. For example, Sadacca *et al.* (356) noted that the picture on which interjudge reliability was lowest was a white blank which elicited an unusually large variety of themes. Third, Sadacca *et al.* found a tendency for pictures eliciting a low percentage of motive-related Imagery to be more difficult to score (according to the percentage agreement index) than pictures eliciting a high percentage of motive-related Imagery (356). There may be two reasons why "weak cue" pictures are more difficult to score. They may be ambiguous pictures which elicit a large variety of themes. This difficulty was mentioned above. They may, on the other hand, be quite unambiguous pictures which elicit a small variety of themes concerning some motive other than the one being scored. Some of these stories clearly indicating the presence of another motive may also contain imagery for the motive being scored. The decision to score this kind of story for motive-related Imagery is apt to be difficult because the content of these stories which is used as the basis for scoring motive-related Imagery is often minimal or on the borderline.

We conclude that conscientious use of the training procedures and materials described here and contained in the appendix of this book will enable a researcher or research team to learn to score TAT-type protocols for n Achievement, n Affiliation, and n Power with interjudge scoring reliabilities acceptable for research purposes.

CHAPTER 16

Development of a Measure of Complex Motivation

ELIZABETH G. FRENCH[1]

THIS PAPER describes an instrument for the independent measurement of complex motives or acquired drives. The need for such a measure was suggested by the fact that ratings of motivation level made by observers did not seem to relate to subsequent behavior in a meaningful way, and by the theoretical consideration that this lack of relationship could be predicted. Observer judgments are necessarily based on behavior. A man is observed to be working hard, and the observer assumes he is motivated by a desire to succeed in his job. Actually he may be motivated by, for example, a desire to please his wife. Motivation is an intervening variable and as such is completely unobservable. Its presence can only be inferred from behavior. Thus the reasoning becomes circular and the conclusions are often erroneous. A measure independent of the behavior to be studied is necessary.

Other investigators have attacked this problem. McClelland and his co-workers (Chs. 3, 4, and 6; 23, 259, 272, 275) have described a method of measuring achievement motivation which involves a special scoring of TAT-type stories. They score stories for the presence or absence of achievement imagery and break the imagery down into several categories. They report sensitivity of test scores to experimentally-varied motivational conditions plus some data which suggest that subjects who show independent evidence of being success oriented perform differently on the test from those who are primarily concerned with the possibility of failure. Sherriffs (378) has described a projective test which he calls "The Intuition

---

[1] This study was carried out as part of the United States Air Force Personnel and Training Research and Development Program. The opinions expressed, however, are those of the author and are not to be construed as reflecting the views or endorsement of the Department of the Air Force. A slightly different version of this study appears as an AFPTRC publication.

242

Questionnaire," in which the subjects are required to describe the motivation behind an isolated item of behavior given as typical of an hypothetical person with whom the subject can empathize. He used it to identify areas of tension and found high validity against a clinical interview criterion. He also found it to be relatively free from conscious distortion in that college subjects who had had instruction in projective techniques were unable to disguise tension areas.

The present method makes partial use of both these techniques. For several reasons it appeared that a combination of the Sherriffs' type of item with a system of scoring responses such as used by McClelland would be best suited to our purposes. The use of verbal material as stimuli, rather than pictures, seemed desirable from the point of view both of the probable responses of the subjects in a military population and of practicality. There was some indication that responses to pictures given by the airman population would be brief and consist largely of picture descriptions. In a trial run involving 100 subjects this proved to be the case. These same subjects, however, gave productive and varied responses to the verbal stimuli. In addition, verbal material is considerably easier to manipulate to obtain the desired degree of specificity or ambiguity.

The construction of the test involved the assumptions that individuals with high needs will tend to interpret the behavior of others in terms of those needs, and further, that interpretations of people who expect to be successful will be in goal oriented terms and those of individuals who fear failure will be in defensive terms. These assumptions are given support by the results of McClelland and Sherriffs quoted above.

The importance of the expectation or orientation of the individual is emphasized by the fact that differential behavior predictions should be made in the two cases, especially under stress. Rosensweig (351) discusses the dichotomy in terms of need-persistive behavior, in which the individual goes on to satisfy the goal response; and ego-defensive behavior, in which the necessity to protect the ego interferes with performance. Newcomb (318) uses "goal-oriented" and "threat-oriented" to describe the same type of behavior.

Several needs were considered for investigation, among them needs for achievement, affiliation, status, dominance, and protection or support. Achievement need, defined as need for the attainment of a standard of excellence, and affiliation need, defined as need for warm and supporting interpersonal relationships, were finally selected since it was felt that the possibility of measuring both these needs would contribute to prediction of behavior under many circumstances.

DEVELOPMENT OF THE TEST

A number of statements were written, which on an *a priori* basis were expected to give subjects an opportunity to make responses relevant to the needs selected but not to force such responses (e.g., "Joe is always willing to listen," "Bill always lets the 'other fellow' win"), and tests of various lengths were tried out. Ten items proved to make an optimum length test which could be completed in 30 minutes or less. A pool of 50 items was prepared and divided into five sets of ten items each. These were printed, evenly spaced, five to a page, with about two inches of blank space between each, in which responses were to be written. The test was presented to the subjects as a "Test of Insight" which measured their understanding of other people. The directions were:

This is a test of your understanding of the reasons why people behave as they do. You will be given a characteristic behavior of each of a number of men. Your task is to explain why each man behaves as he does. Read each description and then decide what you think would usually be the reason why a man does what this man does. Decide what this man is like, what he wants to have or do, and what the results of his behavior are apt to be. If you think of more than one explanation give *only* the one you think is most likely. Write your answers in the spaces provided.

Each ten-item test was administered to a different group of about 70 Pre-Flight Cadets at Lackland Air Force Base during a regularly-scheduled experimental testing session. The "understanding others" approach proved very successful in eliciting productive and varied responses. The average response was four lines, or about 25 words in length. A wide variety of motives was assigned to most of the items. Items which elicited primarily brief or noncommittal responses and items to which most subjects made the same response were eliminated from further consideration. The remaining items were scored by the author and an assistant, independently, for the presence of achievement or affiliation imagery and for positive or negative, i.e., success or failure, orientation. Items on which there was appreciable disagreement between raters about scoring were discarded. From the 31 items remaining after the two eliminations 20 were selected to make up two ten-item tests as nearly parallel as possible. The first four items of each test were items which had elicited achievement and affiliation imagery approximately equally often and had been scored for one or the other at about 50 per cent of the time. The fifth, eighth, and tenth items had elicited achievement imagery about 50 per cent of the time and the imagery had been about evenly divided between positive and negative. The sixth, seventh, and ninth items of each form duplicated the above for affiliation imagery. The items for Form I are:

1. Bill always lets the "other fellow" win.
2. Ed feels upset if he hears that anyone is criticizing or blaming him.[2]
3. Fred enjoys organizing groups and committees.[2]
4. Joe is always willing to listen.
5. Frank would rather follow than lead.
6. Tom never joins clubs or social groups.
7. John's friends can always depend on him for a loan.
8. Don is always trying something new.[2]
9. George said, "They probably won't ask me to go with them."
10. Pete said, "I'm pretty sure I can do it."

The items for Form II are:

1. Ted never hesitates to express an opinion.
2. Dave likes a good argument.[2]
3. Jerry never keeps anything to himself.
4. John said, "Look what I've done." [2]
5. Sam worries a lot about how he has done on examinations.
6. Peter cares very little about what other people think of him.
7. Larry gives lots of parties.
8. Ray works much harder than most people.
9. Jack enjoys being a member of a large family.
10. George will usually volunteer for a difficult task.

THE SCORING SYSTEM

Although it was likely that there would be a fairly high correlation between the scores obtained by merely tabulating the number of items in which the relevant imagery occurred and scores based on a content breakdown of those items, a scoring system involving such a breakdown was devised for several reasons. One was that increasing the number of possible scores per item would increase the possible range of scores, thus permitting increased sensitivity of the test. The second was that further investigation might reveal some types of responses to be more diagnostic than others. The final consideration was ease, reliability, and objectivity of scoring. Breaking the imagery into categories would permit more precise definitions of what should be scored. Scoring by categories would also provide an objective (numerical index) measure of the amount of imagery in an item and eliminate the necessity of a subjective judgment by the rater. Using McClelland's early scoring method as a point of departure, we set up categories which were comprehensive enough to handle our data and which suited our theoretical formulations. The resulting system is similar in many respects to

[2] Items taken or adapted from Sherriffs (378).

McClelland's recently published version (272), which was not available when this research was being done. The categories and a sample response for each appear in Table 1.

TABLE 1. SCORING CATEGORIES FOR THE TEST OF INSIGHT

Category	Example
1. Desire for goal (A +)	"He is determined he will succeed in everything he does."
2. Goal directed activity (I +)	"He does it to make the 'other fellow' like him."
3. Personal qualifications for goal attainment (Q +)	"He has leadership ability."
4. Expectation of goal attainment (Ga +)	"He will make a name for himself."
5. Goal attainment (G +)	"He has lots of friends."
6. Positive affect to goal attainment (P)	"He has a feeling of satisfaction about a job well done."
7. Desire to avoid failure (A −)	"He hates to do anything wrong."
8. Activity directed toward avoiding failure (I −)	"He lets the 'other fellow' win so he won't get mad."
9. Lack of qualifications for, or possession of qualifications preventing, goal attainment (Q −)	"He hasn't enough ambition." "He is disagreeable."
10. Expectation of failure (Ga −)	"He will never profit much."
11. Defensive statements or rationalization (D)	"He pretends he doesn't care because he knows he can't."
12. Failure to attain goal (G −)	"He is an outcast."
13. Negative affect to failure (N)	"He is upset because he didn't pass."

Once the items have been scored, a number of scores can be computed for a given individual: a total score, which is the sum of all the categories scored for all the items; a total positive score, the sum of all the positive categories for all items; a corresponding negative score; and a score for any given category.

The two raters rescored a number of papers independently, using the new scoring method. They then compared scores and resolved differences until the scoring of two successive samples of 30 and 37 ten-item papers produced category agreement of .88 and .91 respectively.

TEST SCORES AND OBSERVATIONAL JUDGMENTS IN RELATION TO BEHAVIOR

Our purpose was to construct a test which would be a better indicator of the degree of operation of a particular need, or motive, than are observational judgments. One measure of our success would be the degree to which the test predicts behavior dependent in part on the motive being measured as compared with predictions based on observational judgments of the presence or absence of the motive. In order to know whether we were on the right track, even in the developmental stage, we obtained observational judgments and some behavior indications for 135 of the cadets who took the various forms of the test. In making the observational judgments the cadets listed the three or four men in their flights whom they felt rated highest on the following: (1) wants very much to achieve in any undertaking, (2) wants very much to have warm and friendly relations with others, (3) does achieve his goal in any undertaking, and (4) has the most friendly relations with others.

The "behavior" to which both the Test of Insight and the observational judgments were to be related consisted of responses of the subjects to 20 "sentiment" and 20 "questionnaire" items, 10 of each for each need, similar to those of Murray (314). A sample sentiment is, "Achievement is a gallant madness." A sample questionnaire item is, "When I am working toward a goal, nothing is as important as its attainment." The subjects indicated agreement or disagreement with the items. For the purposes of this investigation these responses were considered behavior which was dependent in part on the presence of the needs being studied.

In relating the Test of Insight scores to the other measures we were handicapped by the fact that the subjects had taken varying forms of the test and also that test scores on these preliminary forms would be based in part on inadequate items which were rejected for the final form. To minimize these difficulties as much as possible, standard scores were obtained by making separate distributions of total test scores for the five different test forms (using all 344 papers) and converting each distribution into one with a mean of five and a standard deviation of two. These standard scores were used in relating the test to the other measures. These scores presumably were not as sensitive reflectors as scores based on the final forms would be but it was felt they would give an indication of the relationships under investigation.

Test of Insight scores were correlated with observational judgments of motivation and goal attainment for both achievement and affiliation motivation. The correlations ranged from −.05 to +.05. Those between judgments of motivation and goal attainment correlated .82 and .83 for the two motives, respectively. This supports the hypothesis that observational judgments of motivation, which cannot be directly observed, tend to be based on goal attainment, which can.

Both judgment and Test of Insight scores were then correlated

TABLE 2. CORRELATIONS OF TEST OF INSIGHT SCORES AND NOMINATION SCORES WITH QUESTIONNAIRE RESPONSES

$$N = 135$$

	Achievement Motivation Scores	
	Test of Insight	Nomination
Achievement Sentiments	.19*	.02
Achievement Questionnaire	.19*	.05

	Affiliation Motivation Scores	
	Test of Insight	Nomination
Affiliation Sentiments	.18*	.06
Affiliation Questionnaire	.19*	−.09

* Significant at the .05 level.

with sentiment and questionnaire scores. The results appear in Table 2. Those involving Test of Insight are low but extremely consistent and all significant at the .05 level; those involving judgments fail to reach acceptable significance levels. These results suggest that the present approach may be a fruitful one, especially with the more refined test.[3]

---

[3] Chapters 18 and 29 present evidence of the validity of achievement and affiliation scores obtained by this method. See, also, other studies by French (142) and French and Chadwick (143). Editor.

CHAPTER 17

The Need for Achievement as Measured by Graphic Expression

ELLIOT ARONSON

ALTHOUGH the achievement motive has proved to be a useful concept in the prediction of a variety of behaviors, the verbal nature of the measure has rendered it difficult to apply to such problems as the need for achievement in young children, in certain extinct civilizations, and in many contemporary cultures. It has not been feasible to measure achievement motivation in young children because it is difficult to get them to write connected stories. Many ancient civilizations are beyond reach simply because they have left little or no written material which can be examined for the presence of achievement imagery. Differences in semantics have made it difficult to standardize the measure cross culturally, and thus, the measurement of achievement motivation in cultures other than our own has not been practicable.

Furthermore, although the imaginative measure of n Achievement appears to be a valid instrument, there is some evidence which indicates that the validity of the measure is limited by its verbal nature. It seems very possible that many individuals who in fact have a high degree of achievement motivation may score low when tested because they experience anxiety in relation to achievement and failure, which inhibits the verbal expression of achievement imagery (272).

For these reasons, an attempt was made to develop an alternative method of measuring n Achievement. The general area of expressive movements was chosen for investigation, primarily because it is nonverbal and may provide an adequate solution to the problems mentioned above. Expressive behavior has been considered more indicative of the underlying personality structure (i.e., less conscious, less situationally influenced) than problem solving or coping behavior

(252). Thus it seemed particularly well suited to our purposes. Since graphic expression lends itself both to quantification and to careful and leisurely scrutinization, it appeared a desirable mode of expressive behavior for this investigation.

PROCEDURE

The subjects were 196 male college students. They were divided into five separate groups: Group I ($N = 26$), Group II ($N = 18$), Group III ($N = 26$), Group IV ($N = 51$), and Group V ($N = 75$).

First, n Achievement scores, based upon four pictures, were obtained for all subjects according to the standard n Achievement testing procedure (272).

In order to elicit graphic expression, an abstract design (Fig. I) consisting of the basic scribble patterns described by Kellogg (207) was tran-

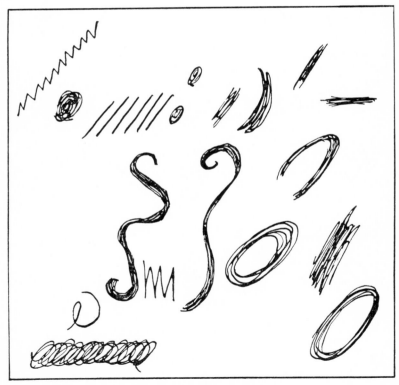

Fig. I. Stimulus Design I

scribed on a $3'' \times 4''$ lantern slide and then tachistoscopically exposed for 1.8 seconds. The size of the projected image was approximately $36'' \times 48''$. The subjects were given two minutes in which to reproduce what they saw, on $8\frac{1}{2}'' \times 11''$ unlined paper. Just prior to the presentation of the design, the following instructions were read to the subjects:

In a few moments, a very complex design will be projected on the screen for a fraction of a second. You will then be allowed two minutes in which to reproduce it on the paper in front of you. Obviously, a fraction of a second is not enough time for you to establish an exact conception of the design. You are to reproduce the design to the best of your ability. If you are not certain of various aspects of the design, draw what you think was there, or what might well have been there. Do not be discouraged by the complexity of the projected design; simply do the best you can. Please focus your attention upon the screen.

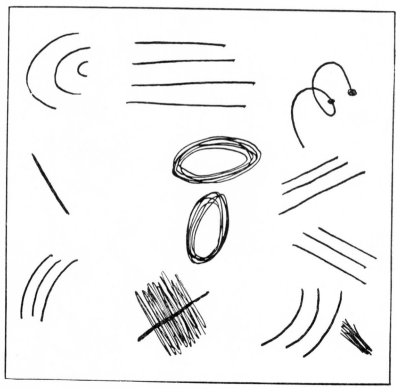

Fig. II. Stimulus Design II

For Group I, only one design was projected. For Groups II, III, IV, and V, the same design was used, plus a second, basically different one (Fig. II). The same instructions and testing procedure were used for both designs and for all five groups.

In addition, a measure of performance, the Lowell Scrambled Words Test (241) was administered to Group II.

There were no particular hypotheses concerning the relation of n Achievement to graphic expression. The design of this study was to discover empirical relationships between n Achievement and various modes of graphic expression, and then to test the validity of these relationships in several cross-validating groups. After administering the test to Group I, the drawings of the 13 subjects above the median n Achievement score and of the 13 below the median n Achievement score were segregated. A content analysis was then performed, i.e., the drawings were carefully examined for differences between the "highs" and the "lows." The major distinction perceived was that the drawings of the "highs" contained a preponderance of single, unattached, discrete lines, while those of the "lows" seemed more overlaid, fuzzier.

Several additional [1] relationships were found.[2] These were

Space. Individuals with high n Achievement tended to leave a smaller margin at the bottom of the page than those with low n Achievement.

Diagonal Configurations. The drawings of the subjects with high n Achievement contained more diagonal configurations than those of the subjects with low n Achievement.

S-shaped Lines. Individuals with high n Achievement drew more S-shaped (two directional, nonrepetitive) lines than did those with low n Achievement.

Multiwave Lines. The drawings of the "highs" contained less multiwave lines (lines consisting of two or more crests in the same direction).

Based upon these findings, a scoring system was devised.

SCORING OF GRAPHIC EXPRESSIONS FOR N ACHIEVEMENT[3]

I. *Discreteness vs. Fuzziness*

1a. Each single, discrete, ungrouped line is scored $+1$.
1b. Each multiple overlaid, ungrouped line is scored -1.

---

[1] These graphic properties are termed "additional" and set apart from the discrete-fuzzy property, because they are less fundamental than discrete-fuzzy; i.e., each line is either discrete or fuzzy regardless of whether it is S-shaped, diagonal, vertical, horizontal, etc.

[2] These were actually derived from a content analysis of the drawings of the 26 subjects in Group III.

[3] Several sample designs and their respective scores may be found in the appendix.

Examples:

/ or —— or \ or ~ or ʃ or (etc. = +1

or ═══ or or or etc. = −1

2a. Each parallel group (3 or more lines) of single discrete lines is scored +1.

2b. Each parallel group (3 or more lines) of multiple overlaid lines is scored −1.

Examples:

///// or ≡≡≡ or /// or ʃʃʃ = +1 ((or // = +2

(2 single lines, see 1a)

//// or ≡≡≡ or /// = −1, but // or ʃʃ = −2

(2 multiple overlaid lines, see 1b)

Note: The major differentiating characteristic between discrete and fuzzy, as scored in 1 and 2, is whether or not the individual lifted his pencil from the page in drawing the lines. Thus, in cases where it is difficult to discriminate whether a line is discrete or fuzzy, the deciding factor is whether the lines are attached at the ends (fuzzy) or not (discrete). Thus /// = +1, and

/// = −1.

3a. Each undulating line (consisting of two or more crests) where the length of the line is greater than three times the height of the highest crest; and where lines do not overlap is scored +1.

3b. Each undulating line (consisting of two or more crests) where length of line is equal to or less than three times the height of the highest crest; *or* where lines overlap at any point is scored −1.

Examples:

4. Each geometric, or near geometric, figure is scored +1. This includes circles, rectangles, parallelograms, trapezoids, spirals, stars, triangles, etc. This does *not* include all intersecting lines such as $\times$ or #.

Examples:

5. Each group (three or more) of geometric, or near geometric, figures (concentric or clustered) is scored +1.

Examples:

(2 circles, see 4)

6a. Each multiple circumference circle is scored +1.
6b. Each multiple overlaid circle is scored −1.

Examples:

Note: The basic difference between multiple circumference and multiple overlaid circles is that the former has an identifiable empty center, while the latter does not.

7a. Each single dot is scored +1.
7b. Each overlaid dot is scored −1.

Examples:

• = +1   ⊚ = −1

8a. Each group of three or more dots is scored +1.
8b. Each group of overlaid dots is scored −1.

General Notes:

1. A group is defined as three or more parallel lines, in approximately the same plane, and similar in size and shape. Thus,

would be considered a group and would each be scored +1. However, the following lines cannot be considered groups

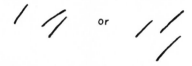

and each line is scored separately as +1.

2. For each individual, a discrete-fuzzy score is obtained by totaling all the scores.

II. *Unused Space*

The amount of blank space from the lowermost point of the drawing to the bottom of the page is measured. The number of centimeters in the lower margin is the score.

III. *Diagonal Configurations*

Each diagonal configuration (whether discrete or fuzzy) is totaled. A diagonal is herein defined as any straight line forming an angle with the horizontal of between 15° and 75°. A diagonal line which is part of another configuration is *not* scored. Thus:

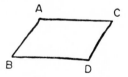

lines AB and CD are not scored, because they are part of another configuration. For the same reason, lines AB, BC, CD, and DE are not scored in the following configuration:

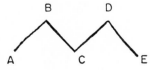

Note that it is each *diagonal configuration* which is scored, *not* each diagonal line. Thus:

/ is scored +1, // is scored +1, and /////// is scored +1; but

// | is scored +2, because it is counted as two separate configurations.

IV. *S-shaped Lines*

All lines which consist of two crests, each pointing in opposite directions, are scored.

Thus,

etc. are scored. When an S-shaped line is part of another configuration, it is not scored as S-shape, but is scored according to criterion I-4.

Thus,

is not scored in criterion IV.

Note: Unlike the diagonal, *each occurrence* of this line is scored.

V. *Multiwave Lines*

All undulating lines consisting of 2 or more crests, pointing in the same direction, are scored. Thus,

etc. are all scored.

When a multiwave line is part of another configuration, it is not scored in criterion V, but in criterion I-4. Thus,

is not scored in V, but is scored in criterion I-4.

Note: Each occurrence of this line is scored.

Note: All lines are scored as either discrete or fuzzy. The same line *may* then be scored as either diagonal, S-shaped, or multiwave. Thus, some lines will be scored in two categories, some in only one. It is obvious that no line can be scored in more than two categories, since criteria III, IV, and V, are, by definition, mutually exclusive.

Scoring reliability. The scoring system can be used reliably. Four months after the drawings were originally scored, the present researcher rescored those of Group V. The score-rescore correlation for all categories was .93 ($N = 75$). Also, an independent scorer, after spending a few hours studying the scoring manual, and receiving 15 minutes of verbal instruction, scored the drawings of 31 subjects for the discrete-fuzzy variable. The correlation between his scoring and that of the present author was .89.

RESULTS

Designs I and II are basically different in composition. The actual difference is shown in Table I, which depicts the scores of the stimulus designs for all of the graphic variables. The major difference is that Design I contains a preponderance of fuzzy lines, while Design II is largely composed of discrete lines.

TABLE I. THE SCORING OF STIMULUS DESIGNS I AND II

	Discrete	Fuzzy	Dis.-Fuz.	Space	Diag.	S-shape	M.W.
Design I	4	14	−10	?*	4	0	4
Design II	10	5	5	?*	6	0	1

* Space is, of course, a function of the size of the projected image.

The product moment correlations between n Achievement and the discrete-fuzzy variable in all five groups are presented in Table II. All of the correlations are in the predicted direction. Three of the

TABLE II. THE RELATION BETWEEN TAT n ACHIEVEMENT SCORE AND DISCRETENESS-FUZZINESS IN GRAPHIC EXPRESSION

Group	N	1 Design I	2 Design II	3 I + II
I	26	.49*+		
II	18	.51*	.50*	.51*
III	26	.26	.24	.27
IV	51	.27*	.09	.33**
V	75	.34**	.18*	.34**

* $p < .05$.
** $p < .01$.
+ Used in determining the scoring criteria.

TABLE III. CORRELATIONS BETWEEN CRITERIA OF GRAPHIC EXPRESSIONS AND TAT n ACHIEVEMENT SCORE

Group	N	n Achievement		Additional Categories				Combined Categories		
					n Achievement			n Achievement		D-F
		D-F	Space	Diagonal	S-shaped	Multiwave	TQS—All Categ.	TQS—Additional Categories	
		+	–	+	+	–	+	+	+
I	26	.49*+	–.29	–.15	.13	–.31	.41*+	.34*	.21+
II	18	.51*	–.12	.61**	.06	.09	.38*	.26	.15
III	26	.27	–.61**+	.43*+	.23+	–.47*+	.62**+	.56**+	.29+
IV	51	.33**	–.02	.37**	.25*+	–.38**+	.37**+	.53**+	.24*+
V	75	.34**	–.17*	.25*	.19*	–.01	.36**	.35**	.29*

D-F = discrete-fuzzy.
TQS = total quartile score.
Categ. = categories.

* $p < .05$.
** $p < .01$.
+ used in determining the scoring criteria.

258

four validating correlations for Design I are significant; two of the validating correlations for Design II are significant. The correlations derived by combining Design I and Design II are, in each group, as high as or higher than those of either design taken separately.

The correlations between n Achievement and the additional scoring categories are listed in Table III. In column 6 are the correlations between n Achievement and the total quartile score (TQS)[3] of all five graphic measures. Column 7 shows the correlations between n Achievement and the TQS of the additional graphic categories. Column 8 lists the correlations between the TQS of the additional categories and the discrete-fuzzy score.

Examination of Table III reveals that 12 of the 14 validating correlations involving the additional graphic categories are in the predicted direction. Five of them are statistically significant.

Correlations between n Achievement and each of these additional categories are rather unstable. The correlations between n Achievement and the total quartile scores, however, are stable and substantial. Two of the three "pure" validating correlations[4] between n Achievement and the TQS of the additional categories are significant; both of the "pure" validating correlations between n Achievement and the TQS of all the categories are significant. The correlations between discrete-fuzzy and the total quartile score of the additional categories are all in the expected direction; two of these are significant.

Table IV lists the means and standard deviations of all of the graphic variables for each group. It can be seen that these are similar for each variable throughout the five groups.

Internal consistency. The internal consistency of the graphic indices has been measured in two ways. Table V is a matrix of the intercorrelations of the five graphic indices (Group V, N = 75), for each design. Fifteen of the 20 resulting correlations are in the pre-

---

[3] The total quartile score was used rather than a more powerful method of combining the various categories (e.g., the multiple-regression equation) because the relationships between the variables and the criterion measure were so unstable that a more powerful method did not seem suitable. The total quartile score is derived by converting the scores for each category into quartile units. For those categories which correlate positively with n Achievement, 4 points are assigned to the highest quartile, 3 points to the next highest, etc. . . . For those which correlate negatively with n Achievement, 1 point is assigned to the highest quartile, 2 points to the next, etc. . . . These are then totaled.

[4] As is indicated in Table III, the correlations involving the TQS of the additional categories (column 7) cannot be considered pure in Groups III and IV, as they involve a total quartile score which includes at least one variable which was derived from the content analysis of that particular group. This is true for Groups I, III, and IV of the TQS for all categories (column 6).

TABLE IV. MEANS AND S.D.'S FOR EACH GRAPHIC EXPRESSION CATEGORY
(DESIGN I + DESIGN II)

Group		D-F	Space	Diag.	S-shape	M.W.	Number of Scored Units**
I	Mean	4.73*	11.23*	1.97*	.39*	1.84*	13.19*
	S.D.	5.12*	6.49*	2.42*	.89*	2.29*	6.01*
II	Mean	9.04	26.38	3.61	.89	5.17	20.81
	S.D.	7.15	9.89	2.16	.97	4.47	5.93
III	Mean	10.38	16.81	4.11	1.01	3.29	25.12
	S.D.	8.31	10.01	2.27	1.23	2.02	7.21
IV	Mean	10.92	21.61	3.02	.88	2.84	23.27
	S.D.	6.73	8.97	1.88	1.60	2.38	8.79
V	Mean	8.81	17.48	5.39	1.31	4.60	22.25
	S.D.	9.95	10.45	2.81	1.60	1.87	7.64

* Based on Design I only.
** Derived by adding number of discrete lines to number of fuzzy lines.

dicted direction; of these, 9 are statistically significant. Table VI
depicts the correlations between the major aspects of graphic expression produced in response to stimulus Design I and those produced
in response to stimulus Design II. Thirteen of the fifteen resulting
correlations are significant.

A further test of the validity of the graphic expression indices of n
Achievement involved relating them to a performance measure of
achievement motivation. The correlation between improvement on
the Lowell Scrambled Words test (see 241) and the discrete-fuzzy
variable is .50 ($p < .05$). The correlation between improvement in
scrambled-words performance and the total quartile score for all
measures is .53 ($p < .05$). The correlation between improvement in
scrambled-words performance and TAT measure of n Achievement is
.46 ($p < .05$).

DISCUSSION

The results indicate that two variables of graphic expression are
consistently good predictors of n Achievement. Both the discrete-
fuzzy score and the total quartile score of the additional categories

TABLE V. THE MATRIX OF THE INTERCORRELATIONS OF THE
GRAPHIC EXPRESSION VARIABLES
(GROUP V, N = 75)

Design I

	D-F	S-Shaped	Diag.	M.W.
S-Shape	−.14			
Diagonal	.15	.23*		
M.W.	.10	−.62**	−.03	
Space	−.19*	−.25*	−.03	−.19*

Design II

	D-F	S-Shaped	Diag.	M.W.
S-Shape	.07			
Diagonal	.33**	.31*		
M.W.	−.40**	.10	−.29*	
Space	−.12	−.42**	−.03	−.18*

* $p < .05$.
** $p < .01$.

TABLE VI. THE CORRELATION OF THE MAJOR GRAPHIC INDICES OF
DESIGN I WITH THOSE OF DESIGN II

Group	N	D-F	TQS (Additional)	TQS (Total)
I	26	.43*	.40*	.41*
II	18	.37*	.39*	.37*
III	26	.29	.41*	.31
IV	51	.50**	.48**	.52**
V	75	.38**	.53**	.47**

* $p < .05$.
** $p < .01$.

have correlated significantly with n Achievement in separate validating samples. Furthermore, both of these graphic measures are significantly related to a performance variable which is, in turn, related to n Achievement.

The total quartile scores have a consistently significant correlation with n Achievement despite the fact that the correlations between n Achievement and each of the additional graphic categories are unstable. This is probably due to the fact that quartiling the scores and then combining them has decreased the variance, thus minimizing the effect of an occasional inconsistency. For example, if a given individual scores "high" on three of the graphic variables but "low" on the fourth, his total quartile score will still be relatively high—higher than that of the individual who scores around the mean on all four measures.

One of the purposes of this study was to develop a measure of the achievement motive which might be an improvement upon the thematic apperceptive procedure developed by McClelland and his associates. Anxiety may inhibit achievement-oriented verbal responses and thus distort the findings. The graphic expression test was specifically designed to circumvent the anxiety variable. But we are forced to validate our measures on the basis of their correlations with n Achievement, which is admittedly an imperfect measure. That the correlations are for the most part significant is a strong indication that the graphic expression test and the n Achievement test are measuring roughly the same thing. That the correlations are not larger than they are may be caused by the fact that the measures of graphic expression are not inhibited by anxiety the way the verbal measure may be. There is no evidence in these data to support this hypothesis, but the possibility is worth further study.

Internal consistency. The correlations between the designs produced in response to stimulus Design I and those produced in response to stimulus Design II (Table VI), although for the most part significant, are not very high. There is evidence, however, to indicate that this may not be a fair index of consistency. In each group, the correlation between n Achievement and discreteness-fuzziness is higher for Design I than for Design II. This can mean either of two things. It may be that Design I is a better stimulus than Design II; that is, Design I may have just the right amount of complexity to elicit the predicted response. An alternative explanation is that an alternation effect may be involved. Since the subjects were asked to reproduce Design II immediately after they had drawn Design I, they may have become satiated with certain configurations and switched to another style of drawing for this reason. This possibly is in line with findings by Atkinson (see Ch. 46) who, in analyzing the content of TAT stories, discovered evidence for the existence of a cyclical effect in the occurrence of achievement imagery in successive stories by the same individual. This would also account for the superiority of the correlations involving Design I, since it seems that once a particular configuration was made in Design I, the possibility of its occurrence in Design II became more remote. It is regrettable that Design II was not presented first in one of the samples. In any case, the data suggest that the correlations may represent underevaluations of the consistency of the graphic measures.

The matrix of the intercorrelations of the categories of graphic expression shows that the categories are generally consistent with one another. The only major exception to this trend is the significant negative correlation between *space* and *multiwave* lines; although both of these categories are negatively related to *n* Achievement, they correlate negatively with each other. They can thus be considered *alternative manifestations*[5] of the need for achievement. That is, it is unlikely for an individual to leave a great deal of blank space, and, at the same time, draw a large number of multiwave lines; he either expresses his low *n* Achievement by filling the page with multiwave scribbles or by leaving the page relatively blank.

The general consistency of the graphic variables receives some confirmation from the invariably positive (albeit low) correlations between the discrete-fuzzy variable and the total quartile score of the additional categories (Table III, column 8). Still further confirmation of this interrelationship is evinced by the fact that adding the highly significant discrete-fuzzy score to the total quartile score (Table III, column 6) does not substantially increase the size of the correlation of the latter with *n* Achievement. If these two indices were unrelated, one would expect to find a substantial increase. The fact that the various categories of graphic expression are interrelated is of great advantage in the application of this method to areas of study where one of the graphic indices may be inapplicable.

The relationships between graphic expression and *n* Achievement have been empirically derived, and the efficacy of the graphic measures depends entirely upon these findings. Nevertheless, it may be of some value to look at these relationships and make a *post hoc* attempt to attach some common sense meaning to them in the hope that this may serve to generate hypotheses for further research. An examination of the scoring categories reveals that they have much in common and seem to reflect several differences between individuals with high

---

[5] The concept of alternative manifestations has been described and discussed by Frenkel-Brunswick (144) and McClelland (Ch. 1) among others.

n Achievement and those with low n Achievement. The drawings of the "highs" suggest motion, are non-repetitive, unrestricted in space, and economical in movement; those of the "lows" seem to be immobile, restricted in space, and redundant in movement. This interpretation may become more understandable to the reader after a careful perusal of the scoring system. The following is a general statement of these factors in terms of each scoring classification:

Discrete-fuzzy. Discrete lines are intrinsically simple and their drawing involves a greater economy of motion than does that of the overlaid lines; one can make the same "statement" with a few discrete lines that requires several strokes in an overlaid fuzzy line. A group of parallel discrete lines are spread out and thus imply motion, and, by the same token, they are unrestrained in space. Overlaid lines, on the other hand, are, by nature, piled one on top of the other, redundant, restricted in movement.

Space. The drawings of "highs" are spread out over the paper; those of the "lows" are confined to a relatively small area.

Diagonality. Diagonal lines are not at rest in either the vertical or horizontal position with respect to gravity. They are "leaning forward," "falling," "off balance"; in short, they suggest motion.

S-shaped and multiwave. The difference between S-shaped and multiwave lines is a good example of what is meant by economy of motion. An S-shaped line is moving in two directions simultaneously; there is no waste motion involved, because it is doing so in the most economical way. The multiwave line is also moving in two directions, but it is redundant. It unnecessarily repeats the two-directional motion and thus represents a waste of energy. Nothing is determined here concerning relative restrictions in space, since it is possible for either line to rove all over the page or to be confined to a restricted space.

The results of this experiment seem to justify its purposes. A method of measuring achievement motivation has been developed which may be of great consequence in the investigation of relationships which were previously unexplorable.

Cross-cultural studies. With these graphic measures, it may be possible, for the first time, to compare the achievement motivation of individuals in different cultures. This was previously impracticable, because of semantic problems which are inherent in a verbal measure.

Study of archaic cultures. A recent study by Berlew (39; also in Ch. 37) suggests that n Achievement as reflected by the literature of a culture is related to its growth and development. There are cultures, however, which have left no written record and are, therefore, inaccessible to this kind of analysis. By examining their art through the criteria of graphic expression, it may be possible to make inferences about their achievement motivation.

Genesis of achievement motivation. Winterbottom (Ch. 33) has found that n Achievement in male children is related to parental attitudes toward independence training, a belief in early independence training being associated with high n Achievement. Due to the limitations of a verbal measure, Winterbottom was unable to study children under 8 years of age; thus, it was impossible to determine exactly when the need for achievement begins to develop. By making the study of preliterate children possible, the graphic expression test may provide a solution to this problem. Furthermore, although the relationship between need for achievement and independence training exists, it is not entirely clear whether early independence training leads to the development of high n Achievement, or whether children with high n Achievement demand early independence training. By studying the child when he is closer in time to the onset of training, it may be possible to ascertain causality in the development of n Achievement.

Underlying these implications is the necessary, but perhaps unjustified, assumption that data gathered from the study of 20th-century college freshmen are applicable to a 20th-century French farmer, a five-year-old American child, and a 15th-century B.C. Egyptian pot-painter. Nevertheless, it seems that a step has been made toward the possible solution of some very intriguing problems.[6]

---

[6] In two recent studies, the graphic expression test has been successfully applied to an analysis of ancient Greek vase painting and to the study of n Achievement in young children. The results of these studies are reported in Chs. 21 and 37 of this volume.

PART THREE

Motivation and Behavior

THE PURPOSE of seeking a valid method for the analysis of imaginative stories is to provide a basis for measuring individual differences in the strength of particular motives. Thereby the difficult question of the relationship between an individual's motives and his behavior can be studied in a systematic way. A variety of studies dealing with the effects of individual differences in the strength of motivation and aiming at a valid method of analysis are presented here under four headings.

A. Towards a Theory Relating Individual Differences in Motive Strength to Performance.

An early investigation by Clark and McClelland (74) and one by Lowell (241) showed that individual differences in n Achievement scores obtained from stories are positively related to performance of simple laboratory tasks. But it soon became apparent in many experiments reviewed in *The Achievement Motive* (272) that factors in the situation at the time of performance strongly influence the relationship between strength of motive (as measured) and performance. Atkinson (23) showed that recall of interrupted tasks, which is conventionally viewed as indicative of strength of motivation, is positively related to the strength of n Achievement in individuals only when tasks are presented as tests on which it is important to do well. This suggested that the achievement motive should be thought of as a *latent* disposition which is aroused and manifested in overt goal striving only when the cues of a situation clearly indicate that performance is instrumental to accomplishment.

Subsequent studies have sought to refine the conception of the interaction between motive, conceived as disposition of the personality, and situation in the determination of overt action.

Papers by French and by Atkinson and Reitman highlight the need to distinguish between the strength of an individual's *motive* (referred to by French as "the individual's typical level of motivation") and the strength of *motivation* that is aroused in a particular situation and manifested in overt performance. Essentially the same inference is to be drawn from other studies by Wendt (430)

267

and Atkinson and Raphelson (27) which deal with the same issue elsewhere.

Next come four studies which direct attention to the relationship of n Achievement to risk-taking behavior and its theoretical interpretation. McClelland's investigations of achievement motivation and entrepreneurship (260, 262, 263) have suggested that the person who is highly motivated to achieve is disposed to take moderate or calculated risks in preference to very speculative or very safe undertakings. Two methods of studying risk-taking tendencies are presented. An investigation by Atkinson of performance in relation to probability of winning a monetary incentive is followed by a related study of the level of aspiration in children by McClelland. Then a theoretical model is presented which links the relative strength of achievement motive and motive to avoid failure to both level of aspiration and performance level under conditions of uncertainty or risk. An important assumption in the application of the theoretical model to the experimental results presented is that individuals who are relatively low in n Achievement are disposed to be more fearful of failure. The final paper in this set, by Raphelson, presents clear-cut evidence that n Achievement and the tendency to experience anxiety in test situations as measured by other tests and by psychogalvanic skin reaction is negative, as assumed.

B. Motivation and Perceptual Sensitivity.

Moulton *et al.* show that the theoretical distinction between strength of motive and strength of aroused motivation is applicable to the relationship between n Achievement and perceptual behavior as well as to the relationship between n Achievement and goal-directed performance. And Atkinson and Walker present evidence that n Affiliation sensitizes the individual to affiliation-related stimuli. This result enhances the validity of the measure of n Affiliation and also suggests that the theoretical picture which has been developed chiefly in studies of n Achievement will apply as well to other kinds of motivation.

C. Personality Correlates of Achievement and Affiliation Motives.

Not all of the studies dealing with the behavioral effects of particular motives are specifically concerned with the theoretical details of the interaction between the motives of the individual and the situation in determining his behavior. Some of them have attempted to explore uncharted territory in search of meaningful relationships, which then become the factual basis for extensions and elaborations of theory.

Three particularly suggestive investigations are presented. Knapp discovers a relationship between n Achievement and aesthetic preference and interprets its significance. Martire relates individual differences in strength and generality of achievement motivation to an individual's conception of himself and his ideals. And Groesbeck begins the study of the behavioral correlates of particular combinations or configurations of achievement and affiliation motives within individuals. His research points the way towards a descriptive system for studies of personality, in which individuals are classified according to the configuration of several different motives rather than in terms of single motives at a time.

D. Complex Interactions Between Motivation and Situation.

French investigates the effect on subsequent performance of different types of feedback to groups engaged in a problem-solving task. The groups are comprised of persons who are all highly motivated to achieve or all highly motivated to affiliate. Her results show the importance of motivationally-relevant feedback. Hardy investigates the role of affiliative motivation in conformity to group pressure and attitude change and discovers an important interaction between n Affiliation and conditions of social support. And in a related study, Samelson calls attention to the varied meanings a situation involving group pressure to conform may have for different persons, depending upon the relative strengths of their needs for achievement and affiliation.

These studies raise many questions for future research. In particular, they call attention to the need for methods of assessing the motivational relevance of various features of the situation in which the behavior of an individual is observed.

CHAPTER 18

Some Characteristics of Achievement Motivation*

Elizabeth G. French[1]

This study represents an attempt to investigate systematically: (a) the relationship between the administration of verbal instructions designed to vary achievement motivation and changes in scores on an independent measure of motivation, and (b) the relation of the first two variables, motivating conditions and measured motivation, to performance on a simple task. Since it is apparent that all individuals do not react in a uniform way to attempts to vary motivation by means of verbal instructions, a variable, or variables, in addition to the instructions must be operating. An hypothesis advanced here is that the individual's typical level of motivation is one of those variables. It is suggested that those Ss who fail to respond to cues such as verbal instructions designed to raise achievement motivation are those with generally low need for achievement. Thus the typical level of achievement need, as well as the stimuli present designed to vary need level, must be taken into account in predicting motivation level in a given situation.

Two related hypotheses follow from this line of reasoning. One is that a greater amount of the variance in performance which is mainly a function of motivation rather than of skill will be due to this resultant total motivation than to environmental cues provided to raise the level of motivation. The second is that the degree of relationship between motivation level in one situation and both motivation level and performance level in another will depend in part on the degree of similarity between the situations with respect

* Reprinted by permission of author and publisher from the *Journal of Experimental Psychology,* 1955, **50**, 232-236. Copyright 1955 by the American Psychological Association, Inc.

[1] The research was carried out as part of the United States Air Force Personnel and Training Research and Development program. The opinions expressed, however, are those of the author and are not to be construed as reflecting the views or endorsement of the Department of the Air Force. Portions of this paper were read at the 1954 meeting of the American Psychological Association.

to motivational cues. The present experiment was designed to test these hypotheses.

METHOD

Instruments. The motivation measure used was a device developed by the author for the measurement of complex motivations. It involves an adaptation of McClelland's (272) motivation imagery scoring system to responses to verbal items similar to those of Sherriffs' "Intuition Questionnaire" (378). The items are single-sentence descriptions of behavior which are presented as typical of hypothetical individuals with whom Ss can identify (i.e., "Tom always lets the 'other fellow' win.") The Ss are instructed to "explain" the behavior. The assumption is that an S with high achievement motivation, for example, will project that motivation into his interpretation of another's behavior when the cause of that behavior is unclear and when an interpretation in achievement terms is not unreasonable (or even, sometimes, when it is). The work of McClelland and of Sherriffs and preliminary work of the author indicate that this approach to the measurement of motivation has validity. The present instrument is disguised as a "Test of Insight." Two equivalent forms have been developed.[2]

The performance test was a digit-letter substitution test which was very simple and primarily a speed test. The number of items completed could be assumed to be, at least in part, a function of the amount of effort expended. The test was of such a length that it could not be completed in the 5-min. time limit allotted. The Ss were instructed to work for both speed and accuracy.

Subjects. The Ss were 90 male students in the Officer Candidate School at Lackland Air Force Base.[3]

Procedure. Two experimental sessions were involved. In the first, regular Air Force test administrators gave all Ss one form of the Test of Insight during a regularly scheduled testing program which all candidates undergo at the start of the course. The scores ranged from 0 to 12 with a mean of 5.30 and SD of 2.02. The median was 4.5. The group was then dichotomized at the median of the achievement motivation scores and three experimental groups, each containing 15 high- and 15 low-scoring Ss, were formed. The value of F for the between-group variance in motivation scores was .13.

In the second session, which took place approximately five months after the first, Ss took one form of the digit-letter code test with no orientation other than instructions pertinent to the test itself, in order to establish a control performance level for each S. Then the verbal instructions designed to vary achievement motivation level were introduced.

---

[2] See Ch. 16.

[3] The author acknowledges with sincere appreciation the assistance of Dr. Walter Borg of the USAF Officer's Military School in obtaining and scheduling Ss.

The Ss in the first group, designated the relaxed group, were told by E (the author) in a casual and friendly way while she collected the code test papers:

"We are just experimenting today and we appreciate your cooperation very much. We want to find out what kinds of scores people make on these tests. The next test you are going to take you will recognize as being like one you took when you first came to OCS. We're asking you to take this second form today to try out the new items. After that you will take one more code test. If anyone has any questions, I'll be glad to answer them at the end of the period."

The second or task-motivated group was told the following, in a formal and serious manner, by a male airman after the code tests had been collected with obvious care:

"The test which you have just taken measures a critical ability—the ability to deal quickly and accurately with unfamiliar material. It is related to general intelligence, and will be related to your future career. Each man should try to perform as well as possible. In a little while you will be given a chance to better your score. But first, you will take a second form of an experimental test you took several months ago."

The third or extrinsically motivated group was given these instructions by a male airman after the code tests had been collected.

"We want to see how fast it is possible to work on a code test like the one you have just taken, without making errors. You are familiar with it now and know just what has to be done. Next you will spend 25 min. on a second form of a test you took several months ago. Then you will take a second 5-min. code test. The five men who make the best scores in that time will be allowed to leave right away—as soon as I can check the papers. The others will have more practice periods and more tests."

The total time scheduled for this group was so arranged that it would be immediately apparent to Ss that the five men who would be allowed to leave early would have an hour of free time, not an inconsiderable incentive for an OCS student.

The second form of the Test of Insight was given immediately following the instructions. When all Ss had finished (about 25 min.) the second code test was given. The E's manner was in keeping with the particular instructions.

The Test of Insight papers were alphabetized without regard for experimental group and scored by the author. Unfortunately, a second scorer, who had assisted in the development of the test, was unavailable for this phase. In view of the high scorer agreement found (.88 and .91 for successive samples), however, it was felt that scoring could be done safely by one person. The scorer, of course, had no knowledge of the group from which any paper came.

RESULTS

The main hypothesis stated that motivation under particular environmental conditions was a function of the typical motivation level of the individual as well as the cues in the environment introduced to vary motivation level. Tables 1 and 2 include the data relevant to this hypothesis. The mean achievement motivation scores for the six subgroups (two levels of initial motivation × three experimental conditions) appear in Table 1. Bartlett's test for

TABLE 1. MEAN ACHIEVEMENT MOTIVATION AND PERFORMANCE SCORES AS A FUNCTION OF INITIAL MOTIVATION LEVEL AND EXPERIMENTAL CONDITIONS

Initial Moti-vation	Experimental Conditions					
	Relaxed		Task		Extrinsic	
	Moti-vation	Perform-ance	Moti-vation	Perform-ance	Moti-vation	Perform-ance
	Mean $\quad$ SD	Mean $\quad$ SD	Mean $\quad$ SD	Mean $\quad$ SD	Mean $\quad$ SD	Mean $\quad$ SD
High	4.20 $\quad$ 1.68	17.73 $\quad$ 16.59	6.27 $\quad$ 2.07	29.80 $\quad$ 16.30	5.40 $\quad$ 2.56	18.20 $\quad$ 15.51
Low	2.80 $\quad$ 1.34	15.40 $\quad$ 17.70	4.40 $\quad$ 2.18	16.66 $\quad$ 14.20	5.67 $\quad$ 1.39	22.47 $\quad$ 14.33
r^*	.17	.03	.45**	.48**	$-.06$	.02

* Correlations with initial motivation.
** $P < .01$.

homogeneity of variance indicated that analysis of variance was not inappropriate for these data. The analysis (Table 2) shows initial achievement motivation level significant at the 5% level, as well as verbal instructions at the 1% level. While motivation level for the groups as a whole was affected by the experimental conditions, efforts to increase or decrease motivation did not override initial levels. Those who had high scores on the first test tended to have high scores on the second test and vice versa. Lack of significant interaction between the experimental conditions and initial moti-

TABLE 2. ANALYSIS OF VARIANCE OF SECOND ACHIEVEMENT MOTIVATION SCORES

Source of Variance	df	MS	F
Initial level of achievement motivation....	1	22.51	5.25*
Experimental conditions..............	2	37.68	8.78**
Interaction.........................	2	9.43	2.20
Within (error)......................	84	4.29	

* $P = .05$
** $P = .01$.

vation level suggests that the apparent reversal for the extrinsic group is a result of chance fluctuation.

The first related hypothesis stated that a greater amount of performance variance would be due to motivation as measured in the situation than to the environmental cues per se. Data in support of this hypothesis are presented in Tables 3 and 4. Performance

TABLE 3. PERFORMANCE IMPROVEMENT MEANS AS A FUNCTION OF
SECOND ACHIEVEMENT MOTIVATION SCORES

Motivation	Experimental Conditions					
	Relaxed		Task		Extrinsic	
	Mean	SD	Mean	SD	Mean	SD
High..........	16.60	17.58	29.53	16.58	26.40	14.98
Low..........	16.60	16.75	16.93	13.51	14.27	12.61
r..........	.00		.48**		.51**	

* Correlation between motivation and performance.
** $P < .01$.

improvement scores were obtained by subtracting each S's first code test score from his second. New subgroups of 15 Ss each were formed by dichotomizing the experimental groups at the median of the Test of Insight scores obtained under the experimental conditions. The means for performance improvement for these groups appear in Table 3. The analysis of variance (Table 4) shows that the F for achievement motivation scores is significant at the 5% level. That for experimental conditions does not reach conventional standards of significance. Motivation, as measured in the situation, did prove to be more closely related to task performance than did the motivational set created by instructions alone. In fact, had the experimental conditions been the only measure of motivation used,

TABLE 4. ANALYSIS OF VARIANCE OF PERFORMANCE IMPROVEMENT SCORES
WHEN SECOND ACHIEVEMENT MOTIVATION SCORE IS A VARIABLE

Source of Variance	df	MS	F
Achievement motivation scores..........	1	1529.34	5.92*
Experimental conditions..............	2	331.74	1.28
Interaction.........................	2	382.75	1.48
Within groups (error).................	84	258.36	

* $P < .05$.

it would have been necessary to conclude that achievement motivation did not affect the task performance even though we know that, due to the nature of the task, this is highly unlikely.

The last hypothesis was concerned with the degree of relation between motivation level in one situation and motivation level and performance in another as a function of the similarity of the motivation cues in the two situations.

It should be pointed out here that the original design of the experiment called for the administration of the first motivation test as an experimental test on a day when other experimental tests were being given, in order to minimize achievement cues. However, it actually was given along with the Career Counselling Battery which the men knew was important for their future assignments. This was a real situation similar to the one the task-motivated directions tried to create. Given these conditions, the expectation was that the relation between original motivation level and both final motivation level and performance scores would be greatest in the task-motivated group, somewhat less in the relaxed group where no achievement cues were provided by the environment, and least in the extrinsically motivated where an entirely different set of motivational cues was introduced. The interaction value in Table 2 and a corresponding one computed for the performance data in Table 1 provide the over-all test of this hypothesis. The F ratio of 2.20 found in Table 2 and the one of 2.16 obtained for the performance data do not reach the .05 level of significance. They are large enough to be suggestive, however, and the differences in the table are in the predicted direction. Therefore, correlations between original motivation scores and the other sets of scores were obtained to provide more information. These are presented in Table 1. Those for the task-motivated group are both significant beyond the .01 level; those for the other groups do not reach the .05 level. In addition, according to expectation, both correlations for the task-motivated group are significantly greater than the corresponding ones for the extrinsically motivated group. The difference between the correlations for the task-motivated and relaxed groups is significant for the performance scores but not for the motivation test scores. These results give support to the hypothesis that similarity of motivation level from situation to situation is most likely to be found when environmental cues relevant to motivation are similar, and that performance can best be predicted under those circumstances as well.

DISCUSSION

Only one point needs further discussion. Although the interaction given in Table 4 also proved to be nonsignificant, examination of the means in Table 3 raised a question concerning the relaxed group. Correlations computed between second achievement scores and performance scores separately for the three conditions yielded values for the two motivated groups that were significantly higher than the zero value obtained for the relaxed group. This was contrary to prediction. An explanation advanced here is that this finding could be due to the nature of the instructions to this group. The task was presented to Ss in such a way that it might have appeared uninteresting to those with high achievement motivation but stimulating to those with high affiliative motivation. The achievement or goal-attainment aspect of the situation was de-emphasized by the instructions. But the female E was friendly in dealing with the group and asked for cooperation. Achieving high scores could be perceived as a way of pleasing E. Under these circumstances Ss with high affiliative motivation would be expected to work hard on the task. Atkinson (23) has suggested such a possibility in the interpretation of his experimental results. This hypothesis was tested by rescoring the Test of Insight papers for affiliation imagery and correlating these scores with performance. These correlations were .48, .02, and $-.13$ for the relaxed, task, and extrinsic groups, respectively. The relationships expressed are the exact reverse of those for achievement motivation shown in Table 3. Apparently the relaxed situation was not only lacking in achievement motivation cues but contained cues relevant to affiliation as a motive.

In general our findings were in support of the hypotheses proposed: that what has been described as typical level of achievement motivation is a significant variable affecting the degree to which a desired level of motivation can be aroused by introducing appropriate cues into an experimental situation; and that this resultant motivation, as it was measured, was related to performance. The findings suggest that an independent measure of motivation and a knowledge of the characteristics of the stimulus situation are both essential for predicting performance. The incidental finding, not specifically predicted, that it is possible to some extent to identify in advance which Ss are more likely to increase output under a given set of stimulus conditions, is of considerable interest.

The final point to be made is that the results, which are in accordance with the hypotheses proposed, provide additional validation for the Test of Insight as a method of measuring achievement motivation.

SUMMARY

An independent measure of motivation and a performance test were given under three different verbally created conditions of achievement motivation: relaxed, task motivated, and extrinsically motivated.

The results, consistent with hypotheses proposed, may be summarized as follows:

1. Increase in achievement motivation score was a function of both previous motivational level and the experimental conditions.

2. Performance scores were more closely related to motivation scores than to the experimental conditions.

3. Performance scores in one situation tended to be most closely related to motivation scores in another when the situations presented similar motivational cues.

4. In addition, when affiliation cues were more prominent in the situation than achievement cues, performance was related to affiliation motivation scores rather than achievement motivation scores.

CHAPTER 19

Performance as a Function of Motive Strength and Expectancy of Goal-Attainment*

JOHN W. ATKINSON AND WALTER R. REITMAN[1]

THE RESULTS of recent studies that have related thematic apperceptive measures of achievement (272) and affiliation motives (Ch. 5) to performance have been consistent with a principle of performance adapted from Tolman's (414) expectancy theory: the goal-directed action tendency is a joint function of the strength of the motive and of the expectancy aroused by situation cues that performance is instrumental to attainment of the goal of the motive (24). Our purpose is to elaborate this idea as it applies to the relation of performance to measures of individual differences in human motives and to present an experimental test of a prediction when more than one motive and one expectancy are involved.

Earlier studies (23, 27, Ch. 18, 241, 430) have shown a positive relationship between performance and n-Achievement scores obtained from thematic apperceptive stories when the cues of the performance situation arouse the expectancy that a feeling of personal accomplishment will accompany a good performance. On the other hand, when the cues for performance are deliberately manipulated so that Ss are given no reason to expect they will experience pride in accomplishment, there is no relationship between performance and n-Achievement scores (23, 27, Ch. 18). On two occasions (27 and Ch. 18), the E's explicit appeal for cooperation in situations not related to achievement has apparently served to engage another motive. Performance level, while unrelated to strength of n Achievement, has

* Reprinted by permission of author and publisher from *The Journal of Abnormal and Social Psychology,* 1956, **53**, 361-366. Copyright 1956 by the American Psychological Association, Inc.

[1] This study was accomplished during the term of a Social Science Research Council fellowship to JWA and a National Science Foundation fellowship to WRR. We should like to acknowledge, also, assistance provided by the Center for Advanced Study in the Behavioral Sciences.

been found positively related to n Affiliation. French (Ch. 18)[2] has also shown that when an incentive unrelated to either n Achievement or n Affiliation is offered, no systematic relationship is found between performance and either of these motives.

We conceive a *motive* as a latent disposition to strive for a particular goal-state or aim, e.g., achievement, affiliation, power. The strength of a particular motive is assessed by thematic apperception under *neutral*[3] conditions. The term *motivation* can then be used to designate the aroused state of the person that exists when a motive has been engaged by the appropriate expectancy, i.e., an expectancy that performance of some act is instrumental to attainment of the goal of that motive. If more than one of an individual's motives are engaged by expectancies that the same act will lead to several different goals, the *total motivation* for performance of that act will be the sum of the contributions made by the particular motives which have been engaged. An overdetermined action tendency, i.e., one which will serve to satisfy more than one motive, is likely to be relatively strong.

This conception implies that a positive relationship between a particular motive (e.g., n Achievement) and performance can be maximized by engaging that motive and no others in performance and can be minimized either (*a*) by failing to engage that motive at all as in (23, 27, Ch. 18) or (*b*) by systematically engaging other motives in performance *as well*, as suggested in (Ch. 18, 430). In the latter case, the person who is weak in the motive the *E* may have measured may be strong in other unmeasured (ulterior) motives that are engaged in performance of the same act.

The missing link among the studies already accomplished is a demonstration that the relationship between n Achievement and performance can be substantially reduced even *when the achievement expectancy is explicitly aroused* by systematic arousal of other motives to perform the same act. This should occur, assuming an asymptote for performance, when the total motivation of a low n-Achievement group approximates that of a high n-Achievement group. Our experimental task, then, is to engage the achievement motive *in two different situations* by instructions that are known to arouse it. But then we must manipulate other features of the two situations so that

---

[2] French's motive scores were obtained through content analysis of responses made to a series of single-sentence descriptions of behavior which *S*s were asked to explain as a "Test of Insight." The categories of response are directly comparable to those employed in the analysis of TAT stories.

[3] A *neutral* condition is one in which no experimental attempt is made either to arouse the motive or to create an especially relaxed state prior to the writing of stories (see 272).

expectancies of attaining other goals are relatively weak or absent in one situation and strong in the other.

Taking a lead from Wendt (430), we designed a group test situation in which two examiners would stalk about the room with watches in hand, pacing performance with a signal every minute and, to the best of their ability, casting disapproving glances at anyone who seemed to be gazing around or not taking the task seriously. These innovations, in addition to the usual type of achievement-orienting instructions, were introduced to engage the affiliation motive, the desire to please the experimenter. Finally, in an appeal to the motivational structure of persons who might be low in both n Achievement and n Affiliation, a substantial monetary reward ($5.00) was offered to the person getting the best score on the test.

In another condition, the same achievement-orienting instruction was used to engage the achievement motive, but to minimize the arousal of other goal-expectancies, the Ss were assigned individually to small test rooms and left to work alone without even the competitive cues provided by the sight and sound of other persons working. In this condition, the *E* was not present during performance, and there was no monetary incentive.

The performance level of persons who are high in n Achievement should be substantially higher than that of persons who are low in n Achievement in the group given achievement-orienting instructions and then left on their own to work without expectancies of satisfying other motives. The difference should be substantially reduced (or removed completely) in the other group given achievement-orienting instructions but in whom expectancies of attaining other goals (affiliation and money) were also aroused. No relationship is expected between n Affiliation and performance in either condition. In one group, only the expectancy of achievement was aroused, while in the other, expectancies of achievement and a monetary reward were also present to confound the simple relationship to n Affiliation that might otherwise have resulted from the introduction of affiliation-related cues.

METHOD

Subjects were 96 male college students selected from a group of several hundred introductory psychology students for whom measures of both achievement and affiliation motives were available.

Measurement of achievement and affiliation motives. Eight four-minute imaginative (TAT-type) stories were written under neutral (272) classroom conditions one to three months before the experimental sessions. The results of a methodological study run concurrently indicate that the first four stories in a series of eight, irrespective of pictures used, provide the greatest predicative validity for n Achievement.[4] The motive scores of the present study were therefore based only on the first four stories. The rank-order score-rescore reliability was .88 for n Achievement (272) and .89 for n Affiliation (Ch. 5). The distributions of scores of the larger population from which the sample was drawn were divided at the median to yield high and low groups with respect to n Achievement and n Affiliation.

Experimental conditions. Fifty-one Ss in groups of six to ten were assigned to the *Achievement-Orientation* condition. The E emphasized the importance of doing well on the tasks by alluding to them as similar to tests of important abilities (executive capacity, leadership, intellectual alertness) developed by psychologists in the past. The Ss were urged to do their best and were told, "your work will be taken as the full measure of your ability" (see 23). They were also told that they would be assigned to individual test rooms to prevent distractions.

Following this general achievement-orienting instruction, and before being assigned to individual test rooms, Ss were given a short story to read and told to memorize its content for later recall. This task, part of another study not reported here,[5] took three minutes. It was introduced to take advantage of the aroused motivational state of the Ss on the assumption that it would in no way affect the performance of Ss on the subsequent tasks of the present experiment. As it turned out, this assumption was probably incorrect.

The Ss were then assigned to individual test rooms. The first task, which consisted of drawing Xs inside of circles, was explained to them. When the test was delivered to each S, he was told to begin and urged, "do your best," or, "see how good you are at this one." The E then noted on a stop watch the exact time the S started working and recorded this time in seconds immediately after leaving the room. He then allowed 10-15 seconds to elapse before delivering a test to the next S in an adjacent room to make it possible for him to stop each S exactly 14 minutes after his own starting time. The E entered each room and stopped each S within five seconds of 14 minutes after he had started.

Instructions for the second task, a set of simple three-step arithmetic problems, were then distributed and explained. The delivery of the second task followed the same procedure. Each S was told, "this one will demand a little more brain power," or, "this one will be a lot harder," when the test itself was delivered. The same procedure of timing Ss was employed.

Forty-five Ss were assigned to the *Multi-Incentive* condition. The Ss in this condition met in groups of 10-20 and stayed together in a large classroom for performance of both tasks. The same general achievement-orienting instruction was given followed by the three-minute memorization task. The E then said, "Since we are interested in seeing your very best performance when you are actually putting out, we are going to award a prize of $5.00 to the person having the highest score on each of the tests.

---

[4] See Ch. 46.

[5] Reitman, W. R., Motivation and recall of meaningful material under achievement-orientation. (Unpublished paper) University of Michigan, 1955.

So you could stand to walk off with $10.00 for your efforts today." Finally, Ss were told they would be asked to skip an item from time to time throughout the test period.

Throughout the performance of each test, the Es walked about the room, stop watches in hand, as if evaluating the seriousness of each S's effort. At the end of each minute, one of the Es called out, "skip," at which point the Ss stopped, skipped an item, and moved on to the next one.

Fourteen minutes were given for each task, and the monetary incentive with a reminder, "do your best," was repeated before the second task which was also paced.

The tasks. The first task consisted of a 15-page booklet containing row after row of $\frac{1}{2}$ inch circles in which the S was instructed to draw Xs (27). The second task, arithmetic problems, required solution of a series of three-step problems. There were 14 pages, each containing 24 problems. The operations consisted of adding or subtracting three digits, remembering the solution while adding or subtracting another set of three digits, and then finally adding or subtracting the two solutions (430).

RESULTS

Drawing Xs in circles. The mean number of Xs drawn in circles was 1255.5 for the Multi-Incentive condition ($N = 45$) and 1149.1 for the Achievement-Orientation condition ($N = 51$). The difference of 106.4 between the two conditions is significant ($t = 3.62$, $p <$ .01), but there was no difference between high and low n-Achievement groups within either condition.

We suspect that performance of the first task was confounded by continued attempts to practice the memory material that had been introduced at the beginning of the test period. When queried about possible effects of the memory task after the experimental session, a number of Ss indicated that they had continued to practice recall during the first task. In light of the results of one earlier study (27) and another in preparation that show the Xs-in-circles task to be a sensitive measure of effort and significantly related to differences in n Achievement under appropriate conditions, we assume that many of the Ss felt it more important to concentrate on the memory material than to do their best at the relatively simple motor task that followed. Continued rehearsal of the memory material would be sufficiently distracting to influence the level of performance.

The achievement motive and arithmetic performance. The results for the second task are presented in Table 1. The arithmetic problems, which demanded continued attention and concentration, would not encourage continued attempts at memorization. We therefore view the results presented in Table 1 as a less confounded test of the initial hypothesis.

TABLE 1. ARITHMETIC PERFORMANCE AS A FUNCTION OF ACHIEVEMENT MOTIVE AND EXPERIMENTAL CONDITION

Achievement Motive	Condition					
	Achievement Orientation			Multi-Incentive		
	N	Attempted Solutions	Correct Solutions	N	Attempted Solutions	Correct Solutions
High..........	21	M 78.1	71.6		M 67.1	60.3
		σ 24.8	24.1	24	σ 19.6	19.3
Low...........	30	M 60.3	55.5		M 69.1	60.1
		σ 15.7	16.4	21	σ 22.3	23.0
Diff.......... (H-L)		17.8	16.1		−2.0	.2
σ diff........		5.93*	5.96		6.23	6.26
t............		3.00	2.70		n.s.	n.s.
p............		.01	.01			

* σ diffs. derived from estimate of within group variance, $df = 92$.

In the Achievement-Orientation condition, the performance level of the high n-Achievement group was significantly higher ($p < .01$) than that of the low n-Achievement group on both number of solutions attempted and number correct. In the Multi-Incentive condition, there was no difference between the performance levels of the two motivation groups. The difference between the differences is 19.8 for attempted solutions and 15.9 for correct solutions. Both are significant in the direction predicted ($ts = 2.30$ and 1.84 respectively, $p < .05$). In other words, the relationship between achievement motive and arithmetic performance was eliminated by systematically engaging other motives in the same performance.

An unanticipated fault in our method of pacing is chiefly responsible for the failure of over-all performance level to increase in the Multi-Incentive condition. When E called out, "skip," at the end of each minute, Ss had to stop working on partially solved problems and move immediately to the next one. On the earlier task, they had merely to skip one circle. Since there were 13 such interruptions, the performance of the high n-Achievement group would suffer a decrement if it were already nearly asymptotic in the Achievement-Orientation condition. And the net gain of the low n-Achievement group, which should profit most by the arousal of other motives, would also be depressed. The high n-Achievement group actually dropped 11.0 in number of attempts and 11.3 in number correct. The low n-Achievement groups showed net gains of 8.8 in number of attempts and 4.6 in number correct. The extent to which the decrease of the high n-Achievement group may be a real decrement accompanying very intense motivation is, unfortunately, indeterminate.

Joint effect of motivation and aptitude on arithmetic performance. Lowell (241, 272) found no relationship between n Achievement and quantitative aptitude among college students. His results can be checked in the present study.

Quantitative Aptitude Scores (Q scores) from the American Council of Education Test were available for 38 Ss in the present Achievement-Orientation condition. The data for 20 additional Ss for whom Q scores could be obtained were added. These 20 Ss had been run under the same Achievement-Oriented condition but as part of a methodological study (Ch. 46). They were divided into high and low n-Achievement groups according to the median score of a much larger group who had taken a different and somewhat less sensitive form of the thematic apperceptive test of motivation. The obtained distribution of 58 Q scores (percentile rank using local norms) was divided into thirds to provide High, Middle, and Low aptitude groups.

The mean Q score was 64.6 for this high n-Achievement group ($N = 29$) and 57.2 for the low n-Achievement group ($N = 29$). The difference, 7.4, is insignificant ($t = 1.05$), confirming Lowell's finding.

The mean number of arithmetic problems attempted by this high n-Achievement group ($N = 29$), irrespective of aptitude, was 71.2; the mean for the low n-Achievement group ($N = 29$) was 61.7. The difference, 9.5, while less than the comparable difference in the experiment proper (Table 1) as a consequence of the less sensitive measure of achievement motive for the 20 additional Ss, is nevertheless significant ($t = 2.06$, $p < .05$). Similarly, the performance levels of High ($N = 18$), Middle ($N = 22$), and Low ($N = 18$) aptitude groups, independent of motive strength, are significantly different as normally expected ($F = 3.23$, $df = 2$ and 55, $p < .05$).

Table 2 shows that the highly motivated groups were uniformly higher in performance than the less motivated groups at the three levels of aptitude. But the effect of motivation was most pronounced in the group that was lowest in aptitude. Here the difference between high and low n-Achievement groups in number of attempted solutions was 14.0 ($t = 1.71$, $p < .05$ in predicted direction). It is less than half as large at the middle level of aptitude (diff. $= 5.9$, σ diff. $= 7.4$) and at the high level of aptitude (diff. $= 4.5$, σ diff. $= 8.4$). The difference between the differences of High and Low aptitude groups, 9.5, is not significant (σ diff. $= 11.8$). The result

Expectancy of Goal Attainment   285

TABLE 2. ARITHMETIC PERFORMANCE AS A JOINT FUNCTION OF
ACHIEVEMENT MOTIVE AND QUANTITATIVE APTITUDE
(Achievement-Orientation Condition)

| Quantitative Aptitude (Percentile Rank) | Achievement Motive | | | | | | Diff. | σ diff. | t | p |
| | High | | | Low | | | | | | |
	N	Attempted Solutions	Correct Solutions	N	Attempted Solutions	Correct Solutions				
High 80-99th	11	76.9	70.5	7	72.4	68.5	4.5 / 2.0	8.4 / 8.5	n.s. / n.s.	
Middle 53-75th	10	65.7	61.2	12	59.8	54.7	5.9 / 6.5	7.4 / 7.5	n.s. / n.s.	
Low 3-48th	8	70.4	62.8	10	56.4	49.0	14.0 / 13.8	8.2 / 8.3	1.71 / 1.66	.05** / .05**
Diff. (H-L)		6.5	7.7		16.0	19.6				
σ diff.		8.1*	8.2		8.6	8.7				
t		—	—		1.86	2.25				
p		—	—		.05**	.05**				

* σ diffs. derived from estimates of within group error, $df = 52$.
** One-tailed tests.

nevertheless suggests that persons who are low in aptitude profit most by strong motivation. The trends for number of correct solutions are very similar, as Table 2 shows, but the differences are somewhat smaller.

Table 2 shows a comparable result regarding the effect on performance of differences in aptitude, viz., the effect is greatest when motivation is low. The difference between High and Low aptitude groups also low in n Achievement was 16.0 for attempted solutions (σ diff. = 8.6, $t = 1.86$, $p < .05$ in expected direction). The comparable difference in the group who were highly motivated to achieve is only 6.5 (σ diff. = 8.1). The result is essentially the same, though in this case slightly more pronounced, for number of correct solutions. In neither case is the difference between the differences significant.

The affiliation motive and arithmetic performance. No systematic relationship between n Affiliation and performance is expected in either of the experimental conditions. Table 3 shows that none of the differences is significant when a two-tailed t-test is made. The tendency for the low n-Affiliation group to perform at a somewhat higher level under Achievement-Orientation can probably be at-

TABLE 3. ARITHMETIC PERFORMANCE AS A FUNCTION OF AFFILIATION MOTIVE AND EXPERIMENTAL CONDITION

Affiliation Motive	Condition					
	Achievement Orientation			Multi-Incentive		
	N	Attempted Solutions	Correct Solutions	N	Attempted Solutions	Correct Solutions
High..........	28	M 63.3	57.7	17	M 75.1	68.3
		σ 15.8	15.9		σ 22.5	22.9
Low..........	23	M 73.0	67.5	28	M 66.1	57.4
		σ 26.4	25.8		σ 18.6	18.3
Diff..........		−9.7	−9.8		9.0	10.9
(H-L)						
σ diff........		6.0*	5.9		6.5	6.3
t............		1.62	1.66		1.38	1.72
p............		n.s.	n.s.		n.s.	.10

* σ diffs. derived from estimate of within group error, $df = 92$.

tributed to the low negative correlation ($-.20$ to $-.25$) between n Achievement and n Affiliation when scores are taken from the same four stories (Ch. 46). In light of this, the *positive* trend between n Affiliation and performance in the Multi-Incentive condition, particularly for correct solutions ($p = .10$), may mean that we were not completely successful in our attempt to eliminate the relationship between performance and a particular motive by systematically arousing other motives. The positive trend, while statistically very tenuous, suggests that the expectancy of pleasing the Es by working hard was most salient in the Multi-Incentive condition. Comparison of changes in performance between the two conditions supports this view, as Ss in the Multi-Incentive condition high in n Affiliation and low in n Achievement ($N = 8$) averaged 16.7 more attempted solutions than Ss with comparable motive scores in the Achievement-Orientation condition ($N = 20$); all other Ss in the Multi-Incentive condition ($N = 37$) averaged 5.8 *fewer* attempted solutions than the comparable Achievement-Oriented Ss ($N = 31$). The difference, 22.5, is significant (σ diff. $= 10.0$, $t = 2.25$ $p < .05$). The correct solutions result is very similar. The greatest increase in performance due to the presence of the Es and the monetary reward was among Ss highly motivated to affiliate but weak in motivation to achieve.

DISCUSSION

Genotype and phenotype. We interpret the results as consistent with the conception of motivation and behavior elaborated in the introductory section. The distinction between strength of particular motives (latent dispositions) and strength of motivation to perform a particular act (the sum of all aroused motives) highlights the genotype-phenotype distinction that is often made in treatments of motivation and behavior. An obvious implication of the results of this and earlier, related studies (23, 27, Ch. 18, 430) is that psychologists should stop expecting to find measures of *particular* motives and performance criteria like academic performance, leadership, etc., to be more highly related than they have been found in the past (for example 301). From the present viewpoint, most performance criteria in real-life situations can be considered overdetermined, i.e., acts or accomplishments for which several of the individual's motives have been engaged.

The role of the situation. The present formulation calls for a good deal more thought than is commonly given the question of conceptualizing and ultimately measuring the properties of the situation in which behavior occurs. Our difficulty in attempting to create an experimental situation that would make the expectancies of achievement, affiliation, and monetary prize nearly equal in salience, as evidenced by the positive trend between n Affiliation and performance in the Multi-Incentive condition, illustrates the need for adequate methods of assessing situations in terms of the expectancies of goal-attainment they provoke. Rotter (354) and his colleagues have begun to make substantial strides in this direction.

SUMMARY

Particular motives, (Achievement, Affiliation, Power, etc.) are conceived as latent dispositions to strive for certain goal states (aims) that are engaged in performance of an act when the cues of the situation arouse the expectancy that performance of an act is instrumental to attainment of the goal of the motive. The total *motivation* to perform the act is conceived as a summation of strengths of all the *motives* that have been aroused by appropriate expectancies of goal-attainment cued-off by the situation. The relationship of achievement motive (as measured by imaginative TAT stories) to performance is shown to be significantly positive when the expectancy that performance is instrumental to producing a feeling of pride in accomplishment is aroused and few if any other expectancies of goal-attainment are aroused. When motives for other goals (affiliation and money) are *also* aroused by deliberate manipulation of situational cues that activate the Ss' expectancies, there is no relationship between achievement motive and performance. The joint effect of quantitative aptitude and achievement motive on arithmetic performance is illustrated in a subsidiary analysis of the data.

CHAPTER 20

....

Towards Experimental Analysis of Human Motivation in Terms of Motives, Expectancies, and Incentives

JOHN W. ATKINSON[1]

EXPERIMENTS which have dealt chiefly with the effects of individual differences in strength of n Achievement and n Affiliation on performance show fairly clearly that both a disposition to strive for a particular goal (a motive) and an expectancy that an act will be instrumental in attaining the goal must be present for the motive to be aroused and expressed in performance of the act. The crude qualitative nature of experimental attempts to manipulate the expectancies of Ss has unavoidably confounded two variables which are given independent status by Tolman (414) and in other expectancy theories (244, 415). These two variables are the strength of *expectancy*, an appropriate measure of which would normally be some index of the probability that performance of the act will have a certain consequence, and the amount of *incentive*, i.e., the magnitude of the reward or potential satisfaction offered should the expected consequence occur.

The distinction between expectancy and incentive is exemplified in the animal experiment in which the probability of reaching food by turning left or right in a maze can be varied independently of the amount of food that is present in the goal box. Given any amount of hunger, the motive, a half-dozen food pellets constitutes a greater incentive than only one.

---

[1] This experiment was conducted during the term of a Social Science Research Council Faculty Research Fellowship. Allan Rubin, Marshall Rosenberg, and Judson Mills assisted in conducting the experimental sessions or in the analysis of results. I wish to acknowledge, also, the time made available by the Center for Advanced Studies in the Behavioral Sciences for developing some of the ideas in this paper.

The present experiment represents an attempt to begin to isolate the effects of differences in the strength of expectancy and incentive on human motivation. This is done within the framework of the kind of experiment which has already proven useful in the study of the effects of differences in strength of motive on performance.

Given our interest in motives for achievement, affiliation, and power, an ideal experiment would be one in which individual differences in the strength of one of these motives, the relevant expectancy, and incentive are measured or varied independently. Our measures of strength of motive and a suitable index of the relative amount of satisfaction of that motive offered as an inducement to perform (incentive) would together constitute an empirical basis for inferences about the "subjective value" or what in decision theory (114) is called the "utility" of the consequence of the act for particular persons. And variations in strength of expectancy reduced to some index of probability would bring our experiments that much closer to a probability-utility model for decision and action (114) that is implied in a motive-expectancy-incentive formulation of the problem.

But at this time, it is difficult to imagine exactly how to go about producing variations in incentives that would be appropriate for the particular human motives we are currently able to measure in thematic apperception. What would constitute a variation in achievement, affiliation, or power incentives? This is a question for future research.

The immediate issue is to find an incentive that permits meaningful variation in experiments with human subjects. A monetary reward obviously meets the requirement. Consequently, our initial attempt focuses primarily upon the effect of variations in monetary incentive and expectancy of attaining the incentive through performance in randomly constituted groups of subjects. In the absence of independent measures, the groups are assumed to be equal in strength of motives for which money is an effective incentive.

The plan. Subjects are offered monetary incentives of either $1.25 or $2.50 to work at two different tasks. The strength of expectancy of "winning" the monetary prize, i.e., the probability of winning, is controlled by informing each S of the number of persons with whom he is in competition for the monetary prize and how many of the persons in his group will be paid for good performance. There are four variations in the probability of winning. These are represented as fractions in which the numerator specifies the number of monetary prizes to be awarded and the denominator the number of persons in competition for the prize. The four conditions are 1/20, 1/3,

1/2, and 3/4. If a S is in the condition which calls for a monetary incentive of $2.50 and a probability of 3/4, he is told, for example: "You are one of a group of 4 persons. The 3 persons in your group with the highest scores will win $2.50. In other words, your chances of winning $2.50 are 3 out of 4."

To create the impression that winning a monetary prize is largely contingent upon how hard the person tries, the Ss are told, . . . "the tasks are as sensitive to effort as to any particular skills or abilities, so the person who tries the hardest is likely to have the best score." The incentive and probability are the same for each of two tasks a S performs. The point of using two distinctly different types of tasks —one calling for concentration in solving simple three-step arithmetic problems, the other requiring only that S draw Xs inside of small circles—is to provide a composite performance score which can be taken as an index of goal-directed effort that is relatively independent of the skill required for a particular kind of task. Even though the experimental procedures are not particularly appropriate for studying the effect of individual differences in strength of achievement motive, in light of other experimental findings (See Ch. 19), a thematic apperceptive measure of n Achievement is obtained for each S to allow at least an exploration of the joint effects of this motive, monetary incentive, and expectancy of goal attainment upon performance.

METHOD

Subjects. The Ss were 124 female college students. They were selected at random from a much larger group of students in an introductory psychology course who had indicated a willingness to participate in an experiment.

Experimental procedure. The Ss were called to a large classroom in groups of 10-20 at assigned hours. They were seated in every other seat so that there would be minimum opportunity to see directly what another person was doing or the instructions given to another person. Within each of these groups of 10-20, the distribution of instructions which defined the various conditions of the experiment was arranged so that persons sitting next to each other would never be in the same experimental condition. In any particular group, the incentive was held constant at either $1.25 or $2.50, but all degrees of probability were represented.

The following preliminary instruction sheet was read by each S at the beginning of the period:

"You are one of approximately 100 students who are participating in psychology laboratory work this week. We have arranged to divide the total group into smaller subgroups of various sizes. There will be competition for monetary rewards within these various subgroups.

You will be given a certain task to perform and told what the amount of the monetary reward will be for good performance and how many people you are in competition with for the reward. For example, you might be told that you are one of a group of 30 persons and that the monetary reward for the highest performance in that group of 30 is 25 cents. This would mean that the prize to be won was 25 cents and your chances of winning were 1 out of 30, depending, of course, upon how hard you work at the tasks. If you were told that you were 1 of a group of 10 persons, your chances would be 1 out of 10, etc.

The tasks you will be asked to perform are as sensitive to effort as to any particular skills or abilities, so the person who tries the hardest is likely to have the best score.

The subgroups were arrived at in a random manner, so it is a matter of sheer chance that you are in one subgroup and not another. You may or may not be in the same subgroup as the persons in the positions next to you. Some of the persons you are competing with have already worked on the tasks; others are still to work on them some time this week. But we shall arrange, before you leave, a suitable method for getting in touch with you if you are one of the winners.

Please raise any general questions you may have before you are given specific instructions for your first task."

Without waiting for the question to be asked, the E reassured the Ss that the monetary prizes would be paid. He said that he wanted to make certain that everyone understood the instructions meant exactly what they said.

Following this, a second instruction sheet clipped to a 14-page booklet of arithmetic problems adapted from Düker and Wendt (430) was distributed. This instruction sheet first informed the S of the amount of monetary incentive and his chance of winning:

"Please do not talk to anyone during the experimental period. This time, you are one of a group of ____ persons. The person(s) who fills in the highest number of correct answers to the problems described in the task below will win _____. In other words, your chances of winning _____ are _____ out of _____."

The Ss were urged to read the instruction a second time to make certain they understood. Then the instruction for solving the arithmetic problems was presented and discussed until everyone understood the procedure. This task is described elsewhere (430). The problems each appeared in this form: $\frac{8-4+2}{9+5-6}$. The S was required to solve the top line and remember it without writing it down. Then he was to solve the bottom line and remember it. If the top solution was larger, he was to subtract the bottom from the top. If the top solution was smaller, he was to add the two and to write down only the final solution. There were 24 such problems on each of the 14 pages of the task booklet. The final instruction to the S was to place a check mark next to the problem on which he was working whenever the E called out "check."

The E gave the signal to begin and called, "check," at the end of each two-minute period. At the end of 20 minutes the Ss were told to stop.

A second task was immediately distributed. A printed instruction which repeated the same monetary incentive and probability of winning for each S was distributed with the instruction for the second task. And the Ss were reassured that they had another chance to win, i.e., that two prizes would be paid, one for each task. The second task required Ss to draw Xs inside of $\frac{1}{2}$ inch circles arranged in rows on regular $8\frac{1}{2} \times 11$ inch paper. There were approximately 300 circles on each page and many more pages than anyone could finish in the twenty-minute period. The procedure of calling "check" at the end of each two-minute period was repeated during the second task.

During the experimental period, the E tried to conduct himself in a relaxed and casual manner. He sat at the front of the room, smoking, with his feet on a desk a good portion of the time. He called "check" in an informal way without making any show of the stop watch. A deliberate attempt was made to minimize the extent to which Ss would feel any particular obligation to work hard at the tasks because of the E's presence as in some other experiments (Ch. 19) and to minimize, if possible, the degree to which Ss would consider the two tasks as important tests on which they should perform well.

Measurement of Achievement Motive. As part of a methodological study reported elsewere (Ch. 46), all of the Ss had written imaginative stories in response to eight pictures under neutral classroom conditions one to three months earlier. The first four stories were analyzed by a team of scorers who had established their scoring reliability at approximately .90 before scoring these stories. In a secondary analysis of results, the Ss of this experiment were divided into high and low n Achievement groups in terms of the median n Achievement score of the larger population from which they were drawn.

RESULTS

A preliminary analysis of results showed that differences in performance level accompanying variations in probability of winning and amount of monetary incentive were very similar (not significantly different) for the two tasks. Consequently, each S's performance score on the arithmetic task (number of correct solutions in twenty minutes) was converted to a standard score based on the mean and standard deviation of all the arithmetic scores. To eliminate negative numbers and decimal points in the presentation of results, the T score conversion, in which the mean is 50 and the standard deviation 10, was used. In a similar manner, each S's raw score representing total number of Xs drawn in circles in twenty minutes was converted to a T-score based on the mean and standard deviation of all scores for this task. Then the average of each S's two T-scores was taken as the single, most reliable index of the effortfulness of his performance over a twenty-minute period.

The effects of monetary incentive and expectancy of winning on motivation as expressed directly in the speed and effort expended in performance are summarized in Table 1 and Figure 1. Performance is greater when the incentive is $2.50 than when it is $1.25 no matter what the probability of winning. The effect of greater monetary incentive is most pronounced when the probability of winning is either very high (3/4) or very low (1/20).

TABLE 1. EFFECT OF MONETARY INCENTIVE AND EXPECTANCY OF WINNING ON PERFORMANCE

| Incentive | | *Expectancy of Winning (Probability)* | | | | |
		1/20	1/3	1/2	3/4	Incentive Means
$2.50	N	18	18	18	18	
	M	50.25	51.81	54.09	51.70	51.96
	S.D.	6.18	8.05	8.94	4.24	
$1.25	N	13	13	13	13	
	M	44.96	50.81	52.00	45.69	48.37
	S.D.	8.30	6.12	5.56	9.72	
Probability Means		48.03	51.39	53.21	49.18	

Analysis of Variance

Source	d.f.	Mean Squares	F	p
Incentive............	1	395.75	6.93	.01
Expectancy..........	3	161.86	2.83	.05
I × E..............	3	46.10		
Error..............	116	57.10		

Note: The performance score for each S represents an average of his standard, T-scores for 20 minutes of arithmetic and 20 minutes of drawing X's in circles.

Of greater interest is the nature of the effect of differences in expectancy of winning on performance. The relationship, as shown in Figure 1, is curvilinear. When the stated probability of winning is very low, 1/20, the level of performance is lowest. It increases as the chance of winning improves, reaching a maximum when the stated probability of winning is 1/2. And then it decreases as the stated probability of winning is increased further to 3/4. In other words, the Ss in both incentive conditions try hardest when they are *most uncertain,* probability 50-50, about the outcome.

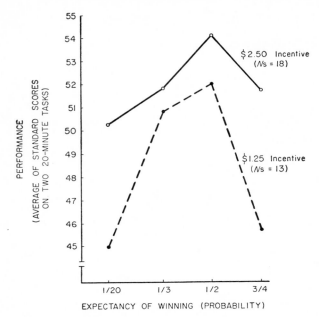

Fig. 1. Motivation directly expressed in performance as a function of monetary incentive and expectancy of winning (probability).

Table 1 shows that the effects of incentive and stated probability of winning are statistically significant ($p < .01$ and $p < .05$).

Effect of Differences in Strength of n Achievement. Table 2 shows very little difference between performance levels of high and low n Achievement groups[2] when the monetary incentive is high ($2.50). But there is a suggestive difference between the performance levels of high and low n Achievement groups when the monetary incentive is low ($1.25) and the probability of winning is also low. Figure 2 shows that when the monetary incentive is low, Ss who are highly motivated to achieve, work harder when the odds are against them (i.e., either 1/20 or 1/3) than Ss who are less motivated to achieve. While the difference is not statistically significant at either the 1/20

---

[2] The unequal number of Ss in various high and low n Achievement groups is the result of random assignment of Ss to conditions before their standing above or below the median score of a larger population of college women was known. No n Achievement score was available for nine of the Ss, and one S who had been run in the $1.25 — ¾ condition but removed by a random method to keep the Ns equivalent in the earlier analysis (Table 1) was added to bolster the N in this analysis.

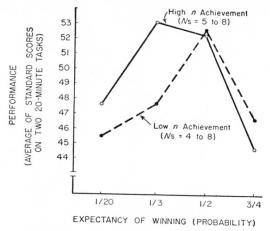

Fig. 2. Motivation directly expressed in performance when the monetary incentive is low ($1.25) as a function of n Achievement.

or 1/3 points taken separately, it approaches the conventional criterion of statistical significance when the 1/20 and 1/3 groups are combined. The mean of this combined high n Achievement group ($N = 13$) is 50.85 and the mean of the combined low n Achievement group is ($N = 11$) 46.13. The chance probability of the difference, 9.42 (σ diff. $= 6.30$), is .07 in the generally expected direction.

DISCUSSION

The results raise more questions than they answer. On the face of it, they show that persons try harder in an interpersonal, competitive situation the greater the monetary incentive and the greater the degree of uncertainty concerning goal attainment, i.e., when the odds are near 50-50. But this simple generalization tends to mask the problem which requires clarification. It will surprise no one that college students are willing to work harder to win $2.50 than $1.25. Had this not occurred, we should have serious reason to doubt the sensitivity of our performance measures of motivation. But why is there a greater willingness to work hard when the outcome is most in doubt?

The curvilinear relationship between expectancy of winning and performance can be translated nicely into common sense. When the chance of winning seems remote even if a great effort is made, it doesn't seem worth the effort. When the chance of winning is almost virtually assured by very favorable odds, in this case 3 out of 4, there is little point in expending more effort than is necessary to assure

TABLE 2. THE EFFECT OF n ACHIEVEMENT ON PERFORMANCE UNDER VARIOUS CONDITIONS OF MONETARY INCENTIVE AND EXPECTANCY OF WINNING

		Expectancy of Winning (Probability)			
$2.50 Incentive		1/20	1/3	1/2	3/4
High n Achievement	N	4	9	9	11
	M	48.50	52.56	54.95	51.28
	S.D.	4.20	9.10	9.09	3.94
Low n Achievement	N	11	9	8	4
	M	49.28	50.89	55.50	51.00
	S.D.	5.90	7.10	7.74	5.49
	Diff. (H-L)	−.78	1.67	−.55	.28
$1.25 Incentive					
High n Achievement	N	5	8	7	6
	M	47.30	53.07	52.21	44.67
	S.D.	8.70	6.20	5.45	9.42
Low n Achievement	N	7	4	6	8
	M	45.43	47.38	52.59	46.38
	S.D.	6.11	8.44	6.39	8.59
	Diff. (H-L)	1.87	5.69	−.38	−1.71

Note: Performance score for each S represents an average of his standard, T-scores for 20 minutes of arithmetic and 20 minutes of drawing Xs in circles.

performing better than the worst of three competitors. But when the odds of winning or losing are near equal, there seems a good chance that a real burst of effort will throw the balance your way.

The Disutility of Effort. Unmeasured, and virtually ignored in planning the experiment, is the general tendency of individuals to avoid fatigue. This idea has been summarized in the psychological literature as the "law of least effort." In the Hullian theory, the avoidance of fatigue is given motivational status in the concept of reactive inhibition which acts as a drive for rest (187). It is necessary to assume, within the framework of an expectancy theory, a disposition within Ss to avoid fatigue having properties similar to those of other motives (See 414). Individuals undoubtedly differ in the strength of this disposition. Some, in other words, tend to be lazier than others. The expectancy of fatigue as a consequence of hard work should engage the fatigue-avoidance disposition. And the individual should be motivated to minimize exertion. Not performing, i.e., resting, is here viewed as functionally equivalent to any other kind of instrumental act.

Unfortunately, there seems to be little more we can say of the possible effect of what decision-theorists would call the "disutility of effort," except hopefully to assume that it was held constant among our experimental groups by virtue of the random selection of Ss. At the very least, it suggests one basis for "explaining" why the Ss offered three chances out of four of winning might have worked no harder than they thought necessary to win.

Can any other suggestions be offered which point towards a systematic statement of the relationships between expectancy of goal attainment, amount of incentive, and motivation as expressed in goal-directed effort?

Satisfaction in Winning as a Function of Probability of Winning. Another idea can be advanced to make some sense of the two primary results: the bell-shaped relationship between performance and expectancy of winning; and the increased level of performance with a flattening out of the curvilinear relationship when monetary incentive is increased. This interpretation will also provide a basis for explaining the suggestive difference between the performance levels of high and low n Achievement groups when the monetary incentive and probability of winning is low.

First, it must be assumed that despite the attempt to minimize the intrinsic achievement relatedness of the tasks in this experiment, any type of task requiring interpersonal competition is likely to be perceived by college students as a possibility for achieving.

Second, in our society a greater sense of accomplishment is experienced the more difficult the feat. This assumption is commonly made in theories about level of aspiration (231).

Third, it must be acknowledged that there is an asymptote, i.e., an upper limit, on performance. Trying harder will produce an increase in performance score up to a certain point beyond which additional effort will produce no increment. Until recently, for example, it seemed that four minutes defined the asymptote for running a mile. The discovery of new techniques of breathing and pacing performance has changed this asymptote, but only by a few seconds.

Leaning on these general assumptions, borrowing a few ideas from probability-utility theories of decision (114), and continuing to ignore the possible differential role of fatigue or the expectancy of fatigue in the experiment, I offer the following:

1. The incentive value of an achievement, i.e., the relative amount of satisfaction to be experienced in any personal accomplishment, is a positive function of the difficulty of the task. In the present experiment, difficulty is inversely related to the probability of winning (p). In other words, the amount of satisfaction to be experienced in winning, *qua* winning, is a positive function of $1-p$, where p is a positive function of the stated probability of winning. When the probability of winning is high—an easy task—the amount of satisfaction experienced in winning is low. When the probability of winning is low—a difficult task—the amount of satisfaction in winning is high.

2. The extent to which motivation is aroused to approach any goal is a joint function of the probability of goal attainment (p) and the incentive value, or amount of satisfaction accompanying attainment of that goal. (In decision theories, the product of probability and utility is referred to as "expected utility" (114).)

3. The product of probability (p) and incentive value of winning ($1-p$), as here defined, is maximal when $p = .50$. If we simply use the probabilities stated in the instructions to the Ss as values for p, the "expected value of winning" in the four probability conditions —1/20, 1/3, 1/2, and 3/4—are .05, .22, .25, and .19. The ordering of the means for performance level as a function of probability of winning in Table 1 corresponds exactly to this order of "expected value of winning."

Now, the argument runs, when the monetary incentive is increased from $1.25 to $2.50, the value of money becomes a more *salient* feature of the goal to be attained than when little money is offered as prize. The incentive value of money, whatever it is, is constant among our experimental groups irrespective of the stated probability of winning it. The expected value of the monetary incentive would of course be greater the higher the probability of winning it. As a consequence, when the monetary incentive is increased, motivation to perform should increase the most when the probability of winning is three out of four. And the asymptote for performance will prevent the 1/2 group from showing the amount of increase in performance that might have been expected of them. As a result, the curvilinear relationship between performance and probability of winning should begin to flatten out as it, in fact, did.

Now what sense can be made of the tendency of Ss who are high in n Achievement to work harder than Ss who are lower in n Achievement when the odds are stacked against them, viz., 1/3 and 1/20?

Several earlier findings provide some basis for thinking that Ss who are high in *n* Achievement might tend to feel that their chances of winning are actually better than the stated odds, i.e., that the *subjective* probabilities would be higher than the stated (*objective*) probabilities. Pottharst (334), for example, has found that Ss who are high in *n* Achievement tend to state higher levels of expectation for performance of a task at which they have had no previous experience than Ss who are low in *n* Achievement. Her findings confirm an earlier one showing that when cues which define a person's past level of performance are ambiguous or in conflict, Ss who are high in *n* Achievement set their level of expectation higher than Ss who are low in *n* Achievement (272). Furthermore, it has been found that Ss who are high in *n* Achievement tend to overestimate their previous grade point averages in college (272). Together, these findings suggest that a person who is high in *n* Achievement, when faced with a novel task and stated odds concerning his chances of winning, might feel subjectively that his chances are a little better. If this were the case, and an upwardly biased "subjective probability of winning" rather than the stated odds is used to calculate the "expected value of winning," i.e., $(p) \times (1-p)$, it is expected that the point of maximum effort by the high *n* Achievement group will fall somewhere below the 50-50 point on the scale of objectively stated odds.

Figure 3 shows arbitrary curves for "expected value of winning." In one, (A in Fig. 3), incentive value of winning is equal to 1 minus the stated (objective) probability. Expected value is greatest when objective $p = .50$. In another, (B in Fig. 3), it is assumed that the

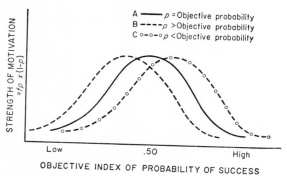

Fig. 3. Hypothetical curves showing strength of motivation as a function of the probability of success. Motivation assumed to be some function of the expected value of winning. Value of winning assumed to be some function of 1-p where p is the subjective probability of success.

subjective probability of winning is higher than the stated odds. Expected value is greatest when the *objective* p is less than .50. There is a suggestion of such a shift in the performance curve of the high n Achievement group when the monetary incentive is low ($1.25).

The "Discrepancy Hypothesis." In this discussion we are following a slightly different tack from one suggested by McClelland and Clark (272, pp. 42-67) in their proposals to account for the antecedents of affective arousal, i.e., pleasure and pain. Combining ideas from Hebb (172) and Helson (176), they have asserted that affective arousal is a function of the size of the discrepancy between the stimulus (perception) and the adaptation level (expectation) of the organism. This "discrepancy hypothesis" accounts very well for a number of experimental findings pertaining to preferences for stimuli which vary along a number of simple dimensions of sensory discrimination. And it produces a number of interesting and testable implications concerning discrepancies between more complex perceptions and exceptations based on prior learning experience. According to the discrepancy hypothesis, pleasure is maximal when the event, as perceived, is a moderate discrepancy from the adaptation level or stable level of expectation of the organism. In effect, the hypothesis suggests that in a competitive situation like the present one, the event —winning—confirms an expectation that might have been very strong (high probability), moderately strong (intermediate probability), or very weak (low probability). The discrepancy between the actual occurrence of the event ($p = 1.00$) and the level of expectation (some $p < 1.00$) is very small in the first instance, moderate in the second instance, and very large in the third instance. The amount of pleasure accompanying the "victory," when plotted against the degree of certainty (probability) of the expectation, should take the very form that the performance curve has taken in this experiment.

The "discrepancy hypothesis" predicts that persons will experience more satisfaction when the prior expectation of winning has been at some intermediate level between very high and very low: "If the expectations are of low probability, then confirmation should produce negative affect as in 'fear of the strange.' If they are of moderate probability, precise confirmation should produce pleasure (as in reading a detective story or playing solitaire). If the expectations are of high probability, then precise confirmation produces boredom or indifference (as in reading over again the detective story one has just finished) to use Hebb's example" (272, p. 62).

The discrepancy hypothesis presumes that the strength of the tendency to approach the goal, i.e., the vigor of performance, indicates directly the amount of pleasure to be experienced in winning. Pleasure in winning is hence presumed greatest when the subjective probability of winning is near 50-50. The arousal of motivation to perform, ignoring for the moment individual differences in strength of motive, is accounted for solely in terms of the incentive value.

An analogy in terms of food incentives may clarify the point. The discrepancy hypothesis seems to imply that the degree of satisfaction accompanying winning when you have been certain of winning all along is comparable to the degree of satisfaction you might experience in eating the familiar liverwurst sandwich. The pleasure accompanying winning when the odds have been near 50-50 is more like what you might experience in eating a novel french pastry. The experience accompanying victory when the odds have been very much stacked against you is like the experience you might have in eating an octopus for the first time—you are too shocked really to enjoy it!

The alternative interpretation offered for the present results *does not* assume that the relationship between amount of pleasure accompanying accomplishment and strength of prior expectancy of winning is bell shaped. Rather it assumes that winning when the odds are 1000 to 1 against you is an immensely enjoyable experience, not one producing a negative affective reaction as the discrepancy hypothesis applied to achievements seems to presume. Furthermore, the hypothesis that the incentive value of achievement is a positive function of $1-p$ states that the amount of pleasure in accomplishment decreases as the odds become more favorable. Finally, it attempts to account for two different effects of probability of winning: (a) *as an index of the strength of the expectancy* that an act will have a certain consequence and (b) as an index of the relative degree of difficulty of the feat which allows *an estimate of the degree of satisfaction $(1-p)$ that would be experienced if the person did win.*

According to this formulation, the person tries harder when uncertain about winning ($p = .50$), not because he will feel more satisfied if he should win than he would feel if the odds were stacked against him, but because the "expected value" or "expected satisfaction"—the product of expectancy (p) and incentive ($1-p$)—is greatest at this point.

An illustration from the field of professional baseball in which subjective probabilities of success are constantly changing as a function of the abilities of the opposition illustrates the central idea. Let us compare the amount of satisfaction a player like Ted Williams might experience in hitting a home run in a pre-season exhibition game against minor league opposition with the amount of satisfaction he would experience hitting a home run in the mid-season All

Star game when opposed by one of the best pitchers in the other league. In the preseason game, his subjective probability of hitting a home run is much greater, but the degree of satisfaction in the accomplishment much less than in the All Star game.

n Achievement and Performance. Granted, the statistical significance of the difference between performance levels of high and low n Achievement groups hardly justifies the construction of a theoretical edifice! Nevertheless, there are several reasons to consider it suggestive of a real difference, worthy of some speculation and of careful follow-up study.

In the first place, other experiments have shown that the relationship between n Achievement and performance is maximized when a "sense of achievement" is the only real incentive for performance. When other incentives are offered and other motives are engaged in performance, the relationship between measures of n Achievement and performance is greatly reduced or washed out completely as in (Ch. 19). As explained elsewhere (Ch. 42, Ch. 19), this does not mean that the achievement motive is not aroused. Rather it means that when other motives are also aroused in the same performance, the simple relationship between strength of achievement motive and performance is confounded in unknown ways.

In the present experiment, no systematic attempt was made to encourage *Ss* to expect that a good performance on these particular tasks had any intrinsic merit. They were not presented, for example, as tests of intelligence. Instead, the monetary incentive was emphasized and the assumption made that motives for which money is a potential satisfier would be aroused in performance. In this connection, it is interesting to note that there is no relationship between measures of n Achievement and performance when the monetary incentive is increased ($2.50). It might be argued that the simple relationship between n Achievement and performance in this trivial competitive game is washed out, as in the earlier experiment (Ch. 19), by the arousal of other motives. The suggestive relationship between n Achievement and performance, when the monetary incentive is lower ($1.25), is consistent with the idea that motives for which money is an incentive have not yet been sufficiently engaged by this amount of money to mask the relationship between n Achievement and performance. Presumably, a much greater amount of money would be required to mask the effects of differences in n Achievement in a competitive situation having greater social, and hence, personal significance.

Finally, our research using the TAT measure of n Achievement during the past eight years has indicated that the instrument is more sensitive to achievement motivation in men than in women. So finding any relationship at all between n Achievement and performance in women, particularly when it occurs where it might have been expected, is suggestive that such a relationship exists. Of course, only follow-up studies—with male subjects—will resolve the doubt one way or the other.

Concluding Comments: Motivation Theory and Decision Theory. As a guide for research in experiments like the present one, it may be helpful simply to list a series of proposals having to do with the use of various terms and possible linkages between a motive-expectancy-incentive conception of human motivation and the probability-utility model for decision and action:

1. The term, *incentive,* has been used to refer to some potential reward or goal that can be manipulated by the experimenter—the amount of food, the amount of money, the difficulty of the task as an index of achievement-incentive, etc. It has been suggested that the incentive to achieve is greater the more difficult the task and specifically that achievement-incentive value equals 1 minus probability of success. It is a problem for future research to discover what constitutes a basis for varying the strength of affiliation, power, and other kinds of incentives.

2. The term, *motive,* has been used to refer to the disposition within the person to strive to approach a certain class of positive incentives (goals) or to avoid a certain class of negative incentives (threats). The definition of a particular class of incentives constitutes the general aim of a particular motive. At present, we infer the strength of various motives through content analysis of thematic apperception.

3. The term, *expectancy,* has been used to refer to a particular kind of cognitive association aroused in the person by situational cues. In the expectancy learning theory, an expectancy is designated S-R-S (244, 415). The initial S refers to the situational cue which arouses a chain of associations involving an act, the R, and the consequence of the act, the final S. We are interested in expectancies which signify consequences which are incentives, i.e., potential satisfiers of some motive. A crude inference can be made of the strength of certain expectancies, i.e., the probability of certain consequences, from qualitative experimental arrangements like variations in instructions given to a group for performance of a task. But better methods for measuring expectancies are needed.

4. Given an objectively-defined incentive for a group of Ss, e.g., a glass of water, the subjective value or utility of that incentive for a particular individual depends upon the strength of his motive, e.g.,

thirst. The utility of a positive incentive is a positive function of the strength of the motive to approach. The disutility of a negative incentive is a positive function of the strength of the motive to avoid.

5. Given an objective basis for inferring the average strength of an expectancy within a group of Ss, the subjective probability of the consequence in a particular individual is influenced by the strength of his motive. The subjective probability of goal attainment is a positive function of the strength of the motive to approach. The subjective probability of a threatening or painful consequence is a positive function of the strength of the motive to avoid.

6. The arousal of motivation to approach, i.e., to perform the act, is equivalent to the expected positive utility of the consequences. Here, the term *motivation* is used to designate the activated state of the person which occurs when the cues of a situation arouse the expectancy that performance of an act will lead to an incentive for which he has a motive.

7. The arousal of motivation to avoid, i.e., not to perform the act, is equivalent to the expected negative utility of the consequences.

8. The resultant motivation, which is expressed directly in performance, is a summation of motivation to approach and motivation to avoid. In decision theory this summation is referred to as the overall expected utility of the consequences.

These suggestions are offered to bring a rather loosely stated theory of human motivation into contact with the more rigorously stated ideas of decision theory. They obviously contribute nothing to the problem of exact measurement of subjective probabilities and utilities which is currently engaging a good deal of experimental interest in the field of decision making. The objective is a very limited one: to try to make some theoretical sense of the observed relationships between thematic-apperceptive measures of the strength of motives and the expression of motivation directly in the vigor and persistence of goal-directed effort. The immediate objective is to increase the theoretical relevance of our future experiments.

The concept of "subjective probability" implies that future-oriented cognitions may differ from person to person *when the objective basis for these cognitions is the same for all persons.* This concept directs attention to the same problem that psychologists have examined in studying the effects of motives on perception and cognition. We have made an assumption that is consistent with empirical findings on the relation of motives to perception and which embraces the idea of subjective probability: any motive to approach a goal— e.g., hunger, thirst, achievement, affiliation, etc.—will heighten the subjective expectancy of attaining the goal of the motive. This means that the expected utility, or expected satisfaction, determined by a multiplicative combination of subjective probability and utility, will be different among individuals who differ in the strength of motive. The assumption, in other words, provides *one* basis for predicting that persons who differ in strength of motive will behave differently when faced with identical objective cues for performance.

This particular assumption does not mean that the strength of motivation as directly expressed in performance will always be reflected in a bell-shaped curve when plotted against the probability of goal attainment. For the subjective probability of goal attainment will usually play no role at all in determining the incentive value at it does in the case of incentives to achieve. The special assumption that difficulty of a task determines the incentive value of *achievement* and the definition of difficulty as an inverse function of the subjective probability of success accounts for the bell-shaped relationship between performance and probability of achievement.

The assumption that avoidance motives, e.g., fear, will bias the subjective expectancy of painful consequences in a similar manner has a number of testable implications. In the present experiment, for example, the person who is disposed to be fearful of failure should have a higher subjective probability of losing and a lower subjective probability of winning than is given in the stated odds. The curve labeled "C" in Figure 3 suggests the predicted effect on performance for a group of persons who are particularly fearful of failure in an experiment like the present one.

The concept of "subjective value" or utility implies that individuals may differ in the degree of satisfaction or dissatisfaction accompanying certain kinds of events. It serves one of the same explanatory functions as the concept of motive. In assuming that the utility of an incentive will vary as a function of the strength of the motive for incentives of that class, we discover then a sound basis for predicting that the expected utility, and hence performance, will be greater for persons who have strong motives *when the objective circumstance (in this case the incentive offered) is the same for everyone.* Winterbottom (Ch. 33) has found that children who are strong in achievement motive are rated by their teachers as showing more pride and pleasure in success than children who are weak in achievement motive. This suggests that the strength of a motive determines the capacity for satisfaction in goal attainment. In the case of avoidance motives—fears, fatigue, guilt, etc.—the assumption will account for greater negative expected utility, and hence stronger avoidant behavior, the stronger the motive in the individual.

CHAPTER 21

....

Risk Taking in Children with High and Low Need for Achievement

DAVID C. McCLELLAND[1]

PREVIOUS RESEARCH in this series has argued that n Achievement is a key factor in accounting for the behavior of entrepreneurs, particularly business entrepreneurs who play a large part in determining the extent of economic development of a country (260, 263). One of the striking characteristics of such entrepreneurs is their willingness to take calculated risks, to innovate in ways that have reasonable chances of success. If n Achievement is in fact related to such entrepreneurial behavior, it ought to predispose people in favor of taking moderate risks as opposed to either the extremely speculative or the extremely safe ones. The rationale for predicting such a linkage runs something like this: in an extremely safe undertaking at which anyone can succeed, the person with high n Achievement can get little achievement satisfaction out of accomplishing his objective. In an extremely speculative one, on the other hand, he not only is almost certain to frustrate his achievement aspirations, he also may feel that if he should by some outside chance succeed, his success could not be attributed to his own personal efforts but to luck or circumstances beyond his control.

A previous experiment has shown that subjects with high n Achievement do in fact tend, more than subjects with low n Achievement, to like those occupations which involve some risk or which are part of the entrepreneurial role (263). This preference exists apparently in male subjects over an age range of roughly 18 to 45, and both in Germany and America. Furthermore, Atkinson has shown in a preliminary experiment that female subjects with high n Achievement tend to perform somewhat better at longer odds

[1] I am deeply indebted to the Office of Naval Research for funds necessary to carry out this project, to Roberta Cohen, Leon Gross, and Elliot Aronson for running the subjects and for helping score the protocols.

306

where the chances of winning are 1 out of 3 than do subjects with low n Achievement whose peak performance comes when the chances of winning are 1 out of 2 (Ch. 20). The experiments to be reported here extend the range of risk phenomena to be investigated from occupational preferences and from performance under odds to the choice of the degree of risk under which a person prefers to operate. These are probably all coordinate phenomena, but free choice of the risk to be taken is an essential part of the behavior of entrepreneurs, who must actually seek out certain types of risk situations as well as perform well in them.

The research was performed on young children because the theory of achievement motivation presented elsewhere (272) argues that the motive is formed roughly between the ages of 5 and 9, and if so, its effect on risk-taking behavior should already be apparent at these ages and perhaps in purer form than later when the subjects may have learned all sorts of things about what risks one *ought* to take. Measuring n Achievement at such early ages has only recently become potentially feasible through the development by Aronson (Ch. 17) of a method for scoring for it from expressive "doodles" or scribbles. The words "potentially feasible" need underlining. Aronson found that certain doodle characteristics were fairly consistently correlated with n Achievement scores obtained in the usual way from written stories (272) across a number of samples of subjects, but he worked with male college students, and it is a very large jump indeed from them to five-year-old boys and girls on whom the main experiment to be reported here was performed. The measurement is feasible because five-year-olds can scribble while they cannot be easily got to tell stories yet; there is no certainty that their scribbles will reflect n Achievement at this age the way college student scribbles do at age 18. In fact, there are so many uncertainties or risky assumptions in the design of this experiment that it may be worth summarizing them in advance. It must be assumed 1) that stable individual differences in n Achievement have been formed by age five, 2) that these differences will be reflected in the scribbles children produce, 3) that fairly stable preferences for certain types of risk-taking have also been developed by age five, and 4) that the hypothesized connection between n Achievement and risk-taking exists and has already been developed by this time. Only if all of these assumptions hold can positive results be obtained to support the hypothesis that children with high n Achievement will prefer moderate risks as contrasted with children with low n Achievement who should show more variability in risk-taking behavior with greater choice of extremely safe or speculative risks.

PROCEDURE

Two groups of subjects were employed. The group on which the main experiment was performed consisted of 26 five-year-old children in kindergarten, 13 boys and 13 girls, who were tested individually by a female graduate student. While their background was essentially middle class, it varied widely, some of the children coming from homes of college professors and others from the Italian and Polish lower middle class or lower class homes typical of a city school district in New England. The second group of subjects consisted of 32 eight- and nine-year-olds from a third grade class in a Connecticut manufacturing city. They were tested in a group by a male college undergraduate.

The tests given the children consisted of the following: *the "doodle" measure of n Achievement*. The children were shown very briefly (for about three seconds) a large white piece of cardboard on which the first set of doodles used by Aronson (Design 1) had been drawn in black ink. They were supplied with a standard piece of blank typewriting paper, a box of colored crayons, and instructed to, "Let me see if you can make scribbles like these. If you can't remember all of them, you can make up your own." They were given as much time as they needed to produce some scribbles, and if necessary, were reminded not to draw pictures of things. The same procedure was followed a second time with a different set of doodles (Design 2), also used by Aronson. In the group experiment with the third graders, the only difference was that the doodles had been drawn on slides which were projected briefly on a screen in front of the class. The scribbles produced by the children were scored for the characteristics developed and described elsewhere by Aronson (Ch. 17). These characteristics may be described briefly as follows without going into the details of scoring definitions: *Line*—the number of scribbles (or scorable units) composed of "discrete" lines (characteristic of high n Achievement) minus the number of units composed of "fuzzy" or repetitious lines (characteristic of low n Achievement). *Space*—amount of unused space (characteristic of low n Achievement), computed as the maximum distance from any margin to the nearest mark on the paper. Aronson used the unused space at the bottom of the paper only, and this procedure was followed with the third graders, but with the five-years-olds it could not be used because it was not always clear what was the bottom of the paper since the children frequently changed their orientation with respect to the page. *Form*—the number of diagonals and S-shapes (characteristic of high n Achievement), and the number of multiple waves (characteristic of low n Achievement). The general principle underlying the differences in the scribbling characteristics of high and low n Achievement seems to be an avoidance by the "highs" of repetition, a tendency to use up space, to avoid going over the same line twice, etc., although it should be emphasized that the scoring system was established entirely empirically simply by correlating various characteristics with the standard n Achievement score obtained from content analysis of stories written to pictures. Additionally, since colored crayons were used with the five-year-olds (instead of pencils as in the Aronson experiment and as in the third grade experiment here), there was an opportunity to check a finding reported by Knapp (Ch. 26) that subjects with high n Achievement prefer blues and greens over reds and yellows. So a new measure was obtained, consisting simply of the number of blue or green units minus the number of red or yellow units, with those colors being omitted which were not easily classifiable as belonging either in one category or in the other.

Risk-taking tasks. (1) Ring toss. In the kindergarten study, one of the original Lewin "level of aspiration" tasks was used in which the subject is simply given a rope ring and asked to try and throw it over a peg placed on the floor. The subject is allowed to stand wherever he wants to and can, of course, stand right next to the peg or as far away as six or seven feet. He was given ten trials and the distance at which he stood for each trial was recorded. Obviously the risk of failure increases the further he stands from the peg. (2) The tilting maze board. In this commercial children's toy, a ball is placed at the start of a maze, and the child is supposed to roll it through the maze by manipulating two wheels which control separately the right-left or up-down tilt of the board. The difficulty is that holes are punched at various points throughout the maze path, and the objective is to see how far one can roll the ball before it drops through a hole. The holes are numbered in sequence and the child was asked to trace with his finger through the path to the point he was going to try to reach on the next trial. Each child in the kindergarten group was given ten trials. Again, the further along the path he set his level of aspiration, the greater he risked failure. (3) Dot connection. In the group experiment with the third graders it was not possible to use ring toss, but a group task as much like it as possible was developed. Subjects were instructed to put down as many or as few dots as they wanted to on a piece of paper and then to try and connect them with a line that does not cross itself. The procedure was repeated twice and the score was simply the number of dots that the person put down each time. It appeared obvious to the subjects that the fewer dots he puts down, the easier the task will be just as in the case of ring toss the closer he stands to the peg, the easier it will be to succeed. The fact is, however, that it is impossible to fail at the dot connection task. Any number of dots can be connected by a line that does not cross itself; but it was hoped that subjects would not discover this in the two trials they were given. (4) Word memory. The third graders were asked to write down a list of words which they were to be asked to recall at some later date in the testing. Again, they could put down as many or as few words as they liked. The procedure was repeated twice, and the score was simply the number of words they put down, and also the number which they correctly remembered. This task was more like ring toss in that the subjects could clearly fail, but it had the marked disadvantage that subjects could defeat the purpose of the test by putting down connected phrases or sentences. Other performance tasks were given to both groups of subjects as part of another study.

310   *Motivation and Behavior*

RESULTS

The first question to settle is whether there is any evidence that the scribbles are reflecting n Achievement among the five-year-olds. The most important evidence on this point will be supplied by the relationship between the doodle measure of n Achievement and risk taking, but there are also two other questions which should be answered in the affirmative, if the doodle score is valid. Is it internally consistent or reliable? And does the mean score increase with age as it should according to the general theory of how the

TABLE 1. MEAN NUMBER OF DETERMINANTS OF n ACHIEVEMENT SCORE IN "DOODLES" PRODUCED BY SUBJECTS OF DIFFERENT AGE LEVELS

	Male College Students, aged around 18 ($N = 75$). After Aronson (Ch. 17)			Boys and Girls in Third Grade, aged around 9 ($N = 32$)			Boys and Girls in Kindergarten, aged around 5 ($N = 26$)		
	Doodle Design			Doodle Design			Doodle Design		
	1	2	Total	1	2	Total	1	2	Total
Total units scored	12.25	10.00	22.25	11.58	11.45	23.03	8.54	9.00	17.54
S D			7.64			7.51			8.23
No. "discrete" minus No. "fuzzy" lines $(+)^*$	3.16	5.65	8.81	2.67	4.55	7.22	.23	3.00	3.23
S D			9.94			9.32			7.72
Space from bottom in cm. $(-)$	8.68	8.80	17.48	12.09	10.55	22.64	not comparable		
S D			10.45			13.40			
Total "forms"	6.81	4.49	11.30	3.55	2.34	5.89	2.49	2.80	5.29
S D			5.09			3.41			4.90
Diagonals $(+)$	2.88	2.51	5.39	1.03	.64	1.67	.42	1.19	1.61
S-shapes $(+)$	.77	.54	1.31	.79	.55	1.34	.15	.23	.38
Multiple waves $(-)$	3.16	1.44	4.60	1.73	1.15	2.88	1.92	1.38	3.30

$*$ $+$ = scored positively, $-$ = scored negatively for n Achievement.

achievement motive develops (272)? The answer to the second question is contained in Table 1, which presents the mean number of scorable units and of the determinants of n Achievement score for each of the two doodle Designs for groups of subjects with modal ages of 5, 9, and 18 years. The total number of scorable units does not differ between ages 9 and 18, but the five-year-olds are significantly ($p < .02$) less productive on the average. The *line* score based on the number of "discrete" minus the number of "fuzzy" lines is the best single index of n Achievement developed by Aronson because it correlates highest by itself with n Achievement, probably because it is based on every scorable unit in the subject's protocol. Also, it should not be influenced by sheer quantity of output nor by the capacity of the subjects to produce various shapes. So in the present instance it permits the most unambiguous comparison of changes in mean n Achievement at different age levels. The mean increase it shows from age 5 to 9, though large, is of borderline significance ($t = 1.76$, $p < .10$) because of some extreme scores which make the variability large, but if a simple measure is taken of the proportion of individuals in each group who score above the mean for all 134 cases combined, it turns out that only 18.2% of the five-year-olds are above the mean as compared with 51.5% of the nine-year-olds ($X^2 = 8.28$, $p < .01$) and 54.7% of the 18-year-olds. Obviously this score shows its big increase between age 5 and age 9, which it should if it is really reflecting n Achievement, since this is supposedly the crucial period for the development of the achievement motive. Furthermore, the much smaller and insignificant increase between the ages of 9 and 18 is entirely consistent with the theory that the motive should be largely complete in its development in most people by the age of 9. Actually, of course, the comparison between the 9-year-olds and the 18-year-olds is not really very meaningful because the 18-year-olds are all males and they are from higher socioeconomic status on the average. Either one or both of these factors might be responsible for the slightly larger mean score in the 18-year-old group over and beyond age as such. Since use of space was measured differently for the 5-year-olds, it can be used only to compare the 9- and 18-year-olds. Here the difference is in the same direction as for the line index, showing more use of space (indicating higher n Achievement) at a near significant level ($t = 1.94$, $p \sim .05$) for the older group. The *form* determinants show age trends like those of the other two determinants, although some recomputations are necessary because the younger age groups show many fewer identifiable forms ($p < .001$). This difference in form output can be equated for by converting each of the form subtype means into the proportion they represent of the total form mean. If this is done, the following clearcut results are obtained. At age 18, 59% of the total form mean is accounted for by high n Achievement forms (diagonals and S-shapes) and 41% by low n Achievement forms (multiwave); at age 9 the proportions are 51% to 49%, and at age 5 they are 38% to 62%, respectively, yielding differences in favor of high n Achievement forms of 18%, 2% and -24% at ages 18, 9, and 5, respectively. Again, as in the case of the line score, the increase in high n Achievement indicators between ages 5 and 9 (26%) is larger than the increase between ages 9 and 18 (16%). So far as the figures in Table 1 go then, they support the hypothesis that the doodle measure is reflecting n Achievement since it increases with age just as it should if it were measuring n Achievement.

The other fact of importance to emerge from Table 1 is that the mean number of identifiable forms in both of the children's groups is much smaller and very significantly so ($t < .001$ in each case) than the mean number of identifiable forms for the college students. This finding has a direct bearing on the computation of the total n Achievement score from doodles and, also, on its reliability. Aronson had obtained his total score by simply quartiling the distribution of scores for a given scoring variable in response to the combined doodle Designs 1 and 2 and summing across the quartile scores (reversed in value, of course, for the negative indicators— i.e., use of space, and multiwaves). In the present instance the use of a separate quartile score for each of the three form determinants when they were so much less frequent would possibly weight random variations much more heavily than desirable, particularly as compared with the "discrete-minus-fuzzy line" score which is based on large numbers of instances. Therefore, a new composite "form" score was devised which consisted of the number of diagonals plus the number of S-shapes minus the number of multi-waves. If this score is quartiled and added to the quartile scores for the other two determinants—line and space—the much less frequent forms contribute only 1/3 to the total score instead of a less justifiable 3/5 of the total score for children who have difficulty making identifiable forms. A check of the new composite form score against n Achievement with the 75 subjects in the college student group used by Aronson (see the first column in Table 1) yielded a correlation of $+.23$ ($p < .05$), a value which is higher than the correlation of two of its components with n Achievement in this sample and slightly lower than the other. While the use of the composite form score thus seemed justified on both theoretical and empirical grounds, it had the disadvantage of curtailing somewhat the range of total doodle n Achievement scores by reducing the number of determinants from five to three. This was corrected by quartiling the distributions of scores for each of the three determinants *on each doodle Design separately* and then adding the resulting six quartile scores to obtain the final total score for an individual. This new method of obtaining the total n Achievement score from doodles was also checked against the regular n Achievement score in the same sample of 75 college students and the resulting correlation was .36, which is exactly the same value obtained by Aronson using his method of combining determinants to get a total score.

The internal consistency of the quartile scores can be obtained by correlating those obtained for doodle Design 1 with those for doodle Design 2. For the kindergarten group the correlation proved to be .13, for the 9-year-olds it was .38, which is more nearly comparable to that obtained by Aronson ($r = .44$). The value for the kindergarten group is discouragingly low and insignificant, but it probably is a serious underestimate of the true correlation caused by the coarse grouping of results into quartiles and also by two deviant cases in a very small sample. Several lines of evidence support this conclusion. First, the correlations of the determinant scores between doodle Design 1 and doodle Design 2 before being quartiled are .58 for discrete minus fuzzy lines, .53 for space, and .46 for the combined form score, each of these correlations being significant well beyond the .05 level. Secondly, if the split is made not between doodle Design 1 and doodle Design 2 but between a score made up of a combination of odd vs. even determinants, regardless of which doodle Design they come from, the resultant split-half correlation is $+.30$ (or $+.43$ if one extremely deviant case is discarded). Thirdly, the scores obtained separately from each doodle correlate about the same with a measure of risk-taking behavior explained below. In short, the evidence tends to support the belief that the true reliability of the doodle measure of n Achievement is somewhere around .40 as a conservative estimate, which, corrected for halving the test, comes to between .55 and .60 for the total score. Such a value is not high enough to give one much faith in the test score for a given individual, but it is high enough to demonstrate that there is significant internal consistency in this measure even in young children and to permit using the measure for studies of group differences.

The most important results on risk-taking among subjects with high and low n Achievement are summarized in Figure 1, which shows where the 5-year-olds stood in relation to the peg in the ring-toss task and what the probability of success was at various distances from the peg. The distributions of choice points for throwing are plotted separately for the 12 subjects above and the 14

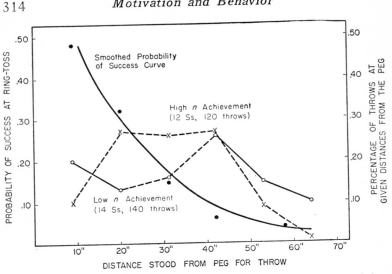

Fig. 1. Percentage of throws made by 5-year-olds with high and low "doodle" n Achievement at different distances from the peg and smoothed curve of probability of success at those distances. 26 Ss, 10 throws each. Plotted at midpoints of intervals of 11 inches beginning with closest distance stood (4"-14", 5"-15", etc.)

subjects below the mean doodle n Achievement score. Obviously the variance of the throwing distances for the "lows" is considerably larger than the variance for the "highs" ($F = 1.83$, $p < .01$). Also, it is clear that, as predicted, the "highs" tend to concentrate their throws in the middle distance ranges (from 20 to 40 inches) where there is moderate probability of success (varying from around $p = .11$ to $p = .30$ to judge by the smoothed curve) whereas the "lows" show a disproportionate tendency to concentrate their shots either very close to the peg or very far away. Actually the grouping necessary to get large enough numbers to plot this graph obscures somewhat how different the "highs" and "lows" are at the extremes. For example, out of the 11 throws made standing as close to the peg as one could get (about 4 inches), 10 of them were made by "lows," whereas at the other extreme, of the 11 throws made at a distance of five feet or more (actually up to seven feet in one case), 10 of 11 of these throws were again made by "lows." While chi-square tests of significance are not strictly legitimate because of the unknown amount of correlation among the observations, they are of some interest as a rough test of significance. For example, if the frequencies in the two extremes of the distribution (farthest and nearest to the peg) are combined, it appears that 30% of the throws made by the "lows" are in these categories, whereas only 11% of the throws made by the "highs" are (chi-square $= 12.8$, $p < .01$). Or if the second farthest category is also added in, nearly 1/2 of the throws (45%) of the "lows" are from extreme positions, whereas only 1/5 of the "highs" are. Differences at each extreme taken separately are also significant. If the frequencies in the nearest or safest category are compared with those in the moderately safe middle distances from 15 to 36 inches, the "lows" show significantly more throws from the safest distance and the "highs" more from the moderately safe distances (chi-square $= 10.74$, $p < .01$). At the other extreme, if the throws from a moderately far distance (37 to 47 inches) are compared with the throws in the "very far" distances (48 inches and up), again the "highs" show significantly more "moderation" and the "lows" more "wild speculation" (chi-square $= 4.70$, $p < .05$).

The results for the tilting maze task are similar except that the distribution of estimates as to how far they could roll the ball is more nearly J-shaped rather than normal as in the case of ring-toss, which means that there is little or no opportunity for a difference between the "highs" and "lows" to show up at the "safe" end of the distribution of risks. That is, the task was so difficult that on 75% of 260 trials the subjects never got beyond the first hole and therefore there was a tendency to pile up levels of aspiration at the low end of the distribution. Nevertheless the difference between the "highs" and the "lows" at the "speculative" end of the distribution could and did show up. A split at the median of the distribution of estimates of how far they would roll the ball on the next trial show that 64% of the estimates of the "lows" were for hole 5 or beyond whereas only 43% of the estimates of the "highs" were this far out (chi-square $= 10.7$, $p < .01$).

To return for a moment to the ring-toss task, one might expect that the subjects with high n Achievement might be more influenced by the actual success that they were having and might tend to gravitate toward a central tendency of the successful throws. Below such a midpoint, success would be easier but less satisfying, while above it, success would be more satisfying but too rare. The mean distance for the successful throws was 23 inches. The average distance at which a child stood on his ten throws was then computed and subtracted from 23 inches to get his deviation from this central tendency of the successful tries. The resulting distribution of deviation scores was badly skewed as inspection of Figure 1 would demonstrate and had to be normalized by a square root transformation. The transformed deviation scores correlated with n

Achievement score $-.40$, $p < .05$, indicating that the higher the subject's n Achievement score, the closer he tended to approximate in his risk-taking the central tendency of the successful throws. The n Achievement score based on each doodle Design is contributing about equally to this correlation, the correlations being $-.32$ for Design 1 alone and $-.28$ for Design 2 alone. Consequently, despite the low correlation between n Achievement scores based on Design 1 and Design 2, there is evidence they are both measuring the same characteristic because each correlates about the same with a third variable—e.g., tendency to take moderate risks.

TABLE 2. FREQUENCIES AND PERCENTAGES OF DIFFERENT NUMBERS OF DOTS PUT DOWN TO BE CONNECTED BY Ss WITH HIGH AND LOW n ACHIEVEMENT

No. of Dots	High (16 Ss, two trials each)		Low (16 Ss, two trials each)	
3-8	2	6%	5	15%
9-14	12	38%	7	22%
15-20	11	34%	6	19%
21-26	3	9%	5	15%
27 & up	4	13%	9	28%

Very similar results were obtained with the third graders, although they are somewhat less dramatic because the tasks used were not as adequate for testing the hypothesis as ring toss was. Table 2 summarizes the distribution of the numbers of dots the subjects with high and low n Achievement put down for themselves to connect. The frequencies are much smaller, but again 43% of the tasks set for themselves by the "lows" fall either in the easiest or the hardest category whereas only 19% of the tasks set for themselves by the "highs" fell in these extreme positions (chi-square $= 4.7$, $p < .05$). There is unfortunately no central tendency of success with this task, and so it was necessary to compute a deviation score simply from the mean number of dots put down for the two trials combined after this distribution of scores had been normalized by a square root transformation. The correlation of n Achievement score with the size of the individual's deviation from the means of these transformed scores was $-.35$, $p < .05$, indicating again that the higher the n Achievement, the closer the subject tended to approximate "moderation" in setting a task for himself to accomplish. It may be noted in passing that in following the principle of transforming scores only when necessary because of an extreme skew in the distribution, *deviations* were transformed in the ring-toss experiment, whereas *raw scores* were transformed in the dot task *before* deviations were computed. However, if the transformations are made the other way in each case, the two resulting correlations of deviation scores with n Achievement do not differ from those reported by more than .01, ($-.41$ for ring toss and $-.34$ for the dot connection task).

Finally, the correlation between n Achievement and the deviation score from the central tendency of the average number of words listed for recall on the two trials in the word memory task was in the predicted direction ($r = -.20$), but insignificant. The reason why it is not larger appears to lie partly in the fact that the distribution of words put down does not show much variability and partly because some of the children put down phrases (e.g., "I love you") which really defeated the purpose of the task as a method of estimating the degree of risk a subject would take in setting an easy or a difficult task for himself.

Could the results obtained be due simply to intelligence? Perhaps the way in which the doodles are scored for n Achievement simply reflects the intelligence of the child, and the more intelligent he is, the more likely he is to take moderate or sensible risks in setting tasks for himself. Unfortunately intelligence test scores were not available on the 5-year-olds, but Otis I.Q.'s were obtainable on 24 of the 32 subjects in the third-grade group. The correlation of these I.Q.'s with the doodle n Achievement score was .08 and with the deviation score estimate of moderate risk taking in the dot connection task was $-.28$. Both fall short of the .40 correlation needed for significance at the 5% level with this number of cases, although the latter correlation suggests that intelligence may also be a factor in influencing children to take calculated or moderate risks.

A final point of interest is the relationship between the doodle n Achievement score and the preference for blues and greens over reds and yellows discovered by Knapp (see Ch. 26). With the 5-year-olds who used colored crayons in making their doodles the correlation was a substantial .45, $p < .05$, suggesting that this color preference may appear quite early in life and perhaps should be added as a determinant of the total n Achievement score obtained from doodles along with line, space, and form. It was added in the present experiment, and the correlation with the deviation score from the mean of the successful throws was recomputed. It dropped from $-.40$ to $-.30$, which is below the level of significance with this number of subjects. Unfortunately the sample is so small that it is hard to evaluate the significance of this drop, but the safest conclusion would appear to be that color preference in the doodle task ought to be correlated with the standard n Achievement score in several cross-validating groups as Aronson did with the other determinants before it is added to them.

DISCUSSION

This study itself represents a rather risky enterprise in that it involved a chain of at least four rather dubious assumptions, any one of which might not have been correct. The fact that positive results were obtained tends to strengthen confidence in all four of the assumptions, namely that individual differences in n Achievement have appeared by age 5, that doodles will sufficiently reflect those differences, that individual differences in risk taking have also appeared by age 5, and that n Achievement tends to predispose children even at this age toward taking moderate risks. Of particular importance is the evidence that n Achievement may be measured in children from their scribbles because the standard method of measuring n Achievement is not readily applicable during the crucial time period when the motive is supposed to be developed. To summarize, this evidence consists of a number of facts. First, there is significant internal consistency in the individual characteristics that make up the total doodle n Achievement score by age 5, indicating that children have developed characteristic ways of scribbling by the age of 5 which are stable from doodle to doodle. Secondly, the shift in mean scores for the determinants with age corresponds to the way n Achievement should increase with age, even to the point of there being a larger shift from age 5 to 9 than from age 9 to 18 (although this last comparison is not really legitimate because the groups are not matched). Third, the n Achievement score based on children's doodles will correctly predict which ones will tend to take moderate risks and which ones will swing between extremely safe and extremely speculative undertakings. It is of further interest to note that in the ring-toss experiment the distance at which the "highs" and "lows" differed most—namely, a median distance of 20 inches—showed a probability of success ($p = .32$) that was practically identical with the odds in Atkinson's experiment ($p = .33$) at which his subjects with high n Achievement (measured in the standard way) showed the greatest superiority in performance over subjects with low n Achievement (Ch. 20).

As an additional piece of evidence for this point it is worth noting in passing that the five-year-olds were also given the task of sorting 20 ESP cards into their respective suits in 30 seconds as part of another study and that subjects who were above the median in their performance on this task were also significantly more often above the median in n Achievement score based on doodles (chi-square $= 3.89$, $p < .05$). In other words, the subjects with presumed higher n Achievement based on their doodles actually performed better at a card-sorting task, and since faster performance was one of the basic validating criteria initially for the verbal n Achievement score, this may be taken as a fourth fact in support of the belief that what is being measured in the doodles is really n Achievement. As a fifth bit of supporting evidence for this belief, one could also cite the fact that the relationship between doodle n Achievement score and risk-taking was found not only once with five-year-olds but a second time with an older group of third graders. A sixth reason for accepting the doodle score as a measure of n Achievement lies in the fact that a possible alternative explanation of the results as being due to intelligence has apparently been ruled out by the zero order correlation of the score with intelligence. A seventh reason is the confirmation of the preference for blues and greens over yellows and reds among subjects with high n Achievement, a finding originally obtained by Knapp with the standard n Achievement score (Ch. 26). Finally, of course, one might reasonably expect that since Aronson found that the doodle score was significantly correlated with the verbal n Achievement score around age 18, the two measures should also correlate at earlier ages.

If we may accept the fact for the moment that we are really dealing with n Achievement in the doodle score, then the obtained relationship to risk-taking behavior has very important social and economic implications. What it suggests is that countries characterized by a low general level of n Achievement will contain a very high percentage of individuals who would be attracted simultaneously to very safe undertakings (as in traditionalist agriculture) and to fairly wild speculations in which the gain is very great but the probability of winning very small (as in lotteries). On the other hand, they will contain a very small percentage of individuals with high n Achievement who will be attracted to moderate risks with smaller gains but with greater probability of success. Yet it is this very class of entrepreneurs taking moderate risks who play a key role in successful social innovation and economic development. Furthermore, that both n Achievement and risk-taking propensities seem to be developed so early in life, too early for them to be part of the conscious ideational system of the child in all probability, is a fact which suggests the difficulty that later learning may have in modifying these early and partly unconscious tendencies. Consequently, even thorough knowledge of the value of moderate risk-taking, if acquired by subjects with low n Achievement later in life, may have little or no effect on the risks that they actually choose to take. In short, the data suggest that if one wants to modify n Achievement and risk-taking behavior at the time they are most easily influenced—e.g., at the time they are being formed —one will have to begin early, probably with the kind of independence and mastery training found by Winterbottom (Ch. 33) to be correlated with high n Achievement if it occurred roughly before the age of 8. The development of socially and economically backward areas by an indigenous class of entrepreneurs may then ultimately depend on changes in the home and in the preschool and early school years, rather than on adult education of the sort usually supported in foreign aid programs.

Finally, one may ask why it is that subjects with high n Achievement should prefer moderate risks, although the data do not admit of a really definitive answer. At the safe end of the continuum one may speculate that they take somewhat longer risks than the "lows" either because their confidence in their own ability is such that the subjective probability of success is increased over what it actually is or because their higher achievement drive would not be sufficiently rewarded by such a "safe" success, or both (cf. Ch. 20). At the speculative end of the continuum, they may reject some of the more extreme risks taken by the "lows" either because failure is more painful to them with their higher achievement drive or because they may be able to take very little personal credit for success if it comes in such a lucky enterprise, or both.

SUMMARY

The relationship of n Achievement to risk taking was studied in two groups of boys and girls, one consisting of 26 children in kindergarten, the other of 32 in third grade. The method of measuring n Achievement involved a technique of scoring doodles developed by Aronson which turned out to be applicable to younger children provided a slight change was made in the method of combining scores on the separate determinants to take account of the significantly lower number of identifiable forms in the protocols of the children. This method of assessing achievement motivation seems to be reasonably adequate since it showed: internal consistency, mean increases in determinant scores with age, no relationship to I.Q., in both groups tested a significant relationship to risk taking as predicted from previous research and theory on the achievement motive, and the capacity to discriminate those subjects who did well in a card-sorting task from those who did not. Confirmation of a tendency found by Knapp for subjects with high n Achievement to prefer blues and greens over reds and yellows was also obtained suggesting that color may be an additional determinant that can be added to the use of lines, space, and forms which currently goes to make up the doodle n Achievement score.

With both groups of subjects, individuals with high n Achievement (as measured by the doodle technique) tended to take moderate risks while subjects with low n Achievement preferred significantly more often either very safe or very speculative enterprises. The possible psychological reasons for this association and its implications for the development of backward countries are briefly discussed.

CHAPTER 22

....

Motivational Determinants of Risk-Taking Behavior*

JOHN W. ATKINSON[1]

THERE ARE two problems of behavior which any theory of motivation must come to grips with. They may finally reduce to one, but it will simplify the exposition which follows to maintain the distinction in this paper. The first problem is to account for an individual's selection of one path of action among a set of possible alternatives. The second problem is to account for the amplitude or vigor of the action tendency once it is initiated and for its tendency to persist for a time in a given direction. This paper will deal with these questions in a conceptual framework suggested by research which has used thematic apperception to assess individual differences in strength of achievement motivation (24, 260, 272).

The problem of selection arises in experiments which allow the individual to choose a task among alternatives which differ in difficulty (level of aspiration). The problem of accounting for the vigor of response arises in studies which seek to relate individual differences in strength of motivation to the level of performance when response output at a particular task is the dependent variable. In treating these two problems, the discussion will be constantly focused on the relationship of achievement motivation to risk-taking behavior, an important association uncovered by McClelland (263) in the investigation of the role of achievement motivation in entrepreneurship and economic development.

Earlier studies have searched for a theoretical principle which would explain the relationship of strength of motive, as inferred from thematic apperception, to overt goal-directed performance. The

*Reprinted by permission of author and publisher from the *Psychological Review*, 1957, **64**, 359-372. Copyright 1957 by the American Psychological Association, Inc.
[1] I wish to acknowledge the stimulation and criticism of colleagues at the Center for Advanced Study in the Behavioral Sciences (1955-56) and current support for this research by a grant from the Ford Foundation.

effect of situation cues—e.g., of particular instructions—on this relationship was detected quite early (24), and subsequent experiments have suggested a theoretical formulation similar to that presented by Tolman (414) and Rotter (353). It has been proposed that *n* Achievement scores obtained from thematic apperception are indices of individual differences in the strength of achievement motive, conceived as a relatively stable disposition to strive for achievement or success. This motive disposition is presumed to be latent until aroused by situation cues which indicate that some performance will be instrumental to achievement. The strength of *aroused* motivation to achieve as manifested in performance has been viewed as a function of both the strength of motive and the *expectancy* of goal attainment aroused by situation cues. This conception has provided a fairly adequate explanation of experimental results to date, and several of its implications have been tested (24; Ch. 19).

The similarity of this conception to the expectancy principle of performance developed by Tolman, which also takes account of the effects of a third variable, *incentive,* suggested the need for experiments to isolate the effects on motivation of variations in strength of expectancy of success and variations in the incentive value of particular accomplishments. The discussion which follows was prompted by the results of several exploratory experiments (Chs. 20 and 21). It represents an attempt to state explicitly how individual differences in the strength of achievement-related motives influence behavior in competitive achievement situations. A theoretical model will be presented first, and then a brief summary of some experimental evidence will be introduced to call the reader's attention to the kinds of research problems it raises and the scope of its implications.

Three variables require definition and, ultimately, independent measurement. The three variables are *motive, expectancy,* and *incentive.* Two of these, expectancy and incentive, are similar to variables presented by Tolman (414) and Rotter (353). An expectancy is a cognitive anticipation, usually aroused by cues in a situation, that performance of some act will be followed by a particular consequence. The strength of an expectancy can be represented as the subjective probability of the consequence, given the act.

The incentive variable has been relatively ignored or at best crudely defined in most research. It represents the relative attractiveness of a specific goal that is offered in a situation or the relative unattractiveness of an event that might occur as a consequence of some act. Incentives may be manipulated experimentally as, for example, when amount of food (reward) or amount of shock (punishment) are varied in research with animals.

The third variable in this triumvirate, motive, is here conceived differently than, for example, in the common conception of motivation as nondirective but energizing *drive* (48). A motive is conceived as a disposition to strive for a certain kind of satisfaction, as a capacity for satisfaction in the attainment of a certain class of incentives. The names given motives—such as achievement, affiliation, power—are really names of classes of incentives which produce essentially the same kind of experience of satisfaction: pride in accomplishment, or the sense of belonging and being warmly received by others, or the feeling of being in control and influential. McClelland (see Ch. 32 and 258, pp. 341-352) has presented arguments to support the conception of motives as relatively general and stable characteristics of the personality which have their origins in early childhood experience. The idea that a motive may be considered a *capacity for satisfaction* is suggested by Winterbottom's (272; Ch. 33) finding that children who are strong in achievement motive are rated by teachers as deriving more pleasure from success than children who are weak in achievement motive.

The general aim of one class of motives, usually referred to as appetites or approach tendencies, is to maximize satisfaction of some kind. The achievement motive is considered a disposition to approach success.

The aim of another class of motives is to minimize pain. These have been called aversions or avoidant tendencies. An avoidance motive represents the individual's capacity to experience pain in connection with certain kinds of negative consequences of acts. The motive to avoid failure is considered a disposition to avoid failure and/or a capacity for experiencing shame and humiliation as a consequence of failure.

The principle of motivation. The strength of motivation to perform some act is assumed to be a multiplicative function of the strength of the motive, the expectancy (subjective probability) that the act will have as a consequence the attainment of an incentive, and the value of the incentive: Motivation = f (Motive × Expectancy × Incentive). This formulation corresponds to Tolman's (414) analysis of performance except, perhaps, in the conception of a motive as a relatively stable disposition. When both motivation to approach and motivation to avoid are simultaneously aroused, the resultant motivation is the algebraic summation of approach and avoidance. The act which is performed among a set of alternatives is the act for which the resultant motivation is most positive. The magnitude of response and the persistence of behavior are functions of the strength of motivation to perform the act relative to the strength of motivation to perform competing acts.

Recent experiments (Ch. 19) have helped to clarify one problem concerning the relationship between measures of the strength of a particular motive (*n* Achievement) and performance. Performance is positively related to the strength of a particular motive only when an expectancy of satisfying that motive through performance has been aroused and when expectancies of satisfying other motives through the same action have not been sufficiently aroused to confound the simple relationship. This is to say no more than when expectancies of attaining several different kinds of incentives are equally *salient* in a situation, the determination of motivation to perform an act is very complex. Performance is then overdetermined in the sense that its strength is now a function of the several different kinds of motivation which have been aroused. The *ideal situation* for showing the relationship between the strength of a particular motive and behavior is one in which the only *reason* for acting is to satisfy that motive.

The theoretical formulation which follows pertains to such an *ideal achievement-related situation,* which is at best only approximated in actual experimentation or in the normal course of everyday life. The discussion will deal only with the effects of the two motives, to achieve and to avoid failure, normally aroused whenever performance is likely to be evaluated against some standard of excellence.

Behavior directed towards achievement and away from failure. The problem of selection is confronted in the level of aspiration situation where the individual must choose among tasks which differ in degree of difficulty. The problem of accounting for the vigor of performance arises in the situation which shall be referred to as *constrained performance.* Here there is no opportunity for the individual to choose his own task. He is simply given a task to perform. He must, of course, decide to perform the task rather than to leave the situation. There *is* a problem of selection. In referring to this situation as constrained performance, it is the author's intention to deal only with those instances of behavior in which motivation for the alternative of leaving the situation is less positive or more negative than for performance of the task that is presented. Hence the individual does perform the task that is given. The level of performance is the question of interest.

Elaboration of the implications of the multiplicative combination of motive, expectancy, and incentive proposed to account for strength of motivation will be instructive if we can find some reasonable basis for assigning numbers to the different variables. The strength of expectancy can be represented as a subjective probability ranging from 0 to 1.00. But the problem of defining the positive incentive value of a particular accomplishment and the negative incentive value of a particular failure is a real stickler.

In past discussions of level of aspiration, Escalona and Festinger (see 231) have assumed that, within limits, the attractiveness of success is a positive function of the difficulty of the task and the unattractiveness of failure is a negative function of difficulty, when the type of activity is held constant. The author will go a few steps farther with these ideas and assume that degree of difficulty can be inferred from the subjective probability of success (P_s). The task an individual finds difficult is one for which his subjective probability of success (P_s) is very low. The task an individual finds easy is one for which his subjective probability of success (P_s) is very high. Now we are in a position to make simple assumptions about the incentive values of success or failure at a particular task. Let us assume that the incentive value of success (I_s) is a positive linear function of difficulty. If so, the value $1 - P_s$ can represent I_s, the incentive value of success. When P_s is high (e.g., .90), an easy task, I_s is low (e.g., .10). When P_s is low (e.g., .10), a difficult task, I_s is high (e.g., .90). The negative incentive value of failure (I_f) can be taken as $-P_s$. When P_s is high (e.g., .90), a very easy task, the sense of humiliation accompanying failure is also very great (e.g., $-.90$). However, when P_s is low (e.g., .10), a very difficult task, there is little embarrassment in failing (e.g., $-.10$). We assume, in other words, that the (negative) incentive value of failure (I_f) is a negative linear function of difficulty. It is of some importance to recognize the dependence of incentive values intrinsic to achievement and failure on the subjective probability of success. One cannot anticipate the thrill of a great accomplishment if, as a matter of fact, he faces what seems a very easy task. Nor does an individual experience only a minor sense of pride after some extraordinary feat against what seemed to him overwhelming odds. The implications of the scheme which follows rest heavily upon the assumption of such a dependence.

In Table 1, values of 1 have been arbitrarily assigned to the achievement motive (M_s) and the motive to avoid failure (M_f). Table 1 contains the strength of motivation to approach success ($M_s \times P_s \times I_s$) and motivation to avoid failure ($M_f \times P_f \times I_f$) through performance of nine different tasks labeled A through I. The tasks differ in degree of difficulty as inferred from the subjective probability of success (P_s). The incentive values of success and failure at each of the tasks have been calculated directly from the assumption that

TABLE 1. AROUSED MOTIVATION TO ACHIEVE (APPROACH) AND TO AVOID FAILURE (AVOIDANCE) AS A JOINT FUNCTION OF MOTIVE (M), EXPECTANCY (P), AND INCENTIVE (I), WHERE $I_s = (1 - P_s)$ AND $I_f = (-P_s)$

	Motivation to Achieve				Motivation to Avoid Failure				Resultant Motivation
	$M_s \times P_s \times I_s =$			Approach	$M_f \times P_f \times I_f =$			Avoidance	(Approach- Avoidance)
Task A	1	.10	.90	.09	1	.90	$-.10$	$-.09$	0
Task B	1	.20	.80	.16	1	.80	$-.20$	$-.16$	0
Task C	1	.30	.70	.21	1	.70	$-.30$	$-.21$	0
Task D	1	.40	.60	.24	1	.60	$-.40$	$-.24$	0
Task E	1	.50	.50	.25	1	.50	$-.50$	$-.25$	0
Task F	1	.60	.40	.24	1	.40	$-.60$	$-.24$	0
Task G	1	.70	.30	.21	1	.30	$-.70$	$-.21$	0
Task H	1	.80	.20	.16	1	.20	$-.80$	$-.16$	0
Task I	1	.90	.10	.09	1	.10	$-.90$	$-.09$	0

incentive value of success equals $1 - P_s$ and incentive value of failure equals $-P_s$; and P_s and P_f are assumed to add to 1.00.

Table 1 may be considered an extension of ideas presented in the *resultant valence* theory of level of aspiration by Escalona and Festinger (231). The present formulation goes beyond their earlier proposals (*a*) in making specific assumptions regarding the incentive values of success and failure, and (*b*) in stating explicitly how individual differences in strength of achievement motive and motive to avoid failure influence motivation.[2]

When the achievement motive is stronger $(M_s > M_f)$. The right-hand column of Table 1 shows the resultant motivation for each of the tasks in this special case where achievement motive and motive to avoid failure are equal in strength. In every case there is an approach-avoidance conflict with resultant motivation equal to 0. This means that if the achievement motive were stronger than the motive to avoid failure, for example if we assigned it a value of 2, the resultant moti-

---

[2] In the resultant valence theory of level of aspiration, the resultant force (f*) for a particular level of difficulty equals probability of success (P_s) times valence of success (Va_s) minus probability of failure (P_f) times valence of failure (Va_f). It is assumed that the valence of a goal [$Va(G)$] depends partly on the properties of the activity and specific goal (G) and partly on the state of need [$t(G)$] of the person, [$Va(G) = F(G,t(G))$] (230, p. 273). In the present conception, the relative rewarding or punishing properties of specific goals (i.e., incentives) and the more general disposition of the person towards a class of incentives (i.e., his motive) are given independent status.

vation would become positive for each of the tasks and its magnitude would be the same as in the column labeled Approach. Let us therefore consider only the strength of approach motivation for each of the tasks to see the implications of the model for the person in whom the need for achievement is stronger than his disposition to avoid failure.

One thing is immediately apparent. Motivation to achieve is strongest when uncertainty regarding the outcome is greatest, i.e., when P_s equals .50. If the individual were confronted with all of these tasks and were free to set his own goal, he should choose Task E where P_s is .50, for this is the point of maximum approach motivation. The strength of motivation to approach decreases as P_s increases from .50 to near certainty of success ($P_s = .90$), and it also decreases as P_s decreases from .50 to near certainty of failure ($P_s = .10$).

If this person were to be confronted with a single task in what is here called the constrained performance situation, we should expect him to manifest strongest motivation in the performance of a task of intermediate difficulty where P_s equals .50. If presented either more difficult tasks or easier tasks, the strength of motivation manifested in performance should be lower. The relationship between strength of motivation as expressed in performance level and expectancy of success at the task, in other words, should be described by a bell-shaped curve.

When the motive to avoid failure is stronger $(M_f > M_s)$. Let us now ignore the strength of approach motivation and tentatively assign it a value of 0 in order to examine the implications of the model for any case in which the motive to avoid failure is the stronger motive. The resultant motivation for each task would then correspond to the values listed in the column labeled Avoidance.

What should we expect of the person in whom the disposition to avoid failure is stronger than the motive to achieve? It is apparent at once that the resultant motivation for every task would be negative for him. This person should want to avoid all of the tasks. Competitive achievement situations are unattractive to him. If, however, he is constrained (e.g., by social pressures) and asked to set his level of aspiration, he should *avoid* tasks of intermediate difficulty ($P_s = .50$) where the arousal of anxiety about failure is greatest. He should choose either the easiest ($P_s = .90$) or the most difficult task ($P_s = .10$). The strength of avoidant motivation is weakest at these two points.

In summary, the person in whom the achievement motive is stronger should set his level of aspiration in the intermediate zone where there is moderate risk. To the extent that he has any motive to avoid failure, this means he will voluntarily choose activities that *maximize* his own anxiety about failure! On the other hand, the person in whom the motive to avoid failure is stronger either should select the easiest of the alternatives or should be extremely speculative and set his goal where there is virtually no chance for success. These are activities which *minimize* his anxiety about failure.

How does the more fearful person behave when offered only a specific task to perform? He can either perform the task or leave the field. If he chooses to leave the field, there is no problem. But if he is constrained, as he must be to remain in any competitive achievement situation, he will stay at the task and presumably work at it. But how hard will he work at it? He is motivated to avoid failure, and when constrained, there is only one path open to him to avoid failure—success at the task he is presented. So we expect him to manifest the strength of his motivation to avoid failure in performance of the task. He too, in other words, should *try hardest*[3] when P_s is .50 and less hard when the chance of winning is either greater or less. The 50-50 alternative is the last he would choose if allowed to set his own goal, but once constrained he must try hard to avoid the failure which threatens him. Not working at all will guarantee failure of the task. Hence the thought of not working at all should produce even stronger avoidant motivation than that aroused by the task itself.

In other words, irrespective of whether the stronger motive is to achieve or to avoid failure, the strength of motivation to perform a task when no alternatives are offered and the individual is constrained should be greatest when P_s is .50. This is the condition of greatest uncertainty regarding the outcome. But when there are alternatives which differ in difficulty, the choice of level of aspiration by persons more disposed to avoid failure is diametrically opposite to that of persons more disposed to seek success. The person more motivated to achieve should prefer a moderate risk. His level of aspiration will fall at the point where his positive motivation is strongest, at the point where the odds seem to be 50-50. The fearful person, on the other hand, must select a task even though all the alternatives are threatening to him. He prefers the least threatening of the available alternatives: either the task which is so easy he cannot fail or the task which is so difficult that failure would be no cause for self-blame and embarrassment.

The tendency for anxious persons to set either extremely high or

---

[3] I do not mean to exclude the possibility that the very anxious person may suffer a performance decrement due to the arousal of some "task-irrelevant" avoidant responses as proposed in the interpretation of research which has employed the Mandler-Sarason Measure of Test Anxiety (248).

very low aspirations has been noted over and over again in the literature on level of aspiration (231). Typically, *groups* of persons for whom the inference of greater anxiety about failure seems justified on the basis of some personality assessment show a much greater variance in level of aspiration than persons whose motivation is inferred to be more normal or less anxious. When the details of behavior are examined, it turns out that they are setting their aspiration level either *defensively* high or *defensively* low.

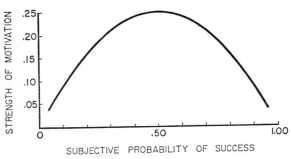

Fig. 1. Strength of motivation to achieve or to avoid failure as a function of the subjective probability of success, i.e., the difficulty of the task.

Without further assumptions, the theory of motivation which has been presented when applied to competitive achievement activity implies that the relationship of constrained performance to expectancy of goal attainment should take the bell-shaped form shown in Figure 1 whether the predominant motive is to achieve or to avoid failure. Further, the theory leads to the prediction of exactly opposite patterns for setting the level of aspiration when the predominant motivation is approach and avoidant as shown in Figure 2.

Both of these hypotheses have been supported in recent experiments. The author (Ch. 20) offered female college students a modest monetary prize for good performance at two 20-minute tasks. The probability of success was varied by instructions which informed the subject of the number of persons with whom she was in competition and the number of monetary prizes to be given. The stated probabilities were 1/20, 1/3, 1/2, and 3/4. The level of performance was higher at the intermediate probabilities than at the extremes for subjects having high thematic apperceptive n Achievement scores and also for subjects who had low n Achievement scores, presumably a more fearful group.

McClelland (Ch. 21) has shown the diametrically opposite tendencies in choice of level of aspiration in studies of children in kindergarten and the third grade. One of the original level-of-aspiration experiments, the ring-toss experiment, was repeated with five-year-olds, and a nonverbal index of the strength of achievement motive was employed. Children who were high in n Achievement more frequently set their level of aspiration in the intermediate range of difficulty. They took more shots from a modest distance. Children who were low in n Achievement showed a greater preponderance of

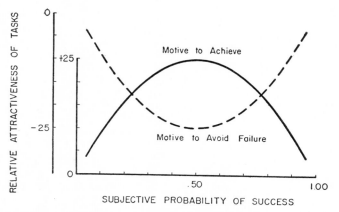

Fig. 2. Relative attractiveness of tasks which differ in subjective probability of success (i.e., in difficulty). Avoidance curve is inverted to show that very difficult and very easy tasks arouse less fear of failure and hence are less unattractive than moderately difficult tasks.

choices at the extreme levels of difficulty. They more often stood right on top of the peg or stood so far away that success was virtually impossible. the same difference between high and low n Achievement groups was observed on another task with children in the third grade. McClelland views these results as consistent with his theoretical argument concerning the role of achievement motivation in entrepreneurship and economic development (260). He has called attention to the relationship between achievement motivation and an interest in enterprise which requires moderate or calculated risks rather than very safe or highly speculative undertakings.

In an experiment designed for another purpose, Clark, Teevan, and Ricciuti (Ch. 41) have presented results with college students comparable to those of McClelland. Immediately before a final examination in a college course, students were asked a series of questions pertaining to grade expectations, affective reactions to grades, and the grade they would *settle for* if excused from taking the exam.

A number of indices were derived from responses to these questions to classify the students as *hopeful of success,* i.e., if the *settle-for* grade was near the maximum grade the student thought he could possibly achieve; *fearful of failure,* i.e., if the *settle-for* grade was near the minimum grade the student thought he might possibly drop to; and *intermediate,* i.e., if the *settle-for* grade fell somewhere between these two extremes. Previously obtained n Achievement scores were significantly higher for the *intermediate* group than for the two groups who set either extremely high or low levels of aspiration.

In terms of the model presented in Table 1, the two extreme patterns of aspirant behavior which are here designated *hope of success* and *fear of failure* are to be considered two *phenotypically* dissimilar alternatives that are *genotypically* similar; that is, they both function to avoid or reduce anxiety for the person in whom the motive to avoid failure is stronger than the motive to achieve.

A question may arise concerning the legitimacy of inferring relatively stronger motive to avoid failure from a low n Achievement score in thematic apperception. The inference seems justified on several counts. First, the kind of learning experience which is thought to contribute to the development of a positive motive to achieve (Ch. 33) seems incompatible with the kind of experience which would contribute to the development of an avoidant motive. In any specific early learning experience in which successful independent accomplishment is encouraged and rewarded, it seems impossible for incompetence, at the same time, to be punished. Second, even if it is assumed that high and low n Achievement groups may be equal in the disposition to be fearful of failure, the fact that one group does not show evidence of a strong motive to achieve (the group with low n Achievement scores) suggests that fear of failure should be *relatively* stronger in that group than in the group which does show evidence of strong n Achievement (high n Achievement scores). Finally, Raphelson (Ch. 23) has presented evidence that n Achievement, as measured in thematic apperception, is *negatively* related to both scores on the Mandler-Sarason Scale of Test Anxiety and a psychogalvanic index of manifest anxiety obtained in a test situation. Test anxiety scores and the psychogalvanic index of manifest anxiety were *positively* correlated, as they should be if each is an effective measure of fear aroused in a competitive situation.

Although a low n Achievement score can hardly be viewed as a direct index of the disposition to avoid failure, there seems good presumptive evidence that fear of failure is *relatively* stronger than the achievement motive in such a group. And this presumption is all the theory demands in order to explain the pattern of goal setting which focuses upon the extremes in the range of difficulty among persons low in *n* Achievement.

The details of the exploratory experiments suggest that one further assumption be made. In both experiments, the high *n* Achievement groups showed evidence of maximum motivation when the observed or stated probability of success was approximately .33. At this point, the high *n* Achievement group showed the highest level of constrained performance. And this point was most favored by the high *n* Achievement group in setting level of aspiration in the McClelland experiment. The assumption to be made seems a reasonable one: the relative strength of a motive influences the subjective probability of the consequence consistent with that motive—biases it upwards. In other words, the stronger the achievement motive relative to the motive to avoid failure, the higher the subjective probability of success given stated odds. The stronger the motive to avoid failure relative to the achievement motive, the higher the subjective probability of failure, given stated odds or any other objective basis for inferring the strength of expectancy. Some evidence from two earlier studies is pertinent. When subjects stated the score they *expected* to make on a test with very ambiguous or conflicting cues from past performance (272, p. 247) or when faced with a novel task at which they had no experience (334), the stated level of *expectation* was positively related to *n* Achievement. The biasing effect of the motive on subjective probability should diminish with repeated learning experience in the specific situation.

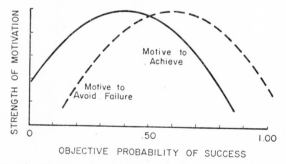

Fig. 3. Strength of motivation to achieve and to avoid failure as a function of the *objective* probability of success. It is assumed that the subjective probability of the consequence consistent with the stronger motive is biased upwards.

When this assumption is made, the point of maximum motivation to achieve now occurs where the stated (objective) odds are somewhat *lower* than .50; and the point of maximum motivation to avoid failure occurs at a point somewhat higher than stated odds of .50, as shown in Figure 3. The implications of this assumption for constrained performance in somewhat novel situations are evident in the figure. When the achievement motive is stronger than the motive to avoid failure, there should be a tendency for stronger motivation to be expressed in performance when the objective odds are long, i.e., below .50. When the motive to avoid failure is stronger than the achievement motive, there should be greater motivation expressed when the objective odds are short, i.e., above .50.

The effects of success and failure. Let us return to the model and ask: What are the effects of success and failure on the level of motivation? We may refer back to Table 1 to answer this question. First, let us consider the effects of success or failure on the level of motivation in a person whose motive to achieve is stronger than his motive to avoid failure. In the usual level of aspiration situation, he should initially set his goal where P_s equals .50. In Table 1, this is Task E. If he succeeds at the task, P_s should increase. And assuming that the effects of success and failure generalize to similar tasks, the P_s at Task D which was initially .40 should increase towards .50. On the next trial, P_s at Task E is now greater than .50, and P_s at Task D now approaches .50. The result of this change in P_s is diminished motivation to achieve at the old task, E, and increased motivation to achieve at Task D, *an objectively more difficult task.* The observed level of aspiration should increase in a steplike manner following success because there has been a change in motivation.

A further implication of the change in strength of motivation produced by the experience of success is of great consequence: given a single, very difficult task (e.g., $P_s = .10$), the effect of continued success in repeated trials is first a gradual increase in motivation as P_s increases to .50, followed by a gradual decrease in motivation as P_s increases further to the point of certainty ($P_s = 1.00$). Ultimately, as P_s approaches 1.00, satiation or loss of interest should occur. The task no longer arouses any motivation at all. Why? Because the subjective probability of success is so high that the incentive value is virtually zero. Here is the clue to understanding how the achievement motive can remain insatiable while satiation can occur for a particular line of activity. The strength of motive can remain unchanged, but interest in a particular task can diminish completely. Hence, when free to choose, the person who is stronger in achievement motive should always look for new and more difficult tasks as he masters old problems. If constrained, the person with a strong achievement motive should experience a gradual loss of interest in his work. If the task is of intermediate difficulty to start with ($P_s = .50$), or is definitely easy ($P_s > .50$), his interest should begin to wane after the initial experience of success.

But what of the effect of failure on the person who is more highly motivated to achieve than to avoid failure? Once more we look at the Approach column of Table 1. If he has chosen Task E ($P_s = .50$) to start with and fails at it, the P_s is reduced. Continued failure will mean that soon Task F (formerly $P_s = .60$) will have a P_s near .50. He should shift his interest to this task, which was *objectively less difficult* in the initial ordering of tasks. This constitutes what has been called a lowering of the level of aspiration. He has moved to the easier task as a consequence of failure.

What is the effect of continued failure at a single task? If the initial task is one that appeared relatively easy to the subject (e.g., $P_s = .80$) and he fails, his motivation should increase! The P_s will drop towards .70, but the incentive value or attractiveness of the task will increase. Another failure should increase his motivation even more. This will continue until the P_s has dropped to .50. Further failure should then lead to a gradual weakening of motivation as P_s decreases further. In other words, the tendency of persons who are relatively strong in achievement motive to persist at a task in the face of failure is probably attributable to the relatively high subjective probability of success they start with. Hence failure has the effect of increasing the strength of their motivation, at least for a time. Ultimately, however, interest in the task will diminish if there is continued failure. If the initial task is perceived by the person as very difficult to start with ($P_s < .50$), motivation should begin to diminish with the first failure.

Let us turn now to the effect of success and failure on the motivation of the person who is more strongly disposed to be fearful of failure. If the person in whom the motive to avoid failure is stronger has chosen a very difficult task in setting his level of aspiration (e.g., Task A where $P_s = .10$) and succeeds, P_s increases and his motivation *to avoid* the task is paradoxically increased. It would almost make sense for him to deliberately fail in order to keep from being faced with a stronger threat on the second trial. If there are more difficult alternatives, he should raise his level of aspiration to avoid anxiety! Fortunately for this person, his strategy (determined by the nature of his motivation) in choosing a very difficult task to start with protects him from this possibility because P_s is so small that he will seldom face the paradoxical problem just described. If he fails at the most difficult task, as is likely, P_s decreases further, P_f increases further, and the aroused motivation to avoid failure is reduced. By continued failure he further reduces the amount of anxiety about failure that is aroused by this most difficult task. Hence, he should continue to set his level at this point. If he plays the game long enough and fails continuously, the probability of failure increases for all levels of difficulty. Sooner or later the minimal motivation to avoid failure at the most difficult task may be indistinguishable from the motivation to avoid failure at the next most difficult task. This may ultimately allow him to change his level of aspiration to a somewhat less difficult task without acting in gross contradiction to the principle of motivation proposed.

If our fearful subject has initially chosen the easiest task (Task I where $P_s = .90$) and he fails, P_s decreases towards .80 and his motivation to avoid the task also increases. If there is no easier task, the most difficult task should now appear least *unattractive* to him and he should jump from the easiest to the most difficult task. In other words, continued failure at a very easy task decreases P_s towards .50; and, as Table 1 shows, a change of this sort is accompanied by increased arousal of avoidant motivation. A wild and apparently irrational jump in level of aspiration from very easy to very difficult tasks, as a consequence of failure, might be mistakenly interpreted as a possible effort on the part of the subject to gain social approval by seeming to set high goals. The present model predicts this kind of activity without appealing to some extrinsic motive. It is part of the strategy of minimizing expected pain of failure after one has failed at the easiest task.

If our fear-disposed subject is successful at the most simple task, his P_s increases, his P_f decreases, and his motivation to avoid this task decreases. The task becomes less and less unpleasant. He should continue playing the game with less anxiety.

Table 1, when taken in its entirety, deals with the special case of the person in whom the two motives are exactly equal in strength. The implications are clear. In the constrained performance situation, he should work hardest when the probability of success is .50 because motivation to achieve and motivation to avoid failure will summate in the constrained instrumental act which is at the same time the pathway towards success and away from failure. (This summation should also occur in the cases where one motive is stronger.) But in the level-of-aspiration setting where there is an opportunity for choice among alternatives, the avoidance motivation exactly cancels out the approach motivation. Hence the resultant motivation for each of the alternatives is zero. His choice of level of aspiration cannot be predicted from variables intrinsic to the achievement-related nature of the task. If there is any orderly pattern in this conflicted person's level of aspiration, the explanation of it must be sought in extrinsic factors, e.g., *the desire to gain social approval*. Such a desire can also be conceptualized in terms of motive, expectancy, and incentive, and the total motivation for a particular task can then be attributed to both achievement-related motives and other kinds of motives engaged by the particular features of the situation.

In recent years there has been something of a rebirth of interest in the problems of level of aspiration, particularly in pathological groups. The tendency for anxious groups to show much greater variability in level of aspiration, setting their goals either very high or very low relative to less anxious persons, was noted in early studies by P. Sears, Rotter, and others (231). D. R. Miller (287), Himmelweit (182), and Eysenck and Himmelweit (124) have produced substantial evidence that persons with affective disorders (neurasthenia or dysthymia) typically set extremely high goals for themselves; hysterics, on the other hand, show a minimal level of aspiration, often setting their future goal even below the level of past performance. In all of these studies, normal control groups have fallen between these two extremes, as might be expected from the present model if *normals* are relatively more positive in their motivation in achievement-related situations.

In the work of Eysenck (123) and his colleagues, both dysthymics and hysterics show greater *neuroticism* than normal subjects. Eysenck's interpretation of this factor as autonomic sensitivity is consistent with the implications of the present model, which attributes the setting of extremely high or low levels of aspiration to relatively strong motivation to avoid failure. A second factor, *extraversion-introversion*, discriminates the affective disorders and hysterics where the present model, dealing only with motives intrinsic to the competitive achievement situation, does not. An appeal to some other motivational difference, e.g., in strength of n Affiliation, might also predict the difference in pattern of level of aspiration.

Probability preferences. The present analysis is relevant to another domain of current research interest, that specifically concerned with the measurement of subjective probability and utility. Edwards (113, 114), for example, has reported probability preferences among subjects offered alternative bets having the same expected value. We[4] have repeated the Edwards type experiment (e.g., 6/6 of winning 30 cents versus 1/6 of winning $1.80) with subjects having high and low n Achievement scores. The results show that persons high in n Achievement more often prefer intermediate probabilities (4/6, 3/6, 2/6) to extreme probabilities (6/6, 5/6, 1/6) than persons low in n

---

[4] Atkinson, J. W., Bastian, J. R., Earl, R. W., and Litwin, G. H. The achievement motive, goal setting, and probability preferences (in preparation).

Achievement. What is more, the same differential preference for intermediate risk was shown by these *same* subjects when they were allowed to choose the distance from the target for their shots in a shuffleboard game. In other words, the incentive values of winning *qua* winning and losing *qua* losing, presumably developed in achievement activities early in life, generalize to the gambling situation in which winning is really *not* contingent upon one's own skill and competence.

Social mobility aspirations. Finally, the present model may illuminate a number of interesting research possibilities having to do with social and occupational mobility. The rankings of occupations according to their prestige in Western societies clearly suggests that occupations accorded greater prestige are also more difficult to attain. A serious effort to measure the perceived probability of being able to attain certain levels on the occupational ladder should produce a high negative correlation with the usual ranking on prestige. If so, then the present model for level of aspiration and the implications of the model for persons who differ in achievement-related motives can be applied to many of the sociological problems of mobility aspiration. A recent paper by Hyman (195) has laid the groundwork for such an analysis.

SUMMARY

A theoretical model is presented to explain how the motive to achieve and the motive to avoid failure influence behavior in any situation where performance is evaluated against some standard of excellence. A conception of motivation in which strength of motivation is a joint multiplicative function of motive, expectancy (subjective probability), and incentive is offered to account for the selection of one task among alternatives which differ in difficulty (level of aspiration) and to account for performance level when only one task is presented. It is assumed that the incentive value of success is a positive linear function of difficulty as inferred from the subjective probability of success; and negative incentive value of failure is assumed to be a negative linear function of difficulty. The major implications of the theory are (a) performance level should be greatest when there is greatest uncertainty about the outcome, i.e., when subjective probability of success is .50, whether the motive to achieve or the motive to avoid failure is stronger within an individual; but (b) persons in whom the achievement motive is stronger should prefer intermediate risk while persons in whom the motive to avoid failure is stronger should avoid intermediate risk and prefer instead either very easy and safe undertakings *or* extremely difficult and speculative undertakings. Results of several experiments are cited, and the implications of the theoretical model for research on probability preferences in gambling and studies of social mobility aspirations are briefly discussed.

CHAPTER 23

The Relationships Among
Imaginative, Direct Verbal,
and Physiological Measures
of Anxiety in an Achievement
Situation*

ALFRED C. RAPHELSON[1]

SEVERAL independent attempts have been made to relate different measures of anxiety (or fear) to performance in competitive achievement situations. In one series of studies (128, 390, 391, 404), anxiety level has been assessed by the Manifest Anxiety Scale (MAS), composed of refined MMPI items which have been classified by clinical psychologists as being indicators of general manifest anxiety. The experimental results indicate that subjects who score high in manifest anxiety condition faster in a classical type of experiment than low-scoring subjects, but show poorer performance in more complicated learning situations.

Mandler and Sarason (248) have developed a Test Anxiety Questionnaire (TAQ) which indicates the extent to which a subject experiences anxiety before, during, and after three typical kinds of testing situations, thus having more specific situational reference than the MAS. Using the TAQ, Sarason, Mandler and Craighill (363) obtained results indicating that as the expectation of failure is increased, the high-anxiety subjects show a decrement in performance, whereas the low-anxiety subjects show an increment.

* Reprinted by permission of author and publisher from *The Journal of Abnormal and Social Psychology,* 1957, **54,** 13-18. Copyright 1957 by the American Psychological Association, Inc.

[1] This article is a portion of a dissertation submitted in partial fulfillment of the requirements for the degree of Doctor of Philosophy to the faculty of the University of Michigan. The writer wishes to express his deep gratitude to Drs. John W. Atkinson and Carl R. Brown for their patient direction and cooperation.

McClelland *et al.* (272) placed subjects in situations differing in aroused motivation to achieve and asked them afterward to write stories to TAT-like pictures. From these stories a scoring system was developed to capture the thought content reflecting the degree to which a subject was motivated to excel in an achievement situation. This need-Achievement (n Ach) score related to behavior in a way that suggests that qualitative differences in thought content of persons who score high and low in n Ach represent real differences in expectancies concerning competitive situations (24). McClelland (258) speaks of the high scorers as showing a positive hope of success. He infers a defensive fear of failure from the relative absence of achievement imagery and relative preponderance of negative categories in the stories of the low scorers.

The present study attempts to investigate the interrelationships among these three measures and to test their relative effectiveness in accounting for reactions at another level of observation, i.e., physiological activity. All three measures give rise to distributions of scores described in terms of the amount of fear or anxiety that characterizes an individual generally (MAS) or specifically in competitive achievement situations (TAQ, n Ach). Traditionally, increases in skin conductance have been found to be correlated with emotional states. It is expected, therefore, that groups characterized as anxious on the individual difference measures (high MAS, high TAQ, low n Ach), if validly classified, will show conductance changes that are more consistent with the patterns expected in an emotional state than the groups classified as nonanxious (low MAS, low TAQ, high n Ach).

METHOD

Apparatus. The data were obtained in a room, $9 \times 9 \times 10$ feet, in which was located the complex structure housing the essential apparatus. These essentials consisted of (*a*) a ground-glass screen 24 inches in diameter on which a ¾-inch spot of light moved, (*b*) a device which provided for a very irregular pattern of movement of this spot, (*c*) a recording polygraph, (*d*) a galvanometer, (*e*) a pneumograph, and (*f*) a red signal light.

The movement of the spot was accomplished by the projection of a ¾-inch spot on the screen by a mirror arrangement which was driven by two motor-driven cams in a highly irregular manner. A hand lever was connected in opposition to this device. A larger circle (3 inches in diameter) was also projected on the screen.

The recording galvanometer was used in conjunction with an electric network which automatically kept constant the current passing through the skin of S at 40 microamperes and measured the apparent resistance in terms of the potential difference across the electrodes. A continuous record of the changes in resistance of the skin was maintained by connecting the galvanometer to a stylus on the polygraph. One electrode was attached to the palm of the left hand, the other to the underside of the wrist on the same hand. Each electrode was made of a fritted glass filter of fine porosity, filled with physiological salt solution in which a loose coil of anodized silver wire was emersed.

The pneumograph was strapped to the abdominal region of S and connected to the polygraph.

A red signal light, located above the screen, indicated when S had allowed an error to occur. The errors were also indicated on the polygraph.

Subjects. The Ss were 25 volunteer male students enrolled in various schools in the University of Michigan. Their class status ranged from freshman to graduate, and their age from 18 to 25.

General Plan. The general plan was to establish a testlike situation in which S was asked to keep the moving spot of light within a small area by manipulating the hand lever. In a brief introduction, the apparatus was described as being like devices used by the Air Force to test intellectual and motor abilities. The following test instructions were given:

> I am going to give you a series of reasoning problems that I want you to solve as best you can. I am not going to ask you for a solution; I do not care whether or not you can verbalize it. But I want you to show me you know the answer by your responses. Each problem consists of a sequence of movements of this spot of light over the screen. I will start the machine which controls the movements of the spot and your task is to discover what the sequence of movements is that the light follows. Now the lever-stick on your right works in opposition to the machine. If the machine moves the spot up you can counter the movement by moving the lever so that the spot moves in the opposite direction. Therefore, if you are able to solve the problem correctly, you will be able to anticipate each subsequent movement of the light, and by manipulating the lever correctly, you can keep the spot from moving very far. In the center of the screen you can see a ring outlined. Your task is to keep the spot of light from wandering out of the limits of this ring. It is an error if you allow the spot to leave that area. Your task is to make a good score by making as few errors as you can. The errors will be recorded on my tape here and after the session we will compare your score to that of others who have been through this test. You are to try your best to make as few errors as possible.

> Now in this problem you will have several other cues to aid you. First, the ring will always be there to indicate where the safe-area ends and the error-area begins. Second, every time you make an error this red light above the screen will flash on. It not only will indicate that you are in error but will also aid you in keeping a running count as to how well you are doing. Before you begin the test, I am going to begin the sequence, and I want you just to observe it for awhile so you can see what the problem is like and try to figure out the pattern of movements. I will tell you when I will begin the sequence and when you are to begin avoiding making errors. Do you have any questions?

Continuous records were taken of skin conductance and respiration during the entire experimental session.[2] The session consisted of the following four periods: *Null 1 Period*—a five-minute period in which S actively manipulated the lever but was not yet given the test instructions. *Anticipation Period*—a two-minute period which immediately followed the test instruction. The S watched the movements of the spot but did not yet begin to avoid making errors. *Solution Period*—a ten-minute period in which S actively attempted to make as few errors as he could by controlling the movements of the spot. *Null 2 Period*—a five-minute period after the Solution Period which was similar to the Null 1 Period. No problem was presented while the S simply manipulated the lever. The first and last periods were conceived of as relatively free of anxiety-arousing cues. It was not expected that the subgroups differentiated by the various dispositional measures would be different in their physiological reactions in these periods.

Since the spot actually moved in an irregular manner and no solution was possible, errors are not a meaningful variable in this experiment. An attempt was made to keep the frequency of errors as constant as possible for each S by manipulating the amplitude of the spot's movement in relation to S's actual performance.

Measures of Individual Difference. Following the motor task, Ss wrote the n-Ach stories while still connected to the recording equipment. They were disengaged before taking the other two tests. To be consistent with the literature on these measures, each distribution of scores was broken into high, middle, and low thirds for comparison on the physiological indices. The n-Ach measure consisted of four TAT-like pictures, presented to elicit imaginative responses from which a score was determined according to the coding procedure described by McClelland, *et al.* (272). The experimenter and another trained coder scored all the stories. The reliability coefficient between the two sets of scores was .82. Differences were resolved by reference to a third expert.[3] The scores for the high-n-Ach third ranged from 8 to 14; for the low third, -3 to 2.

The Test Anxiety Questionnaire has been fully described by Mandler and Sarason (248). A high score indicates a tendency to reflect feelings of anxiety in a testing situation. The scores for the high-TAQ third ranged from 23-31; for the low-TAQ third, 1-13.

The Manifest Anxiety Scale has been described by Taylor (403). The scores for the high-MAS third ranged from 15-22; for the low third, 1-7.

Skin Conductance Measure. The skin resistance records were analyzed in the following way: Samples from the records were taken at the beginning of each period and at the end of each subsequent minute. These

---

[2] No significant relationships were found between any of the other variables in these experiments and any of the characteristics of respiration activity (amplitude, rate, volume). Hence no respiratory data will be reported.

[3] The writer is indebted to Mr. Berne Jacobs and Dr. Joseph Veroff for their cooperation in this scoring.

readings were converted into units of conductance (micromho) and an average based on these samples was computed to represent the entire period. Analyses were done on the average level in each period in terms of variation in conductance within each period expressed as a percentage change over the Null 1 Period average. The percentages were calculated as follows:

$$\frac{\text{Mean Conductance in period}}{\text{Mean Conductance in Null 1}} \times 100.$$

These percentages were converted into angles by the arc sin $\sqrt{\text{percentage}}$ transformation to insure the independence of means and variances (383).

Statistical Analysis. The error estimates used to evaluate the mean differences were derived from analyses of variance designated Type III by Lindquist (235). Since there were twenty-five Ss in this study, it was impossible to have equal numbers in each of the three subgroups for each measure. The numbers in each subgroup, therefore, were equalized by randomly eliminating one case from the subgroup that contained the unequal number.

RESULTS

Interrelationships Among Measures of Individual Differences. The product-moment correlations among the three measures of individual differences are given in Table 1. The two measures of reactions

TABLE 1. PRODUCT-MOMENT CORRELATIONS AMONG THREE MEASURES OF INDIVIDUAL DIFFERENCES

Measure	Test Anxiety	N	Manifest Anxiety	N
n Achievement............	$-.43^*$	24†	$-.25$	25
Test Anxiety..............			.53	24

* r's of .39 and .50 are significant at .05 and .01 levels of confidence respectively.
† One subject failed to fill out the Test Anxiety Questionnaire correctly and was eliminated from all Test-Anxiety analyses.

TABLE 2. MEAN ABSOLUTE CONDUCTANCE IN NULL 1 PERIOD

Measure	High ($n = 8$)	Middle ($n = 8$)	Low ($n = 8$)	σ diff.
n Achievement................	23.9^*	20.7	17.5	6.42
Test Anxiety Questionnaire......	17.3	22.2	23.5	6.40
Manifest Anxiety Scale..........	17.7	22.4	22.0	6.35

* Units in micromhos.

TABLE 3. MEAN VARIATION IN CONDUCTANCE EXPRESSED AS PERCENTAGE
OF NULL 1 LEVEL
($N = 8$ for all subgroups)

Measure	Subgroup	Period		
		Antici-pation	Solution	Null 2
n Achievement	High	102.5*	95.4	68.9
	Middle	101.1	106.5	85.0
	Low	100.1	110.0	79.4
Test Anxiety Questionnaire	High	104.2	109.2	79.6
	Middle	101.0	103.1	86.8
	Low	103.8	89.5	66.8
Manifest Anxiety Scale	High	106.0	109.6	82.8
	Middle	94.0	98.8	71.2
	Low	103.2	101.8	78.6

* The σ diff. for each measure is as follows: n Ach: between = 16.4, within = 7.4; TAQ: between = 16.3, within = 6.4; MAS: between = 16.5, within = 7.6.

specific to achievement (n Ach, TAQ) were significantly correlated, as were the two measures concerned with negative reactions towards general situations (MAS, TAQ). This pattern of relationships is consistent with the specifications set for the measures by the theories to which they are related. The TAQ was developed to measure anxiety symptoms specific to an achievement situation. The MAS was developed to measure general feelings of anxiety which may or may not occur in an achievement situation. A significant positive correlation is expected between them. The n-Ach measure is thought to reflect the degree to which S has expectancies of goal attainment in an achievement situation; such expectancies are incompatible with any anxiety reactions associated with the setting. A high negative correlation is expected with TAQ and a low negative correlation with MAS.

Absolute Conductance Level in Null 1 Period. The initial Null 1 levels of conductance in relation to the several measures of individual differences are presented in Table 2. In this period, the anxiety-arousing instructions had not yet been introduced. However, on each of the three measures, the subgroup which is presumed to be composed of relatively nonanxious Ss showed the highest conductance level. Although even the largest difference, that obtained between the subgroups scoring high and low on n Ach, was not significant (σ diff. = 6.42, $t = .997$), the consistency of the trends in each of the comparisons may be worth noting. They are consistent with the notion that a high conductance level may be indicative of psychological states other than anxiety.

Skin Conductance Variation in Experimental Periods. The mean variation in conductance, expressed as a percentage change over Null 1 level in three experimental periods, is presented in Table 3 for each of the subgroups differentiated by the three measures. The subgroups differentiated by measures of n Ach and TAQ showed significantly different conductance patterns. Though none of the between-subgroup differences were significant at any particular period, there were meaningful differences between subgroups in the direction of the trend of skin conductance through the different experimental periods. The subgroups considered relatively "anxious" (low n Ach, high TAQ) showed an increase in conductance from the Anticipation to the Solution Period. The subgroups considered relatively nonanxious (high n Ach, low TAQ) showed a decrease. The differences between these particular differences with both measures were significant in the predicted direction (n Ach: diff. $= 17.0$, σ diff. $= 10.5$, $t = 1.62$, $p = .05$; TAQ: diff. $= 19.3$, σ diff. $= 9.1$, $t = 2.12$, $p = .025$).

The subgroup designated as anxious by the more general MAS did not show any pattern of change in conductance that was significantly different from the subgroup designated as nonanxious.

A final analysis was made, comparing only those Ss scoring both high in TAQ and low in n Ach (both treated in the past as symptomatic of a disposition to be anxious in achievement situations) with Ss who scored both low in TAQ and high in n Ach (both treated in the past as symptomatic of the relative lack of a disposition to be anxious in an achievement situation). The significant negative correlation between the two measures implied that by examining S's score on both measures, it would be possible to obtain a more reliable estimate of the degree to which he might be anxious or nonanxious in a

TABLE 4. MEAN VARIATION IN CONDUCTANCE EXPRESSED AS A PERCENTAGE CHANGE OF NULL 1 LEVEL FOR SUBJECTS DESIGNATED ANXIOUS OR NONANXIOUS*

Subgroup	N	Period		
		Anticipation	Solution	Null 2
Anxious	7	104.4	112.1	83.7
Nonanxious	9	101.7	89.0	67.6
Difference		2.7	23.1	16.1
σ diff		12.42	12.22	9.05
t		.22	1.89	1.78
p (one-tailed)		—	.04	.05

* On the basis of scores on both the Test Anxiety and the n Achievement measures.

competitive situation. On each measure, the distribution was divided as near as possible to the median. Only Ss who fell in the corresponding high and low anxiety halves of both distributions were selected for comparison. Mean variations in conductance for these subgroups are presented in Table 4. It can be seen that by this method of classifying Ss, the trends observed between subgroups in the separate analyses were further emphasized and were significant in the Solution and Null 2 Periods. The directional change between the Anticipation and Solution Periods observed, significantly different in the separate analyses, was also significant here (diff. $= 20.4$, σ diff. $= 10.1$, $t = 2.01$, $p = .03$).

The trends observed in the earlier analyses concerning the initial level of conductance in Null 1 were further emphasized in this method of classification. The subgroup designated nonanxious showed a significantly higher initial level of conductance than the subgroup designated anxious (diff. $= 7.2$, σ diff. $= 2.88$, $t = 2.50$, $p = .02$).

DISCUSSION

Skin conductance, having been traditionally considered a physiological index of anxiety, is here viewed as a criterion against which discriminations made by the three dispositional indices of anxiety may be checked. The findings imply that the more specific an assessment technique is to the situation in which the predicted behavior is to occur, the more accurate is the prediction. This point is emphasized by the results obtained when Ss were classified according to their standing on both the n-Ach and the TAQ measures. By this method, the nonsignificant between-subgroup trends observed in the individual analyses were further emphasized, reaching a significant level in two of the three experimental periods. Further, the difference in the amount of change between the two subgroups from the Anticipation to the Solution Periods was accentuated as predicted.

An important question is raised by the present result: Of what importance are measures which are designated to be "general indicators" of anxiety? Behavior always occurs in specific situations. If an individual is termed "generally anxious," does it imply that he is anxious in all specific kinds of situations or just in a greater than average number? These results suggest that particular anxiety reactions are associated with specific situations. An assessment technique constructed to reflect response tendencies peculiar to a certain limited class of situations will probably have a predictive advantage over more generally oriented methods.

The analyses made in terms of the initial level of conductance in the Null 1 Period showed that in each of the individual difference measures, the subgroup considered to be the least anxious generally had the highest level of absolute conductance. Though these differences between subgroups in the individual analyses were not significant, they did reach statistical significance when Ss were classified on the combined n-Ach-TAQ indices—presumably the most reliable estimate of individual differences in disposition for achievement test anxiety. Since the Null 1 Period occurred before the experimental instructions were given, the differences must be due to initial reactions to the experimental situation itself, unless differences in conductance are a stable correlate of the individual difference measures.

Schlosberg (366) has argued that conductance levels should be considered an indicator of the degree of energy mobilization or "activation" of the individual in a particular situation. Activation has no particular "sign" or direction; it may stand either for positive interest in the task or for fear motivating avoidance. The Ss with a higher conductance level on entering the experimental room may be reacting to the situation with positive anticipatory interest cued off by the complex apparatus that immediately faces them. This interpretation is consistent with the contention of McClelland *et al.* (272) that the high n-Ach subgroup is likely to be challenged by a problem situation. Burdick (58) similarly reported a significantly greater tendency for persons high in n Ach to volunteer to participate in psychological experiments.

If Schlosberg's theory of activation is correct, it may mean that the increased conductance level that the high n-Ach subgroup shows initially has quite a different "sign" than the change the low n-Ach subgroup shows later. The conductance measure itself is not capable of giving the direction of behavior implied by increased activation, but it is possible to infer direction from the way the two subgroups are conceptualized according to n-Ach theory. It is possible, therefore, to look at the conductance measure as an indicator of the degree to which an individual is activated by the cues of the situation. The direction of this activation, either positive (approach) or negative (avoidance), can be inferred through an analysis of the content of human thought (272, p. 33). Neither the MAS nor TAQ allow this possibility since there is no direct way of obtaining evidence of positive orientation from them (see Part VI-A).

SUMMARY

This study investigated relationships among three dispositional measures and two physiological indices of anxiety in a competitive achievement situation. The disposition measures were relatively weak motivation to achieve as measured through content analysis of imaginative stories (low need Achievement), the Mandler-Sarason Test Anxiety Questionnaire, and the Taylor Manifest Anxiety Scale.

The physiological indices were skin conductance and respiratory volume.

Twenty-five male college students were placed in a competitive test situation and instructed to perform a complex perceptual-motor task. They were informed when they made errors and were given cues to aid in performing the task accurately. The physiological indices were recorded before the ego-involving instructions were given and immediately before, during, and after the performance task. The three dispositional measures were obtained after the performance task.

The correlation between need Achievement and Test Anxiety was −.43; between Test Anxiety and Manifest Anxiety, .53; between Achievement and Manifest Anxiety, −.25. The two measures specifically concerned with reactions in competitive achievement situations (n Achievement, Test Anxiety), were both related to changes in skin conductance during the performance task. The relationship was clearest when the subjects were classified on both of these measures as anxious (i.e., high Test Anxiety and low n Achievement) or nonanxious (low Test Anxiety and high n Achievement). The more anxious group increased in conductance while the relatively nonanxious group decreased. The Manifest Anxiety Scale did not relate to conductance change and no consistent relationships were found between respiratory activity and any of the other measures. These results suggest the advantage of situational over general measures of anxiety in accounting for changes in skin conductance in a particular situation.

It was also found that the highest initial level of conductance was obtained by the subgroup designated as nonanxious on each of the three dispositional measures respectively. These differences occurred before the introduction of the anxiety-arousing instructions. These findings are interpreted in terms of Schlosberg's theory of activation level.

CHAPTER 24

....

The Achievement Motive and Perceptual Sensitivity Under Two Conditions of Motive-Arousal

ROBERT W. MOULTON, ALFRED C. RAPHELSON,
ALFRED B. KRISTOFFERSON, AND JOHN W. ATKINSON[1]

THIS STUDY investigates the extent to which the relationship between strength of achievement motive (n Achievement) and perceptual sensitivity to achievement-related words, originally reported by McClelland and Liberman (272, p. 257; 275), depends upon arousal of motivation at the time of the measurement of recognition thresholds. Recent experiments (23, 24, 27) have shown that differences in strength of achievement motive are reflected in overt behavior only when instructions or other cues engage the motive by arousing the expectancy that performance is instrumental to the goal of personal accomplishment. Atkinson has argued that the achievement motive inferred from content analysis of imaginative (TAT) stories is a "latent characteristic of personality which is manifested in behavior only when engaged or supported by appropriate environmental cues" (23, p. 387). If motivational selectivity in perception requires that a motive be aroused at the time of perceiving, then expected differences in perceptual sensitivity between groups of individuals who differ in strength of achievement motive should be more evident when recognition thresholds are measured immediately after a motive-arousing test experience than when recognition thresholds are measured without any prior arousal of the motive.

The experiment to be reported was conducted twice, first with a group of high school students and again, following several refine-

_____

[1] The present report is based in part on an experiment by RWM as part of his undergraduate Honors thesis at the University of Michigan, 1952, (304). Part of this work was conducted during the term of an SSRC fellowship to JWA.

350

ments in procedure, with a group of college students. In each case, the strength of achievement motive was measured by having subjects (Ss) write imaginative stories under neutral experimental conditions (i.e., without any attempt by the experimenters (Es) to arouse or reduce motivation). Then Ss were divided into two groups to allow measurement of recognition thresholds for achievement-related words under two different experimental conditions on a later occasion. In one condition (Neutral), threshold measurement was preceded only by instructions directly pertinent to the perceptual task. In the other condition (Motive-Aroused), a deliberate attempt was made to arouse the achievement motive, prior to measurement of thresholds, by having Ss take a pencil and paper test under instructions which stressed the importance of doing well.

It is expected that recognition thresholds for achievement-related words will be inversely related to strength of achievement motive and that the effects of differences in motive strength will be accentuated (i.e., greater) in the motive-aroused condition.

METHOD

Procedure with high school sample

Male high school students (aged 14-17) were divided into Neutral ($N = 16$) and Motive-Aroused ($N = 25$) perception conditions. The division was made on the basis of which of two periods the Ss attended study hall. All Ss were volunteers.

Measurement of motivation. The thematic apperception measure of n Achievement was administered to each group under neutral conditions (272, Ch. 3) in a small classroom where both phases of the experiment were run on successive days. Four-minute stories were written in response to the following pictures, listed by code numbers: (A) The heads of two men, (B) Two men working in a shop, (D) Older man standing and handing papers to younger man seated at desk, (H) Boy seated at desk with head in his hand. Stories were scored for n Achievement (Ch. 12) by judges (RWM and JWA) whose scoring reliability is above .90.

Experimental conditions. On the second day, the Neutral group came into the experimental room and was immediately given instructions for the perceptual task.

The Motive-Aroused group were first asked to put names, addresses, and estimates of average grade on the cover of a small test booklet distributed as soon as they were seated. They were told that they would be given a test that was the most important part of the research being done. They were told the test would measure such things as the ability to work hard and efficiently to get things done with a minimum of mistakes, traits which would help a person be successful at almost anything he did, and they were urged to try hard. They were then given a five-minute scrambled-words task. The amount of time allowed very little progress in solving the words. The point of this procedure was to arouse the achievement motive. When the test was completed, the experimenter (E) indicated that now something completely different, which would be of more interest to the Ss, would be done. From this point forward, the procedure was identical in the two conditions.

Measurement of recognition thresholds. Illumination in the experimental room was controlled as well as possible by pulling the shades. Words were projected from a standard 35mm. slide projector on a movie screen 15 feet from the projector at the front of the room. The Ss were seated at random on either side of the projector. The exposure duration was set at .01 sec. Each word was exposed 14 times, with each successive exposure equal to the increase in illumination accompanying a 2% increase on the dial of a series-wired variac. The illumination of the first exposure was based on pretesting and was set to allow recognition of all words within the span of 14 exposure trials. On the fifteenth trial for each word, the illumination was doubled to ensure that most or all Ss would recognize every word. Two practice words (marble, plural) were given to enable Ss to become familiar with the procedure and timing of trials. Following the practice words, four failure words (worst, unable, failure, incapable), four success words (accomplish, competent, surpass, achieve), and five motivationally-neutral control words (malaria, southwest, daytime, actual, reality) were given in a predetermined random order. The three groups of words were approximately matched for frequency of usage in the English language (408).

The Ss were instructed to write down the word they saw each time, to guess, and to continue writing down the word even after they were certain they had seen it correctly. This portion of the work was represented to them as an attempt to learn something about visual acuity in connection with identifying aircraft. Names were not required on the task booklets.

The measure of recognition threshold. The neutral words were used to establish each S's baseline threshold measure. This was done in order to control for the effects of individual differences in tachistoscopic acuity which were accentuated in this experiment by less than adequate control of location of Ss in relation to the screen, variation of illumination between conditions, and other factors independent of motive strength. The criterion of recognition was one correct response.

In the tabulation of results, the neutral word, *malaria,* was eliminated completely since only half of the Ss in the Motive-Aroused group recognized that word by the fourteenth trial. Since the plan was to assign Z scores to success and failure words based on each individual's threshold and variability for neutral words as in (275), the criterion established for elimination of Ss was that these two parameters of the distribution of neutral thresholds had to be determinate. The median rather than the mean was used as a measure of central tendency for success and failure words to prevent further loss of data.

Ten Ss in the Motive-Aroused condition and two in the Neutral condition were eliminated for failing to recognize all five remaining neutral words. An equal number of these were high and low in n Achievement. The relative thresholds (Z scores) used in the analysis of data are equal to the mean number of trials for recognition of neutral words minus the median number of trials for success or failure words divided by the standard deviation for neutral words. A positive Z score indicates greater sensitivity for critical words; a negative Z score indicates less sensitivity for critical words.

Subjects. Fourteen Ss in the Neutral condition and 15 in the Motive-Aroused condition met the stated criteria. The division of the distribution of 29 n Achievement scores at the median produced seven Highs with a mean of 9.6 and seven Lows with a mean of 1.7 in the Neutral condition, and eight comparable Highs with a mean of 8.9 and seven comparable Lows with a mean of 2.0 in the Motive-Aroused condition.

Procedure with college sample[2]

Twenty-six male college students in introductory experimental psychology courses were randomly assigned to Neutral and Motive-Aroused conditions following the measurement of motivation in a neutral group situation. Recognition thresholds were then obtained individually under more refined laboratory conditions approximately a month later.

Measurement of motivation. Subjects wrote six short, two and one-half minute stories under neutral experimental conditions in response to the following pictures: (G) Boy standing before surgical mural; (46) A man skiing rapidly down hill; (9) Man at desk after hours; (64) Two men talking, one rubbing his forehead; (B)

---

[2] We wish to acknowledge the assistance of E. Peretz in running the experiment.

Two men working in a shop; (50) Elderly man with pipe reading something he has just typed. Stories were again scored for n Achievement by judges (ACR and JWA), whose scoring reliability exceeds .90 (numbers refer to code designations of pictures).

Experimental conditions. Each S came individually to the laboratory at an appointed time. On arrival, Ss in the Neutral condition were taken into a small experimental room and seated before a standard Gerbrand's tachistoscope where the E conversed informally with them before giving instructions for threshold determination.

Immediately before the perceptual task, subjects in the Motive-Aroused condition were given a short test presented as an attempt to standardize items for exams in a course they were taking. When Ss in this condition arrived at the laboratory, they were told that a few adjustments had to be made on the tachistoscope, and they were asked if they would mind doing something else for a few moments. Each S was then led into a small room across the hall from the experimental room where the E explained that he was attempting to develop some better tests in the course and wondered if the student would be willing to see how well he could do on various items. The S was then given a series of difficult analogies-type questions. As the E left the room, he told the S there was a key available to see how well he had done and some norms on a few people who had taken the items so far. The E always returned before the S had finished and urged him to finish while looking over his shoulder to heighten his involvement in the test. Since the Es were instructors in the lab courses, the S faced the possibility of making a good or poor impression with his performance. When the S finished, the key was used to grade the paper quickly and the norms were discussed briefly. The scores on the test were such that everyone clustered together, and the small number of cases on the norm sheet made it impossible for the S to judge clearly whether he had done well or poorly. The measurement of recognition thresholds followed immediately.

Measurement of recognition thresholds. Words typed in capital letters and reproduced as a photographic negative appeared in a space indicated by two dots in the center of the projection screen as white on a less white background. The illuminance of both the "target" and the background was controlled by a powerstat and was the same for all Ss. Each word was presented in an ascending series using step intervals of .03 secs. Three practice words (reality, daytime, structural) were given to establish the S's range and familiarize him with the procedure. The Ss were instructed to report their responses verbally to the E, who recorded each one. Guessing was encouraged. Subjects were permitted to relax and look around the room between words. The criterion of recognition was one correct response, although the series was continued until two successive correct responses were obtained. This time, six success words (competent, achieve, mastery, excel, surpass, accomplish), six failure words (defeated, failure, unable, incapable, worst, unskillful), and six motivationally-neutral control words (insect, marble, element, plural, malaria, actual) were given in a random series. The words in different classifications were approximately equated for frequency of usage (408).

The measure of recognition threshold. As with the high school sample, the distribution of threshold scores for neutral words was used to estimate individual differences in performance of the perceptual task. The median threshold score for success and for failure words was converted to a Z score representing deviation from the S's mean threshold for the neutral words. A positive Z score indicates greater sensitivity and a negative Z score less sensitivity for experimental than control words.

Two Ss were eliminated for extreme deviations of 4.85 and 5.00 standard deviations from the mean recognition threshold of the total group for either success or failure words. No other subject deviated more than 2.69 standard deviations from the overall mean threshold of the group.

Subjects. Twelve Ss in the Neutral condition and 14 Ss in the Motive-Aroused condition were divided into High and Low n Achievement groups by splitting the distribution of 26 n Achievement scores as near to the median as possible. Seven Ss in the Neutral condition and five in the Motive-Aroused condition had comparably high scores. The respective means were 9.6 and 9.0. The mean scores of five Lows in the Neutral condition and nine Lows in the Motive-Aroused condition were $-.2$ and 1.7.

RESULTS

Recognition thresholds for neutral control words. An analysis of variance of the number of trials taken to recognize the neutral words by High and Low n Achievement subgroups of the high school sample in the two experimental conditions showed no significant differences among the groups ($F = 1.13$, d.f. $= 3$ and 25). A similar analysis for the college sample also failed to show any differences in recognition thresholds for the control words ($F = 1.40$, d.f. $= 3$ and 22).

Recognition thresholds for success and failure words. Since the same trends were present in high school and college samples and there were no significant differences between the groups in recognition thresholds for success or failure words, the two samples were combined to simplify the presentation of results. Table 1 presents the combined data with t-tests of the most pertinent differences.

TABLE 1. RECOGNITION THRESHOLDS FOR SUCCESS AND FAILURE WORDS BY HIGH AND LOW n ACHIEVEMENT GROUPS UNDER NEUTRAL AND MOTIVE-AROUSED PERCEPTUAL CONDITIONS. HIGH SCHOOL AND COLLEGE SAMPLES COMBINED.

Strength of n Achievement		Perceptual Condition					
		Neutral			Motive-Aroused		
		N	Success Words	Failure Words	N	Success Words	Failure Words
High.........	M	14	−.03*	.25	13	−.12	.06
	σ		.65	.60		.70	.72
Low.........	M	12	−.40	.01	16	−.73	−1.07
	σ		.69	.69		1.19	1.25
Diff. (H-L)...			.37	.24		.61	1.13
σ diff......			.35	.36		.33	.34
t..........			1.08	.67		1.82	3.29
p..........			n.s.	n.s.		.05**	.001**

* Recognition thresholds expressed as Z scores based on the distribution for neutral control words. Z = Mean control wds.-Mdn. critical wds./σ control wds. A positive Z score indicates relatively greater sensitivity for critical than control words.
** One-tailed t-test. Error term for particular t-tests derived from variance within groups, $d.f.$ = 51.

The point of primary interest is the relative size of the differences in recognition threshold between comparable High and Low n Achievement groups in the two experimental conditions. The High n Achievement groups in both conditions have relatively lower recognition thresholds (greater sensitivity) for both success and failure words than the low n Achievement groups, but the differences are most pronounced and are statistically significant for both success ($p < .05$) and failure words ($p < .001$) when the motive has been aroused immediately prior to the determination of thresholds.

In the case of success words, the difference of .61 between High and Low n Achievement groups in the Motive-Aroused condition is not significantly greater than the difference of .37 between comparable groups in the Neutral condition (Diff. $= .24$, σ diff. $= .48$). However, the difference between the High-Low n Achievement group differences is significant for failure words (Diff. $= .89$, σ diff. $= .50$, $t = 1.78$, $p < .05$ in predicted direction). This result is a consequence of a significant decrease in sensitivity to failure words (elevation of threshold) between the Neutral and Motive-Aroused conditions in the Low n Achievement group (Diff. $= -1.08$, σ diff. $= .35$, $t = 3.08$, $p < .01$). The decrease in sensitivity to failure words shown by the Low n Achievement group is almost significantly greater than the decrease shown by the High n Achievement group (Diff. $= .89$, σ diff. $= .50$, $t = 1.78$, $p < .10$) and is larger than the decrease shown by the Low n Achievement group in sensitivity to success words (Diff. $= .75$, σ diff. $= .48$, $t = 1.56$, $p < .10$).

DISCUSSION

The results indicate that a difference can be shown to exist between recognition thresholds for success and failure words of High and Low n Achievement groups following experimental arousal of the motive but not when the motive has not been experimentally aroused before the determination of thresholds. In the case of failure words, the difference between recognition thresholds of High and Low n Achievement groups following motive arousal is significantly larger than in the Neutral condition. The present findings present much clearer evidence of a relationship between n Achievement and recognition threshold for need-related words than the earlier exploration of McClelland and Liberman (272, p. 257) and in general support their interpretation of the result.

These results agree indirectly with the findings of recent studies of performance which have shown little or no relationship between measures of strength of n Achievement and performance unless the achievement motive has been engaged by environmental cues at the time of the performance (see Chs. 18 and 19).

The implications of the findings may become clearer if generalized to the case of hunger. Two individuals known by their friends to differ in the strength of their desire for food at mealtime would normally be expected to reveal this motivational difference most clearly in performances that were instrumental in producing the satisfactions of eating when the motive was aroused, i.e., after a period of food privation. The present results suggest furthermore that differences in perceptual sensitivity to food-related stimuli would be minimal shortly after the noon meal when the cues for arousal of motivation to eat had temporarily subsided. However, very real differences in threshold for food-related stimuli, betraying the difference in strength of motive, should be evident later just before the evening meal when motivation to eat had once more been aroused.

The arousal of the motive to eat is usually attributed to the internal cues accompanying food privation, but external cues may also play a role. However, in the case of the achievement motive, the cues which arouse motivation in the individual are usually external and situational. It is assumed, in the present experiment, that the test situation immediately before the measurement of thresholds in the Motive-Aroused condition introduced more achievement-demanding cues than the normal cues of the classroom or laboratory to which the subjects were exposed in the Neutral condition. Further, it was assumed that individual differences in strength of motivation to achieve which reflect differential experiences in situations similar to those reproduced in the experimental conditions would be systematically aroused. Once the motive is aroused, perceptual and instrumental response dispositions acquired in previous sequences of behavior leading to the same goal are selectively strengthened (24, p. 85). One expected result, then, of *systematic* arousal of a motive in a group of subjects is greater motivational support for a particular class of perceptual response dispositions (hypotheses) the stronger the motive in the individual. Consequently, there will be a greater difference between groups differing in motive-strength in recognition thresholds for stimuli of this class.

An important implication of these results is that thematic apperception can detect *potential* differences in strength of motivation without the motive actually being aroused by situational cues before the measure is administered. This has been explained by assuming that even under neutral testing conditions the picture cues used to elicit imaginative stories to a certain extent arouse motivation and initiate a chain of associations which are symptomatic of the individual's previous learning experience in situations like the ones portrayed. The inference of motive strength from this chain of associations is, apparently, a valid estimate of how motivated the individual will be when actually in real-life situations similar to the ones portrayed in the pictures (24, pp. 81-91), that is, when the motive is strongly aroused.

Finally, the significant decrease in perceptual sensitivity to failure words by the Low *n* Achievement group in the Motive-Aroused condition may be taken as further suggestive evidence that persons low in achievement motive are likely to be more fearful about failure in competitive achievement settings. This phenomenon is usually labeled perceptual defense. The trend is consistent with similar results concerning a decrease in the ability of persons low in n Achievement to recall failures when competitively aroused (23) and with Raphelson's (Ch. 23) recent finding that n Achievement score is correlated −.43 with scores on the Mandler-Sarason Scale of Test Anxiety (see also Ch. 39).

SUMMARY

Strength of motive to achieve in groups of male high school and college students was inferred from imaginative stories the students wrote under neutral classroom conditions. The Ss were divided into two experimental groups. Recognition thresholds for achievement-related words were determined in the usual (Neutral) way for one group. In the other group (Motive-Aroused), the determination of thresholds was preceded by a short test experience deliberately designed to arouse motivation to achieve in the Ss.

It is assumed that the achievement motive, as measured through content analysis of stories written when the Ss are not necessarily in a motivated state, is a disposition of the personality which is expressed in instrumental acts and perceptual behavior only when it is aroused, or engaged, by appropriate environmental cues. Thus it was expected that differences between Ss having high and low n Achievement scores in recognition thresholds for success and failure words would be greater in the Motive-Aroused than the Neutral perceptual condition. The results are viewed as consistent with this hypothesis.

CHAPTER 25

The Affiliation Motive and Perceptual Sensitivity to Faces*

JOHN W. ATKINSON [1] AND EDWARD L. WALKER

THE PRESENT INVESTIGATION is an attempt to predict from imaginative measures of the affiliation motive (n Affiliation) the frequency with which a subject (S) selects human faces from similar but nonhuman figures in a perceptual task. It was undertaken with several objectives in mind. The sensitizing effect of motives on perception has been demonstrated in numerous studies (330), but in many instances the results have admitted reasonable alternative interpretations. For example, McClelland and Liberman (275, 272, p. 257) have reported a study in which n Achievement scores obtained from imaginative (TAT) stories proved to be related to recognition thresholds for achievement-related words. Farber (127), in a careful analysis of the role of motivation in verbal learning and performance, points out quite correctly that these results can be interpreted as a function of verbal habits common to the imaginative story performance and the word-threshold measuring situation. It was hoped that in the present study we could examine the relationship between a verbal-imaginative measure of motivation and sensitivity to relevant stimuli in perception in a situation which would not admit Farber's alternative interpretation or explanation in terms of the word-frequency variable discussed by Solomon and Howes (386).

The second objective was to obtain further evidence of the validity of the method of scoring imaginative (TAT) stories designed to measure motivation for social acceptance or n Affiliation (Ch. 5).

---

* Reprinted by permission of author and publisher from *The Journal of Abnormal and Social Psychology*, 1956, 53, 38-41. Copyright 1956 by the American Psychological Association, Inc.

[1] This research was conducted during the period of a Social Science Research Council Faculty Research Fellowship.

360

The demonstration of a positive relationship between n-Affiliation scores obtained from imaginative stories and perceptual sensitivity to stimuli related to affiliation would be further evidence that a motivational disposition is being measured.

The senior investigator has discussed elsewhere (24, p. 90) the theoretical basis for an expectation that when the motive is measured in a neutral situation (i.e., one in which no special operation has been performed either to arouse the motive or to create an especially relaxed condition), a relationship can be expected with dependent perceptual and performance variables only when arousal operations are performed immediately before the S begins the criterion task. A recent study by Moulton *et al.* (Ch. 24) has found a clear inverse relationship between n-Achievement scores and recognition thresholds for success and failure words when the motive was aroused before the dependent variable performance, but a similar relationship of lesser magnitude with neutral conditions preceding the perceptual task. The difference between the two conditions was statistically significant, however, only in the case of failure words.

In the experiments to be reported, the strength of the affiliation motive was measured by having several groups of male college students write imaginative stories under normal (neutral) classroom conditions. These groups were subsequently subjected to procedures designed to measure perceptual sensitivity to affiliation-related stimuli. Some groups performed the perceptual task under affiliation-neutral conditions; other groups were exposed to procedures designed to arouse the affiliation motive prior to the measurement of perceptual sensitivity for affiliation-related stimuli.

METHOD

Subjects. The Ss were 93 male undergraduates who at the time of their participation in the experiments were members of an introductory experimental psychology course at the University of Michigan. They constituted nearly the entire population of men in three semesters of this course in the years 1952, 1954, and 1955.

Measurement of motive strength. In each class from four to six pictures were used to elicit imaginative stories which were scored for affiliation-related imagery to obtain measures of individual differences in strength of n Affiliation. The instructions used and evidence of the validity of the scoring system may be found elsewhere (Ch. 5). Stories were scored by J. W. A., whose scoring reliability is above .90 (Ch. 5). The affiliation motive is best defined in terms of the content of imagery scored in the imaginative stories the essence of which is concern over establishing, maintaining, or restoring positive affective relations with other persons.

Experimental conditions. Approximately a month after the motive measures were obtained, the groups were introduced to the perceptual task. One whole class was introduced to this task with no immediately preceding attempt to arouse the affiliation motive. A second class participated in a sociometric rating procedure immediately before being introduced to the perceptual task. In this procedure, while all Ss were seated together around a large room, each S was required to place before him a card bearing a code number. Then he was required to make a series of ratings of his classmates of more than a month's acquaintanceship. First they were asked to rank-order a list of traits according to the degree to which possession of the trait would make a person likable. Then each was asked to pick from the list the two traits which best described each other person in the room. Finally, each was asked to write down the code numbers of the three persons whom he would most like to have as close personal friends. This task took about 20 minutes. In another year, half of the class was run under the neutral condition and the other half under a similar aroused condition. In an effort to keep the sociometric rating task and the perceptual task close together in time without establishing an apparent relationship between them, the perceptual task was introduced immediately without the usual break in the two-hour laboratory period. The excuse given was that time was running out and that there was one other task to be completed within the regular laboratory period. It was implied that the two tasks were unrelated.

The perceptual task. The Ss were randomly seated before a screen placed in the front of the room with their backs to a slide projector with a camera-type exposure diaphragm located at the back of the room. They were told that pictures would be projected on the screen before them at a speed and illumination inadequate for clear recognition. They were told that a picture would appear in each of four quadrants (top, bottom, left, and right), and though the image they received was very fuzzy and inadequate for recognition, they would be asked to designate in which of the four quadrants the picture *stood out the most* or was *most clear* to them. They were asked to write down a symbol for the appropriate quadrant after each of 80 exposure trials.

The psychophysical method, adopted from Blackwell (44), is suitable for measuring discrimination without conscious awareness. Blackwell has reported detection thresholds of a highly reliable character obtained with this method when the S was quite positive that no stimulus difference actually existed in the situation. In the present experiment, the exposure interval and level of screen illumination were both deliberately set at very low values on an empirical basis in pretest trials with other Ss, so that nothing more than a faint blur could be seen by the Ss. Many Ss refused to believe that there was any picture on the screen during the exposure interval. Subsequent questioning of the Ss failed to reveal any who could give an adequate description of the composition of the exposure stimuli. For the most part, it can then be assumed that most Ss were performing their task at a perceptual level somewhat below the recognition threshold.

The stimuli. Each slide had four figures somewhat removed from the fixation point and equal distances up, down, left, and right from it. On every slide, one figure was that of a single face or several faces, and the other three figures were presumably neutral in the sense that they were not stimuli related to n Affiliation. Most of the neutral stimuli were pictures of home furnishings, e.g., a lamp, a plate about the size of a face, and in as far as possible having perceptual properties roughly equivalent to the pictures of faces.

There was a total of five face-pictures and 15 neutral pictures. Each face-picture appeared on four slides, once in each available position, and neutral stimuli appeared at random in the other three positions. This arrangement produced five sets of four slides each, for a total of 20 slides. The 20 slides were presented in a predetermined random order, then in a second and independently selected random order for a total of 40 trials. These two orders were repeated to make a total of 80 trials. Each exposure was preceded by a verbal signal, "Ready now," in order to permit the Ss to focus on the fixation point in the middle of the screen.

Treatment of the data. The conditions under which the perceptual task was executed varied somewhat from group to group because the experiment was carried out in a classroom in which adequate control of ambient illumination could not be exercised. For this reason each experimental group was treated separately. For each S, the number of times he selected the face or faces in 80 trials was determined. Z scores were obtained for each of these distributions and it was then possible to place together groups which experienced slightly different conditions.

The n-Affiliation score in different groups was obtained from slightly different sets of pictures and from either four or six pictures. For this reason the n-Affiliation scores for each condition-homogeneous group was broken into High (above the median), and Low (below the median) n-Affiliation groups, and also into High, Middle, and Low (thirds) n-Affiliation groups.

RESULTS

The primary result may be seen in Table 1. Those Ss who are high in n Affiliation tend to choose faces more frequently than those Ss who are low in n Affiliation. The difference is significant at the .02 level. Although not reported here in tabular form, a similar difference at approximately the same significance level appears when the group is divided into High, Middle, and Low on n Affiliation.

Our treatment of the data permits us to compare all Ss who performed the perceptual task under neutral conditions with all those who performed it under aroused conditions even though each total group is composed of one semester's whole class and a half of another. The results of this analysis may be seen in Table 2. Here

TABLE 1. n AFFILIATION AND THE PERCEPTION OF FACES
(Frequency that quadrant containing face(s) was reported most
salient in terms of Z scores from neutral and motive-aroused
conditions combined)

	n-Affiliation Score	
	High	Low
Mean z score	.20	−.23
σ	1.01	.94
N	50	43
σ diff	.205	
t	2.09	
p	.02 (one-tailed test)	

the original finding is seen again in the aroused condition but to a
smaller and not significant extent in the neutral condition. This
difference between aroused and neutral conditions, although large
to the eye, .58 as compared to .25, is not statistically significant
(σ diff. = .53). Furthermore, when this comparison is made with
only a High-Low break of the n-Affiliation distribution the apparent
difference is even smaller.

TABLE 2. PERCEPTION OF FACES AS A FUNCTION OF STRENGTH OF
AFFILIATION MOTIVE AND EXPERIMENTAL CONDITION
(Frequency that quadrant containing face(s) was reported most
salient, in terms of Z scores from neutral and motive-aroused
conditions presented separately)

	Perceptual Condition			
n-Affiliation Score	Neutral		Aroused	
	N	Mean z Score	N	Mean z Score
High	16	.14	17	.21
Middle	11	.15	20	−.01
Low	13	−.11	16	−.37
σ diff. (High vs. Low)		.38*		.35*
t		.66		1.67
p		n.s.		.05 (one-tailed)

* Derived from estimate of variance within groups = 1.0267 with $df = 87$.

DISCUSSION

The clear relationship found between n-Affiliation scores and the tendency to select faces rather than neutral stimuli in a perceptual task seems to support a relationship between motivation and perceptual selection of motive-relevant stimuli. Since the measure of perceptual sensitivity in this case did not involve words, it seems reasonable to reject as an explanation any alternative based on verbal habits as suggested by Farber (127) or one based on frequency of word usage such as that offered by Solomon and Howes (386). Indirectly, this study lends support to the original interpretation in terms of motivation and perceptual selection of some of the studies that have involved the use of words. For example, the McClelland and Liberman study (275) relating n Achievement to recognition threshold for achievement-related words could properly be explained on the basis of verbal habits when considered alone. However, when they are viewed in comparison with the present study where words were not a factor in perceptual selection, it seems doubtful if an appeal to verbal habits constitutes a sufficient explanation.

The clear-cut primary results seem also to add to the evidence for the validity of the n Affiliation scoring system, since the scoring system yields statistically significant results in the expected direction on another variable.

The findings with respect to neutral and aroused conditions were not significantly different from chance. However, they are in the expected direction and the magnitude of the difference is approximately what was expected in comparison to the primary result. That is, there is some relationship in the neutral condition and more in the aroused condition. Since this is the second study in which the identical finding has been obtained (see Moulton *et al.,* Ch. 24), it seems likely that the theoretical expectation (24, p. 90) will eventually be substantiated on the basis of frequency of appearance of the finding or in a study in which there is a very large N.

SUMMARY

Thematic apperception measures of n Affiliation were obtained from 93 male members of a class in elementary experimental psychology. Subsequently they were asked to say which of four figures which were flashed on a screen in the four quadrants from the fixation point of up, down, left, and right, stood out the most or was clearest. The exposure speed and level of illumination was such that the stimuli were below the recognition threshold. On each trial one of the four stimuli was a face or faces and the others were similar but affiliation-neutral stimuli. It was found that those high in n Affiliation selected faces significantly more frequently than Ss low in n Affiliation. The expectation that arousal of the affiliation motive just prior to participation in the perceptual task would produce greater differences between High and Low n Affiliation Ss was confirmed but not to a statistically significant degree. This study is interpreted as supporting the predicted relationship between motivation and the perceptual selection of motive-relevant stimuli, and as lending indirect support to this interpretation of similar findings using word-recognition thresholds.

CHAPTER 26

n Achievement and Aesthetic Preference

ROBERT H. KNAPP

THE *a priori* case to be made for the proposition that aesthetic preference is an excellent index of temperament and personality is thoroughly convincing. Certainly aesthetic preference draws directly upon motivation and affect, taps many unconscious determinants, is directly involved in the operation of at least several defense mechanisms, and shows wide variation between and marked consistency within persons. The average layman, unencumbered by formal psychological theory, rightly feels that he may judge another with quick and intuitive confidence by observing his dress, his car, his home, and his wife, and by inferring from an evaluation of his "taste" the psychological qualities behind them. Yet for all this, we have as yet no well-standardized instrument of personality assessing based upon aesthetic preference. It is the purpose of the present article to present the preliminary form of a test of aesthetic preference and to relate performance on this instrument to the well-established psychological variable, *n* Achievement.

The instrument alluded to above is called the Tartan Test. It consists of photographic reproductions in color of thirty Scottish Tartans, each mounted upon a 6 × 10 inch cardboard. For some years the author has been seeking for material suitable for psychological test of aesthetic taste. Earlier efforts to use reproductions of paintings met with serious objections. Object identification, variation in technique, size, and shape made them unsatisfactory materials. The chance discovery of a small book of Scottish Tartans proved, therefore, a fortunate event for tartans possess a number of attributes particularly desirable for the purpose specified. First, they vary in design only in certain specific and measurable ways, i.e., predominant color, number of colors, fineness of texture, symmetry, complexity, brightness contrast, etc. Each of these is objectively measurable. Again, they are of uniform size. Third, they do not contain object representation with its attendant distractions.

367

Finally, there are over 200 recognized clan tartans from which selection may be made.

In evolving the Tartan Test, 30 tartans were selected out of the 200 represented in Bain's *The Clans and Tartans of Scotland* (29). This was accomplished in the following manner. Initially all 200 were examined, and from this number 48 were selected, including a wide variety from which patently unattractive or repetitious specimens were eliminated. These 48 tartans were then submitted to 40 judges, who arranged them into six categories according to preference and general appeal. Then the average ranking for each tartan was computed, and the nine most popular and the nine least popular were eliminated. This left 30 highly varied "controversial" tartans and constitutes the group employed in the present study.

Thus far preference for these 30 tartans has been correlated with over a dozen psychological variables, yielding some highly promising results with respect to such variables as the scales of the Minnesota Multiphasic, the factors of the Strong Vocational Interest Test, etc. Here we wish to confine ourselves to one result, namely, that pattern of tartan preference correlating with *n* Achievement, and to discuss some of the theoretical problems raised by these findings. It will not be necessary here to indicate the nature of *n* Achievement, which has been discussed extensively elsewhere in this volume and in the writings of McClelland *et al.* (272).

PROCEDURE

The subjects employed in the present inquiry were Wesleyan undergraduates approximately equally divided between the freshman and sophomore classes and numbering 68. At the beginning of the freshman year each class had been given the standard, group-administered, *n* Achievement measure as devised by McClelland and associates. Thus, for the sophomores, the *n* Achievement scores had been obtained a year and a half earlier while for the freshmen, only six months earlier. We mention this because our results clearly suggest, among other things, the stability of this measure over a considerable period.

The Tartan Test was administered in the following fashion. The mounted tartans were placed in random order along a long bulletin board at approximately eye height. The subjects were instructed to inspect the entire number for a few moments from a distance of from three to five feet and then to record their preferences according to the following system. The total number were to be assigned initially to six groups of five each. Then the one most liked and the one most disliked were singled out. This yielded us an eight-step scale with a forced distribution of 1, 4, 5, 5, 5, 5, 4, 1, a compromise between a normalized and rectilinear distribution which appeared to be reasonably satisfactory for our purposes without further adjustments.

TABLE 1

Code No.	Tartan	Correlation with n Ach.	Description
26	Campbell of Broadalbane	+18	Subdued blue-green with fine small yellow lines, open design.
48	Elliot	+18	Predominantly deep blue with dark open figure, very fine brown line.
6	Anderson	+17	Complex, fine-textured asymmetrical with many colors but predominantly light blue.
22	MacDonell of Glengarry	+15	Somber, fine-textured tartan with black and brick-brown predominant color.
7	Macpherson, Hunting	+08	Fairly open grey-black tartan with inconspicuous brick-red grill.
18	Cameron of Erracht	+08	Predominantly green-black tartan of fine texture with brown-yellow overlaid grill.
24	Ogilvie	+07	Bright orange and bluish-green tartan, highly complex, fine-textured, asymmetrical.
37	Clergy	+07	Very somber, deep blue and green tartan.
41	Sutherland, Ancient	+07	Predominantly blue-green, fairly open with brick-brown and white grill overlay.
20	Oliphant	+07	Open, asymmetrical, blue-green tartan with a black and white overlay grill.
16	Drummond	−20	Predominantly bright red tartan, moderately fine-textured, green secondary color.
47	Hay	−20	Generally similar to No. 16 above save dominant red less saturated.
13	Sinclair	−16	Predominantly red, monotonously symmetrical with open design and secondary green.
5	Brodie	−14	Predominantly bright red laced with dramatic black and yellow powerful contrasting design.
15	Cumming	−13	Predominantly green with secondary bright red, fairly fine design, peculiar mossy texture.
43	Stewart	−12	Predominantly bright red-brown tartan with white and blue-grey inconspicuous grills.
17	Barclay	−12	Bold, open, yellow and black tartan with strong contrast.
19	Ramsay	−09	Bold open red and black tartan in very open design, striking contrast.
3	Balmoral	−07	Light grey, fine-textured tartan with red and black overlay grill.
21	Steward of Appin	−07	Predominantly red, secondary green tartan, moderate complexity and asymmetry.

369

RESULTS

The next step was to establish the correlation between the n Achievement measure and the preference ranking assigned each of the tartans. Here product-moment correlations were employed. Given in Table 1 are the names of the ten tartans yielding the highest *positive* correlations and the ten yielding the highest *negative* correlations with n Achievement. Bearing in mind that the number of cases was 68, one might be discouraged at the low order of these correlations and dismiss the entire matter as unprofitable. However, when we examined the attributes of the ten "positive" and the ten "negative" tartans, we found some clear differences in stimulus properties which cannot be ignored and which quite surely cannot be explained as a chance deviation from a null relationship. In passing, moreover, we might mention two considerations which may partly explain the low order of the correlations reported here. First, these correlations are not corrected for discontinuity in the distribution of preference rankings; second, the n Achievement scores had been obtained under different conditions, at different times, with different pictures, and from six months to a year and a half earlier.

Let us now consider what distinguished the ten positive from the ten negative tartans. First and most obvious, the positive tartans are almost uniformly somber while the negative tartans are almost uniformly bright. This impression is immediate and overwhelming. On closer analysis it will be seen that the predominant color differs markedly for the two groups. As shown in Table 2, of the ten negatives, seven are dominantly red, while among the positives only one could doubtfully be so described.

TABLE 2. PRESENCE OF RED IN TARTANS FOR WHICH
PREFERENCE IS POSITIVELY AND NEGATIVELY
ASSOCIATED WITH n ACHIEVEMENT

	Red	Not Red	
Positive........................	1	9	10
Negative........................	7	3	10
	8	12	

$x^2 = 5.20$ (with Yates correction) $p < .03$

On the other hand, as shown in Table 3, blue appears in significant degree in seven of the positives and in none whatever of the negatives.

TABLE 3. PRESENCE OF BLUE IN TARTANS FOR WHICH
PREFERENCE IS POSITIVELY AND NEGATIVELY
ASSOCIATED WITH *n* ACHIEVEMENT

	Blue	Not Blue	
Positive........................	7	3	10
Negative........................	0	10	10
	7	13	

$x^2 = 7.50$ (with Yates correction) $p < .01$

It would appear that this chromatic difference constitutes the most
significant basis for separation between our two groups of tartans, and
that preference for red is consistently associated with low *n* Achievement while preference for blue is associated with high *n* Achievement.
The examination of other features of stimulus quality, such as fineness of texture, symmetry, etc. do not yield decisive further findings
(though with respect to other psychological variables, configurational
and not chromatic properties are definitive).

DISCUSSION

It is now appropriate that we discuss the significance of this interesting pattern relating color preference to *n* Achievement, a relationship which has subsequently been confirmed in McClelland's analysis
of children's doodles (see Ch. 21). It appears to the writer that *n*
Achievement may indeed be thought of not only as a need in the
traditional sense but also as an ego strategy. As an ego strategy, it
may be defined as a general policy of pursuing well-being through
adopting an active manipulatory role with respect to the environment.
Thus, the person with high *n* Achievement wishes to "do unto" his
environment, and one with low *n* Achievement wishes to have his environment "do unto" him. Commitment to one or the other of these
basic strategic policies is obviously a most basic parameter of personality structure and may well be established autogenetically with the
separation and consolidation of the ego in early childhood. Indeed,
present data suggest that *n* Achievement is both measurable and
identifiable at the preschool age.

Now, how may we relate the preference for subdued bluish tartans
and the dislike of red and bright tartans to an ego strategy committed
to playing an active role towards its environment, to "do unto" its
environment rather than the contrary? The answer to this may, I believe, be contained in a consideration of some of the perceptual
properties of these two colors. First, we may note as an established

psychophysical fact that red is inherently brighter than blue, more rarely found in nature, more commanding of attention generally. Beyond this we may take note of the Gestalt observation that blue is a "soft" color, and red a "hard" color, as Liebmann (232) designated them some thirty years ago. It will be recalled that according to this observation, blue holds form poorly, is malleable, and is a preferred "ground" color. Red, by way of contrast, is a "figure" color, resists perceptual distortion, and imposes itself as figure in the perceptual field. We may now tentatively assert that the preference for somber bluish tartans and the dislike of red by individuals with high n Achievement follows. For such persons require that their environment be "soft" while they are "hard"; they wish to exert their will effectively—to manipulate, not be manipulated. They will seek a "passive" environment and eschew strong, intrusive stimuli.

If this interpretation of n Achievement is valid and if our explanation of our tartan results is correct, we may see our way to several further speculative excursions. We venture, as a general hypothesis, that individuals and cultures fostering high achievement motivations will dislike strong and assertive stimuli generally in their fashions, dress, and ornament. They will regard with distaste and aversion bright colors, strong contrasts, and prefer subdued, even monotonous, decor. Now it has been demonstrated that n Achievement is *ceteris paribus* higher among middle class children than among lower class children, and it has also been frequently observed that middle class propriety and conservatism in matters of dress distinguish them from the more colorful taste of lower socioeconomic classes. The "man in the grey flannel suit" expresses the quintessence of the middle class subdued taste.

Again, there is a reasonable quantity of evidence to suggest that n Achievement is higher in Northern European Protestant cultures than in Catholic Mediterranean cultures. If we examine the dress, architecture, and decor of such achievement-oriented cultures as the Germans, the Dutch, and the British, we find a consistent somberness in the use of color when contrasted with Mediterranean peoples. But it is perhaps in the history of 17th-century England that we have the most striking contrast of the two tastes and the two character styles. The Puritans, imbued with very strong achievement motivation, eschewed all but the somberest of dress and ornament, imposed fines for the wearing of bright colors, destroyed the stained glass windows of churches, and cultivated unconditional austerity in dress and decor. They stand in dramatic contrast to the Cavaliers with their feudal and chivalric traditions of ascribed status, colorful dress, and fondness for indulgent living.

CHAPTER 27

....

Relationships Between the Self Concept and Differences in the Strength and Generality of Achievement Motivation*

JOHN G. MARTIRE[1]

THIS STUDY is an investigation of the nature of the differences in self concept among four groups of Ss classified according to the strength and generality of achievement motivation. The plan of the experiment was to obtain n Achievement scores for Ss under two environmental conditions, Neutral and Achievement Oriented, and to relate these scores to measures of the Self, the self-Ideal, and the discrepancies between these self measures.

A secondary interest was to discover any relationships existing between Wishful and Realistic level-of-aspiration estimates and both the n Achievement scores and the self measures.

Relationships between both the integrative and conflictive aspects of self and other personality factors or variables have been the concern of many investigators (7, 53, 59, 67, 180, 197, 258, 310, 346, 384). There is general agreement that there may exist conscious or unconscious conflict between aspects of the self which will show itself in behavioral terms. In the present study, it was expected that self-conflict would be related to high generalized achievement motivation. Such a prediction was made on the basis of the results of Wein-

* Reprinted with minor abridgement by permission of author and publisher from the *Journal of Personality*, 1956, **24**, 364-375. Copyright 1956 by Duke University Press.

[1] This study is based on a doctoral dissertation presented to the faculty of the University of Michigan. It was reported, in abbreviated form, at the 1953 meetings of the MPA.

The writer acknowledges his appreciation to Dr. John W. Atkinson and the other members of his committee for assistance in the completion of this study. Dr. I. E. Farber and Dr. H. P. Bechtoldt of the State University of Iowa were of considerable critical and statistical assistance.

373

berger's study (425) which suggested that Ss with high motivation for achievement rated achievement-related traits as important more frequently than Ss having low achievement motivation. However, these high n Achievement Ss rated these same traits as not characteristic of them. This implied dissatisfaction with the self was a general feature of the high n Achievement people but was not found in the low n Achievement group. The achievement-related traits employed by Weinberger were traits judged in advance of the study to be those in a list most intimately related to successful accomplishment. They were viewed as either defining the goal of accomplishment (General Success) or as being instrumental to achievement (Intelligence, Initiative, Motivation, Creativeness).

Specifically, it was expected in the present investigation that Ss who showed high generalized achievement motivation, i.e., Ss who obtained high n Achievement scores whether achievement-related cues were present or not, the HH's, would show a significantly greater discrepancy between their self-Ideal and Self ratings on the five achievement-related traits than Ss in three other categories. For an approach-avoidance analysis of some personality characteristics of the four groups of Ss to be isolated in this study, applications of achievement theory have been employed and may be found in (24) and (231).

METHOD

Subjects. The Ss were 53 male undergraduate and graduate volunteers with an age range of 18 to 43, and a median age of 25.3. When recruited, Ss were told, in rather vague terms, that they would participate in a personality experiment in which the investigator was standardizing some tests.

Experimental Conditions. Ss were run in each of the two experimental conditions, Neutral and Achievement Oriented, in six separate groups. These conditions were defined in terms of the external or situational cues presented in each of the experimental sessions.

Under the Neutral condition (always the first session) E made every effort to refrain from any behavior which might be perceived as an achievement-related cue. No demands were made and informality was the keynote. Ss were seated facing a screen and told that the tests to be administered were in the developmental stage and that it was of little concern to E how they were completed. After this introduction was completed, Ss were administered the short form of Lowell's (241) Scrambled Words Test which consists of a series of 48 items, each of which is composed of four, five, or six letters arranged in a meaningless order. The task is to make a common word from these scrambled letters. *Ss* were allowed to work at their own paces (about 15 minutes) and were then asked to set the booklets aside without writing their names.

The *Ss* were next asked to respond to pictures with thematic stories and the usual procedure for measuring n Achievement (272, Ch. III) was followed. The four pictures, which are denoted by the standard letters used in *The Achievement Motive* (272), were presented in the order C, E, D, H.

The measures of self concept were adapted from those used by Weinberger (425). For the measure of the self-Ideal, *Ss* were asked to place each of 26 traits[2] in one of five categories running from "personally most important to stand high on" to "least important." For the measure of the Self, the same traits were to be arranged according to the extent to which each *S* saw them as characteristic of himself. In both cases, a forced distribution was employed so that, for each *S*, six traits were assigned to the midpoint and five traits were assigned to each of the other positions.

Ss used anchoring trait definitions supplied to them and successively made the self-Ideal and Self ratings with the proviso that each set of ratings was to be independent of the other. The whole rating procedure took about 25 minutes.

Under the Achievement-Oriented condition, the purpose of the procedure was to arouse the *Ss'* achievement-related motives. This was done by insisting on formality, by making specific achievement demands and by presenting many achievement-related verbal cues. For example, in the "directions" and the "explanation" of the long form of the Scrambled Words Test, the test was related to such factors as verbal ability, intelligence, college success, reasoning ability, flexibility, accuracy, speed, competition, leadership, and executive capacity.

This second experimental session was held about six to eight days later in the same classroom or fraternity dining room. *Ss* were again seated facing a screen and were given a long form of the Scrambled Words Test; they were asked to write their names on the booklets. This long form of the test consisted of 192 meaningless items similar to those used on the short form. The eight pages, with 24 items to

---

[2] These traits were adapted from Brownfain (53). Each trait was defined in terms of a high and a low end of the trait continuum. In the following list the five traits judged to be achievement-related are in italics: *Intelligence,* Emotional Maturity, Social Poise, Physical Attractiveness, Dominance, Sportsmanship, Prestige, Sociability, Sincerity, *Initiative,* Trustfulness, Flexibility, Individuality, Self-Understanding, Interest in Opposite Sex, Dependability, *Motivation,* Understanding of Others, Self-Acceptance, Popularity, *Creativeness,* Over-all Adjustment, Self-Confidence, Autonomy, Security-Minded, and *General Success.*

a page, were arranged in a Latin Square design to randomize differences in item difficulty. *Ss* were told to follow very closely the instructions on time and test speed. As part of the effort to arouse achievement motivation, *Ss* made their *level of aspiration* estimates just before beginning the Scrambled Words Test. They did not have knowledge of previous performances but were given, as a frame of reference, a range of possible scores from 0 to 192, with a mean for the eight pages set at 90. These indices, adapted roughly from Lowell (272), included an average page score of 10 to 12 for a two-minute period. *Ss* were instructed to keep this framework in mind and to write at the bottom of the direction sheet the scores they would "Like to make . . ." and those they would "Expect to make . . ." on the test that followed. These numbers will be referred to as the Wishful and the Realistic level of aspiration estimates.[3]

After a review of the instructions for the Scrambled Words Test, *Ss* were told to go ahead and "do the best you can." As a part of the effort towards producing an achievement-motivating condition, the specific test instructions as to time and page turning were strictly and emphatically enforced. *E* continually walked about the room, peered over shoulders, and acted vitally interested in the *Ss'* progress.[4]

Following the Scrambled Words Test, a fairly equivalent form of the *n* Achievement measure was administered in precisely the same manner as under the Neutral condition. Four different pictures were presented in the order B, A, G, J. The product moment correlation previously reported (272, Ch. VII) between *n* Achievement scores on three of these (B, A, G) and three pictures (C, E, D) from the Neutral condition was .64. The estimated reliability of the measure obtained in response to all six pictures (Spearman-Brown) was reported as .78. The fourth picture (J) contained cues somewhat similar to those of the fourth picture (H) of the first session.

Design. The separate total *n* Achievement scores obtained from stories written by each *S,* under each condition, were used to categorize all *Ss* into four subgroups, Low-High, High-High, High-Low and Low-Low. McClelland *et al.* report a correlation of .95 on *n* Achievement scores obtained by two experienced judges, a score-rescore correlation of .95 for the same judge on two occasions six months apart and scoring reliabilities in the neighborhood of .90 for graduate students with some limited experience. Using the rank differ-

---

[3] It is assumed, in Ch. 22, that responses to the question, "What score do you *expect* to make," will indicate the subjective probability of success. Editor.

[4] See Ch. 19 for a discussion of the effects of procedures of this sort on the relation of *n* Achievement to performance. Editor.

ence correlational method, a scoring reliability of .80 was found between the writer and one of the authors of the scoring system on n Achievement scores obtained from 18 Ss.

The median n Achievement score in each condition was used to separate Ss into a high and a low group for that condition. The Neutral median was 3.7 with a range of -4 to $+17$, and the Achievement-Oriented median was 5.5 with a range of -3 to $+14$. A t-test was computed for the 53 Ss for the difference between the Neutral mean n Achievement score of 4.50 and the Achievement-Oriented mean n Achievement score of 5.30. The difference of .80 was in the expected direction but not significant ($p = .16$). In view of the fact that scores in response to pictures B, A, G, used in the Achievement-Oriented condition, normally average about 1.00 lower than pictures C, E, D, used in the Neutral condition (272, Ch. VI), we may have increased confidence that the trend reflects the influence of the experimental condition, and represents the arousal of motivation in the former group.

Following the initial categorization into groups according to the high and low scores, seven Ss within the median interval of the Neutral condition, and two doubtful Ss were reassigned according to an inspection technique which emphasized the relative distance between high and low scores (see 250, Ch. II). This procedure resulted in 15 LH's, 12 HH's, 14 LL's and 12 HL's.

DISCUSSION OF RESULTS

In order to obtain a single index to be employed to investigate the *self-Ideal and Self ratings on the achievement-related traits,* the mean of each $S's$ importance ratings (self-Ideal) and characteristic ratings (Self) on the five achievement-related traits was computed. The medians of these mean ratings on achievement-related traits for each subgroup are presented in Table 1. When these data were analyzed by the Mann-Whitney U Test, no significant differences were found

TABLE 1. MEDIAN SELF-IDEAL AND SELF-RATINGS AND MEDIAN SELF-IDEAL SELF-DISCREPANCIES ON ACHIEVEMENT-RELATED TRAITS

	N ACHIEVEMENT SUBGROUP			
	HH	LH	LL	HL
N	12	15	14	12
Self-Ideal	3.70	3.20	3.43	3.40
Self	2.70	2.84	3.23	3.20
Discrepancies (Self-Ideal minus Self)	.90	.22	.30	.30

among groups on the self-Ideal or Self ratings on the combined achievement-related traits.

On the basis of the *discrepancy* between his self-Ideal minus Self ratings of the combined achievement-related traits, each S was assigned a positive or negative discrepancy score. The median of the distribution of discrepancy scores for each subgroup is also shown in Table 1. In the case of the HH subgroup, the distribution (Mann-Whitney U-Test) of the self-Ideal—Self discrepancy scores on the achievement-related traits was higher than the LH ($p = .01$), HL ($p = .01$), and LL ($p = .02$) subgroups on similar distributions. No other significant differences were found.

The self-Ideal—Self rating discrepancy in the HH subgroups means that people with high generalized achievement motivation desire those traits associated with achievement (self-Ideal) but do *not* see themselves as possessing those traits (Self). This finding supports the theoretical consideration that it is the discrepancy between the self-Ideal and the Self concepts in the realm of personal achievement which differentiates Ss with high generalized achievement motivation, the HH's, from those in the other three subgroups. A relationship has been established between a *kind* of motivational pattern and a *kind* of self concept discrepancy.

Winterbottom's (Ch. 33) findings are pertinent here. She suggests that people with high generalized achievement motivation, our HH group, have probably had very general achievement demands made on them early in life and have obtained rewards for accomplishment. It is possible that such people might have developed high achievement expectations for themselves which might, in reality, be difficult to meet and satisfy. Dissatisfaction may arise when personal limitations (for example, low intelligence) or when reality limitations (such as lack of financial support) prevent the person from fully meeting his high standards and satisfying his achievement need. Such dissatisfaction may show itself in a discrepancy between an ideal and an actual self picture.

Subgroup Intercorrelations for Self-Ideal and for Self Ratings. The intercorrelations (rhos) among all subgroups for the self-Ideal ratings and for the Self ratings range from .51 to .87. All correlations with one exception ($p < .02$) are at the .01 confidence level. This fact suggests that the four subgroups tend to have quite similar self-Ideal and Self concepts. It follows that we cannot account for expected self concept differences among subgroups on the basis of either the self-Ideal rating or the Self rating *alone*.

Table 2 shows that the r's (inferred from obtained rhos) between the self-Ideal and Self ratings *within each group* are moderately high

TABLE 2. INFERRED PEARSON $r's$ BETWEEN THE SELF-IDEAL AND SELF-RATINGS FOR EACH GROUP *on All Traits* (26) AND SIMILAR $r's$ WITH THE *Achievement-Related Traits* EXCLUDED (21 TRAITS)

Subgroup	All Traits (26)	Achievement-related Traits Excluded (21 Traits)
HH.	.46	.64
LH.	.72	.69
LL.	.79	.84
HL.	.80	.81

when the achievement-related traits (26 traits) are included and somewhat higher when the achievement-related traits are excluded. In all cases $p < .03$.

These findings are interpreted to mean that each group tends to see as characteristic, to some degree, those traits which they consider important. In more general terms, the Ss in each subgroup demonstrate a relatively high degree of congruence between their self-Ideal and Self concepts.

This interpretation applies equally when the achievement-related traits are excluded, with the possible exception of the HH subgroup, although the correlation of .64 for 26 traits is not significantly greater than the correlation of .46 for the 21 traits.

There are significant differences in the expected direction between the self-Ideal—Self correlation of the HH subgroup (.46) for all 26 traits and similar correlations of .79 for the LL (x/SD = 1.96, $p < .03$) and .80 for the HL (x/SD = 2.05, $p < .02$) groups. When the achievement-related traits are part of the self ratings, the HH's have a significantly greater discrepancy, i.e., significantly lower correlation, between the self-Ideal and the Self concepts than two of the other three subgroups. None of the other correlational differences is significant.

There were no significant differences between the HH self-Ideal—Self correlation when the achievement-rated traits were excluded, leaving 21 traits and similar correlations for the other three subgroups. The difference between the HH correlation (.64) and the highest correlation of the other three subgroups (.84 for the LL's) was at the .06 confidence level. These results are seen as a further support of the statement that it is the achievement-related traits which contribute most to the discrepancy between the self-Ideal and the Self concepts for the HH subgroup.

Need Achievement and Level of Aspiration. Table 3 shows the median Wishful and Realistic level of aspiration estimates, the

TABLE 3. MEDIANS OF THE WISHFUL AND REALISTIC LEVEL OF ASPIRATION ESTIMATES AND OF THE DISCREPANCIES BETWEEN THEM FOR EACH GROUP; MEDIAN PERFORMANCE SCORES* FOR EACH GROUP

	HH	LH	LL	HL
N	12	15	14	12
Wishful (Like to make)	140.1	150.0	140.0	115.0
Realistic (Expect to make)	109.8	99.6	100.0	90.3
Discrepancy (Wishful - Realistic)	29.8	40.0	30.0	25.0
Performance	108.0	106.0	121.0	117.0

* Long Form of Scrambled Words Test.

median of their discrepancies (Wishful minus Realistic) and the Performance Scores for each subgroup on the Long Form of the Scrambled Words Test.

The HL's, Ss with strong generalized achievement motivation but presumed to be anxious about failure in a stressful situation, have a distribution of Wishful level of aspiration estimates which is different from the combined distributions of the other three subgroups (x/SD = 2.59, $p < .01$) as computed by the Mann-Whitney U-Test.

The Realistic level of aspiration distributions, as defined by their medians, fall into three groupings with the HH subgroup the highest (Table 3), LH and LL subgroups virtually the same (99.6 and 100.0), and the HL lowest. The distribution of Realistic level of aspiration estimates for the HL subgroup is again different from the combined distributions of the other three subgroups (x/SD = 2.42, $p < .01$).

It is apparent that the HL Ss are a unique group in terms of both their Wishful and Realistic levels of aspiration. It is inferred that these Ss have strong generalized achievement motivation but are anxious about failure. In both cases, Wishful and Realistic, they are consistently *lower* in their estimates than the other three subgroups combined. Their fear of failure is defended against, it is suggested, by the lowering of the level of aspiration. This interpretation is in line with Allport's (7) claim that in level of aspiration studies Ss behave so as to maintain their self-esteem at the highest possible level. Self-protection, i.e., defensiveness, is evidenced when these people are placed in an Achievement-Oriented situation where actual performance may result in failure.

No relationships were discovered between level of aspiration estimates and self concept discrepancies, nor were any performance differences found.

Age Differences Among n Achievement Subgroups. The HH group is younger than the other three groups. The median HH age was 20.5 with a range of 19 to 26 years. The LH group had a median of 27.8 with a range of 19 to 36. The LL and HL groups each had medians of 27.5 and ranges of 18 to 43 and 20 to 40 respectively. Differences between the HH group and each of the others were computed using the Mann-Whitney U-Test. The x/SD values were: LH, 3.37 ($p <$ .01); LL, 1.75 ($p <$ .04); and HL, 3.06 ($p <$ .01).

Comparable groups ($N = 5$) of younger Ss, forming a subgroup, were compared to the total number of Ss in each group on the self-Ideal, Self and Discrepancy median ratings of the achievement-related traits. Trends for these subgroups (Table 4) were quite similar

TABLE 4. MEDIAN SELF-IDEAL, SELF AND DISCREPANCY RATINGS FOR YOUNGER SUBGROUPS ($N = 5$) AND FOR TOTALS Ss WITHIN EACH GROUP

	Self-Ideal	Self	Discrepancy
HH ($N = 5$)	4.20	2.40	1.20
HH ($N = 12$)	3.70	2.70	.90
LH ($N = 5$)	3.40	2.80	.40
LH ($N = 15$)	3.20	2.84	.22
LL ($N = 5$)	3.00	3.40	.20
LL ($N = 14$)	3.43	3.23	.30
HL ($N = 5$)	3.40	3.20	.40
HL ($N = 12$)	3.40	3.20	.30

to the trends evidenced for the total Ss in each group, suggesting that age alone did not account for the obtained self concept differences.

Taken separately, the fact that high generalized achievement motivation is a phenomenon associated with youth or late adolescence suggests another possible explanation of the HH dissatisfaction mentioned earlier. It is at this age that standards of achievement must face the reality of personal limitations and competition with peers. The necessary reorganization of standards may cause a temporary dissatisfaction.

SUMMARY

The primary purpose of this study was to investigate the nature of differences in self concept among four groups of Ss classified according to strength and generality of achievement motivation. A subsidiary interest was to discover the relationships between level of aspiration concerning a specific achievement task and measures of both self concept and achievement motivation.

Previous work on the origins of achievement motivation provided some basis for the expectation that people with strong generalized achievement motivation would show a discrepancy between self-Ideal and Self ratings on five selected traits (Intelligence, Initiative, Creativeness, Motivation, General Success) judged to be related to personal achievement.

Thematic apperception measures of achievement motivation were obtained for 53 male college students under both Neutral and Achievement-motivating conditions. Self-Ideal and Self measures were obtained by having Ss rank 26 traits according to their *importance* and again in terms of how *characteristic* of them each trait was. Wishful and Realistic levels of aspiration were obtained for a specific pencil and paper task.

The general finding was that Ss who obtained high n Achievement scores under both Neutral and Achievement-motivating conditions were found to have a significantly greater discrepancy between their self-Ideal and Self ratings on the five achievement-rated traits combined than Ss in three other categories. These other categories were also based upon measures of strength and generality of n Achievement.

Ss having strong generalized achievement motivation but presumed to be also anxious about failure when in a stressful achievement situation reported significantly lower Wishful and Realistic levels of aspiration for a specific task than other Ss.

While both self concept and level of aspiration measures were meaningfully related to projective measures of achievement motivation, they could not be readily related to each other.

CHAPTER 28

....

Toward Description of Personality in Terms of Configuration of Motives

Byron L. Groesbeck[1]

THE DESCRIPTION of personality in terms of the joint effects or interactions of several motives within the individual has been suggested by many persons. Murray, for example, has pointed to particular kinds of actions which can be accounted for in terms of "fusions" of several motives (314). The present paper summarizes the results of a more comprehensive analysis of personality attributes that tend to be associated with particular configurations or combinations of achievement and affiliation motives within individuals (158).

The indices of strength of n Achievement and n Affiliation were derived from content analysis of stories written in response to TAT pictures. As described elsewhere (Chs. 12 and 13), the measure of achievement motive focuses upon imaginative concern over doing well in relation to standards of performance; the measure of affiliation motive focuses upon imaginative concern over establishing, maintaining, or restoring positive affective relationships with other persons.

The intent of this study is to begin to fill out the descriptive picture of the person in whom motives to achieve or to affiliate are relatively strong and to begin to explore the subtle differences in personality, as manifested to others, of particular configurations of these two motives within individuals. The plan was to classify persons as relatively strong or relatively weak in each of these motives, giving a fourfold typology, and then to discover what particular attributes of personality, as revealed in ratings by the self and others or as measured by standard instruments, would tend to be

---

[1] This paper is based on a thesis submitted to the Department of Psychology of the University of Michigan in partial fulfillment of the requirements for the degree of Doctor of Philosophy. The writer wishes to express his appreciation to Drs. E. L. Kelly and J. W. Atkinson.

383

associated chiefly with a particular motivational configuration or type.

Selection of the Data. In order to investigate the degree to which a rich assortment of personality measures were associated with persons characterized by the four motive configurations, use was made of the data collected at the University of Michigan during the summer of 1947 on which was based part of the report of *The Prediction of Performance in Clinical Psychology* by Kelly and Fiske (208). One-hundred-thirty-seven new trainees in the Veterans' Administration Training Program in Clinical Psychology were assessed in six classes of 24 students each.[2] Each assessment period lasted seven days.

The n Achievement and n Affiliation scores were obtained from six-minute stories written for each of eleven pictures from the TAT set developed by Murray (314). Pictures 1, 7BM, 14, and 17BM had been used in some previous studies of achievement motivation; 3BM, 4, 6BM, 10, and 13MF had been used in affiliation motive research. Pictures 8GF and 11 were also included in the data. The TAT was administered to groups of five or six students at a time. Cues for the arousal of the achievement motive were implicit in the testing situation from which students were taken to write TAT stories. In addition, the students were likely to become infused with a spirit of competition as a result of being associated with a few trainees who were n Achievement-aroused throughout the assessment period.

It can be presumed that the affiliation motive also was situationally aroused. Most of the students were among strangers, far from home. A strong desire for friendship was manifest in that the students went off together in small groups at their first free moments and often thereafter, and a large number of bull sessions and other social interactions took up their free time.

All 11 stories were scored for each of the motives since, at the time, there was no sound rationale for selecting a picture as more appropriate to the measurement of one motive than the other. The writer scored the pictures for the affiliation motive, using the June, 1953 draft of the scoring manual (Ch. 13). The standard for scoring reliability, a rank-difference correlation of .90 between the writer's scoring of a set of sample stories and the scoring of the authors of the system, had been met. Dr. Joseph Veroff, who had extensive prior experience with the scoring system for n Achievement, obtained n

---

[2] One-hundred-twenty-eight males were assessed. The TAT protocol of one student and several scores for two other students were unobtainable. Differences between the achievement motive in males and females (Ch. 3) led us to exclude the data on the nine women.

Achievement scores from the stories. He used scoring system C as described in *The Achievement Motive* (and Ch. 12). The ranges of scores for both measures approximated the ranges usually obtained in studies of these motives.

The reliabilities of comparable forms for n Achievement scores vary from .48 for a three-picture measure to .78 for a six-picture measure. However, two forms of the measure have shown a percentage agreement near 75 (72.5 and 78.1 per cent in two studies) in placing subjects above and below the median total score (272, Ch. VII). It was decided to use the high-low division of the subjects usually made in previous studies of these motives. The n Achievement variable was dichotomized at the median, 2.56, so that 64 persons high in n Achievement and 63 persons low in n Achievement were separated. The median n Affiliation score was 16.22, and the division placed 61 subjects in the high and 66 in the low n Affiliation groups. The gross difference between the n Achievement and n Affiliation median scores can be attributed with reasonable confidence to (1) the much heavier weighting of affiliative and other interpersonal cues than achievement-related cues in the standard TAT pictures that were used and (2) the differences in scoring procedures which gave a -1 score to stories devoid of achievement imagery and a 0 score to stories with no affiliation imagery.

The 2×2 chi-square table of the relationship between n Achievement and n Affiliation yielded 36 persons in the high n Achievement–high n Affiliation cell, 28 in the high n Achievement–low n Affiliation cell, 25 in the low n Achievement–high n Affiliation cell, and 38 in the low n Achievement–low n Affiliation cell. The tetrachoric r for this relationship was .24 ($p < .07$). Since the degree of association between the motives was low, the classification of subjects was made on nearly orthogonal dimensions.

Selection of the Measures. Six different types of data were collected during the assessment period in the summer of 1947: trait ratings of trainees by themselves, by peers, and by the assessment staff; various tests of ability (e.g., the Miller Analogies Test); self-report questionnaires (e.g., the Allport-Vernon Study of Values); sociometric choices by peers; projective tests including the Rorschach and others as well as the TAT; personal history materials. Of these, only the trait ratings, certain self-report questionnaires, and the sociometric questionnaire were selected for this initial analysis.

Trait Ratings. The trait ratings (see Table 1) provided the most complete coverage of personality of any of the measures. The Scale A ratings were "intended to cover primarily phenotypic variables, *descriptive* of the subject as seen by the staff at the time of assessment. Scale B was intended to provide judgments of more genotypic variables, i.e., *evaluative* judgments of broader underlying variables . . ." (208, p. 41). In addition, self, peers, and assessment staff made ratings on Degree of Liking. The peer and self ratings were made on the last (seventh) day of the assessment period. Each of the traits were described in a short paragraph defining the extremes; and ratings were made on an 8 point scale.

The median reliability of the final pooled staff ratings (the only

TABLE 1. PERSONALITY TRAIT RATINGS

Scale A—Phenotypic Traits

1. Readiness to Cooperate	-v-	Obstructiveness
2. Consistent	-v-	Inconsistent
3. Assertive	-v-	Submissive
4. Depressed	-v-	Cheerful
5. Irresponsible	-v-	Serious
6. Gregarious (Adient toward people)	-v-	Nongregarious (abient from people)
7. Easily Upset	-v-	Unshakable
8. Narrow Interests	-v-	Broad Interests
9. Suspicious	-v-	Trustful
10. Generous	-v-	Self-Centered, Selfish
11. Silent	-v-	Talkative
12. Cautious	-v-	Adventurous
13. Socially Poised and Adept	-v-	Socially Clumsy, Awkward in Social Situations
14. Rigid	-v-	Adaptable, Flexible
15. Dependent	-v-	Self-Sufficient
16. Placid	-v-	Worrying, Anxious
17. Conscientious	-v-	Not Conscientious
18. Imaginative	-v-	Unimaginative
19. Marked Overt Interest in Opposite Sex	-v-	Slight Overt Interest in Opposite Sex
20. Frank	-v-	Secretive
21. Dependent Minded	-v-	Independent Minded
22. Limited Overt Emotional Expression	-v-	Marked Overt Emotional Expression

Scale B—Genotypic Traits

23a. Ability to Develop and Maintain Warm Interpersonal Relationships
23b. Social Adjustment
24. Appropriateness of Emotional Expression
25. Characteristic Intensity of Inner Emotional Tension
26. Sexual Adjustment
27. Motivation for Professional Status
28. Motivation for Scientific Understanding of People
29. Insight into Others
30. Insight into Himself
31. Quality of Intellectual Accomplishments

staff ratings used in this study) was .84. To estimate the reliabilities of peer ratings on Scale A variables, an intraclass r was computed with the median $r = .75$ (208, p. 132).

Self-Report Scales. The self-report scales (9, 156, 162, 163, 164, 396) used in this study are listed together with their reliabilities in Table 2. These scales were chosen for the appropriateness of the concepts measured for the description of normal personality.

TABLE 2. SCALES FROM SELF-REPORT QUESTIONNAIRES AND THEIR RELIABILITIES

Strong Vocational Interest Blank (.85 to .94)
    Group I   Interest in Science
    Group II   Interest in Science
    Group V   Working with people for their presumed good
    Group VIII   Business Detail
    Group IX   Business Contacts
    Group X   Language
Study of Values (.49 to .84)
    Theoretical
    Aesthetic
    Economic
    Political
    Social
    Religious
Gough Scales (from MMPI) (.48 to .74)
    Dominance
    Social Status
    Social Participation
    Social Responsibility
    Psychological Interests
    Effective Intellectual Functioning
    Graduate Student
Guilford-Martin Battery of Personality Inventories (.89 to .92)
    Social Extraversion
    Thinking Introversion
    Freedom from Depressive Tendencies
    Freedom from Cycloid Tendencies
    Rhathymia
    Agreeableness
    Cooperativeness
    Objectivity

Sociometric Questionnaire. The sociometric questionnaire was concerned with student preferences among their peers as camping companions, immediate superiors in a psychological clinic, intimate friends, teachers of clinical psychology, and therapists to whom they would send their wives. Two other questions asked were, "Which person do you think understands you best?" and "Which persons did you find most difficult to analyze or size up?" The number of choices of each student for the items mentioned and two other scores, number of times chosen positively in the entire questionnaire and number of individuals choosing an assessee positively, constituted the sociometric data. These data were selected because of their expected negative relationship to strength of affiliation motivation (Chs. 4 and 5).

The other data available were not used because (1) previous research on the motives had elicited relatively little information from projective measures and tests of ability (272) and (2) preliminary exploration on a sample of 35 of the 127 trainees by the writer suggested that few significant relationships to motives would be discovered in personal history data.

Treatment of the Data. As described above, the 127 subjects were divided into four groups according to the following classifications: high n Achievement–high n Affiliation (N = 36), high n Achievement–low n Affiliation (N = 28), low n Achievement–high n Affiliation (N = 25), or low n Achievement–low n Affiliation (N = 38). A frequency distribution of the scores of all 127 subjects was also made for each correlate measure. A high-low division of scores on the correlate measure was made as near as possible to the median of the total distribution. An even high-low division was often not possible because all scores were in single-digit, coded form. A table of the following form was then prepared:

	Low on Correlate (below median)	High on Correlate (above median)
1. High n Achievement–High n Affiliation	. . .	. . .
2. High n Achievement–Low n Affiliation	. . .	. . .
3. Low n Achievement–High n Affiliation	. . .	. . .
4. Low n Achievement–Low n Affiliation	. . .	. . .

The analysis consisted of a comparison of one subgroup with all of the others combined. Thus, characteristics of a subgroup were identified by showing how the subgroup stood out in relation to all other subgroups with respect to the characteristic involved. Phi coefficients were used to give some idea of the relative degree of association. (The relationship of each of the variables to n Achievement and n Affiliation considered separately is presented elsewhere (158).)

Since this kind of analysis is relatively insensitive, only strong trends appear statistically significant ($p < .05$). No curvilinear trends are manifest. However, the high-low division of the distribution of motive scores follows a practice established in light of the relatively low reliability of the measures.

The tables which follow contain only the attributes which were associated with a particular motive configuration to a significant degree, i.e., with a p of .05 or less in a two-tailed test. Furthermore, the tables contain a matrix of tetrachoric correlation coefficients representing the degree of association among the variables which characterize a particular motive configuration. The N for each of these correlation matrices is 125 because the self-report data was incomplete for two subjects.

RESULTS

High n *Achievement–High* n *Affiliation Group.* In Table 3, phi coefficient (ϕ) represents the degree of association of each attribute with the motive configuration ($N = 127$). The attributes are grouped according to their correlations with one another.

The first four characteristics form a cluster which might be characterized as a *strong ethical sense.* The two staff ratings, seriousness and conscientiousness, define a factor found by Kelly and Fiske in a factor analysis of the staff ratings which they termed "Ethical Sense" (208). Persons with high scores on the Social Responsibility scale (developed by Gough from MMPI items) have been described as responsible, conscientious, dependable, and as demonstrating integrity (156).

Two other qualities associated with this group are revealed in self-report scales. Scores on the Effective Intellectual Functioning scale have been known to be correlated with ratings of intellectual competence and ability to communicate ideas effectively (156). Persons with strong Social Values manifest concern for human rights and the welfare of others (9).

According to the assessment staff, the students who were high in both *n* Achievement and *n* Affiliation appeared cheerful, sexually adjusted, and at peace with themselves. Peers of members of this group were less favorable in their opinions, however, and thought them relatively dependent on others for decisions and insensitive to other trainees.

High n *Achievement–Low* n *Affiliation Group.* The first four attributes listed in Table 4 form a cluster of traits, all of which suggest *a facility for working with people.* The two staff ratings, social poise and unshakability, defined a factor in the previously mentioned factor analysis by Kelly and Fiske, which was termed "Social Poise" (208). Peers perceived members of this group as having a minimum of persistent inner tension. The expressed interests of this group can be characterized as showing a "preference for working with others for their presumed good" (396). Personnel managers, school super-

TABLE 3. PERSONALITY CHARACTERISTICS ASSOCIATED WITH A HIGH ACHIEVEMENT—HIGH AFFILIATION CONFIGURATION OF MOTIVES

	ϕ^*	1	2	3	4	5	6	7	8	9	10	11	12
1. Conscientious; honest, unselfish (PSR)	25**	79											
2. Serious; accepts responsibilities (PSR)	20	37	54										
3. Social Responsibility (SRS)	18	57	38	34									
4. Liked very much (PSR)	18	29	18	42	37								
5. Effective Intellectual Functioning (SRS)	30**	−12	00	02	00	31							
6. Strong Social Values (SRS)	18	24	10	−02	15	10	17						
7. Easy to size up (Soc)	20	02	−19	08	19	19	08	51					
8. Cheerful; optimistic; enthusiastic (PSR)	19	22	−03	16	10	16	−17	08	52				
9. Little inner emotional tension (PSR)	17	38	19	31	18	19	−17	15	30	63			
10. Sexual needs enhance overall adjustment (PSR)	20	18	28	26	10	03	07	01	23	17	37		
11. Sexual needs enhance overall adjustment (SR)	19	−03	18	−03	18	−19	−07	02	00	−34	12	−09	
12. Thinks things out for himself (PR)	−18	−05	−10	−21	01	03	09	03	01	02	−03	14	10
13. Understanding of his peers (Soc)	−20												

Note: SR = Self Rating; PR = Peer Rating; PSR = Pooled Staff Rating; SRS = Self Report Scale; Soc = Sociometric Rating.
* Only variables associated at the $p = .05$ level are listed.
** $p = .01$.

intendents, and ministers have interests like those of students in the high-low group.

Another component of the personalities of students with this motive configuration is insight into others (as judged by the "others" involved) and the possession of personal qualities associated with a high degree of social status, for example, conversational facility, an ability to communicate ideas effectively, and self-acknowledged ambition (156). These students gave themselves higher ratings on motivation for professional status than did other students.

Finally, trainees with high n Achievement and low n Affiliation appeared to the staff to be consistent and predictable; i.e., they appeared to behave in the same general way from day to day.

Low n *Achievement–High* n *Affiliation Group.* According to Table 5, three sociometric scores and two peer ratings, all of which were fairly highly intercorrelated, characterized the group with weak achievement and strong affiliation motives. This group was less often chosen as intimate friends, as superiors, or as trusted therapists than other students. It should be noted, however, that this group was *not* chosen as *least* preferred as intimate friends more often than other students. They tended, according to peers, to be over-cautious and to fail to adapt their emotional responses to the needs of the situation.

Subjects in other studies with scores on the Psychological Interest and Intellectual Funtioning scales like those of this group have been described as conforming, having slow personal tempos, and lacking the ability to communicate well (156).

However, the members of this group described themselves as socially adjusted and insightful into the underlying dynamics of their own attitudes, emotions, and motivations. Peers, on the other hand, tended to judge this group as *lacking* in self-insight [$p < .10$ in (158)].

Peers also felt that this group included more students who were difficult to size up or to analyze than any of the other groups.

Low n *Achievement–Low* n *Affiliation Group.* It can be seen in Table 6 that assessees in whom both motives were weak had relatively negative self-concepts where interpersonal relations and intellectual work were concerned. They felt themselves to be inconsiderate of others, to have difficulty in gaining the acceptance of peers, and to be clumsy in social interaction.

Their peers, on the contrary, thought them considerate, and they would have been willing to trust members of this group as psychotherapists for their future wives.

The cluster of measures in Table 3 which described the high-high group as having strong ethical values and as being responsible, i.e.,

TABLE 4. PERSONALITY CHARACTERISTICS ASSOCIATED WITH A HIGH ACHIEVEMENT–
LOW AFFILIATION CONFIGURATION OF MOTIVES

	ϕ^*	1	2	3	4	5	6	7	8
1. Socially poised and adept (PSR)	20	51							
2. Unshakable, self possessed (PSR)	18	34	37						
3. Preference for working with people (SRS)	18	31	30	42					
4. Little inner emotional tension (PR)	17	18	24	31	17				
5. Social status (SRS)	23	24	27	27	16	41			
6. Insight into others (PR)	19	15	19	08	17	24	26		
7. Understanding of his peers (Soc)	23	13	27	31	22	22	25	09	
8. Consistent; predictable (PSR)	21	10	28	20	03	10	16	-09	
9. Motivated for professional status (SR)	20								18

Note: SR = Self Rating; PR = Peer Rating; PSR = Pooled Staff Rating; SRS = Self Report Scale; Soc = Sociometric Rating.
* Only variables associated at the $p = .05$ level are listed.

TABLE 5. PERSONALITY CHARACTERISTICS ASSOCIATED WITH A LOW ACHIEVEMENT–
HIGH AFFILIATION CONFIGURATION OF MOTIVES

	ϕ^*	1	2	3	4	5	6	7	8	9	10	11
1. Chosen as a superior in a psychological clinic (Soc)	-19											
2. Chosen as therapist for one's wife (Soc)	-18	73										
3. Chosen as an intimate friend (Soc)	-22	58	54									
4. Appropriate and spontaneous emotional expression (PR)	-20	52	42	38								
5. Cautious; does the safe thing (PR)	18	-38	-21	-52	-40							
6. Interests like those of psychologists (SRS)	-23	32	-05	13	00	-15						
7. Effective intellectual functioning (SRS)	-18	28	13	-07	07	-06	49					
8. Strong social values (SRS)	-20	24	36	02	-18	04	10	31				
9. Insight into self (SR)	30**	-02	-26	01	14	-22	-37	-22	-21			
10. Good social adjustment (SR)	26**	26	10	23	03	07	-13	-07	05	40		
11. Broad interests (SR)	23**	-02	-13	-16	-03	-08	08	-31	-14	32	10	
12. Easy to size up (Soc)	-21	11	03	19	12	-27	09	10	17	-11	-06	23

Note: SR = Self Rating; PR = Peer Rating; SRS = Self Report Scale; Soc = Sociometric Rating.
* Only variables associated at the p = .05 level are listed.
** p = .01.

TABLE 6. PERSONALITY CHARACTERISTICS ASSOCIATED WITH A LOW ACHIEVEMENT–LOW AFFILIATION CONFIGURATION OF MOTIVES

	ϕ^*	1	2	3	4	5	6	7	8	9	10	11	12	13	14	15
1. Good social adjustment (SR)	−27**															
2. Appropriate and spontaneous emotional expression (SR)	−21	84														
3. Generous; considerate (SR)	−26**	64	42													
4. Socially poised and adept (SR)	−19	52	48	57												
5. Motivated for professional status (SR)	−32**	27	44	34	41											
6. High quality of intellectual work (SR)	−18	24	20	17	47	52										
7. Conscientious; honest; unselfish (PSR)	−19	08	−09	20	−08	10	−13									
8. Serious; accepts responsibilities (PSR)	−18	06	03	25	03	26	20	79								
9. Social responsibility (SRS)	−22	−08	−09	12	19	24	40	37	54							
10. Liked very much (PSR)	−22	11	04	05	−10	14	25	57	38	34						
11. Trustful; accepts statements of others (PSR)	−17	06	22	06	14	18	−08	55	16	31	55					
12. Unshakable; self possessed (PSR)	−20	30	36	−01	16	28	03	00	18	00	37	26				
13. Preference for working with people (SRS)	−19	18	29	−01	22	20	−08	15	00	08	06	24	37			
14. Chosen as therapist for wife (Soc)	18	10	08	−18	03	−22	03	−01	00	−13	07	01	27	07		
15. Generous; considerate (PR)	19	07	07	−04	10	02	−20	−04	−06	−30	14	30	02	02	17	
16. Frank; expresses feelings readily (PR)	19	−07	01	−04	−16	09	13	−04	07	−23	08	04	09	08	11	22

Note: SR = Self Rating; PR = Peer Rating; PSR = Pooled Staff Rating; SRS = Self Report Scale; Soc = Sociometric Rating.
* Only variables associated at the $p = .05$ level are listed.
** $p = .01$.

conscientiousness, seriousness, social responsibility, and likeability, was less characteristic of the low-low group than of the other three groups combined. Thus, this personality component seems to be associated with the *joint* influence of the achievement and affiliation motives.

The assessment staff felt that members of the group weak in both motives were relatively suspicious, that they believed on insufficient grounds that people disliked them. The judgment is consistent with the pattern of self and peer ratings mentioned above. The staff also judged this group to be easily embarrassed and confused in an emergency.

DISCUSSION

Analysis of the motive configurations has provided us with more precise information about correlates of the motives. Thirty-two measures were related significantly to *n* Achievement and *n* Affiliation, taken separately (158). Configurational analysis showed that in 22 of these cases at least one of the four subgroups was characterized by the trait to a significantly greater degree than all other subgroups combined.

Second, more information about the motives was obtained by motive configuration analysis than was possible by separate analyses of the correlates of each motive. Twelve significant correlates of the motive configurations were found which were not related to either motive measure alone.

Third, it was possible to study interaction effects of the motives in relation to all the variables using a crude kind of scatter plot of the data, i.e., a 2×4 chi-square table. For the purposes of an exploratory research such as this one, a study of plots gives the investigator a more concrete picture of relationships than would a single index, e.g., a partial correlation coefficient. Furthermore, an interval scale need not be assumed as when use is made of the partial correlation coefficient technique of analysis.

Despite the relatively low phi coefficients obtained (the highest was $\phi = .32$), a sufficient number of significant relationships were obtained to allow a comparison of the results to expectations we might have had from earlier findings.

High n *Achievement–High* n *Affiliation Group.* An expectation that diligence (conscientiousness in these data) would characterize the high-high group was confirmed by the ratings of the assessment staff. The corresponding result did not appear in peer ratings. This lack of comparability between staff and peer ratings was a general characteristic of the results.

An analysis of the correlates of each motive in these data produced seven correlates of the achievement motive in staff ratings compared to one correlate in the peer ratings, and eight correlates of the affiliation motive in peer ratings as against two correlates in the staff ratings (158). An exact test was made of the relationship between rating source and motive to which ratings were significantly related. The p value was less than .05.

One interpretation of the lack of correspondence between correlates in staff rating data follows from Atkinson's contention that achievement motives are relatively quiescent until situational cues, i.e., test-taking in this case, arouse them (24). Since the students were probably more involved in their tasks than they were in observing peers during the assessment periods, peers would be less likely to perceive the behavior characteristic of persons with strong achievement motivation than would the staff. Contrariwise, affiliation motives would be aroused in the bull sessions and during other free time when peers were able to observe the characteristic behavior of the strongly affiliation-motivated students, but when the assessment staff was often absent.

Another interpretation is that the staff was predisposed to look upon the trainees as prospective students of clinical psychology, which would lead them to make more discriminations among trainees in terms of achievement-related behaviors than in terms of affiliation-related behaviors. Peers, on the other hand, would be more likely to think of each other as companions and friends, and to make their discriminations primarily in terms of expressions of affiliation motivation.

The association of attributes of responsibility and concern for the welfare of others and strength in both n Achievement and n Affiliation corresponds to a positive relationship between clinical ratings on superego development and n Achievement found by McClelland et al. (272). These attributes also tend to corroborate Murray's suggestion that persons high in n Achievement and n Affiliation would prefer to collaborate with others in attaining their own goals (314). In order to interact effectively with others in achieving goals, it seems necessary that a person be responsible for his share of the work and show some concern for the others involved.

A possible source of the apparent moral uprightness of this group might be an intensive Protestant training. The interpretation is suggested by McClelland's report that diligence and self-reliance, traits encouraged by the Protestant ethic, as described by Weber in *The Protestant Ethic* (424), are also used to characterize the n Achievement disposition (272).

Further, useful insights into the personality characteristics of persons high in n Achievement and n Affiliation might come from interviews with peers since they consider this group "easy to size up."

High n *Achievement–Low* n *Affiliation Group.* It was expected that high n Achievement with low n Affiliation would be associated with self-reliance (independent minded or self-sufficient in these data). There was, however, no indication of this expectation being met in the array of significantly-related attributes of this group reported in Table 4. Independent mindedness tended to be attributed by both peers and staff (p about .06) to the group whose motivation to achieve and to affiliate was weak (158). Self-sufficiency also tended to be associated with the low-low group in peer ratings ($p < .10$), but the staff judged the high n Achievement–low n Affiliation group to be more self-sufficient than the other groups combined ($p < .10$) (158). Only one of these four relationships was in the expected direction.

The high n Achievement–low n Affiliation group was rated more understanding of others and as having more insight into others by their peers. Peers did not, however, single them out as intimate friends. This suggests that the social relationships of this group tend to be less affective and more impersonal. The superior ability to communicate which characterizes these students probably facilitates their social interaction and enhances their social poise.

The positive association of social status and self-acknowledged motivation for professional status with the high n Achievement–low n Affiliation configuration might be attributed to explicit praise and increased status among peers as a result of attaining achievement goals. But conclusive evidence that this group is objectively more successful than the group high in both motives has yet to be presented.

"Insight and self-integration" previously found to correlate $+.34$ with n Achievement alone (272, p. 312) is here found to be particularly characteristic of persons high in n Achievement but low in n Affiliation. The traits of consistency, self-possession, and a lack of inner emotional tension attributed to this group together point to the characteristic of self-integration in the earlier study.

Low n *Achievement–High* n *Affiliation Group.* Students with weak achievement motives and strong affiliation motives were less often chosen on several sociometric scales than other students, as had been expected. The description of these students included such traits as cautiousness, lack of spontaneity of emotional expression, lack of conversational facility, and conformity. This pattern of traits is consistent with an interpretation of the behavior of persons highly motivated to affiliate which has been presented by Atkinson, Heyns, and Veroff (Ch. 5). They suggested that the cues which signify satisfactory rapport with another person or group may be more ambiguous and less consistent than cues signifying successful achievement of a task. As a result, persons high in n Affiliation will tend to be cautious in affiliative relationships, feeling their way through the maze of implications which they perceive in what other persons say, the tone of voice used in saying it, the other person's general demeanor, and any other information perceived to be relevant. It is possible that persons in this subgroup were careful about their own comments, taking care not to alienate friends and seeking approval of friends before making their own decisions. A deficiency in independent mindedness attributed to this subgroup by the staff at a level which barely misses our criterion of significance ($p = .06$) is in accord with such an interpretation (158).

The discrepancy between self and teammate ratings in the low n Achievement–high n Affiliation group can be interpreted in at least two ways. Persons in this group might be overestimating their own social adjustment, self-insight, and breadth of interests. In this case, peers might consider them egotistical, a quality associated with n Affiliation in the results of Atkinson, Heyns, and Veroff (Ch. 5). However, the unpopularity of this group with peers might lead to a negative halo effect in peer ratings, i.e., an underrating of persons in this group on attributes desirable by their peers.

Low n *Achievement–Low* n *Affiliation Group.* The "ethical strength and responsibility" component was not characteristic of students with weak achievement and affiliation motives. However, this group did not appear to be happy-go-lucky (i.e., rhathymic) either, although a slight trend in that direction ($p < .15$) was manifest in the more extensive analysis (158).

No clear evidence of concern with influencing others was present as might have been anticipated on the assumption that a power motive would characterize those low in both n Achievement and n Affiliation.

The striking characteristic of persons in this group is their relatively low opinion of themselves in relation to both interpersonal relationships and intellectual output. The low staff ratings on seriousness and conscientiousness suggest that members of this group may have been preoccupied with their own problems and therefore less able to concern themselves with other people and the assessment tasks than other trainees. Some evidence for this interpretation is a trend ($p < .10$) in the ratings of *both* peers and staff showing this subgroup above all others in degree of inner conflict (158).

SUMMARY

In an attempt to obtain new insights in the description of personality, measures of the strength of achievement and affiliation motives were dichotomized and four configurations of motive strength were distinguished. Attributes of each of the four groups of subjects thus formed were identified by comparing one group to the other three groups combined on the basis of several personality measures. The measures, including TAT stories from which the motive scores were derived, were selected from a large amount of data collected during the assessment of clinical psychology trainees by E. L. Kelly and associates. They included (1) behavioral ratings by trainees of themselves and their teammates and ratings by the assessment staff, (2) selected personality questionnaire scales, and (3) sociometric choices.

Outstanding characteristics of persons high in both n Achievement and n Affiliation were conscientiousness and responsibility, effectiveness in intellectual functioning, and freedom from emotional tension. They were liked by the staff. But peers thought of them as relatively dependent minded and lacking understanding of others.

The group with strong n Achievement and weak n Affiliation received relatively high ratings from the staff in social poise and insight and in consistency of behavior. These trainees also tended to possess qualities associated with high social status. Peers judged them to be relaxed and understanding of others.

Cautiousness, lack of spontaneity in emotional expression, and peer rejection from intimate friendship were associated with a configuration of weak n Achievement and strong n Affiliation. Tendencies toward conformity and poor ability to communicate with others were additional characteristics of persons in this group. However, they had a relatively high opinion of their own social adjustment and self-insight.

The group whose scores on both motive measures were low was rated by the staff as easily upset, relatively suspicious, and lacking in responsibility; this group was least liked by the staff. These trainees had relatively low opinions of their own social adjustment and intellectual accomplishments. But peers judged them to be considerate and generous.

It was found that peers (teammates) discriminated among subjects chiefly in terms of the affiliation motive, while the assessment staff usually discriminated among subjects on the basis of the achievement motive.

CHAPTER 29

....

Effects of the Interaction of
Motivation and Feedback on
Task Performance

ELIZABETH G. FRENCH[1]

RECENT WORK of Gibb and his associates (239)[2] has led them to conclude that feeling-oriented feedback, that is, feedback dealing with the personal interaction of the group members, produces higher task efficiency than feedback directly related to the accomplishment of the group task. The feeling-oriented feedback, they hypothesize, reduces defensiveness and permits effective action. Earlier studies by the present author, while not directly comparable, suggest circumstances in which Gibb's finding might not hold. In one experiment (142) the situation was so structured that the S was required to choose as a work partner either a friend who had demonstrated lack of competence on the task to be performed or a man he didn't especially like who had demonstrated competence. When the kinds of choices made were tabulated according to previously obtained motivation scores of the choosers, it was found that Ss high in achievement and low in affiliation motivation tended to choose for competence rather than friendship. On the other hand, Ss high in affiliation and low in achievement motivation chose their friends. The experiment was not set up to permit ratings of effectiveness of the friendly and nonfriendly pairs, but the high achievement-motivated Ss indicated by their choices that they didn't expect to be disturbed by a certain amount of lack of friendliness in the work situation—at least not to the extent of giving up the best chances to succeed. The affiliation-motivated Ss were not willing to expose

---

[1] This study was carried out as part of the United States Air Force Personnel and Training Research and Development Program. The opinions expressed, however, are those of the author and are not to be construed as reflecting the views or endorsement of the Department of the Air Force.

[2] See also 152 and 343.

400

themselves to possible unfriendliness even at the risk of task failure.

In another experiment (141) it was shown that when Ss could satisfy achievement goals when working on tasks in which success was primarily dependent on the effort S was willing to expend, task scores were related to achievement motivation. When the task was presented in such a way that working on it could satisfy affiliation goals, then performance was related to affiliation motivation and not to achievement.

These findings lead to the prediction that the two kinds of feedback would affect achievement-motivated and affiliation-motivated Ss differently. Affiliation-motivated Ss should react as did Gibb's Ss since there is evidence that they are the ones who show concern for friendly relations even in a working group. In addition, feeling feedback could conceivably serve the function of making good group relations at least a subsidiary task goal since the task is discussed in group relations terms. Then, to the extent that success on the task depends on the Ss' efforts, affiliation-motivated Ss should do better. Achievement-motivated Ss would be expected to do better with task feedback. Since they are less concerned over interpersonal relations, they would be indifferent to efforts to reduce tension. Also they would be expected to respond with lessened effort toward a primarily affiliation goal and heightened effort to an achievement one. And finally, they would attend more to the task feedback and so profit from it.

The specific hypothesis to be tested is that Ss high in achievement and low in affiliation motivation will perform better on a task when given task relevant feedback than when given feeling feedback. Ss with the opposite motivation pattern will perform better when given feeling rather than task feedback.

Also tested was the hypothesis that achievement-motivated Ss would get higher scores if the problem appeared to them to be more of an individual than a group task and that the reverse would be true for affiliation-motivated Ss. The reasoning behind this hypothesis is that the possibility of a feeling of individual accomplishment would provide the achievement oriented with additional incentive plus freedom from frustration and from the feeling of being dependent on others. The sense of belonging to the group is more important to the affiliation motivated, on the other hand, and minimizing the group aspects of the task might be expected to be disturbing to them and reduce their efficiency.

These two hypotheses were tested experimentally by subjecting groups of Ss of known motivation patterns to both kinds of feedback under both kinds of task orientation.

METHOD

Groups of four Ss worked together on a story assembly problem. The subjects in any given group all had the same motivation pattern: either they were all high in achievement and low in affiliation or all the reverse. While giving the initial instructions to the Ss, the E established the task as either group or partly individual, as appropriate. The groups worked for a specified amount of time, during which the E interrupted twice to record scores and give the appropriate feedback, either task or feeling. A final task score, taken at the expiration of the time limit, provided the performance measure. The interim solutions were taken merely to provide an easy opening for the feedback discussions.

Formation of motivation groups. Before their scheduled reporting for the experimental session, flights of basic airmen at Lackland Air Force Base were given the Test of Insight (141) as a measure of achievement and affiliation motivations. A total of 128 men with achievement motivation scores above the median score of 6 and affiliation scores below the median score of 5 were selected as the high-achievement-motivation Ss. A like number of men with affiliation scores above 5 and achievement below 6 were selected for the high-affiliation-motivation Ss. In both cases the additional criterion that the two scores for a particular man must be three points apart or more was used. Ss with similar motivation patterns were assembled in groups of four. Inevitably there were variations in the average motivation scores for the groups. Care was taken to assign groups to conditions in such a way that the distribution of group scores was the same for all conditions. Likewise the Armed Forces Qualifications Test (AFQT) scores, which indicate intelligence level, varied from group to group. Again care was taken to assure similar distributions of AFQT scores in all conditions. With these restrictions in mind eight High-Achievement and eight High-Affiliation groups were assigned to each of the following experimental conditions: Task Feedback–Group Orientation and Task Feedback–Individual Orientation, Feeling Feedback–Group Orientation and Feeling Feedback–Individual Orientation. F tests demonstrated that the equating of motivation and intelligence across experimental conditions was adequate.

The task. The suggestion for the task also came from Gibb *et al.* (152), though the actual problem was constructed by the author. It consisted of 20 phrases or short sentences which made up a little story when put together correctly. Each S was given five cards with one phrase on each card. The Ss' task was to reconstruct the story, with the restriction that it must be done at the verbal level. No S could show another his cards and no one was permitted to write anything down. In scoring, one point was given for each phrase used, and an additional point if it followed its correct predecessor. In addition, five extra points were given if the complete and correct sequence was given before the time limit expired. This procedure provides a possible range of scores of zero to 45.

Motivation, Feedback, and Task Performance 403

Instructions to the group. The Ss' perception of the group or individual nature of the task was created at the same time that the general instructions were given. The main part of the instructions was the same for all groups and read:

"The problem today is to fit together the parts of a story. I have here four packs of five cards each. There is a sentence or a part of a sentence written on each card. When they are all fitted together in the proper order, they will tell a sensible story. All the cards fit in and there is only one right way to do it. Each one of you will get a packet. The task is to decide in what order the cards should be read to tell the story. No one person will have cards which he can put together; each man has to fit his in with all the others. *But* you must do this without showing the cards to each other. It must all be done by conversation. You may read aloud and discuss all you like, but each man keeps his own cards and shows them to no one. You work out the proper order by discussion.

"You will work for 10 minutes, and I will stop you and ask for your solution as far as you've gone; then we'll talk about how you are getting along. After that you'll work 10 minutes longer, stop again to read your solution and discuss progress; and finally you'll work a third 10 minute period. At the end of that period I'll ask you for your final solution. You may, of course, make changes from one solution to the next as well as additions."

For the Group problem orientation the Ss were then told:

"I'll give you two minutes warning before the final time limit so you will be prepared to give the best single solution you can."

The Individual orientation was provided by the instruction:

"I'll give you two minutes warning before I call for your final solution. I should say here that either on the final solution or on either of the other two it is not necessary that you all agree. One or more of you may submit different versions, if you like."

The feedback periods. During the working periods the groups were observed and desirable task behavior or interpersonal behavior, according to the condition to which the group was assigned, was checked against a prepared list as it occurred. Only positive feedback was used since positive and negative feedback have been found to have different effects (152) and it seemed best not to include an additional variable. At the end of 10 minutes the E interrupted the group, asked that the Ss read whatever parts they had put together, and recorded the phrases read. Then, for the Task Feedback groups the two-minute discussion was introduced by, "This group is working very efficiently." Following that, five of the specific behaviors previously noted by the E were mentioned. These included such points as: reading off all cards immediately, trying to rough out possible plots, making use of grammatical cues, identifying characters in the story, etc.

For the Feeling Feedback groups the introductory phrase was, "This group works very well together." The specific behaviors mentioned included: praising each other for making good suggestions, giving everyone a chance to contribute, not becoming impatient with poor suggestions, failing to argue or keeping arguments friendly, etc.

After two minutes the Ss returned to the task and worked 10 minutes longer, at the end of which the recording of the phrases and the feedback discussion were repeated. Essentially the same points were made, but the wording was sufficiently different to avoid a feeling of repetition.

Ss then worked for a final 10 minutes and read off the final solution. This concluded the experiment except for the reading of the correct solution by E, which was invariably demanded by the Ss.

RESULTS

Although several of the Ss in the individual condition took advantage of the opportunity to give separate solutions the first and second times, none of them did in giving the final solution. This fact greatly simplified the handling of the data even though it did suggest that the second hypothesis might not be completely tenable. The performance score means, standard deviations, and ranges for the eight experimental groups are given in Table 1 and the analysis of variance of the interactions in Table 2. The test of

TABLE 1. TASK-SCORE MEANS, STANDARD DEVIATIONS, AND RANGES FOR THE EIGHT EXPERIMENTAL CONDITIONS

		Achievement		Affiliation	
		Grp.	Ind.	Grp.	Ind.
Task	Mean.........	40.50	39.38	29.12	25.12
	SD...........	3.68	4.48	5.14	3.44
	Range........	36-45	33-45	24-36	20-32
Feeling	Mean.........	29.25	30.87	38.38	31.50
	SD...........	3.86	3.34	4.45	8.43
	Range........	25-37	27-36	30-45	19-45

the main hypothesis is, of course, the interaction between kind of motivation and kind of feedback. This is significant at well beyond the .001 level. The second hypothesis was tested by the interaction between kind of motivation and kind of orientation to the problem. This F ratio was significant at the .05 level. In interpreting these F ratios attention should perhaps be called to the very small ratio which would be obtained for the interaction between feedback and orientation. A ratio as small as this would occur by chance only about 4 times in 100, which circumstance suggests the possibility that some unspecified variable is affecting the results. No ready

TABLE 2. ANALYSIS OF VARIANCE OF TASK SCORES

Source	df	MS	F	P
Motivation	1	252.02	12.25	
Feedback	1	17.02	—	
Orientation	1	107.64	5.23	
M × F	1	1251.38	60.83	.001
M × O	1	129.39	6.29	.05
F × O	1	.02	—	
M × F × O	1	31.64	1.54	
Within	56	20.57		

idea of what it might be comes to mind, and as the other Fs present no unusual problems, the results are discussed as if this small ratio is actually one of the four in 100 that would occur by chance. The other possibility should not be completely ignored, however. When the means are examined, it appears that three—Achievement-Task-Group, Achievement-Task-Individual, and Affiliation-Feeling-Group —form a cluster at the upper end of the range and that the Affiliation-Task-Individual group is considerably lower than the others. Tukey's gap test defines a significant gap in the first instance and identifies the low group as a straggler. These results give clear support to the first hypothesis that performance is more favorably influenced by feedback which is relevant to the S's primary motivation than by feedback not so relevant. The second hypothesis was partially substantiated. The significant interaction appears to be due entirely to the effect of the Group versus Individual orientation on the high-affiliation Ss. The Achievement-Motivation groups failed to perform better under the Individual condition and, as pointed out earlier, failed to submit individual solutions in the final period. The Affiliation-motivated groups, on the other hand, did perform more poorly under the Individual orientation. The Affiliation-Feeling-Individual mean was significantly lower, as indicated by the gap, than the Affiliation-Feeling-Group mean. The lowest mean of all was that for the Affiliation-Task-Individual condition.

DISCUSSION

The results concerned with the first hypothesis are in complete accord with the prediction and require little discussion. The achievement-motivated Ss did respond with better performance to the heightened achievement cues provided by task feedback than to the introduction of affiliation cues by feeling feedback. The affiliation-motivated Ss apparently did find the atmosphere created by the feeling feedback easier to work in. While the study provided no systematic measure of lessening tension, observations of the behavior of the affiliation Ss when good group relations were pointed out to them supported the tension-reduction notion. The achievement Ss tended to show lack of interest or even impatience with the feeling feedback, though they listened carefully to discussions of their task performance.

The second hypothesis was substantiated only as it related to affiliation-motivated Ss. There was no difference in the Achievement groups associated with the Ss' perception of the task as group or individual. That those in the Individual groups remembered that part of the instructions is attested to by the fact that some individual interim solutions were given. Possibly the instructions weren't enough to overcome the essentially cooperative nature of the task. Or perhaps this dimension cuts both ways, with the more capable Ss seeing a group product as a disadvantage and the less capable as an advantage. At any rate, the prediction that achievement-motivated Ss would profit by being permitted to give individual products was not upheld. The affiliation Ss, however, did markedly less well under the Individual condition, especially, of course, with task feedback. Since their primary motivation is by definition social, taking away the sense of belonging may be assumed to reduce their interest and effort as well as cause discomfort.

At this point the variance in the Affiliation-Feeling-Individual condition should be pointed out (Table 1). Although the chi-square yielded by Bartlett's test for homogeneity of variance did not reach the customary .05 level of significance, it did approach the .10 level. The possibility that the large standard deviation for the aforementioned condition may represent a true difference should not be overlooked. The actual scores for that series were 45, 39, 38, 35, 27, 24, and 19. There seem to be two sets of scores separated by a gap about as wide as the range for either set. These Ss, of course, were given conflicting information. On the one hand they were told they could—and maybe some interpreted this to mean they should—give individual answers. But the feedback was all in terms of their behavior as a group. One may speculate that some groups resolved the seeming incompatibility by ignoring the implication of the instructions and some by ignoring the implications of the feedback. This is given some support by the observation that the Ss in the group making the score of 38 agreed explicitly that they would work together and give a single solution. Possibly the other high-scoring groups in this condition reacted in the same way without verbalizing their reaction.

In conclusion, some behavioral observations of considerable interest might be mentioned. The E went to the experimental sessions without knowledge of the motivational characteristics of the groups in order to keep any bias from influencing treatment of the groups. However, it soon became apparent that in most cases the behavior of the Ss in the situation was quite different for groups with different motivation. Achievement groups were eager to get on with the task, timed themselves, argued violently (with one coming to physical contretemps), etc. The Affiliation groups failed to show these forms of behavior, were quieter and less intense about the task, and in some cases definitely quite interested in being friendly with each other and E. When differences began to appear, E kept a record of her predictions of the motivational composition of the group. Twenty-nine of the 32 Achievement groups were correctly identified. Thirteen of the Affiliation groups were correctly identified because they showed affiliative behavior, and eight more because they failed to show the behavior typical of the Achievement groups; eight were not predicted, and three were misclassified. Apparently, especially among the Achievement groups, a real and observable variable is operating. Had the groups been brought together for social purposes, identification of Affiliation groups might have been more positive and that of the Achievement groups less so.

One further finding which, if it holds up under systematic study, is of real importance, is the relation between intelligence, motivation, and group score. The AFQT level was equated across conditions on the assumption that intelligence would be related to performance. Out of curiosity, a rough estimate of the extent of this relationship was made by putting all 64 performance scores into a single distribution and correlating them with three sets of AFQT scores: average of the four group members, highest of the four, and lowest of the four. All coefficients were essentially zero. A fourth correlation, between performance scores and the AFQT score of the man with the highest achievement motivation (Achievement groups only), had a value of .35, significant at the .05 level. Admittedly, these obtained figures are distorted representations of the actual relationships since the differences in performance due to the experimental conditions are ignored. They do suggest as an hypothesis for systematic testing that group performance tends to be keyed to the ability level of the group's highly motivated member.

SUMMARY

This experiment tested the hypothesis that task-relevant feedback for achievement-motivated subjects and "feeling" feedback for affiliation-motivated subjects would produce higher performance scores than the reverse. In addition to the motivational and feedback variables, the extent to which the task was presented as a group or as an individual problem was varied. The results included a highly significant interaction between kind of motivation and kind of feedback in the predicted direction and a significant interaction between kind of motivation and perceived nature of the task with subjects with high affiliation motivation doing less well under the individual orientation. Findings also suggested that group performance may be keyed to the intellectual level of the S with the highest achievement motivation.

CHAPTER 30

··

Determinants of Conformity
and Attitude Change*

KENNETH R. HARDY[1]

AN ADEQUATE UNDERSTANDING of human social behavior requires the simultaneous study of the nature of social influence and the causes of individual variations in susceptibility to that influence. A notable example of the recent trend to study these concomitantly is seen in the work of S. Asch on independence and submission to group pressure (21, Ch. 12). The study reported here had two objectives: First, to extend the work of Asch from perceptual to attitudinal judgments, from public conformity to attitude change as well. Specifically, this objective was to compare the effects upon conformity and attitude change of unanimous group pressure as contrasted with near-unanimous group pressure. The second objective was to investigate the role of affiliative motivation in affecting susceptibility to group normative pressure.

Attitude change is here considered to include any change in the organization of "motivational, emotional, perceptual, and cognitive processes with respect to some aspect of the individual's world" (221, p. 152). Attitude change arises from changes in perceived social reality, or from other influences which are thought to dependably reflect "objective" reality, such as the opinions of experts or other prestigeful persons, the evidence of research, personal experience, and the like. The importance of "social reality" (132,

* Reprinted by permission of author and publisher from *The Journal of Abnormal and Social Psychology,* 1957, **54,** 289-294. Copyright 1957 by the American Psychological Association, Inc.

[1] This report is based upon a doctoral dissertation, University of Michigan, 1954, which is on file with University Microfilms, Ann Arbor, Michigan, as publication No. 8311 (price $1.56), and which contains the raw data, instruments used, and a fuller discussion of theory, method, and results.

The author wishes to express his appreciation to Dr. Daniel Katz and the other members of his committee for their counsel and encouragement. He is also grateful to Dr. J. W. Atkinson, Dr. J. D. Birch, Joseph Veroff, and Robert Hamblin for assistance in special phases of the research.

317), defined in terms of the shared consensus of (significant) people in the person's environment, is now widely acknowledged as a determinant of social attitudes.

Conformity is here defined as the public avowal of a belief or attitude at variance with one's prior position, which avowal tends to correspond to the position approved by the group in which the avowal occurs. It may occur as an accompaniment of attitude change based upon a shift in perceived social reality. It may also occur in the absence of attitude change in situations where it is believed to be instrumental to the satisfaction of such motives as sex, achievement, affiliation, power, or hunger.

The type of social situation under investigation is one in which a small group of men meet informally. They state their opinions on a given topic, expressing unity of opinion. What will a person do whose position on the issue has hitherto been at variance with that of the others? Will he change his mind about the issue, or will he, at the least, publicly express agreement with the group? What will he do if another person in the group expresses a similarly deviant position? Our predictions were as follows: First, there would be (a) greater conformity and (b) greater attitude change under conditions of unanimous opposition to the subject's prior position than where the subject has a "partner" who shares his opinion. This is presumed because in the "partner" situation the pressures toward conformity are less, and the criterion of social reality loses much of its force when there is a difference of opinion expressed within the group. Secondly, there would be (a) greater conformity and (b) greater attitude change by those who have greater affiliative motivation than by those with lesser affiliative motivation. This prediction is based partly on their greater desire to be accepted and well thought of, combined with the common realization of the tendency of groups to reject those deviant from group norms (365), and partly on their presumably greater intellectual dependence upon social reality.

METHOD

The fundamental plan of the research was to submit a subject to a social influence situation wherein his own attitude would be opposed by all or, alternatively, by all but one of the other persons present. The focus of study was the subject's public reaction to this situation—and his private (attitudinal) response.

In order to accomplish this objective, a three-stage design of pre-test, experimental manipulation, and post-test was used. Male subjects were recruited from classes in introductory psychology and general chemistry at the University of Michigan. They were asked to volunteer two hours of their time to a study of the relative efficacy of various methods of measuring attitudes. The attitude object to be studied was that of divorce, and considerations of control and expedience led to the elimination of all Catholic, married, and Negro volunteers.

Pretest. The pretest, administered to small groups of subjects at a time, consisted of four instruments (discussed below), all ostensibly representing methods of measuring attitudes. Actually, the major purpose of the pretest was to secure data on the subjects' affiliative motivation and attitudinal position respecting divorce so that they could be assigned to the appropriate experimental variation.

The first instrument given was the TAT-type measure of affiliative motivation (n *Affil*) developed by Atkinson, Heyns, Shipley, and Veroff (Ch. 5, Ch. 4). The experimenter said, "The first thing we'd like you men to do is to write some stories." The standard story blanks were distributed, and standard instructions for administering a projective measure of motivation were then read (cf. 272). Four pictures were shown in the following sequence: (a) Two men conversing; (b) Group of seven men around a table; (c) Older woman seated, looking away from young man by window; (d) Man by lamppost (TAT 20).

It was our intention to structure a situation which would be only mildly arousing of affiliative motivation, so that affiliation imagery would be aroused mostly by the pictures shown. Our small groups consisted of strangers or relatively casual acquaintances meeting in a seminar room on campus. The testing was usually preceded by a minor amount of "small talk" as the men arrived in the room. Our own guess would be that this situation was about as affiliatively arousing as the "neutral" condition of Shipley and Veroff (Ch. 4). This guess is substantiated by a comparison of scores obtained in the present study with those obtained on a similar population by these investigators.

Following the completion of the stories, the men were asked to write their names on the back of each sheet. Assurances were given of the confidential treatment of this and other material collected during the study. The blanks were then collected, and a questionnaire booklet, containing the other three instruments, was distributed.

The first questionnaire was the California "F" scale (3, pp. 255-257), introduced as dealing with general public opinion. This scale, and the self-ratings discussed below, were primarily used to bolster the facade that the study was investigating various methods of measuring attitudes, at the same time drawing attention away from the divorce issue. They were also used to explore possible relationships they might have with the experimental variables.[2]

The second questionnaire, which pertained to the divorce issue, was introduced as dealing with a specific attitude quite intensively rather than dealing superficially but extensively with many attitudes as the preceding questionnaire had done. The first page asked the subject to write "your attitude and feelings toward divorce and the reasons you feel the way you do about it." He was allowed about ten minutes to do this. The objective of this section was to provide arguments which the subject's supporter could use in the group situation. The next section consisted of three parts. The first part was a nine-point graphic scale of a continuum of leniency toward divorce, on which the subject indicated his own position and those of his parents and friends. This scale was also used in the group influence situation, where the subject had to publicly state his position. A comparison of these two positions the subject took provided us with our operational definition of conformity. The second part consisted of twelve Likert-type attitude statements dealing with various aspects of divorce: the nature of the marital contract, divorce as a solution to an unhappy marriage, effect of divorce upon children and society generally, the degree of present abuse of divorce, and the obligation partners should feel to remain married. There were six "liberal" and six coordinate "conservative" statements. This set of statements, also given after the group situation, provided our operational definition of attitude change. For example, if a subject marked "−" (mildly disagree) to a given statement initially, but afterward marked "+" (mildly agree), this would be scored as a change of two units. If he marked "++" (strongly agree) initially and "−" later, three units of change would be recorded. If the change occurred in the direction of the group influence, it was scored positively; if in the opposite direction, it was scored negatively. The algebraic sum of these shifts over the twelve statements was the subject's attitude change score. The third part of this questionnaire contained two questions which assessed the strength and certainty of the subject's attitude toward divorce.

The final instrument in the questionnaire booklet was a series of ratings for twenty-three personality traits. Most of the traits were adapted from Fiske (137), who in turn adapted them from a longer list used by Cattell (64). In Fiske's factor analytic study, seven

---

[2] Analysis of results showed no relationships between the "F" scale and either conformity or attitude change. Negative results were also found between the "conformity" factor of the self-ratings and these dependent variables.

of the self-rated traits had loadings of .40 or better on a centroid factor he labeled "conformity."

Experimental manipulation. The group influence situation came after an interval of four to eleven weeks following the pretest. In the interim, the n *Affil* scores were computed and the resulting distribution divided into high and low n *Affil* groups.[3] These groups were then assigned to the partner or no-support variations so as to control for initial position on the divorce issue (as indicated in the graphic scale) and for time elapsing since the pretest. Each subject met with a group of six other students, all of whom were presumably subjects. Actually these six were confederates—that is, they knew the true purpose of the study, and they had been instructed to give standardized "arguments" using five kinds of appeals: emotional, personal contact or experience, scientific evidence, appeal to authority, and acceptability of change as a result of further thought and investigation. The content of each argument centered around some aspect of divorce sampled by the attitude statements in the questionnaire.

As an example, the antidivorce argument appealing to authority and dealing with the effectiveness of divorce as a solution to an unhappy marriage is as follows: "Some people say that a couple ought to get divorced if they are incompatible. A psychiatrist who is a friend of the family told me that the real reason marriages are unhappy is that the couples have not really learned how to solve their problems. The definition of a happy marriage is not one that has no differences or problems; it is one where the husband and wife know how to solve their problems as they arise. Getting divorced and later remarrying doesn't help people to learn these techniques. What they need to be happy is to learn how to get along together." The confederate was free to state the argument in his own words.

It should be noted that this technique of not only stating a judgment but also buttressing it with "reasons" represents a methodological innovation, one which represents more faithfully, in the author's opinion, the ordinary social influence situation. With the perceptual phenomena studied by Asch (21) and Sherif (375), the judgment is immediately given, and there is no room for discussion. This is surely not true with social phenomena generally nor with the attitudes which derive therefrom.

The group situation was structured in the following way. The

---

[3] Reliability was established by comparing the author's scoring of two samples of stories obtained by previous research with the pooled scoring of the authors of the n *Affil* manual (Ch. 5) on these same stories. The average rho for the two samples was .80 for total scores.

men were seated in a semicircle (the confederates were free to take any seat) facing the experimenter, who began by stating, "During the first hour we worked with several methods of measuring attitudes. Today we are going to work with another method which I might call a 'group interview.' What I shall do is call on each of you in turn and ask you to tell me how you feel about a particular topic and why you feel the way you do about it. The topic is divorce. I shall write down in summary form what you say, and then attempt to restate it to see if I have it accurately."

After each interview was completed, the experimenter held up a large placard on which was the graphic scale used during the pretest. After the person stated his position, together with any reasons for placing himself there, the experimenter called on the next individual in his list of names. This procedure was repeated until all the confederates, and finally the subject, had spoken.

In the no support variation, all of the confederates opposed the subject's previously indicated position. Since two sets of arguments had been constructed—one favorable, the other unfavorable to divorce—the set used was the one opposed to the subject's position as indicated on the pretest. A position on the graphic scale paralleled each argument. The arguments were always given in the same sequence. In each case the fifth man "agreed" with the others but added no arguments to those already given. In the partner variation, the fifth man opposed the others, giving arguments the subject had used during the pretest; he placed himself at the subject's initial position on the graphic scale. By this procedure the amount of new ideas presented to the subject was kept constant across the variations. We used the fifth man so that the group norm would be clearly established by the first four men and maintained by the sixth person.

Upon completion of the "group interview," the experimenter said, "Now there is one other thing I'd like you men to do before we are through and that is to fill out a short questionnaire for me individually. In order to do this, I will assign you to separate rooms." Each man was handed a (post-test) questionnaire as he went to his room, but the subject, of course, was the only one who filled it out.

Post-test. This questionnaire, which was filled out privately, contained measures of liking of the group, perception of the group situation, and repeat measures of the attitude toward divorce. Upon completion of the questionnaire, the experimenter interviewed the subject and explained to him the real nature of the study. At this time the subject was given the opportunity to serve as a confederate (which most subjects were eager to do, especially those most affected by the group situation). The major source of confederates, however, was volunteers from classes in Social Psychology and Human Relations.

Although a total of 45 "group interviews" were conducted, in 13 cases the experimental conditions were not met by the failure of one or two confederates to appear, and in one case there were two supporters due to a mix-up in instructions. The results are based upon the 31 remaining cases.

RESULTS

The first question which should be answered is, "Did the situation really provoke conformity and changes in attitude?" With regard to conformity, fourteen men (45%) shifted two or more scale points on the graphic scale, in the direction of the group influence. (The average distance from initial position to the group norm was 4.36 scale points.) In contrast, only three men shifted in the opposite direction, and none of them changed more than one point. Similarly, fourteen men had a positive attitude change score of six or more points; that is, they changed their position on at least half of the attitude statements (or the equivalent). Only two men had a negative score this high. It should be noted here that the correlation between conformity and attitude change was .51. Our observations of these men confirmed those of Asch in detecting more or less severe signs of emotional activation in the group situation. One subject, for example, spoke very rapidly (atypical of him) in pronouncing his agreement with the others, then blurted, "Boy, it's hot in here; can't we open a window?" He was the only one to notice the "heat"!

The Effect of Social Support. Results of t tests indicated that the absence of social support was significantly related to attitude change, but the relationship to conformity fell short of significance, as shown in Table 1. The hypothesis regarding the effect of social support upon attitude change thus received confirmation, but the evidence is ambiguous respecting the effect of support upon conformity.

The Effect of Affiliative Motivation. A comparison of high and low n *Affil* groups showed no differences between these groups on either conformity or attitude change. However, before rejecting this variable as predictive of conformity or attitude change, we felt that two possibilities should be investigated; first, that social support might be interacting with n *Affil* in such a way as to cancel out differences between the affiliation groups; and second, that an

416   *Motivation and Behavior*

TABLE 1. EFFECT OF SOCIAL SUPPORT ON CONFORMITY AND
ATTITUDE CHANGE

	No Support $(N = 16)$	Partner $(N = 15)$	t	p
Conformity				
Mean...............	1.81	1.16	1.30	.11
S.D................	1.55	1.12		
Attitude change				
Mean...............	6.97	2.00	1.79*	.05
S.D................	9.44	5.05		

* A formula recommended by Dixon and Massey (100, pp. 104-105) was used here because of heterogeneity of variance between the two groups.

alternative division of the n *Affil* distribution might show positive relationships.

This second possibility recommended itself from some research done on n *Achievement* by Lowell (241), McClelland and Liberman (275), and Moulton (Ch. 39), who found more clear-cut relationships with certain perceptual and behavioral phenomena on the basis of a high-medium-low division than with a dichotomization of the n *Ach* distribution. They found the high group, which is conceived to be positively motivated toward achievement, to suffer no decrement in performance nor perceptual defense under achievement-arousing conditions. The middle n *Ach* group, which is conceived to be ambivalently motivated toward achievement, *does* show defensiveness to perception of failure words and a performance decrement under arousal conditions.

The Interaction of Social Support and n Affil. To examine these two possibilities, an analysis of variance design was employed, using the two categories of social support, and three categories of n *Affil* based upon a division of that distribution into three groups as nearly equal in size as possible. Table 2a reports the N's, means, and SD's of the six resulting cells for conformity; Table 3a the corresponding data for attitude change. Before analyses of variance were made, the cell frequency (with the accompanying sums of squares) of the "Low n *Affil*, No support" cell was adjusted to make possible an analysis procedure based upon proportional cell frequencies (cf. 234, pp. 151-155). Also, before each analysis, the assumption of homogeneity of variance within cells was checked by using Bartlett's test, and was verified in each case. Table 2b gives the results of the variance analysis for conformity, Table 3b for attitude change.

Conformity and Attitude Change 417

TABLE 2. EFFECT OF n AFFILIATION AND SUPPORT ON CONFORMITY

2a. Conformity in Variations of n Affiliation and Support

Degree of Support	n Affiliation		
	High	Medium	Low
No support			
Mean..................	1.97	2.97	−.175
S.D...................	1.41	.58	.43
N.....................	6	6	4
Partner			
Mean..................	.06	1.83	1.58
S.D...................	.76	1.15	.59
N.....................	5	5	5

2b. Results of Variance Analysis

Source	df	Mean Square	F
Support..................	1	1.51	1.49
n Affiliation..............	2	9.88	9.77
Interaction...............	2	20.85	20.62
Within cells..............	25	1.01	

$F_{.01} = 5.57$ for 2 and 25 df.

The results on the conformity variable indicate that both n $Affil$ and the interaction component are highly significant factors, but support is not. Within the table the following results were obtained:

1. n $Affil$ is significant within each support variation. In the no-support condition, the high and medium groups are significantly more conforming than the low group. In the partner variation, however, the medium and low groups are significantly more conforming than the high group.

2. If the support variations are combined, then the medium n $Affil$ group is more conforming than either the high or low groups.

3. The no-support variation is more comformity-producing for the high need group, less conformity-producing for the low need group than the partner variation. There is no difference between the support variations for the middle need group.

From these results it would appear that conformity is a joint function of the social conditions and the affiliative motivation of the individual. For those high in n $Affil$ the presence of a partner results in the disappearance of conformity which is definitely present under conditions of no support. Those in the middle range of the n $Affil$ distribution do not drop significantly in conformity with the

418 *Motivation and Behavior*

TABLE 3. EFFECT OF n AFFILIATION AND SUPPORT ON ATTITUDE CHANGE

3a. Attitude Change in Variations of n Affiliation and Support

Degree of Support	n Affiliation		
	High	Medium	Low
No support			
Mean	6.75	11.00	1.25
S.D.	7.37	11.37	3.36
N	6	6	4
Partner			
Mean	.40	1.20	4.40
S.D.	4.84	4.26	5.08
N	5	5	5

3b. Results of Variance Analysis

Source	df	Mean Square	F
Support	1	153.78	2.51
n Affiliation	2	43.44	
Interaction	2	242.85	3.96
Within cells	25	61.35	

$F_{.05} = 3.38$ for 2 and 25 df.

presence of a partner. Those in the low n *Affil* group, who do not conform at all under conditions of no support, show a significant *increase* in conformity when a partner is present.

Before interpreting these data, let us look at the results for the other dependent variable, attitude change. Here somewhat similar fluctuations in mean values occur, but none of the factors is statistically significant. (If we test the between-groups variance before the interaction component is accepted as significant (cf. 234, p. 166), the resulting F ratio is 2.37, which leaves the interaction of doubtful significance.)

Though there are somewhat similar patterns for conformity and attitude change, there is one important difference which should be noted. The medium need group conformed whether or not a partner was present; but they tended to change less in attitude in the partner situation than in the no-support situation (p about .05).

These results can reasonably be interpreted in a way comparable to that indicated above for achievement motivation. The high-scoring person is conceived to be positively motivated toward affiliation. When he is unanimously opposed in attitude, he changes his attitude to join his potential friends. When this group of people is divided in attitude, the social reality of the opposing position is much less compelling, as is also the perceived necessity to conform to gain social acceptance. Under these conditions, his thinking and outward actions change but little.

The person obtaining a moderate score on $n\ Affil$ is conceived to be ambivalently and anxiously motivated toward affiliation. His fear of rejection leads to a more pronounced conformity. His thinking, as in the case of the positively motivated person, leans heavily on social reality, so that he shifts attitudinally in the no-support situation, but much less so under conditions of support. In contrast to the positively motivated person, however, his anxiety for approval tends to maintain his conformity even in the support situation, since he derives less assurance from the presence of a lone partner.

If the low-scoring person experiences a negligible arousal of affiliative motivation in the social influence situation, then his behavior should be a function of other factors present, in particular the content of the influential communications. To the extent that he is less dependent upon social reality, he will be more free to develop beliefs based on other considerations. Hovland, Lumsdaine, and Sheffield (185) report that for those initially opposed to a point of view being advocated, greater opinion change resulted when both sides of the issue were presented (with the favored view given preponderant consideration) than when only the favored position was considered. This difference was especially pronounced for those of high school education or better. It is apparent that their situation and results are similar to those of the low-affiliation group in the present study, where greater attitude change occurred upon presentation of both sides of the issue, i.e., under conditions of support. The conformity of this group is interpreted as a by-product of attitude change.

Analyses of individual cases, the post-test questionnaire and interview, and the pretest self-ratings give equivocal support to these interpretations, which are highly tentative, of course. Atkinson, in a personal communication, reports data indicating a curvilinear relationship between $n\ Ach$ and $n\ Affil$, with the high $n\ Affil$ group also high on $n\ Ach$, but the medium $n\ Affil$ group low on $n\ Ach$. Since McClelland (272) found a strong negative relationship between $n\ Ach$ and independence from group pressures (with subjects from Asch's studies), Atkinson believes the greater conformity of the medium $n\ Affil$ group in the present study to be due to their lower $n\ Ach$. It is probable that acceptance of social influence is mediated sometimes by the desire to be "right" or accurate (which is linked to $n\ Ach$), sometimes by the desire for social acceptance ($n\ Affil$), and sometimes by other factors. Which factors are involved will depend on the type of issue and the nature of the situation, as well as on the motivational structure of the person. The task set for Asch's subjects, for example, stressed accuracy (cf. 21, p. 452), while our task did not.

Future research should systematically vary the nature of the task situation and the importance of the issue under study, among other variables, to clarify the relationships involved.

SUMMARY

This investigation studied the effect of affiliative motivation and social support upon conformity and attitude change. College males varying in affiliative motivation were subjected to a group influence situation where their previously measured attitude toward divorce was either unanimously opposed or opposed with the exception of one supporter. The subject's public reaction (conformity) and private response (attitude change) were measured. The results indicated conformity to be a joint function of affiliative motivation and conditions of social support, with roughly similar but less significant results for attitude change. The medium need group, interpreted to be ambivalently motivated toward social acceptance, conformed under both conditions but changed in attitude only in the no support situation. The high need group, conceived to be positively motivated toward affiliation, conformed and changed in attitude under conditions of no support, but not under support conditions. The low need group, which was least affected, changed more under conditions of support than no support but was considered as responding more to the content of the influence situation than to its social structure.

CHAPTER 31

....

The Relation of Achievement and Affiliation Motives to Conforming Behavior in Two Conditions of Conflict with a Majority[1]

FRANZ SAMELSON

IN THE HOPE to learn more about the complex forces determining human behavior, modern psychology is making extensive use of the ambiguous stimulus situation. In this situation, the subject (S) is forced to go, in his response, beyond the physically given and/or to decide between alternative courses of interpretation or action. In one application of this method, ambiguous stimuli are used for projective tests, like the Rorschach or the TAT, to furnish information about personality structure or the strength of motives. A somewhat different use is made of the ambiguous situation if we present conflicting stimuli and observe which part of the total stimulus complex dominates the selection of responses. An example of this type is the experiment by Witkin *et al.* on the perception of the vertical (437).

A similar situation, complicated by the addition of social variables, is used in the classical studies of Sherif (375) and Asch (21). Here the S has to respond to more or less ambiguous task stimuli while being exposed to predetermined and often incorrect evaluations of the same stimuli by other Ss who in reality are secretly instructed accomplices of the experimenter. A number of studies have explored the parameters of this type of situation. Usually a sizable amount of change toward the presented norm, or conformity, was obtained.

---

[1] This paper is based on a doctoral dissertation at the University of Michigan, completed in 1955 under the chairmanship of Daniel Katz. The research was carried out under a research training fellowship from the SSRC. The major results have been reported in (357).

421

The temptation was naturally great to try to define the personality of the conformer and the independent, although the results of earlier attempts to account for the suggestible person should have been a warning that the solution might not be a simple one. Several experiments (32, 177, 305) have provided data about a number of personality correlates of conformity, often using a variant of the Ascendance-Submission dimension. The nature of the processes responsible for the observed effects, however, has not yet been too well specified.

Projective measures of motivation, viz., n Achievement and n Affiliation, were recently linked to behavior in the conformity situation. McClelland's theory of the development of the achievement motive holds that the person high in n Achievement has internalized the standards of excellence with which he is competing, and McClelland compares this person to Riesman's "inner-directed" type (272, p. 286). From this theory it seems to follow that Ss with high n Achievement scores should be less susceptible to social influence in the conformity situation. The results of an analysis of stories written by Asch's Ss seemed to substantiate this deduction. An association of high n Achievement scores with independence was found.

On the other hand, n Affiliation appears, at first glance, quite likely to be related in a positive direction to yielding to social pressure. A closer inspection of the possible interpretation of n Affiliation scores raises several questions, however. Is the concern over positive affective interpersonal relations a general one, or is it focused on special classes of persons or even specific individuals? In the conformity situation, will the person high in n Affiliation be concerned about his relation to the other Ss or about approval from the authority figure (the experimenter)? The data supporting either of these interpretations are sparse. One study by Hardy (Ch. 30) found high and medium n Affiliation scores to be associated with greater attitude change than low scores in a situation where Ss were confronted with a unanimous majority. But after receiving support from one partner, the high scores conformed least. Need Achievement was not controlled in this experiment.

We should remember that n Achievement and n Affiliation are by definition, not specific habitual response tendencies, but motives which should or could combine with specific situational factors to produce different and even seemingly contradictory behavioral outcomes. Despite McClelland's conception of the person with a strong achievement motive as an independent, inner-directed individual, Burdick (58) has already suggested that this person should *conform* in situations in which he perceives conformity as leading to achievement. Beyond these suggestions for the interpretation of the two motives taken separately, recent results obtained in an analysis of personality assessment data indicate that the combination of both motives may be much more meaningful and productive than their use as separate dimensions (Ch. 28). The present study attempts such a "motive-configuration" analysis of behavior in the conformity situation, a situation in which both motives seem to be of crucial importance.

The conformity experiment may be considered a variant of the ambiguous stimulus situation. Even when the task stimuli are *un*-ambiguous, as in Asch's original experiment in which obvious differences between lengths of lines are to be judged, the total situation is quite ambiguous, or unstable. The unanimous (incorrect) judgment of the majority is just as clear and definite as the S's perception of the task stimuli, and no explanations of this contradiction are available to the naive S. Based on this argument, our study attempts to test the hypothesis that it is not only social pressure, i.e., the fear of social sanctions, which induces a sizable amount of conformity, but that conformity is in part due to cognitive conflict stemming from the apparently equal validity of the S's own perception and the contradictory majority response in the absence of additional information indicating how to reconcile the contradiction. Therefore, a condition was devised in which the naive Ss were given, prior to the test for conformity, some indirect information potentially enabling them to explain the disagreement as due to errors by the majority. The details of the principal aspect of the study are reported elsewhere (357, 358). The present report will concentrate on the results in their relation to the motive measures. But a description of the major features of the experiment is required for this purpose.

PROCEDURES[2]

Two conditions were designed under which the naive Ss found themselves in disagreement with a secretly instructed majority. Their task was to identify simple visual stimuli which were presented tachistoscopically but *above* threshold duration. In the Full Conflict condition, Ss were confronted with the wrong majority judgments without any additional information. In the Reduced Conflict condition, the Ss were first given some information allowing the inference that they were faster at recognition than the other observers. Subsequently they found themselves in the same conflict with the majority as did Ss in the Full Conflict condition.

The Ss were 50 beginning psychology students, all freshmen and

---

[2] For a more detailed description of procedures, see (357).

sophomores. They were assigned at random to one of the two conditions. Each of them met with four other students, ostensibly other *S*s but in fact secretly instructed stooges, for an experiment "on the span of apprehension." Their task was to recognize a nonsense syllable presented at .2 seconds and to select it from four (numbered) alternatives shown one second afterwards and displayed until all responses had been made. The three wrong alternatives had been constructed by changing one of the four letters and/or its position. All five participants announced their choice publicly in a fixed sequence by calling out the number of the "correct" alternative. The naive *S* was always fourth in line to report. Twenty different slides were presented. To eight of them (trials 1, 3, 7, 8, 11, 14, 15, and 19) the majority gave the correct answer. On the twelve *critical* trials, all four stooges agreed on a predetermined wrong alternative. The *S*s were seated in a row, separated from each other by small screens in order to reduce the demands on the stooges' acting skill.

The experimental treatment, designed to provide *S*s in the Reduced Conflict condition with information which would reduce the conflict between their own perceptions and wrong majority responses, used the following procedure. Prior to the test trials, groups in the Reduced Conflict condition were given some trials "for practice." Three slides with five-digit numbers were shown to the group at decreasing speeds, beginning with .01 seconds. *S*s were told to report, out of sequence, whenever they had been able to recognize the stimuli or parts of them. The stooges, however, acted as though they were unable to recognize the stimuli at the initial fast speed and gave correct responses only after the naive *S* had made an accurate report and the speed of presentation of the same slide had been decreased twice. The *S*s presumably gained the impression that their recognition thresholds were lower than those of the majority. A postexperimental rating by the *S*s of their ability for the task showed clearly that these manipulations had the intended effect. While only three *S*s in the Full Conflict condition, who had no such practice, rated themselves as above average, 15 *S*s in the Reduced Conflict condition did so ($p < .001$).

In addition to this question, *S*s answered several others about the difficulty of the task, their visual acuity, and their perception of social influence. During the experiment, they were asked to give ratings of their uncertainty about the correct response on a five-point rating scale. This was done to see whether they would differentiate between trails on which they conformed to the majority response and the neutral trials on which the responses of all observers were also in agreement. Practically all *S*s in both conditions rated their conforming responses as more uncertain, on the average, than their correct agreements with the majority on neutral trials.

At the end of the session, Ss were interviewed about their experiences and their perception of the events. Finally, the procedures were fully explained to them because they were all more or less disturbed about the surprising course the events had taken.

Some weeks before the experiment, Ss had written stories in response to n Affiliation and n Achievement pictures under standard neutral conditions. A description of the eight pictures used is given in (Ch. 46). The affiliation- and achievement-related pictures were presented in an alternating sequence. Scores for n Achievement were obtained according to scoring system C (Ch. 12) from the four relevant pictures; n Affiliation scores were obtained from the other set of four pictures (Ch. 13).

In addition to these projective measures, other personality data were available for most of our Ss in the form of scores on the SA-S personality inventory. Answers to the eighty items of this questionnaire-type inventory are analyzed in terms of two approximately orthogonal dimensions which are defined as: a) "Stability-Anxiety" (S), presumably a measure of free-floating anxiety; and b) "Social Approach" (SA) or "permeability or fluidity of structure rigidity," also described as "sociability *vs.* independent self-sufficiency" (382). Actually the questions are rather straightforward, and responses are probably a better index of the self-percept than of actual behavior. The inventory is an experimental device, and its behavioral correlates are not yet well established.

The personality data had not yet been evaluated at the beginning of our experiment. Therefore Ss in the two conditions could not be matched. This resulted in some imbalance between the numbers of cases in different categories. However, no significant differences between conditions were later found on any of the personality measures, intelligence—as measured by scores on the American Council of Education (ACE) test—or age.

RESULTS

An over-all comparison of the frequency of conforming responses in the two conditions supports our hypothesis. The mean number of conforming responses per S on twelve trials is 4.7 in the Full Conflict and 3.5 in the Reduced Conflict condition. Two different analyses, by Ss and by trials, indicate that the difference between conditions is statistically significant ($p < .05$ and .01, respectively, for one-tailed tests). The analysis by trials shows also that on the first two critical trials only a few Ss in either condition conform. (Conformity in the Reduced Conflict condition is actually higher, though only slightly, in these two instances.) This result means that the difference between conditions which is substantial on the third critical trial is not due simply to a better adaptation of the Reduced Conflict Ss to the *physical* features of the task as a result of their earlier practice with a similar one.

In spite of its statistical significance, the absolute mean difference between conditions is not very large, and variation between Ss in both conditions is substantial. In the Full Conflict condition, the range extends from 2 to 11 conforming responses (out of 12 possible), and in the Reduced Conflict condition from 0 to 11.

A correlational analysis of these data and the personality measures (see Table 1) shows no relation between n Affiliation and amount of conformity. The S (Anxiety) score is not related to conformity, nor is intelligence (ACE scores). But n Achievement seems to be correlated with the behavior in the experimental situation. The surprising result, however, is that the direction of the relationship is different for the two conditions. It is negative, as expected, in the Full Conflict condition, but positive in the Reduced Conflict condition. Here high n Achievement scores are associated with relatively high conformity. Only the latter correlation is statistically significant, as Table 1

TABLE 1. THE RELATIONSHIP BETWEEN CONFORMITY AND SEVERAL PERSONALITY VARIABLES IN THE FULL AND REDUCED CONFLICT SITUATIONS

	Full Conflict		Reduced Conflict		Prob. of Diff.
	N	r	N	r	
n Achievement.........	25	$-.05$	22	$+.51**$	.05
n Affiliation............	25	$-.09$	22	$+.08$	n.s.
Social Approach (SA).....	24	$-.36$	23	$+.33$	.02
Anxiety (S).............	24	$+.01$	23	$+.23$	n.s.
Intelligence (ACE).......	24	$-.08$	21	$+.03$	n.s.

$**\ p = .02.$

shows. Yet the *difference* between the two coefficients is significant. The Social Approach measure yields results of the same form, and again the difference between correlations in the two conditions is significant. In other words, a personality factor *interacted* with the experimental conditions.

This result raises a number of questions. Why is the negative relationship between conformity and n Achievement in the Full Conflict condition so much smaller, though in the right direction, than in Asch's experiment, which had been assumed to be rather similar to this condition? There are a number of differences between the features of the two experiments, the populations sampled, and the methods of obtaining the projective stories. But a closer inspection of our data shows that in our Full Conflict condition the relation between conformity and n Achievement seems to be curvilinear. The Ss in the middle range of n Achievement show the largest amount of conformity. Furthermore, this curvilinearity seems to be due largely to a few quite independent Ss very low in n Achievement. Deletion of the four Ss with extremely low scores raises the correlation to $-.40$. Since the results reported for Asch's experiment are based only on a chi-square analysis of data for Ss on the extremes of the conformity variable, the results may actually be less divergent than they seem at first glance. The relationship between n Achievement and conformity in this condition may be curvilinear when the full range of n Achievement scores is sampled. Or possibly our Ss with very low n Achievement scores were "false negatives," i.e., for some reason, like briefness of record or temporary interference of another motive, their stories did not contain any scorable achievement material.[3] This interpretation of the difference between present results and those of Asch is supported by the fact that a replication of the Full Conflict condition by several undergraduate students subject to our stimulus material under the direction of R. A. Clark, produced a correlation of $-.37$ between n Achievement and conformity ($p < .05$, $N = 28$). Their sample contained only one S with a very low n Achievement score.

The more interesting result is the *reversal* of the relationship between n Achievement and conformity in the Reduced Conflict condition. This result was not expected, but the correlation is sizable and statistically significant. The rather similar pattern of results for the SA variable supports the assumption that the reversal is not a spurious result.

Analysis of variance of the conformity scores for three levels of achievement motivation shows the additional fact that the reversal of the relationship between conformity and n Achievement, as well as the over-all reduction in conformity from Full to Reduced Conflict condition, seems to be due exclusively to a large shift among Ss with medium and low n Achievement scores. The amount of conformity shown by the Ss high in n Achievement is approximately the same in both conditions. But for the medium and low scorers on n Achievement, the difference in conforming responses between Full Conflict and Reduced Conflict condition increases with decreasing achievement motivation ($p = .05$ and $.01$). As a consequence of this shift of the medium and low groups, the *relative* position of the high n

---

[3] For an earlier discussion of the possibility of such results, see (272, pp. 181 and 216).

Achievement group changes. In the Full Conflict condition they conform least, but in the Reduced Conflict condition they show more conformity than the other two groups.

Need Affiliation is not significantly related to conformity in an analysis of variance, though there is some variation of the subgroup means. This disappointing result may be partly attributable to the fact that the measure did not differentiate very well among our Ss. More than a third of them had received a zero score, probably because of an unfortunate choice of the pictures used to elicit n Affiliation stories (cf. Ch. 46). Nonetheless, an analysis using both motive measures in combination was carried out. For this purpose the Ss were divided into high and low scorers on each of the motives at the median for the larger population from which our sample had been drawn.[4] A direct three-dimensional analysis of the effects of experimental condition, n Achievement, and n Affiliation was impossible since the number of cases varied from cell to cell. Therefore, three different two-dimensional analyses had to be carried out, each setting one of the main factors against a combination of the remaining two. The mean values for the different motive configurations are given in Table 2.

TABLE 2. MEAN PERCENTAGE OF CONFORMING RESPONSES FOR GROUPS DIFFERING IN n ACHIEVEMENT AND n AFFILIATION IN TWO EXPERIMENTAL CONDITIONS

Motive Configuration		Full Conflict Condition		Reduced Conflict Condition	
n Ach — n Aff		N	Mean	N	Mean
Low — Low		4	54.0*	6	27.0
Low — High		7	34.4	5	12.8
High — Low		7	30.5	4	35.1
High — High		5	45.2	6	45.6

* *arc sin* $\sqrt{percentage}$ on twelve critical trials.

The results of our analyses (not presented here) show that the interaction between treatment and n Achievement, and the interaction between n Achievement and n Affiliation are statistically significant. A simple chi-square analysis for each condition separately shows the same effects of the motive configurations. Table 3 shows that n Affiliation by itself is not related to conformity, but its combination with n Achievement produces a significant differentiation between

---

[4] Three Ss, whose scores fell on the median were omitted from the subsequent analysis.

subgroups. The association of motive configuration with conformity is pronounced in the Full Conflict condition; it is smaller in the Reduced Conflict condition. There, instead, the difference between the two levels of n Achievement is rather large, yet the interaction between the two motives is still present.

TABLE 3. ASSOCIATION OF MOTIVE CONFIGURATIONS WITH CONFORMITY IN TWO EXPERIMENTAL CONDITIONS

Motive Configuration	Full Conflict Condition		Reduced Conflict Condition	
n Ach — n Aff	Low*	High	Low*	High
High — High	1	4	1	5
High — Low	5	2	2	2
Low — High	5	2	5	0
Low — Low	0	4	4	2
x^2 (3 d.f.)	10.1		10.1	
p	.02		.02	
High vs. Low n Ach	n.s.		.05	
High vs. Low n Aff	n.s.		n.s.	

* 0 to 3 conforming responses were classified as low conformity.

The effect of the experimental treatment is most pronounced in the group low in both motives and almost as pronounced in the low n Achievement–high n Affiliation groups. On the other hand, both groups which are high in n Achievement are apparently little affected by the experimental treatment.

DISCUSSION

The differential effect of the treatment is the major result of the analysis of our personality data. It was not expected, and it is difficult to explain in a satisfactory way.

For both n Affiliation groups low in n Achievement, we find a significant reduction in conformity as a result of the experimental treatment. This is in correspondence with our hypothesis. During the practice, these persons realize that they are performing better than the other observers. This evaluation reduces the ambiguity of the situation and gives them a boost in self-confidence. They are able to assume, when they find themselves in conflict with the majority, that the latter's response might be wrong and that they might well stick to their own choice. This behavior is associated with a tendency to rate the task as easier in the Reduced Conflict condition ($p = .05$).

The difference between these two low n Achievement groups remains approximately constant from one condition to the other. The Low-Lows conform the most in the Full Conflict condition. While this may reflect a lack of motivation for the task since they were not motivated either to do well or to please the experimenter, Groesbeck's (Ch. 28) description of such persons as conflict-ridden, self-deprecating, and lacking in responsibility may throw more light on the results. Once this group is reassured that they are doing quite well in comparison with the other observers, they rarely conform.

The trend in the low n Achievement–high n Affiliation group is identical. In the Reduced Conflict condition, this group is quite independent. This suggests that their affiliative need does not invariably tie them to the shackles of majority opinion. Perhaps they become assured in the practice period of the (presumed) appreciation of the authority figure (the E) if they give their own—and correct—answers. Groesbeck's results depict such persons as cautious; they tend to look over all aspects of the situation and to keep their opinions to themselves (Ch. 28). This description may again help us understand why they might conform in the ambiguous situation but not when they think their judgments are better than those of the other observers. Here, we assume that the affiliative need is directed toward the E and not toward their fellow students—an assumption which seems plausible but is without support from other data.

Summing up, we have argued that the two groups low in n Achievement *did* react to the difference in situations as predicted, presumably because their expectations about achievement situations were not sufficiently general and stable to make them insensitive to the cues of this specific situation. An additional possibility, that the practice period made them react negatively to the majority judgments in the Reduced Conflict condition, i.e., that they chose *on principle* answers at variance with the majority in order to have a better chance to be correct, finds no support in the data. The occasional wrong answers in disagreement with the majority (on critical or neutral trials) were too infrequent to indicate such a trend.

The result that requires but seems to defy explanation is the performance of the groups high in n Achievement. They did not conform any less after being given some basis for assuming they had greater ability. Of course, not every S in the Reduced Conflict condition rated himself, postexperimentally, as above average in ability. Yet there was no difference in this respect between the low and high n Achievement groups (nor is the association of "better" ratings with better actual performance statistically significant). How can we reconcile this result with an interpretation of the person who is high in n Achievement as independent, self-reliant, and one to act according to his own standards? Why was the intermediate amount of conformity shown by these groups in the Full Conflict condition not reduced by the treatment? What happened to them as result of the treatment?

As indicated above, there is no support for the interpretation that they simply were not aware of the meaning of the practice. The other alternative is either that the treatment was too weak to influence their performance or that its effect was different from the one intended by the E. The possibility that their superiority had become clear to everyone in the practice and that they therefore stopped competing with the majority during the test trials seems rather unlikely. The general conception of the person high in n Achievement as a hardworking individual does not make this sudden loss of interest appear plausible. Furthermore, the conflict in the experimental situation was quite strongly felt by all Ss.

Before we attempt another interpretation, it might be well to point out that the result obtained for the group high in n Achievement but low in n Affiliation is the most ambiguous result in these data. The High-Low group consisted of only four Ss, and its variance was largest in the Reduced Conflict condition (although Bartlett's test for homogeneity of variances did not result in rejection of the null hypothesis). Therefore our discussion deals primarily with the High-High subgroup. Ss in this group conformed frequently in both conditions. Can we assume that the Reduced Conflict condition did not, in fact, succeed in reducing the conflict for these Ss?

These individuals are presumably highly motivated to be successful, and it is assumed that their expectations of success have been confirmed frequently in the past. During the practice, they again receive confirmation of these expectations. They may have expected this situation to continue. But instead they find themselves in almost continuous disagreement with a solid majority. Having also a strong need for affiliation, these Ss must have experienced considerable conflict. While the presence of both needs seems likely to create conflict in many situations in everyday life, they probably can often reach a satisfactory compromise solution.

What do we know about such persons from other sources? Groesbeck's (Ch. 28) results for this group with strong motivation on both dimensions are curious. The self-ratings as well as the ratings by their teachers sound rather favorable. They see themselves as "unshakeable" and "independent-minded"; the teaching staff considers them as high in ethical sense and as relatively free from emotional tensions. But their fellow students paint a different picture. Their peers tend to reject them and to judge them as lacking integrity and independent mindedness.

These findings suggest that while motivated to achieve and to please by meeting the demands of authority figures, the High-High may compromise himself *if put under strong pressure*. Davage (87) has proposed this interpretation in a study in which a High-Low and a High-High S with different opinions were brought together and required to reach a common solution to a problem. Davage found that the High-High person retains the upper hand more often by manipulating the other S skillfully to change his mind. Here we find a solution to the problem of how to reconcile the two motives. But Davage's experiment deals with a two-person situation in which the disagreement can be discussed and the opponent can be manipulated into changing his opinion. The present experiment, however, involves a situation in which the High-High person is confronted with a solid phalanx of opponents which shows no signs of breaking up under the impact of his disagreement with them. It is a situation in which he seems no longer able to satisfy both needs at the same time. He has no opportunity to persuade the others to change.[5] He is motivated to do well, but he may also be unable to tolerate disagreement with the majority. We find in the Reduced Conflict condition that the High-High group starts with complete independence on the first trial but quickly increases the number of conforming responses as the experimental period progresses. In other words, still being in conflict about how to satisfy their two needs, these Ss choose the only compromise possible in the given situation—to vacillate back and forth between independence and conformity.

The High-Low group is also motivated to achieve and presumably has stable expectations in achievement situations based on earlier experiences. Therefore, the practice trials probably have little influence on their self confidence. In the test trials, the original stimulus is no longer present when they have to make their choice. They therefore have to rely on immediate memory. This may make them just sufficiently insecure about their own judgment to accept the majority report as correct on some occasions. In other words, their high motivation to be correct may induce them to change their report to that of the majority whenever they are not completely sure that their own choice is the correct answer. In the Full Conflict condition, this degree of conformity is below that of the low n Achievement Ss who presumably feel they have even less chance of being correct by going it alone; in the Reduced Conflict condition the situation is reversed. The High-Highs conform more than the High-Lows in

---

[5] He may in general be more helpless in a situation where he is not dealing with a single person on whom he can use his social skills but would have to address himself to several persons at the same time—which would make intimate relations with the other individuals impossible.

both instances because they are forced to agree more often with the majority because of their greater sensitivity to disagreement.[6]

Thus our results suggest that conforming is not a stable habit of certain personalities, irrespective of the situation, but that different personality variables may be associated with conforming responses under different conditions. Several other studies have produced results pointing in the same direction (Ch. 30; 209, 305). Regarding the interpretation of n Achievement, the implication seems to be that to assume a stable association between achievement motive and independence may be erroneous. In our culture, achievement may be more dependent on the evaluation of performance by other persons than on the success of independent striving for private and self-set goals. The individual high in n Achievement may be the person most sensitive to external demands for good performance. This is why he works harder and better in the usual situation where he is complying more than others with the instructions to apply oneself and where the task is perceived as competitive but free from direct conflict with other individuals. He may be independent when he believes that independent effort will bring him the desired success. But if a strong effort is not particularly efficient for the task, he may perceive agreement with the majority as instrumental to success, at least part of the time, and his motivation to be correct may induce him to change his report.

SUMMARY

This paper attempts to analyze the relationship of n Achievement and n Affiliation to conforming behavior under a condition of Full Conflict with a majority and another condition in which prior experimental manipulations had presumably reduced this conflict to some extent. The findings show that in the first condition n Achievement is negatively related to conformity (though weakly). In the Reduced Conflict condition, Ss low in n Achievement become substantially more independent while those high in n Achievement show no change in conformity. Need for affiliation is not directly related to conformity but interacts with n Achievement in a consistent way across the two conditions. The tentative interpretation assumes that in a very ambiguous situation strong motivation to be successful may induce a person to conform to majority opinion in order to satisfy the desire to be correct.

---

[6] This interpretation receives support from an analysis of the uncertainty ratings given after each trial. These ratings show that the group high in n Achievement is about equally uncertain about conforming and independent responses in both conditions. The group low in n Achievement, however, while indicating the same conflict in the Full Conflict condition, is significantly more certain about independent than about conforming responses in the Reduced Conflict condition.

PART FOUR

The Social Origins of Human Motives

THE THEORETICAL CONCEPTION of motivation and behavior which has begun to emerge from experimental studies (Part III) makes a distinction between the *strength of a motive* and the *strength of motivation* to strive for a particular goal that is aroused in some specific situation. A motive is considered a relatively stable characteristic of the personality after the period of early socialization during which it develops. The arousal of motivation to perform some act is attributed to an interaction between the motives of the individual and factors in the situation which confront him. The situation is conceived in terms of the particular cognitive expectancies it elicits regarding the consequences of alternative acts and the specific goals or incentives it presents. Particular cognitive expectancies and the relative value of incentives are also learned. But it is assumed that they are learned later in life under conditions which make them more situation bound and more modifiable than motives.

There can be little question that expectancies and incentives vary greatly from situation to situation. The individual's motivation to achieve, for example, is not aroused to the same extent as he lies sunning himself on a beach as when he enters his office on the day of an important business transaction. It is presumed, however, that the strength of his *motive* to achieve—that is, his tendency to strive for achievement when the situation offers an opportunity for achievement—does not change. His basic personality is the same whether on the beach or at the office, though his momentary interest and behavior will differ in these two situations.

The theoretical distinction between stable motives and changing level of aroused motivation calls attention to early childhood experience as the probable source of very general and stable motive dispositions and to more recent life experiences as the source of specific and more transient situational meanings and relative incentive values of different activities and goals. The distinction presents a methodological problem, the need for independent measures of motives, relative incentive values, and the cognitive expectations aroused in the person

435

in particular situations. This issue will be taken up again in Part VI.

Alternative theories which have been proposed to account for the origins and development of human motives cannot be reviewed here (see 258, 272). But an important question, "Why should early childhood experience be so important in the formation of motives?", can be answered. It is answered in McClelland's analysis of the conditions of early childhood experience in terms of well-known principles of learning. There may be no clear-cut dichotomy between the conditions of early childhood learning and the conditions of learning later in life. Yet it is useful to accentuate differences in degree in order to appreciate why tendencies acquired early in life remain as very general and stable dispositions of the person.

The empirical investigations of this section represent two different methods of uncovering factors in early childhood experience that are associated with the development of particular motives. Winterbottom questions mothers about their methods of child rearing and then relates their replies to thematic apperceptive measures of achievement motivation in their children. The same method of obtaining information about training in independence and mastery has been employed in studies of various ethnic and religious groups by McClelland *et al.* (277) and Strodtbeck (395). Child, Storm, and Veroff employ the method of an earlier investigation by McClelland and Friedman (274). They relate indices of child-rearing practices in different cultures to indices of achievement imagery obtained from analysis of the folk tales of those cultures. Their results, which are based on a larger sample of cultures and improved indices of child training and which differ from the results of the earlier study by McClelland and Friedman, provide a concrete basis for discussion of the interpretation of different substantive findings and of some of the methodological issues in cross-cultural research.

As yet, except for several exploratory studies of early life experience as recalled by college students (174, 392), there are no comparable studies having to do with the origins of *n* Affiliation or *n* Power.

CHAPTER 32

....

The Importance of Early Learning in the Formation of Motives*

DAVID C. McCLELLAND

LET US BEGIN where most theories of motivation have begun in recent years: with two simple assumptions—namely, that the important psychogenic motives are learned (not instinctual), and that they are somehow acquired by association with primary biological pleasure and pain. For the moment let us put aside the pleasure-pain problem and ask what it is that makes this particular kind of learning so persistent and powerful. Psychologists have studied the learning process in the laboratory in great detail. They have set up nonsense syllable pairs for human beings to associate, distinctive goal boxes for rats to associate with food pellets, and token rewards for chimpanzees to associate with oranges or bananas. In all of these learning situations, what the organism acquires is rather rapidly forgotten. Certainly it shows none of the persistence which we must assume characterizes human motivation. Yet the stubborn fact remains that psychologists believe motives are learned in the same way as other responses are learned. What is the solution to this apparent paradox?

So far, the only clue we have mentioned is that avoidance learning is harder to extinguish than other kinds of learning—a clue which, as we have just seen, has led to the elaboration of a theory of secondary motivation which is based on the notion of anxiety reduction and which we have found inadequate on other grounds. But suppose we take a closer look at avoidance learning. Why is it relatively harder for the rat to unlearn an avoidance response? Naïvely we could say that he keeps running to avoid a nonexistent shock simply because he doesn't know it has been turned off. His learned response *prevents*

---

* Reprinted from *Personality* by David C. McClelland, by permission of the author and The Dryden Press, Inc. Copyright 1951 by David C. McClelland. The excerpt, which appears as part of Ch. 12 in *Personality,* has been given the above title for this volume.

him from finding out that conditions have changed. But can't this situation be generalized? Are there not many situations in which the rat or the human being would have difficulty in discovering that conditions are now changed from what they were before—conditions that do not necessarily involve avoidance learning? In general we might predict that the more disorderly and confused the original conditions of acquisition were, the harder it would be to set up conditions which were sufficiently different from them for the organism to perceive the difference and unlearn a response no longer appropriate.

Let us follow this clue a little further: very few laboratory experiments are sufficiently "messy" and disorderly to make the discrimination between learning and extinction difficult for the animal. In their zeal for experimental control, psychologists may have over-reached themselves. They have usually provided *one* cue that is always relevant, *one* response which is always appropriate to the reward, and *one* particular set of time relations between the events in the cue-response-reward sequence. The reasons for such careful control are excellent. If psychologists are to be able to determine the relations among their analytic units (cue-response-reward) they must control some while they systematically vary others. But it is just this control which may be creating the difficulties for explaining the persistence of certain types of "real life" learning. For the fact of the matter is that in life there is seldom any such regularity in the conditions of learning as we introduce normally into laboratory experiments. Stimulus, response, and reward do not occur in any regular sequence. Sometimes a response is rewarded, sometimes not; sometimes it is punished. Sometimes a reward is so delayed that it is difficult or impossible for the organism to determine what response was instrumental in producing it. In fact, learning in natural life situations often takes place under such irregular, changing, and inconsistent conditions that an experimenter who is absorbed in his consistent cue-reward sequences might wonder how anything is *ever* learned under such conditions. But things *are* learned under such conditions and when they are, they should be very hard to unlearn because the learning is so general in the first place, so compounded of different cues, responses, rewards, and punishments, that it will be hard for the person ever to discover that conditions have changed, that some general expectation he has formed is no longer being confirmed.

Fortunately the mature organism has developed its symbolic and anticipatory capacities to the point where such irregularities in external conditions are usually not so important. Language is a great help to human beings. Thus Johnny has no difficulty in learning that he is being punished for having filched some cookies three hours earlier rather than for riding his tricycle, which is what he is doing when his father discovers his theft. A rat might have trouble figuring out what the punishment was for. But Johnny's father simply tells Johnny that he is punished because he stole the cookies, and, if Johnny understands language, the act of stealing cookies will be symbolically redintegrated and directly associated with the punishment that follows. So it is with many situations. Our symbolic capacities free us from too great a dependence on external regularities and enable us to produce the same kind of regularities internally as the experimenter produces by control of external conditions.

But not always. Sometimes associative connections must be formed under such irregular conditions that they should be very difficult to regularize symbolically. This should be particularly true of early childhood before symbolic control has developed to any very great extent. Following our clue has now led us back to the position taken [earlier] that early childhood ought to be the time when the opportunity to form strong, generalized, and persistent associations is greatest. As we discovered, there are many reasons based on learning theory why early childhood experiences should have the great importance assigned to them by the psychoanalysts. Many of these same reasons would lead us to expect that these experiences may form the basis we have been seeking for the formation of the strong secondary motives that obviously persist for long periods in a person's life. In the first place, if we accept the principle of mass action or the greater over-all responsiveness of the infant to stimulation, it would be logical to assume that many more of the infant's associations would have an affective component. Since pleasure and pain (or affective arousal) are easier to produce in an organism which has not yet developed its discriminatory or symbolic capacities, it should follow that many more situations in infancy would get associated with affective states than would be true later on.

In the second place, the connection for the infant between a situation or response and the state of affective arousal must be very vague and general at best, before symbolic control has been achieved. Whatever else can be said about the behavior of parents, it must be much more irregular than the behavior of an animal experimenter trying to get a rat to acquire a strong secondary drive. There are inevitably delays, inconsistencies, and indeterminacies in the association of situations and responses to primary pleasure and pain. For example, if Johnny gets praised occasionally for doing a variety of things like building blocks, throwing a ball, saying a new word, etc., a general connection is set up between "doing something" and pleasure. Johnny is probably not quite sure what the "something" is that leads to pleasure because the reward occurs in a hit-or-miss fashion and because he can't tell the difference very well between one response and the next, but a very general connection is made. Because it is so general, the connection will also be hard to extinguish. Perhaps he isn't rewarded for throwing the ball on several different occasions. But in the first place, he may not perceive this (the lack of reward may be associated with some other act out of the many he is performing) and in the second, even if he did perceive it, that would be no reason to give up, since he was also not rewarded during the acquisition of the association. Furthermore, there are many other acts in the hierarchy associated with this type of reward which have not been extinguished.

For an older child, on the other hand, the specific connection between a particular response and reward would be much more easily formed and also more easily extinguished since a new (nonrewarded) situation could be more easily distinguished from the old, particularly after the use of language had developed to the point where the parents could explain the situation was different. In short, early childhood would seem to be the ideal time to form strong, affective associations which are so general that they will be hard to extinguish. So we now have a hypothesis as to how persistent secondary motives are acquired and why childhood is so important in their formation. Our next problem is to attempt to state more precisely what conditions lead to the development of (a) strong and (b) general associations of an affective nature. Actually there will be some overlap in our treatment of these two attributes of motivational associations for the simple reason that resistance to extinction is commonly used to measure *both* strength of an association and its generality. Nevertheless, each attribute has also some different measuring operations: strength may also be measured by amplitude, frequency of occurrence in competition with other responses, and latency; generality may be inferred from the irregularity of the conditions of learning. Hence the two attributes will be treated separately in the following discussion, although they are inseparable in some cases.

CONDITIONS INFLUENCING PRIMARILY THE STRENGTH OF AFFECTIVE ASSOCIATIONS

(1) Primacy. [Earlier] we discussed briefly why early associations should have some advantage over later ones just because they occurred first and would not therefore be assimilated into a preexisting apperceptive mass. But we did not specifically discuss the problem of strength. As a matter of fact, there are a number of animal experiments which show that early associations are stronger.

Hunt's initial study of feeding frustration in young rats (190) is a case in point. He found that if rats were irregularly deprived of food in infancy they tended to hoard more as adults, when deprived of food again, than did rats whose initial feeding frustration occurred after the organism had matured. Why should this be so? An explanation apparently requires the notions that deprivation cues get associated with anxiety or affective arousal, that hoarding is an instrumental response which reduces this anxiety, and that *the affective arousal is more intense in infancy than later.* Consequently, when the cues are reinstated in adulthood they arouse a greater anxiety in the rats deprived in infancy, which in turn motivates more instrumental hoarding behavior. Similar results have been obtained by Wolf (440), who has reported the relatively greater permanent effect of early over late sensory deprivation in rats. Animals whose eyes or ears had been temporarily sealed off during the nursing period consistently performed less well in a competitive situation in adulthood which required the use of these sense modalities, despite the fact that tests of the sensitivity of sight or hearing under noncompetitive situations showed no impairment. Rats which had been deprived later in life did not show the same inadequacy in the face of adult frustration. While the results of this experiment cannot be interpreted with any great certainty, they can be understood in terms of a hypothesis which states that the early-deprived rats had formed a strong association between frustration and dependence responses involved in nursing which was reinstated when frustration occurred in later life. Again the evidence is that the early association has a stronger or more permanent effect.

Unfortunately it is difficult to perform comparable experiments on human infants and to observe their effect in later life. Most reports at the human level have dealt with motor and intellectual rather than motivational phenomena. Thus Dennis has reported (99) that marked deprivation of social stimulation in young human infants had little effect on their motor development. In a very well-known study McGraw compared the development of a pair of identical twins, Johnny and Jimmy, after treating Johnny to very unusual, accelerative training techniques. She found that the untaught twin caught up very quickly with his brother and the two showed no marked differences later in motor coordination and intellectual capacity. Nevertheless, she did find (280, 281) that the special training had had rather marked effects on such personality variables as self-confidence and initiative. Jimmy remained much more cautious than his accelerated brother. This suggests that generalized learning in infancy involves primarily affective pleasure-pain associations which will influence the motivational or emotional aspects of personality in later life more than the purely intellectual or motor aspects.

(2) *Involvement of the Autonomic Nervous System.* We have been arguing that affective arousal (pleasure and pain) is somehow at the root of motivational associations. Affective arousal is normally accompanied by some kind of discharge over the autonomic nervous system which is characteristically conceived as both *intense* and *diffuse.* From this we may infer that one of the reasons why affective learning is stronger or harder to extinguish is that it is more intense, more diffuse, perhaps more "primitive" than associations involving more highly differentiated cortical control. Mowrer (307) has been so impressed by the differences between learning which involves the autonomic as compared with the central nervous system that he has been led to the conclusion that different kinds of learning are mediated by the two systems. He argues that learning proceeds according to the contiguity principle in the autonomic system and according to the law of effect in the central nervous system. The evidence which he accumulates for two kinds of learning is considerable but it does not lead necessarily to his conclusion that the distinction between the two depends on whether the autonomic or the central nervous system is involved. On anatomical grounds one simply cannot make as sharp a distinction between the two nervous systems as Mowrer's theory requires. Nevertheless, autonomic discharge *can* be taken as a sign of the fact that a central state of considerable intensity and diffuseness has been aroused and one can reason from this that associations involving the autonomic effector system will be stronger and harder to extinguish than those which do not lead to such a discharge. The exact reason why this is so is not known but a suggestion can be made: perhaps affective states are less under cortical control and are therefore less easily aroused symbolically in their full intensity. If this were so, one could argue that they will be harder to extinguish, just as it is hard to extinguish any response which cannot readily be evoked symbolically. One of the benefits of psychotherapy may be that affective states are sufficiently reinstated to become associated with symbolic cues, which can then be attached to new responses which will take the place of the old, maladaptive, affective ones.

Whatever the reason for the apparently greater intensity of affective states associated with autonomic discharge, it again seems likely that they are more apt to be aroused in early childhood (cf. Jersild, 199). Prior to the development of cortical control, nearly any stimulus will involve some autonomic discharge. As the child matures, the affective component apparently gets less and less and more and more specifically attached to certain cues or responses. This suggests that motives may become progressively harder to form with age although clearly a traumatic incident at any age should be sufficient to form the kind of strong affective association that is required. The only difficulty is that even here the association is apt to be much more specific (e.g., a phobia) than the generalized hedonic associations required for "true" motivation. Aside from their greater susceptibility to autonomic involvement, children are also more apt to be subjected to the kinds of experiences which lead directly to affective arousal. They are less able to protect themselves against relatively intense pains such as being stuck by a pin, severe colic, falling out of bed, etc. They are subjected to a great deal more direct reward and punishment by parents, etc. It is in these terms that we can best understand McGraw's finding that generalized associations involving affective arousal from early reward and punishment for roller-skating, climbing boxes, etc., had more permanent effects than the rather specific instrumental associations involved in acquiring such particular motor skills.

(*3*) *Time Discrimination and Intensity.* The psychoanalysts have not been slow to recognize the greater affective intensity of early childhood experiences, but as might be expected they tend to attribute them to other, more subjective factors. Chief among these has been the suggestion that the intensity of pleasure and pain is greater because the infant has not as yet learned to discriminate time, to anticipate in particular that certain experiences will come to an end. Affective states for the infant should have in consequence a certain "timeless" quality which is difficult for adults to comprehend and which psychoanalysts have tried to get them to comprehend by stepping up the vividness of the language they use to describe the infant's phenomenal world. Perhaps Flugel (139) presents the most common-sense description of the infant's inferred states of mind, based on much stronger statements made by child analysts like Susan Isaacs and Melanie Klein. "The very young child, with no more than a minimal appreciation of time, is unable to bear tension; he does not possess the knowledge, so consoling to older human beings, that loss, frustration, pain, and discomfort are usually but temporary and will be followed by relief. Consequently a very small change in a situation (e.g., a less comfortable posture or pressure of his clothes, a less easy grasp of a nipple or a less ready flow of milk) will convert a pleasant satisfying stimulus into an unpleasant dissatisfying one." (139, p. 109.) "In moments of satisfaction everything is well, and the breast—and later the mother—is an entirely good object, the prototype perhaps of the fairy godmother or genie who fulfills all wishes completely and instantaneously. At moments of dissatisfaction the child feels that all is lost, that he is overwhelmed by distress, and that the object or parent is entirely bad, hostile, and frustrating." (139, p. 117.) While many experimentalists (cf. 321) would doubtless object to the anthropocentric language used by Flugel and the psychoanalysts in an attempt to explain the child's world of experience, yet they could certainly agree that the absence of time discrimination would give an "all-or-nothing" characteristic to pleasure or pain experiences which would probably serve to make them more intense than for older organisms that can anticipate the cessation of either pleasure or pain. This lack of discrimination alone would go a long way toward explaining why it is that associations formed between events and pleasure and pain in early childhood should have a persistence and affective intensity that would be hard to equal in the laboratory.

(4) *The Paradoxical Effects of Frequency of Reward.* Nearly all learning theorists assume that the frequency of occurrence of an association has something to do with increasing its strength, even though they may disagree as to whether frequency causes or merely carries the influences which produce an increase in strength. They also commonly assume that persistence or resistance to extinction is a measure of the strength of an association. Yet there have always been some facts that do not fit both of these assumptions. Sometimes, the more frequently a response has been reinforced the *easier* it is to extinguish. How can an operation both strengthen and weaken a response at the same time? Pavlov (326) found that conditioned salivary responses which had been greatly overlearned could sometimes be extinguished on a single trial. Under these circumstances, how could trials to extinguish be a measure of the strength of a connection? Obviously, one or the other of the original assumptions must be in error. The question has come up again and again in learning theory in the controversy over whether a partially learned discrimination can be reversed without loss of learning time (cf. 181). The so-called "continuity" theorists have accepted both of the two assumptions just stated and argued that the more frequently one response to a discrimination situation has been reinforced, the longer it will take to extinguish that response and shift to the opposite one. The noncontinuity theorists have argued that this does not seem to be necessarily so.

Without going into the intricacies of this particular argument, we can note that frequency of reward has two effects which should influence the extinction process differently. In the first place, frequency probably permits the association to be strengthened as the continuity theorists argue. However, in the second place, the more frequent the reward has been, the easier it is for the organism to perceive that there has been a change in conditions when the reward is withdrawn in the extinction condition. The stronger the original association, the more distinctive and specific it is and the greater the contrast with the new situation in which the animal no longer receives reward under the same conditions. Consequently the animal should find it easier to discriminate the new (extinction) situation from the old (acquisition) situation. Really the animal is faced with a *problem in successive discrimination* which will be easier in direct relation to the distinctiveness of the difference between conditions of learning and extinction. The greater the frequency of reward during acquisition, the more distinctively different a series of non-rewarded trials and the easier extinction should be. If original learning is pushed far enough, as in the case of Pavlov's overlearning experiments, a single nonreinforced trial may be sufficient to distinguish the new situation from the old and to produce the appropriate response of not responding. To summarize, the more frequently an association is reinforced, the stronger it will become, but also the more specific and in consequence the more easily extinguished. Evidence for these two conflicting effects of the frequency of reward has been discovered by Gwinn (166) working with the fear response in rats. He found that when he increased the frequency of strong shocks which mature rats received in a compartment, the rats ran out of the compartment faster on the first few extinction trials, which is consistent with the first assumption that frequency of an association increases its strength. But he also found, paradoxically, that the same rats *extinguished more quickly,* which is consistent with the second assumption that these rats were able to distinguish the non-shock situation in extinction from the shock situation in training more easily than the rats who had only been shocked a few times during training.

The bearing of this point on the formation of motives in human beings is interesting, although somewhat conjectural at this stage. Learning psychologists who have attempted to apply their principles to child rearing have up to now usually argued that the way to strengthen a desirable habit or attitude is to reward it consistently. Thus it might be suggested that if Johnny's father wants Johnny to strive for achievement, he ought to reward Johnny for any little efforts toward achievement that he makes. In the light of our present analysis this might strengthen the specific response of achieving for daddy's approval, but if Johnny ever found himself in a situation where approval was not forthcoming, we might expect that the response would also extinguish rather rapidly. It is on just such a basis that we could distinguish between a *habit* of achieving in response to specific situations to get a specific reward and an achievement *motive* which is based on a generalized association between *various* responses and *possible* achievement rewards.

Again, age at which stress is placed on achievement (or other forms of adjustment) seems important. A parent may be extremely consistent in stressing achievement (from his viewpoint) but may begin his consistent disciplining at too early an age for the child to discover and symbolize the consistency. If so, he will tend to develop what we have just called an achievement motive rather than an achievement habit. Thus Friedman (149), in studying the extent to which children in various cultures were required to do things for themselves, found that early stress on independence training was significantly related to the amount of achievement motivation expressed in the mythology of the cultures concerned. Later stress, however, was not as closely related to mythological n Achievement, which suggests that children in such cultures did not develop the strong *generalized* affective associations needed for high imaginative n Achievement but developed instead achievement "habits" which, as in the hypothetical case of Johnny, would be more specifically tied by language to particular situations and rewards.

CONDITIONS AFFECTING PRIMARILY THE GENERALITY
OF AFFECTIVE ASSOCIATIONS

Frequency of reward is a good transition from conditions increasing strength to those increasing generality of associations since, as we have seen, it serves simultaneously to increase strength and decrease generality, particularly if continued long enough. What are some of the other conditions influencing generality of associations, particularly as they may be present in childhood, when motives are presumably learned? Linton has considered the problem in a general way as follows:

"The more specific a response the easier it is to extinguish it. The reason for this is fairly obvious. Laboratory experiments have shown that habits are extinguished either when they fail to achieve the desired ends or when they expose the individual to too much punishment. Owing to environmental or other changes, a response which is linked with a single situation or with a very small number of situations, can easily become subject to the conditions which will lead to extinction. More generalized responses on the other hand, are likely to be rewarded in connection with some situations even when they are unrewarded or punished in connection with others. It is a common experience that while specific patterns of overt behavior are fairly easy to extinguish, value-attitude systems are extremely hard to extinguish. Such systems tend to survive even when their overt expressions have been inhibited in many situations and to reassert themselves with almost undiminished vigor when new situations involving the particular value factor arise." (238, p. 115.) If the word *motive* is substituted for the phrase "value-attitude system" in this quotation, it summarizes in a general way one of the main reasons why motives are so persistent.

Furthermore, Linton goes on to link the formation of generalized value-attitudes to early childhood. They "seem to be easy to establish in childhood but exceedingly difficult to establish in adult life" possibly because of "some inability on the part of the small child to differentiate between related situations" (238, p. 116). In short, he has stated our general thesis that affective associations laid down in childhood are often so exceedingly general because of the child's undeveloped powers of discrimination that they persist because it is difficult to produce the conditions that would make it possible to extinguish them. This argument assumes that associations do not decay simply through disuse, which seems a safe assumption in view of the fairly overwhelming evidence that it is what happens *in time* rather than time itself that causes forgetting (279). What more specifically are some of the conditions that promote generality of initial learning?

1. Lack of Symbolic Control. We have already discussed above the great advantages that human beings have in being able to free themselves from environmental sequences by symbolic manipulation. The use of symbols, especially language, favors specificity of learning largely because it enables the child to make the discrimination much more easily between when it is appropriate to make a response and when it is not. He can group together what would otherwise be a large number of complex experiences, often separated by varying time intervals, under a single heading and say, for instance, "Oh, mummy loves me if I try hard." The younger child does not have this advantage: all he can learn is that there is a vague class of activities which is followed by something pleasant (e.g., "mummy's love"). Since he cannot define the boundaries of the class very well or decide whether a given act belongs to it or not, he may, if pressure for achievement is put on him at this age, learn to "be kept on his toes by a nameless, shapeless, unlocated hope of enormous achievement," as Bateson so nicely phrases it. Language also makes it easier to decide when effort is *not* called for. If the child has named the class of activities which require effort (e.g., schoolwork), he can the more readily distinguish activities that do not require effort (e.g., household chores). But if the independence training is itself so general that no such specific learning is possible, or if it occurs so early in life that adequate symbolization is impossible, then we have the conditions for the formation of an extremely general achievement association which will be very hard to extinguish.

2. Generalized Threats and Promises. We have also already mentioned the fact that avoidance learning may be hard to extinguish because it leads to a response which does not permit the person to discover that the situation is changed. Technically this is somewhat different from general learning, but it delays extinction in the same way. Furthermore, it suggests a type of learning situation which may prevent unlearning because the responses are instrumental to goals which are so high, vague, or indeterminate that *it is impossible for the person to evaluate how well he is doing.* At one extreme, a child may be punished regularly for stealing candy. He knows he will be spanked if he takes it and may learn to inhibit this response. Later on he may try taking it again and if he goes unspanked will soon extinguish the inhibitory response. At the other extreme, a child may be told if he steals candy that "something bad" will happen to him, his conscience will hurt him, God will disapprove, etc. This too will in time inhibit his response but now if he breaks through this inhibition at any time he has no way of knowing accurately whether he is being punished or not. "Something bad" may not happen immediately, but it may later; sins may be stored up in heaven, etc. In short, prohibitions established on the basis of vague threats are much harder to unlearn than those established by direct punishment, just as Mackinnon discovered (cf. 314). The same argument holds for vague promises of reward. The vaguer and more general they are, the harder it will be for the child to discover whether the achievement behavior (for instance) he is showing does or does not lead to the promised gratifications.

3. Irregularity of Original Learning Conditions. For a number of years learning theorists have known that random reinforcement during learning will delay extinction over what it is for 100 per cent reinforcement (189). Many studies summarized by Jenkins and Stanley (198) have shown that this phenomenon is very general and occurs whether reinforcement is periodic (e.g., every second minute), aperiodic (e.g., randomly distributed around two minutes), or in fixed ratio (e.g., for every third response). An explanation of the delay in extinction can readily be made in terms of our analysis of the influence of frequency of reinforcement on the distinctiveness of acquisition as compared to extinction conditions. Whenever reinforcement occurs with less than 100 per cent regularity, acquisition conditions become more similar to extinction conditions and it gets harder for the animal to discriminate between the two and learn to stop responding. Stated in its most general form, our proposition is that *any method of increasing the similarity between acquisition and extinction will delay extinction.*

But randomizing reinforcement is only one way of making the discrimination between learning and extinction difficult. Many other kinds of irregularities may be introduced. Even in these experiments the correct *response* is never varied (as it often would be in life situations), nor are the revelant *cues*. In other words, in a typical experiment bar-pressing remains the response which produces the food, although it may not bring food on a particular occasion. McClelland and McGown (276) performed an experiment in which the reinforcement factor was held constant at 100 per cent but the relevant cues and responses to receiving food were varied. They trained two groups of white rats to associate a goal box with food, one in the standard specific way and the other in an irregular, "general" way. The goal box consisted of a circular alley. In the specific alley-trained group a barrier was inserted in the alley and food reward on the training days was *always* placed just in front of this barrier. Consequently the rats in this group learned to enter the circular alley, turn left, and run a certain fixed distance to find a food pellet. They learned to associate a particular left-turning response, a particular location in the alley, and a particular time delay with food reward.

The group of rats which received generalized reinforcement training were treated quite differently. They too were always fed in the circular alley but there was no barrier in it and the reinforcement was given in such a way as to prevent the animal from associating any particular response, or portion of the alley, or time delay with food reward. This was done by leaving the food rewards in different sections of the circular alley and by sometimes feeding the animal only when he *stopped* in a certain section of the alley. In other words, the occurrence of the food reward in the goal alley was so irregular with respect to time and place and so inconsistent with respect to the response reinforced that the rats must have formed only a very general association between the circular alley and food reward. After both groups of rats had received 100 per cent reinforcement in the goal alley on three successive days in this fashion, the crucial test was made of determining which group would continue to run into the alley longer when the food reward was withdrawn. Both groups showed evidence of the fact that the goal alley, by being associated with food, had attained some secondary reinforcing power. That is, both groups ran into the goal alley more often and faster on the test day than did control groups which had not received reinforcement in it. The group which had been rewarded for a specific response during training extinguished rather rapidly as in all other experiments of this sort. But the general group behaved quite differently. In the first place, the rats in this group ran into the goal alley significantly faster than the specific animals did, showing that the generalized training had developed a more powerful secondary reward. In the second place, they showed little evidence of extinction in the twenty-five extinction trials given them. On the contrary, they showed slight evidence of a tendency to run faster at the time when the "specific" animals had definitely begun to extinguish.

So far then as this experiment goes, it confirms the hypothesis that generalized learning is stronger (speed-of-running measure) and will persist longer than specific learning. It tests the hypothesis, however, only in an over-all fashion. Actually three factors associated with reward were controlled in the specific group and varied in the general group—namely, the response, the time delay, and the place where the food was. Each of these should be studied separately to discover whether it is the variation in the responses rewarded or the place rewarded or the delay of reward which accounts for the persistence of the secondary reinforcing power of the goal alley. Needless to say, all these factors are varied under the normal conditions in which the child is learning something. Prior to the development of language there must be a good many associations which can best be described as "something good" following "something" else at some time or other.

A peculiarly important form of irregularity in learning not so far mentioned is that in which both reward and punishment (or pleasure and pain) get mixed up in the same association. Suppose the rats in McClelland and McGown's experiment had also been shocked occasionally just as they were eating the food. What would have happened then? Would this have delayed extinction still more? As a matter of fact there is some evidence on this point: Drew (106) found that electrifying the food a rat was eating greatly increased the rate of consumption. What is being built up here is an association which involves elements both of pleasure and pain—an association which appears to be "stronger" and should be harder to extinguish by non-reward if Farber's previously reported similar experiment (125) may be taken as indicative of what would happen.

Such associations have very great importance in psychoanalytic theory and in understanding the problems of neurosis. In these areas the term *ambivalence* is commonly applied to them. How such mixed, ambivalent associations are supposed to be acquired in early childhood is again clearly described by Flugel (139). After pointing out that a very small change in the situation may "convert a pleasant satisfying stimulus into an unpleasant dissatisfying one," he states "Thus the child can both love and hate the same objects in rapid succession or alternation and his love and hate alike tend to work on the all-or-nothing principle—there are not the qualifications and quantitative variations that are found in later life." (139, p. 109.) The breast which does not supply the milk may be regarded as "bad" or frustrating one moment and as "good" the next, when milk flows and satisfies hunger. Thus many objects must in the beginning be associated *with both pleasure and pain* in ways that the infant is incapable of separating. As both Lewin (229) and Miller (290) have pointed out, ambivalence or an approach-avoidance conflict is one of the most serious and insoluble types of conflict. As such it may create a secondary disturbance or tension which becomes an important and persistent new motive with tension reduction as its goal. But note in particular that associations which contain pain and punishment to begin with should be exceedingly difficult to extinguish by additional punishment or non-reward later on. Theorists have wondered why a child's love for his mother may persist despite all sorts of discouragements, punishment, evidence of dislike and rejection, etc. One of the reasons may well be that the child acquired his original regard for his mother under conditions which contained a good deal of punishment to begin with. So the "new" punishing situations are not sufficiently different from the "old" learning conditions to make the unlearning of the old response likely or even possible. Ambivalent associations should be harder to unlearn than nonambivalent ones, if this reasoning is correct.

4. Unreproducibility of the Conditions of Learning. A related but somewhat different reason why early learning may be so general that it is hard to extinguish arises from the fact that many of the discriminations a child subsequently makes have not been made at the time the learning in question took place. Chief among these is the distinction between self and not-self, between inner and outer sensations. In Flugel's words, "There is no adequate distinction between sensations and their accompanying feelings and impulses, nor —more important still—between these feelings and impulses and the associated outer objects." (139, p. 110.) In short, things happen in the child's life—pleasurable things and painful things—and the child has no clear notion as to whether the pain comes from within (proprioceptive sensations) or without (sensations from the eye or other distance receptors). Thus the pleasure from sucking may become associated *both* with internal hunger sensations and with external visual ones (the breast). We could expect then a kind of generalized association between eating pleasure and a set of cues not yet discriminated into inner and outer sources which we might label *proto-perceptive.* Later on, however, the child discriminates quite clearly between what happens inside him and what happens in the outside world. Now suppose we had the job of extinguishing an association involving proto-perceptive cues after the inner and outer discrimination had been clearly established. Would it not be difficult? How could we go about reestablishing the cue situation which was present when the association was learned? What we would be most likely to do is to reproduce the external part of the cue compound (e.g., the mother) and expect that new associations learned to this aspect of the compound would replace the old ones. But such a procedure would probably not be very efficient, although some retroactive inhibition through partial similarity in the cue situations should occur. In short, it may be hard to unlearn some early affective associations because they were learned *under cue conditions which cannot be reinstated and attached to new responses.* This point need not only apply to inability to distinguish inner from outer stimuli, of course; it should hold for any peculiar cue conditions of infancy that are hard to reinstate. In fact, the same argument was presented in a more general way [earlier when] we pointed out that as children grow larger it becomes difficult to reinstate exactly what they perceived when they were small and looking at the underneath surfaces of the world. And if cue patterns cannot be reproduced with a fair degree of accuracy, it will be difficult to unlearn the associations involving them.

For all these reasons and for others which are closely related, affective associations formed in early childhood are apt to be strong and very resistant to unlearning or forgetting. From the theoretical viewpoint there is no reason why such associations could not be formed *at any time in life* but more of the conditions we have laid down are apt to occur in childhood, particularly at the preverbal level. Thus we have made a beginning at least toward solving one of the two major difficulties associated with contemporary theories of motivation—namely, the difficulty of explaining their extraordinary persistence and strength in the light of our knowledge of the transitoriness of most laboratory learning.

CHAPTER 33

The Relation of Need for Achievement to Learning Experiences in Independence and Mastery[1]

Marian R. Winterbottom

RESEARCH INTO the origins of motives revealed in fantasy has been directed towards at least two kinds of determinants. One direction has been towards a psychoanalytic understanding of the experience of the person in relation to perceptions of his body as sources of motivation and conceptualization. Another direction has been towards the investigation of environmental factors and has stressed the motivational and conceptual development engendered by experiences with parents, siblings, and the external world in general. These two kinds of determinants are by no means separated in most theoretical discussions, though more or less attention may be paid to each in accordance with the psychologist's theoretical or research interests. The second orientation, the examination of environmental contributions to fantasy, has been favored by psychologists trained in experimental rather than clinical techniques of investigation and has characterized research into the origins of motives such as the achievement motive, as defined and discussed by McClelland *et al.* (272).

Research regarding the origins of the need for achievement has focused on the social conditions in which the growing person learns to be motivated for achievement. For example, McClelland and Friedman (274) have found significant correlations between *n* Achievement scores obtained from the folk tales of eight American Indian tribes and the age and severity of independence training in

---

[1] This article is based on a dissertation submitted in partial fulfillment of the requirements for the degree of Doctor of Philosophy in the University of Michigan, 1953 (436). The writer wishes to express her appreciation to Dr. J. W. Atkinson for his valuable guidance throughout the research.

453

those cultures. McClelland (258, 259) has derived from a theory of motivation a list of variables to be related to achievement motivation. His discussion directs attention to the number of experiences in independent mastery, the age at which the training is given, and the emotional accompaniments of the training as important conditions for the development of an achievement motive in the child.

In order to investigate further these hypotheses within an American community, the author studied a group of twenty-nine eight-year-old boys and their mothers, living in a small, middle-class, midwestern community in 1952. The group was relatively homogeneous economically and socially. The children all attended the same school and were in the same grade and same range of intelligence. The strength of n Achievement in the boys was related to dimensions of independence and mastery training as reported by their mothers in interviews conducted by the experimenter. Mothers were chosen as the initial group for study because of their close contact with children during the early formative years and because of the strong emotional ties of children to their mothers. Later in the paper we will discuss the importance of father and siblings in this learning, but the evidence presented will primarily be concerned with mothers and sons.

THE HYPOTHESES AND PROCEDURE

Mother's Standards of Training in Independence and Mastery (Demands). The hypotheses relevant to this aspect of training state that mothers of boys who are high in n Achievement (a) will make a greater number of demands for independence and mastery, (b) that they will reward the child more frequently and more intensely, and (c) that they will give this training at an earlier age than mothers of boys who are low in n Achievement. These hypotheses are in accordance with McClelland's (258, 259) argument that as achievement cues are followed frequently by emotional changes, the cues take on the characteristic of arousing these emotional changes in an anticipatory way. McClelland has further specified that experiences early in life will be more decisive in this respect because there will be greater generalization of the learning and because emotional responses to parents are more intense at earlier ages.

Information regarding this aspect of training was obtained through interviews with each mother. The data presented comes from a questionnaire which each mother filled out and which included a list of twenty kinds of independence and mastery behaviors that she might consider as goals of her training. A mother was asked to put a check beside each item she considered to be a goal of her training and to indicate the age by which she expected her child to have learned the behavior. The demands were:

To stand up for his own rights with other children.
To know his way around his part of the city so that he can play where he wants without getting lost.
To go outside to play when he wants to be noisy or boisterous.
To be willing to try new things on his own without depending on his mother for help.
To be active and energetic in climbing, jumping, and sports.
To show pride in his own ability to do things well.
To take part in his parents' interests and conversations.
To try hard things for himself without asking for help.
To be able to eat alone without help in cutting and handling food.
To be able to lead other children and assert himself in children's groups.
To make his own friends among children his own age.
To hang up his own clothes and look after his own possessions.
To do well in school on his own.
To be able to undress and go to bed by himself.
To have interests and hobbies of his own. To be able to entertain himself.
To earn his own spending money.
To do some regular tasks around the house.
To be able to stay alone at home during the day.
To make decisions like choosing his clothes or deciding how to spend his money by himself.
To do well in competition with other children. To try hard to come out on top in games and sports.

The emotional consequences of the training were also assessed in the questionnaire. The hypotheses were that children who are more intensely and frequently rewarded for accomplishment are more highly motivated and that children who are more frequently and intensely punished for failure are more highly motivated. (There were some reservations about the latter part of this hypothesis, since it was expected that extreme punishment might lead ultimately to avoidance of thoughts and behavior related to achievement.)

Following the demands scale, there were two lists of alternative parental reactions to the child's behavior. One list is concerned with what the mother does when the child fulfills her expectations. The other list is concerned with what she does when he does not fulfill her demands. The list of alternative reactions to "good" performance in the child is made up of three rewarding reactions:

1. Kiss or hug him to show how pleased you are.
2. Tell him what a good boy he is. Praise him for being good.
3. Give him a special treat or privilege.

and three relatively neutral reactions:

4. Do nothing at all to make it seem special.
5. Show him you expected it of him.
6. Show him how he could have done better.

The list of alternative reactions to the "bad" performance in the child is made up of three punishment items:

1. Scold or spank him for not doing it.
2. Show him you are disappointed in him.
3. Deprive him of something he likes or expects, like a special treat or privilege.

and three relatively neutral items:

4. Don't show any feeling about it.
5. Point out how he should have behaved.
6. Just wait until he does what you want.

The items in each scale were randomized, and mothers were asked to make three choices among the six possibilities.

Two measures can be obtained from each scale. First, the number of rewards or punishments chosen from the six items. This measure can vary from zero to three. For example, a parent may make three choices all neutral, three choices all rewarding, or choices of one or two rewards. Second, the rewards and punishments are assumed to vary in intensity. It is assumed that direct physical rewards or punishments are affectively more intense than less personal reactions on the part of the mother. Verbal praise or punishment is assumed to be second in affective intensity; rewards or punishments which involve objects or privileges, least intense. The rewards and punishments have been listed above in their assumed order of intensity.

The final part of the mothers' questionnaire listed the twenty independence or achievement activities again and asked the mothers to indicate the independence and success which their children had achieved relative to other children. Mothers were asked to rate their children as showing a particular behavior more, less, or to the same degree as other children the same age. This measure was included in order to obtain the mother's picture of the child's achievements. It was expected that the mothers of boys who are high in n Achievement would rate their sons higher than the mothers of boys who are low in n Achievement.

Mother's Restrictions in Training for Independence and Mastery (*Restrictions*). The discussion so far has been concerned with relating n Achievement to accomplishment in the positive sense, and except for the hypothesis that boys high in n Achievement will have experienced greater punishment for failure, the negative aspects of the training have not yet been considered.

In addition to failure to achieve mastery, there are certain aspects of independence and mastery that a mother may prohibit, and these prohibitions are likely to effect the achievement motivation of her child. To test the hypothesis that restrictions will have an effect opposite to that of demands, a list of twenty behaviors that a mother might want to discourage was added to the questionnaire. Each of these restrictions corresponded in content to one of the demand items. For example, the demand "standing up for his rights with other children" was converted to the restriction "not to fight with other children." As with the demands, the mother was asked to check a restriction if she considered it a goal of her training and to indicate the age by which she expected it to be learned. The restrictions were:

Not to fight with children to get his own way.
Not to play away from home without telling his parents where he is.
Not to be noisy and boisterous in the house.
To be cautious in trying new things on his own when his parents aren't around.
Not to run and jump a lot.
Not to try to be the center of attention. Not to boast or brag.
To be respectful and not interfere with adults.
Not to try to do things himself that others can do better.
Not to be sloppy at the table or eat with his fingers.
Not to boss other children.
Not to play with children he doesn't know or of whom his parents don't approve.
Not to leave his clothes lying around or his room untidy.
Not to fail at school work.
Not to stay out after dark.
Not to depend on his mother for suggestions of what to do.
Not to earn money or take a job without his parent's consent.
Not to whine or cry when his mother leaves him alone.
Not to try to do things around the house where he will be in the way.
Not to make important decisions like choosing his clothes or deciding how to spend his money without asking his parents.
Not to try to beat other children in play.

The restrictions were followed by a list of rewarding and punitive reactions identical to those following the demands. The specific hypotheses to be tested were that boys who are high in n Achievement experience fewer restrictions, later in training, and with less intense rewards and punishments.

The reader will note that for the two kinds of negative achievement-related experiences—failure to achieve in relation to parental demands and prohibitions on achievement behavior—we have offered different hypotheses. We predict the high n Achievement group will experience *more* intense punishment for failure to meet demands for achievement but *less* intense rewards and punishments for obeying restrictions. The reason for this difference in the hypotheses is evident if one considers the nature of the effect on the child of the two kinds of negative experience in training. Failure to meet a demand for independent accomplishment can be avoided in at least two ways: first, by not trying and leaving the situation physically or psychologically; second, by putting forth more effort and finally succeeding. We think a child is more likely to learn the former mode of resignation and giving up when failure is a terminal experience—that is, when success does not follow failure. If success often follows failure, then an experience of failure may itself contain cues which arouse anticipations of ultimate achievement. Failure is least likely to be a terminal experience when the mother has made demands which define positive achievement goals for the child. In this case the mother won't stop with failure but will insist that the child try until he succeeds. Extreme punishment for failure may lead to resignation, but moderate punishment probably serves as a goal to harder striving since the fear of failure and anticipation of pleasure in success are not channelled into the same mastery response. Achieving becomes the only sure way of avoiding failure.

On the other hand, if the child learns that a number of his attempts at independent mastery are wrong (i.e., punished) and there is no further definition of the correct response by the parent, he will be less likely to learn to want to achieve as a result of his failure experience. He will be more likely to fear attempting to achieve and will avoid thinking of it. Terminal failure experiences in the achievement training of the child are most likely to be introduced by a parent who phrases most of her goals in relation to independence training in terms of "don'ts," as wrong responses which she wants the child to inhibit. If she rewards the child for avoiding attempts at independence and mastery and if she punishes their occurrence, she is creating conditions which favor the development of a motive to avoid and inhibit achievement-directed thought and action. We expect this type of restrictive training to be reflected in a lower n Achievement score, since the score is primarily a function of the number of imaginative thoughts indicating continued striving towards achievement.

One consideration, however, must be taken into account. If a child has already learned the independent response (e.g., he can already dress or eat by himself), restrictions are less likely to lead to avoiding the situation completely since there will always be something he can do. It is important, then, to consider the sequence of demands and restrictions in studying the effects of restrictions on the strength of the motive to achieve. This is especially true when we consider the age at which restrictions are imposed. It is not age *per se* that is important, but what, if any, learning has preceded the imposition of restrictions. If no learning has preceded it, restrictive training will be more likely to contribute to a motive to avoid attempts at independence and mastery than if some mastery techniques have already been learned.

In summary, the measures obtained from the mother's questionnaire are:

1. Number of demands for independent accomplishment reported as goals of training by the mother.
2. The age at which the mother reported wanting the demands learned.
3. Rewarding or punishing consequences of success or failure in learning demands.
   (a) Number of affective vs. number of nonaffective consequences reported.
   (b) Intensity of affective consequences reported.
4. Mother's opinion of her child compared with other children on his independence and successfulness.
5. Number of restrictions upon independent activity reported as goals of training by the mother.
6. The age at which the mothers reported wanting the restrictions learned.
7. Rewarding or punishing consequences of success or failure in learning restrictions.
   (a) Number of affective vs. number of nonaffective consequences reported.
   (b) Intensity of affective consequences reported.

The Imaginative Measure of n *Achievement.* Some young children showed that they often find it difficult to give imaginatively rich stories in four minutes (the standard time) when pictures are used to elicit thematic apperception. Lowell (272) has used verbal cues with this age group with much more success and without the distracting description-provoking effects of pictures. Hence, two sets of verbal cues, similar but not identical to Lowell's, were used in this study. One set of four was given under what has been called Relaxed Orientation, where every effort is made to put the subject at ease and instructions are given to reduce as much as possible any "test atmosphere." The experimenter said: "What I have for you today is a sort of game. I'm interested in storytelling and I'd like you to tell some stories. It would be hard to make up stories about just anything, so I'm going to tell you what to make up a story about. I'll give you an idea, and you tell me a story about it. Make up a real story with a beginning and an end just like the ones you read. Tell me as much about your story as you can, and I'll write down what you say. Let's try one for practice. Tell me a story about a little boy who is in school."

During the practice story the experimenter asked leading questions similar to those usually printed on the story form when stories are written, i.e., What is happening in this story? What happened before? How did the story begin? What is the boy thinking about—how does he feel? What will happen—how will the story end?

At the end of the practice story, the experimenter said: "Now you have the idea. You can tell me the rest of your stories in the same way. I'll ask you what is happening, what happened before, how the people think and feel, and how the story ends. You can tell the story by answering my questions."

The verbal cues about which the child was to tell the story were (1) A mother and her son. They look worried. (2) Two men standing by a machine. One is older. (3) A boy who has just left his house. (4) A young man sitting at a desk.

At the end of the "relaxed" stories, another condition was introduced: Achievement Orientation. The child was told that he would be given a puzzle test[2] which would tell how smart he was and on which he should try his best because he was to be compared to others in his class. After three minutes of work on the test and during a "rest period," a second set of stories was collected in response to the following verbal cues: (1) A father and son talking about something important. (2) Brothers and sisters playing. One is a little ahead. (3) A young man alone at night. (4) A young man with his head resting on his hands.

The stories were scored according to the criteria for achievement-related imagery developed by McClelland *et al.* (272). Scoring reliability was checked on twenty stories. These were scored by the experimenter and another person who had considerable experience with the scoring system. The product-moment correlation between the two scorings was .92. The over-all percentage agreement in scoring particular categories was 73 per cent.

The median n Achievement score of 5.0 for the 29 boys under Achievement Orientation was greater ($p < .06$ in the expected direction) than the median score of 3.8 under Relaxed Orientation. But since there is no evidence that the two forms of the measure were equivalent, little can be made of this difference except to note that it is in the expected direction.

---

[2] A form of the Carl Hollow Square test was used which was difficult enough so that no child completed it in three minutes.

Treatment of the Data. For the analysis of results presented in this paper, the distributions of both Relaxed and Achievement-oriented n Achievement scores are divided at the medians forming high and low n Achievement groups on each measure. Results are reported in terms of each of these measures and also in terms of another division of subjects into a group ($N = 10$) who were high (i.e., above the median scores) on both Relaxed and Achievement-oriented scores versus a group ($N = 10$) who were low (i.e., below the median scores) in both conditions. This particular breakdown isolates a group who, as Martire has argued elsewhere (Ch. 27), show strong generalized motivation to achieve irrespective of the situation cues and a group who are relatively low in motivation to achieve irrespective of situation cues.

RESULTS

n *Achievement and Demands for Independence and Mastery.* The hypothesis that mothers of the high n Achievement group would report more demands was not confirmed. The median number of demands made by mothers of both high and low n Achievement groups was 19-20 in each of the comparisons, a result indicating that almost all of the mothers chose all of the items as goals of training by age ten.

However, the hypothesis that mothers of boys who are high in n Achievement would make these demands *earlier* is supported. By the age of eight, approximately half the demands of the total group were made. If we consider the demands made before the age of eight as *early* demands, we can compare mothers of high and low n Achievement groups on the number of early demands they make. Table 1 shows the median number of early demands made by mothers

TABLE 1. MEDIAN NUMBER OF EARLY DEMANDS (THROUGH AGE SEVEN) REPORTED BY MOTHERS OF BOYS WHO WERE HIGH AND LOW IN n ACHIEVEMENT

	Measure of n Achievement					
n Achievement	Relaxed Orientation		Achievement Orientation		Both	
	N	Md.	N	Md.	N	Md.
High..........	15	10	14	11	10 (HH)	15.5
Low..........	14	7	15	6	10 (LL)	5.5
p^*...........		.01		.004		.002

* Probability of the difference in predicted direction by Mann-Whitney U Test (303).

of high and low n Achievement groups. It is clear in each of the three comparisons that the mothers of boys who had high n Achievement scores reported significantly more demands through the age of seven than the mothers of boys who were low in n Achievement.

Figure 1 shows the cumulative curves for demands over all ages by the mothers of the boys who were above and below the median n Achievement scores on both measures. This particular figure

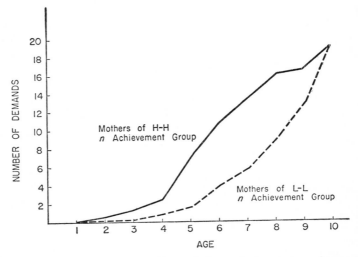

Fig. 1. Cumulative average number of demands for independence and mastery at each age (1-10 years) by mothers of boys who were high ($N = 10$) and low ($N = 10$) on both Relaxed and Achievement Orientation measures of n Achievement.

dramatizes an effect that is also apparent but slightly less pronounced in cumulative curves drawn in terms of either Relaxed or Achievement-oriented n Achievement scores taken separately (436).

When the number of demands made from age eight to ten are considered, the relationship is reversed. Mothers of boys who are high in n Achievement choose fewer items beyond the age of eight than mothers of boys who are low in n Achievement. This relationship is undoubtedly a function of the limited number of items to be chosen. The mothers of boys who are high in n Achievement have already used up significantly more of the items in the list by age eight and hence there are fewer remaining to be chosen.

Rewards for Fulfilled Demands and n *Achievement.* The emotional consequences of demands training are summarized in Table 2. The hypotheses are that mothers of boys who are high in *n* Achievement will be more frequently and intensely rewarding when demands for independence and mastery are fulfilled and will be more frequently and intensely punishing when these demands are not fulfilled.

More mothers of boys who are high in *n* Achievement report using all three types of rewards—verbal, object, and physical—than mothers of boys who are low in *n* Achievement ($p = .05$-$.10$). It is assumed that some form of physical affection like hugging or kissing is more in-

TABLE 2. REWARDS AND PUNISHMENTS ADMINISTERED IN CONNECTION WITH DEMANDS FOR INDEPENDENCE AS REPORTED BY MOTHERS OF BOYS WHO ARE HIGH AND LOW IN *n* ACHIEVEMENT

	Measure of *n* Achievement					
	Relaxed Orientation		Achievement Orientation		Both	
n Achievement:	High	Low	High	Low	High-High	Low-Low
N	15	14	14	15	10	10
Reward						
Verbal	15	13	14	14	10	9
Object	11	8	8	11	6	7
Physical	11	5*	10	5*	9	3*
All three types	8	5	8	3*	6	1*
Punishment						
Verbal	15	12	13	14	7	10
Object	10	12	11	12	8	9
Physical	6	3	4	5	4	2
All three types	1	2	1	2	1	2

* $p < .05$ in predicted direction.

Note: Significance of differences tested by exact probabilities for 2 $\times$ 2 contingency tables.

tensely rewarding than either verbal praise or object rewards. There are no differences between mothers of high and low *n* Achievement boys in frequency of verbal or object rewards. However, mothers of high *n* Achievement boys report more physical affection as reward for fulfilled demands than mothers of low *n* Achievement boys ($p < .05$).

Punishments for Unfulfilled Demands and n *Achievement.* None of the comparisons between mothers of high and low *n* Achievement boys in use of punishment for unfilled demands reveals a significant difference. Apparently mothers of high and low n Achievement children are much the same in their reactions to the child's failure to fulfill demands, at least as we have measured these reactions.

Mother's Evaluation of Son's Accomplishments. We may turn now to the mother's evaluation of her son's accomplishments in relation to those of other children. The hypothesis that mothers of boys who are high in n Achievement will be more likely to rate their children as more skillful is confirmed. An index of the favorableness of each mother's judgments of her son was obtained by subtracting the number of times the son was rated worse than average from the number of times he was rated better than average on the list of twenty demands. A plus score indicates a predominance of positive judgments; a minus score indicates a preponderance of negative judgments. The median scores of mothers of high and low n Achievement boys are shown in Table 3. In each of the comparisons, the mothers of high n Achievement boys are more positive in their evaluations than mothers of low n Achievement boys ($p = .025$-$.05$).

TABLE 3. JUDGMENTS OF MOTHERS CONCERNING THE SKILL OF THEIR SONS IN MASTERY AND INDEPENDENCE RELATIVE TO THE SKILL OF OTHER CHILDREN THE SAME AGE

(Number of times rated more skillful than others minus number of times rated less skillful than others)

	Measure of n Achievement					
	Relaxed Orientation		Achievement Orientation		Both	
n Achievement:	High	Low	High	Low	High-High	Low-Low
N	15	14	14	15	10	10
Md	1.83	−1.00	2.87	−.50	2.50	−1.00
p^*	.04		.005		.003	

* Probability of difference between medians in the predicted direction obtained by the Mann-Whitney U Test (303).

It is difficult to say whether the difference in judgments corresponds to a real difference in achievement levels in the two groups, or whether the mother's own evaluation of her son's achievement has influenced the ratings. Several behavioral ratings made by the boys' teachers in another phase of this study (see Table 9) provides some independent evidence of observable differences in the behavior of the two groups. According to the ratings of teachers, the boys who were high in n Achievement appeared significantly more motivated for success in school work, more independent, more successful in social groups (i.e., popular), and more pleased when they did succeed than the boys who were low in n Achievement. But ratings of success in school work, sports and games, and in leadership did not discriminate significantly between the two motivation groups, although the trend always favored the high n Achievement group. However, there still may be some justification for considering the ratings of a mother as more indicative of her general evaluation of the child's performance. In this light, the data provide additional suggestive evidence that the mothers of boys who are high in n Achievement tend to be more rewarding, i.e., they take a more positive view of the child's behavior.

n *Achievement and Restrictions Upon Independent Activity.* The first hypothesis to be tested is that mothers of high n Achievement children are less restrictive than mothers of low n Achievement children. Table 4 shows that this hypothesis is confirmed. By the age of ten, mothers of the high n Achievement group have selected only 12 to 13 of the restrictions; mothers of the low n Achievement group have selected 16 to 17, significantly more in each of the three comparisons.

It was further hypothesized that the restrictions imposed by the mothers of the high n Achievement group would come later than the demands for independent accomplishment. A comparison between mothers of high and low n Achievement groups in making early

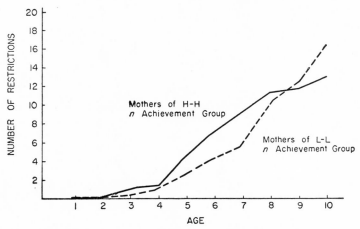

Fig. 2. Cumulative average number of restrictions upon independence and mastery at each age (1-10 years) by mothers of boys who were high $(N = 10)$ and low $(N = 10)$ on both Relaxed and Achievement Orientation measures of n Achievement.

restrictions, i.e., through the age of seven, shows that mothers of the high n Achievement boys actually impose more early restrictions than mothers of the low n Achievement group (Table 4 and Figure 2). But the question is, Do the mothers of the high n Achievement group make more demands or restrictions at any early age? The number of demands and restrictions made by each mother through age seven

TABLE 4. MEDIAN NUMBER OF TOTAL RESTRICTIONS (THROUGH AGE TEN) AND EARLY RESTRICTIONS (THROUGH AGE SEVEN) REPORTED BY MOTHERS OF BOYS WHO WERE HIGH AND LOW IN n ACHIEVEMENT

	Measure of n Achievement					
	Relaxed Orientation		Achievement Orientation		Both	
n Achievement:	High	Low	High	Low	High-High	Low-Low
N	15	14	14	15	10	10
Total restrictions. .	12.17	16.5*	13	16*	12.25	17.25*
Early restrictions. .	9.0	6.4*	9.0	6.5*	10.25	6.25*

* p of difference $<$ .05 in predicted direction by Mann-Whitney U Test (303).

was compared. Table 5 shows that mothers of boys who are high in n Achievement make more demands than restrictions during the early years ($p = .05$). But mothers of boys who are low in n Achievement do not. In other words, mothers of the high n Achievement boys report fewer restrictions through age ten but more early restrictions (through age seven) than mothers of boys who are low in n Achieve-

TABLE 5. RELATIVE EMPHASIS UPON DEMANDS VERSUS RESTRICTIONS IN EARLY TRAINING. NUMBER OF MOTHERS OF BOYS IN HIGH AND LOW n ACHIEVEMENT GROUPS WHO MADE MORE DEMANDS FOR INDEPENDENCE THAN RESTRICTIONS UPON INDEPENDENT ACTIVITY BEFORE THE AGE OF EIGHT

	Measure of n Achievement					
	Relaxed Orientation		Achievement Orientation		Both	
n Achievement:	High	Low	High	Low	High-High	Low-Low
N	15	14	14	15	10	10
More demands than restrictions.	10*	6	10*	5	8*	4

* $p <$ .05 in the predicted direction.
Note: Tests for the high and low n Achievement groups were accomplished separately using the Wilcoxon Matched Pairs Signed Ranks test (303).

ment. However, the restriction training of the high n Achievement group does not precede their demand training; through age seven their training is characterized by a preponderance of positive demands.

Rewards and Punishments Administered in Restrictive Training. The emotional consequences of complying or failing to comply with restrictions are presented in Table 6. The pattern of rewards and punishments in connection with restrictions tends to be similar to the pattern for demands (Table 2) but is less consistent in the three comparisons. There is no evidence to support the hypothesis that the boys who are high in n Achievement experience less frequent and less intense reward and punishment in connection with restrictions. On the contrary, Table 6 shows that the mothers of boys who are high in n Achievement report administering all three types of rewards and using some form of physical affection to reward restrictive training more frequently than mothers of boys who are low in n Achievement. These differences are not significant, however, when the Achievement-Orientation score is the index of strength of n Achievement.

TABLE 6. NUMBER OF MOTHERS OF BOYS HIGH AND LOW IN n ACHIEVEMENT
WHO REPORTED VARIOUS TYPES OF REWARDS AND PUNISHMENTS
IN CONNECTION WITH RESTRICTIONS PLACED UPON
INDEPENDENT ACTIVITY

	Measure of n Achievement					
	Relaxed Orientation		Achievement Orientation		Both	
n Achievement:	High	Low	High	Low	High-High	Low-Low
N	15	14	14	15	10	10
Reward						
Verbal	15	12	13	14	10	9
Object	9	9	8	10	5	7
Physical	11	4*	9	6	8	3*
All three types	8	2**	6	4	5	1
Punishment						
Verbal	13	13	12	14	9	10
Object	12	12	10	14	8	10
Physical	6	4	5	5	4	2
All three types	1	2	1	2	1	2

* $p = .08$ (two-tail test).
** $p = .12$ (two-tail test).

TABLE 7. NUMBER OF MOTHERS OF BOYS HIGH AND LOW IN n ACHIEVEMENT WHO REPORTED MAKING THE DEMANDS EARLY (THROUGH AGE SEVEN)

Demands	n Achievement of Son	No. of Mothers Reporting Demand		No. of Mothers Reporting Early Demand	
		High	Low	High	Low
1. To stand up for his own rights with others	R#	15	13	11	4*
	A	14	14	9	6
	R-A	10	9	7	2
2. To know his way around the city	R	14	11	12	3**
	A	14	11	10	5
	R-A	10	8	9	2**
3. To go outside to play	R	13	14	10	4*
	A	12	15	9	5
	R-A	8	10	7	2**
4. Trying new things on his own	R	14	14	7	4
	A	13	15	8	3*
	R-A	9	10	6	2
5. Being active and energetic	R	13	12	8	4
	A	14	11	11	1**
	R-A	10	8	8	1**
6. Showing pride in his ability to do well	R	13	14	6	5
	A	13	14	8	3*
	R-A	10	9	6	2
7. Taking part in his parents' interests	R	13	13	7	5
	A	12	14	7	5
	R-A	9	10	6	4
8. Trying hard things for himself	R	14	13	12	3**
	A	12	15	10	5*
	R-A	9	10	9	2**
9. Eating well alone	R	15	14	9	7
	A	14	15	8	8
	R-A	10	10	6	5
10. Leading other children	R	12	13	10	4*
	A	13	12	8	6
	R-A	9	9	8	4
11. Making his own friends	R	15	14	10	4*
	A	14	15	10	4*
	R-A	10	10	8	2*
12. Looking after his own possessions	R	15	14	6	6
	A	14	15	6	6
	R-A	10	10	6	6
13. Doing well in school	R	14	14	8	5
	A	14	14	9	4
	R-A	10	10	7	3
14. Going to bed by himself	R	15	14	10	8
	A	14	15	9	9
	R-A	10	10	8	7

TABLE 7 (CONT'D). NUMBER OF MOTHERS OF BOYS HIGH AND LOW IN n
ACHIEVEMENT WHO REPORTED MAKING THE DEMANDS EARLY
(THROUGH AGE SEVEN)

Demands	n Achieve-ment of Son	No. of Mothers Reporting Demand		No. of Mothers Reporting Early Demand	
		High	Low	High	Low
15. Having interests of his own..	R	13	13	10	5
	A	14	12	10	5
	R-A	10	9	8	3
16. Earning his own spending money..................	R	13	9	6	4
	A	12	10	6	4
	R-A	10	7	5	3
17. Doing tasks around the house	R	15	14	6	6
	A	14	15	6	6
	R-A	10	10	5	5
18. Staying at home alone (day).	R	15	13	6	6
	A	14	14	7	5
	R-A	10	9	4	3
19. Making own decisions.......	R	11	14	6	3
	A	12	13	7	2*
	R-A	8	10	6	2*
20. Doing well in competition...	R	14	14	11	4*
	A	14	14	11	4*
	R-A	10	10	9	2**

\# *Measure of* n *Achievement*
R (Relaxed) High $N = 15$; Low $N = 14$.
A (Achievement-oriented) High $N = 14$; Low $N = 15$.
R-A (Both) High-High $N = 10$; Low-Low $N = 10$.
* $p = <.05$ in predicted direction.
** $p = <.01$ in predicted direction.

Item Analysis of the Demands and Restrictions. The particular demand items that distinguish reliably between the two groups are starred in Table 7. These items all indicate differences in the expected direction; the demand is made earlier by the mothers of the high n Achievement group. McClelland *et al.* (272) have suggested, in their summary of this research, that the items which do not distinguish the two motivation groups are of the "caretaking" variety, i.e., independent behaviors that when learned would relieve the mother of some routine responsibility as well as contributing to the child's growing self-competence.

This appears more clearly when items which *do not* differentiate the two groups in any one of the three comparisons are considered. These items are:

7. To take part in his parents' interest and conversations.
9. To be able to eat alone without help in cutting and handling food.
12. To hang up his own clothes and look after his own possessions.
14. To be able to undress and go to bed by himself.
16. To earn his own spending money.
17. To do some regular tasks around the house.
18. To be able to stay alone at home during the day.

Of these items, numbers 7, 16, and 18 were items for which the median age reported by the group as a whole was beyond nine years. Since the upper limit was ten years, these were all required relatively late by both groups of mothers. The others had median ages of eight and below and do seem to reflect simple child care items where independence is primarily a help to the mother.

Table 8 presents the restrictive items. Here the differences in total number imposed as well as in those required early are of some interest. The mothers of the low n Achievement group tend to choose the restrictions as goals of training more frequently than the mothers of the high n Achievement group but in only two cases is the difference significant in more than one of the High-Low n Achievement breakdowns we have made. These two items are:

11. Not to play with children parents don't know or approve.
19. Not to make important decisions.

The restriction on choice of playmates and friends to those whom the parents know and approve may be one source of the association between strength of n Achievement and score on the F-scale measure of authoritarian personality, an indirect measure of prejudice, reported by Brown (52). He found that college students in the lower two-thirds of the distribution of n Achievement scores were significantly higher on the F-scale than the highest third in n Achievement.

Let us now examine the items in which a sizeable number of mothers of high n Achievement boys impose the restriction earlier in all three of the comparisons we have made. There are seven such items. Numbers 1, 6, and 7—not to fight with other children, not to boast or brag, to be respectful and not to interfere with adults—sound like necessary checks on what might otherwise become unbridled self-assertion. Numbers 13 and 15—not to fail at school and not to depend on mother for suggestions—are intimately related to the predominant tendency of this group of parents to foster self-reliance and independent accomplishment. The other two items, 9 and 12—not to be sloppy at the table and not to leave clothes around or be untidy—are from the list of "caretaker" items and do not fit the orientation implied by the other five.

TABLE 8. NUMBER OF MOTHERS OF BOYS HIGH AND LOW IN n ACHIEVEMENT
WHO REPORTED MAKING THE RESTRICTIONS EARLY (THROUGH AGE SEVEN)

Restrictions	n Achieve-ment of Son	No. of Mothers Reporting Restrictions		No. of Mothers Reporting Early Restrictions	
		High	Low	High	Low
1. Not to fight with other children	R#	12	14	8	6
	A	12	14	9	5
	R-A	8	10	7	4
2. Not to play away from home	R	15	14	7	8
	A	14	15	8	7
	R-A	10	10	6	6
3. Not to be noisy and boisterous in the house	R	13	14	10	6
	A	12	15	8	8
	R-A	8	10	6	4
4. To be cautious in trying new things	R	13	13	4	4
	A	12	14	3	5
	R-A	9	10	3	4
5. Not to run and jump	R	4	6	3	2
	A	4	6	2	3
	R-A	3	5	2	2
6. Not to boast or brag	R	15	14	11	7
	A	14	15	10	8
	R-A	10	10	9	5
7. To be respectful and not to interfere with adults	R	15	14	8	6
	A	14	15	9	5
	R-A	10	10	7	4
8. Not to try things that others can do better	R	3	1	2	1
	A	2	2	2	1
	R-A	2	1	2	1
9. Not to be sloppy at table	R	15	14	9	4
	A	14	15	9	4*
	R-A	10	10	8	3*
10. Not to boss other children	R	9	12	7	5
	A	9	12	6	6
	R-A	6	9	5	4
11. Not to play with children parents don't approve of	R	4	9*	1	6
	A	2	11**	1	6
	R-A	2	9**	1	6
12. Not to leave clothes around or untidy	R	15	14	8	6
	A	14	15	10	4*
	R-A	10	10	7	3
13. Not to fail at school	R	9	12	7	4
	A	9	12	7	4
	R-A	6	9	5	2*
14. Not to stay out after dark	R	9	13*	5	6
	A	9	13	5	6
	R-A	5	9	3	4

TABLE 8 (CONT'D). NUMBER OF MOTHERS OF BOYS HIGH AND LOW IN n ACHIEVEMENT WHO REPORTED MAKING THE RESTRICTIONS EARLY (THROUGH AGE SEVEN)

Restrictions	n Achievement of Son	No. of Mothers Reporting Restrictions		No. of Mothers Reporting Early Restrictions	
		High	Low	High	Low
15. Not to depend on mother for suggestions..............	R	11	13	9	5
	A	12	12	8	6
	R-A	8	9	6	3
16. Not to earn money without parents' consent...........	R	6	8	2	5
	A	5	9	3	4
	R-A	4	7	2	4
17. Not to whine or cry when left alone...................	R	13	12	5	7
	A	12	13	7	5
	R-A	8	8	4	4
18. Not to do things in house where he's in the way.......	R	7	10	7	2
	A	7	10	6	3
	R-A	5	8	5	7
19. Not to make important decisions.................	R	3	10**	3	3
	A	5	8	3	3
	R-A	2	7*	2	2
20. Not to try to beat other children in play..............	R	4	6	2	1
	A	3	7	2	1
	R-A	2	5	1	0

 # Measure of n *Achievement*
  R (Relaxed) High $N = 15$; Low $N = 14$.
  A (Achievement-oriented) High $N = 14$; Low $N = 15$.
  R-A (Both) High-High $N = 10$; Low-Low $N = 10$.
* $p = <.05$ in predicted direction.
** $p = <.01$ in predicted direction.

A Note on the Relationship of n *Achievement to Overt Behavior in These Children.* This paper is primarily concerned with the relationship between *n* Achievement in children, as measured in thematic apperception, and childhood training as reported by their mothers. But a brief word is in order concerning some of the relationships discovered between *n Achievement* and overt behavior in these children. The question of whether or not the thematic apperceptive index of achievement motive has the same "meaning" for children as for the college-aged subjects of many other experiments is best answered by a summary of the behavioral correlates of achievement motivation in these children. A description of the procedures and fuller discussion of these findings is presented elsewhere (436).

Two kinds of behavior measures were obtained. The first consisted of ratings of the children by their teachers in school. The second consisted of observations made by the E during the child's performance under achievement orientation. The test situation had been especially conttived to enable the E to make observations of a number of achievement-related decisions and behaviors in the child.

The teachers used a five-point scale to rate children on the following questions. Each point on the scale was designated by an appropriate qualitative statement which represented a difference in degree from "most to least." The items were randomized in the list given teachers but are organized into several categories here.

Achievement Motivation

1. Generally, how much do you think he wants to do well?
2. How hard does he *try* to do well or win in sports or game (even though he may or may not win)?
3. How hard does he *try* to do well in schoolwork (even though he may or may not succeed)?

Objective Success

1. Generally, how successful is he?
2. How well does he do in schoolwork?
3. How popular a child is he with other children?
4. How well does he do in sports or games?
5. How much leadership does he show with other children?

Independence

1. Generally, how would you rate his overall independence?
2. How is he at entertaining himself or keeping himself occupied if necessary?
3. How well does he stand up for his rights with other children?
4. How is he about doing things in school on his own?
5. How well is he able to look after himself in eating, putting on his own clothes, coming and going from school, etc?

Two other questions asked about the degree of pleasure and pride the child took in success and the degree to which he persisted or gave up in the face of failure:

How does he react when he does well in something?

How does he react when he fails at something or has difficulty with a task?

The behaviors rated by the teachers were obviously selected on the theoretical presumption that they ought to be positively related to strength of *n* Achievement. The results in Table 9 speak for themselves. From the teachers' point of view, the children who are high in *n* Achievement appear more independent in general, as experi-

TABLE 9. TEACHERS' RATINGS OF THE BEHAVIOR OF BOYS WHO WERE
HIGH AND LOW IN n ACHIEVEMENT

(Number of boys scoring above and below the median
rating on a five point scale)

n Achievement: N:	Relaxed Orientation		Achievement Orientation		Both	
	High	Low	High	Low	High	Low
Teachers' Rating						
Strength of Achievement *Motivation*						
In general...............	11	7	10	8	8	3*
In sports................	11	6	10	8	8	2*
In schoolwork............	10	7	11	6*	9	4*
Success						
In general...............	9	6	9	6	7	3
In schoolwork............	8	5	8	5	7	3
In popularity............	10	4*	10	4*	8	1**
In sports................	4	2	4	2	3	1
In leadership.............	6	5	7	4	5	2
Independence						
In general...............	8	4	9	3*	7	1**
In entertaining self........	7	6	7	6	6	4
In doing things in school...	10	9	11	8	8	5
In standing up for self.....	10	10	10	10	8	7
In eating, dressing........	7	4	5	6	5	3
Pleasure in success..........	8	4	9	3*	7	1**
Persistence after failure......	9	8	10	7	8	4

$* p < .05.$
$** p < .01.$

encing more pleasure and pride in success, and, especially the group
who were above the median score on both Relaxed and Achievement-
oriented imaginative measures, more motivated for success. The objective success of the two groups does not appear significantly different except in social relations where the high n Achievement group
is demonstrably more popular. This particular result is of special
interest in light of the finding that mothers of the low n Achievement
group had imposed restrictions upon choosing friends.

Table 10 presents the results of the E's observations of children
in the puzzle-solving situation. During the test period, each child was
offered help and rest at intervals and could spontaneously ask for
help if he wanted it. The results show that boys who are high in n

TABLE 10. BEHAVIOR OF HIGH AND LOW n ACHIEVEMENT BOYS IN AN ACHIEVEMENT-ORIENTED TEST SITUATION AS OBSERVED BY THE EXPERIMENTER

n Achievement: N:	Measure of n Achievement					
	Relaxed Orientation		Achievement Orientation		Both	
	High	Low	High	Low	High	Low
Behavior						
Refused offer of help........	7	4	6	5	7	2*
No requests for help........	9	10	12	7*	8	6
Refused offer for rest.......	8	4	9	3*	4	3
Preferred hard to easy task.	8	5	8	7	7	4
Level of aspiration (below median)................	7	7	7	6	6	6
Positive instructions recalled (above median) ...	7	6	6	8	5	5
Negative instructions recalled (below median)....	10	4*	8	6	7	3

* $p = < .05$.

Achievement on the stories told immediately after the puzzle-solution period (i.e., under Achievement Orientation) less frequently asked for help and more often refused an invitation to stop work and rest than boys who were low in n Achievement. And boys who were high in n Achievement on both Relaxed and Achievement-oriented measures more often refused help even when it was offered.

Two different puzzles were used, one more difficult than the other. The high and low n Achievement groups did not differ in preference for easy versus more difficult task, as might have been expected. Nor did they differ in stated level of aspiration for the puzzle task. A statement of level of aspiration was obtained only once, and there is some doubt as to its value since the children were asked to estimate how long it would take them to do the puzzle. Time estimates may be particularly hard to make at this age.

A series of specific instructions were given at the beginning of the puzzle task with the intention of asking the child to recall them at the end. Some instructions were stated positively (as demands), others negatively (as restrictions) with a view to testing the hypothesis that the high n Achievement group would recall more positive and fewer negative instructions. There is no difference in recall of positive instructions, but the trend is as predicted for negative instructions ($p = .05$ on the Relaxed index).

These results present some evidence that boys who are high in n Achievement appear more independent, more popular, and more motivated to succeed than boys who are low in n Achievement. The refusal of help and the offer to rest may be taken as indices of persistence at an achievement task. Assuming that scoring high on both Relaxed and Achievement-oriented measures of n Achievement indicates more generalized motivation to achieve (Ch. 27), it makes sense that the teachers' ratings which must have been based on very general impressions should relate most clearly to the combined index of n Achievement. In general, these attempts to detect expressions of motivation to achieve in overt behavior show that we are measuring in fantasy an attribute of the child that is manifested both in specific tasks and in the kinds of general impressions which emerge from extensive observation of his behavior in a variety of settings.

DISCUSSION

The data presented provide a basis for description of the differences in the learning experiences of boys who have relatively high or low n Achievement scores on the fantasy measure used. The high n Achievement group have earlier training in our list of independence and mastery behaviors. They have fewer experiences in being restricted in these areas, and though restriction training comes earlier for them, it has been preceded by a good deal of training in independence. Their mothers take a more positive view of their accomplishments and are more often and more affectively rewarding. There is no evidence that the high n Achievement group is more frequently punished. All of these conclusions are limited by the measures used. Interviews and questionnaires from mothers may not give an accurate representation of what actually went on during training. The sample of fantasy we used may often miss important kinds of fantasies which may relate to achievement behavior but which are not easily verbalized, or which are not elicited in this situation.

Though it is difficult to evaluate the meaning of our questionnaire data and how it relates to the actual behavior of the mother, there is some possibility of examining the stories of the two groups of children in order to understand the context of fantasy in which the achievement imagery occurs and what clues it may give to other determinants which we have not considered. In order to do this fairly systematically, though without any check on reliability, twenty-five stories that were scored for achievement imagery were selected from the lowest and highest scorers. These stories were analyzed for differences in the stories other than in achievement imagery itself.

Most of the stories were centered around competitiveness. Both the high and low groups had nine stories each, involving competition with children though the resolutions of the stories were different. The high group resolved all the stories with someone winning. Four stories mentioned instances of aggression and cheating in the process of winning, though never leading to success. The low group had instances of resolution by the winner giving up the prize, or the loser refusing to play, or someone getting hurt or changing the theme of the story.

Competition between a young man and an older man occurred seven times in the stories of high n Achievers but not at all in the low group. The stories of the high group contained four references to aggression between the two, two references to someone being hurt, two references to helping each other, and no resolutions where the younger lost out. The low group, when they used the younger-older man theme, structured the stories twice as the older man helping the younger, once as the younger man admiring the older man's accomplishment, and three times as the young man being fired or worried about the possibility. There were no instances of aggression, bragging, or open competition.

These stories suggest that the context of the achievement imagery is limited more for the low group than the high group. Competitiveness is restricted to their own age group and does not get expressed with older men. Also cheating and aggression are not themes which accompany the achievement fantasy of the low group. It may be that the occurrence of such possibilities and subsequent avoidance of their expression may reduce the expressions of ambitions involving them. These stories lead one to believe that a son's relationship with his father may be as important an area to investigate as his relationship with his mother, especially in an attempt to understand the restriction of fantasies that may be present and unexpressed or avoided. The emotional meaning of achievement fantasies is not well understood and is likely far more complex than our data suggest. Investigation of the determinants of achievement motives that have their sources in the psychosexual nature of the child may be helpful.[3] The competitiveness with older men certainly suggests this as a direction for research. The age of independence and mastery training of the child would then be seen in relation to his developmental level. The results which indicate the importance of training before the age of eight do not justify the assertion that the earlier the training the more it contributes to the development of achievement motivation and fantasy. There may be particular age ranges during which an environment which encourages independence and achievement fits particularly well the needs of the growing child.

---

[3] The lack of correspondence between the research on n Achievement in young men and women suggests this direction as well as an investigation of different methods of training.

Another area for investigation is the parent's response to the child's fantasies, especially if the child expresses them in play or conversation. The parental response may be directly encouraging or inhibiting of certain types of fantasy. There is some suggestive evidence in a few cases that the n Achievement of parents (measured by using pictures) is related to the n Achievement of their children.[4] The available evidence, while not conclusive, reinforces the notion that certain kinds of fantasies are expressed in families and that these may vary and affect the child's expression of similar ideas.

The discussion of these other leads which require investigation indicates the author's belief that the determinants of n Achievement are undoubtedly very complex. Within the framework of all the possible determinants, this study has shown the importance of the nature of the child's experience in gaining independence and mastery as his learning is guided by his mother. The kinds of goals she chooses to train the child for, the age at which she wants them learned, and her general evaluation of her child's performance have been shown to be of some importance in contributing to the development of his motivation to achieve.

SUMMARY AND CONCLUSIONS

The results indicate that mothers of children with strong achievement motivation differ from mothers of children with weak achievement motivation in the following respects:

a. They make more demands before the age of eight.
b. They evaluate their children's accomplishments higher and are more rewarding.
c. The total number of restrictions made through age ten is less but the total number of restrictions made through age seven is greater.
d. Even though they make more restrictions through age seven the number of demands they make at this early age exceeds the number of restrictions.

No difference between the two groups was found in the total number of demands made, the number and intensity of punishments for demands and restrictions. It is concluded that early training in independence and mastery contributes to the development of strong achievement motivation.

---

[4] From the initial analysis of data collected by Miss Joanne Steger at Connecticut College, New London, Connecticut.

CHAPTER 34

··

Achievement Themes in Folk Tales Related to Socialization Practice

Irvin L. Child, Thomas Storm, and Joseph Veroff[1]

With the development of a technique for analyzing stories —a technique which has some established validity for individual differences in personality—it is natural to test whether this technique may be usefully applied to cultural differences. McClelland and Friedman (274) made an initial test of this sort for the n Achievement measure. They applied it to a small group of North American Indian tribes which all have folk tales of a similar general pattern (concerned with Coyote as a trickster character). The n Achievement measure obtained from a sample of Coyote tales from each tribe was then related to the most relevant measures then available on the socialization practices of that society, measures concerned with training in independence. The substantial correlations obtained provided evidence that the folk tale analysis is measuring something which is coherent with other aspects of the culture. At the same time these correlations suggested tentative hypotheses about the variables of childhood experience having an influence on personality variables, of which the n Achievement measure is an index.[2]

---

[1] This research is part of a larger project for which financial support was provided by the Social Science Research Council and the Ford Foundation. Partial support was also provided by Grant M-808 from the Institute of Mental Health of the National Institutes of Health, Public Health Service. We are greatly indebted to the other collaborators and assistants who have contributed to the analysis reported here. We are especially grateful to Margaret K. Bacon and Herbert Barry III, who analyzed socialization practices; to Robert J. Drechsler and Elliott M. Marcus, who helped locate and select folk tales; to Arnold J. Kaplin, who helped analyze the folk tales; and to Barbara S. Cohen, Sandra A. Dunn, and Britton K. Ruebush, who did most of the tabulations and computations.

[2] A study by Wright (443), analyzing aggressive content of folk tales from a larger sample of cultures and relating it to the socialization of aggression, while not using the technique of analysis discussed in this volume, also increases one's

Of what personality variable is the score for n Achievement, when applied to folk tales, to be taken as a probable index? One possibility, in line with interpretations made elsewhere in this book, is that the score for n Achievement indicates the general strength of motive for achievement in the people from whose culture the folk tales come. Another possibility, involving less of an inferential leap from the data, is simply that the score for n Achievement reflects the extent to which the thoughts of the people are preoccupied with the theme of achievement. A high degree of such preoccupation might result from a strong motive for achievement, or it might have other sources, such as great frustration of an only moderately strong motive for achievement. We do not at present have any means of confidently predicting different consequences, for our data, from these two views of what the scores might mean.

But how can one justify considering folk tales as a cultural product likely to reflect either the motives or the general preoccupations of a society? The easy explanation would be to suggest that folk tales like other fantasy productions are produced and maintained because of their expression of need satisfactions or their expression of preoccupations, which are salient in the personality of typical members of a society. This explanation, however, meets with a special difficulty. Folk tales can also reflect a cultural lag in a society. A given folk tale may have been expressing characteristics of the members of a society at one time but be presently maintained because of a need to preserve a tradition. Nevertheless, tales that are part of a cultural lag may show modulations which are in keeping with the personality of present members of the society. And it is hoped that these modulations would be picked up by a sensitive measuring device. The general rationale for taking literary content, oral or written, as possibly indicative of personality characteristics common in a society, is more fully presented in a paper by McClelland (Ch. 37) in the present volume.

The study to be reported here grew out of cross-cultural research on socialization in which, among other things, ratings were made for various cultures on socialization pressures relevant to the development of achievement-oriented behavior. Having at hand these ratings, we were encouraged by the results of previous research to believe that n Achievement analysis of folk tales might provide a measure of the characteristic strength of achievement motive or preoccupation in the adult culture and thus permit a test of the consistency between adult culture and socialization practices. Hence

---

confidence in the probable fruitfulness of folk tale analysis for studying culture and personality.

we decided to attempt a more extensive and meticulous sampling of folk tales than had been made in the earlier studies.

SELECTION OF TALES

Our analysis of socialization had been applied to 110 cultures. For each of these we attempted to locate in the ethnographic literature the single collection of tales (or, where necessary, two or more collections) which had most the appearance of generally representing the oral literature of the culture (that is, not selected to make a point nor restricted to a single type of tale). For many cultures we could locate no such collection or no tales at all.

Having located such a collection for a culture, we then attempted to select a sample of 12 folk tales. We omitted certain kinds of stories, principally factual stories and myths of apparently religious significance. We took careful steps to ensure that selection from the rest of the collection would be purely random. In an attempt to reduce variation in length, we decided that for folk tales more than four pages long, only a single episode not exceeding that length would be used. The selection was made by persons not associated with the analysis of socialization, who made a deliberate effort not to become acquainted with other aspects of the culture and followed detailed rules set down in advance.[3]

By these procedures we obtained a sample of 12 tales for each of 46 cultures. We also obtained a smaller number of tales, from 8 to 11, for an additional six cultures for which the sample, though smaller, appeared likely to be fairly representative.

ANALYSIS OF FOLK TALES

We analyzed the folk tales by applying to them the instructions available to us for scoring TAT stories for *n* Achievement, substantially as they are presented elsewhere in this volume. While perhaps new problems arise in applying these instructions to new material, we prepared no special rules to cover them, merely leaving each analyst to solve those problems by repeated reference to the instruction manuals.

The analysis for *n* Achievement was first done by Thomas Storm, who had previously used it on over 1000 TAT stories. It was then

---

[3] A more detailed account of the selection of tales, and an annotated bibliography of the sources used, is presented in a manuscript by Thomas Storm, Elliott H. Marcus and Irvin L. Child, entitled *A Selection of Folktales for Cross-Cultural Research*. It may be obtained by ordering Document No. 5437 from ADI Auxiliary Publications Project, Photoduplication Service, Library of Congress, Washington 25, D. C., remitting in advance $1.25 for microfilm or $1.25 for photocopies. Make checks payable to Chief, Photoduplication Service, Library of Congress.

done independently by Arnold J. Kaplin, who had had no experience with TAT stories. Joseph Veroff, finally, analyzed the tales after long experience in the application of this analysis to TAT stories. Storm could recognize the provenance of some of the tales, as he had selected many of them. The other two analysts did their work with no identification of the tales and with the tales mixed up in more or less random order.

Despite our attempts to reduce variation in length, it became obvious that scores on n Achievement were substantially correlated with the length of tales in our sample. This variable needed urgently to be controlled, as it probably does not with TAT stories written with a uniform time limit. We arranged the entire body of tales in order of length, and classified them into successive fifths (i.e., the shortest 20% of tales, the next shortest 20%, etc.). For the tales in each fifth, we converted one judge's n Achievement scores into normalized z scores. The z scores thus obtained for all the tales from a single culture were then averaged. We used this average z score to test interjudge agreement. Having decided to pool the judgments of the 3 judges for n Achievement, we did the pooling by adding the averaged z scores of the 3 judges. This measure was used for testing substantive hypotheses. This normalizing procedure was successful in eliminating the correlation of length with the content measure.

RELIABILITY

Interjudge agreement. Different judges can show excellent agreement in their analysis of TAT stories. But it does not follow that the same will be true of folk tales. Folk tales are much more variable in themes and other content than are TAT stories. A scorer develops a set for scoring responses to a picture or verbal cue presented to a subject. No such set is present in scoring folk tales.

The intercorrelations between judges for average scores on each culture were $+.64$ (TS vs. JV), $+.59$ (TS vs. AK), and $+.36$ (AK vs. JV). These are much lower than typical correlations for interjudge agreement on samples of TAT stories from individual subjects. There appears, however, to be a usable degree of agreement among judges, and we decided to pool the judgments of all 3 judges.

Internal consistency of the sample of tales from a culture. Given some evidence or presumption of a satisfactory degree of agreement between judges, an equally crucial question of reliability is whether there is satisfactory agreement among the tales from a single culture in what they tell us about that culture. In evaluating the internal consistency of our sample of tales, we used as datum the average of the z scores obtained for each tale by the 3 judges. We first randomly divided the tales for each culture into two groups equal in number, determined the average z score for each group, and plotted a split-half correlation. The reliability coefficient so obtained was so low as to suggest almost no internal consistency. It occurred to us, however, that with so small a number of items (12 at most), the accidents of division into halves might have a considerable influence. Hence we decided to use a measure of internal consistency which does not depend on splitting items into two groups (the measure presented by Gulliksen [165, p. 224] as formula 11). This measure of internal consistency yielded a value of $+.54$ for n Achievement. This is very substantially higher than comparable coefficients for samples of TAT stories from individual subjects in one study in which such measures are computed (69). They indicate, however, that we are dealing here with a measure of such low consistency that relationships to other variables close enough to be statistically significant for the small number of cultures available are not likely to be found.

Conclusion. The interjudge agreement and the internal consistency of our cultural samples of tales are discouragingly low. Clearly, no definitive findings can reasonably be expected from a study using a measure of such low reliability with a sample as small as is available here. The most that can be looked for in the substantive findings to follow is suggestive confirmation or tentative rejection of hypotheses. Such tentative conclusions as we reach can be drawn with no more confidence than our statistical tests indicate. As guides to further research, however, they may well be taken with more seriousness than if our measures were highly reliable. For the unreliability of the measures means that even a very close intrinsic relationship between the underlying variables cannot lead to a very close relationship in our data.

RELATION OF n ACHIEVEMENT SCORES TO SOCIALIZATION VARIABLES

The socialization practices of these cultures were analyzed in relation to achievement-oriented behavior. We were guided by Murray's definition of achievement (314, p. 164) and emphasized orientation toward attaining a high standard of performance. The analysts judged four aspects of socialization related to achievement.

(1) Positive training (a joint function of reward for achievement-oriented behavior and punishment for its absence).

(2) Punishment for absence of achievement-oriented behavior. (Though a part of positive training as defined above, this aspect was also analyzed separately.)

(3) Punishment for presence of achievement-oriented behavior (including disapproval, ridicule, or sacrifice of other goals).

(4) Conflict over achievement (an intuitive judgment of the extent to which the pattern of training analyzed above would be likely to produce conflict over achievement).

Each of these variables was rated on a seven-point scale, separately for the socialization of boys and girls. The ratings of both sexes by two independent judges were averaged to give an over-all measure of each of these aspects. The judges indicated their judgments as confident or doubtful, and for each variable we have used only those cultures for which at least one judge was confident for each sex.

We expected that the n Achievement score from folk tales might be positively related to each of these four aspects of socialization of achievement-oriented behavior. For the variables of positive training and of punishment for absence of achievement-oriented behavior, this prediction seems to follow clearly, regardless of whether the n Achievement score is assumed to measure motive strength or extent of preoccupation. Conflict over achievement should perhaps be especially expected to influence a measure of preoccupation with thoughts about achievement; but it might also influence a measure of strength of achievement motive, in so far as conflict is an important source of acquired motive strength. Punishment for the presence of achievement-oriented behavior, as a source of anxiety, should be expected to be conducive to preoccupation with thoughts about achievement (if we are right in assuming that conditions of human life tend continually—at least in those societies in which such punishment is present—to produce some instigation to achievement-oriented behavior). The argument for a positive effect of such punishment on a motive for achievement is less clear; but such an argument might be based on the considerations mentioned above for conflict, or on some specific version of the general thesis that motivation consists of affective arousal (McClelland *et al.*, 272). At any rate, it should be noted that these four aspects of achievement socialization are all positively correlated with each other. For the 31 societies for which we have both folk tale analyses and ratings of all four socialization variables, the correlation of positive training in achievement is $+.80$, $+.27$, and $+.16$ with the other three variables, in the order of their appearance in Table 1. The correlation of punishment for absence is $+.42$ and $+.23$ with the last two variables in order. The correlation between punishment for presence and conflict is $+.86$. (Though all these correlations are positive, they indicate two clusters of two variables each. Positive training and punishment for absence form one cluster, while conflict and punishment for presence form another. Despite the high correlation within each cluster, we have reported on each variable separately, since there is some degree of independence.)

TABLE 1. RELATION OF n ACHIEVEMENT MEASURE ON FOLK TALES TO VARIABLES OF SOCIALIZATION

Form of Behavior	Relation of n Achievement to Variable of							
	Positive Training		Punishment for Absence		Punishment for Presence		Conflict	
	r	N	r	N	r	N	r	N
Achievement.......	+.34	33	+.24	31	+.34	31	+.09	31
Obedience.........	−.05	45	−.28	46	−.33*	44	−.17	44
Responsibility......	+.06	51	−.19	49	−.19	49	−.19	49
Self-reliance.......	−.02	48	−.19	48	−.18	48	−.12	49
Nurturance........	−.01	28	−.36	27	−.11	27	−.01	28

* Significant at the 5% level.

For comparison with the results thus obtained, we also have parallel ratings of these same four variables of socialization for four other behavior systems: obedience, responsibility, self-reliance, and nurturance (i.e., the child's nurturance toward the younger or more helpless). For these other behavior systems we did not on theoretical grounds predict any consistent relation to the n Achievement scores.

The results are presented in Table 1. While far from conclusive, they provide suggestive confirmation of the predictions. All of the four correlations with achievement socialization variables are in the predicted direction and three of them are among the highest correlations in the table. The correlations with positive training in achievement and with punishment for presence of achievement are just barely short of significance at the 5% level (by a two-tailed test). The correlation with judged conflict in achievement socialization is close to zero, however, where we expected it might be especially high. That conflict may nevertheless have something to do with the matter is perhaps suggested by the fact that the multiple correlation of n Achievement with positive training and punishment for presence of achievement, for the cases for which both measures are available, is +.45, which is significant at the 2% level; this mechanical way of estimating conflict thus yields results different from those obtained with the intuitive estimate.

In general, the socialization of other forms of behavior appears to have a negative relation to n Achievement. As shown in the last four lines of Table 1, all but one of the 16 correlations are negative, though only the largest of them reaches significance at the 5% level. The negative correlations with self-reliance socialization are particularly striking, in view of the fact that judgments of socialization of self-reliance and achievement are positively related to each other. The tentative suggestion might be drawn out that training in self-reliance may somewhat discourage preoccupation with thoughts of achievement unless there is added to it specific training in achievement. To check on this possibility we have calculated partial correlations of n Achievement with variables of achievement and self-reliance socialization, with the corresponding variable of self-reliance training partialed out for achievement training and vice versa. The effect is to increase the size of all the correlation coefficients, leaving the direction the same. The partial correlations for achievement socialization are $+.42$ for positive training (significant at the 2% level), $+.33$ for punishment for absence, $+.35$ for punishment for presence, and $+.11$ for conflict. The corresponding coefficients for self-reliance socialization are, in order, $-.26$, $-.25$, $-.19$, and $-.13$.

Relation to general rigidity of training. Another consistency that appears in Table 1 is the tendency for punishment for absence of each form of behavior (other than achievement) to be negatively correlated with the n Achievement score. Separately for each form of behavior, this might be said to indicate that rigid or compulsive training in it tends to discourage preoccupation with themes of achievement. We have tried to estimate the magnitude of this relationship in general by adding together the punishment-for-absence scores for obedience, responsibility, self-reliance, and nurturance (for the 23 cultures for which all 4 are available) and correlating this sum, as an over-all measure of rigidity of other training, with the n Achievement score. The result is a coefficient of $-.56$, significant at the 1% level (though not much weight should be attached to the statistical significance of such a compound *post hoc* result).

It occurred to us to investigate whether variations in this general rigidity of training in other areas might influence the relationship between achievement socialization and later preoccupation with achievement (as measured by the content of folk tales). Accordingly, we divided societies into those above and below the median on rigidity of training in the other four areas together. For each of these two groups we separately calculated the correlation between n Achievement and each aspect of achievement socialization. The results are presented in Table 2. While the small number of cases available for

TABLE 2. RELATION OF n ACHIEVEMENT MEASURE ON FOLK TALES TO VARIABLES OF ACHIEVEMENT SOCIALIZATION, SEPARATELY FOR CULTURES HIGH AND LOW IN GENERAL RIGIDITY OF TRAINING IN OTHER AREAS

	Variable of Achievement Socialization with Which Folk Tale Measure Is Correlated							
	Positive Training		Punishment for Absence		Punishment for Presence		Conflict	
	r	N	r	N	r	N	r	N
Cultures high in general rigidity	+.57	9	+.58	9	+.68*	9	+.44	9
Cultures low in general rigidity	+.24	10	−.39	9	−.53	9	−.16	9

* Significant at the 5% level.

this test prevents us from being very confident about any conclusion, the results do suggest a much higher positive correlation for the cultures with more rigid training, and perhaps even a negative correlation for the cultures with less rigid training; the difference in correlation even reaches a significant magnitude in the case of punishment for presence, where it is significant at the 2% level. Where socialization in later childhood tends generally to be rigid or compulsive, then, in the sense of enforcing requirements by severely punishing their absence, later preoccupation with themes of achievement seems to be highly correlated with the specific pressures on children in relation to achievement. Where socialization is less rigid in nature, adult preoccupation with themes of achievement is evidently determined by other influences than the specific pressures exerted on children in relation to achievement orientation.

What may these other influences be? One possibility is that they may reside largely in identification with adults and the cultural characteristics they exhibit, and the taking on of adult characteristics without the necessity of specific training. We accordingly looked for relevant characteristics of the adult culture, in the various analyses of these cultures that had been done in the larger project of which this study is a part. The analyses which seemed most likely to be relevant were ratings of two aspects of the economic activity of adults. One was a rating of the extent to which the culture was characterized by competition in acquisition of wealth. The other was a rating of the extent to which adults display pride in their economic skills. Both these ratings are of aspects of the adult culture which might be taken as indices of amount of achievement-oriented behavior. For pride in economic skills, results are obtained which are consistent with the hunch that with low rigidity of training, identification with the adult culture might be a major source of influence on personality. For the 7 societies low in general rigidity and available for this test, the correlation between n Achievement in folk tales and pride in economic skills is $+.75$, whereas for the 8 societies high in general rigidity the correlation is only $-.14$. For competition in acquisition of wealth, however, this tendency is reversed, the correlations being $-.32$ and $-.17$. Thus no inference can safely be drawn from these results alone, and it is only because of consistency with results to be reported later that they are mentioned here.

In showing, above, that the dependence of n Achievement on specific training in achievement seems to vary with a general variable of training which we have called rigidity, we have chosen "rigidity" as one of several labels which might have been applied to that general variable. We do have some justification for choosing that label rather than "punitiveness." It will be recalled that another kind of punitiveness was also rated for each form of behavior— punishment for its presence rather than for its absence. Table 1 indicates that there is a general tendency for these ratings also to be negatively related to n Achievement in the folk tales. When the punishment-for-presence ratings are added up for the four forms of behavior other than achievement, for the 19 cultures for which they are all available, this sum has a correlation of $-.45$ with n Achievement (significant at the 5% level). This would tend to justify a conclusion that general punitiveness of any sort discourages preoccupation with achievement. But when cultures are divided into those high and low on this measure, there is no suggestion of any resulting variation in the relation between n Achievement and measures of achievement socialization. Thus the variation of this sort which we have reported above seems to be specifically related to punitiveness for *absence* of various desired responses, and this variable seems appropriately labeled as *rigidity* of training.

Relation to general indulgence. If rigidity of training appears to have certain relationships, direct and indirect, with n Achievement in folk tales, it would seem that general permissiveness or indulgence might have opposite relationships. In a sense this follows directly, in so far as permissiveness or indulgence may be regarded as defined by the lower end of the scale of rigidity. In our analysis of socialization, however, we did make certain other ratings which provide another operational definition of permissiveness or indulgence, which has by no means a perfect negative correlation with the scale of rigidity and has the advantage of being available for a larger number of societies. Ratings were made of degree of indulgence during infancy and during childhood, and of the severity of socialization involved in the transition from infancy to childhood. We averaged the first two, as positive ratings of indulgence, and subtracted from that average the third rating (as a measure of absence of indulgence during the critical transition period). The resultant measure is what we will term "general indulgence." For the 21 cultures for which both this and the rigidity measure are available, the correlation between them is $-.71$.

General indulgence shows a correlation of only $+.29$ with n Achievement for 39 cultures (several points short of being significant at the 5% level). When cultures are divided into those above and below the median on general indulgence, however, all the tendencies observed with the rigidity measure are confirmed. As shown in Table 3, n Achievement shows much more substantial evidence of

TABLE 3. RELATION OF n ACHIEVEMENT MEASURE ON FOLK TALES TO VARIABLES OF ACHIEVEMENT SOCIALIZATION, SEPARATELY FOR CULTURES HIGH AND LOW IN GENERAL INDULGENCE

	Variable of Achievement Socialization with Which Folk Tale Measure Is Correlated							
	Positive Training		Punishment for Absence		Punishment for Presence		Conflict	
	r	N	r	N	r	N	r	N
Cultures low in general indulgence	$+.34$	13	$+.47$	11	$+.80^{**}$	11	$+.66^*$	11
Cultures high in general indulgence	$+.47$	13	$+.08$	13	$-.03$	13	$+.04$	13

** Significant at 1% level.
* Significant at 5% level.

positive relation to achievement for cultures low in indulgence than for cultures high in indulgence. (One variable, positive training for achievement, provides an exception here.) The reverse is true for relevant features of adult economy. The relation of n Achievement to pride in economic skills is $+.66$ for 13 cultures high in indulgence, and only $+.22$ for 14 cultures low in indulgence. The relation of n Achievement to competition in acquisition of wealth is $+.27$ in the cultures high in indulgence, and $+.13$ in the cultures low in indulgence. While none of these differences in correlations are statistically significant, their consistency argues for giving some attention to the tentative inferences that may be drawn from them.

These tentative inferences have to do, of course, with the role of general parent-child interaction as creating a milieu which in turn determines the nature of specific socialization. If parent behavior is indulgent and nonrigid, specific socialization appears to be accomplished by the child's taking on by identification important and valued characteristics of the behavior of his parents and other adults in the community, and this appears to be achieved for the most part without the necessity of conspicuous training in those directions as a part of the specific socialization procedures of the society. If parent behavior is rigid and non-indulgent, on the other hand, it would appear that the process of identification does not work as dependably to ensure the taking on by children of the characteristics of their parents, and specific socialization pressures are needed to force the personality of children in any particular direction.

DISCUSSION

Relation to previous results. The only previous study directly comparable with ours is that by McClelland and Friedman (274). They found n Achievement scores on folk tales to be positively related to measures of strength and earliness of independence training, while having no measures of achievement training available. Since our variables of "self-reliance" socialization might equally well have been labeled "independence," our results reported in Table 1 seem to disconfirm the findings of McClelland and Friedman. Though the correlations of n Achievement with the four variables of self-reliance socialization are so small that nothing can safely be made of their consistent negative direction, there is certainly no suggestion of a positive relation.

Fortunately, we are able to make a more direct test of the general validity of McClelland and Friedman's findings. Of the 52 cultures for which we analyzed folk tales, 25 are among the cultures included in the Whiting and Child study (432) from which McClelland and Friedman drew their measures of independence training. For these 25 cultures, therefore, we are able to test the relation between our n Achievement measure and the very measures of independence training which were used by them. For 23 cultures for which a rating of initial indulgence of dependence was made, we obtained an r of $+.12$ (compared with their tau of $-.56$). For 18 cultures for which an estimate of earliness of beginning independence training is available, we obtained an r of $+.20$ (compared with their tau of $+.84$). For 23 cultures for which a rating of severity of independence training was made, we obtained an r of $-.11$ (compared with their tau of $+.64$).

None of these correlations are statistically significant, and only that with earliness of training is even in the same direction as the results obtained by McClelland and Friedman.

This disconfirmation of McClelland and Friedman's findings was unexpected, and we have sought for possible reasons. Three differences between their study and ours offer themselves as specially likely to be involved. First, they used only a group of related cultures and only tales of a single type. It is quite likely that with this uniformity of background, differences in achievement content might be more dependably scored and also be a genuinely more sensitive index of cultural differences. Second, they evidently did not take thorough precautions against the possible influence of bias in the scoring of the tales, as they say only that "the person who scored the folk tales had no accurate knowledge of the independence-training ratings when he was scoring them." Third, the n Achievement scores used by McClelland and Friedman were not corrected for length of folk tale. Of the 8 cultures used in their study, 6 are included in our sample too and afford some possibility of checking on the effect of these three differences between the studies. For these 6 cultures, one of us (TS), with no knowledge whatever of the socialization ratings or of the ethnographic data on which they were based, scored n Achievement in the particular Coyote stories used by McClelland and Friedman and in all the Coyote stories in the collections from which their sample was drawn. He had already scored the sample of tales used in our study, and these results could be expressed either in raw-score form or corrected for length. We rank-ordered the 6 cultures for these various measures, as well as for our own final n Achievement score corrected for length. The rank-order correlation with our final corrected score was $+.81$ for TS's raw scoring of our own sample of tales, $+.77$ for the same scoring adjusted for length, $+.71$ for TS's scoring of the entire collection of Coyote tales, $+.60$ for McClelland and Friedman's sample of Coyote tales as scored by TS, and $+.09$ for McClelland and Friedman's own scoring of their sample. Differences of this magnitude among correlations based on only 6 cases provide a very unsatisfactory basis for drawing conclusions. The tentative inference is, however, that the lack of adjustment for length and the restricted nature of the tales in the earlier study account for only a part of the difference in results and that the unconscious bias of the analyst which was evidently possible in the earlier study may well be a more important factor in accounting for the difference.[4]

---

[4] Our other two analysts unfortunately did not score any but our own sample of tales. It is possible, however, to compare their separate scoring of these tales with McClelland and Friedman's scoring of a sample of Coyote tales, for these 6 cultures, to see whether the discrepancy in results was produced primarily by

Conclusions. Our analysis of *n* Achievement in folk tales has led to no very conclusive results, and this may be due to the various important sources of unreliability in the gathering, selection, and analysis of the folk tales. It has led to several tentative conclusions, which at the very least may serve as guides to further research on factors influencing thematic content of imaginative productions. One is that *n* Achievement score gives some evidence of being positively related to variables of socialization which have to do with the attachment of affect (either positive or negative) to achievement-oriented behavior. Another is that this evidence is stronger for those societies where parent behavior is characterized by general rigidity and non-indulgence. In societies where parent behavior is characterized by indulgence and lack of rigidity, *n* Achievement score shows tentative evidence of being more related to the importance of achievement-oriented behavior in adult life; here too, affective arousal might be the mediating event, by way of children's identification with adults. Both of these findings seem to be most easily interpreted if the *n* Achievement score is considered as a measure of the extent to which people's thoughts are preoccupied with ideas about achievement-oriented behavior; they are not, however, necessarily inconsistent with the more specific assumption that the *n* Achievement score measures the strength of a motive for achievement. A third tentative conclusion is that *n* Achievement score is negatively related to general rigidity of socialization and perhaps positively related to general indulgence. Conceivably this may indicate that low rigidity and high indulgence (within the range of variation found among cultural practices) favor the child's identification with adults and thus tend to produce preoccupation with achievement just because conformity to adult standards of excellence in skill is everywhere difficult or impossible for children to achieve.

These tentative findings, which from this study alone emerge only as suggestions, are capable of being tested not only in further cross-cultural research but also in studies of individual differences within our own society.

---

our less experienced judges. For our analysts' raw scores, the rank-order correlations with the McClelland and Friedman scores are $+.20$ (AK), $-.44$ (TS), and $-.10$ (JV). When our analysts' scores are adjusted for length, the corresponding correlations are in order $+.26$, $-.49$, and $+.03$. Thus even the scores of our most experienced analyst (JV) show no evidence of a positive relation to the McClelland and Friedman scores, and the only suggestion of a positive relation appears in the scores of our least experienced analyst (AK).

PART FIVE

Motivation and Society

CAN A METHOD for measuring human motivation which has been developed in the experimental laboratory add anything to our understanding of the problems of human motivation that arise in society? The three studies presented here provide an affirmative answer to that question.

Both Rosen and Douvan find differences in strength of motivation to achieve related to differences in social class background. Milstein (298), also, reports this difference. To the extent that for some this provides a confirmation of what they had expected from other investigations using other techniques, we may conclude that the "thermometer" works when applied to a societal problem. However, for some who may have doubted the need to take account of the constituents of personality in various social groups in theoretical accounts of social mobility and other sociological problems, the results of these studies present substantial evidence that human motives are not randomly distributed among the various segments of a society.

The various indices which have to do with the position of a person in the social structure (social class, religion, ethnic background, etc.) may be related to the theoretical conception of motivation which has been advanced in three—perhaps more—ways:

First, these indices provide a basis for grouping persons who have had similar early life experiences and hence should have similar configurations of motives. The indices, in other words, produce groups of individuals who are similar in basic personality structure.

Second, indices of social position group persons who have had similar kinds of later learning experience—institutional training, verbal indoctrination, and comparable day to day experience in particular kinds of situations after early childhood. Hence, particular subgroups within a society should share certain kinds of expectations regarding the consequences of actions in various situations. They should, in other words, be relatively homogeneous in their conscious beliefs and values.

Third, indices of position in society help us define the kinds of situations in which the behaving adult finds himself from day to day. In addition to pointing to common learning experiences, these indices also account for relative stabilities in the day to day environment of the adult, the environment in which the behavior we seek to explain actually occurs.

In the third paper of this section, which deals with the potential contribution of the psychology of motivation to an understanding of problems in history and economics, McClelland discusses a number of issues which arise in the use of methods of measuring human motivation in studies of society. His exploration broadens the research horizon of social psychology in pointing to problems which are not conventionally viewed as within the domain of empirical psychological inquiry. His demonstration of the relevance of psychological methods to a problem in economic history suggests that many other "new" facts for historians to consider remain to be uncovered in future motivational analyses of historical documents.

CHAPTER 35

The Achievement Syndrome: A Psychocultural Dimension of Social Stratification*

BERNARD C. ROSEN[1]

THE EMPIRICAL GENERALIZATION that upward mobility is greater among members of the middle class than those of the lower strata has been explained in several alternative ways (4, 254, 348). It has been suggested, for example, that social strata possess different physical characteristics which affect mobility, that as a result of certain selective processes persons in the upper and middle strata are, on the average, more intelligent, healthier, and more attractive than those in the lower strata (388).[2] More frequently, differential mobility is described as a function of the relative opportunities available to individuals in the social structure. This structural dimension of stratification is explicit in the "life chances" hypothesis in which it is argued that money, specialized training, and prestigeful contacts—factors which affect access to high position—are relatively inaccessible to individuals in the lower social strata.[3] Such explanations are

---

* Reprinted with minor abridgement by permission of author and publisher from the *American Sociological Review*, 1956, **21**, 203-211. Copyright 1956 by The American Sociological Society.

[1] Expanded version of paper read at the annual meeting of the American Sociological Society, September, 1955.

The author wishes to express his appreciation for the assistance and encouragement of August Hollingshead of Yale University, and David McClelland of Wesleyan University. He is greatly indebted to Marian Winterbottom of the Connecticut College for Women for her work in scoring the TAT protocols, and to George Psathas for his help in the field work. This paper has been influenced by the writer's experience as a former staff member of the project "Cultural Factors in Talent Development" under the general direction of Fred L. Strodtbeck.

[2] For the relationship of intelligence to social mobility, see C. A. Anderson *et al.* (15).

[3] Factors of this sort have been abundantly studied. See H. Pfautz (328), especially pages 401-404.

495

relevant and consistent with one another. They lack exhaustiveness, however, since neither explanation takes into account the possibility that there may be psychological and cultural factors which affect social mobility by influencing the individual's willingness to develop and exploit his talent, intelligence, and opportunities.

It is the thesis of this paper that class differential rates of vertical mobility may be explicated also in terms of a psychocultural dimension of stratification, that is, as a function of differences in the motives and values of social classes.[4] More specifically, this study examines empirically the notion (long current in sociology, but for which there is as yet insufficient empirical verification) that social classes in American society are characterized by a dissimilar concern with achievement, particularly as it is expressed in the striving for status through social mobility.[5] It is hypothesized that social classes possess to a disparate extent two components of this achievement orientation. The first is a psychological factor involving a personality characteristic called *achievement motivation* (or, in Murray's terminology, *need achievement*) which provides an internal impetus to excel. The second is a cultural factor consisting of certain *value orientations* which define and implement achievement motivated behavior. Both of these factors are related to achievement; their incidence, we suggest, is greater among persons of the middle class than those in the lower class.

The task of this paper is threefold: (1) to make a preliminary attempt at determining whether social strata are dissimilar with respect to these two factors by examining their incidence among a group of randomly selected adolescents stratified by social position, (2) to indicate the significance of these factors for differential occupational achievement, and (3) to suggest some class related origins of achievement motivation and values.

---

[4] A review of recent investigations of some psychocultural dimensions of social stratification can be found in H. Pfautz, *op. cit.* While a number of personality correlates of social class have been delineated, there have been no studies of the relationship of class to achievement motive as such, though C. W. Mills' notion of the "competitive personality" comes closest to approximating the personality characteristic examined in this study. See his *White Collar* (296). Of the many studies of the cultural correlates of social class, two which have particular relevance for the problem examined in this paper are H. Hyman (195) and T. Parsons (324).

[5] A. Green in his introductory text, *Sociology* (157), regards the middle class' high level of achievement drive, as expressed through status striving, as its single most pronounced characteristic. However, the data to support this conclusion are largely of an anecdotal, or highly qualitative nature. See C. W. Mills (296); Davis, Gardner, and Gardner (93).

RESEARCH PROCEDURE

The universe from which the study sample was drawn is the entire male population of sophomores in two large public high schools in the New Haven area. This group was stratified by the social position of the main wage-earner in the family (in most cases the father) through data secured by questionnaire and according to a scheme developed by Hollingshead.[6] His Index of Social Position utilizes three factors: (1) occupation, (2) education, and (3) ecological area of residence. Each factor is scaled and assigned a weight determined by a standard regression equation. The combined scores group themselves in five clusters (social strata) and to each of these a numerical index is assigned. The highest status group is labeled Class I; the others follow in numerical order, Class V being the lowest. Respondents were drawn randomly from each stratum: 5 subjects from Class I (the entire Class I Sophomore population in the two schools), 25 from Class II, and 30 each from Classes III, IV, and V. In all there are 120 subjects, all of them white, ages 14 through 16; the modal age is 15.

It was hypothesized that social strata are dissimilar with respect to two factors related to achievement: that is, achievement motivation and achievement value orientation. By achievement motivation we mean an anticipation of an increase in affect aroused by cues in situations involving standards of excellence. The behavior of people highly motivated for achievement is persistent striving activity, aimed at attaining a high goal in some area involving competition with a standard of excellence. In relation to these standards of excellence the achievement oriented person directs his efforts towards obtaining the pleasure of success and avoiding the pain of failure. Value orientations are defined (following the manner described in William's *American Society*) as meaningful and affectively charged modes of organizing behavior, as principles that guide human conduct. They establish the criteria which influence the individual's preferences and goals; they act as spectacles through which the individual sees himself and his environment. Two techniques were employed to measure these factors. A projective test (a technique which does not rely upon the person's self knowledge) was used to measure the adolescent's achievement motivation (272); the direct questionnaire was used to measure his values.

The projective test was administered to the subjects in the following standardized way. Subjects were assembled during the school day

[6] For a fuller exposition of this scheme see A. Hollingshead and F. C. Redlich (184).

in small groups (20 to 30 persons) in a school room equipped with a screen and a slide projector. The test administrator explained to the students that they were going to see a series of pictures and that their task was to write a story about each picture. In his instructions to the subjects the administrator made no effort to manipulate the motive of the students. Since all testing was done in the school, it was expected that each boy would bring to the test his normal achievement motivation level induced by the cues of the school. The same administrator was used throughout the tests.[7]

Following the test, the subjects were asked to fill out a structured questionnaire, part of which contained items (the content of which is described in a later section of this paper) designed to index their value orientations. These items took the form of statements with which the subjects were asked to agree or disagree, and are centered around certain kinds of values that we felt are related to scholastic and vocational achievement.

RESEARCH FINDINGS

Social Stratification and the Achievement Motive. The findings of this study support the hypothesis that social strata differ from one another in the degree to which the achievement motive is characteristic of their members. Furthermore, the data indicate that members of the middle class tend to have considerably higher need achievement scores than individuals in the lower social strata. Plotted on a graph, the mean achievement scores of the social classes fall along a regression curve: the highest mean score in Class II (the group most likely to be described as middle class when the trichotomy of upper, middle, and lower class is used), a somewhat lower score in Class I, and progressively lower scores in an almost linear fashion in Classes III, IV, and V. Reading in numerical order from Class I to V, the mean score

---

[7] Experiments have shown that motivation scores vary with the conditions under which the test is given. The kind of instructions preceding the test are known to affect the test scores. These instructions are basically of three kinds: *achievement-oriented* instructions which produce cues aimed at increasing the score; *relaxed* instructions which tend to de-emphasize the arousal of the motive; and *neutral* instructions that are aimed at obtaining a measure of the normal level of motivation a subject brings to a situation. Instructions used in this study were of the neutral type. The impact the school situation had upon the scores is unknown, but we believe that in effect this factor was controlled since all subjects were tested in the same situation. Further information on the various methods for administering this test, and their significance for the test results, can be found in D. McClelland, *et al.,* (272, Ch. 2). The test protocols were scored by two judges. The Pearson product moment correlation between the two scorings was plus .89, an estimate of scoring reliability similar to those reported in earlier studies with this measure.

for each class is 8.40, 8.68, 4.97, 3.40, and 1.87. The mean score for Class II is more than four times as great as the score for Class V.[8]

A test of the statistical significance of this association between social position and achievement motivation is shown in Table 1.

TABLE 1. ACHIEVEMENT MOTIVATION BY SOCIAL CLASS

Achievement Motivation Score	Social Class			
	I and II	III	IV	V
	Per cent	Per cent	Per cent	Per cent
Low.........................	17	57	70	77
High.........................	83	43	30	23
Number......................	(30)	(30)	(30)	(30)

χ^2: 26.6.
P < .001.

In order to simplify presentation, subjects whose scores fall below the approximate median for the entire sample are categorized as having low achievement motivation;[9] Classes I and II are collapsed into one group because of the scarcity of cases in Class I.[10] The data indicate a clear relationship between social position and motivation score. For example, 83 per cent of the subjects in Classes I and II have high motivation scores, as compared with 23 per cent in Class V, a difference that is statistically significant at the .001 level.

---

[8] In a study of personality and value differences between upper-class Harvard freshmen (private-school graduates) and middle-class freshmen (public-school graduates), C. McArthur (257) found that the need achievement level of the middle class was significantly higher than that of the upper class. The difference between the two groups in the writer's study was in the same direction noted by McArthur, but was not statistically significant. However, since sampling methods, TAT pictures, and scoring procedures used in the two studies are different, the data are not comparable.

[9] Four pictures were used in this study. The approximate median score for the entire sample was +4. Sixty-six subjects have a score of +4 or less; fifty-four subjects a score of +5 or more. Scores ranged from −4 to +15. It should be understood that the terms "high" and "low" used in this study do not refer to absolute standards but to relative ranks for individuals in this sample. As yet there are not sufficient data to permit the setting up of norms for broad cross-sections of the population for either achievement motivation or value orientation.

[10] Analysis of the data in which persons in Classes I and II are examined together in one cell or part reveals that the conclusions noted above are not affected when the cells are collapsed.

Social Stratification and Value Orientation. In itself the achievement motive is not a sufficient cause of upward mobility. Obviously the lack of innate capacity and/or structural opportunities may frustrate the achievement drive, but in addition there are cultural factors which are related to mobility. Among these factors are certain values which affect mobility in that they provide a definition of goals, focus the attention of the individual on achievement, and prepare him to translate motive into action. For example, before the achievement motive can be translated into the kinds of action that are conducive to culturally defined achievement (and hence operate as a factor in social mobility), there must be some definition of the kinds of situations in which achievement is expected and of the goals to which one should or may aspire.

Achievement-oriented situations and goals are not defined by the achievement motive; it may provide the impetus to excel, but it does not delineate the areas in which such excellence should or may take place (Editor's Italics). Achievement motivation can be expressed through a wide range of behavior, some of which may not be conducive to social mobility in our society. The achievement motive can be, and perhaps frequently is, expressed through non-vocational behavior, for example lay religious activity of an individual whose drive to excel finds release through piety or mastery of sacred literature; or it may find an outlet in non-professional "hobby-type" behavior. Even when expressed through vocational activity, the achievement motive may be canalized into culturally defined deviant occupations (e.g. the criminal), or into low status vocations (e.g. the individual whose achievement drive is expressed and satisfied through his desire to be the *best* welder among his peers). Whether the individual will elect to strive for success in situations which facilitate mobility in our society will, in part, be determined by his values.

Furthermore, before the achievement motive can be expressed in culturally defined success behavior, there needs to be more than a desire to achieve success; there must also be some awareness of and willingness to undertake the steps necessary for achievement. Such steps involve, among other things, a preparedness to plan, to work, and to make sacrifices. Whether the individual will understand their importance and accept them will, in part, be affected by his values. It must follow, therefore, that differential inter-class rates of mobility cannot be entirely explained as a function of differences in achievement motivation; social classes must also be shown to differ in their possession of these implementary values necessary to achievement.

The notion that social classes possess dissimilar values as part of their distinctive sub-cultures has been suggested by a number of investigators, for example, the Kluckhohns, who have delineated a wide range of differences in the value systems of social strata in American society (154, 217).[11] In Florence Kluckhohn's schema (216) these values are part of a configuration of value orientations which grow out of man's effort to solve five basic problems that are everywhere immanent in the human situation. While all five of Kluckhohn's orientations are relevant to the problem of achievement, three were selected as especially pertinent for examination in this study: (1) what is the accepted approach to the problem of mastering one's physical and social environment, (2) what is the significant time dimension, and (3) what is the dominant modality of relationship of the individual to his kin. We were interested in determining whether social classes are dissimilar in their possession of these orientations. A brief description of their content (modified somewhat from the way in which they appear in the Kluckhohn schema), and examples of the items used to index each of them, are as follows:[12]

1. *Activistic-passivistic orientation* concerns the extent to which a society or sub-group encourages the individual to believe in the possibility of his manipulating the physical and social environment to his advantage. In an activistic society the individual is encouraged to believe that it is both possible and necessary for him to improve his status, whereas a passivistic-orientation promotes the acceptance of the notion that individual efforts to achieve mobility are relatively futile.

Item 1. "All I want out of life in the way of a career is a secure, not too difficult job, with enough pay to afford a nice car and eventually a home of my own."

Item 2. "When a man is born the success he is going to have is

---

[11] Other investigators are cited in H. Pfautz, *op. cit.*, pp. 403-404.

[12] In all, fourteen items were used to index certain of the adolescent's values and perceptions. The nine additional items are as follows:

1. Even though parents often seem too strict, when a person gets older he will realize it was beneficial.
2. If my parents told me to stop seeing a friend of my own sex, I'd see that friend anyway.
3. Parents seem to believe that you can't take the opinion of a teenager seriously.
4. Parents would be greatly upset if their son ended up doing factory work.
5. It's silly for a teenager to put money in a car when the money could be used to get started in a business or for an education.
6. The best kind of job is one where you are part of an organization all working together, even if you don't get individual credit.
7. Education and learning are more important in determining a person's happiness than money and what it will buy.
8. When the time comes for a boy to take a job, he should stay near his parents even if it means giving up a good job.
9. Even when teenagers get married their main loyalty still belongs to their mother and father.

already in the cards, so he might just as well accept it and not fight against it."

2. *Present-future orientation* concerns a society's attitude toward time and its impact upon behavior. A present-oriented society stresses the merit of living in the present with an emphasis upon immediate gratifications; a future-oriented society urges the individual to believe that planning and present sacrifices are worthwhile, or morally obligatory, in order to insure future gains.

Item 3. "Planning only makes a person unhappy since your plans hardly ever work out anyway."

Item 4. "Nowadays with world conditions the way they are the wise person lives for today and lets tomorrow take care of itself."

3. *Familistic-individualistic orientation* concerns the relationship of the individual to his kin. One aspect of this orientation is the importance given to the maintenance of physical proximity to the family of orientation. In a familistically-oriented society the individual is not urged, or perhaps not permitted, to acquire independence of family ties. An individualistically-oriented society does not expect the individual to maintain the kinds of affective ties which will impede his mobility.

Item 5. "Nothing in life is worth the sacrifice of moving away from your parents."

Responses which indicate an activistic, future-oriented, individualistic point of view (the answer "disagree" to these items) are considered those which reflect values most likely to facilitate achievement and social mobility. These items were used to form a value index, and a score was derived for each subject by giving a point for each achievement oriented response.[13]

An analysis of the data supports the hypothesis that the middle class is characterized by a larger proportion of persons with achievement oriented values than are the lower social strata. The plotting of mean value scores for each class reveals an almost linear relationship between social position and values: the higher the class the higher the value score. Thus the mean scores for the five social strata are in descending order, with Class I first and Class V last, 4.6, 4.1, 3.8, 3.0 and 2.5. This relationship is shown to be statistically significant in Table 2 in which social position is cross-tabulated with value score. To simplify presentation value scores are dichotomized: respondents whose score falls above the approximate median for the entire sample are designated as having a high score. The data reveal that of those adolescents in Class I or II, 77 per cent score high on the value scale,

---

[13] The writer is indebted to an earlier, somewhat different scale (based in part on work done by the writer as a member of the "Cultural Factors in Talent Development" Project), put together by Fred L. Strodtbeck.

TABLE 2. VALUE ORIENTATIONS BY SOCIAL CLASS

Value Score	Social Class			
	I and II	III	IV	V
	Per cent	Per cent	Per cent	Per cent
Low	23	30	67	83
High	77	70	33	17
Number	(30)	(30)	(30)	(30)

χ^2: 28.9.
P < .001.

as compared with 17 per cent of the adolescents in Class V. For the entire table, the probability of this level of association occurring by chance is less than one out of a thousand.

Achievement Correlates of Achievement Motivation and Values. Achievement motivation and value orientation were found to be related to different kinds of behavior that affect social mobility. We have stated that the achievement motive expresses itself in concern with performance evaluated against a standard of excellence. In the school situation this performance may be canalized within the framework of scholastic achievement. That this is probably frequently the case can be seen in Table 3 in which motivation scores are cross-

TABLE 3. AVERAGE SCHOOL GRADE BY ACHIEVEMENT MOTIVATION

Average School Grade	Achievement Motivation Score		Value Orientation Score	
	High	Low	High	Low
	Per cent	Per cent	Per cent	Per cent
"B" or above	69	35	54	46
"C" or below	31	65	46	54
Number	(54)	(66)	(59)	(61)

χ^2: 13.5. χ^2: .833.
P < .001.   P > .30.

tabulated with average school grades. The data show that subjects with high motivation scores are proportionately more likely to achieve grades of "B" or better than are adolescents with low motivation scores: 69 per cent of the former as against 35 per cent of the latter. Value scores, however, proved not to be related to academic achievement, although they are associated with a kind of behavior that is, if not in itself an act of achievement, at least a factor in social mobility in our society. It was found that the individual's value score, but *not* his motivation score, is related to educational aspiration. Thus the data in Table 4 indicate that subjects with high value scores are

TABLE 4. SCHOOL ASPIRATION BY VALUE ORIENTATION

School Aspiration	Value Orientation Score		Achievement Motivation Score	
	High	Low	High	Low
	Per cent	Per cent	Per cent	Per cent
Aspires to go to college..........	61	33	51	46
Does not aspire to go to college..	39	67	49	54
Number.....................	(59)	(61)	(54)	(66)

χ^2: 13.3. χ^2: 1.2.
P < .001.   P > .20.

proportionately more likely to want to go to college than are those with low scores: 61 per cent of the former as compared with 33 per cent of the latter. The relationships between motivation and grades, and between values and aspiration level are statistically significant at the .001 level.

Since high need achievement and value scores tend to occur more frequently among members of the upper and middle than in the lower strata, it is not surprising to find that social strata are different in their academic achievement and educational aspiration levels. This is particularly marked in the case of educational aspiration level, which was found to be considerably higher for adolescents in the upper and middle strata than for those in the lower strata. Thus when subjects were asked, "If you could arrange things to suit yourself, how far would you go in school?" 92 per cent of respondents in the combined category of stratas I, II, and III aspired to continue their education beyond high school, either in college or in a technical school; whereas of the combined stratas IV-V only 47 per cent aspired to go beyond high school.[14]

The hypothesis that this differential in education aspiration is, in part at least, a function of value orientation differences is supported by the data shown in Table 5 in which under- and over-aspirers are

---

[14] Class differentials in educational aspiration level have been noted by a number of investigators. See, for example, J. A. Kahl (203).

TABLE 5. VALUE SCORE BY ASPIRATION LEVEL AND SOCIAL CLASS

Aspiration Level	Social Class			
	I–II–III		IV–V	
	Under-Aspirers	Other-Aspirers	Over-Aspirers	Other-Aspirers
Value Score	Per cent	Per cent	Per cent	Per cent
Low....................	57	23	65	79
High....................	43	77	35	21
Number..................	7	53*	17	43†

* Includes those individuals whose aspiration level represents the modal choice for their status group.

† Includes those subjects whose aspiration level is below or at the modal choice for their group.

examined. Under-aspirers are those respondents in strata I, II, or III whose educational aspiration level is lower than the modality for their group (i.e. those who do not aspire to go beyond high school); over-aspirers are those adolescents in strata IV-V whose aspiration level -is higher than the norm for their group (i.e. those who aspire to go beyond high school). The data in Table 5 in which over- and under-aspirers are compared with one another, and with other members of their class, in terms of their value scores show a clear relationship between over-under-aspiration level and value orientations. Thus fewer under-aspirers have high value scores than do other members of their strata—43 per cent of the former as compared with 77 per cent of the latter; whereas over-aspirers are more likely to have high value scores than are other members of their class—35 per cent as compared with 21 per cent. Furthermore, the class differences in value scores shown in Table 2 virtually disappear when aspiration level is held constant: an earlier difference of more than 40 per cent between categories I-II-III and IV-V is reduced to 8 per cent when over- and under-aspirers are compared with one another; whereas it is increased when the "other" categories are compared.

The relationship between academic achievement (as measured by average grades) and social class appears to reflect to a considerable extent strata differentials in achievement motivation. Class differences in academic achievement which appear significant on first inspection (e.g., 17 per cent of the subjects in the combined category of Classes I-II-III have average grades of "A"; only 3 per cent of those Classes IV-V have grades this high; also 54 per cent of the former have average grades of "B" or higher, as compared with 42 per cent of the

TABLE 6. SCHOOL GRADES BY ACHIEVEMENT MOTIVATION AND SOCIAL CLASS

Achievement Motivation Score	Social Class			
	I–II–III		IV–V	
	High	Low	High	Low
Average School Grades	Per cent	Per cent	Per cent	Per cent
"B" or above.................	66	32	75	36
"C" or below.................	34	68	25	64
Number......................	38	22	16	44

lower status category) are markedly altered when need achievement score is introduced as a test variable. As can be seen in Table 6 the earlier relationship between class and grades is virtually erased for those with low achievement motivation and slightly reversed for those with high motivation. However, although the differences *between* strata are reduced to a statistically insignificant level, *within* strata differences between individuals with high and low motivation scores remain, thus pointing up the relationship between motivation and academic achievement.

Achievement motivation and achievement oriented values are not, of course, the only factors related to academic success and educational aspiration. The fact that *all* the cells in the contingency tables described here contain some cases clearly indicates that other variables are at work. Among these variables may be such factors as sibling rivalry, the operation of ego defense mechanisms, or motives other than need achievement, for example, the need for power. Furthermore, social classes may be dissimilar in ways other than in their motives or values, and these differences can have significance for achievement. Classes are said to be different in manners, richness of cultural-esthetic experiences, and possibly with respect to intelligence, to a general sense of well being, power, and past history of successful endeavor. All of these factors may contribute to differential class rates of mobility by affecting academic and vocational success and aspiration level. The task of this paper, however, has been to focus upon the factors of achievement motivation and values, although probably in the empirical situation many of the above factors are operative and interactive at the same time.

Whatever the importance present and future studies may show the other factors listed above to have for achievement, the fact remains that this study reveals a significant relationship between achievement motivation and grades, and between values and educational aspiration. This fact is of more than academic interest. There is a nexus, though it is of course not a perfect one, between educational and vocational achievement in our society. Furthermore, the college degree is becoming an increasingly important prerequisite for movement into prestigeful and lucrative jobs; hence an aspiration level which precludes college training may seriously affect an individual's opportunity for social mobility. Since we have shown that achievement-oriented motives and values are more characteristic of the middle than the lower strata, it is reasonable to suggest that these variables are, in part at least, factors which tend to create differential class rates of social mobility.

Class Related Origins of Achievement Motivation and Values. The achievement motive and values examined here, while related, represent genuinely different components of the achievement syndrome, not only in their correlates but also in their origins. Value orientations, because they tend to be on a conceptual level, are probably acquired in that stage of the child's cultural training when verbal communication of a fairly complex nature is possible. Achievement motivation, on the other hand, probably has its origins in certain kinds of parent-child interaction that occur early in the child's life and are likely to be emotional and unverbalized. Analytically, then, the learning of achievement-oriented values can be independent of the acquisition of the achievement motive, though empirically they often occur together.

Several empirical studies have shown that achievement motivation is most likely to be high when the child is urged to obtain, and rewarded for achieving, independence and mastery, accompanied by few restrictions after mastery has been acquired. Winterbottom's study (Ch. 33), for example, indicates that mothers of children with high achievement motivation differ from mothers of children who have low motivation in that they: (1) make more demands (particularly for evidences of independence, maturity, and achievement) at early ages; and (2) give more intense and frequent rewards for fulfilled demands.

These are the patterns which are believed to be especially characteristic of middle-class families, although it must be emphasized that the data to substantiate this conclusion are still tentative and often conflicting and that child-rearing practices, like other aspects of American culture, are in constant flux.[15] From babyhood on much of

---

[15] The uncertain character of data relating to class differences in child rearing is pointed up in the article by R. J. Havighurst and A. Davis (171). See also M. C. Ericson (117) and A. Davis (91).

the middle-class child's affect is likely to be associated with achievement related behavior structured for him by the training practices and values of his parents. In the pre-school period the tendency for middle-class parents to make early demands upon their children is reflected in such practices as early toilet training and the intense concern with cleanliness. As the child grows he is frequently urged and encouraged to demonstrate his developing maturity (e.g., early walking, talking, and self care). Signs of precocity are signals for intense parental pride and often lavish rewards. It is precisely this atmosphere which provides, if Winterbottom is correct, a most fertile environment for the growth of the achievement motive.

When the child starts his formal schooling, the achievement-oriented demands and values of his parents tend to be focussed on the school situation. From the beginning of his school career the middle-class child is more likely than his lower-class counterpart to have standards of excellence in scholastic behavior set for him by his parents. In fact, the relatively higher position which scholastic attainment has in the middle-class than in the lower-class value system means that more frequently for the middle- than for the lower-class child parental demands and expectations, as well as rewards and punishments, will center around school performance.

Associated with the stress on scholastic achievement are other achievement-oriented values that are more characteristic of the middle than the lower class. While it is probably true that the notion that success is desirable and possible is widespread in our society, the implementary values—those which encouraged behavior that facilitate achievement—have long been more associated with the culture of the middle than of the lower class. Middle-class children are more likely to be taught not only to believe in success but also to be willing to take those steps that make achievement possible: in short, to embrace the achievement value system which states that *given the willingness to work hard, plan and make the proper sacrifices, an individual should be able to manipulate his environment so as to ensure eventual success* (Editor's Italics).

CHAPTER 36

....

Social Status and Success Strivings*

Elizabeth Douvan[1]

Systematic differences between child-training procedures employed in the two major social classes have been reported by several investigators (89, 109, 117). These differences cluster in two related areas of training: development of internalized controls and learning of achievement motivation. Davis (89) has noted the critical role of anxiety as a reinforcement for achievement strivings in the middle class training scheme, and Ericson's study (117) reveals a picture of the environment of the middle class child as making early and consistent demands for personal attainment.

Since middle class society not only places great stress on accomplishment, but imposes demands earlier than does the working class (117), we would expect the need for achievement to be more generalized in middle class children than in children of lower status.[2] Success-failure cues in any situation should, among middle class children, elicit a relatively consistent reaction, irrespective of the reward conditions of the specific situation. Since working class children are taught achievement strivings neither so early nor so systematically their reactions to success-failure cues should be more responsive to changes in the reward potential of the situation in which such cues occur.

The present study was designed to contrast members of the two social groups with respect to the degree of achievement motivation

* Reprinted by permission of author and publisher from *The Journal of Abnormal and Social Psychology,* 1956, **52,** 219-223. Copyright 1956 by the American Psychological Association, Inc.

[1] This article is based on a doctoral dissertation submitted to the University of Michigan. The author is indebted to Theodore M. Newcomb, Max L. Hutt, and other members of her doctoral committee for their able guidance.

[2] The importance of time of training has been highlighted by McClelland (258). He hypothesizes that behavior patterns learned in the preverbal period will be particularly generalized and intractable since the original learning cues are unavailable to consciousness.

they manifest in two success-failure situations which differ in reward potential. In one situation success was defined as achieving an abstract norm; in the other successful performance offered, in addition, a material reward. The specific hypothesis to be tested was that working class youth would manifest a significantly greater difference in achievement strivings under the two reward conditions than would youngsters from the middle class.

METHOD

Subjects

The Ss for this experiment were adolescents in the senior year of high school in a medium-sized midwestern community. Of the original group of 336, 23 were excluded from the analysis because of incompletions in at least one of the measures used in the study.

School children were used as Ss because the schools provide established groups of individuals from both social classes under similar objective conditions. In addition Ss of this age were especially suitable because of the likelihood of finding among them a substantial proportion who had been subject to the influences of their class subcultures during the crucial early training period.

The schools in which the study was done provided a good cultural setting for an investigation of class differences. The social situation in these schools is characterized by relatively good apparent chances for mobility and by strong pressures exerted toward mobility by teachers and by the middle class satisfactions reflected in the well-kept and expensive homes surrounding the schools. Working class students who do not yield to such pressures—who identify with the working class even in this situation—should be stable representatives of people with working class values and goals.

Measures and Controls

Class membership. Two types of indices were used in defining Ss' class position. The first was an occupational index based on data derived from school records and a questionnaire in which S was asked to describe his father's work and conditions of employment. The second index was a subjective class assignment based on a variation of Centers' technique.[3] Only those Ss for whom the two indices agreed on the middle or working class were used in the test of the study's central hypothesis.

Independent placements of each S on the basis of father's occupation

---

[3] In addition to the Centers' question, and preceding it, Ss were asked: "Which one of the following social classes (middle, lower, working, upper) would you like to be a member of?" and "Which one . . . do you think you'll be a member of in ten years?" By including these questions, it was hoped to reduce elements of fantasy and aspiration in Ss' answers to the question on present class membership.

were made by two judges, with a percentage agreement of .95. The criteria for assigning occupations to the two classes are listed below.[4]

Middle Class

a. Addresses self to people.

b. Exerts control over people either in a disciplinary capacity within the business power unit, or as an active agent of control over people outside the business unit. In either case the exertion of control serves the interest of the business unit.

c. Income can be increased through individual efforts—some degree of effect on the market for his services and skills.

Working Class

a. Addresses self to tools.

b. Exerts control over no one in the job situation.

c. Income relatively fixed. No control over market for his labor, the only source of his income.

d. Easily replaceable skill.

Most occupations were relatively easily placed by means of these criteria. If a job met two of the three criteria for the middle class, it was assigned this position. Most commonly discrepancies occurred between the first criterion and later ones. Thus a surgeon might be said to address himself primarily to tools, but he exerts control over others (patients, nurses, secretarial help) and has some power over the market for his skills. The factory set-up man represents the opposite case of this discrepancy. Fewer than five per cent of the occupations rated revealed any such inharmonious elements.

Need Achievement. McClelland, Atkinson, and co-workers have developed a method for measuring achievement motivation based on a special scoring of an adapted TAT. Their measure, which made possible an experimental test of the hypothesis of the present study, is presented in detail in a recent publication (272).

Scoring was done by two judges, trained by a psychologist experienced in the use of the system. A number of indices of agreement were obtained between each judge and the instructor and between the two judges. Percentage agreements on scoring specific categories ranged from .83 to .96; eight rank-order correlations between total scores assigned by two judges to twenty-five Ss all yielded values above .91. Score-rescore reliabilities computed on 150 protocols were .87 for one judge and .94 for the other.

Procedure

The Ss were assigned by a system of random numbers to one of the two motivation conditions. Limitation of funds for material rewards

---

[4] The rationale for this classification system is presented fully in the original report from which this article is drawn (104). Placements made on the basis of this scheme have been shown to correlate highly with those based on Warner's more complex system (322).

dictated the decision to distribute the sample two-to-one in favor of the symbolic reward condition.

The Ss were given tests, tasks, and questionnaires in the following order:

a. questionnaire on subjective class identification

b. anagrams "test"

c. motor "test"

d. Need Achievement measure

e. questionnaire on father's occupation

The experiment was introduced in the following manner in all groups:

A group of psychologists is administering a series of tests to high school students in different parts of the country. These tests tell us about various abilities of people. We're going to give the tests to you now. I'll describe the ability each test measures . . . before we give it. After each test I'll give you the average score of high school students on that test, so you'll know how you're doing as we go along.

In the material reward condition this introduction was followed by a short statement concerning the fact that we had found that students often did not do as well as they might because they didn't always try hard. For this reason, they were told, ten dollars would be given to any student whose over-all score on the tests reached a certain value:

We'll announce the winning scores tomorrow, but in the meantime, you'll have the average scores of students we've already tested in (*name of city*) so you'll know how you're doing.

The effectiveness of this device for increasing motivation was attested by the excitement which followed the announcement. A questionnaire asking each S to estimate the relative magnitude of his own and others' desire for the prize corroborated the impression of the Es.

The anagrams and motor tasks were used to create failure experiences and thus establish a nonsatiated state of the achievement motive. Before each of the "tests," Ss were told what it measured and how much time they would be given. They were admonished against any discussion during the testing period, and also against "giving up" if they did poorly on early tests. Since the important thing was the over-all score, success on later tests might compensate for humble beginnings.

Following a 4-minute trial on each "test," a falsely high average was announced for "high school students in your city," and we guided Ss rapidly into the next experimental step.

The n Achievement "test" was dissociated from the two previous ones. A different E administered it, and Ss were told that this test would not be counted in their scores. It was introduced as a test of creative imagination, and the instructions conformed closely to those used by McClelland *et al.* (272).

At the end of the testing period it was necessary to relieve anxieties created by the experimentally induced failure. The previously announced high school norms were inaccessibly high, and our desire was to substitute for them more reasonable standards which would leave Ss with the feeling that they had performed well relative to their peers. To effect this substitution, a minor drama was staged.

An experimental assistant came into the room near the close of the hour and hurriedly whispered something to Es. Following this communication, one E announced with obvious embarrassment that because of a last-minute rush in preparations, he had by mistake been given supplies intended for the team of psychologists giving the tests at the local college. The norms he had previously announced for the tests had not, therefore, been the scores of a high school group, but were scores obtained by college students. He now had the correct high school norms, and would read them to Ss.

These belated but "correct" norms were quite moderate, having been established on the basis of pretest experience to be within the near-reach of even the slow high school senior. A free question and discussion period followed and concluded the experiment.

RESULTS

Summary data for tests of hypotheses are presented in Table 1. There is, we see, a significantly greater difference between the n Achievement scores of working class Ss under the two reward conditions than between those of middle class Ss. This finding confirms our hypothesis that middle class youngsters would manifest more gen-

TABLE 1. ACHIEVEMENT MOTIVATION OF WORKING CLASS, MIDDLE CLASS, AND MARGINAL Ss UNDER TWO REWARD CONDITIONS

Class	Material Reward						D_1-D_2	SE of Diff.	t	p
	Present			Absent						
	N	M	SD	N	M	SD				
Working....	34	8.06	3.61	53	4.89	2.89	2.43*	1.05	2.31	.02
Middle......	37	8.30	3.71	73	7.56	3.76				
Marginal....	36	7.85	3.72	71	7.71	4.93	.60†	1.14	.53	.25

* Here D_1 refers to the mean difference for working class Ss under the reward conditions, D_2 to the mean difference for middle class Ss.

† In this case D_1 refers to the mean difference for middle class Ss, D_2 to mean difference for marginals.

eralized achievement strivings, thus showing themselves more impervious to immediate situational demands.

One might ask whether the greater relative shift in striving among working class children does not simply reflect the fact that money is scarcer in their environment and therefore more highly desirable to them. The material reward offered might, according to this argument, be sufficient to trigger additional motivation in the working class child but insufficient to bring into play in the middle class youth any comparable increment of striving.

Results of the questionnaire on the desirability of the ten dollar reward oppose this interpretation—there was no class difference in conscious desire for the reward. The sum of ten dollars was used specifically to guard against differential subjective responses to the material reward.

The n Achievement scores of the class groups under the two reward conditions can be viewed in another way. The fact that under the material reward condition there is substantially no difference in the mean scores of the two class groups ($t = .27$; $p > .30$), indicates that the measure of n Achievement as such is not seriously class biased. We might consider the condition of material reward a control situation designed to establish the applicability of the n Achievement measure to both groups. On this interpretation, results in the situation characterized by the absence of material reward can be generalized thus: In response to a failure, defined as not achieving an abstract standard, middle class individuals manifest a significantly higher need to achieve than working class individuals ($t = 4.3$; $p < .01$).

Since each S knew only his own scores, success did not entail any immediate gratification of prestige strivings or needs for recognition from the group. This extreme limitation of the satisfactions to be gained by success in the nonreward situation leads to the conclusion that the manifestation of a high need to achieve under such conditions attests to the independent and central nature of success as a motivating factor in the individuals responding in this manner.

Marginality. The results reported to this point were obtained when social class was defined on the basis of both objective occupational criteria and a subjective measure. Possibly the most provocative groups defined by this dual scheme are those comprising individuals whose self-assigned social class differs from their objective position in the social structure. From the present analysis it is not possible to make even tentative remarks about downward identifying middle class Ss, since there were too few of these cases. Consider, however, upward identifying working class Ss.

Because of the variety of factors which may underlie such a misidentification (e.g., ambiguity in the status structure, simple ignorance, status anxiety, defensive resistance against one's actual position), no specific predictions were made about the relative achieve-

Social Status and Success Strivings 515

ment motivation of this group under the two reward conditions. However, several general possibilities were explored.

Steiner (393) found a tendency for these marginal cases to behave like middle class individuals, but more extremely. The present study posed two questions relating to this observation: (a) Do marginals obtain higher n Achievement scores than middle class Ss under low reward conditions? and (b) Do marginals react to the two reward conditions with more consistent achievement motivation than middle class Ss?

This analysis did not yield any significant findings. While the mean n Achievement for the marginal group under the symbolic reward condition is higher than the mean of the middle class group (Table 1), the difference is not reliable ($t = .20$; $p > .40$). Nor do the marginals show greater consistency in response to the two situations. There was substantially no difference between middle class and marginal Ss with respect to the relative shift in achievement strivings ($t = .53$; $p > .25$).

Another inquiry into the behavior of this group followed from Davis' distinction (89) between original socialization and adaptive acculturation, and his description of the differential demands and effects of these two kinds of learning. Since the marginal Ss were probably not uniformly socialized in the middle class value pattern, wide variation was anticipated in the extent and accuracy of their incorporation of middle class behavior patterns. Some might have overlearned, some not yet have learned the accepted middle class responses to success-failure cues in a symbolic reward situation. Greater heterogeneity should therefore be manifested in the responses of this group under the condition of absence of material reward.

The findings confirm this expectation. The standard deviation of the marginal group was not compared to that of the working class group, since their means were too different to allow the assumption that the groups derived from the same universe. But the test which could be made—between middle class and marginal variances—reveals that the marginal group is significantly less homogeneous than the middle class group (F ratio $= 1.6$; $p < .05$).

DISCUSSION

The extent and nature of achievement responses have been shown to depend on social class membership. More autonomous and generalized success strivings characterize members of the middle class, while achievement motivation of working class individuals is more highly dependent on the reward loading of the task situation.

The present results, in conjunction with observations made by others (65, 90, 183, 243, 433), suggest that the nature of achievement motivation among adolescents in the two classes is functional to the dominant values and behavior expectations of the class subcultures. The occupational role of the middle class adult requires a high degree of competitive performance, the product is individual, and responsibility for success and failure is personal. To meet these demands successfully the individual must be equipped with generalized and stable internal motivation to achieve. The industrial manual worker, on the other hand, is more familiar with nonpersonal causality and the effect of external factors (e.g., layoffs) on individual goal attainment. His labor contributes to a group product, and the value of personal competitiveness is minimal in his occupational role. Success and failure are less highly personalized so there is little need to strive unless success involves some meaningful and apparent reward (90).

A caveat should be entered against over-interpretation of these findings. They are not concerned with the way in which achievement striving fits into the total psychological structure of the individual. Thus while Davis (89) attributes to anxiety a major role in the determination of success strivings in the middle class, the present data do not permit conclusions about the kind of learning process which underlies them. Nor are assertions justified about the relative rationality, efficiency, or rigidity of the two patterns of behavior observed, since the psychological economics of individual Ss have not been studied. In any case Brown (52) has pointed to the danger that terms like efficiency may serve as screens for evaluation.

The conclusion is warranted, however, that achievement motivation is conditioned by and appropriate to the cultural context in which it develops. The middle class child is urged to individual achievement, is compared to age mates by his parents, and is taught to respond to symbolic as well as material rewards. He develops, accordingly, strong and well-internalized desires for accomplishment, and responds consistently to success-failure cues even when achievement offers little or no substantial reward. The working class child, on the other hand, is not pressed for individual attainment as early or as consistently, and his motivation to succeed in a given task is more clearly related to the rewards such success entails. These differential patterns of response conform to values and life conditions in the two subcultures and to the behavior expectations which will be imposed when the subjects of this study reach adult status in their respective class cultures.

SUMMARY

Previous research has indicated that the two major social classes differ with respect to norms and values in the area of personal achievement. Middle class parents, in rearing their children, assert demands for individual success earlier and more regularly than do parents in the working class. On this basis it was anticipated that achievement striving would be a more central motivational factor in middle class children, and that their responses to situations containing success-failure cues would be relatively consistent despite variations in rewards offered for success. Since children in working class homes are not so vigorously urged to personal attainment, it was hypothesized that their motivation to succeed would vary more directly with changes in the reward potential of task situations.

High school students from both social classes were given a series of tasks under two reward conditions. In one, reward was limited to personal satisfaction derived from attaining a norm; in the other a material reward was added to this satisfaction. Following failure experiences (to induce deprivation) Ss in each condition were given McClelland's projective test for achievement motivation.

As predicted, the mean n Achievement scores for working class Ss under the two reward conditions showed greater variation than did the means for middle class Ss. Though members of both class groups responded similarly to the material reward condition, the achievement strivings of working class Ss dropped significantly when the material reward was absent, while the motivation of middle class Ss remained at approximately the same high level.

The Ss who were placed by an objective criterion in the working class, but identified themselves as middle class, were considered marginal and were excluded from the main analysis. It was predicted that the n Achievement scores of these Ss under the symbolic reward condition would be marked by greater variability than those of other groups. The prediction was confirmed.

From the results it is concluded that the pattern of achievement motivation a child develops depends on the class subculture in which he is trained, and is functional to the values and behavior requirements with which he will be confronted as he assumes adulthood within that setting.

CHAPTER 37

The Use of Measures of
Human Motivation in the
Study of Society

DAVID C. MCCLELLAND

PSYCHOLOGY as the basic science of human behavior ought to be able to contribute to other disciplines interested in man like history and economics, but to date its contributions have not been very impressive. It has made attempts to be helpful, but they have nearly always involved such extensive extrapolations beyond observed facts that social scientists have by and large remained unimpressed. For example, Dodge discovered years ago (101) that human beings showed a built-in variability of response, that the same response—e.g., the knee jerk reflex—could not be elicited twice in succession without a short pause. He tied this in on the one hand with the refractory phase of the nerve impulse and on the other with the observed tendency of societies to avoid doing the same thing twice in a row. He suggested, for instance, that the fact that the United States holds a national election only once every four years might reflect the basic human tendency to avoid immediate repetition of an act, a tendency which should incidentally contribute to the survival of the species by leading to discontinuance of unsuccessful responses. No political scientist that I know of has ever made anything of Dodge's suggestion, even though his argument on the face of it sounds rather plausible. The reason is not hard to find: Dodge made no suggestions as to how the variables in his hypothesis might be measured nor did he suggest any concrete series of intervening behavioral events by which refractory phase in reflex behavior gets transformed into refractory phase in social institutions. So his extrapolation from simply human behavior remains untested and perhaps even untestable.

More recent attempts to generalize psychological observations have not been conspicuously more successful, even though they have, since Freud, often dealt with what would appear to be more relevant

518

characterological variables. To choose an example which at least caused some stir among social scientists, Gorer and Rickman (155) reasoned that keeping Russian babies tightly swaddled during infancy and unswaddling them to kick freely during nursing might well lay down certain basic tendencies in Russian personality structure which would express themselves politically as a desire for firm social control punctuated by periods of great emotional release. Many social scientists—historians, political scientists, Russian experts—simply branded the hypothesis as patently absurd. How could one infer anything about complex social behavior with concrete historical antecedents from what happened to babies during the first year of life? The fact is, however, that the hypothesis is neither more nor less absurd than Dodge's. It is simply not easily testable. Neither Gorer nor Rickman nor anyone else has gone about systematically testing what the reactions to swaddling are in Russia or elsewhere and attempting to build a concrete series of empirically established links between such reactions and social institutions. Until we can measure both psychological reactions to swaddling and degree of "firmness of political control," the hypothesis cannot be tested and social scientists have a right to remain sceptical about it.

Recent advances in methods for measuring human motivation have, however, opened some new possibilities. They make it potentially feasible to get estimates of the average motivational level of social groups—estimates which are independent of the behavior of those groups and which therefore can be used to test empirically hypotheses about the relationships between group motivation and social behavior. To argue, for example, that an increase in the average level of achievement motivation in a group leads to the growth of civilization is either a tautology or an untestable hypothesis unless we have a measure of achievement motivation which is independent of the growth of civilization. But, as a matter of fact, we do have a measure of achievement motivation (272) which might be applied with a few additional assumptions to a group of people since it involves essentially content analysis of what people are thinking about. We are, therefore, in a position to test an hypothesis about the connection between achievement motivation and the rise of civilization.

Since we are treading new ground, and ground that has so often before proven treacherous when psychologists have tried to generalize their findings on individuals to society, let us review in detail how such an hypothesis comes to be formulated and how it is tested. To bring the discussion down to the level where historians and other social scientists can debate the usefulness of the approach in understanding a concrete instance of social change, we will present the methods and results of a study of the relationship between the measured level of achievement motivation and the rise and fall of ancient Greece.[1] By discussing the way methodological problems in this study were solved and by presenting its results, we hope to persuade social scientists generally that the methods of measuring human motivation recently developed by psychologists have real promise for contributing to the understanding of society and social change.

FORMING THE HYPOTHESIS

It will first be necessary to get some idea of the empirical findings which suggested an hypothesis about the relationship of achievement motivation to the growth and decline of civilizations. What, to begin with, does the psychologist mean by "achievement motivation"? The best way to answer the question is to explain how it is measured and what its effects are on people's behavior. The measure was derived by comparing the thought processes of people under the influence of achievement motivation with the thought processes of people not under its influence (272). "Thought processes" were sampled by asking subjects to write imaginative stories to pictures. It was found that they introduced more ideas of a certain kind into their stories when their motivation to achieve—to do well—was aroused than when it was not aroused.

An objective coding definition has been worked out for detecting those "ideas" with high agreement among different observers. Nearly all of the "ideas" can be classified under the heading of "desiring to do well" or "competing with a standard of excellence." This then became the scoring definition for a variable which was named technically n Achievement to distinguish it from other common-sense measures of achievement motivation such as one would get from a subjective report of how well a person said he was trying. The n Achievement score for an individual is simply a sum of the number of instances of achievement "ideas" or images and their subtypes (272), and the score for a group of individuals is some measure of central tendency (the average, the mode) of the scores of individuals who make up the group. In this way it can be determined, for example, that the average n Achievement of a group of teen-age German boys is slightly but significantly lower than the average n Achievement of a carefully matched group of American boys (278), or that American boys from lower class backgrounds have lower average n Achievement than boys from middle-class backgrounds (Ch. 35).

---

[1] Most of the data to be reported were collected by Berlew on an undergraduate research stipend from the Social Science Research Council for work on this problem with the present author and an ancient historian, Professor N. O. Brown. Berlew's report (39) contains many more details than can be included here and owes much, as does this paper, to the advice of Professor Brown.

By this time we know a good deal about how people with high n Achievement scores tend to behave as compared with people with low n Achievement scores. The "highs" work harder at laboratory tasks, learn faster (272), do somewhat better school work in high school even with I.Q. partialled out (342), and seem to do their best work when it counts for their record and not when other special incentives are introduced such as pressure from the outside to do well (Ch. 19), money prizes (Ch. 20), or time off from work (Ch. 18). They are more resistant to social pressure (272), choose experts over friends as work partners (142), and tend to be more active in college or community activities (96, 204), like risky occupations (263), perform better under longer odds (Ch. 20), and choose moderate risks over either safe or speculative ones (Ch. 21). Finally they come from families in which there has been stress on early self-reliance and mastery (Ch. 33), and oddly enough, they cannot report accurately when asked whether they have a high n Achievement or not (96, 272).

What comes out of this fairly large collection of research findings from various psychological laboratories is a composite portrait of a person with high n Achievement as someone who wants to do well at what he undertakes, who is energetic, non-conforming, and tends to be predisposed toward innovations, toward working at tasks which are not safe and traditional but involve some element of risk—perhaps because only then can he feel enough subjective satisfaction from succeeding. What would happen if a large number of such individuals collected in a given society at a given time? If our many empirical studies of their characteristics mean anything at all, we should expect that they would form a class of entrepreneurs who would as a group be extremely busy, who would tend to innovate, and who would probably be more successful than the average at whatever they attempted. There is even some further evidence that they would be particularly likely to be active and successful in business enterprises because business involves risk, personal responsibility (possibilities of credit for success), and measurable results, all of which are characteristics that appear to attract people with high n Achievement (263). We are now in a better position to understand why an hypothesis about the role of achievement motivation in the growth of civilization would seem reasonable and better able to state this hypothesis more precisely as follows: a society with a relatively high percentage of individuals with high n Achievement should contain a strong entrepreneurial class which will tend to be active and successful particularly in business enterprises so that *the society will grow in power and influence*. Or the reverse: a society with a relatively low percentage of individuals with high n Achievement will have a weak entrepreneurial class and will, therefore, tend either not to grow in influence or to lose influence if it already has it. In short, we are predicting that a high level of n Achievement in a society will *precede* its growth, and a decrease will precede its decline. The chief point to observe from this review is that the hypothesis is based, not on an inspired guess or on extended extrapolation from a single finding, but on a whole series of interrelated experimental results.

TESTING THE HYPOTHESIS

Now that the hypothesis has been stated, one might well consider first why it needs to be tested at all. Isn't it a self-evident proposition? An historian might reason like this for example: if a civilization grows, it by definition must have contained a lot of energetic people with high achievement motivation. Or if a civilization declines, of course its people must have lost some of their "zip" or "drive." What could an empirical study of the relationship add to what we already know? Even if we leave aside the obvious answer that in science there are no "of courses," that no hypothesis —however reasonable—can be accepted until it is subjected to empirical test, there are still many questions left unanswered by our common sense knowledge in this instance. For example, is it certain that it is n Achievement measured in this particular way which is associated with the rise and fall of civilization? This is by no means a self-evident proposition. We know, for example, that consciously valuing achievement is not associated with the same behavior characteristics as are n Achievement scores. Which of these two variables is associated with economic growth? And anyway, might it not be another motive altogether, such as the need for power? Furthermore, do we know on the basis of common sense whether changes in n Achievement *precede or accompany* the predicted social change? Perhaps both are the result of some third factor, and only by precise measurement of motivation level at different time intervals in the history of a civilization can we determine the sequence of events.

Psychologists might regard the hypothesis as self-evident from a different point of view. Many of them have been brought up in the tradition of the biological unity of mankind, which can safely assume that a body functions more or less in the same way regardless of time, place, or social conditions. For example, if you drink enough hemlock, you will die just as Socrates did. It doesn't matter that you are living nearly 2000 years later, that he was a Greek and you a white, middle-class American. Bodies functioned then as they do now, and so anything that you learn about the way the body functions here and now will apply to its functioning anywhere else under almost any conditions. Some of the relationships established by psychology seem to have this universal character. It was established in the 1880's and has been confirmed many times since that if a person learns something which is similar to something else he has learned previously, he will subsequently have difficulty in recalling the first thing. No psychologist has spent much time wondering whether retroactive inhibition (as this phenomenon is called) also occurs in the same way among ancient Greeks, modern bushmen, Peruvian old maids, or Orthodox rabbis. He simply assumes the universality of generalizations governing human behavior, and by and large his assumption seems to have been justified. So he might carry it one stage further in the present instance and believe that if it has been demonstrated that male, white college students with high n Achievement behave in the ways described above, it can be accepted without question that any group of other people with high n Achievement will behave in the same way whenever and wherever they happen to live. Of course, such people will be active, energetic, and more successful, just as subjects with high n Achievement in the laboratory are. Why is it necessary to test findings obtained with one group of human beings on another group of human beings since they are all human beings and we assume that they function similarly? In other words, many psychologists raised in the tradition of the biological sciences have little curiosity about testing their empirical findings under different social conditions.

But, in the case of something like achievement motivation, the problem seems much too complicated to be solved by assumption. We need concrete evidence that n Achievement has the same behavioral effects at a different time and place and among a different people as it has in our small groups of experimental subjects. We may be permitted to wonder whether its effects as discovered and reported above are not after all the result of a special combination of personality variables to be found among twentieth-century Americans. If some of those other variables change, perhaps the effect of n Achievement on something like risk taking would be quite different. When we move from the laboratory to society, we also take a big jump. Even though we might assume that n Achievement would, for example, interest people in certain moderately risky enterprises, could not certain social institutions block completely their activity in this direction? In this case n Achievement might or might not lead to the growth of a civilization, depending on other unknown social conditions. Or is it possible that if high n Achievement occurs fairly frequently, there must have been a certain linked set of other social conditions to produce the high-frequency conditions which ought also be favorable to business enterprise? In this case n Achievement would be part of a complex of factors favorable to growth, and might, therefore, have some predictive value for the society as a whole.

All of these possibilities—and many others—simply point to the absolute necessity of an empirical test of the hypothesis. Here, as elsewhere in science, the only way to refine one's theory—to cut down on the number of possible interpretations—is to collect some more data. So, in the present instance we will test whether or not the hypothesis applies to ancient Greece. It was chosen for empirical study because as a civilization it waxed and waned, because it left behind a fairly complete set of written documents to which our measures of motivation can be applied, and because it has already been so thoroughly studied that we would be in a position to profit much from the work of others.

Our hypothesis, stated more specifically in terms of ancient Greece, is as follows: the level of achievement motivation in Greece should have been high before its period of maximum growth and should have fallen significantly before the subsequent decline of the civilization. In other words, the level of n Achievement precedes and presumably determines the changes in general activity level in the culture. Presumably it takes some time for an active and energetic entrepreneurial class to build up a great civilization, though it may take less time for their children and grandchildren with lower achievement motivation to "let things go" so that the civilization collapses, especially when it is under pressure from without.

Before proceeding to a description of the specific methods of testing the hypothesis, it may be worth while to take time out to consider some objections that historians are certain to raise, particularly now that the hypothesis is to be tested on a particular civilization with which many of them are familiar in great detail. To those who really know Greek history, it may well seem the height of absurdity to try and explain the rise of Greece in terms of any single factor like n Achievement. Obviously the situation is much more complex. What if there had been no discovery of the iron which permitted individual Greeks to make their own weapons instead of relying on a central authority for bronze? What if there had been no silver mine near Athens which could be used as a regular source for money, the basis for an expanded economy? What if Cretan civilization had not decayed? What if Athenians had not regarded a man who worked with his hands, an artisan, more highly than had many of their contemporaries? What if Solon had not set up a system of laws which protected private property and thus made it more likely that people were to get the just rewards of their efforts? What if Themistocles had not tricked the

Persian fleet into attacking his disorganized forces at a time and place favorable to victory for his side? So many factors seem to have been involved in the development of Greece that it seems ridiculous to try and single out any one factor.

Historians who raise such objections might mean several things by them. They might mean, for example, that accurate and complete descriptions of what happened in history is their business, that the history of any particular event or country is unique, and that they have discharged their duty when they have described a particular historical sequence in all its uniqueness. In other words, they are simply not interested in generalizations, in attempts to compare different civilizations, or what happened in the same civilization at two different periods in time. To such people it is simply a matter of no concern whether achievement motivation, a change in climate, or any other general factor can be associated with the rise and fall of civilization. Of course not all historians fall into this group. The most notable exception in recent times is Toynbee (417), who has attempted to describe and compare the course of all civilizations in trying to arrive at generalizations about stages in their rise and fall.

But some historians go beyond a mere statement of disinterest in making generalizations. They contend that no generalizations are really possible, that any attempt to find common factors or common stages in growth—even Toynbee's—so distorts the unique qualities of the separate events classed together that the whole enterprise is not worthwhile. There are two answers to this argument. First, any generalization, any attempt to classify two events belonging in the same category, inevitably overlooks some of the unique qualities of each event. When a biologist or any man, for that matter, decides to classify two individual animals as belonging to the category of "cow," he is inevitably doing violence to some of the unique characteristics of each of them—the fact that one is lovable, the other stubborn; that one has curly horns and brown spots, the other no horns and black spots; etc. The search for generalizations means the search for similarities, and in finding similarities differences have to be overlooked. So if an historian is too disturbed by the unique qualities of events which have to be neglected in the search for generalizations, his only correct recourse is to reject an interest in generalizing and stick to concrete description. Secondly, he has no right to complain that generalizations are not possible since this is a matter which can be put to the empirical test. If generalizations are really not possible, then attempts to check specific hypotheses as in the present instance must fail. That is, it will not be possible to demonstrate that high achievement motivation precedes the rise of Greek civilization and that a drop in achievement motivation precedes its fall.

So once again our curiosity is sharpened as to whether our hypothesis will hold in the present instance and, in particular, as to how we are going to find methods for testing it empirically. Two key methodological problems must be solved: how can we measure the general level of achievement motivation in the population of ancient Greece at different time periods and how can we measure the rise and fall of Greek civilization? To begin with the first question, we cannot, as we might like to, administer our picture-story test for measuring n Achievement to a representative group of Greeks in 650 B.C., 450 B.C., and 250 B.C., and compare the mean n Achievement score at those dates. Even if we could, it might be a little difficult to decide how to make up the samples of subjects. Should they be chosen at random? If so, we would include more citizens in 650 B.C. and more slaves at the later periods. Would this be desirable? Should it contain an equal representation from city and country, and from different city-states like Sparta, Athens, or Boeotia? The task of collecting such a sample of individual protocols looks so difficult, even with modern survey research techniques, that we can almost feel relieved that it cannot be done.

Fortunately another simpler approach is possible. It involves analyzing the "fantasies" of a culture—its myths, plays, songs, and stories—at different time periods. Many other investigators have done just that in attempting to assess the themes or values of a culture. Freud popularized the method by uncovering in Sophocles' play *Oedipus, the King,* certain themes in family interrelationships which he held to be basic in all human society. Many others have followed his lead, and more recent investigators like Kardiner and Linton (205) have argued quite persuasively that the imaginative fantasies of a culture (for example, religious myths) may well reflect the basic personality structure of members of the culture. In the same tradition Wolfenstein and Leites (441) have performed analyses of all the Grade A movies produced in the United States, France, and England at a given time period in order to pick out themes which characterize a given country and differentiate it from others.

More directly relevant to our immediate problem are a study by Brown (51) which demonstrates convincingly that the content of the *Homeric Hymn to Hermes* reflects the aspirations of the rising Greek middle class toward the close of the 6th century B.C., and a study by McClelland and Friedman (274) demonstrating that the amount of n Achievement imagery in Coyote folk tales told in various American Indian tribes is significantly associated with the stress in the tribe on early independence training. The last study comes the closest to our present concern since, unlike the others mentioned, it involves actual measurement rather than intuitive judgment and tests quantitatively an hypothesis formed on the basis of prior research on the origins of the achievement motive in early independence training (272). It is particularly encouraging methodologically because the same relationship was obtained using group measures (folk tales for measuring n Achievement and ethnographic reports for measuring age of independence training), as had previously been obtained when both measures were obtained from individuals (picture-story tests for measuring n Achievement and questionnaires for measuring age of independence training).

But if we are to use the imaginative literature of ancient Greece to obtain a measure of n Achievement, all kinds of questions arise. It varies considerably in style from period to period, e.g., poetry was common early, plays in the middle period. It was written for different purposes—to celebrate victories, or the charms of love, to urge the populace on to a greater war effort, to satisfy philosophical curiosity—and yet we know on the basis of our experimental studies that the amount of achievement imagery in imaginative material depends very much on the state of mind of the person at the time he writes it (272). Furthermore, what right do we have to assume that if we take material produced by a particular author—say Hesiod, Aristotle, or Xenophon—that he is in any way representative of the general level of achievement motivation in the population at the time? That is, we assume that what he puts into his writing will reflect his personality, but how can we also assume that his personality structure is typical of others of his time? Hesiod was a farmer, Aristotle a philosopher, and Xenophon a general. Their thought patterns may have been conditioned by their position in life, by their early and different childhood training, or by other unknown factors. How can their writings be compared on the assumption that each is typical of his time?

To minimize such difficulties as much as possible, it is necessary to select samples of literature to be scored according to a strict set of criteria. In the present instance they were as follows:

1) Samples of material which were written as nearly as possible for the same purpose should be chosen to represent different time periods. Table 1 shows how this requirement was met by the samples of material used by Berlew (39). That is, Greeks at different periods in their history had similar goals in mind when writing—to describe man's relationship to his gods, to honor the dead, to describe principles for farm and estate management, etc. The form which an author chose to accomplish his purpose might be different: Hesiod

TABLE 1. SAMPLES OF LITERATURE SCORED CLASSIFIED BY LITERARY TYPE, AUTHOR, CITY-STATE, AND DATE. LENGTH OF SAMPLE REPORTED IN NUMBER OF TEN-WORD LINES.

Period	Man and His Gods	Farm and Estate Management	Public Funeral Celebrations	Poetry (Excluding Victory Odes)	Epigrams (Greek Anthology)	War Speeches of Encouragement
GROWTH 900 B.C. to 475 B.C.	Hesiod (Boeotia) fl. 720 B.C. c. 745 lines from *Thogony*	Hesiod (Boeotia) fl. 720 B.C. c. 367 lines from *Works and Days*	Homer (Ionia?) fl. 9th century B.C.? c. 353 lines from *The Iliad,* Book 23	Sappho (Ionia) fl. c. 600 B.C. c. 452 lines Alcaeus (Ionia) fl. c. 600 B.C. c. 398 lines Tyrtaeus (Sparta) fl. 7th century c. 136 lines Solon (Athens) fl. c. 600 B.C. c. 287 lines TOTAL: c. 1273 ll.	Sample composed of works of 9 Greek writers of the 6th and 7th centuries B.C. TOTAL: c. 127 ll.	Homer (Ionia?) fl. 9th century B.C.? c. 203 lines All instances of a man encouraging others to fight in *The Iliad.*
CLIMAX 475 B.C. to 362 B.C.	Aeschylus (Athens) 525-456 B.C. c. 745 lines from *Prometheus Bound*	Xenophon (Athens) fl. c. 430-354 B.C. c. 367 lines from *The Economist*	Pericles (Athens) c. 500-429 B.C. c. 353 lines from funeral oration recorded by Thucydides, Bk II, XXXV ff.	Pindar (Boeotia) fl. c. 450 B.C. c. 400 lines Simonides (Ionia) fl. c. 470 B.C. c. 400 lines Bacchylides (Ionia) fl. c. 460 B.C. c. 309 lines Timotheus (Ionia) fl. c. 375 B.C. c. 200 lines TOTAL: c. 1309 ll.	Sample composed of works of 5 Greek writers. TOTAL: c. 127 ll.	Pericles (Athens) c. 500-429 B.C. c. 198 lines from speech recorded by Thucydides, Bk II, LX ff.
DECLINE 362 B.C. to 100 B.C.	Callimachus (Cyrene) Born 310 B.C. c. 745 lines from *Hymns to the Gods*	Aristotle (Athens?) 384-322 B.C. c. 367 lines from *Economics and Politics*	Demosthenes (Athens) 384-322 B.C. c. 353 lines from *Funeral Speech*	Sample composed of works of 35 Greek poets. TOTAL: c. 1260 ll. from *Greek Anthology*	Sample composed of works of 14 Greek poets TOTAL: c. 127 ll.	Demosthenes (Athens) 384-322 B.C. c. 200 lines from *Second Olynthiac*

described man's relationship to the gods in narrative form, Aeschylus in dramatic form, Callimachus in the form of hymns to the gods. But if the comparisons are made of material written for the same purpose, regardless of style, the amount of variation in achievement imagery attributable to such an extraneous situational factor should be minimized and that attributable to internal motivational factors in the author maximized. The basis for this assumption is contemporary studies which show that temporary goal states markedly influence the amount of achievement imagery in protocols, although within limits the form of the protocol does not (see Ch. 18, 272).

Furthermore, comparisons were made of material written for several different purposes because the culture might have emphasized achievement in connection with one goal at one time—say man's relationship to the gods in the early period—and in connection with another goal at another time—say farm and estate management in the late period. If this happened to be true, we might get a very distorted picture of the average level of achievement motivation in any period by sticking within too narrowly a prescribed set of goals for which the written material was produced. The number of categories represented in Table 1 seems to be sufficiently large and varied to rule out the possibility that the average level of achievement motivation for different time periods could be attributable to any such accidents of selection.

2) The material to be scored should be chosen to reflect the attitudes and aspirations of as many individuals as possible to increase its representativeness. While it is dangerous to assume that a single author—say Hesiod—had a personality structure typical for his time, the greater the number of such authors included, the less the danger of unrepresentativeness. For example, in Table 1 nine different authors of epigrams from the early period are included as are 35 poets from the late period. Even so, the number of individuals whose works are included is small. Are we prepared to argue that a sample of the thoughts of 15 men will give us an adequate measure of the level of achievement motivation in the Greek population from roughly 900 to 500 B.C.?

Obviously credulity would be strained to the limit if these were ordinary men. But they are not. Homer and Hesiod, who are each represented in the Table twice, were extraordinary men. They captured the spirit of their times as their popularity by the sixth century attests, and, in fact, that popularity may have helped *create* the spirit of the times. In other words, popularity[2] becomes another

---

[2] We have avoided in this discussion the question of popularity *with whom*. Actually for our purposes it is popularity with an educated or an élite group that matters since we know from contemporary studies that the *n* Achievement

and probably better guarantee of representativeness than sheer numbers of authors. Homer and Hesiod were classics during the rise of Greek civilization and continued to be quoted throughout its course, though as a basis for further commentary in later centuries.[3] Why? The assumption is that they were popular because they somehow managed to express what many of the early Greeks were feeling and wanted to hear and read about. So the level of achievement motivation in Homer's and Hesiod's works should be about what the audience expected. If it had been more or less, the members of the audience would have been less satisfied with the characters in Homer's epics or with Hesiod's comments on life and the material would have been less popular. To be sure, it might have been popular *later,* but then it would be a better measure of motives and attitudes at that time.

There is still a further sense in which the Homeric material may be considered especially representative. It is thought that some of it at least was told and retold by various individuals before it finally got written down. Thus, while it was probably the work of a single author in the end, parts of it had been shaped and reshaped by many minds. Thus, as in the case of the folk tales used by McClelland and Friedman (274), the final product available for scoring is already probably the creation of many individuals in the culture rather than of the single person who tells the final tale.

3) The literature to be scored should be chosen for its imaginativeness rather than its realism. The reason for this requirement stems in part from the fact that n Achievement is at the present time measured in individuals from their imaginative stories—not, for example, from their autobiographical statements (82)—and in part from a theoretical consideration. If the material is simply a descriptive, factual account of events that occurred—for example,

---

score distribution is skewed with relatively fewer people classified as "high" than as "low" (272). Furthermore, these few tend to come more often from families which because of their energy and emphasis on mastery have achieved at least moderate status in the community (Ch. 35). Consequently, even if songs which have not come down to us were *more* popular with the masses than Homer and Hesiod, they would probably not be as representative of the motivation of the middle status group from which subjects with high n Achievement tend to be disproportionately drawn.

[3] If their popularity was as great during the decline of Greece, why should they not be taken as representative of that period? There are two arguments against this: (1) Generally in the later periods they are used as jumping-off points for modification and commentary, which often changes their emphasis and (2) while the time at which something is written is not a *guarantee* that it reflects the spirit of that time without some evidence of popular acceptance, it is certainly worth something as evidence that the work is representative of that time.

Xenophon's *Anabasis*—there will be little opportunity for the author's motives, values, attitudes, and aspirations to show themselves. The general rule is that the more external reality determines the content of verbal material, the less the material is able to reflect internal determinants like motives.

4) Finally, the number of lines of each sample of material within a given category should be roughly the same to equalize the opportunity for achievement imagery to appear. The number of ten-word lines in each sample is given in Table 1 and refers to the number of lines of English translation in the definitive Loeb Classical Library of translations of Greek literature.

Having chosen his samples of literature to be scored according to these four criteria and without having read them for content, Berlew was then ready to apply the formal system of content analysis used for determining the amount of *n* Achievement each sample contained. Since the scoring system had been developed to deal with brief written stories with a beginning, a middle, and an end, some adaptations of it were necessary to deal with such different material as epigrams, narrative poems, and plays, but the adaptations were not extensive. According to the usual procedure, once it has been determined that a story contains achievement imagery, a number of different subcategories are scored according to the way the achievement imagery is expressed. But these subcategories are defined in terms of the simple story form of material obtained from individuals and do not apply to such forms as epigrams and poems. So Berlew had to drop the subcategories and noted only each instance of achievement imagery as it appeared in a given passage.

To give a more concrete understanding of how the scoring was done, instances of achievement imagery were scored a) where "one of the characters in the story is engaged in some competitive activity in which winning or doing as well or better than others is *actually stated* as of primary concern"—e.g., "I am not ashamed of it; with this methinks I shall rather surpass the world"; b) where concern for doing well in competitive activity is not explicitly stated, but its importance is definitely implied by affective concern over goal attainment or references to the quality of instrumental acts (e.g., thoroughness, foresight) needed for success—e.g., "Do you, then, providently resolving that yours shall be honor in ages to come and no dishonor in the present, achieve both by prompt and zealous efforts"; or c) where some unique accomplishment is mentioned—e.g., "It was I and none other who discovered ships, the sail-driven wagon that the sea buffets" (after Berlew, 39).

These scoring criteria are the same as the ones used for stories written by individuals today except that one other criterion sometimes used was not applicable to the Greek material—namely, long-term involvement (272). That is, in stories written by college students in our culture it is quite possible to infer that a person wants to do well if his story contains references to a series of acts over time which involve a person's career such as studying for an exam, going on to law school, and becoming a successful lawyer. This criterion was also specific to the story-type material in our culture and did not lend itself to the Greek analysis (see Ch. 12).

It might be objected that the scoring was done of the English translations rather than of the original Greek. Might not the achievement motivation of the translator creep in to mar the results? Of course, to the extent that it does, it will tend to introduce random error into the measurement and make confirmation of the hypothesis less likely, but there is reason to believe that the use of translations did not seriously distort the picture. In the first place, each translator in the Loeb Classical Library is an expert on the author he is translating and did his best to give the literal meaning of the Greek in terms of his extensive knowledge of the style of that particular author. Thus he may have rendered the original meaning more exactly in English than it would have been understood by someone reading and scoring in the original Greek, but who did not understand a particular author as well. In the second place, a number of instances of achievement imagery scored in the English translation were checked against the Greek to make certain that the Greek would also have been scored for *n* Achievement. In no case was there a discrepancy.

The second major methodological problem is to get some measure of the rise and fall of Greek civilization. It is not so easy to solve as one might think. In the first place, was there any such thing as "Greek" civilization? To be sure, there was a collection of city-states spread all over the eastern end of the Mediterranean which shared a common language and religion, but the differences among them might appear to outweigh the similarities. Certainly the social organization, child training practices, and economic development of Sparta and Athens were markedly different. And what did the "backwoods" Macedonians have in common with the cosmopolitan Athenians? Weren't Ionians different from Dorians, who in turn differed from Aeolians? Even more serious is the fact that different city-states in Greek civilization enjoyed prosperity at quite different time periods. Generally speaking, the peak of development which occurred around Athens in the 5th century B.C. moved southeast toward Egypt in succeeding decades so that islands like Rhodes and Delos enjoyed their greatest prosperity as much as a century or so later (389). But since Athens was generally regarded then as the economic and cultural center of Greek civilization, it was decided to choose documents and economic indices as much as possible from Athens and a few other city-states of particular importance in the early period—e.g., Ionia, Boeotia, and Sparta.

The next problem is to set the time limits for the periods of growth, climax, and decline in the development of civilization in this area. Ancient historians are in full agreement that Athens reached her highest point of development in the 5th century B.C. during the "Golden Age" of Pericles. The development of Ionia, where Homer may have lived, was earlier; and that of Sparta and Boeotia, home of Hesiod, was perhaps a little later, at least to judge by their subsequent military successes over Athens. Consequently the year 475 B.C. was chosen rather arbitrarily as the precise date dividing the period of growth from the period of climax—a time that would not be too late for Ionia and Athens or too early for Sparta and Boeotia. It also corresponds to the time when Athens succeeded in organizing the League of Delos, a great maritime federation of Greek city-states which finally succeeded in decisively chasing the Persians out of the Aegean. By the end of the 5th century, Athens had lost the Peloponnesian War to Sparta and had begun her decline. Sparta in turn was defeated by the Thebans of Boeotia under Epaminondas in 369 B.C., but with his death in 362 B.C. the Thebans lost their influence to Philip of Macedon from the "backwoods" up North. So 362 B.C. was arbitrarily chosen as marking the end of the period of climax for the city-states under consideration, though it comes a little late for Athens and Ionia. These decisions set the time limits for the three periods as follows:

Period of growth—around 900 B.C. to 475 B.C.
Period of climax—475 B.C. to 362 B.C.
Period of decline—362 B.C. to around 100 B.C.

But what has happened to Alexander the Great, who expanded the Greek empire to its greatest extent in our period of "decline"— namely, from 326 B.C. to 323 B.C.? Alexander's influence was ignored in the calculations for two reasons: first, he and the influence he represented came, not from the culture area to which it had been decided to limit attention, but from a region on the periphery of Greek city-states—namely, Macedonia; second, his influence was too short-lived to be detectable in the crude economic indices that had to be used to measure the extent of the commercial power of central Greece. It can be argued, of course, that another peak of Greek economic development occurred as late as the first half of the 3rd century B.C., but it was located in a different part of Greece (Asia and the islands to the southeast), from which we had neither written documents nor adequate economic measures. This latter "burst" of activity is worth study in its own right, but we decided to concentrate on the rise and fall of central or "Athenian" Greece.

The final methodological problem is to find some quantitative index of the growth and decline of "civilization" in the area chosen for study. It might be thought that such an index is really not necessary because historians generally agree that the peak of Athens comes in the 5th century B.C. so that anything which occurs before then is in the period of growth and anything which occurs after is in the period of decline. But the difficulty arises when one tries to define more precisely just what is meant by the "peak" of a civilization. Does it refer to the extent of military influence? If so, one really has no right to deal so cavalierly with the conquests of Alexander. Does it refer to cultural achievements? If so, how can one say that Aristotle represents a "decline" over previous philosophers? Is it a matter of the sum total of achievements—political, cultural, military, and economic? If so, how is one to sum such things together and how is one to decide what constitutes a superior achievement? Are the plays of Aeschylus "superior" to the epics of Homer?

It was decided to avoid such embarrassing questions as much as possible by sticking strictly to economic development. Doing so has two further advantages: first, economic prosperity is generally the basis for many other sorts of achievement—whether cultural or military. Certainly this was true of Ancient Greece (see 70, p. 227). Second, people with high achievement motivation appear on the basis of our contemporary empirical studies to be especially attracted to business and commercial enterprises, in which they apparently have a maximum opportunity to express the behavioral characteristics associated with high n Achievement. So choosing an economic measure of the growth and decline of a civilization narrows our hypothesis to one predicting a relationship between n Achievement and Greek economic development, with the additional supposition that economic development was generally correlated with changes in other aspects of classical civilization.

The best measure of the economic prosperity of a country is probably something like income per capita, but the scarcity of data makes the computation of such an index for given periods in Greek history completely out of the question. Even cruder measures like the value or volume of foreign trade, the amount of taxation or tribute, the size of cities or market places are not available in comparable form for different time periods. So it was necessary to derive an index in an indirect way. To understand its significance, one must remember that the economic life of the Greek city-states was organized around agriculture and overseas trade. Above all, it was maritime commerce which brought prosperity; and Athens and her seaport, Piraeus, were at the very center of Greek commerce. Here it was that the bankers and middlemen, the enterprising *naukleroi* and *emporoi,* could be found in greatest numbers making arrangements with sea captains for buying or selling cargo. Here it was that some of the strictest laws were enforced governing fairness in economic dealings and the use of money, weights, and measures. Here it was that ships laden with goods from all over the Mediterranean found their chief port of call. It is small wonder that Isocrates and Xenophon could compare Piraeus to the center of the world (153, Vol. 2, p. 419).

What Athenian Greece had to trade with in addition to her entrepreneurial skills was largely surplus wine and olive oil produced on specialized farms. These she sent overseas to trade for grain from Sicily, rugs from Persia, the perfumes of Arabia, foodstuffs like dried fish and salted meat, and basic materials like iron, leather, wood, and ivory. Olive oil and wine were carried in large earthenware jars, which fortunately from our point of view did not disappear as their contents were used in the cities to which they had been transported by enterprising sea captains and traders. These jars, many of which were made by potters in or near Athens, have been found in regions all around the Mediterranean, and many of them have been dated at least within the century of their production and use. Heichelheim in his definitive study of the economic life of ancient Greece (175, Vol. 1, pp. 324-325) has listed the places where jars have been found which can be classified as belonging to the 6th, 5th, or 4th centuries B.C., centuries which correspond closely enough to the periods of growth, climax, and decline of Greek civilization.

From the location of these vase remains, Berlew reconstructed rough maps of the area within which Athenian Greece traded for each of these three centuries. In quantitative terms the area of trade roughly covered 1.2 million square miles in the 6th century B.C., 3.4 million square miles in the 5th century B.C., and 1.9 million square miles in the 4th century B.C. (39). In descriptive terms, Athenian trade in the 6th century B.C. covered an area beginning with Alexandria on the east and running in a fairly narrow band along the North shore of the Mediterranean westward to Spain. In the 5th century B.C. the area extended south to include the north shore of Africa, East into Persia and Northeast around the Black Sea. By the 4th century B.C. trade was lost with the Italian peninsula where the Roman Empire was developing, with the Black Sea area, and with much of the Persian Empire to the East.

Area of trade is, of course, not a perfect index of economic development: loss of a trading area may be compensated for by intensity of trade within the remaining area or by shifting to manufacturing; trade can be carried on over a wide area with little profit. But in the case of Athenian Greece, the figures on the extent of foreign trade agree rather well with estimates by historians of her economic position based on a consideration of all the factors involved (70, 153). Also, if this index is not accepted, there is always the problem of finding a better one—an extremely difficult task in view of the scantiness of quantitative, comparable data for the three time periods in question. So, rough though it is, the measure of the economic rise and fall of classical Greece was taken to be the area with which she traded, in millions of square miles, as determined by the location of unearthed vases in which her chief export commodities were transported. If this index seems to depend too much on commerce, it must be remembered that the prosperity of central Greece was based to a considerable extent on commerce, and that, in any case, her other economic activity of importance—namely, agriculture—depended on exporting surpluses for profits.

The way in which measures of n Achievement and of economic development were obtained has been described, but it is certain to leave experts in the history of Greece dissatisfied at a number of points. Were all of the vase remains really from central Greece? Suppose by some mischance that all of the vases sent in trade to the Black Sea area in the 4th century B.C. were either destroyed or have not yet been unearthed? Is there not the possibility that the measure of economic activity adopted might be in error by several hundred thousand square miles because of such accidents?

Similarly, not all the samples of literary material can be classified as they have been without question. There are many possible sources of error. Can Sappho really be classified as Ionian when she was born in Lesbos, a territory close to Ionian cities but probably itself Aeolian, and when she lived for a time in Sicily? Is it really right to include Tyrtaeus, a Spartan, along with Ionian and Athenian authors, when Sparta had such a unique social system and mode of bringing up its young? Or, how can Callimachus be included at all when he comes from a state (Cyrene) outside the Athenian central region and a state which at that developed much later economically than the others? Is it not incorrect to classify Xenophon as belonging to the period of climax when he flourished and wrote after Athens had begun her fall? Is the description of the funeral games in *The Iliad* really comparable to the funeral orations of Pericles and Demosthenes? One might question scoring Pericles' funeral oration anyway since it was recalled from memory by Thucydides, although this is not a serious problem since Thucydides belongs roughly to the same historical period as Pericles, and his thoughts are therefore as valuable for our purposes as whatever Pericles may originally have said.

Many more such methodological questions could be raised, but it is unnecessary to go into them and to answer them all here in detail because the answer in every case is the same. Some methodological errors have undoubtedly been made because the requirements of the research design were difficult to fill exactly with the data available. But errors, unless they are systematically made, can only make it *less likely that the hypothesis will be confirmed by the statistical test.* They introduce random variations which make it more difficult to obtain a statistically significant association. For example, suppose Xenophon really belongs to the period of decline in Athens rather than the period of climax where he was assigned. Then his written material should lower the *n* Achievement score for the climax period below what it should be according to the hypothesis. Similarly, if Callimachus should have been classified in the climax period because Cyrene prospered much later than Athens, then his material should raise the *n* Achievement score for the "decline" period over what it should be according to the hypothesis.

In other words, ancient historians who may be shocked by the arbitrary way in which authors and their works are classified together or in which crude indexes of economic development are computed should remember that all such methodological errors, if they are truly random, should only serve to decrease the likelihood that the hypothesis will be confirmed. And the possibility of a non-random bias influencing the results was minimized so far as possible (1) by choosing samples of literature to be scored without knowledge of their achievement content, (2) by making completely arbitrary selections of lines from the samples, and (3) by defining the periods of growth, climax, and decline in terms of an arbitrary, quantitative index of economic influence.

RESULTS

The results of Berlew's analysis (39) can be presented much more quickly and succinctly than his methodology. They are summarized in Table 2 and Figure 1. The number of instances of achievement imagery in a given sample of material was reduced to a common base by dividing by the number of lines in each sample and multiplying by a hundred to express the results in terms of number of instances of achievement imagery per hundred lines. For example, there were 2.01 instances of achievement imagery per hundred lines in Hesiod's *Theogony* and only .81 instances per

TABLE 2. NUMBER OF n ACHIEVEMENT IMAGES PER 100 LINES BY TYPE OF SAMPLE BY TIME PERIOD

Period	Man and His Gods	Estate Manage-ment	Funeral Cele-brations	Poetry	Epi-grams	War Speeches	Average
Growth 900-475 B.C.	2.01	3.54	7.93	2.87	4.72	7.38	4.74
Climax 475-362 B.C.	1.21	.82	5.94	.38	2.36	5.55	2.71
Decline 362-100 B.C.	.81	.00	2.54	.16	1.57	3.00	1.35

Analysis of Variance

	$df.$	Sum of Squares	Mean Square	F	p
Total..............	17	102.15			
Time period.........	2	35.03	17.52	24.0	$<.01$
Type of sample......	5	59.83	11.97	16.4	$<.01$
Interaction..........	10	7.29	.73		

hundred lines in the hymns to the gods by Callimachus. In every category of material scored, the highest incidence of achievement imagery occurs in the growth period, the next highest in the climax period, and the lowest in the period of decline. An analysis of variance shows that the decline over time summarized in the means at the extreme right of Table 1 and in Figure 1 could hardly have arisen by chance. It also shows according to expectation that the purpose for which the material is written makes a significant difference ($p < .01$) in the amount of achievement imagery which it contains. Obviously poems contain much less achievement imagery at any time period than do public funeral celebrations or war speeches of encouragement.

Figure 1 plots n Achievement score against the measure of economic development adopted. The level of n Achievement is highest in the early period when economic growth is still low. By the time economic development has reached its maximum (pushed along by the high level of n Achievement if the hypothesis is correct), the over-all level of n Achievement has dropped, foreshadowing, as hypothesized, the subsequent economic decline. In other words, so far as Ancient Greece is concerned, the hypothesis is confirmed: a high level of achievement motivation precedes economic growth, a lower level of achievement motivation precedes economic decline.

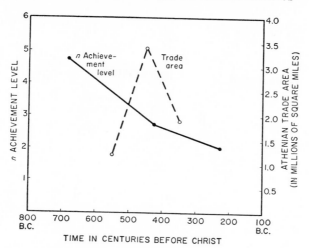

Fig. 1. Average *n* Achievement level plotted at midpoints of periods of growth, climax, and decline of Athenian civilization as reflected in the extent of her trade area (measured for 6th, 5th, and 4th centuries only).

While the quantitative evidence is clearcut, it does not by itself give a very adequate impression of the changes that were going on in the way authors dealt with achievement themes during the period under study. So some qualitative illustrations may be helpful. Consider, for example, how farm and estate management is treated by the three authors compared—Hesiod, Xenophon, and Aristotle. Their spirit is very different. Hesiod, writing in the earliest period, is very conscious of man's achievement strivings. He says, for example, "For when he that has no business looks on him that is rich, he hastens to plow and to plant and to array his house; and neighbor vies with neighbor hastening to be rich: good is this strife for man. So potter contends with potter; the hewer of wood with the hewer of wood; the beggar jealous of the beggar; the minstrel jealous of the minstrel." He takes it for granted that competition—the desire to excel—is natural to man.

Xenophon, writing in the period of climax, reports a dialogue Socrates had with Critobulus on estate management. Socrates spends a good deal of his time demonstrating how difficult it is to manage an estate properly and in fact argues that even if a man does gain something, he very often wastes it. "And so hard rule these passions over every man who falls into their clutches, that so long as they see that he is strong and capable of working, they force him to pay over all the profits of his toil, and spend it on their own desires."

In other words, what use is there in struggling to get ahead? He points out that while he, Socrates, is poor and his friend, Critobulus, is rich by the world's standards, still Critobulus is worse off than he is in many ways because Critobulus has much heavier responsibilities. To be sure, Xenophon attributes to Critobulus the desire to improve the management of his estate, and Socrates contends that one can always learn something—especially from the bad examples of others. So there is some achievement imagery present, but it is less often mentioned than in Hesiod and most of the emphasis is on the difficulty of really achieving anything of lasting worth.

In Aristotle's treatment of estate management from the period of decline, there is practically no mention of achievement striving at all. Aristotle is, as always, concerned with doing what is proper, natural, or suitable to man. A man should be careful so that others working for him will be careful, he should not give wine to his employees because it makes them insolent, he should avoid mistreating his wife as she too is part of the household. In discussing slaves he says, "Three things make up the life of a slave: work, punishment, and food. To give them food but no punishment and no work makes them insolent and that they should have work and punishment but no food is tyrannical and destroys their efficiency. It remains, therefore, to give them work and sufficient food; for it is impossible to rule over slaves without offering rewards, and a slave's reward is his food." Nothing here about potter contending with potter or the hewer of wood with the hewer of wood! No suspicion, at least so far as slaves are concerned, that food isn't everything and that a man may feel rewarded by doing a good job or by doing better than someone else. In fact, Aristotle discredits slaves who are too energetic and comes out here as elsewhere for moderation in all things: "The high spirited are not easy to control."

In other words, the quantitative data neither here nor in the other comparisons distort the impression one gets from reading the material for qualitative differences. Despite the artificial way in which numbers of instances of achievement imagery are counted up, they reflect accurately the way in which achievement themes are handled at different times. And the advantage of dealing with numbers rather than subjective impressions is, of course, that it permits a completely objective test of the hypothesis which any observer trained in the scoring system can check for himself.

FURTHER EVIDENCE

Since Berlew had both selected and scored the passages himself, it is possible that an unconscious bias in favor of the hypothesis influenced his application of the scoring system, despite its objectivity. He knew what period a given selection came from and might have tended to overlook images in some passages and to search more carefully for them in others. For this reason a second judge was trained in the scoring system who had no idea what period a selection was from and who subsequently rescored all the samples of material for n Achievement. The correlation between his scores per sample of material and Berlew's scores was $+.89$; the means for the early, middle, and late periods were 3.48, 2.10, and .48; and an analysis of variance of his data shows that the differences attributable to time periods would have arisen by chance less than one in a hundred times. The second scorer systematically noted fewer achievement images in all of the material than Berlew did, but otherwise his results were identical (39).

There is still another possibility of error: the original selection of triads of material to be scored had to be made in many instances on the basis of some knowledge of the content of the passages. Perhaps this knowledge unconsciously influenced choices in favor of the hypothesis. But two categories of comparisons could not possibly have been influenced by such knowledge—namely, the poetry and epigrams categories, samples for which were drawn largely from the Greek anthology simply by including all lines from the beginning until the quota for the particular time period had been filled. The variance associated with time period for these two categories alone (omitting the other categories as possibly biased) is still significant ($p < .01$) when tested against an estimate of error based on the interaction either in the whole Table or in the six cells of the restricted analysis (39).

But perhaps the unmistakable decline in achievement imagery over time is not its exclusive property. Perhaps almost any category one would score in these samples of material would show the same decline. Berlew also actually scored for a number of other "value orientations" (taken largely from F. Kluckhohn, 216), results for the most important of which are presented in Table 3. For none of these categories does an analysis of variance performed as in Table 2 yield significant trends over time, and for none of them except "future orientation" does even the same decline over time appear as in the case of achievement imagery. In Table 3 a somewhat different and less adequate test of significance is therefore reported, based on the assumption that the total number of instances of a given category should be equally distributed over the three time periods.

If such an assumption is valid, a Chi-square test can be computed which will estimate the likelihood that the obtained distribution

TABLE 3. FREQUENCIES OF SELECTED VALUE ORIENTATIONS FOR
TOTAL SAMPLES FROM EACH TIME PERIOD
(after Berlew, 39)

Period	Future Orientation*	Man over Nature	Impulse Control	Ascribed Status
Growth 900-475 B.C.	136	33	37	32
Climax 475-362 B.C.	99	27	37	16
Decline 362-100 B.C.	56	36	11	32
Chi-square	68.2	1.3	16.01	6.34
p	<.01	insig.	<.01	<.05

* Number of future minus past references plus 100.

of frequencies deviates from the theoretically equal distribution by
an amount which could have arisen by chance only infrequently.
Actually, since many of the observations come from the same passage by the same author in each cell, they are not independent, the
theoretical distribution cannot be accurately estimated, and the Chi-
square test is not strictly speaking legitimate; but it has nevertheless been included to give some idea, however crude, of the significance of the results. It is interesting to note that the category
which comes closest to giving the same results as were obtained for
achievement imagery is "future orientation" because Zatzkis has
shown (272) that subjects with high n Achievement in a college
population today tend to use significantly more future tenses and
anticipatory clauses. So it looks as if "future orientation" might
well be a corollary of n Achievement, which shows the same declining
trend over time.

On the other hand, a value orientation like "man over nature"
shows no trends, despite the fact that F. Kluckhohn and others
have argued (216) that it goes with an individualistic achievement
orientation in our time. Certainly one would think that the more
achievement-oriented a person was, the more likely he would be to
believe that he could control nature rather than be controlled by
it, but the results in this case do not support the hypothesis, however reasonable it may sound. "Impulse control", or the tendency
to stress self-discipline as a means to achievement, might similarly
be thought of as a prerequisite for achievement, but it is not
mentioned in our material more often during the period of growth
than during the period of climax. Actually two forms of impulse
control are perhaps unfairly lumped together in this score. During

Measures of Motivation in Social Studies 543

the period of growth most of the references to impulse control had to do with ascetic self-discipline for the purpose of character-building, while during the period of climax the references were to moderation or avoiding excess. Both types of impulse control tended to be mentioned less often during the period of decline.

The results for "ascribed status" are, theoretically, perhaps the most interesting of all. Included under this category were all references to status or rank based on factors over which the individual had no control—such as sex, age, family connections, and physique. The opposite of ascribed status is achieved status, in which rank is accorded in terms of what the individual has actually done to merit it. To speak in very general terms, during both the periods of growth and decline, Athenian Greece was more "authoritarian" (e.g., power more concentrated in the hands of a few) in political and social structure than it was during the period of climax when it was more "democratic" (e.g., power more dispersed). In authoritarian social systems rank is more commonly based on ascribed factors such as birth order and lineage than in a democracy where, in theory at least, anyone can achieve high rank by his own efforts, even though he may be a younger son or the son of an artisan. So the results for "ascribed status" appear to reflect fairly accurately the way the social system was organized in Greece at the three time periods in question. It is mentioned frequently in the period of growth, less often in the democratic period of climax, and with increased frequency during the period of decline when Greece became less democratic again.

What is especially noteworthy is that in this case the scored value orientation simply *reflects* political and social changes and does not *precede* them, as in the case of *n* Achievement. In short, not all the elements in what might be thought of as an "achievement value complex" appear simultaneously in the thought patterns of members of a society. In this instance, a case can be made for believing that the appearance of high *n* Achievement—while the society was still fairly autocratic and evaluating people in terms of, not achieved, but ascribed, status—was the critical factor in moving the society toward a democracy in which status was awarded on the basis of actual achievement. At any rate, it is well documented (51, 70, 153) that the rising entrepreneurial class of businessmen did force a change in the social system and it is they who, if our current empirical evidence is to be believed, were most probably the ones with high *n* Achievement.

So, the evidence, as far as it goes, is that among the variables measured changes in achievement motivation and only achievement motivation or its correlate, future orientation, foreshadowed both the rise and fall of Greece in this sample of material. Yet one can still ask for more evidence despite all the tests of statistical significance because a conclusion about a whole civilization is after all being based on the analysis of 18 samples of literary material which just might have been chosen with extraordinary good luck. Fortunately a quite independent confirmation of the main result is available. Aronson has recently discovered that subjects with high n Achievement "doodle" in characteristically different ways from subjects with low n Achievement and has cross-validated his findings with several samples of male college students (Ch. 17). He has developed an objective scoring system for the way lines, shapes, and space are used when spontaneous "doodles" are produced by subjects. He found that he could apply with very little modification the scoring definitions for the shape variables and for use of space to the designs appearing on Greek vases as photographed in the *Corpus Vasorum Antiquorum.* He selected his sample of vases to be scored from Cambridge Fascicules 1 and 2 (Great Britain Fascicules 6 and 11) and from Reading Fascicule 1 (Great Britain Fascicule 12), including, from the first two Fascicules for the time periods in question, all whole vases which were clearly enough marked to be scored and contained at least one of the shapes associated with high or low n Achievement, and enough such vases from the third Fascicule to bring the total to over 100 vases for the first two time periods. The number of vases from the third period of decline is only 34, but the results for this period are less crucial for testing the hypothesis that designs characteristic of high or low n Achievement foreshadow economic growth or decline respectively.

Table 4 presents the results of his scoring the vases[4] for four of the design characteristics he had found to be associated with n Achievement. It doesn't include data for a fifth characteristic—namely, the number of discrete minus the number of fuzzy or overlaid lines—because this distinction could not be made with vase designs. Since the details of the scoring system cannot be given in full here, it will perhaps be enough to indicate that by "diagonals" he meant lines that were at least 15 degrees off the vertical or horizontal and that by "S-shapes" he meant lines that reversed direction but did not continue to undulate. If either of these "forms" or the "multiple wave" form appeared in a group of two or more, they were scored twice but no more, and as many sides of a vase were scored as were photographed in the *Corpus.* Both "diagonals" and "S-shapes" are characteristic of male college students with high n Achievement and just like the n Achievement scores based on literary productions, they appear most frequently in 6th century B.C. Greece, next most frequently in the 5th

---

[4] The scoring was of course done "blindly"—i.e., without knowledge until afterward of the period to which a vase belonged.

Measures of Motivation in Social Studies   545

TABLE 4. PERCENTAGE OF VASES FROM DIFFERENT TIME PERIODS WITH
MORE THAN THE MEDIAN NUMBER OF VARIOUS DESIGN
CHARACTERISTICS ASSOCIATED WITH n ACHIEVEMENT

		Characteristic of			
		High n Achievement		Low n Achievement	
Period	Number of Vases	Diagonals 4 or More	S-Shapes 3 or More	Multiple Waves 2 or More	Unused Space at Bottom 12% or More
Growth 900-500 B.C.	103	61.2%	68.9%	57.3%	35%
Climax 500-400 B.C.	105	41.9%	47.6%	54.3%	64.8%
Decline 400-100 B.C.	34	14.7%	14.7%	67.6%	47.1%
Chi-square		23.51	31.63	1.90	18.58
p		<.01	<.01	NS	<.01

century B.C., and least frequently in the 4th century B.C. The Chi-square tests show that such differences over time could hardly have arisen by chance. The results for these categories strongly support the hypothesis that n Achievement was high early and declined steadily.

If the S-shape continues to undulate, it becomes a "multiple wave," a characteristic appearing significantly more often in the doodles of contemporary college males with low n Achievement. No significant trend for this characteristic was found for the vase designs, although it does most often appear as predicted during the period of decline.

Since Aronson had found (Ch. 17) that subjects with low n Achievement tended to fill up less of the space at the bottom of a piece of paper with doodles, he also measured the amount of unused space at the bottom of the Greek vases, dividing in each instance by the vertical height of the vase in the photograph to get the *proportion* of space that was unfilled. As in the case of "diagonals" and "S-shapes," the proportion of space unused followed the n Achievement trend in Greek history quite closely for the first two periods. It was lowest in the period of growth (only about $1/3$ of the vases left 12% or more of the bottom blank) and highest in the period of climax (about $2/3$ of the vases left 12% or more of the bottom blank). The sample of vases for the third period is so small that with only one measure coming from each of them, the shift back toward more use of space cannot be taken to mean very much.

In short, on the whole, the results in Table 4 provide independent support for the hypothesis: the signs of high n Achievement are most frequent (more diagonals and S-shapes, less unused space) in the period of growth and significantly less frequent in the period of climax. In case the findings should appear too mysterious or at least too flatly empirical, it is fairly easy to give them a reasonable interpretation. The designs the person with high n Achievement makes are not completely meaningless: what they suggest is that in movement as in everything else he is energetic (tends to use up space, prefers "dynamic" diagonals to static verticals and horizontals) and likes variety or tends to innovate (prefers S-shapes to redundant multiple waves). Furthermore, the functional similarity between painting vases and making doodles is greater than one might at first suspect. The artist is as free as the "doodler" in many respects to make whatever designs he likes. For example, in making the figure of a man, he may want to outline the inside of an earlobe. In doing so he is producing a "doodle" which, so far as reality is concerned, might just as well be an "S-shape" or a "multiple wave." So whether he gives it an extra twist or not depends, as a "doodle" does, on an inner motivational state which has established his preference for variety or redundancy. As a matter of fact, S-shaped earlobes in vase paintings are more common in the period of the growth of Greek civilization than in the period of climax!

Finally, as with the verbal material, the quantitative results do not appear to distort seriously the qualitative generalizations art historians make in describing the styles of vase designs in these different periods. The vases of the early period are frequently described as having a geometric or dynamic quality in which diagonals, stylized figures, and S-shaped grapevines are frequent (i.e., black-figured style). During the period of climax the style is characterized by a striving for balance, harmony, naturalness in presenting figures, and a tendency to redundancy (i.e., red-figured style).

DISCUSSION

The fact that the empirical findings confirm the hypothesis tends to support all the assumptions that went into testing it—namely, 1) that n Achievement level for a culture can be estimated from popular literary or artistic productions of the culture; 2) that when n

Achievement level is estimated for Greeks living 2500 years ago by applying the same scoring systems to verbal or artistic materials developed on contemporary American males, n Achievement so measured seems to have had the same effect on the behavior of ancient Greeks as one would have predicted from contemporary empirical studies—that is, higher n Achievement then as now appears to have made people more active, energetic, and enterprising, particularly in the economic sphere; 3) that the number of people with high n Achievement (e.g., the entrepreneurial class) in early Greece was sufficiently large to overcome whatever social and environmental obstacles to development there may have been and to produce marked economic and cultural growth.

The last assumption is much too simply stated, of course; n Achievement is not an isolated phenomenon which should be thought of as separate from and acting on the social and political environment rather than being acted on by it. Certainly n Achievement should not be conceived of as some sort of a "first cause," which if strong enough will overcome all obstacles. What is more correct is to think of n Achievement as an outcome of one social institution (the family) which has far-reaching effects on other social institutions (economics and politics). But economics and politics in turn, of course, affect family life so that wherever one picks up the causal chain, it is a circle, or more properly, a spiral, if one takes into account the fact that the mutual influences cannot occur simultaneously but only over time through succeeding generations.

To be more specific, suppose we apply some more of our knowledge about the achievement motive based on contemporary studies to the situation in Ancient Greece, since the application of such information has already been so successful. Do we know anything that would account either for the initial high level of achievement motivation in early Greece or for its subsequent decline? One empirical study has demonstrated that sons whose parents stress early independent mastery of whatever problems life presents tend to develop high n Achievement (272). Furthermore, early self-reliance training tends to occur more often cross-culturally in nomadic or hunting cultures, where survival may often depend on early mastery by males of certain skills.[5] Finally, according to Whiting and Child, early independence training is significantly associated with early weaning (432), and early weaning is associated with high protein content of the diet.[5] That is, the higher the protein content of the diet, the sooner the mother can safely wean her child since he is no longer dependent on the protein supply in her milk.

[5] Personal communication of research results from Professors Irvin Child and J. W. M. Whiting.

The Achaeans, who invaded the Greek peninsula sometime around 2000 B.C. and started Greek civilization on its upward course, both were nomadic, raising cattle and horses (153, Vol. 1, p. 74), and had plenty of meat to eat, making early weaning and independence training possible. So they possessed the background characteristics which have been found to be associated with early self-reliance training, but more than this cannot be said at the present time. There have doubtless been other such cattle-raising tribes which have not developed early self-reliance training and high n Achievement, and the difficulty of finding out the real level of their achievement motivation before Homer is very great in view of the scarcity of written records. The only possibility is to score for n Achievement vase designs produced in earlier centuries by the various subcultures that contributed to the rise of Greek civilization (Achaean, Dorian, Cretan, etc.). This should settle which group contributed the most in n Achievement and might even shed light on the sources of n Achievement by permitting a comparison of the background characteristics of groups high and low in it.

It is easier to find an explanation for a decrease in early self-reliance training in the subsequent history of Greece. Democratic though the Greeks were in many ways, they never thought of extending their democracy to slaves. Slaves had probably been common in the households of great Mycenaean and other early Greek chieftains as the legitimate spoils of war (see, for example, Odysseus' nurse mentioned by Homer); but the growing group of middle-class entrepreneurs did not become wealthy enough to purchase and maintain slaves in large numbers until toward the end of the 6th century B.C. (70, pp. 199-201; 228-229). In the period of greatest prosperity during the 5th century B.C., the son of a well-to-do Athenian family typically had a nurse of his own from birth onward to care for his wants (153, Vol. 2, p. 582) and a pedagogue, literally to walk him to school, to stay there with him, and to bring him home (153, Vol. 2, p. 591). It does not take much imagination to suppose that the nurse and the pedagogue between them, both being normally slaves and dependent on the favor of the family, would scarcely be the ones to insist on early self-reliance for the child. On the contrary, their very existence at his side tended to make the child more dependent on others for a longer period of time than perhaps his father had been, whose father had not, in turn, been rich enough to support so many slaves.

Much has been written about the way slavery undermined Greek economic life by making labor appear degrading (*banausic*) and by reducing local markets for goods through low wages (70, p. 200), so that in a sense there is nothing original in pointing to slavery as a source of Greece's subsequent difficulties. What is new is that there is now evidence for another way in which slavery undermined Greek life by causing "character" to "degenerate." It enabled parents to provide slaves to care for their children, which deprived the children of the early self-reliance training the parents may themselves have received in less wealthy homes. And certainly by the 5th century B.C. the use of slaves was widespread in households throughout Athens, so that the decrease in self-reliance training should have been general rather than restricted to a few chieftains as in earlier generations. Estimates differ as to the number of slaves in Athens, but there were probably almost as many as there were freemen and their families, although contemporary Greeks were apt to put the figure much higher (153, Vol. 2, p. 228).

It is tempting to speculate that one reason why practically all great civilizations of the past have declined after a few generations of "climax" is because families have nearly always used their increased prosperity to turn over the rearing of their children to slaves or other dependents who "spoil" the children or keep them dependent too long. For a time a civilization may draw its leaders with high n Achievement from the periphery, from portions of the society which have not as yet become wealthy enough to support slaves, but if prosperity becomes too general, the effect may be to diminish the number of children with high n Achievement below some critical point needed to maintain the civilization.

Such theorizing about the causes of changes in the level of achievement motivation in Greece has one important theoretical value: it serves to put n Achievement level back in its social context. Thus, we have argued that the initial high level of motivation was the function of the way the early Greeks earned their living and that its decline was at least in part a function of a general prosperity and a social system which permitted and encouraged the use of household slaves. So while n Achievement modifies society, it is itself also modified by society. But the chain of influence is more of a spiral than a circle, with early family life providing the means by which changes are mediated over generations in time. That is, social and economic conditions influence the extent to which one generation provides early self-reliance training for its children.

Early or late self-reliance training presumably generates a relatively fixed characteristic in the children, n Achievement, which determines the energy and success with which they will start enterprises, particularly economic ones, that in turn will modify social and economic conditions which may affect the rearing of the next generation. The process has been described as if it occurs in three generations, but of course in actuality it may take much longer. Child-rearing attitudes are not so easily changed. Parents try to raise their children as they were raised, slaves or no slaves. Economic wealth, no matter how high the n Achievement, cannot be built up for a whole society in one generation. But the sequence of interaction between man and society should be as described no matter how many generations it takes, if the general interpretation of the results obtained so far is correct.

Whatever their final interpretation, it is to be hoped that the presentation of a study of the contribution of achievement motivation to the rise and fall of Greece has succeeded in making a case for the value of applying recently developed methods of measuring human motivation to the study of society and social change. The methods used for assessing the level of achievement motivation from either literary or artistic products are completely general and can be applied to any civilization, including our own. They might shed light on the rise and fall of other great civilizations, centered in Rome, Venice, or Central America. It is not even a handicap that Mayan records cannot as yet be deciphered since their art can be scored by the Aronson technique. The methods might be used to discover which countries are today on the verge of economic development if the level of achievement motivation can be taken as a sign of impending change.

Furthermore, objective scoring systems have also been devised for motives other than n Achievement (Chs. 13, 14). What patterns of changes in group level of n Power or n Affiliation would appear if the Greek material was scored for these motives? Theories of economic development such as Max Weber's hypothesis that the rise of capitalism in the West was associated with Protestantism can be explored by applying methods for scoring n Achievement and other motives to Catholic and Protestant writings or to literary material produced by predominantly Catholic or Protestant countries. Certainly one would expect that n Achievement level among Protestant groups should have been higher if the line of evidence presented in this paper is correct and if Weber is correct in arguing that Protestants were more active economically. Certainly the number of interesting and important social and historical questions on which these methods for measuring the motivation level of groups can shed light is almost limitless. Whatever results they turn up, and however they are interpreted, the methods themselves should provide the social scientist with an important new tool for collecting data on which to base generalizations about the behavior of man in society.

The existence of such a tool may furthermore redress a rather one-sided interpretation of history which received its chief impetus from Darwin about a century ago. By focusing attention on the role of the environment in natural selection, Darwin set the tone for nearly all social scientists—historians, anthropologists, sociologists, psychologists—who have tended since to think of man as *reacting to* the demands and pressures of the environment rather than as actively molding and reshaping it to suit his needs. The tendency to interpret human history in terms of the external demands of the environment has also been strong because the characteristics of the environment have until now been more measurable than the characteristics of man or any given group of men. So Huntington, using quantitative records of temperature and rainfall (191), could attempt, for example, to make a case for civilization arising only in temperate zones, and Toynbee (417) could attempt to explain the rise of civilization as a response to a challenge from an environment which was neither too great nor too small.

Despite his strong, activist Protestant emphasis and his contention that no simple explanation of the course of civilizations in terms of environment can work, Toynbee remains essentially a Darwinian in viewpoint by starting his explanations with a description of the environment rather than with the characteristics of the men who inhabit it. For example, he argues that the climatic and psychological challenge of Northern Ireland was just right to evoke the maximum response from the Scots who came down from their highlands, whereas the Appalachian fastnesses of North America were too much for the same group of people and destroyed their initiative. In theorizing in this way he is still thinking in terms of external factors as a place to start because he can to some extent measure and describe them. He recognizes that the psychological response to the environmental challenge from without is of great importance but rejects the notion that it can ever be measured. "This unknown quantity is the reaction of the actors to the ordeal when it actually comes. These psychological momenta, which are inherently impossible to weigh and measure, and therefore to estimate scientifically in advance, are the very forces which actually may decide the issue when the encounter takes place" (417, p. 68).

But Toynbee has spoken too soon; it is always dangerous to predict in advance what science will be unable to do. Precisely what this paper purports to demonstrate is that "these psychological momenta" can be scientifically measured and estimated in advance so that the reaction of the civilization to a challenge can, to some extent, be predicted. So the theoretical significance of the new methods of measuring human motivation is that they open up the possibility that man's contribution—or more precisely, the contribution of a group of men, a culture—to history can be estimated independently of the contribution of the environment, the characteristics of which have been more easily measured or described for some time. What will result, let us hope, will not be a psychological interpretation of history —which would be as one-sided as economic and other environmentalist interpretations have been—but a genuinely balanced interpretation in which generalizations will be based on established empirical relationships among either psychological or environmental variables, both of which we are now in a position to measure.[6]

---

[6] See Ch. 22 for a theory of achievement motivation which begins to take account of the influence of *both* "psychological momenta" and "environmental challenge." Editor.

PART SIX

Analysis of the Thematic Apperceptive Measuring Instrument

THIS SECTION points toward the improvement of thematic apperceptive indices of motivation. The studies which follow acknowledge that we are at a very primitive level in our understanding of the factors which influence the characteristics of the "thought sample" obtained from stories told about pictures. They strive for clarification of the issues and refinement of ideas about what the manifest content of thematic apperception actually reveals. The studies included deal specifically with the measures of motivation presented in this volume. Lindzey and his co-workers (236, 237) have examined similar questions in a more general survey of the uses of thematic apperception.

The first four studies try to isolate the separate effects of approach and avoidance motives on thematic apperception. The problem of approach-avoidance conflict, dealt with by Clark in studies of sexual motivation, is a general one. Our earliest studies of achievement motivation suggested the possibility that the method of content analysis used to assess the strength of achievement motive might be confounding indices of a positive motive to achieve and indices of fear of failure, an avoidance tendency. The papers by McArthur; Moulton; Scott; and Clark, Teevan, and Ricciuti illustrate different approaches to the problem of isolating approach and avoidant motives.

The initial paper of the second set of four, by the editor, provides a general summary of the facts to be explained in an analysis of the thematic apperceptive instrument as it has been employed in this research. The instrument is then examined within the context of the theory of motivation which has been developed. An attempt is made to define in theoretical terms the "ideal" test situation for the assessment of any motive.

The three investigations which follow deal with the role of pictures and test situation in the assessment of motives. These studies by Jacobs; Birney; and Haber and Alpert illustrate the methods that

553

are being employed to answer questions concerning factors that influence the content of thematic stories and are so often glossed over or completely ignored in the applied use of thematic apperception.

We conclude with a survey by Reitman and Atkinson of other methodological issues. It provides at least some tentative conclusions concerning the powers and limitations, revealed in this research on motivation, of the thematic apperceptive measuring instrument.

These papers ask many more questions than they answer. They represent, we hope, a springboard for a renewed and more sophisticated attack, now guided by the experience of a decade's work, on the original problem—the effect of experimental arousal of motivating states on thematic apperception.

CHAPTER 38

....

The Effects of Need Achievement on the Content of TAT Stories: A Re-Examination*

AS ONE RESULT of a series of studies of the projection of inner needs and especially of need Achievement, McClelland (Ch. 3) has stated that increases in the narrator's need Achievement led to his telling stories containing more:

1. Mention of mastery
2. Failures by the hero
3. Acts to overcome failure
4. Statements of the need for mastery by the hero
5. Press hostile to mastery
6. Wishes for mastery by the hero
7. Anxiety over mastery by the hero
8. Mastery images in the story, especially vocational ones.

We infer that McClelland postulates at least four kinds of relationships between the needs possessed by his storytellers and the needs they attribute to their story heroes. These relationships include:

a. Heroes with needs like the narrator's
b. Heroes with needs opposite to the narrator's
c. Heroes with needs complementary to (e.g., likely to stimulate) the narrator's
d. Heroes with needs instrumental to the narrator's.

---

* Reprinted by permission of author and publisher from *The Journal of Abnormal and Social Psychology,* 1953, **48**, 532-536. Copyright 1953 by the American Psychological Association, Inc.
[1] This paper was made possible as a part of the research program of the Department of Hygiene, Harvard University.

Murray[2] has labelled the first three Self, Contrast, and Complementary Projection. The fourth is labelled Instrumental Projection by McClelland.

That an increase in strength of need should set off all these processes is quite possible; nature offers causal patterns of far greater complexity. Yet such a conceptualization lacks parsimony. Might we not explain McClelland's data with a simpler, intellectually "prettier" paradigm?

TAT workers have traditionally and successfully interpreted the test in terms of Self Projection, which equates the narrator with his story people, need for need and press for press. For instance, narrators who had been dominated (or who felt themselves to be dominated) were expected to create heroes who were also dominated. If the narrator's response to domination was to develop ambition, then the story hero was expected to respond to press Dominance by need Achievement. We had:

Narrator: p Dom → n Ach
Hero: p Dom → n Ach

Then we spoke of a "theme," as we do in the title of the test.

In short, the kind of projection that we would like to invoke as an alternative hypothesis to McClelland's view is "Thematic Self Projection." We thereby greatly simplify the relation between narrator and hero, reducing the possibilities from four to one. Our one postulate remains in the classical tradition of TAT analysis.

But will such a simple, classical theory explain McClelland's data? We think it will. His items 1, 4, 6, and 8 (increased mentions of and desires for mastery) are already apparent as Self Projection and need no further explanation. Item 2, the increased failure of the hero, is the critical problem. A statement that narrators whose need Achievement has increased will therefore tell more stories in which the heroes fail is in direct contravention to our hypothesis of "Thematic Self Projection." Its explanation lies hidden in McClelland's experimental design: in order to "increase need Achievement" he made his subjects (Ss) fail! So we know *two* things about his narrators: their ambition and their most recent press. That press, as our hypothesis predicts, they projected directly into their Thematic Apperception Tests.

They also projected actions to overcome failure, but that need not surprise us. If these Ss were even a usually ambitious sample of middle-class, success-culture, doing-oriented college students, many

---

[2] Murray, H. A. Mimeographed notes for Social Relations 277, Harvard University, 1951-52.

of them must have been feeling a strong need to "do something" about that recently imposed failure. They would have been living out the theme:

p Failure → n Counteraction

and that theme (or segments of it emphasized by their various personalities) would be projected into their tests.

Similarly, we can argue that stories including both press hostile to mastery and anxieties over mastery were to be expected as Self Projections of a recently induced press and state. Indeed, theoretical interest may attach to McClelland's experiment just because he demonstrated how completely the TAT is responsive to recent and psychodynamically "superficial" needs.

PREDICTIONS FROM SELF PROJECTION HYPOTHESIS

This alternative conceptualization of McClelland's experiment leads to very different predictions from his about what would happen should his list of eight items be applied as an index of need Achievement in another experimental setting. McClelland implies that wherever need Achievement is maximized, *all eight* variables will increase in the stories. We suggest that if need Achievement is maximized without S having any experience of failure, only McClelland's points 1, 4, 6, and 8 (mentions of and desires for mastery) will be affected. Contrariwise, we suggest that if failure is induced in Ss who are low on need Achievement, McClelland's point 2 (failure by the hero) will consequently be high!

In short, we predict that McClelland's eight items will not covary, except where need Achievement and press Failure happen to occur simultaneously in the conditions of the experiment.

Conditions that separate ambition and failure occur in the American college. There, ambitious students regularly achieve beyond their predicted "aptitude" by dint of hard work; such "overachievers" will not usually fail. They therefore form a ready-made experimental group. Similarly, a group that is presumably low in need Achievement but has not yet tasted failure exists in those "underachievers" who have been rewarded by satisfactory grades. A third group, containing failures who came well endowed with scholastic aptitude, is likely to run low in need Achievement; the mechanics of college administration almost guarantees us this. Such a tripartite division is not so perfect as one might make in the laboratory, yet it should roughly serve. A legitimate demand on any theory is that it work in practical application. If it doesn't, we at least ought to ask why.

558   *The Thematic Apperceptive Measure*

TEST OF SELF PROJECTION HYPOTHESIS WITH OVER- AND UNDERACHIEVERS

We gave our alternate version of the effect of need Achievement a practical trial at predicting the stories told by Harvard freshmen who were academic over- and underachievers. Two samples of entering classes had been invited to "test the test" in the course of the development of a group instrument, the Visual Impressions Test, that included five self-administered TAT pictures. We can argue on both theoretical and empirical (120) grounds that the written stories thus collected are validly interpretable by the usual TAT principles. The pictures used were:

1   The violin picture
4   Young couple and "pin-up"
6BM   Young man and old lady
14   Silhouette in opening
7BM   Young man and old man

Academic overachieving and underachieving were measured by the difference between a man's Predictive Rank List, an effective measure of scholastic aptitude based on college board scores and preparatory school records that was developed by Harvard's Office of Tests (110), and his attained Rank List, based on his June grades. Following the Office of Tests usage, the boy was classified as an overachiever if his June grades attained one full rank above that predicted for him, but if his grades fell a full rank below prediction he was labelled an "underachiever." The middle class, which was accurately predicted, was put in a neutral category.

TABLE 1. PERCENTAGE OF TESTS "HIGH" ON MCCLELLAND VARIABLES AMONG ACADEMIC OVER- AND UNDERACHIEVERS, BOTH SAMPLES*

Variable	Over-achievers ($N = 41$)	Neutral Achievers ($N = 126$)	Under-achievers ($N = 32$)	Total Occurrence ($N = 199$)
1. Mastery central........	32%	24%	19%	25%
2. Hero fails.............	15%	18%	19%	18%
3. Acts to overcome.......	12%	16%	19%	16%
4. Hero states need†.......				
5. Obstacles..............	15%	19%	13%	17%
6. Hero wishes............	24%	26%	13%	24%
7. Hero anxious..........	12%	21%	9%	17%
8. Imagery in tale‡........	61%	50%	29%	53%

* A test was "high" on a variable if that variable was scored in two of the five tales, except that three of the five were required for variable 1.
† Not tested.
‡ Tested in second sample only.

Need Achievement: A Re-Examination 559

Table 1 shows the results. It gives the percentages of overachievers, predictable achievers, and underachievers telling sets of five stories that were high in each of McClelland's list of characteristics. Item 4, the hero's stating his need for achievement, did not occur in this material. The remaining items show the predicted trends. We may be encouraged that only items 1 (mention of mastery), 6 (wishes for mastery), and 8 (mastery images), for which we predicted increases, vary in the predicted directions, while no trends occur in the remaining items. This outcome is more like our predictions than like McClelland's hypothesis that all eight items should reflect need Achievement.

The trends were small, however. Only item 8 (mastery images) was statistically significant. And they are unreliable. For example, mastery was the theme central in .41 of the tests written by boys from our later sample (N = 101) but in only .08 of the tests collected in the earlier (N = 98).

Why this shift? Most likely, there may have been an accident of sampling. Although neither sample differed significantly from the composition of the class it represented, the two samples differ from each other. More boys who prepared for college in an Eastern private preparatory school are found in the earlier sample, while more boys who prepared in public high schools are found in the later one. Could that factor underlie the great difference observed in the frequency of achievement tales?

It should. "Public school boys" at Harvard come from the middle class and possess those values, attitudes, and needs prescribed for them by rearing in the American "success culture." Many of Harvard's "private school boys" come, by contrast, from the Eastern upper class and have been reared to regard academic achievement as less important than certain other kinds (216) of approved behavior.

It would seem, then, that our ethnocentric assumption that college overachievers are high in need Achievement was demonstrably applicable chiefly to the public school group. It will be the *overachievers among public school boys* who are most frequently and fiercely driven by ambition. This proposition has been empirically demonstrated (255) elsewhere. Our statistics, therefore, must be rerun, using only the public school group.

When this re-examination is made, no new trends emerge, but there is increased clarity in the trends. Statistical significance is reached by item 1 (mention of mastery) and item 8 (mastery images). Item 6 (hero's wishes) improves, though it does not reach statistical significance. The combined result, shown in Table 2, increasingly confirms our alternative theory about the properties of TAT stories told by narrators who are high in need Achievement.

TABLE 2. PREDICTED TRENDS IN PUBLIC SCHOOL OVERACHIEVERS

Variable	Over-achievers	Neutral Achievers	Under-achievers	p
1. Mastery central.......	46%	25%	9%	.02
6. Hero wishes..........	31%	26%	18%	not significant
8. Vocational images*.....	69%	41%	0%	<.01

* Tested on second sample only.

TEST OF SELF PROJECTION HYPOTHESIS WITH COLLEGIATE FAILURES

One proposition of McClelland's was markedly different from our alternative formulation: McClelland stated that an increase in need Achievement led to an increase in stories of failure by the hero. We have already seen that in at least one presumably mastery-minded group, overachievers, this proposition was false. We have further proposed that the appearance of failures in the stories collected by McClelland and his collaborators was an artifact resulting from the induced failures that were part of his experimental procedure. We therefore suggest that high incidence of failure can be found in the stories told by members of any group who have had a recent experience of failing, even if the group is demonstrably *low* on need Achievement.

Such a group is provided by student referrals that the author has tested in the course of his duties as psychologist to Harvard's student health service. From the nature of the University's administrative machinery, two statements can be made about students who come for testing. First, they all have had the subjective experience (and many the administrative label) of failure. Second, they are nearly all low on need Achievement.

For this failure group, McClelland's theory would predict low scores on all eight variables. Our alternative theory of Self Projection would predict low scores on items 1 (mention of mastery), 6 (wishes for mastery by hero), and 8 (mastery images in stories) but a high score on item 2 (failures by hero). Since these students have not taken constructive action to ameliorate their problems, the theory of Self Projection would also predict low scores for this failure group on item 3 (acts to overcome failure). As to the other items on McClelland's list, it does not seem to the writer that there are sufficiently valid reasons for assuming that this group will systematically vary one way or another.

All except one of our predictions about the failure group come true. Item 2 (failure by the hero) is high in one-third of these tests, but only in one-sixth of those collected from the nonfailing samples. What is more, failure is a high variable in *every one* of the tests from this group that mentions mastery at all!

On the other hand, mastery is a central theme (item 1) in only one of these "failure" tests, which is also the only one in which vocational images (item 8) are frequent. Nor do these failing heroes created by failing narrators very often restrive (item 3). They do so, as predicted, less frequently than the nonfailure narrators, although p for this difference only goes down to .09. Table 3 summarizes these facts.

TABLE 3. PERCENTAGE OF TESTS HIGH ON CERTAIN ITEMS

Variable	Hygiene Failures ($N = 53$)	Nonfailure Samples ($N = 199$)	p
1. Mastery central.	2%	25%	<.001
2. Hero fails.	32%	18%	.02
3. Acts to overcome.	9%	16%	.09
6. Hero wishes.	30%	24%	not significant
8. Vocational images*.	2%	53%	<.001

* Tested on second sample only.

Our prediction was incorrect for item 6 (wishes for mastery), which both our alternative and McClelland's original theory predicted as running lower in failure than in nonfailure cases. The fact that heroes who wish for mastery are just as common among failing as among nonfailing narrators scores as a breakdown of both hypotheses. The Self Projection hypothesis does, however, offer an explanation after the fact: we may have at last run into the problem of psychological "levels" within the TAT story. It is often important to know whether the hero expressed his need by phantasy or by action. Tomkins (416) regards level analysis as one of the essential parts of any TAT scoring scheme. In our instance, may not the failing group have been Self Projecting when they created heroes who *wished* for mastery but did not *act* to attain it?

Perhaps we should point out that McClelland's hypothesis, which breaks down badly on the more delicate distinction between academically acceptable groups who are over- and underachieving, does a better job of describing the grosser differentiations between failures and nonfailures. Failures do tell stories that are lower on six of Mc-Clelland's eight items. That is, they less frequently discuss every aspect of achievement except failure and daydreaming. That finding gives McClelland's list some validity for making the broader distinctions between successful and nonsuccessful narrators, but it is a finding equally consonant with the simpler hypothesis of Self Projection, which will also explain the two items that seem in McClelland's theory to be exceptions.

SUMMARY

There is now no exact knowledge of the relationship between the traits of a man telling a TAT story and the traits he ascribes to the story people he creates. Three possibilities are Self Projection, Contrast Projection, and Complementary Projection. McClelland has suggested a fourth, Instrumental Projection. It is here hypothesized that Self Projection accounts for all or nearly all of the content of stories told to the TAT.

If we accept the theory of Self Projection, McClelland's list of eight effects of heightening the narrator's need Achievement becomes suspect. It is suggested that four of his items (1, More mastery tales; 4, Hero states need for mastery; 6, Hero wishes for mastery; 8, More mastery images, especially vocational images in story) are theoretically sound, while the other four (2, Failure by the hero; 3, Actions to overcome failure; 5, Press hostile to mastery; 7, Anxiety about mastery) are artifacts of his experimental design.

This hypothesis is tested against a group of academic overachievers, who are presumably higher in need Achievement than their controls. Positive trends occur in items 1, 6, and 8, with item 4 being untestable. No trends were found in items 2, 3, 5, and 7. When the experiment is run on a purer experimental group, two of these trends (all three of which are in the direction predicted) attain statistical significance.

A second trial is made by contrasting the above nonfailing groups with a failing group. The prediction is that all of McClelland's items will run low except item 2 (failure by the hero), which will be high among the failures. This proved to be the case, except that item 6 (wishes for mastery) remained constant. The latter finding had been predicted by neither theory, though it can be explained on the theory of Self Projection.

Our conclusions are: (*a*) that McClelland's eight variables do not necessarily reflect high need Achievement nor do they necessarily covary, and (*b*) that their variations in our two experimental groups fit very well the assumption that TAT stories are Self Projections.

It is suggested that the premise of Self Projection (if made to include projection of both needs and press) is sufficient to explain and predict a large portion of the content of TAT stories.

CHAPTER 39

....

Notes for a Projective
Measure of Fear of Failure

ROBERT W. MOULTON

THE WORK REPORTED here is an attempt to develop a measure of fear of failure. It will utilize the general method of content analysis developed by McClelland and his associates to measure the achievement motive. The impetus for this study is provided by the recurrence of curvilinear relationships between n Achievement scores and certain kinds of behavior. In several investigations of performance (52), perception (275), and memory (272, p. 269), persons in the mid-third of the n Achievement distribution have shown performance decrements—attributed to anxiety about failure—relative to the highest and lowest thirds. Exploratory analyses of the content of stories of the mid-third group has suggested the presence of more negative achievement-related categories of response (I−, Ga−, Bp, Bw, G−) in their stories. These categories may be indicative of an avoidance motive rather than a positive motive to achieve. The scoring system for n Achievement may confound these two tendencies and hence produce artifactual curvilinear relationships which are difficult to interpret. The present inquiry will search for a method of coding stories which will isolate the motive to avoid failure, or as it is commonly referred to, fear of failure.

This inquiry is limited to a reanalysis of stories in one study which showed quite clearly the curvilinear relationship between n Achievement score and behavior that has been attributed to greater fear of failure in the mid-third of the n Achievement distribution. In a study of the recall of completed and interrupted tasks performed under three different instructions, Atkinson (23, 272) found that Ss in the mid-third n Achievement group showed high recall of interrupted tasks under Relaxed Orientation but lower recall of interrupted tasks than the high or low thirds of the n Achievement distribution when the tasks were performed under achievement orientation and hence could be interpreted as failures when not completed.

PROCEDURE

The imaginative stories of the twenty-four subjects in the Achievement Orientation group of Atkinson's (23, 272) study were used as source material for the development of the f Failure measure. *Inability to recall incompleted tasks is assumed to be a manifestation of f Failure.*

The initial stage in the development of the scoring system involved assessing the four stories written by each subject for manifestations of fear of failure or avoidance of the achievement situation. These rather intuitive judgments provided a crude basis for predicting relative standing on recall of incompleted tasks. Next, an attempt was made to define various categories of response which had been used in the rough initial assessment. The negative categories of the n Achievement scoring system were found to be useful in this attempt and thus were incorporated. After some discussion, clarification, and revision, the following scoring system was devised.

F Failure Scoring Method. Each story is first examined to determine if it meets any of the definitions of fear imagery. If this is not the case, the story is scored no further and is given a value of zero. To avoid overweighting stories with a minimal indication of f Failure it was decided that a story which meets one of the fear imagery criteria but contains only one subcategory is to be scored for fear imagery only. This practice is also logical in view of the fact that the imagery definitions are for the most part simply broader definitions of the various subcategories. Any story which is found to contain more than one identifiable subcategory is scored for imagery as well as for all the subcategories present. Each subcategory is to be scored just once, although it may appear in various parts of the same story. The f Failure score is the simple summation of the imagery and subcategories, each scored +1.

Fear of Failure Imagery. (1) Any indication of poor performance in a situation where performance is customarily evaluated. For example: a school room, library, shop, inventor's laboratory, etc.

A. A standard of aspiration is established in the story, and either one of the characters does not meet it or he, or someone else, doubts his ability to attain the goal. Example: a boy dreaming of becoming a famous surgeon eventually becomes an ordinary physician. There need be no overt indication of negative affect resulting from the failure to meet the standard.

B. Any mention of failure, or speculation or doubt about the success or competence of any character. This can be inferred by *criticism* of a character in regard to his performance.

C. *Any* evidence of discouragement or negative affect when there is the possibility of achievement evaluation. Here negative affect can be inferred from unpleasant circumstances, such as being a laughing stock or being badly beaten.

(2) A desire to leave a situation in which achievement evaluation might take place.

A. An expressed preference for some other type of activity.

B. Daydreaming in the achievement situation unless the subject of the daydream is of some kind of successful achievement.

(3) Any indication of achievement activity which is not or has not been going smoothly.

Need. A desire for help of some type which would ease the threat or pain of failure. In general this category includes statements of desires or hopes whose fulfillment would circumvent adverse achievement evaluation. These needs can refer to leaving the situation or securing help in circumventing an achievement obstacle.

Instrumental Activity. Mental or physical departure from or avoidance of the achievement situation (leaving the field). Daydreams which occur in the achievement situation are scored unless they are of some successful achievement.

Anticipations of Failure. Someone anticipates possible failure or doubts someone else's ability.

Negative Affective State. Someone experiences a negative affective (emotional) state which seems to be a result of poor performance or low evaluation. Almost any negative affect which occurs in the achievement situation will be scored unless specifically attributed to other non-achievement-related factors. Negative affect may be inferred from unpleasant achievement-related incidents like "flunking the exam."

Hostile Press. Overt criticism of one character by another for inadequate performance. This includes predictions of failure.

Personal Obstacles. Various types of obstacles located in the individual. These obstacles can be:

(1) Impediments to avoidance of the achievement sequence. For example: "he would like to skip school but *feels that he must go.*"

(2) Impediments to an achievement sequence; for example: confusion while taking an exam, failure to study sufficiently.

(3) Any mention of personal inadequacy, including lack of preparation or any lack of effective instrumental action whether or not it can be determined if the action is approach- or avoidance-oriented.

Environmental Obstacles. Impediments to the failure avoidance response which are external, for example: the nasty teacher, societal regulations, etc. Also, any external block of achievement activity which does not merely define the task.

Fear Thema. A story meets the definition of fear imagery and contains no reference to any positive striving whatsoever. (Nothing in the story would be scored for the achievement motive.)

Discussion of Scoring System. A good many of the definitions of this system as it is presently constituted are arbitrary. A general question concerning the imagery category and many of the sub-categories is whether a distinction needs to be made between difficulties which occur in the positive achievement-directed (approach) sequence and those which hinder the characters in their attempts to avoid failure. This is a particular problem in scoring stories in which there appears some difficulty in an otherwise positive achievement sequence. Possibly obstacles of this sort should not be as highly weighted as a direct statement of failure or a desire to escape an achievement situation. The same kind of dichotomy occurs in the Need category. Frequently in the case of the Need category it is impossible to determine on the basis of the phraseology whether the statement of motivation is approach or avoidance in intent. One possibility in this case is to view the Need statement as part of the most prominent behavioral sequence in the story, i.e., either hope of success or fear of failure.

It is helpful to consider the range of possibilities within which the approach or avoidance nature of an achievement story can vary. The following is an approximation of the presumed probable order of the strength of fear of failure indicated by a story of a given type.

1. Completely achievement (approach)-oriented (minimal fear of failure).

2. A minimal block in a story otherwise concerned completely with the approach sequence.

3. A serious obstacle to the achievement sequence, but in a story in which the achievement goal is reached.

4. A serious obstacle to the achievement sequence in a story in which there is doubt as to the eventual success of the characters.

5. The obstacle dominates the story and success is obviously never attained.

6. The story is mainly concerned with negative doubts, accounts of failure, etc.

7. The story is concerned with escape from the achievement situations, like daydreaming, preference for some other activity, etc.

8. Some block of the escape from the achievement situation is

constructed. The character is impeded even in the avoidance response (maximal fear of failure).

The present f Failure scoring system begins to score stories of the sort described in 2 above. With this procedure, it may be that rather minimal indications of f Failure are given an unduly heavy weight. However, these stories do not usually contain as great a density of fear subcategories as do those described in points 6, 7, and 8, a point which argues for the present system.

Empirical test of the scoring system. The 24 n Achievement protocols of the Achievement Orientation condition and 27 protocols from the Relaxed Orientation condition of the interrupted tasks experiment were scored for f Failure.[1]

For purposes of the present study, a refined measure of positive achievement-related motivation, called Hope of Success (h Success), will consist of the positive categories of the original n Achievement scoring system. These include achievement imagery, positive anticipations of success (Ga+), positive emotional concomitants of achievement (G+), external assistance for characters in an ongoing achievement activity (NuP), successful instrumental activity leading to achievement (I+), and absence of a competing theme not related to achievement (Ach. th.). The sum of these categories will comprise the h Success score.

What is to be called a *net* Hope of Success score was derived for each subject by subtracting his f Failure score from his Hope of Success score. This value should provide an improved prediction of instrumental behavior, which is thought to be a function of the resultant of approach (h Success) and avoidance (f Failure).

The rank-order correlations between the various scores and recall of incompleted and completed tasks under Relaxed and Achievement Orientation conditions are shown in Table 1. Obviously a cross validation of the system should be made before these relationships are accepted with confidence. However, the obtained results provide a preliminary basis for evaluation of the scoring system proposed.

If recall of incompleted tasks under Achievement Orientation is equivalent to recall of *failures,* then it appears that the f Failure scoring system is measuring a tendency to avoid recall of failures. Under both conditions the f Failure score is negatively related to recall of incompleted tasks (Table 1).

Recall of completed tasks might be construed as defensive behavior

---

[1] The achievement-related motivation scores of the present study are based on four stories written by each subject. In earlier reports of this experiment (23, 272), n Achievement scores were based on only *three* stories for reasons explained fully elsewhere (See 272, p. 191 and 265).

TABLE 1. RANK ORDER CORRELATIONS BETWEEN VARIOUS
ACHIEVEMENT MOTIVATION SCORES AND RECALL OF
INCOMPLETED AND COMPLETED TASKS*

Score	Achievement Orientation ($N = 24$)		IR–CR
	Recall of Incompleted Tasks (IR)	Recall of Completed Tasks (CR)	
net Hope of Success..........	.69***	−.07	.45**
n Achievement..............	.61***	.05	.25
Hope of Success.............	.67***	.18	.31
f Failure...................	−.38	.47**	−.61***

Score	Relaxed Orientation ($N = 27$)		IR-CR
	Recall of Incompleted Tasks (IR)	Recall of Completed Tasks (CR)	
net Hope of Success..........	.23	.29	.01
n Achievement..............	.20	.14	.01
Hope of Success.............	−.03	.13	−.05
f Failure...................	−.32	−.25	−.05

* Reanalysis of data collected by Atkinson (23; 272, p. 264).
** $p < .05$.
*** $p < .01$.

so that the person motivated by a f Failure might tend to retain awareness of the tasks on which he believed himself to have succeeded. This assumption would account for the positive relationship found between f Failure and recall of completed tasks in the Achievement Orientation condition. The negative relationship found between these same variables in the Relaxed condition is not easily interpreted. Possibly low recall of both incompleted and completed tasks in the Relaxed condition is a function of a general lack of interest where there is no necessity for defensive recall of "successes" and avoidance of "failures" as there presumably would be when f Failure is aroused, as in the Achievement Orientation condition.

One possible interpretation of the negative relationship between recall of incompleted tasks and f Failure is that all this newly developed instrument is measuring is a general lack of interest in achievement. This interpretation seems inadequate in view of the significant positive relationship between the f Failure score and the recall of completed tasks in the Achievement Orientation condition where f Failure should be aroused.

The number of completed tasks recalled was subtracted from the number of incompleted tasks recalled (IR-CR) and the various motivation scores were correlated with this value, an index of the Zeigarnik effect. Again the scoring systems show an appreciably greater predictive efficiency under Achievement Orientation condition than in the Relaxed condition. The relationships in the Achievement Orientation group are in the expected direction.

One of the general problems in the research involving the n Achievement measure is the frequently found curvilinear relationship. Removal of the confounding effect of a n Achievement score based on a summation of positive and negative categories is possible by utilization of the *net Hope score*. For example, in Atkinson's study (272), the middle third on n Achievement showed the Zeigarnik effect to a greater extent than did the upper third under Relaxed Orientation. In the Achievement Orientation condition, the mid-third group showed less recall of incompleted tasks than did the lower third.

The three way breakdowns of the relationship between original n Achievement scores and the net hope of success scores of both these experimental conditions are given in Table 2. In the Achievement Orientation condition, four of the eight subjects placed in the mid-third by the n Achievement scoring system are placed in the lower third of the distribution by the net Hope score.

TABLE 2. THE RELATIONSHIP BETWEEN THE n ACHIEVEMENT SCORE AND THE NEWLY-DEVELOPED NET HOPE OF SUCCESS SCORE IN TERMS OF HIGH, MIDDLE, AND LOW THIRDS

		Achievement Orientation ($N = 24$)			Relaxed Orientation ($N = 27$)		
		Net Hope of Success Score			Net Hope of Success Score		
		high	middle	low	high	middle	low
Original	high	7	1	0	4	1	3
n Achievement	middle	1	3	4	5	3	1
Score	low	1	1	6	1	5	4

In the original study, the mid-third of the n Achievement distribution was high in recall of incompleted tasks under Relaxed Orientation and low under Achievement Orientation. Table 3 compares the median recall of incompleted tasks for the thirds of the n Achievement and net Hope distributions in the Relaxed and Achievement Orientation conditions. Recall of incompleted tasks increases in a linear manner plotted against net Hope scores in both conditions. Compare this to the curvilinear relation between n Achievement and recall of incompleted tasks. It appears that the net Hope of Success score orders subjects on achievement motivation in a more linear manner than the original n Achievement score—at least when recall of incompleted tasks is the behavioral criterion of achievement motivation.

TABLE 3. MEDIAN RECALL OF INCOMPLETED TASKS FOR THIRDS OF THE n ACHIEVEMENT AND NET HOPE OF SUCCESS DISTRIBUTIONS

	Achievement Orientation $(N = 24)$		Relaxed Orientation $(N = 27)$	
	n Ach.	net Hope	n Ach.	net Hope
high third............	6.15	5.78	4.69	5.03
middle third..........	4.72	4.89	4.86	4.75
low third.............	4.76	4.32	4.52	4.59

Note: Recall scores are standard scores based on forms, plus a constant of 5, of arc sin transformations of percentages of completed and incompleted tasks recalled. This table differs from a comparable table in *The Achievement Motive* (272, p. 269), where the original results are given, in that the division into high, middle, and low thirds of the n Achievement distribution is here based on scores from four stories rather than only three as in the earlier report.

It should be expected that a measure of achievement-related motivation would show an appreciable mean increase between two experimental conditions which vary in the degree to which *they are designed* to arouse this motivation. Table 4 summarizes the mean increases between conditions for the various scores. The f Failure score increases in the correct direction, but not dramatically ($p < .50$). There is a slight increase in the n Achievement ($p < .20$) and h Success scores ($p < .20$). The most marked increase, however, is noted in the *sum* of the h Success and f Failure scores where an increase of 2.17 is observed ($p < .10$). This suggests that there is a measurable increase in *total* motivation which is brought about by situational manipulation. There is no reason to expect an increase in the net Hope of Success score between conditions since an increase in achievement involvement in the experimental situation might be expected to differentially affect hope and fear motivation.

The rank-order correlations between the original n Achievement scores and the f Failure and h Success scores of the present inquiry support the inference that n Achievement, as presently measured, is a positive disposition to achieve. In the Achievement Orientation con-

TABLE 4. MEAN VALUES OF THE VARIOUS SCORES UNDER RELAXED AND ACHIEVEMENT-ORIENTED CONDITIONS AND MEAN INCREASES BETWEEN CONDITIONS

	Relaxed Orientation ($N = 27$)		Achievement Orientation ($N = 24$)		$M_{diff.}$	$\sigma_{diff.}$	t	p
	Mean	σ	Mean	σ				
n Achievement	5.70	5.17	7.38	5.16	1.68	1.48	1.14	.50
net Hope	−.85	4.71	−.96	4.92	.11	1.38	.06	.90
h Success	4.48	2.79	5.79	3.74	1.31	.95	1.38	.20
f Failure	5.93	3.52	6.79	2.89	.86	.92	.93	.50
h Success + f Failure	10.41	4.54	12.58	4.28	2.17	1.26	1.72	.10

dition ($N = 24$) the correlation between n Achievement score and h Success score is .96, between n Achievement score and f Failure score is −.02. between h Success score and f Failure score is −.16. The average h Success scores of the upper ($N = 7$), middle ($N = 9$), and low ($N = 7$) n Achievement groups in this condition are 10.6, 5.4, and 1.7 respectively. The average f Failure scores of these same groups are 6.0, 7.2, and 7.3 respectively.

Unfortunately, the scoring for f Failure was accomplished without control for the theoretical expectancy, on the part of the scorer, of a greater incidence of f Failure in the achievement-oriented group and among persons who have difficulty recalling interrupted tasks. The present exploratory results are therefore presented as a basis for future hypotheses rather than as a basis for firm conclusions.[2]

[2] A definitive answer to the question of how to code thematic content for separate indices of approach and avoidance motives should be one of the more important goals of future research. The editor has assumed, in Ch. 22, that a relatively high n Achievement score implies that the motive to achieve, i.e., to approach, is relatively stronger within the individual than the motive to avoid failure (here called fear of failure). It was further assumed that a relatively low n Achievement score implies that the motive to avoid failure is relatively stronger than the motive to achieve within the individual. In addition to the evidence of the present investigation, which shows a heavier saturation of imagery having to do with escape from or avoidance of achievement situations in the stories of persons who normally score low in n Achievement, the reader is reminded that subjects having low n Achievement scores show more evidence of test anxiety as measured by questionnaire responses and psychogalvanic reaction (Ch. 23), increased thresholds for failure-related words when the situation is test-like (Ch. 24), avoidance in recall of interrupted (i.e., failed) tasks (23), and greater rigidity in problem-solving behavior (52). The theoretical model which employs this assumption (Ch. 22) accounts for observed differences in the risk-taking behavior of persons having high and low n Achievement scores. Editor.

CHAPTER 40

The Avoidance of Threatening Material in Imaginative Behavior*

WILLIAM ABBOTT SCOTT[1]

SINCE ITS ORIGINAL development as an aid to clinical assessment of global personality configurations, the Thematic Apperception Test has gained increasingly widespread use in laboratory studies of personality traits. Modifications in administering and scoring procedures have been devised to yield relatively objective measures of various specific traits, which are studied one at a time, rather than as aspects of more complex configurations.

Perhaps the most extensive use of the TAT approach within an experimental setting has been in the investigation of complex human motives, such as the need for achievement (24, 72, 272, 250). Focusing on a single trait at a time has permitted researchers to specify in relatively precise fashion certain determiners of imaginative behavior deemed relevant to that trait and to its manifestations in the imaginative stories. The research to be reported here likewise deals with isolated personality traits, measured by specific categories of story content. Its approach is not primarily motivational, however, but stems more from a perceptual or cognitive point of view.

In the studies cited, the theoretical formulations from which the scoring categories were derived have generally posed the problem in some such terms as: "What sorts of personal and situational factors

* Reprinted by permission of author and publisher from *The Journal of Abnormal and Social Psychology,* 1956, **52,** 338-346. Copyright 1956 by the American Psychological Association, Inc.

[1] This report is based on a dissertation submitted to the Doctoral Program in Social Psychology, University of Michigan (see 367). The study of "Anxiety over War Catastrophe" was done while the author was associated with the Survey Research Center, and several of the Center's staff members participated in its planning and execution. I am especially indebted to Professors J. W. Atkinson, G. S. Blum, and S. B. Withey for their contributions to the suggested theoretical formulations.

572

lead subjects to approach a given class of goal objects?" Accordingly, these formulations have, for the most part, dealt with factors that could account for the "approach" of an S toward the critical thematic content under investigation; and the picture stimuli have most frequently been designed to represent positively valenced situations.

Recently certain investigators (see, for example, 24, 72) have become concerned with the problem: "What happens when a person is confronted with a pictorial situation that represents a threat rather than a goal, or represents simultaneously a goal and a threat?" The present research deals with this problem, by means of the following experimental paradigm: The Ss are asked to write or tell imaginative stories about series of ambiguous pictures under two different conditions. The first condition (low cues) provides no intentional suggestion as to what the content of the stories should be. The second condition (high cues) for the same Ss focuses their attention on a particular event, which may be threatening to some of them.

What is the probability of the S's producing stories with the critical thematic content in response to high cues, as compared with low cues? Here a formulation of the problem is considered which represents a generalization of Miller's approach-avoidance conflict theory (290). Data are then presented from three separate studies which tend to support the suggested formulation.

Miller (290), in describing the overt behavior of animals with respect to an object that represents, simultaneously, a goal and a threat, has used the concepts of goal and threat gradients to account for the observed tendencies of animals to approach the object and at the same time to avoid it. These gradients may be represented schematically as sloping lines on a set of coordinates, the abscissa indicating units of distance from the object (origin of the coordinates), and the ordinate indicating the strength of the animal's approach or avoidance tendency. Tendency to approach or to avoid is at a maximum at the origin (in the presence of the object), and falls to a minimum at some distance away. It is assumed that the threat gradient is steeper than the goal gradient, so that as the animal comes nearer to the critical object from any suitable distance, his tendency to run away from it increases more rapidly than does his tendency to approach it. Differences in heights of the gradients (depending on levels of fear and drive) determine where the two slopes cross (if at all) and, accordingly, at what range on the abscissa approach behavior occurs, and at what range avoidance. Miller has suggested (291, 293) that "distance from the goal" need not be restricted to the physical space between the animal and the object, but may usefully be applied to other dimensions of stimulus generalization.

The approach-avoidance formulation can be applied to the present problem if the concept "cue strength" be regarded as the inverse equivalent of "distance from the goal-threat." From such an extrapolation follows the hypothesis that, if an S is sufficiently afraid of an event represented in the pictures, the stronger the cues for it become, the less likely will he be to talk or write about it in his imaginative stories (since, for him, the threat gradient is higher than the goal gradient in the neighborhood of strong cues). If an S has relatively little (or no) fear of the event, an increase in cue strength should be accompanied by an increased likelihood of his telling stories about it.

Three independent studies, dealing with two different kinds of events, yielded data on which this general hypothesis could be tested. The first was a study of imaginative stories told in response to increasingly clear cues relating to war catastrophe; the second and third dealt in similar manner with imaginative responses to competition cues. In all three studies there were sizable proportions of Ss (17%, 37%, and 48%) who exhibited *decreased* tendencies to talk or write about the critical events in the presence of *increased* cues. The Ss who displayed such a response pattern will be called *avoiders;* all other Ss are called *nonavoiders.* To support the approach-avoidance formulation it is necessary to show that the avoidance pattern is associated with fear of the critical event. Evidence of fear was obtained from a content analysis of the imaginative stories.

Evidences of Fear Within Stories. The test of the general hypothesis that fear results in avoidance lies in a comparison of the stories about the threatening event told by avoiders with those told by nonavoiders. Avoidance of critical thematic content in a TAT-type story is regarded as a symbolic defense against anxiety, equivalent to an animal's running away from a fear-arousing object. On those occasions when an avoider remains in the presence of the threatening event, by telling a story about it, he should display symptoms of continuing fear, or anxiety. However, if he escapes from it, by telling a story about another kind of event, the anxiety (and symptoms of it) should be reduced. (The terms *fear* and *anxiety* are here used interchangeably to refer to the S's reactions to a specific, external event which is threatening.)

Current theories of anxiety (146, p. 114; 253, pp. 88, 199) and conventional clinical testing practices (1, p. 203; 35, p. 115; 335, p. 404) suggest that TAT-type stories of an anxious S may be identified with the following general characteristics: (*a*) impoverished content, blocking of imaginative production, relatively short length, lack of involvement in the story; (*b*) failure to describe problem-solving behavior of the characters in the story; (*c*) failure to describe a successful outcome. Various operational measures of these general "maladaptive" characteristics were therefore designated for each of the studies. In each case it was predicted that when avoiders *do* tell stories about the threatening event, these critical stories will be more likely to display the designated characteristics than the stories which nonavoiders tell about the threatening event. However, when avoiders tell stories about other kinds of events (nonthreatening), no excess of fear symptoms is expected, since they have removed themselves from the threatening situation; so these nonthreatening stories should not differ from those of nonavoiders on the characteristics mentioned.

FEAR OF WAR CATASTROPHE

The Interview. Four pictures of varying cue strength were presented to 139 respondents in New York and Philadelphia during an interview about problems related to civil defense.[2] Two of them were shown at the beginning of the interview, before there had been any mention of war or civil defense. The remaining two pictures were presented about halfway through the interview, following a series of open questions covering such matters as likelihood of war, danger of enemy attack, degree of damage expected, mortality radius of the atom bomb, amount of personal concern, items of information on attack and defense methods, etc.

The relative cue strengths of the pictures were assessed by twenty-one judges who ranked them according to "the degree to which the picture suggests war catastrophe." Mean ranks were ordered as follows: A (weakest), C, B, and D (strongest). Half of the respondents were shown A and B before the interview, then C and D following the first ten questions; the other half received the pictures in the order, C—D—interview—A—B. The cues from the interview are assumed to have contributed to the total cue strength (re war catastrophe) at the time the second pair of pictures was presented. Accordingly, the war-catastrophe cues were presumably stronger at the time of presentation of the last picture (D or B, depending upon sequence) than for any preceding picture. (This assumption was supported by the data on frequency of war-catastrophe themes for each picture. The frequencies were arranged in precisely the order indicated by the judges.)

The interviewer suggested:

---

[2] The pictures are on file in the Survey Research Center, University of Michigan, Ann Arbor. They were drawn to represent:
A. Woman looking at sky with birds (or planes).
B. Man on hill overlooking city, with mushroom-like cloud in sky.
C. Woman running with two children.
D. Man standing by gutted house.

We're interested in finding out what people can see or imagine in these pictures. I wonder if you'd look at each one and try to imagine what kind of a story might go with it. Just use your imagination in doing this and say whatever comes into your mind. I'll show each of them to you for a few seconds, and then take it away and ask you to tell me about it.

The interviewer took a *verbatim* record of the respondent's story, using the following probes as necessary: "What is this picture about? What is the person thinking? What do you think will happen next? What do you think other people might say it's about?"

Content Analysis of Protocols. The code for analysis of the protocols included various dimensions referring to the content of the story and to the manner in which it was told. Within each dimension were categories relevant to the hypotheses about differences between avoiders' and nonavoiders' protocols. (See Table 1 for descriptions of the dimensions.) The protocols were coded by the regular coding staff of the Survey Research Center, for the most part undergraduate and graduate students untrained in clinical psychology.

Coding reliability indices[3] ranged from $\pi = .30$ to $.75$, with a mean of $.57$. These low figures suggest that the categories were not very well defined for the coders, and that considerable subjective judgment entered into their discriminations.

The theme (situation) of each story was classified as either (a) war catastrophe (actual or impending), or (b) any other theme (including nonwar catastrophes) or "Don't know." The "avoidance" group is composed of respondents who gave war-catastrophe themes for one or more of the first three pictures, but not for the last one (where cues were strongest). The nonavoidance theme patterns are those which include a war-catastrophe theme for the last picture. Twenty-four of the 139 respondents in the sample (17%) were categorized as avoiders of war-catastrophe themes, and 110 were categorized as nonavoiders.

Although the percentage of war-catastrophe themes mentioned by the avoiders was necessarily lower than that of the nonavoiders, the proportion of *all* catastrophe (both war and nonwar) themes was similar for both groups (78% and 80%). Where avoiders failed to mention war catastrophe, they tended to give other than war-ca-

---

[3] The reliability index (368) represents the extent to which obtained agreement between two coders exceeds that which could be expected on the basis of chance alone. $\pi = \dfrac{P_o - P_e}{1 - P_e}$, where P_o is the percentage of judgments on which the two coders agree; and P_e is the "expected agreement" (on the basis of chance alone), given the particular distribution of responses among the m categories of the dimension. $P_e = \sum_{a=1}^{m} P_a^2$ where P_a is the proportion of cases assigned to the ath category.

tastrophe interpretations (fire, explosion, etc.). The "avoidance" dimension would thus seem to represent fear of *war* catastrophe, specifically, and not generalized fear of all kinds of catastrophic situations.

Results of War Catastrophe Study. The first two columns of Table 1 report the results of the analysis of war-catastrophe protocols. The significant differences between avoiders' and nonavoiders' stories were: (*a*) avoiders tended to tell shorter stories; (*b*) avoiders were less likely to mention spontaneously thinking of the central figure or outcome of the story before these were specifically probed for by the interviewer; (*c*) avoiders were less likely to mention problem-oriented activity of the central figure (e.g., get to shelter, protect others, give relief or aid to others); (*d*) avoiders told fewer stories with successful outcomes. The remaining differences between avoiders' and nonavoiders' protocols were in the predicted directions, but did not reach acceptable levels of significance.[4]

When avoiders and nonavoiders told stories about nonwar catastrophes (e.g., fire or flood), no differences between their protocols were expected, with respect to the characteristics coded here. The first two columns of Table 2 indicate that this expectation was borne out: none of the differences reaches the .05 level of confidence, and the directions of differences are inconsistent.

FEAR OF COMPETITIVE SITUATIONS

Procedure. The general design of the competition studies[5] involved the presentation to the same Ss of TAT-type pictures under "relaxed" or "neutral" conditions and also under "aroused" or achievement-oriented conditions (Ch. 27; 272). The neutral condition of Study A was produced as follows: On the first day of the semester members

---

[4] Since protocol length was related to the avoidance criterion, and was, in turn, correlated with some of the other dimensions of the content analysis, it seemed advisable to control for the effects of protocol length when computing the relationship between avoidance and other protocol characteristics. This was done by grouping the protocols according to number of words (two groups in the war catastrophe study, two groups in competition study A, three groups in competition study B), and computing the significance of the difference between avoiders' and nonavoiders' protocols within each group. The significance levels were then combined (234, p. 46). Tables 1 and 2 report the "combined" significance levels, with protocol length controlled, for each of the dimensions which was correlated with protocol length. The codes for content analysis and data from which these summary tables were constructed may be seen in the original report of the research (367).

[5] I am indebted to John Martire (250) and Alfred C. Raphelson for the use of protocols which they had previously collected for research on the achievement motive.

of an undergraduate psychology class at the University of Michigan were shown a series of pictures, projected one by one on a screen, and asked to write stories about them. They were given no particular information about the nature of the task. Then the instructor left the room and returned a few minutes later to create the aroused condition. He implied that the class was overcrowded, so it would be desirable for all students to take a general psychology qualifying examination in order to determine whether everyone had the requisite background for the course. Following a fifteen-minute examination period, a second series of pictures was administered, and stories were written as before.

The relaxed condition of Study B was created by the experimenter's presenting some "interesting" tasks to the Ss (undergraduate psychology students at the University of Iowa), so that he could get data "to see what might be made of them" as tests. The atmosphere was informal and achievement demands were minimized prior to the writing of stories. After a scrambled-words task the pictures were projected on a screen one at a time and Ss wrote imaginative stories about them. In the aroused condition, a week or more later, Ss were informed that the tests were measures of "leadership and executive qualifications" and were urged to do their best on them. A different form of the scrambled-words test was given, followed by a second series of pictures and imaginative stories. Throughout this second pretest period, formality and specific achievement demands were emphasized.

Thirty-five Ss from Study A and 62 Ss from Study B are represented in this analysis. A few Ss had to be excluded because of incomplete protocol sequences.

Both of these experiments differ from the war-catastrophe study in the lack of systematic grading of pictures in strength of cues with respect to the threatening event. The condition of increasing cue strength required by the theory must therefore be met entirely by a shift in condition from relaxed (or neutral) to aroused.

The subjects were divided into two groups: (a) those who gave more competition themes under neutral than under aroused conditions (13 Ss in Study A; 30 Ss in Study B); and (b) all other Ss (22 and 32 Ss in Studies A and B, respectively). The first response pattern constitutes the operational definition of avoidance for these two studies.

The protocols were coded by the writer and one assistant. Contamination with the avoidance criterion was precluded, since a given S's theme pattern was not known at the time his stories were analyzed. Coding reliability indices ranged from $\pi = .30$ to .82, with a mean of .67.

Results of Competition Studies. The right-hand part of Table 1 presents results of the analysis of competition stories. For each of the two studies, separately, the protocols of avoiders and nonavoiders are compared on characteristics similar to those used in the analysis of war-catastrophe stories. Significant differences in Study A were: (*a*) avoiders tended to tell shorter stories; (*b*) avoiders told fewer stories which were judged as indicating a realistic acceptance of the competition situation; (*c*) avoiders were less likely to mention problem-oriented activity of the central figure (e.g., try to win the contest, build a good tool, etc.); (*d*) avoiders told fewer stories with successful outcomes; (*e*) when failure did occur in the *Ss'* stories, avoiders were less likely than nonavoiders to describe a competitive reaction to it on the part of the central figure—e.g., he was more likely to give up than to evidence renewed striving for success. The remaining differences between avoiders' and nonavoiders' protocols in Study A were in the predicted directions, but did not reach the .05 level of significance.

In Study B the hypotheses did not fare so well. In the first place, the average length of avoiders' and nonavoiders' competition stories differed—but in the opposite direction to that predicted: the avoiders tended to tell longer competition stories. When story length is controlled, two of the predicted differences reach the .05 level of significance: (*a*) avoiders were less likely to evidence a realistic acceptance of the competition situation; (*b*) avoiders were less likely to mention problem-oriented activity. All the rest of the differences, though in the predicted direction, were small and unreliable. It is quite likely that the failure of Study B to yield results as supportive as those of Study A is due to the time-lag between the two series of pictures: the neutral and aroused conditions were separated by a period of about a week, and many extraneous factors could intervene to muddy the results. Hypothesis strength and fear strength are not likely to remain constant for that long a time; this would lead to misclassification of avoiders and nonavoiders, and to a consequent attenuation of the predicted relationships.

When avoiders and nonavoiders told stories about noncompetitive situations, their protocols did not differ according to the characteristics coded here. The right-hand side of Table 2 compares the two groups' noncompetition stories. None of the differences reaches the .05 level of significance, and the directions of differences are inconsistent.

DISCUSSION

In the three studies reported here, it was possible to make repeated independent tests of several of the specific hypotheses con-

TABLE 1. COMPARISON OF AVOIDERS' AND NONAVOIDERS' PROTOCOLS DEALING WITH THREATENING SITUATIONS

(Entries represent proportions of protocols in each group showing a given characteristic)

Characteristic	War Catastrophe Protocols			Competition Protocols									Combined p-value*
				Study A			Study B						
	Avoiders	Non-avoiders	p	Avoiders	Non-avoiders	p	Avoiders	Non-avoiders	p	
% of stories judged to indicate realistic acceptance of situation	53	72	NS	6	24	.05	18	24	.05	.01
% of stories judged to evidence much imagination	29	34	NS	7	24	NS	30	32	NS	.20
% of stories where thinking or outcome was volunteered before probe	15	30	.05	(not codable in competition protocols)						
% of stories with problem-oriented thinking	25	35	NS	39	55	NS	60	62	NS	.30
% of stories with problem-oriented activity	27	43	.05	22	45	.01	46	60	.05	.001
% of stories with successful outcomes	6	26	.05	13	36	.01	45	59	NS	.005
% of stories with competitive reaction to success	(not coded)			0	18	NS	15	19	NS	.10
% of stories with competitive reaction to failure	(not coded)			8	35	.05	33	45	NS	.02
Mean number of words	(58)	(74)	.01	(46)	(55)	.01	(104)	(94)	.996†	.01

* Significance levels were combined according to the procedure suggested by Lindquist (234, p. 46).

† Significant difference, opposite to predicted direction.

Note.—Significance levels reported here represent the relations between the avoidance criterion and the specified protocol characteristics, with protocol length held constant in every case where it could be a contaminating factor in the relationship. Since directions of differences were predicted, one-tailed t tests were used throughout. See Kish (214, p. 207) and Scott (367, p. 119) for a description of the sampling-error formula used to correct for intercorrelation among several responses from the same subject.

TABLE 2. COMPARISON OF AVOIDERS' AND NONAVOIDERS' PROTOCOLS DEALING WITH NONTHREATENING SITUATIONS

(Entries represent proportions of protocols in each group showing a given characteristic)

Characteristic	Nonwar Catastrophe Protocols		Noncompetition Protocols				Combined p-value
			Study A		Study B		
	Avoiders	Non-avoiders	Avoiders	Non-avoiders	Avoiders	Non-avoiders	
% of stories indicating realistic acceptance of the situation	(not coded)	25	6	11	24	25	.50
% of stories evidencing much imagination	20	25	20	22	46	40	.80
% of stories where thinking or outcome was volunteered before probe	27	24	(not coded)				
% of stories with problem-oriented thinking	37	35	40	55	75	79	.70
% of stories with problem-oriented activity	42	48	26	30	52	44	.60
% of stories with successful outcomes	33	35	4	17	41	34	.40
% of stories with problem-oriented reaction to success	(not coded)		0	0	4	5	
% of stories with problem-oriented reaction to failure	(not coded)		25	22	18	15	.80
Mean number of words	(62)	(65)	(48)	(54)	(102)	(100)	.30

Note.—Significance levels were computed from one-tailed t tests, which test the hypothesis that nonwar-catastrophe or noncompetition problem stories of avoiders and nonavoiders differ in the same manner as was predicted for war-catastrophe and competition stories. None of the differences reported here reaches the .05 level of confidence.

cerning differences between avoiders' and nonavoiders' stories about threatening events. Altogether, Table 1 represents 23 tests of specific predicted relationships. Eleven of the differences surpass the .05 level of confidence in the predicted direction; one (protocol length in Competition Study B) is significantly opposite to the predicted direction; the remaining eleven differences are in the predicted direction, but fail to attain an acceptable level of significance. Where similar predictions were tested on two or three different studies, it is possible to combine the significance levels of the separate results into combined p values, according to the procedure suggested by Lindquist (234, p. 46). The last column of Table 1 reports these composite results, from which the following conclusions can be drawn:

When avoiders *do* tell stories about events which are presumably threatening to them, their stories differ from those which nonavoiders tell about the same kinds of events. The most reliably discriminating characteristics are: (*a*) protocol length, (*b*) degree of acceptance of the situation described in the story, (*c*) nature of activity described (adaptive, as opposed to nonadaptive or no activity), (*d*) nature of outcome of the situation (successful, as opposed to unsuccessful or no outcome). The rest of the characteristics coded in these studies either did not reliably discriminate avoiders and nonavoiders, or yielded results which were not replicated. Since the directions of differences were quite uniformly as predicted, it may be assumed that the other characteristics are potential discriminators, provided the empirical categories can be refined and clarified.

These results are specific to stories about the threatening events. When avoiders tell stories about nonthreatening events, their protocols do not differ significantly or consistently from stories which nonavoiders tell about similar kinds of events. Consequently, it cannot be maintained that avoiders react similarly to all kinds of projective story situations. They manifest symptoms of fear within their stories only when these stories deal with threatening events.

The findings thus lend credibility to the approach-avoidance model on which the analyses were based. They are also consistent with findings from certain other recent studies of perceptual and imaginative behavior. Blum (45) demonstrated that *S*s whose attention had been focused on presumably traumatic sexual stimuli were less able to locate these stimuli when presented tachistoscopically at close-to-conscious level (one-fifth of a second) than they were to locate nontraumatic stimuli presented in the same manner, although at a faster speed (.03 sec.) increased perceptual vigilance for the former had occurred. Clark (72) showed a series of TAT pictures to a group of Ss after they had been subjected to conditions calculated to arouse sexual motivation. Their protocols were analyzed to determine the amount of manifest sex imagery contained in them, and the results from this group were compared with the protocols of Ss who saw the same pictures under "neutral" conditions (no deliberate sex-arousal). The *aroused* group exhibited significantly less manifest sex imagery than the *neutral* group. This finding indicated that the focusing of an S's attention on sex could arouse enough anxiety to require partial suppression of sex-related symbolic behavior.

Though the model for the present research has been reported in terms of approach-avoidance conflict theory, it is possible to state it in terms compatible with Bruner and Postman's hypothesis-information theory of perception and cognition (54, 329). To their formulation of the approach aspects of cognitive processes one may add variables to account for the avoidance aspects investigated here, resulting in a theory which applies to either threatening or non-threatening events, as follows:

The net tendency to report the presence of event X in a stimulus situation is the resultant of two opposite tendencies, approach and avoidance. When the avoidance tendency is stronger, X is not reported. When the approach tendency is stronger, X is reported, providing other net approach tendencies are not still stronger. (It is necessary to consider alternative approach tendencies, since a single stimulus may include cues relevant to two or more kinds of events, say $X, Y,$ and Z. So an S's report of Y does not necessarily indicate an avoidance of X, but may merely mean that Y is more salient than X; or, in the present terminology, that his net approach tendency with respect to Y is stronger than that with respect to X.)

The approach tendency with respect to X is a function of (a) the strength of the S's hypothesis that X will occur and (b) the degree of structuring of the cues with respect to X.

The avoidance tendency with respect to X is a function of (a) the amount of fear associated with X, and (b) the degree of structuring of the cues with respect to X.

For a given level of hypothesis strength, the approach tendency increases monotonically as the cue strength is increased. For a given level of fear, the avoidance tendency also increases monotonically as the cue strength is increased. But with increasing cue strength, the avoidance tendency increases more rapidly (has a greater acceleration) than the approach tendency. Thus, as strength of cues is increased, from very weak to very strong, the avoidance tendency *may* overtake the approach tendency, so that the net tendency shifts from positive to negative. Whether or not this occurs depends on the relative strengths of hypothesis and fear.

If an S has no fear of event X, the net tendency in the presence of adequate cues is always positive. And it remains positive even in the face of a minimal amount of fear, providing there is a moderate degree of hypothesis strength, and that the cues do not become too strong.

Given considerable fear of X, it is possible, at least theoretically, to increase the cue strength to the point where the avoidance tendency becomes predominant, and the S no longer reports the presence of X. (The qualification, "at least theoretically," is introduced because in the present TAT-type experiment, it may be impossible to make any picture represent the threatening event well enough to elicit the requisite amount of fear.)

If an S is characterized by extreme fear of X, it is possible that any level of cue strength, no matter how weak, may elicit an avoidance tendency which is stronger than the approach tendency. Thus, the two gradients do not cross, and the S never reports the presence of X.

From a consideration of the relative heights of these approach and avoidance gradients at any given level of cue strength, it is possible to interpret various thematic response patterns to a graded set of TAT-type pictures, so as to yield information about both hypothesis strength and fear strength with respect to event X. However, such an interpretation is valid within the present framework only if other cues (re events Y and Z) are held constant while cues re X are increased through the sequence of pictures. Usually this requirement can only be approximately satisfied. Moreover, if the picture sequence is extended beyond a rather small number, it is to be expected that "theme fatigue" or "desire for new imaginative experience" will produce a shift in theme, even in nonanxious Ss.

Within such limitations, however, the above formulation may prove useful in interpreting thematic responses to projective tests. It was used to predict the relationships reported in the present studies of imaginative behavior. It might conceivably be extended to areas of perceptual and cognitive behavior as well; for the concept of avoidance tendency in the present schema appears quite analogous to the concept of perceptual defense and to the concepts of repression and distortion in memory.[6]

SUMMARY

The Ss in three different studies were asked to write or tell imaginative stories about series of ambiguous pictures under two conditions. The first condition (low cues) provided no intentional suggestion as to what the content of the stories should be. The second condition (high cues), for the same Ss, focused their attention on a particular event, which might be threatening to some of them. One of the studies presented war catastrophe as the potentially threatening event; the other two studies focused on competition with a standard of excellence. In all three studies sizable proportions of the Ss (though in no case a majority) exhibited *decreased* tendencies to tell stories about the threatening event under

---

[6] The approach-avoidance distinction dealt with in this paper has arisen in a number of other studies included in this book. See also Chs. 23, 24, 38, 39, 41, and 42; also 72.

high-cue, as compared with low-cue, conditions. These Ss are called *avoiders*.

According to the proposed theoretical interpretation, avoidance results from fear of the critical event. Therefore, when avoiders do tell stories about the event, they should display symptoms of fear within those stories. But when they "get out of the threatening situation" by telling stories about some other, nonthreatening, event, these symptoms of fear should disappear.

Content analysis of the imaginative stories provided support for this interpretation. Comparison of avoiders' and nonavoiders' stories about the threatening event yielded eleven out of twenty-three instances in which the former showed significantly more evidences of fear. All the other differences, save one, were in the predicted direction. But when these two groups were compared on their stories dealing with nonthreatening events, no significant differences were found, and the directions of differences were inconsistent.

The most reliable discriminators of avoiders' and nonavoiders' stories about threatening events were: (*a*) protocol length, (*b*) degree of acceptance of the situation described in the story, (*c*) nature of activity described, and (*d*) outcome.

CHAPTER 41

....

Hope of Success and Fear of Failure as Aspects of Need for Achievement*

RUSSELL A. CLARK, RICHARD TEEVAN
AND HENRY N. RICCIUTI[1]

RESEARCH by McClelland and his associates (272) on a group TAT measure of need for achievement (n Achievement) yielded evidence suggesting that this measure involves two recognizable aspects of achievement motivation, *hope of success* (HS) and *fear of failure* (FF). One is an approach motive involving anticipation of reward, the other an avoidance motive involving anticipation of punishment. The main source of evidence for this distinction (summarized in [272]) consists of the repeated finding that individuals with moderate or low n Achievement scores appear fearful or defensively oriented whereas individuals with high scores appear hopeful. For example, those with moderate or low scores inhibit the recall of tasks failed, and are slow to recognize the tachistoscopic presentation of achievement-related words connoting failure, obstacles to achievement, etc. Subjects with high n Achievement scores, on the other hand, are especially quick in the recognition of achievement-related success words and show none of the defensive characteristics of the moderate group.

Clarification of these suggested relationships requires the measurement of fear of failure and hope of success, and several attempts have been made to arrive at such measures. The senior investigator first sought to arouse fear of failure and hope of success experimentally, administering the group TAT to subjects after they had been led to anticipate doing either very well or very poorly on the

---

* Reprinted by permission of author and publisher from *The Journal of Abnormal and Social Psychology,* 1956, **53**, 182-186. Copyright 1956 by the American Psychological Association, Inc.

[1] This study was supported by a grant from the Office of Naval Research under the supervision of David C. McClelland.

586

examination that they were about to take. Results failed to support the expectation that certain of the subcategories composing the total n Achievement score, singly or in combinations, would distinguish between these two experimentally different groups.

Another attempt involved a factor analysis of the intercorrelations among these subcategories in the hope that fear of failure and hope of success might emerge clearly in such an analysis, and that categories or combinations of categories proving to be heavily saturated with the two respective factors could then be used for indices. Several such analyses were made involving somewhat different categories, combinations of categories, and criterion measures. This approach in turn was unsuccessful.

A fresh approach to the problem, a measure of these two aspects of n Achievement, was therefore sought that was independent of the measurement of the achievement motive. Studies of level of aspiration seemed to offer a way of isolating the cautious, defensive individual (FF) as opposed to the hopeful person (HS). A questionnaire on level of aspiration was therefore designed for the present purpose.

Because of recognized complexities in the measurement of level of aspiration, it had been given low priority in our previous approach to the problem. Our experience with such a measure seems worth reporting, however, not only because it yielded some positive results but also because it shed light on one plausible reason why some of the previous attempts had failed.

METHOD

The group TAT measure of n Achievement had been administered to three classes of Swarthmore freshmen under so-called neutral conditions about five weeks prior to the final examination. The level-of-aspiration questionnaire was administered to these classes immediately before the examination. It read as follows:

You are asked to cooperate in a study of students' attitudes toward examinations by answering several questions which are explained below. The information you record will be held in strict confidence, and *will not* be seen by your instructors, or by anyone concerned with your course grades. Please express yourself as honestly and candidly as you can since the success of the study will depend upon your giving your frank and best opinion.

Question 1. On the grade scale in the table below, you are to indicate the two grades between which you are *practically certain* your final examination grade will fall. Make this as objective a judgment as you can, following these directions.

Lower Extreme: The lower grade you mark would answer this question: "I'm practically certain I will get at least a ———."

Upper Extreme: The higher grade you mark would answer this question: "I'm practically certain I won't get a better grade than a ———."

Grade Scale

E   D—   D   D+   C—   C   C+   B—   B   B+   A—   A   A+

Question 2. For *each* of the grades in the table above, indicate how you believe you would feel if you made that particular grade on your final examination. Do this by placing *below each grade from E to A+*, the number of the most appropriate statement below, which would describe how you would feel. Do this on the line marked "Question 2."

+3 I would feel extremely good and very satisfied with my grade.
+2 I would feel quite good and quite satisfied.
+1 I would feel somewhat satisfied.
 0 I would feel about neutral—neither good nor bad.
−1 I would feel somewhat disappointed.
−2 I would feel quite disappointed and dissatisfied.
−3 I would feel extremely bad, and very much dissatisfied with my grade.

Question 3. Supposing that it were possible for you to be excused from taking the final examination you are about to take. In that case, would you be willing to settle for an A+? For *each of the remaining grades* from E to A+, indicate whether you *would* (Y) or *would not* (N) be willing to settle for that grade rather than take the examination, if that were possible. Do this by marking a Y or N under each grade.

Question 4. What grade are you really going to try to make on the examination?

Thank you very much for your cooperation. When you have finished, please put this sheet in the envelope and seal the envelope.

In the questionnaire, Question 1 calls for a realistic estimate of the limits within which the students' grades will fall. Question 2 calls for the *affect* that would be experienced upon receiving any particular grade. Question 3, which is somewhat of an innovation in level-of-aspiration studies, asks for the lowest grade that the student would "settle for" in lieu of taking the final exam. The fourth question is one frequently asked in level-of-aspiration studies. It asks for the grade that the individual is "really going to try to make."

How can these items be used to distinguish FF from HS? Several possibilities were entertained. First, we expected that an FF student might settle for a grade that was farther below his upper realistic limit than would an HS person (Index I). Such a defensive, fearful person should accept a lower grade in relation to his realistic expectations because doing so minimizes possibility of failure. An HS student, however, is optimistic and should be unwilling to settle for a grade very far removed from his realistic upper limit. An equally meaningful index would take into consideration the range of expected scores. A second index, therefore, was obtained by dividing Index I by the range. Still another index follows from the consideration that, other things being equal, the affect associated with the grade "settled for" should be more positive for the HS person than for the FF person. The HS person should not settle for a grade unless he is fairly well satisfied with it, while an FF individual should be willing to compromise in this respect. A fourth index is related to the third, and attempts to correct for differences in realistic expectations. The difference between the affect associated with the upper limit grade and the grade "settled for" should be less for the HS group than for the FF group. For example, an HS person who realistically expects to get a poor grade might settle for a grade close to this level without being highly pleased with it, provided that he anticipates that it would give almost as much satisfaction as the upper realistic limit. This formulation permits HS subjects to have low or negative absolute levels of affect, but requires that these levels be close to the level of affect associated with the upper limit.

In treating responses to Question 1, adjacent grades were considered to be one unit apart. The distribution of scores for Index I (Upper Limit minus Settle For) was grouped into seven class intervals, with a value of seven being assigned to the smallest difference. Since the prediction is that for the HS person the quantity (Upper Limit minus Settle For) will be small, the data were coded so that HS subjects would receive the highest scores. The results for the other three indices were treated in parallel fashion.

RESULTS

Table 1 presents intercorrelations showing the internal consistency of these indices. It shows that the correlations are all positive and highly significant. For establishing further relations with the HS–FF continuum all four categories were summed in order to obtain

TABLE 1. RELATIONSHIP AMONG FOUR INDICES OF HOPE OF
SUCCESS AND FEAR OF FAILURE*

(Each index is correlated with the sum of the other three)

Index	Correlation with Remaining Three Indices
Upper Limit minus Settle For	.85
Upper Limit minus Settle For Range	.82
Affect over Settle For	.58
Affect over Upper Limit minus Affect Settle For	.83

* For $N = 45$ a correlation of .38 is significant at the .01 level of confidence.

a more stable though crude measure. This distribution was divided into thirds with the high third showing hope of success in clearest form and the low third showing the most consistent fear of failure. The middle third might be characterized either in terms of conflict or of realistic orientation, alternatives that we are not at present in a position to distinguish.

Table 2 presents the relationship between this three-way categorization and four separate questionnaire responses: Upper Limit, Lower Limit, Settle For, and Level of Aspiration. We had made no prior predictions concerning these relationships, but, other things

TABLE 2. RELATIONSHIP BETWEEN THE HOPE OF SUCCESS–FEAR OF FAILURE CONTINUUM AND QUESTIONNAIRE RESPONSES

(χ^2 test of independence)

Questionnaire Items	χ^{2*}	p
Settle For	27.45	<.01
Level of Aspiration	9.12	.06
Upper Limit	1.57	—
Lower Limit	8.20	<.10

* χ^2 was calculated using the method of maximum likelihood.

being equal, one would expect that the HS subjects would have higher absolute levels of Settle For and Level of Aspiration. In our prediction we had used Settle For, but the contention was that it would be closer to the Upper Limit for the HS students and not necessarily at a higher absolute value. In any event both the Settle For and Level of Aspiration turn out to be higher for the HS than for the FF subjects.

We had no expectations about the relationship with Upper Limit and Lower Limit. The HS group and the Middle group have about the same distribution at upper and lower limits, whereas the FF group is lower in upper and lower limits than either of the other groups.

Turning now to the relationship with the TAT measure of n Achievement let us first examine the relationship between the HS-FF continuum and the total n Achievement score. Table 3 presents an analysis of variance of this threefold relationship. It is quite clear that the Middle group has the highest scores with HS and FF groups scoring at about the same level. In previous work persons with high scores had showed HS characteristics, with moderate or low scores being associated with signs of fear of failure. The present results are in obvious disagreement.[2]

---

[2] However, the present results are consistent with the theoretical model presented in Ch. 22 which was developed after this study was completed. Editor.

TABLE 3. TOTAL N ACHIEVEMENT SCORES FOR THE HOPE OF SUCCESS, MIDDLE, AND FEAR OF FAILURE GROUPS
(F_1 = between groups/within groups; F_2 = Middle and combined HS, FF group/within groups)

Group	N	Mean n Achievement Score
HS	14	11.57
Middle	16	18.00
FF	15	10.73
	$F_1 = 4.26$	$F_2 = 8.44$
	$p < .05$	$p < .01$

With respect to subcategories in the measurement of n Achievement, the McClelland scoring system includes several clearly positive and negative categories, which are given below. The positive categories represent what McClelland has earlier termed "Goal Imagery"; the negative categories represent what he has called "Deprivation Imagery."

Goal Imagery

Positive Categories

 I+ Successful Instrumental Activity
 GA+ Anticipations of Success
 G+ Positive Affect over Goal Achievement

Deprivation Imagery

Negative Categories

 I− Unsuccessful Instrumental Activity
 GA− Anticipation of Failure
 G− Negative Affect over Failure to Achieve Goal
 B Blocks or Obstacles in Path to Achievement

The following analyses involve the use of positive and negative subtotals computed from the scored protocols of each individual.

Table 4 presents an analysis of variance for both the positive and negative subscores. The Middle group employs significantly more negative categories than either the HS or FF groups. In regard to the positive subscores the three group means are very similar. The group differences in total n Achievement score are thus accounted for mainly in terms of the negative categories.

Because the Middle group has a much higher number of achieve-

592 *The Thematic Apperceptive Measure*

TABLE 4. POSITIVE AND NEGATIVE N ACHIEVEMENT SUBSCORES FOR THE HS, MIDDLE, AND FF GROUPS
(F_1 = between groups/within groups; F_2 = middle and combined HS, FF group/within groups)

Groups	Mean n Achievement Subscores		
	N	Negative	Positive
HS........................	14	1.78	1.43
Middle...................	16	3.81	1.37
FF........................	15	1.87	1.47
	$F_1 = 4.22$	$F_2 = 8.43$	F_1, n.s.;
	$p < .025$	$p < .01$	F_2, n.s.

ment-related stories, however, this group should tend to show a higher frequency for all categories. To take account of this difference the total positive and negative scores for each individual were divided by the number of his achievement-related stories. Table 5 presents the results of a median test for the number of positive and negative categories per achievement-related story. The median test is appropriate to the present data since it makes no assumptions about the variances, which would be dubious in the case of ratio scores. These results show that the HS and FF groups are about equal in relative frequency of positive categories, but are significantly higher than the Middle group. The findings for relative negative frequency are just the reverse except that the differences are not highly reliable.

TABLE 5. MEDIAN ANALYSIS OF HS–FF IN RELATION TO FREQUENCY OF POSITIVE AND NEGATIVE CATEGORIES

Group	Number of Subjects Above or Below Median with Respect to:			
	Negative Categories		Positive Categories	
	Above Median	Below Median	Above Median	Below Median
HS.................	6	8	10	4
Middle..............	11	5	4	12
FF.................	11	9	9	6
	$\chi^{2*} = 3.13$		$\chi^{2*} = 7.41$	
	$p = .20$		$p = .03$	

* χ^2 was calculated using the method of maximum likelihood.

DISCUSSION

Let us first examine the treatment of this general problem offered by McClelland (258). After a thorough review of the evidence related to the effects of different levels of intensity of motivation, McClelland presents the hypothetical functional relationships which are reproduced in Fig. 1. It can be seen that these curves are very similar to those in Fig. 2 which represent a plot of the results obtained from the analysis of the number of positive and negative categories per achievement-related story. McClelland's "Wish Fulfillment" stage, which corresponds to our HS group, represents a condition of satisfaction and no anxiety over failure to attain the goal in question. His "Push Toward Reality" stage corresponds to what we have called the Middle group. Here there is decreasing optimism and satisfaction and a moderate increase in anxiety over goal attainment. His final "Defense" stage is analogous to our FF group. Here anxiety is so great and hope of goal attainment so small that the individual must repress deprivation-imagery stimuli and enhance goal-related imagery. The interested reader should consult McClelland (258) for the complete treatment of this problem.

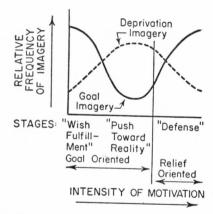

Fig. 1. The hypothetical effect of increased motive intensity on thought processes. (Reproduced by permission from McClelland [258] Copyright by William Sloane Assoc.)

One general implication strongly suggested by this study is that the level of n Achievement score *cannot* be used as an index of the FF-HS continuum. It is quite probable that the total n Achievement scores obtained by groups along this continuum are a function of the pictures used to obtain the n Achievement scores. The dis-

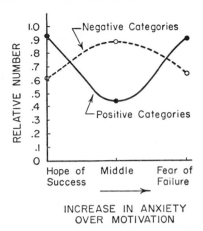

INCREASE IN ANXIETY
OVER MOTIVATION

Fig. 2. The number of positive and negative categories per achievement-related story as a function of the HS-FF continuum. Because there were five negative categories and only three positive categories used in this analysis, the number of positive categories has been multiplied by five-thirds in order to make the two curves directly comparable.

crepancy between the present results and earlier results could easily result from the fact that of the eight pictures used in this study, only one was the same as that used in the earlier work.

The present research also indicates why some of the earlier work failed to distinguish fear of failure and hope of success as aspects of achievement motivation. The present research shows that FF subjects are *phenotypically* similar to subjects characterized by Hope of Success. With regard to the TAT measure of n Achievement the total score and the positive and negative subscores are similar for both of these extreme groups. It is the inclusion of the Middle group that gives rise to significant differences. In the initial attempt to arouse hope of success and fear of failure experimentally, successful arousal would lead only to the two extreme groups. Since no Middle group was provided for, the expected differences could not be found.[3]

---

[3] To apply the theoretical model presented in Ch. 22, it is assumed that a high n Achievement score implies that the motive to achieve is relatively stronger than the motive to avoid failure within the individual; and conversely, it is assumed that a low n Achievement score implies a stronger motive to avoid failure. With these assumptions, the model predicts that persons who prefer intermediate risk will have higher n Achievement scores than persons who prefer either very safe or very speculative undertakings. In terms of this model, the aspirant behaviors which in the present study are called *hope of success* and *fear of failure* represent alternative (*phenotypic*) expressions of the same underlying (*genotypic*) motive to avoid failure. In other words, the TAT

SUMMARY

Previous research has suggested that McClelland's TAT measure of n Achievement involves two recognizable aspects—hope of success (HS) and fear of failure (FF). A level-of-aspiration questionnaire related to grades on a course examination was designed to give an independent measure of the HS-FF continuum, and administered to college students in conjunction with the examination. Relations between this measure and both total n Achievement score and various n Achievement subscores were investigated. In brief, the findings were these: (a) Students at the extremes of the continuum have lower n Achievement scores than students in the middle of the continuum. (b) In terms of positive subscores (goal imagery) on the n Achievement measure, the extremes have higher scores than subjects in the middle of the HS-FF continuum. (c) In terms of negative subscores (deprivation imagery) the Middle group tends to score more highly than the extremes.

---

measure is accepted as a measure of the underlying or genotypic motivation while stated levels of aspiration are considered the phenotypic expressions. In the present article, the authors lean heavily on just the opposite assumption, that stated levels of aspiration can be used to identify two groups that are genotypically different, i.e., hopeful of success or fearful of failure, and that these two groups turn out to be phenotypically similar, viz., in having relatively low n Achievement scores.

The other important result of the present study, that the stories of the intermediate level of aspiration group contain relatively more "deprivation imagery" and relatively less "goal imagery," needs to be considered in light of the studies by Scott (Ch. 40) and Moulton (Ch. 39). Scott found that anxious subjects were prone to avoid producing the kind of thematic content that made them anxious. And Moulton argues that an adequate thematic apperceptive measure of fear of failure, i.e., the motive to avoid failure, will have to embrace imagery expressing escape-from and avoidance-of achievement situations, categories not presently included in the "negative" categories which constitute part of the scoring for n Achievement.

If one accepts the alternative explanation of the Clark-Teevan-Ricciuti results which is here proposed, their finding more "deprivation imagery" in the stories of persons having higher n Achievement scores seems to indicate quite clearly that deprivation imagery which appears in stories otherwise concerned with positive achievement striving *cannot by itself* be taken as a very reliable index of the over-all strength of the motive to avoid failure. In light of results to be reported by Birney in Chapter 44, which show a significant relationship between the qualitative characteristics of pictures and the affective tone of achievement-related imagery in stories, it might be expected that the imagery produced to certain kinds of pictures by persons highly motivated to achieve would often be negatively toned.

This important issue is still very much up in the air. The present study nicely defines the problem and offers an insightful set of proposals for its solution. In this footnote, I have attempted to call attention to a more recently proposed solution to the same problem. Editor.

CHAPTER 42

Thematic Apperceptive Measurement of Motives Within the Context of a Theory of Motivation

JOHN W. ATKINSON

CAN WE TURN NOW to the measuring instrument and see it in the context of ideas about motivation and behavior suggested by the empirical findings of studies which have used it to assess the strength of motivation? Thematic apperception is, after all, a particular kind of behavior. One test of the adequacy of some of the ideas which have been advanced is to see whether or not they can be used to provide at least the outline of a theory of the measuring instrument, one which will help to define the path for further research aimed at increasing the validity of inferences about motivation drawn from imaginative behavior.

One potential value of an analysis of the measuring instrument is coming face to face with the fact that the problems of assessing individual differences in motivation and the problems faced in the search for general laws relating motivation and behavior are completely intertwined. Lewin has made the oft-neglected point as clearly as anyone: "A law is expressed in an equation which relates certain variables. Individual differences have to be conceived as various specific values which these variables have in a specific case. In other words, general laws and individual differences are merely two aspects of one problem; they are mutually dependent on each other and the study of one cannot proceed without the study of the other" (230, p. 243).

Three important questions are to be considered: What is a need or motive?[1] How is the strength of a particular motive related to

---

[1] These two terms have been used interchangeably throughout the book. The term, motive, however, is preferred because it does not imply that activation and direction of behavior is necessarily linked to conditions of deprivation Of all the other alternatives available, the term motive seems the most general in its connotation.

overt adaptive behavior? And how is the fact of a changing level of motivational content in thematic apperceptive stories, both as a function of systematic changes in the situation at the time of testing and of the pictures used to elicit stories, to be reconciled with the conception of a motive, or need, as a relatively stable and enduring attribute of personality? (A fourth question, the historical issue of how motives are acquired, has been dealt with more fully elsewhere by McClelland *et al.* (272, Ch. II and IX) and is reviewed also in Part IV of this volume.)

The only feasible way to deal with all three questions is to take them one at a time and to try to keep the others from intruding until it is their turn for discussion. The plan is to review ideas which have been presented in earlier portions of this book and to present rather dogmatically what is admittedly an incomplete conceptual scheme. In the process, we shall point to the empirical findings which seem, at the moment, to demand such a scheme. Along the way, we shall try to uncover the problems for future research which the scheme suggests.

WHAT IS A NEED, OR MOTIVE?

The conception of a need, or a motive, as a relatively enduring disposition of personality was developed by Murray (314) in an attempt to formulate a comprehensive system for description of personality. The core of personality, as viewed by Murray, is a configuration or hierarchy of basic needs. McClelland (258) has extended and elaborated the general argument for this theoretical position, particularly in his analysis of the origins of motivational dispositions in the primary learning experiences of childhood.

A motive, or need, is a disposition to strive for a particular kind of goal-state or aim, e.g., achievement, affiliation, power. The aim of a particular motive is a particular kind of *effect* to be brought about through some kind of action. The aim of a motive defines the *kind* of satisfaction that is sought, e.g., pride in accomplishment, a positive affective relationship with another person, a sense of being in control of the means of influencing the behavior of other persons. The attainment of a goal-state is accompanied by feelings of satisfaction; disruption of goal-directed activity, or non-attainment of a desired goal-state, is accompanied by feelings of dissatisfaction. The aim of a motive is not identified with performance of particular kinds of acts such as approval seeking or attempts at influence, or with particular qualities of instrumental action like persistence or rigidity. A particular kind or quality of instrumental action may, however, come to be associated with attainment of the aim of a particular motive and hence provide a fairly reliable clue to the presence of that motive.

The question of how many basic motives it may be useful to consider and the problem of what criteria are relevant for deciding upon a limited set of basic motives are matters beyond the scope of the present discussion. These issues have been dealt with at length by both Murray (314) and McClelland (258). It is doubtful whether anything new can be added to their discussion of this problem before empirical studies directly pertinent to it are undertaken to provide something concrete to talk about.

The linkage between affective reactions and the attainment or nonattainment of goals has made it possible to clarify the definition of the aims, or goal-states, of particular motives by experiment (See Part I). When a particular kind of motivation is experimentally aroused, thematic apperceptive stories produced by the motivated person contain elaborate imaginative descriptions of the kinds of circumstances which will produce feelings of satisfaction and dissatisfaction in him. The definitions of the goal-states of the three motives presented in Part II are hence to be viewed as *empirically-derived* generalizations from analysis of hundreds of thematic apperceptive stories produced by persons in whom these motives had been experimentally aroused. In some cases, the initial task of clarifying the definitions of the aim of a motive has taken one to two years of repeated trial and check analysis of the material. The write-ups of experiments often fail to communicate the trial-and-check nature of the procedure.

McClelland, in Ch. 32, has produced a number of cogent arguments rooted in accepted principles of learning to support the view, advanced chiefly in psychoanalytic writings, that motives are developed early in childhood and become relatively stable attributes of personality which are highly resistant to change. Implicit in the studies reported in this book is an assumption that the motives of an individual are relatively stable dispositions which he carries about with him from situation to situation. This conception of a motive poses two problems: a) How are motives related to overt adaptive behavior? b) If the strength of a motive is a relatively stable thing, how can it be measured through thematic apperception when the motivational content of thematic apperception is extremely sensitive to situational influences?

HOW IS THE STRENGTH OF A PARTICULAR NEED OR MOTIVE RELATED TO OVERT ADAPTIVE (I.E., INSTRUMENTAL) BEHAVIOR?

Let us, for the moment, assume that the index of the strength of a particular motive as obtained from thematic apperception in a "neutral" situation *is* a valid measure of the strength of a relatively stable disposition, acquired early in life, to strive for a particular goal-state. We shall make a thorough analysis of the measuring rod, itself, in the next section and examine this assumption critically. But for now, let us accept it in order to turn to the question of the relation of motives to behavior.

Do we always expect the individual's motives to be clearly manifested in his overt behavior? Do we expect the person who is highly motivated to achieve always to show concentration in the task at hand, a heightened desire to perform well, a willingness to persist in the face of obstacles? Do we expect the person who is strong in the need for affiliation constantly to display approval-seeking tendencies in his actions? Do we expect the person who is high in the power motive invariably to attempt to influence the behavior and opinions of others?

The intuitive answer to these questions, when put in so bald a form, is obviously no; and experimental findings (Part III) confirm our intuition that the answer should be no. We find that the situation at the time of performance somehow defines the relevance or functional significance of alternative paths of action for the individual. Our theoretical task, then, is to conceptualize the effect of the situation in a way that will clarify the problem for further experimental analysis. This, hopefully, may lead to a technique for independent and more precise assessment of the salient features of situations which have a profound influence on behavior. Here we come face to face with the stubborn problem of the interaction of personality and situation as it arises in studies of the effects of human motives on behavior. And to solve the problem, we have adapted several ideas developed over the years chiefly by Tolman (413, 414). Our analysis of the situation pursues a course that is similar in many respects to that also developed in the recent writings of Rotter (353, 354).[2]

Our experiments have suggested that a particular motive (e.g., *n* Achievement) is aroused or engaged in the performance of an act when the cues of the situation can be interpreted to mean that performance of the act will be instrumental in attaining some satisfaction (an incentive) of that particular motive. In other words, when the situation seems to arouse in the person a *cognitive expectancy* (now to use Tolman's concept) that performance of the act will produce an effect he is generally interested in bringing about, his motive is aroused and manifested in overt performance of the act. The influence of the situation seems to be reducible to the kinds and relative strengths of the cognitive expectancies it arouses in a person (given his recent life history) concerning the possible rewarding or punish-

---

[2] See also the clarifications of expectancy theory presented by MacCorquodale and Meehl (244, 245).

ing consequences (given his motives) of this versus that path of action. Rotter (354) has directed attention to the central role of the situation in defining the *expectancies* and *reinforcement values* (incentives) which determine behavior. The present conception tends to highlight the role of individual differences in the strength of motives.

To simplify the present analysis of the interaction between personality (motive) and situation (expectancy of goal-attainment), we will assume that incentive, i.e., the amount of satisfaction of a motive offered in a situation, is held constant. Obviously the amount of satisfaction of a motive can vary from situation to situation just as the degree to which any satisfaction expected from that motive can vary from situation to situation. But the present "limited" conception will ignore possible variations in the value of the incentive. (Several earlier chapters, viz., Chs. 20 and 22, have attempted to deal with the specific effects of variations in the incentive to achieve, the special case where incentive value is dependent upon the strength of expectancy.)

Where does our conception of the role of the situation in the determination of behavior lead us? It can be assumed that every individual has acquired a number of different kinds of motives. And any particular situation in which he may find himself, e.g., a college classroom, a business office, a walk in the park with a friend, a luncheon with strangers, is likely to arouse a number of different cognitive expectancies concerning possible consequences of performing this or that act. It may be expected, for example, that a pleasant comment about the weather will provoke a positive reaction in a stranger at lunch but have little, if any, rewarding consequence if produced while one is working alone late at night in one's business office. On the other hand, it may be expected that silent concentration on the task at hand will move one closer to that sense of pride in accomplishment sought on the job; but the same degree of silent concentration on the task of eating one's lunch may be expected to heighten interpersonal tension rather than to contribute to the affiliative satisfaction of a friendly luncheon conversation.

Some situations arouse expectancies of satisfying different motives through performance of different acts: the college student torn between continued study in his room and going to the movie with his friends. In such cases, the individual experiences a conflict between the two tendencies to act which have been aroused in him: one instrumental to achievement, the other to affiliation. When, on the other hand, the cues of a situation arouse expectancies of simultaneously satisfying several different motives through performance of the same act, these several different motives should be engaged in performance of the same act. The resultant behavior should then reflect the combined strengths of the several motives which have been engaged. The total strength of motivation to perform the act will be greater than the strength contributed by any one of the particular motives which has been engaged. The behavior, in other words, is *overdetermined*.

This discussion of how the motives of an individual are engaged by expectancies aroused in a situation may seem to imply that the person is completely conscious of his decision-making processes. Such an implication is certainly not intended. Both the motives of the individual and the expectancies aroused in him are inferences to be made from relevant and independent observations of his past behavior, i.e., from a survey of his developmental history or from behavior as recorded on some instrument especially designed for assessment of motives or expectancies. What a person consciously experiences when a motive is aroused is an interesting empirical question for future study. Our hunch is that the motivated person will report only the feeling of wanting to perform some act and certain images pertaining to the consequences of the act when asked to describe his inner experience.

We see here the need for a distinction in terminology. The term *motive* (or need) has been used to refer to dispositions to strive for rather general goal-states, kinds of satisfaction, or effects. These dispositions, it is assumed, have their origins in childhood experience and are relatively stable and enduring after childhood. They are carried about from situation to situation by the adult and constitute the core of what is called personality. Our discussion has suggested that these dispositions be thought of as latent, with respect to overt adaptive behavior, until the cues of a situation arouse the appropriate expectancy of goal-attainment through performance of some act. The cognitive expectancies cued-off in particular situations are also acquired. But we assume that specific expectancies of attaining this or that goal through performance of this or that act in a particular situation are normally acquired later than motives, that expectancies can be acquired through verbal training, as well as through actual experience, and that the more situationally-defined expectancies are more amenable to change than the more general motive dispositions. Expectancies, in other words, are the stuff of which beliefs, social norms, and social roles are made.

But to return to the need for a distinction in terminology: if the term motive refers to the more general and relatively stable disposition, what shall we call a person's *temporarily aroused state* produced when the cues of a situation elicit an expectancy of goal-attainment which engages the motive? I should like to use the term which immediately comes to mind to designate the aroused state, *motivation*.

The term motivation refers to the arousal of a tendency to act to produce one or more effects. The term motivation points to the final strength of the action tendency which is experienced by the person as an "I want to ———." The particular aim of the momentary state of motivation is situationally defined. It is specific and concrete; it is the aim of the moment, e.g., to get a high score on this test, to be warmly received by that person. The aims of the one or more motives which may be contributing to the momentary strength of motivation, on the other hand, are more general and refer to the kinds of experience of satisfaction that may be sought on the particular occasion. For example, one may experience strong *motivation* to eat a hamburger or a piece of lemon pie; the general aim of the *motive* is the satisfaction that accompanies eating something.

One may be strongly motivated to complete a task; the general aim of the motive may be a sense of personal accomplishment. The term motivation points to the over-all strength of the tendency to strive which has been aroused on this particular occasion. The term motive is used to define the functional significance of the striving in relation to the more general and relatively enduring dispositions of the individual. The term motive points to the one or more "meanings" of the act for the individual, *of which meanings he may be completely unaware.*

The distinction intended between motive as disposition and motivation as aroused state is presented schematically in Figure 1.[3]

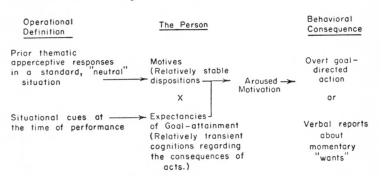

Fig. 1. The interaction of the motives of an individual with the situation in the determination of the momentary strength of motivation to perform some act.

---

[3] As mentioned earlier, the effect of *incentive,* i.e., the *amount* of satisfaction of the motive offered in the situation, is not included in the present formulation. But the reader may note that many of the points which are made concerning the influence of expectancies on strength of motivation can be repeated concerning the effects of variations in incentive value.

This conception of motivation to perform an act as a joint function of the motives of the individual and the expectancies of motive-satisfying consequences elicited by situational cues is supported by a number of experimental facts which can be summarized briefly:

1. Performance is positively related to the thematic apperceptive index of the strength of a particular motive when the situation cues have aroused the expectancy of attaining the goal state of that motive through performance of the act and few or no other expectancies of goal attainment have been aroused. In this case, the strength of motivation to perform the act, as measured by response output or some equivalent index, should largely be a function of the strength of the one motive which has been systematically engaged.

2. Performance is unrelated to the strength of a particular motive when the cues of the situation have been deliberately rigged to minimize the probability that any one would expect to satisfy *that* motive through performance of the act. In this case, motivation to perform the act must be attributed to various other unmeasured motives which are unsystematically engaged in performance of the act.

3. When the cues of a situation are deliberately controlled to arouse the expectancy of attaining the goal of a particular motive, but expectancies of satisfying other motives through performance of the same act are also systematically aroused, the relationship between performance and thematic apperceptive indices of the strength of the particular motive of interest is greatly reduced or washed out completely. In this case, the person who is weak in the particular motive which has been measured may be strong in some other motive which has also been systematically aroused. To the extent that several different motives are now contributing to the total motivation to perform the same act, a simple relationship between the strength of any one of them and performance is confounded.

These are the main facts of the experiments presented in Part III-A. Can we now point to other empirical findings that also fit the scheme?

One of the important results of Groesbeck's (158) analysis of the personality correlates of thematic apperceptive indices of n Achievement and n Affiliation in the data accumulated by Kelly and Fiske (208) in their assessment of clinical psychology trainees illustrates another implication of this conception. In the course of the assessment program, a group of prospective clinical trainees were brought together for a week-long period of testing and observation. During this period, they lived together and spent most of their leisure time in each other's company. Towards the end of the week, each individual was rated by his peers on a number of personality traits. Each individual was also rated on these same traits by a group of staff psychologists who had observed the trainees in a number of test situations and in interviews throughout the week.

Staff ratings were made chiefly in terms of behavior observed in achievement-oriented contexts, while trainees presumably had their best opportunity to size each other up in the interpersonal contexts of their leisure hours. When Groesbeck examined the personality correlates of these motives taken singly, he found that the *staff* ratings of the trainees were related almost exclusively to differences in n Achievement. Ratings by *peers,* on the other hand, were related almost as exclusively to differences in n Affiliation (158, pp. 26 and 28). This result can reasonably be attributed to the different kinds of expectancies of goal-attainment normally aroused in the situations in which the most reliable observations by the two groups were likely to be made. The staff observed behavior aroused in the various test situations and so motivated to a great extent by n Achievement; the peers, on the other hand, were presumably basing their ratings on behavior motivated chiefly by n Affiliation and other interpersonal motives engaged in the off-duty hours when they were more free to observe their associates. One may wonder, in the light of these suggestive findings, how general a description of personality in terms of behavioral ratings is ever likely to be when the behavior observed occurs in fairly circumscribed situations which are capable of arousing expectancies which make a limited appeal to the motivational structure of the individual.

One of the findings in a project dealing with conformity reported by Walker and Heyns (422) is also consistent with the present scheme. They report that subjects were put into a conflict in which continued hard work at a task, instrumental to personal accomplishment, was pitted against slowing up to satisfy the appeal of a friend and partner who was being put in a position of invidious comparison by the subject's high level of performance. A group of subjects who were classified high in n Affiliation but low in n Achievement showed the greatest tendency to be influenced by the appeal of the friend to slow down. In this case, expectancies of satisfying two different motives through performance of incompatible acts were aroused. A willingness to slow down should be expected in a group who are strong in n Affiliation but relatively weak in n Achievement. Along the same line, French (142) has found that persons highly motivated to achieve but low in n Affiliation prefer a successful stranger to an unsuccessful friend as a work partner, while just the reverse is true of persons high in n Affiliation but low in n Achievement.

In light of the present conception of the relationship between particular motives and overt behavior, it is not at all surprising that the correlations which have been reported between thematic apperceptive measures of particular motives and complex performance criteria like academic grade average are, at best, low to moderate (301, 342) and vary from school to school. A high grade point average in school or college is an *accomplishment* requiring performances which undoubtedly are overdetermined in the sense of involving more than one of the individual's motives. The strength of motivation to get good grades in school, for example, is in part a function of the strength of the achievement motive, but few will quarrel with the idea that performance in school is also perceived by many students as instrumental to gaining the approval of parents (affiliation) or as the path to an influential vocation (power), to list but two other possible "meanings" that working hard in school may have for particular individuals.

A more promising approach to investigation of factors which contribute to academic accomplishment, in light of the present analysis, would be to assess the expectations of particular individuals regarding the consequences of their working to get good grades. Such an assessment of expectations together with thematic apperceptive measurement of the various motives which, as a result, may be engaged in academic work should bring us much closer to the accurate prediction of academic success from motivational variables that we have been seeking for so long in a relatively blind empirical way. The same idea may be applied to many other instances in which an overdetermined performance criterion is to be predicted.

A THEORETICAL CONCEPTION OF THE THEMATIC APPERCEPTIVE INDEX OF MOTIVE STRENGTH

Let us turn now to the questions which we put aside earlier: How is the conception of motives as relatively enduring and stable dispositions to be reconciled with the fact that the level of motive-related imagery in thematic apperception, which provides the index of the strength of a motive, is not constant but varies as a function of systematic changes in the situation prior to administration of the test and of the pictures used to elicit stories? How, in other words, can the strength of a stable disposition be inferred from the frequency of particular kinds of imaginative responses when the frequency of such responses is known to vary?

These questions can be satisfactorily answered if the distinctions between *motive, expectancy,* and *aroused motivation* which we are forced to make in an analysis of instrumental action are now applied to the imaginative response of the subject to a particular picture. The fact that changes in average level of motivational imagery in stories occur as a result of certain experimental procedures and the idea of a relatively stable strength of motive can be reconciled if imaginative content is thought of as an expression of the *momentary state of aroused motivation* in the person.

According to our theoretical formulation, the momentary state of motivation is a changing thing. It is a joint function of a stable element, the motive, and a transient or changing element, the momentary expectancy of attaining some degree of satisfaction of the motive, which has been aroused by situational cues. When we refer to the total score for a particular kind of motivation (e.g., *n* Achievement score) as obtained from a series of thematic apperceptive stories, we are referring to a summation of the amounts of that kind of motivation which has been expressed in a series of stories *in a particular situation, e.g., under certain experimental conditions*. The strength of motivation aroused by expectancies cued-off by the situation is assumed to remain fairly constant throughout the 20 to 30 minute test period. When, on the other hand, we view the changing level of motive-related imaginative response from picture to picture *within* the test period, we are observing an additional effect on the level of motivation of particular expectancies aroused by the cues of different pictures. Our theoretical task, then, is to define the conditions, both situation-wise and picture-wise, under which the inferring of individual differences in strength of *motive* from observed differences in an index of strength of *motivation* is reasonably valid and to discover the conditions under which inferences about the strength of motive from this motivation score might be very erroneous.

Let us start with a generalization of the findings of experiments dealing with the effects of experimental arousal of motives on thematic apperception (Part I): when reasonable and generally acceptable procedures are used to arouse experimentally a particular kind of motivation by controlling the motivating cues prior to the test, the imaginative thought sequence is increasingly saturated with imagery which is expressive of that kind of motivation. The arousal of a particular *kind* of motivation is, in other words, accompanied by an increase in a particular *kind* of imaginative content.

According to the present theoretical formulation, the experimental procedures employed in these studies can be described as manipulating the cues which arouse particular kinds of expectancies, e.g., of having performance evaluated in terms of standards of excellence (achievement), of being liked or disliked by others (affiliation), etc. If we consider the over-all frequency of a particular kind of motivational content in a series of stories to be a measure of the strength of that kind of motivation in the person at the time of writing the stories, the index obtained in the so-called "neutral" or standard situation for assessing individual differences must represent the strength of that kind of motivation which has been aroused in that situation. In experiments dealing with the relationship of individual differences in strength of particular motives to behavior, the thematic apperceptive measure has normally been administered in a college classroom or some similar situation, and stories are written without any attempt by the experimenter either to arouse a particular motive prior to the test or deliberately to relax the subjects. Nevertheless, this so-called "neutral" situation is obviously not neutral with respect to the motives of the individual. The cues of a college classroom should arouse particular kinds of expectancies by virtue of the relatively limited range of kinds of satisfactions that have been experienced by individuals in such a situation.

We have been willing to proceed on the assumption that the kinds of expectancies cued-off in the so-called neutral situation are very similar, i.e., relatively constant, among the individuals tested. It is not too bad an assumption in most cases. There are few situations which can make a greater claim of being illustrative of what is meant by a common or shared learning experience in our society than the average classroom situation. It is the geographic locus of activity of all members of the society for six hours a day, five days a week from age five to sixteen or beyond. To the extent that the assumption is warranted, the state of motivation at the time of writing thematic apperceptive stories, following our theoretical scheme, should be largely a function of the relative strengths of various motives in the individuals. Let us check this assumption, tentatively, as one to be scrutinized carefully a little later on and proceed, for the moment, to a discussion of the instrument itself. The reader who finds it difficult to grant the assumption—even tentatively—may simply imagine an "ideal" standard situation for assessment of motives in a number of individuals. This is one in which the expectancies aroused by the situation cues are the same for all individuals so that differences in the aroused state of a particular kind of motivation can be unambiguously attributed to differences in the strength of motive.

In the neutral situation, or for that matter in any situation, the average score of a group of individuals for a particular kind of motivation varies significantly from picture to picture (see subsequent chapters). Pictures of men working in a shop or of a young man seated at his desk in school, for example, elicit more achievement-related responses than relatively unstructured or obviously non-achievement-related pictures. Similarly, pictures of a group of persons sitting in a clubroom or of two young people apparently conversing are the kinds of pictures which provoke the greatest affiliative response. The pictures which produce the greatest amount of imagery symptomatic of a particular motive are, in other words, pictures of situations which normally arouse expectancies of satisfying that particular motive through some kind of action (Figure 2).

If the situation portrayed in a picture arouses the expectancy that evaluation of performance in terms of standards of excellence is the normal consequence of behavior in that setting, we should expect the achievement motive to be engaged and the motivational content of the imaginative story to contain a variety of associations related to the achievement-directed sequence of behavior. The characters of the story should be trying to achieve something. They should experience feelings of satisfaction when they have performed well and unpleasant

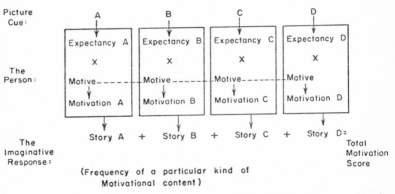

Fig. 2. A conception of the determinants of the imaginative response in which the strength of motive is constant throughout a series of stories, and the expectancies aroused by the cues of the real-life situation (not included in diagram) are constant throughout the test period, but the expectancies of goal-attainment aroused by the cues of particular pictures vary. As a consequence, the momentary strength of motivation expressed in particular stories varies.

feelings when their efforts to accomplish are thwarted in some way. Similarly, if the picture portrays a situation which normally elicits expectancies having to do with the attainment of power, the stories written in response to such a picture should be saturated with associations related to the power-directed sequence of behavior. The motivational content of the story should, in other words, reveal the kinds of motives normally aroused in real-life situations similar to those contained in the picture.

The imaginative story, however, tells us more about the state of motivation than does simple observation of the vigor of acts in a real-life situation; the imaginative story contains specific statements of aim and imagery related to the subtleties of feeling that are never directly observed in action. *The imaginative story defines the motive by describing the kinds of circumstances which produce affective reactions in the characters of the stories.*

If it were plausible to assume that the expectancies aroused by the distinctive cues of a particular picture were the same for all subjects, it would be reasonable to treat differences in the frequency of a particular kind of motivational content appearing in stories written to that picture as a fair index of the strength of the motive in various individuals. If, in other words, the expectancies aroused by a picture were constant for all subjects, then observed differences in a particular kind of motivational content could be directly attributed to differences in the strength of the motive.

We need not make this assumption, however, since the index we use as our estimate of the strength of a motive is the total score obtained from a series of pictures. The total score, you will recall, is a summation of a particular kind of motivational content which appears in *all* the stories the individual has written. To infer differences in the strength of motive from differences in total motivation score, we need only assume that the *average strength* of a particular expectancy (e.g., the expectancy of achievement, or of power, etc.) aroused by *all* of the pictures in the series is approximately equal for all subjects. When such an assumption is warranted, every subject has had a fair opportunity to reveal his motive in the test as a whole.

The point may be clarified by an example. Let us take two hypothetical young men known to have had the kinds of early childhood experiences which would account for their having developed equally strong motives to achieve (see Part IV). But let us suppose that the later cultural experience of one of these men had emphasized apprenticeship training for a job as a skilled machinist. He has quit school very early and has had expectations of achieving strengthened in the "blue-collar" work situation. The other young man, however, has had a different kind of later indoctrination and experience. His father is in business, and the son has had a number of influences play upon him at home and in summer jobs as a clerk in an office which point towards the long-term goal of an executive role in business.

How do we expect these two young men to respond in thematic apperception when confronted with pictures of a "man working in a shop" and a "business office scene"? For the first young man, achievement-related expectancies should be relatively strong in response to the blue-collar picture and relatively weak in response to the white-collar picture. Just the reverse should be true of the second young man. Given equally strong motives to achieve, the frequency of achievement-related imaginative responses should be greater in response to the blue-collar picture for the first young man and greater in response to the white-collar picture for the second young man. But their total scores from the two stories should be very comparable. They both should have higher total scores, for example, than young men who have had similar *later* cultural learning experiences which define cognitive expectations in these particular situations, but who have not had the significant *early* affective experiences of childhood which contribute to the development of a strong motive to achieve at something.

In summary, our conception of the determinants of the imaginative response is directly analogous to our conception of the joint role played by motives and situationally-aroused expectancies in the determination of adaptive, instrumental acts. The cues preceding the test period and of the test situation itself are thought to arouse certain expectancies in each individual. This accounts for a base level of motivation before the first picture is even presented. (In the "ideal" test situation, the expectancies aroused would be the same in all of the persons tested.) The pictures used to elicit stories are conceived as arousing particular kinds of expectancies of goal attainment which engage particular motives of the individual. These are expressed in the motivational content of the imaginative story. The story reveals the kinds of associations that situations similar to the one portrayed in the picture would elicit in the person in real life. Inferring individual differences in strength of a motive from the total motivation score is justified only when it can be assumed that all individuals tested have had an equal opportunity to express that motive in the test as a whole. This condition is likely to be *approximated* when the situations portrayed in the pictures are representative of a wide variety of life situations in which people can satisfy the particular motive. But the "ideal" instrument, and this point is worth repeating, is one in which the average strength of the expectancies of attaining the goal of a particular motive aroused by all of the pictures is equal for all individuals tested. And the "ideal" test situation is one which arouses the same goal expectancies in everyone.

We can organize most of the known facts about the index of motivation derived from thematic apperception in terms of this scheme. In the first place, the assumption that the thematic content related to a particular aim, e.g., achievement imagery or affiliation imagery, corresponds to the state of motivation rather than directly to the strength of the motive, enables us to account for the fact that we are able to develop valid scoring procedures by defining the particular kinds of content which increase in frequency in imaginative stories when a particular kind of motivation is experimentally aroused. The motive, conceived as a relatively stable disposition, cannot change when motivating cues are introduced; but the state of motivation can change. Secondly, the assumption that picture cues also arouse expectancies of goal attainment which engage particular motives and heighten the momentary strength of that kind of motivation enables us to account for a number of facts concerning the average response to particular pictures. For example:

1. In college students, the average n Achievement score is greater in response to pictures of culturally-defined achievement situations than to pictures of unstructured or unrelated situations (272). The same is generally true of n Affiliation and n Power scores, although systematic studies have not been performed except for achievement.

2. Rosenstein (350) has shown that a group of physical education majors and a group of chemistry majors obtain nearly equal high average n Achievement scores in response to pictures of athletic competition situations, a fairly universal achievement training experience for all males in this society; but the chemistry majors had a significantly higher n Achievement score than physical education majors in response to pictures portraying laboratory situations. It seems reasonable to attribute this difference to the rather specialized kinds of learning experiences a group of young men who decide to major in chemistry have had, experiences which would account for their having stronger achievement-related expectancies in laboratory situations.

3. The average n Achievement scores of American male and female students in high school and college are significantly greater in response to pictures of *men* in culturally-defined achievement settings than in response to pictures of *women* in very comparable settings (420). Mead (284) has argued that ideas of achievement are defined out of the female role in our society at about the time of adolescence. The girl begins to realize that trying to achieve puts her in competition with men and elicits a negative reaction from these potential marriage partners. As a result, we should expect that expectations of achievement are stronger, even in women, in response to pictures of men rather than women in work situations.

A CONCEPTION OF CONFLICT WHICH INHIBITS THE EXPRESSION OF MOTIVE IN THEMATIC APPERCEPTION

We have been lucky in our choice of the achievement motive for most of these early experimental excursions. Had we started our research with sex or aggression, the motives which interest clinicians most in societies which have made them special problems, we would not have been led so easily to as simple a scheme as that outlined in the preceding paragraphs. Our society does not generally punish the expression of a motive to achieve. Quite the contrary. So we have been able to avoid, to this point, discussing a question that frequently arises concerning the ultimate utility of thematic apperception for measuring the strength of motives about which the individual is seriously conflicted.

Let us see what happens when we impose the motive-expectancy distinction on the classic motivations, sex and aggression. Our scheme would lead us to look to early childhood for experiences which contribute to the development of these two motives, conceived as dispositions to attain certain kinds of gratifying effects or aims. The sense of having injured another person might serve, tentatively, as a definition of the aim of the aggressive motive; and sensuous pleasure will serve as a definition of the general aim of the sex motive. The question of type of act is, as in the cases of the other motives, left out of the definition of the aim.

Now, we might ask, when are these two motives expressed in overt action? Our theoretical answer is that these motives, like all others, are engaged when the cues of the situation, as a result of prior learning, arouse the expectancy of satisfying the motive through performance of some instrumental act. These two motives, like all others, are aroused by expectancies of satisfaction.

But, and this is an important *but,* there is a tremendous accumulation of evidence which indicates that overt expression of these motives is often inhibited. And, as Clark (72) has shown, even direct expression in thematic apperception is inhibited or distorted. We cannot expect, so the argument runs, to infer the strength of these motives simply by counting the frequency of *manifest,* motive-related responses as is the case for achievement, affiliation, and hunger.

The expression of sexual or aggressive motivation is inhibited when some other motive has also been engaged and the resultant motivations are incompatible. The conception of approach-avoidance conflict introduced by Lewin (228), extended and refined by Miller (293) within the framework of S-R reinforcement theory, and employed by Clark (72) has become the conventional model for discussion of inhibition produced by conflict. We can employ this general model. But instead of accounting for the relative strengths of the competing tendencies in terms of the concepts of drive and habit, as in the Miller (293) scheme, we shall appeal to a multiplicative relationship between motive and expectancy (and incentive) as outlined in earlier paragraphs.

What are the motives for avoidance? Fear or anxiety over painful consequences is the by now well-documented general answer to this question. Is there any reason that we cannot conceive of pain-avoidance as the general aim of a family of avoidance dispositions? McClelland (258) has stated affirmatively the argument for a two factor theory of motivation. And the distinction between appetites and aversions, pleasure-seeking and pain-avoidance, hopes and fears has been advanced in the writings of Tolman (413), Mowrer (308), Murray (314), and others. One can look to early childhood for the antecedents of pain-avoidance motives, e.g., a rejection-avoidance motive, a failure-avoidance motive, etc., just as easily as one can look there for antecedents of approach dispositions like achievement, affiliation, and aggression. It may be less cumbersome in discussion to call these avoidance dispositions fears, as McClelland (258) has suggested, and to define them in terms of the particular kinds of punishing consequences that are to be avoided, e.g., fear of punishment, fear of rejection, fear of failure, etc.

Conflict will occur when an approach motive and an avoidance motive are simultaneously engaged by different expectancies cued-off in a situation. For example, the same cues which arouse the expectancy of satisfying the aggressive impulse may serve also to arouse the expectancy of punishment. If so, two mutually incompatible *motivations* are aroused—to hit and not to hit. The person is in a state of conflict. Under such circumstances, the expression of the approach tendency is likely to be weakened or inhibited completely as many experiments have shown. What will be expressed in its place? The answer to this question requires a theory of how particular conflicts are resolved by the person. It is at this particular point that the simple conception of motivation and behavior offered here must make contact with ideas about conflict and its resolution.

Does this mean that we cannot hope to measure a motive through the manifest content of thematic apperception if it happens to be one about which the individual often experiences conflict? The theoretical answer is: *not necessarily*. What is now clearly required, however, is specification of the conditions—in theoretical terms—under which the approach motive can be expressed without disguise, and the conditions under which conflict with its attendant distortion of the approach tendency is to be expected. It is at least theoretically possible to imagine a situation which will arouse the expectancy of satisfying the approach motive without simultaneously arousing the expectancy of punishing consequences which would engage the avoidance disposition and hence inhibit expression of the approach tendency. The concept of displacement points to such conditions. And work of Sears (373) and others with doll play in children suggests the possibility of kinds of situations which allow fairly free reign to an otherwise inhibited approach tendency. The task for those who would like to extend the thematic apperception method to the point of fairly accurate assessment of sexual and aggressive motives is to construct a test situation and choose a set of pictures which meet the requirement of arousing the expectancy of satisfying the approach tendency without also arousing the expectancy of punishment for its expression. The experimental problem may be difficult, but it need not be decided in advance that it is impossible to solve.

The experiment by Clark (72) on expression of sexual motivation in thematic apperception has shown that arousal of fear of punishment, or guilt, which inhibits free expression of sexual motivation, is reduced by alcohol. And Mussen and Scodel (Ch. 8) have shown that the strength of the expectancy of punishment, and hence strength of the inhibiting motivation, can be increased and decreased by subtle changes in situational variables, viz., a stern versus a permissive experimenter.

Another hopeful possibility is that as our understanding of how conflicts are resolved advances (e.g., see McClelland and Apicella,

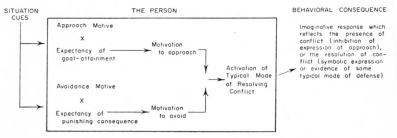

Fig. 3. A conception of approach-avoidance conflict as it effects the attempt to assess the strength of an approach motive from manifest motive-related imagery in thematic apperception. (Suggested by the earlier conception and experimental evidence of Clark [72] and the current conception of conflict and defense by Miller and Swanson [288].)

267; and the recent work of Miller and Swanson, 288), it may be possible to assess the relative strengths of the competing tendencies directly from the distorted expression which represents a particular mode of resolving the conflict. The studies of Clark and Sensibar (Ch. 7) and Beardslee and Fogelson (Ch. 9), for example, point the way to reading the strength of a motive from the frequency and extent of symbolic expressions of it. There is every reason to believe that continued experimental analysis of this problem will lead to the development of valid and reliable techniques for *latent* content analysis.

In any case, the ultimate solution of this problem will require independent assessment of the expectancies aroused by both situation and picture cues. For unless there is some way of knowing in advance what the situation "means" to the individual, any attempt to infer motives from expressed motivations will continue to involve two unknown quantities—the motive and the expectancy aroused by momentary cues.

Figure 3 summarizes the conception that is advanced for thinking about conflict in terms of simultaneously aroused approach and avoidance motives. Better than anything else, it defines the need for independent assessment of expectancies aroused by situation cues as a first step towards teasing out the effect of motives on thematic material and on instrumental activity.

INDEPENDENT ASSESSMENT OF EXPECTANCIES AROUSED BY SITUATIONAL AND PICTURE CUES

Rotter's (353) social-learning theory gives a central role to the concept of expectancies aroused by situational cues. His own analysis of the directive role of situation cues has begun to produce a series of theoretically-relevant attempts to assess expectations (354). Our own attempts along the same line, presented in subsequent chapters, have focused chiefly upon the problem of defining the cue characteristics of the pictures used in thematic apperceptive measurement of motives. And while the empirical research to date has dealt only with picture cues, the methodological implications would seem to hold as well for attempts to assess the cognitive meaning, in expectancy terms, of the cues of any real-life situation in which the behavior of a person might be observed.

The few excursions we have taken in trying to assess the cognitive meaning of the situation for a person suggest the possibility of constructing fairly standard conditions for the measurement of any human motive. In our use to date of the thematic apperception method, we have felt compelled to hold the *physical* stimulation of situation cues and pictures as constant as possible for purposes of comparing individuals or groups presumed to differ in strength of a particular motive. If it is actually possible to obtain an independent measure of the particular cognitive expectancies aroused by both situation and picture cues, the experimenter will be in a position to loosen his control of the physical stimuli and substitute instead his readings taken on the cognitive meanings of these stimuli for particular subjects or particular groups of subjects. *The ideal test of strength of a particular motive may ultimately consist of different pictures for different individuals—pictures more alike in the expectancies they arouse than in their physical properties.* When and if we reach this stage of precision, we shall be controlling the psychological environment rather than having to assume some kind of rough equivalence produced by constant physical cues.

FINAL COMMENT

If nothing else, this theoretical analysis supports Rotter's (354) emphasis of the need for an adequate technique for assessing the cue characteristics of the stimulus situation to which the individual responds. In adapting Tolman's (414) concept of expectancy to deal with the "causal texture of the environment," I have deliberately sought a concept which captures the central idea of the Lewinian lifespace, or psychological environment, as distinct from the geographic or physical environment.

Embedding the problem of assessing human motives in an expectancy theory of motivation and action tends, furthermore, to bring us a step nearer to the probability-utility model for decision making, which has had a durable history in economics and is currently engaging the interest of modelbuilders with an empirical slant (114). The possible fruits of a union between a method for assessing the strength of basic motives in an individual and a mathematical model for decision making seems worth the effort of a try.

The decision to employ the concept of expectancy to carry the burden of the meaning of the situation for the person is the result of another consideration. It is an appreciation of the extent to which an appeal to cognitive expectations is the core of what social scientists in other fields have in mind when they speak of the *norms* of a society and the definitions of *roles* within a society. Working in his own bailiwick, the psychologist has become sensitive to the need— argued forcefully by Sears (372)—for a conception of personality which makes contact with a theory of action, so that the individual will be described in terms of potentialities for action for which there are known principles. The psychologist may also be susceptible to another kind of argument. It should influence his choice of concept when there are admittedly many different alternatives open to him. The ultimate point of contact between psychological and sociological conceptions lies in the analysis of the behavior of persons in particular concrete situations. The choice of concept and the development of methods for treating the effect of the situation on the individual can enhance or hinder the possibility of integrating the conception of personality and the conception of social structure in concrete research. The idea of measuring cognitive expectancies aroused in particular real-life situations seems to me a promising mediating link.

CHAPTER 43

A Method for Investigating
the Cue Characteristics
of Pictures

BERNE JACOBS, JR.[1]

THE PURPOSE of this study is to develop a method for determining the cue characteristics of pictures used in the projective measurement of motivation. The importance of having a measure of the cue value of the pictures which is independent of the procedure for assessing motivation has been cited in the preceding chapter and elsewhere (272, 24). Briefly, a knowledge of the cue value of the pictures is important for at least two reasons: first, in any considerations of the projective device as a measurement instrument, it is important to know the role of the pictures in contributing to the motivation score; second, from the point of view of an experimenter who is designing a study, information about the cue value of the pictures would be helpful so that he might select pictures most useful for his purpose.

Two sets of experimental results cited in *The Achievement Motive* (272, pp. 197-207) describe the effect that the cues in pictures have on the *n* Achievement score. First, it was found that the effect of increasing the achievement-relatedness of cues in the pictures is to increase the mean *n* Achievement score per picture. Second, it was found that increasing the strength of motivation by experimental procedures has the effect of increasing the mean *n* Achievement score to both high- and low-cue pictures, the amount of increase being practically identical for both types of pictures. In each case, the cue strength of pictures was based on the intuitive judgment of the *E* as to whether or not they were "suggestive" of achievement. A "suggestive" picture was one which showed characters in a rather obvious work situation.

---

[1] This paper is based on an unpublished Honors thesis, University of Michigan, 1953. The writer wishes to express his gratitude to Dr. J. W. Atkinson for his encouragement and helpful criticism, and to Dr. Alfred Raphelson for his assistance in scoring stories for *n* Achievement.

617

McClelland *et al.* (272) assert that the cues which arouse the achievement motive are those which have been associated with affective changes accompanying success and failure in competing with standards of excellence. Atkinson asserts (24, p. 86) that "the arousal of a motive is equivalent to the arousal of a family of perceptual and instrumental response dispositions whose strength may be accounted for in terms of the principles of associative learning." In the situation in which motivation is measured, the perceptual response dispositions are manifested in the imaginative responses that appear in a subject's protocol. Both situational and picture cues may arouse the family of perceptual response dispositions associated with a particular motive.

From these considerations, we might define the cue value of a picture for a given motive as the probability that the picture will engage some or all of the family of perceptual response dispositions which have been associated with attainment of the aim or goal state of that motive. Thus, the greater the number of persons who give responses characteristic of a given motive to a picture, the higher the cue value of the picture for that motive.

This study attempts 1) to develop a method for determining the cue value of pictures that is independent of the imaginative response from which strength of motive is inferred, 2) to determine by the use of this method the cue value of twelve pictures which have been used in previous experimental work, and 3) to discover the extent to which the indices obtained by this method are statistically independent of the motivation scores derived from content analysis of thematic material.

METHOD

The basic idea is to obtain judgments from a number of people about what might be the dominant concerns of characters portrayed in a given picture. A more systematic assessment of the "meaning" of the picture should yield more stable and standard results than would an *a priori* rating by any single experimenter before he begins an experiment.

To this end, an attempt was made to compile a fairly comprehensive list of the goals of human behavior and to arrange for subjects to rank these goals in the order that seemed appropriate for situations portrayed in each of twelve pictures. The goals were expressed in phrases beginning with the words "concerned over" or "concerned with," and subjects were asked to decide what persons in a situation like the one portrayed were most likely to be concerned about.

Cue Characteristics of Pictures   619

The list of goals. The list of "concerns" was derived from Murray's list of needs (314), and White's list of goals (431). It was designed to be fairly comprehensive with a minimum of overlapping meanings. The result was the list of fourteen given below. The descriptive word or phrase in parentheses, which did not appear in the list given *S*s, will be used to refer to these concerns throughout the paper.

1. Concerned with influencing and controlling the opinions or behavior or others (power or influence).
2. Concerned with getting food or water to satisfy hunger or thirst (hunger and thirst).
3. Concerned over not doing poorly at something, with avoiding failure (avoidance of failure).
4. Concerned with attracting attention, gaining praise and commendation (attention).
5. Concerned over being liked or loved by the opposite sex, or with associating with a member of the opposite sex (sex).
6. Concerned over gaining knowledge and understanding (knowledge).
7. Concerned with establishing and maintaining warm friendly relations with others (affiliation).
8. Concerned with complying with the wishes of persons in authority (compliance).
9. Concerned with resting, physical relaxation (relaxation).
10. Concerned over doing something well, with excellence of performance, achieving (achievement).
11. Concerned over not being accepted and liked by others, with avoiding social rejection (avoidance of rejection).
12. Concerned over physical security, with avoiding physical pain (safety).
13. Concerned with harming, punishing, or belittling someone else (aggression).
14. Concerned over having done something bad or unacceptable, with easing feeling of guilt (guilt).

Four of the concerns are designed to represent the approach and avoidance aspects of achievement and affiliation motives: achievement versus avoidance of failure, affiliation versus avoidance of rejection.

Pictures. The twelve pictures used are described below. In the course of the work with these pictures, they have been given identifying names. A brief description of the pictures is given along with names which will be used to identify them in the rest of this paper. The source of the picture is noted; the four original pictures used for the study of the achievement motive are designated with an asterisk (*).

I. *Conference*—A group of men, about 25-35 years old, sitting around a conference table, talking (179).

II. *Crumpled Figure*—Figure, crumpled on floor, with head resting on arm on the seat of a divan (TAT 3BM).

III. *Boy and Mural*—A boy, 10-15 years old, in foreground; scene of "operation" in background. This scene or mural is of two men in white, "operating" on a prone figure. At the left of the boy is a gun (TAT 8BM).*

IV. *Father-Son*—The heads of two men, one about 60 years old, the other about 35-40. The older is above and to the left. They both look serious (TAT 7BM).*

V. *Man in Doorway*—Man looking out doorway of house. Only his back can be seen. Through the doorway is seen a tree, shrubs, and a sidewalk or a street (179).

VI. *Club Scene*—Four men, about 55-65 years old, standing and sitting in a lounge or club atmosphere (179).

VII. *Basketball*—A basketball game; one of the players jumping to shoot a basket, another trying to stop him (350).

VIII. *Two Young Men Talking*—Head and shoulders of two young men talking; between 20 and 30 years old (179).

IX. *Streetlight*—A man in overcoat and hat, standing under a streetlight (TAT 20).

X. *School*—Young boy, 15-18 years old, sitting at a desk in school, looking away from an open book (272).*

XI. *Feet*—Two legs from the knees down, climbing a flight of stairs. Wearing dress trousers (215).

XII. *Inventors*—Two men, 35-50 years old, working at a machine. Time probably about 1850-1870 (272).*

These pictures were selected for various reasons. *Boy and Mural, Father-Son, School,* and *Inventors* were used in the original study of the achievement motive (272) and in many later studies. *Basketball* was used by Rosenstein (350) in a study which found that practically all persons respond with achievement stories to pictures of athletic competition. It was included as an example of a picture supposedly very high in achievement cue value.

Conference, Crumpled Figure, Man in Doorway, Club Scene, Two Young Men Talking, and *Streetlight* were included because they had been used in studies of the affiliation motive (Ch. 4, Ch. 5). *Feet* was chosen as an example of a minimally structured picture (215).

Design and instructions to subjects. The present investigation consisted of two separate experiments. Experiment 1 was designed to determine the cue value of the twelve pictures. Experiment 2 was conducted to determine whether or not the measures of the cue value of pictures were independent of the strength of motivation in the subjects.

The Ss for Experiment 1 were 20 male undergraduate college students who had volunteered for the experiment. They had not seen the pictures before; the rankings were obtained in a classroom, but not during a regular class period.

For Experiment 2, the Ss were 27 male undergraduate college students taking laboratory courses in psychology. They had written stories in response to some of the pictures several months earlier. The rankings were obtained during the regular laboratory meeting of the class.

The Ss were given a booklet with instructions and pages for rankings. In *Task 1,* the Ss looked at each picture separately and then ranked the fourteen concerns according to the following instruction:

You will be shown a series of pictures, one at a time. *Please examine each one in detail.* One or more persons will be portrayed in each picture. *You are asked to decide what the person(s) in that situation is (are) most likely to be concerned about.* Following each picture will be a list of concerns (e.g., influencing others' opinions, being liked and accepted, personal accomplishment). You are asked to rank the concerns by assigning a rank of 1 to the concern you would expect to be dominant in the minds of most people in the given situation, a rank of 2 to the concern you would expect to occur next most frequently, and so on, assigning a rank of 14 to the concern you would least often expect a person in that situation to have.

The same concerns are given following each picture. Put the rank you assign to a concern in the space before it. Please try to decide while you are looking at the picture what persons in identical situations in real life might be concerned about and then go to the check list for ranking.

Use all the available cues—the situation, the facial cues, etc.—to arrive at your judgment. We are trying to find out what these particular pictures suggest.

Even though it will be difficult in some instances, you must rank all 14 items for every picture. You will find that some of the concerns seem to apply to a picture and some are not clearly related. I would like you to circle the last rank which seems to you to be clearly related to the picture or which is easy for you to rank for that picture.

In the space at the top of the page, put the letter corresponding to the picture you are working on.

The order of the concerns was the same for all Ss. The pictures were passed around among the Ss. There was no standard order in which they were received. There was no time limit for the ranking.

After the Ss had completed this task, they were shown all twelve pictures at once and asked to rank the pictures for the extent to which they suggested a particular concern. The pictures were ranked for four different concerns: achievement, avoidance of failure, affiliation, and avoidance of rejection. Half the Ss ranked the pictures for achievement and affiliation; the other half ranked the pictures for avoidance of failure and avoidance of rejection.

The directions were as follows:

I would now like you to rank the pictures on the basis of one of the concerns. This time you will rank all the pictures for one concern, whereas before you ranked all the concerns for one picture.

The concern you are now being asked to rank the pictures by is that of being concerned over ————————————————. Rank the pictures by assigning a rank of 1 to the situation in which most people would be concerned over this, a rank of 2 to the situation showing the next greatest concern, and a rank of 12 to the situation where people are least concerned. For example, if picture A shows more concern than picture B, you would rank A above B; and if A shows more concern than any other picture, you would rank A number 1.

It is not assumed that every person has necessarily had personal experiences in every situation shown in the picture, but everyone has opinions and expectations, based on a general knowledge of his culture, about situations like these. Thus, when people are asked to indicate what concerns might be characteristic of the situations shown in the pictures, each responds on the basis of what he sees in the picture and of his learning experience—sometimes as participant, sometimes as observer—in situations like those shown. When the judgments of a group of people are summated, the result is a cultural consensus about the concerns of people in situations like those portrayed. It is this consensus of opinion which becomes the operational definition of the cue value of the pictures.

RESULTS

Experiments 1 and 2 yielded results which were analyzed with four questions in mind: 1) What is the relative cue value of each picture of each of the concerns in the list? 2) Do the pictures differ in ambiguity, and can this difference be assessed? 3) What is the relative strength of the picture cues for achievement and affiliation? and 4) Is the S's judgment of the pictures in this ranking task influenced by his own motivation?

1. *Cue value of the pictures.* The relative cue value of each picture in regard to the fourteen concerns may be determined by ordering the concerns according to the mean rank assigned to each concern for that picture. Table I shows the relative cue value of each picture in terms of the fourteen concerns. The pictures are listed in order of the cue values for achievement.

We may examine the cue values of pictures in the light of assumptions made about them in earlier studies. For example, the

TABLE I. MEAN RANK ASSIGNED TO EACH MOTIVATIONAL CONCERN ON EACH PICTURE BY 20 Ss IN TASK 1

Mean Rank

Goal Concerns	Picture VII Basket-ball	Picture XII Inven-tors	Picture X School	Picture I Confer-ence	Picture III Boy and Mural	Picture VIII Two Young Men Talking	Picture IV Father-Son	Picture VI Club Scene	Picture V Man in Doorway	Picture XI Feet	Picture II Crum-pled Figure	Picture IX Street-light
10 Achievement	1.55	1.80	3.25	4.00	4.15	4.70	5.85	6.05	6.45	6.85	8.10	8.20
4 Attention	2.45	5.05	6.05	4.25	6.10	7.60	8.10	4.45	7.75	5.95	9.00	8.65
3 Avoidance of failure	4.85	5.00	3.90	6.85	5.80	6.90	5.50	7.10	6.40	6.60	6.65	7.10
7 Affiliation	5.95	8.10	9.20	3.65	8.90	6.15	7.05	3.75	6.55	6.20	7.60	11.25
1 Power or influence	6.15	5.70	8.75	2.05	7.05	2.70	4.05	2.10	7.25	5.75	9.15	7.50
8 Compliance	6.70	6.30	6.35	7.55	7.20	3.00	4.90	9.00	7.95	5.20	5.65	8.35
11 Avoidance of rejection	6.90	9.60	6.30	7.45	6.35	6.80	6.50	7.20	6.65	9.05	4.10	4.50
5 Sex	7.25	12.20	8.40	10.55	11.45	10.90	10.65	11.90	5.60	7.60	6.35	8.10
12 Safety	9.30	9.65	11.00	9.60	7.95	7.90	5.85	8.75	11.75	11.50	7.90	4.75
6 Knowledge	9.35	3.15	2.80	4.85	5.05	4.75	6.40	4.55	7.15	4.00	11.10	10.60
13 Aggression	10.10	8.20	9.10	10.40	4.55	10.60	8.65	8.90	7.95	8.75	6.10	6.80
9 Relaxation	10.45	10.60	10.10	9.50	10.25	12.40	11.95	8.00	2.80	10.05	8.55	7.00
14 Guilt	11.40	9.80	7.90	11.30	8.50	7.15	6.20	9.95	7.05	9.15	2.80	3.65
2 Hunger and thirst	12.60	9.80	11.90	12.35	11.60	13.35	13.20	13.30	13.15	8.35	11.70	8.65

assumption (in 272) that the picture of *Father-Son* (IV) is weaker in achievement-related cues than the picture of *Inventors* (XII) is supported. The average ranks assigned to achievement is 5.85 for picture IV and 1.80 for picture XII. It is interesting to note that these two pictures are near equal in failure-avoidance cue strength. The average rank is 5.50 for picture IV and 5.00 for picture XII. The other two pictures from the initial studies of n Achievement have intermediate achievement cue value. The average rank for achievement is 3.25 for picture X (*School*) and 4.15 for III (*Boy and Mural*).

The results also confirm an assumption made by Atkinson, Heyns, and Veroff (Ch. 5) in order to reconcile their findings concerning n Affiliation with those reported in an earlier study by Shipley and Veroff (Ch. 4). The scoring criteria for n Affiliation proposed by Shipley and Veroff had centered on separation imagery and the negative consequences of rejection. In their argument for a broader conception of the affiliation motive, Atkinson *et al.* pointed out that the particular pictures used by Shipley and Veroff emphasized the affiliation-deprivation situation. Two of the pictures used by Shipley and Veroff were used in this study. The average rank assigned to rejection-avoidance is higher than the average rank for affiliation on both of them. For the *Crumpled Figure* (II) the rank of rejection-avoidance is 4.10 and the rank for affiliation, 7.60. For *Streetlight* (IX), the average rank for rejection-avoidance is 4.50 and for affiliation 11.25. Both pictures, in other words, are more strongly cued for affiliation-deprivation.

On the other hand, all four of the pictures from the Atkinson *et al.* study that were included here have lower ranks for affiliation than rejection-avoidance. The ranks, with the affiliation rank stated first, were: *Conference* (I)—3.65 and 7.45; *Man in Doorway* (V)—6.55 and 6.65; *Club Scene* (VI)—3.75 and 7.20; *Two Young Men Talking* (VIII)—6.15 and 6.80. The assumption that the cues in the pictures used to elicit thematic stories can play an important role in defining the content of imaginative manifestations of the motive is supported in terms of this independent measure of the cue value of the pictures.

2. Do the pictures differ in ambiguity? A stimulus can be referred to as ambiguous when it is subject to a wide variety of interpretations, i.e., when it gives rise to many different responses because it lacks characteristics which produce agreement or consensus among a number of persons.

The responses of a number of people to any single picture might fall anywhere on a continuum ranging from complete agreement to complete lack of agreement. Pictures near the lack-of-agreement end of this continuum might then be called *ambiguous*.

Ambiguity is operationally defined in this manner. Using a formula presented in Guilford (159, p. 369), the average intercorrelation between the rankings of the same picture by all of the judges was determined. This average intercorrelation between the rankings of the concerns for each picture indicates the average interjudge agreement as to the meaning of the situation portrayed. Table II shows the average intercorrelation between the rankings of concerns for each picture.

TABLE II. AVERAGE INTERCORRELATIONS (r) BETWEEN THE
RANKINGS OF 14 GOAL CONCERNS FOR EACH OF
12 PICTURES BY 20 SUBJECTS

Picture	r
VIII—Two Young Men Talking	.60
VII—Basketball	.58
I—Conference	.58
VI—Club Scene	.54
XII—Inventors	.50
X—School	.43
IV—Father-Son	.38
III—Boy and Mural	.29
V—Man in Doorway	.29
II—Crumpled Figure	.29
IX—Streetlight	.23
XI—Feet	.20

Let us consider the manner in which these pictures might differ to result in these differences in ambiguity. We are reminded of the hypothesis that what is being tapped in the ranking task is the S's opinions and expectations about what is likely to happen in a situation like the one portrayed. In order for him to arrive at a definite conclusion about any given situation, there would have to be a sufficient number of cues present in the picture. The cues which would be relevant to the task of deciding what is going on in a picture fall into three general classes: the environmental situation portrayed, the activity that is going on, and the facial and postural cues of persons in the pictures. When the pictures are considered in terms of degree of ambiguity as in Table II, it is found that the pictures higher in the list (less ambiguous) have rather definite cues from one or more of these three classes of cues. The pictures lower in the list (more ambiguous) lack these cues. Examination of the last five pictures, for example, shows that in only one of them can facial expressions be seen at all; in none of them is there a definite goal-directed activity taking place; and none have very definite environmental cues. In Bruner's terms (54), there is a lack of "relevant" information to aid in the confirmation or infirmation of an hypothesis about the situation shown. The S has little information to use in making his judgments. Therefore, the possibility of different responses by different Ss is greatly increased.

This definition of ambiguity should prove of some use in the choice of pictures for further experimentation. If the experimenter desires to determine what perceptual response dispositions are aroused independently of picture cues, the use of an ambiguous picture which allows many various interpretations would appear to be a feasible procedure.

Another use of an ambiguous picture would be as an independent check on the efficacy of experimental procedures for the arousal of a specific motive. If, following experimental conditions designed to arouse a specific type of motivation, an ambiguous picture were inserted at the beginning of the measurement procedure, then the variability of response to the ambiguous picture, compared to the variability under "normal" or "neutral" conditions, could define the success of the procedure for arousing a specific motive. An ambiguous picture, by definition, is one which results in little agreement of response. If there were greater agreement of response among Ss following arousal procedures, we would hypothesize that this was due to the cues of the experimental situation. The variability of response under arousal conditions, compared with the variability under neutral conditions, could be quantified as an "index of arousal."

On the other hand, a well-structured picture is also useful. When a particular motive is being studied, the use of a well-structured picture with a high cue value for that motive should insure at least minimal response from most of the subjects. This would be useful when it is desirable to get a good spread of scores for a given motive, instead of having a cluster of Ss near the lower end of the distribution of scores resulting from many responses unrelated to the motive being studied.

3. *Specific achievement and affiliation cue value of the pictures.* The second rankings of the pictures (see Table III) for the four "concerns" designed to represent the approach and avoidance aspects of the achievement motive and the affiliation motive indicate the relative cue value of each of the pictures for these four tendencies. For example, *Basketball* (VII) has a higher achievement cue value than any of the other pictures, and *Club Scene* (VI) has a higher affiliation cue value than *Man in Doorway* (V).

TABLE III. ORDER OF PICTURES ACCORDING TO THEIR MEAN RANK (M.R.) FOR ACHIEVEMENT- AND AFFILIATION-RELATED GOAL CONCERNS

Achievement		Avoidance of Failure		Affiliation		Avoidance of Rejection	
Picture	M.R.	Picture	M.R.	Picture	M.R.	Picture	M.R.
VII	2.8	VII	2.6	I	2.2	II	1.5
X	3.1	X	2.7	VI	3.1	IX	4.6
XII	3.8	XII	4.6	VIII	3.6	IV	4.9
I	4.7	III	5.0	IV	5.2	X	5.7
III	6.1	IV	5.5	VII	5.5	I	6.4
VIII	6.4	IX	6.5	V	6.4	VIII	6.5
V	7.3	I	6.8	II	7.3	V	6.6
IV	7.5	VIII	6.8	XII	8.0	III	7.0
VI	7.5	II	8.6	III	8.7	VII	7.1
II	9.3	VI	8.8	X	8.9	VI	8.5
IX	9.7	XI	9.8	IX	9.7	XII	9.1
XI	9.8	V	10.3	XI	9.7	XI	10.1

Limiting the discussion to the three highest and three lowest pictures in each case, we find that there is considerable agreement between the cue values of pictures for achievement and avoidance of failure. The pictures most suggestive of achievement are *Basketball* (VII), *School* (X), and *Inventors* (XII). Least suggestive of achievement are *Feet* (XI), *Streetlight* (IX), and *Crumpled Figure* (II).

Most suggestive of avoidance of failure are the same three: *Basketball* (VII), *School* (X), and *Inventors* (XII). Least suggestive of avoidance of failure are *Man in Doorway* (V), *Feet* (XI), and *Club Scene* (VI). The pictures most suggestive of achievement are also most suggestive of avoidance of failure. The rank-order correlation between average rank for achievement and avoidance of failure is .79.

The result is quite different in the case of the approach and avoidance aspects of affiliation. The pictures which are suggestive of affiliation do not also suggest avoidance of rejection. Most suggestive of affiliation are *Conference* (I), *Club Scene* (VI), and *Two Young Men Talking* (VIII). Least suggestive of affiliation are *Feet* (XI), *Streetlight* (IX), and *School* (X).

On the other hand, most suggestive of avoidance of rejection are *Crumpled Figure* (II), *Streetlight* (IX), and *Father-Son* (IV). Least suggestive of avoidance of rejection are *Feet* (XI), *Inventors* (XII), and *Club Scene* (VI). In each case, a picture high on one list appears low on the other list. The rank-order correlation between average rank for affiliation and avoidance of rejection is .03. The cue values for approach and avoidance aspects of affiliation are uncorrelated in this data.

4. *Does the subject's motivation influence the judgment of concerns suggested by pictures?* In order to answer this question, Experiment 2 was carried out. The two ranking tasks were given to 27 Ss who had written imaginative stories to several of the pictures about six weeks before making the cognitive rankings.

If the motivation of Ss has an effect on the cognitive judgments, this should be reflected in the rank assigned to the concern which represents that kind of motivation. Thus, if n Achievement affects the judgment, it is expected that the rank assigned the achievement concern will vary systematically in relation to n Achievement in the Ss. We examined the correlations between n Achievement scores and n Affiliation scores obtained from the imaginative stories and the average rank for each S on achievement, avoidance of failure, affiliation, and avoidance of rejection.

The 27 Ss had written stories in response to nine of the twelve pictures used in the rankings of concerns. Need Affiliation scores were obtained from stories written in response to pictures V, VI, VIII, and IX by an experienced scorer (JWA). The stories written in response to pictures III, IV, VII, X, and XII were scored for n Achievement by the author and another reliable judge (AR) who resolved scoring differences after their initial independent scorings. The average of the ranks assigned to achievement, affiliation, avoidance of failure, and avoidance of rejection on all pictures was also determined for each S.

The rank-difference correlation between the imaginative measure of n Achievement and average rank for achievement concern on all pictures was found to be .17. The correlation between n Achievement score and average rank for avoidance of failure concern over all pictures was .05. When only the five pictures to which stories had been written were used as the basis for computing the average rank on achievement and avoidance of failure concerns, the correlations were .02 and $-.02$ respectively.

The correlation between n Affiliation score and average rank for affiliation concern on all pictures was found to be .23. The correlation between n Affiliation score and average rank for avoidance of rejection concern over all pictures was .15. When only the pictures to which stories had been written were used to compute the average rank on affiliation and avoidance of rejection concerns, the correlations with n Affiliation were .18 and .32 respectively.

Only one of the correlations, viz., that between n Affiliation and the ranking on concern over avoidance of rejection, approaches the value necessary for rejection of the hypothesis of independence at the 10 per cent level of confidence. From these results it may be concluded that the method used to determine the cue value of pictures is relatively independent of the motivation in Ss. The method for assessing the cue characteristics of pictures produces indices of cue value for particular motives that are statistically independent of measures of individual differences in strength of motivation obtained from analysis of thematic content written in response to the same cues.

CHAPTER 44

....

Thematic Content and the Cue
Characteristics of Pictures

ROBERT C. BIRNEY

RESEARCH ON PROJECTIVE TEST PICTURES

BEFORE DISCUSSING our current knowledge of the role of picture
cues in the achievement motive measure, it seems appropriate to
review some of the past picture research by others who have constructed picture projective tests. In general, very little work has
been done. The major evidence concerning the stimulus characteristics of the pictures can be found in studies to determine the
normative nature of projective responses to the pictures. Norms
imply some commonness of response due, in part, to the stimulus
properties of the pictures. Normative data on the Murray TAT
has been published by Rosenzweig and Flemming (352) and Eron
(119). These studies show that the majority of the 20 pictures
elicit stories of hostility, affiliative loss, and anxiety. Only three
pictures—the boy-violin, No. 1; the boy-surgical mural, 8BM; and
the silhouetted figure, No. 14—commonly elicit stories about achievement and success. However, normative data are so rare that Bellak
(37) says, "No experimentally derived performance standards for
'normal' or even for various diagnostic groups have as yet been
fully established, although much work is currently being carried out
to provide evidence of modal performance for members of various
groups (p. 205)."

Very few studies have been done on dimensions of the TAT
score other than the theme of the stories. But it should be recognized
at the outset that Murray does not feel that this type of research
should be emphasized. Rather he feels that the TAT should be
used to perfect the interpreter, whom Murray calls psychology's
forgotten instrument.

Eron *et al.* (121), and Wittenborn and Eron (439), have established that the TAT pictures differ in their elicitation of
"emotional tone," most being negatively toned despite wide picture
differences. In another study Eron (118) found that cards with

figures in social situations provided most themes of aggression, hostility, conflict, and occasional aspiration, while cards without clear social significance provided stories of a descriptive, impersonal, and symbolic nature.

To some extent the demonstration that the TAT cards do have distinctive and unique suggestive character is merely a proof of the obvious. Certainly such results must validate the unpublished notions of Murray's co-workers who selected the pictures by trying out several hundred cards until they found a set that gave "good" responses. The basic issue is one of determining how to predict the modal response to pictures so that pictures can be devised for specific problems in important areas of personality research.

The construction of new picture tests has provided some research on picture differences. Wekstein (429) believed that children give their most revealing responses when being as fanciful as possible. Therefore he created pictures of extreme symbolic and bizarre appearance, and asked the children to tell fairy tales. He reported that he obtained very elaborate tales of diagnostic value.

Various researchers have changed the appearance of the figures in the pictures to correspond to those of the subjects on whom the tests were to be used. Thompson (407) changed the TAT to figures of Negroes and reported an immediate increase in meaningful material. Subsequent work on this "identification" variable with Negroes has proved equivocal, both success and failure with such efforts being reported. Henry (178) adapted the TAT situations for use with American Indians by creating pictures with Indian figures in situations unique to their culture. He also reports success in obtaining useful protocols. Briggs (47) reports similar success with a modification for Naval personnel. Weisskopf (428) made the most drastic changes in pictures by superimposing actual pictures of the subjects being tested and also, in another study, by altering the physique of the figures to match the subjects' (427), and in neither case did he find any change in the amount of projective (stimulus free) responses.

Weisskopf (426) studied the problem of picture ambiguity by using pictures under low and high illumination, and found no differences in protocols. She also used pictures with complete vs. incomplete lines, and found the complete pictures to be far superior. From this she concluded that the physical ambiguity of a picture has to do with the perceptual completeness of the picture. Thus a fragmented picture presents the subject with the task of organizing it into something meaningful, while the complete picture permits him to interpret the familiar figures. Weisskopf is among the first to give operational meaning to the term "ambiguous." Another attack on this problem by Kenny and Bijou (212) used the method of having judges rank-order the TAT cards according to ". . . the estimated number of interpretations . . ." the judges thought could apply to the cards. Protocols obtained from male college students were then sorted (Q technique) by two clinicians according to the ". . . amount of personality factors revealed . . ." Here the basic finding was that pictures of medium ambiguity gave the greatest amount of personality material. In a follow-up study Kenny (211) found that Weisskopf's transcendence index (a measure of stimulus-free responses) showed significant correlation with his ambiguity indices for pictures taken from the clinicians judgements of protocols described above. Also the transcendence index was much higher for protocols obtained from cards viewed for two minutes as opposed to cards viewed for five seconds. Finally, Weisskopf's transcendence index also proved to be highest for pictures of medium ambiguity.

A similar kind of study by Kogan (220) required the construction of pictures relating to the central theme of aggression between young boys. He found that pictures most suggestive of aggression elicited more stories of aggression from boys who were rated as overtly aggressive than from boys rated low in overt aggression. There were no differences between the groups on the least suggestive pictures.

These studies on the general problem of picture ambiguity all suggest that there exists a definable range of picture cue salience for the most predictive protocols.

To the writer's knowledge only Symonds (399) has published a detailed report on the selection of pictures for a new picture test. In selecting pictures for adolescents he first set up on *a priori* grounds criteria by which to judge the usefulness of imaginative products. These stated that the stories should have within them a variety of themes, a minimum of description of the picture, and little commonality across the subjects. Stories written to the pictures were then rated by judges on these criteria, and the pictures given a rating on a five point scale of "goodness" as a function of the stories they elicited. Next he set out dimensions on which to rate the pictures. These were (a) emotionality, (b) amount of detail, (c) age relevance to subjects, (d) ongoing action, (e) familial involvement, and (f) commonplaceness of setting. The same judges then rated the pictures on these dimensions, and correlations were run between the ratings of stories and ratings of pictures.

Symonds reports that pictures rated high on the "goodness" scale showed high ratings on three picture dimensions, namely, amount of detail, age relevance, and commonplaceness of setting. The results are based on a sample of 81 pictures.

This review of the literature permits some general conclusions. First, it appears that pictures do differ in their suggestiveness of themes and emotions. Also, the nature of the stories may vary with both the physical and the social cues in the picture. There is some agreement between investigators on these points. None of the literature thus far has dealt with the basic problem of establishing a method for the selection of pictures so as to obtain stories with predictable fantasy material in them. It is in this area that the work of this study begins.

PICTURES FOR THE ACHIEVEMENT MOTIVE

Turning to the picture work done in relation to studies of the achievement motive, we find that the same basic procedures of picture selection and usage were followed here as with the measures just reviewed. The experimenters looked through popular magazines for pictures which seemed relevant to their ideas of the cultural definition of achievement. These, plus the boy-surgical mural (8 BM) and the father-son (7 BM) from the Murray TAT were among the original pictures used (272). The choices proved to be happy ones since adequate amounts of achievement imagery were obtained from the stories written about them. Subsequently, Atkinson (272) refined the selection of pictures by doing a response analysis study, wherein pictures were assessed by the extent to which scores made on them agreed with scores made on the rest of the battery. Eight pictures were used in this study. The original four pictures were supplemented by four new ones thought to be parallel to them. One of these pictures, the boy-violin (TAT card 1), was found to be non-parallel. It was Atkinson's guess at the time that the failure of this child picture stemmed from its tendency to stimulate recall, rather than fantasies of the future or present as demanded by his theory of motivation. But the difficulty may well have been the failure to distinguish the achievement strivings of parent and child in scoring this picture (See Lindzey [236] for a comprehensive review of interpretative assumptions in the use of thematic apperception).

Some preliminary work by Rosenstein (350) indicated that pictures depicting scenes in the college student's field of concentration did elicit some differential effects. College majors in chemistry produced more achievement imagery to pictures of men in laboratories than did physical education majors, but there were no differences between the groups when they wrote stories to pictures of athletic events.

Jacobs' research, reported in the preceding chapter, was the first attempt in this program of research to provide a definition of the pictures' cues that was independent of the stories written to the pictures. The present study represents a further inquiry into the characteristics of pictures.

Traditionally, stimuli have been defined in three ways: (a) the experimenter takes the role of expert and defines the stimulus, (b) the stimulus is defined in terms of the responses it elicits, and (c) a group of judges, chosen either because they are experts or because they are representative of the population to be tested, have been asked to judge what the characteristics of the stimulus may be. This last method has been used extensively in the construction of attitude scales where each item is analogous to a picture in a projective test. It is the method employed in the present study.

Implicit in the selection of pictures in past studies of n Achievement has been the assumption that the pictures were in some way relevant to past achievement experiences of the subjects. The most reliable way to assure ourselves of such relevance is to have the judgments made by persons similar to the subjects who will be asked to write stories. Therefore, we proposed to have a large sample of college students rate the pictures in order to provide us with a definition of the stimulus characteristics of the pictures.

However, we faced a problem in trying to determine what kind of a rating task would provide the data we needed. The answer seemed to be that we should give the raters as explicitly as possible the very attributes which go to define the achievement scoring system. Fortunately, these attributes can be stated in a language which is meaningful to our subjects (a circumstance which might not occur if we used a system of latent content analysis).

From the above argument we concluded that when judges rated pictures for achievement relevance, we would obtain primarily a cognitive estimate of the stimulus character of the pictures. But when subjects wrote stories about the pictures and made achievement references, we would obtain primarily an estimate of the achievement motivation of the subjects.

In the statement of hypotheses to follow it should be borne in mind that *none of the subjects who wrote stories acted as judges of the pictures.*

HYPOTHESES

1. There will be a positive correlation between the rank order of pictures determined by judges' ratings of achievement strength and the rank order of pictures determined by the percentage of stories scored for n Achievement.

2. There will be a positive correlation between the rank order of pictures determined by judges' ratings of achievement-related affect

and the rank order of pictures determined by the proportion of positive affect scores.

The decision to use the proportion of positive affect scores as the index of achievement-related affect was determined by an assumption made about the ratings. This assumption was that the rater, when faced with a picture having both positive and negative affective possibilities, would arrive at a kind of algebraic balance, e.g., a strong positive and a strong negative affect cue would result in the picture being placed in the middle of the positive to negative range. Should the picture in fact elicit an equal number of both positive and negative affect scores, the index derived from the proportion of positive to total affect scores would also put it in the middle of the range.

3. There will be positive correlations between the rank order of pictures as determined by judges' ratings of how suggestive the picture is of subcategories in the achievement scoring system and the corresponding rank orders of pictures determined by the percentage of such scores obtained from imagery counts in stories written to those pictures.

This hypothesis must be restricted to the upper two-thirds of the strength distribution of pictures since the low third of pictures will provide too few subcategories.

PROCEDURE

Rating Tasks. The procedures used for obtaining picture ratings were modifications of those developed by Jacobs. Five pictures were mounted on a large card and placed directly in front of five or more persons. Each person was given a booklet with instructions and pages for his rankings. The experimenter then read the instructions to the subjects as follows:

You will be shown a number of pictures and asked to examine them carefully. One or more persons will be portrayed in each picture. You are to decide what situation the picture portrays, and you will be asked to judge these pictures in a variety of ways. Two methods will be used. One will be the simple rank order method in which you will be asked to rank the statements or pictures on some attribute. The other method will be the "pick-five" method, in which you are asked to pick the five pictures or statements that most clearly show some attribute and the five that show the attribute least. The first five are designated by a "1," the second five by a "2," and the last five by a "3." Then after that is done you will go back and rank all of them, ordering the first five from 1 to 5, the second five from 6 to 10, and the last five from 11 to 15.

An example was then given. The experimenter continued to read with the subjects:

Task 1. Read the definitions of the situations given below, and then, drawing on your knowledge of how people behave and feel in situations similar to those portrayed in the pictures, you are to:

1. First use the "pick-5" method.
2. Rank the situations as described in the instructions. A rank of "1" is "most appropriate," and a rank of "15" is "least appropriate." Read the complete list of situations before you begin.

Picture ————   The situation portrayed deals with:

Group   Rank

————   ————   *influence,* interest in controlling the opinions or behavior of others.

————   ————   *attention,* interest in securing the attention, praise, or interest of others.

————   ————   *authority,* interest in legal or social control over action of others.

————   ————   *avoiding rejection,* interest in avoiding social rejection by others.

————   ————   *achievement,* interest in doing well on a unique task of personal importance or on a long-term career basis.

————   ————   *physical safety,* interest in restoration or maintenance of physical well-being.

————   ————   *guilt feelings,* interest in reducing guilt over wrong doing.

————   ————   *friendship,* interest in the restoration or maintenance of warm, interpersonal relations.

————   ————   *knowledge,* interest in knowing about oneself and the world in which one lives.

————   ————   *sexual gratification,* interest in being loved and esteemed by one of the opposite sex.

————   ————   *avoiding failure,* interest in avoiding poor performance, either on a unique task or in a long-term career.

————   ————   *relaxation,* interest in rest and relaxation from one's duties.

————   ————   *submission to authority,* interest in submitting to and complying with the wishes of someone in authority.

————   ————   *reputation,* interest in the preservation or restoration of one's reputation.

————   ————   *health,* interest in the maintenance and restoration of good health.

Task 2. Still considering picture ————, look at it as portraying *achievement,* interest in doing well in a unique task of personal importance or in a long-term career.

Now rank the behaviors and experiences listed below for likelihood of occurrence in the pictured situation. If, in other words, we assume the chief interest to be achievement, which of the following descriptions of behavior and feelings is most appropriate. Let a rank of "1" be most likely and a rank of "10" be least likely. Read the entire list before you begin.

Rank

_____ wanting to achieve
_____ striving successfully to achieve
_____ striving unsuccessfully to achieve
_____ being helped to achieve
_____ anticipating success
_____ anticipating frustration
_____ facing environmental obstacles to achievement
_____ facing personal shortcomings
_____ experiencing the satisfaction accompanying success
_____ experiencing the dissatisfaction of failure

Task 3. Still regarding the picture as portraying an achievement situation, now consider the three emotional possibilities listed below. Rank the picture for achievement-related emotional tone, using a rank of "1" for most appropriate and a rank of "3" for least appropriate.

_____ success, happiness, satisfaction, elation, optimism
_____ neutral
_____ unsuccessful, unhappy, dissatisfaction, dejected

Each booklet contained the numbers of the pictures the subject was to consider, and these were ordered differently across subjects so as to minimize serial position effects. The subject then considered each picture in turn as he made his rankings. After doing four pictures, the subjects were stopped, and the cards containing the pictures were combined to provide ten pictures in front of the subjects. They then turned to the last page of the booklet where the Task B picture rankings on achievement strength and achievement-related affect were made. Once again the experimenter read the instructions with the subjects as follows:

This time your task is to consider ten pictures and compare them, first grouping them into the five most appropriate and the five least appropriate, and then ranking them from 0 to 10 on their appropriateness to a situation which portrays

achievement, i.e., interest in excellence of performance on a unique task or on a long-term career.

Simply use the pick and rank method on the ten pictures compared for appropriateness to the achievement situation.

Still considering the pictures for appropriateness to achievement, now use the pick and rank method to indicate the emotional tone of the pictures—rank 1 being the most successful and happy, rank 10 being the least.

The raters were 150 college students in the introductory psychology course at the University of Michigan. Both male and female subjects took part.

These procedures provided two ways of obtaining the rank orders of pictures on appropriateness to achievement situations. Thus we obtained for each picture the median value of the achievement statement from the list of 15 need statements. Then the pictures were ordered by these median values. In the second procedure the ordering of the pictures on achievement strength is obtained directly, with the median rank assigned to each picture used to combine each group of ten pictures into one total ranking.

It is quite possible that the ordering of pictures obtained from the two rating tasks could disagree. Thus, a picture could be very unsuggestive of anything, but to the extent that it had any cues at all, the cues are relevant to achievement. Such a picture would have achievement interest ranked high on Task A but low on Task B. In order for the two rating tasks to give identical results each picture must be strong on some dimensions, weak on others, but all equally suggestive of something.

Finally, there was the problem of which ordering of pictures to use in comparing ratings with stories. We wanted the procedure which is most comparable to the story writing situation so that the two situations differed only in the crucial aspect of rating on a provided dimension versus free response in writing. In writing the stories the subject looks at each picture for 20 seconds. Then he is given four and one-half minutes to write his story. At no time does he see all the pictures simultaneously. Task A, in which fifteen need statements are ranked for one picture, is most like the story writing situation. Provided the two rating tasks showed adequate correlation, Task A was the one we wished to use. However, Task B facilitated the ranking of pictures by medians of affect ratings. Hence this method was used after ascertaining that we had high agreement between the two tasks.

Preliminary analysis of results showed there were no sex differences in ratings, ten raters showed as much interjudge reliability as twenty, and the agreement between Task A and Task B ratings of achievement interest was high—a product moment correlation of $+.82$ for the 19 pictures having the highest number of raters and a correlation of $+.61$ for all 54 pictures on which ratings were obtained (41).

Most of the pictures used were obtained from magazines, although one group of about 12 had been especially photographed by the writer.

Projective Testing. Three sets of six pictures were chosen from the total sample of pictures. Each subject was to write stories to six pictures. The three sets of pictures were chosen so as to be equivalent on strength and affective sign according to the raters' judgments. Table 1 contains a description of each picture and gives

TABLE 1. COMPARISON OF COGNITIVE JUDGMENTS OF ACHIEVEMENT-RELATEDNESS OF PICTURES AND OBTAINED FREQUENCIES OF ACHIEVEMENT IMAGERY IN IMAGINATIVE STORIES

Code No.	Pictures — Description	Median Rank* Achievement (Task A)	% Stories Containing Achievement Imagery
	Set I	Group 1 ($N = 22$)	
14	Inventors....................	1.20	.45
32	Potter working clay............	1.21	.76
50	Student taking notes...........	2.25	.04
7	Small school boy..............	2.28	.45
19	Four men in lounge............	4.50	.14
4	Father-son, TAT 7BM..........	6.50	.36
	Set II	Group 2 ($N = 23$)	
66	Louis Pasteur.................	1.37	.78
24	Colonial printers..............	1.41	.57
54	Men in mailing room..........	1.50	.04
17	Office boy....................	2.50	.26
21	College classroom.............	4.00	.17
41	Two young men talking........	6.75	.17
	Set III	Group 3 ($N = 27$)	
34	Four students in lecture........	1.17	.61
2	Schoolroom..................	1.75	.19
53	Elderly mechanic.............	2.00	.44
64	Salesman....................	3.00	.30
69	Man talking on kitchen phone...	3.30	.00
12	Two young men in blueprint shop	4.00	.22

* Not less than 10 Ss per picture. Range of ranks 1-15.

the median rank of achievement interest (Task A) for each picture.

In an effort to control for serial position effects, the six pictures of each set were arranged in a Latin Square design taken from Fisher (136). The Latin Square requirement dictated one change in the standard administration procedure. The general practice is to project pictures on a large screen. Here, however, it was necessary to test as many persons as possible under the same working conditions. Therefore, pictures were presented to the subjects in booklet form. This administration permits the simultaneous use of as many pictures in as many orders as the experimenter desires. The booklets were arranged before the subjects arrived at the auditorium in which the testing took place, so that a random assignment of subjects was accomplished.

The subjects who wrote stories were 72 college males from undergraduate courses in psychology at the University of Michigan. The administration of the measure of achievement motive was part of a testing session which also involved certain performance tasks described elsewhere (41). These performance tasks were given under high achievement arousal instructions, and the TAT measure was administered in the middle of the testing session. Hence, stories were written under "aroused" or achievement-oriented conditions. The test booklet contained the usual instruction for story-writing (Ch. 4) and two additional statements:

DO NOT LOOK BACK AT THE PICTURE AFTER STARTING.

DO NOT GO ON TO THE NEXT PAGE UNTIL THE SIGNAL IS GIVEN.

The writer's competence with the n Achievement scoring system was established by his scoring stories of twenty-seven subjects (four stories per subject) used in a previous study. These stories had been independently scored by an experienced judge (JWA). The rank-order correlation between the two n Achievement score distributions was $+.92$.

The Latin Square design on each of the three sets of pictures was employed to control for any systematic positional or sequential differences on the n Achievement score. Analysis of scores indicated that there were sizeable picture differences but that no systematic trends appeared in either the ordinal or sequence means. A test of the difference between the most disparate group means showed no reliable difference (41).

It also developed that six of the pictures produced so little achievement imagery that it was necessary to restrict the test of the second hypothesis concerning achievement-related affect to only twelve pictures.

RESULTS

Table 1 shows that none of the pictures was very low in rated achievement interest since the range of medians covers only about half that possible. Despite this restriction on range, we find a correlation $(tau_a)^1$ of $+.41$ between rated achievement strength and the percentage of subjects whose stories contained achievement imagery. The size of this relationship, however, suggests that the use of ratings alone to predict "picture pull" or achievement imagery will lead to considerable error.

Our second hypothesis asserts that raters can anticipate the sign of the achievement-related affect found in the stories. The correlation (tau_a) here is $+.59$ between rating of affective tone and an index[2] of the affective tone of stories. The raters were apparently able to anticipate the sign of the emotional references in the stories more accurately than the actual primary theme. This finding calls to mind the fact that Eron (121) found the Murray TAT pictures differed most reliably in their elicitation of emotional tone. Pictures of people in social settings may provide rather "conventional" cues to emotionality which determine the emotional tone of any story written about the picture.

TABLE 2. CORRELATIONS (TAU_a) BETWEEN COGNITIVE JUDGMENTS OF ACHIEVEMENT-RELATED BEHAVIORS SUGGESTED BY PICTURES AND THE FREQUENCY OF THESE BEHAVIORS IN ACHIEVEMENT STORIES WRITTEN ABOUT THE PICTURES

tau_a	Need $+.03$	I+ $+.08$	I− $+.14$	Ga+ $+.03$	Ga− $+.11$	G+ $+.50*$	G− $+.24**$

* P < .01, one tailed.
** P < .15, one tailed. $n = 12$ pictures in all cases.

Table 2 contains the correlations (all tau_a) between the raters' estimates of various aspects of the normal behavioral sequence that are subcategories of the achievement scoring system and the ordering of pictures according to the obtained frequencies of subcategories in the stories. Here it appears that cognitive judgments about the pictures do not anticipate the kinds of imaginative content which will appear in the stories. The implication of these findings taken together seems to be that cognitive judgments predict moderately well the general emotional tone of the story and the general theme, but that details of expression of motivation cannot be predicted from the raters' estimates. The only exception to this is found in

[1] The use of tau_a was dictated by the desire to know how the order of pictures obtained from ratings reproduced that given by obtained scores.

[2] This index was computed by taking the proportion of positive affect scores to total number of affect scores. This was done on the rationale that the rater's efforts to balance off positive and negative cues would reflect a similar weighting system.

affect scoring categories (G+ and G−), which refers again to the finding already noted about achievement-related affect.

Additional analyses. Another question of interest can be examined: do cognitive judgments about the subcategories of achievement-related behavior (e.g., need, instrumental activity, etc.) predict the likelihood of achievement imagery in the stories? Atkinson (Ch. 42) has argued that pictures which arouse expectancies of goal-attainment are likely to engage a motive. There is, therefore, some basis for expecting that pictures judged as "suggestive" of the possibility of goal satisfaction (Ga+ and G+) might provide the best prediction of the likelihood of achievement imagery in the stories.

TABLE 3. CORRELATIONS (TAU$_a$) BETWEEN COGNITIVE JUDGMENTS OF ACHIEVEMENT-RELATED BEHAVIORS IN PICTURES, AND THE FREQUENCY OF ACHIEVEMENT IMAGERY IN STORIES WRITTEN ABOUT THE PICTURES

Categories:	Need	I+	I−	Ga+	G+	G−
Values of tau$_a$	+.29*	+.06	−.14	+.28	+.09	−.37**

* P < .07, one tailed.
** P < .03, one tailed. $n = 15$ pictures.

Table 3 contains the correlations (tau$_a$) between cognitive judgments of pictures by scoring category and the frequency of achievement imagery in stories to those pictures. Here we see that both the *Need* (*N*) and the *Positive anticipatory goal state* (*Ga+*) categories show some relationship to frequency of achievement imagery in stories. Although the correlations are not high, they are of some theoretical interest since they give some support to Atkinson's argument. Even more interesting, however, is the fact that pictures judged to be suggestive of *Negative affective state* (*G−*) elicit less achievement imagery. It has been argued by McArthur (Ch. 38) and Moulton (Ch. 39) that the negative categories of the *n* Achievement scoring system may reflect negative expectancies associated with a disposition to avoid failure. Since the presence of such a motive would imply a very different kind of performance than that implied by the achievement motive, the use of these negative scoring categories (Bp, Bw, Ga−, G−) in the achievement scoring system has been questioned. The present result, that the raters' designation of a picture as suggestive of negative achievement-related affect is associated with low frequency of achievement imagery, lends some support to the above arguments.

SUMMARY

This chapter presents further exploratory work on the problem of how characteristics of the picture affect thematic content of stories written in response to it. Some of the previous literature on this general problem is reviewed. The actual prediction of thematic content from ratings made of the pictures is shown to be feasible. It is shown that ratings of the affective tone of the picture predict the affective tone of achievement-related stories best and the likelihood of achievement-related themes moderately well. In addition it is found that ratings of *negative* achievement-related affect are correlated negatively with the presence of achievement imagery in imaginative stories.

CHAPTER 45

....

The Role of Situation and Picture Cues in Projective Measurement of the Achievement Motive

RALPH NORMAN HABER AND RICHARD ALPERT [1]

THE PURPOSE of this paper is to present a theoretical discussion and experimental method for an analysis of certain variables in the projective measurement of the achievement motive. We feel such a reanalysis of the measure is called for because it is theoretically possible to distinguish several determinants of an individual's score, whereas the present test yields only one score which appears to confound these determinants. The justification for the theoretical analysis which follows lies in the increased sensitivity in measurement of motivation through fantasy which we believe will result. While this paper considers the measurement of the achievement motive specifically, the identification of the determinants which elicit fantasy should be applicable to projective measures of other motives as well.

In the n Achievement test developed by McClelland and his associates, Ss are asked to write TAT-like stories to specially selected pictures. To measure an S's achievement motive, his stories are then scored according to an empirically derived scoring system for amount

---

[1] We wish to express our gratitude to the National Science Foundation, who provided a grant for this research, and to Robert R. Sears, who administered the grant in a most helpful and encouraging manner. For the theoretical aspects of this paper, we also are deeply indebted for guidance and wise council to John W. Atkinson, and in the statistical aspects to Quinn McNemar and Joseph K. Adams. We wish to emphasize, however, that the responsibility for the paper rests solely with the authors. In addition, we would like to express appreciation and thanks to James R. Bowditch, J. Merrill Carlsmith, Robert N. Geddes, and Jan R. and Robert C. Pierce, who worked with us during various aspects of the research. Parts of this study are reported in the Ph.D. thesis by the first author (167).

of achievement imagery and the detail of its elaboration. McClelland *et al.* infer the relative magnitude of an S's achievement motive by the number of achievement-related thoughts he produces in a small sample of his responses to a standard set of picture cues. They hypothesize that an S's achievement thoughts are highly correlated with his achievement behavior in situations where achievement cues are present. Thus, an S who writes stories containing high achievement imagery should respond more quickly, intensely, or accurately in an actual achievement situation. In general, the data have supported this hypothesis, although the findings cast some doubt on the adequacy of such a simple formulation.

While we agree in principle with this hypothesis, we feel it is necessary to be more specific about the determinants of an S's score. It is our belief that only if the cue conditions connected with the motive measurement are comparable to those of the performance measurement can there be accurate prediction from one to the other. We have, therefore, defined within the testing situation the types of cues which might affect an S's production of achievement-related thoughts. By applying the results of an analysis of the specifications of the situational cues and individual differences in the effect of these cues on each S, we believe we can both increase the efficiency of this method of measuring motivation and add to our knowledge about the way cues affect behavior.

VARIABLES DEMANDING SEPARATE TREATMENT

The testing situation consists of (1) cues provided by the immediate external situation, e.g., task instructions, the experimenter, the room used, immediate past achievement experiences. We postulate individual differences in the Ss' sensitivity to these situation cues. Given such individual differences, in order to predict accurately a S's imagery score we have to have independent measures of the amount and intensity of motivating cues actually present in the situation, and we have to know how sensitive an individual is to situational motivation cues.

(2) Then there are cues in the test pictures employed to elicit the thought samples. There is ample evidence (272) that some pictures elicit more achievement imagery than others. A picture of a sleeping elephant will bring out considerably fewer images of achievement than a college graduation scene. In addition to these differences between pictures, there are individual differences among Ss in sensitivity (i.e., in the production of achievement imagery) to the cues in any one picture. We need to know the amount or number or intensity of the achievement cues in each picture used and the sensitivity of each S to these achievement cues.

In addition to individual differences in sensitivity to various situational cues, there are individual differences in the disposition to make achievement responses. This disposition to respond with a specific class of behaviors, in this case achievement behaviors, can be operationally defined in terms of the number of appropriate cues (i.e., achievement cues) that must be present in the environment before the individual will make an achievement response. In effect, we are thinking in terms of a lower threshold. A person highly disposed to make an achievement response will do so when merely a minimum number of achievement cues are present in the environment; conversely, a person with little disposition to respond with achievement behavior will only do so when there are a great many achievement cues present in the environment. Individual differences in the disposition presumably reflect differences in early life training of the sort Winterbottom (Ch. 33) has pointed out in her study of the genetic development of the achievement motive. Hence, if a S's thought processes are continually involved with achievement, even when such thoughts appear to be inappropriate to the situation, we say his achievement disposition has become generalized. The best way to assess the generality of the disposition is to measure achievement responses (achievement imagery) when there are very few cues present which might make such responses appropriate to the situation.

These are the determinants of the score on the test for n Achievement that we have attempted to isolate. It is possible to conceptualize the motivational determinants of achievement performances—such as taking a final examination, running a track race, building a business—in terms of the same variables. There are a series of external cues specifying the importance of the tasks, the amount of evaluation good performance will have, and so forth; and there are also individual differences in the degree to which these cues will motivate Ss to try to do well. Furthermore, some Ss work hard on tasks even when the external cues are minimal. Finally, there are Ss who try primarily to avoid failure (rather than to gain success) or to deny the instructions to do well, either of which motives results in irrelevant behavior on the tasks and thus lowers the efficiency of performance.[2]

METHOD

Our general procedure calls for Ss to be tested twice on the picture measure of the achievement motive, the first time under a relaxed

---

[2] Another variable which also influences achievement response is anxiety or avoidance reactions to the cues associated with achievement-related behaviors. The present research also included an especially designed test of achievement anxiety. The effect of this variable on both thematic apperceptive response and performance is presented elsewhere (13).

orientation—where all attempts are made to de-emphasize the importance of the task—and then under an achievement orientation—where the importance of the task is emphasized. In each session, six pictures are used to elicit achievement imagery. Three of the pictures are high in achievement cues, and three are low in achievement cues. Thus, we will test each S under relaxed conditions (low situation cues) with both low- and high-achievement cue pictures, and under aroused conditions (high situation cues) with both low- and high-achievement cue pictures.

Pictures. Two comparable six-picture batteries were developed to elicit the thought samples. Each battery contained three high-achievement cue pictures and three low-achievement cue pictures. Three criteria were used to select the pictures.

(1) *Frequency of achievement imagery elicited by pictures in pre-tests. High-cue picture:* at least 75 per cent of the Ss had to write stories containing achievement imagery. *Low-cue picture:* at least 25 per cent, but not more than 50 per cent, of pre-test Ss had to write stories containing achievement imagery.

(2) *Consensus among a group of pre-test raters that the picture was high or low in suggested concern with achievement.* This was measured with a modification of the technique introduced by Jacobs (Ch. 43). A group of pre-test Ss was given a definition of achievement taken directly from the scoring definition (272): competition with a standard of excellence, affective concern over goal attainment, evaluation of performance, some statement of unique accomplishment, or attainment of a long term achievement goal. Situational examples of each were given to make the task more concrete. Then 10 pictures were presented in pairs, with all possible combinations of the 10 shown, a total of 45 pairs. For each pair, Ss had to choose the picture having more achievement cues, according to the definition of achievement they were given. From the 45 choices, we derived a rank order of the 10 pictures according to each S. We also obtained an estimate of the transitivity of the judgments for each S by counting the number of intransitive triads $(A > B, B > C, C > A)$ with a test devised by Kendall (210). All Ss tested by this procedure were able to make highly transitive judgments. The three pictures highest and the three lowest in achievement cues were listed for each S. Only those pictures unanimously agreed upon as high or low were selected.

(3) *A picture had to be primarily concerned with the achievement motive and could not have any significant number of cues pertaining to other motives.* This criterion was ascertained by a modification of a technique developed by Jacobs (Ch. 43). Ss were given a list of 17

"concerns," of which six were achievement related, three were affiliation related, two were power related, and the rest were related to other needs. The Ss were then shown a series of ten pictures, one at a time. First, they were to check all the concerns they thought relevant to the characters in the picture. Second, they were to pick the five most relevant concerns, assigning a rank of 1 to the most relevant and 5 to the least relevant of the five. *To be selected for this study, the first three concerns ranked by every S for that picture must have been achievement-related.*

TABLE 1. LIST OF CONCERNS USED FOR JUDGING CUES IN PICTURES

(* = achievement-related concerns)

1. Concerned with influencing and controlling the behavior and opinions of others.
2.* Concerned about the future and long-term involvements connected with the future.
3. Concerned with attracting attention, gaining praise and commendation.
4.* Concerned over not doing poorly at something, with avoiding failure.
5. Concerned over being liked or loved by the opposite sex, or with associating with the opposite sex.
6.* Concerned with success in competition with others.
7.* Concerned over gaining knowledge and understanding.
8. Concerned with establishing and maintaining warm and friendly relationships with others.
9. Concerned with complying with the wishes of persons in authority.
10.* Concerned about fulfilling one's own standards of excellence.
11. Concerned with resting, physical relaxation (but not necessarily recovery from fatigue).
12. Concerned over not being accepted and liked by others, with avoiding social rejection.
13.* Concerned with achieving uniquely or creatively, as with an invention or a painting.
14. Concerned with harming, punishing, or belittling someone else.
15. Concerned over physical security, with avoiding physical pain.
16. Concerned with gaining independence.
17. Concerned over having done something bad or unacceptable, with easing feelings of guilt.

We pre-tested a total of 120 pictures with these criteria. The pictures included all those used in earlier studies of n Achievement and a large number culled by the authors from periodicals. The percentage of Ss telling stories containing achievement imagery following standard, neutral story-writing instructions (272) was determined for all 120 pictures. All pictures satisfying Criterion 1 were then ranked by paired comparison. Those which met Criterion 2 were then rated on the multiple-concerns questionnaire. Two-hundred Ss were used in these three pre-tests.

Fifteen pictures satisfied the three criteria, eight of these high in achievement cues and seven low in achievement cues. Twelve of these were finally selected and then divided into two forms, with three high- and three low-achievement cue pictures in each form (Table 2). The only basis used in making this decision was to try to avoid duplication of specific content in the same session, e.g., two pictures of athletic events were not put in the same forms. The presentation order for both forms was low, high, high, low, high, low. This is the best possible balance for taking into account any alternation phenomena or general decrease in imagery toward the end of the sequence of pictures (261).

TABLE 2. PICTURE FORMS I AND II WITH PRESENTATION ORDER INDICATED

Form I

A man painting or writing at an easel in a log cabin	Low
A young boy watching an airplane take off	High (25)
A foot-racer on his mark preparing to start	High
A young student in a checked shirt in a class room	Low (8)
A chemist in a white coat holding up a test tube	High
A business executive looking out over his factory	Low (59)

Form II

A pioneer chopping down a tree for a cabin	Low
Three foot-racers straining to cross the finish line	High
An engineer making an adjustment on a piece of apparatus	High
A man at a crossroad trying to decide on directions	Low (20)
Two men working on an invention	High (2)
A cub reporter being handed papers by an older man	Low (4)

Note: High or low indicates the final rating of cue strength in terms of the three criteria. The last numbers in the parentheses refer to the numbers in the McClelland numbering system; all other pictures were selected by the authors from periodicals.

Some pre-test results. In the process of selecting the twelve pictures, we collected a great deal of peripheral data on these criteria, which we will consider here.

Eighty pictures of the 120 failed to meet the imagery criteria percentage and were not used again. The forty remaining pictures were then tested for rank of achievement cues (Criterion 2). For these forty, there is a correlation of .71 ($p < .001$) between the achievement imagery percentage (Criterion 1) and the achievement-cue rank each picture gets. This correlation was based upon independent samples, since different Ss were used for the two criteria.

Thirty pictures were tested for both achievement imagery percentage (Criterion 1) and for concerns ratings (Criterion 3). There is a correlation of .58 ($p < .001$) between the percent achievement imagery and the number of achievement concerns checked. Here again, different Ss were used in the determination of each score.

These results support Birney (Ch. 44) and Jacobs (Ch. 43), who also found a high relationship between average objective rankings of the pictures for achievement concerns and the average amount of imagery elicited by the pictures in the *total group*.

We had two small samples of Ss, $N = 12$ and 13, write stories to the pictures *and* rank the same pictures for achievement cues. This allows us to study the relation between these two criteria for the subject. We can check Jacobs' proposition (Ch. 43) that there should be no relationship between the cognitive judgment a S makes of a picture and the amount of achievement imagery (n Achievement score) that the same S produces in response to that picture. For both samples, the Ss were first told to write stories to the six pictures under the standard neutral instructions. The n Achievement scores for the six pictures were ranked for each S. Then the same six pictures were presented in pairs of all possible combinations, and the Ss were asked to pick the member of each pair that had the highest cues. This provided a second set of rankings of the six pictures for each S. We calculated a rho for each S based on his six pairs of scores. With the two samples combined, the mean of the 25 rho's is .169, with a sigma of .304. The range is from $+.785$ to $-.443$. This probably indicates a slight positive correlation between the rank an S gives a picture on the strength of its achievement cues and the amount of achievement imagery he actually puts into a story about the picture. The correlations are undoubtedly influenced by serial position effects which were uncontrolled.

We also did a picture by picture analysis. Here we could not combine the samples, since they were administered different pictures. The data, therefore, contain an N of 13 for six pictures, and a different N of 12 for six other pictures, thus providing 12 pictures for the analysis. For each picture, we correlated the rank each S assigned it and the n Achievement score he obtained in response to the same picture. Hence, for each of the 12 pictures, we have either 12 or 13 pairs of scores. The mean of these 12 correlations is $+.076$, with a sigma of .221. The range of the correlations is from $+.466$ to $-.281$, with eight of the twelve correlations positive. Thus, there seems to be a *very* slight tendency for a picture that is judged by a person as highly achievement related to draw more achievement imagery in the stories of that person.

In summary: (1) We have the average rank assigned to pictures by a group of Ss and the percentage of Ss in a similiar group that tell stories containing achievement imagery in response to the same pictures. With $N = 40$ pictures, the correlation is $+.71$. This says that pictures that receive high ranking by a group of Ss will tend to draw more imagery in a group of Ss. (2) We have the rank each S assigns every picture and the amount of achievement imagery he produces to the same picture. This gives a correlation for each S between the objective rank he gives pictures and the relative amount of achievement imagery he projects into his stories to those pictures. With $N = 25$ Ss, we found an average correlation of $+.17$, with a sigma of $.30$. This says there is a slight tendency for an S to give more imagery to pictures he ranks higher. (3) We have the ranks Ss assign to a picture and the amount of achievement imagery the same Ss produce in stories about the picture. This gives a correlation *for each picture* between the ranking Ss give a picture and the amount of imagery elicited from them by the picture. With $N = 12$ pictures (and $N = 12$ and 13 Ss), the average correlation is $+.08$, with a sigma of $.22$. There seems to be a *very* slight tendency for a picture that is ranked high to draw more imagery.

The general conclusions we draw from these three results are (1) the average judgment of a group about the relevance of achievement is positively related to the amount of imagery elicited by pictures. This is a comforting result because it means that a picture, when measured objectively, has the same amount of achievement cue in it relative to other pictures as does the imagery it elicits when measured projectively. (2) there is very little relation between rankings and imagery for *individual* Ss or for *individual* pictures. Hence, one cannot substitute an S's objective rankings of the pictures for his projective imagery scores and maintain the same ordering of individuals on an achievement dimension.

While we have used these criteria for some objective estimates of the achievement-cue content of pictures, it should be noted that these techniques have a potentially wide range of application. They may be used appropriately with cues related to needs other than achievement, such as affiliation and power. Furthermore, they are techniques for analysis of the cue configurations operating in other test media such as story stems and cartoons. This generality of application to other needs and methods is important in view of the recently increased interest in the analysis of situational factors which affect behavior (see also Rotter, 353).

Task instructions. The two sets of instructions finally employed in this experiment were also the result of extensive purification and pretesting. From the literature, and unpublished research on the achievement motive, we collected instructions used both to relax and to achievement-orient Ss. After examining these we constructed several sets of relaxed and several sets of achievement-oriented instructions, which were used in our pilot studies. We picked the present sets after examining the comment sheets of the Ss, talking more extensively to some of the Ss and examining the data for indices of change between the relaxed- and achievement-oriented sessions that could not be accounted for by practice or fatigue effects.

The attitudes of the E also seemed very important. (See Birney, 42, for some of these dimensions.) We attempted, therefore, to specify exactly the nonverbal components of the instructions and to minimize the arousal of other motives, such as affiliation. Since we were not measuring this motive, we wanted to avoid its operation altogether. We based this decision on Atkinson (Ch. 19), who found that when the affiliation motive is aroused, n Affiliation scores will predict performance, while n Achievement scores will not.

In the relaxed sessions, the E presented himself as a graduate student, working on a research project. He was dressed very informally and did not appear to be highly motivated himself. There was a definite attempt to de-emphasize the importance of the tasks. Since dress clearly discriminates students from faculty at Stanford, the authority of E, who was dressed as a student, was low. In the achievement-oriented sessions, the E acted in both his manner and dress so as to be taken for either part of the administration or as a faculty member of the psychology department. There was continual reference to the importance of the tasks, and any actions or comments on the part of the Ss indicating lack of achievement involvement were counteracted with reminders about their being evaluated. Thus, we hoped to have utilized the full potential of E as a cue, relaxed in the first session and achievement oriented in the second.

We also manipulated the physical testing situation of the two sessions. For the relaxed session, each group of Ss met in a large experimental room, with many more seats than Ss. Thus, no S should have felt himself singled out for attention. Ss were allowed to sit anywhere, rather than in alternate seats, which would connote being tested. The E entered and left the room in a random fashion during the session. When he was present, he would sit up in front of the Ss engrossed either in working along with them or reading a magazine or newspaper.

For the achievement-oriented sessions, Ss were taken to a small experimental room, which had four seats at a long table. A divider was placed between Ss, so they could not see each other. The Ss were told to put all books, etc., under their chairs so the table top would be clear. E sat behind the Ss, where he could see them but where they could not see him without turning around, and at times he walked around watching the Ss. The screen for the slide presentation was in front of the Ss, and E always went to the front of the room to give instructions and pass out forms.

Thus, we hoped also to use physical situational cues to supplement the instructions. The setting for the relaxed sessions was as nontest-oriented as possible within the confines of the study. The achievement-oriented sessions, on the other hand, emphasized a testing atmosphere, where strong safeguards were being taken against cheating. The Ss were told in the instructions that a smaller room was being used so that there would be less disturbance, thus allowing them to do their best work.

Session I: Relaxed Orientation. An informally-dressed graduate student gave the following instructions at the outset:

The next hour or so will be very different from previous times you have been in a classroom setting. We are not interested in you. We are not interested in how you do on anything we give you today. We are trying to find out some things about these tasks themselves. These data are purely for research purposes, and you are not in any way going to be evaluated on them. In fact, there is no reason or need to put your name on the papers. However, so we can keep each of your papers together, let me give each of you a number so you can put it at the top of your papers. (Pointing)— you are number one, you are number two, (and so forth). This will be a much more palatable experience if you just relax . . . in fact, that will probably be the only way you can enjoy it at all.

The blanks for the stories were then passed out. The cover sheet contained the standard neutral instructions (272), with an additional sentence inserted: "In other words, write a complete story, a story with plot and characters. We are trying to find out the kinds of stories and ideas *these pictures* suggest to people." Six pictures were then presented, following the standard procedure (272).

After the last picture, the specific instructions dealing with the performance measures were given. Then the four performance measures were admininstered. After the last task, a comment sheet was distributed, which included, among other things, a question about how relaxed or achievement-oriented a S felt. The performance measures and the comment sheet are described elsewhere (167).

Four groups were run under the relaxed orientation. The two smaller groups were designated as control groups, and the two larger as experimental groups. There were no changes in size or composition of the control groups for the second session, which met three weeks later. They were given a different picture form and different forms of the performance tests by a different experimenter. The instructions, attitudes, and general setting were the same. However, for the experimental groups, in addition to the different forms of the pictures and tests and a different experimenter, the Ss were run in much smaller groups (fourteen groups of four Ss each) and the instructions were radically altered.

For the experimental groups, Session II was conducted under Achievement Orientation. An experimenter dressed in a business suit administered the instructions and ran the session. After the four Ss were seated, they were given an achievement anxiety test developed by Carlsmith.[3] This test was given at the outset as a further method of arousal, since it uses pictures dealing with college students involved in anxiety-provoking achievement situations. For each picture, Ss are given a list of adjectives from which they have to select those that best describe the student. After the Carlsmith test, the following achievement-orientating instructions were given by E:

What we are going to do for the remainder of this period is quite important. Let me start by telling you a little bit about the study in which you are participating. Considerable research at another university has led to a finding which is startling and of great significance. You will recall having written some stories to a set of pictures in the last session. The responses made to a similar set of pictures has been found to be related highly to aptitude scores derived from the college boards. In addition to a general intelligence, they measure your capacity to organize material and your ability to evaluate situations quickly and accurately. The pictures you took last time were a practice set to familiarize you with the process involved. Today, you will be shown the actual set of pictures that were sent to us from this other school.

We are doing this study for the administration, which is most interested in determining the relationship of this new measure to *your* college board aptitude scores. Therefore, on all of the things you take today, sign your name in the same way in which it appears at the registrar's office—last name first, first name last. This will allow the administration to relate this to your grades, your aptitude scores, and other measures in your academic folders. Following these stories, you will be given a set of tests which are taken from various college boards and graduate record examinations. These will also be familiar to you, since we gave you a practice set during the last session. Since you will be interested in how well you do on these tests, we have made arrangements for the posting of the results on the sign-up bulletin board and for personal interviews to discuss their meaning with you in more detail. I can make such appointments with you at the end of the session. We are testing you in small groups in this room in order to provide suitable conditions for your best work. Do not make any comments while these tests are in progress. We will take a brief break after

---

[3] Unpublished test by J. Merrill Carlsmith, Stanford University, 1956.

the picture presentation. Here are the blanks for the intelligence test. Remember to sign your name in the upper right corner, last name first.

The neutral picture instructions were then read. After the last picture, achievement-orienting instructions for several performance measures were given (167). After the last performance test was finished, a comment sheet similar to the first one was distributed. Then we explained to the Ss the nature of the experimental manipulations to which they had been subjected and that our main interest was in the reactions of individuals to achievement stress when placed under pressure to do well on important tasks.

Analysis of stories. Stories were scored by the authors and one of their assistants. All three have a reliability of about .90 for the presence of achievement imagery with the standard scoring manual (272). Every story was scored *twice,* each time by a different scorer. There were a total of 960 stories, and therefore, each scorer scored 640 stories in all. The average reliability for the initial scoring for the presence or absence of achievement imagery alone was 87 per cent agreement. The average reliability for the initial scoring of total *n* Achievement scores was .83. Whenever there were disagreements, either as to whether a story should be scored at all or about the scoring of any subcategory, the story was read again by the appropriate scorers and a correct score decided between them. Our scoring reliability figures, therefore, do not adequately represent the amount of care and precision in the final scoring. The final scores represent complete agreement between the two scorers.

Subjects. The Ss were 80 male undergraduate students from the introductory course in psychology at Stanford University. Since the introductory course requires that each student serve as a subject, Ss were selected at random from the entire class. They were run in two sessions of one and one-half hours each, separated by three weeks. The two Es in these sessions were the authors.

TABLE 3. EXPERIMENTAL DESIGN OF PICTURE PRESENTATION

A fourfold table showing the design of the experiment, with the independent variable and the four measurement conditions for each S specified.

Picture Cues	Situational Cues	
	Relaxed Orientation (Form I)	Achievement Orientation (Form II)
High achievement cues in pictures	Cell C	Cell D
Low achievement cues in pictures	Cell A	Cell B

Operational Definitions and Design. Our design can be conceived as a fourfold table (Table 3), with three pictures being given every subject under the conditions represented by each cell.

Definitions

(1) *Cues in the immediate external environment.* We have two different configurations of cues, one pertaining to a relaxed orientation and the other to an achievement orientation. In terms of the design above, this involves the labels of the two columns.

(2) *S's responsiveness to cues in the immediate external situation.* We have imagery scores under relaxed cues and under achievement-oriented cues. We shall define the difference score between these two imagery scores as a measure of an S's responsiveness to such cues. This difference can be measured in the responses between the six relaxed pictures and the six aroused pictures $[(D + B) - (C + A)]$; or between the responses to the high pictures only, three in each session $(D - C)$; or between the responses to the low pictures only, three in each session $(B - A)$.

(3) *Cues in the pictures used to elicit the thought samples.* In terms of design, this involves the labels of the two rows.

(4) *S's responsiveness to cues in the pictures used to elicit the thought samples.* We have imagery scores for the low-cue pictures and for high-cue pictures. We define the difference score between these two imagery scores as a measure of a S's responsiveness to such cues. This difference can be measured in the responses between the six high-cue pictures and the six low-cue pictures $[(C + D) - (A + B)]$; or between the three high-cue and the three low-cue pictures in the relaxed session $(C - A)$; or between the three high-cue and the three low-cue pictures in the aroused session $(D - B)$.

(5) *S's responsiveness with achievement imagery in the absence of strong achievement cues.* This is defined as the imagery score in the relaxed session elicited by the three low-cue pictures. This is the minimal cue situation in this experiment. It is defined by responses to cell A alone.

DISCUSSION OF RESULTS

These operations provide a number of scores which we shall now consider. Each of the scores represents the over-all amount of achievement-related imagery, i.e., the *n* Achievement score. Nine scores are for totals: four of them are for the cells A, B, C, and D, which have three pictures each; two more are for the relaxed session total and the aroused session total on six pictures each; another two

TABLE 4. MEANS, STANDARD DEVIATIONS, AND SIGNIFICANCE TESTS FOR ALL PICTURE-STORY SCORING CATEGORIES

Variable	Experimental Mean	Control Mean	p value	Experimental Sigma	Control Sigma	p value
Total score on all 12 pictures	22.87	17.65	$p = .05$	9.72	11.77	n.s.
First session total 6 pictures (relaxed orientation)	10.11	9.27	n.s.	5.63	6.86	n.s.
Second session total 6 pictures (achievement oriented for experimental group)	12.78	8.38	$p < .01$	5.82	6.53	n.s.
Low picture total 6 pictures	6.65	5.27	n.s.	5.42	7.10	n.s.
High picture total 6 pictures	16.26	12.38	$p < .02$	5.96	7.05	n.s.
Cell A (Low-Rel)	2.22	3.27	n.s.	3.15	4.13	$p = .05$
Cell B (Low-Ach.)	4.42	2.00	$p < .001$	3.72	3.19	n.s.
Cell C (High-Rel)	7.89	6.00	$p < .05$	3.81	3.86	n.s.
Cell D (High-Ach.)	8.37	6.38	$p < .05$	3.26	4.11	n.s.
Responsiveness to picture cues—relaxed sessions $(C - A)$	+5.67	+2.73	$p < .001$	4.14	4.10	n.s.
Responsiveness to picture cues—second session (aroused for experimental) $(D - B)$	+3.94	+4.38	n.s.	3.89	3.37	n.s.
Responsiveness to picture cues—both sessions combined $(C + D) - (A + B)$	+9.80	+7.12	$p < .06$	6.02	5.96	n.s.
Responsiveness to situational cues—low pictures $(B - A)$	+2.24	−1.31	$p < .001$	4.29	4.29	n.s.
Responsiveness to situational cues—high pictures $(D - C)$	+0.48	+0.38	n.s.	3.84	3.62	n.s.
Responsiveness to situational cues—all pictures $(B + D) - (A + C)$	+2.72	−0.90	$p < .02$	6.04	6.45	n.s.

for the high-cue pictures total and the low-cue pictures total on six pictures each; and a final one for a grand total on twelve pictures. In addition, we have the three difference scores for responsiveness to arousal cues, cells $(B - A)$, cells $(D - C)$, and cells $(B + D) - (A + C)$; three difference scores for responsiveness to picture cues, cells $(C - A)$, cells $(D - B)$, and cells $(C + D) - (A + B)$; and a difference score for the combined responsiveness to both arousal and picture cues, cells $(D - A)$.

A more extensive analysis of the results of this study will be reported in another paper by Haber and Alpert (167), which will consider the performance measures as criteria variables. And the relationship of achievement anxiety to the variables of the present report is discussed elsewhere by Alpert (13). The results presented here have interest mainly for their methodological importance. These deal with the effects of the picture cues, the effects of arousal of achievement orientation, form and experimenter differences, and the reliability of the test.

Table 4 reports the means and sigmas for all the measures for the experimental group, $N = 54$, and the control group, $N = 26$.

Table 5 presents the results of the analysis of variance of the four

TABLE 5. ANALYSIS OF VARIANCE TESTING THE SIGNIFICANCE OF THE EFFECTS OF SITUATION CUES AND PICTURE CUES UPON THE AMOUNT OF ACHIEVEMENT IMAGERY FOR THE EXPERIMENTAL GROUP

	Relaxed orientation	Achievement orientation	
High achievement cues in pictures	7.89	8.37	16.25
Low achievement cues in pictures	2.22	4.42	6.64
	10.11	12.79	22.87

Source	Sums of Squares	Degrees of Freedom	Variance Estimate	F	
Picture cues..........	1247.042	1	1247.042	140.60	$p < .001$
Situational cues........	97.338	1	93.338	9.828	$p < .005$
Individual Differences....	1273.833	53	24.034		
P × S...............	40.041	1	40.041	5.531	$p < .05$
P × I...............	473.509	53	8.934		
S × I...............	524.912	53	9.904		
P × S × I............	383.652	53	7.239		
Total...............	4024.884	215			

Role of Situation and Picture Cues 659

cells for the experimental group. Table 6 presents the results of the analysis of variance of the four cells for the control group.

Both analyses of variance show a significant difference in imagery between low-cue and high-cue pictures. The Experimental Group shows a significant difference in imagery between the relaxed and aroused sessions, with more imagery in the aroused sessions. The Control Group shows no significant difference between first and second relaxed sessions. This difference between the Experimental and Control groups indicates the effectiveness of our instructions and

TABLE 6. ANALYSIS OF VARIANCE TESTING THE SIGNIFICANCE OF THE EFFECTS OF PICTURE CUES AND REPEATED MEASUREMENT (RELAXED ORIENTATION) UPON THE AMOUNT OF ACHIEVEMENT IMAGERY FOR THE CONTROL GROUP

	First Session	Second Session	
High achievement cues in pictures	6.00	6.38	12.38
Low achievement cues in pictures	3.27	2.00	5.27
	9.27	8.38	17.65

Source	Sums of Squares	Degrees of Freedom	Variance Estimate	F	
Picture cues	329.09	1	329.09	33.67	$p < .001$
Repeated Measurement	5.09	1	5.09	0.49	n.s.
Individual Differences	899.97	25	37.00		
P × R	17.77	1	17.77		
P × I	230.66	25	9.23		
R × I	266.66	25	10.67		
P × R × I	135.98	25	5.44		
Total	1885.22	103			

general arousal procedure. These results are in complete agreement with earlier findings concerning the effects of picture and situational cues on achievement-related thematic content (272, Ch. VII).

The interaction of picture × situation among the experimental group calls attention to a possible "ceiling effect" in cell D (high-cue pictures under aroused conditions). No matter how many cues we put in the situation, the scoring system imposes a limit on the possible upper score. The mean score for the experimental Ss in cell D was 8.37 on the three pictures, or 2.79 per picture. While this does not approach the maximum possible score, it is a very high score for a large group of Ss. We expect that no one would get a maximum score on a group of pictures because of phenomena such as alternation set in telling stories or because of tendencies not to repeat categories, both of which would tend to lower score from the maximum. The argument for a ceiling effect is further supported by the smaller variance in cell D, smaller than any other cell except cell A, which is naturally curtailed at the other end of the distribution.

It should be noted that our procedure in giving achievement-orienting instructions for the task of writing stories is a deviation from almost all of the previous studies. The usual procedure involves preceding the story-writing period with a series of achievement tests. Thus the arousal of achievement cues for the stories, which are given with neutral instructions, is accomplished by carry-over from the performance task. In one earlier study, when the story writing itself was presented as an achievement test, McClelland *et al.* (272) report that the stories contained very little imagery; it seemed that the Ss "froze" and became so concerned about how to write a good story that they didn't write sufficiently elaborate stories. We felt that our procedure would not cause Ss to freeze since the achievement arousal occurred in the second session when the Ss were already familiar with the task of writing stories. The results clearly show a significant increase in achievement imagery after this arousal procedure in the second session.

Test for form differences. In the Relaxed session, for the Experimental and Control Groups combined, 38 Ss were given Set I of the pictures and 42 Ss were given Set II. The difference between mean n Achievement scores obtained from the two sets is only .58, $t = .05$, n.s. The forms, therefore, may be taken as equivalent.

Test for differences between the experimenters. In the Relaxed session (experimentals and controls combined), Haber ran 47 Ss and Alpert ran 33 Ss. The difference between mean n Achievement scores of these two groups is 1.62, $t = 1.06$, $p < .25$. In the Achievement-Oriented sessions (experimentals only), Haber ran 29 Ss and Alpert ran 25 Ss. The difference between the mean scores of these two groups is .49, $t = .30$, n.s. There is, in other words, no evidence that the experimenters had any differential effects on the results.

Intercorrelations among scores for Control Group (repeated tests under Relaxed Orientation). Table 7 presents the intercorrelations among scores in the four cells of the experimental design and the total scores on the first and second tests under Relaxed Orientation for the Control Group. The latter correlation may be taken as an index of test-retest reliability since the second session is a retest with a comparable set of pictures and an equivalent experimenter. The correlation between scores on the first and second tests is .54. When this correlation is corrected by the Spearman-Brown formula for the full length test (i.e., 12 stories), the corrected reliability coefficient is .70. Atkinson (272) has reported a corrected reliability of .65 for an eight-story measure and a corrected reliability of .78 for a six-story measure after removing two pictures that failed to relate to the total score in an item analysis. His estimates were for split-half presentations. The present figure is a test-retest correlation *with a three week interval,* and hence it is susceptible to trait variation as well as instrument variation.

TABLE 7. THE INTERCORRELATIONS AMONG VARIOUS ACHIEVEMENT IMAGERY SCORES IN THE CONTROL GROUP ($N = 26$)

	First Session	Second Session	Low-cue Pictures	High-cue Pictures	Cell A	Cell B	Cell C
First Session	—						
Second Session	54	—					
Low-cue Pictures	77*	69	—				
High-cue Pictures	78	82	57	—			
Cell A	78	42	84	49	—		
Cell B	54	60	51	61	36	—	
Cell C	85	52	47	88	48	57	—
Cell D	57	92	54	34	39	53	59

$p \leq .05$ for $r \geq .41$.
$p \leq .01$ for $r \geq .54$.
* Italicized r's indicate spuriousness due to whole-part contamination.

We also have a measure of the reliability of the low-cue pictures taken separately. The correlation between cells A and B is .36, which corrected by the Spearman-Brown formula becomes .53 (six pictures). The reliability of the high-cue pictures taken separately (cells C and D) is .59. When corrected to provide an estimate of reliability of six pictures, this correlation becomes .74, about the same as that reported earlier by Atkinson for six pictures, which according to our criteria would be classified relatively high in achievement cues. The correlation between six high-cue pictures and six low-cue pictures is .57.

Comment sheets were administered to all Ss in both sessions to provide an independent estimate of the difference in degree of arousal of achievement interest in the two test sessions. Subjects were asked to state how relaxed or concerned about achieving they were in each of the sessions. Their responses were reliably coded in terms of a five-point scale by two coders ($r = .92$). Table 8 reports the results of this independent check on degree of achievement-arousal. The results support the conclusion that the Experimental Group was aroused in the second session relative to the first session. The Control Group, however, shows no evidence of greater arousal the second time. The slight decrease in score for the Control Group,

TABLE 8. MEAN RATINGS ON DEGREE OF ACHIEVEMENT AROUSAL FROM Ss' COMMENT SHEETS (1 = LOW AROUSAL, 5 = HIGH AROUSAL)

	N	First Session	Second Session	Difference	p
Experimental Group	54	1.8	4.1	+2.3	.001
Control Group	26	1.9	1.6	−.03	n.s.
Difference		−0.1	+2.5		
p		n.s.	.001		

while not significant, probably indicates adaptation to the testing procedure. A similar slight decrease in achievement imagery in response to low-cue pictures (cell B) on the second test may be noted for this group in Table 6. Because of the restrictions on variance in the ratings (using only a five-point scale), no significant differences between the variances appeared.

Intercorrelations among scores for the Experimental Group (second test taken under conditions of Achievement Orientation). Table 9

TABLE 9. INTERCORRELATIONS AMONG VARIOUS ACHIEVEMENT IMAGERY SCORES IN THE EXPERIMENTAL GROUP ($N = 54$)

	Relaxed Session	Aroused Session	Low-cue Pictures	High-cue Pictures	Cell A	Cell B	Cell C
Relaxed Session..	—						
Achievement-aroused Session	45	—					
Low-cue Pictures	69*	74	—				
High-cue Pictures	76	72	46	—			
Cell A.........	76	27	75	30	—		
Cell B.........	34	86	83	41	24	—	
Cell C.........	85	44	39	87	30	31	—
Cell D.........	40	80	38	81	20	38	42

$p \leq .05$ for $r \geq .41$.
$p \leq .01$ for $r \geq .54$.
* Italicized r's indicate spuriousness due to whole-part contamination.

presents the intercorrelations among the various scores for the Experimental Group.

Of particular interest here is the correlation between first test (Relaxed Orientation) and second test (Achievement Orientation).

This correlation is .45 as compared to .54 (in Table 7) when the second test was also given under Relaxed Orientation. The correlation between six high-cue pictures and six low-cue pictures (half of each given under Relaxed Orientation and half under Achievement Orientation) is .46. This correlation is also lower than the comparable correlation, which was .57 when the two tests were given under the same condition (Table 7). While these two correlations are significant, indicating that persons who score relatively high under Relaxed Orientation tend also to score relatively high under Achievement Orientation, they account for only 20% of the variance in scores. And even when the reliability of the test is taken into account, less than half the variance in scores is accounted for. The intercell correlations in Table 9 are all lower than in Table 7. The fact that so much of the variance in scores is left unaccounted for serves to illustrate the main point of this study, namely, that cognizance must be taken of individual differences in responsiveness to the achievement cues which the experimenter controls if the test is to be used for effective prediction of achievement-related behaviors.

The purpose of this paper has been to call attention to and to specify ways of isolating some of the individual differences which influence thematic apperceptive scores. Results concerning the relationship of the various achievement imagery scores reported here and performance measures which can be used to test the effectiveness of the instrument will be reported at a later date by Haber and Alpert (167). It is anticipated that refinement of the measure of achievement motivation in the ways suggested by the present paper will enhance the prediction of performance variables.

CHAPTER 46

....

Some Methodological Problems in the Use of Thematic Apperceptive Measures of Human Motives

WALTER R. REITMAN AND JOHN W. ATKINSON[1]

THIS PAPER reviews experimental studies of several methodological problems that have arisen in the use of thematic apperceptive measures of motives. Research in the past few years has included an increasing number of studies of the *intrinsic* properties of thematic apperceptive tests and of the effects of these intrinsic properties upon inferences in regard to motives drawn from the stories. Many of these variables are delineated by McClelland *et al.* in *The Achievement Motive* (272, pp. 185-217), and several preliminary studies of their effects are also reported there.

The effects upon imaginative stories of variations in *picture cues* was the first of these variables to be studied, perhaps because this is the methodological factor most obviously related to problems of content interpretation. The preceding papers by Jacobs, Birney, and Haber and Alpert review the steps that have been taken to develop an operation to give picture cues a definition independent of the thematic imagery they elicit.

More recent work has also dealt with the effects of picture cues and the serial position of the pictures upon the predictive efficiency of motive indices derived from the thematic apperceptive stories. Evidence also is available as to the optimal length of thematic apperceptive measures.

The development of measures for an increasing number of motives has promoted an interest in the intercorrelations obtained when indices of the strengths of several different motives are derived by

---

[1] This study was accomplished during the term of a National Science Foundation Fellowship to WRR and a Social Science Research Council fellowship to JWA.

means of several scorings of a single set of protocols. In addition to evaluating the effects of such multiple scoring, the present paper also evaluates the reliability of objectively-scored thematic apperceptive measures and describes a quick and effective method for training reliable scorers.

No conclusive statements can be made as to the effects of the several factors considered here. The purpose of this paper is rather to indicate the extent to which these factors have been found to affect the results obtained on thematic apperceptive measures, and to draw whatever conclusions seem probable in the light of the available evidence. In view of the many fascinating content problems which these measures have opened up, it is not surprising that so little work has been devoted to methodological considerations; it is clear, however, that studies utilizing thematic apperceptive measures can contribute little to real psychological progress until such time as these studies proceed from a firm factual knowledge of the basic intrinsic properties of the instrument. By calling attention to the existence of these problems and the possible limitations of the instrument, we hope to sensitize researchers to them so that they are enabled to make more effective use of the thematic apperceptive method.

EFFECTS OF SERIAL POSITIONS OF PICTURES UPON THEMATIC APPERCEPTIVE STORIES

The complete TAT originally consisted of twenty pictures, although ". . . for practical reasons it has become more and more the custom to use only ten or twelve pictures" (38, p. 39). Although serial position might be expected to have some effect in a test of this length, to the writers' knowledge there are no experimental studies of the effect of picture position upon clinical interpretation of the story. Bellak, for example, simply lists the pictures he considers essential for testing men and adds, without further comment, that "they should be shown in this order" (38, p. 100). With the development of experimentally-validated thematic apperceptive measures for several different motives (e.g., achievement motive, affiliative motive, etc.) and with each typically employing a special set of pictures, batteries intended to measure several motives at once have increased in length to eight or more pictures, thus making the possibility of serial position effects upon the motive indices derived from the measures an important consideration in experimental work with thematic apperceptive tests.

One of the first studies to investigate the effects of serial position (22) made use of a Latin Square design, such that each picture appeared once and only once in a given serial position. An analysis of variance, which considered only the variation of scores about a common mean and ignored any orderly trend of the scores, revealed no significant effect of ordinal position upon achievement-motive scores. Subsequent examination of the data, however, revealed an unexpected saw-toothed phenomenon; mean achievement-motive scores from stories written by 32 college men to pictures in even serial positions were uniformly higher than those written to pictures in odd serial positions.

The difference between mean achievement-motive scores for odd and even serial positions, adjusted to removed systematic differences attributable to the pictures, is significant at the $p = .01$ level (22, p. 27).[2]

Further analysis of these data has revealed a second significant position effect: there is a significant relationship between the Ss' mean achievement-motive scores for the first four positions and the size of the decrease from these scores to the achievement-motive scores based on the last four positions (rho $= .66$), with scores again equated for systematic differences due to pictures. The product-moment correlation for this relationship, corrected by Thomson's formula (159, p. 373) for the unreliability of the measures of initial status and of the gains, is $r = .60$. The mean achievement-motive score is lower for the second four positions, but not significantly so. Even a significant difference, however, would in no wise account for the observed relationship.

One possible explanation of this result is that ". . . achievement motivation might be reduced through the fantasy in early stories leading to a decrease in the amount of achievement imagery appearing in later stories" (22, p. 12).

Since no independent criterion measure was employed in this investigation, it was impossible to determine whether the effects of serial position influenced predictions from achievement-motive scores to behavior.

Effects of serial positions of pictures upon predictions to behavior from motive scores. The present authors have attempted to determine whether the same pictures in different subsets of serial positions within a larger series of pictures yield equally valid measures of motives, as inferred from the relationship of the achievement-motive indices derived from such subsets to a behavioral criterion. The full details of the experimental procedure are described in a study of performance as a function of motive strength and expectancy of goal

---

[2] Stories in this study were later rescored using an improved form of the n Achievement scoring system, with several minor changes in this result (272, p. 188).

attainment, run concurrently with the present study and reported elsewhere (Ch. 19).

In the present study, three different eight-picture forms were used. In the first (Form I), four pictures, chosen *a priori* for their apparent relatedness to achievement and normally used to measure the achievement motive (272, p. 375: 1B, two men, "inventors," working in a shop at a machine; 1A, "father and son"—TAT card 7BM; IH, boy in checkered shirt at desk with open book; 1G, boy with vague operation scene in background—TAT card 8BM), were followed by four pictures selected from those normally used to measure the affiliation motive (see Ch. 5: 3A, the heads of two young men facing each other in conversation; 3I, a man standing in an open doorway looking away from the viewer at the landscape outside; 3O, a group of men around a table as if in conference; and see Ch. 4: 3F, a man standing under a lamppost—TAT card 20). In the second form (Form II), the four affiliation-related pictures came first, followed by the four achievement-related pictures. In the third form (Form III), the affiliation-related pictures appeared in odd serial positions, alternating with the achievement-related pictures. The sequential order of the four achievement-related pictures, as well as that of the four affiliation-related pictures, was constant for all three forms. The four affiliation-related pictures used were somewhat weak in affiliation-related cues; a set of pictures containing somewhat stronger affiliation-related cues probably would have permitted better differentiation among Ss having low and moderate affiliation motives.

As the present study utilized three arbitrary forms, rather than a Latin Square design, stories could not be equated for picture differences and thus no attempt could be made to replicate the earlier sawtoothed finding. On the other hand, by preserving the conventional four-picture forms, the present procedure facilitates comparison with other studies which have utilized them.

Subjects taking part in this experiment were from a larger group ($N = 133$) of male college students who wrote stories to these forms under "neutral" conditions (272, p. 101); in this, the most common assessment condition, no attempt is made to manipulate the motivation which Ss would normally have in a serious laboratory demonstration situation. Large, 18×20 inch, pictures were held up before the student subjects in very large classrooms. All eight stories were scored for both achievement motive and affiliation motive. Score-rescore reliabilities (to be discussed in detail later) were .88 for achievement motive and .89 for affiliation motive.

The behavioral criterion employed was a set of three-step arithmetic problems (430). This performance criterion is particularly suitable as quantitative aptitude scores have been found to be uncorrelated with achievement-motive scores (Ch. 19, 272), while both are correlated with performance on the arithmetic problems (Ch. 19). The performance measures were obtained one to three months after the thematic apperceptive measures.

Subjects worked at the tasks under conditions which were optimal from a theoretical standpoint. The theoretical argument is developed at length elsewhere (Ch. 19); suffice it to say that the relationship between strength of achievement motive inferred from thematic apperceptive stories and performance on the criterion measure should be at its maximum when the experimental conditions are such as to arouse selectively only expectations that adequate performance will lead to the attainment of an achievement goal. Subjects were given competitive-test (i.e. achievement-orienting) instructions in small groups and then worked alone at the problems in small test rooms. A significantly higher relationship between achievement-motive scores and performance was found for these Ss than for another group where irrelevant incentives were introduced in order to engage other motives in the performance as well (Ch. 19).

We first tested the effect of serial position upon prediction of arithmetic performance by comparing the predictive efficiency of achievement-motive scores derived from stories written to the four achievement-related pictures in each of the three eight-picture forms. Table 1 presents the mean number of correct solutions of the arith-

TABLE 1. THE EFFECT OF SERIAL PLACEMENT OF PICTURES UPON PREDICTION OF MEAN CORRECT ARITHMETIC PROBLEMS FOR Ss ABOVE (HIGH) AND BELOW (LOW) MEDIAN ACHIEVEMENT MOTIVE SCORES BASED ON STORIES WRITTEN TO FOUR ACHIEVEMENT-RELATED PICTURES IN EACH FORM

Achievement Motive	Serial Positions of Achievement-related Pictures					
	1st, 2nd, 3rd, 4th (Form I)		5th, 6th, 7th, 8th (Form II)		2nd, 4th, 6th, 8th (Form III)	
	N	M	N^*	M	N	M
High..........	9	67.33	15	65.40	15	65.13
Low..........	15	51.87	11	64.73	9	53.55
Diff. (H-L).....		15.46		.67		11.58
σ diff.**........		8.82		8.30		8.82
t..............		1.75		.08		1.31
p^{***}..........		.04		n.s.		.10

* One S who did not complete all four stories is excluded.
** σ diffs. derived from estimate of variance within groups = 437.19, with 68 d.f.
*** In the predicted direction.

metic problems in a 14-minute test period for Ss above (high) and below (low) their respective median achievement-motive scores as a function of the serial position of the achievement-related pictures.

There is a significant difference ($p = .04$) in mean arithmetic performance of Ss with high vs. low achievement-motive scores when these scores are based on the achievement-related pictures in the first four serial positions. There is practically no difference, on the other hand, in mean arithmetic performance of high and low achievement-motive groups if predictions are made from the same achievement-related pictures when they are in the last four serial positions. The difference in performance ($p = .10$) predicted with achievement-motive scores obtained from Form III, which has two achievement-related pictures in the first and two in the last four ordinal positions, falls midway between the differences predicted with the first two forms, as might be expected if the first four serial positions are more valid sources of motive scores than the last four. This supposition is not clearly supported by these data, however, as the difference between the differences predicted with Forms I and II, 14.79, is not significant (σ diff. $= 12.10$, $t = 1.22$).

A more comprehensive test compared the predictive efficiency of the first four positions, as opposed to the last four, for the three forms combined. Stories written to the four affiliation-related pictures by all Ss in the larger populations from which these samples were drawn, were scored for the achievement motive. The achievement motive scores obtained from the first and last four serial positions were thereby made available for all Ss, although, of course, each of the three forms had a different combination of pictures in the first and in the last four serial positions. Subjects above and below their respective median achievement-motive scores for each of the three combinations of first four vs. last four stories were lumped together to form combined high and low groups. Mean arithmetic performance for Ss having high and low achievement-motive scores was computed and a comparison made of predictions to behavior based on first as opposed to last four positions.

The difference in arithmetic performance predicted from achievement-motive scores based on the first four positions is significant at the $p = .01$ level. Again, furthermore, the size of the difference drops virtually to zero when predicted from achievement-motive scores based on the last four positions.

To remove any possible biasing of the result due to the uncontrolled difference in the content of the pictures between the first and second halves of Form III, the same comparison was made for those Ss who had written stories in response to Form I or Form II only. For this combined group, the same pictures appeared an almost equal number of times on both the first and second halves of the eight-picture measure—essentially the A-B, B-A design. The results of this comparison are given in Table 2.

TABLE 2. THE EFFECT OF SERIAL PLACEMENT OF PICTURES UPON PREDICTION OF MEAN CORRECT ARITHMETIC TASKS FOR Ss ABOVE (HIGH) AND BELOW (LOW) THEIR RESPECTIVE MEDIAN ACHIEVEMENT MOTIVE SCORES FROM FORMS I AND II

Achievement Motive	Serial Position of Pictures			
	1st, 2nd, 3rd, 4th		5th, 6th, 7th, 8th	
	N	M	N^*	M
High.	21	71.57	29	62.24
Low.	30	55.47	18	61.00
Diff. (H-L).		16.10		1.24
σ diff.		5.79		6.70
t.		2.78		.19
p^{**}.		.005		n.s.

* Three Ss (Form I) and one S (Form II) who had incomplete sets of stories were eliminated.

** In the predicted direction.

This comparison emphasizes still further the trends which were evident in the two previous ones. The difference in arithmetic performance predicted from achievement-motive scores based on pictures occurring in the first half of the series of eight is again highly significant. By contrast, scores based on the very same pictures appearing in the last four positions seem to be quite invalid if judged by their ability to predict performance on the arithmetic problems criterion measure. Finally, it should be noted that on this, the most balanced and comprehensive of the three comparisons, the difference between the differences in performance predicted with indices of achievement-motive strength derived from the first four and from the last four positions attains to borderline statistical significance (diff. = 14.86, σ diff. = 8.80, t = 1.70, p = .09).

Effects of serial positions of pictures upon split-half reliability coefficients for motive scores. Another test of the effects of the serial positions of the pictures upon the motive indices derived from them was made by comparing the split-half reliability coefficients for the achievement-motive scores obtained with each of the three forms. These reliability coefficients were obtained by correlating separately for each form the achievement-motive scores from the four achievement-related pictures with those from the four affiliation-related pictures. In other words, although in all three cases the scores were derived from the identical two sets of pictures, for the first two forms the scores obtained from the first four pictures were correlated with those obtained from the last four of the eight-picture form, whereas for Form III the correlation was one between scores from the same two sets of pictures in alternate serial positions.

All of the achievement-related pictures were scored for the affiliation motive. This made possible a corresponding test of serial-position effects upon affiliation-motive scores. Just as with the achievement-motive indices, this was accomplished by computing the split-half reliability coefficients for the motive scores for each of the three forms and comparing them. The results of these two sets of comparisons are presented in Table 3. The Ns in these comparisons include all the subjects for whom performance measures were available plus others who had written thematic apperceptive stories, but for whom no performance measures were obtained.

TABLE 3. CORRELATIONS BETWEEN MOTIVE SCORES OBTAINED SEPARATELY FROM ACHIEVEMENT-RELATED AND AFFILIATION-RELATED PICTURES AS A FUNCTION OF SERIAL POSITIONS OF THE TWO SETS OF FOUR PICTURES

Serial Position of Pictures	Achievement Motive Scores r	Affiliation Motive Scores r
Form I: ($N = 44$)................ Achievement-related, 1-4 Affiliation-related, 5-8	.32	−.06
Form II: ($N = 48$)............... Affiliation-related, 1-4 Achievement-related, 5-8	.28	.05
Form III: ($N = 41$).............. Affiliation-related, 1, 3, 5, 7 Achievement-related, 2, 4, 6, 8	.38	.56

For affiliation-motive scores, the differences between the correlation coefficient from Form III, where position effects should be minimal due to the alternation of pictures, and those from the first two forms, where the scores come from first vs. last four positions, were highly significant. A test of these differences, with r's converted into Fisher's z coefficients (160, pp. 224-25), yielded a difference of .69 between z's for Forms I and III (σ diff. = .225, $t = 3.07$, $p = .005$) and a difference of .58 between z's for Forms II and III (σ diff. = .217, $t = .267$, $p = .01$). The corresponding differences for the achievement-motive coefficients, while not significant (difference between I and III is .07, σ diff. $= .225$, $t = .31$; difference between II and III is .11, σ diff. $= .217$, $t = .51$), were in the same direction. Taken as a whole, these comparisons constitute further evidence of the effect of serial position upon motive scores.

Implications of the results from studies of serial-position effects upon motive scores. In interpreting the results presented above, care must be taken to point out that these studies cannot be considered entirely conclusive from a statistical point of view for two reasons. In all three tests of predictions made from motive scores in regard to performance on the arithmetic problems criterion measure it was found that motive scores derived from pictures in the first four positions of an eight-picture form predicted significant differences, whereas those derived from pictures in the last four positions essentially did not predict to performance at all. Now, the difference in predictive efficiency between the first four vs. the last four serial positions, while quite sizeable in all cases, nonetheless attained to borderline statistical significance in only one of the three comparisons. In the second place, although the differences between the reliability coefficient for affiliation-motive scores from Form III and those from Form I and II were highly significant and provided clear-cut evidence of serial-position effects upon the motive scores, the corresponding differences in reliability coefficients for achievement-motive scores from the three forms, while in the same direction, were quite small.

However, taken together with earlier findings of serial-position effects (22), the experimental comparisons, presented here, of predictions to performance from achievement-motive scores derived from the first four vs. the last four positions seem quite clearly to indicate that different subsets of serial positions *do not in fact yield equally valid measures of the achievement motive.*

Furthermore, as there surely is no *a priori* reason why these effects should be limited to the scores from which the strength of the achievement motive is inferred, it seems quite probable that measures of other motives derived from pictures in later serial positions also may be relatively invalid, at least with respect to their ability to predict to differences in behavior. Should this in fact be the case, it would of course seriously affect the interpretation of research utilizing such measures. The absence of a suitable behavioral criterion made it impossible in our experiment to obtain direct evidence for this supposition with regard to affiliation-motive scores (i.e., to evaluate predictions to performance from affiliation-motive scores based on different subsets of serial positions). Yet, the striking differences in the reliability coefficients for these scores as a function of serial position strongly suggest that the above conclusion applies with equal force to measures of the affiliation motive derived from different subsets of serial positions.

The results of these studies would seem to have important implications not only for the experimental use of thematic apperceptive measures but also for the clinical use of such instruments. It is certainly reasonable to suppose that serial position may have comparable effects upon the many variables obtained from the TAT by means of systems of content analysis such as Murray's (315). The studies reviewed here suggest that these variables quite possibly may have one meaning when coded from stories written early on the TAT and quite another when coded from later stories, *entirely apart from any effects of the cues of the specific pictures upon the stories they elicit.* It will be recalled that the results from our studies were obtained with forms consisting of eight pictures. The extent to which the position effects reported here are multiplied and further complicated on ten-, twelve-, or twenty-picture forms cannot be estimated from the data presently available. These findings, however, surely constitute a *caveat* of some importance for those who must make interpretations to personality dynamics from tests of this length.[3]

Effects of picture cues upon the predictive efficiency of motive scores. One alternative to the use of longer forms, with separate subsets of pictures for each motive to be measured, is to score the same set of pictures for several motives. Such a procedure raises several new problems. One of these concerns the predictive efficiency of

---

[3] A study by H. N. Ricciuti and R. A. Clark (341) comparing need-achievement stories written by experimentally "relaxed" and "achievement-oriented" subjects also may be relevant to this discussion. They found that the increment in mean achievement-motive scores obtained under achievement-oriented as opposed to relaxed administration conditions was significant at $p = .05$ or better for scores derived from two and one-half minute stories written to each of the first eight pictures of their 12-picture form. Only one of the last four pictures yielded mean achievement-motive scores significantly different for the two conditions (341, p. 16). As it is impossible to partial out from these results the possible effects of differential picture content upon the amount of increment in mean achievement-motive score, these results in themselves, while suggesting a serial position effect similar to that described in this paper, do not, of course, constitute strong evidence for such an effect.

Ricciuti and Clark also call attention to another problem not treated here. When only two and one-half minutes are allowed for writing each story, verbal productivity differentiates "relaxed" and "aroused" groups and is also correlated with n Achievement scores within the groups. This problem, which has not arisen in studies of college groups when four minutes are allowed and leading questions are employed to elicit the story, may require special attention when there are gross differences in the length of protocols. The reader may consult Ricciuti and Clark (341) and Chapters 10 and 34 of this volume for discussions of how to remove the effects of gross differences in length of stories when the problem arises.

motive scores when they are derived from pictures originally chosen to measure another motive. Early experiments with thematic apperceptive measures of motives utilized pictures chosen *a priori* on the basis of their apparent relatedness to the motive to be measured, i.e., on the basis of the anticipated ability of the picture cues to evoke associations having some particular content. The question of the extent to which such picture cues actually affect the predictive efficiency of motive scores assumes increased importance due to the fact that serial-position effects would seem to impose a serious limitation upon the number of pictures which may be utilized in such measures.

Results have been presented which show that cognitive judgments of the relatedness of a picture to a particular motive can, at least in the case of the achievement motive, predict the relative frequency of achievement imagery with some success (Ch. 44, Ch. 45). The problem to be considered here is a related one: to what extent does the amount or frequency of a specific imagery content elicited by a picture affect the predictive efficiency of the corresponding motive score. Are "related" pictures necessary for a valid measure of a motive?

Atkinson (22) classified 32 male Ss as high or low in achievement motive on the basis of total scores for eight stories. He then computed the mean difference in achievement-motive score between high and low Ss for three pictures with strong achievement cues and compared this with the corresponding mean difference in achievement-motive score between high and low Ss in response to two pictures with moderately weak achievement cues. For the three strong-cue pictures, which elicited an average of 93% stories containing achievement imagery, the difference between high and low Ss was 1.90. For the two weak-cue pictures, which elicited an average of 42% stories containing achievement imagery, the difference between high and low Ss was 1.94. Atkinson concluded that: "The effect of suggesting achievement situations in pictures containing adult characters is equivalent to the addition of a constant value to what the n Ach [-ievement, i.e., achievement-motive] score would be in response to pictures having comparable adult characters but an unstructured or unrelated situation" (22, p. 33).

Another opportunity to evaluate the effects of picture cues upon predictive efficiency was afforded by the present investigation. We were able to test predictions to arithmetic performance from achievement-motive scores based on stories written to affiliation-related pictures in the first four positions of an eight-picture form (Form II). The results were then compared with those obtained when predictions to performance were made from achievement-motive scores based on stories written to achievement-related pictures in the first four positions of an eight-picture form (Form I). The choice of a comparison utilizing only scores from the first four serial positions was made in view of the finding that these positions seemed to yield the most efficiently predicting motive scores. Results are presented in Table 4.

TABLE 4. PREDICTION OF MEAN CORRECT ARITHMETIC PROBLEMS FOR Ss ABOVE (HIGH) AND BELOW (LOW) THE MEDIAN ACHIEVEMENT MOTIVE SCORES FROM STORIES BASED ON ACHIEVEMENT-RELATED AND AFFILIATION-RELATED PICTURES IN THE FIRST FOUR POSITIONS OF AN EIGHT PICTURE FORM

Achievement Motive	Source of Achievement Motive Scores			
	Achievement-related Pictures (Form I, 1-4)		Affiliation-related Pictures (Form II, 1-4)	
	N	M	N	M
High	9	67.33	12	74.75
Low	15	51.87	15	59.07
Diff. (H-L)		15.46		15.68
σ diff.*		8.62		7.92
t		1.79		1.98
p**		.04		.025

* σ diff. derived from estimate of variance within groups 418.16, with 47 d.f.
** In the predicted direction.

The significant difference ($p = .025$) predicted from achievement-motive scores based on affiliation-related pictures in the first four positions is actually slightly larger than the comparable difference ($p = .04$) predicted from achievement-motive scores based on achievement-related pictures in the same positions. Our data thus provide no indication whatsoever that the cognitively judged "relatedness" of a set of pictures to a particular motive has any effect upon the predictive efficiency of achievement-motive scores derived from stories written to those pictures (see also 340, 341, 342).

Further research is required before this conclusion can be generalized to other measures of motives with any degree of certainty; the present finding does suggest, however, that it may prove possible to measure several motives with a single set of four pictures, thus obviating the need for longer forms. This finding does not mean, on the other hand, that the predictive efficiency or validity of motive scores is entirely independent of all aspects of picture content. It has been found (22), for example, that achievement-motive scores from pictures containing only child characters may be relatively invalid, judging from the relation between these scores and the ones from the rest of the pictures in an eight-picture thematic apperceptive measure. On the basis of this finding, the suggestion was made that such pictures might promote regressive identifications and might result in a relatively larger proportion of stories based directly on past experience, and that this in turn might interfere with the future-oriented anticipatory thought sequence which seems most symptomatic of the motivation of the contemporary individual (p. 34).

Optimal length for thematic apperceptive measures. Position effects tend to reduce drastically the predictive efficiency of motive scores derived solely from stories written to pictures occurring relatively late on thematic apperceptive measures. Therefore, in attempting to find an optimal length for such measures, it is important to know whether stories to pictures in such positions contribute anything at all to the predictive efficiency of scores based on the total form; if they do not, there would seem to be little point in utilizing measures of this length.

We computed achievement-motive scores on the basis of all eight pictures and compared the mean performance on the arithmetic problems for Ss with high and with low achievement-motive scores, median scores for each of the three forms being determined on the basis of the larger populations. The results for the three forms separately and combined are given in Table 5.

TABLE 5. MEAN CORRECT ARITHMETIC PROBLEMS FOR Ss ABOVE (HIGH) AND BELOW (LOW) MEDIAN ACHIEVEMENT MOTIVE SCORES BASED ON ALL EIGHT STORIES IN EACH OF THREE FORMS OF THE TEST

Achievement Motive	Form						Three Forms Combined	
	I		II		III			
	N^*	M	N^*	M	N	M	N	M
High........	12	61.58	15	69.27	15	63.87	42	65.14
Low........	9	52.33	11	59.45	9	59.44	29	57.24
Diff. (H-L)..		9.25		9.82		4.43		7.90
σ diff........		8.86**		7.98		8.47		4.86
t..........		1.04		1.23		.52		1.63
p^{***}........		.15		.11		.30		.06

* Three Ss on Form I and one S on Form II whose sets of stories were incomplete are excluded.
** σ diffs. derived from estimate variance within groups = 404.14 with 65 d.f.
*** In the predicted direction.

A comparison of these results with those obtained when predictions are made from only the first four stories shows that, for the three forms considered separately, in two out of three cases the difference in performance predicted from all eight stories is smaller than that predicted from the first four. For the three forms combined, the difference predicted from the scores based on all eight stories is 7.90, while that predicted from the scores based on only the first four stories is 11.51. Although all of these differences are small, they suggest that combining the scores from the first four pictures with those from the last four tends, instead of increasing predictive efficiency, actually to *decrease* it somewhat. It should be emphasized that this finding in connection with a thematic apperceptive measure contrasts considerably with that obtained in nonprojective test situations, where an increase in the length of a test typically acts to increase its correlation with a criterion.

Insofar as the evidence obtained is hardly compelling, and in the absence of similar comparisons of predictions from initial positions and total forms for any other motive index, it would be premature to recommend that longer forms be dispensed with. If such forms are used, however, and a good, independent criterion variable is not available, these findings certainly suggest that relationships between motive scores and other variables be investigated in terms of the motive scores derived from the initial stories written by the Ss.

A study by Lindzey and Heinemann (237) also is relevant here. They gave all of their Ss both group and individual TAT's. Half of the Ss were allowed to write only five minutes to each picture in the group administration, while the other half were allowed eight minutes per story. Using as their criterion for optimal length the amount of similarity between scores for the same individual from group and individual administrations, they found that the five-minute group scores showed a higher correlation with the individual TAT scores than did the eight-minute group scores. While the eight-minute group test was more similar to the individually administered test in means and variances and in number of words and ideas produced, Lindzey and Heinemann considered these variables less important, and they concluded: "Consequently, although a conservative interpretation of our findings would suggest that there is no clear evidence for the superiority of one group method over the other, the available evidence implies that, if anything, the five-minute test may be the more valuable" (p. 51).

Effect of multiple scorings upon relationships between motive scores. The studies considered above indicate that valid measures of motives, at least in terms of the predictive efficiency of the motive indices, may only be obtained from stories written to pictures occurring early on the thematic apperceptive measure. No evidence was found which would suggest that longer forms provided more efficient scores than the shorter ones.

On the other hand, since picture content was shown in at least one case to have little effect upon the predictive efficiency of motive scores, it may be that, even in the absence of longer thematic apperceptive forms, valid indices for several different motives can be obtained from the same three or four pictures by means of multiple scorings. The possibility exists, however, that such multiple scoring introduces as artifacts relationships between the different motive scores which otherwise would have been absent.

In order to determine whether spurious relationships between the inferred motives were actually introduced by multiple scoring, we computed three sets of intercorrelations between the achievement and affiliation motives from the data obtained in the experiment described earlier. The first intercorrelation was computed from scores obtained, for each motive, from the related pictures only, i.e., the two scores were derived from separate and nonoverlapping sets of stories. The second was computed with both scores derived from all eight pictures. The third was computed with both scores derived from the first four pictures of each form only. The results appear in Table 6.

TABLE 6. THE CORRELATION BETWEEN ACHIEVEMENT MOTIVE SCORES AND
AFFILIATION MOTIVE SCORES AS A FUNCTION OF THE
SOURCE OF THE MOTIVE SCORES

	Serial Order of Pictures			
Source of Motive Scores	Form I ($N = 44$)	Form II ($N = 48$)	Form III ($N = 41$)	Weighted* Average
Four related pictures only (no overlap)	−.03	−.21	−.04	−.10
All eight pictures	−.15	−.20	.13	−.08
First four pictures only	−.24	−.21	.13	−.12

* According to the procedure suggested in Guilford (159, pp. 355-56).

None of the obtained correlations or weighted averages was significant. None of the differences between correlations or weighted averages was significant. There was no apparent change in the correlation between achievement and affiliation-motive scores as a function of multiple scorings.

The finding that achievement- and affiliation-motive scores are essentially uncorrelated confirms the results of previous studies.

Groesbeck, for example, obtained a correlation of $r = +.16$ for 125 Ss, with both sets of scores obtained from the same TAT pictures (Ch. 28; 158, p. 13).

Reliability. There are two aspects to reliability as the concept applies to scores derived by means of content analysis from thematic apperceptive measures. The first involves the reliability of the measure, as estimated by split-half statistics or test-retest correlations. The second concerns the reliability of the system of content analysis used in scoring, as measured, for example, by the correlation between two sets of scores obtained from the same stories by two different scorers. Both kinds of reliability are important for those who make use of such scores, either experimentally or in the clinic.

Few equivalent-form coefficients have been computed for these measures. Atkinson (272, p. 191) reported a correlation of .64 between achievement-motive scores from two equivalent sets of three pictures each; corrected by the Spearman-Brown formula (159, pp. 418-19) this yielded an estimated reliability of .78 for the achievement-motive scores obtained from these six pictures.

Other split-half and test-retest correlations have generally been somewhat lower (e.g., Table 3 above; 272, pp. 187-194). In a recent discussion of the relatively low test-retest reliability of the achievement-motive score, McClelland[4] suggests, particularly in view of the reasonably high validity coefficients reported for the measure, that in part the paradox may result from Ss' avoidance of response repetition in successive performances. McClelland cites Atkinson's finding of a saw-toothed phenomenon (cf. above) as an illustration of this, and he also notes that data reported by Rogers and Dymond (347, pp. 132-134), although not explicitly noted by these authors, show the same kind of cyclical alternation effect over three successive test administrations. Reasoning from the established validity of these measures and from the fact that the observed changes in performance on successive administrations of thematic apperceptive measures are definitely *systematic and cyclical in nature,* McClelland concludes that the apparently low test-retest reliability of scores derived from such measures apparently is a function of "a set for response variability." We shall want to return to this problem in our concluding discussion (see also Ch. 45).

A number of estimates of interscorer and score-rescore reliability are available. When used by experienced scorers, the measures not uncommonly yield reliability coefficients above .90 (see Ch. 15). Achieving high scorer reliability is like learning to read a radar

---

[4] McClelland, D. C. Note on cyclical effects in successive administrations of the TAT to the same persons. Unpublished paper, Wesleyan University, 1956.

screen. Both activities require the learning of a series of fine discriminations, which then must be used in making coding decisions.

An attempt to develop a rapid and efficient method of instruction in scoring was made in an experimental seminar on the scoring of the achievement motive conducted at the University of Michigan in the fall of 1954. The participants, six undergraduate honors students and first year graduate students in psychology with no previous experience in the use of the system, were given copies of the scoring manual (272, Ch. IV) and two practice sets of thirty four-story protocols. The protocols were scored individually, and then each individual's scorings of the stories were compared with scores previously assigned by experienced scorers. A total of about four hours, over a period of several weeks, was spent in the seminar in ironing out scoring problems under the direction of an experienced scorer. A reliability check was then made, using a third set of four-story protocols. Percentage agreement on achievement imagery ranged from .78 to .91 ($N = 6$). (An index of agreement on the most important scoring decision was made by taking twice the number of agreements between each student's scores and the criterion scores assigned by experienced coders and dividing it by the number of categories scored by both.) The average percentage agreement was .87.

A similar seminar on instruction in scoring for the affiliation motive was held in the spring of 1955. Several but not all of the eight participants had also participated in the earlier seminar. After a similar training sequence, percentage agreement on the basic decision required by the system—whether or not to score for affiliation imagery —was computed and was found to range from .89 to .95 ($N = 8$). The average percentage agreement was .92. Some of these scorers, joined by several others who had had previous experience, were assigned the task of scoring all of the stories written in response to a particular picture in the present study. The achievement-motive scores and the affiliation-motive scores in this study were thus composites of scores obtained by several different scorers. The authors rescored stories written to the four motive-related pictures to provide a rescore reliability check on the total scores for four stories. The scoring reliability coefficients were .88 for achievement-motive ($N = 24$) and .89 for affiliation-motive ($N = 41$).

Two morals may be drawn from this story. First, previously untrained persons can learn to score thematic apperceptive protocols for motives in a very short span of time, provided that they can talk over their errors in discrimination with experienced scorers. Second, there is no reason to believe that experienced scorers could not be replaced by more detailed and comprehensive scoring manuals.[5]

---

[5] See Ch. 15 by Feld and Smith.

CONCLUDING DISCUSSION

Preliminary investigations invariably raise many more questions than they answer; we shall briefly try to consider a few of the most pressing of these in the discussion which follows.

One of the more fascinating findings reported by the studies reviewed here was the discovery of a marked serial-position effect upon motive scores. The suggestion (22, p. 12) that motivation may be reduced through fantasy in writing earlier stories gains plausibility in the light of a recent study by Feshbach (Ch. 11). This experimenter aroused the Ss' hostility to the E and found that Ss who expressed their aggression in thematic apperceptive stories to pictures were subsequently significantly less hostile and aggressive on a questionnaire than were Ss who were not given the opportunity to write stories and who thus were unable to reduce aggression in fantasy prior to filling in the questionnaire. On the other hand, any such reduction in motivation would seem to be quite transient and specific, since a number of studies have demonstrated differences in performance between Ss high and low in the achievement-motive when the dependent performance variable was measured immediately after the administration of the measure of the motive (e.g., 23).

The cyclical saw-toothed phenomenon described previously is a second unexplained position effect. McClelland's interpretation of this effect has already been mentioned; we might add that the effect is analogous, at least superficially, to alternation phenomena studied years ago by Thorndike and Dodge under the rubric of "refractory phase" and more recently examined by Dennis, Montgomery, and Walker—and by others—and this effect may well be related to such phenomena.

A second plausible explanation of position effects has been proposed which, although essentially quite simple, may nonetheless have a number of consequences for the general use of the TAT. Subjects usually are told that the TAT is a test of "creative imagination," and it may be that "some of them, in the interest of being creative and imaginative, might tend to inhibit the repetition of particular aspects of plots similar to ones appearing in earlier stories" (22, p. 12). At the present time, no evidence is available which might be brought to bear for or against this possibility.

Three basic methodological problems among the many which urgently require further investigation stand out as particularly important. The study of change in the motive structure of the individual presupposes the validity of motive reassessment by means of the original measuring instrument. No systematic data are available on the relative validity—as measured by their predictive efficiency—of motive scores obtained from a retest with a thematic apperceptive measure of motivation. It is possible that the instrument is effective for the first few pictures only and that thereafter some Ss adapt to the method in some way. In other words, our finding which showed the relative invalidity of scores from the last four positions may be only indirectly a function of "serial position"; *all* subsequent measures may be equally invalid for some Ss who adapt to the test.

On the other hand, in the absence of any evidence on the problem, the opposite condition is equally likely. Retest scores may predict as efficiently as the original measurement, and a pause of fifteen minutes between the first and last four pictures of an eight-picture measure may render scores from the last half as valid as those from the first, although in view of McClelland's observation the latter possibility seems somewhat unlikely.

The second basic methodological problem is simply the absence of adequate knowledge of the effects of picture content upon thematic apperceptive stories and, particularly, upon the motive scores derived from such stories. Lacking such knowledge, our selection of pictures for thematic apperceptive measures becomes a hit-or-miss affair. Rosenstein (24, 350) has reported one pertinent finding: college students who major in chemistry obtain higher achievement-motive scores in response to pictures of men working in laboratory situations than do physical education majors; the two groups do not differ in response to pictures of athletic competition. This result suggests that achievement-motive scores in response to a particular kind of content in the pictures should correspond to competitive interest in that particular kind of activity. The systematic follow-up of this lead might well add a new dimension to our understanding of the relationships between the stimuli presented to the individual and the complex processes which eventuate in his thematic apperceptive story.

The third problem is to determine the extent to which experimental findings obtained with group administrations of thematic apperceptive measures, such as those reported here, may be generalized to the individual administration of the test. The results of two recent studies may be mentioned briefly in this connection. Lindzey and Heinemann call attention to Eron and Ritter's finding, in a comparison of a group and a set of individual administrations of the TAT, that, despite some differences in the formal qualities of the stories, "in content—i.e., actual thematic material elicited—the two groups are almost identical" (120, pp. 60-61). In their own study described earlier, Lindzey and Heinemann conclude:

"Considering the measurement shortcomings that at present inhere in the instrument and our procedures, the findings seem to us strongly positive in suggesting that the group test may be a reasonable substitute for the individual test" (237, p. 42).

Further progress in the gradual development of an instrument for assessment of total motivational structure waits upon further basic methodological research. Studies of position effects, for example, as they appear in thematic apperceptive measures, clearly serve also as an avenue for an experimental approach to the dynamics of motivation; knowledge of the changes which take place in the course of taking the test will provide new insight into the laws and mechanisms of such changes.

It may be predicted with confidence that not only will such basic methodological research result in more efficient and useful measures of human motives but in the process it will also contribute to our knowledge of the fundamental characteristics of motivation and of related psychological processes. For it is likely that with further refinement, what first appeared to be disadvantages of the technique, the richness and complexity of the thematic apperceptive method, will be more than compensated for as progressive study of the instrument itself ultimately provides new insights into the nature of language and thought and into the relation of language and thought processes to motivational variables.

APPENDIX I

How to Learn the Method of Content Analysis for n Achievement, n Affiliation, and n Power[1]

CHARLES P. SMITH AND SHEILA FELD

APPENDIX I CONTAINS instructions and practice materials for learning the method of content analysis for n Achievement, n Affiliation, and n Power. The practice materials are divided into three sections, one for each motive. In each section may be found (a) a "Self-Test" on the scoring manual for that particular motive, (b) descriptions of the pictures used to elicit the practice stories, (c) seven sets of practice stories (30 stories in a set), and (d) expert scoring for the practice stories. The first four sets of practice stories (A, B, C, and D) for each motive correspond exactly to the sets designated by the same letters in the study of scoring reliability reported in Chapter 15. The remaining three sets (E, F, and G) for each motive, however, are not the same as the sets designated E, F, and G in Chapter 15. In order to make optimum use of the limited amount of practice material that could be included in this appendix, three new sets were compiled for each motive from Sets A, B, C, and D of the other two motives. Consequently, these appendix materials provide the opportunity for practice with a greater variety of pictures than the practice materials used in the study reported in Chapter 15. The implications of this change in the practice materials will be discussed in detail in the section "How to Evaluate Your Progress."

Conscientious use of these practice materials should enable the user to learn to score imaginative stories for n Achievement, n Affiliation, or n Power with interjudge scoring reliability acceptable for research purposes after approximately twelve hours of practice. This training procedure was developed so that persons could learn to score without having to discuss scoring problems with an expert, i.e., a person who has had extensive previous experience with the

---

[1] The development of these training procedures was supported by a grant from the Ford Foundation (J. W. Atkinson, Project Director).

scoring system.[2] The procedure calls for studying the appropriate scoring manual (see Chapters 12, 13, or 14) and then scoring seven sets of practice protocols.

INSTRUCTIONS

Seven sets of practice stories are to be scored in five different practice sessions, with approximately two days between sessions. Score Set A during the first session (about three hours). Score Set B during the second session (about an hour and a half). During the third session (about two hours) score Sets C and D. During the fourth session (about two hours) review errors in the manner to be suggested and then score Set E. During the fifth session (about two hours) score Sets F and G.

The Practice Stories and How They Were Elicited. Imaginative stories may be obtained from individuals singly or in groups. The usual procedure is to show a group of persons a picture for twenty seconds, then to ask them to write a story about it using as an outline the four questions listed below. A minute is allowed for each question. The questions are equally spaced on an otherwise blank sheet of $8\frac{1}{2} \times 14$ inch paper. Four to six pictures are customarily used. This provides a sufficient sample of the subject's imaginative thought process for most research purposes. Detailed discussion of instructions and other procedures which have been used may be found in *The Achievement Motive* (272, pp. 97-106).

Four questions are used to guide the subject's storywriting: (1) What is happening? Who are the persons? (2) What has led up to this situation? That is, what has happened in the past? (3) What is being thought? What is wanted? By whom? (4) What will happen? What will be done? The stories are reproduced here so that the answers to the four questions are numbered 1, 2, 3, and 4. Proper names have been deleted in these stories; otherwise they are reproduced here exactly as they were written: *errors in grammar and spelling, etc.,* have not been changed. The stories were selected from typical samples of protocols which have been used for research purposes. Most of the stories included here were written by college students since college populations have been sampled most frequently in past research.

Preparation. Read the scoring manual (Ch. 12, 13, or 14) carefully. Next, without consulting the manual, write your answers to

---

[2] For the "expert scoring" of the practice stories included in Appendix I we wish to acknowledge the combined efforts of John W. Atkinson, Berne Jacobs, Edward Lichtenstein, George Litwin, Charles Mahone, Joan Munson, Patricia O'Connor, Clara Oppenheimer, Walter Reitman, and Joseph Veroff.

the questions on the "Self-Test" for the manual you are studying. Then carefully check your answers with the manual. It is a waste of time to begin practice scoring until you have mastered the scoring definitions.

Scoring Sheet. Make a scoring sheet on which you can record your scoring of the 30 stories in each practice set. Down the left side of the sheet number 1 through 30, and across the top of the sheet designate a column for each scoring category: Imagery, Unrelated Imagery, Need, $I+$, $I?$, $I-$, and so on. At the head of each column also write the numerical value that each category contributes to the total score. This is important for two reasons: First, the total score will be used for checking scoring reliability; it should be computed and recorded for each story. Second, the categories given values of $+1$, 0, or -1 are not always the same in the n Achievement, n Affiliation, and n Power scoring systems. To avoid confusion in the calculation of the total score for a story it is helpful to have the numerical value of each category for that particular scoring system on the scoring sheet. After the Thema column, designate a column in which to enter the total score for each story and another column in which to enter the rank for each story in order to facilitate the computation of rank-order reliability. Mark an X in the appropriate cell on your scoring sheet when a particular category is present in a story and a dash (—) when that category is absent.

Set A. This is a set of 30 stories which is to be scored *one category* at a time. First, score all 30 stories for Imagery. The expert has written out explanations for his scoring decisions, and these explanations follow the last set of practice stories. Check your scoring with that of the expert *after each story,* and carefully read the expert's explanation. These explanations supplement the examples in the scoring manuals. To avoid looking ahead at the expert's scoring of the next stories, cover the part of the page you are not working on.

After scoring all the stories for Imagery, score those stories in which the expert found motive-related Imagery to be *present* for the next category, Need (N). Once again, check your scoring with that of the expert after each story. After scoring these stories for Need, repeat this procedure for each of the other subcategories: Instrumental Acts (I), Anticipatory Goal States (Ga), Obstacles or Blocks (Bp, Bw), etc.

On this and every other set of stories, *refer to the scoring manual whenever necessary* while scoring. Do not trust your memory if you are in doubt. Make use of the criteria and examples which the manual provides.

Set B. This is a set of 30 stories which is to be scored *one story* at a time. That is, score each story for every category before going on to the next story. (When the scoring system is used for research purposes, each story is scored for all categories before the next story is considered.) Score the *first ten* stories in the set, then carefully check your scoring with that of the expert. Pay particular attention to stories on which errors were made. *Refer to the manual* or to Set A whenever necessary. Review examples of difficult categories in Set A.

Repeat this procedure for the next ten stories, then for the last ten stories. As before, record your scores by placing an X when you think a category is present and a dash (—) when you think a category is absent in a particular story. This procedure of noting either presence or absence insures that each category will be considered for each story.

For Sets B through G compute your agreement with the expert on the following two criteria after scoring *each set* of stories and checking your scoring with that of the expert. The first index of agreement is the *percentage agreement* between you and the expert on the presence of motive-related Imagery. This index is the ratio of twice the number of times that you and the expert agree in scoring the *presence* of motive-related Imagery divided by the number of times you have scored Imagery present plus the number of times the expert has scored Imagery present. For example, in a set of 30 stories you may think 10 contain motive-related Imagery and the expert may think that 20 contain motive-related Imagery. There may be agreement between you and the expert on seven of these cases. The index would then be as follows:

$$\frac{2 \quad (7)}{10 + 20} = \frac{14}{30} = .47$$

The second index of agreement is a *rank-order correlation*[3] between your ranking and the expert's ranking of the protocols according to the total score for each story.[4]

---

[3] To find out how to compute a rank-order correlation, consult any general statistics text, e.g.: (423, p. 278 ff.).

[4] In the practice sets of stories included in this Appendix there is only one story for each of 30 Ss in a set. Consequently, the 30 Ss are ranked according to a one-story score. Typical research data, however, would consist of four or more stories for each S. In this case, the grand total of all four or more stories written by an S would be obtained. Then the Ss would be ranked according to these grand totals in computing scoring reliability.

Sets C through G. Each of the following sets of stories is to be scored story by story. Sets C through G consist of 30 stories each. Score all stories in a set at one scoring session. Do not refer to the expert scoring of a set of stories until *all* stories in that set have been scored. *Refer to the manual and/or previously scored sets of stories whenever necessary.* In checking your scoring with that of the expert, pay particular attention to stories on which errors were made. Try to determine the basis for the expert's scoring, and reread the section of the manual regarding the category involved.

Before scoring Set E, conduct a systematic review of your errors. Beginning with Set B, look at your scoring sheets and write down the numbers of the first 20 stories in which you made any errors. Rescore these one by one, checking with the expert after each story. If you still disagree with the expert, reread his explanation and the relevant sections of the scoring manual in order to try to see his point of view. After rescoring these stories, see if there are particular categories with which you consistently have difficulty. If so, review the stories in which you have made errors in the scoring of these categories and reread the relevant sections in the scoring manual. After this review of errors, proceed to Sets E, F, and G.

It is recommended that you score all the sets of stories included here even if you attain a satisfactory scoring reliability after the first set or two. Considerable practice is necessary before the scoring system can be used with speed and accuracy and can be remembered over a long period of time. The amount of practice afforded by these materials must be considered minimal. It is essential for most scorers to review the manual carefully before scoring if a period of several weeks or more has elapsed since previous scoring.

After becoming proficient with the scoring system, you may want to disregard the practice of designating the absence of a category from a story. This practice, which was suggested for purposes of learning with the practice materials, is of little value after a scorer has become proficient with a scoring system.

How to Evaluate Your Progress. Since it was not possible to match exactly the practice sets of stories for scoring difficulty, your scoring reliability may not increase consistently from set to set. However, by Set D you should have some idea of your progress and general level of scoring reliability. You can compare your scoring reliability on Sets A through D with Table 1 of Chapter 15, which gives the scoring reliabilities of 12 volunteer graduate students on these sets of stories. (Sets E, F, and G in Chapter 15, however, are *not the same* as Sets E, F, and G in Appendix I and do not provide any basis for comparison.)

Table 1 of Chapter 15 shows that on Set D, 8 of the 12 graduate Ss attained scoring reliabilities of .80 or better on both indices. An additional group of undergraduate volunteers who scored Sets A through D after the study reported in Chapter 15 was completed attained slightly lower reliabilities on these sets of stories. Results from both graduate and undergraduate scorers show that the Affiliation scoring system produces higher interjudge scoring reliabilities than the Achievement or Power scoring systems.

Table 1 of Chapter 15 also indicates that after Set D, practice with stories written to the same pictures brings little additional improvement in coding reliability. Hence, these stories (Sets E and F of Chapter 15) were not included when it became necessary to limit the number of practice stories in this book. Instead, three new sets of stories—designated E, F, and G—were compiled for each motive. The new sets were made up from stories in Practice Sets A through D for the *other* motives. For example, Sets E, F, and G for n Achievement were made up from stories contained in Sets A through D for Power and Affiliation. This means that for each motive the stories in Sets E, F, and G were elicited by different kinds of pictures than the stories in Sets A through D.

In view of the change to novel pictures after Set D, a decrease in scoring reliability on Sets E, F, and G may be expected. A significant decrease in scoring reliability from familiar to novel pictures is reported in Chapter 15. Among the undergraduate Ss on whom the new practice sets E, F, and G of Appendix I were tried out, the decrease in coding reliabilities was particularly evident among the Ss who scored stories for n Achievement ($N = 3$). The median percentage agreement in scoring Imagery dropped from .90 on Set D to .59 (E), .48 (F), and .64 (G); the median rank-order correlation dropped from .83 on Set D to .43 (E), .44 (F), and .67 (G). For Affiliation and Power Sets E, F, and G, scoring reliabilities remained virtually the same as they had been on Set D. For Affiliation, ($N = 3$), both indices of scoring reliability were above .80 throughout; for Power, ($N = 6$), both indices of scoring reliability were around .70 to .75 throughout.

As a final test of their scoring proficiency, these undergraduate scorers were given an additional set of 60 stories (Set F of Chapter 15) which had been elicited by the same pictures as the stories of Sets A through D. The results showed that practice with novel stories did not interfere with previously-attained scoring reliabilities. For Set F of Chapter 15 the undergraduate Ss attained the following scoring reliabilities for the percentage agreement in scoring Imagery index and the rank-order correlation index respectively: Achievement, .82 and .80; Affiliation, .86 and .81; and Power, .81 and .81.

Eight of the 12 undergraduates in our sample attained scoring reliabilities of .80 or above on both indices on this final criterion set of 60 stories immediately following their completion of Appendix I Practice Sets A through G. Nine of the 12 graduate Ss attained this level of scoring reliability on Set F of Chapter 15. In other words, approximately three out of four persons who complete the training procedures outlined here can be expected to be ready to score protocols for research purposes with very little additional practice. Interjudge reliability in the .90's is, of course, desirable, but a number of useful studies have been conducted with scoring reliabilities in the .80's. Further improvement in scoring probably requires discussion of difficult scoring questions between scorers and agreement concerning conventions which are not adequately covered in the manuals.

The decrease in scoring reliability on *n* Achievement Sets E, F, and G points up an important problem. The expert scoring of these stories was re-examined, and in a few cases errors were discovered in the original scoring. These were corrected. Further examination of Achievement Sets E, F, and G showed that very often Achievement Imagery, when present, represented only a minor concern in the story and that most of the novice scorers seemed to have particular difficulty in spotting the minimal evidence of Achievement Imagery in these stories. Unlike stories in Achievement Sets A through D, which contain a profusion of Achievement Imagery, these stories rarely contain more than one or two subcategories. We wish to sensitize the novice coder to stories which contain minimal imagery because the primary theme of the story is not motive-related. For a discussion of other issues which arise in scoring novel materials see Chapter 15.

Scoring stories written to novel pictures is, in some respects, analogous to scoring other imaginative materials, such as folk tales (cf. Chapter 34), on which scoring reliabilities have been much lower. Consequently, practice with Sets E, F, and G should be valuable since it provides expert scoring for examples of a sort which may not be found in the scoring manuals and should introduce the scorer to the problems which arise when the scoring systems are extended to new types of materials.

SOME RULES OF THUMB FOR RESEARCH

There are several important final recommendations to be made regarding rules for coding in research.

1. If protocols are obtained under more than one experimental condition (e.g., nonaroused and aroused), then the scorer should *not* be aware of the condition under which the protocols he is

scoring were obtained. This may be accomplished by removing any means of identification and by mixing protocols obtained under various conditions.

2. When scoring a particular story for a subject, the scorer should *not* be aware of that subject's scores on other stories (or have any other information regarding that subject's behavior) since such knowledge might easily induce a specious relationship (i.e., bias) among the scores of the various stories written by that subject. This precaution may be taken by observing the following conventions: (a) Score all the stories written in response to one picture before going on to another picture. Try, also, to score all stories written to one picture in one or two sittings so as to preserve approximately the same set for that picture. (b) Shuffle the protocols before scoring each picture. This means you will score the subjects in a different order for each picture. (c) *Never* look back at a subject's scores on previous pictures in making a decision about a picture being scored!

3. Refresh your memory by studying the scoring manual before starting to score, and *refer to the manual while scoring whenever necessary*. We strongly recommend that even experienced scorers use at least one set of practice materials for warm-up before coding a set of stories for research purposes.

4. After a reasonable interval of time (at least one week), rescore the material in order to provide a score-rescore reliability check, *or,* preferably, have the material scored by another person and report the rank-order correlation between the two independent scorings as your estimate of the reliability of coding.

5. Even experienced scorers (i.e., reliabilities above .85) differ in the degree to which they are conservative or liberal in the use of the scoring manuals. The differences may amount to one or two points for average scores obtained from four to six stories for a group of subjects, and may be even larger if the scoring reliability coefficients are lower. To prevent constant differences between scorers from having an erroneous influence on results when different experimental groups are to be compared or when scores obtained by different judges are to be pooled in one final distribution, the following procedures are recommended: (a) If several experimental groups are to be compared, each scorer should be assigned the same number of cases (randomly selected) from each experimental group. (b) If scores obtained by different judges are to be pooled in a common distribution for purposes of making high-low breaks within the distribution, constant differences between judges can be removed by first converting scores obtained by each judge to z scores based on his own mean and standard deviation (assuming that stories have been assigned to separate judges by a random method). (c) When a large number of

protocols has to be scored by several judges, each judge can be assigned all the stories to a particular picture so that the biases of all judges influence the scoring of every subject's stories.

ACHIEVEMENT SECTION *

SELF-TEST: *n* ACHIEVEMENT MANUAL (CH. 12)

After reading the scoring manual, write out your answers to the following questions without consulting the manual. Then check your answers to see if you are correct.

Imagery. What is the goal of the achievement motive? What are the three general criteria for scoring Achievement Imagery? What are the specific kinds of statements that would satisfy each of these criteria? What kinds of stories are scored Doubtful Achievement Imagery?

Need. What is the criterion for scoring N? What two types of statements of desire are not scored N? What is the relationship between instrumental activity and the scoring of N?

Instrumental Activity. What is the criterion for scoring I? What types of statements of instrumental activity in the past tense would be scored I and what types would not be scored I? What determines whether I is scored $+$, $?$, or $-$?

---

* The scorer who desires practice with additional *n* Achievement stories besides those included in Appendix I may find four stories for each of 30 Ss and the expert scoring for those stories in *The Achievement Motive* (272, pp. 335-374). The additional stories and the practice stories presented here are scored according to Scoring System C (Ch. 12).

Another version of the *n* Achievement scoring system which represents an attempt to revise and elaborate the present scoring system may be found, together with illustrative practice materials, in Sadacca, R., Clark, R. A., and Ricciuti, H. N., *Content Analysis of Achievement Motivation Protocols: A Working Manual,* Princeton: Educational Testing Service, 1957. This working manual presents a number of provocative leads for future research designed to improve the assessment of achievement motivation from imaginative materials.

The results of an experimental validation study of the modified scoring definitions (System D-2) by Ricciuti and Clark (341), unfortunately not available in time for inclusion here, provide additional evidence of the validity of scoring definitions presented in Ch. 12. But, in addition, they (a) call attention to "explicit evaluation of performance" and "affective involvement in a task" as the most sensitive criteria for Achievement Imagery, (b) isolate the most valid categories in the system, and (c) call attention to the relationship between length of protocol and *n* Achievement scores when the time allowed for writing is two and one-half rather than four minutes. (See Ch. 10 for one method of treating the relationship between motive score and length of protocol.) Editor.

Anticipatory Goal States. When is Ga scored? What is done with anticipatory goal statements in which the outcome is doubtful or uncertain? What is the distinction between covert, or mental, activity which is scored I and that which is scored Ga?

Obstacles or Blocks. What is meant by obstacles or blocks? What is the distinction between Bp and Bw? What is done when it is doubtful whether a block is to be scored Bp or Bw? What "apparent environmental blocks" are not scored?

Nurturant Press. What is meant by Nup?

Affective States. What are the two criteria for scoring G? What is the distinction between Ga and G? What is the relationship between I and G?

Thema. When is Th scored? Can Th be scored if no other subcategories are scored?

PICTURES USED TO ELICIT STORIES SCORED FOR n ACHIEVEMENT

The pictures used to elicit the stories for Sets A through D were as follows: Stories 1-10 in each set were written to a picture of two men in a shop working at a machine (Picture B, "inventors"). Stories 11-20 in each set were written to a picture of a boy in a checked shirt at a desk, with an open book in front of him (Picture H). Stories 21-30 in each set were written to a picture of an adolescent boy looking straight out of the picture; the barrel of a rifle is visible at one side, and in the background is the dim scene of a surgical operation, like a reverie-image (Picture G, TAT card 8 BM).[1]

Since Sets E, F, and G are composed of stories in the Affiliation and Power sections of this Appendix, the descriptions of the pictures used to elicit the stories for Sets E-G can be found in those sections of this Appendix. These pictures are not normally used to obtain achievement imagery. They have been scored for n Achievement and are included here to provide further practice and experience in transferring the meaning of various subcategories to novel material.

Note: Errors in grammar and spelling in these stories have not been changed.

SET A: ACHIEVEMENT STORIES

A–1　　1. A worker is putting a hot plate of metal back in the oven with a pair of tongs in order to heat it up again. The gentleman beside him is a helper.

---

[1] The description of the Murray TAT picture is from the *Thematic Apperception Test Manual* by H. A. Murray (315).

2. The metal cooled off and they want to reheat it. They were making some sort of metalic object.

3. They are a little expectant waiting for some sort of invention that they are working on to be realized and the hot piece of metal is necessary for the completion of the object.

4. The workman putting the metal into the oven will heat it up and the two will go to the object they are working on in hopes of completing their invention successfully.

A–2 1. The persons are the apprentice and the instructor. The instructor is evidently hitting the machine which was stopped up by the apprentice.

2. The apprentice has made a mistake and has jammed the machine and the instructor is hitting the object to loosen it.

3. The apprentice wants better instructions on how to operate the machine.

4. The situation will be settled with the machine running again in order. The apprentice will be more careful.

A–3 1. The apprentice has made a blunder at his machine and now he is trying to get it remedied. The persons are the apprentice at the machine and his teacher watching him.

2. The apprentice has been clumsy in the past and it has finally gotten the teacher mad. He is disgusted with the apprentice.

3. The apprentice is confused and nervous and wishes the teacher would help him. The teacher thinks that the apprentice is a clumsy oaf.

4. The teacher will finally help him but the apprentice will be fired and he will feel very bad for he really wanted to succeed.

A–4 1. The character on the right is completing an invention that he's been working on for a long time. The person on the left is his assistant, who is rather cynical about the whole thing.

2. All his life the person on the right has wanted to become known as an inventor. He thinks this job of a new tool will do the trick for him. In the past he has had several failures.

3. The person on the left is ready to give up in despair but the person on the right still has that last spark of hope pushing him on.

4. The invention will again be a failure, the cynic will still keep on helping the inventor, but neither will ever achieve glory or fame, yet their whole lives are spent on this task.

A–5 1. Two men are inventing a revolutionary type of new machinery. They are brothers working together to fulfill one of their dreams of success as a team.

2. In the past, they have been encouraged to do things together and have been rewarded for doing so. Now in later life they seek rewards of admiration together.

3. Some difficulty has been met, but a solution seems to have been found by one of the brothers, while the other appears to be quite puzzled.

4. The two brothers will continue successfully to solve the problem and create the new piece of machinery. They will be rewarded with praise and some financial success and continue their inventiveness.

A–6   1. One man is hammering at a machine. The men are shop workers.

2. Broken machine. Machine broke.

3. Nothing, wanted to fix machine, don't care who.

4. Fix machine. A part will be put in machine.

A–7   1. The two men are testing a new type of metal alloy in an electric arc furnace.

2. They have had a long period of experimentation in trying to find a special alloy which will resist very high temperatures. They have met with little success in the past.

3. Each is of course wondering if the specimen being tested will meet very high standards so as to be accepted by the government.

4. The metal will not meet the test and will be rejected. The men will then continue to search for another alloy which they can test.

A–8   1. A man is attempting to fix a machine. The workers are two men who work on the line.

2. The machine has broken down.

3. Neither is thinking. One is watching, the other doing, (ever work in a factory? You don't experience emotion—you just solve puzzles).

4. Probably the machine will start. Then one of the men can go back to his work.

A–9   1. Two workers are beside a machine, the function of which is beyond my imagination. The person on the left is fairly new on the job. He is the operator.

2. The person at the right hasn't seen the machine in operation before. He is curious. The operator is somewhat nervous because he is new on the job.

3. Each one awaiting outcome of the operation. The operator is hoping everything will pan out properly. The other feels sympathy and apprehension.

4. Everything will turn out all right. The man on the left will do O.K. The value of the machine remains in question.

A–10   1. Two persons are in workshop, there has just been a great discovery made. The man has just found a way to make a new kind of shoe leather for shoes. This will be a great boon to mankind.

2. These men have been working for many years on their invention.

3. They now know that they have something that will be useful to all mankind.

4. This invention will turn these two men into bitter enemies with the result that one will die by the other's hand, while the killer will go unpunished.

A–11   1. A young boy is meditating on his present plight.

2. He has been going to school for the past 7 years, hating everything he has learned, being forced by the family to continue, and consistently considering running away.

3. He is now planning never to return to school, to lead the life of an adventurer, a pirate, a thief.

4. He will not do his homework, console himself by going out to play ball, and resignedly return to school next day continuing to dream of his plot against society.

A–12   1. This chap is doing some heavy meditating. He is a sophomore and has reached an intellectual crisis. He cannot make up his mind. He is troubled, worried.

2. He is trying to reconcile the philosophies of Descartes and Thomas Aquinas—and his tender age of 18. He has read several books on philosophy and feels the weight of the world on his shoulders.

3. He wants to present a clear-cut synthesis of these 2 conflicting philosophies, to satisfy his ego and to gain academic recognition from his professor.

4. He will screw himself up royally. Too inexperienced and uninformed, he has tackled too great a problem. He will give up in despair, go down to the G—— and drown his sorrows in a bucket of beer.

A–13   1. The boy in the checkered shirt whose name is Ed is in a classroom. He is supposed to be listening to the teacher.

2. Ed has been troubled by his father's drunkeness and his maltreatment of Ed's mother. He thinks of this often and worries about it.

3. Ed is thinking of leaving home for a while in the hope that this might shock his parents into getting along.

4. He will leave home but will only meet further disallusionment away from home.

A–14   1. A student in a classroom is listening to a teacher explain the contents of a book which lies before the student. He is very interested in the subject.

2. He has passed through all preceding school years, and is an intelligent boy. He entered the classroom with his fellows and is now listening to the teacher.

3. He is trying to understand the subject which is new to him. The teacher also is trying his best to make the students understand.

4. The student will understand the subject and will go out of the class happy about his success in grasping it. He will be a success in life.

A–15   1. A boy in a checkered sport shirt holds his head and stares dismally and miserably out through the open window of the schoolroom.

2. A number of reasons can be found to have caused his present

unhappiness. For a long time now he has wanted to become a garage mechanic, to get away from the dullness of Cicero and Caesar. But no! They won't let him.

3. He feels miserable and trapped. He cannot get out of a mesh of emotional thought, and daydreams and worries himself to a nervous-shattering point.

4. Soon he will leap from his chair, go completely berserk and be led away in a large wagon where he will sit on a piece of toast believing himself a fried egg.

A–16   1. Ed is daydreaming and worrying.

2. Ed lost a baseball game because of a blundering error.

3. He now wonders what would have happened had he made the catch.

4. He will star in the next game although he does not know it.

A–17   1. This is a student in a study hall, trying to solve a problem—however there is every likelihood that he has gone off on a tangent—daydreaming.

2. Before entering the school that day, he participated in an argument with his . . .

3. The boy is trying to solve his problem and at the same time ascertain the emotional problem disturbing him. They both remain unsolved.

4. The student will enter his classroom—unprepared, be called on by the teacher, give an incorrect answer, attempt to justify his error by claiming that he did study.

A–18   1. The student, Peter, is flunking a Physics exam which is very important to get into dent school.

2. He fooled around at the beginning of a semester and got two E's on tests and has since studied rather . . .

3. He is frightfully afraid as he wants an A to balance the E's. His mind is thus confused as he can't understand the problems. He fears that he will fail.

4. By a stroke of luck, the class average is very low and Peter gets a B. He is thus encouraged and fights bravely on to get a B at the end of the semester.

A–19   1. The boy in a classroom who is day dreaming about something.

2. He is recalling a previously experienced incident that struck his mind to be more appealing than being in the classroom.

3. He is thinking about the experience and is now imagining himself in the situation. He hopes to be there.

4. He will probably get called on by the instructor to recite and will be embarrased.

A–20   1. This brings to mind T. Edison who is dreaming of possible inventions rather than turning to his studies. A poor student Edison is probably worried about his future.

2. Probably he is doing poorly in school or is thinking of his girl

or perhaps he is being reprimanded by the teacher for inferior work.

3. I think he is dreaming of some childhood invention that he would much rather be working on than studying the boring subjects of grammar school.

4. He is destined to become one of the greatest of American inventors devoting his entire life to things such as the light bulb, phonograph.

A-21   1. This pensive fellow we here look upon is the grandson of the late ——— who is today being honored by the ——— universities' dedication of the new medical school.

2. Fifty-five years ago his grandfather came to this part of the country where his practice was begun and where through his efforts the first hospital was built.

3. Young Edward is wondering if he could ever be able to reach the level of personal knowledge and bravery to be so ———.

4. Following this momentous occasion he shall view his future with an ever increasing intent upon medicine and the study and practice of surgery.

A-22   1. There are 3 persons and a boy. One of the men is taking a knife out of another man in bed. The boy is looking through a window.

2. There was probably a hot argument and it turned to bloodshed. There is also a rifle indicating the weapons were easy at hand.

3. The boy is wondering if the man which may be his father is going to die. He wants his mother, but she may have been the cause.

4. The father may live, the mother may be put to trial.

A-23   1. The people are members of the underground, one of the members has just been shot. The boy is standing guard at the door.

2. They are trying to dig out the bullet. The injured member blew up a convoy and was shot while getting away.

3. The doctor is thinking that the wound is not too bad if only they don't get caught. They want to save the man's life and also escape the enemy.

4. The man dies because he doesn't get the proper care. The underground wants now to get even.

A-24   1. A young boy is dreaming of his future profession, that of a surgeon. The surgeon with the knife he is in his older age.

2. He has been considering medical school for a long time and can't quite decide whether he wants or rather likes the idea of cutting up another person.

3. He is somewhat worried wondering whether he will be capable of such a feat. He remembers the blood and nauseous feeling he had.

4. He will formulate his opinions one way or another, and

eventually decide balancing out the relative weights of his decision to be a surgeon and distaste for blood, etc.

A-25   1. Jim Newman is standing in his father's den wondering whether to become a famous hunter like his father was. He has just placed his fathers favorite rifle . . .

2. Jim's father was gored by an African water buffalo in his latest expedition, and lost his life. Because of it, although operated upon, the conditions . . .

3. Jim is thinking of the operation that took place in Africa and he wishes his father had been in a hospital where better conditions could have saved his life.

4. Jim becomes a hunter like his father was. But he never is hurt on any trips and lives to be the greatest hunter of wild life the world has ever known a title his father always wanted.

A-26   1. The boy, Dave, visualized his life as surgeon.

2. His parents have instilled in him the idea of becoming a great surgeon like his father.

3. He is frustrated. He wants to be an inventor like his friend Ed, but his father has his mind set.

4. He grows up, frustrated, does only average in school because of his dislike of becoming a surgeon. He goes into Med school by pull, flunks out, and becomes a hopeless alcoholic.

A-27   1. The fellow is trying to decide what profession to go into. The gun, symbolic of soldier—in background are symbols of doctor, teacher, and other professions.

2. The fellow has grown up in a good home, gone to Sunday School and has been well sheltered. Now he has his decisions to make about what to do.

3. The fellow is weighing the relative merits of each profession, the glory, the work, the pay—what it will do for mankind.

4. He will make a decision, whether good or bad. Might be just to fall into business. But he is growing up and cannot escape working for a living. College is probably in the future.

A-28   1. This a boy named Mike. He is visiting a nurse. He has just looked at a display on medicine. He is dreaming of becoming a doctor.

2. This boy come from a good middle class family and is fairly intelligent. His family has always wanted him to be a lawyer though. His father is a lawyer.

3. He is thinking that some day he will be a great surgeon and save many lives.

4. Then a psychologist will step in tell the parents and the boy will enter pre med. He will not be a success he dreamed of—but he will be a good doctor.

A-29   1. In the foreground there is a young boy on the right and a gun. In the background are 3 figures, one lying on the table and the other two bending over him and they seem to be giving him plasma.

2. The young boy in the foreground of the picture has probably been reading war stories.

3. The boy is probably imagining the situation in the background and possibly putting himself in the position of the young fellow administering plasma to the wounded man.

4. The boy probably has an interest to some degree in medicine and might become a doctor later in life. However, this situation he is imagining will be forgotten soon.

A–30   1. A boy is dreaming about becoming a doctor when he grows up.

2. In his vision he sees an emergency operation taking place in which he plays the key role of surgeon.

3. Some fatal shooting has recently taken place, in which the victim died before aid could reach the man. "When I am grown-up" thinks the boy, "I shall be a great surgeon and be able to prevent fatalities like this if I am near."

4. The boy will die of polio a year later.

SET B: ACHIEVEMENT STORIES

B–1   1. These two scientists that we see working in the workshop of their laboratory are anxiously testing the fruits of their research.

2. In the approach to the problem at hand, much of their research and experimentation has taken place within their minds which

3. Each man is wondering primarily will their new substance withstand the conditions which will be required by the war.

4. After the successful testing of their new compound they will take steps to simplify the processes and make it suitable for manufacture on a large scale.

B–2   1. The workers are repairing some type of generator.

2. The generator must have burned out or an accident occurred which put it out of commission.

3. The workers are attempting to discover what is the trouble with the generator.

4. They are desirous of finding its breakdown. They will find the breakdown and repair it.

B–3   1. These two men are working with a machine, perhaps a printing press. It might be Tom Paine and an assistant working on the publication of his famous booklet advocating freedom for America.

2. Oppression by the British has angered Paine into writing a pamphlet expressing the grievence of the Americans which is destined to make history.

3. The two men are perhaps disturbed by the failure of their primative press and are discussing possibilities of repairing it so that their important document can be published.

4. The pamphlet of T. Paine is destined to become one of the

greatest of revolutionary documents and was instrumental in arousing the colonists to fight for their freedoms.

B–4   1. Machine has broken down and is being fixed. Man fixing it is the boss of the shop. Other man is worker who broke machine.

2. Boss has told worker to be careful in handling machine because it operates with difficulty.

3. Man fixing the machine thinks breakage good have been avoided. The worker is just plain angry because the damn thing broke and he is watching with disgust.

4. The machine will be repaired. Worker will be fired if it happens again.

B–5   1. The man with the wrench is a plumber who is fixing a leak in the laboratory of the other man who is.

2. The inventor has been experimenting with pressure valves for running the machine and the pipe burst due to faulty packing in the joint ruining the experiment and irking the inventor.

3. The inventor is thinking what the heck went wrong and why doesn't the plumber hurry up. The plumber is thinking about how will the whole operation seems. The plumber will fix the leak and then stand around to watch the experiment.

4. The experiment will come off very well and the plumber will become chief engineer for the great concern that will be built up by this new discovery.

B–6   1. The two workmen clad in aprons seem to be adjusting the slide valve of a steam engine.

2. The place seems to be a small poor but efficient factory with the engine probably furnishing power for this factory. Therefore when anything happens to the engine it is of critical concern for all the men because they lose money from lost work.

3. It seems that some trouble is being had either with the adjustment or functioning. Perhaps they are adjusting it as it runs.

4. It will probably happen that engine will run right again but not nearly as right as one of a large concern that can employ applicants for work like this.

B–7   1. There are two men here, John the younger, Bill the older. The machine on which John is working has broken in some way. Bill will try to fix it.

2. John has worked in this lab only 6 months and is unfamiliar with the machine except to run it.

3. John wants to learn to fix the machine. Bill wants the machine fixed so that he may do it himself (J.) next time.

4. The machine will be fixed. John will go back to work. Bill will return to his supervising job.

B–8   1. Two craftsmen are in a workshop. The one on the right seems to be about to engage the machine, while the one on the left is watching him.

2. I would assume that both men have worked to arrange the piece held now by the machine so it obtains the proper results.

3. Both men hope that the piece of work will be machined correctly. The one on the right is temporarly occupied by thoughts of correctly engaging the piece.

4. I think it is a printing press where copy will be made.

B-9   1. Two inventors are working against time to complete their machine. Something has happened and a vital part is broken, with no spare parts they seem to be hopelessly stuck.

2. They have contracted to deliver this particular invention at a certain date, but cannot now do so because of the breakdown.

3. The first man is angry and disheartened, but the second is making a desperate attempt to repair the damage. Both are under great nervous strain.

4. The break will be repaired in time, and the additional knowledge thereby gained will enable them to perfect an even better invention in the future.

B-10   1. Repairing the machine—machinist that are inventing it.

2. An experiment has failed and they have to make improvements.

3. Wondering how to do it—man on right is in doubt of thing left man is doing.

4. Mutual compromise and the machine will be successful.

B-11   1. School taking an exam.

2. He didn't study the night before and isn't doing too well because he had a date.

3. He is trying to figure out a good way to pass the test—also trying to answer one specific problem and also about the date he had last night.

4. He will flunk the exam and will go on pro.

B-12   1. The persons are studying. The central object is daydreaming, not concentrating. He is probably in a world of fantasy, or reliving some past experience.

2. The boy attended classes and got assignments to do. He has balanced his time so he has a little extra. He should be studying but he is not. Some problem is bothering him, probably lack of concentration.

3. The boy wants to remember something pleasant. Perhaps he is not—perhaps reliving his past summer and the fun he had.

4. The outcome will be snap out of it and get back to work. The daydreaming will surely become part of his subconscious to be relived again at some future time.

B-13   1. Peter is in class and he has to write a quiz.

2. The day before Peter instead of studying for the quiz went to the movies with some friends.

3. Peter thinks now how foolish it was to go to the movies, he wants now to know the answers for the quiz.

4. Peter will have a poor grade in his quiz and should work harder to make up his grade.

B-14 1. This is a picture of a student in high school day-dreaming.

2. His mother died recently and he cannot seem to get his mind on his work.

3. He is very depressed and wants to see his mother just once again.

4. He will probably be called upon to answer a question by the teacher, which will leave him very confused and he will stammer and hem and haw not even having heard the question.

B-15 1. Boy (student) is taking an exam but has his mind on an external difficulty.

2. His father has just been fired from a job because of drunkeness.

3. Boy is trying to find a bright spot in the future and also trying to forget and get down to work.

4. Boys father will get a new job, reform and then slip back.

B-16 1. An engineer is taking an open book exam and he is finding the exam too difficult.

2. The student is not stupid, but he has a girl and didn't study as hard as he should have.

3. He wishes that he had studied harder and wishes the correct answers. He would cheat, but it is an honor exam and he has too much character.

4. He will get a "D" in the exam and will turn over a new leaf and devote the proper time to study.

B-17 1. Jim Doakes is taking his final exam in economics, and has reached a problem needing quite a bit of thought.

2. The other problems were rather simple for Jim, but this one is the toughest one of the whole exam. He is trying to work it out logically in his mind.

3. What is the answer to this problem? Oh, yes, I have it now! But wait a minute! I'm missing something yet.

4. John will work out his problem in his mind and will continue with his economic exam without too much difficulty.

B-18 1. This has all the markings of an examination, but the presence of the opened book suggests otherwise. The boy is about 16, and is having difficulty in following the instructions of the teacher.

2. The boy hasn't been too punctual in his home assignments. He is tired. It is about 11:17 A.M. He is hungry. He is thinking of spring and all of its manifestations.

3. He wants to get the class over with. He is bored. The subject is dry, disinteresting.

4. The class will finally end. The students will close their books and get out of here as fast as possible.

B-19   1. The young student seems to be perplexed with some problem and then finding no solution appears to daydream.

2. The young student was asked a question about which he didn't know the answer, so he felt rather discourage and disgusted.

3. The student is wondering whether school work is necessary "stuff" or not. He hopes he were doing something else.

4. He will continue in school, perhaps graduate; if not, he will soon quit school and look for adventure elsewhere perhaps in a trade school.

B-20   1. A youngster is trying to do homework, but can't because it's a beautiful day and he'd rather play baseball.

2. He was once ill and will recovering he was told to play games to strengthen himself and he became interested in baseball.

3. He is thinking how dull school is, and would rather quit.

4. He is going to come across a book on chemistry. He finds it interesting, goes on to college and becomes a famous chemist.

B-21   1. Two medical men are working on a wounded or injured person. Perhaps they are giving a blood transfusion.

2. There has been a war as shown by the gun on the side. This man has been wounded in battle.

3. The men are thinking of saving the life of the wounded person. They are wise men and see the tragedy of the situation.

4. There are two possibilities. Either the young boy on the left will also go into war and be in the same position as the wounded, or he man, in the event of war, go on to something more productive—the study of medicine for cure.

B-22   1. Two doctors are hovering over a sick patient. The boy pictured is the patient when he was younger, in good health.

2. The patient's chances of living through the proposed operation are very slim. He will probably die. Maybe he is already dead. Maybe the patient is corpse, about to have a P.M.

3. The doctors feel no emotion. The body before them is just a mass of organs. The boy is innocent, looking hopefully to the future.

4. If the patient is dead, I suppose the body will decay. I hope some one will bury the poor devil. The boy is but a memory.

B-23   1. The boy is thinking of some incident that has happened in a book which he just read. The persons other than the boy are characters of the book he has read.

2. The boy has read a book in which the incidents are constantly playing on his mind.

3. The boy is thinking of how these two men have just murdered another man for talking too much.

4. The two men will continue in their schemes and bury their dead man, while the boy will probably have nightmares.

B-24   1. The young boy is day dreaming of what he is expecting to happen to him.

2. He has just been drafted into the service and actually has a deadly fear of leaving home so young in life. He has been pampered at home.

3. He is thinking that he will be wounded where there are no good doctors. They will have to operate without anesthetic and he can almost feel the pain now.

4. He will go to war. Become very timid among the other more forward men. He will easily be led astray by bad men and will eventually get caught robbing the P.X. Then he will be court martialed and sent to prison where he will try to escape only to be shot.

B–25　1. A choice has been presented to the lad. A career as a doctor and entering the Army.

2. A war in progress necessitates some time to be spent in the Army. The war shows promise of lasting some time.

3. His problem is whether to enter the service at once or go to school and take a chance that the war would be over when he finished. Also the problem of facing his friends who did go into the Army at once.

4. He will ponder over the question. Choose the one that will fit his emotional state.

B–26　1. Some poor guy is being operated on by two doctors and the boy in the foreground is thinking about a medical career.

2. The boy has experienced something associated with medicine and surgery and has taken a liking to it.

3. The boy is thinking of how he would like to be a great surgeon.

4. He will probably end up being a great doctor and everybody will be happy.

B–27　1. The young boy is imagining himself a great physician. In background are the Drs. M—— carrying the torch of modern sterilized medicine.

2. The young lad has been inspired by something he has seen or read, and wants very much to be a doctor.

4. He will leave his brown study, return to it eventually and apply to college for admission.

B–28　1. The boy (Mal) probably has a yearning to become a doctor and pictures himself as one performing one which is very delicate.

2. He probably saw a Doctor save his mother when he was very young and because he loved his mother so much he decided to help other mothers.

3. He wants to become a Doctor to save other mothers and people from being sick.

4. I really don't know, if the impression made by the Doctor which saved his mother was strong enough. Mal might become a Doctor. But it may turn out that its just a passing idea with him.

B–29　1. A young boy thinks about a doctor in years gone by—the crude implements he had to use.

2. The boy has been told that his grandfather who was in the Civil War died from an appendectomy operation because the doctor was unable to remove the appendix in time, while in the tent on the battlefield.

3. The boy thinks of the scene where the doctor takes a pencil and marks off on the skin the approximate distance from the hip to navel where the appendix should be.

4. The boy will then write a composition for an English class about his grandfather's heroic deeds without injury, and the irony of dying from a mere appendectomy.

B–30 1. The young boy is a displaced person. He has lost his family. In his wanderings sights such as the operation are common to him.

2. He sees the man being operated upon as his father, though in reality it is merely another soldier.

3. The boy recalls days in the past and he longs to find his family again.

4. Since his family is all dead, the boy spends his life wandering aimlessly.

SET C: ACHIEVEMENT STORIES

C–1 1. It is a machine shop and the two men are taking hot metal out of a furnace.

2. They want to know what the composition of the metal will be after it is water quenched that is what led up to it.

3. They are quite sure they know what the composition will be but there is still some doubt in their minds.

4. The results are slightly different than was expected so they write a book about it.

C–2 1. Two men are working in a machine shop. One seems to be a bit older than the other. I think they are inventing something.

2. Perhaps they are father and son. Both are interested in machines. The son has more knowledge than the father but is more likely to be to impetuous and not think things out. The father holds him down—both have mutual respect for each other.

3. The older man is performing the crucial test. The young man out of deference allows him to do so.

4. The invention will succeed—they have put hard work into it. The invention is something that will benefit the inventors and humanity.

C–3 1. Two men are working near a drilling machine, in what seems to be a workshop. The piece of metal go red hot, and as the worker is inspecting it; and holds it in a pair of plairs.

2. Something has gone wrong with one man's automobile.

3. The hole drilled is being inspected, and they are wondering whether it is sufficient.

4. It will be decided to be redrilled, or some future work on that metal will be performed.

C–4   1. The boy is watching the older man do something that the boy is trying to learn to do.

2. The boy was trying to do this but he was doing it wrong and the old man is showing how now.

3. The boy is a little downhearted. He knows he can do it if he tries a little harder. The man is calm and patient with the boy and is try to teach him.

4. The boy will watch and the man will allow the boy to try again and the boy will do well because I think he is determined to do it.

C–5   1. The boss is provoked at his helper for not performing the work properly and has come over to show the helper how it should be done.

2. The worker's product did not please the boss, so the boss had to finish the work properly.

3. The boss thinks he ought to get some new man to replace this dullard he has now.

4. The whole product will be ruined, and the boss will place the whole blame on the younger man.

C–6   1. One person is using a drill press wrongly. The men are fellow shop workers.

2. The operator has boasted of a proficiency with this tool (to his cohort).

3. The observer thinks badly of the operator for employing wrong techniques. The operator wants the position permanently.

4. The operator will be removed to a job for which he better suited.

C–7   1. The picture has in it a foreman and a ———— worker. The foreman is just about ready to bawl out the worker for making a mistake. The worker

2. Also the foreman has a personal grievance against the worker for stealing his girl.

3. The worker is worried. The foreman is mad. The foreman wants to catch his worker making this mistake. The worker knows he will.

4. The worker will lose his job—join a communist group and ———— Bill the foreman in an uprising of the proletariet.

C–8   1. Machinists are engaged in making some sort of article.

2. The article has been heated and the one worker is handling it at a distance.

3. The workers are hesitating momentarily to allow the object to cool.

4. The heated object will be placed in the machine to be pressed or tooled toward further refinement.

C–9   1. One man is working on a machine in a tool shop while another man is standing with hands on hips watching him. Tools are hanging in front of a window in the background, and both men are attired in aprons.

2. The young man watching seems to be learning the trade, and the older fellow is teaching him how to handle the machine.

3. The young man is disgusted and impatient, while the older man is quite absorbed in his work.

4. The young man will lose interest and leave the job. The older fellow will continue his work for the rest of his life.

C–10 1. appears that the two men are machinists and one is giving instructions to the fellow standing by.

2. The men are working

4. The man who was watching the other at work will feel enlightened.

C–11 1. It's a beautiful day in Ann Arbor for a golf game today, thought the young pupil as he gazed out of the window.

2. Ben Brown was here yesterday and "Jake" was sure happy to be able to watch this guest golfer.

3. He would sure give a lot to be able to play golf like that. Then he would tour the country as a gentlemen.

4. Suddenly his day-dreaming was climaxed with the knelling of the Tower's bell signifying the end of class.

C–12 1. The boy is thinking about a problem. He and the man in the background are the principles.

2. He has come upon some problem which is new, and is trying to think it through.

3. "Now let me see. If . . . ." Either a mathematical answer or a glittering phrase for English. By *le garcon*

4. He'll get it worked out. Then he'll go on to the next one.

C–13 1. The boy is apparently a student, and is looking up from his work. Class is going on.

2. He is distracted by something. Someone has called him from a nearby seat. It looks as if a test was being given.

3. The boy is wondering what his caller wants. He listens, and is asked by his friend for some of the test answers.

4. He will smile and shake his head as if in doubt about the answers himself. Then he will return to his work.

C–14 1. Obviously an examination. A person who does not quite understand the question asked.

2. Fellow has natural dislike for course and has not prepared for the exam properly.

3. What is the ——— of a sphere 4/3 pi r3 or 4pi? Answer. The follow of course.

4. He will pass the test, he has a photographic memory.

C–15 1. The boy is in school studying supposedly, but his mind is wandering. He is thinking about what an adventurous life he could lead outside of this musty classroom.

2. He is a high school student. His mother wants him to be a doctor, but he'd rather fly planes or raise horses.

3. He is thinking about whether he will ever achieve his goal. He wants to do what mother wants, but still his own ambitions keep returning.

4. He will continue on to college. He will become a rather prosperous doctor, marry, have children, but alway there will be that burning, unsatisfied desire to travel and see what the world is like.

C–16   1. It is a kid in college—awfully tired of his books.

2. He was sent to college against his will, at his parents' command.

3. He wants to leave school—figures the only way to do it is flunking out. Here there will be no way in which his folks can continue their frustrating activities.

4. He flunks out, joins the Navy for a while, comes out with new ideas, tries to get back in school. This proves impossible. Gets manual labor job, works very half-heartedly, reflecting in the stupidity of his past, tries to commit suicide, fails. Returns to job with new life, works happily and industriously after being widely awakened from his trauma.

C–17   1. The young man pictured at his desk is not attending to the textbook before him.

2. This boy is probably dwelling on thoughts of what he could be doing outside school, remembering the fine times he's had out of school and the irksomeness of school.

3. The boy pictured wants to be free of the regimentation of the classroom.

4. He wants to get outside where he can be his own master. School will let out for the day and the boy's resentment at having had to stay there will disappear.

C–18   1. The boy is taking an hour written. He and the others are high school students. The test is about two thirds over and he is doing his best to think it through.

2. He was supposed to study for the test and did so. But because it is factual there were some items he saw but did not learn.

3. He knows he has studied the answers he can't remember and is trying to summon up the images and related ideas to remind him of them.

4. He may remember one or two but he will miss most of the items he can't remember. He will try hard until five minutes is left, then give up, go back over his paper, and be disgusted for reading but not learning the answers.

C–19   1. A young boy dressed in a black and white checkered shirt is leaning on one arm—lost in deep thought. His face is set in a serious way, and he is ignoring the book before him.

2. He just heard from the National Bird Assoc. that his long-lost friend, the "Bodini" bird had been shot down in a skirmish over Pango-Pango.

3. He can't decide whether or not he should fly down to Zulu Islands for the funeral or hop a pogo stick.
4. He will abandon both of these ideas and go by means of a baby carriage on land and water skis for the ocean.

C-20   1. Taking an exam, and can't think of answer. One boy.
2. He has forgotten the answer to the question. He did not concentrate on that part too much before.
3. Nothing. The answer. The boy.
4. He will recall the answer, He will put it down on the paper.

C-21   1. Peter wants to be a surgeon and is daydreaming.
2. Peter has been cutting classes just walking around in a daze.
3. He thinks how great being a surgeon would be.
4. Peter flunks out of school and becomes a sailor.

C-22   1. The boy is looking at a photo or painting of a wounded soldier and a doctor attempting to operate on him.
2. The boy has gone to the art museum with his high school class to see there paintings.
3. The boy thinks of war and of wounded men. He feels sympathy for the wounded. It fills him with desire to do good for mankind.
4. He decides to become a doctor. He becomes a doctor, and soon the country is at war. At the front the boy takes care of the wounded. Five hundred men are in his hospital, and one night planes bomb it, killing all the men, including the boy.

C-23   1. This boy is dreaming about being a doctor and saving a life in an emergency. He imagines his best playmate as his assistant.
2. He has already formulated ideas and attitudes toward helping others and has greatly respected the family physician.
3. He is thinking primarily of the great honor attending the saving of a human life and this has become his most vital desire for the future.
4. He will strive toward this goal and will succeed unless his respect and admiration turns toward another profession or vocation within the next five years.

C-24   1. A young man wants to be a doctor, but he cannot stand the sight of blood. The hunting accident to his father makes him hate medicine.
2. Not too much leading to this, except as related in #1.
3. He has his dreams shattered—realizes he will never make a physician.
4. Goes to college, takes up medical biology. Serves medicine in useful capacity, feels he is satisfying his desires, lives happily working in a field so closely related to medicine.

C-25   1. The boy is remembering the time when he saw a man being operated on with a rusty poket knife for a gun wound.
2. The man was hunting on the boys fathers farms up in the

wilds of Canada and shot himself while climbing a tree to get away from a red bear.

3. The boy is thinking of this because he is standing on the threshold of his pre-medical training.

4. Although he has a very brilliant mind he fools around through his first year and so flunks out and is a bum the rest of his life.

C–26 1. There are 4 people in the picture. On of the persons is having a bullet probed for by 2 others. Actually nothing has happened. The young boy who has a vivid imagination—seeing the rifle has allowed his imagination to wander somewhat morbidly.

2. The situation in the boy's imagination was that he had the rifle and shot someone he didn't like. Perhaps his best friend.

3. The boy is thinking of his imagined act. He thought it would be satisfying but it wasn't. The other people are impersonal.

4. The boy will stop his phantasy, but feel slightly worried about his morbid thoughts. He probably indulges in them occasionally.

C–27 1. The boy is standing in front of a picture with a rifle leaning against the picture.

2. The boy is modeling for an artist. He has stook thru for a while and is beginning to feel tired.

3. He is thinking about things he could be doing instead of studying there. He wants the time to go faster so he can relax for a while.

4. He will stand there a while longer and then he will be allowed to leave and do the things he wants to.

C–28 1. A teenager is day dreaming about an emergency operation being performed under terrible conditions behind the battle lines in the war. He is dreaming he is helping the old Army surgeon.

2. The boy has read a story of medical corps heroism and now transports himself into an active role as a hero and man of experience.

3. He thinks how fascinating it would be to be at such an operation, and how tough it would be and how impervious and stoic would be his action through it all.

C–29 1. George, a young boy, is daydreaming

2. He has been reading the comic books again, and that always start him to daydreaming.

3. He is not sure whether he wants to be a surgen or a soldier, but right now he is sure that it is one of these.

4. He will probably decide to be a teacher in a couple of minutes, if he isn't interrupted, but actually he will probably be a lawyer or an engineer.

C–30 1. Young boy is watching during emergency operation to his friend, scene is reflected in window.

2. Boy has appendicitis, and took ill suddenly

3. Observing boy wants everything to come out o.k.

4. This is really just a picture of a dream the observing boy had concerning his friend. He will wake up before any conclusion has taken place.

SET D: ACHIEVEMENT STORIES

D-1
1. Jim and his father are working on an invention that was thought of by Jim's uncle John who was killed in the Civil War. He left the idea with his brother Harold who is Jim's father.
2. Harold and John were in the same company and when John was wounded at Gettysburg Harold was at his death bed. It was then . . .
3. The thoughts running through both their minds is that the invention they are trying to construct will save human lives. It is a new type of rifle and they think . . .
4. The opposite of what they think, the rifle proves to be a deadly weapon and in a Cuban revolution it is used by the government forces to massacre the rebels.

D-2
1. The two machinists are about to place the metal into the machine to shape it into their desired shape.
2. The man on the left has picked up the material from the bench with the tongs and has walked over to the machine. The man on the right has walked from the bench to the back of the machine.
3. The thought of getting the piece of metal into the machine without mishap is being expressed by both men. The man on the right shows signs of apprehension as to the action of the process.
4. The piece will be shoved into the machine. The machine will stamp it out. The right hand man will walk over to the bench while the left hand man removes the piece from the machine and places it on the bench again.

D-3
1. These men are working on the first power drill. They are the men who invented it.
2. The world has long needed such a drill of this kind so the men decided to invent something useful.
3. The men have almost completed the drill but have run into an engineering difficulty. They are looking for a solution to their problem.
4. Evidently they will find out what's wrong and fix it, because we have power drills now.

D-4
1. Pete Willow has come over to Jack Barnes machine and is asking him if he is working—for the company or for the Union.
2. Pete hasn't paid much attention to the unions and their ideas and he has needed money badly for his farm. Jack has been promoting the union and is ready to call a strike.
3. Pete wants to work. Jack is trying to talk Pete into joining the union and strike for better conditions. Jack argues that in the long run Pete will be better off.

4. Pete joins the strike unwillingly and is worried that he did because Jack wants to use force against the other non-striking forces.

D-5   1. A broken machine is being repaired. The person whose profile is seen is the repairing technical while the man whose back is toward us is the worker who broke it.

2. The worker by not obeying instructions tried to do something which that machine was not capable of doing. He didn't know the limitations of the machine.

3. The worker is unhappy—he believes it is his fault. The repairman having this particular breakdown happen to him often thinks it is fault of management not to train their workers properly.

4. The technician will repair the machine and will recommend that workers be better instructed in handling that machine, in being taught how to use it and what it can or cannot do.

D-6   1. Two men are working on a machine of some sort. Tim and Dick are the persons.

2. They are trying to develop a time machine.

3. Something is wrong. One person is utterly disgusted. This is Tim.

4. They will not succeed. They both will die an unhappy death.

D-7   1. Two working men are running a milling machine. One is observing the other and offering advice.

2. They have spent a lot of time preparing this part and are nearing its completion.

3. When work is finished, want it to be good job. Both men

4. Part will be completed satisfactory, and new job will be started.

D-8   1. Two men are working at repairing a machine. One is doing the hammering while the other looks on, probably criticizing. Both are machinists.

2. The machine has probably gone on the bum, and now needs to be fixed. The one hammering has probably been called to the task by the other.

3. The one on the right wants the other man to fix his machine because something has gone wrong.

4. The machine will be fixed so that the man on the right can go back to work.

D-9   1. A crude machine has broken down and two factory hands are trying to repair it. The man on the left knows what to do, while the man on the right stands idly by being of little help.

2. The man on the right has carelessly used the machine and is responsible for the damage. He is irked by the anger and disgust of the man on the left concerning his accident.

3. The man on the left desires to repair the machine, and thinks to himself that the man on the right is a blundering idiot. Man on

right watches in disgust at the other's attitude—both are angry.

4. The machine will be fixed unless a fight develops between the two men who are quite angry at one another. At any rate, there will be ill feelings over the incident the rest of the day.

D-10   1. Two men, one of them an embroyo industrialist, "A", are working in A's home workshop.

2. A has had a revolutionary idea in the field of transportation. He is working in his free time developing the first model of his invention.

3. Both men are eagerly anticipating the results of their first experiment. They expect complete success.

4. It will fail. Their funds run out—the idea is left for someone else to develop.

D-11   1. Joe is trying to study—he cannot study. He is running for two offices on campus and is thinking campaign ideas. His girl is also giving him a bad time.

2. Joe has been going along fine. His marks are good and he has had some subordinate position on campus. Now he is at a turning point. If he wins this election he is set. Otherwise he is through.

3. He is thinking of ideas for posters, mimeographing, letters and speeches instead of thinking about classes.

4. He will lose both elections. Because he is not studying he will fail his courses. His girl will leave him—he will turn to drink and become an alchoholic!

D-12   1. A student is attempting to study on a warm spring day, while his mind seems to be wandering toward the possibility of playing ball rather than studying at all.

2. He has always enjoyed playing ball, and seems to resent the fact that school is hindering his being outside at that moment.

3. He is imagining himself hitting a home run, and winning the game for his fellow teamates.

4. He will continue studying and letting his mind wander until the study hour is over. He will not have gained too much knowledge in this study experience.

D-13   1. The boy is a student who is supposed to be studying a very boring subject, but he doesn't want to study.

2. The teacher has told the students that there will be a test over the subject matter at the end of the hour.

3. The weather is certainly beautiful outside, and I certainly would like to be at the old swimming hole. This is the boys thought.

4. He wakes up from his revery just in time to flunk the test.

D-14   1. Ted Markem is wondering whether he is right in coming to college. He hasn't been able to concentrate at all.

2. He got through high school without much effort and he passed the college boards successfully.

3. College—is it all what its cracked up to be—Ted wonders. Nothing is clear. His purpose in life is a complete image of half ideas and dreams, none of them complete and meaningful.

4. Ted made it. He passed. He has developed some self-confidence with which to carry on with. He will now pass everything.

D–15   1. The boy is in school with his book in front of him but he is day dreaming.

2. The boy isn't very interested in the work and he is wandering away from the subject very much.

3. The boy is thinking about some pleasurable incident in his life and is wishing he could get out to do the things he wants to do.

4. He will stop day dreaming and go on and read and study his assignment but he still may wander from it a little.

D–16   1. As any properly adjusted liberal arts student should, we find this gent mulling over the value of Aristotlian thought and ideas in the

2. Following his several weeks work in classes he is now beginning to "see the light," or the worth of such studies.

3. He is a searcher for the truth who feels the whole world may some time profit by his efforts if he continues with sufficient diligence and his personal problems will also receive more understanding treatment.

4. After his initial enthusiasm this idea will become part of his background and make him a more learned and interested student.

D–17   1. The boy is trying to decide whether or not to leave school and enlist in the Army.

2. He has been under a great strain, but he has just about come to a conclusion.

3. He is weighting the possibilities. He realizes that he is well equipped to make a good soldier but feels he should also finish his education. He does not know where his duty lies.

4. He decides to finish high school then enlist, with a view toward becoming an officer.

D–18   1. Jim is trying to study for a psych exam.

2. He elects psych in the fall term and he does not find it too interesting.

3. He is trying to think what his instructor, Mrs. Smith, will okay the exam.

4. He will have to take the exam tomorrow and probably just pass it.

D–19   1. Student is contemplating the value of study.

2. Something ponderous has presented itself in the reading.

3. The question of values is bewildering the student. Is it likely that he can comprehend the material and successfully pass the teacher's examination.

4. Reading will continue after the moment's diversion.

D-20   1. The student is trying to get material for a very involved laborious paper.
2. He is unable to concentrate and finds his thoughts wandering. He thinks about his girl.
3. He isn't really thinking. He is just letting his mind wander. His thoughts, however, betray a want for female companionship.
4. He will fritter away his time and finally at the last minute will in a burst of effort get his paper written. Thoughts about his girl will disappear.

D-21   1. The boy has visions of becoming a surgeon and has projected his mind to the day when he will be performing operations.
2. He has had a concern for people in the past and desires to be of service to mankind.
3. The boy is thinking of the day when he will be a successful surgeon. He is looking forward to that day very serioulsly.
4. It is likely that he will strive and reach his goal.

D-22   1. The boy is thinking of his fortune as a great doctor, or he may be thinking of the time when he may be operated on. He may be a hypochrondriac. He is probably a doctor's son.
2. He has been brought up in a medium of medicine, or he has been brought up in a home full of sickness.
3. He is thinking of how he will obtain the future to a doctor, or he is thinking of the sickness which he will endure.
4. He will either become a great doctor or he will become sickly and through worry become sickly.

D-23   1. A young boy is thinking about a medical operation on a soldier. He pictures the gory details.
2. This young boy's older brother was probably badly injured during the war, and died of his injuries despite medical attention.
3. The young fellow feels sad and lonely without his dead brother, but he is proud of him.
4. The young boy's pride in his brother will assert itself more strongly, for he has now become accustomed to living without his brother. He does not need him, now, but he is proud of him.

D-24   1. This young boy is dreaming of the day he will have completed his training and become a great and famous doctor. Perhaps this portrays someone already famous for research.
2. He has been asked by his father or relative what he wants to do when he grows up and he is trying to tell them the mental picture that he has in his mind of himself in thirty years.
3. The boy is thinking of the great thrill that must be experienced by a doctor when he performs a delicate operation saving someone's life.
4. The boy will go out through college and eventually become a world famous doctor.

D-25   1. The boy, Dale K——, is dreaming of becoming a doctor like his father who was also a doctor. In the background is his view of his father operating on a wounded soldier.

2. Dale's father was an army doctor and was killed in the war.

3. Dale wants to be a doctor because he idolized his father.

4. He will go on to be a successful doctor with a society practice and will forget all the youthful idealism that impelled him toward medicine to begin with.

D-26   1. The boy is a serious-minded high-school student who hopes to go to college and become a doctor.

2. The boy has been in a hospital and seen doctors heal the sick, etc., and he is full of noble ideas of helping the sick and needy.

3. The boy is thinking of all the good that he might do as a doctor and all the prestige that he might get.

4. The boy's father will die he will go to school and have to work to support himself. He will be unable to become a doctor and instead will become a frustrated teacher.

D-27   1. A young man, med. student in college, a veteran, is night-maring over the time he was being operated on and civilian French doctors worked over him with poor instruments and unsanitary conditions.

2. He was parachuted by OSS into German occupied territory, was caught and escaped but badly wounded and now bullet removed in this poor set up.

3. He is reminiscing how lucky he was that his life was saved. He is a med. student in college now and realizes how the odds were against him.

4. He will dedicate his life and energy to preservation of peace and international exchange of medical information.

D-28   1. Allan, a young man, is seeing his dreams what happened when he was a small boy in the old country.

2. The Russians came and found his father ill. They told Allen to go outside. Allan looked through the window and saw his father being operated on.

3. His father died on the table in the interest of science. Allan can't forgive nor forget.

4. He will develop into a neurotic unless modern psychiatry can get ahead of him.

D-29   1. Young fellow is showing anxiety toward impending operation.

2. Some malady has been diagnosed.

3. The doctor has prescribed an operation to remove the source of illness and the boy wonders about the advisability of such a plan.

4. The operation will be performed and successfully.

D-30   1. The boy is thinking seriously about a possible accident.

2. He decided to go hunting with some other young friends and his father has warned him to be careful of accidents.

3. The father's lecture has had some effect because the boy thinks or imagines a shooting accident and the victim being given emergency treatment.

4. The boy will snap out of the daydream and prepare for the trip, but take care to prevent accidents.

SETS E, F, AND G: ACHIEVEMENT STORIES

The stories constituting Achievement Sets E, F, and G were selected from stories in the Affiliation and Power Practice Sets. Turn to the Affiliation and Power Sections of this Appendix to find these stories. The stories which correspond to E–1—E–30, F–1—F–30, and G–1—G–30 of Achievement Sets E, F, and G are listed below in parentheses. For example, to find the tenth story in Set E (E–10) turn to the first story in Affiliation Practice Set C.

The pictures to which these stories were written are described in the Affiliation and Power Sections of this Appendix.

Set E		Set F		Set G	
E–1	(Aff A–1)	F–1	(Aff C–2)	G–1	(Pow D–9)
E–2	(Aff A–2)	F–2	(Aff D–2)	G–2	(Pow D–10)
E–3	(Aff A–6)	F–3	(Aff D–8)	G–3	(Pow A–13)
E–4	(Aff A–7)	F–4	(Aff D–9)	G–4	(Pow A–14)
E–5	(Aff A–10)	F–5	(Aff C–14)	G–5	(Pow A–15)
E–6	(Aff B–3)	F–6	(Aff C–15)	G–6	(Pow A–16)
E–7	(Aff B–4)	F–7	(Aff C–16)	G–7	(Pow B–14)
E–8	(Aff B–7)	F–8	(Aff C–17)	G–8	(Pow B–15)
E–9	(Aff B–8)	F–9	(Aff C–18)	G–9	(Pow B–16)
E–10	(Aff C–1)	F–10	(Aff D–11)	G–10	(Pow C–12)
E–11	(Aff A–11)	F–11	(Aff D–20)	G–11	(Pow C–13)
E–12	(Aff A–12)	F–12	(Pow A–1)	G–12	(Pow C–14)
E–13	(Aff A–13)	F–13	(Pow A–2)	G–13	(Pow C–16)
E–14	(Aff A–15)	F–14	(Pow A–3)	G–14	(Pow D–11)
E–15	(Aff A–17)	F–15	(Pow A–4)	G–15	(Pow D–12)
E–16	(Aff B–14)	F–16	(Pow A–5)	G–16	(Pow A–22)
E–17	(Aff B–15)	F–17	(Pow A–6)	G–17	(Pow A–23)
E–18	(Aff B–16)	F–18	(Pow A–7)	G–18	(Pow A–28)
E–19	(Aff B–19)	F–19	(Pow A–8)	G–19	(Pow A–29)
E–20	(Aff B–20)	F–20	(Pow A–9)	G–20	(Pow B–23)
E–21	(Aff A–22)	F–21	(Pow A–10)	G–21	(Pow B–25)
E–22	(Aff A–23)	F–22	(Pow B–5)	G–22	(Pow B–26)
E–23	(Aff A–27)	F–23	(Pow B–6)	G–23	(Pow B–29)
E–24	(Aff A–28)	F–24	(Pow B–7)	G–24	(Pow C–22)
E–25	(Aff C–23)	F–25	(Pow B–10)	G–25	(Pow C–23)
E–26	(Aff C–27)	F–26	(Pow C–4)	G–26	(Pow C–27)
E–27	(Aff C–28)	F–27	(Pow C–8)	G–27	(Pow D–22)
E–28	(Aff C–29)	F–28	(Pow C–9)	G–28	(Pow D–23)
E–29	(Aff D–21)	F–29	(Pow D–1)	G–29	(Pow D–29)
E–30	(Aff D–22)	F–30	(Pow D–8)	G–30	(Pow D–26)

SET A: ACHIEVEMENT EXPERT SCORING

The expert's scoring decisions for the 30 stories of Set A are briefly explained below, one category at a time. In general, only instances where a subcategory is scored are discussed. When a decision not to score a subcategory is a difficult one, it is also discussed.

Imagery

A–1 *AI.* A unique accomplishment in progress "invention." Also, there is evidence of great concern in "expectant" and "hopes of completing invention successfully." A good example of the unique accomplishment criterion.

A–2 *TI.* Two men working at a machine. A routine mistake. One man wants better instructions, but if he were given better instructions (his desire satisfied), would that amount to having achieved something? No. Since none of the three criteria are met but the story is a concrete work situation where achievement might be involved, we score it Doubtful (*TI*).

A–3 *AI.* Explicit statements of affective arousal contingent upon not performing well. The teacher is "disgusted" and "mad." The apprentice feels bad because he wanted to succeed.

A–4 *AI.* Unique accomplishment in first sentence, "invention."

A–5 *AI.* Unique accomplishment imagery in first sentence, "inventing." Several explicit statements of affective arousal contingent upon achievement.

A–6 *TI.* Routine work. None of the three criteria are met. Yet it is a situation in which achievement involvement could take place, i.e., they are working. So we score it Doubtful (*TI*).

A–7 *AI.* Unique accomplishment underway (invention). Also later explicit statement of achievement intention, "they want it to meet very high standards."

A–8 *TI.* Routine work interruption. It could be achievement related, but there is no explicit statement to justify scoring Achievement Imagery.

A–9 *AI.* Affective arousal in an achievement setting. Both men are expectant and involved in how it comes out: "the operator is hoping everything will pan out properly." Note the concern of both men with performance in relation to a standard of excellence.

A–10 *AI.* "A great discovery" is a unique accomplishment. It makes no difference that the achievement theme is lost in a final burst of aggression. Achievement Imagery very definitely appears.

A–11 *UI.* The achievement-related interest is explicitly denied in the story.

A-12 *AI.* A specific work task which has taken on the aura of a unique accomplishment in "trying to reconcile the philosophies . . ." and "wants to present a clear-cut synthesis . . . to satisfy his ego and to gain academic recognition. . . ." There is also evidence of affective concern "wants to satisfy own ego . . . drown sorrows. . . ."

A-13 *UI.* A boy in a classroom who is concerned about other things than performing well in class.

A-14 *AI.* Suggestion of strong achievement interest in early paragraphs. Later this involvement is confirmed by "happy about his success in grasping it." Here is explicit statement of affective arousal contingent upon achievement, i.e., "happy."

A-15 *AI.* Long-term achievement interest: "he has wanted to become a garage mechanic." Remember in scoring not to impose your own sense of achievement values on the characters. In stories written by some primitive island people, there might be long-term interest of an achievement-related sort in climbing trees for coconuts.

A-16 *AI.* Affective arousal contingent upon a failure. Also evidence of future success: "star in later game." Together these indicate the seriousness of the achievement-related interest.

A-17 *TI.* The boy is in an achievement situation and is going through the motions, but nowhere do we see clear-cut evidence of any achievement concern. No affective arousal. No explicit statement of wanting to do well. So it is Doubtful (*TI*).

A-18 *AI.* Affective arousal contingent upon failure and later upon relative success. For example, he is "encouraged" when he gets a B and then fights bravely for a B on the final. There is also long-term involvement regarding getting into "dent school."

A-19 *UI.* A student goofing off in class. Not even doubtful achievement interest.

A-20 *AI.* Here is the great inventor story (unique accomplishment) with explicit statements of affective concern added as embroidery. Probably the easiest kind of story to score.

A-21 *AI.* The grandfather is being honored for his accomplishment. An example of imagery related to unique accomplishment. The future-oriented expectations and intentions of the young man to follow medicine as a career also meet the criterion of "long-term career involvement."

A-22 *UI.* Lots of imagery related to aggression. No suggestion that any character is achievement involved.

A-23 *UI.* Someone has done something, but there is no evidence of satisfaction contingent upon a job well done. It is not an example of a routine work setting. The imagery is more closely related to aggression and its consequences.

A–24 *AI*. Long term involvement expressed in first sentence. It makes no difference that later in the story there is strong suggestion of sadistic interest. There is Achievement Imagery, even though another kind of imagery shares the stage later in the story.

A–25 *AI*. Affective involvement in first sentence: "wondering whether to become a famous hunter. . . ." Later he becomes the "greatest hunter." Affective arousal contingent upon unique accomplishment.

A–26 *AI*. First sentence has the boy imagining himself a surgeon. Here is imagery related to long-term career goal. Later he "wants to be an inventor." It makes no difference that the story ends in failure. The Achievement Imagery is there.

A–27 *AI*. Again some evidence of long-term career involvement. Future oriented thought about choice of career. One of the kinds of satisfactions he anticipates is "glory."

A–28 *AI*. "he is dreaming of becoming a doctor." Later reiteration of this long-term achievement interest.

A–29 *TI*. This story is like others which are scored *AI*. What is the difference? Until the last paragraph the boy is thinking himself into the medical situation but with no clear-cut identification of it as a career goal, something wonderful he would like to do. When medicine is finally mentioned as a possible career, the author of the story qualifies the degree of interest and then immediately denies it in the last sentence. We are left in a state of doubt as to how to score it, so we score it Doubtful (*TI*).

A–30 *AI* Here the boy is daydreaming about becoming a doctor right off the bat, so it is easy to score Achievement Imagery.

Need

A–1 *N*. "they want to reheat it." Here is an explicit statement of an intention to complete one phase of the achievement-related task. The aim of the intention is specific, but it is achievement-related in the sense of specifying their desire to move ahead to the ultimate goal.

A–3 *N*. In the last line: "he really wanted to succeed." The early statement of a desire for help is not a need for achievement. If he is helped, he has not achieved, that is, he has not done something by himself for which he can be proud.

A–4 *N*. "has wanted to become known as an inventor . . ."

A–5 *No N*.

A–7 *N*. "they want it to meet very high standards."

A–9 *N*. "The operator is hoping everything will pan out properly."

A–10 *No N*.

A–12 *N*. "he wants to present a clear-cut synthesis."

A-14 *No N.*

A-15 *N.* "For a long time now he has wanted to become a garage mechanic."

A-16 *No N.*

A-18 *N.* "He wants an A to balance the Es."

A-20 *No N.*

A-21 *N.* "he shall view his future with ever increasing intent upon medicine and the study and practice of surgery." Manual states: "very strong indications of the presence of the motive are scored *N.*"

A-24 *No N.*

A-25 *N.* "A title his father always wanted." Here the statement of Need refers to the father. He also was interested in unique accomplishment.

A-26 *N.* "he wants to be an inventor."

A-27 *No N.*

A-28 *No N.* The manual explicitly excludes scoring *N* based on a statement by one character which defines an achievement goal for another, e.g., "His family has always wanted him to be a lawyer. . . ."

A-30 *No N.*

Instrumental Activity

Note that the phrases called for here must state actions that have been taken or indicate problem-solving thinking about the task. The outcome depends upon the over-all outcome of all the instrumental acts.

A-1 *I?.* "they are making some sort of metalic object . . . they are working on . . . workman putting the metal box into . . . are working on. . . ." No indication of ultimate success or failure is given.

A-3 *No I.* Do not score "The apprentice has made a blunder" as *I.* All evidences of past failure should be scored *Bp.*

A-4 *I—.* "that he's been working on a long time . . . will again be a failure."

A-5 *I+.* "brothers working together . . . now later in life they seek rewards of admiration . . . continue successfully . . . create the new piece of machinery."

A-7 *I—.* "long period of experimentation . . . trying to find . . . metal will not meet standards."

A-9 *No I.*

A–10   *I+.* "men have been working for many years . . . they have something which is a boon to all mankind." Note that after the success a new subplot develops. This does not cancel the fact that the effect of all achievement-directed acts were successful.

A–12   *I—.* "trying to reconcile . . . has read several books . . . has tackled . . . will give up . . ."

A–14   *I+.* "He entered the classroom . . . and is now listening . . . trying to understand . . . he will understand and be happy about success in grasping it."

A–15   *No I.*

A–16   *No I.* "He will star in the next game" is merely a statement of outcome in the final sentence.

A–18   *I+.* "fights bravely on to get a B . . ." Here the instrumental action and outcome are all given in the last sentence. This is OK to score since there is a clear statement of action. If the story said only "he gets a B at the end of the semester," there is no justification for inferring the actions. The instrumental act (working or thinking) must be explicitly stated.

A–20   *No I.*

A–21   *I+.* "through his efforts the first hospital was built . . . who is today being honored." The outcome is given before the action in this story.

A–24   *I?.* "has been considering medical school . . . remembers the time . . . will formulate his opinions . . . and eventually decide . . ." The instrumental action here is all covert; he is wrestling with a problem. The outcome is never given.

A–25   *I+.* "Jim . . . wondering whether to become a famous hunter like his father was . . . lives to be the greatest hunter." While the statement of action is in the first sentence, it is not the initial descriptive statement.

A–26   *No I.*

A–27   *I?.* "the fellow is weighing alternatives . . . he will make a decision." Again, someone thinking through the achievement-related problem, but without the outcome of these covert actions being clearly stated.

A–28   *No I.*   A–30   *No I.*

Anticipatory Goal States

A–1   *Ga—.* "They are a little expectant waiting for. . . ." But we are never told whether they anticipated success or failure. It is really *Ga?,* but is arbitrarily scored *Ga—.*

A–3   *No Ga.*

A–4   *Ga+*. "He thinks this job of a new tool will do the trick for him . . . last spark of hope. . . ." He anticipates success.

      Ga–. "The person on the left . . . is rather cynical about the whole thing." He anticipates failure.

A–5   *Ga+*. "dreams of success . . ." A dream is future-oriented thought. In this case, the dream is concerned with goal-attainment.

A–7   *Ga–*. "wondering if the specimen will meet the requirements . . ." This doubtful uncertainty is scored *Ga–*.

A–9   *Ga–*. "the operator is nervous . . . each one waiting the outcome."

A–10.   *No Ga.*

A–12   *Ga–*. "he is troubled . . . worried." Presumably about whether or not he can do it. The word "worried" describes his present state. His present state has (by implication) a future reference.

A–14   *No Ga.*

A–15   *Ga–*. "daydreams and worries himself to a nerve-shattering point." Here the future-oriented thought must be negative as indicated by the word, "worries." One doesn't worry about the possibility of being a success. One hopes for that.

A–16   *Ga+*. "He now considers what would have happened had he made the catch." He is daydreaming about what might have been. But his thought is considered equivalent to anticipation of success or a dream of success. He is now anticipating success and its wonderful consequences. Granted, it seems a little unrealistic. But he does go on to fulfill his frustration-inspired dream of glory.

A–18   *Ga–*. "he is frightfully afraid . . . [why] he fears that he will fail."

      Ga+. "Peter gets a B. He is thus encouraged. . . ." That is, his anticipations regarding his wish to get an A become more positive.

A–20   *Ga+*. "T. Edison dreaming of possible inventions . . ."

      Ga–. "is probably worried about his future . . ."

A–21   *Ga+*. "he shall view his future with . . . intent upon medicine."

      Ga–. "wondering if he could" (*Ga?* scored *Ga–*).
When thoughts of goal-attainment dominate future-oriented thought, the person is really thinking positively, i.e., success. When thoughts of negative consequences fill his thought, he is anticipating failure.

A–24   *Ga–*. "A young man is dreaming of his future profession. . . ."
Ga?, thus *Ga–*. Also, "He is somewhat worried, wondering whether he will be capable of such a feat."

A–25   *No Ga.*

A–26   *Ga—.* "He visualizes himself as a surgeon," but to the leading character this is a negative anticipation. His life is a failure if he is forced into that, and his dream visualizes that possibility.

A–27   *No Ga.* The symbols of future professions are being considered in terms of his problem-solving activity, deciding on a career.

A–28   *Ga+.* "He is dreaming of becoming a doctor." "He is thinking that some day he will be a great surgeon."

A–30   *Ga+.* "Daydreaming about becoming a doctor when he grows up . . . when I grow up, I shall be a great surgeon. . . ."

Obstacles

A–1   *No Block.*

A–3   *Bp.* "apprentice has made a blunder." His own inability at an easy task is the obstacle.

A–4   *Bp.* "In the past he has had several failures." Past failures, to be overcome, are always represented as personal obstacles.

A–5   *Bw.* "Some difficulty has been met."

A–7   *Bp.* "have met with little success in the past . . ." Past failure to be overcome always scored *Bp.*

A–9   *No Block.*   A–10   *No Block.*

A–12   *Bw.* "has tackled too great a problem . . ." It is the magnitude of the problem that stops him.

A–14   *No Block.*

A–15   *Bw.* "The dullness of Cicero and Caesar" are an external obstacle to this boy's aspirations. So too, "They won't let him."

A–16   *Bp.* "because of a blundering error . . ."

A–18   *Bp.* "fooled around at beginning of semester . . ."

A–20   *Bp.* "doing poorly . . . reprimanded for inferior work . . ." Any evidence of failure is scored *Bp.*

A–21   *No Block.*

A–24   *Bp.* The boy's distaste for blood is an internal obstacle to medicine as a career.

A–25   *No Block.*

A–26   *Bp.* The boy's dislike of being a surgeon is obstacle in schoolwork. *Bw.* Ed wants to be an inventor but his father has his mind set on his being a surgeon.

A–27   *No Block.*

A–28   *Bw.* "conflict with parents" interferes with his own achievement plans.

A–30   *Bw.* "The boy will die of polio." Quite a final obstacle.

Nurturant Press

A–1 *No Nup.*   A–3 *No Nup.*

A–4 *No Nup.* Don't score "the cynic will keep on helping the inventor," since the apprentice and inventor can be viewed as a team working toward a joint achievement goal.

A–5 *No Nup.*   A–7 *No Nup.*

A–9 *No Nup.*   A–10 *No Nup.*

A–12 *No Nup.*

A–14 *Nup.* "The teacher is also trying his best to make the students understand." The achievement goal of the student is to understand the subject, and the teacher is aiding him.

A–15 *No Nup.*   A–16 *No Nup.*

A–18 *No Nup.*   A–20 *No Nup.*

A–21 *No Nup.*   A–24 *No Nup.*

A–25 *No Nup.*   A–26 *No Nup.*

A–27 *No Nup.*   A–28 *No Nup.*

A–30 *No Nup.*

Affective States

A–1 *No G.*

A–3 *G–.* "teacher mad . . . disgusted . . . apprentice . . . confused . . . he will feel very bad . . ."; all contingent upon poor performance.

A–4 *G–.* "ready to give up hope . . . despair . . ."

A–5 *G+.* "rewarded with praise and some financial success . . ." Objective benefits in addition to description of successful activity.

A–7 *No G.*   A–9 *No G.*

A–10 *G+.* "This will be a *great* boon to mankind." Once more, the author has given a vivid description of the objective concomitants of success. From this vivid description we infer a Positive Affective State. Without the vivid description, *G+* would not be scored.

A–12 *G–.* "give up in despair . . . drown his sorrows . . ."

A–14 *G+.* "interested in subject . . . happy about success . . ."

A–15 *G–.* "present unhappiness . . . feels miserable and trapped . . ." All contingent upon being blocked in own achievement aspirations.

A–16 *G–.* "worrying" following his blundering error. He, in other words, feels bad right now because he has failed immediately before.

A–18 *No G.*

A–20 *G+.* "to become one of the *greatest* of American Inventors . . ." A vivid description of extraordinary success allows the inference of "he feels good."

A–21 *No G.*   A–24 *No G.*

A–25 *G+.* "lives to be the *greatest* hunter of wild life the world has ever known . . ." An accomplishment in the top 10% of all possible success experiences in this area of endeavor.

A–26 *G–.* "He is frustrated" (in his achievement desires) and "he flunks out, and becomes a hopeless alcoholic." The latter is an outcome in the bottom 10% of all possible failure experiences.

A–27 *No G.*   A–28 *No G.*

A–30 *No G.*

Thema

The rule for scoring Thema is to score whenever the *leitmotif* is the achievement behavioral sequence. When, however, achievement imagery is not the dominant tendency in the story, when there is a strong subplot, do not score Achievement Thema.

A–1 *Th.*

A–3 *No Th.* The intensity of the hostility in the teacher is strongly suggested at several points implying a countertheme of aggression.

A–4 *Th.*   A–5 *Th.*

A–7 *Th.*   A–9 *Th.*

A–10 *No Th.* The plot takes a completely different turn at the end. Aggression imagery forges into the foreground.

A–12 *Th.*   A–14 *Th.*

A–15 *No Th.* The present unhappiness and final resolution of the story may have a number of causes (as stated) other than achievement.

A–16 *Th.*   A–18 *Th.*

A–20 *Th.*   A–21 *Th.*

A–24 *No Th.* The concern over sight of blood has become as salient in the story as the achievement plot itself.

A–25 *No Th.* The subplot about concern over father's welfare shares the stage with the achievement plot.

A–26 *No Th.* The interference by father represents a strong countertheme, domination and its resultant ill-feeling towards what the father stands for.

A–27 *Th.*

A–28 *Th*. Thema is scored here despite the parent-child conflict since the conflict concerns a choice of achievement goals.

A–30 *No Th*. The preoccupation with death implies another concern as dominant as achievement in this story.

SET B: ACHIEVEMENT EXPERT SCORING

The expert scoring below may be read as follows: first, the expert's scoring decisions are briefly explained; second, the total score is given; and third, in parentheses, is the rank of that story (with the highest score of the set given a rank of 1 and the lowest score a rank of 30). In general, only instances where a subcategory is scored are discussed. When a decision not to score a subcategory is a difficult one, it is also discussed.

B–1 *AI*. Scientists engaged in unique accomplishment.

I+. "are anxiously testing . . . much of their research has taken place in their minds . . . after successful testing" (the outcome).

Ga–. Early statement: "anxiously testing" paired with "wondering" will their product work, a doubtful anticipation.

Th. No counterplot. 4 (9.5)

B–2 *TI*. A routine breakdown with routine desire to fix it. 0 (20)

B–3 *AI*. A unique accomplishment: "working on famous booklet . . . destined to make history . . . to be greatest."

I+. "working on publication . . . discussing possibilities of repairing it . . ." The outcome is indicated by "the pamphlet is destined to become one of greatest. . . ."

G–. "*disturbed* by the failure . . ."

G+. "The pamphlet becomes one of the greatest of revolutionary documents. . . ." This is top 10% of possible outcomes.

Bw. "failure of primitive press . . ."

Th. Score Thema even though there is a great deal of ideological content. The major action is the unique accomplishment. 6 (1.5)

B–4 *TI*. Some suggestions of possible achievement imagery, e.g., "will be fixed," but no one is concerned about losing his job. Also the "anger" of the worker is affective, but it does not appear to involve a sense of failure so much as sheer frustration provoked by the "damn thing." 0 (20)

B–5 *AI*. "The inventor": unique accomplishment.

I+. "has been experimenting . . . fix leak . . . experiment will come off well."

G+. "become *chief* engineer . . . great concern . . .": top 10% accomplishment.

G–. "irking the inventor . . ."

Bw. "pipe burst . . . ruining experiment . . ."

Th. Achievement is major plot. 6 (1.5)

B–6   *TI.* Work situation, but only stated concern is possible loss of money. 0 (20)

B–7   *TI.* One man wants to learn to run the machine. But this interest in a specific task is not explicitly related to a long-term career goal. Nor is it unique accomplishment. Nor is there explicit affective arousal in relation to some stated standard of excellence. 0 (20)

B–8   *AI.* Concern over meeting a standard of excellence: "hope . . . work will be machined correctly."

N. "hope . . ."

I?. Several statements of work and thoughts about work but no outcome given. e.g. "The one on the right is temporarily occupied by thoughts of (how to) correctly engaging the piece."

Th. No counterplot. 4 (9.5)

B–9   *AI.* "Inventors": unique accomplishment.

I+. "desperate attempt to repair . . . will be repaired . . ."

No Ga. The nervous strain may be worry over outcome, but this is not clear enough to score.

G–. "first man angry and disheartened . . ."

Bw. "Vital part is broken . . . stuck."

Th. Obviously the central plot. 5 (5)

B–10   *AI.* Invention is unique accomplishment.

I+. "wondering how to do it . . . will be successful . . ."

Ga–. Man on right "in doubt" presumably about outcome.

Bw. Experiment has failed, the machine needs repair. Doubtful who's responsible, so score *Bw.* This is a general rule: If it is unclear whether a Block is *Bp* or *Bw*, score *Bw.*

Th. No counterplot. 5 (5)

B–11   *TI.* Some suggestion of possible Achievement Imagery. The boy is apparently trying to overcome his obstacle. But the absence of regret (negative affect) over his unpreparedness and the absence of clear-cut concern over anything other than just meeting the minimal requirement "to pass the test" makes this a Doubtful (*TI*) story. Just passing a test more clearly defines avoidance of failure than achieving, e.g., a good grade. In cases of this sort it is desirable to be conservative rather than to confound the achievement motive and the motive to avoid failure. 0 (20)

B–12   *TI.* He is working part of the time, but unconcerned. More often he is avoiding his potential achievement task in fantasy. 0 (20)

B–13   *AI.* Regret over unpreparedness and stated desire, plus statement of hard work, taken together define "concern" over meeting a standard of excellence.

N. "wants to know the answers for quiz . . ."

No I. There is no statement of action, e.g., he is taking a quiz, he is trying to figure out the answers.

G—. Regret, i.e., "thinks how foolish it was . . ."

Bp. "went to movies . . ." and hence was unprepared.

Th. Achievement-related difficulty is the whole plot of the story. 5 (5)

B–14 *UI.* The main concern is clearly unrelated to achievement. There is no doubt about this not having any Achievement Imagery. —1 (28)

B–15 *TI.* The boy is taking an exam, but he is not concerned about it nor is it explicitly related to a long-term goal. The father is fired and gets back his job, but nowhere is explicitly *concerned* about his job. This story contains a series of "near misses." It does not meet any one of the criteria for scoring *AI.* 0 (20)

B–16 *AI.* Regretting unpreparedness, wishing correct answers, and turning over a new leaf together constitute concern over achievement.

N. "wishes the correct answers"

G—. Regret: "wishes he had studied harder . . ."

Bp. "didn't study as hard as he should . . ."

Th. Achievement difficulty is the *leitmotif.* 5 (5)

B–17 *AI.* Affective arousal in solving the difficult problem is defined by the *Ga+* "Oh, yes, I have it now!"

I+. "trying to work it out . . . will work out problem . . ."

Ga+. "Oh, yes, I have it now!"

No Bw. Block is not scored when the obstacle is the initial problem which defines the achievement goal.

Th. Solving the tough problem is the whole story. 4 (9.5)

B–18 *TI.* It started out as an examination, but the achievement-relatedness is denied by later avoidance of interest and the class itself. 0 (20)

B–19 *TI.* Here the student experiences negative affect as a consequence of his failure, but instead of a positive concern about overcoming his deficiency he seeks to escape the situation. This is suggestive of a motive to avoid failure situations in distinction to a positive motive to overcome obstacles and excel. Score Doubtful (*TI*) since there is no evidence of positive concern. 0 (20)

B–20 *AI.* The Achievement Imagery is all contained in the last sentence, hence Thema is not scored. *Interest* in chemistry, a long-term career goal is the basis for scoring *AI.*

No I. "He goes on to college and becomes a famous chemist" is a statement of outcome only and not action.

No Bw. The things interfering with his school work cannot be considered obstacles to an achievement goal since there is no expressed concern about doing well in school.

G+. "becomes a *famous* chemist": the upper 10% of all possible successes as a chemist defines objective concomitants of success sufficiently clearly to allow scoring *G+.* 2 (13)

B–21   *TI.* There is some imagery related to a specific task (saving a life) that might be achievement-related. And there is a final reference to medicine as a career. But in neither case is the achievement-related concern of some character clearly spelled out. 0 (20)

B–22   *UI.* No reference to the task interest of the doctors. Clearly unrelated to achievement. −1 (28)

B–23   *UI.* The only content has to do with hostility and aggression. −1 (28)

B–24   *UI.* There is no indication of competition with a standard of excellence. −1 (28)

B–25   *AI.* The story has to do with the content of a long-term career decision. The story describes what the central character is thinking about: long-term career involvement. The varied content of his thought argues against also scoring Thema. 1 (14)

B–26   *AI.* Long-term career interest and affective arousal as a consequence of success.

N. "he would like to be a great surgeon."

Ga−. "is thinking about a medical career . . ." From this phrase the content of the anticipation is unclear, thus score *Ga−.*

G+. End up as "great doctor . . . everybody happy . . ."

Th. The successful career story is the plot of the story. 5 (5)

B–27   *AI.* Long-term career interest.

N. "wants to be a doctor . . ."

No I. "and apply to college for admission" is an outcome statement in the final clause.

Ga+. "imagining himself a great physician . . ." *Dreams of glory* as well as realistic expectations are scored *Ga+.*

No Nup. Inspiration from something seen or read is not sufficient. Must have sympathetic, personal help to score *Nup.* 4 (9.5)

B–28   *AI.* Long-term career interest.

N. "yearning to be a doctor . . . wants to become a doctor . . ."

Ga+. "pictures himself as one . . ." Again, dreams of glory. The love of mother and denial of achievement interest at the end argue against scoring Thema.

No Nup. The doctor saving the mother's life is not directly aiding the boy's achievement goal.

No Th. This story has two themes: being a doctor as a career interest and helping people who are sick. 3 (12)

B–29 *TI.* There is a reference to "heroic deeds" of the grandfather. But this mere mention of an accomplishment does not constitute concern over some unique accomplishment. 0 (20)

B–30 *UI.* The content is almost totally concerned with separation from loved ones. −1 (28)

SET C: ACHIEVEMENT EXPERT SCORING

C–1 *AI.* 1 (16.5)
C–2 *AI, I+, G+, Ach Th.* 4 (8)
C–3 *TI.* 0 (22)
C–4 *AI, N, I+, Ga+, Bp, Nup, G−, Ach Th.* 8 (1)
C–5 *AI, I−, Bw, Ach Th.* 4 (8)
C–6 *AI, N, Bp, G−, Ach Th.* 5 (4)
C–7 *TI.* 0 (22)
C–8 *TI.* 0 (22)
C–9 *TI.* 0 (22)
C–10 *TI.* 0 (22)
C–11 *AI, N.* 2 (14)
C–12 *AI, N, I+, Ach Th.* 4 (8)
C–13 *TI.* 0 (22)
C–14 *TI.* 0 (22)
C–15 *AI.* 1 (16.5)
C–16 *AI, I−, Bp, G−.* 4 (8)

C–17 *TI.* 0 (22)
C–18 *AI, I−, Bp, G−, Ach Th.* 5 (4)
C–19 *UI.* −1 (28.5)
C–20 *TI.* 0 (22)
C–21 *AI, N, Ga+, Ach Th.* 4 (8)
C–22 *AI, N.* 2 (14)
C–23 *AI, N, I+, Ga+, Ach Th.* 5 (4)
C–24 *AI, N, I+, Ga−, Bp, G+, Ach Th.* 7 (2)
C–25 *AI, Bp, G−.* 3 (11.5)
C–26 *UI.* −1 (28.5)
C–27 *UI.* −1 (28.5)
C–28 *AI, Ga+, Ach Th.* 3 (11.5)
C–29 *AI, N.* 2 (14)
C–30 *UI.* −1 (28.5)

SET D: ACHIEVEMENT EXPERT SCORING

D–1 *AI, Ga+.* 2 (13)
D–2 *TI.* 0 (21)
D–3 *AI, I+, Bw, Ach Th.* 4 (7.5)
D–4 *TI.* 0 (21)
D–5 *TI.* 0 (21)
D–6 *AI, I−, Bw, G−.* 4 (7.5)
D–7 *AI, N, I+, Ach Th.* 4 (7:5)
D–8 *TI.* 0 (21)
D–9 *TI.* 0 (21)
D–10 *AI, I−, Ga+, Bw, Ach Th.* 5 (3.5)
D–11 *TI.* 0 (21)
D–12 *AI, Ga+.* 2 (13)

D–13 *TI.* 0 (21)
D–14 *AI, Bp, Ach Th.* 3 (10.5)
D–15 *TI.* 0 (21)
D–16 *AI, I+, Ga+, G+, Ach Th.* 5 (3.5)
D–17 *AI, I+, Ga+, Bp, Ach Th.* 5 (3.5)
D–18 *TI.* 0 (21)
D–19 *TI.* 0 (21)
D–20 *TI.* 0 (21)
D–21 *AI, N, Ga+, Ach Th.* 4 (7.5)
D–22 *AI, Ga+.* 2 (13)
D–23 *UI.* −1 (28.5)
D–24 *AI, I+, Ga+, G+, Ach Th.* 5 (3.5)

D–25 $AI, N, Ga+$. 3 (10.5)   D–28 UI. −1 (28.5)
D–26 $AI, N, Ga+, Bw, G−, Ach$ D–29 UI. −1 (28.5)
      Th. 6 (1)   D–30 UI. −1 (28.5)
D–27 AI. 1 (15)

SET E: ACHIEVEMENT EXPERT SCORING

E–1 UI. −1 (25.5)   E–17 $AI, N, G+$. 3 (9)
E–2 $AI, I?, Nup$. 3 (9)   E–18 $AI, I+, Bw, G+, G−$. 5
E–3 TI. 0 (18.5)   (1.5)
E–4 UI. −1 (25.5)   E–19 $AI, N, Ga+, Ga−, Th$. 5
E–5 $AI, I?, Bp, Th$. 4 (4.5)   (1.5)
E–6 $AI, N, I+, Th$. 4 (4.5)   E–20 UI. −1 (25.5)
E–7 TI. 0 (18.5)   E–21 AI, N. 2 (13.5)
E–8 UI. −1 (25.5)   E–22 UI. −1 (25.5)
E–9 $AI, I?, Nup$. 3 (9)   E–23 AI, N. 2 (13.5)
E–10 $AI, I+, G+$. 3 (9)   E–24 $AI, I?, Th$. 3 (9)
E–11 $AI, I?$. 2 (13.5)   E–25 $AI, I?$. 2 (13.5)
E–12 UI. −1 (25.5)   E–26 TI. 0 (18.5)
E–13 TI. 0 (18.5)   E–27 AI. 1 (16)
E–14 UI. −1 (25.5)   E–28 UI. −1 (25.5)
E–15 $AI, N, I+, Bw$. 4 (4.5)   E–29 UI. −1 (25.5)
E–16 UI. −1 (25.5)   E–30 $AI, I+, Bp, Th$. 4 (4.5)

SET F: ACHIEVEMENT EXPERT SCORING

F–1 UI. −1 (28)   F–17 TI. 0 (19)
F–2 $AI, G+$. 2 (11)   F–18 TI. 0 (19)
F–3 TI. 0 (19)   F–19 $AI, I+, Bw, Nup, Th$. 5
F–4 UI. −1 (28)   (2.5)
F–5 TI. 0 (19)   F–20 UI. −1 (28)
F–6 TI. 0 (19)   F–21 TI. 0 (19)
F–7 $AI, I+, Ga+$. 3 (8)   F–22 TI. 0 (19)
F–8 UI. −1 (28)   F–23 TI. 0 (19)
F–9 $AI, Ga+$. 2 (11)   F–24 TI. 0 (19)
F–10 $AI, I?, N, Th$. 4 (5)   F–25 TI. 0 (19)
F–11 $AI, I?$ 2 (11)   F–26 TI. 0 (19)
F–12 TI. 0 (19)   F–27 $AI, N, I+, Th$. 4 (5)
F–13 $AI, I?, Bw, G−, Th$. 5   F–28 UI. −1 (28)
      (2.5)   F–29 $AI, N, I?, Bp, G−, Th$. 6
F–14 $AI, I+, Ga−$. 3 (8)   (1)
F–15 TI. 0 (19)   F–30 $AI, N, I+, Th$. 4 (5)
F–16 $AI, Ga+, Bw$. 3 (8)

SET G: ACHIEVEMENT EXPERT SCORING

G–1 $AI, Bw, Nup, G−, Th$. 5   G–5 $AI, N, I?$. 3 (8)
      (3)   G–6 UI. −1 (26)
G–2 $AI, I+$. 2 (10)   G–7 $AI, N, I+, Ga+, Th$. 5
G–3 $AI, I+, Bw$. 3 (8)   (3)
G–4 UI. −1 (26)   G–8 UI. −1 (26)

G–9   *TI.*   0   (16)
G–10   *TI.*   0   (16)
G–11   *TI.*   0   (16)
G–12   *UI.*   −1   (26)
G–13   *AI, I?, Bw.*   3   (8)
G–14   *UI.*   −1   (26)
G–15   *TI.*   0   (16)
G–16   *TI.*   0   (16)
G–17   *TI.*   0   (16)
G–18   *TI.*   0   (16)
G–19   *UI.*   −1   (26)
G–20   *AI, I+, Ga−, Th.*   4   (5.5)

G–21   *TI.*   0   (16)
G–22   *UI.*   −1   (26)
G–23   *AI, N, I−, Ga+, Ga−, Bp, Th.*   7   (1)
G–24   *TI.*   0   (16)
G–25   *UI.*   −1   (26)
G–26   *AI, N, I+, Th.*   4   (5.5)
G–27   *UI.*   −1   (26)
G–28   *TI.*   0   (16)
G–29   *TI.*   0   (16)
G–30   *AI, I?, Bp, Nup, Th.*   5   (3)

AFFILIATION SECTION

SELF-TEST: *n* AFFILIATION MANUAL (CH. 13)

After reading the scoring manual, write out your answers to the following questions without consulting the manual. Then check your answers to see if you are correct.

Imagery. Define the general basis for scoring Affiliation Imagery. What are the four other more specific bases for scoring Affiliation Imagery? What are the rules governing the scoring of Affiliation Imagery in stories which are about the following relationships: parent-child, marriage, dating, friendship?

Need. What is the criterion for scoring N? What two types of statements are scored N which do not meet the general criterion for scoring N?

Instrumental Activity. What is the criterion for scoring I? What are three fairly common types of actions usually scored I? When is giving advice or asking for advice scored I? What types of statements of Instrumental Activity in the past tense would be scored I, and what types would not be scored I? What determines whether I is scored $+$, $?$, or $-$?

Anticipatory Goal States. When is Ga scored? What is done with doubtful or uncertain anticipatory goal statements? What is the distinction between covert, or mental, activity which is scored I and that which is scored Ga?

Obstacles or Blocks. What is meant by Obstacles or Blocks? What is the distinction between Bp and Bw? What is the most frequent type of statement scored Bw, Bp? Is the occurrence of a disruption of a relationship sufficient grounds for scoring Block?

Affective States. What are the two criteria for the scoring of G? What is the distinction between Ga and G? What is the relationship between I and G?

Thema. When is Th scored? Can Th be scored if no other subcategories are scored?

PICTURES USED TO ELICIT STORIES SCORED FOR n AFFILIATION

The pictures used to elicit the stories for Sets A through D were as follows: Stories 1-10 in each set were written to a picture of the heads of two young men facing each other in conversation (Picture C of n Affiliation series).* Stories 11-20 in each set were written to a picture of a man standing at an open doorway looking away from the viewer at the landscape (Picture B of n Affiliation series).* Stories 21-30 in each set were written to a picture of a group of seven men sitting and standing around a table as if in conference (Picture A of n Affiliation series).*

Since Sets E, F, and G are composed of stories in the Achievement and Power sections of this Appendix, the descriptions of the pictures used to elicit the stories for Sets E-G can be found in those sections of this Appendix. These pictures are not normally used to obtain Affiliation Imagery. They have been scored for n Affiliation and are included here to provide further practice and experience in transferring the meaning of various subcategories to novel material.

Note: Errors in grammar and spelling in these stories have not been changed.

SET A: AFFILIATION STORIES

A-1 1. Apparently a tense moment, or a moment of clash has occurred between the man and his girl. They seem to be arguing over something.

2. The two have gone together for some time and are planning to be married—it is the first time there has ever been a radical difference of opinion between them.

3. They each have different plans—the man feels he should go into the service before they are married, the girl wants to marry now.

4. They will work out a happy solution; some sort of a compromise on taking the step after they know definitely what will happen to him in the service.

A-2 1. The persons in the picture appear to me to be an older brother talking to his younger kid brother about an interesting experience.

---

* These pictures were originally used by Henry and Guetzkow and are reproduced in their article (179).

2. The older brother had, perhaps, been a star athlete and hence is relating an exciting anecdote.

3. The older brother feels that maybe his relating this experience will liven the younger boy's spirit because the latter is entering an important event or contest.

4. The younger brother will give his all to follow in his brother's footsteps whom his expression shows signs of idolization.

A–3   1. Father and son. The son has just told his Dad he enlisted. The father is not pleased.

2. The son has been dominated by his parents since his youth and wants to get away from it.

3. The father can't understand it. The son wants understanding.

4. The son will come out a better man. The parents will have reconciled themselves to the fact that their son is able to stand on his own two feet.

A–4   1. An active is raising the devil with a pledge. These are two fraternity men as indicated above.

2. The pledge has probably done something that irked the active.

3. The active is thinking of doing something "dirty" for the pledge, i.e., the pledge is in for the devil. The pledge is very defiant.

4. The pledge will probably get a bad opinion of the active from this incident and will probably have hostile feelings against him forever throughout activeship.

A–5   1. It seems a father is telling his son what to do and what not to do. The boy appears to be guilty of doing something undesirable and is being reprimanded in a man-to-man talk.

2. Apparently the boy did something that did not comply with the desire of the father.

3. The son feels guilty and wants forgiveness by his father.

4. The son will be more cautious next time. Probably no further punishment will be inflicted on the boy at this time.

A–6   1. Father talking to his son—son is just going to college.

2. Son is just ready to leave for his first year at college.

3. His father is thinking how his son has grown up so quickly. He wants (the father) to assure himself that his son will make the new adjustment at college and continue to make his father proud of him.

4. He will give his son some advice about buckling down, working hard at school and continue making his father proud of him — However the son left alone at school will begin drinking, going out with girls and finally get married in his first year—after first flunking out.

A–7   1. A younger man is approaching a man older than himself for help or advice on a problem.

2. The younger man is worried about his lack of acceptance in the new social group he has just become acquainted into.

3. The young man seeks a restoration of his confidence. He knows his problem.

4. A short conversation will ensue in which the older man will restore the young man's confidence in himself.

A–8
1. Two fellows are having an argument. The one on the left seems to be angry with the one on the right.

2. The one on the right has done something that the one on the left didn't like.

3. The boy on the left is rather puzzled by the accusations.

4. The boys will still be friends after the argument.

A–9
1. Two people are having a serious conversation with each other. They are fraternity brothers and are probably talking about something very close to themselves or their house.

2. A problem has probably developed or perhaps one needs advice. Maybe a pledge is talking to his big brother.

3. The pledge is thinking that in his big brother he can find understanding and worthwhile advice. The younger fellow wants to be put straight and make himself a better fellow and thus wants his big brother to help him in this.

4. The pledge will be enlightened and will proceed to develop into a worthwhile individual.

A–10
1. A father is reprimanding his college-age son.

2. The son has not performed some duty which he was obligated to execute.

3. The father is explaining to the son the importance of doing the job as it is to be accomplished best, and the son is realizing this importance.

4. The son will attempt to perform the duty effectively as per his father's wishes.

A–11
1. The boy is the son of a deceased person probably father. He is thinking alone at the door.

2. The boy has had a very happy family life and the death is a great shock.

3. He is thinking of his childhood and also wondering of the future.

4. He will go on in his father's business and try to make good.

A–12
1. An active is watching some performances being done to a pledge or a group of pledges.

2. Pledges or pledge have violated something that the active or actives don't tolerate.

3. The man in the door (supposedly an active) is not too concerned about the whole matter but is supposed to see that the pledges carry out their "detail."

4. The incident will probably be forgotten by all not too much

after. But incident will provoke a recurrence of pledges activities against house.

A–13   1. It is one of the first days of spring and the man is enjoying the peace and security of his home.

2. It has been a long winter, with many worries and anxieties that have passed—troubles don't seem as big now that spring is here.

3. The man is thinking just how lucky he is and how things perhaps weren't as bad as he thought they were.

4. The man will enjoy himself for awhile and then go back to his work, with a new vigor that was lacking during the bleak months of the winter.

A–14   1. A fellow is looking out the door, at leisure. He is a young fellow.

2. It is spring, and he is wanting to go out in the open. He is waiting for his girl.

3. He is thinking of going for a walk with her. He is waiting for her to come, so they can leave, but he is in no hurry. His posture would indicate relaxation and expectancy at going out.

4. They will go for a walk in the sunshine and enjoy each other's company. They like being together.

A–15   1. Young man who works in an office is standing in doorway of home on Sunday looking at the first sure spring day.

2. He's been cooped up in an office for a year. It's his first job after graduating from college.

3. He's thinking how nice it would be to be able to chuck his job and get away from it all. He wants independence from pressure of his parents which makes him stick to his job.

4. He'll stand there for awhile, then go out and have a few beers on the lawn and dream about the South Seas and native girls. Next day at 6:45 he'll get up, pack his lunch and go to the office.

A–16   1. Man living alone waiting with nothing in particular to do for company who are to arrive at a later time. He is ready for them ahead of time. It is a nice spring day.

2. Whoever is coming is someone he wants very much to see, hence has prepared himself ahead of time for arrival.

3. Man is making effort to be calm and not excite himself. He does this by directing his thinking to the weather and attempting to be nonchalant.

4. Person, or people, will arive late. Man who has become quite agitated by this time rushes out to meet them, is very effusive and demonstrative.

A–17   1. Young man is looking out into the distance thinking of his own thoughts or maybe searching for someone he expects. Person is any young businessman.

2. Troubles in business or expecting arrival or friends or relatives who are late.

3. Thoughts of how pleasant it will be when friends or relatives appear—or how to improve business position. Relief from his tension is wanted by the young man.

4. With arrival of friends tension will be relieved. Thoughts of improvement will eventually come and he will work industriously to carry them out.

A–18   1. A college age boy is home for spring vacation. He is standing in the doorway of a not now used summer cottage.

2. The previous summer this boy met, dated, and fell in love with a girl whose parents were staying at this cottage near his home town. The girl is now far away in Hawaii and the boy is seeking to recapture the previous summer.

3. The boy dreams of last summer and longs for those happy days. Does the girl still love him or does she think it a summer romance? He wishes he knew for sure. She writes that she does but it's been so long and she's young and pretty and so far away.

4. The boy will turn, lock the door and leave. He will feel better somewhat but the unanswered question will remember until she comes home.

A–19   1. The fellow in the picture is looking out of his front door dreaming of the future.

2. He had an interesting book and it has set his mind wandering about his plans for the rest of his life.

3. He is thinking of a wife and a job with good pay. He wants secruity and a happy life.

4. He will probably be a success in his future and will work hard to gain a secure and comfortable life.

A–20   1. This fellow, Tom, has just severely beaten his girl. She had been, at least he thought so, unfaithful to him.

2. Tom had been in the Army. On returning he had planned to marry Janet. Then he found out that she was engaged to someone else.

3. Tom is deciding what to do. Go back and apologize, trying to make the most of a bad situation or to run away.

4. Tom does run away and leave Janet. He rejoins the Army, volunteers for a dangerous mission and is killed. Janet marries her other lover, but is subconsciously unhappy.

A–21   1. A group of young fraternity men are discussing a serious house problem.

2. Certain incidents in the past such as no cooperation within the house and general unrest and the beginning of factions.

3. A remedy to bring the men together and solidify the house is being sought.

4. Bigger and better parties and house functions will be planned.

A–22   1. The boys are just getting up from a fraternity dinner table. The one standing with the glasses is a pledge.

2. They have eaten their dinners and the pledges entertained the actives with their jokes, etc.

3. The pledge is wondering what might happen next and is relieved that dinner is over. He wants to complete training and become active—making a good leader.

A–23   1. A discussion has arisen in a chapter meeting. There are pro and con men for some discussion.

2. Someone has thought up a hot idea which is being "run down" by a voice of dissension.

3. Some radical people won't change their minds and "lose their heads" because the vote has gone against them. Con men still contend for their rights.

4. A split might be involved in the house. Unless something is done, the chapter will go downhill.

A–24   1. A discussion is being held in our house by a bunch of brothers —a bull session—all are amused—some walk in others walk out— but all do not disagree seriously.

2. Nothing in particular—just a desire to "blow off steam" and "sound off" with a bunch of guys we all get along with fairly well.

3. Hard to say—women, girls, alcoholic beverages, nothing desired—just shooting off all talking—mostly one at a time but occasionally all at once.

4. Nothing—will gradually break off when we move on to our studies or the sack—no hard feeling some blowhards and liars but all in good feelings.

A–25   1. A business conference and there has been a major difference of opinion. the president with his hand upraised is restoring order to the confusion brought about by the man at rear left walking out in a fury.

2. The man who has walked out is somewhat of a radical thinker and his ideas have just been rejected by a more normal thinking group.

3. The man who has walked out is angry at himself for not putting over his ideas more shrewdly—the men at the table are thinking he is just a crackpot and perhaps they would be better off without him.

A–26   1. Fraternity bull session, members of the club discussing some topic of interest with one member having the floor at present.

2. Dinner has just been finished and they are sitting around discussing the age-old subjects of sex, past experiences or status with the draft. The member speaking is an old salt giving them the straight way.

3. The younger members want to hear all about his adventures but one member seems to be disturbed about a few of the remarks, maybe he is an idealist or has strong convictions of his own.

4. They will sit there, say the same things over and over again,

answer a few questions, solve no problems and finish off an enjoyable evening of swapping stories.

A–27 1. The fellows are chewing the fat after dinner at a card game. They are a bunch of fellows in a frat.

2. Everyone feels in a talkative mood and probably want to talk about prospective dates or exams etc. So they sit down and talk.

3. They all are thinking about some girls they would like to date, or some bluebook they would like to get a good grade on.

4. They will all talk for a while then play cards and then break up and all go their own way.

A–28 1. There is a council meeting going on in a small firm. The young men involved are the young board of directors.

2. They are just getting started in their business and an important issue or problem is coming up which is of utmost interest to all concerned.

3. The chairman is thinking and relating to the rest what should exactly be done to meet the forthcoming problem.

4. The board will pass on the chairman's advice or veto it. Their expressions convey their intent interest.

A–29 1. A meeting of a high school executive council, trying to decide whether to flaunt the authorities or to do as they say.

2. The school board has refused to allow the Spring Prom. The students want to hold it anyway.

3. They are deciding the consequences of their decision. The vote is split over what to do.

4. They finally hold the prom outside the authorization of the school board. The board raises a fuss but the parents back their children and elect a new, liberal progressive board.

A–30 1. A bull session in a fraternity house is going on. The people are the brothers.

2. The war in Korea led up to this situation.

3. They are thinking of what the future will hold. They want a chance to finish their schooling if possible, and a chance to do something along their line of study.

4. Someone may be stirred up enough to enlist for fear of not getting a good deal.

SET B: AFFILIATION STORIES

B–1 1. An older man is talking to some younger man.

2. The expressions on the faces indicate the older person, that is, on the right, is in the process of bawling out the other for something like wrecking the family car.

3. The younger, on the left, is taken aback, see stance of leaning backwards, by the words and expression of the other. The older is trying to impress on the younger the fact of his wrongness and to realize the importance and not do it again.

4. Restriction to home for some period of time with little or no use of family car.

B–2   1. Father and son—father is chastising son for some action of son's of which he does not approve, such as drinking, smoking, etc.
2. Boy has been caught in act or else conclusive proof of his guilt has been brought to father's attention and he confronts boy with proof—or possibly surprising boy with accusation.
3. Father is much surprised that son should be indulging in this vice—son realizing he has been caught cheating is desperate.
4. Son will stammer—hem and haw try to make up quick excuse which is weak—father much disillusioned. Boy will be punished in___

B–3   1. One is an interviewer from some large firm (one on the left) and the other is a student about to graduate. The student is asking questions about job.
2. The student has made the arrangements for the interview through the school bureau. Student has already had several interviews.
3. The student wants a job and is merely attempting to evaluate the job and asking questions concerning it.
4. The interviewer is well impressed by the student and so indicates by inviting him to come to the plant for further interviews. Student gets the job.

B–4   1. Father is scolding adolescent son—persons are a father and his son.
2. Son has stayed out too late or maybe he has come home with poor marks from school.
3. Son is trying to think of a comeback for father's scoldings. Results are wanted by the father.
4. Son may or may not take father's advice. He may or may not improve or come in earlier. It may all depend on his own needs or wants.

B–5   1. An older brother is speaking to his younger brother rather seriously. They may be any brothers of a family.
2. The younger brother has done something wrong either socially, morally, or lawfully. It appears to be the first time.
3. The younger brother is scared, ashamed and sorry. The older brother is disappointed and is trying to put him straight.
4. The younger brother will accept the advice of his elder.

B–6   1. They are two college buddies who haven't met each other in a long time. A chance meeting. They are very glad to see each other.
2. It is probably a class reunion or frat founders day. They were very close friends in college.
3. They are probably reminiscing of old times.
4. They will have an evening together and make arrangements for future meetings.

B–7   1. Two fellows are arguing. They are 2 fellows who are jealous of each other and always trying to outdo the other.

2. They have had strong antipathy from each other.

3. They are arguing against the other, wanting the other to give in. They are thinking how much they hate or despise the other.

4. They will not fight but walk away burning up inside, probably nursing a grudge.

B–8   1. Two brothers are discussing their future. One is in college, while the other is older, being a pro football player.

2. Jack, the younger brother, is trying to decide if he should finish college and go on with his chosen profession, or go into pro football.

3. Jack's girl wants him to stay clear of football, but Jack thinks he can make more money in pro football. Bill, the other brother, is talking to him about both.

4. Bill convinces Jack to go on with his profession. Jack finally sees the light, marries his girl, and lives happily ever after.

B–9   1. One fellow is telling another his close friend something that surprises him.

2. It came as a shock to the fellow who was being told.

3. The fellow being told isn't too sure what he is being told is such a good idea.

4. They will probably do what the fellow who is talking is wanting to do because of his enthusiasm and sureness.

B–10   1. Two fraternity brothers are talking together. The one on the left is the older of the two. He has just told the younger about some important event that will happen to the youngster.

2. The older one has promised to fix the other up with a blind date. The younger one has previously asked to be "fixed up."

3. The younger one is amazed at what he is learning. The girl he is to go out with is really quite the babe. The younger is thinking how he is going to "make out."

4. The younger one will go on the date, but will be greatly disappointed when he finds out his girl is nothing but a "teaser."

B–11   1. A man is standing in a doorway looking out over the landscape looking into the sun. The place appears to be in the country.

2. The man arose early, dressed and ate prior to the sun rising and since it is a nice day is standing in the doorway watching the early morning break into day.

3. He isn't thinking of anything. He notices the quietness turn to bustle and activity as the day grows older. He is content.

4. He will leave shortly for work in the city and return that night to home.

B–12   1. A man is standing in a doorway thinking of his future. The day is bright and his thoughts are hopeful.

2. The past has been interesting to him but his thinking is towards the future.

3. Nothing is wanted except insight to his future and ——
4. The future will bring much to this young man for his thoughts are bright as this day is for him.

B-13   1. The young man in the door is a senior in college. He is about to enter the army after graduation in a few weeks. He is considering marrying the girl he has been pinned to throughout college.

2. The young man really loves the girl and doesn't want to lose her while he's in the army. He can't make up his mind to marry or not.

3. He is thinking how married life will be if he's away at camp and his wife is home. He really loves her and doesn't want to hurt her by going away.

4. He finally marries the girl and she goes to work while he is away. It all turns out very well.

B-14   1. The people involved are a baby and his brother. The older fellow is baby sitting.

2. The parents have gone out for the evening.

3. The older fellow is thinking of how nice it would be down at the corner with the gang. He seeks escape!

4. He will have to spend a lonesome, uneventful evening with the baby, but perhaps witnessing and experiencing many uneasy moments caused by the baby's crying, etc.

B-15   1. The man is thinking of the good things of life. He is happily married man.

2. He is a rising business man. He has a family, home, contentment, and the fine things of life.

3. He is thankful for his good fortune and wants everything to continue as it has.

4. He will continue to be happily married and keep rising in the business world.

B-16   1. Man just home from work and gazing out at the countryside about him. It is springtime.

2. This man has been disgusted with his position in life until he came home and spent dinner with his wife and children.

3. He is now happy and contented and realized that his disconcern was only a temporary mood and he is in reality fortunate.

4. The man puts forth a better effort at the office and overcomes the obstacle that discouraged him. He does and gets promoted.

B-17   1. The boy is standing in the doorway dreaming and looking out on what seems to be a beautiful day.

2. Something is keeping the boy inside. Apparently he is not allowed to leave the house because of difficulties at home.

3. He is probably fighting his conscience. He is feeling guilt for a misdeed or perhaps sorrow for a mishap. He is waiting for the trouble to blow over.

4. Probably the problem will finally be solved and the boy will be outside again feeling happy with himself again.

B–18　1. The fellow is dreaming.

2. Nothing has led up to the situation, he just happened to stop at the doorway and thoughts began entering his mind.

3. He is dreaming about things he would like to do. Things he would like to have happen.

4. After he gets through dreaming he will resume his everyday chores, and forget about his dreams.

B–19　1. Son about to step out into the world of reality. He is thinking of the prospects of success ahead of him and the events he will have to face.

2. He has graduated from college or high school and is about to start on his own. He wants to be away from the support of his parents and be self-supporting, successful, etc.

3. What will lie ahead of him in the way of opportunities. Will he be able to capitalize on the breaks he receives.

4. He will go out into the real world get settled and married and then spend the rest of his life in the Army.

B–20　1. A young man is lingering lazily in a doorway in a daydreaming type of pose.

2. He evidently is free from care and responsibility. Somewhat the feeling you have on a vacation when there is nothing to do but relax.

3. Thoughts might be drifting toward his friends at home, the job he is away from, and his own sense of complete relaxation.

4. Soon he will find an activity to engage in. Swimming, fishing, or possibly reading.

B–21　1. The boys in the fraternity have been having a drinking party. They're now sitting around the table.

2. Before they were drinking beer—the alarm went off signifying the Campus Cops were coming up the driveway. So they ditched the beer and are trying to act nonchalant.

3. They're thinking what—the University is—they want to be able to enjoy themselves like normal people—not hunted criminals.

4. The Campus men inspect the place, not find any beer and dope, go off grumbling as the Frat boys gleefully pull out the keg from the fire place and proceed to get blasted while cussing the U. up and down.

B–22　1. A group of close friends, and they are discussing something that they are planning to do.

2. Nothing has led up to this situation, it is just an idea that was brought before the group.

3. They are trying to plan their idea and figure out if it is agreeable to all.

4. They will probably end up doing whatever they are discussing after a bit of discussing.

B-23   1. There is a meeting going on at the fraternity, and some of the members, not all, are present.

2. It is a special meeting, called for the purpose of discussing the campus drinking problem.

3. The fellow standing up is saying that there should be no drinking in the house. A couple of fellows are bored. A couple of others are interested and are following what the speaker is saying. They want to reach some conclusion about the drinking situation in fraternity houses.

4. They will continue the discussion and present their conclusions to the rest of the house.

B-24   1. This is a group of guys playing cards. They all work together at the same plant but this is Sunday afternoon. Their wives are in the other room talking and sewing. One of the men has been caught cheating at cards—poker for 5 and 10.

2. The man caught or rather accused and the accuser the man standing have never been very good friends. They have been rivals in the plant for a better position.

3. The others are trying to laugh it off. The man accused is hurt and angry but he is level-headed so he merely stomps away while the other talks.

4. The thing will work itself out for the afternoon, i.e., the incident will not be pressed. The two men will remain enemies.

B-25   1. 7 men or young men are in the picture. 1 is looking out the window or bookcase and 6 others are gathered around the table with one standing speaking to the others.

2. The frat. next door got caught drinking the previous night and some of the fellows are discussing the possibilities of their being caught and possible actions to pursue.

3. The fellow standing is a DRY and won't hear of any alcohol being in the house. The others are thinking of a rebuttal or support for his argument.

4. All are interested in some solution that will benefit all parties. Formal discussion will be brought up at next chapter meeting with house going wet or dry.

B-26   1. A group of fraternity men discussing the problem of drinking or not drinking in the house. The speaker is a wet.

2. The university's attitude on the subject of drinking. Although most parents want their children to drink at home if at all, the University assumes the role of a parent and protector.

3. That the drys are submissive, cautious, and afraid of the University. A little self assertion.

4. They will vote dry and the house will be in the good graces of the guiding, protecting, self-asserting University.

B-27   1. Some of the boys are sitting around the table talking. One of the young men has gone out for something in the other room.

2. The meeting of these young men is for the purpose of deciding something of importance that concerns them all.
3. In the other room is a box of cigars for the men to smoke.
4. They will continue talking and finally reach their decisions.

B–28 1. Some fellows are waiting for someone else to arrive. They are in some sort of trouble.
2. They all run around together. They like to raise hell occasionally.
3. They are all worried. They want to be cleared of the trouble They want the other person(s) to arrive.
4. Other person(s) will arrive and they will discuss their problem.

B–29 1. The six boys have gotten together for a poker game and are now discussing differences.
2. The game probably fell through as the boys became tired and and wanted to find something else to do.
3. They are thinking of having a party, and the boy at the head of the table is giving his ideas.
4. They will have a party and each will do some of the work.

B–30 1. A group of fraternity men holding an informal discussion of some matter of great interest and importance—something that will affect the policy of the house—house is split over issue.
2. The problem has been slyly introduced into the thinking of the men by whomever wants to see the action taken by the house.
3. Some men are thinking seriously of the effects the issue will have—weighing it pro and con—others (those talking violently) are arguing with little solid thought.
4. Issue will cause tempers to rise and cause some ill feeling. It will be decided equitably in meeting, but feelings will linger on.

SET C: AFFILIATION STORIES

C–1 1. Father and son are talking. The son has done something to please his father. He is somewhat proud of himself and wishes his father's approval.
2. The boy may have done well in school and is showing his father his marks.
3. The father is approving of his son's work and is pleased as a father.
4. The son will continue to do good work with his [incomplete]

C–2 1. Two people are talking friendly to each other. They are two boys meeting each other on campus.
2. They are probably discussing a game they saw the other night. a hockey game which was very thrilling.
3. They are thinking over the various high points of the game. The taller boy wants the short one to agree on the best play.
4. They finally agree on the high point and will split up each in his own direction.

C-3   1. An older man is talking to a young boy. It looks as if he might be giving some kind of advice.

2. Perhaps some incident which the boy has been unable to fully understand and he seeks advice.

3. Elderly advice is being given. The boy seeks such advice.

4. The boy will have his problem solved and profit by the older man's advice.

C-4   1. Father and son. Father appears to be talking to his son about something especially important and interesting to the son as shown by his expression.

2. Well probably the most obvious answer is that the son is seeking knowledge about some unknown fact, he doesn't understand sex, machines, etc.

3. Son is enraptured by the talk of his father and evidently wants the full details of the lecture.

4. The father will fulfill his talk to his son and then the son will ask questions of the father.

C-5   1. A college student is looking up with an amazed expression at his brother who has stopped by to see him. The college boy the one on the right, is surprised.

2. The fact that his brother has come to see him unexpectedly.

3. The college boy is wondering, "what is brother doing here?" The brother just came by to say "hello!"

4. They will be pleased to see each other again. The college boy will be happy and they will laugh and talk for a while.

C-6   1. One fellow is accusing the other of doing something. The fellows look like college students.

2. The one took something that belonged to the other.

3. One wants to find out if the other took it and what he did with it, the other is looking for a way out.

4. The act will be decried and nothing done.

C-7   1. These are two fellows (possibly students) having an argument about something more or less intellectual.

2. They were talking about something which happened in a classroom and showed opposite viewpoints on this subject.

3. The fellow in the left has just started an argument and expects the other fellow to believe it. But the other one just laughs as if the fellow on the left were stupid.

4. The fellow on the left will become angry. And possibly they will argue heatedly. Until one of them will become disgusted; the argument will end and they will go on being friends anyway.

C-8   1. The father is talking to his son.

2. The son has just wrecked his father's car. It was while he was out on a date with his girl. The father had expressly told the boy not to go out of town because he had only gotten his license a week before. The boy disobeyed and wrecked the car. No one was hurt, however.

3. The father is furious. In his initial shock over the loss of his car which he needs to go to work, he has forgotten so far what might have been the more tragic results. Tomorrow he will remember.

4. The father will settle down eventually and require the boy to work to help pay for the car.

C–9   1. Two brothers arguing.

2. Disagreement on who gets the car that night.

3. Larger brother thinks he ought to get it because of seniority.

4. Might end in fight. Depends on how strong feeling is. Father probably won't let either have it.

C–10   1. John Doe is telling off Bill Smith, I associate a slightly drunk Don Brown talking to a completely drunk me.

2. I have been drinking and he has accused me of pinching his wife in the buttocks—he says he saw me do it.

3. He wants me to "lay off" or he will "teach me"—I have an urge to give him a push, hit him or kick him down the stairs which he is standing at the head of. I know I only tapped her on the shoulder.

4. I at the time realize that if I do the house will suffer so I turned and walked away without saying any thing.

C–11   1. A young man is passing the time of day dreaming. The person may be any young man.

2. The young man has been away for some time and is home on vacation. There are no friends around at present and he is looking for something to do.

3. He wishes there were someone to chum with, to play a game of golf or some sport.

4. He decides to go for a walk and just mosey around town.

C–12   1. I see my eternally dreaming roommate—Remy—staring off into space—his mind a 100,000,000,000—0 miles away.

2. He is continually wanting what he doesn't have at the present and wants a change of scenery and new things to do—he has passed over the last hill and wants new worlds to conquer.

3. He is probably roaming in greener pastures than his present stamping grounds and is thinking of moving on.

C–13   1. A young man is looking wistfully out of the door at the countryside.

2. He became tired of the party going on inside.

3. He thinks he will go for a walk and get away from the confusion.

4. He will go for a walk.

C–14   1. Young fishing addict wants to go fishing or golfing but studies interfere. Eight months of absence of these sports. In the past has gotten enjoyment from same.

3. He is thinking that teachers should not give homework during spring vacation.

4. He will probably study for the present but will do these things spring vacation anyway.

C–15 1. A man is standing by an open door gazing out to the countryside.

2. He has just got up from studying.

3. He just wants a few moments relaxation.

4. He will go back to his studies.

C–16 1. Young man on vacation enjoying doing nothing. He is just enjoying the beauty of the countryside. He is probably home for vacation.

2. He has studied hard for several months and now he has a chance to relax and he is making the most of it. He is resting his mind and eyes as he looks off into the distance.

3. He is probably dreaming of the good marks he received on mid-terms and of the girl he is with while home. He wants relaxation and a good time.

4. He will be rudely awakened and have to go back to school and final exams in a few days, but he realizes that the time spent is for his own good in the future.

C–17 1. A man is standing in the doorway watching 2 persons leave the road on the hill in the background.

2. A sudden departure or perhaps a departure that will be lengthy. The three have been quite close in the past.

3. The despair of sudden lonesomeness. The old companionship is wanted by the man.

4. Perhaps a rejoining will come in the future. In the meantime his thoughts will be with them.

C–18 1. The fellow is standing there thinking about many things. The person is probably someone like myself.

2. Several things have happened to make him worry and feel discouraged and left out and feel as if you are the only one that way.

3. He is thinking about being good or excelling at something, so people will accept him and want him around.

4. He thinks a lot about these things and then will just go on as before.

C–19 1. The man is waiting for his sweetheart to come. He's in love and is very anxious to see his girl.

2. He has dated a girl and has fallen in love. He has some kind of arrangement whereby, his girl is supposed to come over to his house today.

3. He is thinking of his girl. He wishes that the time would go faster so he'd be with her.

4. The girl will arrive and he'll go on with his plans and they'll complete their date.

C–20   1. He is just watching a friend leave or maybe standing looking over the hill. He is probably the owner of the house.

2. His friend's leaving or maybe the concentration on a problem has caused him to pause by the door for a moment.

3. He is probably thinking of how lovely things are. He wants what everyone else wants—peace of mind.

4. If there's a problem existing, he will soon face it and try to solve it.

C–21   1. A meeting is being held with seven men appearing. One is looking outside. One is on the floor apparently being clarified by the leader.

2. It seems to be some kind of legislative council going over the error committed by the brother (assuming fraternity). Some punishment must be imposed.

3. They are going over the misdeed to arrive at a just punishment by the council.

4. Some fine or punishment will be imposed if a suitable one is decided upon, if any is needed at all.

C–22   1. A fraternity meeting is taking place. The man at the head of table is president. The one standing is discussing a motion before the floor.

2. The motion that was brought up concerned the spending of money, a large sum, on a reconstruction job.

3. The members are thinking of the comments of the one standing who is against spending money by assessments.

4. Another member, the president, suggests that the members work for the money for the house. It is agreed and all join in to cooperate. Reconstruction job is completed.

C–23   1. This is a business meeting or discussion of some sort—people are conferring to find a solution to some unknown problem.

2. Problem that cannot be solved individually. Must be solved by group itself.

3. How best to solve problem—man looking out of window—preoccupied or disgusted—man with finger pointed and man standing up seem to be trying to get attention of the rest of the group.

4. Problem may or may not be solved depending on personal interest of each individual.

C–24   1. The man in the center is the "rah rah" boy of the fraternity. The men are sitting around having a bull session. They are hearing all about "Romeo's" latest adventure over the weekend.

2. The center man has just come back from a big weekend at another campus. He has quite a reputation as a lover. He really "made out" this weekend.

3. The center man is seeking attention but he isn't getting it.

One man has walked away already. The others are only mildly attentive.

4. As usual nothing will happen. Nobody dares tell him what a bore he is and he just keeps on the same way all through school.

C–25   1. Before scene at all night poker game. Persons are friends in school.

2. Something to do. Good times had in past and enjoyment in getting together to shoot the bull.

3. Nothing in particular is being thought although old times is probably main thought.

4. Party will last until quite late with some refreshments.

C–26   1. We have a group meeting in a somewhat informal atmosphere. A few members are having a jovial time while one member is on his feel with an angry expression on his face.

2. A question has been brought up which most of the group takes lightly, but which is serious to the member standing.

3. The person on his feet is demanding attention and is frustrated that he is not getting it. The other members are not particularly interested.

4. The fellow will sit down still frustrated but will learn from the experience how to keep group attention by better expression next time.

C–27   1. A meeting of some organization is being held. The people are the members themselves.

2. A sudden change of policy has brought about this meeting and a solution is being sought.

3. Disagreement is evident here by the man looking away out of the window. A solution is wanted by all. But all can't agree on how it should be reached.

4. A strong leader will arise who has careful thoughts and will swing the others to working his way if he has a good solution and a good line.

C–28   1. A gang of fraternity brothers are having a bull session after a game of cards. They are relaxing between studies for a break in the monotony of routine.

2. Much work during the day in books and getting through lectures has made them want some means of relaxation without spending money and bull sessions or cards do a good job.

3. Probably talking about the world situation and that they will be able to continue school if their grades are good. Relaxation is wanted by all.

4. Pretty soon the gang will break up and everyone will do something else. Some will study and some will watch T.V. Nothing will come from the session.

C–29   1. It is the usual college "clique" having a bull session and ignoring the guy who they don't think fits into their group. They are discussing what they think are the ways of life.

2. The other boy is somewhat retiring and more intelligent. He was brought up this way. They are typically immature and conceited. They're "know it alls."

3. He is wishing he could join them, for we're all gregarious. They'll finally grow up enough in later life to just accept a man on his merits, not by what group he belongs to.

C–30 1. A bunch of guys in a gang spending an afternoon in the local hangout. Another guy in the distance an outcast is trying to become one of the gang.

2. The bunch of guys were always together and this new fellow just moved into town. The new guy is a good fellow at heart but wants to become one of the tough bunch.

3. The new fellow is debating whether or not he should walk over to them or just wait and see what happens. The bunch of guys on the other hand are not paying attention to him and don't even see him there.

4. The boy will not become one of the gang. He will meet a nice girl and forget about joining the gang. He will marry the girl and live happily. The gang will get into trouble and all go to prison.

SET D: AFFILIATION STORIES

D–1 1. Father is giving son a good talking to. He probably received a ticket or wrecked the car and the father is giving the son a good going over so he will be more careful next time. Probably saying cars cost a lot of money and that if he ever does it again he can't use it any more.

2. Son has been careless. Probably the son has been reckless before.

3. Consideration and carefulness by the father. Father wants son to be more careful. Father telling son.

4. He will get the car again but he must be more careful. He will probably have to pay for the car.

D–2 1. A man is talking to a younger person. The man is probably the Father and the younger person may be the son. It looks as if the older man was congratulating the younger person.

2. The son has done something for which he is being congratulated or praised.

3. The son is thinking about what he has done, and he is proud of his accomplishment. The older person feels good about being able to praise the younger.

4. The praise will help the boy emotionally and his security in family will be strengthened.

D–3 1. An older man is talking with a young man. The older fellow is giving advice to the younger fellow.

2. The reason for their conversation is because the young fellow

has been confronted with a problem and he wants it cleared up or answered by the older fellow.

3. The young man wants the older fellow to give him some "fatherly" advice on the subject which is being conversed.

4. The older man will give the younger fellow some advice.

D–4 1. Father lecturing son. Son being disciplined.

2. Close relation father and son. Not much conflict. Little disipline required.

3. Father desires same relation as past. Son maturing. Desires equality, freedom. Own decisions.

4. Father will be hurt emotionally short while then proud acceptance as young man.

D–5 1. Two boys, one several inches taller than the other, are talking about some happening. Very probably, the taller of the two is criticizing the other.

2. They had an argument, undoubtedly on some current happening.

3. Neither boy wants to give in to the other. Each boy wants the other to concede to his way of thinking. The taller of the two is the most persistant.

4. The two boys will compromise with each other. They will again be on good terms even though they may not think alike.

D–6 1. It is one man looking into a large mirror. He was told by his girl friend to try to grow more hair on his head but he couldn't so he is now buying a wig.

2. He just bought the wig and wants to see how it looks. Ever since he was ill he's been bald so he feels it's time to look better.

3. He thinks that it looks pretty good, but he is scrutinizing it carefully.

4. He decides to buy the wig and eventually will find someone to love him.

D–7 1. Possibly the persons are father and son. The father is frowning indicating something done by the son that disagreed with him.

2. Who knows. The smiling person has done something that obviously disagrees with the frowning one.

3. The frowning person wants something that the other won't give readily.

4. One of them is likely to go away mad (the frowning one).

D–8 1. The larger man is telling the smaller man that he is not doing his job as he had ought to. The larger man is the employer. The smaller man is a bit nervous.

2. The smaller man has been a bit lazy and hasn't been doing his job as he should! He has provoked his employer.

3. The smaller man is nervous and wishing he could disapear. The larger man is angry. The larger man wants the smaller one to get to work.

4. The smaller man will become frightened at the thought of losing his job and will do as he is told.

D-9   1. The father is berating his son for some misdemeanor.

2. The son has probably committed some act which the father has forbidden him to do.

3. The son thinks it is not as serious as the father does. The son wants the father to discontinue his beratement.

4. The father will continue until he feels his point is carried, but the son will become increasingly antagonistic. With this method of correction there will be very little done, by either the father or son in correcting the problem.

D-10   1. Father and son. The father is giving the son a "dressing-down" or mild lecture.

2. The boy did some comparatively minor misdemeanor. Perhaps he kept his girl out too late, and the boy's father heard of it.

3. The father is talking to the boy because he has to. He doesn't care really, about how late the kid stays up. The kid knows he's a little in the wrong, but he looks a bit belligerent, as if to say, "Why's he treating me like a little boy?"

4. Probably nothing will be done about it. The boy will be a little more careful the next time, and forget about it thereafter.

D-11   1. A fellow is looking out into space wondering what is in store for him. He is trying to decide just what his actions should be or what course of life he should follow.

2. He has gone from one interest to another and now has found it is time to make a final and decisive decision as to what he wants to make of his life.

3. He is hashing over in his mind what possibilities there are. He wants to know what course will be the best and which will lead to his becoming the best person.

4. He will finally come out with a decision and strive to the best of his ability to make it the thing for him and make himself a worthwhile person.

D-12   1. The fellow is looking at the scene just outside his door. It is the beginning of full summer. The air tantalizes his nostrils. He would like to walk far and free.

2. He has been at school, just getting home two weeks previous to this scene.

3. He would like to walk and walk. Possibly at night, too. Just get in amongst the green and become a part of it, cool and refreshed.

4. He will probably stay and just look. Dream a little but go to work the next day and remember it. He will see the same scene the next day.

D-13   1. The man is looking from the door of his home, out onto the plains which he would like to roam. He is carefree and has the desire to travel.

2. He has always been a wanderer and his blood just tells him that its time to move on.

3. He is thinking or debating about leaving. He wants to go, but hates to leave the house which he has come to call home.

4. He will decide to go. His wandering spirit will catch up to him.

D-14 1. The man is waiting for his chance to go out of doors to relax or to enjoy himself.

2. The man has probably been in his office or home for weeks or months and is tired of it. He wants the freedom of the out-of-doors.

3. He is thinking how nice it will or would be to get out of doors. He wants to go out.

4. The man will go out.

D-15 1. A married man is standing in the door way thinking about a problem that has confronted him. He is at home.

2. He has probably had a quarrel or argument with his wife and is trying to decide what to do.

3. He is thinking what it would be like if he would have stayed single and not married.

4. He will look at the "other side of picture" and will finally see his wife's viewpoint.

D-16 1. One nice looking, fairly young man is waiting nonchalantly in the doorway for his friend who will be coming up the walk.

2. He invited his friend over to play cards with him. They have always been buddies and have done this many many times together before.

3. The man in the doorway is glad his friend finally has arrived (even a little unhappy that he is a little late).

4. They will be enjoying the beautiful day together after the house owner pleasantly meets his friend at the door.

D-17 1. Man is standing in doorway watching either the sunset or sunrise.

2. Probably had a very satisfying day and is reminiscing about those past events.

3. Thinking about past events and events and problems that will come up in the future and is trying to solve them beforehand.

4. Will go back inside at peace with himself and more assured of himself.

D-18 1. Man standing in door thinking. Owner of home.

2. A man working hard all of his life to obtain for himself and family a home and a place to raise a family and enjoy life.

3. How lucky he is to have the things he has. How proud he is to have a wonderful family. Nothing.

4. Nothing except to continue to live there and enjoy it. To make his family still happier.

D-19   1. A man, probably depressed, is looking out at the air and is thinking about recent occurences.

2. Someone dear to him has probably died.

3. The man is thinking about the past; he is wishing that certain things could be done over again, and how he could have changed the present.

4. He will get over this feeling in time.

D-20   1. A poeter is standing besides the opened door and looks very pleasant the beautiful view of the country. Probably he watches his child who plays on the ground and feels happy.

2. He was writing or studying something great but when he heard the voice of his child he went to the door to see his own child, his happiness.

3. He is watching the beauty outside and after a while he will go back to his desk and work.

4. This is the happiness of life. To work hard and to enjoy the happiness of the family.

D-21   1. A fraternity meeting is in progress. A pertinent topic is up for discussion and there is some lively discussion about it.

2. The situation has become bigger and bigger and has demanded the attention of the house. It has been a ticklish subject because there were variances of opinion about it.

3. All are striving to establish in their mind what the best policy would be for the house. They desire the resulting policy to be the most worthwhile for the house.

4. They will decide in favor of one policy and because they have looked at all sides of the question they will adopt a favorable policy.

D-22   1. This is a business meeting of young salesmen. The fellow at the head of the table is the head of the department.

2. Their department has been low and they are in serious need of a lift in sales.

3. The head of the department has just given the men the usual pep talk and they are about to leave. He is just winding up with hopes that the men will work efficiently. The men take it as the "same old stuff."

4. The men will go out, a few conscientious men will try hard to get sales, the rest will go along at the same rate. Sales will go up slightly and the *whole* group will be complimented for a few men's work.

D-23   1. The members of a large club have just adjourned from their meeting and are having a few beers at the local bar.

2. The boys have just left their meeting and are debating over some of the motions made at the meeting.

3. The boys don't want anything in particular but are just sitting around making conversation.

4. When everyone has felt he has had enough brews they will go home or out to see their girls.

D-24   1. A group of young men are seated around a table drinking and playing cards.

2. They are members of a fraternity and they are spending the night in an all-night game. A few jokes are also being exchanged.

3. They are all trying to think of a joke to tell and they are all pretty tired. They all want to win.

4. The game will end about five in the morning and they will all go to bed.

D-25   1. A group of young men are sitting around a table and have been drinking for several hours. Their tongues are loose now and everyone is talking at once.

2. They have been together before and are celebrating old times. Perhaps they were boyhood chums, in and out of the army again and are going over old times.

3. They want to bring back the old times and forget the sights and memories of things they have seen in the war.

4. They will gradually forget and settle down in their new life out of the army.

D-26   1. It is a bunch of guys from a fraternity house on a Saturday night after a big football victory. They are singing all the school songs, while getting pleasantly inebriated.

2. The general routine of college life, all the relaxation after a big victory and the general happiness of all.

3. What a great game it was and somebody bring a pitcher of beer. There is no thought of school.

4. Some will get tight and stagger home. The rest will just be gay and everyone will be great friends.

D-27   1. This is a gang of boys who are trying to become a real outlaw gang. The guy at the rear is announcing that one member has been caught and exposed.

2. The exposed member was a pickpocket and was caught by the police. The boy at the rear of the picture saw it.

3. The boy at the rear is about to tell the others about this. He wonders if the caught member will betray them all.

4. The caught member will "sing" and bring and end to the gang.

D-28   1. A small time gang of hoods has just knocked off the Federal Reserve Bank of Phil.

2. The high cost of beer and women. They were all millionnaires but taxes wiped them out.

3. Did we get enough or should we go back after that last billion. To find the most lovely creatures and spend all of their newly acquired fortune on them. By them all.

4. They will take Fort Knox next. The Treasury will go on the good will standard and the head of the gang will become Sect. of Treas.

D-29   1. It is a neighborhood gang—planning some form of malpractice—probably robbery, etc.

2. They have been brought up "on the wrong side of the tracks"—led to believe crime is the way to success.

3. Each is thinking of the job—of the money—of good times later—of possible consequences.

4. They will complete plans—then set out—to meet later and complete their mission of evil.

D-30   1. A group of boys are sitting around talking and partying. A group of going students.

2. They decided—of doing nothing in particular to have this affair.

3. Nothing special—just a good time—fellowship is wanted—by all.

4. They will have a party and overindulge—that is some of them will—then they will go home and plan another one for next year.

SETS E, F, AND G: AFFILIATION STORIES

The stories constituting Affiliation Sets E, F, and G were selected from stories in the Achievement and Power Practice Sets. Turn to the Achievement and Power Sections of this Appendix to find these stories. The stories which correspond to E–1—E–30, F–1—F–30, and G–1—G–30 of Affiliation Sets E, F, and G are listed below in parentheses. For example, to find the first story in Set E (E–1) turn to the fourteenth story in Achievement Practice Set B.

The pictures to which these stories were written are described in the Achievement and Power Sections of this Appendix.

Set E		Set F		Set G	
E–1	(Ach B–14)	F–1	(Pow A–1)	G–1	(Pow B–11)
E–2	(Ach B–15)	F–2	(Pow A–9)	G–2	(Pow B–12)
E–3	(Ach C–11)	F–3	(Pow A–10)	G–3	(Pow B–13)
E–4	(Ach C–12)	F–4	(Pow C–1)	G–4	(Pow B–14)
E–5	(Ach C–13)	F–5	(Pow C–2)	G–5	(Pow B–15)
E–6	(Ach C–14)	F–6	(Pow C–3)	G–6	(Pow B–16)
E–7	(Ach C–15)	F–7	(Pow C–4)	G–7	(Pow B–17)
E–8	(Ach D–13)	F–8	(Pow D–2)	G–8	(Pow B–18)
E–9	(Ach D–20)	F–9	(Pow D–6)	G–9	(Pow B–19)
E–10	(Ach B–25)	F–10	(Pow D–7)	G–10	(Pow B–20)
E–11	(Ach B–26)	F–11	(Pow C–11)	G–11	(Pow C–19)
E–12	(Ach B–27)	F–12	(Pow C–12)	G–12	(Pow C–20)
E–13	(Ach B–28)	F–13	(Pow C–13)	G–13	(Pow C–29)
E–14	(Ach B–29)	F–14	(Pow C–14)	G–14	(Pow B–21)
E–15	(Ach B–30)	F–15	(Pow C–15)	G–15	(Pow B–22)
E–16	(Ach C–29)	F–16	(Pow C–16)	G–16	(Pow B–23)

E–17	(Ach C–30)	F–17	(Pow C–17)	G–17	(Pow B–26)
E–18	(Ach D–23)	F–18	(Pow C–18)	G–18	(Pow B–27)
E–19	(Ach D–24)	F–19	(Pow D–11)	G–19	(Pow D–13)
E–20	(Ach D–25)	F–20	(Pow D–12)	G–20	(Pow D–14)
E–21	(Pow A–11)	F–21	(Pow A–27)	G–21	(Pow C–30)
E–22	(Pow A–12)	F–22	(Pow A–28)	G–22	(Pow D–21)
E–23	(Pow A–13)	F–23	(Pow A–29)	G–23	(Pow D–22)
E–24	(Pow A–14)	F–24	(Pow A–30)	G–24	(Pow D–23)
E–25	(Pow A–15)	F–25	(Pow C–23)	G–25	(Pow D–24)
E–26	(Pow A–16)	F–26	(Pow C–24)	G–26	(Pow D–25)
E–27	(Pow A–17)	F–27	(Pow C–25)	G–27	(Pow D–26)
E–28	(Pow A–18)	F–28	(Pow C–26)	G–28	(Pow D–27)
E–29	(Pow A–19)	F–29	(Pow C–27)	G–29	(Pow D–28)
E–30	(Pow A–20)	F–30	(Pow C–28)	G–30	(Pow D–29)

SET A: AFFILIATION EXPERT SCORING

The expert's scoring decisions for the 30 stories of Set A are briefly explained below, one category at a time. In general, only instances where a subcategory is scored are discussed. When a decision not to score a subcategory is a difficult one, it is also discussed.

Imagery

A–1   *Aff Im.* There is concern over marriage: "are planning to be married . . . The man feels he should go into the service before they are married, the girl wants to marry now."

A–2   *Aff Im.* This is a difficult scoring decision. The following considerations lead to scoring *Aff Im.*: the role of brother is not one in which giving help is prescribed; there seems to be small talk, a sharing of experiences, e.g., "the older brother is talking to his younger brother about an interesting experience . . . is relating an exciting anecdote . . ." to "liven his spirit."

A–3   *Aff Im.* "The son wants understanding." Wanting understanding implies wanting a positive affective reaction from another person.

A–4   *U Im.* Though this is a fraternity situation, there is no concern over affiliation expressed.

A–5   *Aff Im.* "The son feels guilty and wants forgiveness." Once again, the son's affective concern with his father's reactions seems to go beyond cultural prescriptions.

A–6   *U Im.* Advice giving by father to son is considered as part of the cultural definition of a father's role. The mere statement of someone being married is not a basis for scoring *Aff Im.* There must be concern about marriage. The son's attempt to make his father proud of him seems too tied in with achievement to be scored *Aff Im.*

A-7   *Aff Im.* "The younger man is worried about his lack of acceptance in the new social group. . . ." There is concern over a separation from an affiliation object, the group.

A-8   *Aff Im.* "The boys will still be friends after the argument." This implies that there was a friendship relationship and this is the primary criterion for scoring *Aff Im.*

A-9   *Aff Im.* "The pledge is thinking that in his big brother he can find understanding. . . ." The basis for scoring *Aff Im.* is the conception of understanding implying a positive affective relationship, not the fraternity situation.

A-10   *U Im.* There is no indication of a warm, affectionate relationship between father and son; rather the story is about the son's duty to do a task well.

A-11   *Aff Im.* "The boy has had a *happy family life* and the death (of his father is a *great shock.*" Here there is affective concern over the loss of an affiliative object.

A-12   *U Im.* This is a fraternity situation in which an aggressive rather than an affiliative theme is presented.

A-13   *U Im.* There is no evidence of affiliative concern.

A-14   *Aff Im.* "He is waiting for his girl. They will go for a walk in the sunshine and *enjoy each other's company.*" This is an instance of a dating relationship characterized by the participants enjoying each other's company, a convivial, companionate activity.

A-15   *U Im.* No affiliative concern. Dreams about the South Seas and native girls represent sexual interest.

A-16   *Aff Im.* Here a man living alone is eagerly awaiting the arrival of company, and we infer he anticipates affiliation.

A-17   *Aff Im.* Here a man is awaiting the arrival of friends and is concerned about his separation from them.

A-18   *Aff Im.* Here a dating relationship extended into one of love, and we infer by this a relationship that normally implies more than sex.

A-19   *Aff Im.* "his mind is wandering about his plans for the rest of his life. He is thinking of a wife . . . He wants . . . a happy life." Here there is concern about marriage.

A-20   *Aff Im.* "On returning he planned to marry Janet." Here again, there is concern about marriage.

A-21   *Aff Im.* "A remedy to bring the men together and solidify the house is being sought." This appears to be a desire for maintaining or restoring affiliative ties.

A-22   *Aff Im.* "He (the pledge) wants to complete training and become an active (member)." Here is desire to affiliate. "The boys are just getting up from a fraternity dinner table." Here is convivial, companionate activity.

A–23   *U Im.*   In this house meeting, unlike that of story A–21, the problem under discussion could be nonaffiliative in nature.

A–24   *Aff Im.*   "A discussion is being held in our house . . . just a desire to blow off steam and sound off with a bunch of guys we all get along with fairly well." This is an example of convivial, companionate activity, relaxed small talk.

A–25   *U Im.*   The dissension within the ranks of this group does not seem to be viewed from the point of view of broken affiliative ties by the story writer.

A–26   *Aff Im.*   "Fraternity bull session . . . they are sitting around discussing the age-old subjects . . . They will sit there . . . solve no problems and finish off an enjoyable evening of swapping stories." Once again, this is an example of convivial, companionate activity, relaxed small talk.

A–27   *Aff Im.*   "The fellows are chewing the fat after dinner at a card game." Normal, convivial, companionate activity is indicated.

A–28   *U Im.*   Once again, a group is discussing a nonaffiliative problem.

A–29   *Aff Im.*   There is concern over the planning of normally affiliative activity, the spring prom.

A–30   *U Im.*   The phrase "bull session" does not seem to be describing an affiliative gathering so much as a problem-oriented discussion concerning an issue of great importance to all persons. Affiliative interest is again not stated.

Need

A–1   *N.*   "the girl wants to marry now."

A–2   *No N.*   We cannot infer desire for approval from "will give his all to follow in his brother's footsteps." Do not infer *N* from instrumental acts.

A–3   *N.*   "the son wants understanding."

A–5   *N.*   "The son . . . wants forgiveness by his father."

A–7   *No N.*   It is not clear what is meant by the sentence "The young man seeks a restoration of his confidence." It might be interpreted as indicating that he knows his problem in being accepted is lack of self-confidence, and he wants to remedy this in order to affiliate, *but* this is very ambiguous. Hence *N* is not scored.

A–8   *No N.*

A–9   *No N.*   The statement "The younger fellow wants to be put straight" is not clearly a desire relevant to affiliation.

A–11   *No N.*   A–14   *No N.*

A–16   *N.*   "Whoever is coming is someone he wants to see very much."

A–17   *N.*   "Relief from his tension is wanted by the young man." This is clearly tension relevant to affiliation as indicated by "With arrival of friends tension will be relieved."

A–18   *N.* "the boy is seeking to recapture the previous summer," during which he had an affiliative relationship.

A–19   *No N.* It is not clear that "wanting . . . a happy life . . ." is a purely affiliative desire.

A–20   *No N.*

A–21   *N.* "A remedy to bring the men together and solidify the house is being sought."

A–22   *N.* "He wants to complete training and become an active."

A–24   *N.* "just a desire to blow off steam and sound off with a bunch of guys we all get along with fairly well."

A–26   *No N.* "The younger members want to hear all about his adventures" is not clearly *n* Affiliation; perhaps it's *n* Excitement.

A–27   *N.* "Everyone . . . wants to talk about prospective dates or exams etc." They want to participate in affiliative activity.

A–29   *N.* "The students want to hold it anyway." The spring prom is a normally convivial activity.

Instrumental Activity

A–1   *I+.* "are planning to be married . . ." This is problem-solving thought directed towards an affiliative end. "They will work out a happy solution" indicates a successful outcome, thus *I+.*

A–2   *I?.* The nurturant act by the older brother of trying to cheer up the younger one is scored *I.* The small talk is also scorable as *I.* The outcome of the nurturant act isn't clear, though the small talk seems to have a positive outcome. On the basis of all instrumental acts, *I?* is scored.

A–3   *No I.*

A–5   *I?.* "The son will be more cautious next time" is the statement of an act whose goal is affiliative, i.e., approval of father. The outcome is not clear.

A–7   *I?.* "A younger man is approaching a man older than himself for help or advice on a problem . . . A short conversation will ensue" is a statement of the act of seeking help for what is described elsewhere as an affiliative problem. The scoring of the outcome is made with regard to whether this conversation brought the boy closer to his affiliative goal of group acceptance. On this basis *I?* is scored.

A–8   *No I.*

A–9   *No I.* The conversation here is clearly not small talk with an affiliative end. Rather, it seems to be problem solving: "a serious conversation . . . a problem has developed or perhaps one needs advice."

A–11   *No I.*

A–14   *I+.* "They will go for a walk in the sunshine" is the act and "enjoy each other's company" indicates the outcome.

A–16   *I+.* "He is ready for them ahead of time . . . has prepared himself ahead of time for arrival" is the act statement. The outcome is inferred from "Person . . . will arrive late. Man . . . is very effusive and demonstrative."

A–17   *I+.* "Young man is . . . searching for someone he expects" is the act statement. "With arrival of friends tension is relieved" is the outcome.

A–18   *I?.* "She writes that she does (love him)" is the act statement, its outcome is in doubt: "but its been so long and she's young and pretty and so far away . . . He will feel better somehow but the unanswered question will remember. . . ."

A–19   *No I.*

A–20   *I–.* "On returning he had planned to marry Janet" is one *I* in the story. The other is "Tom is deciding what to do. Go back and apologize, trying to make the most of a bad situation or to run away." Both have negative outcomes. The marriage plans don't materialize, he runs away, gets killed, and Janet is unhappy.

A–21   *No I?.* Instrumental Activity with questionable outcome might have been scored from the first and last sentences. But a conservative interpretation of the rule not to score a statement of the situation or of the outcome argues against it.

A–22   *I+.* "They have eaten their dinners and the pledges *entertained* the actives with their jokes, etc." This is an example of convivial, companionate activity with a positive (see italicized portion) outcome.

A–24   *I+.* "A discussion is being held in our house by a bunch of brothers—a bull session—*all are amused* . . . blow off steam and sound off with a bunch of guys . . . gradually break off . . . *all in good feelings.*" This is another example of convivial, companionate activity with a positive (see italicized portions) outcome.

A–26   *I+.* "Fraternity bull session . . . Dinner has just finished and they are sitting around discussing the age old subjects . . . and finish off an *enjoyable evening* of swapping stories." Again, there is convivial, companionate activity with a positive outcome (see italicized portion).

A–27   *I+.* "The fellows are chewing the fat after dinner at a card game . . . Everyone feels in a talkative mood . . . So they sit down and talk . . . They will talk for a while then play cards.

. . ." Here again is convivial, companionate activity. The outcome is inferred from this kind of affiliative small talk which is an end in itself.

A–29 *I+*. Here, an affiliative problem is being discussed, the block to the holding of a spring prom, and a decision is reached so that the prom is held. Both the discussion of the problem and the actual holding of the prom are instrumental acts. The outcome of the discussion is positive in that the block to an affiliative activity is overcome.

Anticipatory Goal States

A–1 *No Ga.*

A–2 *Ga+*. "The older brother feels that maybe his relating this experience will liven the younger boy's spirit. . . ." This is the older brother anticipating the success of his nuturant act.

A–3 *No Ga.* A–5 *No Ga.*

A–7 *No Ga–*. "The younger man is worried about his lack of acceptance in the new social group" describes contemporary concern about a past state of affairs and thus is scored *G–* not *Ga–*.

A–8 *No Ga.*

A–9 *Ga+*. "The pledge is thinking that in his big brother he can find understanding. . . ."

A–11 *No Ga–*. "He is . . . wondering of the future" is not clearly an anticipation of *affiliative* goal attainment or frustration.

A–14 *Ga+*. "He is waiting for his girl . . . His posture would indicate relaxation and expectancy at going out."

A–16 *Ga+*. "Man living alone waiting . . . for company who are to arrive at a later time . . . Whoever is coming is someone he wants to see very much . . . Man is making effort to be calm and not excite himself."

A–17 *Ga+*. "Thoughts of how pleasant it would be when friends or relatives appear . . ."

A–18 *Ga+*. "The boy dreams of last summer and longs for those happy days."

Ga–. "Does the girl still love him or does she think it a summer romance? He wishes he knew for sure."

A–19 *Ga+*. "The fellow . . . is . . . dreaming of the future . . . He is thinking of a wife . . . He wants . . . a happy life."

A–20 *No Ga.* A–21 *No Ga.*

A–22 *No Ga–*. "the pledge is wondering what might happen next. . . ." This is not clearly anticipation of affiliative goal attainment or frustration.

A–24 *No Ga.* A–26 *No Ga.*

A–27 *No Ga.* "They are thinking about some girls they would like to date. . . ." The dating relationships being anticipated are not fully enough described to be considered affiliative.

A–29 *No Ga.*

Obstacles or Blocks

A–1 *Bw.* "Apparently a tense moment, or a moment of clash has occurred between the man and his girl. They seem to be arguing over something."

A–2 *No Block.*

A–3 *Bw.* "The father can't understand it." This is disruptive to the affiliative relationship in view of the son's desire for understanding. It is scored *Bw* since the character who desires to affiliate is the son, and the obstacle is not his actions, but his father's.

A–5 *Bp.* "The boy appears to be guilty of doing something undesirable and is being reprimanded . . . The son feels guilty and wants forgiveness by his father." The character concerned with affiliating has misbehaved in such a way as to lead to a disruption of the affiliative relationship.

A–7 *Bw.* "The younger man is worried about his lack of acceptance in the new social group. . . ." The lack of acceptance is the *Bw.* Do not score *Bp* based on his lack of confidence. It is not clear whether this is the cause of his lack of acceptance.

A–8 *Bp.* Two friends are having an argument traceable to something one of them has done which angered the other. This is *Bp* rather than *Bw* because the fault is attributable to one of the characters, who, we infer, desires to affiliate since he has been and remains a friend of the other one.

A–9 *No Block.*

A–11 *Bw.* "The boy is the son of a deceased person probably father . . . the death is a great shock." Here is an example of a physical separation about which the character is concerned.

A–14 *No Block.*

A–16 *Bw.* "Person, or people, will arrive late. . . ." There is a prolonged physical separation about which the character concerned with affiliation is concerned: "Man . . . waiting . . . for company . . . someone he wants to see very much."

A–17 *Bw.* "Person is . . . expecting arrival of friends or relatives who are late." Here again is physical separation about which the character concerned with affiliating is upset: "Relief from his tension is wanted . . . with arrival of friends tension will be relieved."

A-18   *Bw.* Here again is a story about physical separation of a person desiring to affiliate from the desired object of his affiliation.

A-19   *No Block.*

A-20   *Bw.* The character who indicates a desire to affiliate, Tom, has been blocked by others, Janet and her other lover, from the object of his affiliation. His own behavior also contributes to the "separation."

A-21   *Bw.* "a serious house problem. Certain incidents in the past such as no cooperation within the house and general unrest and the beginning of factions."

A-22   *No Block.*   A-24   *No Block.*

A-26   *No Block.*   A-27   *No Block.*

A-29   *Bw.* "The school board has refused to allow the Spring Prom."

Affective States

A-1   *G+.* "they will work out a *happy* solution. . . ."

A-2   *G+.* "his expression shows signs of idolization." The author seems to be describing the younger boy's feelings in terms of his expression. Idolization seems to involve a mixture of fondness and pride. The fondness component is the basis of scoring *G+.*

A-3   *No G−.* "The father is not pleased" is not scored since there is no indication that the father wants to affiliate. His displeasure may stem from thwarted power wishes or other sources.

A-5   *G−.* "The son feels guilty" about action leading to a disruption of his affiliative relationship with his father.

A-7   *G−.* "The younger man is worried about his lack of acceptance in the new social group. . . ."

A-8   *No G−.* "The one on the left seems to be angry with the one on the right" is not scored *G−* since it is not clear whether his anger is connected with affiliative goal attainment.

A-9   *No G.*

A-11   *G+.* "The boy has had a very happy family life. . . ." This is a description of an affective state which occurred in the past.
       G−. "and the death is a great shock."

A-14   *G+.* "They will . . . enjoy each other's company."

A-16   *G−.* The "agitation" following the obstacle (delay) represents negative affect.

A-17   *G+.* "With arrival of friends tension will be relieved."

A-18   *G+.* "He will feel better" after receiving her letter of assurance.

A-19   *No G.*

A–20   *G–*. "Janet . . . is subconsciously unhappy." It is assumed that the loss of her old beau—the final separation—is the cause.

A–21   *No G.*

A–22   *No G–*. The pledge's relief about the end of dinner may be positive affect, but it is not clearly related to his affiliative goal.

A–24   *G+*. "will gradually break off . . . all in *good feelings . . .*"

A–26   *G+*. "finish off an enjoyable evening of swapping stories . . ." Do not score "one member seems to be disturbed about a few of the remarks, maybe he is an idealist" as *G–* since the negative affect is not affiliation-related.

A–27   *No G.*   A–29   *No G.*

Thema

A–1   *Th*. This story is scored *Th* despite concern over entering the service since the functional significance of this seems to be as a block to affiliation, about which the story seems to center.

A–2   *No Th*. The last sentence points to other than affiliative feelings that the younger brother has for the older brother: awe, pride, etc. Furthermore, there is a good deal of achievement imagery sharing this stage.

A–3   *No Th*. There are indications of a power in addition to an affiliative relationship between father and son: "The son has been dominated by his parents . . . reconciled themselves to the fact that their son is able to stand on his own two feet."

A–5   *No Th*. The following statements indicate some concern other than affiliation: "a father is telling his son what to do and what not to do. The boy . . . is being reprimanded . . . Apparently the boy did something that did not comply with the desire of the father."

A–7   *Th*. This whole story is centered about the younger man's concern over his lack of acceptance and what he tries to do about it.

A–8   *No Th.*

A–9   *No Th*. The following statements indicate nonaffiliative concerns in this story: "The pledge is thinking that in his big brother he can find . . . worthwhile advice. The younger fellow wants to be put straight and make himself a better fellow . . . The pledge will be enlightened."

A–11   *No Th*. *Th* is not scored because of a twist in the plot at the end in the direction of achievement.

A–14   *Th*. The entire story seems to be about an affiliative relationship.

A–16   *Th*. The whole story seems to be about someone who desired, is expecting, and experiences an affiliative relationship.

A–17 *No Th.* The alternative interpretations of the picture in terms of both business and affiliative concerns prevents scoring *Th.*

A–18 *Th.* The entire story is about someone who desires to affiliate and who is worried about the outcome of his affiliative desires.

A–19 *No Th.* There are several indications of nonaffiliative concerns: "He is thinking of . . . a job with good pay. He wants security . . . He will probably be a success in his future and will work hard. . . ." This appears to be an additional theme, an achievement concern.

A–20 *No Th.* There are several other possible themes, e.g., aggression and sex are indicated: "Tom has just severely beaten his girl. She has been, at least he thought so, unfaithful to him."

A–21 *Th.* The entire story appears to be about an attempt to mend a disrupted affiliative relationship among the fraternity members.

A–22 *Th.* The story takes place in a normally affiliative setting, the fraternity dining hall, and one of the characters indicates a desire to affiliate. The only other possibly nonaffiliative concern in the story is the sentence: "The pledge is wondering what might happen next . . . ," but this isn't clearly enough nonaffiliative to prevent scoring *Th.*

A–24 *Th.* The entire story seems to be a description of a convivial, companionate situation.

A–26 *Th.* The major portion of this story is about a convivial, companionate situation.

A–27 *Th.* The entire story is a description of convivial, companionate activity.

A–29 *No Th.* In addition to the affiliative concern in this story there is a power struggle: "trying to decide whether to flaunt the authorities. . . ."

SET B: AFFILIATION EXPERT SCORING

The expert scoring below may be read as follows: first, the expert's scoring decisions are briefly explained; second, the total score is given; and third, in parentheses, is the rank of that story (with the highest score of the set given a rank of 1 and the lowest score a rank of 30). In general, only instances where a subcategory is scored are discussed. When a decision not to score a subcategory is a difficult one, it is also discussed.

B–1 *U Im.* There is no indication of warmth or affection nor any desire for them. 0 (22.5)

B–2 *U Im.* Again, there is no indication of a warm, affectionate relationship between father and son. 0 (22.5)

B–3   *U Im.* This is a simple job interview, conducted on a business-like basis. There are no warm, affectionate relationships here. 0 (22.5)

B–4   *U Im.* This is a father-son relationship with no indication of warmth or affection existing or desired by either. 0 (22.5)

B–5   *Aff Im.* "The younger brother is scared, *ashamed, sorry.* The older brother is disappointed. . . ." There is affective concern about the disruption of a relationship.

No I. Giving advice is not *I* unless it is advice concerning an affiliative problem.

Bp. The younger brother has done something which disrupts the relationship.

G–. "The younger brother is . . . *ashamed, sorry.*"

No Th. There is too much concern with the wrong act. 1 (13)

B–6   *Aff Im.* "a class reunion or frat founders day. They were very close friends in college."

I+. The meeting of the two buddies *during which they reminisce* is companionate activity. The outcome is indicated by "They are very glad to see each other . . . make arrangements for future meetings."

No Ga+. "reminiscing of old times" represents contemporary affiliative activity. Hence *I+* rather than *Ga+* is scored.

Bw. "haven't met each other in a long time . . ." The fact of separation causes the story to be scored *Bw.*

G+. "They are very *glad* to see each other."

Th. The whole story concerns the restoration and maintenance of an affiliative relationship. 5 (1.5)

B–7   *U Im.* There is certainly no affiliative concern here. 0 (22.5)

B–8   *Aff Im.* The decision regarding future occupation has a bearing on an affiliative relationship: marriage. There is concern about establishing this relationship and the affective arousal when it is established.

I+. The brothers are discussing this decision which has relevance to the proposed marriage. The outcome is "Jack finally sees the light, marries his girl, and lives happily ever after."

Bw. "Jack's girl wants him to stay clear of football, but Jack thinks he can make more money in pro football." There is a disagreement between Jack and his affiliative object.

G+. "and lives happily ever after . . ."

No Th. There is too much concern with a future career to score *Aff Th.* 4 (3.5)

B–9   *Aff Im.* "One fellow is telling another his *close friend.* . . ." This friendship relationship is the only basis for scoring Imagery.

No I. There is no indication that the conversation is affiliative rather than problem oriented. 1 (13)

B–10 *Aff Im.* "The older one has promised to fix the other up with a blind date." This is a friendly nurturant act.

No N. The statement "The younger one has previously been asked to be 'fixed up' " is not grounds for scoring N. The younger boy is asking for help with what may be an affiliative problem, but we cannot *infer N* from an instrumental act.

I+. "The older one has promised to fix the other up with a blind date . . . The younger one is amazed at what he has learned." The act of helping his friend out with a date is assumed to cement the relationship, despite the later dating trouble.

No G. The statement "The younger one will go on the date but will be greatly disappointed" is not scored as $G-$ since the negative affect appears to be concerned with sexual rather than affiliative desires.

No Th. The rest of the story is concerned with the sexual possibilities in such a date. The story is not scored further. 2 (9.5)

B–11 *U Im.* There is no indication of affiliation at all. 0 (22.5)

B–12 *U Im.* Again, there is no possible affiliation concern. 0 (22.5)

B–13 *Aff Im.* "He is considering marrying the girl he has been pinned to . . . the young man really loves the girl and doesn't want to lose her." There is concern about marriage, a normally affiliative relationship.

N. "doesn't want to lose her . . . doesn't want to hurt her . . ."

I+. "He is considering marrying . . . He finally marries the girl . . . all turns out well." Note that considering marriage is problem-solving thought rather than goal anticipation.

Ga−. "He is thinking how married life will be if he's away at camp and his wife is home." It is unclear whether these are $+$ or $−$ anticipations. Score $Ga-$ by convention.

No G+. G should not be inferred from successful I, e.g., "It all turns out well."

Bw. Having to enter the army is perceived as a block to marriage.

Th. The entire story is about an affiliative problem, whether to marry now or not. The army is relevant only as a block to marriage. 5 (1.5)

B–14 *Aff Im.* "The older fellow is thinking of how nice it would be to be down at the corner with his gang . . . He will have to spend a lonesome evening." Affective concern over separation from objects of affiliation (gang) is present.

No N. "He seeks escape" is not a statement of desire to affiliate.

Ga+. "The older fellow is thinking of how *nice* it would be to be down at the corner with his gang."

Bw. "The older fellow is baby sitting . . . thinking of how nice it would be to be down at the corner with his gang."

G—. "He will have to spend a *lonesome* evening."

Th. The entire story concerns blocked efforts to affiliate. 4 (3.5)

B–15 *Aff Im*. "He is a happily married man." The affective word makes the statement more than a mere mention of the occurrence of marriage and indicates concern about the type of relationship.

N. "He wants everything (including the affiliative satisfactions already stated) to continue as it has."

G+. "He is *happily* married . . . he will continue to be *happily* married."

No Th. Business concern prevents scoring this *Aff Th*. 3 (6)

B–16 *Aff Im*. "spent dinner with wife and children . . . is now happy and contented . . ." This is affective arousal in connection with loved ones. The dinner hour is normally an occasion for warm interpersonal relationships.

No I+. "disgusted . . . until he came home and spent dinner with his wife and children" is not scored *I* because it is merely the statement of the results of a previous act.

G+. "He is now *happy* and *contented*. . . ." This is affect contingent on affiliating.

No Th. "He is disgusted with his position in life . . . man puts forth better effort at office. . . ." 2 (9.5)

B–17 *U Im*. There is no indication that what he feels bad about is an affiliative problem. 0 (22.5)

B–18 *U Im*. There is no indication of an affiliative problem. 0 (22.5)

B–19 *U Im*. There is no affiliative concern. The mere mention of getting married someday is not a sufficient basis for scoring *Aff Im*. 0 (22.5)

B–20 *Aff Im*. "Thoughts might be drifting to his friends at home." The mention of a friendship relationship is in itself sufficient ground for scoring *Aff Im*, despite the lack of any other indication of affiliative concern.

Ga+. "Thoughts might be drifting to his friends at home. . . ." 2 (9.5)

B–21 *Aff Im*. "The boys in the fraternity have been having a drinking party." A party is normally affiliative in nature.

No I. "They were drinking beer. . . ." It isn't clear that beer drinking is affiliative in view of the rest of the story concerning defiance of authority. The party is considered minimally affiliative, but it is mentioned only in the first sentence. 1 (13)

B–22 *Aff Im.* "A group of close friends . . ."

I+. "they are discussing something that they are planning to do . . . just an idea . . . trying to plan their idea and figure out if it is agreeable to all . . . They will probably end up doing (it). . . ." What they are planning seems to be a group activity, some companionate activity.

Th. The entire story is about affiliative activity, a group of friends discussing things with one another. 3 (6)

B–23 *U Im.* This is a fraternity meeting clearly concerned with a specific nonaffiliative problem, drinking. 0 (22.5)

B–24 *Aff Im.* "This is a group of guys playing cards . . . Their wives are in the other room talking and sewing." This is normally convivial, companionate activity.

I?. The same action which is the basis for scoring *Aff Im* is scored *I*. The outcome of the get-together is questionable: "One of the men has been caught cheating . . . The others try to laugh it off."

Bw. The cheating accusation disrupted the companionate activity. 2 (9.5)

B–25 *U Im.* This is a fraternity situation where the main concern of the members is the drinking problem, not affiliation with one another. 0 (22.5)

B–26 *U Im.* Again, this is a fraternity situation where problem solving regarding the drinking question is the concern. 0 (22.5)

B–27 *U Im.* This is a discussion, but of a problem-solving, rather than of an affiliative, small-talk, nature. 0 (22.5)

B–28 *U Im.* The sentence "They all run around together" raises the possibility of affiliative relationships, but it isn't spelled out sufficiently to cause this to be scored *Aff Im*. The meeting is problem solving, rather than affiliative, in nature. 0 (22.5)

B–29 *Aff Im.* This is a story about companionate activity, a poker game, then a party.

I+. "They are thinking of having a party, and the boy at the head of the table is giving his ideas" is the activity. The outcome is "They will have a party."

No Bw. Not knowing what to do doesn't seem to disrupt the affiliative relationships.

Th. The entire story is about the occurrence and planning of companionate activity. 3 (6)

B–30 *U* Im. Again, this is a fraternity situation where the concern of the members is directed towards problem solving that is not indicated to be affiliative in nature. 0 (22.5)

SET C: AFFILIATION EXPERT SCORING

C–1 *Aff Im, N, I+.* 3 (7.5)
C–2 *Aff Im, I+, Th.* 3 (7.5)
C–3 *Aff Im.* 1 (14)
C–4 *U Im.* 0 (23)
C–5 *Aff Im, I+, G+, Th.* 4 (4.5)
C–6 *U Im.* 0 (23)
C–7 *Aff Im, Bw.* 2 (10.5)
C–8 *U Im.* 0 (23)
C–9 *U Im.* 0 (23)
C–10 *U Im.* 0 (23)
C–11 *Aff Im, N, Bw, Th.* 4 (4.5)
C–12 *U Im.* 0 (23)
C–13 *U Im.* 0 (23)
C–14 *U Im.* 0 (23)
C–15 *U Im.* 0 (23)
C–16 *U Im.* 0 (23)

C–17 *Aff Im, N, Bw, G—, Th.* 4 (4.5)
C–18 *Aff Im, N, G—.* 2 (10.5)
C–19 *Aff Im, N, I+, Ga+, Th.* 5 (2)
C–20 *Aff Im.* 1 (14)
C–21 *U Im.* 0 (23)
C–22 *U Im.* 0 (23)
C–23 *U Im.* 0 (23)
C–24 *U Im.* 0 (23)
C–25 *Aff Im, G+.* 2 (10.5)
C–26 *Aff Im.* 1 (14)
C–27 *U Im.* 0 (23)
C–28 *Aff Im, I+.* 2 (10.5)
C–29 *Aff Im, N, I?, Bw, Th.* 4 (4.5)
C–30 *Aff Im, N, I+, Bw, G+, Th.* 6 (1)

SET D: AFFILIATION EXPERT SCORING

D–1 *U Im.* 0 (22.5)
D–2 *Aff Im, I+, G+.* 3 (6)
D–3 *Aff Im.* 1 (14)
D–4 *Aff Im, N, Bw, G—.* 3 (6)
D–5 *U Im.* 0 (22.5)
D–6 *Aff Im, I+.* 2 (10.5)
D–7 *U Im.* 0 (22.5)
D–8 *U Im.* 0 (22.5)
D–9 *U Im.* 0 (22.5)
D–10 *U Im.* 0 (22.5)
D–11 *U Im.* 0 (22.5)
D–12 *U Im.* 0 (22.5)
D–13 *U Im.* 0 (22.5)
D–14 *U Im.* 0 (22.5)
D–15 *Aff Im, Bw.* 2 (10.5)
D–16 *Aff Im, I+, Bw, G+, Th.* 5 (1)

D–17 *U Im.* 0 (22.5)
D–18 *Aff Im, G+.* 2 (10.5)
D–19 *Aff Im, N, Bw, G—, Th.* 4 (3)
D–20 *Aff Im, I+, G+.* 3 (6)
D–21 *U Im.* 0 (22.5)
D–22 *U Im.* 0 (22.5)
D–23 *Aff Im, I+.* 2 (10.5)
D–24 *Aff Im, I+.* 2 (10.5)
D–25 *Aff Im, I+.* 2 (10.5)
D–26 *Aff Im, I+, G+, Th.* 4 (3)
D–27 *U Im.* 0 (22.5)
D–28 *U Im.* 0 (22.5)
D–29 *U Im.* 0 (22.5)
D–30 *Aff Im, N, I+, Th.* 4 (3)

SET E: AFFILIATION EXPERT SCORING

E–1 *Aff Im, N, Bw, G—.* 3 (5)
E–2 *U Im.* 0 (22.5)
E–3 *U Im.* 0 (22.5)
E–4 *U Im.* 0 (22.5)
E–5 *Aff Im.* 1 (12)

E–6 *U Im.* 0 (22.5)
E–7 *Aff Im, N, Bw.* 3 (5)
E–8 *U Im.* 0 (22.5)
E–9 *Aff Im, I+.* 2 (8.5)
E–10 *Aff Im, I?, Ga—.* 1 (12)
E–11 *U Im.* 0 (22.5)

E–12 *U Im.* 0 (22.5)
E–13 *Aff Im.* 1 (12)
E–14 *U Im.* 0 (22.5)
E–15 *Aff Im, N, Bw, G–, Th.* 4 (1.5)
E–16 *U Im.* 0 (22.5)
E–17 *Aff Im, N, Th.* 3 (5)
E–18 *Aff Im, G–.* 1 (12)
E–19 *U Im.* 0 (22.5)
E–20 *U Im.* 0 (22.5)
E–21 *U Im.* 0 (22.5)

E–22 *Aff Im, I+, G+.* 3 (5)
E–23 *U Im.* 0 (22.5)
E–24 *U Im.* 0 (22.5)
E–25 *Aff Im, I+, Th.* 3 (5)
E–26 *Aff Im, I+, G+, Th.* 4 (1.5)
E–27 *Aff Im, G+.* 2 (8.5)
E–28 *U Im.* 0 (22.5)
E–29 *U Im.* 0 (22.5)
E–30 *Aff Im.* 1 (12)

SET F: AFFILIATION EXPERT SCORING

F–1 *U Im.* 0 (23)
F–2 *Aff Im, I+, Ga+, Th.* 4 (2.5)
F–3 *U Im.* 0 (23)
F–4 *Aff Im, I+, Th.* 3 (6)
F–5 *U Im.* 0 (23)
F–6 *Aff Im.* 1 (11.5)
F–7 *U Im.* 0 (23)
F–8 *U Im.* 0 (23)
F–9 *Aff Im.* 1 (11.5)
F–10 *U Im.* 0 (23)
F–11 *U Im.* 0 (23)
F–12 *Aff Im.* 1 (11.5)
F–13 *Aff Im, I?, Ga+, Bw, Th.* 4 (2.5)
F–14 *U Im.* 0 (23)
F–15 *Aff Im, I+, G+, Th.* 4 (2.5)

F–16 *U Im.* 0 (23)
F–17 *Aff Im, I+, G+.* 3 (6)
F–18 *Aff Im.* 1 (11.5)
F–19 *Aff Im, I+, Th.* 3 (6)
F–20 *U Im.* 0 (23)
F–21 *U Im.* 0 (23)
F–22 *U Im.* 0 (23)
F–23 *Aff Im.* 1 (11.5)
F–24 *Aff Im.* 1 (11.5)
F–25 *Aff Im.* 1 (11.5)
F–26 *U Im.* 0 (23)
F–27 *U Im.* 0 (23)
F–28 *Aff Im, I+, Ga+, Th.* 4 (2.5)
F–29 *U Im.* 0 (23)
F–30 *Aff Im.* 1 (11.5)

SET G: AFFILIATION EXPERT SCORING

G–1 *Aff Im, I+, Th.* 3 (3)
G–2 *U Im.* 0 (21)
G–3 *Aff Im.* 1 (9.5)
G–4 *U Im.* 0 (21)
G–5 *U Im.* 0 (21)
G–6 *U Im.* 0 (21)
G–7 *Aff Im, I+, Th.* 3 (3)
G–8 *Aff Im, I+, Th.* 3 (3)
G–9 *U Im.* 0 (21)
G–10 *U Im.* 0 (21)
G–11 *Aff Im, G+.* 2 (6)
G–12 *Aff Im, I?.* 1 (9.5)
G–13 *Aff Im, I+, Ga–, Bw, G+, G–, Th.* 5 (1)
G–14 *Aff Im, N.* 2 (6)
G–15 *U Im.* 0 (21)

G–16 *U Im.* 0 (21)
G–17 *U Im.* 0 (21)
G–18 *U Im.* 0 (21)
G–19 *U Im.* 0 (21)
G–20 *U Im.* 0 (21)
G–21 *Aff Im.* 1 (9.5)
G–22 *U Im.* 0 (21)
G–23 *U Im.* 0 (21)
G–24 *Aff Im.* 1 (9.5)
G–25 *U Im.* 0 (21)
G–26 *U Im.* 0 (21)
G–27 *U Im.* 0 (21)
G–28 *U Im.* 0 (21)
G–29 *Aff Im, I+.* 2 (6)
G–30 *U Im.* 0 (21)

POWER SECTION
SELF-TEST: n POWER MANUAL (CH. 14)

After reading the scoring manual, write out your answers to the following questions without consulting the manual. Then check your answers to see if you are correct.

Imagery. What is the general basis for scoring Power Imagery? What are the three criteria for scoring Power Imagery? What kinds of statements would satisfy each of these criteria? What are the rules governing the scoring of Power Imagery in stories about solicited advice, physical power, parent-child relationships?

Need. What is the criterion for scoring N? What kinds of statements of desire are not scored N?

Instrumental Activity. What is the criterion for scoring I? What are typical examples of I? What determines whether I is scored $+$, $?$, or $-$?

Anticipatory Goal States. When is Ga scored? How are comments by the author of the story dealt with? How is a statement about a goal already attained dealt with?

Blocks. What is meant by *Blocks*? How is failure to obtain the goal dealt with? What is the distinction between Bp and Bw?

Affective States. What are the two criteria for scoring G? What is the distinction between Ga and G? What affective statements are not scored G?

Thema. When is Th scored? Can Th be scored if no other subcategories are scored?

PICTURES USED TO ELICIT STORIES SCORED FOR n POWER

The pictures used to elicit the stories for Sets A through D were as follows: Stories 1-10 in each set were written to a picture of two men standing in a well-furnished office gesturing in conversation (Picture E in the n Achievement series).* Stories 11-20 in each set were written to a picture of four men sitting and lounging informally in a furnished room (Picture E in the n Affiliation series).* Stories 21-30 in each set were written to a picture of two young men standing on the sidewalk of a campus talking to one another, one with books under his arm.*

---

* These pictures were used to elicit stories to be scored for n Power by Joseph Veroff in his study on the development and validation of a projective measure of power motivation (419).

Since Sets E, F, and G are composed of stories in the Achievement and Affiliation sections of this Appendix, the descriptions of the pictures used to elicit the stories for Sets E-G can be found in those sections of this Appendix. These pictures are not normally used to obtain power imagery. They have been scored for n Power and are included here to provide further practice and experience in transferring the meaning of various subcategories to novel material.

Note: Errors in grammar and spelling in these stories have not been changed.

SET A: POWER STORIES

A–1 1. The persons appear to be two businessmen—high executives who are discussing some phase of their business's operation.

2. There has been a discrepancy among these men in their business. This is obviously a conference to hash out the controversy.

3. The older man who may be the wiser is trying to explain his position to the younger, junior executive. This junior executive is trying to get his point over.

4. The older man will win his point. He is not going to hold any grudges against his junior executive. All will turn out for the best interest of the company.

A–2 1. The persons that are talking are business men in a deal or plotting for their own gain.

2. They seem to be discouraged with the results in the past and are trying to come up with some new ideas.

3. The man by the desk is discouraged about something and seems to be giving the man at the window a rough time about it.

4. The person at the window seems doubtful if he knows what is going on and that probably the other man will go ahead with his plans.

A–3 1. One person is an incumbent, or former office holder and the other man is the newly elected candidate. They are discussing the aspects of the just completed election.

2. There has been a rather controversial election, (close) and there is a congratulary or handing down mood in one of the men while the other is contemplating.

3. One is thinking of what has happened while in office, the other what is going to happen. They are discussing aspects of the job to be done.

4. One will retire, the other will go on successfully with the office to which he has been elected. It is a model American scene of (free) political life.

A–4 1. I would say that it was a reverend and probably a politician of some sort. The reverend is telling the man not to worry about whether he will win or lose.

2. It would be the night of a political ballot counting such as this and the man is worried about the disgrace he will have to face.

3. The man wants the reverend to give him sympathy or faith.

4. The reverend will console him that no matter who wins the looser never has to face disgrace, because only a good man can lose in the right manner.

A–5 1. Head officials of some company are arguing over a question of policy. One on left is younger man with new ideas older man has steadfast ones.

2. Personal conflict between two men. Young man thinks others ideas are obsolete—a waste of efficiency.

3. Old man thinks young one wants to run company into ground. Young one is sure he can do things better.

4. Friction will arise as is shown beginning now. Young man will win eventually because of better ideas and approach.

A–6 1. These are two professors having a discussion or argument about some point.

2. There has been some type of theme which has come up, and the two professors are discussing it.

3. Each person is thinking about what the other said, about the topic. They want to come to some type of agreement before the discussion is finished by both.

4. The two men will come to some type of decision. They will then leave the room.

A–7 1. The old man is looking at a watch, while the other stands by the window looking back inquisitively. They are both concerned with the time, because they are waiting for someone to come to their office of business.

2. An appointment was made to discuss a problem, a business problem, no doubt a routine problem that is not crucial.

3. They wonder why he has not shown up. (Or are they waiting for more than one.) They expected him to be on time so that they could get on with business. Waiting is nervewracking.

4. He (or they) will come in a few minutes and they will get on with the matter, and solve the problem partially, or all.

A–8 1. The older person is a well-respected judge who is trying to convince the younger, doubtful man that he should run for governor.

2. The younger man had planned to run for the position of governor and was all set to do so till he learned of some of the hardships needed to be dealt with (his wife became ill also.)

3. The young man is now hesitant. The older man is trying to convince him to go thru with the campaign because it is worth it in the long run and his leadership is needed.

4. The young man will reluctantly agree to run whereby he will win and become a good governor.

A-9 1. The two men are good friends. They have known each other for a long time. One is asking the other for advice.

2. They met each other as boys. One was older and protected the younger against outside aggression.

3. They are discussing old times. Some of the fun they had as boys.

4. They will continue to be friends and seek each other for help when it is needed.

A-10 1. The persons are two important figures in the government.

2. A foreign country (this is funny) has brought a critical situation to bear upon the government represented by these two people.

3. The man on the left is very dubious about the plan or solution presented by gentleman on right. The former originally thought of a plan, but is slowly being convinced of the validity of the latter's argument.

4. The man on the left will accept the other gentlemen's solution and will act upon it.

A-11 1. It looks like a typical group of neighbors getting together to talk over a community problem or current political situation, etc.

2. It could have been that they were having troubles with high taxes or colored people moving into their community and they are going to try solve the problem.

3. The men are trying to find a reasonable solution to the problem which confronts them.

4. By the looks of the wise fellow with the pipe who is doing the speaking, I would say that they would most likely come to a very suitable solution.

A-12 1. Four men in political discussion. Man standing is conservative—apprehensive, man talking is progressive in ideas, others inbetween.

2. Men are close friends, enjoy talks of this sort. Get together after dinner in a club or personal home.

3. Man standing is about to explode with own theories, against the man who is talking other two men will stay out of conversation.

4. Heated debate ending in a friendly parting with neither of the two men swayed, and other two men—talkers undecided. Nothing is accomplished.

A-13 1. The men are political party leaders meeting informally to map strategy before the big coming national convention in Chicago.

2. These men have been connected to a loosing party for the past few years and now are out to pick a real winner for this year's presidential election.

3. They have a fellow in mind whom all agree should be their man and they are thinking of ways to convince the rest of their party.

4. Their man will be hotly debated over at the convention but will win the nomination and the election. His administration will please the wiser party members and displease the rest.

A–14   1. The man seated and speaking is trying to tell the other three men something very important and of much interest to them.

2. The other three men are a bit concerned with what is being told them. They, however, seem to know that this explanation had to come.

3. The man standing by the wall is not sure that he agrees with all that is being said. Others are intensely interested.

4. The seated man will get his point across to the others, however, the standing man will not like it but will go along with the rest.

A–15   1. These are four members of the Shiloh Rod and Gun Club discussing pleasantly the plans for the next meeting and discussing the program for that time.

2. They were given the job of preparing an evening's entertainment and they got together to discuss plans for what type and how much entertainment to procure.

3. They are thinking of various types of recreation that would be beneficial to all their members. They want to put on a good program so that they will be able to do the job again.

4. The time will fly, they'll drink a beer and get the meeting arranged. After that, a card game or some tall tales will be in order. Late the next week they will finish arranging the entertainment for their Sunday meeting.

A–16   1. The persons are a few friends that have gathered at a favorite hangout. The man seated with the pipe in hand is relating an interesting experience that happened to him.

2. The man has had this experience happen to him and thought it interesting enough to be told to his friend.

3. Nothing is wanted. It is just a hash session by a group of men who are good friends.

4. They will have a good laugh and maybe this fellows experience will help them in the future to avoid or do it.

A–17   1. A group of friends have gathered for a bull session. They are connected remotely in business, but they have maintained association and often meet to hash out and compare their ideas. One of them seems to be holding the attention.

2. This is not an unusual occurrence, since they have always

enjoyed these meetings. They happen sort of unexpectedly but they happen.

3. They are discussing the world situation, something of grave concern, but not really having any immediate personal concern. All they want is to pick up more understanding of the situation by exchanging ideas.

4. They will dismiss after a time, having been convinced it was a profitable discussion and look forward to the next.

A–18 1. These men are officers of a mens' club. They are successful men. The one to the left is trying emphatically to make a point to his colleagues. The others are listening attentively.

2. The man talking has been trying to get something across to the others, but his plans have been continually sidetracked.

3. The other men, though listening attentively, are not taking the other seriously. They feel a little sympathy for his view and possibly for him, since he is down on his luck.

4. They will listen and not do anything. The talking man will try again next year or next meeting.

A–19 1. The four men are discussing some plan or problem in one of the men's home. They are four middle-aged family men, meeting for the express purpose of discussion.

2. Something in the municipal government or school system displeases them. The authorities have not been doing things to their liking.

3. The man on the left is presenting his solution or plan and the others are listening with varying degrees of enthusiasm or skepticism.

4. They will eventually work out their course of action and formulate a plan. They will present their plan to the proper authorities.

A–20 1. Four members of a country or social club are having a discussion. They are each respected, successful members of the community.

2. These four men have known each other for quite a long time and probably have sat in similar discussions in the past.

3. They are discussing a controversial matter concerning the local schools. Three of the men have children of school age while the other is not a father and does not want a raise in school taxes.

4. The single dissenter will be won over by his three parental friends and will be brought to realize the benefit to be gained by the entire community through better education.

A–21 1. In this case the men are discussing—it seems as if one is trying to convince the other—perhaps a candidate trying to convince another to vote for him.

2. One man is running in an election—the other is a voter—perhaps an acquaintance whom he's met.

3. The voter is thinking—"Well, he'll have to show me—the candidate is frankly wondering if its worth it with this guy.

4. I believe the voter will at least highly consider the candidate when the time to vote comes—perhaps not vote for him, however.

A–22   1. They are two college students who have just come from class and one is telling something to the other that happened in class that he didn't understand.

2. They have just come from class where the instructor has given them some new material and the one with the books doesn't understand it.

3. The fellow with the books is trying to gain knowledge and the other one is trying to explain it to him so that he can understand it.

4. The fellow will probably in the end grasp the material and be able to add it to his other knowledge or be able to tie it in with what is going on.

A–23   1. This is a typical sight in the past week. It looks like a candidate for a student position stopping a friend on the diag and telling how great he is and that he is the man to vote for.

2. This was just a casual acquaintance and the candidate was not sure that he would receive the vote without a little persuasion or talk.

3. The fellow is probably thinking that these guys are always the same—real friendly when they want something.

4. The person will probably be antagonistic and vote for someone else if he can think of a better person for the office.

A–24   1. A student who is running for office (in the suit with his hand out) is explaining the basis of his campaign to a second student who is not particularly interested.

2. The two probably "walked together" and struck up a conversation about student problems, and now have reached a place where they must part. The last part is still to be explained.

3. The student campaign is explained carefully. The listener is absorbing information but is not actually interested. He's listening to be polite.

4. The campaign will go its way and the listener will maybe make a judgment.

A–25   1. The persons are two students of a University who are engaged in a political argument.

2. Neither of the students has a class at the present or in the near future. They just ran into each other and after the usual greeting became involved in a political argument. They, of course, know each other quite well.

3. The fellow on the right wishes to convince the other fellow that the former is correct in his line of thinking.

4. The fellow on the left will outwardly agree with the other fellow, but inwardly feel different, and they will part soon.

A-26   1. Two young men are talking. One facing us is trying to convince other man about some topic which is important to the man talking.

2. The man being talked to has disagree with other man. He has done this nicely but still the man talking wishes to convince the other.

3. The one man is really disinterested. The man talking wants to convince the other. The man being talked to wants to leave.

4. The man talking will wind up. The other will leave—he has business to attend to while the other will continue on thinking about how he could have convinced the other.

A-27   1. While walking across campus, a faculty member comes across a student who has been walking on grass bearing signs saying "Keep Off". He is explaining to the student the rationale behind the signs.

2. The teacher has always been as anxious to see that signs are obeyed as he is that he is neat and tidy. His mother was always meticulous and made it a point to pass along that virtue to her offspring.

3. The student thinks the teacher is, as usual, getting all excited over nothing, and wishes he would go home. The teacher has only a vague idea of what he wants to accomplish, but continues to scold anyway.

4. Eventually, they will both part, the teacher unsatisfied he has accomplished anything. The student satisfied that the teacher should see a psychiatrist.

A-28   1. Two university students who do not know each other too well are discussing a course in which they both have the same recitation teacher.

2. They met as freshman and have since stopped to talk when they see each other for a moment or two.

3. One boy asked the other what he thought of a recent test given in the course. The other has gone on at some length to explain.

4. Nothing will happen. They will continue in their present relationship.

A-29   1. Man #1 on typical campus scene is trying to express an important point to his friend #2.

2. Man #1 thinks he is an authority on this point. Man #2 is not too sure, but probably doesn't care.

3. Man #1 believes he is convincing man #2 and doing a good job. Actually it is not as hot as he thinks.

4. Man #1 will have been pleased that he talked to #2. But #2 will forget that he even had this conversation with #1.

A-30   1. Fraternity man in back trying to talk undecided freshman into rushing. Freshman is not sure he wants to; fraternity man is using high pressure.

2. Frat man needs good men in house and had this one in orienta-

tion group where he (the freshman) expressed dislike for Greeks.

3. Freshman doesn't want to rush—afraid it will take too much time. Frat man wants not to seem overbearing, but uses high pressure anyway.

4. Freshman will not rush, showing a measure of independence from the picture.

SET B: POWER STORIES

B-1 1. Two professional men, probably lawyers are discussing a case or determining policy—they are in a slight friendly disagreement.

2. The two lawyers have been educated in different environments —therefore their thinking on how to handle the case is different, that is why they are in disagreement.

3. The man who is talking is the one who feels the most strongly, his point of view is probably the morally better one.

B-2 1. Two heads of a firm (business) are talking. The older seems to be giving advice to the younger man.

2. Some kind of problem is on the younger man's mind and he needs some older person to give him advice.

3. Some business deal is not going smoothly.

4. They will talk the situation over and reach some kind of agreement and then everything will be okay.

B-3 1. There are two men standing in a room discussing some subject about which they do not both agree. One is trying to emphasize a particular point.

2. The men have probably talked this situation over with others and are now discussing it between themselves.

3. The man listening does not seem to want to give in to the man making the demand but is willing to listen to reason. The man asking the question must be making an urgent demand.

4. They will probably argue back and forth for a while but the man listening will not give in at this time.

B-4 1. The young man is receiving a present which he doesn't think he deserves.

2. The young man has always wanted this.

3. The young man is thinking that how awful he has been, and now is being treated as though he was a hero.

4. The young man will confess what he has done, at first the old man will be shocked, but later will understand.

B-5 1. It's a story of a lawyer and his client; there has been a misunderstanding of a certain business deal which seems to have perturbed the client and the lawyer is trying to explain.

2. The client has lost a considerable amount of property in a downtown business area and feels the lawyer should do something of this (the time seems to be in early 1900).

3. The client wants the lawyer to sue the firm to which he lost his property because he feels that he has unrightly lost it.

4. The lawyer will seek to put his influence into work but is trying to explain that it will be worthless to try.

B–6　　1. A Father and son, both owners of large business are talking together.

2. The business hasn't been doing very well. The father is pointing out the faults and suggesting remedial procedures. The son is reflecting.

3. The son is evaluating the suggestions offered by the father. The father believes his suggestions are right and wants them adopted.

4. Together they will concur on a common course to take. The effect will be a remedy to the existing state of affairs.

B–7　　1. The younger man has made a mistake in business dealings and is being given a lecture by the older man who is his employer.

3. The older man wants the younger man to do something to correct his mistakes and the younger man is being sulky about it.

4. The younger man will be convinced that he should do as he is advised.

B–8　　1. There are two people, a father and son. The father wants to make a gift of something that has been in the family for a long time.

2. The object has been passed down from generation to generation and it is the son's turn to keep it until he has a son old enough to keep it.

3. The son is thinking about the value and the father is thinking about the past history of the object. The father wants the son to take it.

4. The son will accept the object and keep it until he has a son old enough to keep it.

B–9　　1. A man is showing another man an object in his hand. The persons are probably public officials, and one individual is threatening to expose the other with the damaging evidence in his hand.

2. The man has been in corrupt politics and the other man is trying to expose him, perhaps for blackmail.

3. The man without the evidence is wondering what to do. Whether he should bump him off, or pay the blackmail.

4. The corrupt man will pay the blackmail money, and he will stay in politics.

B–10　　1. There seems to be an oral test given. An old man seems to be quizzing a younger man. An old man and a young man are present.

2. Probably some course in which an oral exam is given.

3. The younger man probably doesn't know the answer and the older man wants an answer.

4. The younger man will probably flunk the exam and he then might be asked to drop out of school.

B-11   1. These four men are having a little card party. They are all bankers and have the afternoon off so they decided to play some cards. They have finished playing and now are talking.

2. It is a miserable day outside and the fellows can't play any golf. They wanted relaxation so decided on cards.

3. The four men are discussing the stock exchange and how the stocks have been fluctuating. They are remembering the old depression of the 1930's.

4. The time will pass—wives will start calling their spouses home for dinner. Their party will be ended.

B-12   1. A group of mediocre politicians who are discussing their political beliefs and who will win the coming elections.

2. The year is a national election year and the candidates have all come out with their campaign speeches.

3. The speaker is talking in behalf of his candidate and he wants to convince the others of the strength of his candidate but is lacking.

4. From the looks of the situation, two of the group are interested in what the speaker is saying yet are seeming disgusted and has his own political thoughts that are opposed to those of the speaker.

B-13   1. A discussion of current events is being held by 4 men who have known each other for some time.

2. They have just finished Sunday dinner, and their wives are washing dishes in the kitchen.

3. One of the men is trying to put across his point and the others are listening with reserved skepticism.

4. The discussion will break up with each participant holding the views he started with.

B-14   1. People look like business men. One has stumbled on an idea and is telling the rest about it. They seem enthused.

2. These four men have worked together, and had been searching for a particular idea. Their success may depend on outcome.

3. The fellow is trying to convince the others about it. He wants them to invest their money in it. He has to capture their enthusiasm.

4. He probably will succeed. The others seem eager enough, and want something good.

B-15   1. A group of men who have known each other for a long time are discussing politics.

2. They have known each other for a long time and feel free to express their opinions.

3. Three men are thinking about the views of the fourth man. They want to decide how they should vote or convince others to vote the same as they will.

4. They will finish the discussion and no one may change his

mind. They will go to the polls and vote as they were going to before the talk.

B-16   1. Four men are discussing a business arrangement. They are all probably businessmen.

2. They have probably finished dinner and are trying to reach some conclusion as to a possible solution to a business or world problem.

3. One man is doing the talking and one other man is agreeing with him because of the smile on his face. The other standing is thinking—he doesn't know whether to accept the proposition or not. The other has his back towards us.

4. They may reach a decision or they may not, depending on the complexity of situation. They may all decide to have a drink and be done with it.

B-17   1. The scene is a party at someone's home. The party is a mixed one and the males have retired to a corner to talk "on the sly" and perhaps tell a few jokes.

2. Invitations by the host toward some of his married friends have prompted the couples to attend this party. It is a casual one of friends, not a large extravaganza put on for a great celebration. Just a little get together.

3. The man squatting (or sitting on a chair, I've forgotten which) is telling a joke and the other three men are waiting for the punch line so they can laugh.

4. The man telling the joke will eventually finish it and the other men will laugh. They will then resume talking, tell more jokes, or perhaps join their wives.

B-18   1. Four men are grouped around together and one is at this time telling a probably not too serious story to the others. The others are very interested in what he has to say.

2. The men have probably been telling each other stories for some time now, each one telling one as he thinks of it.

3. The man telling the story is thinking of the incident he is talking about. The others are, as well as listening to him, thinking of a story to tell next.

4. They will probably go on for some time like this with the subject matter and type of stories constantly changing.

B-19   1. Three men probably professors, are listening to another professor give his opinion about the subject.

2. Probably some problem about a concept or principle. Maybe they are talking about school affairs.

3. The three men think this man is an authority on the subject. An answer or explanation is wanted by the three men from the man with the pipe.

4. They will probably come to a conclusion. Some drastic measure might be taken to remedy the bad situation.

B–20   1. There are four persons, probably all from the same firm. One has just come back from a vacation and is explaining his vacation to the individuals present.

2. The individual went on a vacation, and is now telling them about it.

3. The men listening are wondering about the man's vacation. They wonder if his fish really was that big, the story teller is wondering if he is getting his story over. That is what the story teller wants. The others want him to finish the story.

4. The story teller will finish his story, and the men will go back to work.

B–21   1. The person in the striped suit is attempting to explain a point to the other person. He is square because of his striped suit. He looks like a student running for S.G.C.* [Ed. note: * Student Gov't. Council].

2. The talking fellow probably wants to be popular and has failed to do so and/or wants to be a big man on campus.

3. The fellow in the ugly suit is telling the other one about his qualifications and about the reforms he will incite.

4. He won't get elected because he is wearing that ugly suit. He will become bitter and never make a happy family man.

B–22   1. Two average people have met on the diag. and have become embroiled in a discussion of a certain subject.

2. The two people happened to meet on the diag., and probably disagreeing in a previous discussion are continuing that disagreement.

3. One doesn't agree with the other. Both want the other to be impressed by their side of the argument.

4. The discussion will continue with little or no results and the two will continue on their way largely unsatisfied.

B–23   1. The one in the pin-striped suit is campaigning for an office of his senior college class, probably vice-president. The other, because he once knew him has to listen.

2. The pin-striped campaigner has gone through four years of college without accomplishing any more than a 2.5 average and thinks he should do something for the school and himself.

3. One listening dislikes his policies. They both secretly think he will lose the election.

4. He will lose. After this he will give up any attempts to do anything but study and he will end up with a 3.2 on his final grades.

B–24   1. 2 college students are discussing a particular course, probably a law school.

2. The man talking is the older, and he has known the other individual since his freshman days.

3. Man talking feels he is a great sage, giving advice about a course he has taken, other man is just taking course. He wants info. about it, but feels that his friend is a trifle pedantic.

4. Advice will be taken with a grain of salt. Both men will go their own way without much regard for the conversation.

B–25   1. There is a chance meeting between an instructor and a student who is asking him about a problem he doesn't know how to solve.

2. The student was in the instructor's class but they have chanced to meet outside of the school and the child wishes some help with a problem given in the class.

3. The pupil is wanting help or explanation of the problem and the instructor is helping him and explaining the problem to him.

4. The student will understand the problem and they both will be grateful—one for having received help and the other for being able to help and for the interest shown by the student.

B–26   1. These are two students. The time of the year is the end of March. The weather is just starting to be nice. They are discussing the weather and how beautiful it is.

2. The two fellows were in the same high school and graduated together. They are wondering just what the other has been doing since graduation.

3. The fellows are asking each other the familiar question, "Well, how are you doing this semester?"

4. The two boys will depart. One will go home to his studies and the other will go home and decide he would like a nice cold bottle of beer. The weather is warm and it would taste good.

B–27   1. A student is being talked to by another student who is running for office in the campus elections.

2. The first student was on his way to a class when he was accosted by the candidate.

3. The candidate is trying to convince him that he should vote for him. The student is listening politely.

4. The student will excuse himself politely, without committing his vote.

B–28   1. An instructor is explaining something to a student on the U. of M. campus.

2. Probably the student stopped the instructor and asked him a question. The student thinks the instructor is right and the instructor thinks the student wants to learn.

3. The instructor will give an explanation and the student will accept it and then they will go merrily on their own way.

B–29   1. A teacher and a student are talking. The teacher is telling the student about his past grades, and what the exam will be like.

2. The student's failing grades made him wonder what the exam was going to be like, and whether he still had a chance to pass.

3. The student is thinking that he still might pass. The teacher is thinking that he will fail. The student wants to pass, and the teacher undoubtedly wants him to pass also.

4. The student will take the exam and fail. He will take the course over again next semester.

B–30   1. The scene: a college campus. The person left is a student, the other an instructor. The pupil has met this teacher accidentally out of class and has asked him a question relative to the course he teaches.

2. The student has read or heard something relative to the course which he does not understand and wishes to clarify.

3. They are both thinking about the question in mind and the teacher is trying to give an answer to it which the student wants.

4. The teacher will answer the question which may provoke discussion or another question or the student may be satisfied and they will part.

SET C: POWER STORIES

C–1   1. This is a father and son in law combination. He is telling an incident that occurred during the day that he found amusing. He is evidently relating it with great gusto.

2. He had an amusing incident with an employee of his in the office. The picture behind him denotes that he is of wealth. The story concerns a mistake that was not crucial but one which he found interesting.

3. This is just a friendly meeting. The thoughts are of good company and relaxation. There is the time to get away from the hurry of business life.

4. The story will end with a good laugh. The feeling of comradeship will grow between the two and help them to better understand each other in the future.

C–2   1. The people are a man and his father-in-law. The father-in-law is giving his son some advice.

2. Although the son-in-law is a wealthy man, he has somehow become involved in a shady transition in business. He has come to the father-in-law for help.

3. The elder gentleman, also a well-to-do businessman, is trying to straighten out the problem confronting his son-in-law. He is reading from a book which contains sound philosophical thought.

4. The son-in-law will take the advice of the father-in-law and face the issue squarely. Everything will turn out well.

C–3   1. The first man is a lawyer and his friend with a watch in his hand is a business man. They are talking about the value of time.

2. The lawyer has been telling his friend that there is plenty of time for everything and his friend is disagreeing.

3. The lawyer is thinking of an answer to his friend's lecture on the value of time and while still not convinced is being swayed.

4. The lawyer will be swayed by his friend's arguments and will

see his viewpoint that time is valuable and there isn't time for everything.

C–4 1. The two people are law partners. The one man is slightly older than the other. He is advising the other man on a law case in his office.

2. The two men have been handling the law case. The one man isn't quite sure about a legal point, so asks the advice of the other.

3. The younger looking man asks advice from the slightly older one on the law case. He is uncertain about a point.

4. The point will be fully discussed, and the younger man will handle the law case accordingly.

C–5 1. The people in this picture are college officials. The older man on the right is a professor, and the man by the window is the president or an administrator. They are discussing a problem.

2. Something has happened that displeased the professor.

3. The administrator does not agree with the professor's point of view. The professor is trying to convince the administrator.

4. Probably the professor will not achieve his goal. He will not get what he wants.

C–6 1. Two men, probably friends, or business associates are talking. The one is trying to sell or convince the other about the object in his hand.

2. The meeting had been previously arranged. The one man was not particularly interested but the other is trying to convince him.

3. Man #1 wants to convince man #2 with regards to the object in his hand.

4. Man #1 will accomplish whatever it is he is trying to sell or convince to man #2. Man #1 will not like it.

C–7 1. It looks like there is a discussion over what is being held in the one gentleman's hand. I think they look like a couple of aristocrats.

2. There was some difficulty between the two of them of what should be the use of the article or of who should be the owner.

3. The one gentleman wants the other's opinion on the matter.

4. They will eventually come to some solution as to its use or owner.

C–8 1. Two elderly gentlemen are discussing something which is being measured in time—since the wristwatch in one gentleman's hand—perhaps one is rehearsing a speech.

2. Probably there has been some thought preparation by the gentleman who is doing the talking.

3. The speech is being carefully explained to the listener who is judging it for effectiveness. Their idea is probably to make it most effective in the limited time that is provided.

4. No doubt they will together arrive at what they think can best be put across in the limited time.

C-9   1. There are three men in the picture (you can't see one). It looks as though the man by the window is in trouble. The old visible man looks like a lawyer. It seems as though they are trying to get him out of trouble or solve a problem.

2. It looks as though the man by the window has done something like a crime, etc. or that he has a serious problem that the older man are advising him on.

3. The man by the window looks like he is not in complete agreement. The man with the book seems to think he is right. The man's hands visible seems to make one think of a father etc. who is worried about young man.

4. Who knows?

C-10   1. These two persons are my uncle Grover Jackson and the Firth of Forth. This object that Grover is holding is the secret key to the world of happiness.

2. The Firth of Forth, who is an imaginative thinker, has believed the wild story that there is such a key. Grover has perhaps pulled the biggest surprise of the year 1806; completely pulling the wool over the eyes of the Firth.

3. The Firth of Forth has suddenly realized his serious blunder and position. He sees that Grover has played him for a complete fool. What can he do now?

4. The Firth of Forth finally hits upon a solution. He thanks Grover for his sincerity and tells him he is writing a book concerning happiness. He was trying to find out what the reaction to such a key would be. Grover now feels rather foolish, and wishes him luck on the book.

C-11   1. The seated gentleman is telling a rather unpleasant experience of his past. He is relatively clear about it—smoking a pipe—yet quite emphatic in stating what he believes. The listeners are very attentive.

2. Apparently what the story is about was interesting enough to compel the listeners to come over and stand calmly while listening. They are quite concerned.

3. The seated speaker is probably carefully thinking out the story. The other gentlemen are listening for the complete story.

4. After all the information has been given it will then be discussed by the group. Some discussion will be reached at to clear the story.

C-12   1. These four men are club members of the same lodge. They are discussing the up and coming club elections.

2. Since the one with a pipe has been a previous officer, he is commenting on the capabilities of the prospective in light of what will be expected of them.

3. The one standing in the rear is rather doubtful as to the qualification of the particular man in question. The one closest to the speaker is bringing out a new point. The man on the couch is taking everything in.

4. Most likely all will finally agree on a capable set of candidates. These men have been friends for years and they each respect the opinions of the others.

C-13   1. These men are business associates who are planning a hunting trip. They are discussing the time of departure. They will go north to hunt birds.

2. They have met and become friends by working together as executives for a large industrial firm. This association forms their only friendships.

3. They are thinking how they will enjoy the trip, but they are also (some of them) somewhat concerned if they can get away because of business conflicts.

4. They will go on the trip. One or at most two won't make it because of business responsibilities.

C-14   1. Here is an informal discussion between 4 teachers about some modern day topic. Something like politics or something to that effect.

2. One of the four men said something which started the discussion. All four men had something to say on the subject so it developed into a full discussion about topic.

3. Each man is thinking something different, but some of their ideas are similar. They want to discuss the subject fully, but no swaying of their opinions is wanted.

4. Nothing will happen except they will have a good discussion and it will end for some other time.

C-15   1. The four men are in one of their homes. They are relaxing in the living room after just finishing eating. Their wives are doing dishes in the kitchen.

2. These four couples know each other quite well. They enjoy each other's company, and frequently do things together. The one couple has invited the other three to their house.

3. The men are not thinking of anything in particular. They are just relaxing and smoking after enjoying a good big dinner.

4. The evening will continue in a friendly, enjoyable mood. After the wives finish the dishes, they will discuss their affairs by themselves, as the men are doing.

C-16   1. A meeting of the top nuclear scientists in the world. Dr. Comet, Dr. Hott, Dr. Zilch, and Dr. Hopkins. A new development in the hydrogen bomb; the islands around the last atomic blast have begun to sink into the ocean.

2. Dr. Hott was originally afraid of such an occurrence. It was fairly obvious that the nuclear blast would start eruptions on nearby islands and cause a sinkage. What about Japan? All the other scientists had disbelieved him.

3. The other scientists are now afraid Dr. Hott was right. They are worried about Japan. It is decided by Dr. Comet, the oldest scientist, to take a trip to Japan to test for tremors.

4. The session has just been closed. Dr. Hott has just said, "I told you so." Dr. Comet has given his last ultimatum, "Stop fighting among ourselves and find a solution to the problem."

C–17   1. A group of business men are talking over plans for something in an informal, though effective manner. The plans could be for a business project, or a weekend fishing trip.
2. The situation is a result of past, pleasant experiences together. They can obviously relax with each other.
3. One man is attempting to gain the approval of his plan or suggestion by the others.
4. He will be successful for they have a friendly spirit towards each other.

C–18   1. They are personal acquaintances, at a social affair at one's home. They are involved in a discussion about world affairs with some difference of opinion or ignorance of the situation.
2. Nothing much has happened in the past except arrangements, invitations, etc. to the guests to the host's house.
3. Looks like one who has some definite opinions about some world affair is expounding on them.
4. Probably the net result will be a little more information gained by the others about some situation.

C–19   1. This is a friendly discussion of men on the best ways to handle the economic situation in America. They are neighborhood men.
2. These men are neighbors and meet often informally to talk and have bull sessions.
3. The men are considering the man who is speaking's ideas on foreign markets and are about to make their own contributions to the discussion.
4. Nothing will be decided finally, but all will express opinions and have a good time.

C–20   1. Tom, Dick, Harry and Bill are meeting each other in a hotel during a convention and are telling dirty stories. They have known each other since college and are catching up on all news and jokes.
2. The convention is to decide the national chairman and these four are all in contention; however Bill has the backing of a big city will probably come out on top tho Harry is also strong.
3. Bill wants the job but Tom knows some scandal that would ruin Bill's chances, he is undecided as to whether or not he should tell but he wants Harry.
4. Harry gets the job over Bill but Tom doesn't talk because Dick has something over him and Dick wants to be Harry's vice chairman.

C–21   1. These two people are teaching fellows in psychology. They are posing.
2. The psych. dept. is conducting a test and the two men are

posing for a picture to be given on an exam testing thought-picture associations under stress.

3. The man on the right is an egoist and feels he is doing just right in his gesture but the man on the left thinks the other man is too artificial.

4. They'll drop the pose and go back to their work, and the candidates will be tested.

C–22   1. Two people are talking on a sidewalk on a college campus. The one on the left is a student most likely, and the one on the right is an instructor.

2. The instructor has apparently failed to put across a point in class, and the student has followed him out, seeking clarification of the point.

3. The instructor is trying to put across some point, and is concentrating on so doing. The student is having difficulty grasping the point.

4. The instructor will be more or less successful in explaining his point, and they will part after not too much discussion, the student and professor both satisfied.

C–23   1. Two campus acquaintances have met each other and are discussing a matter of importance to the university.

2. Much publicity has been given to this controversial question. Each has been aware of this and are set in their opinions.

3. The boy in the suit is the more informed, possibly since he has personally worked with the controversial problem. He is trying to explain the facts as he sees them to his friend.

4. The boys will hold their opinions after the end of the discussion but the one who was least informed (book under arm) will be a little doubtful that he is correct in his theory.

C–24   1. The people are college students. They are walking between classes, and see each other. So, they stop to talk. The one is obviously older and more experienced than the other.

2. The two people have known each other in the past. They come from the same town. The younger one trusts the older one.

3. The older one is trying to explain something to the younger. The younger one is interested in what the older one is saying and listens intently.

4. The discussion will be short, because they are between classes. They will continue to their next class.

C–25   1. Here two students have met in center of campus and are having an argument about some topic they had in class.

2. During their class session the teacher said something and they are now debating it outside of class.

3. Each one thinks he is right and the argument is not swaying either side. Each wants to put his 2 cents worth in.

4. The two will continue their discussion for a while and then will leave each other to go to their corresponding places.

C–26   1. Two friends have just met on one of the campus walks. They are just saying hello and talking over last weekend's party.

2. The party the previous week that they both attended.

3. The thought is that it was a good party and nothing particular is wanted.

4. The two will probably agree to get together with their dates again this weekend for another party.

C–27   1. This is a D—— technician telling a spring graduate what job opportunities are at the company. He tells him of the positions and the advancements he received in five years with them.

2. He graduated, got a job, worked, and is now busy showing graduates how to come to D——. The other is a student, attended 15 years of school before and is ready to graduate.

3. A job is wanted by the student. A good man is wanted by D——. Money is wanted by both of them. Money is on the brain.

4. D—— wins out. The graduate goes to them and in five years returns to the same place for the same metamorphosis.

C–28   1. Jim, the one facing us, is running for J Hop and is trying to convince Joe to vote for him.

2. Jim has been interested in dance organization for many years and now wants to run and so is soliciting votes from all his friends.

3. Jim wants Joe's vote. Joe is analyzing Jim's platform, and stand on a certain issue concerning J Hop.

4. Joe will be convinced by Jim's frank manner and will vote for Jim for J Hop.

C–29   1. Don Smith of the Trojans Football Team is trying to talk Jerry Jones into going out for football. Jerry is afraid of physical contact because of his leg, which had been afflicted with polio.

2. Jerry had been afraid that his friends would not accept him back into the "gang" because of his long illness. Mr. Jones had asked Jerry's idol, Don Smith, to persuade him to participate in sports.

3. Jerry still feels "left out" and is afraid of himself. Don reassures him that he has a fine physique and a good mind to play quarterback on the hometown team.

4. Jerry decides to give it a whirl. The other fellows on the team give him every break they can. He makes second string quarterback on the team. Although he did not get to play much, Jerry has finally found himself and feels a part of the "gang."

C–30   1. The man in the suit is looking for a certain house and he is asking the student where the fraternity house is located.

2. The man is a member of the fraternity from another chapter who has come down for the weekend for a big party and sports event (his girl is waiting in a car).

3. The fraternity man is wondering why the student doesn't know the information right off—he thinks everyone should know where it is located.

4. The fraternity man will not find the information here and will go to a drug store down the street where he will find out and get to the house.

SET D: POWER STORIES

D–1   1. The scene is set in the office of a man who is the head or important in some business. The man at the right is this man. He is a superior of the office worker who is at the left as is indicated by his manner and appearance.

2. The man at the left, the office worker has performed his duties poorly and has been called in to answer to his superior.

3. The head man, the boss, is demanding answers for the poor work. He demands a better standard of work from his employee who looks dejected.

4. He threatens that if a better standard of work is not forthcoming, then he will have no other alternative than to fire his employee! This visibly affects the employee.

D–2   1. One person is explaining something to another one is older and probably his father. Telling him what he should do.

2. Something has taken place.

3. The older man is asking it of the younger man to do it, to take over, to continue.

4. The son will do it and try to carry out the old mans wishes. He will succeed.

D–3   1. The younger is over a barrel. The old man has some evidence on him that will put him in hot soup. He holding an object in his hand which is the evidence.

2. The young man has led a restless life, probably got involved with a woman. The old man is holding the proof.

3. The old man is thinking of not taking the young man into the business. The young fellow seems pretty peeved and mad.

4. The young man will probably turn on the old fellow, maybe kill him. He has the young man in quite a spot.

D–4   1. Two men talking about the object in the man on the right's hand. The two people look well to do. I can't make the object out.

2. Anything may have led up to it.

3. One man (the one holding the object) is trying to interest the second man in it and he is contemplating.

D–5   1. Two persons are discussing something. It appears to me as if one man whom I shall call Sid is talking to another man (Sam) about a speech. He seems to be timing it.

2. It appears that there has been an argument about something.

3. Sid seems to want Sam to take the watch.

4. Nothing that I can see.

D–6   1. There are lawyers and clients discussing a case they are about to defend and prosecute respectively.

2. The lawyers have worked on cases together in the past and have become friends. The case at present has brought them together.

3. One lawyer is stressing his case while the other listens thoughtfully.

4. The lawyer has told his client that he has a good chance but must convey to him all the important factors.

D-7   1. A rather bald man who is wearing glasses is showing another man who also wears glasses but has a busht crop, some undistinguishable object. He holds something, maybe a book, in his left hand.

2. Probably the "visitor" has asked to "host" if he might see the particular object discussed.

3. Both men appear happy. Perhaps the before mentioned object is being handed from the partly bald man to his visitor.

4. The "donor" will give the other man the object, the other man will look at it, and then give it back.

D-8   1. It is a meeting in the executive's office of a big firm. The firm is G—— corporation and the 1 man is trying to convince Herbert Wilson, the president, of a new production method.

2. Nothing has led up to the situation with the exception of a new idea that was submitted by an employee.

3. The idea is being thought for its soundness. Improve on the assembly is wanted by the executives.

4. The method will be tested for a short period. It will be successful.

D-9   1. There is a clergyman and a business executive in the executives office. The executive is receiving spiritual guidance from the clergyman.

2. The executive has not received the position of advancement he thought he was entitled to. He has become very skeptical.

3. The executive is beginning to see some meaning in the clergymans words. The executive of course, is seeking spiritual comfort.

4. The executive will regain his faith in his fellow man and will continue to better himself in the corporation.

D-10   1. The old man is a retiring president of a firm, probably a bank, the young man is the prospective president. The older one is explaining to the younger about executive policy.

2. The old man has reached his pension or retirement age. The younger has advanced from a low position since his college days to the top of the latter.

3. The young man thinks the policy should be modified. The older one wishes the young to continue the present policy.

4. After the old man retires, first gradual and then definite changes in the executive policy will come about.

D-11   1. There is what I would term a good old bull session going on. The gentlemen involved are friends and are either remember the good old days or trying to top each others story of what they had done when they were young.

2. They got together for a few drinks or a card game or maybe both.

3. The thoughts are just the relating of old adventures and the only thing wanted is to top the other guy's story.

4. The session will continue until all the yarns are spun. Nothing particular will be done.

D-12   1. There is a discussion of an interesting topic going on. The persons look like library men.

2. The one seated on the left has background knowledge of his subject, research perhaps. The man standing and leaning over is very interested as the man seated on sofa. The man standing away alone seems like he has also some research or has background on the subject being discussed.

3. The man standing on the rt. alone is jealous—he wants to let other men know he knows something about subject too. The other men seem just interested although man on sofa seems like he wants to get up and move around.

4. There will be a longer discussion—man standing to right will talk and bother others. Man on sofa will get up. Discussion will end.

D-13   1. The persons are four fathers. They are carrying on a discussion which all are vitally interested in.

2. Something has happened to their family or some member in it in a common way to the four situations. Perhaps they are discussing a sports event which their sons are to be involved in.

3. All are discussing the relative merits of their respective interests in the conversation. Each is vitally interested in the other but also interested in his own cause.

4. They will have a good hash on the subject, have a few drinks, laugh it up, then proceed to observe what is about to happen (which they have been discussing.)

D-14   1. The four men belong to the same civic club. They are deciding an important issue, probably whether or not to install more parking meters in town.

2. They met at the request of the General council to render a decision based on good conversational investigation. The town has some meters, but not enough.

3. The committee head, man on left with gavel, has raised disapproval over whether or not they should get a certain amount. He is being heard by the rest.

4. They will hash and re-hash until meter goes out of style or become illegal.

D-15   1. Four men are discussing a new political development. The one on the left is putting across his ideas—the rest are listening. They are probably businessmen.

2. A new change in policy, resulting from a change in government has led to this.

3. The man on the left is against the new policy. The others listen, the one in the back seems opposed to the speaker.

4. The discussion will terminate with nobody's mind being changed. Nothing more than talk will result and the policy no doubt will still be carried out by the gov't.

D-16   1. The group of four men are involved in a political discussion. The men are all related and are at a family "get together."

2. The men have various party beliefs. That is they do not all support the same political party.

3. The man standing next to the fireplace disagrees with the speaker but will not challenge his statement. The man bending over next to the speaker is deeply interested in his statement and will counter it when he is finished.

4. There will be one final agreement among the four men.

D-17   1. The persons are four men who are attending a party and whose wives are, at the moment, in the ladies' room. The man on the left is telling a very interesting story.

2. The four gentlemen arrived at the party earlier with their wives, and their wives just left to get their coats.

3. Nothing is wanted by anybody—the man on the left is telling an interesting and rather serious story, and the other men are very attentive.

4. The man will finish his story, several comments will be made by other men present, and then they will hear their wives' voices and return to them.

D-18   1. Four businessmen are talking.

2. One of them (the one by the fireplace) has called them to his home to discuss the sales force in their small business.

3. One of them feels (the one talking) that more money should be spent on sales personnel to increase activity.

4. The older two will express conservatist views but the group will come around and adopt the plan on a trial basis.

D-19   1. These four men are engaged in a violent but fruitless political argument, which has been raging for some time—they are ordinary middle class Americans.

2. It is election time early November and 2 men are eager Republicans the other 2 liberal democrats. All have followed the campaigns.

3. The man shaking his fist (a Republican) spars with the man standing (a Dem.). He thinks that his opponent is too liberal and in fact crazy in his views toward labor he wants a Republican victory.

4. Regardless of the hours spent in argument no one's views are changed. They go to the polls and vote on the party line.

D-20   1. The man on the right has taken a stand on some problem which all four men are interested in.

2. There has been a problem which all feel is important to judge by their looks. The man on the right feels he has a solution.

3. The one on the right is trying desperately to convince the others. They are trying to turn him down but by this point feel so engrossed in his side that they think maybe he's right.

4. They will defeat his argument.

D-21   1. Joe has just met his professor of psychology and they are discussing problems in the course. Joe is puzzled because he doesn't understand the course scope.

2. Lessons in class have led up to the situations.

3. Joe wants to know when he will get the feeling of learning psychology. So far the course has been not as Joe thought it would be.

4. Joe will continue to try to appreciate the course more. Further lectures will probably bring out interest.

D-22   1. A rather tough individual, probably a football player, is picking on a meek, good-natured "weenie," on the way to classes.

2. The situation is probably that the weenie has done something which annoyed the other.

3. The "tough guy" is typical—just looking for trouble—and he picks on the "weenie" because he knows society will back him up, and anyway, he has nothing to fear from *that* character.

4. Probably no blows will be struck, since the "weenie" is not of the pugilistic cast, and the affair will end—no one being better for having begun.

D-23   1. Graduate student meets undergraduate. Older one is giving advice to the younger. Identify each by type of clothing worn.

2. They probably knew each and while out walking accidently bumped into each other. Chance meeting on spring day.

3. The younger student asks older about vocation, both pursuing the same vocation. The older is only too glad to give advice.

4. The younger will probably go home, tell friends or folks about meeting and ideas. May forget them when better idea comes in view.

D-24   1. This High School student has stopped to talk with his guidance counselor about a future career. This counselor, also the local X company representative, has suggested a career with the X company.

2. In the past, Y company has taken most of the promising students. The teacher is explaining the X company retirement plan as an inducement.

3. The student is thinking, wouldn't it be better for me to go to college? But he is afraid to say. The guidance counselor is controlling the situation.

4. The lad will become lost in a maze of desks and the X guid-

ance counselor will eventually become V. P. in charge of employment.

D–25   1. The minister of a certain church has just stopped a young acquaintance of his and asked him if he will come to church next Sunday.

2. The minister met the young man a few days before and found out that he belonged to no church in town.

3. The minister would like him to join the church someday. The youth is thinking that it's nice that the minister should take such concern.

4. So he goes to the church the following Sunday and finds he likes it very much.

D–26   1. A college adviser or professor has stopped one his boys on campus and is trying to get a point across about the boys work, either that he has to do better or he is explaining some brief phase of work not understood.

2. The boy has made a mistake somewhere either in general conduct or performance in the classroom.

3. The adult wants to help the boy to be helped.

4. The boy will see the light and do what he has to do better or at least fully as well as he can so as not to hurt the professors feelings and to justify his own pride.

D–27   1. Election for school president at college. George Williams out campaigning mingling with the pro of student.

2. George has been ambitious, powerful speaker. His rule for life is not money but power and what it can get him. His previous work in high school showed this.

3. But he is smart he never showed it. He will rise to new heights by trusting people and using them.

4. Yet George will almost do this. Then he will become class president or rise to greater heights. Yet inhibition and moderation will catch up with him and he will choke in the mase of his own power.

D–28   1. Two college students have stopped on the sidewalk to have a chat.

2. They were walking opposite directions and when they met, they stopped and shook hands. Then they began to talk about "how long its been since . . ." and did you see? . . ." etc.

3. They are thinking about the appointments they are nearly late for, and wish to get going.

4. They will stand and talk a while longer just to be sociable and then will part and go their own ways.

D–29   1. An instructor is talking to a student on a college campus.

2. The student is in the instructor's class and so the instructor knows him.

3. The instructor is thinking about something the student has

asked. The student wants to know something and that is why he has asked the question.

4. The instructor will answer the question. The student will find out what he wanted to know.

D–30   1. Two students meet on campus. One, having camera, is presenting a thinking to the other.

2. The, back to camera, student has faith in the other students thinking and has solicited his aid. Probably has had trouble in mutual class and can't seem to right a tipped canoe.

3. The, facing camera, person is trying to aid the other, but meets obstacles in the slowness of the others mind. Both want to be heard and understood.

4. Both will hold some ideas as held before. Bright student will enlighten someday.

SETS E, F, AND G: POWER STORIES

The stories constituting Power Sets E, F, and G were selected from stories in the Achievement and Affiliation Practice Sets. Turn to the Achievement and Affiliation Sections of this Appendix to find these stories. The stories which correspond to E–1—E–30, F–1—F–30 and G–1—G–30 of Power Sets E, F, and G are listed below in parentheses. For example, to find the second story in Set E (E–2) turn to the third story in the Achievement Practice Set A.

The pictures to which these stories were written are described in the Achievement and Affiliation Sections of this Appendix.

Set E		Set F		Set G	
E–1	(Ach A–1)	F–1	(Aff A–1)	G–1	(Aff C–2)
E–2	(Ach A–3)	F–2	(Aff A–2)	G–2	(Aff C–3)
E–3	(Ach B–1)	F–3	(Aff A–4)	G–3	(Aff C–4)
E–4	(Ach B–2)	F–4	(Aff A–5)	G–4	(Aff C–5)
E–5	(Ach B–3)	F–5	(Aff A–6)	G–5	(Aff C–6)
E–6	(Ach B–4)	F–6	(Aff A–7)	G–6	(Aff C–7)
E–7	(Ach B–5)	F–7	(Aff A–8)	G–7	(Aff C–8)
E–8	(Ach C–1)	F–8	(Aff A–9)	G–8	(Aff C–9)
E–9	(Ach C–4)	F–9	(Aff A–10)	G–9	(Aff D–1)
E–10	(Ach C–5)	F–10	(Aff B–1)	G–10	(Aff D–2)
E–11	(Ach C–7)	F–11	(Aff B–3)	G–11	(Aff D–3)
E–12	(Ach C–9)	F–12	(Aff B–4)	G–12	(Aff D–4)
E–13	(Ach D–1)	F–13	(Aff B–5)	G–13	(Aff D–5)
E–14	(Ach D–4)	F–14	(Aff B–6)	G–14	(Aff D–6)
E–15	(Ach A–11)	F–15	(Aff B–7)	G–15	(Aff D–7)
E–16	(Ach A–12)	F–16	(Aff B–9)	G–16	(Aff D–8)
E–17	(Ach A–13)	F–17	(Aff B–10)	G–17	(Aff D–9)
E–18	(Ach A–14)	F–18	(Aff C–1)	G–18	(Aff D–10)

E–19	(Ach A–15)	F–19	(Aff A–23)	G–19	(Aff C–21)
E–20	(Ach A–16)	F–20	(Aff A–24)	G–20	(Aff C–22)
E–21	(Ach B–11)	F–21	(Aff A–25)	G–21	(Aff C–23)
E–22	(Ach B–12)	F–22	(Aff A–26)	G–22	(Aff C–24)
E–23	(Ach C–16)	F–23	(Aff A–27)	G–23	(Aff C–25)
E–24	(Ach C–17)	F–24	(Aff A–28)	G–24	(Aff C–26)
E–25	(Aff A–12)	F–25	(Aff A–29)	G–25	(Aff C–27)
E–26	(Aff A–15)	F–26	(Aff B–22)	G–26	(Aff D–21)
E–27	(Aff B–19)	F–27	(Aff B–23)	G–27	(Aff D–22)
E–28	(Aff C–12)	F–28	(Aff B–24)	G–28	(Aff D–23)
E–29	(Aff C–14)	F–29	(Aff B–25)	G–29	(Aff D–24)
E–30	(Aff D–11)	F–30	(Aff B–30)	G–30	(Aff D–25)

SET A: POWER EXPERT SCORING

The expert's scoring decisions for the 30 stories of Set A are briefly explained below, one category at a time. In general, only instances where a subcategory is scored are discussed. When a decision not to score a subcategory is a difficult one, it is also discussed.

Imagery

A–1   *Pow Im.* Criterion 2. Both men in this story are trying to get something across to each other (trying to explain his position and trying to get his point across). Both these instrumental statements are sufficient to decide to score this story for *Pow Im.* Note that the story could also be scored under Criterion 3. The men are perceived in status hierarchy—executive, junior executive.

A–2   *Pow Im.* Here the only thing which makes the story scorable for *Pow Im* under Criterion 2 is the word "plotting." This is a word from which it would be safe to assume that there are thoughts about controlling the means of influence.

A–3   *Pow Im.* Criterion 1. The man being congratulated on winning the election can be assumed to feel some positive affect in regard to having just won. Inferring a positive affect state like this will be rare. Only when it is clear-cut should you infer it.

A–4   *Pow Im.* Concern about winning an election (worried about the disgrace he will have to face) makes this story scorable under Criterion 1.

A–5   *Pow Im.* Here we have disputes over the control of decision making in a company. First of all, the head officials are arguing over policy. This is sufficient for scoring *Pow Im.* But there are further elaborations which make this a highly loaded story for *Pow Im.* The third paragraph deals with the thoughts of the two men who are oriented around who has control of the means of influence. Criterion 2.

A-6 *U Im.* Although there is some hint of an argument going on between these two people, there are no direct statements of influence *activity*. They are having an argument is not a sufficient statement of activity that can be scored. This assumption is backed up in this story by the elaboration that these men want to reach agreement, which is not the goal of argumentation in a power-related story.

A-7 *U Im.* Imagery has to do with problem solving and waiting for a person. Neither of these are scorable imageries.

A-8 *Pow Im.* There are two different power-related imageries in this story. First of all there is the judge attempting to convince the younger man to run for governor. And then there is the man who actually does run for governor and *wins*. Both of these imageries meet Criterion 2.

A-9 *U Im.* Soliciting advice is not scored. Otherwise this is an affiliation-related story.

A-10 *Pow Im.* Here there is direct evidence of influence activity although there is no direct statement of influence activity: "is slowly being convinced of the validity of the latter's argument. . . ." Hence this will be scored under Criterion 2.

A-11 *U Im.* Problem-solving behavior with no mention of influence attempts or status differentiation. Hence not scored for *Pow Im.*

A-12 *Pow Im.* The man exploding with theories against the other man is the imagery that is the basis for scoring this story under Criterion 2.

A-13 *Pow Im.* Party *leaders* thinking of ways to *convince* the members of the party. The role differentiation and the concern about influencing others are the two reasons for scoring this story.

A-14 *Pow Im.* Criterion 2. "The seated man will get his point across to the others" is the only statement in this story which makes this story scorable.

A-15 *Pow Im.* Criterion 1. "They want to put on a good program so that they will be able to do the job again." This statement of wanting a job which controls decision making makes this story scorable for *Pow Im.*

A-16 *U Im.* Convivial activity; nothing there to score for power concerns.

A-17 *U Im.* Discussion of ideas with no influence behavior. Not scored.

A-18 *Pow Im.* "Trying emphatically to make a point" and "trying to get something across" are both instrumental activities that allow this story to be scored under Criterion 2.

A-19 *U Im.* Although there is some statement about the role differentiation of authorities and members of the community, the story should not be scored on that basis because there is no direct interaction of the two status positions. Presenting a solution is not enough to have this scorable for Power Imagery. If the man was specifically trying to put his solution across to the others, then this story would be scored.

A–20   *Pow Im.* The dissenter being *won over* makes this story relevant to power and hence scorable under Criterion 2. This is the only power reference in the story.

A–21   *Pow Im.* Again statements of trying to convince another makes this story clearly scorable for *Pow Im.*

A–22   *U Im.* Although there is some teaching imagery in this story (trying to explain it to him), the explanation was solicited. Hence, do not score.

A–23   *Pow Im.* A candidate for office attempting to influence a voter. Scorable under Criterion 2.

A–24   *U Im.* Although there are a number of statements about explaining the basis of the campaign of a candidate for office, there are no direct statements of trying to get points across or trying to convince others. So this story should not be scored.

A–25   *Pow Im.* Again mere mention of an argument would not have made this story scorable. What does, is that one student wants to convince the other.

A–26   *Pow Im.* Wishing to convince, trying to convince: both are direct statements in this story allowing the scorer to code *Pow Im* under Criterion 1 or 2.

A–27   *Pow Im.* Criterion 3. The teacher-student relationship used to enforce regulation.

A–28   *U Im.* Casual talk; no power-related interaction. Not scored.

A–29   *Pow Im.* "Trying to express an important point" by itself would not be sufficient to allow this story to be scored. However when the *S* introduces the statement that "Man #1 believes he is convincing man #2," then we have some assurance that it is an influence attempt, and then the story can be scored under Criterion 2.

A–30   *Pow Im.* Although the goal of getting the other man into the fraternity can be thought of as the goal state of the influence behavior in the imagery of this story, there is enough concern about mentioning the pressure applied to the student that this story should still be scored for *Pow Im.*

Need

A–1   *No N.*   A–2   *No N.*

A–3   *No N.*

A–4   *No N*. The man wants the reverend to give him sympathy. This need statement is irrelevant to the power concern.

A–5   *No N*.

A–8   *No N*. "Planned to run for position of governor" is a statement of activity rather than need.

A–10   *No N*.   A–12   *No N*.

A–13   *No N*.   A–14   *No N*.

A–15   *N*. "They *want* to put on a good program so that they will be able to do the job again." Without the last part of the sentence, which clarifies the goal of the need, this statement would not have been scored. With the statement, it will be scored.

A–18   *No N*.   A–20   *No N*.

A–21   *No N*.

A–23   *No N*. "Real friendly when they want something" is a phrase that should not be scored for Need. It is expressed as the thought of someone else and hence should not be scored.

A–25   *N*. "*Wishes to* convince the other fellow that the former is correct . . ."

A–26   *N*. "The man talking *wants to* convince the other."

A–27   *N*. "*Anxious* to see that signs are obeyed."

A–29   *No N*.   A–30   *No N*.

Instrumental Activity

A–1   *I?*. "trying to explain his position to the younger, junior executive. This jr. executive is trying to get his point over." The first act is successful; the second, unsuccessful. Therefore, the scoring is a compromise *I?*.

A–2   *I?*. "plotting for their own gain": *I?* because it is not clear how this works out.

A–3   *I+*. "They are discussing aspects of the job to be done." This discussion has to do with how best to carry out the office, in this case a position of control, a political office. Since he is successful, *I+* is scored.

A–4   *No I*. There are no statements of power-related instrumental activity here.

A–5   *I?*. "are arguing . . ." One wins; one loses, and so this story is scored *I?*.

A–8   *I+*. "is trying to convince the younger" and such are all *I+*.

A–10   *No I*. Although "is slowly being convinced of the validity of the latter's argument" is a statement implying instrumental activity, there is no direct statement in the story. The reason for not scoring I here is not because of the passive voice. If the story read "is slowly convinced by the latter," the story would be scored. This is a subtle distinction.

A–12 $I-$. "is about to explode with his own theories" is the I scored here. Note that this statement is future oriented. But that does not mean it should not be scored.

A–13 $I+$. "They are thinking of ways to convince the rest of the party" is the most obvious Instrumental Activity in this story.

A–14 $I+$. "is trying to tell the other three men something important" and "will get his point across to the others" are statements that enable the scorer to code $I+$.

A–15 $I?$. "They are thinking of various types of recreation that would be beneficial to all their members." This is activity that is engaged in for gaining control of the affairs of the club. Not an obvious I.

A–18 $I-$. "is trying emphatically to make a point . . ."

A–20 $I+$. "The single dissenter will be won over by his three parental friends. . . ."

A–21 $I?$. "trying to convince the other," with dubious results.

A–23 $I-$. "telling how great he is and that he is the man to vote for . . ."

A–25 $I?$. "are engaged in a political argument . . ." Outward agreement but inward reservations make this code $I?$.

A–26 $I-$. "trying to convince the other man . . ."

A–27 $I-$. "explaining the rationale behind the sign . . ."

A–29 $I-$. "is trying to express an important point . . ."

A–30 $I-$. "trying to talk undecided freshman into rushing" and "is using high pressure" are statements which allow this story to be scored for I. The activity is unsuccessful, and hence scored $I-$.

Goal Anticipation

A–1 *No Ga.*   A–2   *No Ga.*

A–3 *No Ga.*

A–4 $Ga-$. "is worried about the disgrace he will have to face . . ."

A–5 $Ga+$. "Young one is sure he can do things better." Here the man is anticipating the control he could exert.

A–8 *No Ga.*   A–10 *No Ga.*

A–12 *No Ga.* "Man standing is about to explode with own theories" should not be scored. If it were prefaced by "The man is thinking he will explode," then it would be in the *Ga* form that is scorable.

A–13   *No Ga.*   A–14   *No Ga.*

A–15   *No Ga.*   A–18   *No Ga.*

A–20   *No Ga.*   A–21   *No Ga.*

A–23   *No Ga.*   A–25   *No Ga.*

A–26   *No Ga.* "Thinking about how he could have convinced the other" should not be scored. It is a statement of regret over past action, reminiscence, which is not scored under *Ga*. Only score anticipations of future events.

A–27   *No Ga.*

A–29   *Ga+.* Man #1 believes he is convincing man #2.

A–30   *No Ga.*

Blocks

A–1   *No Block.* The elaboration of the two sides in the argument is not sufficient for scoring *Bw*.

A–2   *No Block.*   A–3   *No Block.*

A–4   *No Block.*

A–5   *No Block.* "Friction will arise" is just an elaboration of the beginning arguing situation; nothing new added, hence not scorable.

A–8   *Bw.* "His wife became ill." This is a Block to his ongoing interest in attaining a political position.

Bp. "The young man is now hesitant" is scored for *Bp*. The hesitancy is a Block to his political career. You might also look at this as a *Bw* to the man trying to convince him to run. Since the same imagery cannot be used to score both categories, and since *Bw* was scored above, score this phrase *Bp*.

A–10   *No Block.*   A–12   *No Block.*

A–13   *No Block.*   A–14   *No Block.*

A–15   *No Block.*

A–18   *Bw.* "his plans have been continually sidetracked" is a Block to the man's desire for influence.

A–20   *No Block.*

A–21   *Bp.* This is a very arbitrary code. The imagery "the candidate is frankly wondering whether if it's worth it with this guy" can be coded either as a *Ga—* or a *Bp*. It has both the elements of Goal Anticipation (a doubtful one, *Ga—*) and of a Block to the ongoing influence behavior. There is no rationale for considering it one or the other predominantly. *De gustibus*. But don't score both in a case like this.

A–23   *No Block.*   A–25   *No Block.*

A–26 *Bw.* "The man being talked to wants to leave." This need interferes with the main character's influence attempts. Hence it is scored *Bw.* Note that this statement is over and above the situation of a man resisting influence.

A–27 *No Block.*   A–29 *No Block.*

A–30 *No Block.*

Affective States

A–1 *No G.*   A–2 *No G.*

A–3 *G+.* "Congratulatory mood" is not a specific statement of affect, but the affect associated with this statement is so clear that it should be scored.

A–4 *No G.*   A–5 *No G.*

A–8 *No G.*   A–10 *No G.*

A–12 *No G.*   A–13 *No G.*

A–14 *No G.*   A–15 *No G.*

A–18 *No G.*   A–20 *No G.*

A–21 *No G.*

A–23 *No G.* "Antagonistic" is not scored. The affect can be as a result of not wanting to be influenced, but since one can offer other hypotheses, don't score it.

A–25 *No G.*   A–26 *No G.*

A–27 *No G.*

A–29 *G+.* Man #1 will have been pleased that he talked to #2.

A–30 *No G.*

Thema

A–1 *Th.* No competing thematic material.

A–2 *No Th.* There are a number of references to a vague discouragement, which might have little to do with power, hence not scored.

A–3 *No Th.* So much of this story can be interpreted as an achievement theme running parallel with the power concern, that the scorer is advised not to score it. If there are shades of meaning to the imagery that is scored, and yet the coder has decided to score for *Pow Im,* then show the judgment of ambiguity for the story in general by not scoring Thema.

A–4 *No Th.*

A–5 *Th.* The whole story has to do with a struggle for power.

A–8 *Th.* Both characters have Power Imagery present in their concerns. The sidetrack (wife's illness) is introduced in the context of the Power Imagery.

A–10   *No Th.*

A–12   *Th.* All interactions are within the power imagery context.

A–13   *Th.* No competing themes.

A–14   *No Th.* There is too much emphasis in this story on the effect of the content of what is being put across for this story to be scored for Thema.

A–15   *No Th.*

A–18   *Th.* Again all the interactions have to do with the influence theme.

A–20   *No Th.*

A–21   *Th.* All about someone trying to convince another.

A–23   *Th.* The last paragraph is the only contradictory thematic material to this power concern—hostility. And yet this is a reaction to an influence attempt, and so you would still be safe in scoring Thema.

A–25   *Th.* All about an argument and the concerns about winning a point.

A–26   *Th.* All about an argument and the concerns about winning a point.

A–27   *No Th.* Thema is not scored because of the vague statement of the power concern to begin with.

A–29   *Th.* Again all the interactions have to do with the influence theme.

A–30   *No Th.* The emphasis on the desires of the person being influenced takes this story out of the Thema category.

SET B: POWER EXPERT SCORING

The expert scoring below may be read as follows: first, the expert's scoring decisions are briefly explained; second, the total score is given; and third in parentheses, is the rank of that story (with the highest score of the set given a rank of 1 and the lowest score a rank of 30). In general, only instances where a subcategory is scored are discussed. When a decision not to score a subcategory is a difficult one, it is also discussed.

B–1   *U Im.* Although there is some mention of an argument going on, nowhere in the story is there a statement that would indicate that one of the parties is trying to convince the other. There is no direct statement of instrumental activity to meet Criterion 2. 0   (23)

B–2   *U Im.* Solicited advice (the young man had a problem on his mind); not scored. 0   (23)

B–3   *Pow Im.* Criterion 2. There are many statements in this story which fulfill this criterion: (1) "trying to emphasize a particular point," (2) "man making the demand," (3) "making an urgent demand."

I?. All those listed above are scorable for Instrumental Activity. The final sentence indicates that the outcome of the activity is in doubt.

Need. "Does not seem to want to give in . . ."

No Bw. The foregoing Need statement might also be interpreted as a block to the goal of the other man. But since it does not necessarily interfere with the ongoing activity directly, it is not scored.

Th. No other theme in evidence. 4 (3.5)

B–4 *U Im.* A guilt-over-achievement story; no indication of power concern. 0 (23)

B–5 *Pow Im.* This story is scored just for the last sentence. "Seek to put his influence into work" meets Criterion 2.

I?. The above is also scored for *I*. 2 (14)

B–6 *Pow Im.* Criterion 2. Unsolicited advice from the father to the son.

Need. "the father believes his suggestions are right and *wants them adopted.*"

I+. "is pointing out faults and remedial procedures . . ." Concurrence suggests a positive outcome to the advice giving. 3 (9)

B–7 *Pow Im.* Criterion 3. Boss-employee relationship explicitly stated and elaborated upon.

No Need. "The older man wants the younger man to do something to correct his mistakes. . . ." This is *not* scored since it is not a statement of an influence goal. If the statement read "The older man wants to be able to get the younger man to do something," then it would be scored for Need.

I+. "is being given a lecture by the older man" is scored for *I*, although it is in the passive voice. The employer is carrying out his role in the power domain.

Bw. The younger man is being sulky about it.

Th. The employer-employee relationship is the mainspring of the imagery in the story. No other concerns mentioned in the story. 4 (3.5)

B–8 *U Im.* Giving a gift; no mention of influence behavior. 0 (23)

B–9 *Pow Im.* Criterion 2: the man is trying to expose the other; an attempt to control the means of influence. Although blackmail is listed as a goal, this is not an exclusive structuring of the story.

I+. "is trying to expose him . . ." This activity works, so it is scored plus.

Th. You might be hesitant in scoring Thema because of the blackmail reference, but actually this story is completely structured in the power relationship, and the blackmail motif can be incorporated into it. 3 (9)

B–10 *U Im.* Testing situation is one that is not scorable under Criterion 2. 0 (23)

B–11 *U Im.* Affiliative story; no indication of power concerns. 0 (23)

B–12 *Pow Im.* "He wants to convince the others." Criterion 1.

Need. Above statement is also scored for Need.

I?. "is talking in behalf of his candidate . . ."

No Bw. The whole last statement in the story is not a disruption of the ongoing influence attempt. It is an elaboration of the need to convince. Hence, not scored for *Bw.*

No G. "are seeming disgusted" is an affective statement, but not in regard to lack of control of the means of influence. So this too is not scored.

No Th. Too much emphasis on the political race for this story to be scored for Thema. 3 (9)

B–13 *Pow Im.* "is trying to put across his point . . ." Scorable, Criterion 2.

I—. The above statement is what is scored for *I,* and since it fails, it is scored *I—.*

Bw. "the others are listening with reserved skepticism" is scored for *Bw.*

No Th. The affiliative activity in the story is a competing theme which makes this story not scorable for Thema. 3 (9)

B–14 *Pow Im.* "The fellow is trying to convince the others about it." Clearly meets Criterion 2.

I?. The above statement works as an instrumental act. The outcome is doubtful: "He probably will succeed."

No Need. "He wants them to invest their money. He has to capture their enthusiasm." Neither of these statements are scored for Need. The first one explains the object of the influence, which should not be scored. If it read "He wants to try to convince them to invest their money," it would be scored. The second explains a need that the character has, but it is not a direct statement from *his* point of view. Scorable would be the statement "He wants to capture their enthusiasm." 2 (14)

B–15 *Pow Im.* "they want to decide how they should . . . convince others." This statement meets the scoring demands of Criterion 1.

Need. The above statement is also scored for Need.

I—. "thinking about the views of the fourth man" is a statement of *I*, a thinking through for means of attempting to control. "vote as they were going to before their talk" makes this scored *I—.*

Th. No interfering themes in this story. 4 (3.5)

B–16 *U Im.* No mention of someone directly trying to put across a view. The whole story is a merely problem-solving situation. 0 (23)

B–17 *U Im.* Camaraderie; no power mentioned 0 (23)

B–18 *U Im.* Storytelling without any mention of trying to put across the point. 0 (23)

B–19 *U Im.* Giving an opinion is not enough to warrant scoring for *Pow Im.* There must be clear indication that the person giving the opinion wants another to adopt his point of view. And, although there is some mention of the man being an authority on the subject, this is not a clear case of a status-role situation. 0 (23)

B–20 *Pow Im.* The only Power Imagery in this predominantly affiliative story is the one reference to the fact that the storyteller wants to get his story across: concern over control of the means of influence (Criterion 1).

Need. "wondering if he is getting his story across. That is what the storyteller wants."

No I. "is explaining his vacation" is not specific enough to the Instrumental Activity of getting a story across to warrant scoring this story for Instrumental Activity.

Ga—. "is wondering whether he is getting his story across . . ."

No Th. Too much emphasis on the interests of the other people in this story to score Thema. 3 (9)

B–21 *Pow Im.* "attempting to explain a point . . ." Criterion 2. "wants to be a big man on campus . . ." Criterion 1. This is a more ambiguous basis for scoring. There are a number of goal satisfactions in being a BMOC, but if this were the only Power Imagery mentioned, it still would be scorable. There are enough power overtones to the BMOC concept to warrant scoring it.

Need "wants to be a big man on campus . . ."

I—. "is attempting to explain a point to the other person . . . is telling the other about his qualifications and about the reforms he will incite . . ." Both of these statements are scorable as instrumental acts. Since they fail, *I—* is scored.

Bp. "He is wearing that ugly suit," a Block to his election according to the story writer.

No Th. No other themes mentioned, but there are enough other interpretations present in the story to keep from scoring *Th.*

That is, the popularity theme, a happy-family-man theme, and whatever other meanings can be ascribed to the BMOC theme. 4 (3.5)

B–22   *Pow Im.* "Both want the other to be impressed by their side of the argument." Criterion 1.

Need. Above also scorable for Need.

I–. "Continuing their disagreement" which doesn't sway either, scored *I–*.

G–. "Continue on their way largely unsatisfied . . ." The implication here is that they are unsatisfied because they did not sway the other person.

Th. No other themes brought up in the story. 5 (1)

B–23   *Pow Im.* "is campaigning for the office . . ." Criterion 2.

I–. The above statement is the instrumental act, and it doesn't work, so it is scored *I–*.

Ga–. "think he will lose . . ."

No Bw. "One listening dislikes his policies" is a statement which does not actively interfere with the ongoing power attempt, so it is not scored.

No Th. Achievement references makes this story unscorable for Thema. 3 (9)

B–24   *Pow Im.* Unsolicited advice in this story is the only reason why this story is scored at all.

I?. "giving advice," taken with a grain of salt, makes this scored *I?.* 2 (14)

B–25   *U Im.* Solicited explanation. 0 (23)

B–26   *U Im.* Casual small talk. 0 (23)

B–27   *Pow Im.* "trying to convince . . ." Criterion 2.

I?. The above statement plus "accosted by the candidate" are instrumental acts which have doubtful outcome ("the student will excuse himself politely, without committing his vote").

Th. No interfering themes present in this story. 3 (9)

B–28   *U Im.* Solicited explanation; not scored. 0 (23)

B–29   *U Im.* Concern about academic failure; no influence interactions in the story. 0 (23)

B–30   *U Im.* Solicited explanation. 0 (23)

SET C: POWER EXPERT SCORING

C–1	*U Im.* 0 (23)	C–5	*Pow Im, N, I–, Th.* 4 (2.5)
C–2	*U Im.* 0 (23)		
C–3	*Pow Im, I+.* 2 (11)	C–6	*Pow Im, N, I+, Th.* 4 (2.5)
C–4	*U Im.* 0 (23)		

C-7   *U Im.* 0 (23)
C-8   *Pow Im, I+, Th.* 3 (5.5)
C-9   *U Im.* 0 (23)
C-10 *Pow Im, I+.* 2 (11)
C-11 *U Im.* 0 (23)
C-12 *Pow Im, I?.* 2 (11)
C-13 *U Im.* 0 (23)
C-14 *U Im.* 0 (23)
C-15 *U Im.* 0 (23)
C-16 *Pow Im, I+.* 2 (11)
C-17 *Pow Im, I+.* 2 (11)
C-18 *Pow Im, I+.* 2 (11)
C-19 *U Im.* 0 (23)

C-20 *Pow Im, N, Th.* 3 (5.5)
C-21 *U Im.* 0 (23)
C-22 *Pow Im, I+.* 2 (11)
C-23 *U Im.* 0 (23)
C-24 *U Im.* 0 (23)
C-25 *Pow Im, N, I—, Th.* 4 (2.5)
C-26 *U Im.* 0 (23)
C-27 *Pow Im, I+.* 2 (11)
C-28 *Pow Im, N, I+, Th.* 4 (2.5)
C-29 *Pow Im, I+.* 2 (11)
C-30 *U Im.* 0 (23)

SET D: POWER EXPERT SCORING

D-1   *Pow Im, I?, Th.* 3 (4.5)
D-2   *Pow Im, I+.* 2 (11)
D-3   *Pow Im, I?.* 2 (11)
D-4   *Pow Im, I?.* 2 (11)
D-5   *U Im.* 0 (23)
D-6   *U Im.* 0 (23)
D-7   *U Im.* 0 (23)
D-8   *U Im.* 0 (23)
D-9   *U Im.* 0 (23)
D-10 *Pow Im, N, I?.* 3 (4.5)
D-11 *U Im.* 0 (23)
D-12 *U Im.* 0 (23)
D-13 *U Im.* 0 (23)
D-14 *Pow Im, I?.* 2 (11)
D-15 *Pow Im, I—, Th.* 3 (4.5)
D-16 *Pow Im, I+.* 2 (11)
D-17 *U Im.* 0 (23)

D-18 *U Im.* 0 (23)
D-19 *Pow Im, I—, Th.* 3 (4.5)
D-20 *Pow Im, I—, Bw, Th.* 4 (1.5)
D-21 *U Im.* 0 (23)
D-22 *Pow Im, I?.* 2 (11)
D-23 *U Im.* 0 (23)
D-24 *Pow Im, I+.* 2 (11)
D-25 *Pow Im, I+.* 2 (11)
D-26 *Pow Im, I+.* 2 (11)
D-27 *Pow Im, N, Bp, Th.* 4 (1.5)
D-28 *U Im.* 0 (23)
D-29 *U Im.* 0 (23)
D-30 *U Im.* 0 (23)

SET E: POWER EXPERT SCORING

E-1   *U Im.* 0 (22.5)
E-2   *Pow Im, I+.* 2 (9)
E-3   *U Im.* 0 (22.5)
E-4   *U Im.* 0 (22.5)
E-5   *Pow Im, I+, Bw.* 3 (3.5)
E-6   *Pow Im, I+.* 2 (9)
E-7   *U Im.* 0 (22.5)

E-8   *U Im.* 0 (22.5)
E-9   *Pow Im, I+.* 2 (9)
E-10 *Pow Im, I?, Th.* 3 (3.5)
E-11 *Pow Im, I?.* 2 (9)
*E-12 *U Im.* 0 (22.5)
E-13 *U Im.* 0 (22.5)
E-14 *Pow Im, N, I+, Th.* 4 (1)

---

* E-12. Although this story contains imagery of someone teaching another person, it is not scored for *Pow Im* because there is no emphasis on the teacher's *desires* to or *attempts* to teach. The manual states that attempting to teach is scorable. This should be amplified to state that only statements of *attempts* to teach are scorable for *Pow Im* (e.g., the professor *is trying* to teach his students).

E–15 *Pow Im, I?, Ga+.* 3 (3.5)
E–16 *U Im.* 0 (22.5)
E–17 *U Im.* 0 (22.5)
E–18 *Pow Im, I+.* 2 (9)
E–19 *Pow Im.* 1 (13.5)
E–20 *U Im.* 0 (22.5)
E–21 *U Im.* 0 (22.5)
E–22 *U Im.* 0 (22.5)

E–23 *Pow Im, I—, Bw.* 3 (3.5)
E–24 *Pow Im, N.* 2 (9)
E–25 *Pow Im.* 1 (13.5)
E–26 *Pow Im, N.* 2 (9)
E–27 *U Im.* 0 (22.5)
E–28 *U Im.* 0 (22.5)
E–29 *U Im.* 0 (22.5)
E–30 *U Im.* 0 (22.5)

SET F: POWER EXPERT SCORING

F–1 *Pow Im, I?.* 2 (12)
F–2 *Pow Im, I+, Ga+.* 3 (5)
F–3 *Pow Im, I—, Bw.* 3 (5)
F–4 *Pow Im, I+.* 2 (12)
F–5 *Pow Im, I?.* 2 (12)
F–6 *U Im.* 0 (23.5)
F–7 *U Im.* 0 (23.5)
F–8 *U Im.* 0 (23.5)
F–9 *U Im.* 0 (23.5)
F–10 *Pow Im, I?.* 2 (12)
F–11 *U Im.* 0 (23.5)
F–12 *Pow Im, I?, Th.* 3 (5)
F–13 *Pow Im, I?.* 2 (12)
F–14 *U Im.* 0 (23.5)
F–15 *Pow Im, N, I—, G—, Th.* 5 (1)

F–16 *U Im.* 0 (23.5)
F–17 *U Im.* 0 (23.5)
F–18 *U Im.* 0 (23.5)
F–19 *Pow Im, I?, Bw, Th.* 4 (2)
F–20 *U Im.* 0 (23.5)
F–21 *Pow Im, G—, Th.* 3 (5)
F–22 *U Im.* 0 (23.5)
F–23 *U Im.* 0 (23.5)
F–24 *Pow Im, I?.* 2 (12)
F–25 *Pow Im, I+.* 2 (12)
F–26 *U Im.* 0 (23.5)
F–27 *Pow Im, I?.* 2 (12)
F–28 *U Im.* 0 (23.5)
F–29 *Pow Im, I?.* 2 (12)
F–30 *Pow Im, I?, G—.* 3 (5)

SET G: POWER EXPERT SCORING

G–1 *Pow Im, N.* 2 (11)
G–2 *U Im.* 0 (23)
G–3 *U Im.* 0 (23)
G–4 *U Im.* 0 (23)
G–5 *U Im.* 0 (23)
G–6 *Pow Im, I?, Ga+, G—, Th.* 5 (2)
G–7 *U Im.* 0 (23)
G–8 *Pow Im, I?.* 2 (11)
G–9 *Pow Im, I?.* 2 (11)
G–10 *U Im.* 0 (23)
G–11 *U Im.* 0 (23)
G–12 *Pow Im, N, I—, G—, Th.* 5 (2)
G–13 *Pow Im, N, I?, Th.* 4 (4.5)
G–14 *U Im.* 0 (23)
G–15 *U Im.* 0 (23)

G–16 *Pow Im, I+.* 2 (11)
G–17 *Pow Im, Ga+, Bw.* 3 (6)
G–18 *Pow Im, I?, Bw, Th.* 4 (4.5)
G–19 *Pow Im, I+.* 2 (11)
G–20 *Pow Im, I+.* 2 (11)
G–21 *Pow Im, I?.* 2 (11)
G–22 *U Im.* 0 (23)
G–23 *U Im.* 0 (23)
G–24 *Pow Im, I—, Bw, G—, Th.* 5 (2)
G–25 *Pow Im, I?.* 2 (11)
G–26 *U Im.* 0 (23)
G–27 *Pow Im, I+.* 2 (11)
G–28 *U Im.* 0 (23)
G–29 *U Im.* 0 (23)
G–30 *U Im.* 0 (23)

APPENDIX II

Practice Materials for Analysis of Graphic Expression to Assess the Achievement Motive

ELLIOT ARONSON

Figures 1 through 10 contain samples of graphic expression. In Figures 1 through 5, the appropriate scoring of each separate design is indicated. The symbol for the appropriate scoring is contained within a small circle immediately adjacent to the design. The appropriate scoring is not given for Figures 6 through 10. These may be used for practice. The complete scoring of each figure is given at the end of the set in Table 1.

The symbols used to designate the various characteristics of a design are: (D) Discrete; (F) Fuzzy; (GD) Group Discrete; (GF) Group Fuzzy; (DC) Diagonal Configuration; (S) S-shaped; (MW) Multiwave. Complete descriptions are given in Chapter 17.

(Since the practice materials have been scaled down from $8\frac{1}{2}'' \times 11''$ sheets to about half that size, it will be necessary to double the amount of unused space measured in each of the figures. Editor.)

819

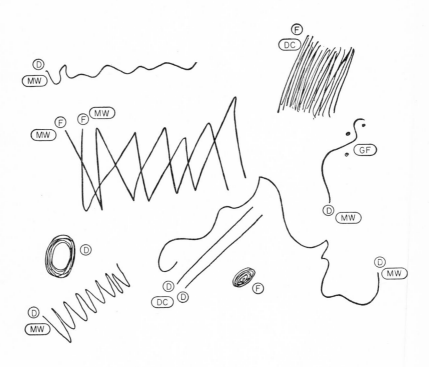

Fig. 1.

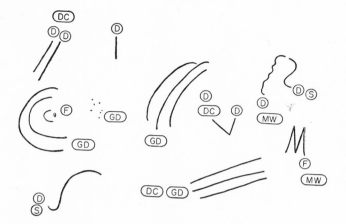

Fig. 2.

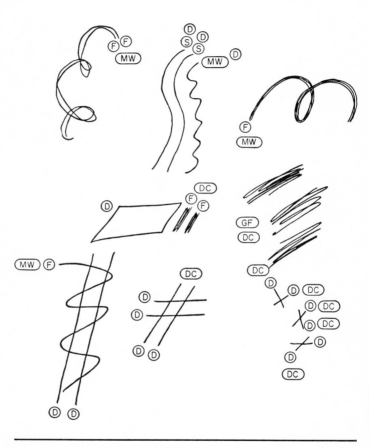

Fig. 3.

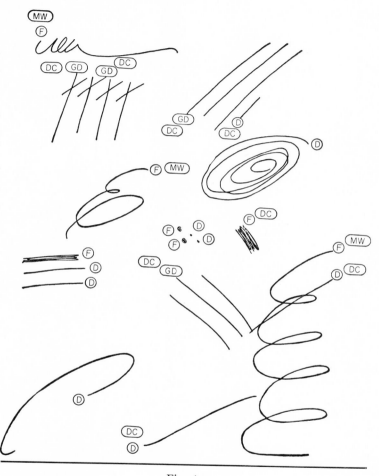

Fig. 4.

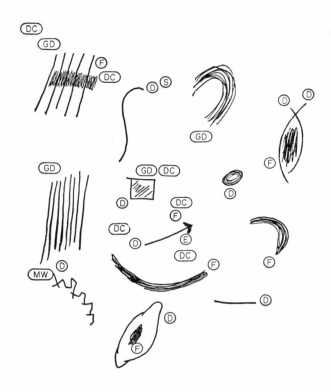

Fig. 5.

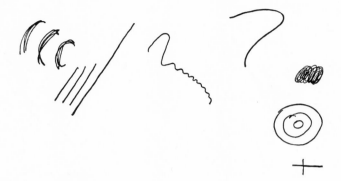

Fig. 6.

Fig. 7.

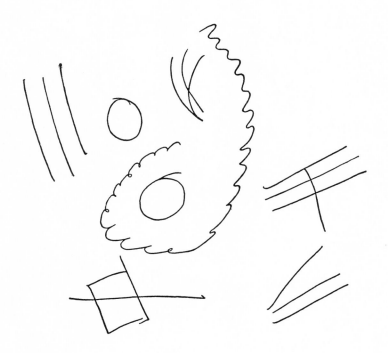

Fig. 8.

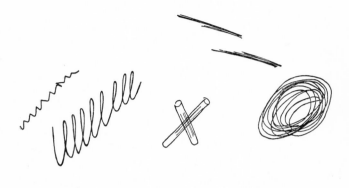

Fig. 9.

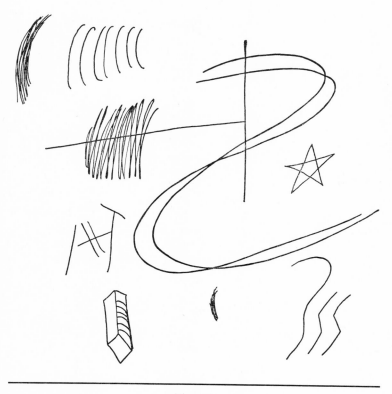

Fig. 10.

TABLE 1. SCORES ASSIGNED TO FIGURES 1 THROUGH 10

#	Discrete	Fuzzy	Dis.-Fuz.	Space	Diagonal Config.	S-shaped	Multi-Wave
1	7	5	2	7	2	0	6
2	12	2	10	14	3	2	2
3	16	7	9	1	8	2	4
4	13	7	6	0	8	0	3
5	13	7	6	6	6	1	1
6	7	2	5	13	2	0	1
7	13	7	6	2	4	2	0
8	13	1	12	4	2	0	1
9	2	7	−5	15	2	0	2
10	15	5	10	1	4	4	1

APPENDIX III

....

Pictures Used to Elicit Stories, and Other Considerations

Not enough is known about the effects of pictures, serial positions, and other factors intrinsic to the thematic apperceptive method to recommend a single set of pictures as a test of motivation suitable for all types of research. Current evidence shows a loss in predictive validity of stories late in a series of eight or more (Ch. 46; see also Ricciuti and Clark, 342). This suggests that until more definitive results are available, thematic apperceptive measures of motivation should probably not exceed about six pictures in length. The researcher who ordinarily uses longer sets of pictures, for example, the *Thematic Apperception Test,* should realize that motive-scores obtained from pictures after the first 20 to 25 minutes of testing may be invalid.

The confusion among results of studies using the present methods of content analysis with female subjects (see Ch. 3, fn. 9) has produced frank recognition that there are still important questions to be answered before assuming that the measures presented are equally valid for women. Under no circumstances should the results of male and female subjects be lumped together until the equivalence of the measures has been amply demonstrated. Any investigator who plans to study some substantive problem with female subjects should review the several studies cited in Footnote 9 of Chapter 3 for suggestions concerning the kinds of pictures that have been employed.

The use of verbal cues to elicit thematic apperceptive content is discussed in Chapters 16 and 33.

RECOMMENDED PICTURES

Below are descriptions of a number of pictures which can be recommended for use in research on n Achievement, n Affiliation, and n Power with male subjects of at least high-school age. The investigator may wish to use one of the sets of pictures for which some useful normative information is available, or he may prefer to construct a set of pictures to meet specific requirements of his own research. The pictures listed were selected from a much larger number that have been studied (see Ricciuti, Clark, and Sadacca, 341, 342; the validation studies in Chs. 3, 4, 5, 6, and 45; and 272). The identifying numbers (1 through 82) were taken from David C. McClelland's catalog of pictures employed in studies of n Achievement. Negatives of pictures which are not already available in

831

published sets have been deposited with the American Documentation Institute, making them generally available at a modest cost.

The source of each picture is listed following its descriptive title. The reader is referred to five general sources:

1. (TAT) Murray, Henry A. *Thematic Apperception Test and Manual.* New York (522 Fifth Avenue): Psychological Corporation, 1956. $6.30 (pictures listed below as 1, 7, 81, 89, 90, 91).

2. (HG) Henry, W. E., and Guetzkow, Harold. Group projection sketches for the study of small groups. *J. soc. Psychol.*, 1951, **33**, 77-102. Reproduction of the cards ($21'' \times 18''$) may be obtained from the University of Michigan Press, Ann Arbor, Michigan, for $2.50 a set (pictures listed below as 83, 84, 85, 86, 87).

3. (AM) McClelland, D. C., Atkinson, J. W., Clark, R. A., and Lowell, E. L. *The Achievement Motive.* New York: Appleton-Century-Crofts Inc., 1953, pp. 100-101 (pictures listed below as 2, 8).

4. (SR) Survey Research Center, University of Michigan, Ann Arbor, Michigan. Attn. Drs. Gerald Gurin and Joseph Veroff (pictures listed below as 101, 102, 103).

5. (ADI) American Documentation Institute. Address: Chief, Photo-duplication Service, Library of Congress, Auxiliary Publications Project, Washington 25, D. C. Order Document No. 5500 and state the number and description of each picture desired, remitting $.75 for each $8'' \times 10''$ photoprint, or $1.00 for each $2'' \times 2''$ positive slide. Make check or money order payable to Chief, Photo-duplication Service, Library of Congress (pictures listed below as 3, 4, 5, 9, 11, 20, 24, 25, 26, 28, 33, 46, 48, 52, 53, 59, 60, 62, 88, 92, 93, 94, 95, 96, 97, 98, 99, 100). Minor imperfections in some prints and slides, which in no way limit their use for projective testing, are attributable to imperfections in the negatives deposited with the ADI.

PICTURES

1. Father-son. Picture A of the original n Achievement series (Ch. 3; 272, 341). Source: Card 7 BM from TAT.

2. Two men ("inventors") in a shop working at a machine. Picture B of the original n Achievement series (Ch. 3; 272, 341, 342). Source: AM.

3. Two men, in colonial dress, printing in a shop. Picture C of the extended n Achievement series (272, 342). Source: ADI.

4. "Cub reporter" scene: older man (standing) handing papers to a younger man. Picture D of the extended n Achievement series (272). Source: ADI.

5. "Lawyers" office: two men talking in a well-furnished office. Picture E of the extended n Achievement series (272). Source: ADI.

7. Boy with vague operation scene in background. Picture G of the

original n Achievement series (Ch. 3; 272, 341). Source: Card 8 BM from TAT.

8. Boy in checked shirt at a desk, an open book in front of him. Picture H of original n Achievement series (Ch. 3; 272, 341, 342). Source: AM.

9. Good work, Bill! Man working on papers at office desk. (See Ricciuti, Clark, Sadacca, 341, 342.) Source: ADI.

11. Engineer with apparatus in lab. (See Ricciuti, Clark, Sadacca, 341, 342.) Source: ADI.

20. Crossroads. Man's face superimposed on a crossroad. (See Haber and Alpert, Ch. 45.) Source: ADI.

24. "Homeland." Man and youth chatting outdoors. (See Ricciuti and Sadacca, 342.) Source: ADI.

25. Boy watching large airliner. Source: ADI.

26. Foreman and worker standing near machine in shop. (See Ricciuti, Clark, Sadacca, 341, 342.) Source: ADI.

28. Man seated at drafting board. (See Ricciuti and Sadacca, 342.) Source: ADI.

33. Boy, smiling, at desk at home. (See Ricciuti, Clark, Sadacca, 341, 342.) Source: ADI.

46. Man skiing down steep hill. (See Ricciuti, Clark, Sadacca, 341, 342.) Source: ADI.

48. Hardest story: man working with typewriter and books. (See Ricciuti, Clark, Sadacca, 341, 342.) Source: ADI.

52. The price of success: man working at office desk at night. (See Ricciuti and Sadacca, 342.) Source: ADI.

53. Man relaxing on plane. Source: ADI.

59. Industrialist gazing out office window at factory. (See Haber and Alpert, Ch. 45.) Source: ADI.

60. Truck driver operating large van at night. (See Ricciuti and Sadacca, 342.) Source: ADI.

62. Man and woman in trapeze act. (See Ricciuti and Sadacca, 342.) Source: ADI.

81. Figure under street lamp at night. (See Shipley and Veroff, Ch. 4.) Source: Card 20 from TAT.

83. Conference group. Seven men variously grouped around a conference table. (See Atkinson *et al.*, Ch. 5.) Source: HG.

84. Man standing in a doorway. (See Atkinson *et al.*, Ch. 5.) Source: HG.

85. The heads of two men facing each other, the older on the left and the younger on the right. (See Atkinson *et al.*, Ch. 5.) Source: HG.

86. Informal group. Four men in a room which looks like a clubroom. (See Atkinson *et al.*, Ch. 5.) Source: HG.

87. Woman and man. Older woman sitting. To her left by a window is a young man. (See Atkinson *et al.*, Ch. 5.) Source: HG.

88. Group of young men seated, with one man standing outside of and away from group. (See Shipley and Veroff, Ch. 4.) Source: ADI.

89. Older woman and young man. (See Shipley and Veroff, Ch. 4.) Source: Card 6 BM from TAT.
90. Figure crumpled on floor, resting head on divan. (See Shipley and Veroff, Ch. 4.) Source: Card 3 BM from TAT.
91. A young woman's head against a man's shoulder. (See Shipley and Veroff, Ch. 4.) Source: Card 10 from TAT.
92. Instructor in classroom with students. (See Birney, Ch. 44; Veroff, Ch. 6.) Source: ADI.
93. Two young men meet on campus. (See Birney, Ch. 44; Veroff, Ch. 6.) Source: ADI.
94. Political scene. (See Veroff, Ch. 6.) Source: ADI.
95. A man painting or writing at an easel in a log cabin. (See Haber and Alpert, Ch. 45.) Source: ADI.
96. A foot-racer on his mark preparing to start. (See Haber and Alpert, Ch. 45.) Source: ADI.
97. A chemist in a white coat holding up a test tube. (See Haber and Alpert, Ch. 45.) Source: ADI.
98. A pioneer chopping down a tree for a cabin. (See Haber and Alpert, Ch. 45.) Source: ADI.
99. Three foot-racers straining to cross the finish line. (See Haber and Alpert, Ch. 45.) Source: ADI.
100. An engineer making an adjustment on a piece of apparatus. (See Haber and Alpert, Ch. 45.) Source: ADI.
101. Four men seated at a table with coffee cups. One man is writing on sheaf of papers. Source: SR.
102. Man (father) and children seated at breakfast table. Source: SR.
103. Woman in foreground with man standing behind and to the left. Source: SR.

RECOMMENDED SETS

The results presented below were obtained under "neutral" test conditions, that is, nothing was done before the administration of the test either to deliberately arouse a particular kind of motivation or to relax the subjects. Four minutes were allowed for writing each story.

In making use of this normative information about different sets of pictures, as in the design of research requiring comparisons between average scores of different groups, the investigator must consider the tendency of even well-trained scorers to differ in the degree to which they are conservative or liberal in the use of the scoring manuals. Two scorers may agree very well in detecting imagery and in rank ordering subjects within a group for purposes of high-low comparisons and yet differ one or two points in the average score assigned to a group of subjects (see the discussion of this problem in Appendix I).

For n Achievement only. A. The set of four pictures used in the original validation studies and probably most often employed in studies of college groups: pictures 2, 8, 1, 7 in that order. Combining several distributions of scores obtained from groups of male introductory psychology students at the University of Michigan (between 1949-1955) yields the following information: $N = 207$; Mean $= 6.10$; $\sigma = 4.81$; Median $= 6.08$; Range -2 to $+25$; $Q_1 = 10$ and above; $Q_2 = 7$ to 9; $Q_3 = 3$ to 6; $Q_4 = 2$ and below. Percentage Achievement Imagery in response to each picture: $2 = 69.1$ per cent; $8 = 51.2$ per cent; $1 = 28.5$ per cent; $7 = 41.6$ per cent.

B. See also McClelland *et al.* (272, p. 192) for information concerning two equivalent three-picture forms: pictures 2, 1, 7; and 3, 4, 5.

C. Pictures recommended by Ricciuti and Clark (341) for use with male college students: 1, 2, 7, 8, 11, 33, 46, 48.

D. Pictures 33, 26, 9, 24 in that order. Data obtained by B. Rosen, from an unpublished paper, "Race, ethnicity, and achievement motive $=$ value syndrome," on heterogeneous group of boys aged 8–14 yield the following information: $N = 427$; Mean $= 4.74$; $\sigma = 5.11$; $Q_1 = 9$ and above; $Q_2 = 4$ to 8; $Q_3 = 1$ to 3; $Q_4 = 0$ and below. Percentage Achievement Imagery in response to each picture ($N = 76$, data collected by D. C. McClelland): $33 = 49$ per cent; $26 = 59$ per cent; $24 = 38$ per cent; $9 = 41$ per cent.

E. See also Chapter 45 of this volume by Haber and Alpert for information concerning two equivalent six-picture forms: pictures 95, 25, 96, 8, 97, 59; and 98, 99, 100, 20, 2, 4.

For n Affiliation only. Of several different sets developed to measure only *n* Affiliation, pictures 85, 83, 87, and 81 employed by Hardy (Ch. 30) yielded the best distribution of scores. The subjects were male college students: $N = 79$; Mean $= 4.99$; $\sigma = 3.11$; Median $= 4.5$; Range 0 to 12; High third $= 7$ to 12; Mid third $= 4$ to 6; Low third $= 0$ to 3.

Multiple purpose set for n Achievement and n Affiliation. Six pictures— 2, 1, 7, 85, 81, 87—administered in that order. All pictures scored for both *n* Achievement and *n* Affiliation. The subjects were male college students ($N = 190$) taking introductory psychology at the University of Michigan in the fall, 1956, and spring, 1957.

n Achievement: Mean $= 1.55$; $\sigma = 4.47$; Median $= 1.00$; Range $= -6$ to $+17$; $Q_1 = 5$ and above; $Q_2 = 2$ to 4; $Q_3 = -1$ to $+1$; $Q_4 = -2$ and below. Percentage Achievement Imagery to pictures: $2 = 75$ per cent; $1 = 14$ per cent; $7 = 28$ per cent; $85 = 14$ per cent; $81 = 10$ per cent; $87 = 6$ per cent.

n Affiliation: Mean $= 4.20$; $\sigma = 3.17$; Median $= 3.78$; Range $= 0$ to 15; $Q_1 = 7$ and above; $Q_2 = 4$ to 7; $Q_3 = 2$ to 3; $Q_4 = 0$ to 1. Percentage Affiliation Imagery to pictures: $2 = 5$ per cent; $1 = 16$ per cent; $7 = 19$ per cent; $85 = 35$ per cent; $81 = 24$ per cent; $87 = 61$ per cent.

Multiple purpose sets for n Achievement, n Affiliation, and n Power. A. A set recently developed by D. C. McClelland consisting of six pictures —5, 28, 83, 9, 24, and 53—in that order. Administered to 50 adult businessmen. The same stories were coded for three motives yielding the following results:

n Achievement: Mean $= 7.46$; $\sigma = 5.98$; $Q_1 = 12$ and above; $Q_2 = 7$ to 11; $Q_3 = 4$ to 6; $Q_4 = 3$ and below. Percentage Achievement Imagery in response to pictures: $5 = 46$ per cent; $28 = 48$ per cent; $83 = 26$ per cent; $9 = 64$ per cent; $24 = 40$ per cent; $53 = 52$ per cent.

n Affiliation: Mean $= 6.08$; $\sigma = 3.89$; $Q_1 = 10$ and above; $Q_2 = 6$ to 9; $Q_3 = 3$ to 5; $Q_4 = 2$ and below. Percentage Affiliation Imagery in response to pictures: $5 = 14$ per cent; $28 = 70$ per cent; $83 = 32$ per cent; $9 = 22$ per cent; $24 = 44$ per cent; $53 = 38$ per cent.

n Power: Mean $= 6.74$; $\sigma = 3.64$; $Q_1 = 9$ and above; $Q_2 = 7$ to 8; $Q_3 = 5$ to 6; $Q_4 = 4$ and below. Percentage Power Imagery in response to pictures: $5 = 90$ per cent; $28 = 0$ per cent; $83 = 56$ per cent; $9 = 14$ per cent; $24 = 48$ per cent; $53 = 14$ per cent.

B. Another set of six pictures, developed by Joseph Veroff, for use in a national survey study conducted by the Survey Research Center, University of Michigan (Project Director: Gerald Gurin). The analysis of results is in progress as the current volume goes to press. However, some preliminary information is available from a sample of male college students ($N = 49$).

The recommended order of presentation is 2, 101, 102, 28, 83, 103. The results reported here combine scores from six different orders of presentation (Latin Square Design with $N_s = 7$ to 10 in each sequence).

n Affiliation: Mean $= 4.67$; $\sigma = 3.45$; $Q_1 = 8$ and above; $Q_2 = 5$ to 7; $Q_3 = 3$ to 4; $Q_4 = 0$ to 2. Percentage Affiliation Imagery in response to pictures: $2 = 8$ per cent; $101 = 14$ per cent; $102 = 24$ per cent; $28 = 66$ per cent; $83 = 26$ per cent; $103 = 40$ per cent.

n Power: Mean $= 3.47$; $\sigma = 2.72$; $Q_1 = 6$ and above; $Q_2 = 4$ to 5; $Q_3 = 2$ to 3; $Q_4 = 0$ to 1. Percentage Power Imagery in response to pictures: $2 = 20$ per cent; $101 = 6$ per cent; $102 = 50$ per cent; $28 = 4$ per cent; $83 = 18$ per cent; $103 = 34$ per cent.

n Achievement: Mean $= .43$; $\sigma = 7.55$; $Q_1 = 3$ and above; $Q_2 = 1$ to 2; $Q_3 = -1$ to 0; $Q_4 = -2$ and below. Percentage Achievement Imagery in response to pictures: $2 = 63$ per cent; $101 = 35$ per cent; $102 = 4$ per cent; $28 = 16$ per cent; $83 = 6$ per cent; $103 = 0$ per cent. (Note: The mean *n* Achievement score drops considerably in sets of pictures containing cues for other motives because -1 is scored for unrelated imagery. This practice is not followed in scoring *n* Affiliation and *n* Power. When 0 is scored for both "doubtful" and "unrelated" imagery in this data, the mean *n* Achievement score is 3.61 and σ is 6.13. The correlation between the two sets of scores is .95.)

OTHER CONSIDERATIONS

A. *Administration.* Story booklets contain a cover sheet with instructions and a separate page ($8\frac{1}{2}''$ x $14''$) for each story. A modification of the original instruction (272, Ch. 3) by Ricciuti, Clark, Sadacca (341, 342)[1] is recommended:

---

[1] See also Sadacca, R., Clark, R. A., and Ricciuti, H. N. Content analysis of achievement motivation protocols: A working manual. Princeton, N. J.: *Research Bull. Educ. Testing Service,* July, 1957.

Picture Interpretations: Instructions

"You are going to see a series of pictures, and your task is to tell a story that is suggested to you by each picture. Try to imagine what is going on in each picture. Then tell what the situation is, what led up to the situation, what the people are thinking and feeling, and what they will do.

"In other words, write as complete a story as you can—a story with plot and characters.

"You will have 20 seconds to look at a picture and then 4 minutes to write your story about it. Write your first impressions and work rapidly. I will keep time and tell you when it is time to finish your story and to get ready for the next picture.

"There are no right or wrong stories or kinds of pictures, so you may feel free to write whatever story is suggested to you when you look at a picture. Spelling, punctuation, and grammar are not important. What is important is to write out as fully and as quickly as possible the story that comes into your mind as you imagine what is going on in each picture.

"Notice that there is one page for writing each story. If you need more space for writing any story, use the reverse side of the paper."

On each story sheet these four questions are printed with about a three-inch space for writing following each question:

1. What is happening? Who are the persons?
2. What has led up to this situation? That is, what has happened in the past?
3. What is being thought? What is wanted? By whom?
4. What will happen? What will be done?

The picture is presented for 20 seconds and then removed. Four minutes are allowed for writing the story. At the end of each minute, the investigator says informally, "It is about time to go on to the next question." About 30 seconds before the end of the fourth minute, the investigator says, "Will you try to finish up in about 30 seconds?" At the end of four minutes he says, "All right, here is the next picture." (Review other statements of this procedure in [272, Ch. 3] and in the various chapters of this volume.)

B. *Effect of length of protocol on motive-scores derived from content analysis.* The obtained correlations between number of words per story and motive scores obtained from content analysis have been insignificant and negligible in homogeneous college groups when leading questions are employed and four minutes is allotted for each story (see Chs. 2, 3, 4, 5, 6). However, when the same kind of instrument is employed in a very heterogeneous population (see Chs. 10 and 34), or when a shorter time (two and one-half minutes) is allotted for writing stories without leading questions, as in Ricciuti and Clark (342), a significant correlation between number of words per story and motive scores is obtained.

The investigator should check the relationship between length of protocol and motive scores. When it occurs, the references cited may be consulted for methods of correcting motive scores to remove the influence of gross differences in length of protocol.

References

[Studies using methods described in this book are indicated by (*).]

1. ABT, L. E., and BELLAK, L. *Projective psychology.* New York: Knopf, 1950. P. *574.*†
2. ADLER, A. *Understanding human nature.* New York: Greenberg, 1927. Pp. *106, 113.*
3. ADORNO, T. W., FRENKEL-BRUNSWIK, ELSE, LEVINSON, D. J., and SANFORD, R. N. *The authoritarian personality.* New York: Harper, 1950. Pp. *411, 547.*
4. ALBRECHT, R. Social class in old age. *Social Forces,* 1951, **29,** 400-405. P. *495.*
5. ALEXANDER, H. W. A general test for trend. *Psychol. Bull.,* 1946, **43,** 533-557.
6. ALLPORT, G. W. *Personality.* New York: Holt, 1937. Pp. *17, 161.*
7. ALLPORT, G. W. The ego in contemporary psychology. *Psychol. Rev.,* 1943, **50,** 451-478. Pp. *373, 380.*
8. ALLPORT, G. W., and POSTMAN, L. *The psychology of rumor.* New York: Holt, 1947. P. *60.*
9. ALLPORT, G. W., and VERNON, P. E. *Manual of directions for study of values.* New York: Houghton-Mifflin, 1951. Pp. *108, 113, 387, 389.*
10. ALLPORT, G. W., VERNON, P. E., and LINDZEY, G. *Study of values: manual of directions.* Boston: Houghton-Mifflin, 1951. P. *23.*
11. ALPER, THELMA G. Memory for completed and incompleted tasks as a function of personality: an analysis of group data. *J. abnorm. soc. Psychol.,* 1946, **41,** 403-420.
12. ALPER, THELMA G. Task-orientation vs. ego-orientation in learning and retention. *Amer. J. Psychol.,* 1946, **59,** 236-248. Pp. *64, 67, 76.*
13. ALPERT, R., and HABER, R. N. Studies of the effects of stress on academic performance. Unpublished manuscript, Stanford Univer., 1957. Pp. *646, 658.*
14. ALTUCHER, N. Conflict in sex identification in boys. Unpublished doctoral dissertation, Univer. of Michigan, 1956.
15. ANDERSON, C. A., *et al.* Intelligence and occupational mobility. *J. political Econ.,* 1952, **60,** 218-239. P. *495.*

---

† Numbers in italics refer to pages of this book where a reference to the book or article here listed is to be found.

16.*ANGELINA, A. L. Un novo método par avaliar a motivação humana. Unpublished doctoral dissertation, Universidade de São Paulo, Brazil, 1955. Pp. *13, 77.*

17. ANSBACHER, H. Perception of number as affected by the monetary value of the objects. *Arch. Psychol.,* 1937, **30,** No. 215.

18. APPLEZWEIG, DEE G. An investigation of the interrelationships of several measures of rigidity under varying conditions of security. Unpublished doctoral dissertation, Univer. of Michigan, 1951 P. *13.*

19.*ARONSON, E. The need for achievement as measured by graphic expression. Unpublished master's thesis, Wesleyan Univer., 1956.

20. ASCH, S. E. Forming impressions of personality. *J. abnorm. soc. Psychol.,* 1946, **41,** 258-290.

21. ASCH, S. E. *Social psychology.* New York: Prentice-Hall, 1952. Pp. *409, 413, 420, 421.*

22.*ATKINSON, J. W. Studies in projective measurement of achievement motivation. Unpublished doctoral dissertation, Univer. of Michigan, 1950. Pp. *19, 32, 665, 666, 672, 674, 676, 681.*

23.*ATKINSON, J. W. The achievement motive and recall of interrupted and completed tasks. *J. exp. Psychol.,* 1953, **46,** 381-390. Also in D. C. McClelland (Ed.), *Studies in motivation.* New York: Appleton-Century-Crofts, 1955. Pp. *23, 91, 234, 242, 267, 276, 278, 279, 287, 350, 359, 563, 564, 568, 571, 681.*

24.*ATKINSON, J. W. Explorations using imaginative thought to assess the strength of human motives. In M. R. Jones (Ed.), *Nebraska symposium on motivation, 1954.* Lincoln: Univer. of Nebraska Press, 1954. Pp. *278, 322, 323, 341, 350, 358, 361, 365, 374, 396, 572, 573, 617, 618, 682.*

25.*ATKINSON, J. W., HEYNS, R. W., and VEROFF, J. The effect of experimental arousal of the affiliation motive on thematic apperception. *J. abnorm. soc. Psychol.,* 1954, **49,** 405-410.

26.*ATKINSON, J. W., and MCCLELLAND, D. C. The projective expression of needs. II. The effect of different intensities of the hunger drive on thematic apperception. *J. exp. Psychol.,* 1948, **38,** 643-658.

27.*ATKINSON, J. W., and RAPHELSON, A. C. Individual differences in motivation and behavior in particular situations. *J. Pers.,* 1956, **24,** 349-363. Pp. *268, 278, 279, 282, 287, 350.*

28.*ATKINSON, J. W., and REITMAN, W. R. Performance as a function of motive strength and expectancy of goal attainment. *J. abnorm. soc. Psychol.,* 1956, **53,** 361-366. Pp. *39, 234, 235.*

29. BAIN, R. *Clans and tartans of Scotland.* London and Glasgow: Collins, 1954. P. 368.

30. BALDWIN, A. L. *Behavior and development in childhood.* New York: Dryden, 1955. P. 8.

31. BALDWIN, A. L., KALHORN, J., and BREESE, F. H. Patterns of parent behavior. *Psychol. Monogr.,* 1945, **58,** No. 3.

32. BARRON, F. Some personality correlates of independence of judgment. *J. Pers.,* 1953, **21,** 287-297. P. *422.*

33. BARTLETT, F. C. *Remembering: a study in experimental and social psychology.* Cambridge: Cambridge Univer. Press, 1932.

34. BASS, B. M. Authoritarianism or acquiescence? *J. abnorm. soc. Psychol.,* 1955, **51**, 616-623. P. *25.*

35. BELL, J. E. *Projective techniques.* New York: Longmans, Green, 1948. P. *574.*

36. BELLAK, L. The concept of projection. *Psychiatry,* 1944, **7**, 353-370. Pp. *1, 46, 58, 61, 72, 79, 80.*

37. BELLAK, L. The thematic apperception test in clinical use. In L. E. Abt and L. Bellak, *Projective psychology.* New York: Knopf, 1950. P. *630.*

38. BELLAK, L. *The TAT and CAT in clinical use.* New York: Grune and Stratton, 1954. P. *665.*

39.*BERLEW, D. E. The achievement motive and the growth of Greek civilization. Unpublished honors thesis, Wesleyan Univer., 1956. Pp. *34, 264, 520, 527, 531, 535, 537, 541, 542.*

40.*BIRNEY, R. C. The effect of threat on thematic apperception. Unpublished honors thesis, Wesleyan Univer., 1950. Pp. *83, 86.*

41.*BIRNEY, R. C. Studies in the role of picture cues in projective measurement of achievement motivation. Unpublished doctoral dissertation, Univer. of Michigan, 1955. Pp. *107, 640.*

42.*BIRNEY, R. C. Experimenter effect on the achievement motive. Unpublished manuscript, Amherst College, 1956. P. *35.*

43.*BIRNEY, R. C. Notes for a single picture measure of achievement motivation. Unpublished manuscript, Amherst College, 1957. P. *19.*

44. BLACKWELL, H. R. Psychophysical thresholds: Experimental studies of methods of measurement. *Engng. Res. Instit. Bull.,* No. 36. Ann Arbor: Univer. of Michigan Press, 1953, p. 227. P. *362.*

45. BLUM, G. S. An experimental reunion of psychoanalytic theory with perceptual vigilance and defense. *J. abnorm. soc. Psychol.,* 1954, **49**, 94-98. P. *582.*

46. BLUM, G. S., and MILLER, D. R. Exploring the psychoanalytic theory of the oral character. *J. Pers.,* 1952, **20**, 287-304. P. 103.

47. BRIGGS, D. L. A modification of the Thematic Apperception Test for naval enlisted personnel (N-TAT). *J. Psychol.,* 1954, **37**, 233-242. P. *631.*

48. BROWN, J. S. Problems presented by the concept of acquired drives. In M. R. Jones (Ed.), *Current theory and research in motivation.* Lincoln: Univer. of Nebraska Press, 1953. Pp. *8, 11, 324.*

49. BROWN, J. S., and FARBER, I. E. Emotions conceptualized as intervening variables—with suggestions toward a theory of frustration. *Psychol. Bull.,* 1951, **48**, 465-495. P. *16.*

50. BROWN, J. S., and JACOBS, A. The role of fear in the motivation and acquisition of responses. *J. exp. Psychol.,* 1949, **39**, 747-759. P. *15.*

51. BROWN, N. O. *Hermes, the thief.* Madison: Univer. of Wisconsin Press, 1947. Pp. *526, 543.*

52.*BROWN, R. W. A determinant of the relationship between rigidity and

842 *References*

authoritarianism. *J. abnorm. soc. Psychol.*, 1953, **48**, 469-476. Pp. *470, 516, 563, 571.*

53. BROWNFAIN, J. J. Stability of the self-concept as a dimension of personality. *J. abnorm. soc. Psychol.*, 1952, **47**, 597-606. Pp. *373, 375.*

54. BRUNER, J. S. Personality dynamics and the process of perceiving. In R. R. Blake and G. V. Ramsey (Eds.), *Perception: an approach to personality.* New York: Ronald Press, 1951. Pp. *538, 626.*

55. BRUNER, J. S., and GOODMAN, C. C. Value and need as organizing factors in perception. *J. abnorm. soc. Psychol.*, 1947, **42**, 33-44.

56. BRUNER, J. S., and POSTMAN, L. Emotional selectivity in perception and reaction. *J. Pers.*, 1947, **16**, 69-77. P. *125.*

57. BRUNER, J. S., and POSTMAN, L. On the perception of incongruity: a paradigm. *J. Pers.*, 1949, **18**, 206-223.

58.*BURDICK, H. A. The relationship of attraction, need achievement and certainty to conformity under conditions of a simulated group atmosphere. Unpublished doctoral dissertation, Univer. of Michigan, 1955. Pp. *18, 348.*

59. CAMERON, N. A. *The psychology of behavior disorders.* Boston: Houghton-Mifflin, 1947. P. *373.*

60. CARMICHAEL, L., KENNEDY, J. I., and MEAD, L. L. Some recent approaches to the experimental study of human fatigue. *Proc. nat. Acad. Sci.*, 1949, **35**, 691-696. P. *24.*

61. CARTWRIGHT, D. Toward a social psychology of groups. Presidential address delivered before SPSSI, Cleveland, Ohio, 1953. P. *106.*

62. CATTELL, R. B. Projection and the design of projective tests of personality. *Charact. & Pers.*, 1944, **12**, 177-194. Pp. *58, 60.*

63. CATTELL, R. B. The riddle of perseveration. I. "Creative effort" and disposition rigidity. *J. Pers.*, 1946, **14**, 229-238.

64. CATTELL, R. B. Confirmation and clarification of primary personality factors. *Psychometrika*, 1947, **12**, 197-220. P. *412.*

65. CENTERS, R. Attitude and belief in relation to occupational stratification. *J. soc. Psychol.*, 1948, **27**, 159-185. P. *516.*

66. CENTERS, R. Motivational aspects of occupational stratification. *J. soc. Psychol.*, 1948, **28**, 187-217. P. *108.*

67. CHEIN, I. The awareness of self and the structure of the ego. *Psychol. Rev.*, 1944, **51**, 304-314. P. *373.*

68. CHILD, I. L. Personality. *Annu. Rev. Psychol.*, 1954, **5**, 149-170. P. *22.*

69.*CHILD, I. L., FRANK, KITTY F., and STORM, T. Self-ratings and TAT: their relations to each other and to childhood background. *J. Pers.*, 1956, **25**, 96-114. Pp. *41, 483.*

70. CHILDE, V. G. *What happened in history* (rev. ed.). Harmondsworth, Eng.: Penquin Books, Ltd., 1954. Pp. *534, 536, 543, 548.*

71. CLARK, R. A. The problem of closure in mental organization. Unpublished honors thesis, Wesleyan Univer., 1947.

72.*CLARK, R. A. The projective measurement of experimentally induced levels of sexual motivation. *J. exp. Psychol.*, 1952, **44**, 391-399. Pp. *44, 95, 101, 117, 130, 132, 139, 178, 572, 573, 582, 584, 612, 613.*

References

843

73.*CLARK, R. A. The effects of sexual motivation on phantasy. In D. C. McClelland (Ed.), *Studies in motivation.* New York: Appleton-Century-Crofts, 1955. Pp. *132, 138.*

74*CLARK, R. A., and MCCLELLAND, D. C. A factor analytic integration of imaginative and performance measures of the need for achievement. *J. gen. Psychol.,* 1956, **55**, 73-83. Pp. *35, 39, 67, 267.*

75.*CLARK, R. A., RICCIUTI, H. N., and TEEVAN, R. C. An investigation of the hope of success and fear of failure aspects of need for achievement. *J. abnorm. soc. Psychol.,* 1956, **53**, 182-186.

76.*CLARK, R. A., and SENSIBAR, MINDA R. The relationships between symbolic and manifest projections of sexuality with some incidental correlates. *J. abnorm. soc. Psychol.,* 1956, **50**, 327-334.

77. CLARK, R. M. A method of administering and evaluating the Thematic Apperception Test in group situations. *Genet. Psychol. Monogr.,* 1944, **30**, 3-55. P. *49.*

78. COCHRAN, W. G. Some methods for strengthening the common X^2 tests. *Biometrics,* 1954, **10**, 417-451. Pp. *155, 156.*

79. COHEN, A. R. The effects of individual self-esteem and situational structure on threat-oriented reactions to power. Unpublished doctoral dissertation, Univer. of Michigan, 1953.

80. COHEN, A. R., STOTLAND, E., and WOLFE, D. M. An experimental investigation of need for cognition. *J. abnorm. soc. Psychol.,* 1955, **51**, 291-294.

81. COLEMAN, W. The Thematic Apperception Test. I. Effect of recent experience. II. Some quantitative observations. *J. clin. Psychol.,* 1947, **3**, 257-264. Pp. *1, 46, 61, 79.*

82. COMBS, A. W. A comparative study of motivation as revealed in thematic apperception stories and autobiography. *J. clin. Psychol.,* 1947, **3**, 65-75. Pp. *25, 530.*

83. CONGER, J. J. The effects of alcohol on conflict behavior in the albino rat. *Quart. J. Stud. Alcohol,* 1951, **12**, 1-29.

84. COX, F. N., and SARASON, S. B. Test anxiety and Rorschach performance. *J. abnorm. soc. Psychol.,* 1954, **49**, 371-377. P. *24.*

85. CRONBACH, L., and MEEHL, P. E. Construct validity in psychological tests. *Psychol. Bull.,* 1955, **52**, 281-302. Pp. *8, 20, 26, 27, 30.*

86. CUTLER, R. L. The therapist's personality and his psychotherapy: a study of countertransference. Unpublished manuscript, Univer. of Michigan, 1956. P. *29.*

87.*DAVAGE, R. H. Effect of achievement-affiliation motive patterns on yielding behavior in two person groups. Unpublished doctoral dissertation, Univer. of Michigan, 1956. P. *432.*

88. DAVIDS, A. Comparison of three methods of personality assessment: direct, indirect, and projective. *J. Pers.,* 1955, **23**, 423-440. P. *18.*

89. DAVIS, A. Socialization and adolescent personality. *Adolescence, Forty-third Yearb., Part I.* Chicago: National Society for the Study of Education, 1944. Pp. *509, 515, 516.*

90. DAVIS, A. The motivation of the underprivileged worker. In W. F.

Whyte (Ed.), *Industry and society*. Chicago: Univer. of Chicago Press, 1946, pp. 84-106. P. *516*.

91. DAVIS, A. *Social-class influences upon learning*. Cambridge: Harvard Univer. Press, 1948. P. *507*.

92. DAVIS, A., and DOLLARD, J. *Children of bondage*. Washington: American Council on Education, 1940.

93. DAVIS, A., GARDNER, B., and GARDNER, M. *Deep South*. Chicago: Univer. of Chicago Press, 1941. P. *469*.

94. DAVIS, A., and HAVIGHURST, R. J. Social class and color differences in child rearing. *Amer. soc. Rev.*, 1946, **11**, 698-710.

95. DAVIS, A., and HAVIGHURST, R. J. *Father of the man; how your child gets his personality*. Boston: Houghton-Mifflin, 1947.

96.*DECHARMS, R. C., MORRISON, H. W., REITMAN, W. R., and MCCLELLAND, D. C. Behavioral correlates of directly and indirectly measured achievement motivation. In D. C. McClelland (Ed.), *Studies in motivation*. New York: Appleton-Century-Crofts, 1955, p. 414. Pp. *22, 23, 24, 36, 37, 39, 234, 521*.

97. DEESE, J., and LAZARUS, R. S. The effects of psychological stress upon perceptual-motor performance. *USAF, Hum. Resour. Res. Cent., Res. Bull.*, 1952, No. 52-19.

98. DEMBO, TAMARA. Anger as a problem of dynamics. In Translations of eight experimental studies in personality, directed by Kurt Lewin. Unpublished manuscript, Yale Univer. Library, 1940. P. *161*.

99. DENNIS, W. Infant development under conditions of restricted practice and of minimum social stimulation: a preliminary report. *J. genet. Psychol.*, 1938, **53**, 149-158. P. *441*.

100. DIXON, W. J., and MASSEY, F. J., JR. *Introduction to statistical analysis*. New York: McGraw-Hill, 1951.

101. DODGE, R. *Conditions and consequences of human variability*. New Haven: Yale Univer. Press, 1931. P. *518*.

102. DOLLARD, J., DOOB, L. W., MILLER, N. E., MOWRER, O. H., and SEARS, R. R. *Frustration and aggression*. New Haven: Yale Univer. Press, 1939. Pp. *12, 24, 126, 127*.

103. DOLLARD, J., and MILLER, N. E. *Personality and psychotherapy*. New York: McGraw-Hill, 1950. P. 173.

104.*DOUVAN, ELIZABETH. The influence of social class membership on reactions to failure. Unpublished doctoral dissertation, Univer. of Michigan, 1951.

105.*DOUVAN, ELIZABETH. Social status and success strivings. *J. abnorm. soc. Psychol.*, 1956, **52**, 219-223.

106. DREW, G. G. The function of punishment in learning. *J. genet. Psychol.*, 1938, **52**, 257-267. P. *450*.

107. DUBOIS, C. *The people of Alor*. Minneapolis: Univer. of Minnesota Press, 1944.

108. DUKES, W. F. Psychological studies of values. *Psychol. Bull.*, 1955, **52**, 24-50. P. *23*.

109. DUVALL, EVELYN M. Conceptions of parenthood. *Amer. J. Soc.*, 1946, **52**, 193-203. P. *509*.

110. DYER, H. S. *The proper use of objective test scores.* Cambridge: Office of Tests, Harvard Univer., 1951. P. *558.*

111. EDWARDS, A. L. *Statistical analysis.* New York: Rinehart, 1946.

112. EDWARDS, A. L. *Edwards Personal Preference Schedule.* New York: Psychol. Corp., 1954. Pp. *8, 22, 25.*

113. EDWARDS, W. Probability preferences in gambling. *Amer. J. Psychol.,* 1953, **66,** 349-364. P. *337.*

114. EDWARDS, W. The theory of decision making. *Psychol. Bull.,* 1954, **51,** 380-417. Pp. *289, 298, 337, 616.*

115. ELLIS, H. *The psychology of sex.* New York: New American Library, 1954. P. *132.*

116. ERIKSON, C. W., and DAVIDS, A. The meaning and clinical validity of the Taylor Anxiety Scale and the Hysteria-Psychesthenia Scales from the MMPI. *J. abnorm. soc. Psychol.,* 1955, **50,** 135-137. P. *25.*

117. ERICSON, MARTHA C. Social status and child-rearing practices. In T. M. Newcomb and E. L. Hartley (Eds.), *Readings in social psychology.* New York: Holt, 1947, pp. 494-501. Pp. *507, 509.*

118. ERON, L. D. Frequencies of themes and identifications in stories of patients and non-hospitalized college students. *J. consult. Psychol.,* 1948, **12,** 387-395. P. *630.*

119. ERON, L.D. A normative study of the TAT. *Psychol. Monogr.,* 1950, **9,** 64. P. *630.*

120. ERON, L. D., and RITTER, ANNE M. A comparison of two methods of administration of the Thematic Apperception Test. *J. consult. Psychol.,* 1951, **15,** 55-61. Pp. *558, 681.*

121. ERON, L. D., TERRY, D., and CALLAHAN, R. The use of rating scales for emotional tone of TAT stories. *J. consult. Psychol.,* 1950, **14,** 473-478. Pp. *630, 641.*

122. ESCALONA, SIBYLLE. Play and substitute satisfaction. In R. G. Barker, J. S. Kounin, and H. F. Wright (Eds.), *Child behavior and development.* New York: McGraw-Hill, 1943, pp. 363-378. P. *161.*

123. EYSENCK, H. J. A dynamic theory of anxiety and hysteria. *J. ment. Sci.,* 1955, **101,** 28-51. P. *337.*

124. EYSENCK, H. J., and HIMMELWEIT, H. T. An experimental study of the reactions of neurotics to experiences of success and failure. *J. gen. Psychol.,* 1946, **35,** 59-75. P. *337.*

125. FARBER, I. E. Response fixation under anxiety and non-anxiety conditions. *J. exp. Psychol.,* 1948, **38,** 111-131. P. *450.*

126. FARBER, I. E. Anxiety as a drive state. In M. R. Jones (Ed.), *Nebraska symposium on motivation, 1954.* Lincoln: Univer. of Nebraska Press, 1954. Pp. *8, 15, 22, 23.*

127. FARBER, I. E. The role of motivation in verbal learning and performance. *Psychol. Bull.,* 1955, **52,** 311-327. Pp. *10, 30, 365.*

128. FARBER, I. E., and SPENCE, K. W. Complex learning and conditioning as a function of anxiety. *J. exp. Psychol.,* 1953, **45,** 120-125. P. *340.*

129. FARBER, I. E., and SPENCE, K. W. Effects of anxiety, stress and task variables on reaction time. *J. Pers.,* 1956, **25,** 1-18. pp. *19, 23.*

130. FESHBACH, S. The drive reducing function of fantasy behavior. *J. abnorm. soc. Psychol.*, 1955, **50**, 3-11.

131. FESTINGER, L. Development of differential appetite in the rat. *J. exp. Psychol.*, 1943, **32**, 226-234. P. *76.*

132. FESTINGER, L. Informal social communication. *Psychol. Rev.*, 1950, **57**, 271-282. P. *409.*

133. FIELD, W. F. The effects of thematic apperception upon certain experimentally aroused needs. Unpublished doctoral dissertation, Univer. of Maryland, 1951. Pp. *13, 77.*

134. FINNEY, D. J. The Fisher-Yates test of significance in the 2×2 contingency tables. *Biometrika*, 1948, **35**, 145-156.

135. FISHER, R. A. *Statistical methods for research workers* (7th ed.). Edinburgh: Oliver & Boyd, 1938.

136. FISHER, R. A. *The design of experiments.* New York: Hafner, 1951. P. *136.*

137. FISKE, D. W. Consistency of the factorial structure of personality ratings from different sources. *J. abnorm. soc. Psychol.*, 1949, **44**, 329-344. P. *412.*

138.*FITZGERALD, J. E. The effect of pre-dental anxiety on thematic apperception. Unpublished honors thesis, Harvard Univer., 1950. P. *13.*

139. FLUGEL, J. C. *Man, morals, and society.* New York: Internat'l Universities Press, 1945. Pp. *443, 444, 451.*

140. FORD, C. S., and BEACH, F. A. *Patterns of sexual behavior.* New York: Harper, 1951. P. *126.*

141.*FRENCH, ELIZABETH G. Some characteristics of achievement motivation. *J. exp. Psychol.*, 1955, **50**, 232-236. Pp. *34, 401, 402.*

142.*FRENCH, ELIZABETH G. Motivation as a variable in work-partner selection. *J. abnorm. soc. Psychol.*, 1956, **53**, 96-99. Pp. *34, 248, 400, 521.*

143.*FRENCH, ELIZABETH G., and CHADWICK, IRENE. Some characteristics of affiliation motivation. *J. abnorm. soc. Psychol.*, 1956, **52**, 296-300. Pp. *34, 178, 248.*

144. FRENKEL-BRUNSWIK, ELSE. Motivation and behavior. *Genet. Psychol. Monogr.*, 1942, **26**, 121-265. Pp. *16, 26, 263.*

145. FREUD, ANNA. *The ego and mechanisms of defense.* New York: Internat'l Universities Press, 1946. P. 161.

146. FREUD, S. *The problem of anxiety.* New York: Norton, 1936. P. *574.*

147. FREUD, S. *The basic writings of Sigmund Freud.* New York: Random House, 1938. Pp. *126, 134.*

148. FREUD, S. The relation of the poet to day-dreaming. In *Collected Papers.* Vol. IV. London: Hogarth, 1949, pp. 173-183. P. 160.

149.*FRIEDMAN, G. A. A cross-cultural study of the relationship between independence training and *n* Achievement as revealed by mythology. Unpublished honors thesis, Harvard Univer., 1950. P. 446.

150. GESELL, A., et al. *The first five years of life.* New York: Harper, 1940.

151. GESELL, A. and ILG, FRANCES L. *Infant and child in the culture of today.* New York: Harper, 1943.

152. GIBB, J. R., SMITH, E. E., and ROBERTS, A. H. Effects of positive and negative feedback upon defensive behavior in small problem-solving groups. *Amer. Psychologist*, 1955, **10**, 335. (Abstract) Pp. *400, 402, 403.*

153. GLOTZ, G. *Histoire Grecque* (2 vols.). Paris: Les Presses Universitaires de France, 1925. Pp. *535, 536, 543, 548, 549.*

154. GORDON, M. M. *Kitty Foyle* and the concept of class as culture. *Amer. J. Soc.*, 1947, **53**, 210-217. P. *501.*

155. GORER, G., and RICKMAN, J. *The people of Great Russia.* New York: Chanticleer Press, 1950.

156. GOUGH, H. G. A preliminary guide for the use and interpretation of the California Psychological Inventory. Unpublished manuscript, Univer. of California, 1954. Pp. *389, 391.*

157. GREEN, A. *Sociology.* New York: McGraw-Hill, 1952. P. *496.*

158.*GROESBECK, B. L. Personality correlates of the achievement and affiliation motives in clinical psychology trainees. Unpublished doctoral dissertation, Univer. of Michigan, 1956. Pp. *383, 388, 391, 395, 396, 397, 398, 603, 604, 679.*

159. GUILFORD, J. P. *Psychometric methods.* New York: McGraw-Hill, 1936. Pp. *625, 666, 678, 679.*

160. GUILFORD, J. P. *Fundamental statistics in psychology and education* (2nd ed.). New York: McGraw-Hill, 1950. P. *671.*

161. GUILFORD, J. P., CHRISTENSEN, P. R., BOND, N. R., JR., and SUTTON, M.A. A factor analysis of human interests. *Psychol. Monogr.*, 1954, **68**, 1-38. P. *22.*

162. GUILFORD, J. P., and GUILFORD, RUTH B. Personality factors S, E, and M and their measurement. *J. Psychol.*, 1936, **2**, 109-127. P. *387.*

163. GUILFORD, J. P., and GUILFORD, RUTH B. Personality factors D, R, T, and A. *J. abnorm. soc. Psychol.*, 1939, **34**, 21-36. P. *387.*

164. GUILFORD, J. P., and MARTIN, H. G. *Manual for Guilford-Martin Personnel Inventory.* Beverly Hills, Calif.: Sheridan Supply Co., 1943. P. *387.*

165. GULLIKSEN, H. *Theory of mental tests.* New York: Wiley, 1950. P. *483.*

166. GWINN, G. T. Resistance to extinction of learned fear drives and avoidance behavior. Unpublished manuscript, 1950. P. *445.*

167.*HABER, R. N. The prediction of achievement behavior by an interaction of achievement motivation and achievement stress. Unpublished doctoral dissertation, Stanford Univer., 1957. Pp. *644, 653, 655, 658.*

168. HALL, C. S. A cognitive theory of dream symbols. *J. gen. Psychol.*, 1953, **48**, 169-186. P. *120.*

169. HANAWALT, N. G. Memory trace for figures in recall and recognition. *Arch. Psychol.*, 1937, **31**, 1-89.

170.*HARDY, K. R. The influence of affiliative motivation and social support upon conformity and attitude change. Unpublished doctoral dissertation, Univer. of Michigan, 1954.

171. HAVIGHURST, R. J., and DAVIS, A. A comparison of the Chicago and Harvard studies of social class differences in child rearing. *Amer. soc. Rev.*, 1955, **20**, 438-442. P. *507.*

172. HEBB, D. O. *The organization of behavior.* New York: Wiley, 1949. P. *300.*

173.*HEDLUND, J. L. Construction and evaluation of an objective test of achievement imagery. Unpublished doctoral dissertation, State Univer. of Iowa, 1953. P. *32, 33, 37, 39.*

174.*HEENEY, J. The relation of childhood experiences as recalled by college women to n Affiliation and n Achievement. Unpublished honor thesis, Univer. of Michigan, 1955. P. *436.*

175. HEICHELHEIM, F. *Wirtschaftsgeschichte des altertums* (2 vols.). Leiden: A. W. Sijthoff, 1938. P. *535.*

176. HELSON, H. Adaptation level as frame of reference for prediction of psychophysical data. *Amer. J. Psychol.*, 1947, **60**, 1-29. P. *300.*

177. HELSON, H., BLAKE, R. R., MOUTON, JANE S., and OLMSTEAD, J. A. Attitudes as adjustments to stimulus, background, and residual factors. *J. abnorm. soc. Psychol.*, 1956, **52**, 314-322. P. *422.*

178. HENRY, W. E. The Thematic Apperception Test technique in the study of culture-personality relations. *Genet. Psychol. Monogr.*, 1947, **35**, 3-135. P. *631.*

179. HENRY, W. E., and GUETZKOW, H. Group projection sketches for the study of small groups. *J. soc. Psychol.*, 1951, **33**, 77-102. Pp. *620, 736.*

180. HILGARD, E. R. Human motives and the concept of the self. *Amer. Psychologist*, 1949, **4**, 374-382. P. *373.*

181. HILGARD, E. R., and MARQUIS, D. G. *Conditioning and learning.* New York: Appleton-Century-Crofts, 1940. P. *444.*

182. HIMMELWEIT, H. T. A comparative study of the level of aspiration of normal and neurotic persons. *Brit. J. Psychol.*, 1947, **37**, 41-59. P. *337.*

183. HOLLINGSHEAD, A. B. *Elmtown's youth.* New York: Wiley, 1949. P. *516.*

184. HOLLINGSHEAD, A. B., and REDLICH, F. C. Social stratification and psychiatric disorders. *Amer. soc. Rev.*, 1953, **18**, 163-169. P. *497.*

185. HOVLAND, C. I., LUMSDAINE, A. A., and SHEFFIELD, F. J. *Experiments on mass communication.* Princeton, N. J.: Princeton Univer. Press, 1949, P. *419.*

186. HULL, C. L. Goal attraction and directing ideas conceived as habit phenomena. *Psychol. Rev.*, 1931, **38**, 487-506. P. *79.*

187. HULL, C. L. *Principles of behavior.* New York: Appleton-Century-Crofts, 1943. Pp. *16, 296.*

188. HULL, C. L. *A behavior system.* New Haven: Yale Univer. Press, 1952.

189. HUMPHREYS, L. G. The effect of random alternation of reinforcement on the acquisition and extinction of conditioned eyelid reactions. *J. exp. Psychol.*, 1939, **25**, 141-158. P. *448.*

190. HUNT, J. McV. The effects of infant feeding-frustration upon adult

hoarding in the albino rat. *J. abnorm. soc. Psychol.*, 1941, **36**, 338-360.

191. HUNTINGTON, E. *Civilization and climate.* New York: Yale Univer. Press, 1915. P. *551.*

192.*HURLEY, J. R. The Iowa Picture Interpretation Test: a multiple choice variation of the TAT. *J. consult. Psychol.*, 1955, **19**, 372-376. Pp. *22, 39.*

193.*HURLEY, J. R. Achievement imagery and motivational instructions as determinants of verbal learning. *J. Pers.*, 1957, **25**, 274-282.

194. HUTT, M. L. A clinical study of "consecutive" and "adaptive" testing with the revised Stanford-Binet. *J. consult. Psychol.*, 1947, **11**, 93-103.

195. HYMAN, H. The value system of different classes: A social psychological contribution to the analysis of stratification. In R. Bendix and S. Lipset (Eds.), *Class, status and power.* Glencoe, Ill.: The Free Press, 1953. Pp. *338, 496.*

196.*JACOBS, B. A method for investigating the cue characteristics of pictures used in projective measures of motives. Unpublished honors thesis, Univer. of Michigan, 1953.

197. JAMES, W. *The principles of psychology.* Vol. 1. New York: Holt, 1890. P. *373.*

198. JENKINS, W. O., and STANLEY, J. C. Partial reinforcement: a review and critique. *Psychol. Bull.*, 1950, **47**, 193-234. P. *448.*

199. JERSILD, A. T. *Child psychology* (3rd ed.). New York: Prentice-Hall, 1947. P. *442.*

200. JOHNSON, P. O. *Statistical methods in research.* New York: Prentice-Hall, 1949. P. *121.*

201.*JOHNSTON, R. A. The effects of achievement imagery on maze-learning performance. *J. Pers.*, 1955, **24**, 145-152. P. *39.*

202.*JOHNSTON, R. A. A methodological analysis of several revised forms of the Iowa Picture Interpretation test. *J. Pers.*, 1957, **25**, 283-293.

203. KAHL, J. A. Educational and occupational aspirations of "Common Man" boys. *Harvard educ. Rev.*, 1953, **23**, 186-203. P. *504.*

204.*KALTENBACH, J. E., and MCCLELLAND, D. C. Achievement and social status in three small communities. Chapter 3 in Report on the Committee on Identification of Talent. New York: Social Science Research Council, 1957. P. *521.*

205. KARDINER, A. Psychological frontiers of society. New York: Columbia Univer. Press, 1945. P. *526.*

206.*KAROLCHUCK, P., and WORELL, L. Achievement motivation and learning. *J. abnorm. soc. Psychol.*, 1956, **53**, 255-257. P. *234.*

207. KELLOG, R. *What children scribble and why.* San Francisco: Author, 1955. P. *250.*

208. KELLY, E. L., and FISKE, D. W. The prediction of performance in clinical psychology. Ann Arbor: Univer. of Michigan Press, 1951. Pp. *384, 386, 387, 389, 603.*

209. KELMAN, H. C. Effects of success and failure on "suggestibility"

in the autokinetic situation. *J. abnorm. soc. Psychol.*, 1950, **45**, 267-285. P. *433*.

210. KENDALL, M. G. *Rank correlation methods.* London: Chas. Griffin, 1948. P. *210*.

211. KENNY, D. T. Transcendence indices, extent of personality factors in fantasy responses and the ambiguity of TAT cards. *J. consult. Psychol.*, 1954, **18**, 345-348. P. *632*.

212. KENNY, D. T., and BIJOU, S. W. Ambiguity of pictures and extent of personality factors in fantasy responses. *J. consult. Psychol.*, 1953, **17**, 283-288. P. *632*.

213. KINSEY, A. C., POMEROY, W. B., MARTIN, E. C., and GEBHARD, F. H. *Sexual behavior in the human female.* Philadelphia: Saunders, 1953. P. *140*.

214. KISH, L. Selection of the sample. In L. Festinger and D. Katz (Eds.), *Research methods in the behavioral sciences.* New York: Dryden, 1953. P. *580*.

215.*KLAUS, D. J. The effect of experimentally produced guilt on thematic apperception. Unpublished honors thesis, Univer. of Michigan, 1951. P. *620*.

216. KLUCKHOHN, FLORENCE R. Dominant and substitutive profiles of cultural orientations: their significance for the analysis of social stratification. *Social Forces,* 1950, **28**, 376-393. Pp. *541, 542, 559*.

217. KLUCKHOHN, C., and KLUCKHOHN, FLORENCE R. American culture: Generalized orientations and class patterns. In L. Bryson (Ed.), *Conflicts of power in modern culture.* Harper, 1947.

218. KNAPP, R. H. Experiments in serial reproduction and related aspects of the phsychology of rumor. Unpublished doctoral dissertation, Harvard Univer., 1948. P. *60*.

219. KOFFKA, K. *Principles of Gestalt Psychology.* New York: Harcourt, Brace, 1935, p. 127.

220. KOGAN, J. The measurement of overt aggression from fantasy. *J. abnorm. soc. Psychol.*, 1956, **52**, 390-393. P. *632*.

221. KRECH, D., and CRUTCHFIELD, R. *Theory and problems of social psychology.* New York: McGraw-Hill, 1948. P. *409*.

222. LANGER, W. *Psychology and human living.* New York: Appleton-Century-Crofts, 1941. P. *80*.

223.*LAZARUS, R. Motivation and personality in psychological stress. ONR Progress Report No. II, Clark Univer., 1956. P. *18*.

224. LAZARUS, R. S., DEESE, J., and OSLER, SONIA F. The effects of psychological stress upon performance. *Psychol. Bull.*, 1952, **49**, 293-317.

225. LEIGHTON, D., and KLUCKHOHN, C. *Children of the people.* Cambridge: Harvard Univer. Press, 1947.

226. LEVINE, R., CHEIN, I., and MURPHY, G. The relation of the intensity of a need to the amount of perceptual distortion: a preliminary report. *J. Psychol.*, 1942, **13**, 283-293. Pp. *10, 43*.

227. LEVY, D. M. Primary affect hunger. *Amer. J. Psychiat.*, 1937, **94**, 643-652.

228. LEWIN, K. Environmental forces in child-behavior and development.

In C. Murchison (Ed.), *A handbook of child psychology.* Worcester, Mass.: Clark Univer. Press, 1931. P. *612.*

229. LEWIN, K. *A dynamic theory of personality.* New York: McGraw-Hill, 1935. Pp. *11, 161, 451.*

230. LEWIN, K. *Field theory in social science.* D. Cartwright (Ed.). New York: Harper, 1951, p. 243. P. *596.*

231. LEWIN, K., DEMBO, TAMARA, FESTINGER, L., and SEARS, PAULINE S. Level of aspiration. In J. McV. Hunt (Ed.), *Personality and the behavior disorders.* Vol. 1. New York: Ronald Press, 1944, pp. 333-378. Pp. *297, 326, 327, 330, 337, 374.*

232. LIEBMANN, S. Uber das verholten forgiger forman bei helligkeits-gleichheit von figur und grund. *Psychol. Forsch.,* 1927, **9**, 300-353. P. *372.*

233. LINDNER, H. Sexual responsiveness to perceptual tests in a group of sexual offenders. *J. Pers.,* 1953, **21**, 364-374. P. *126.*

234. LINDQUIST, E. F. *Statistical analysis in educational research.* New York: Houghton-Mifflin, 1940. Pp. *416, 418, 577, 580, 582.*

235. LINDQUIST, E. F. *Design and analysis of experiments in psychology and education.* Boston: Houghton-Mifflin, 1953. P. *344.*

236. LINDZEY, G. Thematic Apperception Test: interpretive assumptions and related empirical evidence. *Psychol. Bull.,* 1952, **49**, 1-25. Pp. *553, 633.*

237.*LINDZEY, G., and HEINEMANN, S. H. Thematic Apperception Test: individual and group administration. *J. Pers.,* 1955, **24**, 34-55. Pp. *19, 20, 32, 34, 35, 36, 37, 38, 553, 677, 683.*

238. LINTON, R. *The cultural background of personality.* New York: D. Appleton-Century, 1945. P. *447.*

239. LOTT, A. J., SCHOPLER, J. H., and GIBB, J. R. Effects of feeling-oriented and task-oriented feedback upon defensive behavior in small problem-solving groups. *Amer. Psychologist,* 1955, **10**, 335. (Abstract)

240.*LOWELL, E. L. A methodological study of projectively measured achievement motivation. Unpublished master's thesis, Wesleyan Univer., 1950.

241.*LOWELL, E. L. The effect of need for achievement on learning and speed of performance. *J. Psychol.,* 1952, **33**, 31-40. Pp. *252, 260, 267, 278, 284, 374, 416.*

242. LUBORSKY, L., and SARGENT, H. The psychotherapy research project of the Menninger Foundation. V. Sample use of method. *Bull. Menninger Clinic,* 1956, **20**, 263-276. P. *28.*

243. LYND, R. S., and LYND, HELEN M. *Middletown.* New York: Harcourt, Brace, 1929. P. *516.*

244. MACCORQUODALE, K., and MEEHL, P. E. Preliminary suggestions as to a formalization of expectancy theory. *Psychol. Rev.,* 1953, **60**, 55-63. Pp. *288, 303, 599.*

245. MACCORQUODALE, K., and MEEHL, P. E. Edward C. Tolman in *Modern learning theory.* New York: Appleton-Century-Crofts, 1954. P. *599.*

246. MAHLER, W. Studies of the substitute function of different levels of reality. In Translation of eight experimental studies in personality, directed by Kurt Lewin. Unpublished manuscript, Yale Univer. Library, 1940. P. *161.*

247. MAIER, N. R. F. *Frustration.* New York: McGraw-Hill, 1949.

248. MANDLER, G., and SARASON, S. B. A study of anxiety and learning. *J. abnorm. soc. Psychol.,* 1952, **47,** 166-173. Pp. *329, 340.*

249. MARQUIS, D. P. Learning in the neonate: the modification of behavior under three feeding schedules. *J. exp. Psychol.,* 1941, **29,** 263-282.

250.*MARTIRE, J. G. Relationships between the self concept and differences in the strength and generality of achievement motivation. Unpublished doctoral dissertation, Univer. of Michigan, 1953. Pp. *377, 572, 577.*

251.*MARTIRE, J. G. Relationships between the self concept and differences in the strength and generality of achievement motivation. *J. Pers.,* 1956, **24,** 364-375.

252. MASLOW, A. H. *Motivation and personality.* New York: Harper, 1954. P. *250.*

253. MAY, R. *The meaning of anxiety.* New York: Ronald Press, 1950. P. *574.*

254. MAYER, K. B. *Class and Society.* New York: Doubleday, 1955. P. *495.*

255. MCARTHUR, C. C. Cultural values as detrminants of imaginal productions. Unpublished doctoral dissertation, Harvard Univer., 1951. P. *559.*

256.*MCARTHUR, C. C. The effects of need for achievement on the content of TAT stories; a re-examination. *J. abnorm. soc. Psychol.,* 1953, **48,** 532-536.

257.*MCARTHUR, C. C. Personality differences between middle and upper classes. *J. abnorm. soc. Psychol.,* 1955, **50,** 247-254. P. *499.*

258.*MCCLELLAND, D. C. *Personality.* New York: Wm. Sloane Associates, 1951. Pp. *90, 95, 127, 324, 341, 373, 436, 454, 509, 593, 597, 598, 612, 613.*

259.*MCCLELLAND, D. C. Measuring motivation in phantasy: the achievement motive. In H. Guetzkow (Ed.), *Groups, leadership and men.* New York: Carnegie Press, 1951, pp. 191-205. Pp. *242, 454.*

260.*MCCLELLAND, D. C. Note on cyclical effects in successive administration of the TAT to the same persons. Unpublished manuscript, Wesleyan Univer., 1955. Pp. *268, 306, 322, 331.*

261.*MCCLELLAND, D. C. Some social consequences of achievement motivation. In M. R. Jones (Ed.), *Nebraska symposium on motivation, 1955.* Lincoln: Univer. of Nebraska Press, 1955. P. *649.*

262.*MCCLELLAND, D. C. The calculated risk—an aspect of creative scientific performance. In *Collected papers of conference on scientific creativity.* Salt Lake City: Univer. of Utah Press, 1956. P. *268.*

263.*MCCLELLAND, D. C. Interest in risky occupations among subjects with high achievement motivation. Unpublished manuscript, Harvard Univer., 1956. Pp. *38, 268, 306, 322, 521.*

264. McClelland, D. C. Personality. *Annu. Rev. Psychol.,* 1956, **7**, 39-62. Pp. *22, 23, 25.*

265.*McClelland, D. C. Risk-taking in children with high and low need for achievement. Unpublished manuscript available from the author, 1956.

266. McClelland, D. C. Toward a science of personality psychology. In H. P. David (Ed.), *Perspectives in personality theory.* New York: Basic Books, 1957. Pp. *20, 27.*

267. McClelland, D. C., and Apicella, F. S. A functional classification of verbal reactions to experimentally induced failure. *J. abnorm. soc. Psychol.,* 1945, **40**, 376-390. P. *614.*

268. McClelland, D. C., and Apicella, F. S. Reminiscence following experimentally induced failure. *J. exp. Psychol.,* 1947, **37**, 159-169.

269.*McClelland, D. C., Atkinson, J. W., and Clark, R. A. The effect of different intensities of need mastery on thematic apperception. ONR Report, 1947. P. *78.*

270.*McClelland, D. C., and Atkinson, J. W. The projective expression of needs. I. The effect of different intensities of the hunger drive on perception. *J. Psychol.,* 1948, **25**, 205-232. Pp. *9, 30, 31, 43, 46, 47, 59, 64.*

271.*McClelland, D. C., Atkinson, J. W., and Clark, R. A. The projective expression of needs. III. The effect of ego involvement, success and failure on perception. *J. Psychol.,* 1949, **27**, 311-330. Pp. *68, 77, 78, 79.*

272.*McClelland, D. C., Atkinson, J. W., Clark, R. A., and Lowell, E. L. *The achievement motive.* New York: Appleton-Century-Crofts, 1953. Pp. *1, 8, 12, 13, 17, 19, 20, 21, 24, 27, 31, 32, 33, 34, 35, 36, 37, 38, 39, 68, 77, 95, 96, 97, 105, 107, 110, 114, 179, 234, 241, 242, 246, 249, 250, 267, 271, 278, 279, 280, 281, 284, 299, 300, 307, 310, 311, 322, 324, 333, 341, 343, 348, 350, 351, 357, 360, 368, 375, 376, 377, 385, 388, 396, 397, 411, 419, 422, 427, 436, 453, 459, 460, 469, 484, 497, 498, 510, 512, 519, 520, 521, 527, 529, 530, 532, 542, 547, 563, 564, 568, 569, 570, 572, 577, 586, 597, 611, 612, 617, 618, 620, 633, 645, 647, 648, 653, 655, 659, 660, 661, 664, 666, 667, 668, 679, 680, 686, 693, 831, 832, 833, 836, 837.*

273.*McClelland, D. C., Clark, R. A., Roby, T. B., and Atkinson, J. W. The projective expression of needs. IV. The effect of need for achievement on thematic apperception. *J. exp. Psychol.,* 1949, **39**, 242-255.

274.*McClelland, D. C., and Friedman, G. A. A cross-cultural study of the relationship between child-training practices and achievement motivation appearing in folk tales. In G. E. Swanson, T. M. Newcomb, and E. L. Hartley (Eds.), *Readings in social psychology.* New York: Holt, 1952. Pp. *34, 38, 436, 453, 479, 489, 490, 526, 530.*

275.*McClelland, D. C., and Liberman, A. M. The effect of need for achievement on recognition of need-related words. *J. Pers.,* 1949, **18**, 236-251. Pp. *91, 242, 350, 353, 360, 365, 416, 563.*

276. McClelland, D. C., and McGown, D. R. The effect of non-specific food reinforcement on the strength of a secondary reward. Unpublished manuscript, 1950. P. *449*.

277. McClelland, D. C., Rindlisbacher, A., and deCharms, R. C. Religious and other sources of parental attitudes toward independence training. In D. C. McClelland (Ed.), *Studies in motivation.* New York: Appleton-Century-Crofts, 1955. P. *436*.

278.*McClelland, D. C., Sturr, J., and Wendt, H. W. A comparison of values and motives in German and American adolescent boys. Unpublished manuscript available from the atuhors, 1956. P. *520*.

279. McGeoch, J. A. *The psychology of human learning.* New York: Longmans, Green, 1942. P. *447*.

280. McGraw, Myrtle B. *Growth: a study of Johnny and Jimmy.* New York: D.-Appleton-Century, 1935. P. *441*.

281. McGraw, Myrtle B. Later development of children specially trained in infancy. *Child Develpm.,* 1939, **10,** 1-19. P. *441*.

282. McKeachie, W. J. Anxiety in the college classroom. *J. educ. Res.,* 1951, **45,** 153-160.

283.*McKeachie, W. J., Pollie, D., and Speisman, J. Relieving anxiety in classroom examinations. *J. abnorm. soc. Psychol.,* 1955, **50,** 93-98.

284. Mead, Margaret. *Male and female.* New York: Wm. Morrow, 1949. P. *611*.

285. Melton, A. W. Learning. In W. S. Monroe (Ed.), *Encyclopedia of educational research.* New York: Macmillan, 1952. P. *14*.

286. Melton, A. W., and von Lackum, W. J. Retroactive and proactive inhibition in retention: evidence for a two-factor theory of retroactive inhibition. *Amer. J. Psychol.,* 1941, **54,** 157-173.

287. Miller, D. R. Responses of psychiatric patients to threat of failure. *J. abnorm. soc. Psychol.,* 1951, **46,** 378-387. P. *337*.

288. Miller, D. R., and Swanson, G. E. The study of conflict. In M. R. Jones (Ed.), *Nebraska symposium on motivation, 1956.* Lincoln: Univer. of Nebraska Press, 1956. P. *614*.

289. Miller, J. G. Discrimination without awareness. *Amer. J. Psychol.,* 1939, **52,** 562-578.

290. Miller, N. E. Experimental studies of conflict. In J. McV. Hunt (Ed.), *Personality and the behavior disorders.* Vol. 1. New York: Ronald Press, 1944. Pp. *122, 124, 451, 573*.

291. Miller, N. E. Theory and experiment relating psychoanalytic displacement to stimulus-response generalization. *J. abnorm. soc. Psychol.,* 1948, **43,** 155-178. P. *573*.

292. Miller, N. E. Learnable drives and rewards. In S. S. Stevens (Ed.), *Handbook of experimental psychology.* New York: Wiley, 1951, Pp. *10, 15, 143*.

293. Miller, N. E. Comments on theoretical models illustrated by the development of a theory of conflict behavior. *J. Pers.,* 1951, **20,** 82-100. Pp. *101, 573, 612*.

294. Miller, N. E., Bailey, C. J., and Stevenson, J. A. F. Decreased

"hunger" but increased food intake resulting from hypothalamic lesions. *Science,* 1950, **112**, 256-259. P. *17.*

295. MILLER, N. E., and DOLLARD, J. *Social learning and imitation.* New Haven: Yale Univer. Press, 1941. P. *11.*

296. MILLS, C. W. *White collar.* New York: Oxford Univer. Press, 1951. P. *496.*

297. MILNER, E. Effects of sex roles and social status on the early adolescent personality. *Genet. Psychol. Monogr.,* 1949, **40**, 231-325.

298.*MILSTEIN, A. FREDA. Ambition and defense against threat of failure. Unpublished doctoral dissertation, Univer. of Michigan, 1956. P. *493.*

299. MOOD, A. M. *Introduction to the theory of statistics.* New York: McGraw-Hill, 1950. P. *154.*

300.*MORGAN, H. H. A psychometric comparison of achieving and non-achieving college students of high ability. *J. consult. Psychol.,* 1952, **16**, 292-298. P. *234.*

301.*MORGAN, H. H. Measuring achievement motivation with "picture interpretation." *J. consult. Psychol.,* 1953, **17**, 289-292. Pp. *234, 287, 605.*

302.*MORRISON, H. W. Validity and behavioral correlates of female need for achievement. Unpublished master's thesis, Wesleyan Univer., 1954. Pp. *13, 77.*

303. MOSES, L. E. Non-parametric statistics for psychological research. *Psychol. Bull.,* 1952, **49**, 122-143. Pp. *461, 466.*

304.*MOULTON, R. W. Relationship of need for achievement to perceptual sensitivity under two degrees of motive arousal. Unpublished honors thesis, Univer. of Michigan, 1952. P. *350.*

305. MOUTON, JANE S., BLAKE, R. R., and OLMSTEAD, J. A. The relationship between frequency of yielding and the disclosure of personal identity. *J. Pers.,* 1956, **24**, 339-347. Pp. *422, 433.*

306. MOWRER, O. H. An experimental analogue of "regression" with incidental observations on "reaction-formation." *J. abnorm. soc. Psychol.,* 1940, **35**, 56-87.

307. MOWRER, O. H. On the dual nature of learning—a re-interpretation of "conditioning" and "problem-solving." *Harvard educ. Rev.,* 1947, **17**, 102-148. P. *442.*

308. MOWRER, O. H. *Learning theory and personality dynamics.* New York: Ronald Press, 1950. Pp. *11, 613.*

309. MOWRER, O. H., and VIEK, P. An experimental analogue of fear from a sense of helplessness. *J. abnorm. soc. Psychol.,* 1948, **43**, 193-200. P. *145.*

310. MURPHY, G. *Personality.* New York: Harper, 1947. P. *373.*

311. MURPHY, G. Social motivation. In G. Lindzey (Ed.), *Handbook of social psychology.* Cambridge, Mass.: Addison-Wesley, 1954, pp. 601-633. P. *115.*

312. MURRAY, H. A. The effect of fear upon estimates of the maliciousness of other personalities. *J. soc. Psychol.,* 1933, **4**, 310-329. Pp. *60, 145.*

313. MURRAY, H. A. Techniques for a systematic investigation of fantasy. *J. Psychol.*, 1937, **3**, 115-143. Pp. *1, 49, 58.*

314. MURRAY, H. A., et. al. *Explorations in personality.* New York: Oxford Univer. Press, 1938. Pp. *1, 17, 22, 23, 26, 29, 47, 49, 58, 64, 72, 76, 80, 85, 247, 383, 384, 396, 448, 483, 597, 598, 613.*

315. MURRAY, H. A. *Thematic Apperception Test manual.* Cambridge: Harvard Univer. Press, 1943. Pp. *1, 673, 694.*

316. MURRAY, H. A., and STEIN, M. Note on the selection of combat officers. *Psychosom. Med.*, 1943, **5**, 386-391.

317. Newcomb, T. M. Autistic hostility and social reality. *Hum. Relat.*, 1947, **1**, 68-86. P. *410.*

318. NEWCOMB, T. M. *Social psychology.* New York: Dryden, 1950. P. *243.*

319. NICHOLS, R. C. A study of psychoanalytic symbolism in relation to stimulus generalization. *Amer. Psychologist,* 1955, **10**, 351-352. (Abstract) P. *135.*

320. NOWLIS, H. H. The influence of success and failure on the resumption of an interrupted task. *J. exp. Psychol.*, 1941, **23**, 304-325. P. *64.*

321. ORLANSKY, H. Infant care and personality. *Psychol. Bull.*, 1949, **46**, 1-48. P. *444.*

322. ORT, R. S. A study of role-conflicts as related to class level. *J. abnorm. soc. Psychol.*, 1952, **47**, 425-432. P. *511.*

323. Parrish, J., and Rethlingshafer, D. A study of the need to achieve in college achievers and non-achievers. *J. gen. Psychol.*, 1954, **50**, 209-226. P. *35.*

324. PARSONS, T. A revised analytical approach to the theory of social stratification. In R. Bendix and S. Lipset (Eds.), *Class, status and power.* Glencoe, Ill.: The Free Press, 1953. P. *496.*

325. PATRICK, J. K. Studies in rational behavior and emotional excitement. I. The effect of emotional excitement on rational behavior of human subjects. *J. comp. Psychol.*, 1934, **18**, 153-195. P. 10.

326. PAVLOV, I. P. *Conditioned reflexes.* (Transl. by G. V. Anrep) London: Oxford Univer. Press, 1927. P. *444.*

327. PERKY, C. W. An experimental study of imagination. *Amer. J. Psychol.*, 1910, **21**, 422-452.

328. PFAUTZ, H. The current literature on social stratification. Critique and bibliography. *Amer. J. Soc.*, 1953, **58**, 391-418. P. *495.*

329. POSTMAN, L. Toward a general theory of cognition. In J. H. Rohrer and M. Sherif (Eds.), *Social psychology at the crossroads.* New York: Harper, 1951. Pp. *9, 30, 583.*

330. POSTMAN, L. The experimental analysis of motivational factors in perception. In M. R. Jones (Ed.), *Current theory and research in motivation.* Lincoln: Univer. of Nebraska Press, 1953. P. *360.*

331. POSTMAN, L., BRONSON, WANDA C., and GROPPER, G. L. Is there a mechanism of perceptual defense? *J. abnorm. soc. Psychol.*, 1953, **48**, 215-224.

332. POSTMAN, L., and CRUTCHFIELD, R. S. The interaction of need, set,

and stimulus structure in a cognitive task. *Amer. J. Psychol.*, 1952, **65**, 196-217. Pp. *9, 24, 30, 31.*

333. POSTMAN, L., and SCHNEIDER, B. H. Personal values, visual recognition and recall. *Psychol. Rev.*, 1951, **58**, 271-284. P. *24.*

334.*POTTHARST, BARBARA C. The achievement motive and level of aspiration after experimentally induced success and failure. Unpublished doctoral dissertation, Univer. of Michigan, 1955. Pp. *299, 333.*

335. RAPAPORT, D. *Diagnostic psychological testing.* Chicago: Year Book Publishers, 1945-1946. Pp. *1, 574.*

336.*RAPHELSON, A. C. Imaginative and direct verbal measures of anxiety related to physiological reactions in the competitive achievement situation. Unpublished doctoral dissertation, Univer. of Michigan, 1956.

337.*RAPHELSON, A. C. The relationship between imaginative, direct verbal, and physiological measures of anxiety in an achievement situation. *J. abnorm. soc. Psychol.*, 1957, **54**, 13-18.

338. RAZRAN, G. The cognitive evocation of attitudes (cognitive conditioning?) *J. exp. Psychol.*, 1954, **48**, 278-282. P. *141.*

339.*REITMAN, W. R. Selective recall of meaningful material as a function of achievement motivation. Unpublished master's thesis, Wesleyan Univer., 1954.

340.*RICCIUTI, H. N. The prediction of academic grades with a projective test of achievement motivation. I. Initial validation studies. Princeton, N. J.: Educational Testing Service, 1954. Pp. *19, 33, 36, 675.*

341.*RICCIUTI, H. N., and CLARK, R. A. A comparison of need-achievement stories written by experimentally "relaxed" and "achievement-oriented" subjects: effects obtained with new pictures and revised scoring categories. Princeton, N. J.: Educational Testing Service, 1954. Pp. *33, 36, 179, 673, 675, 693, 831, 832, 833, 835, 836.*

342.*RICCIUTI, H. N., and SADACCA, R. The prediction of academic grades with a projective test of achievement motivation. II. Cross validation at the high school level. Princeton, N. J.: Educational Testing Service, 1955. Pp. *36, 521, 605, 675, 831, 832, 833, 836, 837.*

343. ROBERTS, A. H., *et al.* Effects of feeling-oriented classroom teachings upon reactions to feedback. *Amer. Psychologist,* 1955, **10**, 420. (Abstract) P. *400.*

344.*ROBY, T. B. The effect of need for security on thematic apperception. Unpublished master's thesis, Wesleyan Univer., 1948. P. *83.*

345. RODNICK, E. H., and KLEBANOFF, S. G. Projective reactions to induced frustration as a measure of social adjustment. *Psychol. Bull.,* 1942, **39**, 489. Pp. *1, 46.*

346. ROGERS, C. R. The organization of personality. *Amer. Psychologist,* 1947, **2**, 358-368. P. *373.*

347. ROGERS, C. R., and DYMOND, R. F. *Psychotherapy and personality change.* Chicago: Univer. of Chicago Press, 1954. Pp. *19, 679.*

348. ROGOFF, N. *Recent trends in occupational mobility.* Glencoe, Ill.: The Free Press, 1953. P. *495.*

349.*Rosen, B. The achievement syndrome. *Amer. soc. Rev.*, 1955, **21**, 203-211.

350.*Rosenstein, A. J. The specificity of the achievement motive and the motivating effects of picture cues. Unpublished honors thesis, Univer. of Michigan, 1952. Pp. *611, 620, 633, 682.*

351. Rosensweig, S. An experimental study of "repression" with special reference to need-persistive and ego-defensive reactions to frustration. *J. exp. Psychol.*, 1943, **32**, 64-74. P. *243.*

352. Rosensweig, S., and Flemming, E. Apperception norms for the Thematic Apperception Test. II. An empirical investigation. *J. Pers.*, 1949, **17**, 485-503. Pp. *1, 630.*

353. Rotter, J. B. *Social learning and clinical psychology.* New York: Prentice-Hall, 1954. Pp. *323, 599, 615, 651.*

354. Rotter, J. B. The role of the psychological situation in determining the direction of human behavior. In M. R. Jones (Ed.), *Nebraska symposium on motivation, 1955.* Lincoln: Univer. of Nebraska Press, 1955. Pp. *287, 599, 600, 615, 616.*

355. Rotter, J. B., and Willerman, B. The Incomplete Sentence Test as a method of studying personality. *J. consult. Psychol.*, 1947, **11**, 43-48. P. 164.

356.*Sadacca, R., Ricciuti, H. N., and Swanson, E. O. Content analysis of achievement motivation protocols: a study of scorer agreement. Princeton, N. J.: Educational Testing Service, 1956. Pp. *234, 241.*

357.*Samelson, F. Group pressure and conflict in the cognitive field as determinants of conformity. Unpublished doctoral dissertation, Univer. of Michigan, 1955. Pp. *421, 423.*

358. Samelson, F. Conforming behavior under two conditions of conflict in the cognitive field. *J. abnorm. soc. Psychol.*, 1957, **55**, 181-187. P. *423.*

359. Sanford, R. N. The effects of abstinence from food upon imaginal processes: a preliminary experiment. *J. Psychol.*, 1936, **2**, 129-136. P. *43.*

360. Sanford, R. N. The effects of abstinence from food upon imaginal processes: a further experiment. *J. Psychol.*, 1937, **3**, 145-159. P. *43.*

361. Sanford, R. N., Adkins, Margaret M., Miller, R. B., Cobb, E. A., *et al.* Physique, personality and scholarship: a cooperative study of school children. *Monogr. Soc. Res. Child Develpm.*, 1943, **8**, No. 1. P. *1.*

362. Sarason, S. B., and Mandler, G. Some correlates of test anxiety. *J. abnorm. soc. Psychol.*, 1952, **47**, 810-817.

363. Sarason, S. B., Mandler, G., and Craighill, P. C. The effect of differential instructions on anxiety and learning. *J. abnorm. soc. Psychol.*, 1952, **47**, 561-565. P. *340.*

364. Sargent, H. Projective methods, their origins, theory and application to personality research. *Psychol. Bull.*, 1945, **42**, 257-293. Pp. *49, 61.*

365. Schachter, S. Deviation, rejection and communication. *J. abnorm. soc. Psychol.*, 1951, **46**, 190-207, P. *410.*

366. SCHLOSBERG, H. Three dimensions of emotion. *Psychol. Rev.*, 1954, **61**, 81-88. P. *348.*

367.*SCOTT, W. A. The avoidance response to pictorial representation of threatening situations. Unpublished doctoral dissertation, Univer. of Michigan, 1954. Pp. *572, 580.*

368. SCOTT, W. A. Reliability of content analysis: the case of nominal scale coding. *Publ. Opin. Quart.*, in press.

369. SEARS, R. R. Experimental studies of projection: I. Attribution of traits. *J. soc. Psychol.*, 1936, **7**, 151-163. P. *29.*

370. SEARS, R. R. Success and failure: a study of motility. Chapter 13 in *Studies in personality.* New York: McGraw-Hill, 1942. Pp. *12, 64, 76.*

371. SEARS, R. R. Experimental analysis of psychoanalytic phenomena. Chapter 9 in J. McV. Hunt (Ed.), *Personality and the behavior disorders.* New York: Ronald Press, 1944.

372. SEARS, R. R. A theoretical framework for personality and social behavior. *Amer. Psychologist*, 1951, **6**, 476-483. P. *616.*

373. SEARS, R. R. Social behavior and personality development. In T. Parsons and E. A. Shils (Eds.), *Toward a general theory of action.* Cambridge: Harvard Univer. Press, 1951. P. *613.*

374. SHELDON, W. H. *Varieties of delinquent youth: An introduction to constitutional psychiatry.* New York: Harper, 1949.

375. SHERIF, M. A study of some social factors in perception. *Arch. Psychol.*, 1935, **27**, No. 187. Pp. *413, 421.*

376. SHERIF, M. *An outline of social psychology.* New York: Harper, 1948. P. *10.*

377. SHERIF, M., and CANTRIL, H. *The psychology of ego-involvements.* New York: Wiley, 1947.

378. SHERRIFFS, A. C. "The intuition questionnaire": a new projective test. *J. abnorm. soc. Psychol.*, 1948, **43**, 326-337. Pp. *245, 271.*

379.*SHIPLEY, T. E., and VEROFF, J. A projective measure of need for affiliation. *J. exp. Psychol.*, 1952, **43**, 349-356.

380. SIIPOLA, E. M. A group study of some effects of preparatory set. *Psychol. Monogr.*, 1935, **46**, 27-38. P. *25.*

381. SINHA, A. K. P. Experimental induction of anxiety by conditions of uncertainty. Unpublished doctoral dissertation, Univer. of Michigan, 1951.

382. SMITH, D. E. P., *et al.* Reading improvement as a function of student personality and teaching method. *J. educ. Psychol.*, 1956, **47**, 47-59. P. *425.*

383. SNEDECOR, G. W. *Statistical methods.* Ames: The Iowa State Press, 1946.

384. SNYGG, D., and COMBS, A. W. *Individual behavior.* New York: Harper, 1949. P. *373.*

385. SOLOMON, R. L., and BRUSH, E. S. Experimentally derived conceptions of anxiety and aversion. In M. R. Jones (Ed.), *Nebraska symposium on motivation, 1956.* Lincoln: Univer. of Nebraska Press, 1956. P. *143.*

386. SOLOMON, R. L., and HOWES, D. H. Word frequency, personal values and visual duration thresholds. *Psychol. Rev.,* 1951, **58,** 256-270. Pp. *360, 365.*

387. SOPCHAK, A. L. Individual differences in responses to different types of music, in relation to sex, mood, and other variables. *Psychol. Monogr.,* 1955, **69,** No. 11. P. *132.*

388. SOROKIN, P. *Social mobility.* New York: Harper, 1927. P. *495.*

389. SOROKIN, P. *Social and cultural dynamics.* Vol. 3. New York: American Book Co., 1937. P. *532.*

390. SPENCE, K. W., and FARBER, I. E. Conditioning and extinction as a function of anxiety. *J. exp. Psychol.,* 1953, **45,** 116-119. P. *340.*

391. SPENCE, K. W., and TAYLOR, JANET A. Anxiety and strength of the UCS as determiners of the amount of eyelid conditioning. *J. exp. Psychol.,* 1951, **42,** 183-188. P. *340.*

392.*SPENCER, BARBARA J. The relation of birth order to achievement and affiliation motivation. Unpublished honors thesis, Univer. of Michigan, 1953. P. *436.*

393. STEINER, I. A theory and an empirical study of the role of reference groups. Unpublished master's thesis, Univer. of Michigan, 1948. P. *515.*

394.*STRODTBECK, F. L. Family interaction and the transmission of achievement related attitudes. Unpublished manuscript, Univer. of Chicago, 1954.

395.*STRODTBECK, F. L., and SULTAN, F. Ethnic differences in achievement: a contrast of Jews and Italians in the United States. Unpublished manuscript, Univer. of Chicago, 1955. P. *436.*

396. STRONG, E. K., JR. *Vocational interests of men and women.* Stanford, Calif.: Stanford Univer. Press, 1943. Pp. *23, 24, 25, 387, 389.*

397. SUCHMAN, E. A., GOLDSEN, R. K., and WILLIAMS, R. M., JR. Attitudes toward the Korean war. *Publ. Opin. Quart.,* 1953, **17,** 171-184. P. *38.*

398. SULLIVAN, H. S. *Conceptions of modern psychiatry.* Washington: Wm. Alanson White Psychiatric Foundation, 1947. P. *106.*

399. SYMONDS, P. M. Criteria for the selection of pictures for the investigation of adolescent fantasies. *J. abnorm. soc. Psychol.,* 1939, **34,** 271-274. Pp. *61, 632.*

400. SYMONDS, P. M. *The dynamics of human adjustment.* New York: D.-Appleton-Century, 1946. P. *160.*

401. SYMONDS, P. M. *Adolescent fantasy: an investigation of the picture story method of personality study.* New York: Columbia Univer. Press, 1949. P. *1.*

402. TAYLOR, JANET A. The relationship of anxiety to the conditioned eyelid response. *J. exp. Psychol.,* 1951, **41,** 81-92. Pp. *9, 17, 22.*

403. TAYLOR, JANET A. A personality scale of manifest anxiety. *J. abnorm. soc. Psychol.,* 1953, **48,** 285-290. Pp. *143, 343.*

404. TAYLOR, JANET A., and SPENCE, K. W. The relationship of anxiety level to performance in serial learning. *J. exp. Psychol.,* 1952, **44,** 61-64. P. *340.*

405. TEEVAN, R. C., and McKEACHIE, W. J. Effects on performance of different instructions in multiple-choice examinations. *Mich. Acad. Sci., Arts Letters,* 1954, **39**, 467-475.

406. TELFORD, C. W. The refractory phase of voluntary and associative processes. *J. exp. Psychol.,* 1931, **14**, 1-36. Pp. *20, 33.*

407. THOMPSON, C. E. The Thompson modification of the thematic apperception test. *Rorschach Res. Exch. & J. proj. Tech.,* 1949, **13**, 469-478. P. *631.*

408. THORNDIKE, E. L. *A teacher's word book of twenty thousand words.* New York: Teachers Coll., Columbia Univer., 1931. P. *352.*

409. THORNDIKE, E. L., and LORGE, I. *The teacher's workbook of 30,000 words.* New York: Teachers Coll., Columbia Univer., 1944.

410. Thurstone, L. L. *A factorial analysis of perception.* Chicago: Univer. of Chicago Press, 1944. P. *66.*

411. TINBERGEN, N. *The study of instinct.* Oxford: Clarendon Press, 1951. P. *140.*

412. TOLMAN, E. C. Cognitive maps in rats and men. *Psychol. Rev.,* 1948, **55**, 189-208. P. *80.*

413. TOLMAN, E. C. *Collected papers in psychology.* Berkeley: Univer. of California Press, 1951. Pp. *599, 613.*

414. TOLMAN, E. C. Principles of performance. *Psychol. Rev.,* 1955, **62**, 315-326. Pp. *278, 288, 296, 323, 324, 599, 616.*

415. TOLMAN, E. C., and POSTMAN, L. Learning. *Annu. Rev. Psychol.,* 1954, **5**, 27-56. Pp. *288, 303.*

416. TOMKINS, S. S. *The Thematic Apperception Test.* New York: Grune & Stratton, 1947. Pp. *1, 72, 80, 161, 561.*

417. TOYNBEE, A. J. *A study of history.* (Abridgment of Vols. 1-6 by D. C. Somervell) New York: Oxford Univer. Press, 1947. Pp. *525, 551.*

418.*VEROFF, J. A projective measure of achievement motivation in adolescent males and females. Unpublished honors thesis, Wesleyan Univer., 1950.

419.*VEROFF, J. Development and validation of a projective measure of power motivation. *J. abnorm. soc. Psychol.,* 1957, **54**, 1-8. P. *777.*

420.*VEROFF, J., WILCOX, SUE., and ATKINSON, J. W. The achievement motive in high school and college age women. *J. abnorm. soc. Psychol.,* 1953, **48**, 108-119. Pp. *77, 95, 234, 611.*

421.*VOGEL, MARGARET D. An investigation of the affiliation motive in college age women using low cue strength pictures. Unpublished honors thesis, Univer. of Michigan, 1954. P. *77.*

422.*WALKER, E. L., and HEYNS, R. W. Studies in conformity. Unpublished manuscript, Univer. of Michigan, 1956. P. *604.*

423. WALKER, HELEN M., and LEV, J. *Statistical inference.* New York: Holt, 1953. Pp. *136, 138, 239, 688.*

424. WEBER, M. *The Protestant ethic.* (Transl. by T. Parsons) New York: Chas. Scribner's Sons, 1930. P. *396.*

425.*WEINBERGER, BERNICE. Achievement motivation and self-concept. Unpublished honors thesis, Univer. of Michigan, 1951. Pp. 374, 375.

426. WEISSKOPF, E. A. An experimental study of the effect of brightness and ambiguity on projection in the Thematic Apperception Test. *J. Psychol.*, 1950, **29**, 407-416. P. *631.*

427. WEISSKOPF, E. A., and DUNLEVY, G. P. Bodily similarity between subject and central figure in the TAT as an influence on projection. *J. abnorm. soc. Psychol.*, 1952, **47**, 441-445. P. *631.*

428. WEISSKOPF, E. A., JOELSON, E., and MONEY, L. Facial similarity between subject and central figure in the TAT as an influence on projection. *J. abnorm. soc. Psychol.*, 1953, **48**, 341-344. P. *631.*

429. WEKSTEIN, L. A preliminary outline for a fantasy production technique as a clinical instrument. *J. Psychol.*, 1945, **19**, 341-346. P. *631.*

430.*WENDT, H. W. Motivation, effort, and performance. In D. C. McClelland (Ed.), *Studies in motivation.* New York: Appleton-Century-Crofts, 1955. Pp. *267, 278, 279, 280, 282, 287, 291, 667.*

431. WHITE, R. K. Value-analysis—the nature and use of the method. *Soc. psychol. Stud. soc. Issues,* 1951. P. *619.*

432. WHITING, J. W. M., and CHILD, I. L. *Child training and personality: a cross-cultural study.* New Haven: Yale Univer. Press, 1953. Pp. *490, 547.*

433. WHYTE, W. F. *Street corner society.* Chicago: Univer. of Chicago Press, 1943. P. *516.*

434.*WILCOX, SUE. A projective measure of achievement motivation of college women. Unpublished honors thesis, Univer. of Michigan, 1951.

435. WILLIAMS, J. E. Mode of failure, interference tendencies, and achievement imagery. *J. abnorm. soc. Psychol.*, 1955, **51**, 573-580. Pp. *23, 37, 39.*

436.*WINTERBOTTOM, MARIAN R. The relation of childhood training in independence to achievement motivation. Unpublished doctoral dissertation, Univer. of Michigan, 1953. Pp. *453, 462, 472.*

437. WITKIN, H. A., et al. *Personality through perception.* New York: Harper, 1954. P. *421.*

438. WITTENBORN, J. R. The study of alternative responses by means of the correlation coefficient. *Psychol. Rev.,* 1955, **62**, 451-460. P. *16.*

439. WITTENBORN, J. R., and ERON, L. D. An application of drive theory to TAT responses. *J. consult. Psychol.*, 1951, **15**, 45-50. Pp. *161, 630.*

440. WOLF, A. The dynamics of the selective inhibition of specific functions in neurosis. Chapter 31 in S. S. Tomkins (Ed.), *Contemporary psychopathology.* Cambridge: Harvard Univer. Press, 1943. P. *441.*

441. WOLFENSTEIN, MARTHA and LEITES, N. *Movies: a psychological study.* Glencoe, Ill.: The Free Press, 1950. P. *526.*

442. WOODWORTH, R. S., and SCHLOSBERG, H. *Experimental psychology* (rev. ed.). New York: Holt, 1954. P. *141.*

443. WRIGHT, G. O. Projection and displacement: a cross-cultural study of folk-tale aggression. *J. abnorm. soc. Psychol.*, 1954, **49**, 523-528. P. *479.*

444.*ZATZKIS, J. The effect of the need for achievement on linguistic behavior. Unpublished master's thesis, Wesleyan Univer., 1949.

Index of Subjects

507 *passim;* high school grades, 503; and school aspiration, 504; class-related origins of, 507-508
Acquiescence, 25
Action, theory of, 602
Activation: and skin conductance, 348; Schlosberg theory of 348-349
Activistic-passivistic orientation, 501
Administration of thematic apperceptive measures, 682, 836-837
Aesthetic preference and *n* Achievement, 367-372 *passim*
Affect: in pictures, 634-635, 642; measure of, 582-589
Affective arousal: in achievement training, 492; in childhood, 439; in growth of motives, 442-443
Affective associations: generality of, 446-452; strength of, 440-446
Affective reactions, as symptoms of motive, 598
Affective Goal States (G+, G—), defined: achievement, 199-202; affiliation, 216-217; fear of failure, 565; power, 230-231
Affiliation Imagery (*Aff Im*), defined, 205-210
Affiliation motivation: and approval-seeking, 103; and attitude change, 409-419; and conformity, 409-419, 422, 426, 428, 602; and *n* Achievement, 385; and perception of faces, 364-365; and performance level, 276, 278-279, 285-286, 404; and popularity, 92, 102; and preference for work partner, 602; and ratings of pictures, 628; and staff-versus-peer trait ratings, 395-396; arousal procedures, 83-85, 93, 95-96, 362, 411; comparison of scoring systems, 100-102; cue value of pictures, 627; effect of different arousal conditions, 101; effect of different pictures, 100; effect on thematic apperception, 88-90, 93, 98-99; *n* Affiliation score, 90, 99; original scoring system, 86-87, 97-98; scoring reliability, 234 ff
(*See also* Configuration of motives; Expert coding; Pictures; Practice stories; Reliability; Scoring procedures; Self tests)
Affiliation Thema (*Aff Th*) (*see* Thema)
Aggression: and sexuality, 126-127; displaced, 129; effect on thematic apperception, 126-128, 170-171, 175; in achievement fantasies of children, 476-477; in Sentence Completion

Test, 169; induction of, 161-162; inhibition of, in thematic apperception, 612-615; measures of, 164, 166; motive-expectancy distinction, 612
Aim of motive, 597, 601-602; defined by imaginative story, 608-609
Alcohol: effect on thematic content, 614
(*See also* Sexual motivation)
Allport-Vernon-Lindzey Study of Values, 13, 22-23, 108, 387 ff
Alternation effect: in graphic expression, 262-263
(*See also* Serial position effects)
Alternative manifestations of motive, 16-17, 39, 263
Ambiguity: defined, 624; effect on conformity, 421-422; index for pictures, 625
Ambivalence, 450-451
(*See also* Approach-avoidance; Conflict)
Anticipatory Goal States (*Ga+*, *Ga—*), defined: achievement, 195-197; affiliation, 214-215; fear of failure, 565; power, 228-229
Anxiety: 10-11; about failure, 563; about future, 328-339 *passim;* and respiratory activity, 349; and skin conductance, 341; effect of alcohol on, 119; effect on thematic content, 123, 572-585 *passim*, 594, 595 n3; relations among imaginative, direct verbal, and physiological measures, 340; validity of general measures, 347-348
(*See also* Fear; Manifest anxiety; Test anxiety)
Appetite, 613
Approach-avoidance: activation, 348; conflict, 451, 573-574; distinction, 90, 91, 101-102, 122-124, 304; motives for, 324; motivation for success and fear of failure, 326-339 *passim*, 566 ff, 586; theory applied to thematic apperception, 249, 572-585, 612-616
Arousal of motivation: ratings of, 662; technique, 651-655
Artistic productions, in cross-cultural research, 546-547
Ascribed status, in Greek literature, 542-543
Assessment of individual differences: in clinical psychology trainees, 603-604; theoretical discussion of, 596-616
(*See also* Configuration of motives)
Attitude change: and *n* Affiliation, 409-419; correlation with conform-